Features for Students

MyStatLab provides students with a personalized, interactive environment where they can learn at their own pace and measure their progress.

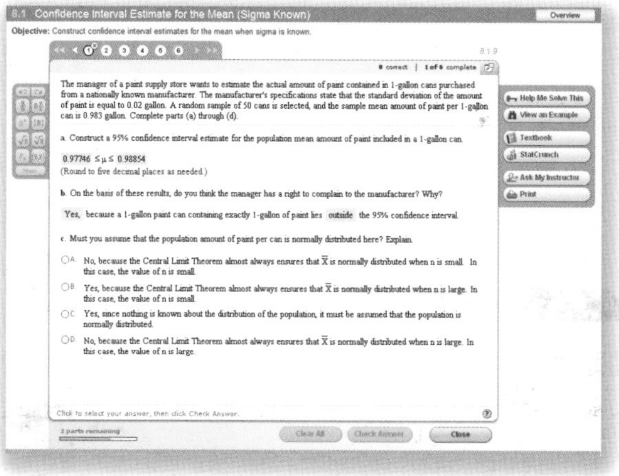

◄ **Interactive tutorial exercises**

MyStatLab's homework and practice exercises, correlated to the exercises in the textbook, are generated algorithmically, giving students unlimited opportunity for practice and mastery. Exercises include guided solutions, sample problems, and learning aids for extra help at point-of-use, and they offer helpful feedback when students enter incorrect answers.

StatCrunch ►

StatCrunch offers both numerical and data analysis and uses interactive graphics to illustrate the connection between objects selected in a graph and the underlying data. In most MyStatLab courses, all data sets from the textbook are pre-loaded in StatCrunch, and StatCrunch is also available as a tool from all online homework and practice exercises.

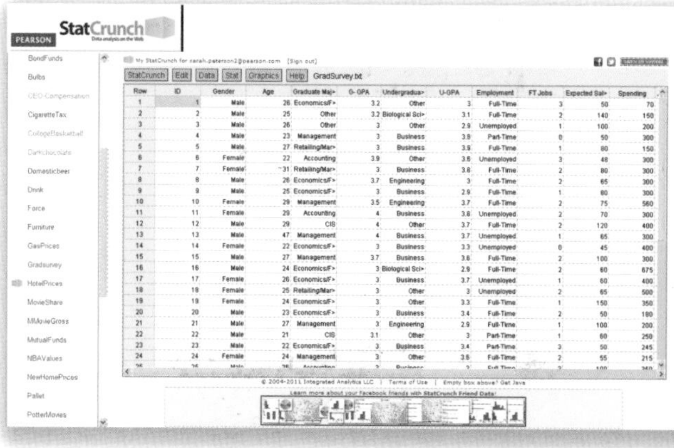

PHStat ►

PHStat is the Pearson Education statistics add-in. PHStat creates working worksheets and chart sheets that are identical to the ones featured in this book. This book features PHStat version 4, which is fully compatible with all current Microsoft Windows and (Mac) OS X versions of Microsoft Excel. (To learn more, see the Excel Guide in the "Big Things to Learn First" chapter.)

Student Purchasing Options

There are many ways for students to sign up for MyStatLab:

- Use the access kit bundled with a new textbook
- Purchase a stand-alone access kit from the bookstore
- Register online through **pearsonmylabandmastering.com**

PEARSON

A Roadmap for Selecting a Statistical Method

ata Analysis Task	For Numerical Variables	For Categorical Variables
escribing a group r several groups	Ordered array, stem-and-leaf display, frequency distribution, relative frequency distribution, percentage distribution, cumulative percentage distribution, histogram, polygon, cumulative percentage polygon **(Sections 2.2 2.4)** Mean, median, mode, geometric mean, quartiles, range, interquartile range, standard deviation, variance, coefficient of variation, skewness, kurtosis, boxplot, normal probability plot **(Sections 3.1, 3.2, 3.3, 6.3)** Index numbers **(bonus eBook Section 16.8)**	Summary table, bar chart, pie chart, Pareto chart **(Sections 2.1, 2.3)**
nference about one group	Confidence interval estimate of the mean **(Sections 8.1 and 8.2)** *t* test for the mean **(Section 9.2)** Chi-square test for a variance or standard deviation **(bonus eBook Section 12.7)**	Confidence interval estimate of the proportion **(Section 8.3)** *Z* test for the proportion **(Section 9.4)**
omparing two groups	Tests for the difference in the means of two independent populations **(Section 10.1)** Wilcoxon rank sum test **(Section 12.5)** Paired *t* test **(Section 10.2)** *F* test for the difference between two variances **(Section 10.4)**	*Z* test for the difference between two proportions **(Section 10.3)** Chi-square test for the difference between two proportions **(Section 12.1)** McNemar test for two related samples **(bonus eBook Section 12.6)**
omparing more han two groups	One-way analysis of variance for comparing several means **(Section 11.1)** Kruskal-Wallis test **(Section 12.6)** Two-way analysis of variance **(Section 11.2)** Randomized block design **(bonus eBook Section 11.3)**	Chi-square test for differences among more than two proportions **(Section 12.2)**
nalyzing the relationship etween two variables	Scatter plot, time series plot (**Section 2.5**) Covariance, coefficient of correlation **(Section 3.5)** Simple linear regression **(Chapter 13)** *t* test of correlation **(Section 13.7)** Time series forecasting **(Chapter 16)**	Contingency table, side-by-side bar chart, PivotTables **(Sections 2.1, 2.3, 2.8)** Chi-square test of independence **(Section 12.3)**
nalyzing the relationship etween two or more variables	Multiple regression **(Chapters 14 and 15)**	Multidimensional contingency tables **(Section 2.7)** PivotTables and business analytics **(Section 2.8)** Logistic regression **(Section 14.7)** Predictive analytics and data mining **(Section 15.6)**

Statistics for Managers

Using Microsoft Excel

SEVENTH EDITION

Statistics for Managers

Using Microsoft Excel

SEVENTH EDITION

David M. Levine

Department of Statistics and Computer Information Systems

Zicklin School of Business, Baruch College, City University of New York

David F. Stephan

Two Bridges Instructional Technology

Kathryn A. Szabat

Department of Business Systems and Analytics

School of Business, La Salle University

PEARSON

Boston Columbus Indianapolis New York San Francisco Upper Saddle River
Amsterdam Cape Town Dubai London Madrid Milan Munich Paris Montreal Toronto
Delhi Mexico City São Paulo Sydney Hong Kong Seoul Singapore Taipei Tokyo

Editor in Chief: Donna Battista
Editorial Project Manager: Mary Kate Murray
Editorial Assistant: Ashlee Bradbury
Director of Marketing: Maggie Moylan
Marketing Manager: Jami Minard
Senior Managing Editor: Judy Leale
Production Project Manager: Jane Bonnell
Operations Specialist: Cathleen Petersen
Creative Director: Blair Brown
Art Director: Steve Frim
Interior Designers: Dina Curro/Suzanne Behnke
Cover Designer: Black Horse Designs
Cover Image: 3DDock/Shutterstock
Cover Art: Spreadsheet: Electragraphics
Associate Media Project Manager, Editorial: Sarah Peterson
Media Producer: Christina Maestri
Media Project Manager, Production: John Cassar
Composition/Full-Service Project Management: PreMediaGlobal
Printer/Binder: Courier/Kendallville
Cover Printer: Lehigh-Phoenix Color/Hagerstown
Text Font: TimesNewRomanPS

Library of Congress Cataloging-in-Publication Data

Levine, David M.
Statistics for managers using Microsoft Excel / David M. Levine, David F. Stephan, Kathryn A. Szabat.—7th ed.
p. cm.
Rev. ed. of: Statistics for managers using Microsoft Excel / David M. Levine … [et al.]. 6th ed.
ISBN 978-0-13-306181-9 (hbk.)
1. Microsoft Excel (Computer file) 2. Management—Statistical methods. 3. Commercial statistics. 4. Electronic spreadsheets. 5. Management—Statistical methods—Computer programs. 6. Commercial statistics—Computer programs. I. Stephan, David. II. Szabat, Kathryn A. III. Statistics for managers using Microsoft Excel. IV. Title.
HD30.215.S73 2014
519.50285'554—dc23

2012043163

10 9 8 7 6 5 4 3 2 1

PEARSON

ISBN 10: 0-13-306181-7
ISBN 13: 978-0-13-306181-9

To our spouses and children,
Marilyn, Mary, Sharyn, and Mark,

and to our parents,
in loving memory, Lee, Reuben, Ruth, Francis, and William,
in honor, Mary

About the Authors

The authors of this book: Kathryn Szabat, David Levine, and David Stephan at a Decision Sciences Institute meeting.

David M. Levine is Professor Emeritus of Statistics and Computer Information Systems at Baruch College (City University of New York). He received B.B.A. and M.B.A. degrees in statistics from City College of New York and a Ph.D. from New York University in industrial engineering and operations research. He is nationally recognized as a leading innovator in statistics education and is the co-author of 14 books, including such best-selling statistics textbooks as *Statistics for Managers Using Microsoft Excel*, *Basic Business Statistics: Concepts and Applications*, *Business Statistics: A First Course*, and *Applied Statistics for Engineers and Scientists Using Microsoft Excel and Minitab*.

He also is the co-author of *Even You Can Learn Statistics: A Guide for Everyone Who Has Ever Been Afraid of Statistics*, currently in its second edition, *Six Sigma for Green Belts and Champions* and *Design for Six Sigma for Green Belts and Champions*, and the author of *Statistics for Six Sigma Green Belts*, all published by FT Press, a Pearson imprint, and *Quality Management*, third edition, McGraw-Hill/Irwin. He is also the author of *Video Review of Statistics* and *Video Review of Probability*, both published by Video Aided Instruction, and the statistics module of the MBA primer published by Cengage Learning. He has published articles in various journals, including *Psychometrika*, *The American Statistician*, *Communications in Statistics*, *Decision Sciences Journal of Innovative Education*, *Multivariate Behavioral Research*, *Journal of Systems Management*, *Quality Progress*, and *The American Anthropologist*, and he has given numerous talks at the Decision Sciences Institute (DSI), American Statistical Association (ASA), and Making Statistics More Effective in Schools and Business (MSMESB) conferences. Levine has also received several awards for outstanding teaching and curriculum development from Baruch College.

David F. Stephan is an independent instructional technologist. He was an Instructor/Lecturer of Computer Information Systems at Baruch College (City University of New York) for over 20 years and also served as an Assistant to the Provost and to the Dean of the School of Business & Public Administration for computing. He pioneered the use of computer classrooms for business teaching, devised interdisciplinary multimedia tools, and created techniques for teaching computer applications in a business context. He also conducted the first large-scale controlled experiment to show the benefit of teaching Microsoft Excel in a business case context to undergraduate students.

An avid developer, he created multimedia courseware while serving as the Assistant Director of a Fund for the Improvement of Postsecondary Education (FIPSE) project at Baruch College. Stephan is also the originator of PHStat, the Pearson Education statistical add-in for Microsoft Excel and a co-author of *Even You Can Learn Statistics: A Guide for Everyone Who Has Ever Been Afraid of Statistics* and *Practical Statistics by Example Using Microsoft Excel and Minitab*. He is currently developing ways to extend the instructional materials that he and his co-authors develop to mobile and cloud computing platforms as well as develop social-media facilitated means to support learning in introductory business statistics courses.

Stephan received a B.A. in geology from Franklin and Marshall College and a M.S. in computer methodology from Baruch College (City University of New York).

Kathryn A. Szabat is Associate Professor and Chair of Business Systems and Analytics at LaSalle University. She teaches undergraduate and graduate courses in business statistics and operations management. She also teaches as Visiting Professor at the Ecole Superieure de Commerce et de Management (ESCEM) in France.

Szabat's research has been published in *International Journal of Applied Decision Sciences, Accounting Education*, *Journal of Applied Business and Economics*, *Journal of Healthcare Management*, and *Journal of Management Studies*. Scholarly chapters have appeared in *Managing Adaptability, Intervention, and People in Enterprise Information Systems*; *Managing, Trade, Economies and International Business*; *Encyclopedia of Statistics in Behavioral Science*; and *Statistical Methods in Longitudinal Research*.

Szabat has provided statistical advice to numerous business, non-business, and academic communities. Her more recent involvement has been in the areas of education, medicine, and nonprofit capacity building.

Szabat received a B.S. in mathematics from State University of New York at Albany and M.S. and Ph.D. degrees in statistics, with a cognate in operations research, from the Wharton School of the University of Pennsylvania.

Brief Contents

Contents

Preface

Over a generation ago, advances in "data processing" led to new business opportunities as first centralized and then desktop computing proliferated. The Information Age was born. Computer science became much more than just an adjunct to a mathematics curriculum, and whole new fields of studies, such as computer information systems, emerged.

More recently, further advances in information technologies have combined with data analysis techniques to create new opportunities in what is more data *science* than data *processing* or *computer* science. The world of business statistics has grown larger, bumping into other disciplines. And, in a reprise of something that occurred a generation ago, new fields of study, this time with names such as informatics, data analytics, and decision science, have emerged.

This time of change makes what is taught in business statistics and how it is taught all the more critical. These new fields of study all share statistics as a foundation for further learning. We are accustomed to thinking about change, as seeking ways to continuously improve the teaching of business statistics have always guided our efforts. We actively participate in Decision Sciences Institute (DSI), American Statistical Association (ASA), and Making Statistics More Effective in Schools and Business (MSMESB) conferences. We use the ASA's Guidelines for Assessment and Instruction (GAISE) reports and combine them with our experiences teaching business statistics to a diverse student body at several large universities.

What to teach and how to teach it are particularly significant questions to ask during a time of change. As an author team, we bring a unique collection of experiences that we believe helps us find the proper perspective in balancing the old and the new. Our lead author, David M. Levine, was the first educator, along with Mark L. Berenson, to create a business statistics textbook that discussed using statistical software and incorporated "computer output" as illustrations—just the first of many teaching and curricular innovations in his many years of teaching business statistics. Our second author, David F. Stephan, developed courses and teaching methods in computer information systems and digital media during the information revolution, creating, and then teaching in, one of the first personal computer *classrooms* in a large school of business along the way. Early in his career, he introduced spreadsheet applications to a business statistics faculty audience that included David Levine, an introduction that eventually led to the first edition of this textbook. Our newest co-author, Kathryn A. Szabat, has provided statistical advice to various business and non-business communities. Her background in statistics and operations research and her experiences interacting with professionals in practice have guided her, as departmental chair, in developing a new, interdisciplinary academic department, Business Systems and Analytics, in response to the technology- and data-driven changes in business today.

All three of us benefit from our many years teaching undergraduate business subjects and the diversity of interests and efforts of our past co-authors, Mark Berenson and Timothy Krehbiel. We are pleased to offer the innovations and new content that are itemized starting on the next page. As in prior editions, we are guided by these key learning principles:

- Help students see the relevance of statistics to their own careers by providing examples drawn from the functional areas in which they may be specializing.
- Emphasize interpretation of statistical results over mathematical computation.
- Give students ample practice in understanding how to apply statistics to business.
- Familiarize students with how to use statistical software to assist business decision making.
- Provide clear instructions to students for using statistical applications.

Read more about these principles on page xxvii.

What's New and Innovative in This Edition?

This seventh edition of *Statistics for Managers Using Microsoft Excel* contains both new and innovative features and content, while refining and extending the use of the DCOVA (**D**efine, **C**ollect, **O**rganize, **V**isualize, and **A**nalyze) framework, first introduced in the sixth edition as an integrated approach for applying statistics to help solve business problems.

Innovations

Let's Get Started: Big Things to Learn First—In a time of change, you can never know exactly what knowledge and background students bring into an introductory business statistics classroom. Add that to the need to curb the fear factor about learning statistics that so many students begin with, and there's a lot to cover even before you teach your first statistical concept.

We created "Let's Get Started: Big Things to Learn First" to meet this challenge. This unit sets the context for explaining what statistics is (not what students may think!) while ensuring that all students share an understanding of the forces that make learning business statistics critically important today. Especially designed for instructors teaching with course management tools, including those teaching hybrid or online courses, "Let's Get Started" has been developed to be posted online or otherwise distributed before the first class section begins and is available from the download page for this book that is discussed in Appendix Section C.1.

Complete Microsoft Windows and OS X Excel-Based Solutions for Learning Business Statistics—Expanding on the contents of previous editions, this book features revised Excel Guides that address differences in current versions and features a new version of PHStat, the Pearson Education statistics add-in, that is simpler to set up and is compatible with both Microsoft Windows and OS X versions of Microsoft Excel. Using PHStat or the expanded set of Excel Guide workbooks that serve as models and templates for solutions gives students two distinct ways of incorporating Excel in their study of statistics. (See Section EG.2 on page 10 in the Excel Guide for "Let's Get Started: Big Things to Learn First" for complete details.)

Student Tips—In-margin notes reinforce hard-to-master concepts and provide quick study tips for mastering important details.

Discussion of Business Analytics—"Let's Get Started: Big Things to Learn First" quickly defines *business analytics* and *big data* and explains how these things are changing the face of statistics. Section 2.8, "PivotTables and Business Analytics," uses standard Microsoft Excel features to explain and illustrate descriptive analytics techniques. Section 14.7, "Logistic Regression," and Section 15.6, "Predictive Analytics and Data Mining," explain and illustrate predictive analytics concepts and techniques.

Digital Cases—In the Digital Cases, learners must examine interactive PDF documents to sift through various claims and information in order to discover the data most relevant to a business case scenario. Learners then determine whether the conclusions and claims are supported by the data. In doing so, learners discover and learn how to identify common misuses of statistical information. Many Digital Cases extend a chapter's Using Statistics scenario by posing additional questions and raising issues about the scenario.

Digital Cases appear at the end of all chapters and are the successors to the Web Cases found in previous editions. (Instructional tips for using the Digital Cases and solutions to the Digital Cases are included in the Instructor's Solutions Manual.)

Chapter—Short Takes Online electronic documents that are available for viewing or download supply additional insights or explanations to important statistical concepts or details about the worksheet-based solutions presented in this book.

Revised and Enhanced Content

New Continuing End-of-Chapter Cases—This seventh edition features several new end-of-chapter cases. Managing Ashland MultiComm Services is a new integrated case about a consumer-oriented telecommunications provider that appears throughout the book, replacing the *Springville Herald* case in the previous edition. New and recurring throughout the book is a case that concerns analysis of sales and marketing data for home fitness equipment (CardioGood Fitness), a case that concerns pricing decisions made by a retailer (Sure Value Convenience Stores), and the More Descriptive Choices Follow-Up case, which extends the use of the retirement funds sample first introduced in Chapter 2. Also recurring is the Clear Mountain State Student Surveys case, which uses data collected from surveys of undergraduate and graduate students to practice and reinforce statistical methods learned in various chapters. This case replaces end-of-chapter questions related to the student survey database in the previous edition. Joining the Mountain States Potato Company regression case of the previous edition are new cases in simple linear regression (Brynne Packaging) and multiple regression (The Craybill Instrumentation Company).

Many New Applied Examples and Problems—Many of the applied examples throughout this book use new problems or revised data. The ends-of-section and ends-of-chapter problem sets contain many new problems that use data from *The Wall Street Journal*, *USA Today*, and other sources.

Checklist for Getting Started to use Microsoft Excel with This Book—Part of the Excel Guide in "Let's Get Started: Big Things to Learn First," the checklist and related material explain for students which Excel skills they will need and where they will find information about those skills in the book.

Revised Appendices Keyed to the Getting-Started Microsoft Excel Checklist—The revised Appendix B discusses the Excel skills that readers need to make best use of the *In-Depth Excel* instructions in this book. The all-new Appendix F presents useful Excel knowledge, including a discussion of the new worksheet function names that were introduced in Excel 2010.

Enhanced Online Resources Appendix—Appendix C presents a complete summary of all the online resources for this book that are available for download. This appendix expands and replaces the sixth edition's Appendix F.

Enhanced Configuring Software Appendix—Primarily designed for readers who maintain their own computer systems, Appendix D helps readers to eliminates the common types of technical problems that could complicate their use of Microsoft Excel as they learn business statistics with this book.

Distinctive Features

We have continued many of the traditions of past editions and have highlighted some of these features below.

Using Statistics Business Scenarios—Each chapter begins with a Using Statistics example that shows how statistics is used in the functional areas of business—accounting, finance, information systems, management, and marketing. Each scenario is used throughout the chapter to provide an applied context for the concepts. The chapter concludes with a Using Statistics, Revisited section that reinforces the statistical methods and applications discussed in each chapter.

Emphasis on Data Analysis and Interpretation of Excel Worksheet Results—We believe that the use of computer software is an integral part of learning statistics. Our focus emphasizes analyzing data by interpreting results while reducing emphasis on doing computations. For example, in the coverage of tables and charts in Chapter 2, the focus is on the interpretation of various charts and on when to use each chart. In our coverage of hypothesis testing in Chapters 9 through 11, and regression and multiple regression in Chapters 12 and 13, extensive computer results have been included so that the *p*-value approach can be emphasized.

Pedagogical Aids—An active writing style is used, with boxed numbered equations, set-off examples to provide reinforcement for learning concepts, student tips, problems divided into "Learning the Basics" and "Applying the Concepts," key equations, and key terms.

Answers—Most answers to the even-numbered exercises are included at the end of the book.

Flexibility Using Excel—For almost every statistical method discussed, this book presents more than one way of using Excel. Students can use *In-Depth Excel* instructions to directly work with worksheet solution details *or* they can use either the *PHStat* instructions *or* the *Analysis ToolPak* instructions to automate the creation of those worksheet solutions.

Visual Explorations—The Excel add-in workbook allows students to interactively explore important statistical concepts in descriptive statistics, the normal distribution, sampling distributions, and regression analysis. For example, in descriptive statistics, students observe the effect of changes in the data on the mean, median, quartiles, and standard deviation. With the normal distribution, students see the effect of changes in the mean and standard deviation on the areas under the normal curve. In sampling distributions, students use simulation to explore the effect of sample size on a sampling distribution. In regression analysis, students have the opportunity to fit a line and observe how changes in the slope and intercept affect the goodness of fit.

Chapter-by-Chapter Changes Made for This Edition

Besides the new and innovative content described in "What's New and Innovative in This Edition?" the seventh edition of *Statistics for Managers Using Microsoft Excel* contains the following specific changes to each chapter. Highlights of the changes to the individual chapters are as follows.

Let's Get Started: Big Things to Learn First—This all-new chapter includes new material on business analytics and introduces the DCOVA framework and a basic vocabulary of statistics, both of which were introduced in Chapter 1 of the sixth edition.

Chapter 1—Measurement scales have been relocated to this chapter from Section 2.1. Collecting data, sampling methods, and types of survey errors have been relocated from Sections 7.1 and 7.2. There is a new subsection on data cleaning. The CardioGood Fitness and Clear Mountain State Surveys cases are included.

Chapter 2—Section 2.1, "Data Collection," has been moved to Chapter 1. The chapter uses a new data set that contains a sample of 318 mutual funds. There is a new section on PivotTables and business analytics that presents Excel slicers. The CardioGood Fitness, More Descriptive Choices Follow-up, and Clear Mountain State Surveys cases are included.

Chapter 3—For many examples, this chapter uses the new mutual funds data set that is introduced in Chapter 2. There is increased coverage of skewness and kurtosis. There is a new example on computing descriptive measures from a population using "Dogs of the Dow." The CardioGood Fitness, More Descriptive Choices Follow-up, and Clear Mountain State Surveys cases are included.

Chapter 4—The chapter example has been updated. There are new problems throughout the chapter. The CardioGood Fitness, More Descriptive Choices Follow-up, and Clear Mountain State Surveys cases are included.

Chapter 5—There is an additional example on applying probability distributions in finance, and there are many new problems throughout the chapter.

Chapter 6—This chapter has an updated Using Statistics scenario and some new problems. The CardioGood Fitness, More Descriptive Choices Follow-up, and Clear Mountain State Surveys cases are included.

Chapter 7—Sections 7.1 and 7.2 have been moved to Chapter 1.

Chapter 8—This chapter includes an updated Using Statistics scenario, additional problems on sigma known in Section 8.1, and new examples and exercises throughout the chapter. The Sure Value Convenience Stores, CardioGood Fitness, More Descriptive Choices Follow-up, and Clear Mountain State Surveys cases are included. The section "Applications of Confidence Interval Estimation in Auditing" has been moved online.

Chapter 9—This chapter includes additional coverage of the pitfalls of hypothesis testing. The Sure Value Convenience Stores case is included.

Chapter 10—This chapter has an updated Using Statistics scenario, increased coverage of the test for the difference between two means assuming unequal variances, and a new example on the paired *t*-test on textbook prices. The Sure Value Convenience Stores, CardioGood Fitness, More Descriptive Choices Follow-up, and Clear Mountain State Surveys cases are included.

Chapter 11—This chapter includes the Sure Value Convenience Stores, CardioGood Fitness, More Descriptive Choices Follow-up, and Clear Mountain State Surveys cases. It now includes an online section on fixed effects, random effects, and mixed effects models.

Chapter 12—The chapter includes many new problems. This chapter includes the Sure Value Convenience Stores, CardioGood Fitness, More Descriptive Choices Follow-up, and Clear Mountain State Surveys cases. The McNemar test is now an online section.

Chapter 13—The Using Statistics scenario has been updated and changed, with new data used throughout the chapter. This chapter includes the Sure Value Convenience Stores, CardioGood Fitness, More Descriptive Choices Follow-up, and Clear Mountain State Surveys cases.

Chapter 14—This chapter now includes a section on logistic regression.

Chapter 15—This chapter now includes a section on predictive analytics and data mining. This chapter includes the Sure Value Convenience Stores, Craybill Instrumentation, and More Descriptive Choices Follow-up cases.

Chapter 16—This chapter includes new data involving movie attendance in Section 16.3 and updated data for The Coca-Cola Company in Sections 16.4 through 16.6 and Wal-Mart Stores, Inc., in Section 16.7. In addition, most of the problems are new or updated.

Chapter 17—This chapter now includes some new problems.

About Our Educational Philosophy

In *Our Starting Point* at the beginning of this preface, we stated that we are guided by these key learning principles:

- Help students see the relevance of statistics to their own careers by providing examples drawn from the functional areas in which they may be specializing.
- Emphasize interpretation of statistical results over mathematical computation.
- Give students ample practice in understanding how to apply statistics to business.
- Familiarize students with how to use statistical software to assist business decision making.
- Provide clear instructions to students for using statistical applications.

The following further explains these principles:

1. **Help students see the relevance of statistics to their own careers by providing examples drawn from the functional areas in which they may be specializing.** Students need a frame of reference when learning statistics, especially when statistics is not their major. That frame of reference for business students should be the functional areas of business, such as accounting, finance, information systems, management, and marketing. Each statistics topic needs to be presented in an applied context related to at least one of these functional areas. The focus in teaching each topic should be on its application in business, the interpretation of results, the evaluation of the assumptions, and the discussion of what should be done if the assumptions are violated.
2. **Emphasize interpretation of statistical results over mathematical computation.** Introductory business statistics courses should recognize the growing need to *interpret* statistical results that computerized processes create. This makes the interpretation of results more important than knowing how to execute the tedious hand calculations required to produce them.
3. **Give students ample practice in understanding how to apply statistics to business.** Both classroom examples and homework exercises should involve actual or realistic data as much as possible. Students should work with data sets, both small and large, and be encouraged to look beyond the statistical analysis of data to the interpretation of results in a managerial context.
4. **Familiarize students with how to use statistical software to assist business decision making.** Introductory business statistics courses should recognize that programs with statistical functions are commonly found on a business decision maker's desktop computer. Integrating statistical software into all aspects of an introductory statistics course allows the course to focus on interpretation of results instead of computations (see point 2).
5. **Provide clear instructions to students for using statistical applications.** Books should explain clearly how to use programs such as Microsoft Excel with the study of statistics, without having those instructions dominate the book or distract from the learning of statistical concepts.

Student Resources

Student Solutions Manual—Written by Professor Pin Tian Ng of Northern Arizona University, this manual provides detailed solutions to virtually all the even-numbered exercises and worked-out solutions to the self-test problems. You can purchase this solutions manual by searching for ISBN 0-13-340129-4 at **www.mypearsonstore.com**. You can also purchase this manual at a reduced price when you buy the manual packaged with this book; search for ISBN 0-13-340764-0 at **www.mypearsonstore.com**.

Online resources—This book comes with a complete set of online resources that are discussed in detail in Appendix C. These resources include the **Excel Data Workbooks** that contain the data used in chapter examples or named in problems and end-of-chapter cases; the **Excel Guide Workbooks** that contain templates or model solutions for applying Excel to a particular statistical method; the **Digital Cases** PDF files that support the end-of-chapter Digital Cases; the **Visual Explorations Workbooks** that interactively demonstrate various key statistical concepts; and the **PHStat Files** that include the Microsoft Windows and (Mac) OS X Excel add-in workbook that simplifies the use of Microsoft Excel with this book, as explained in Section EG.2.

The online resources also include the **Chapter Short Takes** and **Bonus eBook Sections** that expand and extend the discussion of statistical concepts worksheet-based solutions as well as the full text of two bonus chapters, "Statistical Applications in Quality Management" and "Decision Making."

MyStatLab™

MyStatLab provides students with direct access to the online resources as well as the following exclusive online features and tools:

- **Interactive tutorial exercises.** A comprehensive set of exercises have been written especially for use with this book that are algorithmically generated for unlimited practice and mastery. Most exercises are free-response exercises and provide guided solutions, sample problems, and learning aids for extra help at point of use.
- **Personalized study plan.** A plan indicates which topics have been mastered and creates direct links to tutorial exercises for topics that have not been mastered. MyStatLab manages the study plan, updating its content based on the results of online assessments.
- **Pearson Tutor Center (www.pearsontutorservices.com).** The MyStatlab student access code grants access to this online resource, staffed by qualified instructors who provide book-specific tutoring via phone, fax, email, and interactive web sessions.
- **Integration with Pearson eTexts.** iPad users can download a free app at **www.apple.com/ipad/apps-for-ipad/** and then sign in using their MyStatLab account to access a bookshelf of all their Pearson eTexts. The iPad app also allows access to the Do Homework, Take a Test, and Study Plan pages of their MyStatLab course.
- **Mobile Dashboard.** This allows students to use their mobile devices to log in and review information from the dashboard of their courses: announcements, assignments, results, and progress bars for completed work. This app, available for iPhones, iPads, and Android devices, is designed to promote effective study habits rather than to allow students to complete assignments on their mobile devices.

@RISK trial Palisade Corporation, the maker of the market-leading risk and decision analysis Excel add-ins @RISK and the DecisionTools® Suite, provides special academic versions of its software to students (and faculty). Its flagship product, @RISK, debuted in 1987 and performs risk analysis using Monte Carlo simulation. To download a trial version of @RISK software, visit **www.palisade.com/academic/**.

Instructor Resources

Instructor's Resource Center—The Instructor's Resource Center contains the electronic files for the complete Instructor's Solutions Manual, the Test Item File, and PowerPoint lecture presentations (**www.pearsonhighered.com/levine**).

- **Register, Redeem, Login:** At www.pearsonhighered.com/irc, instructors can register to access a variety of print, media, and presentation resources that are available with this text in downloadable, digital format.
- **Need help?** Our dedicated technical support team is ready to assist instructors with questions about the media supplements that accompany this text. Visit http://247pearsoned.com/ for answers to frequently asked questions and toll-free user-support phone numbers.

The following supplements are among the resources available to adopting instructors at the Instructor's Resource Center.

- **Instructor's Solutions Manual.** Written by Professor Pin Tian Ng of Northern Arizona University and checked for accuracy by Annie Puciloski, this manual includes solutions for end-of-section and end-of-chapter problems, answers to case questions, where applicable, and teaching tips for each chapter. Instructors can order the printed solution manual by specifying the ISBN 0-13-306185-X. Electronic versions of the *Instructor's Solutions Manual* are available in both PDF and Microsoft Word (.docx) formats at the Instructor's Resource Center.

- **Lecture PowerPoint Presentations.** PowerPoint presentations, created by Professor Patrick Schur of Miami University and accuracy checked by Annie Puciloski, are available for each chapter. The PowerPoint slides provide an instructor with individual lecture outlines to accompany the text. The slides include many of the figures and tables from the text. Instructors can use these lecture notes as is or can easily modify the notes to reflect specific presentation needs.
- **Test Item File.** Created by Professor Pin Tian Ng of Northern Arizona University and checked for accuracy by Annie Puciloski, the downloadable Test Item File contains true/false, multiple-choice, fill-in, and problem-solving questions based on the definitions, concepts, and ideas developed in each chapter of the text.
- **TestGen.** Instructors can download TestGen, Pearson Education's test-generating software. The software is Microsoft Windows and (Mac) OS X compatible and preloaded with all of the Test Item File questions. You can manually or randomly view test questions and drag and drop to create a test. You can add or modify test-bank questions as needed.
- **Learning Management Systems.** Conversions of TestGens for use in BlackBoard and WebCT are available. Conversions to D2L or Angel can be requested through your local Pearson sales representative.

MathXL®

MathXL for Statistics—MathXL for Statistics is a powerful online homework, tutorial, and assessment system that accompanies Pearson Education statistics textbooks. With MathXL for Statistics, instructors can create, edit, and assign online homework and tests using algorithmically generated exercises correlated at the objective level to the textbook. They can also create and assign their own online exercises and import TestGen tests for added flexibility. All student work is tracked in MathXL's online grade book. Students can take chapter tests in MathXL and receive personalized study plans based on their test results. Each study plan diagnoses weaknesses and links the student directly to tutorial exercises for the objectives he or she needs to study and retest. Students can also access supplemental animations and video clips directly from selected exercises. MathXL for Statistics is available to qualified adopters. For more information, visit **www.mathxl.com** or contact your sales representative.

MyStatLab™

MyStatLab—Part of the MyMathLab and MathXL product family, MyStatLab is a text-specific, easily customizable online course that integrates interactive multimedia instruction with textbook content. MyStatLab gives you the tools you need to deliver all or a portion of your course online, whether your students are in a lab setting or working from home. The latest version of MyStatLab offers a new, intuitive design that features more direct access to MathXL for Statistics pages (Gradebook, Homework & Test Manager, Home Page Manager, etc.) and provides enhanced functionality for communicating with students and customizing courses. Other key features include:

- **Assessment manager.** An easy-to-use assessment manager lets instructors create online homework, quizzes, and tests that are automatically graded and correlated directly to your textbook. Assignments can be created using a mix of questions from the MyStatLab exercise bank, instructor-created custom exercises, and/or TestGen test items.
- **Grade book.** Designed specifically for mathematics and statistics, the MyStatLab grade book automatically tracks students' results and gives you control over how to calculate final grades. You can also add offline (paper-and-pencil) grades to the grade book.
- **MathXL Exercise Builder.** You can use the MathXL Exercise Builder to create static and algorithmic exercises for your online assignments. A library of sample exercises provides an easy starting point for creating questions, and you can also create questions from scratch.
- **eText-MathXL for Statistics Full Integration.** Students using appropriate mobile devices can use your eText annotations and highlights for each course, and iPad users can download a free app that allows them access to the Do Homework, Take a Test, and Study Plan pages of their course.
- **"Ask the Publisher" Link in "Ask My Instructor" Email.** You can easily notify the content team of any irregularities with specific questions by using the "Ask the Publisher" functionality in the "Ask My Instructor" emails you receive from students.
- **Tracking Time Spent on Media.** Because the latest version of MyStatLab requires students to explicitly click a "Submit" button after viewing the media for their assignments, you will be able to track how long students are spending on each media file.

Acknowledgments

We are extremely grateful to the RAND Corporation and the American Society for Testing and Materials for their kind permission to publish various tables in Appendix E, and to the American Statistical Association for its permission to publish diagrams from the *American Statistician*.

A Note of Thanks

We would like to thank William Borders, Troy University; Ozgun C. Demirag, Pennsylvania State University; Annette Gourgey, Baruch College; Hyokyoung Hong, Baruch College; Min Li, California State University; Robert Loomis, Florida Institute of Technology; Mahmood Shandiz, Oklahoma City University; Joe Sullivan, Mississippi State University; Rene Villano, University of New England; and Rongning Wu, Baruch College, for their comments, which have made this a better book.

We would especially like to thank Chuck Synovec, Mary Kate Murray, Ashlee Bradbury, Donna Battista, Judy Leale, Anne Fahlgren, and Jane Bonnell of the editorial, marketing, and production teams at Pearson Education. We would like to thank our statistical reader and accuracy checker Annie Puciloski for her diligence in checking our work; Kitty Wilson for her copy editing; Martha Ghent for her proofreading; and Tammy Haskins of PreMediaGlobal for her outstanding work in the production of this book.

Finally, we would like to thank our families for their patience, understanding, love, and assistance in making this book a reality. It is to them that we dedicate this book.

Concluding Remarks

Please email us at **authors@davidlevinestatistics.com** if you have a question or require clarification about something discussed in this book. We also invite you to communicate any suggestions you may have for a future edition of this book. And while we have strived to make this book both pedagogically sound and error-free, we encourage you to contact us if you discover an error. When contacting us electronically, please include "SMUME edition 7" in the subject line of your message.

You can also visit **davidlevinestatistics.com**, where you will find an email contact form and links to additional information about this book. For technical assistance using Microsoft Excel or any of the add-ins that you can use with this book including PHStat, review Appendices D and G and follow the technical support links discussed in Appendix Section G.1, if necessary.

David M. Levine

David F. Stephan

Kathryn A. Szabat

Statistics for Managers

Using Microsoft Excel

SEVENTH EDITION

LET'S GET STARTED

Big Things to Learn First

Learning Objectives

In this chapter, you learn:

- That the volume of data that exists in the world makes learning about statistics critically important
- That statistics is a way of thinking that can help you make better decisions
- What business analytics is and how these techniques represent an opportunity for you
- How the DCOVA framework for applying statistics can help you solve business problems
- How to make best use of this book
- How to prepare for using Microsoft Excel with this book

Mclek / Shutterstock

USING STATISTICS

"You Cannot Escape from Data"

Not so long ago, business students were unfamiliar with the word *data* and had little experience handling data. Today, every time you visit a search engine website or "ask" your mobile device a question, you are handling data. And if you "check in" to a location, indicate that you "like" something, or otherwise share your preferences and opinions, you are creating data as well.

You accept as almost true the premises of movies, TV series, or novels in which characters collect "a lot of data" to uncover conspiracies, to foretell disasters, or to catch a criminal. You hear concerns about how the government or business might be able to "spy" on you in some ways or how large social media companies "mine" your personal data for profit.

You hear the word *data* everywhere and may even have bought a "data plan" for your smartphone. You know, in a general way, that data are facts about the world and that most data seem to be, ultimately, a set of numbers—that 49% of students recently polled dreaded taking a business statistics course, or that 50% of citizens believe the country is headed in the right direction, or that unemployment is down 3%, or that your best friend's social media account has 835 friends and 202 recent posts that you have not read.

You cannot escape from data in this digital world. What, then, should you do? You could try to ignore data and conduct business by relying on hunches or your "gut feelings." While hunches may sometimes pay off, that's a very different process than the rational process that your business courses are trying to teach you so that you can become a better decision maker. If you only want to use gut feelings, then you probably shouldn't be reading this book or taking business courses in the first place.

You could note that there is so much data in the world—or just in your own little part of the world, that you couldn't possibly get a handle on it. You could avoid thinking about that much data or use other people's summaries of data instead of having to review the data. For example, you could turn over your money to an investment company and only pay attention to how much "richer" you are becoming because of the wonderful and consistent rates of return that your money generates every year. (Read the SHORT TAKES for Let's Get Started to learn a reason for avoiding such a choice.)

Or, you could do things the proper way and realize that you cannot escape learning the methods of statistics, the subject of this book …

Angela Waye / Shutterstock

You've probably done some statistics in the past. Have you ever created a chart to summarize data or calculated values such as averages to summarize data? There's even more to statistics than these commonly taught techniques as the detailed table of contents for this book reveals.

Even if you completed an entire statistics course in the recent past, are you properly prepared for the future? Are you aware of how continuing advances in information technology have shaped statistics in the modern age? Are you familiar with the newer ways of visualizing data that either did not exist, were not practical to do, or were not widely known until recently? Do you understand that statistics today can be used to "listen" to what the data might be telling you rather than just being a way to prove something about what you want the data to say?

And, perhaps most importantly, do you have experience working with new techniques that combine statistics with other business disciplines to enhance decision making? In particular, are you knowledgeable about **business analytics**? This emerging field makes "extensive use of data, statistical and quantitative analysis, explanatory and predictive models, and fact-based management to drive decisions and actions" (see reference 2).

Because you cannot escape these changes, you cannot escape using software that makes these changes possible. This book uses Microsoft Excel to demonstrate how people in business apply statistics in order to make better decisions. You will quickly learn that you need not worry about doing a lot of mathematical calculations when learning statistics. The software does the calculations for you and generally does it better than you could ever hope to do. So, if you "knew" that statistics is just a type of mathematics, you have already learned that you were mistaken. So what is statistics? Read on.

LGS.1 A Way of Thinking

Statistics is a way of thinking that can help you make better decisions. Statistics helps you solve problems that involve decisions that are based on data that have been collected. To apply statistics properly, you need to follow a framework, or plan, to minimize possible errors of thinking and analysis. The **DCOVA framework** is one such framework.

THE DCOVA FRAMEWORK

The DCOVA framework consists of these tasks:

- **Define** the data that you want to study in order to solve a problem or meet an objective.
- **Collect** the data from appropriate sources.
- **Organize** the data collected by developing tables.
- **Visualize** the data collected by developing charts.
- **Analyze** the data collected to reach conclusions and present those results.

The DCOVA framework uses the five tasks **D**efine, **C**ollect, **O**rganize, **V**isualize, and **A**nalyze to help apply statistics to business decision making. Typically, you do the tasks in the order listed. You must always do the first two tasks to have meaningful outcomes, but in practice, the order of the other three can change or appear inseparable. Certain ways of visualizing data help you to organize your data while performing preliminary analysis as well. In any case, when you apply statistics to decision making, you should be able to identify all five tasks, and you should verify that you have done the first two tasks before the other three.

Using the DCOVA framework helps you to apply statistics to these four broad categories of business activities:

- Summarize and visualize business data
- Reach conclusions from those data
- Make reliable forecasts about business activities
- Improve business processes

Throughout this book, and especially in the Using Statistics scenarios that begin the chapters, you will discover specific examples of how DCOVA helps you apply statistics. For example, in one chapter, you will learn how to demonstrate whether a marketing campaign has increased sales of a product, while in another you will learn how a television station can reduce unnecessary labor expenses.

LGS.2 Define Your Terms!

The **D** task in the DCOVA framework—**Define** the data that you want to study in order to solve a problem or meet an objective—initially sounds easy. But defining means communicating a meaning to others, and many analyses have been ruined by not having all those involved share the same understanding of the definition. For example, the word *data* has been already informally defined as "facts about the world"—and while that definition is true, it lacks clarity. The word *data* needs an **operational definition**, a clear and precise statement that provides a common understanding of meaning.

For example, one operational definition of **data** could be "the values associated with a trait or property that help distinguish the occurrences of something." For example, the names "David Levine" and "Kathryn Szabat" are data because they are both values that help distinguish one of the authors of this book from another. In this book, *data* is always plural to remind you that data is a collection, or set, of value*s*. While one could say that a single value, such as "David Levine," is a *datum*, the phrases *data point*, *observation*, *response*, and *single data value* are more typically encountered.

Sometimes creating an operational definition requires thought and consideration of related concepts and leads to further refinement of the original definition. The definition of *data* talks about "a trait or property." So we might ask, "What word can be used to describe 'a trait or property of something'?" In this book, that word is **variable**. By substituting the word *characteristic* for the phrase "trait or property that helps distinguish" and substituting "an item or individual" for the word *something* produces the operational definitions of variable and data used in this book.

Student Tip
Business convention places the data, the *set* of values, for a variable in a column when using a worksheet or similar object. The Excel data worksheet examples in this book follow this convention (see Section EG.5 on page 13). Because of this convention, people sometimes use the word *column* as a substitute for *variable*.

VARIABLE
A characteristic of an item or individual.

DATA
The set of individual values associated with a variable.

Think about characteristics that distinguish individuals in a human population. Name, height, weight, eye color, marital status, adjusted gross income, and place of residence are all characteristics of an individual. All of these traits are possible *variables* that describe people.

Defining a variable called author-name to be the first and last names of the authors of this text makes it clear that valid values would be "David Levine," "David Stephan," and "Kathryn Szabat" and not, say, "Levine," "Stephan," and "Szabat." Be careful of cultural or other assumptions in definitions—for example, is "last name" a family name, as is common usage in North America, or an individual's own unique name, as is common usage in most Asian countries?

Having defined *data* and *variable*, you can create an operational definition for the subject of this book, **statistics**.

STATISTICS
The methods that help transform data into useful information for decision makers.

Statistics allows you to determine whether your data represent information that could be used in making better decisions. Therefore, statistics helps you determine whether differences in the numbers are meaningful in a significant way or are due to chance. To illustrate, consider the following news reports about various data findings:

- **"Acceptable Online Ad Length Before Seeing Free Content" (*USA Today*, February 16, 2012, p. 1B)** A survey of 1,179 adults 18 and over reported that 54% thought that 15 seconds was an acceptable online ad length before seeing free content.
- **"First Two Years of College Wasted?" (M. Marklein, *USA Today*, January 18, 2011, p. 3A)** A survey of more than 3,000 full-time traditional-age students found that the students spent 51% of their time on socializing, recreation, and other activities; 9% of their time attending class/lab; and 7% of their time studying.
- **"Follow the Tweets" (H. Rui, A. Whinston, and E. Winkler, *The Wall Street Journal*, November 30, 2009, p. R4)** In this study, the authors found that the number of times a specific product was mentioned in comments in the Twitter social messaging service could be used to make accurate predictions of sales trends for that product.

Without statistics, you cannot determine whether the "numbers" in these stories represent useful information. Without statistics, you cannot validate claims such as the claim that the number of tweets can be used to predict the sales of certain products. And without statistics, you cannot see patterns that large amounts of data sometimes reveal.

When talking about statistics, you use the term **descriptive statistics** to refer to methods that primarily help summarize and present data. Counting physical objects in a kindergarten class may have been the first time you used a *descriptive* method. You use the term **inferential statistics** to refer to methods that use data collected from a small group to reach conclusions about a larger group. If you had formal statistics instruction in a lower grade, you were probably mostly taught descriptive methods, the focus of the early chapters of this book, and you may be unfamiliar with many of the inferential methods discussed in later chapters.

LGS.3 Business Analytics: The Changing Face of Statistics

As noted in the Using Statistics scenario that opens this chapter, statistics has witnessed the increasing use of new techniques that either did not exist, were not practical to do, or were not widely known in the past. Of all these new techniques, business analytics best represents the changing face of statistics. These methods combine "traditional" statistical methods with methods and techniques from management science and information systems to form an interdisciplinary tool that supports fact-based management decision making. Business analytics enables you to

- Use statistical methods to analyze and explore data to uncover unforeseen relationships.
- Use management science methods to develop optimization models that impact an organization's strategy, planning, and operations.
- Use information systems methods to collect and process data sets of all sizes, including very large data sets that would otherwise be hard to examine efficiently.

Business analytics allows you to interpret data, reach conclusions, and make decisions and, in doing that, it combines many of the tasks of the DCOVA framework into one integrated process. And because you apply business analytics in the context of *organizational* decision making and problem solving (see reference 9), successful application of business analytics requires an understanding of a business and its operations.

Business analytics has already been applied in many business decision-making contexts. Human resource (HR) managers use analytics to understand relationships between

HR drivers and key business outcomes, as well as how employee skills, capabilities, and motivation impact those outcomes. Financial analysts use analytics to determine why certain trends occur so they can predict what the financial environments will be like in the future. Marketers use analytics and customer intelligence to drive loyalty programs and customer marketing decisions. Supply chain managers use analytics to plan and forecast based on product distribution and optimize sales distribution based on key inventory measures.

Going forward, business analytics will continue to be used to help answer the basic questions that help frame the decision-making process: What happened? How many, how often, and where? What exactly is the problem? What actions are needed? What could happen? What if these trends continue? What will happen next? How can we achieve the best outcome? How can we achieve the best outcome, including the effects of variability? (See reference 5.)

"Big Data"

Relatively recent advances in information technology allow businesses to collect, process, and analyze very large volumes of data. Because the operational definition of "very large" can be partially dependent on the context of a business—what might be "very large" for a sole proprietorship might be commonplace and small for a multinational corporation—many use the term **big data**.

Big data is more of a fuzzy concept than a term with a precise operational definition, but it implies data that are being collected in huge volumes and at very fast rates (typically in real-time) and data that arrive in a variety of forms, organized and unorganized. These attributes of "volume, velocity, and variety," first identified in 2001 (see reference 7), make big data different from any of the data sets used in this book.

Big data spurs the use of business analytics because the sheer size of these very large data sets makes preliminary exploration of the data using older techniques impractical to do. While examples of business analytics frequently use big data, such as a mass retailer figuring out how to deduce which of its shoppers are most likely pregnant (see reference 4), you should remember that the techniques of business analytics can be used on small sets of data, too, as Section 2.8 demonstrates.

Statistics: An Important Part of Your Business Education

As business analytics becomes increasingly important in business, and especially as the use of big data increases, statistics, an essential component of business analytics, becomes increasingly important to your business education. In the current data-driven environment of business, you need general analytical skills that allow you to manipulate data, interpret analytical results, and incorporate results in a variety of decision-making applications, such as accounting, finance, HR management, marketing, strategy/planning, and supply chain management.

The decisions you make will be increasingly based on data and not on gut or intuition supported by personal experience. Data-guided practice is proving to be successful; studies have shown an increase in productivity, innovation, and competition for organizations that embrace business analytics. The use of data and data analysis to drive business decisions cannot be ignored. Having a well-balanced mix of technical skills—such as statistics, modeling, and basic information technology skills—and managerial skills—such as business acumen, problem-solving skills, and communication skills—will best prepare you for today's, and tomorrow's, workplace (see reference 1).

If you thought that you could artificially separate statistics from other business subjects, take a statistics course, and then forget about statistics, you have overlooked the changing face of statistics. The changing face is the reason that Hal Varian, the chief economist at Google, Inc., noted as early as 2009, "the sexy job in the next 10 years will be statisticians. And I'm not kidding" (see references 10 and 11).

LGS.4 How to Use This Book

This book helps you develop the skills necessary to use the DCOVA framework to apply statistics to the four broad categories of business activities listed on page 4. Chapter 1 discusses the **D**efine and **C**ollect tasks of the DCOVA framework, the necessary starting point for all statistical activities. The **O**rganize, **V**isualize, and **A**nalyze tasks are threaded throughout the remaining chapters of the book. Chapters 2 and 3 present methods that summarize and visualize business data (the first activity listed in Section LGS.1). Chapters 4 through 12 discuss methods that use sample data to reach conclusions about populations (the second activity listed). Chapters 13 through 16 review methods to make reliable forecasts (the third activity), and the online-only Chapter 18 introduces methods that you can use to improve business processes (the fourth activity).

Each chapter begins with a Using Statistics scenario that places you in a realistic business situation. You will face problems that the specific statistical concepts and methods introduced in the chapter will help solve. Later, near the end of the chapter, a Using Statistics Revisited section reviews how the statistical methods discussed in the chapter can be applied to help solve the problems you faced.

Each chapter ends with a variety of features that help you review what you have learned in the chapter. Summary, Key Equations, and Key Terms concisely present the important points of a chapter. Checking Your Understanding tests your understanding of basic concepts, and Chapter Review Problems allow you to practice what you have learned.

Throughout this book, you will find Excel worksheets that show solutions to example problems and that are available for download to use as templates or models for other problems. You will also find many *Student Tips*, margin notes that help clarify and reinforce significant details about particular statistical concepts. Selected chapters include Visual Explorations features that allow you to interactively explore statistical concepts. And many chapters include a Think About This essay that explains important statistical concepts in further depth.

This book contains a number of case studies that ask you to apply what you have learned in a chapter as well as giving you an opportunity to enhance your analytic and communication skills. Appearing in most chapters is the continuing case study *Managing Ashland MultiComm Services* that details problems managers of a residential telecommunications provider face and a Digital Case, which asks you to examine a variety of electronic documents and then apply your statistical knowledge to resolve problems or address issues raised by these cases. Besides these two cases, you will find a number of other cases, including some that reoccur in several chapters, in this book.

Excel Guides

Immediately following each chapter is an Excel Guide. For this chapter, a special Excel Guide explains how the guides have been designed to support your own learning in two distinct but complementary ways and helps prepare you for using Microsoft Excel with this book. You should fully review this Excel Guide, even if you are an experienced Excel user, to ensure that you understand how this book teaches and uses Excel.

In later chapters, the Excel Guides are keyed to the in-chapter section numbers and present detailed Excel instructions for performing the statistical methods discussed in chapter sections. Most Excel Guide sections begin by identifying the key Excel technique to be used for a statistical method and then state an example that is used as the basis for the detailed instructions.

Don't worry if your instructor does not cover every section of every chapter. Introductory business statistics courses vary in terms of scope, length, and number of college credits earned. Your chosen functional area of specialization (accounting, management, finance, marketing, etc.) may also affect what you learn in class or what you are assigned to read in this book.

REFERENCES

1. Advani, D. "Preparing Students for the Jobs of the Future." *University Business* (2011), **www.universitybusiness.com/article/preparing-students-jobs-future**.
2. Davenport, T., and J. Harris. *Competing on Analytics: The New Science of Winning*. Boston: Harvard Business School Press, 2007.
3. Davenport, T., J. Harris, and R. Morison. *Analytics at Work*. Boston: Harvard Business School Press, 2010.
4. Duhigg, C. "How Companies Learn Your Secrets." *The New York Times*, February 16, 2012, **www.nytimes.com/2012/02/19/magazine/shopping-habits.html**
5. Greenland, A. "The Analytics Landscape." PowerPoint slide show presented at "Leveraging Analytics in Government," Washington, DC, September 16, 2010.
6. Keeling, K., and R. Pavur. "Statistical Accuracy of Spreadsheet Software." *The American Statistician* 65 (2011): 265–273.
7. Laney, D. *3D Data Management: Controlling Data Volume, Velocity, and Variety*. Stamford, CT: META Group. February 6, 2001.
8. Levine, D., and D. Stephan. "Teaching Introductory Business Statistics Using the DCOVA Framework." *Decision Sciences Journal of Innovative Education* 9 (September 2011): 393–398.
9. Liberatore, M. and W. Luo. "The Analytics Movement." *Interfaces* 40 (2010): 313–324.
10. Varian, H. "For Today's Graduate: Just One Word: Statistics." *The New York Times*, August 6, 2009, retrieved from **www.nytimes.com/2009/08/06/technology/06stats.html**.
11. Varian, H. "Hal Varian and the Sexy Profession." *Significance*, March 2011.

KEY TERMS

EXCEL GUIDE

EG.1 WHAT is MICROSOFT EXCEL?

Microsoft Excel is the primary data analysis application of the Microsoft Office suite of programs. Excel evolved from earlier electronic spreadsheets that were first applied to accounting and financial tasks. Excel uses worksheets (sometimes called spreadsheets) to both store data and present the results of analyses. A **worksheet** is a tabular arrangement of data in which the intersections of rows and columns form **cells**, boxes into which you make entries. As noted previously, the data for each variable are placed in separate columns, following standard business practice. Generally, to perform statistical analysis, you use one or more columns of data and then apply the appropriate commands.

Excel saves files that it calls workbooks. A **workbook** is a collection of worksheets and chart sheets, so called because they present charts separately from the worksheet data on which they are based. You save a workbook when you save "an Excel file," typically using either the **.xlsx** or **.xls** file format.

EG.2 HOW CAN I USE EXCEL with this BOOK?

The In-Depth Excel instructions and the Excel Guide workbooks have been developed to work best with the latest versions of Microsoft Excel, including Excel 2010 and Excel 2013 (Microsoft Windows) and Excel 2011 (OS X). Where incompatibilities arise with older versions such as Excel 2007, the incompatibilities are noted in the instructions and alternative worksheets are provided for use as discussed in Appendix Section F.3.

Excel Guides also contain instructions for using the Analysis ToolPak add-in that is included with some Microsoft Excel versions. Because you can use the ToolPak for only a few statistical methods, these instructions appear infrequently throughout the Excel Guides.

You use Excel to learn and apply the statistical methods discussed in this book and as an aid in solving end-of-section and end-of-chapter problems. How you use Excel is up to you (or perhaps your instructor), and the Excel Guides give you two complementary ways to use Excel.

If you are focused more on the results than on the Excel techniques to get those results, if you are in a hurry to get Excel results, or if you want to avoid the time-consuming task of entering and editing all the individual cell entries for a worksheet, consider using PHStat. PHStat, available free for users of this book, is an example of an add-in, an application that extends the functionality of Microsoft Excel. PHStat simplifies the task of operating Excel while creating *real* Excel worksheets that use in-worksheet calculations. With PHStat, you can create worksheets that are identical to the ones featured in this book while avoiding the tedium of—and potential errors associated with—having to create entries for all the cells in a worksheet. (In contrast, most other add-ins create results that are mostly text pasted into an empty worksheet. (To learn more about PHStat, see Appendices D and G.)

For many topics, you may choose to use the *In-Depth Excel* way of using Excel. Most *In-Depth Excel* instructions use pre-constructed worksheets as models or **templates** for a statistical solution. You learn how to make slight changes to the data or structure of a worksheet to construct your own solutions. Many of these sections feature a specific *Excel Guide workbook* that contain worksheets that are, for the most part, *identical* to the worksheets that PHStat creates. If you want to mimic the standard business practice of opening and using predefined worksheet solutions, you should use this way.

Because both of these ways create the same results and the same worksheets, you can use a combination of both ways as you read through this book. You can examine Excel in depth when you want to (or when your instructor asks you!), and you can also create results in a hurry during those parts of your semester in which your available free time is in short supply.

EG.3 WHAT EXCEL SKILLS DOES this BOOK REQUIRE?

From the title of this book, you can guess that you may be "using Microsoft Excel" as you study statistics, but to do that, you will not need to be a Microsoft Excel "expert." This book contains plenty of examples from which you can learn (and copy) and plenty of worked-out Excel solutions that you can use as the basis for your own work. (Modifying an existing solution is much easier than building a solution from scratch, and it also mimics real-world use of Excel.)

There are some basic skills that you will need to master in order to use the Excel instructions, and they are listed in Table EG.A. If you have not mastered the table's "basic computing skills," then read the eBook bonus section "Basic Computing Skills." (Appendix C explains how you can download a copy of this and other eBook bonus sections.) To learn or review the basic Microsoft Office skills listed in the table, read the later sections of this Excel Guide.

TABLE EG.A

Required Basic Skills

Basic Computing Skills	**Specifics**
Identification of Excel application window objects	Title bar, minimize/resize/close buttons, scroll bars, formula bar, workbook area, cell pointer, shortcut menu, and these Ribbon parts: tab, group, gallery and launcher button
Knowledge of mouse operations	Click (also called select), check and clear, double-click, right-click, drag/drag-and-drop
Identification of dialog box objects	Command button, list box, drop-down list, edit box, option button, check box
Basic Microsoft Office Skills	**Specifics**
Excel data entry	Organizing worksheet data in columns, entering numerical and categorical data
File operations	Open, save, print
Worksheet operations	Create, copy

You will want to master the Table EG.A basic skills before you begin using Excel to understand statistical concepts and solve problems. Whether you need to learn more than these basic skills depends on whether you plan to use *In-Depth Excel* or *PHStat* instructions, the two different ways of using Microsoft Excel with this book (see Section EG.2). If you plan to use the *In-Depth Excel* instructions, you will need to master the skills listed in Table EG.B as well. While you do not necessarily need these skills if you plan to use PHStat, knowing them will be useful if you expect to customize the Excel worksheets that PHStat creates or if you anticipate using Excel in later courses or in the workplace.

TABLE EG.B

Required Skills for Using *In-Depth Excel* Instructions

Skill	**Specifics**
Formula skills	Concept of a formula, cell references, absolute and relative cell references, how to enter a formula, how to enter an array formula
Workbook presentation	How to apply format changes that affect the display of worksheet cell contents
Chart formatting correction	How to correct the formatting of charts that Excel improperly creates
Discrete histogram creation	How to create a properly formatted histogram for a discrete probability distribution

Appendix B teaches you the skills listed in Table EG.B. If you start by studying Sections B.1 through B.4 of that appendix, you will have the skills you need to make effective use of the *In-Depth Excel* instructions when you first encounter them in Chapter 1. (You can read other sections in Appendix B as needed.)

If you have absolutely no experience using Microsoft Excel, or if you took a prerequisite course that taught you little about Excel or left you very confused, *don't panic*! You can read *Don't Panic: You Can Quickly Learn Microsoft Excel*. This free eBook bonus section, by the authors of the *Even You Can Learn Statistics* series, helps you get started learning the skills listed in Table EG.A. (Appendix C explains how you can download a copy of this bonus section.)

If you want to learn additional skills that can be helpful when using Microsoft Excel, read Appendix Sections F.1 and F2. This appendix also explains differences between the older and newer worksheet function names and describes the non-statistical functions used in this book.

EG.4 GETTING READY to USE EXCEL with this BOOK

To minimize problems that you may face later, review and complete the Table EG.C checklist as your first step in getting ready to use Microsoft Excel with this book.

TABLE EG.C

Checklist for Getting Ready to Use Excel with This Book

- ❑ Determine how you will use Microsoft Excel with this book (see Section EG.2).
- ❑ Verify your knowledge of the required basic skills. Read and review any necessary material discussed in Section EG.3, if necessary.
- ❑ Read Appendix C to learn about the online resources you need to make best use of this book. Appendix C includes a complete list of the Excel data workbooks that are used in the examples and problems found in this book. Names of Excel data workbooks appear in this distinctive type face—**Retirement Funds**—throughout this book.
- ❑ Download the online resources that you will need to use this book, using the instructions in Appendix C.
- ❑ Use the Appendix Section D.1 instructions to update Microsoft Excel.
- ❑ If you plan to use PHStat, the Visual Explorations add-in workbooks, or the Analysis ToolPak and maintain your own computer system, read the special instructions in Appendix D.
- ❑ Examine Appendix G to learn answers to frequently asked questions (FAQs)

Computing Conventions Used in This Book

The Excel instructions in this book use the conventions presented in Table EG.D to describe common keyboard and mouse pointer operations.

TABLE EG.D

Computing Conventions Used in This Book

Operation and Examples	Notes
Keyboard keys **Enter Ctrl Shift**	Names of keys are always the object of the verb *press*, as in "press **Enter**."
Keystroke combinations **Ctrl+C** **Ctrl+Shift+Enter** **Command+Enter**	Keyboarding actions that require you to press more than one key at the same time. **Ctrl+C** means press **C** while holding down **Ctrl. Ctrl+Shift+Enter** means press **Enter** while holding down both **Ctrl** and **Shift**.
Click or select operations click **OK** select the **first 2-D Bar** gallery item	Mouse pointer actions that require you to single click an onscreen object. Book uses the verb *select* when the object is either a worksheet cell or an item in a gallery, menu, list, or Ribbon tab.
Menu or ribbon selection **File → New** **Layout → Legend → None**	A sequence of Ribbon or menu selections. **File → New** means first select the **File** tab and then select **New** from the list that appears.
Placeholder object ***variable 1 cell range*** ***bins cell range***	An italicized boldfaced phrase is a placeholder for an object reference. In making entries, you enter the reference, e.g., **A1:A10,** and not the placeholder.

EG.5 ENTERING DATA

As first noted on page 6, you place the data for a variable in a worksheet column. By convention, and the style used in this book, when you enter data for a set of variables, you enter the name of each variable into the cells of the first row, beginning with column A. Then you enter the data for the variable in the subsequent rows to create a DATA worksheet similar to the one shown in Figure EG.1.

FIGURE EG.1
An example of a data worksheet

	A	B	C	D	E	F	G	H	I	J	K	L
1	**Fund Number**	**Market Cap**	**Type**	**Assets**	**Turnover Ratio**	**Beta**	**SD**	**Risk**	**1YrReturn%**	**3YrReturn%**	**5YrReturn%**	**10YrReturn%**
2	RF001	Large	Growth	15.00	0.00	2.17	42.42	High	13.88	62.91	-3.12	-2.30
3	RF002	Large	Growth	106.50	34.00	2.05	39.98	High	10.49	54.79	3.25	-0.73
4	RF003	Large	Growth	144.50	76.00	2.05	40.09	High	10.10	54.75	3.33	-0.61
5	RF004	Large	Growth	73.60	11.49	1.10	21.81	Average	13.72	38.84	1.73	6.71

To enter data in a specific cell, either use the cursor keys to move the cell pointer to the cell or use your mouse to select the cell directly. As you type, what you type appears in the formula bar. Complete your data entry by pressing **Tab** or **Enter** or by clicking the checkmark button in the formula bar.

When you enter data, never skip any rows in a column, and as a general rule, also avoid skipping any columns. Also refrain from using row 1 variable headings that could be mistaken for numerical data; if you cannot avoid their use, precede those values with apostrophes. Pay attention to any special instructions that occur throughout the book for the order of the entry of your data. For some statistical methods, entering your data in an order that Excel does not expect will lead to incorrect results.

Most of the Excel data workbooks that you can download and use with this book (see Appendix C) contain a DATA worksheet that follows the rules of this section. You can consult any of those worksheets as an additional model for how to enter data in an Excel worksheet.

EG.6 OPENING and SAVING WORKBOOKS

You open and save a workbook by first selecting the folder that stores the workbook and then specifying the file name of the workbook. In most Excel versions, you select **File → Open** to open a workbook file and **File → Save As** to save a workbook. In Excel 2007, you select **Office Button → Open** to open a workbook file and **Office Button → Save As** to save a workbook. **Open** and **Save As** display nearly identical dialog boxes that vary only slightly among the different Excel versions. Figure EG.2 shows the Excel 2010 Open and Save As dialog boxes. (To see these dialog boxes in Excel 2013, double-click **Computer** in the Open or Save As panels.)

FIGURE EG.2
Excel 2010 Open and Save As dialog boxes

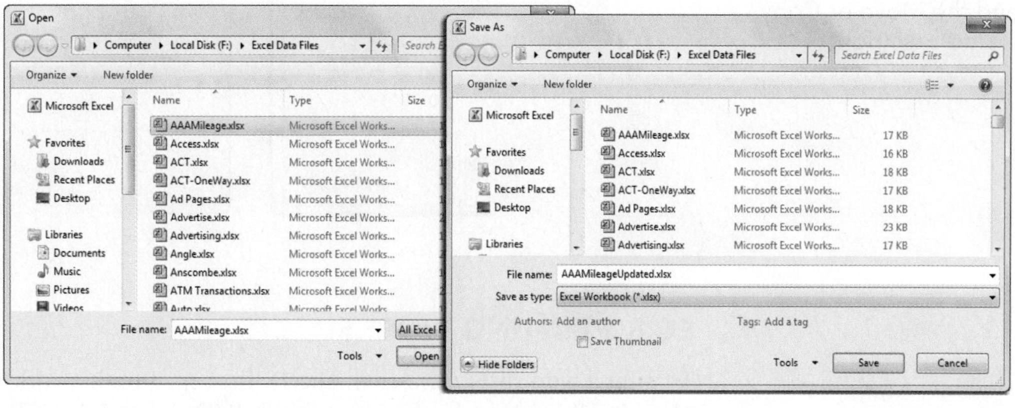

You select the storage folder by using the drop-down list at the top of either of these dialog boxes. You enter, or select from the list box, a file name for the workbook in the **File name** box. You click **Open** or **Save** to complete the task. Sometimes when saving files, you may want to change the file type before you click **Save**.

In Microsoft Windows Excel versions, to save your workbook in the format used by versions older than Excel 2007, select **Excel 97-2003 Workbook (*.xls)** from the Save as type drop-down list (shown in Figure EG.2) before you click **Save**.

To save data in a form that can be opened by programs that cannot open Excel workbooks, you might select either **Text (Tab delimited) (*.txt)** or **CSV (Comma delimited) (*.csv)** as the save type. In OS X Excel versions, the equivalent selections are to select **Excel 97–2004 Workbook (.xls), Tab Delimited Text (.txt)**, or **Windows Comma Separated (.csv)** from the **Format** drop-down list before you click **Save**.

When you want to open a file and cannot find its name in the list box, double-check that the current folder being searched is the proper folder. If it is, change the file type to **All Files (*.*)** (**All Files** in OS X Excel) to see all files in the current folder. This technique can help you discover inadvertent misspellings or missing file extensions that otherwise prevent the file from being displayed.

Although all versions of Microsoft Excel include a **Save** command, you should avoid this choice until you gain experience. Using Save makes it too easy to inadvertently overwrite your work. Also, you cannot use the Save command for any open workbook that Excel has marked as read-only. (Use Save As to save such workbooks.)

EG.7 CREATING and COPYING WORKSHEETS

You create new worksheets by either creating a new workbook or by inserting a new worksheet in an open workbook. In Microsoft Windows Excel versions, select **File → New** (**Office Button → New** in Excel 2007) and in the pane that appears, double-click the Blank workbook icon. In OS X Excel versions, select **File → New Workbook.**

New workbooks are created with a fixed number of worksheets. To delete extra worksheets or insert more sheets, right-click a sheet tab and click either **Delete** or **Insert** (see Figure EG.3). By default, Excel names a worksheet serially, in the form Sheet1, Sheet2, and so on. You should change these names to better reflect the content of your worksheets. To rename a worksheet, double-click the sheet tab of the worksheet, type the new name, and press **Enter**.

You can also make a copy of a worksheet or move a worksheet to another position in the same workbook or to a second workbook. Right-click the sheet tab and select **Move or Copy** from the shortcut menu that appears. In the **To book** drop-down list of the Move or Copy dialog box (see Figure EG.3), first select **(new book)** (or the name of the pre-existing target workbook), check **Create a copy**, and then click **OK**.

FIGURE EG.3
Worksheet tab shortcut menu (left) and the Move or Copy dialog box (right)

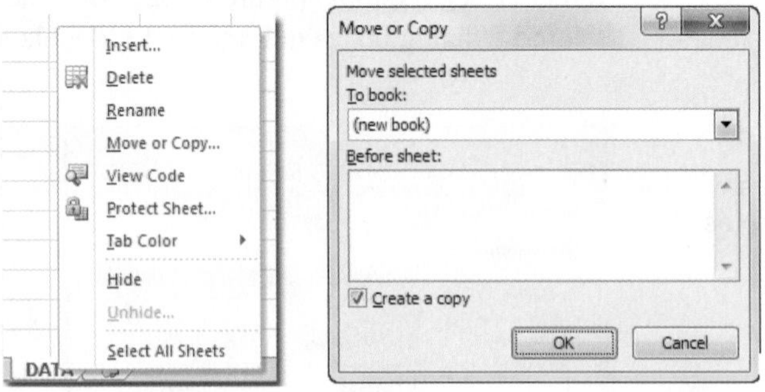

EG.8 PRINTING WORKSHEETS

To print a worksheet (or a chart sheet), first open to the worksheet by clicking its sheet tab. Then, in all Excel versions except Excel 2007, select **File → Print**. If the print preview (partially obscured in Figure EG.4) is acceptable to you, click the **Print button.** To make changes to the worksheet, return to the worksheet by clicking **File** (most Microsoft Windows Excel versions) or **Cancel** (OS X Excel versions).

FIGURE EG.4
Excel 2010 Print Preview and Page Setup (inset) dialog boxes

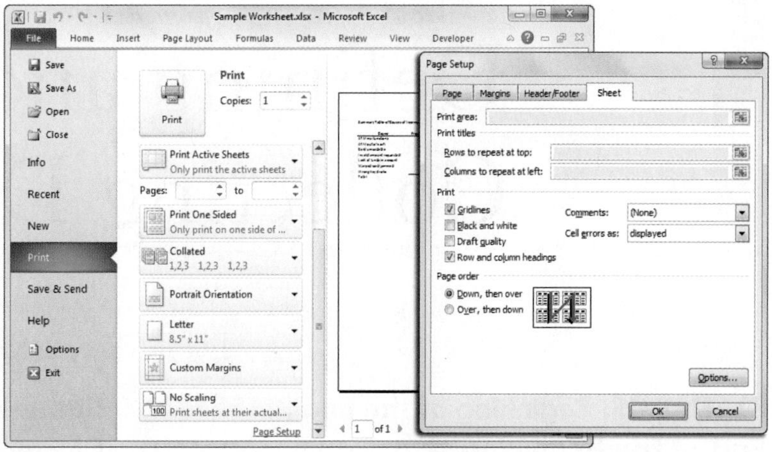

In Excel 2007, the same process requires more mouse clicks. First click **Office Button** and then move the mouse pointer over (but do not click) Print. In the Preview and Print gallery, click **Print Preview**. If the preview (see Figure EG.4) contains errors or displays the worksheet in an undesirable manner, click **Close Print Preview**, make the necessary changes, and reselect the print preview. After completing all corrections and adjustments, click **Print** in the Print Preview window to display the Print dialog box. Select the printer to be used from the **Name** drop-down list, click **All** and **Active sheet(s)**, adjust the **Number of copies**, and click **OK**.

If necessary, you can adjust print formatting while in print preview by clicking **Page Setup** to display the Page Setup dialog box (see Figure EG.4 inset). For example, to print your worksheet with gridlines and numbered row and lettered column headings (similar to the appearance of the worksheet onscreen), click the **Sheet** tab in the Page Setup dialog box, check **Gridlines** and **Row and column headings**, and click **OK**.

Although every version of Excel offers the (print) Entire workbook choice, you get the best results if you print each worksheet separately when you need to print more than one worksheet (or chart sheet).

Printing in Older Excel Versions

Excel versions older than Excel 2007 display a Print dialog box instead of a panel or window that contains a preview when you select **File → Print**. Click **OK** in the Print dialog box to print the worksheet. To see a print preview, select **File → Print Preview** and then click **Print** to print a worksheet.

CHAPTER

1 Defining and Collecting Data

Learning Objectives

In this chapter, you learn:

- The types of variables used in statistics
- The measurement scales of variables
- How to collect data
- The different ways to collect a sample
- About the types of survey errors

USING STATISTICS

Visage / Getty Images

Beginning of the End . . . Or the End of the Beginning?

The past few years have not been kind to Good Tunes & More (GT&M), a business that traces its roots to Good Tunes, a music store that sold music CDs and vinyl records.

GT&M first broadened its merchandise to include home entertainment and computer systems (the "More"), and then underwent an expansion to take advantage of prime locations left empty by bankrupt former competitors. Today, GT&M finds itself at a crossroads. Hoped-for increases in revenues that have failed to occur and declining profit margins due to the competitive pressures of online and "big box" sellers have led management to reconsider the future of the business.

While some investors in the business have argued for an orderly retreat, closing stores and limiting the variety of merchandise, GT&M CEO Emma Levia has decided in a time of uncertainty to "double down" and accept the risk of expanding the business by purchasing Whitney Wireless, a successful three-store chain that sells smartphones and other mobile media devices.

Levia foresees creating a brand new "A-to-Z" electronics retailer but first must establish a fair and reasonable price for the privately held Whitney Wireless. To do so, she has asked a group of analysts to identify, define, and collect the data that would be helpful in setting a price for the wireless business. As part of that group, you quickly realize that you need the data that would help to verify the contents of the wireless company's basic financial statements.

You focus on data associated with the company's profit and loss statement and quickly realize the need for sales and expense-related variables. You begin to think about what the data for such variables would "look like" and how to collect those data. You realize that you are starting to apply the DCOVA framework to the objective of helping Levia acquire Whitney Wireless.

Tyler Olson / Shutterstock

Defining a business objective is only the beginning of the process of business decision making. In the GT&M scenario, the objective is to establish a fair and reasonable price for the company to be acquired. Establishing a business objective always precedes the application of statistics to business decision making. Business objectives can arise from any level of management and can be as varied as the following:

- A marketing analyst needs to assess the effectiveness of a new television advertisement.
- A pharmaceutical company needs to determine whether a new drug is more effective than those currently in use.
- An operations manager wants to improve a manufacturing or service process.
- An auditor wants to review the financial transactions of a company in order to determine whether the company is in compliance with generally accepted accounting principles.

Establishing an objective is the end of what some would label *problem* definition, the formal beginning of any business decision-making process. But establishing the objective also marks a beginning—of applying the DCOVA framework to the task at hand.

Recall from Section LGS.1 that the DCOVA framework uses the five tasks **D**efine, **C**ollect, **O**rganize, **V**isualize, and **A**nalyze to help apply statistics to business decision making. Restated, using the definition of a variable on page 5, the DCOVA framework consists of these tasks:

- **Define** the *variables* that you want to study in order to solve a problem or meet an objective.
- **Collect** the data *for those variables* from appropriate sources.
- **Organize** the data collected by developing tables.
- **Visualize** the data collected by developing charts.
- **Analyze** the data collected to reach conclusions and present those results.

In this chapter, you will learn more about the **D**efine and **C**ollect tasks.

1.1 Establishing the Variable Type

Section LGS.2 introduced you to the importance of establishing operational definitions for the variables you decide to study. To complete the **D**efine task, you establish the type of values your operationally defined variables will have.

Knowing the *variable type* is important because the statistical methods you can use in your analysis vary according to type. The nature of the values for the data associated with a variable determines its type. There are two major variable types:

- **Categorical variables** (also known as **qualitative variables**) have values that can only be placed into categories such as yes and no. "Do you have a Facebook profile?" (yes or no) and Student class designation (Freshman, Sophomore, Junior, or Senior) are examples of categorical variables.
- **Numerical variables** (also known as **quantitative variables**) have values that represent quantities.

Numerical variables are further identified as being either *discrete* or *continuous* variables.

Discrete variables have numerical values that arise from a *counting* process. "The number of premium cable channels subscribed to" is an example of a discrete numerical variable because the response is one of a finite number of integers. You subscribe to zero, one, two, or more channels. "The number of items purchased" is also a discrete numerical variable because you are counting the number of items purchased.

Continuous variables produce numerical responses that arise from a *measuring* process. The time you wait for teller service at a bank is an example of a continuous numerical variable because the response takes on any value within a *continuum*, or an interval, depending on the precision of the measuring instrument. For example, your waiting time could be 1 minute,

LEARN MORE

Read the SHORT TAKES for Chapter 1 to learn more about determining the type of variable.

1.1 minutes, 1.11 minutes, or 1.113 minutes, depending on the precision of the measuring device used. (Theoretically, no two continuous values would ever be identical. However, because no measuring device is perfectly precise, identical continuous values for two or more items or individuals can occur.)

At first glance, identifying the variable type may seem easy, but some variables that you might want to study could be either categorical or numerical, depending on how you define them. For example, "age" would seem to be an obvious numerical variable, but what if you are interested in comparing the buying habits of children, young adults, middle-aged persons, and retirement-age people? In that case, defining "age" as a categorical variable would make better sense. Again, this illustrates the earlier point that without operational definitions, variables are meaningless.

Asking questions about the variables you have identified for study can often be a great help in determining the type of variable you have. Table 1.1 illustrates the process.

TABLE 1.1

Identifying Types of Variables

Question	Responses		Data Type
Do you currently have a profile on Facebook?	❑ Yes ❑ No	→	Categorical
How many text messages have you sent in the past three days?	______	→	Numerical (discrete)
How long did it take to download the update for your newest mobile app?	______ seconds	→	Numerical (continuous)

1.2 Measurement Scales for Variables

Variables can be further identified by the level of measurement, or **measurement scale**. Statisticians use the terms *nominal scale* and *ordinal scale* to describe the values for a categorical variable and use the terms *interval scale* and *ratio scale* to describe the values for a numerical variable.

Nominal and Ordinal Scales

Values for a categorical variable are measured on a nominal scale or on an ordinal scale. A **nominal scale** (see Table 1.2) classifies data into distinct categories in which no ranking is implied. Examples of a nominal scaled variable are your favorite soft drink, your political party affiliation, and your gender. Nominal scaling is the weakest form of measurement because you cannot specify any ranking across the various categories.

TABLE 1.2

Examples of Nominal Scales

Categorical Variable	Categories
Do you have a Facebook profile?	❑ Yes ❑ No
Type of investment	❑ Cash ❑ Mutual funds ❑ Other
Cellular provider	❑ AT&T ❑ Sprint ❑ Verizon ❑ Other ❑ None

LEARN MORE

Read the SHORT TAKES for Chapter 1 for additional examples of nominal and ordinal scales.

An **ordinal scale** classifies values into distinct categories in which ranking is implied. For example, suppose that Good Tunes & More conducted a survey of customers who made a purchase and asked the question "How do you rate the overall service provided by Good Tunes &

More during your most recent purchase?" to which the responses were "excellent," "very good," "fair," and "poor." The answers to this question represent an ordinal scaled variable because the responses "excellent," "very good," "fair," and "poor" are ranked in order of satisfaction. Table 1.3 lists other examples of ordinal scaled variables.

TABLE 1.3

Examples of Ordinal Scales

Categorical Variable	Ordered Categories
Student class designation	Freshman Sophomore Junior Senior
Product satisfaction	Very unsatisfied Fairly unsatisfied Neutral Fairly satisfied Very satisfied
Faculty rank	Professor Associate Professor Assistant Professor Instructor
Standard & Poor's investment grade ratings	AAA AA+ AA AA– A+ A BBB
Course grade	A B C D F

Ordinal scaling is a stronger form of measurement than nominal scaling because an observed value classified into one category possesses more of a property than does an observed value classified into another category. However, ordinal scaling is still a relatively weak form of measurement because the scale does not account for the amount of the differences between the categories. The ordering implies only which category is "greater," "better," or "more preferred"—not by how much.

Interval and Ratio Scales

Values for a numerical variable are measured on an interval scale or a ratio scale. An **interval scale** (see Table 1.4) is an ordered scale in which the difference between measurements is a meaningful quantity but does not involve a true zero point. For example, a noontime temperature reading of 67° Fahrenheit is 2 degrees warmer than a noontime reading of 65°. In addition, the 2° Fahrenheit difference in the noontime temperature readings is the same as if the two noontime temperature readings were 74° and 76° Fahrenheit because the difference has the same meaning anywhere on the scale.

TABLE 1.4

Examples of Interval and Ratio Scales

Numerical Variable	Level of Measurement
Temperature (in degrees Celsius or Fahrenheit)	Interval
ACT or SAT standardized exam score	Interval
File download time (in seconds)	Ratio
Age (in years or days)	Ratio
Cost of a computer system (in U.S. dollars)	Ratio

A **ratio scale** is an ordered scale in which the difference between the measurements involves a true zero point, as in height, weight, age, or salary measurements. If Good Tunes & More conducted a survey and asked how much money you expected to spend on audio equipment in the next year, the responses to such a question would be an example of a ratio scaled variable. A person who expects to spend $1,000 on audio equipment expects to spend twice as much money as someone who expects to spend $500. As another example, a person who weighs 240 pounds is twice as heavy as someone who weighs 120 pounds. Temperature is a trickier case: Fahrenheit and Celsius scales are interval but not ratio scales; the "zero" value is arbitrary, not real. You cannot say that a noontime temperature reading of 4° Fahrenheit is twice as hot as 2° Fahrenheit.

LEARN MORE

Read the SHORT TAKES for Chapter 1 to learn more about interval and ratio scales.

But a Kelvin temperature reading, in which 0° means no molecular motion, is ratio scaled. In contrast, the Fahrenheit and Celsius scales use arbitrarily selected 0° beginning points.

Data measured on an interval scale or on a ratio scale constitute the highest levels of measurement. They are stronger forms of measurement than an ordinal scale because you can determine not only which observed value is the largest but also by how much.

Problems for Sections 1.1 and 1.2

LEARNING THE BASICS

1.1 Four different beverages are sold at a fast-food restaurant: soft drinks, tea, coffee, and bottled water.

a. Explain why the type of beverage sold is an example of a categorical variable.

b. Explain why the type of beverage sold is an example of a nominal scaled variable.

1.2 U.S. businesses are listed by size: small, medium, and large. Explain why business size is an example of an ordinal scaled variable.

1.3 The time it takes to download a video from the Internet is measured.

a. Explain why the download time is a continuous numerical variable.

b. Explain why the download time is a ratio scaled variable.

APPLYING THE CONCEPTS

SELF Test **1.4** For each of the following variables, determine whether the variable is categorical or numerical. If the variable is numerical, determine whether the variable is discrete or continuous. In addition, determine the measurement scale.

a. Number of cellphones in the household

b. Monthly data usage (in MB)

c. Number of text messages exchanged per month

d. Voice usage per month (in minutes)

e. Whether the cellphone is used for email

1.5 The following information is collected from students upon exiting the campus bookstore during the first week of classes.

a. Amount of time spent shopping in the bookstore

b. Number of textbooks purchased

c. Academic major

d. Gender

Classify each of these variables as categorical or numerical. If the variable is numerical, determine whether the variable is discrete or continuous. In addition, determine the measurement scale for each of these variables.

1.6 For each of the following variables, determine whether the variable is categorical or numerical. If the variable is numerical, determine whether the variable is discrete or continuous. In addition, determine the measurement scale for each variable.

a. Name of Internet service provider

b. Time, in hours, spent surfing the Internet per week

c. Whether the individual uses a mobile phone to connect to the Internet

d. Number of online purchases made in a month

e. Where the individual uses social networks to find sought-after information

1.7 For each of the following variables, determine whether the variable is categorical or numerical. If the variable is numerical, determine whether the variable is discrete or continuous. In addition, determine the measurement scale for each variable.

a. Amount of money spent on clothing in the past month

b. Favorite department store

c. Most likely time period during which shopping for clothing takes place (weekday, weeknight, or weekend)

d. Number of pairs of shoes owned

1.8 Suppose the following information is collected from Robert Keeler on his application for a home mortgage loan at the Metro County Savings and Loan Association.

a. Monthly payments: $2,227

b. Number of jobs in past 10 years: 1

c. Annual family income: $96,000

d. Marital status: Married

Classify each of the responses by type of data and measurement scale.

1.9 One of the variables most often included in surveys is income. Sometimes the question is phrased "What is your income (in thousands of dollars)?" In other surveys, the respondent is asked to "Select the circle corresponding to your income level" and is given a number of income ranges to choose from.

a. In the first format, explain why income might be considered either discrete or continuous.

b. Which of these two formats would you prefer to use if you were conducting a survey? Why?

1.10 If two students score a 90 on the same examination, what arguments could be used to show that the underlying variable—test score—is continuous?

1.11 The director of market research at a large department store chain wanted to conduct a survey throughout a metropolitan area to determine the amount of time working women spend shopping for clothing in a typical month.

a. Indicate the type of data the director might want to collect.

b. Develop a first draft of the questionnaire needed in (a) by writing three categorical questions and three numerical questions that you feel would be appropriate for this survey.

1.3 Collecting Data

After defining the variables that you want to study, you can proceed with the data collection task. Collecting data is a critical task because if you collect data that are flawed by biases, ambiguities, or other types of errors, the results you will get from using such data with even the most sophisticated statistical methods will be suspect or in error. (For a famous example of flawed data collection leading to incorrect results, read the Think About This essay on page 29.)

Data collection consists of identifying data sources, deciding whether the data you collect will be from a population or a sample, cleaning your data, and sometimes recoding variables. The rest of this section explains these aspects of data collection.

Data Sources

You collect data from either primary or secondary data sources. You are using a **primary data source** if you collect your own data for analysis. You are using a **secondary data source** if the data for your analysis have been collected by someone else.

You collect data by using any of the following:

- Data distributed by an organization or individual
- The outcomes of a designed experiment
- The responses from a survey
- The results of conducting an observational study
- Data collected by ongoing business activities

Market research companies and trade associations distribute data pertaining to specific industries or markets. Investment services such as Mergent, Inc., provide business and financial data on publicly listed companies. Syndicated services sold by The Nielsen Company provide consumer research data to telecom and mobile media companies. Print and online media companies also distribute data that they may have collected themselves or may be republishing from other sources.

The outcomes of a designed experiment are a second data source. For example, a consumer goods company might conduct an experiment that compares the stain-removing abilities of several laundry detergents. Note that developing a proper experimental design is mostly beyond the scope of this book, but Chapters 10 and 11 discuss some of the fundamental experimental design concepts.

Survey responses represent a third type of data source. People being surveyed are asked questions about their beliefs, attitudes, behaviors, and other characteristics. For example, people could be asked which laundry detergent has the best stain-removing abilities. (Such a survey could lead to data that differ from the data collected from the outcomes of the designed experiment of the previous paragraph.) Surveys can be affected by any of the four types of errors that are discussed in Section 1.5.

Observational study results are a fourth data source. A researcher collects data by directly observing a behavior, usually in a natural or neutral setting. Observational studies are a common tool for data collection in business. For example, market researchers use focus groups to elicit unstructured responses to open-ended questions posed by a moderator to a target audience. Observational studies are also commonly used to enhance teamwork or improve the quality of products and services.

Data collected by ongoing business activities are a fifth data source. Such data can be collected from operational and transactional systems that exist in both physical "bricks-and-mortar" and online settings but can also be gathered from secondary sources such as third-party social media networks and online apps and website services that collect tracking and usage data. For example, a bank might analyze a decade's worth of financial transaction data to identify patterns of fraud, and a marketer might use tracking data to determine the effectiveness of a website.

LEARN MORE

Read the SHORT TAKES for Chapter 1 for a further discussion about data sources.

Sources for "big data" (see Section LGS.3) tend to be a mix of primary and secondary sources of this last type. For example, a retailer interested in increasing sales might mine Facebook and Twitter accounts to identify sentiment about certain products or to pinpoint top influencers and then match those data to its own data collected during customer transactions.

Populations and Samples

You collect your data from either a *population* or a *sample*. A **population** consists of all the items or individuals about which you want to reach conclusions. All the Good Tunes & More sales transactions for a specific year, all the customers who shopped at Good Tunes & More this weekend, all the full-time students enrolled in a college, and all the registered voters in Ohio are examples of populations.

A **sample** is a portion of a population selected for analysis. The results of analyzing a sample are used to estimate characteristics of the entire population. From the four examples of populations just given, you could select a sample of 200 Good Tunes & More sales transactions randomly selected by an auditor for study, a sample of 30 Good Tunes & More customers asked to complete a customer satisfaction survey, a sample of 50 full-time students selected for a marketing study, and a sample of 500 registered voters in Ohio contacted via telephone for a political poll. In each of these examples, the transactions or people in the sample represent a portion of the items or individuals that make up the population.

Student Tip
By convention, the letter *s* represents a sample, and the letter *p* represents a population. To help remember the difference between a sample and a population, think of a pie. The entire *pie* represents the population, and the pie *slice* that you select is the sample.

Data collection will involve collecting data from a sample when any of the following conditions hold:

- Selecting a sample is less time-consuming than selecting every item in the population.
- Selecting a sample is less costly than selecting every item in the population.
- Analyzing a sample is less cumbersome and more practical than analyzing the entire population.

Data Cleaning

Whatever ways you choose to collect data, you may find irregularities in the data you collect. These irregularities might be typographical or data entry errors, values that are impossible or undefined, or values that are "missing," such as a missing response to a survey question. For numerical variables, you may also find **outliers**, values that seem excessively different from most of the rest of the values. Such values may or may not be errors, but they demand a second review. If you discover missing values, you should know that while more sophisticated statistical programs have provisions to process data that contain occasional missing values, Microsoft Excel does not.

When you spot an irregularity, you may have to "clean" the data you have collected. Although a full discussion of data cleaning is beyond the scope of this book (see reference 8), you can learn more about the ways you can use Excel for data cleaning in the SHORT TAKES for Chapter 1. If you only use the Excel data workbooks designed for use with this book and available online (see Appendix C), you will not need to worry about data cleaning as none of those data files contain any irregularities.

Recoded Variables

After you have collected data, you may discover that you need to reconsider the categories that you have defined for a categorical variable or that you need to transform a numerical variable into a categorical variable by assigning the individual numeric data values to one of several groups. In either case, you can define a **recoded variable** that supplements or replaces the original variable in your analysis.

For example, having defined the variable student class designation to be one of the four categories shown in Table 1.3 on page 20, you realize that you are more interested in investigating the differences between lowerclassmen (defined as Freshman or Sophomore) and upperclassmen (Junior or Senior). You can create a new variable UpperLower and assign the value Upper if a student is a Junior or Senior and assign the value Lower if the student is a Freshman or Sophomore.

*The **RECODED worksheet** of the **Recoded workbook** demonstrates the recodings of a categorical variable and a numerical variable. See Section EG1.3 for a discussion of how these recodings were done in Microsoft Excel.*

When recoding variables, be sure that the category definitions cause each data value to be placed in one and only one category, a property known as being **mutually exclusive**. Also ensure that the set of categories you create for the new, recoded variables include all the data values being recoded, a property known as being **collectively exhaustive**. If you are recoding a categorical variable, you can preserve one or more of the original categories, as long as your recodings are both mutually exclusive and collectively exhaustive.

When recoding numerical variables, pay particular attention to the operational definitions of the categories you create for the recoded variable, especially if the categories are not self-defining ranges. For example, while the recoded categories Under 12, 12–20, 21–34, 35–54, 55 and Over are self-defining for age, the categories Child, Youth, Young Adult, Middle Aged, and Senior need their own operational definitions.

Problems for Section 1.3

APPLYING THE CONCEPTS

1.12 The Data and Story Library (DASL) is an online library of data files and stories that illustrate the use of basic statistical methods. Visit **lib.stat.cmu.edu/index.php**, click DASL, and explore a data set of interest to you. Which of the five sources of data best describes the sources of the data set you selected?

1.13 Visit the website of the Gallup organization, at **www.gallup.com**. Read today's top story. What type of data source is the top story based on?

1.14 Visit the website of the Pew Research organization, at **www.pewresearch.org**. Read today's top story. What type of data source is the top story based on?

1.15 Transportation engineers and planners want to address the dynamic properties of travel behavior by describing in detail the driving characteristics of drivers over the course of a month. What type of data collection source do you think the transportation engineers and planners should use?

1.16 Visit the "Longitudinal Employer-Household Dynamics" page of the U.S. Census Bureau website, **lehd.did.census.gov/led/**. Examine the "Did You Know" panel on the page. What type of data source is the information presented here based on?

1.4 Types of Sampling Methods

When you collect data by selecting a sample, you begin by defining the **frame**. The frame is a complete or partial listing of the items that make up the population from which the sample will be selected. Inaccurate or biased results can occur if a frame excludes certain groups, or portions of the population. Using different frames to collect data can lead to different, even opposite, conclusions.

Using your frame, you select either a nonprobability sample or a probability sample. In a **nonprobability sample**, you select the items or individuals without knowing their probabilities of selection. In a **probability sample**, you select items based on known probabilities. Whenever possible, you should use a probability sample as such a sample will allow you to make inferences about the population being analyzed.

Nonprobability samples can have certain advantages, such as convenience, speed, and low cost. Such samples are typically used to obtain informal approximations or as small-scale initial or pilot analyses. However, because the theory of statistical inference depends on probability sampling, nonprobability samples *cannot be used* for statistical inference and this more than offsets those advantages in more formal analyses.

Figure 1.1 shows the subcategories of the two types of samples. A nonprobability sample can either be a convenience sample or a judgment sample. To collect a **convenience sample**, you select items that are easy, inexpensive, or convenient to sample. For example, in a warehouse of stacked items, selecting only the items located on the tops of each stack and within easy reach would create a convenience sample. So, too, would be the responses to surveys that the websites of many companies offer visitors. While such surveys can provide large amounts of data quickly and inexpensively, the convenience samples selected from these responses will consist of self-selected website visitors. (Read the Think About This on page 29 for a related story.)

FIGURE 1.1
Types of samples

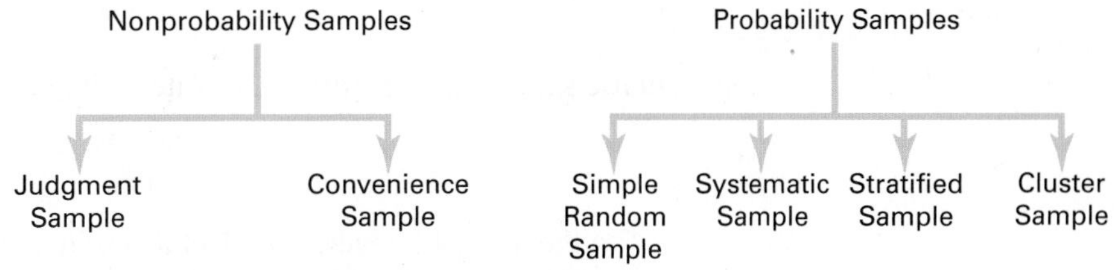

To collect a **judgment sample**, you collect the opinions of preselected experts in the subject matter. Although the experts may be well informed, you cannot generalize their results to the population.

The types of probability samples most commonly used include simple random, systematic, stratified, and cluster samples. These four types of probability samples vary in terms of cost, accuracy, and complexity, and they are the subject of the rest of this section.

Simple Random Sample

In a **simple random sample**, every item from a frame has the same chance of selection as every other item, and every sample of a fixed size has the same chance of selection as every other sample of that size. Simple random sampling is the most elementary random sampling technique. It forms the basis for the other random sampling techniques.

With simple random sampling, you use n to represent the sample size and N to represent the frame size. You number every item in the frame from 1 to N. The chance that you will select any particular member of the frame on the first selection is $1/N$.

You select samples with replacement or without replacement. **Sampling with replacement** means that after you select an item, you return it to the frame, where it has the same probability of being selected again. Imagine that you have a fishbowl containing N business cards, one card for each person. On the first selection, you select the card for Grace Kim. You record pertinent information and replace the business card in the bowl. You then mix up the cards in the bowl and select a second card. On the second selection, Grace Kim has the same probability of being selected again, $1/N$. You repeat this process until you have selected the desired sample size, n.

Typically, you do not want the same item or individual to be selected again in a sample. **Sampling without replacement** means that once you select an item, you cannot select it again. The chance that you will select any particular item in the frame—for example, the business card for Grace Kim—on the first selection is $1/N$. The chance that you will select any card not previously chosen on the second selection is now 1 out of $N - 1$. This process continues until you have selected the desired sample of size n.

When creating a simple random sample, you should avoid the "fishbowl" method of selecting a sample because this method lacks the ability to thoroughly mix the cards and, therefore, randomly select a sample. You should use a more rigorous selection method.

One such method is to use a **table of random numbers**, such as Table E.1 in Appendix E, for selecting the sample. A table of random numbers consists of a series of digits listed in a randomly generated sequence (see reference 9). To use a random number table for selecting a sample, you first need to assign code numbers to the individual items of the frame. Then you generate the random sample by reading the table of random numbers and selecting those individuals from the frame whose assigned code numbers match the digits found in the table. Because the number system uses 10 digits $(0, 1, 2, \ldots, 9)$, the chance that you will randomly generate any particular digit is equal to the probability of generating any other digit. This probability is 1 out of 10. Hence, if you generate a sequence of 800 digits, you would expect about 80 to be the digit 0, 80 to be the digit 1, and so on. Because every digit or sequence of digits in the table is random, the table can be read either horizontally or vertically. The margins of the table designate row numbers and column numbers. The digits themselves are grouped into sequences of five in order to make reading the table easier.

LEARN MORE

Learn to use a table of random numbers to select a simple random sample in a Chapter 1 eBook bonus section.

Systematic Sample

In a **systematic sample**, you partition the N items in the frame into n groups of k items, where

$$k = \frac{N}{n}$$

You round k to the nearest integer. To select a systematic sample, you choose the first item to be selected at random from the first k items in the frame. Then, you select the remaining $n - 1$ items by taking every kth item thereafter from the entire frame.

If the frame consists of a list of prenumbered checks, sales receipts, or invoices, taking a systematic sample is faster and easier than taking a simple random sample. A systematic sample is also a convenient mechanism for collecting data from telephone books, class rosters, and consecutive items coming off an assembly line.

To take a systematic sample of $n = 40$ from the population of $N = 800$ full-time employees, you partition the frame of 800 into 40 groups, each of which contains 20 employees. You then select a random number from the first 20 individuals and include every twentieth individual after the first selection in the sample. For example, if the first random number you select is 008, your subsequent selections are 028, 048, 068, 088, 108, . . . , 768, and 788.

Simple random sampling and systematic sampling are simpler than other, more sophisticated, probability sampling methods, but they generally require a larger sample size. In addition, systematic sampling is prone to selection bias that can occur when there is a pattern in the frame. To overcome the inefficiency of simple random sampling and the potential selection bias involved with systematic sampling, you can use either stratified sampling methods or cluster sampling methods.

Stratified Sample

LEARN MORE

Learn how to select a stratified sample in a Chapter 1 eBook bonus example.

In a **stratified sample**, you first subdivide the N items in the frame into separate subpopulations, or **strata**. A stratum is defined by some common characteristic, such as gender or year in school. You select a simple random sample within each of the strata and combine the results from the separate simple random samples. Stratified sampling is more efficient than either simple random sampling or systematic sampling because you are ensured of the representation of items across the entire population. The homogeneity of items within each stratum provides greater precision in the estimates of underlying population parameters.

Cluster Sample

In a **cluster sample**, you divide the N items in the frame into clusters that contain several items. **Clusters** are often naturally occurring designations, such as counties, election districts, city blocks, households, or sales territories. You then take a random sample of one or more clusters and study all items in each selected cluster.

Cluster sampling is often more cost-effective than simple random sampling, particularly if the population is spread over a wide geographic region. However, cluster sampling often requires a larger sample size to produce results as precise as those from simple random sampling or stratified sampling. A detailed discussion of systematic sampling, stratified sampling, and cluster sampling procedures can be found in reference 2.

Problems for Section 1.4

LEARNING THE BASICS

1.17 For a population containing $N = 902$ individuals, what code number would you assign for

a. the first person on the list?
b. the fortieth person on the list?
c. the last person on the list?

1.18 For a population of $N = 902$, verify that by starting in row 05, column 01 of the table of random numbers (Table E.1), you need only six rows to select a sample of $N = 60$ *without* replacement.

1.19 Given a population of $N = 93$, starting in row 29, column 01 of the table of random numbers (Table E.1), and reading across the row, select a sample of $N = 15$

a. *without* replacement.
b. *with* replacement.

APPLYING THE CONCEPTS

1.20 For a study that consists of personal interviews with participants (rather than mail or phone surveys), explain why simple random sampling might be less practical than some other sampling methods.

1.21 You want to select a random sample of $n = 1$ from a population of three items (which are called A, B, and C). The rule for selecting the sample is as follows: Flip a coin; if it is heads, pick item A; if it is tails, flip the coin again; this time, if it is heads, choose B; if it is tails, choose C. Explain why this is a probability sample but not a simple random sample.

1.22 A population has four members (called A, B, C, and D). You would like to select a random sample of $n = 2$, which you decide to do in the following way: Flip a coin; if it is heads, the sample will be items A and B; if it is tails, the sample will be items C and D. Although this is a random sample, it is not a simple random sample. Explain why. (Compare the procedure described in Problem 1.21 with the procedure described in this problem.)

1.23 The registrar of a college with a population of $N = 4{,}000$ full-time students is asked by the president to conduct a survey to measure satisfaction with the quality of life on campus. The following table contains a breakdown of the 4,000 registered full-time students, by gender and class designation:

	Class Designation				
Gender	**Fr.**	**So.**	**Jr.**	**Sr.**	**Total**
Female	700	520	500	480	2,200
Male	560	460	400	380	1,800
Total	1,260	980	900	860	4,000

The registrar intends to take a probability sample of $n = 200$ students and project the results from the sample to the entire population of full-time students.

a. If the frame available from the registrar's files is an alphabetical listing of the names of all $N = 4{,}000$ registered full-time students, what type of sample could you take? Discuss.

b. What is the advantage of selecting a simple random sample in (a)?

c. What is the advantage of selecting a systematic sample in (a)?

d. If the frame available from the registrar's files is a list of the names of all $N = 4{,}000$ registered full-time students compiled from eight separate alphabetical lists, based on the gender and class designation breakdowns shown in the class designation table, what type of sample should you take? Discuss.

e. Suppose that each of the $N = 4{,}000$ registered full-time students lived in one of the 10 campus dormitories. Each dormitory accommodates 400 students. It is college policy to fully integrate students by gender and class designation in each dormitory. If the registrar is able to compile a listing of all students by dormitory, explain how you could take a cluster sample.

SELF Test **1.24** Prenumbered sales invoices are kept in a sales journal. The invoices are numbered from 0001 to 5000.

a. Beginning in row 16, column 01, and proceeding horizontally in a table of random numbers (Table E.1), select a simple random sample of 50 invoice numbers.

b. Select a systematic sample of 50 invoice numbers. Use the random numbers in row 20, columns 05–07, as the starting point for your selection.

c. Are the invoices selected in (a) the same as those selected in (b)? Why or why not?

1.25 Suppose that 5,000 sales invoices are separated into four strata. Stratum 1 contains 50 invoices, stratum 2 contains 500 invoices, stratum 3 contains 1,000 invoices, and stratum 4 contains 3,450 invoices. A sample of 500 sales invoices is needed.

a. What type of sampling should you do? Why?

b. Explain how you would carry out the sampling according to the method stated in (a).

c. Why is the sampling in (a) not simple random sampling?

1.5 Types of Survey Errors

As you learned in Section 1.3, responses from a survey represent a source of data. Nearly every day, you read or hear about survey or opinion poll results in newspapers, on the Internet, or on radio or television. To identify surveys that lack objectivity or credibility, you must critically evaluate what you read and hear by examining the validity of the survey results. First, you must evaluate the purpose of the survey, why it was conducted, and for whom it was conducted.

The second step in evaluating the validity of a survey is to determine whether it was based on a probability or nonprobability sample (as discussed in Section 1.4). You need to remember that the only way to make valid statistical inferences from a sample to a population is by using a probability sample. Surveys that use nonprobability sampling methods are subject to serious biases that may make the results meaningless.

Even when surveys use probability sampling methods, they are subject to four types of potential survey errors:

- Coverage error
- Nonresponse error
- Sampling error
- Measurement error

Well-designed surveys reduce or minimize these four types of errors, often at considerable cost.

Coverage Error

The key to proper sample selection is having an adequate frame. **Coverage error** occurs if certain groups of items are excluded from the frame so that they have no chance of being selected in the sample. Coverage error results in a **selection bias**. If the frame is inadequate because certain groups of items in the population were not properly included, any probability sample selected will provide only an estimate of the characteristics of the frame, not the *actual* population.

Nonresponse Error

Not everyone is willing to respond to a survey. **Nonresponse error** arises from failure to collect data on all items in the sample and results in a **nonresponse bias**. Because you cannot always assume that persons who do not respond to surveys are similar to those who do, you need to follow up on the nonresponses after a specified period of time. You should make several attempts to convince such individuals to complete the survey. The follow-up responses are then compared to the initial responses in order to make valid inferences from the survey (see reference 2). The mode of response you use, such as face-to-face interview, telephone interview, paper questionnaire, or computerized questionnaire, affects the rate of response. Personal interviews and telephone interviews usually produce a higher response rate than do mail surveys—but at a higher cost.

Sampling Error

When collecting a probability sample, chance dictates which individuals or items will or will not be included in the sample. **Sampling error** reflects the variation, or "chance differences," from sample to sample, based on the probability of particular individuals or items being selected in the particular samples.

When you read about the results of surveys or polls in newspapers or on the Internet, there is often a statement regarding a margin of error, such as "the results of this poll are expected to be within ± 4 percentage points of the actual value." This **margin of error** is the sampling error. You can reduce sampling error by using larger sample sizes. Of course, doing so increases the cost of conducting the survey.

Measurement Error

In the practice of good survey research, you design surveys with the intention of gathering meaningful and accurate information. Unfortunately, the survey results you get are often only a proxy for the ones you really desire. Unlike height or weight, certain information about behaviors and psychological states is impossible or impractical to obtain directly.

When surveys rely on self-reported information, the mode of data collection, the respondent to the survey, and or the survey itself can be possible sources of **measurement error**. Satisficing, social desirability, reading ability, and/or interviewer effects can be dependent on the mode. The social desirability bias or cognitive/memory limitations of a respondent can affect the results. And vague questions, double-barreled questions that ask about multiple issues but require a single response, or questions that ask the respondent to report something that occurs over time but fail to clearly define the extent of time about which the question asks (the reference period) are some of the survey flaws that can cause errors.

To minimize measurement error, you need to standardize survey administration and respondent understanding of questions, but there are many barriers to this (see references 1, 3, and 11).

Ethical Issues About Surveys

Ethical considerations arise with respect to the four types of survey error. Coverage error can result in selection bias and becomes an ethical issue if particular groups or individuals are purposely excluded from the frame so that the survey results are more favorable to the survey's sponsor. Nonresponse error can lead to nonresponse bias and becomes an ethical issue if the sponsor knowingly designs the survey so that particular groups or individuals are less likely than others to respond. Sampling error becomes an ethical issue if the findings are purposely presented without reference to sample size and margin of error so that the sponsor can promote a viewpoint that might otherwise be inappropriate. Measurement error can become an ethical issue in one of three ways: (1) a survey sponsor chooses leading questions that guide the respondent in a particular direction; (2) an interviewer, through mannerisms and tone, purposely makes a respondent obligated to please the interviewer or otherwise guides the respondent in a particular direction; or (3) a respondent willfully provides false information.

Ethical issues also arise when the results of nonprobability samples are used to form conclusions about the entire population. When you use a nonprobability sampling method, you need to explain the sampling procedures and state that the results cannot be generalized beyond the sample.

THINK ABOUT THIS New Media Surveys/ Old Sampling Problems

Imagine that you work for a software distributor that has decided to create a "customer experience improvement program" to record how your customers are using your products, with the goal of using the collected data to make product enhancements. Or say that you are an editor of an online news website who decides to create an instant poll to ask website visitors about important political issues. Or you're a marketer of products aimed at a specific demographic and decide to use a social networking site to collect consumer feedback. What might you have in common with a *dead-tree* publication that went out of business over 70 years ago?

By 1932, before there was ever an Internet—or even commercial television—a "straw poll" conducted by the magazine *Literary Digest* had successfully predicted five U.S. presidential elections in a row. For the 1936 election, the magazine promised its largest poll ever and sent about 10 million ballots to people all across the country. After receiving and tabulating more than 2.3 million ballots, the *Digest* confidently proclaimed that Alf Landon would be an easy winner over Franklin D. Roosevelt. As things turned out, FDR won in a landslide, with Landon receiving the fewest electoral votes in U.S. history. The reputation of *Literary Digest* was ruined; the magazine would cease publication less than two years later.

The failure of the *Literary Digest* poll was a watershed event in the history of sample surveys and polls. This failure refuted the notion that the larger the sample is, the better. (Remember this the next time someone complains about a political survey's "small" sample size.) The failure opened the door to new and more modern methods of sampling discussed in this chapter. Today's Gallup polls of political opinion (**www.gallup.com**) or GfK Roper Reports about consumer behavior (**www.gfkamerica.com/practice_areas/roper_consulting**) arose, in part, due to this failure. George Gallup, the "Gallup" of the poll, and Elmo Roper, of the eponymous reports, both first gained widespread public notice for their correct "scientific" predictions of the 1936 election.

The failed *Literary Digest* poll became fodder for several postmortems, and the reason for the failure became almost an urban legend. Typically, the explanation is coverage error: The ballots were sent mostly to "rich people," and this created a frame that excluded poorer citizens (presumably more inclined to vote for the Democrat Roosevelt than the Republican Landon). However, later analyses suggest that this was not true; instead, low rates of response (2.3 million ballots represented less than 25% of the ballots distributed) and/or nonresponse error (Roosevelt voters were less likely to mail in a ballot than Landon voters) were significant reasons for the failure (see reference 10).

When Microsoft revealed its new Office Ribbon user interface for Office 2007, a program manager explained how Microsoft had applied data collected from its "Customer Experience Improvement Program" to the user interface redesign. This led others to speculate that the data were biased toward beginners—who might be less likely to decline participation in the program—and that, in turn, had led Microsoft to create a user interface that ended up perplexing more experienced users. This was another case of nonresponse error!

The editor's instant poll mentioned earlier is targeted to the visitors of the online news website, and the social network–based survey is aimed at "friends" of a product; such polls can also suffer from nonresponse error, and this fact is often overlooked by users of these new media. Often, marketers extol how much they "know" about survey respondents, thanks to data that can be collected from a social network community. But no amount of information about the respondents can tell marketers who the nonrespondents are. Therefore, new media surveys fall prey to the same old type of error that may have been fatal to *Literary Digest* way back when.

Today, companies establish formal surveys based on probability sampling and go to great lengths—and spend large sums—to deal with coverage error, nonresponse error, sampling error, and measurement error. Instant polling and tell-a-friend surveys can be interesting and fun, but they are not replacements for the methods discussed in this chapter.

Problems for Section 1.5

APPLYING THE CONCEPTS

1.26 A survey indicates that the vast majority of college students own their own personal computers. What information would you want to know before you accepted the results of this survey?

1.27 A simple random sample of $n = 300$ full-time employees is selected from a company list containing the names of all $N = 5{,}000$ full-time employees in order to evaluate job satisfaction.

a. Give an example of possible coverage error.
b. Give an example of possible nonresponse error.
c. Give an example of possible sampling error.
d. Give an example of possible measurement error.

SELF Test **1.28** Results of an AT&T Small Business Tech Poll indicate that 60% of small businesses surveyed plan to spend as much or more in 2012 than they did in 2011 on online marketing (**bit.ly/Oq5n26**). Three in four (75%) small businesses have websites, with nearly one-third (31%) having mobile websites that are designed to be viewed on smartphones. Preferences for various kinds of online marketing were found to vary by gender: Male small business owners are more likely than female owners to rely on their company website for marketing (65% vs. 58%), whereas female small business owners are more likely than their male counterparts to employ social media to market their business (48% vs. 34%). These results are based on an online survey, conducted in November 2011, of 1,232 small business owners and/or employees responsible for Information Technology (IT). Identify *potential* concerns with coverage, nonresponse, sampling, and measurement errors.

1.29 A recent survey indicated that 29% of Americans spent more money in recent months than they used to. But the majority (58%) still said that they *enjoy* saving money more than spending it. (Data extracted from E. Mendes, "More Americans Say Their Spending Is Up," **www.gallup.com**, May 3, 2012.) What additional information would you want to know about the survey before you accepted the results of the study?

1.30 A recent survey points to a wholesale collapse of traditional TV viewing. The study found that the percentage of consumers watching broadcast or cable TV in a typical week plummeted from 71% in 2009 to 48% in 2011. (**onforb.es/zgdZKo**). What additional information would you want to know about the survey before you accepted the results of the study?

USING STATISTICS Beginning . . . Revisited

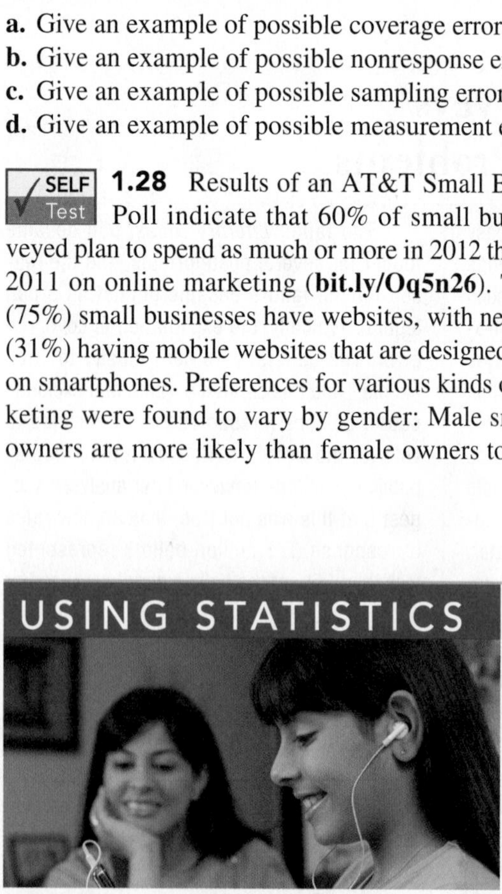

Visage / Getty Images

The analysts charged by GT&M CEO Emma Levia to identify, define, and collect the data that would be helpful in setting a price for Whitney Wireless have completed their task. The group has identified a number of variables to analyze. In the course of doing this work, the group realized that most of the variables to study would be discrete numerical variables based on data that (ac)counts the financials of the business. These data would mostly be from the primary source of the business itself, but some supplemental variables about economic conditions and other factors that might affect the long-term prospects of the business might come from a secondary data source, such as an economic agency.

The group foresaw that examining several categorical variables related to the customers of both GT&M and Whitney Wireless would be necessary. The group discovered that the affinity ("shopper's card") programs of both firms had already collected demographic data of interest when customers enrolled in those programs. That primary source, when combined with secondary data gleaned from the social media networks to which the business belongs, might prove useful in getting a rough approximation of the profile of a typical customer that might be interested in doing business with an "A-to-Z" electronics retailer.

SUMMARY

In this chapter, you learned about the various types of variables used in business and their measurement scales. In addition, you learned about different methods of collecting data, several statistical sampling methods, and issues involved in taking samples. In the next two chapters, you will study a variety of tables and charts and descriptive measures that are used to present and analyze data.

REFERENCES

1. Biemer, P. B. , R. M. Graves, L. E. Lyberg, A. Mathiowetz, and S. Sudman. *Measurement Errors in Surveys*. New York: Wiley Interscience, 2004.
2. Cochran, W. G. *Sampling Techniques*, 3rd ed. New York: Wiley, 1977.
3. Fowler, F. J. *Improving Survey Questions: Design and Evaluation, Applied Special Research Methods Series*, Vol. 38, Thousand Oaks, CA: Sage Publications, 1995.
4. Keeling, K., and R. Pavur. "Statistical Accuracy of Spreadsheet Software." *The American Statistician* 65 (2011): 265–273.
5. McCullough, B. D., and D. Heiser. "On the Accuracy of Statistical Procedures in Microsoft Excel 2007." *Computational Statistics and Data Analysis* 52 (2008): 4568–4606.
6. *Microsoft Excel 2010*. Redmond, WA: Microsoft Corporation, 2010.
7. Nash, J. C. "Spreadsheets in Statistical Practice—Another Look." *The American Statistician* 60 (2006): 287–289.
8. Osbourne, J. *Best Practices in Data Cleaning*. Thousand Oaks, CA: Sage Publications, 2012
9. Rand Corporation. *A Million Random Digits with 100,000 Normal Deviates*. Glencoe, IL: The Free Press, 1955.
10. Squire, P. "Why the 1936 *Literary Digest* Poll Failed." *Public Opinion Quarterly* 52 (1988): 125–133.
11. Sudman, S., N. M. Bradburn, and N. Schwarz. *Thinking About Answers: The Application of Cognitive Processes to Survey Methodology*. San Francisco, CA: Jossey-Bass, 1993.

KEY TERMS

CHECKING YOUR UNDERSTANDING

1.31 What is the difference between a sample and a population?

1.32 What is the difference between a categorical variable and a numerical variable?

1.33 What is the difference between a discrete numerical variable and a continuous numerical variable?

1.34 What is the difference between a nominal scaled variable and an ordinal scaled variable?

1.35 What is the difference between an interval scaled variable and a ratio scaled variable?

CHAPTER REVIEW PROBLEMS

1.36 Visit the official website for Excel, **www.office.microsoft.com/excel**. Read about the program and then think about the ways the program could be useful in statistical analysis.

1.37 Results of an AT&T Small Business Tech Poll indicate that 60% of small businesses surveyed plan to spend at least as much in 2012 as they did in 2011 on online marketing (**bit.ly/Oq5n26**). Three in four (75%) small businesses have websites, and nearly one-third (31%) have mobile websites that are designed to be viewed on a smartphone. Preferences for various kinds of online marketing were found to vary by gender: Male small business owners are more likely than female owners to rely on their company website for marketing (65% vs. 58%), whereas female small business owners are more likely than their male counterparts to employ social media to market their business (48% vs. 34%). These results are based on an online survey, conducted in November 2011, of 1,232 small business owners and/or employees responsible for information technology (IT). The sample of participating small businesses, having between 2 and 99 employees, was drawn from e-Rewards's online business panel of companies.

a. Describe the population of interest.
b. Describe the sample that was collected.

1.38 The Gallup organization releases the results of recent polls at its website, **www.gallup.com**. Visit this site and read an article of interest.

a. Describe the population of interest.
b. Describe the sample that was collected.

1.39 A Gallup poll indicated that 29% of Americans spent more money in recent months than they used to. But the majority (58%) still said they *enjoy* saving money more than spending it. (Data extracted from E. Mendes, "More Americans Say Their Spending Is Up," **www.gallup.com**, May 3, 2012.) The results are based on telephone interviews conducted April 9–12, 2012, with a random sample of 1,016 adults, aged 18 and older, living in all 50 U.S. states and the District of Columbia.

a. Describe the population of interest.
b. Describe the sample that was collected.

1.40 The Data and Story Library (DASL) is an online library of data files and stories that illustrate the use of basic statistical methods. Visit **lib.stat.cmu.edu/index.php**, click DASL, and explore a data set of interest to you.

a. Describe a variable in the data set you selected.
b. Is the variable categorical or numerical?
c. If the variable is numerical, is it discrete or continuous?

1.41 Download and examine the U.S. Census Bureau's "Business and Professional Classification Survey (SQ-CLASS)," available at **bit.ly/OdmpnP** or through the **Get Help with Your Form** link at **www.census.gov/econ/**.

a. Give an example of a categorical variable included in the survey.
b. Give an example of a numerical variable included in the survey.

1.42 Three professors examined awareness of four widely disseminated retirement rules among employees at the University of Utah. These rules provide simple answers to questions about retirement planning (R. N. Mayer, C. D. Zick, and M. Glaittle, "Public Awareness of Retirement Planning Rules of Thumb," *Journal of Personal Finance*, 2011 10(1), 12–35). At the time of the investigation, there were approximately 10,000 benefitted employees, and 3,095 participated in the study. Demographic data collected on these 3,095 employees included gender, age (years), education level (years completed), marital status, household income ($), and employment category.

a. Describe the population of interest.
b. Describe the sample that was collected.
c. Indicate whether each of the demographic variables mentioned is categorical or numerical.

1.43 A manufacturer of cat food is planning to survey households in the United States to determine purchasing habits of cat owners. Among the variables to be collected are the following:

i. The primary place of purchase for cat food
ii. Whether dry or moist cat food is purchased
iii. The number of cats living in the household
iv. Whether any cat living in the household is pedigreed

a. For each of the four items listed, indicate whether the variable is categorical or numerical. If it is numerical, is it discrete or continuous?
b. Develop five categorical questions for the survey.
c. Develop five numerical questions for the survey.

CHAPTER

2 Organizing and Visualizing Data

Learning Objectives

In this chapter, you learn:

- To construct tables and charts for categorical data
- To construct tables and charts for numerical data
- The principles of properly presenting graphs
- To organize and analyze many variables

the SHORT TAKES for Chapter 1 to learn more about this advanced recoding technique.

EG1.4 TYPES of SAMPLING METHODS

Simple Random Sample

Key Technique Use the **RANDBETWEEN(*smallest integer, largest integer*)** function to generate a random integer that can then be used to select an item from a frame.

Example Create a simple random sample *with* replacement of size 40 from a population of 800 items.

In-Depth Excel Enter a formula that uses this function and then copy the formula down a column for as many rows as is necessary. For example, to create a simple random sample with replacement of size 40 from a population of 800 items, open to a new worksheet. Enter **Sample** in cell **A1** and enter the formula **=RANDBETWEEN(1, 800)** in cell **A2**. Then copy the formula down the column to cell **A41**.

Excel contains no functions to select a random sample *without* replacement. Such samples are most easily created using an add-in such as PHStat or the Analysis ToolPak, as described in the following paragraphs.

Analysis ToolPak Use **Sampling** to create a random sample *with replacement*.

For the example, open to the worksheet that contains the population of 800 items in column A and that contains a column heading in cell A1. Select **Data → Data Analysis**. In the Data Analysis dialog box, select **Sampling** from the **Analysis Tools** list and then click **OK**. In the procedure's dialog box (see below):

1. Enter **A1:A801** as the **Input Range** and check **Labels**.
2. Click **Random** and enter **40** as the **Number of Samples**.
3. Click **New Worksheet Ply** and then click **OK**.

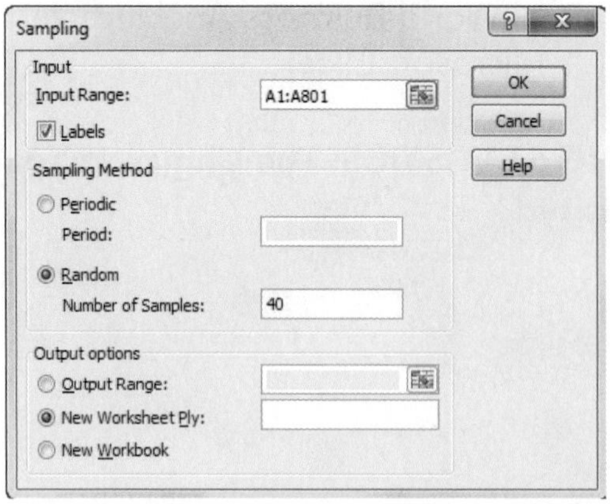

Example Create a simple random sample *without* replacement of size 40 from a population of 800 items.

PHStat Use **Random Sample Generation.**
For the example, select **PHStat → Sampling → Random Sample Generation**. In the procedure's dialog box (shown below):

1. Enter **40** as the **Sample Size.**
2. Click **Generate list of random numbers** and enter **800** as the **Population Size.**
3. Enter a **Title** and click **OK**.

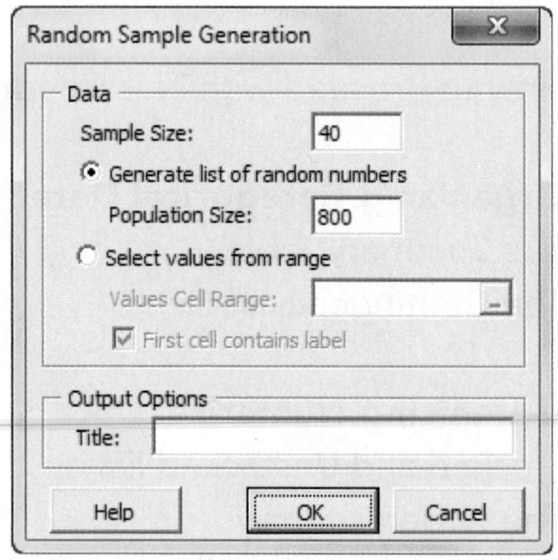

Unlike most other PHStat results worksheets, the worksheet created contains no formulas.

In-Depth Excel Use the **COMPUTE worksheet** of the **Random workbook** as a template.

The worksheet already contains 40 copies of the formula **=RANDBETWEEN(1, 800)** in column B. Because the RANDBETWEEN function samples *with* replacement as discussed at the start of this section, you may need to add additional copies of the formula in new column B rows until you have 40 unique values.

If your intended sample size is large, you may find it difficult to spot duplicates. The **ADVANCED worksheet** in the same workbook adds a formula to the cells in column C to identify whether the integer in column B is unique. Read the SHORT TAKES for Chapter 1 to learn more about this advanced technique.

EG1.5 TYPES of SURVEY ERRORS

There are no Excel Guide instructions for this section.

CHAPTER 1 EXCEL GUIDE

EG1.1 ESTABLISHING the VARIABLE TYPE

Microsoft Excel infers the variable type from the data you enter into a column. If Excel discovers a column that contains numbers, for example, it treats the column as a numerical variable. If Excel discovers a column that contains words or alphanumeric entries, it treats the column as a non-numerical (categorical) variable.

This imperfect method works most of the time, especially if you make sure that the categories for your categorical variables are words or phrases such as "yes" and "no" and are not coded values that could be mistaken for numerical values, such as "1," "2," and "3." However, because you cannot explicitly define the variable type, Excel will occasionally and mistakenly offer or allow you to do nonsensical things such as using a statistical method that is designed for numerical variables on categorical variables. If you must use coded values such as 1, 2, or 3, enter them preceded with an apostrophe, as Excel treats all values that begin with an apostrophe as non-numerical data. (You can check whether a cell entry includes a leading apostrophe by selecting a cell and viewing the contents of the cell in the formula bar. Excel will not display the leading apostrophe inside the cell itself.)

EG1.2 MEASUREMENT SCALES for VARIABLES

There are no Excel Guide instructions for this section.

EG1.3 COLLECTING DATA

Recoded Variables

Key Technique To recode a categorical variable, you first copy the original variable's column of data and then use the find-and-replace function on the copied data. To recode a numerical variable, enter a formula that returns a recoded value in a new column.

Example Using the DATA worksheet of the Recoded workbook, create the recoded variable UpperLower from the categorical variable Class and create the recoded Variable Dean's List from the numerical variable GPA.

In-Depth Excel Use the **RECODED worksheet** of the **Recoded workbook** as a model.

The worksheet already contains UpperLower, a recoded version of Class that uses the operational definitions on page 5, and Dean's List, a recoded version of GPA, in which the value No recodes all GPA values less than 3.3 and Yes recodes all values 3.3 or greater than 3.3.

The **RECODED_FORMULAS worksheet** in the same workbook shows how formulas in column I use the IF function to recode GPA as the Dean's List variable.

These recoded variables were created by first opening to the **DATA worksheet** in the same workbook and then following these steps:

1. Right-click column **D** (right-click over the shaded "D" at the top of column D) and click **Copy** in the short-cut menu.
2. Right-click column **H** and click the **first choice** in the **Paste Options** gallery.
3. Enter **UpperLower** in cell **H1**.
4. Select column **H**. With column H selected, click **Home ➔ Find & Select ➔ Replace**.

In the Replace tab of the Find and Replace dialog box:

5. Enter **Senior** as **Find what**, **Upper** as **Replace with**, and then click **Replace All**.
6. Click **OK** to close the dialog box that reports the results of the replacement command.
7. Still in the Find and Replace dialog box, enter **Junior** as **Find what** (replacing **Senior**), and then click **Replace All**.
8. Click **OK** to close the dialog box that reports the results of the replacement command.
9. Still in the Find and Replace dialog box, enter Sophomore as **Find what**, **Lower** as **Replace with**, and then click **Replace All**.
10. Click **OK** to close the dialog box that reports the results of the replacement command.
11. Still in the Find and Replace dialog box, enter **Freshman** as **Find what** and then click **Replace All**.
12. Click **OK** to close the dialog box that reports the results of the replacement command.

(This creates the recoded variable UpperLower in column H).

13. Enter **Dean's List** in cell **I1**.
14. Enter the formula **=IF(G2 < 3.3, "No", "Yes")** in cell **I2**.
15. Copy this formula down the column to the last row that contains student data (row 63).

(This creates the recoded variable Dean's List in column I.)

The RECODED worksheet uses the **IF** function to recode the numerical variable into two categories (see Appendix Section F.4). Numerical variables can also be recoded using more a complicated form that nests several IF statements together or by using the **VLOOKUP** function. The **ADVANCED worksheet** in the same workbook illustrates the use of VLOOKUP, which can recode a numerical variable into any number of categories. Read

In fact, as you will learn in Section 2.6, charts that incorporate icons as shown on the third page are considered examples of *chartjunk* and would never be used by people seeking to properly visualize data. The use of chartjunk symbols creates the impression that unit sales data are being presented. If the data are unit sales, does such data best support the claim being made, or would something else, such as dollar volumes, be a better indicator of sales at the retailer?

For the moment, let's assume that unit sales are being visualized. What are you to make of the second row, in which the three icons on the right side are much wider than the three on the left? Does that row represent a newer (wider) model being sold or a greater sales volume? Examine the fourth row. Does that row represent a decline in sales or an increase? (Do two partial icons represent more than one whole icon?) As for the fifth row, what are we to think? Is a black icon worth more than a red icon or vice versa?

At least the third row seems to tell some sort of tale of increased sales, and the sixth row tells a tale of constant sales. But what is the "story" about the seventh row? There, the partial icon is so small that we have no idea what product category the icon represents.

Perhaps a more serious issue is those curious chart labels. "Latest twelve months" is ambiguous; it could include months from the current year as well as months from one year ago and therefore may not be an equivalent time period to "two years ago." But the business was established in 2001, and the claim being made is "best sales year ever," so why hasn't management included sales figures for *every* year?

Are the Whitney Wireless managers hiding something, or are they just unaware of the proper use of statistics? Either way, they have failed to properly organize and visualize their data and therefore have failed to communicate a vital aspect of their story.

In subsequent Digital Cases, you will be asked to provide this type of analysis, using the open-ended case questions as your guide. Not all the cases are as straightforward as this example, and some cases include perfectly appropriate applications of statistical methods.

USING STATISTICS

The Choice *Is* Yours

Dmitriy Shironosov / Shutterstock

Even though he is still in his 20s, Tom Sanchez realizes that he needs to start funding his 401(k) retirement plan now because you can never start too early to save for retirement. Sanchez wants to make a reasonable investment choice and believes that placing his money in retirement funds would be a good choice for his current financial situation. He decides to contact the Choice Is Yours investment service that a business professor had once said was noted for its ethical behavior and fairness toward younger investors.

What Sanchez did not know is that Choice Is Yours has already been thinking about studying a wide variety of retirement funds, with the business objective of being able to suggest appropriate funds for its younger investors. A company task force has already selected 318 retirement funds that may prove appropriate for younger investors. You have been asked to define, collect, organize, and visualize data about these funds in ways that could assist prospective clients making decisions about the funds in which they will invest. What facts about each fund would you collect to help customers compare and contrast the many funds?

You decide that a good starting point would be to define the variables for key characteristics of each fund, including each fund's past performance. You also decide to define variables such as the amount of assets that a fund manages and whether the goal of a fund is to invest in companies whose earnings are expected to substantially increase in future years (a "growth" fund) or invest in companies whose stock price is undervalued, priced low relative to their earnings potential (a "value" fund).

You collect data from appropriate sources and use the business convention of placing the data for each variable in its own column in a worksheet. As you think more about your task, you realize that 318 rows of data, one for each fund in the sample, would be a lot for anyone to review. Prospective clients such as Tom Sanchez will be forced to scroll down through several screens to view all the data and will face the challenge of remembering the data that has gone offscreen. Is there something else you can do? Can you organize and present these data to prospective clients in a more helpful and comprehensible manner?

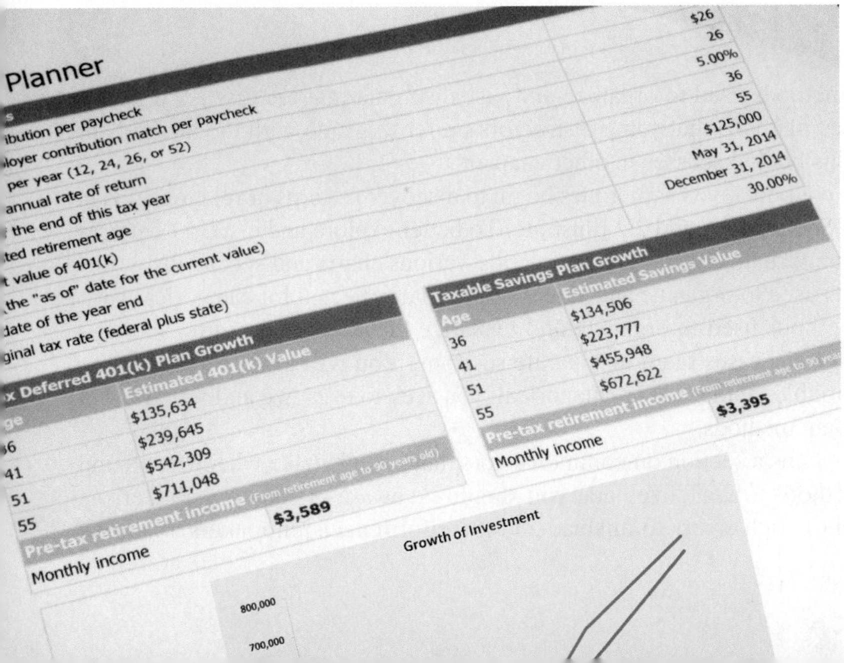

Ryan R Fox / Shutterstock

Arranging data into columns marks the beginning of the third task of the DCOVA framework, **O**rganizing the data collected into tables. While a worksheet full of data columns is a table in the simplest sense, you need to do more for the reasons noted in the scenario.

Designers of the first business computing systems faced a similar problem. Operating under the presumption that the more data shown to decision makers, the better, they created programs that listed all of the data collected, one line at a time in lengthy reports that consumed much paper and that could weigh many pounds. Such reports often failed to facilitate decision making as most decision makers did not have the time to read through a report that could be dozens or hundreds of pages long.

What those decision makers needed was information that *summarized* the detailed data. Likewise, you need to take the detailed worksheet data and organize *summary* tables. Summary tables help provide an efficient way of comprehending the data. Because the contents of most summary tables can be visualized as charts, you can also consider the fourth DCOVA task—**V**isualize the data collected—by developing charts based on the summary tables you construct.

Recently, advances in computing technology have allowed computer analysts, statisticians, and others to recycle the early premise that the more data shown to decision makers the better. Instead of repeating past mistakes, methods from the interdisciplinary field of business analytics enables you to combine the organizing and visualizing tasks with the fifth DCOVA task—**A**nalyze the data collected to reach conclusions and present those results. For this reason, this chapter includes a section that uses worksheet data and standard Microsoft Excel features to demonstrate the principles of business analytics. (Typical applications of business analytics use many large sets of data concurrently and programs much more powerful than Microsoft Excel, but the principles remain the same.)

Student Tip
To avoid confusing these two terms, remember that a *parameter* is for a *population* (two *p* words) and a *statistic* is for a *sample* (two *s* words).

Before you learn how to organize and visualize your data, recall from Section 1.3 that you collect your data from either a population or a sample. As part of the **O**rganize, **V**isualize, and **A**nalyze tasks, you will often create measures that help describe data collected for a variable. If you collected population data, each measure that describes a variable is called a **parameter**. If you collected sample data, each measure that describes a variable is called a **statistic**. In the Choice *Is* Yours scenario, in which you are working with a *sample* of 318 funds, you would need to identify the relevant *statistics* that you could present to the task force for their consideration.

For its examples, this chapter makes extensive use of **Retirement Funds**, an Excel data workbook that contains the sample of 318 funds mentioned in the scenario. (This file is one of many that you use with this book, as explained on page 12 and in Appendix C.) You may want to open the DATA worksheet of this workbook and examine the variables it contains before working the chapter examples. Learn more about retirement funds in general as well as the variables found in the Retirement Funds workbook in a Chapter 2 eBook bonus section.

How to Proceed with This Chapter

Table 2.1 presents the methods used to organize and visualize data that are discussed in this book. This table includes methods that some instructors prefer to group with the methods of this chapter but which this book discusses in other chapters.

When you organize your data, you sometimes begin to discover patterns or relationships in the data, as examples in Sections 2.1 and 2.2 illustrate. To better explore and discover patterns and relationships, you can visualize your data by creating various charts and special displays.

Because the methods used to organize and visualize the data collected for categorical variables differ from the methods used to organize and visualize the data collected for numerical variables, this chapter discusses them in separate sections. You will always need to first determine the type of variable, numerical or categorical, you seek to organize and visualize, in order to choose appropriate methods.

This chapter also contains a section on common errors that people make when visualizing data. When learning methods to visualize data, you should be aware of such possible errors because of the potential of such errors to mislead and misinform decision makers about the data you have collected.

TABLE 2.1

Methods to Organize and Visualize Data

For Categorical Variables:

Summary table, contingency table (in Section 2.1)

Bar chart, pie chart, Pareto chart, side-by-side bar chart (in Section 2.3)

For Numerical Variables:

Ordered array, frequency distribution, relative frequency distribution, percentage distribution, cumulative percentage distribution (in Section 2.2)

Stem-and-leaf display, histogram, polygon, cumulative percentage polygon (in Section 2.4)

Boxplot (in Section 3.3)

Normal probability plot (in Section 6.3)

Mean, median, mode, quartiles, geometric mean, range, interquartile range, standard deviation, variance, coefficient of variation, skewness, kurtosis (in Sections 3.1, 3.2, and 3.3)

Index numbers (in Section 16.8)

For *Two* Numerical Variables:

Scatter plot, time-series plot (in Section 2.5)

For Categorical and Numerical Variables Considered Together:

Multidimensional contingency tables (in Section 2.7)

PivotTables and business analytics (in Section 2.8)

2.1 Organizing Categorical Data

You organize categorical data by tallying the values of a variable by categories and placing the results in tables. Typically, you construct a summary table to organize the data for a single categorical variable and you construct a contingency table to organize the data from two or more categorical variables.

The Summary Table

A **summary table** tallies the values as frequencies or percentages for each category. A summary table helps you see the differences among the categories by displaying the frequency, amount, or percentage of items in a set of categories in a separate column. Table 2.2 presents a summary table that tallies responses to a recent survey that asked adults about the demands their bosses place on them during vacation time. From this table, stored in **Vacation Time**, you can conclude that 31% need to be reachable or are expected to work part time and that 65% face no demands from their bosses.

TABLE 2.2

What Bosses Demand During Vacation Time

Demand	Percentage (%)
No demands	65
Be reachable	18
Work part time	13
Other	4

Source: Data extracted and adapted from "How Does Their Boss Treat Vacation Time?" *USA Today*, July 28, 2011, p. 1B.

EXAMPLE 2.1

Summary Table of Levels of Risk of Retirement Funds

The sample of 318 retirement funds for the Choice *Is* Yours scenario (see page 39) includes the variable risk that has the defined categories low, average, and high. Construct a summary table of the retirement funds, categorized by risk.

SOLUTION From Table 2.3, you can see that almost half the funds have an average level of risk. More funds have a low risk than have a high level of risk.

TABLE 2.3

Frequency and Percentage Summary Table of Risk Level for 318 Retirement Funds

Fund Risk Level	Number of Funds	Percentage of Funds (%)
Low	99	31.13%
Average	145	45.60%
High	74	23.27%
Total	318	100.00%

The Contingency Table

Like worksheet cells, contingency table cells are the intersections of rows and columns, but unlike in a worksheet, both the rows and the columns represent variables. To identify placement, the terms row variable *and* column variable *are often used.*

A **contingency table** cross-tabulates, or tallies jointly, the values of two or more categorical variables, allowing you to study patterns that may exist between the variables. Tallies can be shown as a frequency, a percentage of the overall total, a percentage of the row total, or a percentage of the column total, depending on the type of contingency table you use. Each tally appears in its own **cell**, and there is a cell for each **joint response**, a unique combination of values for the variables being tallied. In the simplest contingency table, one that contains only two categorical variables, the joint responses appear in a table such that the tallies of one variable are located in the rows and the tallies of the other variable are located in the columns.

Student Tip
Remember, each joint response gets tallied into only one cell.

For the sample of 318 retirement funds for the Choice *Is* Yours scenario, you might create a contingency table to examine whether there is any pattern between the fund type variable and the risk level variable. Because the fund type is one of two possible values (Growth or Value) and the risk level is one of three possible values (Low, Average, or High), there would be six possible joint responses for this table. You could create the table by hand tallying the joint responses for each of the retirement funds in the sample. For example, for the first fund listed in the sample you would add to the tally in the cell that is the intersection of the Growth row and the High column because the first fund is of type Growth and risk level High. However, a better choice is to use one of the ways described in the Chapter 2 Excel Guide to automate this process.

Table 2.4 presents the completed contingency table after all 318 funds have been tallied. In this table, you can see that there are 62 retirement funds that have the value Growth for the fund type variable and the value Low for the risk level variable and that the Growth and Average was the most frequent joint response for the fund type and risk level variables.

TABLE 2.4

Contingency Table Displaying Fund Type and Risk Level

	RISK LEVEL			
FUND TYPE	Low	Average	High	Total
Growth	62	113	48	223
Value	37	32	26	95
Total	99	145	74	318

Contingency tables that display cell values as a percentage of a total can help show patterns between variables. Table 2.5 shows a contingency table that displays values as a percentage of the Table 2.4 overall total (318), Table 2.6 shows a contingency table that displays values as a percentage of the Table 2.4 row totals (223 and 95), and Table 2.7 shows a contingency table that displays values as a percentage of the Table 2.4 column totals (99, 145, and 74).

Table 2.5 shows that 70.13% of the funds sampled are growth funds, 29.87% are value funds, and 19.50% are growth funds that have low risk. Table 2.6 shows that 27.80% of the growth funds have low risk, while 38.95% of the value funds have low risk. Table 2.7 shows that of the funds that have low risk, 62.63% are growth funds. From the tables, you see that growth funds are less likely than value funds to have low risk.

TABLE 2.5

Contingency Table Displaying Fund Type and Risk Level, Based on Percentage of Overall Total

	RISK LEVEL			
FUND TYPE	**Low**	**Average**	**High**	**Total**
Growth	19.50%	35.53%	15.09%	70.13%
Value	11.64%	10.06%	8.18%	29.87%
Total	31.13%	45.60%	23.27%	100.00%

TABLE 2.6

Contingency Table Displaying Fund Type and Risk Level, Based on Percentage of Row Total

	RISK LEVEL			
FUND TYPE	**Low**	**Average**	**High**	**Total**
Growth	27.80%	50.67%	21.52%	100.00%
Value	38.95%	33.68%	27.37%	100.00%
Total	31.13%	45.60%	23.27%	100.00%

TABLE 2.7

Contingency Table Displaying Fund Type and Risk Level, Based on Percentage of Column Total

	RISK LEVEL			
FUND TYPE	**Low**	**Average**	**High**	**Total**
Growth	62.63%	77.93%	64.86%	70.13%
Value	37.37%	22.07%	35.14%	29.87%
Total	100.00%	100.00%	100.00%	100.00%

Problems for Section 2.1

LEARNING THE BASICS

2.1 A categorical variable has three categories, with the following frequencies of occurrence:

Category	Frequency
A	13
B	28
C	9

a. Compute the percentage of values in each category.

b. What conclusions can you reach concerning the categories?

2.2 The following data represent the responses to two questions asked in a survey of 40 college students majoring in business: What is your gender? (M = male; F = female) and What is your major? (A = Accounting; C = Computer Information Systems; M = Marketing):

Gender:	M	M	M	F	M	F	F	M	F	M	F	M	M	M	M	F	F	M	F	F
Major:	A	C	C	M	A	C	A	A	C	C	A	A	A	M	C	M	A	A	A	C

Gender:	M	M	M	M	F	M	F	F	M	M	F	M	M	M	M	F	M	F	M	M
Major:	C	C	A	A	M	M	C	A	A	A	C	C	A	A	A	A	C	C	A	C

a. Tally the data into a contingency table where the two rows represent the gender categories and the three columns represent the academic major categories.
b. Construct contingency tables based on percentages of all 40 student responses, based on row percentages and based on column percentages.

APPLYING THE CONCEPTS

2.3 The Gallup organization releases the results of recent polls at its website, **www.gallup.com**. Visit this site and read an article of interest.
a. Describe a parameter of interest.
b. Describe the statistic used to estimate the parameter in (a).

2.4 A Gallup poll that was based on telephone interviews conducted April 9–12, 2012, using a random sample of 1,016 adults aged 18 and older, living in all 50 U.S. states and the District of Columbia, indicated that 29% of Americans spent more money in recent months than they had spent in earlier months. But the majority (58%) still said that they *enjoy* saving money more than spending it. (Data extracted from E. Mendes, "More Americans Say Their Spending Is Up," **www.gallup.com**, May 3, 2012.)
a. Is 29% a statistic or a parameter? Explain.
b. Is 58% a statistic or a parameter? Explain.

2.5 The 2012 Data Breach Investigations Report (DBIR) is a recounting of the many facets of corporate data theft. In this document, the Verizon RISK Team reported that there were 855 data breaches in 2011; various external agents were responsible for 840 of them, summarized as follows:

External Agent Category	Frequency
Organized criminal group	697
Unknown	84
Unaffiliated person(s)	34
Activist group	17
Former employee	8
Relative or acquaintance of employee	0

Source: Data extracted from "The Data Breach Investigations Report," **www.verizonbusiness.com**, March, 2012, p. 20.

a. Compute the percentage of values in each category.
b. What conclusions can you reach concerning the data breaches?

SELF Test **2.6** The following table represents world oil production in millions of barrels a day in the third quarter of 2011:

Region	Oil Production (millions of barrels a day)
Iran	3.53
Saudi Arabia	9.34
Other OPEC countries	22.87
Non-OPEC countries	52.52

Source: International Energy Agency, 2012.

a. Compute the percentage of values in each category.
b. What conclusions can you reach concerning the production of oil in the third quarter of 2011?

2.7 A May 2012 survey of millennials, people aged 18 to 30, explored that group's buying habits. Millennials who were identified as being likely to purchase a computer during the next six months were asked to indicate the brand of the computer they were likely to purchase. The responses were:

Brand	Frequency
Apple	161
HP	77
Dell	81
Toshiba	22
Sony	10
Other	49

Source: Data extracted from "Exclusive Survey: The Hottest Brands Among Millennials," *The Fiscal Times*, May 15, 2012.

a. Compute the percentage of values for each brand.
b. What conclusions can you reach concerning the hottest brands among millennials?

2.8 A survey of 1,085 adults asked "Do you enjoy shopping for clothing for yourself?" The results indicated that 51% of the females enjoyed shopping for clothing for themselves as compared to 44% of the males. (Data extracted from "Split Decision on Clothes Shopping," *USA Today*, January 28, 2011, p. 1B.) The sample sizes of males and females were not provided. Suppose that the results were as shown in the following table:

	GENDER		
ENJOY SHOPPING	**Male**	**Female**	**Total**
Yes	238	276	514
No	304	267	571
Total	542	543	1,085

a. Construct contingency tables based on total percentages, row percentages, and column percentages.
b. What conclusions can you reach from these analyses?

2.9 Each day at a large hospital, hundreds of laboratory tests are performed. The rate of "nonconformances," tests that were done improperly (and therefore need to be redone), has seemed to be steady, at about 4%. In an effort to get to the root cause of the nonconformances, the director of the lab decided to study the results for a single day. The laboratory tests were subdivided by the shift of workers who performed the lab tests. The results are as follows:

LAB TESTS PERFORMED	SHIFT Day	Evening	Total
Nonconforming	16	24	40
Conforming	654	306	960
Total	670	330	1,000

a. Construct contingency tables based on total percentages, row percentages, and column percentages.
b. Which type of percentage—row, column, or total—do you think is most informative for these data? Explain.
c. What conclusions concerning the pattern of nonconforming laboratory tests can the laboratory director reach?

2.10 Do social recommendations increase ad effectiveness? A study of online video viewers compared viewers who arrived at an advertising video for a particular brand by following a social media recommendation link to viewers who arrived at the same video by Web browsing. Data were collected on whether the viewer could correctly recall the brand being advertised after seeing the video. The results were:

ARRIVAL METHOD	CORRECTLY RECALLED THE BRAND Yes	No
Recommendation	407	150
Browsing	193	91

Source: Data extracted from "Social Ad Effectiveness: An Unruly White Paper," **www.unrulymedia.com**, January 2012, p. 3.

What do these results tell you about social recommendations?

2.2 Organizing Numerical Data

You organize numerical data by creating ordered arrays or distributions. To prepare the data collected for organization, you must first decide if you will need to analyze your numerical variables by groups that are defined by the values of a second, categorical variable. Your decision affects how you prepare your data.

Stacked and Unstacked Data

If you decide that you will need to analyze your numerical variables by groups that are defined by the values of a second, categorical variable, then you must decide whether you will use a stacked or unstacked format. In a **stacked** format, all of the values for a numerical variable appear in one column and a second, separate column contains the categorical values that identify to which subgroup each numerical value belongs. In **unstacked** format, the values for a numerical variable are divided by subgroup and placed in separate columns.

For example, for a study of meal costs at restaurants, you might decide to compare costs at restaurants located in the city to costs at restaurants in the suburbs. To prepare this data in stacked format, you would create a column for the variable meal cost and a column for the variable location, a categorical variable with the values City and Suburban. To prepare this data in unstacked format, you would create two columns, one that contains the meal costs for city restaurants and the other that contains the meal costs for suburban restaurants.

While stacked and unstacked data formats are equivalent, sometimes a particular command or function in a data analysis program requires your data to be in a particular format. (Instructions in the Excel Guides note this requirement when it arises.) While you can always manually stack or unstack data to meet such requirements, Section EG2.2 in the Excel Guide discusses a method that can simplify this task.

The Ordered Array

An **ordered array** arranges the values of a numerical variable in rank order, from the smallest value to the largest value. An ordered array helps you get a better sense of the range of values in your data and is particularly useful when you have more than a few values. For example, financial analysts reviewing travel and entertainment costs might have the business objective of determining whether meal costs at city restaurants differ from meal costs at suburban restaurants. They collect data from a sample of 50 city restaurants and from a sample of 50 suburban restaurants for the cost of one meal (in $). Table 2.8A shows the unordered data (stored in **Restaurants**). The lack of ordering prevents you from reaching any quick conclusions about meal costs.

TABLE 2.8A

Meal Cost at 50 City Restaurants and 50 Suburban Restaurants

City Restaurant Meal Costs

27 53 53 65 47 46 47 51 81 57 63 53 30 63 68 29 44 48 57 29 34 42 76 42 53 30
64 88 57 82 51 38 41 32 69 45 55 38 54 57 31 62 44 44 43 53 45 55 92 92

Suburban Restaurant Meal Costs

35 33 48 52 58 51 48 40 48 36 43 42 39 49 38 48 48 56 41 41 47 30 32 54 32 44
48 45 43 36 48 50 48 61 35 30 37 53 36 46 56 44 29 32 46 47 48 35 31 28

In contrast, Table 2.8B, the ordered array version of the same data, enables you to quickly see that the cost of a meal at the city restaurants is between $27 and $92 and that the cost of a meal at the suburban restaurants is between $28 and $61.

TABLE 2.8B

Ordered Arrays of Meal Costs at 50 City Restaurants and 50 Suburban Restaurants

City Restaurant Meal Cost

27	29	29	30	30	31	32	34	38	38	41	42	42	43
44	44	44	45	45	46	47	47	48	51	51	53	53	53
53	53	54	55	55	57	57	57	57	62	63	63	64	65
68	69	76	81	82	88	92	92						

Suburban Restaurant Meal Cost

28	29	30	30	31	32	32	32	33	35	35	35	36	36
36	37	38	39	40	41	41	42	43	43	44	44	45	46
46	47	47	48	48	48	48	48	48	48	48	48	49	50
51	52	53	54	56	56	58	61						

When your collected data contains a large number of values, reaching conclusions from an ordered array can be difficult. In such cases, creating one of the distributions discussed in the following pages would be a better choice.

The Frequency Distribution

A **frequency distribution** tallies the values of a numerical variable into a set of numerically ordered **classes**. Each class groups a mutually exclusive range of values, called a **class interval**. Each value can be assigned to only one class, and every value must be contained in one of the class intervals.

To create a useful frequency distribution, you must consider how many classes would be appropriate for your data as well as determine a suitable *width* for each class interval. In general, a frequency distribution should have at least 5 and no more than 15 classes because having too few or too many classes provides little new information. To determine the **class interval width** [see Equation (2.1)], you subtract the lowest value from the highest value and divide that result by the number of classes you want your frequency distribution to have.

DETERMINING THE CLASS INTERVAL WIDTH

$$\text{Interval width} = \frac{\text{highest value} - \text{lowest value}}{\text{number of classes}} \tag{2.1}$$

For the city restaurant meal cost data shown in Tables 2.8A and 2.8B, between 5 and 10 classes are acceptable, given the size (50) of that sample. From the city restaurant meal costs ordered array in Table 2.8B, the difference between the highest value of \$92 and the lowest value of \$27 is \$65. Using Equation (2.1), you approximate the class interval width as follows:

$$\frac{65}{10} = 6.5$$

This result suggests that you should choose an interval width of \$6.50. However, your width should always be an amount that simplifies the reading and interpretation of the frequency distribution. In this example, an interval width of \$10 would be much better than an interval width of \$6.5.

Because each value can appear in only one class, you must establish proper and clearly defined **class boundaries** for each class. For example, if you chose \$10 as the class interval for the restaurant data, you would need to establish boundaries that would include all the values and simplify the reading and interpretation of the frequency distribution. Because the cost of a city restaurant meal varies from \$27 to \$92, establishing the first class interval as \$20 to less than \$30, the second as \$30 to less than \$40, and so on, until the last class interval is \$90 to less than \$100, would meet the requirements. Table 2.9 contains frequency distributions of the cost per meal for the 50 city restaurants and the 50 suburban restaurants using these class intervals.

TABLE 2.9

Frequency Distributions of the Meal Costs for 50 City Restaurants and 50 Suburban Restaurants

Meal Cost (\$)	City Frequency	Suburban Frequency
20 but less than 30	3	2
30 but less than 40	7	16
40 but less than 50	13	23
50 but less than 60	14	8
60 but less than 70	7	1
70 but less than 80	1	0
80 but less than 90	3	0
90 but less than 100	2	0
Total	50	50

Student Tip

The total of the frequency column must always equal the total number of values.

The frequency distribution allows you to reach some preliminary conclusions about the data. For example, Table 2.9 shows that the cost of city restaurant meals is concentrated between \$40 and \$60, while the cost of suburban restaurant meals is concentrated between \$30 and \$50.

For some charts discussed later in this chapter, class intervals are identified by their **class midpoints**, the values that are halfway between the lower and upper boundaries of each class. For the frequency distributions shown in Table 2.9, the class midpoints are \$25, \$35, \$45, \$55, \$65, \$75, \$85, and \$95. Note that well-chosen class intervals lead to class midpoints that are simple to read and interpret, as in this example.

If the data you have collected does not contain a large number of values, different sets of class intervals can create different impressions of the data. Such perceived changes will diminish as you collect more data. Likewise, choosing different lower and upper class boundaries can also affect impressions.

EXAMPLE 2.2

Frequency Distributions of the Three-Year Return Percentages for Growth and Value Funds

As a member of the company task force in The Choice *Is* Yours scenario (see page 39), you are examining the sample of 318 retirement funds stored in **Retirement Funds**. You want to compare the numerical variable 3YrReturn%, the three-year percentage return of a fund, for the two subgroups that are defined by the categorical variable Type (Growth and Value). You construct separate frequency distributions for the growth funds and the value funds.

SOLUTION The three-year percentage returns for the growth funds are concentrated between 15 and 30 and the value funds are concentrated between 15 and 25 (see Table 2.10).

TABLE 2.10

Frequency Distributions of the Three-Year Return Percentage for Growth and Value Funds

Three-Year Return Percentage	Growth Frequency	Value Frequency
0 but less than 5	1	0
5 but less than 10	2	1
10 but less than 15	16	12
15 but less than 20	52	35
20 but less than 25	101	29
25 but less than 30	33	9
30 but less than 35	13	7
35 but less than 40	2	2
40 but less than 45	0	0
45 but less than 50	0	0
50 but less than 55	2	0
55 but less than 60	0	0
60 but less than 65	1	0
Total	223	95

In the solution for Example 2.2, the total frequency is different for each group (223 and 95). When such totals differ among the groups being compared, you cannot compare the distributions directly as was done in Table 2.9 because of the chance that the table will be misinterpreted. For example, the frequencies for the class interval "10 but less than 15" *look* similar—16 and 12—but represent two very different parts of a whole: 16 out of 223 and 12 out of 95, or about 7% and 13%, respectively. When the total frequency differs among the groups being compared, you construct either a relative frequency distribution or a percentage distribution.

Classes and Excel Bins

To make use of Microsoft Excel features that can help you construct a frequency distribution, or any of the other types of distributions discussed in this chapter, you must implement your set of classes as a set of Excel **bins**. While bins and classes are both ranges of values, bins do not have explicitly stated intervals.

You establish bins by creating a column that contains a list of bin numbers arranged in ascending order. Each bin number explicitly states the upper boundary of its bin. Bins' lower boundaries are defined implicitly: A bin's lower boundary is the first value greater than the previous bin number. For the column of bin numbers 4.99, 9.99, and 15.99, the second bin has the explicit upper boundary of 9.99 and has the implicit lower boundary of "values greater than 4.99." Compare this to a class interval, which defines both the lower and upper boundaries of the class, such as in "*0* (lower) but *less than 5* (upper)."

Because the first bin number does not have a "previous" bin number, the first bin always has negative infinity as its lower boundary. A common workaround to this problem, used in the examples throughout this book (and in PHStat, too), is to define an extra bin, using a bin number that is slightly lower than the lower boundary value of the first class. This extra bin number, appearing first, will allow the now-second bin number to better approximate the first class, though at the cost of adding an unwanted bin to the results.

In this chapter, Tables 2.9 through 2.13 use class groupings in the form "*valueA* but less than *valueB*." You can translate class groupings in this form into nearly equivalent bins by creating a list of bin numbers that are slightly lower than each *valueB* that appears in the class groupings. For example, the Table 2.10 classes on page 48 could be translated into nearly equivalent bins by using this bin number list: –0.01 (the extra bin number is slightly lower than the first lower boundary value 0), 4.99 (slightly less than 5), 9.99, 14.99, 19.99, 24.99, 29.99, 34.99, 39.99, 44.99, 49.99, 54.99, 59.99, and 64.99.

For class groupings in the form "all values from *valueA* to *valueB*," such as the set 0.0 through 4.9, 5.0 through 9.9, 10.0 through 14.9, and 15.0 through 19.9, you can approximate each class grouping by choosing a bin number slightly more than each *valueB*, as in this list of bin numbers: –0.01 (the extra bin number), 4.99 (slightly more than 4.9), 9.99, 14.99, and 19.99.

To use your bin numbers, enter them into an empty column in the worksheet that contains your untallied data. Enter the column heading **Bins** in the row 1 cell of that column and, starting in row 2, enter your bin numbers in ascending order.

The Relative Frequency Distribution and the Percentage Distribution

Relative frequency and percentage distributions present tallies in ways other than as frequencies. A **relative frequency distribution** presents the relative frequency, or proportion, of the total for each group that each class represents. A **percentage distribution** presents the percentage of the total for each group that each class represents. When you compare two or more groups, knowing the proportion (or percentage) of the total for each group is more useful than knowing the frequency for each group, as Table 2.11 demonstrates. Compare this table to Table 2.9 on page 47, which displays frequencies. Table 2.11 organizes the meal cost data in a manner that facilitates comparisons.

TABLE 2.11

Relative Frequency Distributions and Percentage Distributions of the Meal Costs at City and Suburban Restaurants

	City		Suburban	
Meal Cost ($)	**Relative Frequency**	**Percentage (%)**	**Relative Frequency**	**Percentage (%)**
20 but less than 30	0.06	6.0	0.04	4.0
30 but less than 40	0.14	14.0	0.32	32.0
40 but less than 50	0.26	26.0	0.46	46.0
50 but less than 60	0.28	28.0	0.16	16.0
60 but less than 70	0.14	14.0	0.02	2.0
70 but less than 80	0.02	2.0	0.00	0.0
80 but less than 90	0.06	6.0	0.00	0.0
90 but less than 100	0.04	4.0	0.00	0.0
Total	1.00	100.0	1.00	100.0

The **proportion**, or **relative frequency**, in each group is equal to the number of *values* in each class divided by the total number of values. The percentage in each group is its proportion multiplied by 100%.

COMPUTING THE PROPORTION OR RELATIVE FREQUENCY

The proportion, or relative frequency, is the number of *values* in each class divided by the total number of values:

$$\text{Proportion} = \text{relative frequency} = \frac{\text{number of values in each class}}{\text{total number of values}} \quad \textbf{(2.2)}$$

If there are 80 values and the frequency in a certain class is 20, the proportion of values in that class is

$$\frac{20}{80} = 0.25$$

and the percentage is

$$0.25 \times 100\% = 25\%$$

You construct a relative frequency distribution by first determining the relative frequency in each class. For example, in Table 2.9 on page 47, there are 50 city restaurants, and the cost per meal at 14 of these restaurants is between \$50 and \$60. Therefore, as shown in Table 2.11, the proportion (or relative frequency) of meals that cost between \$50 and \$60 at city restaurants is

$$\frac{14}{50} = 0.28$$

> **Student Tip**
> The total of the relative frequency column must always be 1.00. The total of the percentage column must always be 100.

You construct a percentage distribution by multiplying each proportion (or relative frequency) by 100%. Thus, the proportion of meals at city restaurants that cost between \$50 and \$60 is 14 divided by 50, or 0.28, and the percentage is 28%. Table 2.11 presents the relative frequency distribution and percentage distribution of the cost of meals at city and suburban restaurants.

From Table 2.11, you conclude that meal cost is slightly more at city restaurants than at suburban restaurants. You note that 14% of the city restaurant meals cost between \$60 and \$70 as compared to 2% of the suburban restaurant meals and that 14% of the city restaurant meals cost between \$30 and \$40 as compared to 32% of the suburban restaurant meals.

EXAMPLE 2.3

Relative Frequency Distributions and Percentage Distributions of the Three-Year Return Percentage for Growth and Value Funds

As a member of the company task force in The Choice *Is* Yours scenario (see page 39), you want to properly compare the three-year return percentages for the growth and value retirement funds. You construct relative frequency distributions and percentage distributions for these funds.

SOLUTION From Table 2.12, you conclude that the three-year return percentage for the growth funds is higher than the three-year return percentage for the value funds. For example, 7.17% of the growth funds have returns between 10 and 15, while 12.63% of the value funds have returns between 10 and 15. Of the growth funds, 45.29% have returns between 20 and 25 as compared to 30.53% of the value funds.

TABLE 2.12

Relative Frequency Distributions and Percentage Distributions of the Three-Year Return Percentage for Growth and Value Funds

	Growth		Value	
Three-Year Return Percentage	Relative Frequency	Percentage	Relative Frequency	Percentage
0 but less than 5	0.0045	0.45	0.0000	0.00
5 but less than 10	0.0090	0.90	0.0105	1.05
10 but less than 15	0.0717	7.17	0.1263	12.63
15 but less than 20	0.2332	23.32	0.3684	36.84
20 but less than 25	0.4529	45.29	0.3053	30.53
25 but less than 30	0.1480	14.80	0.0947	9.47
30 but less than 35	0.0583	5.83	0.0737	7.37
35 but less than 40	0.0090	0.90	0.0211	2.11
40 but less than 45	0.0000	0.00	0.0000	0.00
45 but less than 50	0.0000	0.00	0.0000	0.00
50 but less than 55	0.0090	0.90	0.0000	0.00
55 but less than 60	0.0000	0.00	0.0000	0.00
60 but less than 65	0.0045	0.45	0.0000	0.00
Total	1.0000	100.00	1.0000	100.00

The Cumulative Distribution

The **cumulative percentage distribution** provides a way of presenting information about the percentage of values that are less than a specific amount. You use a percentage distribution as the basis to construct a cumulative percentage distribution.

For example, you might want to know what percentage of the city restaurant meals cost less than \$40 or what percentage cost less than \$50. Starting with the Table 2.11 meal cost percentage distribution for city restaurant meal costs, you combine the percentages of individual class intervals to form the cumulative percentage distribution. Table 2.13 presents the necessary calculations. From this table, you see that none (0%) of the meals cost less than \$20, 6% of meals cost less than \$30, 20% of meals cost less than \$40 (because 14% of the meals cost between \$30 and \$40), and so on, until all 100% of the meals cost less than \$100.

TABLE 2.13

Developing the Cumulative Percentage Distribution for City Restaurant Meal Costs

From Table 2.11:		
Class Interval	Percentage (%)	Percentage (%) of Meal Costs That Are Less Than the Class Interval Lower Boundary
20 but less than 30	6	0 (there are no meals that cost less than 20)
30 but less than 40	14	6 = 0 + 6
40 but less than 50	26	20 = 6 + 14
50 but less than 60	28	46 = 6 + 14 + 26
60 but less than 70	14	74 = 6 + 14 + 26 + 28
70 but less than 80	2	88 = 6 + 14 + 26 + 28 + 14
80 but less than 90	6	90 = 6 + 14 + 26 + 28 + 14 + 2
90 but less than 100	4	96 = 6 + 14 + 26 + 28 + 14 + 2 + 6
100 but less than 110	0	100 = 6 + 14 + 26 + 28 + 14 + 2 + 6 + 4

Table 2.14 is the cumulative percentage distribution for meal costs that uses cumulative calculations for the city restaurants (shown in Table 2.13) as well as cumulative calculations for the suburban restaurants (which are not shown). The cumulative distribution shows that the cost of suburban restaurant meals is lower than the cost of meals in city restaurants. This distribution shows that 36% of the suburban restaurant meals cost less than $40 as compared to 20% of the meals at city restaurants; 82% of the suburban restaurant meals cost less than $50, but only 46% of the city restaurant meals do; and 98% of the suburban restaurant meals cost less than $60 as compared to 74% of such meals at the city restaurants.

TABLE 2.14

Cumulative Percentage Distributions of the Meal Costs for City and Suburban Restaurants

Meal Cost ($)	Percentage of City Restaurants Meals That Cost Less Than Indicated Amount	Percentage of Suburban Restaurants Meals That Cost Less Than Indicated Amount
20	0	0
30	6	4
40	20	36
50	46	82
60	74	98
70	88	100
80	90	100
90	96	100
100	100	100

Unlike in other distributions, the rows of a cumulative distribution do not correspond to class intervals. (Recall that class intervals are mutually *exclusive*. The rows of cumulative distributions are not: the next row "down" *includes* all of the rows above it.) To identify a row, you use the lower class boundaries from the class intervals of the percentage distribution as is done in Table 2.14.

EXAMPLE 2.4

Cumulative Percentage Distributions of the Three-Year Return Percentage for Growth and Value Funds

As a member of the company task force in The Choice *Is* Yours scenario (see page 39), you want to continue comparing the three-year return percentages for the growth and value retirement funds. You construct cumulative percentage distributions for the growth and value funds.

SOLUTION The cumulative distribution in Table 2.15 indicates that returns are higher for the growth funds than for the value funds. The table shows that 8.52% of the growth funds and 13.68% of the value funds have returns below 15%.The table also reveals that 31.84% of the growth funds have returns below 20 as compared to 50.53% of the value funds.

TABLE 2.15

Cumulative Percentage Distributions of the Three-Year Return Percentages for Growth and Value Funds

Three-Year Return Percentages	Growth Percentage Less Than Indicated Value	Value Percentage Less Than Indicated Value
0	0.00	0.00
5	0.45	0.00
10	1.35	1.05
15	8.52	13.68
20	31.84	50.53
25	77.13	81.05
30	91.93	90.53
35	97.76	97.89
40	98.65	100.00
45	98.65	100.00
50	98.65	100.00
55	99.55	100.00
60	99.55	100.00
65	100.00	100.00

Problems for Section 2.2

LEARNING THE BASICS

2.11 Construct an ordered array, given the following data from a sample of $n = 7$ midterm exam scores in accounting:

68 94 63 75 71 88 64

2.12 Construct an ordered array, given the following data from a sample of midterm exam scores in marketing:

88 78 78 73 91 78 85

2.13 In late 2011 and early 2012, the Universal Health Care Foundation of Connecticut surveyed small business owners across the state that employed 50 or fewer employees. The purpose of the study was to gain insight on the current small business health-care environment. Small business owners were asked if they offered health-care plans to their employees and if so, what portion (%) of the employee monthly health-care premium the business paid. The following frequency distribution was formed to summarize the *portion of premium paid* for 89 (out of 311) small businesses who offer health-care plans to employees:

Portion of Premium Paid (%)	Frequency
less than 1%	2
1% but less than 26%	4
26% but less than 51%	16
51% but less than 76%	21
76% but less than 100%	23
100%	23

Source: Data extracted from "Small Business Owners Need Affordable Health Care: A Small Business Health Care Survey," Universal Health Care Foundation of Connecticut, April 2012, p. 15.

a. What percentage of small businesses pays less than 26% of the employee monthly health-care premium?
b. What percentage of small businesses pays between 26% and 75% of the employee monthly health-care premium?
c. What percentage of small businesses pays more than 75% of the employee monthly health-care premium?

2.14 Data were collected on the Facebook website about the most "liked" fast food brands. The data values (the number of "likes" for each fast food brand) for the brands named ranged from 1.0 million to 29.2 million.

a. If these values are grouped into six class intervals, indicate the class boundaries.
b. What class interval width did you choose?
c. What are the six class midpoints?

APPLYING THE CONCEPTS

2.15 The file BBCost2011 contains the total cost ($) for four tickets, two beers, four soft drinks, four hot dogs, two game programs, two baseball caps, and parking for one vehicle at each of the 30 Major League Baseball parks during the 2011 season. These costs were

174 339 259 171 207 160 130 213 338 178 184 140
159 212 121 169 306 162 161 160 221 226 160 242
241 128 223 126 208 196

Source: Data extracted from **seamheads.com/2012/01/29/mlb-fan-cost-index/**.

a. Organize these costs as an ordered array.
b. Construct a frequency distribution and a percentage distribution for these costs.
c. Around which class grouping, if any, are the costs of attending a baseball game concentrated? Explain.

SELF Test **2.16** The file Utility contains the following data about the cost of electricity (in $) during July 2012 for a random sample of 50 one-bedroom apartments in a large city.

96	171	202	178	147	102	153	197	127	82
157	185	90	116	172	111	148	213	130	165
141	149	206	175	123	128	144	168	109	167
95	163	150	154	130	143	187	166	139	149
108	119	183	151	114	135	191	137	129	158

a. Construct a frequency distribution and a percentage distribution that have class intervals with the upper class boundaries $99, $119, and so on.
b. Construct a cumulative percentage distribution.
c. Around what amount does the monthly electricity cost seem to be concentrated?

2.17 One operation of a mill is to cut pieces of steel into parts that will later be used as the frame for front seats in an automobile. The steel is cut with a diamond saw and requires the resulting parts to be within ± 0.005 inch of the length specified by the automobile company. Data are collected from a sample of 100 steel parts and stored in Steel. The measurement reported is the difference in inches between the actual length of the steel part, as measured by a laser measurement device, and the specified length of the steel part. For example, the first value, -0.002 represents a steel part that is 0.002 inch shorter than the specified length.

a. Construct a frequency distribution and a percentage distribution.
b. Construct a cumulative percentage distribution.
c. Is the steel mill doing a good job meeting the requirements set by the automobile company? Explain.

2.18 A manufacturing company produces steel housings for electrical equipment. The main component part of the housing is a steel trough that is made out of a 14-gauge steel coil. It is produced using a 250-ton progressive punch press with a wipe-down operation that puts two 90-degree forms in the flat steel to make the trough. The distance from one side of the form to the other is critical because of weatherproofing in outdoor applications. The company requires that the width of the trough be between 8.31 inches and 8.61 inches. The widths of the troughs, in inches, collected from a sample of 49 troughs and stored in Trough, are:

8.312	8.343	8.317	8.383	8.348	8.410	8.351	8.373
8.481	8.422	8.476	8.382	8.484	8.403	8.414	8.419
8.385	8.465	8.498	8.447	8.436	8.413	8.489	8.414
8.481	8.415	8.479	8.429	8.458	8.462	8.460	8.444
8.429	8.460	8.412	8.420	8.410	8.405	8.323	8.420
8.396	8.447	8.405	8.439	8.411	8.427	8.420	8.498
8.409							

a. Construct a frequency distribution and a percentage distribution.
b. Construct a cumulative percentage distribution.
c. What can you conclude about the number of troughs that will meet the company's requirements of troughs being between 8.31 and 8.61 inches wide?

2.19 The manufacturing company in Problem 2.18 also produces electric insulators. If the insulators break when in use, a short circuit is likely to occur. To test the strength of the insulators, destructive testing in high-powered labs is carried out to determine how much *force* is required to break the insulators. Force is measured by observing how many pounds must be applied to the insulator before it breaks. The force measurements, collected from a sample of 30 insulators and stored in Force, are:

1,870	1,728	1,656	1,610	1,634	1,784	1,522	1,696
1,592	1,662	1,866	1,764	1,734	1,662	1,734	1,774
1,550	1,756	1,762	1,866	1,820	1,744	1,788	1,688
1,810	1,752	1,680	1,810	1,652	1,736		

a. Construct a frequency distribution and a percentage distribution.
b. Construct a cumulative percentage distribution.
c. What can you conclude about the strength of the insulators if the company requires a force measurement of at least 1,500 pounds before the insulator breaks?

2.20 The file Bulbs contains the life (in hours) of a sample of 40 100-watt light bulbs produced by Manufacturer A and a sample of 40 100-watt light bulbs produced by Manufacturer B. The following table shows these data as a pair of ordered arrays:

Manufacturer A					Manufacturer B				
684	697	720	773	821	819	836	888	897	903
831	835	848	852	852	907	912	918	942	943
859	860	868	870	876	952	959	962	986	992
893	899	905	909	911	994	1,004	1,005	1,007	1,015
922	924	926	926	938	1,016	1,018	1,020	1,022	1,034
939	943	946	954	971	1,038	1,072	1,077	1,077	1,082
972	977	984	1,005	1,014	1,096	1,100	1,113	1,113	1,116
1,016	1,041	1,052	1,080	1,093	1,153	1,154	1,174	1,188	1,230

a. Construct a frequency distribution and a percentage distribution for each manufacturer, using the following class interval widths for each distribution:

Manufacturer A: 650 but less than 750, 750 but less than 850, and so on.
Manufacturer B: 750 but less than 850, 850 but less than 950, and so on.

b. Construct cumulative percentage distributions.
c. Which bulbs have a longer life—those from Manufacturer A or Manufacturer B? Explain.

2.21 The file **Drink** contains the following data for the amount of soft drink (in liters) in a sample of 50 2-liter bottles:

2.109	2.086	2.066	2.075	2.065	2.057	2.052	2.044	2.036	2.038
2.031	2.029	2.025	2.029	2.023	2.020	2.015	2.014	2.013	2.014
2.012	2.012	2.012	2.010	2.005	2.003	1.999	1.996	1.997	1.992
1.994	1.986	1.984	1.981	1.973	1.975	1.971	1.969	1.966	1.967
1.963	1.957	1.951	1.951	1.947	1.941	1.941	1.938	1.908	1.894

a. Construct a cumulative percentage distribution.
b. On the basis of the results of (a), does the amount of soft drink filled in the bottles concentrate around specific values?

2.3 Visualizing Categorical Data

The chart you choose to visualize the data for a single categorical variable depends on whether you seek to emphasize how categories directly compare to each other (bar chart) or how categories form parts of a whole (pie chart), or whether you have data that are concentrated in only a few of your categories (Pareto chart). To visualize the data for two categorical variables, you use a side-by-side bar chart.

The Bar Chart

A **bar chart** visualizes a categorical variable as a series of bars, with each bar representing the tallies for a single category. In a bar chart, the length of each bar represents either the frequency or percentage of values for a category and each bar is separated by space, called a gap.

The left illustration in Figure 2.1 displays the bar chart for the Table 2.2 summary table on page 41 that tallies responses to a recent survey that asked adults about the demands their bosses place on them during vacation time. Reviewing Figure 2.1, you see that respondents are most likely to say that their bosses place no demands on their vacation time, followed by the demand to be reachable. Very few respondents mentioned other.

FIGURE 2.1 Bar chart (left) and pie chart (right) for what bosses demand during vacation time

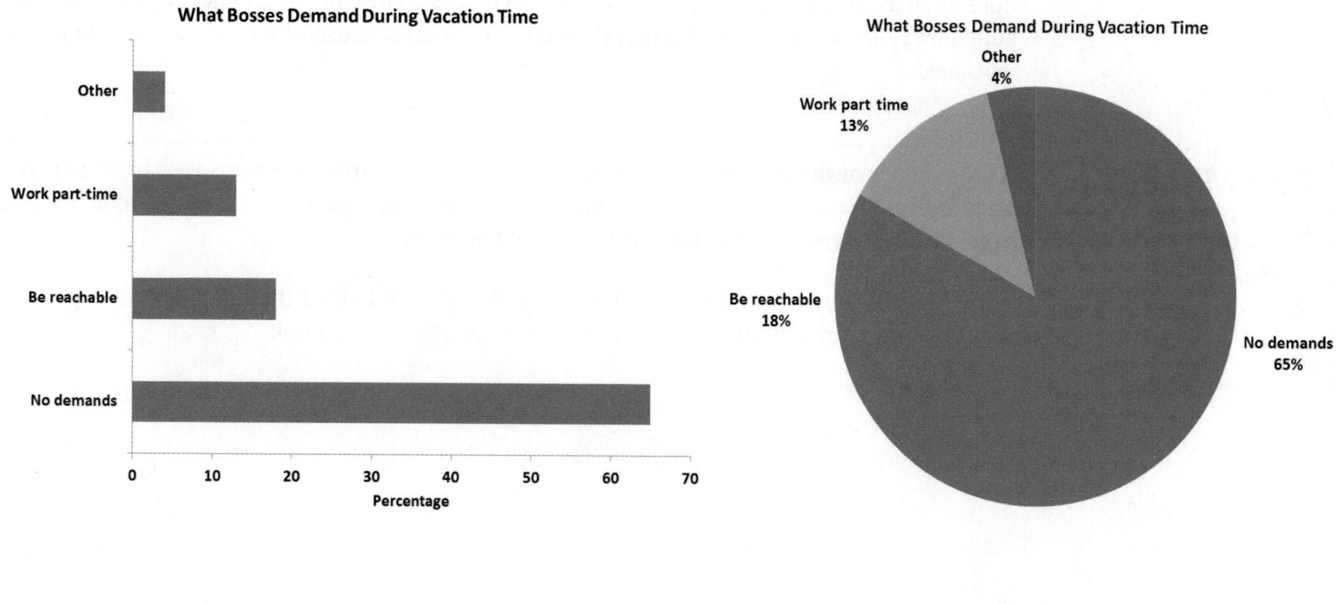

EXAMPLE 2.5

Bar Chart of Levels of Risk of Retirement Funds

As a member of the company task force in The Choice *Is* Yours scenario (see page 39), you want to first construct a bar chart of the risk of the funds that is based on Table 2.3 on page 42 and then interpret the results.

SOLUTION Reviewing Figure 2.2, you see that average risk is the largest category, followed by low risk, and high risk.

FIGURE 2.2

Bar chart of the levels of risk of retirement funds

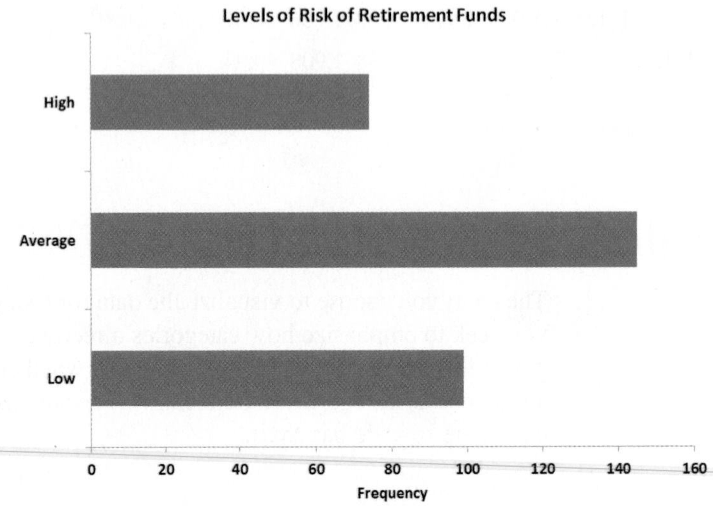

The Pie Chart

A **pie chart** uses parts of a circle to represent the tallies of each category. The size of each part, or pie slice, varies according to the percentage in each category. For example, in Table 2.2 on page 41, 65% of the respondents stated that they could completely check out of work while on vacation. To represent this category as a pie slice, you multiply 65% by the 360 degrees that makes up a circle to get a pie slice that takes up 234 degrees of the 360 degrees of the circle, as shown in Figure 2.1 on page 55. From the Figure 2.1 pie chart, you can see that the second largest slice is being reachable, which contains 18% of the pie.

Today, some assert that pie charts should never be used. Others argue that they offer an easily comprehended way to visualize parts of a whole. All commentators agree that variations such as 3D perspective pies and "exploded" pie charts, in which one or more slices are pulled away from the center of a pie, should not be used because of the visual distortions they introduce.

EXAMPLE 2.6

Pie Chart of Levels of Risk of Bond Retirement Funds

As a member of the company task force in The Choice *Is* Yours scenario (see page 39), you want to visualize the risk level of the funds by constructing a pie chart based on Table 2.3 (see page 42) for the risk variable and then interpret the results.

SOLUTION Reviewing Figure 2.3, you see that almost half of the funds are average risk, about one-third are low risk, and fewer than one-quarter are high risk.

FIGURE 2.3

Pie chart of the risk of retirement funds

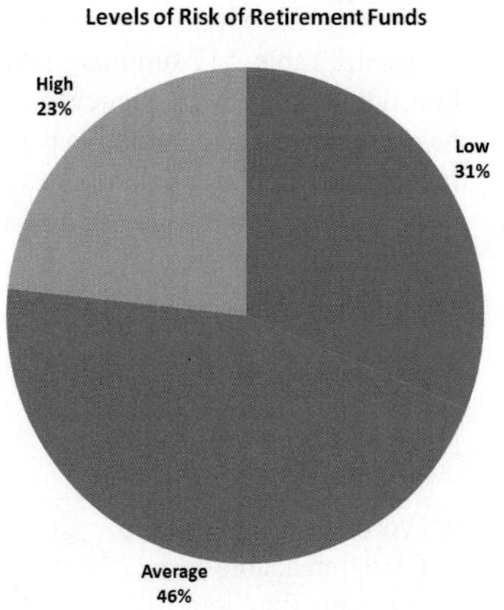

The Pareto Chart

In a **Pareto chart**, the tallies for each category are plotted as vertical bars in descending order, according to their frequencies, and are combined with a cumulative percentage line on the same chart. Pareto charts get their name from the **Pareto principle**, the observation that in many data sets, a few categories of a categorical variable represent the majority of the data, while many other categories represent a relatively small, or trivial, amount of the data.

Pareto charts help you to visually identify the "vital few" categories from the "trivial many" categories so that you can focus on the important categories. Pareto charts are also powerful tools for prioritizing improvement efforts, such as when data are collected that identifies defective or nonconforming items.

The informal "80/20" rule, which states that often 80% of results are from 20% of some thing, such as "80% of the work is done by 20% of the employees," derives from the Pareto principle.

A Pareto chart presents the bars vertically, along with a cumulative percentage line. The cumulative line is plotted at the midpoint of each category, at a height equal to the cumulative percentage. In order for a Pareto chart to include all categories, even those with few defects, in some situations, you need to include a category labeled Other or Miscellaneous. If you include such a category, you place the bar that represents that category at the far end (to the right) of the X axis.

Using Pareto charts can be an effective way to visualize data for many studies that seek causes for an observed phenomenon. For example, consider a bank study team that wants to enhance the user experience of automated teller machines (ATMs). During this study, the team identifies incomplete ATM transactions as a significant issue and decides to collect data about the causes of such transactions. Using the bank's own processing systems as a primary data source, causes of incomplete transactions are collected, stored in ATM Transactions, and then organized in the Table 2.16 summary table.

TABLE 2.16

Summary Table of Causes of Incomplete ATM Transactions

Cause	Frequency	Percentage (%)
ATM malfunctions	32	4.42
ATM out of cash	28	3.87
Invalid amount requested	23	3.18
Lack of funds in account	19	2.62
Card unreadable	234	32.32
Warped card jammed	365	50.41
Wrong keystroke	23	3.18
Total	724	100.00

Source: Data extracted from A. Bhalla, "Don't Misuse the Pareto Principle," *Six Sigma Forum Magazine*, May 2009, pp. 15–18.

To separate out the "vital few" causes from the "trivial many" causes, the bank study team creates the Table 2.17 summary table, in which the causes of incomplete transactions appear in descending order by frequency, as required for constructing a Pareto chart. The table includes the percentages and cumulative percentages for the reordered causes, which the team then uses to construct the Pareto chart shown in Figure 2.4. In Figure 2.4, the vertical axis on the left represents the percentage due to each cause and the vertical axis on the right represents the cumulative percentage.

TABLE 2.17

Ordered Summary Table of Causes of Incomplete ATM Transactions

Cause	Frequency	Percentage (%)	Cumulative Percentage (%)
Warped card jammed	365	50.41%	50.41%
Card unreadable	234	32.32%	82.73%
ATM malfunctions	32	4.42%	87.15%
ATM out of cash	28	3.87%	91.02%
Invalid amount requested	23	3.18%	94.20%
Wrong keystroke	23	3.18%	97.38%
Lack of funds in account	19	2.62%	100.00%
Total	724	100.00%	

FIGURE 2.4

Pareto chart of incomplete ATM transactions

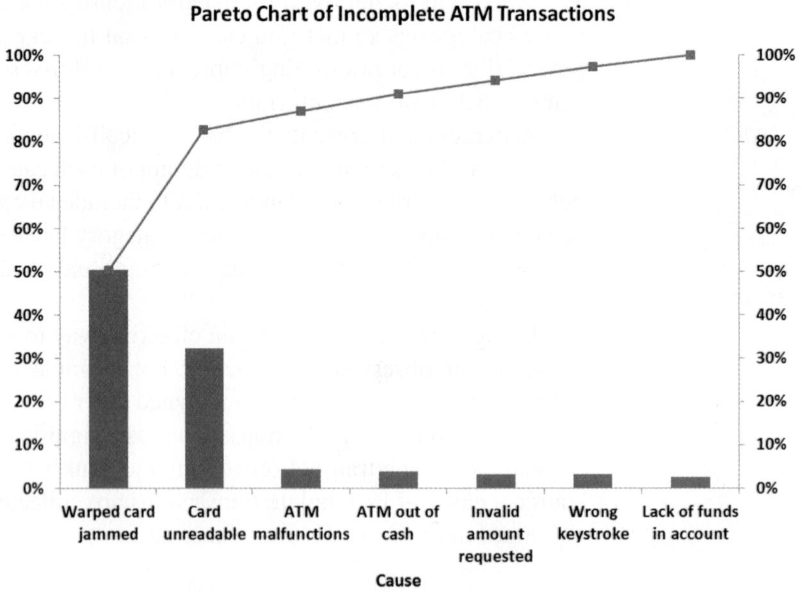

Because the categories in a Pareto chart are ordered by decreasing frequency of occurrence, the team can quickly see which causes contribute the most to the problem of incomplete transactions. (Those causes would be the "vital few," and figuring out ways to avoid such causes would be, presumably, a starting point for improving the user experience of ATMs.) By following the cumulative percentage line in Figure 2.4, you see that the first two causes, warped card jammed (50.41%) and card unreadable (32.32%), account for 82.73% of the incomplete transactions. Attempts to reduce incomplete ATM transactions due to warped or unreadable cards should produce the greatest payoff.

EXAMPLE 2.7

Pareto Chart of What Bosses Demand During Vacation Time

Construct a Pareto chart from Table 2.2 (see page 41), which summarizes what bosses demand during vacation time.

SOLUTION First, create a new table from Table 2.2 in which the categories are ordered by descending frequency and columns for percentages and cumulative percentages for the ordered categories are included (not shown). From that table, create the Pareto chart in Figure 2.5. From Figure 2.5, you see that being able to completely check out of work accounted for 65% of the responses and being able to completely check out of work, being reachable, and being expected to work up to a certain point accounted for 96% of the responses.

FIGURE 2.5
Pareto chart of what bosses demand during vacation time

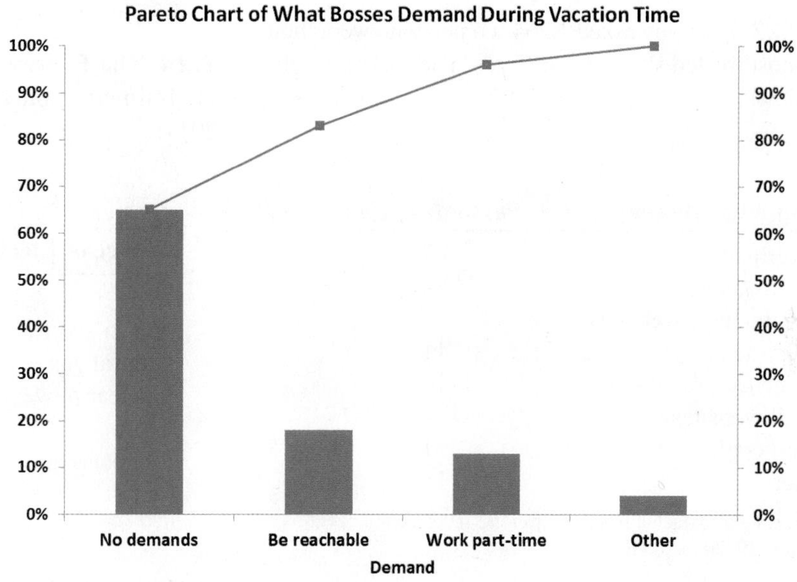

The Side-by-Side Bar Chart

A **side-by-side bar chart** uses sets of bars to show the joint responses from two categorical variables. For example, the Figure 2.6 side-by-side chart visualizes the data for the levels of risk for growth and value funds shown in Table 2.4 on page 42.

FIGURE 2.6
Side-by-side bar chart of fund type and risk level

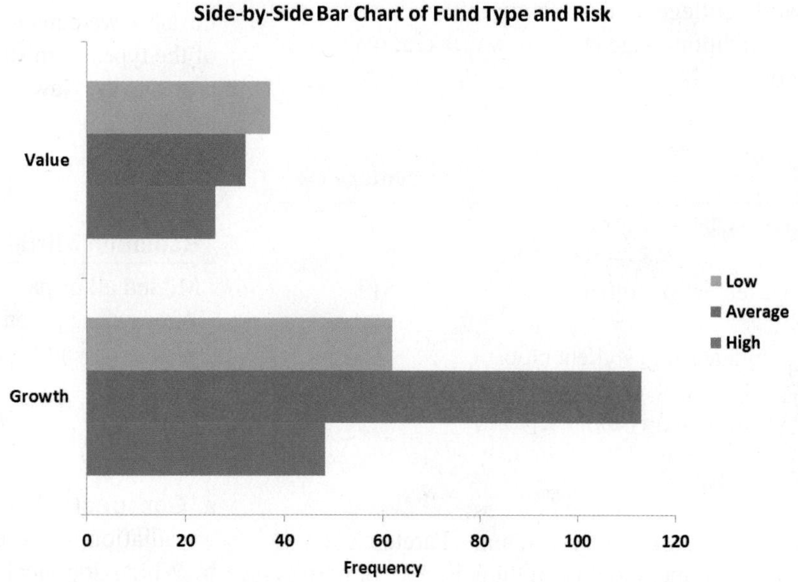

Reviewing Figure 2.6, you see that many more of the growth funds have average risk as compared to low or high risk, while the risk level of the value funds is approximately evenly divided among the three risk categories.

Problems for Section 2.3

APPLYING THE CONCEPTS

SELF Test **2.22** A survey asked 1,264 women who were their most trusted shopping advisers. The survey results were as follows:

Shopping Adviser	Percentage (%)
Advertising	7
Friends/family	45
Manufacturer websites	5
News media	11
Online user reviews	13
Retail websites	4
Salespeople	1
Other	14

Source: Data extracted from "Snapshots," *USA Today*, October 19, 2006, p. 1B.

a. Construct a bar chart, a pie chart, and a Pareto chart.
b. Which graphical method do you think is best for portraying these data?
c. What conclusions can you reach concerning women's most trusted shopping advisers?

2.23 What do college students do with their time? A survey of 3,000 traditional-age students was taken, with the results as follows:

Activity	Percentage (%)
Attending class/lab	9
Sleeping	24
Socializing, recreation, other	51
Studying	7
Working, volunteering, student clubs	9

Source: Data extracted from M. Marklein, "First Two Years of College Wasted?" *USA Today*, January 18, 2011, p. 3A.

a. Construct a bar chart, a pie chart, and a Pareto chart.
b. Which graphical method do you think is best for portraying these data?
c. What conclusions can you reach concerning what college students do with their time?

2.24 The Energy Information Administration reported the following sources of electricity in the United States in 2011:

Source of Electricity	Percentage (%)
Coal	42
Hydro and renewables	13
Natural gas	25
Nuclear power	19
Other	1

Source: Energy Information Administration, 2011.

a. Construct a Pareto chart.
b. What percentage of power is derived from coal, nuclear power, or natural gas?
c. Construct a pie chart.
d. For these data, do you prefer using a Pareto chart or a pie chart? Why?

2.25 An article discussed radiation therapy and new cures from the therapy, along with the harm that could be done if mistakes were made. The following tables represent the results of the types of mistakes made and the causes of mistakes reported to the New York State Department of Health from 2001 to 2009:

Radiation Mistakes	Number
Missed all or part of intended target	284
Wrong dose given	255
Wrong patient treated	50
Other	32

a. Construct a bar chart and a pie chart for the types of radiation mistakes.
b. Which graphical method do you think is best for portraying these data?

Causes of Mistakes	Number
Quality assurance flawed	355
Data entry or calculation errors by personnel	252
Misidentification of patient or treatment location	174
Blocks, wedges, or collimators misused	133
Patient's physical setup wrong	96
Treatment plan flawed	77
Hardware malfunction	60
Staffing	52
Software or network malfunction	24
Override of computer data by personnel	19
Miscommunication	14
Unclear/other	8

Source: Data extracted from W. Bogdanich, "A Lifesaving Tool Turned Deadly," *The New York Times,* January 24, 2010, pp. 1, 15, 16.

c. Construct a Pareto chart for the causes of mistakes.
d. Discuss the "vital few" and "trivial many" reasons for the causes of mistakes.

2.26 The following table indicates the percentage of residential electricity consumption in the United States, in a recent year organized by type of appliance:

Type of Appliance	Percentage (%)
Air conditioning	18
Clothes dryers	5
Clothes washers/other	24
Computers	1
Cooking	2
Dishwashers	2
Freezers	2
Lighting	16
Refrigeration	9
Space heating	7
Water heating	8
TVs and set top boxes	6

Source: Data extracted from J. Mouawad, and K. Galbraith, "Plugged-in Age Feeds a Hunger for Electricity," *The New York Times*, September 20, 2009, pp. 1, 28.

a. Construct a bar chart, a pie chart, and a Pareto chart.
b. Which graphical method do you think is best for portraying these data?
c. What conclusions can you reach concerning residential electricity consumption in the United States?

2.27 IBM's revenue was $24.7 billion in the first quarter of 2012. The revenue categorized by business segment was as follows:

Segment	Revenue per Segment ($billions)
Global technology services	10.1
Global business services	4.6
Software	5.6
Systems and technology	3.7
Global financing	0.5
Other	0.2

Source: Data extracted from "IBM Beats Earnings Target Despite Stalling Revenue," Statista.com, April 17, 2012.

a. Construct a bar chart and a pie chart.
b. What conclusions can you reach concerning IBM's revenue during the first quarter of 2012?

2.28 A survey of 1,085 adults asked "Do you enjoy shopping for clothing for yourself?" The results indicated that 51% of the females enjoyed shopping for clothing for themselves as compared to 44% of the males. (Data extracted from "Split Decision on Clothes Shopping," *USA Today*, January 28, 2011, p. 1B.) The sample sizes of males and females were not provided. Suppose that the results were as shown in the following table:

Enjoy Shopping for Clothing	Gender		
	Male	Female	Total
Yes	238	276	514
No	304	267	571
Total	542	543	1,085

a. Construct a side-by-side bar chart of enjoying shopping and gender.
b. What conclusions can you reach from this chart?

2.29 Each day at a large hospital, hundreds of laboratory tests are performed. The rate of "nonconformances," tests that were done improperly (and therefore need to be redone), has seemed to be steady, at about 4%. In an effort to get to the root cause of the nonconformances, the director of the lab decided to study the results for a single day. The laboratory tests were subdivided by the shift of workers who performed the lab tests. The results are as follows:

	Shift		
Lab Tests Performed	Day	Evening	Total
Nonconforming	16	24	40
Conforming	654	306	960
Total	670	330	1,000

a. Construct a side-by-side bar chart of nonconformances and shift.

b. What conclusions concerning the pattern of nonconforming laboratory tests can the laboratory director reach?

2.30 Do social recommendations increase ad effectiveness? A study of online video viewers compared viewers who arrived at an advertising video for a particular brand by following a social media recommendation link to viewers who arrived at the same video by web browsing. Data were collected on whether the viewer could correctly recall the brand being advertised after seeing the video. The results were as follows:

	Correctly Recalled the Brand	
Arrival Method	**Yes**	**No**
Recommendation	407	150
Browsing	193	91

Source: Data extracted from "Social Ad Effectiveness: An Unruly White Paper," **www.unrulymedia.com**, January 2012, p.3.

a. Construct a side-by-side bar chart of the arrival method and whether the brand was promptly recalled.

b. What do these results tell you about the arrival method and brand recall?

2.4 Visualizing Numerical Data

You visualize the data for a numerical variable through a variety of techniques that show the distribution of values. These techniques include the stem-and-leaf display, the histogram, the percentage polygon, and the cumulative percentage polygon (ogive), all discussed in this section, as well as the boxplot, which requires descriptive summary measures, as explained in Section 3.3.

The Stem-and-Leaf Display

A **stem-and-leaf display** visualizes data by presenting the data as one or more row-wise *stems* that represent a range of values. In turn, each stem has one or more *leaves* that branch out to the right of their stem and represent the values found in that stem. For stems with more than one leaf, the leaves are arranged in ascending order.

Stem-and-leaf displays allow you to see how the data are distributed and where concentrations of data exist. Leaves typically present the last significant digit of each value, but sometimes you round values. For example, suppose you collect the following meal costs (in $) for 15 classmates who had lunch at a fast-food restaurant (stored in **FastFood**):

7.42 6.29 5.83 6.50 8.34 9.51 7.10 6.80 5.90 4.89 6.50 5.52 7.90 8.30 9.60

To construct the stem-and-leaf display, you use whole dollar amounts as the stems and round the cents to one decimal place to use as the leaves. For the first value, 7.42, the stem would be 7 and its leaf would be 4. For the second value, 6.29, the stem would be 6 and its leaf 3. The completed stem-and-leaf display for these data is

Student Tip
If you turn a stem-and-leaf display sideways, the display looks like a histogram.

4	9
5	589
6	3558
7	149
8	33
9	56

EXAMPLE 2.8

Stem-and-Leaf Display of the Three-Year Return Percentage for the Value Funds

As a member of the company task force in The Choice *Is* Yours scenario (see page 39), you want to study the past performance of the value funds. One measure of past performance is the numerical variable 3YrReturn%, the three-year return percentage. Using the data from the 95 value funds, you want to visualize this variable as a stem-and-leaf display.

SOLUTION Figure 2.7 illustrates the stem-and-leaf display of the three-year return percentage for value funds.

FIGURE 2.7
Stem-and-leaf display of the three-year return percentage for value funds

Stem-and-Leaf Display of the Three-Year Return Percentage for Value Funds	
Stem unit	10
1	011234444555555555666666666677777788888888999999
2	0000011111122222222223334444555557789
3	0011123357

Figure 2.7 allows you to conclude:

- The lowest three-year return was approximately 10.
- The highest return three-year was 37.
- The three-year returns were concentrated between 10 and 30.
- Very few of the three-year returns were 30 or above.

The Histogram

A **histogram** visualizes data as a vertical bar chart in which each bar represents a class interval from a frequency or percentage distribution. In a histogram, you display the numerical variable along the horizontal (*X*) axis and use the vertical (*Y*) axis to represent either the frequency or the percentage of values per class interval. There are never any gaps between adjacent bars in a histogram.

The histograms in Figure 2.8 and throughout the rest of this book have been modified using the instructions of Appendix Section B.8 to eliminate the extra, zero-length bar that would otherwise be created due to the Excel quirk that is explained in "Classes and Excel Bins" on page 48.

Figure 2.8 visualizes the data of Table 2.9 on page 47, meal costs at city and suburban restaurants, as a pair of frequency histograms. The histogram for city restaurants shows that the cost of meals is concentrated between approximately \$40 and \$60. Very few meals at city restaurants cost more than \$70. The histogram for suburban restaurants shows that the cost of meals is concentrated between \$30 and \$50. Very few meals at suburban restaurants cost more than \$60.

FIGURE 2.8
Frequency histograms for meal costs at city and suburban restaurants

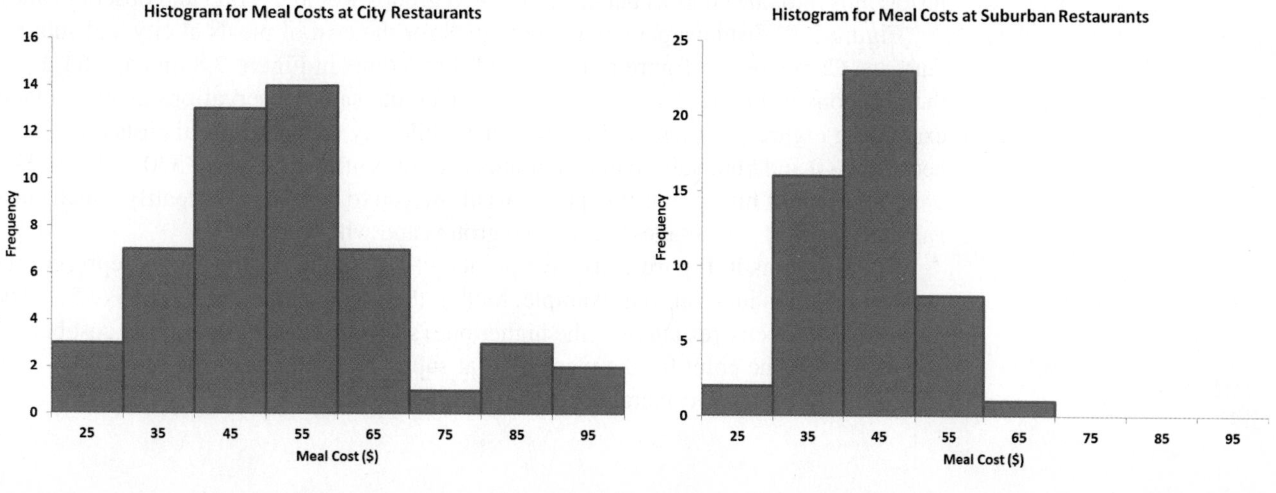

EXAMPLE 2.9
Histograms of the Three-Year Return Percentages for the Growth and Value Funds

As a member of the company task force in The Choice *Is* Yours scenario (see page 39), you seek to compare the past performance of the growth funds and the value funds, using the three-year return percentage variable. Using the data from the sample of 318 funds, you construct histograms for the growth and the value funds to create a visual comparison.

SOLUTION Figure 2.9 displays frequency histograms for the three-year return percentages for the growth and value funds.

FIGURE 2.9

Frequency histograms for the three-year return percentages for the growth and value funds

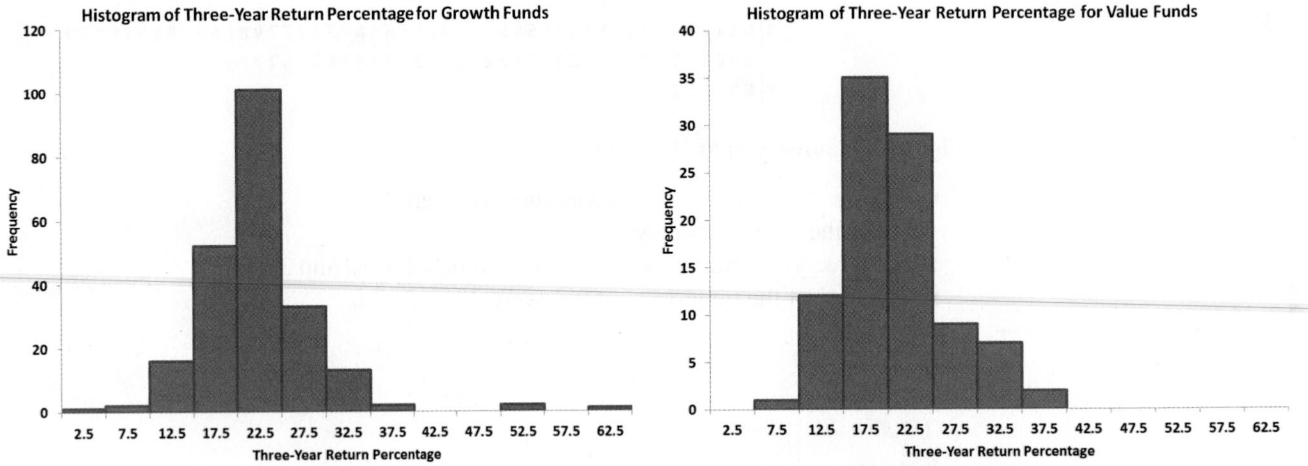

Reviewing the histograms in Figure 2.9 leads you to conclude that the returns were higher for the growth funds than for value funds. The return for growth funds is concentrated between 15 and 30, and the return for the value funds is concentrated between 15 and 25.

The Percentage Polygon

When using a categorical variable to divide the data of a numerical variable into two or more groups, you visualize data by constructing a **percentage polygon**. This chart uses the midpoints of each class interval to represent the data of each class and then plots the midpoints, at their respective class percentages, as points on a line along the X axis. While you can construct two or more histograms, as was done in Figures 2.8 and 2.9, a percentage polygon allows you to make a direct comparison that is easier to interpret. (You cannot, of course, combine two histograms into one chart as bars from the two groups would overlap and obscure data.)

Figure 2.10 displays percentage polygons for the cost of meals at city and suburban restaurants. Compare this figure to the pair of histograms in Figure 2.8 on page 63. Reviewing the polygons in Figure 2.10 allows you to make the same observations as were made when examining Figure 2.8, including the fact that while city restaurant meal costs are concentrated between $40 and $60, suburban restaurants are concentrated between $30 and $50. However, unlike the pair of histograms, the polygons allow you to more easily identify which class intervals have similar percentages for the two groups and which do not.

The polygons in Figure 2.10 have points whose values on the X axis represent the midpoint of the class interval. For example, look at the points plotted at $X = 55$ ($55). The point for meal costs at city restaurants (the higher one) show that 28% of the meals cost between $50 and $60, while the point for the meal costs at suburban restaurants (the lower one) shows that 16% of meals at these restaurants cost between $50 and $60.

FIGURE 2.10
Percentage polygons of meal costs for city and suburban restaurants

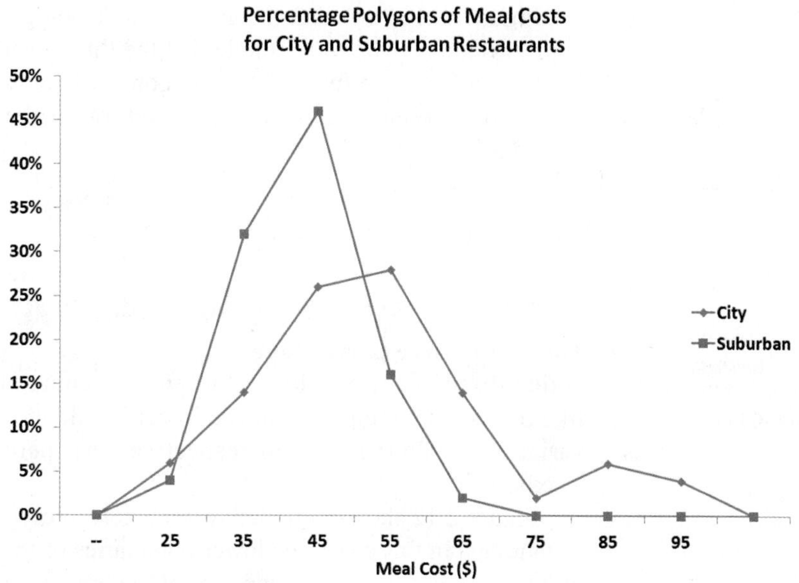

When you construct polygons or histograms, the vertical (Y) axis should include zero to avoid distorting the character of the data. The horizontal (X) axis does not need to show the zero point for the numerical variable, but a major portion of the axis should be devoted to the entire range of values for the variable.

EXAMPLE 2.10

Percentage Polygons of the Three-Year Return Percentage for the Growth and Value Funds

As a member of the company task force in The Choice *Is* Yours scenario (see page 39), you seek to compare the past performance of the growth funds and the value funds using the three-year return percentage variable. Using the data from the sample of 318 funds, you construct percentage polygons for the growth and value funds to create a visual comparison.

SOLUTION Figure 2.11 displays percentage polygons of the three-year return percentage for the growth and value funds.

FIGURE 2.11
Percentage polygons of the three-year return percentages for the growth and value funds

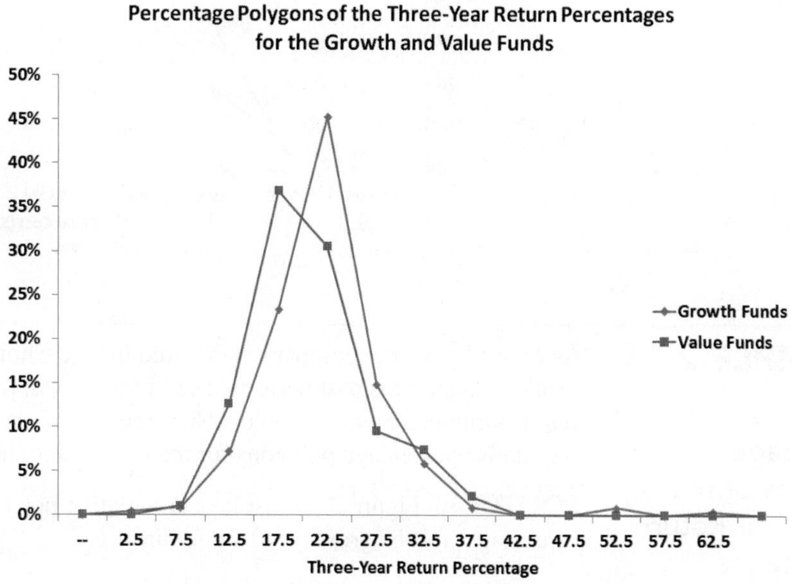

Figure 2.11 shows that the growth funds polygon is to the right of the value funds polygon. This allows you to conclude that the three-year return percentage is higher for growth funds than for value funds. The polygons also show that the return for value funds is concentrated between 15 and 25, and the return for the growth funds is concentrated between 15 and 30.

The Cumulative Percentage Polygon (Ogive)

In Microsoft Excel, you approximate the lower boundary by using the upper boundary of the previous bin.

The **cumulative percentage polygon**, or **ogive**, uses the cumulative percentage distribution discussed in Section 2.2 to plot the cumulative percentages along the *Y* axis. Unlike the percentage polygon, the lower boundary of the class interval for the numerical variable are plotted, at their respective class percentages, as points on a line along the *X* axis.

Figure 2.12 shows cumulative percentage polygons of meal costs for city and suburban restaurants. In this chart, the lower boundaries of the class intervals (20, 30, 40, etc.) are approximated by the upper boundaries of the previous bins (19.99, 29.99, 39.99, etc.). Reviewing the curves leads you to conclude that the curve of the cost of meals at the city restaurants is located to the right of the curve for the suburban restaurants. This indicates that the city restaurants have fewer meals that cost less than a particular value. For example, 46% of the meals at city restaurants cost less than $50, as compared to 82% of the meals at suburban restaurants.

FIGURE 2.12
Cumulative percentage polygons of meal costs for city and suburban restaurants

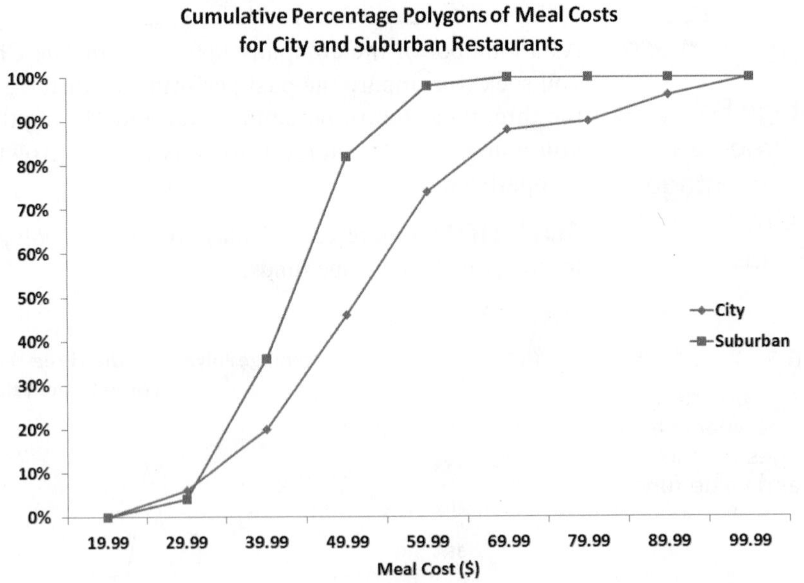

EXAMPLE 2.11

Cumulative Percentage Polygons of the Three-Year Return Percentages for the Growth and Value Funds

As a member of the company task force in The Choice *Is* Yours scenario (see page 39), you seek to compare the past performance of the growth funds and the value funds using the three-year return percentage variable. Using the data from the sample of 318 funds, you construct cumulative percentage polygons for the growth and the value funds.

SOLUTION Figure 2.13 displays cumulative percentage polygons of the three-year return percentages for the growth and value funds.

FIGURE 2.13
Cumulative percentage polygons of the three-year return percentages for the growth and value funds

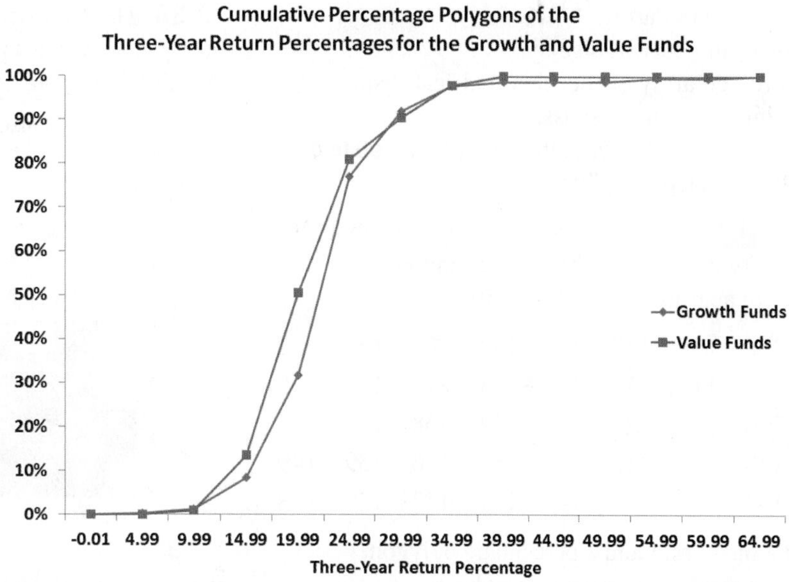

The cumulative percentage polygons in Figure 2.13 show that the curve for the three-year return percentage for the growth funds is located slightly to the right of the curve for the value funds. This allows you to conclude that the growth funds have fewer three-year return percentages that are lower than a particular value. For example, 31.84% of the growth funds had three-year return percentages below 20, as compared to 50.53% of the value funds. Also, 8.52% of growth funds had three-year return percentages below 15, as compared to 13.68% of the value funds. You can conclude that, in general, the growth funds outperformed the value funds in their three-year returns.

Problems for Section 2.4

LEARNING THE BASICS

2.31 Construct a stem-and-leaf display, given the following data from a sample of midterm exam scores in finance:

54 69 98 93 53 74

2.32 Construct an ordered array, given the following stem-and-leaf display from a sample of $n = 7$ midterm exam scores in information systems:

5	0
6	
7	446
8	19
9	2

APPLYING THE CONCEPTS

2.33 The following is a stem-and-leaf display representing the amount of gasoline purchased, in gallons (with leaves in tenths of gallons), for a sample of 25 cars that use a particular service station on the New Jersey Turnpike:

9	147
10	02238
11	125566777
12	223489
13	02

a. Construct an ordered array.

b. Which of these two displays seems to provide more information? Discuss.

c. What amount of gasoline (in gallons) is most likely to be purchased?

d. Is there a concentration of the purchase amounts in the center of the distribution?

2.34 The file BBCost2011 contains the total cost (in $) for four tickets, two beers, four soft drinks, four hot dogs, two game programs, two baseball caps, and parking for one vehicle at each of the 30 Major League Baseball parks during the 2011 season.

Source: Data extracted from **seamheads.com/2012/01/29/mlb-fan-cost-index/**.

a. Construct a stem-and-leaf display.

b. Around what value, if any, are the costs of attending a baseball game concentrated? Explain.

2.35 The file ChocolateChip contains the cost (in $) per serving of 30 grams for a sample of 18 chocolate chip cookies:

0.76 1.75 0.33 0.44 1.14 0.37 0.13 0.17 0.21
0.39 0.19 0.29 0.26 0.35 0.29 0.35 0.33 0.38

Source: Data extracted from "How the Cookie Crumbles," *Consumer Reports,* December 2011, pp. 8–9.

a. Construct an ordered array.
b. Construct a stem-and-leaf display.
c. Does the ordered array or the stem-and-leaf display provide more information? Discuss.
d. Around what value, if any, is the cost of chocolate chip cookies concentrated? Explain.

2.36 The file **Utility** contains the following data about the cost of electricity during July 2012 for a random sample of 50 one-bedroom apartments in a large city:

96	171	202	178	147	102	153	197	127	82
157	185	90	116	172	111	148	213	130	165
141	149	206	175	123	128	144	168	109	167
95	163	150	154	130	143	187	166	139	149
108	119	183	151	114	135	191	137	129	158

a. Construct a histogram and a percentage polygon.
b. Construct a cumulative percentage polygon.
c. Around what amount does the monthly electricity cost seem to be concentrated?

2.37 As player salaries have increased, the cost of attending baseball games has increased dramatically. The following histogram and cumulative percentage polygon visualizes the total cost (in $) for four tickets, two beers, four soft drinks, four hot dogs, two game programs, two baseball caps, and parking for one vehicle at each of the 30 Major League Baseball parks during the 2011 season that is stored in **BBCost2011**.

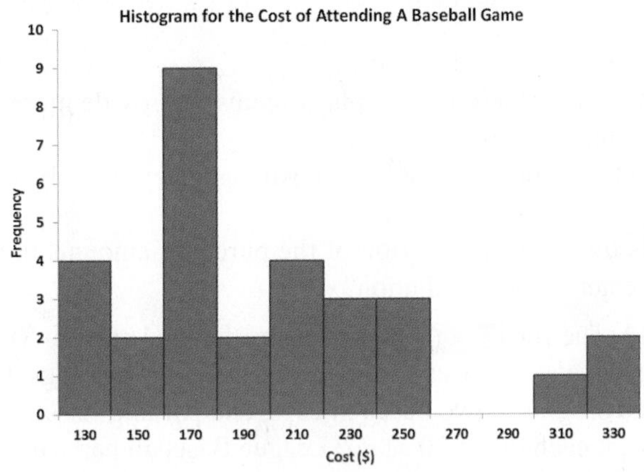

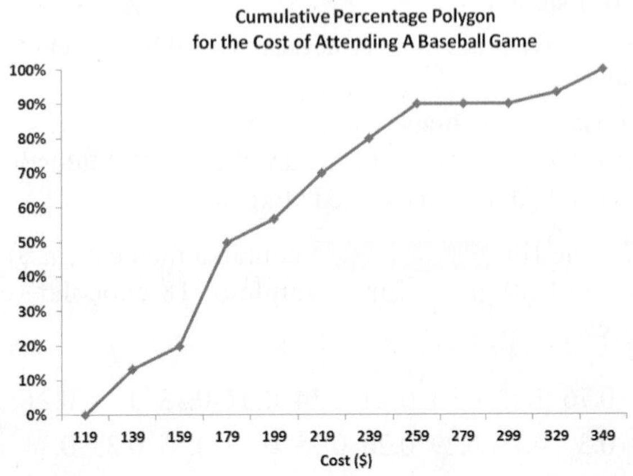

What conclusions can you reach concerning the cost of attending a baseball game at different ballparks?

2.38 The following histogram visualizes the data about the property taxes per capita for the 50 states and the District of Columbia, stored in **Property Taxes**.

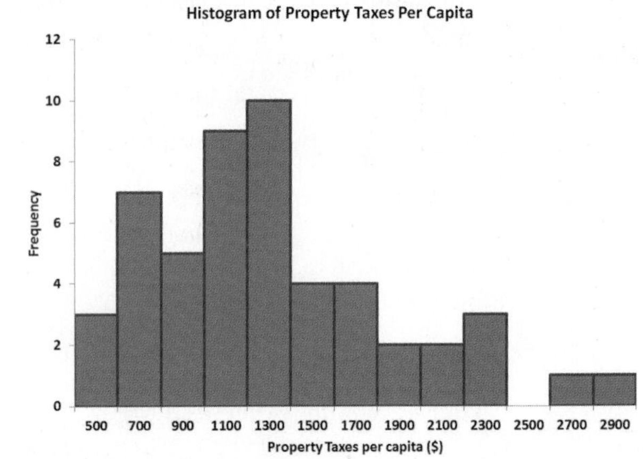

What conclusions can you reach concerning the property taxes per capita?

2.39 One operation of a mill is to cut pieces of steel into parts that will later be used as the frame for front seats in an automobile. The steel is cut with a diamond saw and requires the resulting parts to be within ± 0.005 inch of the length specified by the automobile company. The data are collected from a sample of 100 steel parts and stored in **Steel**. The measurement reported is the difference in inches between the actual length of the steel part, as measured by a laser measurement device, and the specified length of the steel part. For example, the first value, -0.002 represents a steel part that is 0.002 inch shorter than the specified length.
a. Construct a percentage histogram.
b. Is the steel mill doing a good job meeting the requirements set by the automobile company? Explain.

2.40 A manufacturing company produces steel housings for electrical equipment. The main component part of the housing is a steel trough that is made out of a 14-gauge steel coil. It is produced using a 250-ton progressive punch press with a wipe-down operation that puts two 90-degree forms in the flat steel to make the trough. The distance from one side of the form to the other is critical because of weatherproofing in outdoor applications. The company requires that the width of the trough be between 8.31 inches and 8.61 inches. The widths of the troughs, in inches, collected from a sample of 49 troughs, are stored in **Trough**.
a. Construct a percentage histogram and a percentage polygon.
b. Plot a cumulative percentage polygon.
c. What can you conclude about the number of troughs that will meet the company's requirements of troughs being between 8.31 and 8.61 inches wide?

2.41 The manufacturing company in Problem 2.40 also produces electric insulators. If the insulators break when in use, a short circuit is likely to occur. To test the strength of the insulators, destructive testing in high-powered labs is carried out to determine how much *force* is required to break the insulators. Force is measured by observing how many pounds must be applied to the insulator before it breaks. The force measurements, collected from a sample of 30 insulators, are stored in **Force**.

a. Construct a percentage histogram and a percentage polygon.
b. Construct a cumulative percentage polygon.
c. What can you conclude about the strengths of the insulators if the company requires a force measurement of at least 1,500 pounds before the insulator breaks?

2.42 The file **Bulbs** contains the life (in hours) of a sample of 40 100-watt light bulbs produced by Manufacturer A and a sample of 40 100-watt light bulbs produced by Manufacturer B. The following table shows these data as a pair of ordered arrays.

Manufacturer A					Manufacturer B				
684	697	720	773	821	819	836	888	897	903
831	835	848	852	852	907	912	918	942	943
859	860	868	870	876	952	959	962	986	992
893	899	905	909	911	994	1,004	1,005	1,007	1,015
922	924	926	926	938	1,016	1,018	1,020	1,022	1,034
939	943	946	954	971	1,038	1,072	1,077	1,077	1,082
972	977	984	1,005	1,014	1,096	1,100	1,113	1,113	1,116
1,016	1,041	1,052	1,080	1,093	1,153	1,154	1,174	1,188	1,230

Use the following class interval widths for each distribution:

Manufacturer A: 650 but less than 750, 750 but less than 850, and so on.
Manufacturer B: 750 but less than 850, 850 but less than 950, and so on.

a. Construct percentage histograms on separate graphs and plot the percentage polygons on one graph.
b. Plot cumulative percentage polygons on one graph.
c. Which manufacturer has bulbs with a longer life—Manufacturer A or Manufacturer B? Explain.

2.43 The data stored in **Drink** represents the amount of soft drink in a sample of 50 2-liter bottles.

a. Construct a histogram and a percentage polygon.
b. Construct a cumulative percentage polygon.
c. On the basis of the results in (a) and (b), does the amount of soft drink filled in the bottles concentrate around specific values?

2.5 Visualizing Two Numerical Variables

Visualizing two numerical variables together can reveal possible relationships between two variables and serve as a basis for applying the methods discussed in Chapters 13 through 16. To visualize two numerical variables, you construct a scatter plot. For the special case in which one of the two variables represents the passage of time, you construct a time-series plot.

The Scatter Plot

A **scatter plot** explores the possible relationship between two numerical variables by plotting the values of one numerical variable on the horizontal, or *X*, axis and the values of a second numerical variable on the vertical, or *Y*, axis. For example, a marketing analyst could study the effectiveness of advertising by comparing advertising expenses and sales revenues of 50 stores by using the *X* axis to represent advertising expenses and the *Y* axis to represent sales revenues.

EXAMPLE 2.12

Scatter Plot for NBA Investment Analysis

Suppose that you are an investment analyst who has been asked to review the valuations of the 30 NBA professional basketball teams. You seek to know if the value of a team reflects its revenues. You collect revenue and valuation data (both in $millions) for all 30 NBA teams, organize the data as Table 2.18, and store the data in **NBAValues**.

To quickly visualize a possible relationship between team revenues and valuations, you construct a scatter plot as shown in Figure 2.14, in which you plot the revenues on the *X* axis and the value of the team on the *Y* axis.

TABLE 2.18
Revenues and Values for NBA Teams

Team Code	Revenue ($millions)	Value ($millions)	Team Code	Revenue ($millions)	Value ($millions)	Team Code	Revenue ($millions)	Value ($millions)
ATL	105	295	IND	95	269	OKC	118	329
BOS	151	452	LAC	102	305	ORL	108	385
CHA	98	281	LAL	214	643	PHI	110	330
CHI	169	511	MEM	92	266	PHX	147	411
CLE	161	355	MIA	124	425	POR	127	356
DAL	146	438	MIL	92	258	SAC	103	293
DEN	113	316	MIN	95	264	SAS	135	404
DET	147	360	NJN	89	312	TOR	138	399
GSW	119	363	NOH	100	280	UTA	121	343
HOU	153	443	NYK	226	655	WAS	107	322

Source: Data extracted from **www.forbes.com/lists/2011/32/basketball-valuations-11_land.html.**

FIGURE 2.14
Scatter plot of revenue and value for NBA teams

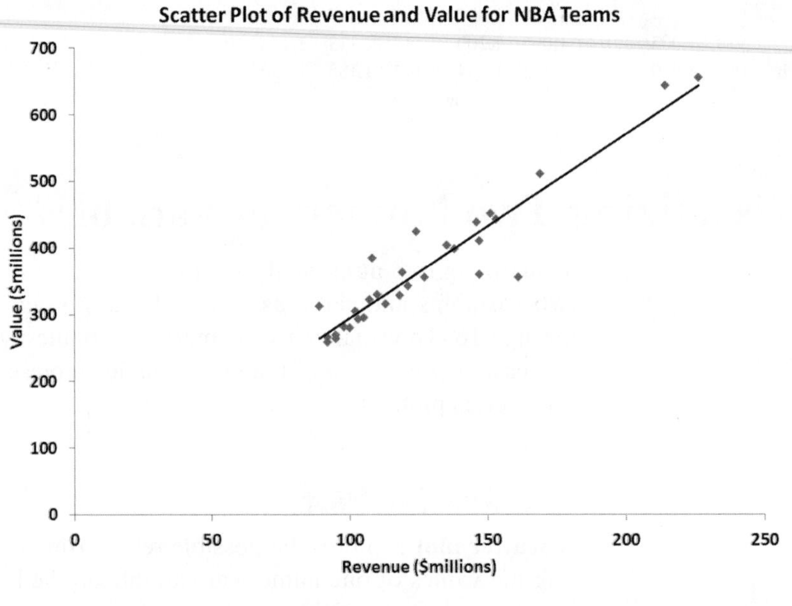

SOLUTION From Figure 2.14, you see that there appears to be a strong increasing (positive) relationship between revenues and the value of a team. In other words, teams that generate a smaller amount of revenues have a lower value, while teams that generate higher revenues have a higher value. This relationship has been highlighted by the addition of a linear regression prediction line that will be discussed in Chapter 13.

LEARN MORE
Read the SHORT TAKES for Chapter 2 for an example that illustrates a negative relationship.

Other pairs of variables may have a decreasing (negative) relationship in which one variable decreases as the other increases. In other situations, there may be a weak or no relationship between the variables.

The Time-Series Plot

A **time-series plot** plots the values of a numerical variable on the Y axis and plots the time period associated with each numerical value on the X axis. A time-series plot can help you visualize trends in data that occur over time.

EXAMPLE 2.13

Time-Series Plot for Movie Revenues

As an investment analyst who specializes in the entertainment industry, you are interested in discovering any long-term trends in movie revenues. You collect the annual revenues (in $billions) for movies released from 1995 to 2011, and organize the data as Table 2.19, and store the data in **Movie Revenues**.

To see if there is a trend over time, you construct the time-series plot shown in Figure 2.15.

TABLE 2.19

Movie Revenues (in $billions) from 1995 to 2011

Year	Revenue ($billions)	Year	Revenue ($billions)
1995	5.29	2004	9.27
1996	5.59	2005	8.95
1997	6.51	2006	9.25
1998	6.77	2007	9.63
1999	7.30	2008	9.85
2000	7.48	2009	10.65
2001	8.13	2010	10.47
2002	9.19	2011	10.20
2003	9.35		

Source: Data extracted from **www.the-numbers.com/market**, April 3, 2012.

FIGURE 2.15

Time-series plot of movie revenue per year from 1995 to 2011

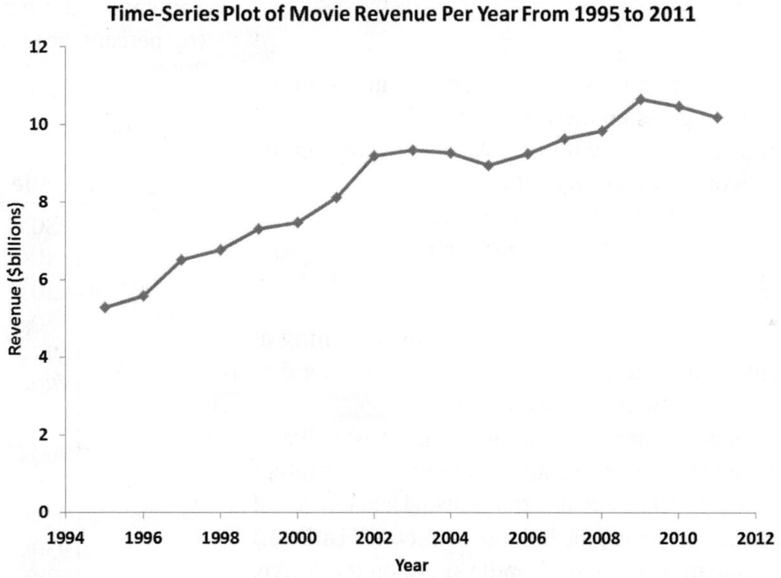

SOLUTION From Figure 2.15, you see that there was a steady increase in the revenue of movies between 1995 and 2009, with a leveling off from 2010 and 2011. During that time, the revenue increased from under $6 billion in 1995 to more than $10 billion in 2009 to 2011.

Problems for Section 2.5

LEARNING THE BASICS

2.44 The following is a set of data from a sample of $n = 11$ items:

X:	7	5	8	3	6	0	2	4	9	5	8
Y:	1	5	4	9	8	0	6	2	7	5	4

a. Construct a scatter plot.

b. Is there a relationship between X and Y? Explain.

2.45 The following is a series of annual sales (in $millions) over an 11-year period (2001 to 2011):

Year:	2001	2002	2003	2004	2005	2006	2007	2008	2009	2010	2011
Sales:	13.0	17.0	19.0	20.0	20.5	20.5	20.5	20.0	19.0	17.0	13.0

a. Construct a time-series plot.

b. Does there appear to be any change in annual sales over time? Explain.

APPLYING THE CONCEPTS

SELF Test **2.46** Movie companies need to predict the gross receipts of individual movies once a movie has debuted. The following results, stored in PotterMovies, are the first weekend gross, the U.S. gross, and the worldwide gross (in $millions) of the eight Harry Potter movies:

Title	First Weekend ($millions)	U.S. Gross ($millions)	Worldwide Gross ($millions)
Sorcerer's Stone	90.295	317.558	976.458
Chamber of Secrets	88.357	261.988	878.988
Prisoner of Azkaban	93.687	249.539	795.539
Goblet of Fire	102.335	290.013	896.013
Order of the Phoenix	77.108	292.005	938.469
Half-Blood Prince	77.836	301.460	934.601
Deathly Hallows Part I	125.017	295.001	955.417
Deathly Hallows Part II	169.189	381.011	1,328.111

Source: Data extracted from **www.the-numbers.com/interactive/comp-HarryPotter.php**.

a. Construct a scatter plot with first weekend gross on the *X* axis and U.S. gross on the *Y* axis.
b. Construct a scatter plot with first weekend gross on the *X* axis and worldwide gross on the *Y* axis.
c. What can you say about the relationship between first weekend gross and U.S. gross and first weekend gross and worldwide gross?

2.47 Data were collected on the typical cost of dining at American-cuisine restaurants within a 1-mile walking distance of a hotel located in a large city. The file Bundle contains the typical cost (a per transaction cost in $) as well as a Bundle score, a measure of overall popularity and customer loyalty, for each of 40 selected restaurants. (Data extracted from **www.bundle.com** via the link **on-msn.com/MnlBxo**.)
a. Construct a scatter plot with Bundle score on the *X* axis and typical cost on the *Y* axis.
b. What conclusions can you reach about the relationship between Bundle score and typical cost?

2.48 College basketball is big business, with coaches' salaries, revenues, and expenses in millions of dollars. The file College Basketball contains the coaches' salary and revenue for college basketball at 60 of the 65 schools that played in the 2009 NCAA men's basketball tournament. (Data extracted from "Compensation for Division 1 Men's Basketball Coaches," *USA Today*, April 2, 2010, p. 8C; and C. Isadore, "Nothing but Net: Basketball Dollars by School," **money.cnn.com/2010/03/18/news/companies/basketball_profits/**.)
a. Do you think schools with higher revenues also have higher coaches' salaries?
b. Construct a scatter plot with revenue on the *X* axis and coaches' salaries on the *Y* axis.
c. Does the scatter plot confirm or contradict your answer to (a)?

2.49 A Pew Research Center survey found that social networking is popular in many nations around the world. The file GlobalSocialMedia contains the level of social media networking (measured as the percentage of individuals polled who use social networking sites) and the GDP at purchasing power parity (PPP) per capita for each of 25 selected countries. (Data extracted from Pew Research Center, "Global Digital Communication: Texting, Social Networking Popular Worldwide," updated February 29, 2012, via the link **bit.ly/sNjsmq.**)
a. Construct a scatterplot with GDP (PPP) per capita on the *X* axis and social media usage on the *Y* axis.
b. What conclusions can your reach about the relationship between GDP and social media usage?

2.50 How have stocks performed in the past? The following table presents the data stored in Stock Performance and shows the performance of a broad measure of stocks (by percentage) for each decade from the 1830s through the 2000s:

Decade	Performance (%)
1830s	2.8
1840s	12.8
1850s	6.6
1860s	12.5
1870s	7.5
1880s	6.0
1890s	5.5
1900s	10.9
1910s	2.2
1920s	13.3
1930s	−2.2
1940s	9.6
1950s	18.2
1960s	8.3
1970s	6.6
1980s	16.6
1990s	17.6
2000s*	−0.5

*Through December 15, 2009.

Source: Data extracted from T. Lauricella, "Investors Hope the '10s Beat the '00s," *The Wall Street Journal*, December 21, 2009, pp. C1, C2.

a. Construct a time-series plot of the stock performance from the 1830s to the 2000s.
b. Does there appear to be any pattern in the data?

2.51 The data in NewHomeSales represent number and median sales price of new single-family houses sold in the United States recorded at the end of each month from January 2000 through April 2012. (Data extracted from www.census.gov, June 1, 2012.)

a. Construct a times series plot of new home sales prices.
b. What pattern, if any, is present in the data?

2.52 The file Movie Attendance contains the yearly movie attendance (in billions) from 2001 through 2011:

Year	Attendance (billions)
2001	1.44
2002	1.60
2003	1.52
2004	1.48
2005	1.38
2006	1.40
2007	1.40
2008	1.36
2009	1.42
2010	1.35
2011	1.30

Source: Data extracted from Motion Picture Association of America, **www.mpaa.org**; and S. Bowles, "Ticket Sales Slump at 2010 Box Office," *USA Today*, January 3, 2011, p. 1D.

a. Construct a time-series plot for the movie attendance (in billions).
b. What pattern, if any, is present in the data?

2.53 The file Audits contains the number of audits of corporations with assets of more than $250 million conducted by the Internal Revenue Service between 2001 and 2011. (Data extracted from **www.irs.gov**.)

a. Construct a time-series plot.
b. What pattern, if any, is present in the data?

2.6 Challenges in Visualizing Data

Visualizing data can provide many benefits to a business decision maker. Visual methods can help a decision maker make preliminary conclusions about data, see patterns in the data that would otherwise be hidden, and begin the process of understanding the reasons for the data values that have been collected. However, these strengths of visualization methods can also be their weaknesses.

Figure 2.16 shows two pie charts of market shares for two industries created in Excel using the default Excel chart style. Use these charts to compare the two industries. Does the dark blue company in the left chart have a greater market share than the dark red company in the right chart? Would the combination of the red and orange companies in the left chart have a greater market share then the combination of the aqua and purple companies in the right chart?

FIGURE 2.16
Market shares of companies in "two" industries

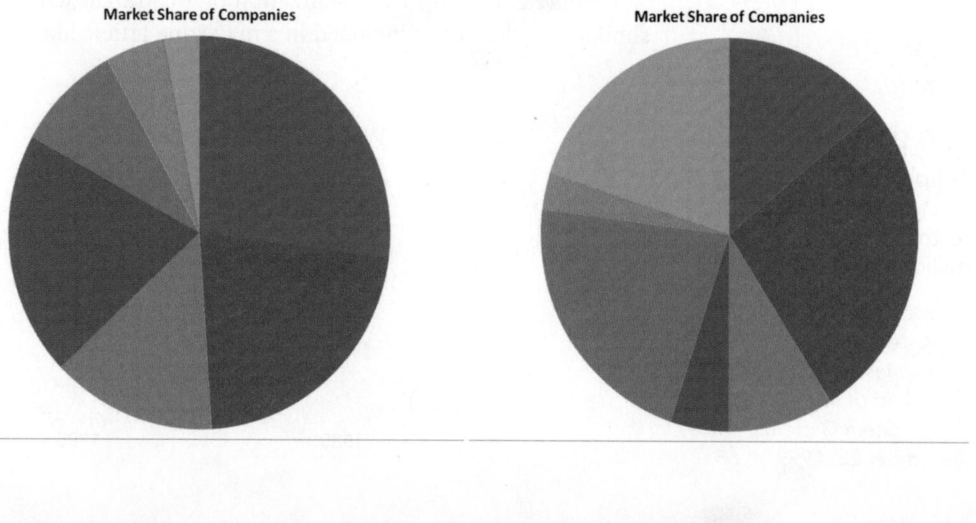

Whatever your answers, have you realized that the two pie charts visualize the identical data? The answers to both questions are "No" as both questions ask you to compare *equal* quantities. Even if you answered the questions correctly, you most likely had a different initial reaction to the two (equivalent) pie charts. These points illustrate that the arrangement of the pie slices as well as the coloring of the pie slices can impose their own patterns on the data collected, confounding a decision maker's analysis.

If you are having a hard time believing that the dark blue slice in the left pie chart is equal to the dark red slice in the right pie, open to the ***TwoPies worksheet*** *in the* ***Challenging workbook*** *and verify the underlying data.*

Figure 2.17 presents a pair of time-series plots that visualize the gross revenues of a motion picture for the first three weeks at a small movie theater. The line chart on the right visualizes the same data but reflects the corrections to the line charts Excel constructs. (These corrections are discussed in Appendix Section B.6.) Only the corrected chart accurately reflects that the gross revenue for the three weeks—11,984, 11,972, and 11,974—vary by only 1%, or, in other words, have been constant for the purposes of preliminary analysis.

FIGURE 2.17

Weekly movie grosses at a small movie theater

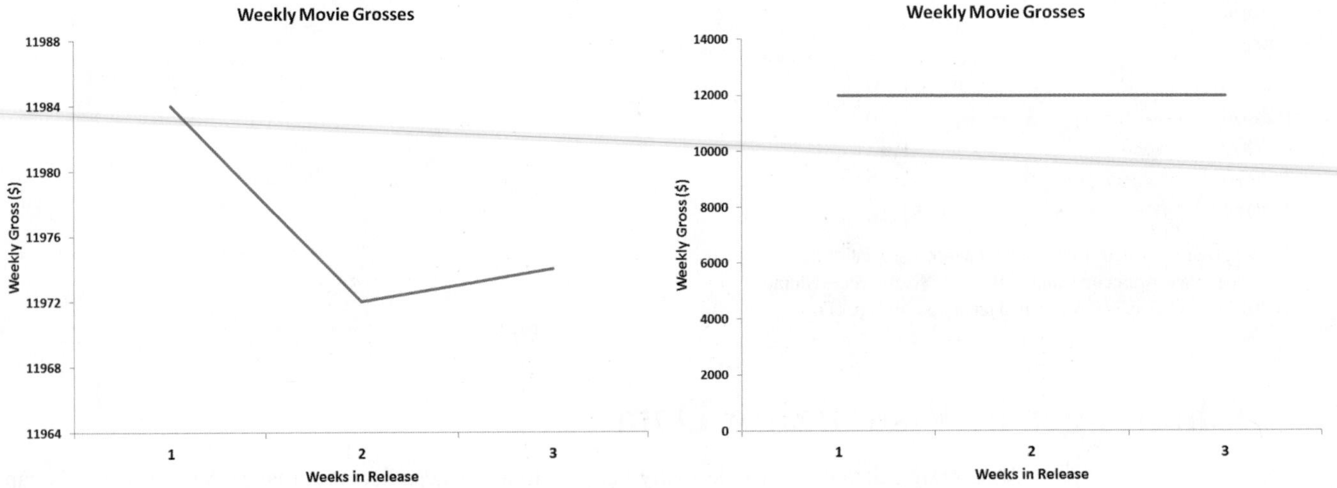

Chartjunk

Visualizing data tempts many people to add visual elements other than the data itself in an attempt to enhance the visualization. While judicious use of visual elements can create a visualization that is more memorable or that more quickly conveys an important point about the data (see reference 1), many add elements that either fail to convey any useful information or that obscure important points about the data. Elements that do the latter are called **chartjunk**.

Figure 2.18 shows a visualization of Australian wine exports to the United States and is similar to a chart once included in a magazine article about the wine industry.

FIGURE 2.18

"Improper" display of Australian wine exports to the United States, in millions of gallons

Source: Based on S. Watterson, "Liquid Gold—Australians Are Changing the World of Wine. Even the French Seem Grateful," Time, *November 22, 1999, p. 68.*

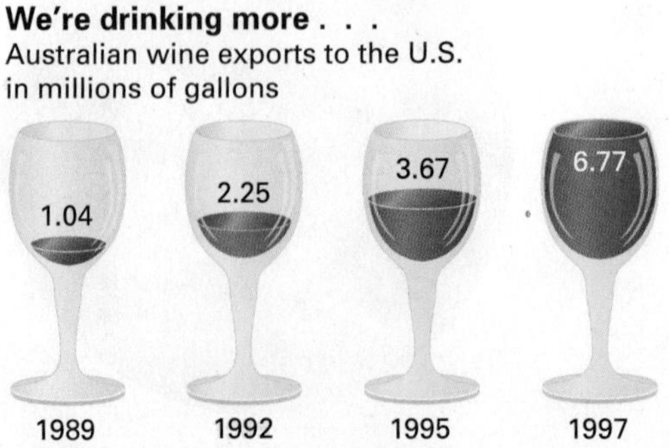

Here, the chartjunk is the wine glasses being used in place of a proper time-series plot. While the wine glasses quickly convey the point that "we're drinking more" Australian wine, the glasses introduce distortions to the data collected. The wineglass that represents the 6.77 million gallons for 1997 does not appear to be almost twice the size of the wineglass representing the 3.67 million gallons for 1995, nor does the wineglass representing the 2.25 million gallons for 1992 appear to be twice the size of the wineglass representing the 1.04 million gallons for 1989. These distortions arise from the problem of using a three-dimensional object drawn in perspective, the volume of a wineglass, to represent the data, the number of gallons exported, that is not itself a three-dimensional volume.

Figure 2.19 presents another visual used in the same magazine article. In this visualization the grape leaves and bunch of grapes convey no meaningful information and, in fact, distract from the data.

FIGURE 2.19
"Improper" display of amount of land planted with grapes for the wine industry

Source: Based on S. Watterson, "Liquid Gold—Australians Are Changing the World of Wine. Even the French Seem Grateful," Time, *November 22, 1999, pp. 68–69.*

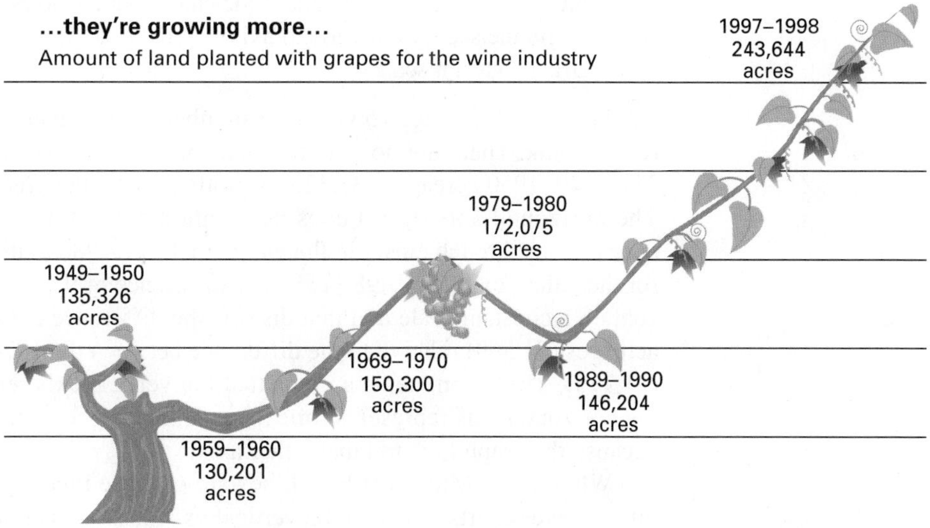

Figure 2.20 visualizes the market share for selected soft drinks. The "fizzy" chartjunk takes up much of the space of the chart and fails to convey any more than a simple bar chart or pie chart would. The soda bottle tops included in the chart confound the viewer; are they "part" of the fizzy "bars," or do they serve to establish a baseline *X* axis?

FIGURE 2.20
"Improper" plot of market share of soft drinks

Source: Based on Anne B. Carey and Sam Ward, "Coke Still Has Most Fizz," USA Today, *May 10, 2000, p. 1B.*

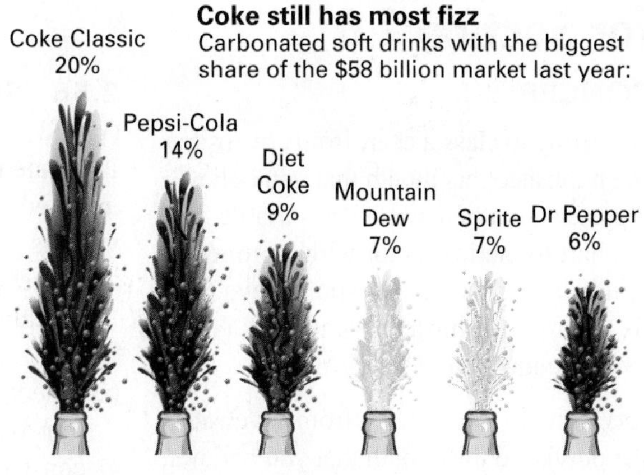

While the chartjunk examples shown in Figures 2.18 through 2.20 derive from print media, chartjunk also exists in electronic media. Most notably, some news and information cable channels compete to present data they collect using innovative visualization techniques that often are expensive examples of chartjunk. Sometimes, the chartjunk proves to be too much for even the on-air commentators, as in the clip that can be seen at **www.mefeedia.com/watch/48082929**.

Guidelines for Developing Visualizations

When you visualize your data, you should always be guided by the goal of not distorting your data. To avoid such distortions and to create a visualization that best conveys your data, you should always

- Avoid chartjunk
- Use the simplest possible visualization
- Include a title
- Label all axes
- Include a scale for each axis if the chart contains axes
- Begin the scale for a vertical axis at zero
- Use a constant scale

Figure 2.19 on page 75 violates a number of these guidelines besides not avoiding the use of chartjunk. There are no axes present, and there is no clear zero point on the vertical axis. The 1949–1950 acreage, 135,326, is plotted *above* the *higher* 1969–1970 acreage, 150,300. The horizontal axis (time) does not contain a constant scale as the value for 1989–1990 appears much, much closer to the value for 1979–1980 (a difference of 10 years) than it does for the value for 1997–1998 (a *smaller* difference of 9 years). The vertical axis also does not contain a constant scale and that distorts the difference between 1979–1980 and 1997–1998 acreages (71,569) relative to the difference between the 1979–1980 and 1969–1970 acreages (21,775). These comments assume that the vertical axis represents the acreage planted and the horizontal axis represents time in years, but, of course, you do not know that is the case because the graph fails to label either axis!

When using Microsoft Excel, beware of these types of distortions. In particular, Excel often creates charts in which the vertical axis does not begin at zero, as illustrated by the left graph shown in Figure 2.17. Excel also tempts you to restyle simple charts by, for example, offering a choice to convert a pie chart into a 3D pie chart with "exploded" slices, and offers uncommon chart choices such as doughnut, radar, surface, bubble, cone, and pyramid charts. You should resist the temptation to restyle a simple chart or use an uncommon chart type because in most cases your choices will distort or obscure the data.

Problems for Section 2.6

APPLYING THE CONCEPTS

2.54 (Student Project) Bring to class a chart from a website, newspaper, or magazine published this month that you believe to be a poorly drawn representation of a numerical variable. Be prepared to submit the chart to the instructor with comments about why you believe it is inappropriate. Do you believe that the intent of the chart is to purposely mislead the reader? Also, be prepared to present and comment on this in class.

2.55 (Student Project) Bring to class a chart from a website, newspaper, or magazine published this month that you believe to be a poorly drawn representation of a categorical variable. Be prepared to submit the chart to the instructor with comments about why you consider it inappropriate. Do you believe that the intent of the chart is to purposely mislead the reader? Also, be prepared to present and comment on this in class.

2.56 (Student Project) The Data and Story Library (DASL) is an online library of data files and stories that illustrate the use of basic statistical methods. Go to **lib.stat.cmu.edu/index.php**, click DASL, and explore some of the various graphical displays.

a. Select a graphical display that you think does a good job revealing what the data convey. Discuss why you think it is a good graphical display.

b. Select a graphical display that you think needs a lot of improvement. Discuss why you think that it is a poorly constructed graphical display.

2.57 Examine the following visual display, adapted from one that appeared in the *World Happiness Report*, distributed by the United Nations in April 2012, as reported by **flowingdata.com**.

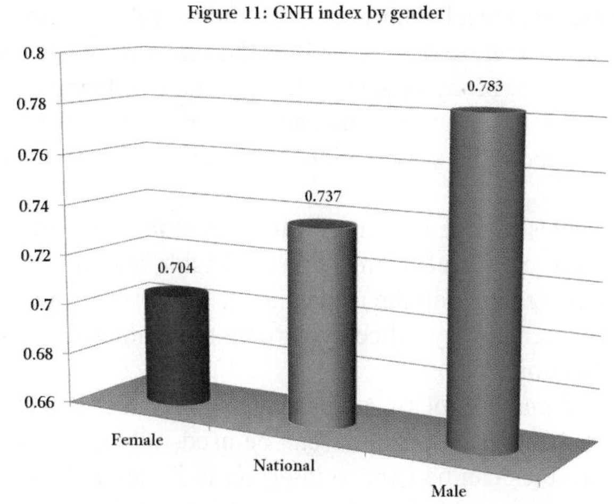

a. Describe at least one good feature of this visual display.
b. Describe at least one bad feature of this visual display.
c. Redraw the graph, using the guidelines given on page 76.

2.58 Examine the following visual display, adapted from one that appeared during a Fox News Channel broadcast in 2011, as reported by **flowingdata.com**.

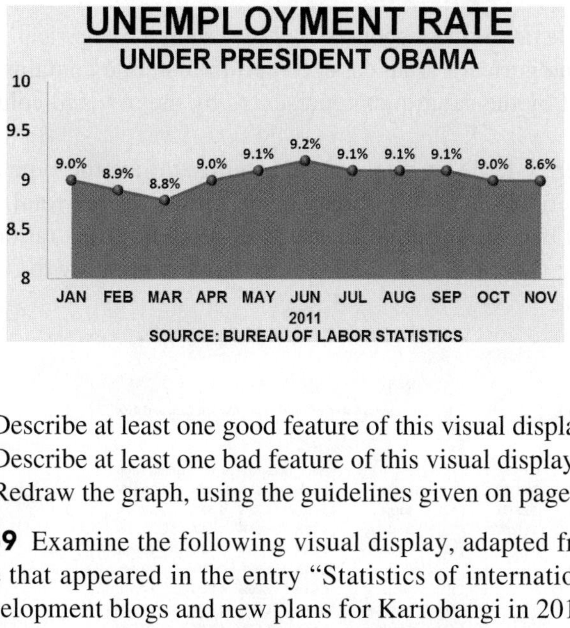

a. Describe at least one good feature of this visual display.
b. Describe at least one bad feature of this visual display.
c. Redraw the graph, using the guidelines given on page 76.

2.59 Examine the following visual display, adapted from one that appeared in the entry "Statistics of international development blogs and new plans for Kariobangi in 2012," on the kariobangi blog, **kariobangi.wordpress.com**, on January 3, 2012.

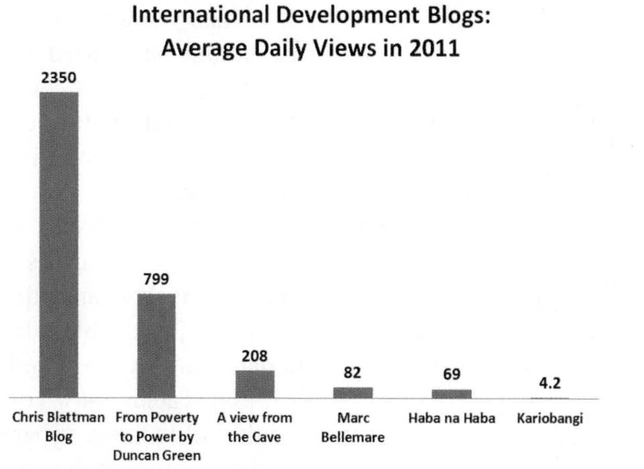

a. Describe at least one good feature of this visual display.
b. Describe at least one bad feature of this visual display.
c. Redraw the graph, using the guidelines given on page 76.

2.60 Professor Deanna Oxender Burgess of Florida Gulf Coast University conducted research on annual reports of corporations (see D. Rosato, "Worried About the Numbers? How About the Charts?" *The New York Times*, September 15, 2002, p. B7). Burgess found that even slight distortions in a chart changed readers' perception of the information. Using online or library sources, select a corporation and study its most recent annual report. Find at least one chart in the report that you think needs improvement and develop an improved version of the chart. Explain why you believe the improved chart is better than the one included in the annual report.

2.61 Figure 2.1 shows a bar chart and a pie chart for what bosses demand during vacation time (see page 55).
a. Create an exploded pie chart, a doughnut chart, a cone chart, or a pyramid chart that shows what bosses demand during vacation time.
b. Which graphs do you prefer—the bar chart or pie chart or the exploded pie chart, doughnut chart, cone chart, and pyramid chart? Explain.

2.62 Figures 2.2 and 2.3 show a bar chart and a pie chart for the risk level for the retirement fund data (see pages 56 and 57).
a. Create an exploded pie chart, a doughnut chart, a cone chart, and a pyramid chart that shows the risk level of retirement funds.
b. Which graphs do you prefer—the bar chart or pie chart or the exploded pie chart, doughnut chart, cone chart, and pyramid chart? Explain.

2.7 Organizing and Visualizing Many Variables

As discussed in Let's Get Started: Big Things to Learn First, spurred by changes in information technology, statistics has seen the increasing use of new techniques that either did not exist, were not practical to do, or were not widely known in the past. Recently, organizing and visualizing many variables at the same time, even variables that represent "big data" (see Section LGS.3), has become practical for business decision makers to do.

PivotTables are technically limited by both the available computer memory (a limit you will never reach while using this book) and the number of rows a worksheet can have (which is approximately 1 million for current Excel versions—again, not a limit you will reach using this book).

When you work with many variables, you must be mindful of the limits of the information technology being used to collect, store, and analyze data as well as the limits of others to be able to perceive and comprehend your results. Many people make a mistake of being overly worried about the former limits—over which, in a typical business environment, they have no control—and forgetting or being naïve about the presentation issues which are often much more critical.

In Microsoft Excel, you use PivotTables to organize many variables at the same time. A **PivotTable** summarizes the variables as a multidimensional summary table and allows you to interactively change the level of summarization and the arrangement and formatting of the variables. PivotTables also allow you to interactively "slice" your data to summarize subsets of data that meet specified criteria (see Section 2.8).

PivotTables allow you to discover patterns and relationships that simpler tables and charts would fail to make apparent. While any number of variables can be used, subject to limits, examples of more than three or four variables can be hard to interpret in Excel and are best left to more specialized Excel add-ins or more sophisticated statistical software such as SAS Institute's JMP.

For each PivotTable you create, you can construct an associated PivotChart in which you can directly manipulate the contents and presentation of a chart in ways that interactively change the PivotTable being used as the source of the chart. Unfortunately, the PivotChart feature in versions prior to Excel 2010 is inconsistently implemented, making PivotCharts less useful in those older Excel versions. And as the Chapter 2 Excel Guide explains, the chart type that the PivotChart feature uses, even in more recent Excel versions, is often the wrong type that you will need to change manually.

Multidimensional Contingency Tables

A **multidimensional contingency table** tallies the responses of three or more categorical variables. In the simplest case of three categorical variables, each cell in the table contains the tallies of the third variable, organized by the subgroups represented by the row and column variables.

Consider the Table 2.5 contingency table on page 43 that jointly tallies the type and risk variables for the sample of 318 retirement funds as percentages of the overall total. For convenience, this table is shown as a two-dimensional PivotTable in the left illustration of Figure 2.21. This table shows, among other things, that there are many more growth funds of average risk than of low or high risk.

FIGURE 2.21

PivotTable showing percentage of overall total for fund type and risk (left) and for fund type, market cap, and risk (right) for the retirement funds sample

Contingency Table of Fund Type and Risk

	RISK			
TYPE	Low	Average	High	Grand Total
Growth	19.50%	35.53%	15.09%	70.13%
Value	11.64%	10.06%	8.18%	29.87%
Grand Total	31.13%	45.60%	23.27%	100.00%

Contingency Table of Fund Type, Market Cap, and Risk

	RISK			
TYPE	Low	Average	High	Grand Total
Growth	19.50%	35.53%	15.09%	70.13%
Large	15.09%	14.78%	2.52%	32.39%
Mid-Cap	3.77%	13.84%	3.14%	20.75%
Small	0.63%	6.92%	9.43%	16.98%
Value	11.64%	10.06%	8.18%	29.87%
Large	9.43%	7.86%	0.00%	17.30%
Mid-Cap	1.57%	1.57%	2.83%	5.97%
Small	0.63%	0.63%	5.35%	6.60%
Grand Total	31.13%	45.60%	23.27%	100.00%

Adding a third categorical variable, the market cap of the fund, creates the multidimensional contingency table shown at right in Figure 2.21. This new PivotTable reveals the following patterns that cannot be seen in the original Table 2.5 contingency table:

- **For the growth funds, the pattern of risk differs depending on the market cap of the fund.** Small cap funds are most likely to have high risk and are very unlikely to have low risk. Mid-cap funds are most likely to have average risk. Large cap funds are most likely to have low risk or average risk and are not very likely to have high risk.

- **The value funds show a pattern of risk that is different from the pattern seen in the growth funds.** Mid-cap funds are most likely to have high risk. Nearly two-thirds of large value funds are low risk, and none of the large value funds had high risk.

Adding Numerical Variables

Multidimensional contingency tables can include numerical variables. When you add a numerical variable to a multidimensional analysis, you use categorical variables or variables that represent units of time as the row and column variables that form the groups by which the data of numerical variable will be presented.

When you include a numerical variable, you typically compute one of the numerical descriptive statistics discussed in Sections 3.1 and 3.2. For example, the multidimensional contingency table that computes the mean, or average, 10-year return percentage for each of the groups formed by the type, risk, and market cap categorical variables is presented in two different ways in Figure 2.22.

FIGURE 2.22
PivotTable of fund type, risk, market cap, showing the mean 10-year return percentage

	A	B	C	D	E
1	Contingency Table of Fund Type, Market Cap, and Risk				
2					
3	Average of 10YrReturn%	RISK			
4	TYPE	Low	Average	High	Grand Total
5	⊞Growth	4.12	5.07	4.72	4.73
6	⊞Value	5.14	4.71	6.87	5.47
7	Grand Total	4.50	4.99	5.48	4.95

	A	B	C	D	E
1	Contingency Table of Fund Type, Market Cap, and Risk				
2					
3	Average of 10YrReturn%	RISK			
4	TYPE	Low	Average	High	Grand Total
5	⊟Growth	4.12	5.07	4.72	4.73
6	Large	3.69	3.65	1.26	3.48
7	Mid-Cap	5.62	6.04	5.77	5.92
8	Small	5.38	6.15	5.30	5.65
9	⊟Value	5.14	4.71	6.87	5.47
10	Large	4.52	4.13		4.34
11	Mid-Cap	6.62	6.27	5.52	6.01
12	Small	10.77	8.12	7.58	7.94
13	Grand Total	4.50	4.99	5.48	4.95

The left table in Figure 2.22 has the market cap categories *collapsed*, or hidden from view. This table highlights that the value funds with low or high risk have a higher mean 10-year return percentage than their growth funds with those risk levels. The right table, with the market cap categories *expanded*, reveals a more complicated pattern including that growth funds with large market capitalizations are the poorest performers and significantly depress the mean for the growth fund category. (Because there are no value funds with large capitalizations and high risk, as shown in Figure 2.22, no mean can be computed for this group and therefore the cell that represents this group is blank.)

Drill-down

Double-clicking a cell in a PivotTable causes Excel to **drill down** and display the underlying data in a new worksheet. The new worksheets that the drill-down creates can be used like any other worksheets, and you can apply statistical methods to the worksheet data without affecting the source PivotTable.

For example, in the PivotTable that presents the percentage of overall total for fund type and risk (shown in the left illustration in Figure 2.21), double-clicking cell D6, which tallies the joint response "value fund and high risk," creates the new worksheet partially shown in Figure 2.23. In this new worksheet, you see the details for the 26 retirement funds with that joint response. (And consistent with earlier observations, you can note that there are no funds with a large market cap in this group.)

FIGURE 2.23
Drill-down worksheet

	A	B	C	D	E	F	G	H	I	J	K	L	M	N
1	Fund Number	Market Cap	Type	Assets	Turnover Ratio	Beta	SD	Risk	1YrReturn%	3YrReturn%	5YrReturn%	10YrReturn%	Expense Ratio	Star Rating
2	RF318	Small	Value	83.6	124	0.85	23.62	High	-3.77	19.06	2.16	9.13	1.6	Three
3	RF316	Small	Value	9	131	0.85	25.14	High	-1.34	20.13	-0.94	6.45	1.87	Two
4	RF315	Small	Value	22.3	127	0.68	24.86	High	4.63	20.9	-0.92	4.44	1.96	Five
5	RF314	Small	Value	1698.9	123	0.95	23.68	High	[illegible]	21.74	1.35	8.43	[illegible]	Three
24	RF228	Mid-Cap	Value	5926.3	95	1.38	25.91	High	-3.26	25.33	-1.41	6.41	0.6	Five
25	RF227	Mid-Cap	Value	1352.3	38	1.44	28.42	High	0.57	29.83	4.82	10.09	1.29	Four
26	RF226	Mid-Cap	Value	28	381	1.57	32.05	High	0.44	30.04	-2.87	2.03	1.54	Five
27	RF225	Mid-Cap	Value	18.3	26	1.46	28.97	High	0.81	35.01	2.73	4.46	2.07	Three

Problems for Section 2.7

APPLYING THE CONCEPTS

2.63 Using the sample of retirement funds stored in RetirementFunds:

a. Construct a table that computes the average three-year return for each type, market cap, and risk.

b. Drill down to examine the large cap growth funds with high risk. How many funds are there? What conclusions can you reach about these funds?

2.64 Using the sample of retirement funds stored in RetirementFunds:

a. Construct a table that tallies type, market cap, and rating.

b. What conclusions can you reach concerning differences among the types of retirement funds (growth and value), based on market cap (small, mid-cap, and large) and the rating (one, two, three, four, and five)?

c. Construct a table that computes the average three-year return for each type, market cap, and rating.

d. Drill down to examine the large cap growth funds with a rating of three. How many funds are there? What conclusions can you reach about these funds?

2.65 Using the sample of retirement funds stored in RetirementFunds:

a. Construct a table that tallies market cap, risk, and rating.

b. What conclusions can you reach concerning differences among the types of funds based on market cap (small, mid-cap, and large), risk (low, average, and high), and the rating (one, two, three, four, and five)?

c. Construct a table that computes the average three-year return for each market cap, risk, and rating.

d. Drill down to examine the large cap funds that are high risk with a rating of three. How many funds are there? What conclusions can you reach about these funds?

2.66 Using the sample of retirement funds stored in RetirementFunds:

a. Construct a table that tallies type, risk, and rating.

b. What conclusions can you reach concerning differences among the types of retirement funds (growth and value), based on the risk (low, average, and high), and the rating (one, two, three, four, and five)?

c. Construct a table that computes the average three-year return for each type, risk, and rating.

d. Drill down to examine the growth funds with high risk with a rating of three. How many funds are there? What conclusions can you reach about these funds?

2.67 Using the sample of retirement funds stored in RetirementFunds:

a. Construct a table that tallies type, market cap, risk, and rating.

b. What conclusions can you reach concerning differences among the types of funds based on market cap (small, mid-cap, and large), based on type (growth and value), risk (low, average, and high), and rating (one, two, three, four, and five)?

c. Which table do you think is easier to interpret, the one in this problem or the ones in Problems 2.64–2.66? Explain.

d. Compare the results of this table with those of Figure 2.21 and Problems 2.64–2.66. What differences can you observe?

2.8 PivotTables and Business Analytics

Excel features used with multidimensional PivotTables can illustrate some of the underlying principles of business analytics, even though those features are not business analytics software in the strictest sense. Recall from Section LGS.3, that business analytics allows you to explore the data to uncover unforeseen relationships. Already, in the various examples in Section 2.7, some unforeseen relationships in the sample of 318 retirement funds have been uncovered by the addition of a third or fourth variable to a multidimensional contingency table.

Some analytics processes work that way: You add variables and see if unforeseen relationships are uncovered. But other analytics processes start with many variables and allow you to *filter* the data by exploring specific combinations of categorical values or numerical ranges. In Excel, using slicers is one way to mimic this filtering operation.

Slicers are not available in Excel 2011 (OS X) and Excel 2007 (Microsoft Windows)

In its simplest form, a **slicer** is a panel of clickable buttons that appears superimposed over a worksheet. Each slicer panel corresponds to one of the variables that is under study, and each button in a variable's slicer panel represents a unique value of the variable that is found in the data under study. You can create a slicer for any variable that has been *associated* with a PivotTable and not just the variables that you have physically inserted into a PivotTable. This allows you to work with more than three or four variables at the same time in a way that avoids creating an overly complex multidimensional contingency table that would be hard to read.

By clicking buttons in slicer panels, you can ask questions of the data you have collected, one of the basic methods of business analytics. This contrasts to the methods of organizing data described earlier in this chapter, which allow you to observe data relationships but not ask about the presence or absence of specific relationships. Because a set of slicers can give you a "heads-up" about the data you have collected, using a set of slicers mimics the function of a business analytics dashboard. Much like the dashboard in automobile, a business analytics **dashboard** summarizes the current state of your data and allows you to see exceptionalities to the data, as they occur often with data visualizations that use chart types discussed in this chapter as well as more novel visualizations that can mimic an automotive dashboard display.

The worksheet in Figure 2.24 shows a PivotTable that has been associated with the variables found in the DATA worksheet of the Retirement Funds workbook. In the PivotTable, the variables type and risk have been inserted as the row and column variables, and slicers for the variables Type, Market Cap, Star Rating, and Expense Ratio have been added to the worksheet.

FIGURE 2.24
PivotTable of fund type and risk with associated slicers

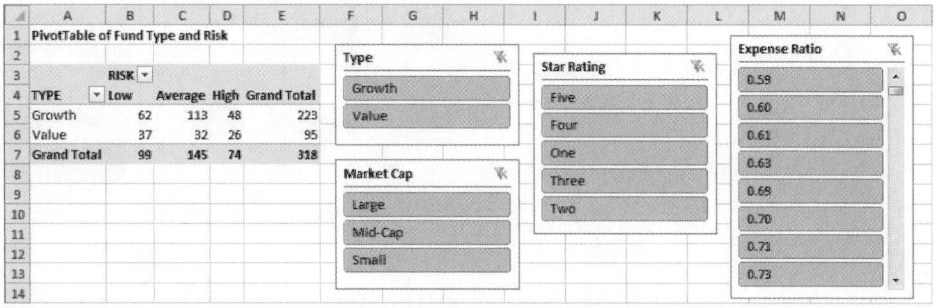

With these four slicers, you can ask such questions as:

1. What are the attributes of the fund with the lowest expense ratio?
2. What are the expense ratios associated with small market cap funds that have a financial rating of five stars?
3. Which fund(s) in the sample have the highest expense ratio?
4. What is the type and market cap of the five-star fund with the lowest expense ratio.

Slicer displays that answer Questions 1 and 4 are shown in Figure 2.25. Note that Excel has dimmed, or disabled, the buttons that represent variable values the current data filtering excludes. This allows you to visually see the answers to questions. For example, the answer to Question 1 is that a **growth** fund with **large** market cap and a **four-**star rating has the lowest expense ratio, **0.59**. (From the PivotTable not shown in Figure 2.25, you can learn that there is only one such fund.) The answer to Question 4 is that a five-star fund with the lowest expense ratio (0.60%) is a mid-cap value retirement fund. (Answers to all four questions can be seen in the Slicer workbook.)

FIGURE 2.25
Slicer displays for Question 1 answer (left) and Question 4 answer (right)

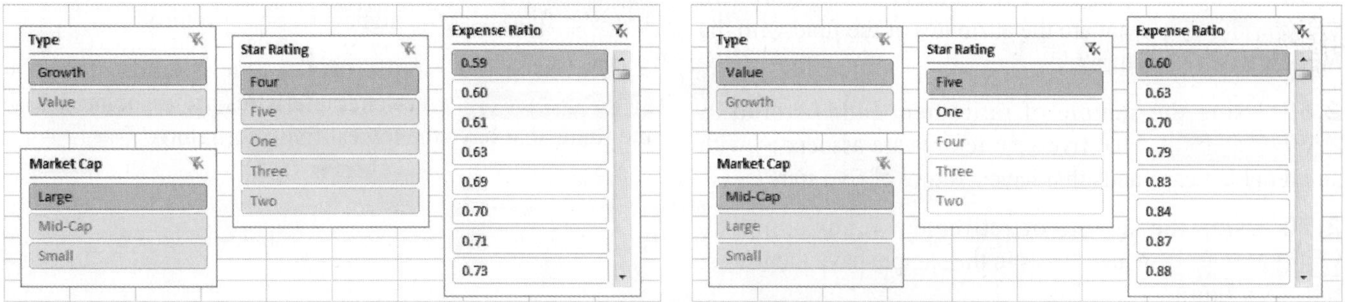

More complicated displays are possible with slicers. In Figure 2.26, the five highest turnover ratio values have been clicked to see which funds are associated with those ratios. Among other things, you can see that the funds associated with these ratios (RF070, RF135, RF177, RF242, and RF272) are rated as either two or five stars. Clicking Five in the Star Rating panel (not shown) leads to the discovery that all but RF135 are five-star funds. That could raise additional questions about what makes the two-star RF135 so unique in the sample of retirement funds.

FIGURE 2.26
A more complex slicer display that identifies the retirement funds with the five highest turnover ratios

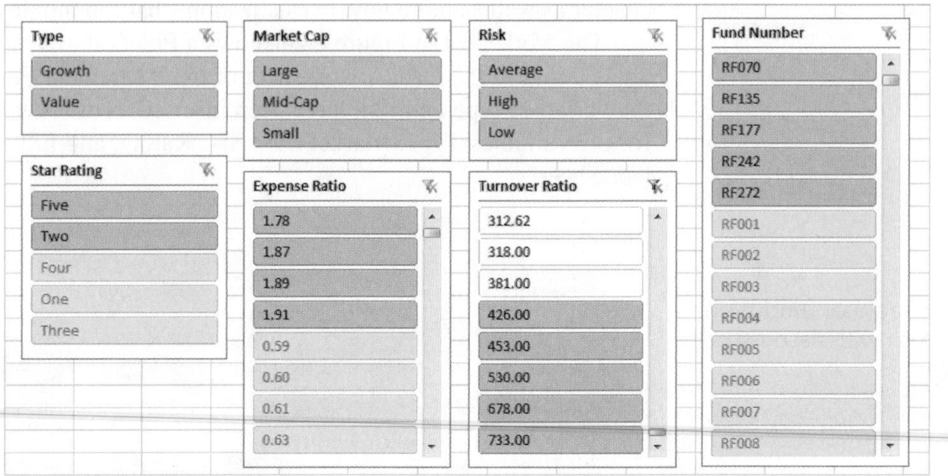

Real-World Business Analytics and Microsoft Excel

The examples in this section serve as an introduction to business analytics, but there are significant differences between the examples and real-world business analytics. Examples in this section use PivotTables that retrieve data from a single worksheet. Real-world business analytics uses very large data sets and retrieves data from corporate databases. The examples in this section use simple filtering based on specific values of variables. Real-world analytics do that, too, but more significantly can filter data based on complex conditional relationships or formulas that calculate values (formulas similar in concept to the worksheet formulas discussed in Appendix Section B.1).

Differences not withstanding, learning about PivotTables can prepare you for "real" business analytics tools. One such tool is the PowerPivot add-in for Excel 2010 and Excel 2013 that Microsoft offers as a free download. As the name of the add-in implies, this add-in extends the basic PivotTable functionality in ways that eliminate the differences noted in the preceding paragraph. Although PowerPivot requires a corporate database as the source of its data, which is beyond the scope of this book, the add-in operates in ways that will be familiar to any user of PivotTables.

Problems for Section 2.8

APPLYING THE CONCEPTS

2.68 Using the sample of retirement funds stored in **RetirementFunds**: what are the attributes of the fund with the highest five-year return?

2.69 Using the sample of retirement funds stored in **RetirementFunds**: what five-year returns are associated with small market cap funds that have a rating of five stars?

2.70 Using the sample of retirement funds stored in **RetirementFunds**: which funds in the sample have the lowest five-year return?

2.71 Using the sample of retirement funds stored in **RetirementFunds**: what is the type and market cap of the five-star fund with the highest five-year return?

2.72 Using the sample of retirement funds stored in **RetirementFunds**: what characteristics are associated with the funds that have the lowest five-year return?

Dmitriy Shironosov / Shutterstock

USING STATISTICS The Choice *Is* Yours, Revisited

In the Using Statistics scenario, you were hired by the Choice Is Yours investment company to assist clients who seek to invest in retirement funds. A sample of 318 retirement funds was selected, and information on the funds and past performance history was recorded. For each of the 318 funds, data were collected on 13 variables. With so much information, visualizing all these numbers required the use of properly selected graphical displays.

From bar charts and pie charts, you were able to see that about one-half of the funds were classified as having average risk, about one-third had low risk, and less than one-quarter had high risk. Contingency tables of the fund type and risk revealed that many more of the growth funds have average risk as compared to low or high risk, while the risk level of the value funds is approximately evenly divided among the three risk categories. After constructing histograms and percentage polygons on the three-year return, you were able to conclude that the three-year returns were higher for the growth funds than for the value funds. The return for the growth funds is concentrated between 15 and 30, and the return for the value funds is concentrated between 15 and 25.

From a multidimensional contingency table, you discovered more complex relationships; for example, for the growth funds, the pattern of risk differs depending on the market cap of the fund. From using data slicers and related techniques from business analytics, you start to identify retirement funds that have unique sets of attributes that may represent exceptional investment opportunities for clients of the investment firm.

With these insights, you can inform your clients about how the different funds performed. Of course, the past performance of a fund does not guarantee its future performance. You might also want to analyze the differences in return in the most recent year and also in the past 5 years and the past 10 years to see how the growth funds, the value funds, and the small, mid-cap, and large market cap funds performed.

SUMMARY

Organizing and visualizing data are the third and fourth tasks of the DCOVA framework. How you accomplish these tasks varies by the type of variable, categorical or numerical, as well as the number of variables you seek to organize and visualize at the same time. Table 2.20 on page 84 summarizes the appropriate methods to do these tasks.

Using the appropriate methods to organize and visualize your data allows you to reach preliminary conclusions about the data. In several different chapter examples, tables and charts helped you reach conclusions about the demands people's bosses place on them during vacation time and about the cost of restaurant meals in a city and its suburbs; they also provided some insights about the sample of retirement funds in The Choice *Is* Yours scenario.

Using the appropriate methods to visualize your data may help you reach preliminary conclusions as well as cause you to ask additional questions about your data that may lead to further analysis at a later time. If used improperly, methods to visualize data can add ambiguity or distortions to your data, as Section 2.6 discusses. And when using Microsoft Excel, you must know about the corrections you can make for the common errors Excel sometimes makes when visualizing data. (The Chapter 2 Excel Guide discusses these corrections in detail.)

Methods to organize and visualize data help summarize data. For numerical variables, there are many additional ways to summarize data that involve computing sample statistics or population parameters. The most common examples of these, *numerical descriptive measures*, are the subject of Chapter 3.

TABLE 2.20

Organizing and Visualizing Data

Type of Variable	Methods
Categorical variables	
Organize	Summary table, contingency table (Section 2.1)
Visualize one variable	Bar chart, pie chart, Pareto chart (Section 2.3)
Visualize two variables	Side-by-side chart (Section 2.3)
Numerical variables	
Organize	Ordered array, frequency distribution, relative frequency distribution, percentage distribution, cumulative percentage distribution (Section 2.2)
Visualize one variable	Stem-and-leaf display, histogram, percentage polygon, cumulative percentage polygon (ogive) (Section 2.4)
Visualize two variables	Scatter plot, time-series plot (Section 2.5)
Many variables together	
Organize	Multidimensional tables (Section 2.7)
Visualize	Excel slicers, methods adapted from business analytics (Section 2.8)

REFERENCES

1. Batemen, S., R. Mandryk, C. Gutwin, A. Genest, D. McDine, and C. Brooks. "Useful Junk? The Effects of Visual Embellishment on Comprehension and Memorability of Charts." April 10, 2010, **www.hci.usask.ca/uploads/173-pap0297-bateman.pdf**.
2. Huff, D. *How to Lie with Statistics*. New York: Norton, 1954.
3. *Microsoft Excel 2010*. Redmond, WA: Microsoft Corporation, 2010.
4. Tufte, E. R. *Beautiful Evidence*. Cheshire, CT: Graphics Press, 2006.
5. Tufte, E. R. *Envisioning Information*. Cheshire, CT: Graphics Press, 1990.
6. Tufte, E. R. *The Visual Display of Quantitative Information*, 2nd ed. Cheshire, CT: Graphics Press, 2002.
7. Tufte, E. R. *Visual Explanations*. Cheshire, CT: Graphics Press, 1997.
8. Wainer, H. *Visual Revelations: Graphical Tales of Fate and Deception from Napoleon Bonaparte to Ross Perot*. New York: Copernicus/Springer-Verlag, 1997.

KEY EQUATIONS

Determining the Class Interval Width

$$\text{Interval width} = \frac{\text{highest value} - \text{lowest value}}{\text{number of classes}} \qquad \textbf{(2.1)}$$

Computing the Proportion or Relative Frequency

$$\text{Proportion} = \text{relative frequency} = \frac{\text{number of values in each class}}{\text{total number of values}} \qquad \textbf{(2.2)}$$

KEY TERMS

CHECKING YOUR UNDERSTANDING

2.73 What is the difference between a statistic and a parameter?

2.74 How do histograms and polygons differ in construction and use?

2.75 Why would you construct a summary table?

2.76 What are the advantages and disadvantages of using a bar chart, a pie chart, and a Pareto chart?

2.77 Compare and contrast the bar chart for categorical data with the histogram for numerical data.

2.78 What is the difference between a time-series plot and a scatter plot?

2.79 Why is it said that the main feature of a Pareto chart is its ability to separate the "vital few" from the "trivial many"?

2.80 What are the three different ways to break down the percentages in a contingency table?

2.81 How can a multidimensional table differ from a two-variable contingency table?

2.82 What type of insights can you gain from a contingency table that contains three variables that you cannot gain from a contingency table that contains two variables?

2.83 What is the difference between a drill-down and a slicer?

CHAPTER REVIEW PROBLEMS

2.84 The following summary table presents the breakdown of the price of a new college textbook:

Revenue Category	Percentage (%)	
Publisher	64.8	
Manufacturing costs		32.3
Marketing and promotion		15.4
Administrative costs and taxes		10.0
After-tax profit		7.1
Bookstore	22.4	
Employee salaries and benefits		11.3
Operations		6.6
Pretax profit		4.5
Author	11.6	
Freight	1.2	

Source: Data extracted from T. Lewin, "When Books Break the Bank," *The New York Times*, September 16, 2003, pp. B1, B4.

a. Using the four categories of publisher, bookstore, author, and freight, construct a bar chart, a pie chart, and a Pareto chart.

b. Using the four subcategories of publisher and three subcategories of bookstore, along with the author and freight categories, construct a Pareto chart.

c. Based on the results of (a) and (b), what conclusions can you reach concerning who gets the revenue from the sales of new college textbooks? Do any of these results surprise you? Explain.

2.85 The following table represents the market share (in number of movies, gross in millions of dollars, and millions of tickets sold) of each type of movie in 2011:

Type	Number	Gross ($millions)	Tickets (millions)
Based on book/short story	80	2,146.6	270.7
Based on comic/graphic novel	12	803.8	101.4
Based on magazine article	19	427.3	53.9
Based on game	1	6.9	0.9
Based on musical/opera	1	0.005	0.0006
Based on play	14	201.4	25.4
Based on real life events	180	418.1	52.7
Disney Ride	1	241.1	30.4
Based on TV	8	821.7	103.6
Compilation	2	1.4	0.2
Original screenplay	350	4,221.9	532.4
Remake	17	396.7	50.0
Traditional/legend/ fairytale	6	271.6	34.3
Spin-off	1	145.7	18.4
Musical group movie	1	0.1	0.01

Source: Data extracted from **www.the-numbers.com/market/Sources2011.php**.

a. Construct a bar chart, a pie chart, and a Pareto chart for the number of movies, gross (in $millions), and number of tickets sold (in millions).

b. What conclusions can you reach about the market shares of the different types of movies in 2011?

2.86 A survey was conducted from 665 consumer magazines on the practices of their websites. The results are summarized in a copyediting table and a fact-checking table:

Copyediting as Compared to Print Content	Percentage (%)
As rigorous	41
Less rigorous	48
Not copyedited	11

Source: Data extracted from S. Clifford, "Columbia Survey Finds a Slack Editing Process of Magazine Web Sites," *The New York Times*, March 1, 2010, p. B6.

a. For copyediting, construct a bar chart, a pie chart, and a Pareto chart.

b. Which graphical method do you think is best for portraying these data?

Fact Checking as Compared to Print Content	Percentage (%)
Same	57
Less rigorous	27
Online not fact-checked	8
Neither online nor print is fact-checked	8

Source: Data extracted from S. Clifford, "Columbia Survey Finds a Slack Editing Process of Magazine Web Sites," *The New York Times*, March 1, 2010, p. B6.

c. For fact checking, construct a bar chart, a pie chart, and a Pareto chart.

d. Which graphical method do you think is best for portraying the fact checking data?

e. What conclusions can you reach concerning copyediting and fact checking of print and online consumer magazines?

2.87 The owner of a restaurant that serves Continental-style entrées has the business objective of learning more about the patterns of patron demand during the Friday-to-Sunday weekend time period. Data were collected from 630 customers on the type of entrée ordered and organized in the following table:

Type of Entrée	Number Served
Beef	187
Chicken	103
Mixed	30
Duck	25
Fish	122
Pasta	63
Shellfish	74
Veal	26
Total	630

a. Construct a percentage summary table for the types of entrées ordered.

b. Construct a bar chart, a pie chart, and a Pareto chart for the types of entrées ordered.

c. Do you prefer using a Pareto chart or a pie chart for these data? Why?

d. What conclusions can the restaurant owner reach concerning demand for different types of entrées?

2.88 Suppose that the owner of the restaurant in Problem 2.87 also wants to study the demand for dessert during the same time period. She decides that in addition to studying whether a dessert was ordered, she will also study the gender of the individual and whether a beef entrée was ordered. Data were collected from 600 customers and organized in the following contingency tables:

	GENDER		
DESSERT ORDERED	**Male**	**Female**	**Total**
Yes	40	96	136
No	240	224	464
Total	280	320	600

	BEEF ENTRÉE		
DESSERT ORDERED	**Yes**	**No**	**Total**
Yes	71	65	136
No	116	348	464
Total	187	413	600

a. For each of the two contingency tables, construct contingency tables of row percentages, column percentages, and total percentages.
b. Which type of percentage (row, column, or total) do you think is most informative for each gender? For beef entrée? Explain.
c. What conclusions concerning the pattern of dessert ordering can the restaurant owner reach?

2.89 The following data represent the pounds per capita of fresh food and packaged food consumed in the United States, Japan, and Russia in a recent year:

	COUNTRY		
FRESH FOOD	**United States**	**Japan**	**Russia**
Eggs, nuts, and beans	88	94	88
Fruit	124	126	88
Meat and seafood	197	146	125
Vegetables	194	278	335
PACKAGED FOOD			
Bakery goods	108	53	144
Dairy products	298	147	127
Pasta	12	32	16
Processed, frozen, dried and chilled food, and ready-to-eat meals	183	251	70
Sauces, dressings, and condiments	63	75	49
Snacks and candy	47	19	24
Soup and canned food	77	17	25

Source: Data extracted from H. Fairfield, "Factory Food," *The New York Times*, April 4, 2010, p. BU5.

a. For the United States, Japan, and Russia, construct a bar chart, a pie chart, and a Pareto chart for different types of fresh foods consumed.
b. For the United States, Japan, and Russia, construct a bar chart, a pie chart, and a Pareto chart for different types of packaged foods consumed.
c. What conclusions can you reach concerning differences between the United States, Japan, and Russia in the fresh foods and packaged foods consumed?

2.90 Several years ago, a growing number of warranty claims on Firestone tires sold on Ford SUVs prompted Firestone and Ford to issue a major recall. An analysis of warranty claims data helped identify which models to recall. A breakdown of 2,504 warranty claims based on tire size is given in the following table:

Tire Size	Number of Warranty Claims
23575R15	2,030
311050R15	137
30950R15	82
23570R16	81
331250R15	58
25570R16	54
Others	62

Source: Data extracted from Robert L. Simison, "Ford Steps Up Recall Without Firestone," *The Wall Street Journal*, August 14, 2000, p. A3.

The 2,030 warranty claims for the 23575R15 tires can be categorized into ATX models and Wilderness models. The type of incident leading to a warranty claim, by model type, is summarized in the following table:

Incident Type	ATX Model Warranty Claims	Wilderness Warranty Claims
Tread separation	1,365	59
Blowout	77	41
Other/unknown	422	66
Total	1,864	166

Source: Data extracted from Robert L. Simison, "Ford Steps Up Recall Without Firestone," *The Wall Street Journal*, August 14, 2000, p. A3.

a. Construct a Pareto chart for the number of warranty claims by tire size. What tire size accounts for most of the claims?
b. Construct a pie chart to display the percentage of the total number of warranty claims for the 23575R15 tires that

come from the ATX model and Wilderness model. Interpret the chart.

c. Construct a Pareto chart for the type of incident causing the warranty claim for the ATX model. Does a certain type of incident account for most of the claims?

d. Construct a Pareto chart for the type of incident causing the warranty claim for the Wilderness model. Does a certain type of incident account for most of the claims?

2.91 One of the major measures of the quality of service provided by an organization is the speed with which the organization responds to customer complaints. A large family-held department store selling furniture and flooring, including carpet, had undergone a major expansion in the past several years. In particular, the flooring department had expanded from 2 installation crews to an installation supervisor, a measurer, and 15 installation crews. A business objective of the company was to reduce the time between when the complaint is received and when it is resolved. During a recent year, the company received 50 complaints concerning carpet installation. The number of days between the receipt of the complaint and the resolution of the complaint for the 50 complaints, stored in **Furniture**, are:

54	5	35	137	31	27	152	2	123	81	74	27
11	19	126	110	110	29	61	35	94	31	26	5
12	4	165	32	29	28	29	26	25	1	14	13
13	10	5	27	4	52	30	22	36	26	20	23
33	68										

a. Construct a frequency distribution and a percentage distribution.

b. Construct a histogram and a percentage polygon.

c. Construct a cumulative percentage distribution and plot a cumulative percentage polygon (ogive).

d. On the basis of the results of (a) through (c), if you had to tell the president of the company how long a customer should expect to wait to have a complaint resolved, what would you say? Explain.

2.92 The file **DomesticBeer** contains the percentage alcohol, number of calories per 12 ounces, and number of carbohydrates (in grams) per 12 ounces for 150 of the best-selling domestic beers in the United States.

Source: Data extracted from **www.beer100.com/beercalories.htm**, June 1, 2012.

a. Construct a percentage histogram for percentage alcohol, number of calories per 12 ounces, and number of carbohydrates (in grams) per 12 ounces.

b. Construct three scatter plots: percentage alcohol versus calories, percentage alcohol versus carbohydrates, and calories versus carbohydrates.

c. Discuss what you learn from studying the graphs in (a) and (b).

2.93 The file **CigaretteTax** contains the state cigarette tax ($) for each state as of January 1, 2012.

a. Construct an ordered array.

b. Plot a percentage histogram.

c. What conclusions can you reach about the differences in the state cigarette tax between the states?

2.94 The file **CDRate** contains the yields for one-year certificates of deposit (CDs) and a five-year CDs for 24 banks in the United States, as of June 21, 2012.

Source: Data extracted and compiled from **www.Bankrate.com**, June 21, 2012.

a. Construct a stem-and-leaf display for each variable.

b. Construct a scatter plot of one-year CDs versus five-year CDs.

c. What is the relationship between the one-year CD rate and the five-year CD rate?

2.95 The file **CEO-Compensation** includes the total compensation (in $millions) for CEOs of 194 large public companies and the investment return in 2011. (Data extracted from **nytimes.com/2012/06/17/business/executive-pay-still-climbing-despite-a-shareholder-din.html**.) For total compensation:

a. Construct a frequency distribution and a percentage distribution.

b. Construct a histogram and a percentage polygon.

c. Construct a cumulative percentage distribution and plot a cumulative percentage polygon (ogive).

d. Based on (a) through (c), what conclusions can you reach concerning CEO compensation in 2011?

e. Construct a scatter plot of total compensation and investment return in 2011.

f. What is the relationship between the total compensation and investment return in 2011?

2.96 Studies conducted by a manufacturer of Boston and Vermont asphalt shingles have shown product weight to be a major factor in customers' perception of quality. Moreover, the weight represents the amount of raw materials being used and is therefore very important to the company from a cost standpoint. The last stage of the assembly line packages the shingles before the packages are placed on wooden pallets. The variable of interest is the weight in pounds of the pallet, which for most brands holds 16 squares of shingles. The company expects pallets of its Boston brand-name shingles to weigh at least 3,050 pounds but less than 3,260 pounds. For the company's Vermont brand-name shingles, pallets should weigh at least 3,600 pounds but less than 3,800. Data, collected from a sample of 368 pallets of Boston shingles and 330 pallets of Vermont shingles, are stored in **Pallet**.

a. For the Boston shingles, construct a frequency distribution and a percentage distribution having eight class intervals, using 3,015, 3,050, 3,085, 3,120, 3,155, 3,190, 3,225, 3,260, and 3,295 as the class boundaries.

b. For the Vermont shingles, construct a frequency distribution and a percentage distribution having seven class intervals, using 3,550, 3,600, 3,650, 3,700, 3,750, 3,800, 3,850, and 3,900 as the class boundaries.

c. Construct percentage histograms for the Boston shingles and for the Vermont shingles.

d. Comment on the distribution of pallet weights for the Boston and Vermont shingles. Be sure to identify the percentages of pallets that are underweight and overweight.

2.97 What was the average price of a room at two-star, three-star, and four-star hotels in cities around the world in 2011? The file HotelPrices contains the prices in English pounds (about US$1.56 as of January 2012). (Data extracted from **press.hotels.com/en-gb/files/2012/03/HPI_2011_UK.pdf**.) Complete the following for two-star, three-star, and four-star hotels:

a. Construct a frequency distribution and a percentage distribution.
b. Construct a histogram and a percentage polygon.
c. Construct a cumulative percentage distribution and plot a cumulative percentage polygon (ogive).
d. What conclusions can you reach about the cost of two-star, three-star, and four-star hotels?
e. Construct separate scatter plots of the cost of two-star hotels versus three-star hotels, two-star hotels versus four-star hotels, and three-star hotels versus four-star hotels.
f. What conclusions can you reach about the relationship of the price of two-star, three-star, and four-star hotels?

2.98 The file Protein contains calorie and cholesterol information for popular protein foods (fresh red meats, poultry, and fish).

Source: U.S. Department of Agriculture.

a. Construct a percentage histogram for the number of calories.
b. Construct a percentage histogram for the amount of cholesterol.
c. What conclusions can you reach from your analyses in (a) and (b)?

2.99 The file Natural Gas contains the monthly average wellhead and residential price for natural gas (dollars per thousand cubic feet) in the United States from January 1, 2008, to January 1, 2012. (Data extracted from "U.S. Natural Gas Prices," **www.eia.gov/dnav/ng/ng_pri_sum_dcu_nus_m.htm**, June 20, 2012.) For the wellhead price and the residential price:

a. Construct a time-series plot.
b. What pattern, if any, is present in the data?
c. Construct a scatter plot of the wellhead price and the residential price.
d. What conclusion can you reach about the relationship between the wellhead price and the residential price?

2.100 The following data (stored in Drink) represent the amount of soft drink in a sample of 50 consecutively filled 2-liter bottles. The results are listed horizontally in the order of being filled:

2.109	2.086	2.066	2.075	2.065	2.057	2.052	2.044	2.036	2.038
2.031	2.029	2.025	2.029	2.023	2.020	2.015	2.014	2.013	2.014
2.012	2.012	2.012	2.010	2.005	2.003	1.999	1.996	1.997	1.992
1.994	1.986	1.984	1.981	1.973	1.975	1.971	1.969	1.966	1.967
1.963	1.957	1.951	1.951	1.947	1.941	1.941	1.938	1.908	1.894

a. Construct a time-series plot for the amount of soft drink on the *Y* axis and the bottle number (going consecutively from 1 to 50) on the *X* axis.
b. What pattern, if any, is present in these data?
c. If you had to make a prediction about the amount of soft drink filled in the next bottle, what would you predict?
d. Based on the results of (a) through (c), explain why it is important to construct a time-series plot and not just a histogram, as was done in Problem 2.43 on page 69.

2.101 The file Currency contains the exchange rates of the Canadian dollar, the Japanese yen, and the English pound from 1980 to 2011, where the Canadian dollar, the Japanese yen, and the English pound are expressed in units per U.S. dollar.

a. Construct time-series plots for the yearly closing values of the Canadian dollar, the Japanese yen, and the English pound.
b. Explain any patterns present in the plots.
c. Write a short summary of your findings.
d. Construct separate scatter plots of the value of the Canadian dollar versus the Japanese yen, the Canadian dollar versus the English pound, and the Japanese yen versus the English pound.
e. What conclusions can you reach concerning the value of the Canadian dollar, Japanese yen, and English pound in terms of the U.S. dollar?

2.102 (Class Project) Have each student in the class respond to the question "Which carbonated soft drink do you most prefer?" so that the instructor can tally the results into a summary table.

a. Convert the data to percentages and construct a Pareto chart.
b. Analyze the findings.

2.103 (Class Project) Cross-classify each student in the class by gender (male, female) and current employment status (yes, no), so that the instructor can tally the results.

a. Construct a table with either row or column percentages, depending on which you think is more informative.
b. What would you conclude from this study?
c. What other variables would you want to know regarding employment in order to enhance your findings?

REPORT WRITING EXERCISES

2.104 Referring to the results from Problem 2.96 on page 88 concerning the weights of Boston and Vermont shingles, write a report that evaluates whether the weights of the pallets of the two types of shingles are what the company expects. Be sure to incorporate tables and charts into the report.

2.105 Referring to the results from Problem 2.90 on page 87 concerning the warranty claims on Firestone tires, write a report that evaluates warranty claims on Firestone tires sold on Ford SUVs. Be sure to incorporate tables and charts into the report.

CASES FOR CHAPTER 2

Managing Ashland MultiComm Services

Recently, Ashland MultiComm Services has been criticized for its inadequate customer service in responding to questions and problems about its telephone, cable television, and Internet services. Senior management has established a task force charged with the business objective of improving customer service. In response to this charge, the task force collected data about the types of customer service errors, the cost of customer service errors, and the cost of wrong billing errors. It found the following data:

Types of Customer Service Errors

Type of Errors	Frequency
Incorrect accessory	27
Incorrect address	42
Incorrect contact phone	31
Invalid wiring	9
On-demand programming error	14
Subscription not ordered	8
Suspension error	15
Termination error	22
Website access error	30
Wrong billing	137
Wrong end date	17
Wrong number of connections	19
Wrong price quoted	20
Wrong start date	24
Wrong subscription type	33
Total	448

Cost of Customer Service Errors in the Past Year

Type of Errors	Cost ($ thousands)
Incorrect accessory	17.3
Incorrect address	62.4
Incorrect contact phone	21.3
Invalid wiring	40.8
On-demand programming errors	38.8
Subscription not ordered	20.3
Suspension error	46.8
Termination error	50.9
Website access errors	60.7
Wrong billing	121.7
Wrong end date	40.9
Wrong number of connections	28.1
Wrong price quoted	50.3
Wrong start date	40.8
Wrong subscription type	60.1
Total	701.2

Type and Cost of Wrong Billing Errors

Type of Wrong Billing Errors	Cost ($thousands)
Declined or held transactions	7.6
Incorrect account number	104.3
Invalid verification	9.8
Total	121.7

1. Review these data (stored in AMS2-1). Identify the variables that are important in describing the customer service problems. For each variable you identify, construct the graphical representation you think is most appropriate and explain your choice. Also, suggest what other information concerning the different types of errors would be useful to examine. Offer possible courses of action for either the task force or management to take that would support the goal of improving customer service.

2. As a follow-up activity, the task force decides to collect data to study the pattern of calls to the help desk (stored in AMS2-2). Analyze these data and present your conclusions in a report.

Digital Case

In the Using Statistics scenario, you were asked to gather information to help make wise investment choices. Sources for such information include brokerage firms, investment counselors, and other financial services firms. Apply your knowledge about the proper use of tables and charts in this Digital Case about the claims of foresight and excellence by an Ashland-area financial services firm.

Open **EndRunGuide.pdf**, which contains the EndRun Financial Services "Guide to Investing." Review the guide, paying close attention to the company's investment claims and supporting data and then answer the following.

1. How does the presentation of the general information about EndRun in this guide affect your perception of the business?
2. Is EndRun's claim about having more winners than losers a fair and accurate reflection of the quality of its investment service? If you do not think that the claim is a fair and accurate one, provide an alternate presentation that you think is fair and accurate.
3. Review the discussion about EndRun's "Big Eight Difference" and then open and examine the attached sample of mutual funds. Are there any other relevant data from that file that could have been included in the Big Eight table? How would the new data alter your perception of EndRun's claims?
4. EndRun is proud that all Big Eight funds have gained in value over the past five years. Do you agree that EndRun should be proud of its selections? Why or why not?

CardioGood Fitness

The market research team at AdRight is assigned the task to identify the profile of the typical customer for each treadmill product offered by CardioGood Fitness. The market research team decides to investigate whether there are differences across the product lines with respect to customer characteristics. The team decides to collect data on individuals who purchased a treadmill at a Universal Fitness retail store during the prior three months. The data are stored in the CardioGood Fitness file. The team identifies the following customer variables to study: product purchased, TM195, TM498, or TM798; gender; age, in years; education, in years; relationship status, single or partnered; annual household income ($); average number of times the customer plans to use the treadmill each week; average number of miles the customer expects to walk/run each week; and self-rated fitness on an 1-to-5 ordinal scale, where 1 is poor shape and 5 is excellent shape.

1. Create a customer profile for each CardioGood Fitness treadmill product line by developing appropriate tables and charts.
2. Write a report to be presented to the management of CardioGood Fitness detailing your findings.

The Choice *Is* Yours Follow-up

Follow up the Using Statistics Revisited section on page 83 by analyzing the differences in 1-year return percentages, 5-year return percentages, and 10-year return percentages for the sample of 318 retirement funds stored in Retirement Funds. In your analysis, examine differences between the growth and value funds as well as the differences among the small, mid-cap, and large market cap funds.

Clear Mountain State Student Surveys

1. The student news service at Clear Mountain State University (CMSU) has decided to gather data about the undergraduate students that attend CMSU. They create and distribute a survey of 14 questions and receive responses from 62 undergraduates (stored in UndergradSurvey). For each question asked in the survey, construct all the appropriate tables and charts and write a report summarizing your conclusions.
2. The dean of students at CMSU has learned about the undergraduate survey and has decided to undertake a similar survey for graduate students at CMSU. She creates and distributes a survey of 14 questions and receives responses from 44 graduate students (stored in GradSurvey). For each question asked in the survey, construct all the appropriate tables and charts and write a report summarizing your conclusions.

CHAPTER 2 EXCEL GUIDE

EG2.1 ORGANIZING CATEGORICAL DATA

The Summary Table

Key Technique Use the PivotTable feature to create a summary table for untallied data.

Example Create a frequency and percentage summary table similar to Table 2.3 on page 42.

PHStat Use **One-Way Tables & Charts**.
For the example, open to the **DATA worksheet** of the **Retirement Funds workbook**. Select **PHStat → Descriptive Statistics → One-Way Tables & Charts**. In the procedure's dialog box (shown below):

1. Click **Raw Categorical Data** (because the worksheet contains untallied data).
2. Enter **H1:H319** as the **Raw Data Cell Range** and check **First cell contains label**.
3. Enter a **Title**, check **Percentage Column**, and click **OK**.

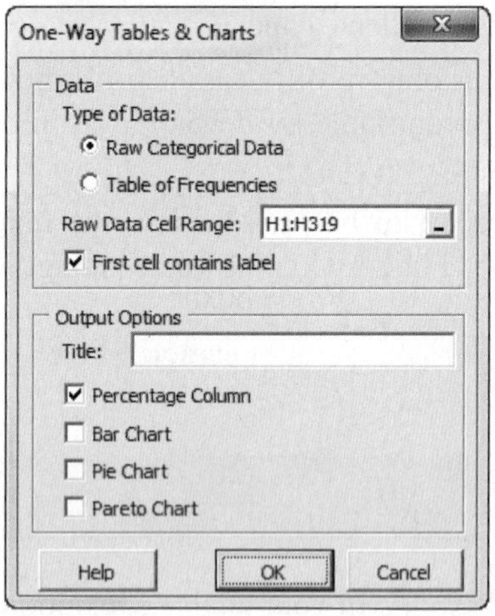

PHStat creates a PivotTable summary table on a new worksheet. For data that have already been tallied into categories, click **Table of Frequencies** in step 1.

In the PivotTable, risk categories appear in alphabetical order and not in the order low, average, and high as would normally be expected. To change to the expected order, use steps 14 and 15 of the *In-Depth Excel* instructions but change all references to cell A6 to cell A7 and drop the Low label over cell A5, not cell A4.

In-Depth Excel (untallied data) Use the **Summary Table workbook** as a model.

For the example, open to the **DATA worksheet** of the **Retirement Funds workbook** and select **Insert → PivotTable**. In the Create PivotTable dialog box (shown below):

1. Click **Select a table or range** and enter **H1:H319** as the **Table/Range** cell range.
2. Click **New Worksheet** and then click **OK**.

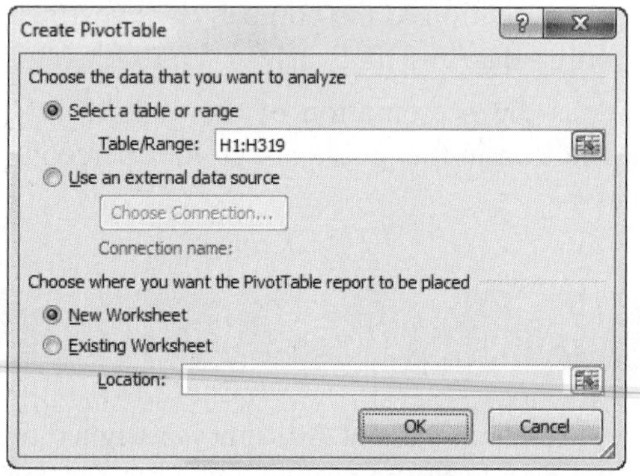

In the PivotTable Field List task pane (shown below) or the similar PivotTable Fields task pane in Excel 2013:

3. Drag **Risk** in the **Choose fields to add to report** box and drop it in the **Rows Labels** (**Rows** in Excel 2013) box.
4. Drag **Risk** in the **Choose fields to add to report** box a second time and drop it in the Σ **Values** box. This second label changes to **Count of Risk** to indicate that a count, or tally, of the risk categories will be displayed in the PivotTable.

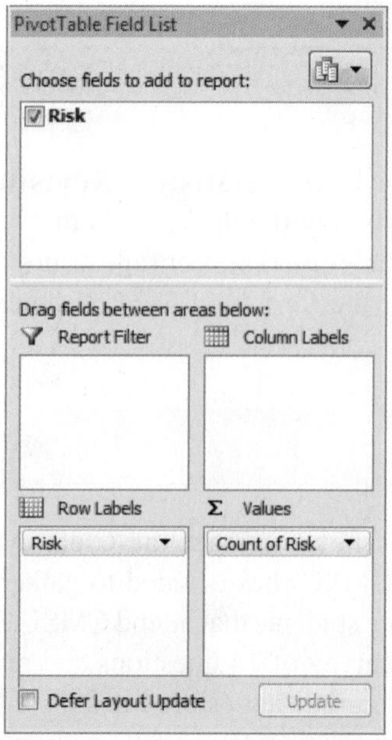

In the PivotTable being created:

5. Enter **Risk** in cell **A3** to replace the heading Row Labels and enter a title in cell **A1**.
6. Right-click and then click **PivotTable Options** in the shortcut menu that appears.

In the PivotTable Options dialog box (shown below):

7. Click the **Layout & Format** tab.
8. Check **For empty cells show** and enter **0** as its value. Leave all other settings unchanged.
9. Click **OK** to complete the PivotTable.

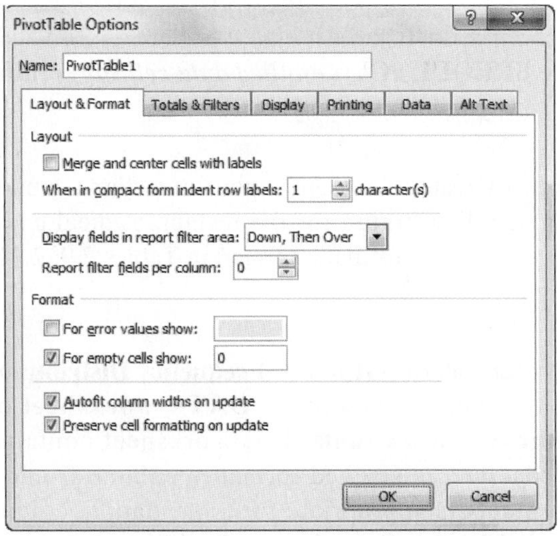

To add a column for the percentage frequency:

10. Enter **Percentage** in cell C3. Enter the formula **=B4/B$7** in cell **C4** and copy it down through row **7**.
11. Select cell range **C4:C7**, right-click, and select **Format Cells** in the shortcut menu.
12. In the **Number** tab of the Format Cells dialog box, select **Percentage** as the **Category** and click **OK**.
13. Adjust the worksheet formatting, if appropriate (see Appendix B).

In the PivotTable, risk categories appear in alphabetical order and not in the order low, average, and high, as would normally be expected. To change to the expected order:

14. Click the **Low** label in cell **A6** to highlight cell A6. Move the mouse pointer to the top edge of the cell until the mouse pointer changes to a four-way arrow.
15. Drag the **Low** label and drop the label over cell A4. The risk categories now appear in the order Low, Average, and High in the summary table.

In-Depth Excel (tallied data) Use the **SUMMARY_SIMPLE worksheet** of the **Summary Table workbook** as a model for creating a summary table.

The Contingency Table

Key Technique Use the PivotTable feature to create a contingency table for untallied data.

Example Construct a contingency table displaying fund type and risk level similar to Table 2.4 on page 42.

PHStat (untallied data) Use **Two-Way Tables & Charts**. For the example, open to the **DATA worksheet** of the **Retirement Funds workbook**. Select **PHStat → Descriptive Statistics → Two-Way Tables & Charts**. In the procedure's dialog box (shown below):

1. Enter **C1:C319** as the **Row Variable Cell Range**.
2. Enter **H1:H319** as the **Column Variable Cell Range**.
3. Check **First cell in each range contains label**.
4. Enter a **Title** and click **OK**.

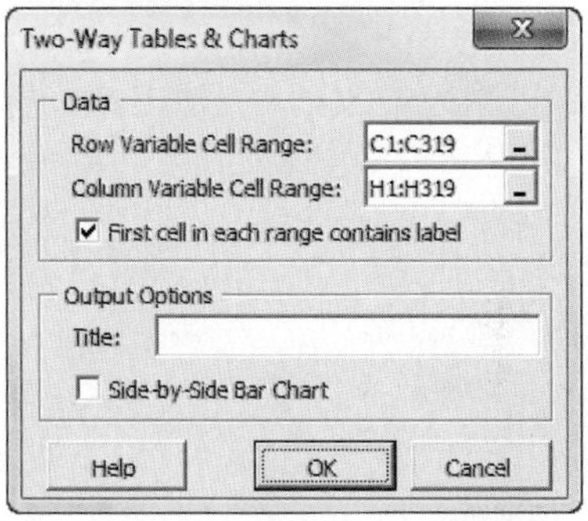

In the PivotTable, risk categories appear in alphabetical order and not in the order low, average, and high as would normally be expected. To change the expected order, use steps 6 and 7 of the *In-Depth Excel* instructions.

In-Depth Excel (untallied data) Use the **Contingency Table workbook** as a model.

For the example, open to the **DATA worksheet** of the **Retirement Funds workbook**. Select **Insert → PivotTable**. In the Create PivotTable dialog box:

1. Click **Select a table or range** and enter **A1:N319** as the **Table/Range** cell range
2. Click **New Worksheet** and then click **OK**.

In the PivotTable Field List (PivotTable Fields in Excel 2013) task pane:

3. Drag **Type** from **Choose fields to add to report** and drop it in the **Row Labels** (**ROWS** in Excel 2013) box.
4. Drag **Risk** from **Choose fields to add to report** and drop it in the **Column Labels** (**COLUMNS** in Excel 2013) box.
5. Drag **Type** from **Choose fields to add to report** a second time and drop it in the **Σ Values** box. (**Type** changes to **Count of Type**.)

In the PivotTable being created:

6. Click the **Low** label in cell **D4** to highlight cell D4. Move the mouse pointer to the left edge of the cell until the mouse pointer changes to a four-way arrow.
7. Drag the **Low** label to the left and drop the label when an I-beam appears between columns A and B. The Low label appears in B4 and column B now contains the low risk tallies.

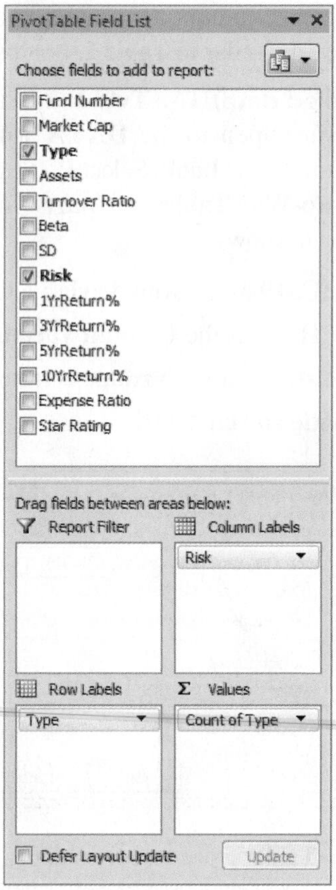

8. Right-click over the PivotTable and then click **PivotTable Options** in the shortcut menu that appears.

In the PivotTable Options dialog box:

9. Click the **Layout & Format** tab.
10. Check **For empty cells show** and enter **0** as its value. Leave all other settings unchanged.
11. Click the **Total & Filters** tab.
12. Check **Show grand totals for columns** and **Show grand totals for rows**.
13. Click **OK** to complete the table.

In-Depth Excel (tallied data) Use the **CONTINGENCY_SIMPLE worksheet** of the **Contingency Table workbook** as a model for creating a contingency table.

EG2.2 ORGANIZING NUMERICAL DATA

Stacked and Unstacked Data

PHStat Use **Stack Data** or **Unstack Data**.

For example, to unstack the 3YrReturn% variable data by the Type variable in the retirement funds sample, open to the **DATA worksheet** of the **Retirement Funds workbook**. Select **Data Preparation → Unstack Data**. In that procedure's dialog box, enter **C1:C319** (the cell range of the Type variable) as the **Grouping Variable Cell Range** and enter **J1:J319** (the cell range of the 3YrReturn% variable) as the **Stacked Data Cell Range**. Check **First cells in both ranges contain label** and click **OK**. The unstacked data appear on a new worksheet.

The Ordered Array

In-Depth Excel To create an ordered array, first select the numerical data to be sorted. Then select **Home → Sort & Filter** (in the Editing group) and, in the drop-down menu, click **Sort Smallest to Largest**. (You will see **Sort A to Z** as the first drop-down choice if you did not select a cell range of *numerical* data.)

The Frequency Distribution

Key Technique Establish bins (see Section 2.2) and then use the **FREQUENCY(*untallied data cell range*, *bins cell range*)** array function to tally data.

Example Create a frequency, percentage, and cumulative percentage distribution for the restaurant meal cost data that contains the information found in Tables 2.9, 2.11, and 2.14, in Section 2.2.

PHStat (untallied data) Use **Frequency Distribution**. For the example, open to the **DATA worksheet** of the **Restaurants workbook**. This worksheet contains the meal cost data in stacked format in column G and a set of bin numbers appropriate for those data in column H. Select **PHStat → Descriptive Statistics → Frequency Distribution**. In the procedure's dialog box (shown below):

1. Enter **G1:G101** as the **Variable Cell Range**, enter **H1:H10** as the **Bins Cell Range**, and check **First cell in each range contains label**.
2. Click **Multiple Groups - Stacked** and enter **A1:A101** as the **Grouping Variable Cell Range**. (The cell range A1:A101 contains the Location variable.)
3. Enter a **Title** and click **OK**.

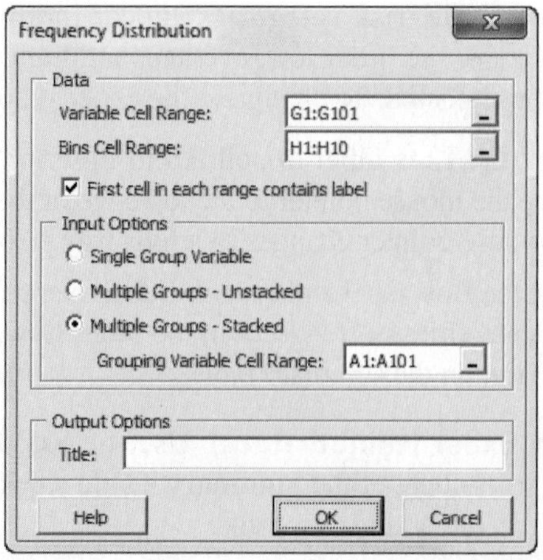

Click **Single Group Variable** in step 2 if constructing a distribution from a single group of untallied data. Click **Multiple**

Groups - Unstacked in step 2 if the **Variable Cell Range** contains two or more columns of unstacked, untallied data. If you plan to construct a histogram or polygon, use **Histogram & Polygons**, discussed in Section EG2.4, instead of **Frequency Distribution**.

Frequency distributions for the two groups appear on separate worksheets. To display the information for the two groups on one worksheet, select the cell range **B3:D12** on one of the worksheets. Right-click that range and click **Copy** in the shortcut menu. Open to the other worksheet. In that other worksheet, right-click cell **E3** and click **Paste Special** in the shortcut menu. In the Paste Special dialog box, click **Values and numbers format** and click **OK**. Adjust the worksheet title as necessary. (Appendix Section B.4 discusses the paste special command in greater detail.)

In-Depth Excel (untallied data) Use the **Distributions workbook** as a model.

For the example, open to the **UNSTACKED worksheet** of the **Restaurants workbook**. This worksheet contains the meal cost data unstacked in columns A and B and a set of bin numbers appropriate for those data in column D. Then:

1. Right-click the **UNSTACKED** sheet tab and click **Insert** in the shortcut menu.
2. In the **General** tab of the Insert dialog box, click **Worksheet** and then click **OK**.

In the new worksheet:

3. Enter a title in cell **A1**, **Bins** in cell **A3**, and **Frequency** in cell **B3**.
4. Copy the bin number list in the cell range **D2:D10** of the **UNSTACKED worksheet** and paste this list into cell **A4** of the new worksheet.
5. Select the cell range **B4:B12** that will hold the array formula.
6. Type, but do not press the **Enter** or **Tab** key, the formula **=FREQUENCY(UNSTACKED!$A$1:$A$51, $A$4:$A$12)**. Then, while holding down the **Ctrl** and **Shift** keys (or the **Command** key on a Mac), press the **Enter** key to enter the array formula into the cell range **B4:B12**. (See Appendix Section B.3 for an expanded explanation about entering array formulas into worksheets.)
7. Adjust the worksheet formatting as necessary.

Note that in step 6, you enter the cell range **UNSTACKED!$A$1:$A$51** and not the cell range **A1:A51** because the untallied data are located on another (the UNSTACKED) worksheet. (Appendix Section B.1 further explains this type of cell reference.)

Steps 1 through 7 construct a frequency distribution for the meal costs at city restaurants. To construct a frequency distribution for the meal costs at suburban restaurants, repeat steps 1 through 7 but in step 6 type **=FREQUENCY (UNSTACKED!$B$1:$B$51, $A$4:$A$12)** as the array formula.

To display the distributions for the two groups on one worksheet, select the cell range **B3:B12** on one of the worksheets. Right-click that range and click **Copy** in the shortcut menu. Open to the other worksheet. In that other worksheet, right-click cell **C3** and click **Paste Special** in the shortcut menu. In the Paste Special dialog box, click **Values and numbers format** and click **OK**. Adjust the worksheet title as necessary. (Appendix Section B.4 discusses the paste special command in greater detail.)

Analysis ToolPak (untallied data) Use **Histogram**.

For the example, open to the **UNSTACKED worksheet** of the **Restaurants workbook**. This worksheet contains the meal cost data unstacked in columns A and B and a set of bin numbers appropriate for those data in column D. Then:

1. Select **Data ➔ Data Analysis**. In the Data Analysis dialog box, select **Histogram** from the **Analysis Tools** list and then click **OK**.

In the Histogram dialog box (shown below):

2. Enter **A1:A51** as the **Input Range** and enter **D1:D10** as the **Bin Range**. (If you leave **Bin Range** blank, the procedure creates a set of bins that will not be as well formed as the ones you can specify.)
3. Check **Labels** and click **New Worksheet Ply**.
4. Click **OK** to create the frequency distribution on a new worksheet.

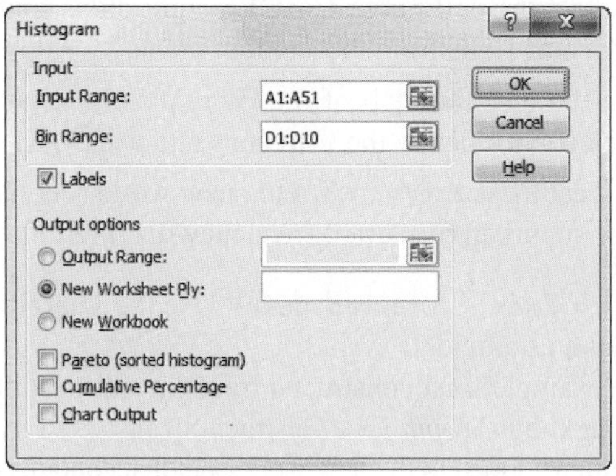

In the new worksheet:

5. Select row 1. Right-click row 1 and click **Insert** in the shortcut menu. Repeat. (This creates two blank rows at the top of the worksheet.)
6. Enter a title for the frequency distribution in cell A1.

The ToolPak creates a frequency distribution that contains an improper bin labeled **More**. Correct this error by using these general instructions:

7. Manually add the frequency count of the **More** row to the frequency count of the preceding row. (For the example, the More row contains a zero for the frequency, so the frequency of the preceding row does not change.)
8. Select the worksheet row (for this example, row 11) that contains the **More** row.

9. Right-click that row and click **Delete** in the shortcut menu.

Steps 1 through 9 construct a frequency distribution for the meal costs at city restaurants. To construct a frequency distribution for the meal costs at suburban restaurants, repeat these nine steps but in step 6 enter **B1:B51** as the **Input Range.**

The Relative Frequency, Percentage, and Cumulative Distributions

Key Technique Add columns that contain formulas for the relative frequency or percentage and cumulative percentage to a previously constructed frequency distribution.

Example Create a distribution that includes the relative frequency or percentage as well as the cumulative percentage information found in Tables 2.11 (relative frequency and percentage) and 2.14 (cumulative percentage) in Section 2.2 for the restaurant meal cost data.

PHStat (untallied data) Use **Frequency Distribution.**
For the example, use the *PHStat* instructions in "The Frequency Distribution" to construct a frequency distribution. Note that the frequency distribution constructed by PHStat also includes columns for the percentages and cumulative percentages. To change the column of percentages to a column of relative frequencies, reformat that column. For the example, open to the new worksheet that contains the city restaurant frequency distribution and:

1. Select the cell range **C4:C12,** right-click, and select **Format Cells** from the shortcut menu.
2. In the **Number** tab of the Format Cells dialog box, select **Number** as the **Category** and click **OK.**

Then repeat these two steps for the new worksheet that contains the suburban restaurant frequency distribution.

In-Depth Excel (untallied data) Use the **Distributions workbook** as a model.
For the example, first construct a frequency distribution created using the *In-Depth Excel* instructions in "The Frequency Distribution." Open to the new worksheet that contains the frequency distribution for the city restaurants and:

1. Enter **Percentage** in cell **C3** and **Cumulative Pctage** in cell **D3.**
2. Enter **=B4/SUM($B$4:$B$12)** in cell **C4** and copy this formula down through row **12.**
3. Enter **=C4** in cell **D4.**
4. Enter **=C5 + D4** in cell **D5** and copy this formula down through row **12.**
5. Select the cell range **C4:D13**, right-click, and click **Format Cells** in the shortcut menu.
6. In the **Number** tab of the Format Cells dialog box, click **Percentage** in the **Category** list and click **OK.**

Then open to the worksheet that contains the frequency distribution for the suburban restaurants and repeat steps 1 through 6.

If you want column C to display relative frequencies instead of percentages, enter **Rel. Frequencies** in cell C3. Select the cell range **C4:C12**, right-click, and click **Format Cells** in the shortcut menu. In the **Number** tab of the Format Cells dialog box, click **Number** in the **Category** list and click **OK.**

Analysis ToolPak Use **Histogram** and then modify the worksheet created.

For the example, first construct the frequency distributions using the *Analysis ToolPak* instructions in "The Frequency Distribution." Then use the *In-Depth Excel* instructions to modify those distributions.

EG2.3 VISUALIZING CATEGORICAL DATA

The Bar Chart and the Pie Chart

Key Technique Use the Excel bar or pie chart feature. If data to be visualized is untallied, first construct a summary table (see the Section EG2.1 "The Summary Table" instructions).

Example Construct a bar or pie chart from a summary table similar to Table 2.3 on page 42.

PHStat Use **One-Way Tables & Charts.**
For the example, use the Section EG2.1 "The Summary Table" *PHStat* instructions, but in step 3, check either **Bar Chart** or **Pie Chart** (or both) in addition to entering a **Title**, checking **Percentage Column**, and clicking **OK.**

In-Depth Excel Use the **Summary Table workbook** as a model.
For the example, open to the **OneWayTable worksheet** of the **Summary Table workbook.** (The worksheet contains a PivotTable that was created by completing the Section EG2.1 "The Summary Table" *In-Depth Excel* instructions.) Then:

1. Select cell range **A4:B6**. (Begin your selection at cell B6 and not at cell A4, as you would normally do.)
2. Click **Insert**. For a bar chart, click **Bar** in the **Charts group** and then select the **first 2-D Bar** gallery item (**Clustered Bar**). For a pie chart, click **Pie** in the **Charts group** and then select the **first 2-D Pie** gallery item (**Pie**).
3. Right-click the Risk drop-down button in the chart and click **Hide All Field Buttons on Chart.**
4. For a bar chart, select **Layout → Axis Titles → Primary Horizontal Axis Title → Title Below Axis (Design → Add Chart Element → Axis Titles → Primary Horizontal** in Excel 2013**)**. Select the words "Axis Title" in the chart and enter the title **Frequency.**

   For a pie chart, select **Layout → Data Labels → More Data Label Options.** In the Format Data Labels dialog box, click **Label Options** in the left pane. In the Label Options right pane, check **Category Name** and **Percentage** and clear the other Label Contains check boxes. Click **Outside End** and then click **Close.** In Excel 2013, select **Design → Add Chart Element → Data Labels → More Data Label Options.** In the

Format Data Labels task pane, check **Category Name** and **Percentage**, clear the other Label Contains check boxes, and click **Outside End**.

5. Relocate the chart to a chart sheet and turn off the chart legend and gridlines (bar chart only) by using the instructions in Appendix Section B.6.

Although not the case with the example, sometimes the horizontal axis scale of a bar chart will not begin at 0. If this occurs, right-click the horizontal (value) axis in the bar chart and click **Format Axis** in the shortcut menu. In the Format Axis dialog box, click **Axis Options** in the left pane. In the Axis Options right pane, click the first **Fixed** option button (for Minimum) and enter **0** in its box and then click **Close**. In Excel 2010, you set this value in the Format Axis task pane by replacing the value in the **Minimum** box. (There is no option button to select.)

The Pareto Chart

Key Technique Use the Excel chart feature with a modified summary table.

Example Construct a Pareto chart of the incomplete ATM transactions similar to Figure 2.4 on page 58.

PHStat Use **One-Way Tables & Charts.**
For the example, open to the **DATA worksheet** of the **ATM Transactions workbook**. Select **PHStat → Descriptive Statistics → One-Way Tables & Charts**. In the procedure's dialog box:

1. Click **Table of Frequencies** (because the worksheet contains tallied data).
2. Enter **A1:B8** as the **Freq. Table Cell Range** and check **First cell contains label**.
3. Enter a **Title**, check **Pareto Chart**, and click **OK**.

In-Depth Excel Use the **Pareto workbook** as a model.
For the example, open to the **ATMTable worksheet** of the **ATM Transactions workbook**. Begin by sorting the modified table by decreasing order of frequency:

1. Select row **11** (the Total row), right-click, and click **Hide** in the shortcut menu. (This prevents the total row from getting sorted.)
2. Select cell **B4** (the first frequency), right-click, and select **Sort & Filter** and, in the drop-down list, click **Sort Largest to Smallest**.
3. Select rows **10** and **12** (there is no row 11 visible), right-click, and click **Unhide** in the shortcut menu to restore row 11.

Next, add a column for cumulative percentage:

4. Enter **Cumulative Pct.** in cell **D3**. Enter **=C4** in cell **D4**. Enter **= D4 + C5** in cell **D5** and copy this formula down through row **10**.
5. Adjust the formatting of column D as necessary.

Next, create the Pareto chart:

6. Select the cell range **A3:A10** and while holding down the **Ctrl** key also select the cell range **C3:D10**.
7. Select **Insert → Column** (in the Charts group) and select the **first 2-D Column** gallery item (**Clustered Column**).
8. Select **Format** (under Chart Tools). In the **Current Selection** group, select **Series "Cumulative Pct."** from the drop-down list and then click **Format Selection**.
9. In the Format Data Series dialog box, click **Series Options** in the left pane and in the **Series Options** right pane, click **Secondary Axis**. Click **Close**.
10. With the cumulative percentage series still selected in the Current Selection group, select **Design → Change Chart Type**, and in the **Change Chart Type** gallery, select the **fourth Line** gallery item (**Line with Markers**). Click **OK**.

Next, set the maximum value of the primary and secondary (left and right) *Y* axis scales to 100%. For each *Y* axis:

11. Right-click on the axis and click **Format Axis** in the shortcut menu.
12. In the Format Axis dialog box, click **Axis Options** in the left pane and in the **Axis Options** right pane, click the **Fixed** option button for Maximum and enter **1** in its box. Click **Close**.
13. Relocate the chart to a chart sheet, turn off the chart legend and gridlines, and add chart and axis titles by using the instructions in Appendix Section B.6.

If you use a PivotTable as a summary table, replace steps 1 through 3 and 6 with these steps:

1. Add a column for the percentage frequency. (See the Section EG2.1 "The Summary Table" instructions steps 10 through 13.) Select the total row, right-click, and click **Hide** in the shortcut menu. (This prevents the total row from getting sorted.)
2. Right-click the cell that contains the first frequency (typically this will be cell **B4**).
3. Right-click and select **Sort → Sort Largest to Smallest**.
4. Select the cell range of only the percentage and cumulative percentage columns (the equivalent of the cell range C3:D10 in the example).

The Pareto chart constructed from a PivotTable using these modified steps will not have proper labels for the categories. To add the correct labels, right-click over the chart and click **Select Data** in the shortcut menu. In the Select Data Source dialog box, click **Edit** that appears under **Horizontal (Category) Axis Labels**. When the Axis Labels dialog box appears, drag the mouse to *select* the cell range **A4:A10** (the categories) to enter that cell range. Do *not* type the cell range in the **Axis label range** box as you would otherwise do for the reasons explained in Appendix Section B.7. Click **OK** in this dialog box and then click **OK** in the original dialog box.

The Side-by-Side Chart

Key Technique Use an Excel bar chart that is based on a contingency table.

Example Construct a side-by-side chart that displays the fund type and risk level, similar to Figure 2.6 on page 59.

PHStat Use **Two-Way Tables & Charts.**
For the example, use the Section EG2.1 "The Contingency Table" *PHStat* instructions, but in step 4, check **Side-by-Side Bar Chart** in addition to entering a **Title** and clicking **OK**.

In-Depth Excel Use the **Contingency Table workbook** as a model.
For the example, open to the **TwoWayTable worksheet** of the **Contingency Table workbook** and:

1. Select cell **A3** (or any other cell inside the PivotTable).
2. Select **Insert → Bar** and select the **first 2-D Bar** gallery item (**Clustered Bar**).
3. Right-click the Risk drop-down button in the chart and click **Hide All Field Buttons on Chart**.
4. Relocate the chart to a chart sheet, turn off the gridlines, and add chart and axis titles by using the instructions in Appendix Section B.6.

When creating a chart from a contingency table that is not a PivotTable, select the cell range of the contingency table, including row and column headings, but excluding the total row and total column, as step 1.

If you need to switch the row and column variables in a side-by-side chart, right-click the chart and then click **Select Data** in the shortcut menu. In the Select Data Source dialog box, click **Switch Row/Column** and then click **OK**. (In Excel 2007, if the chart is based on a PivotTable, you will not be able to click **Switch Row/Column** as that button will be disabled. In that case, you need to change the PivotTable to change the chart.)

EG2.4 VISUALIZING NUMERICAL DATA

The Stem-and-Leaf Display

Key Technique Enter leaves as a string of digits that begin with the ' (apostrophe) character.

Example Construct a stem-and-leaf display of the three-year return percentage for value retirement funds, similar to Figure 2.7 on page 63.

PHStat Use the **Stem-and-Leaf Display**.
For the example, open to the **UNSTACKED worksheet** of the **Retirement Funds workbook**. Select **PHStat → Descriptive Statistics → Stem-and-Leaf Display**. In the procedure's dialog box (shown in the next column):

1. Enter **B1:B96** as the **Variable Cell Range** and check **First cell contains label**.
2. Click **Set stem unit as** and enter **10** in its box.
3. Enter a **Title** and click **OK**.

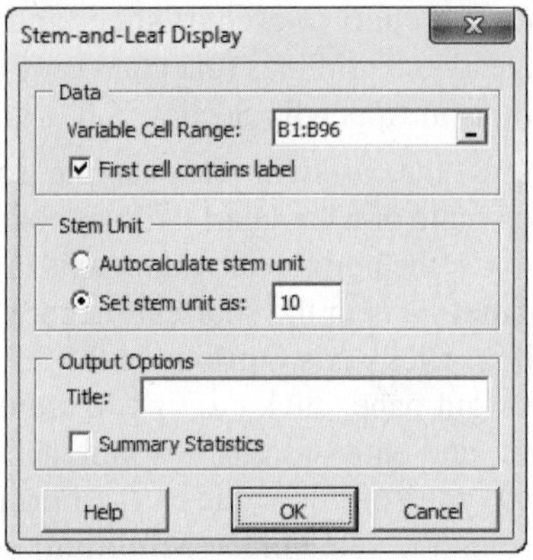

When creating other displays, use the **Set stem unit as** option sparingly and only if **Autocalculate stem unit** creates a display that has too few or too many stems. (Any stem unit you specify must be a power of 10.)

In-Depth Excel Use the **Stem-and-leaf workbook** as a model.

Manually construct the stems and leaves on a new worksheet to create a stem-and-leaf display. Adjust the column width of the column that holds the leaves as necessary.

The Histogram

Key Technique Modify an Excel column chart.

Example Construct histograms for the three-year return percentages for the growth and value retirement funds, similar to Figure 2.9 on page 64.

PHStat Use **Histogram & Polygons.**
For the example, open to the **DATA worksheet** of the **Retirement Funds workbook**. Select **PHStat → Descriptive Statistics → Histogram & Polygons.** In the procedure's dialog box (shown on page 99):

1. Enter **J1:J319** as the **Variable Cell Range, P1:P15** as the **Bins Cell Range, Q1:Q14** as the **Midpoints Cell Range**, and check **First cell in each range contains label**.
2. Click **Multiple Groups - Stacked** and enter **C1:C319** as the **Grouping Variable Cell Range**. (In the DATA worksheet, the three-year return percentages for both types of retirement funds are stacked, or placed in a single column. The column C values allow PHStat to separate the returns for growth funds from the returns for the value funds.)
3. Enter a **Title**, check **Histogram**, and click **OK**.

PHStat inserts two new worksheets, each of which contains a frequency distribution and a histogram. To relocate the histograms to their own chart sheets, use the instructions in Appendix Section B.6.

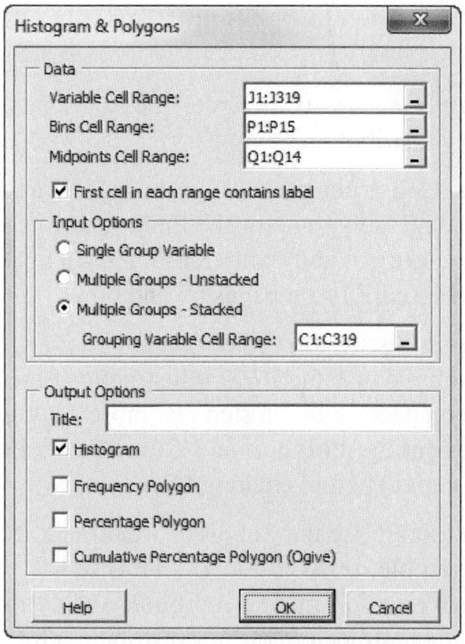

As explained in Section 2.2, you cannot define an explicit lower boundary for the first bin, so the first bin can never have a midpoint. Therefore, the **Midpoints Cell Range** you enter must have one fewer cell than the **Bins Cell Range**. PHStat associates the first midpoint with the second bin and uses **--** as the label for the first bin.

The example uses the workaround discussed in Section 2.2, "Classes and Excel Bins on page 48." When you use this workaround, the histogram bar labeled **--** will *always* be a zero bar. Appendix Section B.8 explains how you can delete this unnecessary bar from the histogram, as was done for the examples shown in Section 2.4.

In-Depth Excel Use the **Histogram workbook** as a model. For the example, first construct frequency distributions for the growth and value funds. Open to the **UNSTACKED worksheet** of the **Retirement Funds workbook**. This worksheet contains the retirement funds data unstacked in columns A and B and a set of bin numbers and midpoints appropriate for those data in columns D and E. Then:

1. Right-click the **UNSTACKED** sheet tab and click **Insert** in the shortcut menu.
2. In the **General** tab of the Insert dialog box, click **Worksheet** and click then **OK**.

In the new worksheet.

3. Enter a title in cell **A1**, **Bins** in cell **A3**, **Frequency** in cell **B3**, and **Midpoints** in cell **C3**.
4. Copy the bin number list in the cell range **D2:D15** of the **UNSTACKED worksheet** and paste this list into cell **A4** of the new worksheet.
5. Enter **'--** in cell **C4**. Copy the midpoints list in the cell range **E2:E14** of the **UNSTACKED worksheet** and paste this list into cell **C5** of the new worksheet.
6. Select the cell range **B4:B17** that will hold the array formula.
7. Type, but do not press the **Enter** or **Tab** key, the formula **=FREQUENCY(UNSTACKED!$A$2:$A$224, $A$4:$A$17)**. Then, while holding down the **Ctrl** and **Shift** keys (or the **Command** key on a Mac), press the **Enter** key to enter the array formula into the cell range **B4:B17**.
8. Adjust the worksheet formatting as necessary.

Steps 1 through 8 construct a frequency distribution for the growth retirement funds. To construct a frequency distribution for the value retirement funds, repeat steps 1 through 8 but in step 7 type **=FREQUENCY(UNSTACKED!$B$1:$B$96, $A$4:$A$17)** as the array formula.

Having constructed the two frequency distributions, continue by constructing the two histograms. Open to the worksheet that contains the frequency distribution for the growth funds and:

1. Select the cell range **B3:B17** (the cell range of the frequencies).
2. Select **Insert → Column** and select the **first 2-D Column** gallery item (**Clustered Column**).
3. Right-click the chart and click **Select Data** in the shortcut menu.

In the Select Data Source dialog box:

4. Click **Edit** under the **Horizontal (Categories) Axis Labels** heading.
5. In the Axis Labels dialog box, drag the mouse to *select* the cell range **C4:C17** (containing the midpoints) to enter that cell range. Do not type this cell range in the Axis label range box as you would otherwise do for the reasons explained in Appendix Section B.7. Click **OK** in this dialog box and then click **OK** (in the Select Data Source dialog box).

In the chart:

6. Right-click inside a bar and click **Format Data Series** in the shortcut menu.

In the Format Data Series dialog box:

7. Click **Series Options** in the left pane. In the Series Options right pane, change the **Gap Width** slider to **No Gap**. Click **Close**.
8. Relocate the chart to a chart sheet, turn off the chart legend and gridlines, add axis titles, and modify the chart title by using the instructions in Appendix Section B.6.

This example uses the workaround discussed in Section 2.2, "Classes and Excel Bins" on page 48. When you use this workaround, the histogram bar labeled **--** will *always* be a zero bar. Appendix Section B.8 explains how you can delete this unnecessary bar from the histogram, as was done for the examples shown in Section 2.4.

Analysis ToolPak Use **Histogram.**
For the example, open to the **UNSTACKED worksheet** of the **Retirement Funds workbook** and:

1. Select **Data → Data Analysis**. In the Data Analysis dialog box, select **Histogram** from the **Analysis Tools** list and then click **OK**.

In the Histogram dialog box:

2. Enter **A1:A224** as the **Input Range** and enter **D1:D15** as the **Bin Range**.
3. Check **Labels**, click **New Worksheet Ply**, and check **Chart Output**.
4. Click **OK** to create the frequency distribution and histogram on a new worksheet.

In the new worksheet:

5. Follow steps 5 through 9 of the *Analysis ToolPak* instructions in "The Frequency Distribution" in Section EG2.2.

These steps construct a frequency distribution and histogram for the growth funds. To construct a frequency distribution and histogram for the value funds, repeat the nine steps but in step 2 enter **B1:B96** as the **Input Range**. You will need to correct several formatting errors that Excel makes to the histograms it constructs. For each histogram:

1. Right-click inside a bar and click **Format Data Series** in the shortcut menu.

In the Format Data Series dialog box:

2. Click **Series Options** in the left pane. In the Series Options right pane, change the **Gap Width** slider to **No Gap**. Click **Close**.

Histogram bars are labeled by bin numbers. To change the labeling to midpoints, open to each of the new worksheets and:

3. Enter **Midpoints** in cell **C3** and **'--** in cell **C4.** Copy the cell range **E2:E14** of the **UNSTACKED worksheet** and paste this list into cell **C5** of the new worksheet.
4. Right-click the histogram and click **Select Data**.
5. In the Select Data Source dialog box, click **Edit** under the **Horizontal (Categories) Axis Labels** heading.
6. In the Axis Labels dialog box, drag the mouse to select the cell range **C4:C17** to enter that cell range. Do not type this cell range in the Axis label range box as you would otherwise do for the reasons explained in Appendix Section B.7. Click **OK** in this dialog box and then click **OK** (in the Select Data Source dialog box).
7. Relocate the chart to a chart sheet, turn off the chart legend and modify the chart title by using the instructions in Appendix Section B.6.

This example uses the workaround discussed in Section 2.2, "Classes and Excel Bins." Appendix Section B.8 explains how you can delete this unnecessary bar from the histogram, as was done for the examples shown in Section 2.4.

The Percentage Polygon and the Cumulative Percentage Polygon (Ogive)

Key Technique Modify an Excel line chart that is based on a frequency distribution.

Example Construct percentage polygons and cumulative percentage polygons for the three-year return percentages for the growth and value retirement funds, similar to Figures 2.11 and 2.12 on pages 65 and 66.

PHStat Use **Histogram & Polygons.**
For the example, use the *PHStat* instructions for creating a histogram on page 98 but in step 3 of those instructions, also check **Percentage Polygon** and **Cumulative Percentage Polygon (Ogive)** before clicking **OK**.

In-Depth Excel Use the **Polygons workbook** as a model.
For the example, open to the **UNSTACKED worksheet** of the **Retirement Funds workbook** and follow steps 1 through 8 to construct a frequency distribution for the growth retirement funds. Repeat steps 1 through 8 but in step 7 type the array formula **=FREQUENCY(UNSTACKED!$B$1:$B$96, $A$4:$A$17)** to construct a frequency distribution for the value funds. Open to the worksheet that contains the growth funds frequency distribution and:

1. Select column **C**. Right-click and click **Insert** in the shortcut menu. Right-click and click **Insert** in the shortcut menu a second time. (The worksheet contains new, blank columns C and D and the midpoints column is now column E.)
2. Enter **Percentage** in cell C3 and **Cumulative Pctage.** in cell **D3**.
3. Enter **=B4/SUM($B$4:$B$17)** in cell **C4** and copy this formula down through row **17**.
4. Enter **=C4** in cell **D4**.
5. Enter **=C5 + D4** in cell **D5** and copy this formula down through row **17**.
6. Select the cell range **C4:D17**, right-click, and click **Format Cells** in the shortcut menu.
7. In the **Number** tab of the Format Cells dialog box, click **Percentage** in the **Category** list and click **OK**.

Open to the worksheet that contains the value funds frequency distribution and repeat steps 1 through 7. To construct the percentage polygons, open to the worksheet that contains the growth funds distribution and:

1. Select cell range **C4:C17**.
2. Select **Insert → Line** and select the **fourth 2-D Line** gallery item (**Line with Markers**).
3. Right-click the chart and click **Select Data** in the shortcut menu.

In the Select Data Source dialog box:

4. Click **Edit** under the **Legend Entries (Series)** heading. In the Edit Series dialog box, enter the *formula* **="Growth Funds"** as the **Series name** and click **OK**.

5. Click **Edit** under the **Horizontal (Categories) Axis Labels** heading. In the Axis Labels dialog box, drag the mouse to select the cell range **E4:E17** to enter that cell range. Do not type this cell range in the Axis label range box as you would otherwise do for the reasons explained in Appendix Section B.7.
6. Click **OK** in this dialog box and then click **OK** (in the Select Data Source dialog box).

Back in the chart:

7. Relocate the chart to a chart sheet, turn off the chart gridlines, add axis titles, and modify the chart title by using the instructions in Appendix Section B.6.

In the new chart sheet:

8. Right-click the chart and click **Select Data** in the shortcut menu.
9. In the Select Data Source dialog box, click **Add**.

In the Edit Series dialog box:

10. Enter the formula **="Value Funds"** as the **Series name** and press **Tab**.
11. With the current value in **Series values** highlighted, click the worksheet tab for the worksheet that contains the value funds distribution.
12. Drag the mouse to select the cell range **C4:C17** to enter that cell range as the **Series values**. Do not type this cell range in the Series values box as you would otherwise do, for the reasons explained in Appendix Section B.7.
13. Click **OK**. Back in the Select Data Source dialog box, click **OK**.

To construct the cumulative percentage polygons, open to the worksheet that contains the growth funds distribution and repeat steps 1 through 13 but replace steps 1, 5, and 12 with these steps:

1. Select the cell range **D4:D17**.
5. Click **Edit** under the **Horizontal (Categories) Axis Labels** heading. In the Axis Labels dialog box, drag the mouse to select the cell range **A4:A17** to enter that cell range.
12. Drag the mouse to select the cell range **D4:D17** to enter that cell range as the **Series values**.

If the *Y* axis of the cumulative percentage polygon counts up to more than 100%, right-click the axis and click **Format Axis** in the shortcut menu. In the Format Axis dialog box, click **Axis Options** in the left pane and in the **Axis Options** right pane, click the **Fixed** option button for Maximum and enter **1** in its box. Click **Close**.

EG2.5 VISUALIZING TWO NUMERICAL VARIABLES

The Scatter Plot

Key Technique Use the Excel scatter chart.

Example Construct a scatter plot of revenue and value for NBA teams, similar to Figure 2.14 on page 70.

PHStat Use **Scatter Plot**.

For the example, open to the **DATA worksheet** of the **NBAValues workbook**. Select **PHStat Descriptive Statistics Scatter Plot**. In the procedure's dialog box (shown below):

1. Enter **D1:D31** as the **Y Variable Cell Range**.
2. Enter **C1:C31** as the **X Variable Cell Range**.
3. Check **First cells in each range contains label**.
4. Enter a **Title** and click **OK**.

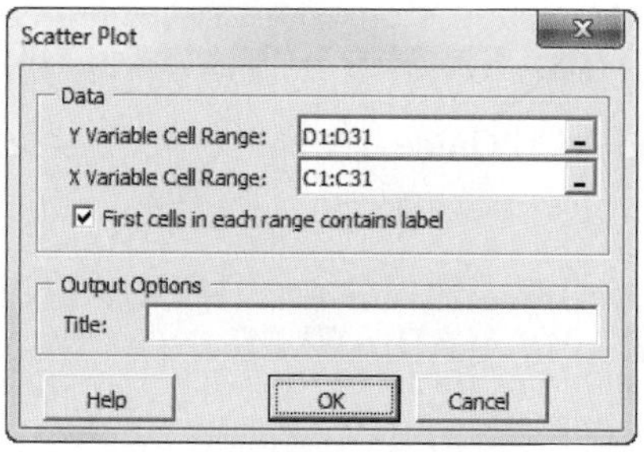

To add a superimposed line like the one shown in Figure 2.14, click the chart and select **Layout → Trendline → Linear Trendline**.

In-Depth Excel Use the **Scatter Plot workbook** as a model.

For the example, open to the **DATA worksheet** of the **NBAValues workbook** and:

1. Select the cell range **C1:D31**.
2. Select **Insert → Scatter** and select the **first Scatter** gallery item (**Scatter with only Markers**).
3. Select **Layout → Trendline → Linear Trendline**.
4. Relocate the chart to a chart sheet, turn off the chart legend and gridlines, add axis titles, and modify the chart title by using the instructions in Appendix Section B.6.

When constructing Excel scatter charts with other data, make sure that the *X* variable column precedes (is to the left of) the *Y* variable column. (If the worksheet is arranged *Y* then *X*, cut and paste so that the *Y* variable column appears to the right of the *X* variable column.)

The Time-Series Plot

Key Technique Use the Excel scatter chart.

Example Construct a time-series plot of movie revenue per year from 1995 to 2011, similar to Figure 2.15 on page 71.

In-Depth Excel Use the **Time Series workbook** as a model.

For the example, open to the **DATA worksheet** of the **Movie Revenues workbook** and:

1. Select the cell range **A1:B18**.
2. Select **Insert → Scatter** and select the **fourth Scatter** gallery item (**Scatter with Straight Lines and Markers**).

3. Relocate the chart to a chart sheet, turn off the chart legend and gridlines, add axis titles, and modify the chart title by using the instructions in Appendix Section B.6.

When constructing time-series charts with other data, make sure that the X variable column precedes (is to the left of) the Y variable column. (If the worksheet is arranged Y then X, cut and paste so that the Y variable column appears to the right of the X variable column.)

EG2.6 CHALLENGES in VISUALIZING DATA

There are no Excel Guide instructions for this section.

EG2.7 ORGANIZING and VISUALIZING MANY VARIABLES

Multidimensional Contingency Tables

Key Technique Use the Excel PivotTable feature.

Example Construct a PivotTable showing percentage of overall total for fund type, risk, and market cap for the retirement funds sample, similar to the one shown in Figure 2.21 on page 78.

In-Depth Excel Use the **MCT workbook** as a model.
For the example, open to the **DATA worksheet** of the **Retirement Funds workbook** and:

1. Select **Insert → PivotTable**.

In the Create PivotTable dialog box:

2. Click **Select a table or range** and enter **A1:N319** as the **Table/Range**.
3. Click **New Worksheet** and then click **OK**.

Excel inserts a new worksheet and displays the PivotTable Field List pane. The worksheet contains a graphical representation of a PivotTable that will change as you work inside the PivotTable Field List (or PivotTable Fields) task pane. In that pane (partially shown in the next column):

4. Drag **Type** in the **Choose fields to add to report** box and drop it in the **Row Labels** (or **ROWS**) box.
5. Drag **Market Cap** in the **Choose fields to add to report** box and drop it in the **Row Labels** (or **ROWS**) box.
6. Drag **Risk** in the **Choose fields to add to report** box and drop it in the **Column Labels** (or **COLUMNS**) box.
7. Drag **Type** in the **Choose fields to add to report** box a second time and drop it in the Σ **Values** box. The dropped label changes to **Count of Type**.
8. Click (not right-click) **Count of Type** and click **Value Field Settings** in the shortcut menu.

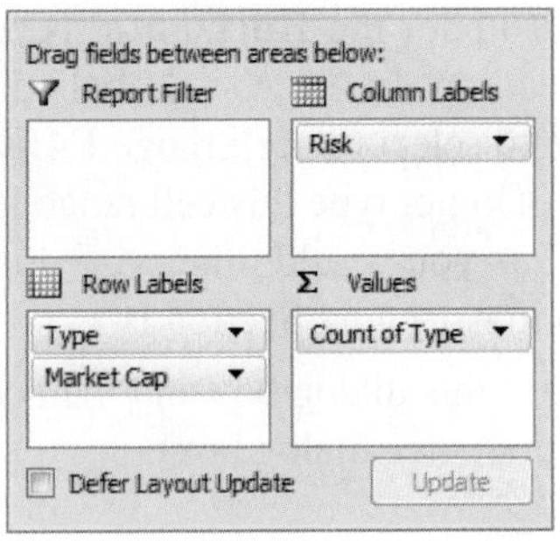

In the Value Field Settings dialog box:

9. Click the **Show Values As** tab and select **% of Grand Total** from the **Show values as** drop-down list (shown below).
10. Click **OK**.

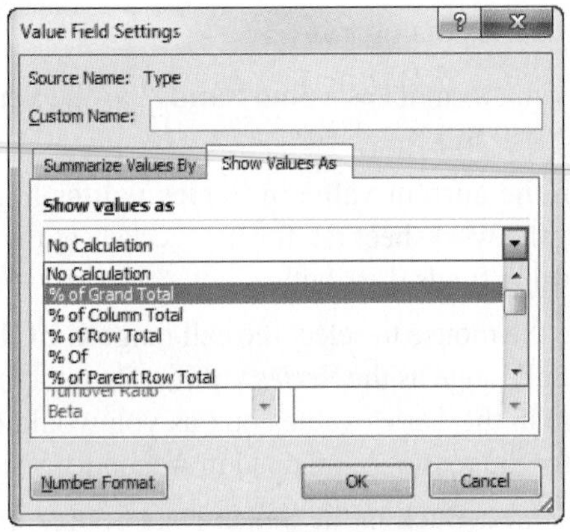

In the PivotTable:

11. Enter a title in cell **A1**.
12. Enter a **space character** in cell A3 to replace the value "Count of Type." Due to a Microsoft Excel quirk, you must use a space character as you cannot delete "Count of Type" directly as you might otherwise do.
13. Follow steps 6 and 7 of the *In-Depth Excel* "The Contingency Table" instructions on page 93 to relocate the Low column from column D to column B.

If the PivotTable you construct does not contain a row and column for the grand totals as the PivotTables in Figure 2.21 contain, follow steps 9 through 13 of the *In-Depth Excel*, "The Contingency Table" instructions to include the grand totals.

Adding Numerical Variables

Key Technique Alter the contents of the Σ Values box in the PivotTable Field List pane.

Example Construct a PivotTable of fund type, risk, market cap, showing the mean ten-year return percentage for the retirement funds sample, similar to the one shown in Figure 2.22 on page 79.

In-Depth Excel Use the **MCT workbook** as a model. For the example, first construct the PivotTable showing percentage of overall total for fund type, risk, and market cap for the retirement funds sample using the instructions of the previous section. Then continue with these steps:

14. If the PivotTable Field List pane is not visible, right-click cell **A3** and click **Show Field List** in the shortcut menu.

In the PivotTable Field List pane:

15. Drag the **blank label** (initially labeled **Count of Type** after step 7) in the Σ **Values** box and drop it outside the pane to delete this label. The PivotTable changes and all of the percentages disappear.
16. Drag **10YrReturn%** in the **Choose fields to add to report** box and drop it in the Σ **Values** box. The dropped label changes to **Sum of 10YrReturn%**.
17. Click **Sum of 10YrReturn%** and click **Value Field Settings** in the shortcut menu.

In the Value Field Settings dialog box (shown below):

18. Click the **Summarize Values By** tab and select **Average** from the list. The **Custom Name** changes to **Average of 10YrReturn%**.
19. Click **OK**.

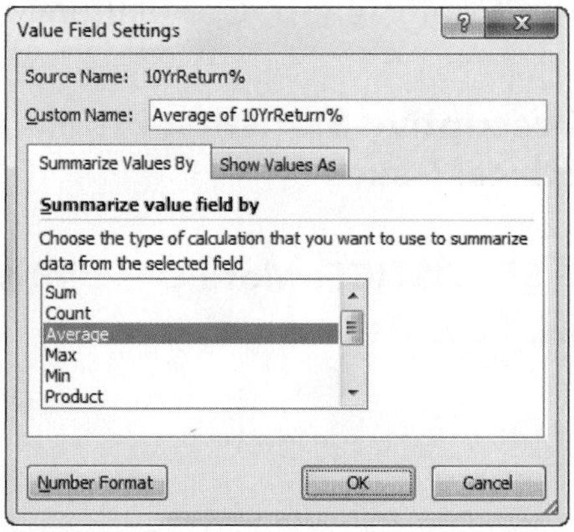

In the PivotTable:

20. Select cell range **B5:E13**, right-click, and click **Format Cells** in the shortcut menu. In the Number tab of the Format Cells dialog box, click **Number**, set the **Decimal places** to **2**, and click **OK**.

EG2.8 PIVOTTABLES and BUSINESS ANALYTICS

Key Technique Use the Excel slicer feature with an already-defined PivotTable.

Example Construct slicers for type, market cap, star rating, and expense ratio to use with a PivotTable of fund type and risk, similar to the slicers shown in Figure 2.24 on page 81.

In-Depth Excel Use the **Slicers workbook** as a model. For the example, first construct a PivotTable using the *In-Depth Excel* "The Contingency Table" instructions on page 93. Click cell **A3** in the PivotTable and:

1. Select **Insert ➔ Slicer**.

In the Insert Slicers dialog box (shown below):

2. Check **Market Cap**, **Type**, **Expense Ratio**, and **Star Rating**.
3. Click **OK**.

4. In the worksheet, drag the slicers to reposition them. If necessary, resize slicer panels as you would resize a window.

Click the value buttons in the slicers to explore the data. For example, to create the display shown in the left illustration of Figure 2.25 on page 81 that answers the first question presented in Section 2.8, click **0.59** in the **Expense Ratio** slicer.

When you click a value button, the icon at the top right of the slicer changes to include a red X (as can be seen in both Expense Ratio slicers in Figure 2.25). Click this icon to reset the slicer. When you click a value button, value buttons in *other* slicers may become dimmed (as have buttons such as Value, Mid-Cap, Small, Five, One, Three, and Two in Figure 2.25). Dimmed value buttons represent values that are not found in the currently "sliced" data, and if you click a dimmed value button, the PivotTable will be empty and show no values.

CHAPTER

3 Numerical Descriptive Measures

Learning Objectives

In this chapter, you learn:

- To describe the properties of central tendency, variation, and shape in numerical data
- To construct and interpret a boxplot
- To compute descriptive summary measures for a population
- To compute the covariance and the coefficient of correlation

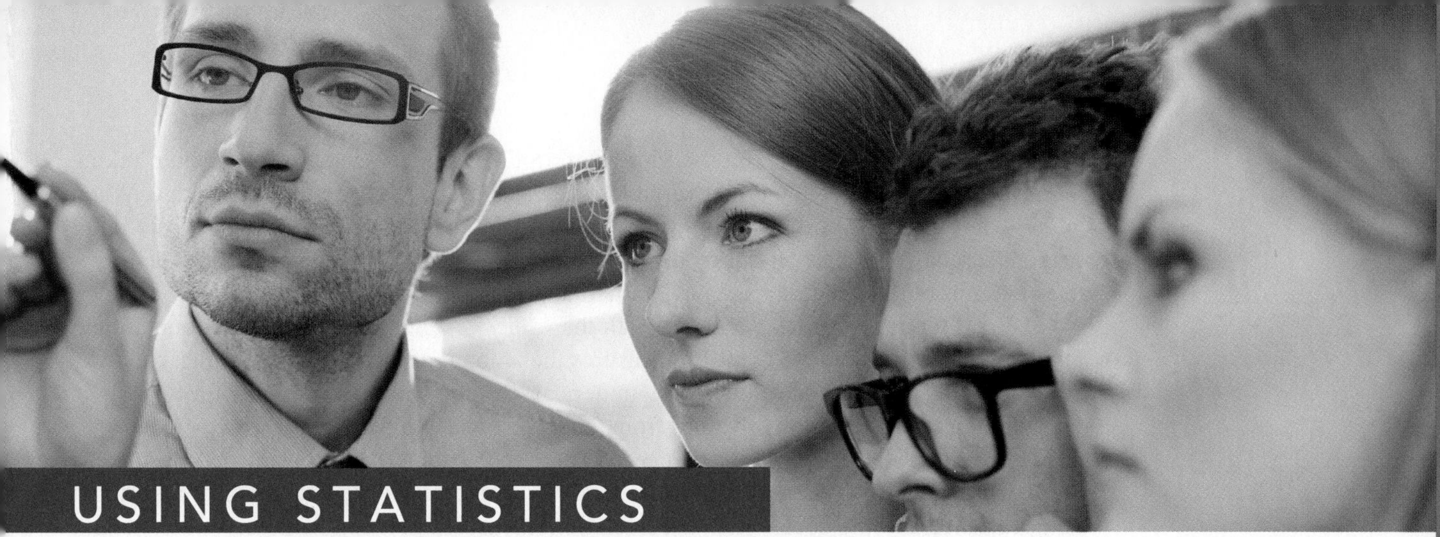

baranq / Shutterstock

USING STATISTICS

More Descriptive Choices

As a member of a task force at the Choice *Is* Yours investment service, you helped organize and visualize the data from a sample of 318 retirement funds. Now, several weeks later, prospective clients such as Tom Sanchez are reviewing this work but want to know more.

In particular, prospective clients would like to able to compare the results of an individual retirement fund to the results of similar funds. For example, while the earlier work your team did shows how the three-year return percentages are distributed, customers would like to know how the value for a particular mid-cap growth fund compares to the three-year returns of all mid-cap growth funds. Prospective clients also seek to understand how the values for the variables collected vary. Are all the values relatively similar? And does any variable have outlier values that are either extremely small or extremely large?

While doing a complete search of the retirement funds data could lead to answers to the preceding questions, you wonder if there are easier ways than extensive searching to uncover those answers. You also wonder if there are other ways of being more *descriptive* about the sample of funds—providing answers to questions not yet raised by prospective clients. If you can help the Choice *Is* Yours investment service provide such answers, prospective clients will be better able to evaluate the retirement funds that your firm features.

Ryan R Fox / Shutterstock

The prospective clients in the More Descriptive Choices scenario have begun asking questions about numerical variables such as the three-year return percentage. When summarizing and describing numerical variables, the organizing and visualizing methods discussed in Chapter 2 are only a starting point. You also need to describe such variables in terms of their central tendency, variation, and shape.

Central tendency is the extent to which the values of a numerical variable group around a typical, or central, value. **Variation** measures the amount of dispersion, or scattering, away from a central value that the values of a numerical variable show. The *shape* of a variable is the pattern of the distribution of values from the lowest value to the highest value.

This chapter discusses ways you can compute these numerical descriptive measures as you begin to analyze your data within the DCOVA framework. The chapter also talks about the covariance and the coefficient of correlation, measures that can help show the strength of the association between two numerical variables. Computing the descriptive measures discussed in this chapter would be one way to help prospective clients of the Choice *Is* Yours service find the answers they seek.

3.1 Central Tendency

Most sets of data show a distinct tendency to group around a central value. When people talk about an "average value" or the "middle value" or the "most frequent value," they are talking informally about the mean, median, and mode—three measures of central tendency.

The Mean

The **arithmetic mean** (typically referred to as the **mean**) is the most common measure of central tendency. The mean can suggest a typical or central value and serves as a "balance point" in a set of data, similar to the fulcrum on a seesaw. The mean is the only common measure in which all the values play an equal role. You compute the mean by adding together all the values in a data set and then dividing that sum by the number of values in the data set.

The symbol $\overline{X}$, called *X-bar*, is used to represent the mean of a sample. For a sample containing n values, the equation for the mean of a sample is written as

$$\overline{X} = \frac{\text{sum of the values}}{\text{number of values}}$$

Using the series $X_1, X_2, \ldots, X_n$ to represent the set of n values and n to represent the number of values in the sample, the equation becomes

$$\overline{X} = \frac{X_1 + X_2 + \cdots + X_n}{n}$$

By using summation notation (discussed fully in Appendix A), you replace the numerator $X_1 + X_2 + \cdots + X_n$ with the term $\sum_{i=1}^{n} X_i$, which means sum all the X_i values from the first X value, X_1, to the last X value, X_n, to form Equation (3.1), a formal definition of the sample mean.

SAMPLE MEAN

The **sample mean** is the sum of the values in a sample divided by the number of values in the sample:

$$\overline{X} = \frac{\sum_{i=1}^{n} X_i}{n} \qquad \textbf{(3.1)}$$

where

$$\bar{X} = \text{sample mean}$$
$$n = \text{number of values or sample size}$$
$$X_i = i\text{th value of the variable } X$$
$$\sum_{i=1}^{n} X_i = \text{summation of all } X_i \text{ values in the sample}$$

Because all the values play an equal role, a mean is greatly affected by any value that is very different from the others. When you have such extreme values, you should avoid using the mean as a measure of central tendency.

For example, if you knew the typical time it takes you to get ready in the morning, you might be able to arrive at your first destination every day in a more timely manner. Using the DCOVA framework, you first define the time to get ready as the time from when you get out of bed to when you leave your home, rounded to the nearest minute. Then, you collect the times for 10 consecutive workdays and organize and store them in **Times**.

Using the collected data, you compute the mean to discover the "typical" time it takes for you to get ready. For these data:

Day:	1	2	3	4	5	6	7	8	9	10
Time (minutes):	39	29	43	52	39	44	40	31	44	35

the mean time is 39.6 minutes, computed as follows:

$$\bar{X} = \frac{\text{sum of the values}}{\text{number of values}}$$

$$\bar{X} = \frac{\sum_{i=1}^{n} X_i}{n}$$

$$\bar{X} = \frac{39 + 29 + 43 + 52 + 39 + 44 + 40 + 31 + 44 + 35}{10}$$

$$= \frac{396}{10} = 39.6$$

Even though no individual day in the sample had a value of 39.6 minutes, allotting this amount of time to get ready in the morning would be a reasonable decision to make. The mean is a good measure of central tendency in this case because the data set does not contain any exceptionally small or large values.

To illustrate how the mean can be greatly affected by any value that is very different from the others, imagine that on day 3, a set of unusual circumstances delayed you getting ready by an extra hour, so that the time for that day was 103 minutes. This extreme value causes the mean to rise to 45.6 minutes, as follows:

$$\bar{X} = \frac{\text{sum of the values}}{\text{number of values}}$$

$$\bar{X} = \frac{\sum_{i=1}^{n} X_i}{n}$$

$$\bar{X} = \frac{39 + 29 + 103 + 52 + 39 + 44 + 40 + 31 + 44 + 35}{10}$$

$$\bar{X} = \frac{456}{10} = 45.6$$

The one extreme value has increased the mean by 6 minutes. The extreme value also moved the position of the mean relative to the all the values. The original mean, 39.6 minutes, had a middle, or *central*, position among the data values: 5 of the times were less than that mean and 5 were greater than that mean. In contrast, the mean using the extreme value is greater than 9 of the 10 times, making the new mean a poor measure of central tendency.

EXAMPLE 3.1

The Mean Calories in Cereals

Nutritional data about a sample of seven breakfast cereals (stored in **Cereals**) includes the number of calories per serving:

Cereal	Calories
Kellogg's All Bran	80
Kellogg's Corn Flakes	100
Wheaties	100
Nature's Path Organic Multigrain Flakes	110
Kellogg's Rice Krispies	130
Post Shredded Wheat Vanilla Almond	190
Kellogg's Mini Wheats	200

Compute the mean number of calories in these breakfast cereals.

SOLUTION The mean number of calories is 130, computed as follows:

$$\bar{X} = \frac{\text{sum of the values}}{\text{number of values}}$$

$$\bar{X} = \frac{\sum_{i=1}^{n} X_i}{n}$$

$$= \frac{910}{7} = 130$$

The Median

The **median** is the middle value in an ordered array of data that has been ranked from smallest to largest. Half the values are smaller than or equal to the median, and half the values are larger than or equal to the median. The median is not affected by extreme values, so you can use the median when extreme values are present.

To compute the median for a set of data, you first rank the values from smallest to largest and then use Equation (3.2) to compute the rank of the value that is the median.

MEDIAN

$$\text{Median} = \frac{n+1}{2} \text{ ranked value} \qquad (3.2)$$

You compute the median by following one of two rules:

- **Rule 1** If the data set contains an *odd* number of values, the median is the measurement associated with the middle-ranked value.
- **Rule 2** If the data set contains an even number of values, the median is the measurement associated with the average of the two middle-ranked values.

To further analyze the sample of 10 times to get ready in the morning, you can compute the median. To do so, you rank the daily times as follows:

Student Tip
Remember that you must rank the values in order from the smallest to the largest in order to compute the median.

Ranked values:	29	31	35	39	39	40	43	44	44	52
Ranks:	1	2	3	4	5	6	7	8	9	10

↑
Median = 39.5

Because the result of dividing $n + 1$ by 2 for this sample of 10 is $(10 + 1)/2 = 5.5$, you must use Rule 2 and average the measurements associated with the fifth and sixth ranked values, 39 and 40. Therefore, the median is 39.5. The median of 39.5 means that for half the days, the time to get ready is less than or equal to 39.5 minutes, and for half the days, the time to get ready is greater than or equal to 39.5 minutes. In this case, the median time to get ready of 39.5 minutes is very close to the mean time to get ready of 39.6 minutes.

EXAMPLE 3.2

Computing the Median from an Odd-Sized Sample

Nutritional data about a sample of seven breakfast cereals (stored in **Cereals**) includes the number of calories per serving (see Example 3.1 on page 108). Compute the median number of calories in breakfast cereals.

SOLUTION Because the result of dividing $n + 1$ by 2 for this sample of seven is $(7 + 1)/2 = 4$, using Rule 1, the median is the measurement associated with the fourth ranked value. The number of calories per serving values are ranked from the smallest to the largest:

Ranked values:	80	100	100	110	130	190	200
Ranks:	1	2	3	4	5	6	7

↑
Median = 110

The median number of calories is 110. Half the breakfast cereals have equal to or less than 110 calories per serving, and half the breakfast cereals have equal to or more than 110 calories.

The Mode

The **mode** is the value in a set of data that appears most frequently. Like the median and unlike the mean, extreme values do not affect the mode. For a set of data, there can be several modes or no mode at all. For example, for the sample of 10 times to get ready in the morning:

29 31 35 39 39 40 43 44 44 52

there are two modes, 39 minutes and 44 minutes, because each of these values occurs twice. However, for this sample of 8 prices for tablet computers (stored in **Tablets-Seven-Inch**[1]):

270 290 300 350 400 430 500 600

there is no mode. None of the values is "most typical" because each value appears the same number of times (once) in the data set.

[1] Price data extracted from "Tablets and e-Book Readers," *Consumer Reports*, September 2011, p. 46

EXAMPLE 3.3

Determining the Mode

A systems manager in charge of a company's network keeps track of the number of server failures that occur in a day. Determine the mode for the following data, which represent the number of server failures per a day for the past two weeks:

1 3 0 3 26 2 7 4 0 2 3 3 6 3

SOLUTION The ordered array for these data is

0 0 1 2 2 3 3 3 3 3 4 6 7 26

Because 3 occurs five times, more times than any other value, the mode is 3. Thus, the systems manager can say that the most common occurrence is having three server failures in a day. For this data set, the median is also equal to 3, and the mean is equal to 4.5. The value 26 is an extreme value. For these data, the median and the mode are better measures of central tendency than the mean.

The Geometric Mean

When you want to measure the rate of change of a variable over time, you need to use the geometric mean instead of the arithmetic mean. Equation (3.3) defines the geometric mean.

GEOMETRIC MEAN

The **geometric mean** is the *n*th root of the product of *n* values:

$$\bar{X}_G = (X_1 \times X_2 \times \cdots \times X_n)^{1/n} \quad \textbf{(3.3)}$$

The geometric mean rate of return measures the average percentage return of an investment per time period. Equation (3.4) defines the geometric mean rate of return.

GEOMETRIC MEAN RATE OF RETURN

$$\bar{R}_G = [(1 + R_1) \times (1 + R_2) \times \cdots \times (1 + R_n)]^{1/n} - 1 \quad \textbf{(3.4)}$$

where

$$R_i = \text{rate of return in time period } i$$

To illustrate these measures, consider an investment of $100,000 that declined to a value of $50,000 at the end of Year 1 and then rebounded back to its original $100,000 value at the end of Year 2. The rate of return for this investment per year for the two-year period is 0 because the starting and ending value of the investment is unchanged. However, the arithmetic mean of the yearly rates of return of this investment is

$$\bar{X} = \frac{(-0.50) + (1.00)}{2} = 0.25 \text{ or } 25\%$$

because the rate of return for Year 1 is

$$R_1 = \left(\frac{50{,}000 - 100{,}000}{100{,}000}\right) = -0.50 \text{ or } -50\%$$

and the rate of return for Year 2 is

$$R_2 = \left(\frac{100{,}000 - 50{,}000}{50{,}000}\right) = 1.00 \text{ or } 100\%$$

Using Equation (3.4), the geometric mean rate of return per year for the two years is

$$\begin{aligned}\overline{R}_G &= [(1 + R_1) \times (1 + R_2)]^{1/n} - 1 \\ &= [(1 + (-0.50)) \times (1 + (1.0))]^{1/2} - 1 \\ &= [(0.50) \times (2.0)]^{1/2} - 1 \\ &= [1.0]^{1/2} - 1 \\ &= 1 - 1 = 0\end{aligned}$$

Using the geometric mean rate of return more accurately reflects the (zero) change in the value of the investment per year for the two-year period than does the arithmetic mean.

EXAMPLE 3.4
Computing the Geometric Mean Rate of Return

The percentage change in the Russell 2000 Index of the stock prices of 2,000 small companies was 25.3% in 2010 and −5.5% in 2011. Compute the geometric rate of return.

SOLUTION Using Equation (3.4), the geometric mean rate of return in the Russell 2000 Index for the two years is

$$\begin{aligned}\overline{R}_G &= [(1 + R_1) \times (1 + R_2)]^{1/n} - 1 \\ &= [(1 + (0.253)) \times (1 + (-0.055))]^{1/2} - 1 \\ &= [(1.253) \times (0.945)]^{1/2} - 1 \\ &= (1.184085)^{1/2} - 1 \\ &= 1.0882 - 1 = 0.0882\end{aligned}$$

The geometric mean rate of return in the Russell 2000 Index for the two years is 8.82% per year.

3.2 Variation and Shape

In addition to central tendency, every data set can be characterized by its variation and shape. Variation measures the **spread**, or **dispersion**, of values in a data set. One simple measure of variation is the range, the difference between the largest and smallest values. More commonly used in statistics are the standard deviation and variance, two measures explained later in this section. The shape of a data set represents a pattern of all the values, from the lowest to highest value. As you will learn later in this section, many data sets have a pattern that looks approximately like a bell, with a peak of values somewhere in the middle.

The Range

The **range** is the difference between the largest and smallest value and is the simplest numerical descriptive measure of variation in a set of data.

RANGE

The range is equal to the largest value minus the smallest value.

$$\text{Range} = X_{\text{largest}} - X_{\text{smallest}} \qquad \textbf{(3.5)}$$

To further analyze the sample of 10 times to get ready in the morning, you can compute the range. To do so, you rank the data from smallest to largest:

29 31 35 39 39 40 43 44 44 52

Using Equation (3.5), the range is 52 − 29 = 23 minutes. The range of 23 minutes indicates that the largest difference between any two days in the time to get ready in the morning is 23 minutes.

EXAMPLE 3.5

Computing the Range in the Calories in Cereals

Nutritional data about a sample of seven breakfast cereals (stored in **Cereals**) includes the number of calories per serving (see Example 3.1 on page 108). Compute the range of the number of calories for the cereals.

SOLUTION Ranked from smallest to largest, the calories for the seven cereals are

80 100 100 110 130 190 200

Therefore, using Equation (3.5), the range = 200 − 80 = 120. The largest difference in the number of calories between any two cereals is 120.

The range measures the *total spread* in the set of data. Although the range is a simple measure of the total variation in the data, it does not take into account *how* the data are distributed between the smallest and largest values. In other words, the range does not indicate whether the values are evenly distributed throughout the data set, clustered near the middle, or clustered near one or both extremes. Thus, using the range as a measure of variation when at least one value is an extreme value is misleading.

The Variance and the Standard Deviation

Being a simple measure of variation, the range does not consider how the values distribute or cluster between the extremes. Two commonly used measures of variation that account for how all the values are distributed are the **variance** and the **standard deviation**. These statistics measure the "average" scatter around the mean—how larger values fluctuate above it and how smaller values fluctuate below it.

A simple measure of variation around the mean might take the difference between each value and the mean and then sum these differences. However, if you did that, you would find that these differences sum to zero because the mean is the balance point in *every* set of data. A measure of variation that *differs* from one data set to another *squares* the difference between each value and the mean and then sums these squared differences. The sum of these squared differences, known as the **sum of squares (*SS*)**, is then used to compute the sample variance (S^2) and the sample standard deviation (S).

The **sample variance** (S^2) is the sum of squares divided by the sample size minus 1. The **sample standard deviation (*S*)** is the square root of the sample variance. Because this sum of squares will always be nonnegative according to the rules of algebra, *neither the variance nor the standard deviation can ever be negative.* For virtually all sets of data, the variance and standard deviation will be a positive value. Both of these statistics will be zero only if every value in the sample is the same value (i.e., the values show no variation).

For a sample containing n values, $X_1, X_2, X_3, \ldots, X_n$, the sample variance (S^2) is

$$S^2 = \frac{(X_1 - \overline{X})^2 + (X_2 - \overline{X})^2 + \cdots + (X_n - \overline{X})^2}{n - 1}$$

Equations (3.6) and (3.7) define the sample variance and sample standard deviation using summation notation. The term $\sum_{i=1}^{n}(X_i - \overline{X})^2$ represents the sum of squares.

SAMPLE VARIANCE

The sample variance is the sum of the squared differences around the mean divided by the sample size minus 1:

$$S^2 = \frac{\sum_{i=1}^{n}(X_i - \overline{X})^2}{n - 1} \quad \textbf{(3.6)}$$

where

$\overline{X}$ = sample mean

n = sample size

X_i = ith value of the variable X

$\sum_{i=1}^{n}(X_i - \overline{X})^2$ = summation of all the squared differences between the X_i values and $\overline{X}$

SAMPLE STANDARD DEVIATION

The sample standard deviation is the square root of the sum of the squared differences around the mean divided by the sample size minus 1:

$$S = \sqrt{S^2} = \sqrt{\frac{\sum_{i=1}^{n}(X_i - \overline{X})^2}{n - 1}} \quad \textbf{(3.7)}$$

Note that in both equations, the sum of squares is divided by the sample size minus 1, $n - 1$. The value is used for reasons having to do with statistical inference and the properties of sampling distributions, a topic discussed in Section 7.2 on page 250. For now, observe that the difference between dividing by n and by $n - 1$ becomes smaller as the sample size increases.

In practice, you will most likely use the sample standard deviation as the measure of variation. Unlike the sample variance, a squared quantity, the standard deviation will always be a number expressed in the same units as the original sample data. For almost all sets of data, the majority of the values in a sample will be within an interval of plus and minus 1 standard deviation above and below the mean. Therefore, knowledge of the mean and the standard deviation usually helps define where at least the majority of the data values are clustering.

To hand-compute the sample variance, S^2, and the sample standard deviation, S:

- Compute the difference between each value and the mean.
- Square each difference.
- Add the squared differences.
- Divide this total by $n - 1$ to compute the sample variance.
- Take the square root of the sample variance to compute the sample standard deviation.

Student Tip
Remember, neither the variance nor the standard deviation can ever be negative.

To further analyze the sample of 10 times to get ready in the morning, Table 3.1 shows the first four steps for calculating the variance and standard deviation with a mean $(\overline{X})$ equal to 39.6. (Computing the mean is explained on page 107.) The second column of Table 3.1 shows step 1. The third column of Table 3.1 shows step 2. The sum of the squared differences (step 3) is shown at the bottom of Table 3.1. This total is then divided by $10 - 1 = 9$ to compute the variance (step 4).

TABLE 3.1

Computing the Variance of the Getting-Ready Times

$\overline{X} = 39.6$

Time (X)	*Step 1:* $(X_i - \overline{X})$	*Step 2:* $(X_i - \overline{X})^2$
39	−0.60	0.36
29	−10.60	112.36
43	3.40	11.56
52	12.40	153.76
39	−0.60	0.36
44	4.40	19.36
40	0.40	0.16
31	−8.60	73.96
44	4.40	19.36
35	−4.60	21.16
	***Step 3:* Sum:**	412.40
	***Step 4: Divide by* $(n - 1)$:**	45.82

You can also compute the variance by substituting values for the terms in Equation (3.6):

$$S^2 = \frac{\sum_{i=1}^{n}(X_i - \overline{X})^2}{n - 1}$$

$$= \frac{(39 - 39.6)^2 + (29 - 39.6)^2 + \cdots + (35 - 39.6)^2}{10 - 1}$$

$$= \frac{412.4}{9}$$

$$= 45.82$$

Because the variance is in squared units (in squared minutes, for these data), to compute the standard deviation, you take the square root of the variance. Using Equation (3.7) on page 113, the sample standard deviation, S, is

$$S = \sqrt{S^2} = \sqrt{\frac{\sum_{i=1}^{n}(X_i - \overline{X})^2}{n - 1}} = \sqrt{45.82} = 6.77$$

This indicates that the getting-ready times in this sample are clustering within 6.77 minutes around the mean of 39.6 minutes (i.e., clustering between $\overline{X} - 1S = 32.83$ and $\overline{X} + 1S = 46.37$). In fact, 7 out of 10 getting-ready times lie within this interval.

Using the second column of Table 3.1, you can also compute the sum of the differences between each value and the mean to be zero. For any set of data, this sum will always be zero:

$$\sum_{i=1}^{n}(X_i - \overline{X}) = 0 \text{ for all sets of data}$$

This property is one of the reasons that the mean is used as the most common measure of central tendency.

EXAMPLE 3.6

Computing the Variance and Standard Deviation of the Number of Calories in Cereals

Nutritional data about a sample of seven breakfast cereals (stored in **Cereals**) includes the number of calories per serving (see Example 3.1 on page 108). Compute the variance and standard deviation of the calories in the cereals.

SOLUTION Table 3.2 illustrates the computation of the variance and standard deviation for the calories in the cereals.

TABLE 3.2

Computing the Variance of the Calories in the Cereals

$\bar{X} = 130$

Calories	*Step 1:* $(X_i - \bar{X})$	*Step 2:* $(X_i - \bar{X})^2$
80	−50	2,500
100	−30	900
100	−30	900
110	−20	400
130	0	0
190	60	3,600
200	70	4,900
	***Step 3:* Sum:**	13,200
	***Step 4: Divide by* $(n - 1)$:**	2,220

Using Equation (3.6) on page 113:

$$S^2 = \frac{\sum_{i=1}^{n}(X_i - \bar{X})^2}{n - 1}$$

$$= \frac{(80 - 130)^2 + (100 - 130)^2 + \cdots + (200 - 130)^2}{7 - 1}$$

$$= \frac{13{,}200}{6}$$

$$= 2{,}200$$

Using Equation (3.7) on page 113, the sample standard deviation, S, is

$$S = \sqrt{S^2} = \sqrt{\frac{\sum_{i=1}^{n}(X_i - \bar{X})^2}{n - 1}} = \sqrt{2{,}200} = 46.9042$$

The standard deviation of 46.9042 indicates that the calories in the cereals are clustering within ± 46.9042 around the mean of 130 (i.e., clustering between $\bar{X} - 1S = 83.0958$ and $\bar{X} + 1S = 176.9042$). In fact, 57.1% (four out of seven) of the calories lie within this interval.

The Coefficient of Variation

The coefficient of variation is equal to the standard deviation divided by the mean, multiplied by 100%. Unlike the measures of variation presented previously, the **coefficient of variation (CV)** measures the scatter in the data relative to the mean. The coefficient of variation is a *relative measure* of variation that is always expressed as a percentage rather than in terms of the units of the particular data. Equation (3.8) defines the coefficient of variation.

LEARN MORE

The Sharpe ratio, another relative measure of variation, is often used in financial analysis. Read the SHORT TAKES for Chapter 3 to learn more about this ratio.

COEFFICIENT OF VARIATION

The coefficient of variation is equal to the standard deviation divided by the mean, multiplied by 100%.

$$CV = \left(\frac{S}{\overline{X}}\right)100\% \quad \textbf{(3.8)}$$

where

S = sample standard deviation

$\overline{X}$ = sample mean

For the sample of 10 getting-ready times, because $\overline{X} = 39.6$ and $S = 6.77$, the coefficient of variation is

$$CV = \left(\frac{S}{\overline{X}}\right)100\% = \left(\frac{6.77}{39.6}\right)100\% = 17.10\%$$

Student Tip

The coefficient of variation is always expressed as a percentage, not in the units of the variables.

For the getting-ready times, the standard deviation is 17.1% of the size of the mean.

The coefficient of variation is especially useful when comparing two or more sets of data that are measured in different units, as Example 3.7 illustrates.

EXAMPLE 3.7

Comparing Two Coefficients of Variation When the Two Variables Have Different Units of Measurement

Which varies more from cereal to cereal—the number of calories or the amount of sugar (in grams)?

SOLUTION Because calories and the amount of sugar have different units of measurement, you need to compare the relative variability in the two measurements.

For calories, using the mean and variance computed in Examples 3.1 and 3.6 on pages 108 and 115, the coefficient of variation is

$$CV_{Calories} = \left(\frac{46.9042}{130}\right)100\% = 36.08\%$$

For the amount of sugar in grams, the values for the seven cereals are

6 2 4 4 4 11 10

For these data, $\overline{X} = 5.8571$ and $S = 3.3877$. Therefore, the coefficient of variation is

$$CV_{Sugar} = \left(\frac{3.3877}{5.8571}\right)100\% = 57.84\%$$

You conclude that relative to the mean, the amount of sugar is much more variable than the calories.

Z Scores

The **Z score** of a data value is the difference between that value and the mean, divided by the standard deviation. Z scores can help identify **outliers**, defined in Section 1.3 as values that seem excessively different from most of the rest of the values. Values that are very different from the mean will have either very small (negative) Z scores or very large (positive) Z scores. As a general rule, a Z score that is less than −3.0 or greater than +3.0 indicates an outlier value.

Z SCORE

The Z score for a value is equal to the difference between the value and the mean, divided by the standard deviation:

$$Z = \frac{X - \overline{X}}{S} \quad \textbf{(3.9)}$$

To further analyze the sample of 10 times to get ready in the morning, you can compute the Z scores. Because the mean is 39.6 minutes, the standard deviation is 6.77 minutes, and the time to get ready on the first day is 39.0 minutes, you compute the Z score for Day 1 by using Equation (3.9):

$$Z = \frac{X - \overline{X}}{S}$$

$$= \frac{39.0 - 39.6}{6.77}$$

$$= -0.09$$

Table 3.3 shows the Z scores for all 10 days.

TABLE 3.3

Z Scores for the 10 Getting-Ready Times

	Time (X)	Z Score
	39	−0.09
	29	−1.57
	43	0.50
	52	1.83
	39	−0.09
	44	0.65
	40	0.06
	31	−1.27
	44	0.65
	35	−0.68
Mean	39.6	
Standard deviation	6.77	

The largest Z score is 1.83 for Day 4, on which the time to get ready was 52 minutes. The lowest Z score is −1.57 for Day 2, on which the time to get ready was 29 minutes. Because none of the Z scores are less than −3.0 or greater then +3.0, you conclude that the getting-ready times include no apparent outliers.

EXAMPLE 3.8

Computing the Z Scores of the Number of Calories in Cereals

Nutritional data about a sample of seven breakfast cereals (stored in **Cereals**) includes the number of calories per serving (see Example 3.1 on page 108). Compute the *Z* scores of the calories in breakfast cereals.

SOLUTION Table 3.4 on page 118 illustrates the *Z* scores of the calories for the cereals. The largest *Z* score is 1.49, for a cereal with 200 calories. The lowest *Z* score is −1.07, for a cereal with 80 calories. There are no apparent outliers in these data because none of the *Z* scores are less than −3.0 or greater than +3.0.

TABLE 3.4

Z Scores of the Number of Calories in Cereals

	Calories	Z Scores
	80	−1.07
	100	−0.64
	100	−0.64
	110	−0.43
	130	0.00
	190	1.28
	200	1.49
Mean	130	
Standard deviation	46.9042	

Shape: Skewness and Kurtosis

The pattern to the distribution of data values throughout the entire range of all the values is called the **shape**. The shape of the distribution of data values can be described by two statistics: skewness and kurtosis.

Skewness measures the extent to which the data values are not **symmetrical** around the mean. In a perfectly symmetrical distribution, the values below the mean are distributed in exactly the same way as the values above the mean, and the skewness is zero. In a **skewed** distribution, there is an imbalance of data values below and above the mean, and the skewness is a nonzero value. Figure 3.1 depicts the shape of the distribution of data values for three sets of data, with the mean for each set plotted as a dashed vertical line.

FIGURE 3.1

The shapes of three data distributions

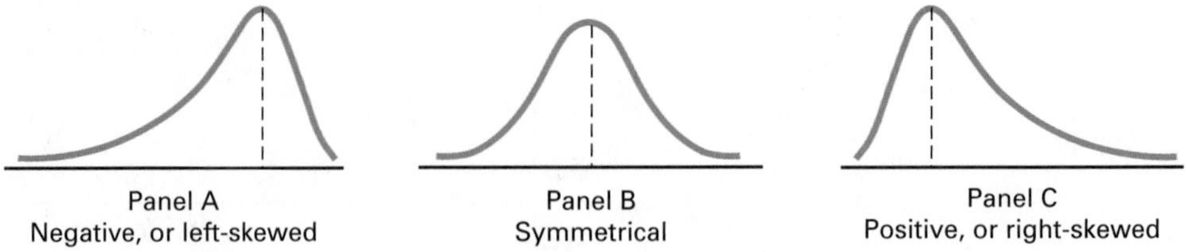

In Panel A, the distribution of data values is **left-skewed**. In this panel, most of the values are in the upper portion of the distribution. A long tail and distortion to the left is caused by some extremely small values. Because the skewness statistic for such a distribution will be less than zero, the term *negative skew* is also used to describe this distribution. These extremely small values pull the mean downward so that the mean is less than the median.

In Panel B, the distribution of data values is symmetrical. The portion of the curve below the mean is the mirror image of the portion of the curve above the mean. There is no asymmetry of data values below and above the mean, the mean equals the median, and, as noted earlier, the skewness is zero.

In Panel C, the distribution of data values is **right-skewed**. In this panel, most of the values are in the lower portion of the distribution. A long tail on the right is caused by some extremely large values. Because the skewness statistic for such a distribution will be greater than zero, the term *positive skew* is also used to describe this distribution. These extremely large values pull the mean upward so that the mean is greater than the median.

The observations about the mean and median made when examining Figure 3.1 generally hold for most distributions of a continuous numerical variable. Summarized, these observations are:

- **Mean $<$ median:** negative, or left-skewed distribution
- **Mean $=$ median:** symmetrical distribution with zero skewness
- **Mean $>$ median:** positive, or right-skewed distribution

Kurtosis measures the extent to which values that are very different from the mean affect the shape of the distribution of a set of data. Kurtosis affects the peakedness of the curve of the distribution—that is, how sharply the curve rises approaching the center of the distribution. Kurtosis compares the shape of the peak to the shape of the peak of a normal distribution (discussed in Chapter 6), which, by definition, has a kurtosis of zero.[2] A distribution that has a sharper-rising center peak than the peak of a normal distribution has *positive* kurtosis, a kurtosis value that is greater than zero, and is called **lepokurtic**. A distribution that has a slower-rising (flatter) center peak than the peak of a normal distribution has *negative* kurtosis, a kurtosis value that is less than zero, and is called **platykurtic**. A lepokurtic distribution has a higher concentration of values near the mean of the distribution compared to a normal distribution, while a platykurtic distribution has a lower concentration compared to a normal distribution.

[2] Several different operational definitions exist for kurtosis. The definition here, which is also used by Microsoft Excel, is sometimes called *excess kurtosis* to distinguish it from other definitions. Read the SHORT TAKES for Chapter 3 for more about how skewness (and kurtosis) are calculated in Excel.

In affecting the shape of the central peak, the relative concentration of values near the mean also affects the ends, or *tails*, of the curve of a distribution. A lepokurtic distribution has *fatter* tails, many more values in the tails, than a normal distribution has. If decision making about a set of data mistakenly assumes a normal distribution, when, in fact, the data forms a lepokurtic distribution, then that decision making will underestimate the occurrence of extreme values (values that are very different from the mean). Such an observation has been a basis for several explanations about the unanticipated reverses and collapses that financial markets have experienced in the recent past. (See reference 4 for an example of such an explanation.)

EXAMPLE 3.9

Descriptive Statistics for Growth and Value Funds

In the More Descriptive Choices scenario, you are interested in comparing the past performance of the growth and value funds from a sample of 318 funds. One measure of past performance is the three-year return percentage variable. Compute descriptive statistics for the growth and value funds.

SOLUTION Figure 3.2 presents a worksheet that computes descriptive summary measures for the two types of funds. The results include the mean, median, mode, minimum, maximum, range, variance, standard deviation, coefficient of variation, skewness, kurtosis, count (the sample size), and standard error. The standard error, discussed in Section 7.2, is the standard deviation divided by the square root of the sample size.

FIGURE 3.2

Descriptive statistics for the three-year return percentages for the growth and value funds

Figure 3.2 shows a worksheet similar to both the **CompleteStatistics worksheet** *of the* **Descriptive workbook** *and the worksheet created by the PHStat Descriptive Summary procedure. The Analysis ToolPak Descriptive Statistics procedure creates a comparable worksheet.*

	A	B	C
1	Descriptive Statistics for 3YrReturn% Variable		
2			
3		Growth	Value
4	Mean	22.44	20.42
5	Median	22.32	19.46
6	Mode	21.65	31.25
7	Minimum	3.39	9.82
8	Maximum	62.91	37.19
9	Range	59.52	27.37
10	Variance	44.1004	32.2427
11	Standard Deviation	6.6408	5.6783
12	Coeff. of Variation	29.60%	27.80%
13	Skewness	1.9175	0.8166
14	Kurtosis	10.0648	0.3180
15	Count	223	95
16	Standard Error	0.4447	0.5826

In examining the results, you see that there are differences in the three-year return for the growth and value funds. The growth funds had a mean three-year return of 22.44 and a median return of 22.32. This compares to a mean of 20.42 and a median of 19.46 for the value funds. The medians indicate that half of the growth funds had three-year annualized returns of 22.32 or better, and half the value funds had three-year annual returns of 19.46 or better. You conclude that the growth funds had a higher return than the value funds.

The growth funds had a higher standard deviation than the value funds (6.6408, as compared to 5.6783). While both the growth funds and the value funds showed right- or positive skewness, the growth funds were much more skewed. The kurtosis of the growth funds was very positive, indicating a distribution that was much more peaked than a normal distribution.

VISUAL EXPLORATIONS Exploring Descriptive Statistics

Open the **VE-Descriptive Statistics workbook** to explore the effects of changing data values on measures of central tendency, variation, and shape. Change the data values in the cell range **A2:A11** and then observe the changes to the statistics shown in the chart.

Click **View the Suggested Activity Page** to view a specific change you could make to the data values in column A. Click **View the More About Descriptive Statistics Page** to view summary definitions of the descriptive statistics shown in the chart. (See Appendix C to learn how you can download a copy of this workbook.)

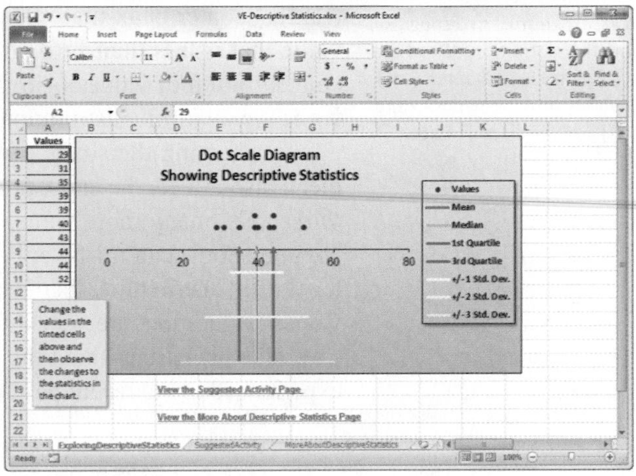

Problems for Sections 3.1 and 3.2

LEARNING THE BASICS

3.1 The following set of data is from a sample of $n = 5$:

7 4 9 8 2

a. Compute the mean, median, and mode.
b. Compute the range, variance, standard deviation, and coefficient of variation.
c. Compute the Z scores. Are there any outliers?
d. Describe the shape of the data set.

3.2 The following set of data is from a sample of $n = 6$:

7 4 9 7 3 12

a. Compute the mean, median, and mode.
b. Compute the range, variance, standard deviation, and coefficient of variation.
c. Compute the Z scores. Are there any outliers?
d. Describe the shape of the data set.

3.3 The following set of data is from a sample of $n = 7$:

12 7 4 9 0 7 3

a. Compute the mean, median, and mode.
b. Compute the range, variance, standard deviation, and coefficient of variation.
c. Compute the Z scores. Are there any outliers?
d. Describe the shape of the data set.

3.4 The following set of data is from a sample of $n = 5$:

7 −5 −8 7 9

a. Compute the mean, median, and mode.
b. Compute the range, variance, standard deviation, and coefficient of variation.
c. Compute the Z scores. Are there any outliers?
d. Describe the shape of the data set.

3.5 Suppose that the rate of return for a particular stock during the past two years was 10% for one of the years and

30% for the other year. Compute the geometric rate of return per year. (*Note:* A rate of return of 10% is recorded as 0.10, and a rate of return of 30% is recorded as 0.30.)

3.6 Suppose that the rate of return for a particular stock during the past two years was 20% for one of the years and −30% for the other year. Compute the geometric rate of return per year.

APPLYING THE CONCEPTS

3.7 A survey conducted by the American Statistical Association reported the following results for the salaries of professors teaching statistics in research universities with four to five years in the rank of associate professor and professor:

Title	Median
Associate professor	90,200
Professor	112,000

Source: Data extracted from **magazine.amstat.org/blog/2011/12/01/academicsurvey2012/**.

Interpret the median salary for the associate professors and professors.

3.8 The operations manager of a plant that manufactures tires wants to compare the actual inner diameters of two grades of tires, each of which is expected to be 575 millimeters. A sample of five tires of each grade was selected, and the results representing the inner diameters of the tires, ranked from smallest to largest, are as follows:

Grade *X*	Grade *Y*
568 570 575 578 584	573 574 575 577 578

a. For each of the two grades of tires, compute the mean, median, and standard deviation.
b. Which grade of tire is providing better quality? Explain.
c. What would be the effect on your answers in (a) and (b) if the last value for grade *Y* was 588 instead of 578? Explain.

3.9 According to the U.S. Census Bureau, in 2011, the median sales price of new houses was $227,200, and the mean sales price was $267,900 (extracted from www.census.gov, June 25, 2012).
a. Interpret the median sales price.
b. Interpret the mean sales price.
c. Discuss the shape of the distribution of the price of new houses.

SELF Test **3.10** The file FastFood contains the amount that a sample of 15 customers spent for lunch ($) at a fast-food restaurant:

7.42	6.29	5.83	6.50	8.34	9.51	7.10	6.80
5.90	4.89	6.50	5.52	7.90	8.30	9.60	

a. Compute the mean and median.
b. Compute the variance, standard deviation, range, and coefficient of variation.
c. Are the data skewed? If so, how?
d. Based on the results of (a) through (c), what conclusions can you reach concerning the amount that customers spent for lunch?

3.11 The file Sedans contains the overall miles per gallon (MPG) of 2012 family sedans:

38 24 26 21 25 22 24 34 23 20 37 22 20 33 22 21

Source: Data extracted from "Ratings," *Consumer Reports*, April 2012, pp. 31.

a. Compute the mean, median, and mode.
b. Compute the variance, standard deviation, range, coefficient of variation, and *Z* scores.
c. Are the data skewed? If so, how?
d. Compare the results of (a) through (c) to those of Problem 3.12 (a) through (c) that refer to the miles per gallon of small SUVs.

3.12 The file SUV contains the overall miles per gallon (MPG) of 2012 small SUVs:

20	22	23	22	23	22	22	21	19
22	22	26	23	24	19	21	22	16

Source: Data extracted from "Ratings," *Consumer Reports*, April 2012, pp. 35–36.

a. Compute the mean, median, and mode.
b. Compute the variance, standard deviation, range, coefficient of variation, and *Z* scores.
c. Are the data skewed? If so, how?
d. Compare the results of (a) through (c) to those of Problem 3.11 (a) through (c) that refer to the miles per gallon of family sedans.

3.13 The file AccountingPartners contains the number of partners in a cohort of rising accounting firms with fewer than 225 employees that have been tagged as "firms to watch." The firms have the following numbers of partners:

24	32	12	13	29	30	26	17	15	21	16	23
21	19	30	14	9	30	17					

Source: Data extracted from **www.accountingtoday.com/gallery/Top-100-Accounting-Firms-Data-62569-1.html**.

a. Compute the mean, median, and mode.
b. Compute the variance, standard deviation, range, coefficient of variation, and *Z* scores. Are there any outliers? Explain.

c. Are the data skewed? If so, how?
d. Based on the results of (a) through (c), what conclusions can you reach concerning the number of partners in rising accounting firms?

3.14 The file **MarketPenetration** contains the market penetration value (that is, the percentage of the country population that are users) for the 15 countries the lead the world in total number of Facebook users:

50.19	25.45	4.25	18.04	31.66	49.14	39.99	28.29
37.52	28.87	37.73	46.04	52.24	38.06	34.91	

Source: Data extracted from **www.socialbakers.com/facebook-statistics/**.

a. Compute the mean, median, and mode.
b. Compute the variance, standard deviation, range, coefficient of variation, and Z scores. Are there any outliers? Explain.
c. Are the data skewed? If so, how?
d. Based on the results of (a) through (c), what conclusions can you reach concerning Facebook's market penetration?

3.15 Is there a difference in the variation of the yields of different types of investments? The file **CD Rate** contains the yields for one-year certificates of deposit (CDs) and five-year CDs for 24 banks in the United States, as of June 21, 2012.

Source: Data extracted from **www.Bankrate.com**, June 21, 2012.

a. For one-year and five-year CDs, separately compute the variance, standard deviation, range, and coefficient of variation.
b. Based on the results of (a), do one-year CDs or five-year CDs have more variation in the yields offered? Explain.

3.16 The file **HotelAway** contains the average room price (in US$) paid in 2011 by people of various nationalities while traveling away from their home country:

171	166	159	157	150	148	147	146

Source: Data extracted from **www.hotel-price-index.com/2012/spring/pdf/Hotel-Price-Index-2011-US.pdf**.

a. Compute the mean, median, and mode.
b. Compute the range, variance, and standard deviation.
c. Based on the results of (a) and (b), what conclusions can you reach concerning the room price (in US$) in 2011?
d. Suppose that the first value was 200 instead of 171. Repeat (a) through (c), using this value. Comment on the difference in the results.

3.17 A bank branch located in a commercial district of a city has the business objective of developing an improved process for serving customers during the noon-to-1:00 P.M. lunch period. The waiting time, in minutes, is defined as the time the customer enters the line to when he or she reaches the teller window. Data collected from a sample of 15 customers during this hour are stored in **Bank1**:

4.21	5.55	3.02	5.13	4.77	2.34	3.54	3.20
4.50	6.10	0.38	5.12	6.46	6.19	3.79	

a. Compute the mean and median.
b. Compute the variance, standard deviation, range, coefficient of variation, and Z scores. Are there any outliers? Explain.
c. Are the data skewed? If so, how?
d. As a customer walks into the branch office during the lunch hour, she asks the branch manager how long she can expect to wait. The branch manager replies, "Almost certainly less than five minutes." On the basis of the results of (a) through (c), evaluate the accuracy of this statement.

3.18 Suppose that another bank branch, located in a residential area, is also concerned with the noon-to-1:00 P.M. lunch hour. The waiting time, in minutes, collected from a sample of 15 customers during this hour, are stored in **Bank2**:

9.66	5.90	8.02	5.79	8.73	3.82	8.01	8.35
10.49	6.68	5.64	4.08	6.17	9.91	5.47	

a. Compute the mean and median.
b. Compute the variance, standard deviation, range, coefficient of variation, and Z scores. Are there any outliers? Explain.
c. Are the data skewed? If so, how?
d. As a customer walks into the branch office during the lunch hour, he asks the branch manager how long he can expect to wait. The branch manager replies, "Almost certainly less than five minutes." On the basis of the results of (a) through (c), evaluate the accuracy of this statement.

3.19 General Electric (GE) is one of the world's largest companies; it develops, manufactures, and markets a wide range of products, including medical diagnostic imaging devices, jet engines, lighting products, and chemicals. In 2010, the stock price rose 17.73%, and in 2011, the stock price rose 1.38%.

Source: Data extracted from **finance.yahoo.com**, June 24, 2012.

a. Compute the geometric mean rate of return per year for the two-year period 2010–2011. (Hint: Denote an increase of 1.38% as $R_2 = 0.0138$.)
b. If you purchased $1,000 of GE stock at the start of 2010, what was its value at the end of 2011?
c. Compare the result of (b) to that of Problem 3.20 (b).

SELF Test **3.20** TASER International, Inc., develops, manufactures, and sells nonlethal self-defense devices known as Tasers and markets primarily to law enforcement, corrections institutions, and the military. TASER's stock price in 2010 increased by 1.08%, and in 2011, it increased by 2.4%.

Source: Data extracted from finance.yahoo.com, June 24, 2012.

a. Compute the geometric mean rate of return per year for the two-year period 2010–2011. (Hint: Denote an increase of 1.08% as $R_1 = 0.0108$.)
b. If you purchased $1,000 of TASER stock at the start of 2010, what was its value at the end of 2011?
c. Compare the result of (b) to that of Problem 3.19 (b).

3.21 The file Indices contains data that represent the yearly rate of return (in percentage) for the Dow Jones Industrial Average (DJIA), the Standard & Poor's 500 (S&P 500), and the technology-heavy NASDAQ Composite (NASDAQ) from 2008 through 2011. These data are:

Year	DJIA	S&P 500	NASDAQ
2011	5.5	−0.0	−1.8
2010	11.0	12.8	16.9
2009	18.8	23.5	43.9
2008	−33.8	−38.5	−40.5

Source: Data extracted from **finance.yahoo.com**, *June 24, 2012.*

a. Compute the geometric mean rate of return per year for the DJIA, S&P 500, and NASDAQ from 2008 through 2011.
b. What conclusions can you reach concerning the geometric mean rates of return per year of the three market indices?
c. Compare the results of (b) to those of Problem 3.22 (b).

3.22 In 2008 through 2011, the value of precious metals fluctuated dramatically. The data in the following table (contained in the file Metals) represent the yearly rate of return (in percentage) for platinum, gold, and silver from 2008 through 2011:

Year	Platinum	Gold	Silver
2011	−21.1	10.2	−9.8
2010	21.5	29.8	83.7
2009	55.9	23.9	49.3
2008	−41.3	4.3	−26.9

Source: Data extracted from A. Shell, "Is Market Poised to Heat Up for a Bull Run in 2012?" *USA Today*, January 3, 2012, pp. 1B, 2B.

a. Compute the geometric mean rate of return per year for platinum, gold, and silver from 2008 through 2011.
b. What conclusions can you reach concerning the geometric mean rates of return of the three precious metals?
c. Compare the results of (b) to those of Problem 3.21 (b).

3.23 Using the three-year return percentage variable in Retirement Funds:
a. Construct a table that computes the mean for each type, market cap, and risk.
b. Construct a table that computes the standard deviation for each type, market cap, and risk.
c. What conclusions can you reach concerning differences among the types of retirement funds (growth and value), based on market cap (small, mid-cap, and large) and the risk (low, average, and high)?

3.24 Using the three-year return percentage variable in Retirement Funds:
a. Construct a table that computes the mean for each type, market cap, and rating.
b. Construct a table that computes the standard deviation for each type, market cap, and rating.
c. What conclusions can you reach concerning differences among the types of retirement funds (growth and value), based on market cap (small, mid-cap, and large) and the rating (one, two, three, four, and five)?

3.25 Using the three-year return percentage variable in Retirement Funds:
a. Construct a table that computes the mean for each market cap, risk, and rating.
b. Construct a table that computes the standard deviation for each market cap, risk, and rating.
c. What conclusions can you reach concerning differences based on the market cap (small, mid-cap, and large), risk (low, average, and high), and rating (one, two, three, four, and five)?

3.26 Using the three-year return percentage variable in Retirement Funds:
a. Construct a table that computes the mean for each type, risk, and rating.
b. Construct a table that computes the standard deviation for each type, risk, and rating.
c. What conclusions can you reach concerning differences among the types of retirement funds (growth and value), based on the risk (low, average, and high) and the rating (one, two, three, four, and five)?

3.3 Exploring Numerical Data

Sections 3.1 and 3.2 discuss measures of central tendency, variation, and shape. An additional way of describing numerical data is through an exploratory data analysis that computes the quartiles and the five-number summary and constructs a boxplot.

Quartiles

Quartiles split a set of data into four equal parts—the **first quartile** (Q_1) divides the smallest 25.0% of the values from the other 75.0% that are larger. The **second quartile** (Q_2) is the median; 50.0% of the values are smaller than or equal to the median, and 50.0% are larger than or equal to the median. The **third quartile** (Q_3) divides the smallest 75.0% of the values from the largest 25.0%. Equations (3.10) and (3.11) define the first and third quartiles.[3]

[3] Q_1, the median, and Q_3 are also the 25th, 50th, and 75th percentiles, respectively. Equations (3.2), (3.10), and (3.11) can be expressed generally in terms of finding percentiles: $(p \times 100)$th percentile $= p \times (n + 1)$ ranked value, where $p =$ the proportion.

FIRST QUARTILE, Q_1

25.0% of the values are smaller than or equal to Q_1, the first quartile, and 75.0% are larger than or equal to the first quartile, Q_1:

$$Q_1 = \frac{n+1}{4} \text{ ranked value} \tag{3.10}$$

THIRD QUARTILE, Q_3

75.0% of the values are smaller than or equal to the third quartile, Q_3, and 25.0% are larger than or equal to the third quartile, Q_3:

$$Q_3 = \frac{3(n+1)}{4} \text{ ranked value} \tag{3.11}$$

Student Tip
As is the case when you compute the median, you must rank the values in order from smallest to largest before computing the quartiles.

Use the following rules to compute the quartiles from a set of ranked values:

- **Rule 1** If the ranked value is a whole number, the quartile is equal to the measurement that corresponds to that ranked value. For example, if the sample size $n = 7$, the first quartile, Q_1, is equal to the measurement associated with the $(7 + 1)/4 =$ second ranked value.
- **Rule 2** If the ranked value is a fractional half (2.5, 4.5, etc.), the quartile is equal to the measurement that corresponds to the average of the measurements corresponding to the two ranked values involved. For example, if the sample size $n = 9$, the first quartile, Q_1, is equal to the $(9 + 1)/4 = 2.5$ ranked value, halfway between the second ranked value and the third ranked value.
- **Rule 3** If the ranked value is neither a whole number nor a fractional half, you round the result to the nearest integer and select the measurement corresponding to that ranked value. For example, if the sample size $n = 10$, the first quartile, Q_1, is equal to the $(10 + 1)/4 = 2.75$ ranked value. Round 2.75 to 3 and use the third ranked value.

To further analyze the sample of 10 times to get ready in the morning, you can compute the quartiles. To do so, you rank the data from smallest to largest:

Ranked values:	29	31	35	39	39	40	43	44	44	52
Ranks:	1	2	3	4	5	6	7	8	9	10

The first quartile is the $(n + 1)/4 = (10 + 1)/4 = 2.75$ ranked value. Using Rule 3, you round up to the third ranked value. The third ranked value for the getting-ready data is 35 minutes. You interpret the first quartile of 35 to mean that on 25% of the days, the time to get ready is less than or equal to 35 minutes, and on 75% of the days, the time to get ready is greater than or equal to 35 minutes.

The third quartile is the $3(n + 1)/4 = 3(10 + 1)/4 = 8.25$ ranked value. Using Rule 3 for quartiles, you round this down to the eighth ranked value. The eighth ranked value is 44 minutes. Thus, on 75% of the days, the time to get ready is less than or equal to 44 minutes, and on 25% of the days, the time to get ready is greater than or equal to 44 minutes.

EXAMPLE 3.10

Computing the Quartiles

Nutritional data about a sample of seven breakfast cereals (stored in **Cereals**) includes the number of calories per serving (see Example 3.1 on page 108). Compute the first quartile (Q_1) and third quartile (Q_3) of the number of calories for the cereals.

SOLUTION Ranked from smallest to largest, the numbers of calories for the seven cereals are as follows:

Ranked values:	80	100	100	110	130	190	200
Ranks:	1	2	3	4	5	6	7

For these data

$$Q_1 = \frac{(n + 1)}{4} \text{ ranked value}$$

$$= \frac{7 + 1}{4} \text{ ranked value} = \text{2nd ranked value}$$

Therefore, using Rule 1, Q_1 is the second ranked value. Because the second ranked value is 100, the first quartile, Q_1, is 100.

To compute the third quartile, Q_3,

$$Q_3 = \frac{3(n + 1)}{4} \text{ ranked value}$$

$$= \frac{3(7 + 1)}{4} \text{ ranked value} = \text{6th ranked value}$$

Therefore, using Rule 1, Q_3 is the sixth ranked value. Because the sixth ranked value is 190, Q_3 is 190.

The first quartile of 100 indicates that 25% of the cereals contain 100 calories or fewer per serving and 75% contain 100 or more calories. The third quartile of 190 indicates that 75% of the cereals contain 190 calories or fewer per serving and 25% contain 190 or more calories.

The Interquartile Range

The **interquartile range** (also called the **midspread**) measures the difference in the center of a distribution between the third and first quartiles.

> INTERQUARTILE RANGE
>
> The interquartile range is the difference between the third quartile and the first quartile:
>
> $$\text{Interquartile range} = Q_3 - Q_1 \qquad \textbf{(3.12)}$$

The interquartile range measures the spread in the middle 50% of the data. Therefore, it is not influenced by extreme values. To further analyze the sample of 10 times to get ready in the morning, you can compute the interquartile range. You first order the data as follows:

29 31 35 39 39 40 43 44 44 52

You use Equation (3.12) and the earlier results in Example 3.10 on page 125, $Q_1 = 35$ and $Q_3 = 44$:

$$\text{Interquartile range} = 44 - 35 = 9 \text{ minutes}$$

Therefore, the interquartile range in the time to get ready is 9 minutes. The interval 35 to 44 is often referred to as the *middle fifty*.

EXAMPLE 3.11

Computing the Interquartile Range for the Number of Calories in Cereals

Nutritional data about a sample of seven breakfast cereals (stored in Cereals) includes the number of calories per serving (see Example 3.1 on page 108). Compute the interquartile range of the number of calories in cereals.

SOLUTION Ranked from smallest to largest, the numbers of calories for the seven cereals are as follows:

80 100 100 110 130 190 200

Using Equation (3.12) and the earlier results from Example 3.10 on page 125, $Q_1 = 100$ and $Q_3 = 190$:

$$\text{Interquartile range} = 190 - 100 = 90$$

Therefore, the interquartile range of the number of calories in cereals is 90 calories.

Because the interquartile range does not consider any value smaller than Q_1 or larger than Q_3, it cannot be affected by extreme values. Descriptive statistics such as the median, Q_1, Q_3, and the interquartile range, which are not influenced by extreme values, are called **resistant measures**.

The Five-Number Summary

The **five-number summary** for a set of data consists of the smallest value (X_{smallest}), the first quartile, the median, the third quartile, and the largest value (X_{largest}).

FIVE-NUMBER SUMMARY

$$X_{\text{smallest}} \quad Q_1 \quad \text{Median} \quad Q_3 \quad X_{\text{largest}}$$

The five-number summary provides a way to determine the shape of the distribution for a set of data. Table 3.5 on page 127 explains how relationships among these five statistics help to identify the shape of the distribution.

TABLE 3.5

Relationships Among the Five-Number Summary and the Type of Distribution

	Type of Distribution		
Comparison	**Left-Skewed**	**Symmetrical**	**Right-Skewed**
The distance from $X_{smallest}$ to the median versus the distance from the median to $X_{largest}$.	The distance from $X_{smallest}$ to the median is greater than the distance from the median to $X_{largest}$.	The two distances are the same.	The distance from $X_{smallest}$ to the median is less than the distance from the median to $X_{largest}$.
The distance from $X_{smallest}$ to Q_1 versus the distance from Q_3 to $X_{largest}$.	The distance from $X_{smallest}$ to Q_1 is greater than the distance from Q_3 to $X_{largest}$.	The two distances are the same.	The distance from $X_{smallest}$ to Q_1 is less than the distance from Q_3 to $X_{largest}$.
The distance from Q_1 to the median versus the distance from the median to Q_3.	The distance from Q_1 to the median is greater than the distance from the median to Q_3.	The two distances are the same.	The distance from Q_1 to the median is less than the distance from the median to Q_3.

To further analyze the sample of 10 times to get ready in the morning, you can compute the five-number summary. For these data, the smallest value is 29 minutes, and the largest value is 52 minutes (see page 125). Calculations done on pages 109 and 125–126 show that the median = 39.5, $Q_1 = 35$, and $Q_3 = 44$. Therefore, the five-number summary is as follows:

$$29 \quad 35 \quad 39.5 \quad 44 \quad 52$$

The distance from $X_{smallest}$ to the median $(39.5 - 29 = 10.5)$ is slightly less than the distance from the median to $X_{largest}$ $(52 - 39.5 = 12.5)$. The distance from $X_{smallest}$ to $Q_1 (35 - 29 = 6)$ is slightly less than the distance from Q_3 to $X_{largest}$ $(52 - 44 = 8)$. The distance from Q_1 to the median $(39.5 - 35) = 4.5)$ is the same as the distance from the median to $Q_3 (44 - 39.5 = 4.5)$. Therefore, the getting-ready times are slightly right-skewed.

EXAMPLE 3.12

Computing the Five-Number Summary of the Number of Calories in Cereals

Nutritional data about a sample of seven breakfast cereals (stored in **Cereals**) includes the number of calories per serving (see Example 3.1 on page 108). Compute the five-number summary of the number of calories in cereals.

SOLUTION From previous computations for the number of calories in cereals (see pages 109 and 125), you know that the median = 110, $Q_1 = 100$, and $Q_3 = 190$.

In addition, the smallest value in the data set is 80, and the largest value is 200. Therefore, the five-number summary is as follows:

$$80 \quad 100 \quad 110 \quad 190 \quad 200$$

The three comparisons listed in Table 3.5 are used to evaluate skewness. The distance from $X_{smallest}$ to the median $(110 - 80 = 30)$ is less than the distance $(200 - 110 = 90)$ from the median to $X_{largest}$. The distance from $X_{smallest}$ to Q_1 $(100 - 80 = 20)$ is more than the distance from Q_3 to $X_{largest}$ $(200 - 190 = 10)$. The distance from Q_1 to the median $(110 - 100 = 10)$ is less than the distance from the median to Q_3 $(190 - 110 = 80)$. Two comparisons indicate a right-skewed distribution, whereas the other indicates a left-skewed distribution. Therefore, given the small sample size and the conflicting results, the shape is not clearly determined.

The Boxplot

The **boxplot** visualizes a five-number summary, thereby helping to identify the shape of the distribution associated with the five-number summary. Figure 3.3 contains a boxplot for the sample of 10 times to get ready in the morning.

FIGURE 3.3
Boxplot for the getting-ready times

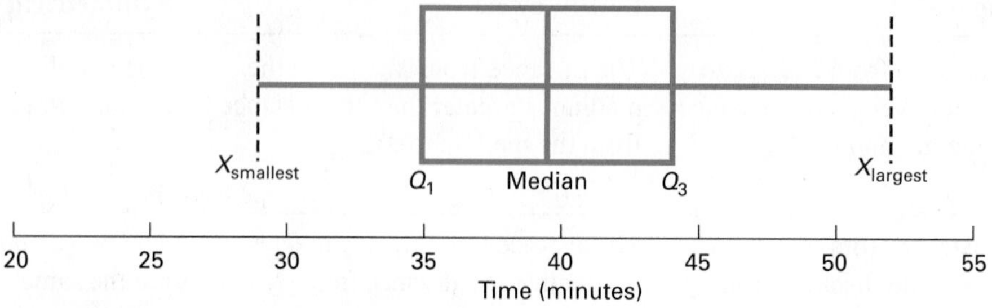

The vertical line drawn within the box represents the median. The vertical line at the left side of the box represents the location of Q_1, and the vertical line at the right side of the box represents the location of Q_3. Thus, the box contains the middle 50% of the values. The lower 25% of the data are represented by a line connecting the left side of the box to the location of the smallest value, $X_{smallest}$. Similarly, the upper 25% of the data are represented by a line connecting the right side of the box to $X_{largest}$.

The Figure 3.3 boxplot for the getting-ready times shows a slight right-skewness: The distance between the median and the highest value is slightly greater than the distance between the lowest value and the median, and the right tail is slightly longer than the left tail.

EXAMPLE 3.13

Boxplots of the Three-Year Returns for the Growth and Value Funds

In the More Descriptive Choices scenario, you are interested in comparing the past performance of the growth and value funds from a sample of 318 funds. One measure of past performance is the three-year return percentage variable. Construct the boxplots for this variable for the growth and value funds.

SOLUTION Figure 3.4 contains the five-number summaries and boxplots for the three-year return percentages for the growth and value funds.

FIGURE 3.4
Five-number summaries and boxplots for the growth and value funds

	A	B	C
1	Five-Number Summary for 3YrReturn%		
2			
3		Growth	Value
4	Minimum	3.39	9.82
5	First Quartile	18.46	15.98
6	Median	22.32	19.46
7	Third Quartile	24.85	23.49
8	Maximum	62.91	37.19

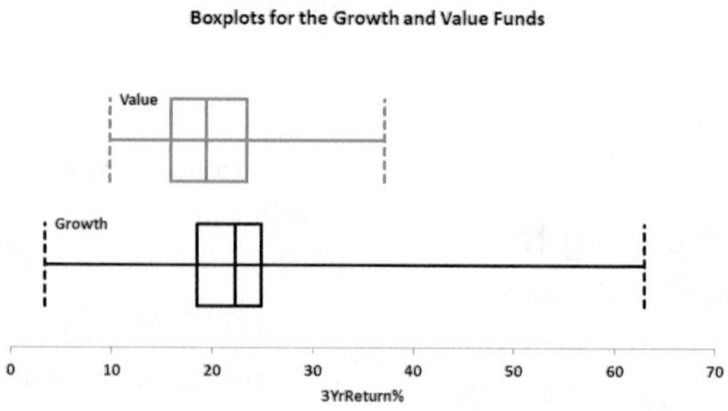

The median return, the quartiles, and the maximum returns are higher for the growth funds than for the value funds. Both the growth and value funds are right-skewed, but the growth funds have a very long tail in the upper part of the range. These results are consistent with the statistics computed in Figure 3.2 on page 119.

Figure 3.5 demonstrates the relationship between the boxplot and the density curve for four different types of distributions. The area under each density curve is split into quartiles corresponding to the five-number summary for the boxplot.

The distributions in Panels A and D of Figure 3.5 are symmetrical. In these distributions, the mean and median are equal. In addition, the length of the left tail is equal to the length of the right tail, and the median line divides the box in half.

FIGURE 3.5

Boxplots and corresponding density curves for four distributions

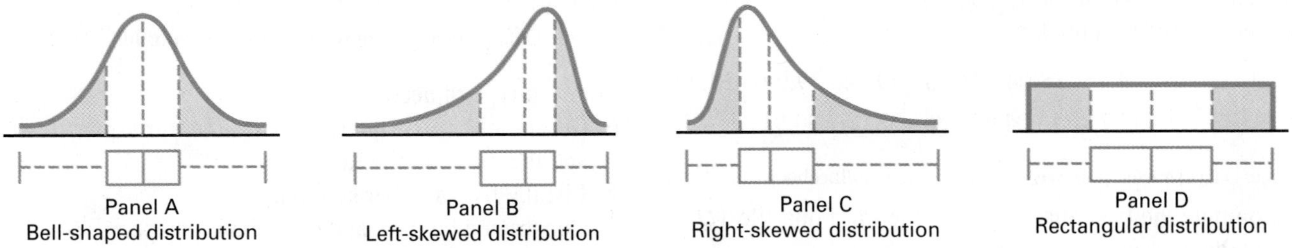

The distribution in Panel B of Figure 3.5 is left-skewed. The few small values distort the mean toward the left tail. For this left-skewed distribution, there is a heavy clustering of values at the high end of the scale (i.e., the right side); 75% of all values are found between the left edge of the box (Q_1) and the end of the right tail (X_{largest}). There is a long left tail that contains the smallest 25% of the values, demonstrating the lack of symmetry in this data set.

The distribution in Panel C of Figure 3.5 is right-skewed. The concentration of values is on the low end of the scale (i.e., the left side of the boxplot). Here, 75% of all values are found between the beginning of the left tail and the right edge of the box (Q_3). There is a long right tail that contains the largest 25% of the values, demonstrating the lack of symmetry in this data set.

Problems for Section 3.3

LEARNING THE BASICS

3.27 The following is a set of data from a sample of $n = 7$:

12 7 4 9 0 7 3

a. Compute the first quartile (Q_1), the third quartile (Q_3), and the interquartile range.
b. List the five-number summary.
c. Construct a boxplot and describe its shape.
d. Compare your answer in (c) with that from Problem 3.3 (d) on page 120. Discuss.

3.28 The following is a set of data from a sample of $n = 6$:

7 4 9 7 3 12

a. Compute the first quartile (Q_1), the third quartile (Q_3), and the interquartile range.
b. List the five-number summary.
c. Construct a boxplot and describe its shape.
d. Compare your answer in (c) with that from Problem 3.2 (d) on page 120. Discuss.

3.29 The following is a set of data from a sample of $n = 5$:

7 4 9 8 2

a. Compute the first quartile (Q_1), the third quartile (Q_3), and the interquartile range.
b. List the five-number summary.
c. Construct a boxplot and describe its shape.
d. Compare your answer in (c) with that from Problem 3.1 (d) on page 120. Discuss.

3.30 The following is a set of data from a sample of $n = 5$:

7 −5 −8 7 9

a. Compute the first quartile (Q_1), the third quartile (Q_3), and the interquartile range.
b. List the five-number summary.
c. Construct a boxplot and describe its shape.
d. Compare your answer in (c) with that from Problem 3.4 (d) on page 120. Discuss.

APPLYING THE CONCEPTS

3.31 The file AccountingPartners contains the number of partners in a cohort of rising accounting firms with fewer than 225 employees that have been tagged as "firms to watch." The firms have the following numbers of partners:

24 32 12 13 29 30 26 17 15 21 16 23
21 19 30 14 9 30 17

Source: Data extracted from **www.accountingtoday.com/gallery/Top-100-Accounting-Firms-Data-62569-1.html**.

a. Compute the first quartile (Q_1), the third quartile (Q_3), and the interquartile range.
b. List the five-number summary.
c. Construct a boxplot and describe its shape.

3.32 The file MarketPenetration contains the market penetration value (that is, the percentage of the country population that are users) for the 15 countries that lead the world in total number of Facebook users:

50.19 25.45 4.25 18.04 31.66 49.14 39.99 28.29
37.52 28.87 37.73 46.04 52.24 38.06 34.91

Source: Data extracted from **www.socialbakers.com/facebook-statistics/**.

a. Compute the first quartile (Q_1), the third quartile (Q_3), and the interquartile range.
b. List the five-number summary.
c. Construct a boxplot and describe its shape.

3.33 The file HotelAway contains the average room price (in US$) paid in 2011 by people of various nationalities while traveling away from their home country:

171 166 159 157 150 148 147 146

Source: Data extracted from **www.hotel-price-index.com/2012/spring/pdf/Hotel-Price-Index-2011-US.pdf**.

a. Compute the first quartile (Q_1), the third quartile (Q_3), and the interquartile range.
b. List the five-number summary.
c. Construct a boxplot and describe its shape.

3.34 The file SUV contains the overall miles per gallon (MPG) of 2012 small SUVs:

20 22 23 22 23 22 22 21 19
22 22 26 23 24 19 21 22 16

Source: Data extracted from "Ratings," *Consumer Reports*, April 2012, pp. 35–36.

a. Compute the first quartile (Q_1), the third quartile (Q_3), and the interquartile range.
b. List the five-number summary.
c. Construct a boxplot and describe its shape.

3.35 The file CD Rate contains the yields for one-year certificates of deposit (CDs) and five-year CDs, for 24 banks in the United States, as of June 21, 2012.

Source: Data extracted from **www.Bankrate.com**, June 21, 2012.

For each type of account:
a. Compute the first quartile (Q_1), the third quartile (Q_3), and the interquartile range.
b. List the five-number summary.
c. Construct a boxplot and describe its shape.

3.36 A bank branch located in a commercial district of a city has the business objective of developing an improved process for serving customers during the noon-to-1:00 P.M. lunch period. The waiting time, in minutes, is defined as the time the customer enters the line to when he or she reaches the teller window. Data are collected from a sample of 15 customers during this hour. The file Bank1 contains the results, which are listed below:

4.21 5.55 3.02 5.13 4.77 2.34 3.54 3.20
4.50 6.10 0.38 5.12 6.46 6.19 3.79

Another bank branch, located in a residential area, is also concerned with the noon-to-1:00 P.M. lunch hour. The waiting times, in minutes, collected from a sample of 15 customers during this hour, are contained in the file Bank2 and listed here:

9.66 5.90 8.02 5.79 8.73 3.82 8.01 8.35
10.49 6.68 5.64 4.08 6.17 9.91 5.47

a. List the five-number summaries of the waiting times at the two bank branches.
b. Construct boxplots and describe the shapes of the distributions for the two bank branches.
c. What similarities and differences are there in the distributions of the waiting times at the two bank branches?

3.4 Numerical Descriptive Measures for a Population

Sections 3.1 and 3.2 discuss the statistics that can be computed to describe the central tendency and variation properties of a sample. When you collect data for an entire population (see Section 1.3), you compute and analyze population *parameters* for these properties, including the population mean, population variance, and population standard deviation.

To help illustrate these parameters, consider the population of the stocks for the 10 companies in the Dow Jones Industrial Average that form the "Dogs of the Dow," defined as the 10 stocks of the 30 stocks that make up the Dow Jones Industrial Average whose dividend is the highest fraction of their price in the previous year. (These stocks are used in an alternative investment scheme popularized by Michael O'Higgins.) Table 3.6 contains the one-year returns (excluding dividends) for the 10 "Dow Dog" stocks in 2011. These data, stored in DowDogs, will be used to illustrate the population parameters discussed in this section.

TABLE 3.6

One-Year Return for the "Dogs of the Dow" in 2011

Stock	One-Year Return	Stock	One-Year Return
AT&T	2.93	DuPont	−8.22
Verizon	12.13	Johnson & Johnson	6.03
Merck	4.61	Intel	15.31
Pfizer	23.59	Procter & Gamble	3.70
GE	−2.08	Kraft Foods	18.57

Source: Data extracted from S. Russolillo and B. Conway, " 'Dogs' Strategy Paid Dividends for Second Year in a Row," *The Wall Street Journal,* January 3, 2012, p. R24.

The Population Mean

The **population mean** is the sum of the values in the population divided by the population size, N. This parameter, represented by the Greek lowercase letter mu, μ, serves as a measure of central tendency. Equation (3.13) defines the population mean.

POPULATION MEAN

The population mean is the sum of the values in the population divided by the population size, N.

$$\mu = \frac{\sum_{i=1}^{N} X_i}{N} \tag{3.13}$$

where

μ = population mean

X_i = ith value of the variable X

$\sum_{i=1}^{N} X_i$ = summation of all X_i values in the population

N = number of values in the population

To compute the mean one-year return for the population of "Dow Dog" stocks in Table 3.6, use Equation (3.13):

$$\mu = \frac{\sum_{i=1}^{N} X_i}{N}$$

$$= \frac{2.93 + 12.13 + 4.61 + 23.59 + (-2.08) + (-8.22) + 6.03 + 15.31 + 3.70 + 18.57}{10}$$

$$= \frac{76.57}{10} = 7.657$$

Thus, the mean one-year return for the "Dow Dog" stocks is 7.657.

The Population Variance and Standard Deviation

The parameters **population variance** and the **population standard deviation** measure variation in a population. The population variance is the sum of the squared differences around the population mean divided by the population size, N, and the population standard deviation is the square root of the population variance. In practice, you will most likely use the population standard deviation because, unlike the population variance, the standard deviation will always be a number expressed in the same units as the original population data.

The Greek lowercase letter sigma, σ, represents the population standard deviation, and sigma squared, σ^2, represents the population variance. Equations (3.14) and (3.15) define these parameters. The denominators for the right-side terms in these equations use N and not the $(n - 1)$ term that is found in Equations (3.6) and (3.7) on page 113 that define the sample variance and standard deviation.

POPULATION VARIANCE

The population variance is the sum of the squared differences around the population mean divided by the population size, N:

$$\sigma^2 = \frac{\sum_{i=1}^{N}(X_i - \mu)^2}{N} \tag{3.14}$$

where

μ = population mean

X_i = ith value of the variable X

$\sum_{i=1}^{N}(X_i - \mu)^2$ = summation of all the squared differences between the X_i values and μ

POPULATION STANDARD DEVIATION

$$\sigma = \sqrt{\frac{\sum_{i=1}^{N}(X_i - \mu)^2}{N}} \tag{3.15}$$

To compute the population variance for the data of Table 3.6, you use Equation (3.14):

$$\sigma^2 = \frac{\sum_{i=1}^{N}(X_i - \mu)^2}{N}$$

$$= \frac{22.3445 + 20.0077 + 9.2842 + 253.8605 + 94.8092 + 252.0791 + 2.6471 + 58.5684 + 15.6579 + 119.0936}{10}$$

$$= \frac{848.3522}{10} = 84.8352$$

From Equation (3.15), the population sample standard deviation is

$$\sigma = \sqrt{\sigma^2} = \sqrt{\frac{\sum_{i=1}^{N}(X_i - \mu)^2}{N}} = \sqrt{\frac{848.3522}{10}} = 9.2106$$

Therefore, the typical percentage return differs from the mean of 7.657 by approximately 9.21. This large amount of variation suggests that the "Dow Dog" stocks produce results that differ greatly.

The Empirical Rule

In most data sets, a large portion of the values tend to cluster somewhere near the median. In right-skewed data sets, this clustering occurs to the left of the mean—that is, at a value less than the mean. In left-skewed data sets, the values tend to cluster to the right of the mean—that is, greater than the mean. In symmetrical data sets, where the median and mean are the same, the values often tend to cluster around the median and mean, producing a normal distribution (discussed in Chapter 6).

The **empirical rule** states that for population data that form a normal distribution, the following are true:

- Approximately 68% of the values are within ± 1 standard deviation from the mean.
- Approximately 95% of the values are within ± 2 standard deviations from the mean.
- Approximately 99.7% of the values are within ± 3 standard deviations from the mean.

The empirical rule helps you examine variability in a population as well as identify outliers. The empirical rule implies that for normal distributions, only about 1 out of 20 values will be beyond 2 standard deviations from the mean in either direction. As a general rule, you can consider values not found in the interval $\mu \pm 2\sigma$ as potential outliers. The rule also implies that only about 3 in 1,000 will be beyond 3 standard deviations from the mean. Therefore, values not found in the interval $\mu \pm 3\sigma$ are almost always considered outliers.

EXAMPLE 3.14

Using the Empirical Rule

A population of 2-liter bottles of cola is known to have a mean fill-weight of 2.06 liters and a standard deviation of 0.02 liter. The population is known to be bell-shaped. Describe the distribution of fill-weights. Is it very likely that a bottle will contain less than 2 liters of cola?

SOLUTION

$$\mu \pm \sigma = 2.06 \pm 0.02 = (2.04, 2.08)$$
$$\mu \pm 2\sigma = 2.06 \pm 2(0.02) = (2.02, 2.10)$$
$$\mu \pm 3\sigma = 2.06 \pm 3(0.02) = (2.00, 2.12)$$

Using the empirical rule, you can see that approximately 68% of the bottles will contain between 2.04 and 2.08 liters, approximately 95% will contain between 2.02 and 2.10 liters, and approximately 99.7% will contain between 2.00 and 2.12 liters. Therefore, it is highly unlikely that a bottle will contain less than 2 liters.

The Chebyshev Rule

For heavily skewed sets of data and data sets that do not appear to be normally distributed, you should use the Chebyshev rule instead of the empirical rule. The **Chebyshev rule** (see reference 2) states that for any data set, regardless of shape, the percentage of values that are found within distances of k standard deviations from the mean must be at least

$$\left(1 - \frac{1}{k^2}\right) \times 100\%$$

You can use this rule for any value of k greater than 1. For example, consider $k = 2$. The Chebyshev rule states that at least $[1 - (1/2)^2] \times 100\% = 75\%$ of the values must be found within ± 2 standard deviations of the mean.

The Chebyshev rule is very general and applies to any distribution. The rule indicates *at least* what percentage of the values fall within a given distance from the mean. However, if the data set is approximately bell-shaped, the empirical rule will more accurately reflect the greater concentration of data close to the mean. Table 3.7 compares the Chebyshev and empirical rules.

TABLE 3.7

How Data Vary Around the Mean

See Section EG3.4 in the Excel Guide for a description of the **VE-Variability workbook** *that allows you to explore the empirical and Chebyshev rules.*

	% of Values Found in Intervals Around the Mean	
Interval	**Chebyshev (any distribution)**	**Empirical Rule (normal distribution)**
$(\mu - \sigma, \mu + \sigma)$	At least 0%	Approximately 68%
$(\mu - 2\sigma, \mu + 2\sigma)$	At least 75%	Approximately 95%
$(\mu - 3\sigma, \mu + 3\sigma)$	At least 88.89%	Approximately 99.7%

EXAMPLE 3.15

Using the Chebyshev Rule

As in Example 3.14, a population of 2-liter bottles of cola is known to have a mean fill-weight of 2.06 liter and a standard deviation of 0.02 liter. However, the shape of the population is unknown, and you cannot assume that it is bell-shaped. Describe the distribution of fill-weights. Is it very likely that a bottle will contain less than 2 liters of cola?

SOLUTION

$$\mu \pm \sigma = 2.06 \pm 0.02 = (2.04, 2.08)$$
$$\mu \pm 2\sigma = 2.06 \pm 2(0.02) = (2.02, 2.10)$$
$$\mu \pm 3\sigma = 2.06 \pm 3(0.02) = (2.00, 2.12)$$

Because the distribution may be skewed, you cannot use the empirical rule. Using the Chebyshev rule, you cannot say anything about the percentage of bottles containing between 2.04 and 2.08 liters. You can state that at least 75% of the bottles will contain between 2.02 and 2.10 liters and at least 88.89% will contain between 2.00 and 2.12 liters. Therefore, between 0 and 11.11% of the bottles will contain less than 2 liters.

You can use these two rules to understand how data are distributed around the mean when you have sample data. With each rule, you use the value you computed for $\overline{X}$ in place of μ and the value you computed for S in place of σ. The results you compute using the sample statistics are *approximations* because you used sample statistics $(\overline{X}, S)$ and not population parameters (μ, σ).

Problems for Section 3.4

LEARNING THE BASICS

3.37 The following is a set of data for a population with $N = 10$:

7 5 11 8 3 6 2 1 9 8

a. Compute the population mean.
b. Compute the population standard deviation.

3.38 The following is a set of data for a population with $N = 10$:

7 5 6 6 6 4 8 6 9 3

a. Compute the population mean.
b. Compute the population standard deviation.

APPLYING THE CONCEPTS

3.39 The file **Tax** contains the quarterly sales tax receipts (in $thousands) submitted to the comptroller of the Village of Fair Lake for the period ending March 2011 by all 50 business establishments in that locale:

10.3	11.1	9.6	9.0	14.5	13.0	6.7	11.0	8.4	10.3
8.0	11.2	7.3	5.3	12.5	8.0	11.8	8.7	10.6	9.5
11.1	10.2	11.1	9.9	9.8	11.6	15.1	12.5	6.5	7.5
10.0	12.9	9.2	10.0	12.8	12.5	9.3	10.4	12.7	10.5
9.3	11.5	10.7	11.6	7.8	10.5	7.6	10.1	8.9	8.6

a. Compute the mean, variance, and standard deviation for this population.
b. What percentage of the 50 businesses has quarterly sales tax receipts within ± 1, 2, or ± 3 standard deviations of the mean?
c. Compare your findings with what would be expected on the basis of the empirical rule. Are you surprised at the results in (b)?

3.40 Consider a population of 1,024 mutual funds that primarily invest in large companies. You have determined that μ, the mean one-year total percentage return achieved by all the funds, is 8.20 and that σ, the standard deviation, is 2.75.
a. According to the empirical rule, what percentage of these funds is expected to be within ± 1 standard deviation of the mean?
b. According to the empirical rule, what percentage of these funds is expected to be within ± 2 standard deviations of the mean?
c. According to the Chebyshev rule, what percentage of these funds is expected to be within ± 1, ± 2, or ± 3 standard deviations of the mean?
d. According to the Chebyshev rule, at least 93.75% of these funds are expected to have one-year total returns between what two amounts?

3.41 The file **CigaretteTax** contains the state cigarette tax (in $) for each of the 50 states as of January 1, 2012.
a. Compute the population mean and population standard deviation for the state cigarette tax.
b. Interpret the parameters in (a).

SELF Test **3.42** The file **Energy** contains the per capita energy consumption, in kilowatt-hours, for each of the 50 states and the District of Columbia during a recent year.
a. Compute the mean, variance, and standard deviation for the population.
b. What proportion of these states has per capita energy consumption within ± 1 standard deviation of the mean, within ± 2 standard deviations of the mean, and within ± 3 standard deviations of the mean?
c. Compare your findings with what would be expected based on the empirical rule. Are you surprised at the results in (b)?
d. Repeat (a) through (c) with the District of Columbia removed. How have the results changed?

3.43 Thirty companies comprise the DJIA. Just how big are these companies? One common method for measuring the size of a company is to use its market capitalization, which is computed by multiplying the number of stock shares by the price of a share of stock. On June 27, 2012, the market capitalization of these companies ranged from Alcoa's $8.9 billion to ExxonMobil's $379.9 billion. The entire population of market capitalization values is stored in **DowMarketCap**.

Source: Data extracted from **money.cnn.com**, June 27, 2012.

a. Compute the mean and standard deviation of the market capitalization for this population of 30 companies.
b. Interpret the parameters computed in (a).

3.5 The Covariance and the Coefficient of Correlation

In Section 2.5, you used scatter plots to visually examine the relationship between two numerical variables. This section presents two measures of the relationship between two numerical variables: the covariance and the coefficient of correlation.

The Covariance

The **covariance** measures the strength of the linear relationship between two numerical variables (X and Y). Equation (3.16) defines the **sample covariance**, and Example 3.16 illustrates its use.

SAMPLE COVARIANCE

$$\text{cov}(X, Y) = \frac{\sum_{i=1}^{n}(X_i - \bar{X})(Y_i - \bar{Y})}{n - 1} \tag{3.16}$$

EXAMPLE 3.16

Computing the Sample Covariance

In Figure 2.14 on page 70, you constructed a scatter plot that showed the relationship between the value and the annual revenue of the 30 NBA professional basketball teams (stored in NBAValues). Now, you want to measure the association between the annual revenue and value of a team by determining the sample covariance.

SOLUTION Table 3.8 provides the annual revenue and the value of the 30 teams.

TABLE 3.8

Revenues and Values for NBA Teams

Team Code	Revenue ($millions)	Value ($millions)	Team Code	Revenue ($millions)	Value ($millions)
ATL	105	295	MIL	92	258
BOS	151	452	MIN	95	264
CHA	98	281	NJN	89	312
CHI	169	511	NOH	100	280
CLE	161	355	NYK	226	655
DAL	146	438	OKC	118	329
DEN	113	316	ORL	108	385
DET	147	360	PHI	110	330
GSW	119	363	PHX	147	411
HOU	153	443	POR	127	356
IND	95	269	SAC	103	293
LAC	102	305	SAS	135	404
LAL	214	643	TOR	138	399
MEM	92	266	UTA	121	343
MIA	124	425	WAS	107	322

Figure 3.6 contains two worksheets that together compute the covariance for these data. From the result in cell B9 of the covariance worksheet, or by using Equation (3.16) directly (shown below), you determine that the covariance is 3,199.8563:

$$\text{cov}(X, Y) = \frac{92{,}795.8333}{30 - 1}$$

$$= 3{,}199.8563$$

FIGURE 3.6

Data and covariance worksheets for the revenue and value for the 30 NBA teams

In Figure 3.6, the covariance worksheet illustration includes a list of formulas to the right of the cells in which they occur, a style used throughout the rest of this book.

	A	B	C	D
1	Revenue	Value	(X-XBar)	(Y-YBar)
2	105	295	-21.8333	-73.7667
3	151	452	24.1667	83.2333
4	98	281	-28.8333	-87.7667
5	169	511	42.1667	142.2333
6	161	355	34.1667	-13.7667
7	146	438	19.1667	69.2333
8	113	316	-13.8333	-52.7667
9	147	360	20.1667	-8.7667
10	119	363	-7.8333	-5.7667
11	153	443	26.1667	74.2333
12	95	269	-31.8333	-99.7667
13	102	305	-24.8333	-63.7667
14	214	643	87.1667	274.2333
15	92	266	-34.8333	-102.7667
16	124	425	-2.8333	56.2333
17	92	258	-34.8333	-110.7667
18	95	264	-31.8333	-104.7667
19	89	312	-37.8333	-56.7667
20	100	280	-26.8333	-88.7667
21	226	655	99.1667	286.2333
22	118	329	-8.8333	-39.7667
23	108	385	-18.8333	16.2333
24	110	330	-16.8333	-38.7667
25	147	411	20.1667	42.2333
26	127	356	0.1667	-12.7667
27	103	293	-23.8333	-75.7667
28	135	404	8.1667	35.2333
29	138	399	11.1667	30.2333
30	121	343	-5.8333	-25.7667
31	107	322	-19.8333	-46.7667

	A	B	
1	**Covariance Analysis of Revenue and Value**		
2			
3	Intermediate Calculations		
4	*XBar*	126.8333	=AVERAGE(DATA!A:A)
5	*YBar*	368.7667	=AVERAGE(DATA!B:B)
6	Σ(*X-XBar*)(*Y-YBar*)	92795.8333	=SUMPRODUCT(DATA!C:C, DATA!D:D)
7	*n*-1	29	=COUNT(DATA!A:A) - 1
8			
9	**Covariance**	**3199.8563**	=COVARIANCE.S(DATA!A:A, DATA!B:B)

The covariance has a major flaw as a measure of the linear relationship between two numerical variables. Because the covariance can have any value, you cannot use it to determine the relative strength of the relationship. In Example 3.16, you cannot tell whether the value 3,199.8563 indicates a strong relationship or a weak relationship between revenue and value. To better determine the relative strength of the relationship, you need to compute the coefficient of correlation.

The Coefficient of Correlation

The **coefficient of correlation** measures the relative strength of a linear relationship between two numerical variables. The values of the coefficient of correlation range from -1 for a perfect negative correlation to $+1$ for a perfect positive correlation. *Perfect* in this case means that if the points were plotted on a scatter plot, all the points could be connected with a straight line.

When dealing with population data for two numerical variables, the Greek letter ρ(*rho*) is used as the symbol for the coefficient of correlation. Figure 3.7 illustrates three different types of association between two variables.

FIGURE 3.7

Types of association between variables

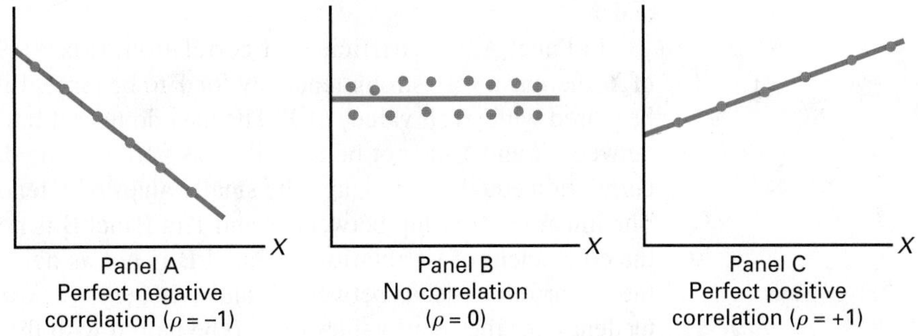

In Panel A of Figure 3.7, there is a perfect negative linear relationship between X and Y. Thus, the coefficient of correlation, ρ, equals -1, and when X increases, Y decreases in a perfectly predictable manner. Panel B shows a situation in which there is no relationship

between X and Y. In this case, the coefficient of correlation, ρ, equals 0, and as X increases, there is no tendency for Y to increase or decrease. Panel C illustrates a perfect positive relationship where ρ equals +1. In this case, Y increases in a perfectly predictable manner when X increases.

Correlation alone cannot prove that there is a causation effect—that is, that the change in the value of one variable caused the change in the other variable. A strong correlation can be produced simply by chance, by the effect of a third variable not considered in the calculation of the correlation, or by a cause-and-effect relationship. You would need to perform additional analysis to determine which of these three situations actually produced the correlation. Therefore, you can say that *causation implies correlation, but correlation alone does not imply causation.*

Equation (3.17) defines the **sample coefficient of correlation (*r*)**.

SAMPLE COEFFICIENT OF CORRELATION

$$r = \frac{\text{cov}(X, Y)}{S_X S_Y} \tag{3.17}$$

where

$$\text{cov}(X, Y) = \frac{\sum_{i=1}^{n}(X_i - \overline{X})(Y_i - \overline{Y})}{n - 1}$$

$$S_X = \sqrt{\frac{\sum_{i=1}^{n}(X_i - \overline{X})^2}{n - 1}}$$

$$S_Y = \sqrt{\frac{\sum_{i=1}^{n}(Y_i - \overline{Y})^2}{n - 1}}$$

When you have sample data, you can compute the sample coefficient of correlation, r. When using sample data, you are unlikely to have a sample coefficient of correlation of exactly +1, 0, or −1. Figure 3.8 presents scatter plots along with their respective sample coefficients of correlation, r, for six data sets, each of which contains 100 values of X and Y.

In Panel A, the coefficient of correlation, r, is −0.9. You can see that for small values of X, there is a very strong tendency for Y to be large. Likewise, the large values of X tend to be paired with small values of Y. The data do not all fall on a straight line, so the association between X and Y cannot be described as perfect. The data in Panel B have a coefficient of correlation equal to −0.6, and the small values of X tend to be paired with large values of Y. The linear relationship between X and Y in Panel B is not as strong as that in Panel A. Thus, the coefficient of correlation in Panel B is not as negative as that in Panel A. In Panel C, the linear relationship between X and Y is very weak, $r = -0.3$, and there is only a slight tendency for the small values of X to be paired with the large values of Y. Panels D through F depict data sets that have positive coefficients of correlation because small values of X tend to be paired with small values of Y, and large values of X tend to be associated with large values of Y. Panel D shows weak positive correlation, with $r = 0.3$. Panel E shows stronger positive correlation, with $r = 0.6$. Panel F shows very strong positive correlation, with $r = 0.9$.

FIGURE 3.8

Six scatter plots and their sample coefficients of correlation, r

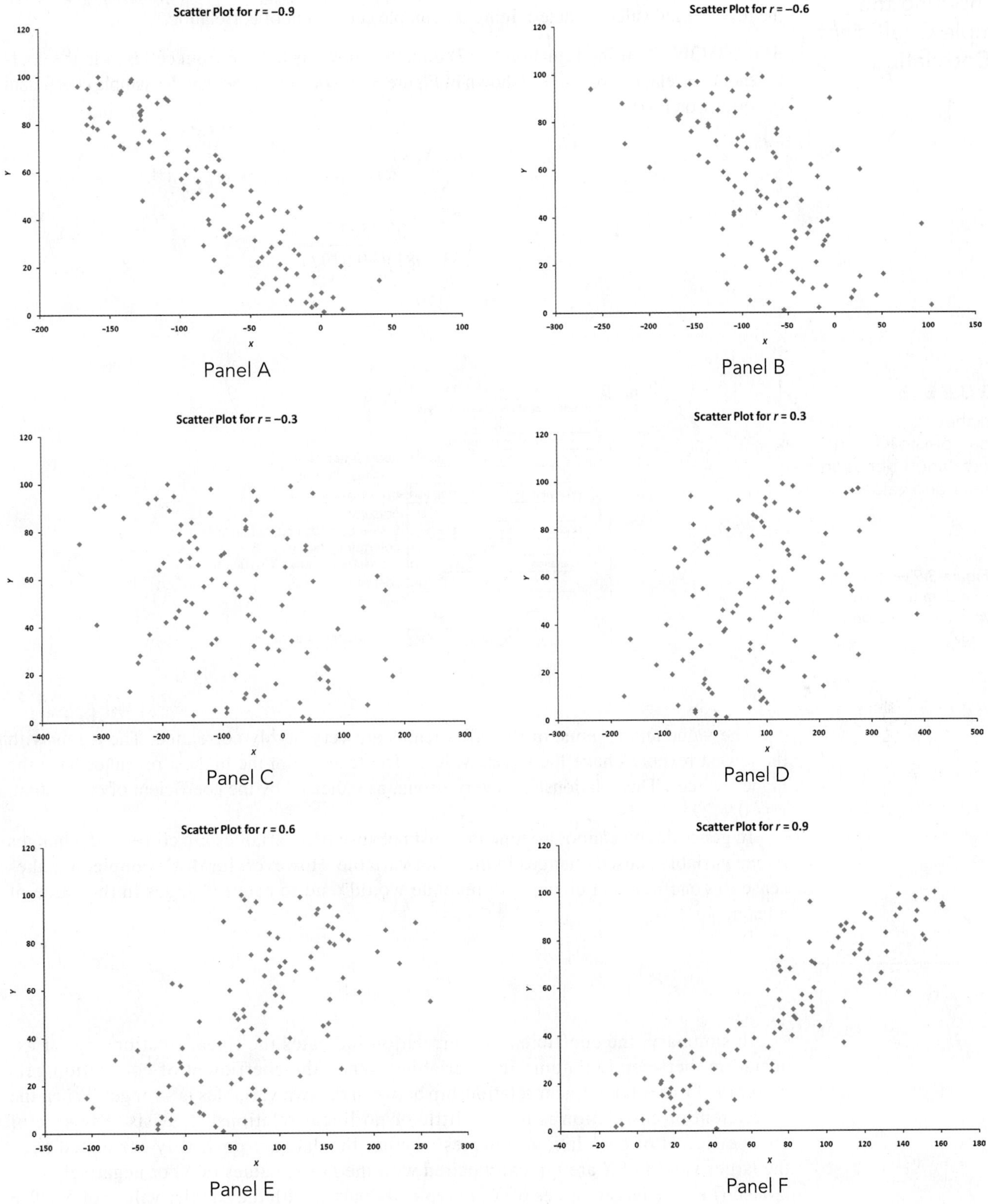

EXAMPLE 3.17

Computing the Sample Coefficient of Correlation

In Example 3.16 on page 136, you computed the covariance of the revenue and value for the 30 NBA teams. Now, you want to measure the relative strength of a linear relationship between the revenue and value by determining the sample coefficient of correlation.

SOLUTION By using Equation (3.17) directly (shown below) or from cell B14 in the coefficient of correlation worksheet (shown in Figure 3.9), you determine that the sample coefficient of correlation is 0.9429:

$$r = \frac{\text{cov}(X, Y)}{S_X S_Y}$$

$$= \frac{3{,}199.8563}{(33.9981)(99.8197)}$$

$$= 0.9429$$

FIGURE 3.9

Worksheet to compute the sample coefficient of correlation between revenue and value

The Figure 3.9 worksheet uses the data worksheet shown in Figure 3.6 on page 137.

	A	B	
1	**Coefficient of Correlation Analysis**		
2			
3	Intermediate Calculations		
4	*XBar*	126.8333	=AVERAGE(DATA!A:A)
5	*YBar*	368.7667	=AVERAGE(DATA!B:B)
6	$\Sigma(X\text{-}XBar)^2$	33520.1667	=DEVSQ(DATA!A:A)
7	$\Sigma(Y\text{-}YBar)^2$	288955.3667	=DEVSQ(DATA!B:B)
8	$\Sigma(X\text{-}XBar)(Y\text{-}YBar)$	92795.8333	=SUMPRODUCT(DATA!C:C, DATA!D:D)
9	*n*-1	29	=COUNT(DATA!A:A) - 1
10	Covariance	3199.8563	=COVARIANCE.S(DATA!A:A, DATA!B:B)
11	S_X	33.9981	=SQRT(B6/B9)
12	S_Y	99.8197	=SQRT(B7/B9)
13			
14	*r*	**0.9429**	=CORREL(DATA!A:A, DATA!B:B)

The value and revenue of the NBA teams are very highly correlated. The teams with the lowest revenues have the lowest values. The teams with the highest revenues have the highest values. This relationship is very strong, as indicated by the coefficient of correlation, $r = 0.9429$.

In general, you cannot assume that just because two variables are correlated, changes in one variable caused changes in the other variable. However, for this example, it makes sense to conclude that changes in revenue would tend to cause changes in the value of a team.

In summary, the coefficient of correlation indicates the linear relationship, or association, between two numerical variables. When the coefficient of correlation gets closer to $+1$ or -1, the linear relationship between the two variables is stronger. When the coefficient of correlation is near 0, little or no linear relationship exists. The sign of the coefficient of correlation indicates whether the data are positively correlated (i.e., the larger values of X are typically paired with the larger values of Y) or negatively correlated (i.e., the larger values of X are typically paired with the smaller values of Y). The existence of a strong correlation does not imply a causation effect. It only indicates the tendencies present in the data.

Problems for Section 3.5

LEARNING THE BASICS

3.44 The following is a set of data from a sample of $n = 11$ items:

X	7	5	8	3	6	10	12	4	9	15	18
Y	21	15	24	9	18	30	36	12	27	45	54

a. Compute the covariance.
b. Compute the coefficient of correlation.
c. How strong is the relationship between X and Y? Explain.

APPLYING THE CONCEPTS

3.45 A study of 218 students at Ohio State University suggests a link between time spent on the social networking site Facebook and grade point average. Students who rarely or never used Facebook had higher grade point averages than students who use Facebook.

Source: Data extracted from M. B. Marklein, "Facebook Use Linked to Less Textbook Time," www.usatoday.com, April 14, 2009.

a. Does the study suggest that time spent on Facebook and grade point average are positively correlated or negatively correlated?
b. Do you think that there might be a cause-and-effect relationship between time spent on Facebook and grade point average? Explain.

SELF Test **3.46** The file **Cereals** lists the calories and sugar, in grams, in one serving of seven breakfast cereals:

Cereal	Calories	Sugar
Kellogg's All Bran	80	6
Kellogg's Corn Flakes	100	2
Wheaties	100	4
Nature's Path Organic Multigrain Flakes	110	4
Kellogg's Rice Krispies	130	4
Post Shredded Wheat Vanilla Almond	190	11
Kellogg's Mini Wheats	200	10

a. Compute the covariance.
b. Compute the coefficient of correlation.
c. Which do you think is more valuable in expressing the relationship between calories and sugar—the covariance or the coefficient of correlation? Explain.
d. Based on (a) and (b), what conclusions can you reach about the relationship between calories and sugar?

3.47 Movie companies need to predict the gross receipts of individual movies once a movie has debuted. The following results, stored in **PotterMovies**, are the first weekend gross, the U.S. gross, and the worldwide gross (in $millions) of the eight Harry Potter movies:

Title	First Weekend	U.S. Gross	Worldwide Gross
Sorcerer's Stone	90.295	317.558	976.458
Chamber of Secrets	88.357	261.988	878.988
Prisoner of Azkaban	93.687	249.539	795.539
Goblet of Fire	102.335	290.013	896.013
Order of the Phoenix	77.108	292.005	938.469
Half-Blood Prince	77.836	301.460	934.601
Deathly Hallows – Part 1	125.017	295.001	955.417
Deathly Hallows – Part 2	169.189	381.011	1,328.111

Source: Data extracted from **www.the-numbers.com/interactive/comp-HarryPotter.php**.

a. Compute the covariance between first weekend gross and U.S. gross, first weekend gross and worldwide gross, and U.S. gross and worldwide gross.
b. Compute the coefficient of correlation between first weekend gross and U.S. gross, first weekend gross and worldwide gross, and U.S. gross and worldwide gross.
c. Which do you think is more valuable in expressing the relationship between first weekend gross, U.S. gross, and worldwide gross—the covariance or the coefficient of correlation? Explain.
d. Based on (a) and (b), what conclusions can you reach about the relationship between first weekend gross, U.S. gross, and worldwide gross?

3.48 College basketball is big business, with coaches' salaries, revenues, and expenses in millions of dollars. The file **College Basketball** contains the coaches' salaries and revenues for college basketball at 60 of the 65 schools that played in the 2009 NCAA men's basketball tournament.

Source: Data extracted from "Compensation for Division 1 Men's Basketball Coaches," *USA Today*, April 2, 2010, p. 8C; and C. Isadore, "Nothing but Net: Basketball Dollars by School," **money.cnn.com/2010/03/18/news/companies/basketball_profits/**.

a. Compute the covariance.
b. Compute the coefficient of correlation.
c. Based on (a) and (b), what conclusions can you reach about the relationship between coaches' salaries and revenues?

3.49 A Pew Research Center survey found that social networking is popular in many nations around the world. The file GlobalSocialMedia contains the level of social media networking (measured as the percentage of individuals polled who use social networking sites) and the GDP at purchasing power parity (PPP) per capita for each of 25 selected countries. (Data extracted from Pew Research Center, "Global Digital Communication: Texting, Social Networking Popular Worldwide," updated February 29, 2012, via the link **bit.ly/sNjsmq**).

a. Compute the covariance.

b. Compute the coefficient of correlation.

c. Based on (a) and (b), what conclusions can you reach about the relationship between the GDP and social media use?

3.6 Descriptive Statistics: Pitfalls and Ethical Issues

This chapter describes how a set of numerical data can be characterized by the statistics that measure the properties of central tendency, variation, and shape. In business, descriptive statistics such as the ones discussed in this chapter are frequently included in summary reports that are prepared periodically.

The volume of information available from online, broadcast, or print media has produced much skepticism in the minds of many about the objectivity of data. When you are reading information that contains descriptive statistics, you should keep in mind the quip often attributed to the famous nineteenth-century British statesman Benjamin Disraeli: "There are three kinds of lies: lies, damned lies, and statistics."

For example, in examining statistics, you need to compare the mean and the median. Are they similar, or are they very different? Or is only the mean provided? The answers to these questions will help you determine whether the data are skewed or symmetrical and whether the median might be a better measure of central tendency than the mean. In addition, you should look to see whether the standard deviation or interquartile range for a very skewed set of data has been included in the statistics provided. Without this, it is impossible to determine the amount of variation that exists in the data.

Ethical considerations arise when you are deciding what results to include in a report. You should document both good and bad results. In addition, when making oral presentations and presenting written reports, you need to give results in a fair, objective, and neutral manner. Unethical behavior occurs when you selectively fail to report pertinent findings that are detrimental to the support of a particular position.

USING STATISTICS More Descriptive Choices, Revisited

baranq / Shutterstock

In the More Descriptive Choices scenario, you were hired by the Choice *Is* Yours investment company to assist investors interested in stock mutual funds. A sample of 318 stock mutual funds included 223 growth funds and 95 value funds. By comparing these two categories, you were able to provide investors with valuable insights.

The three-year annualized returns for both the growth funds and the value funds were right-skewed, as indicated by the boxplots (see Figure 3.4 on page 128). The descriptive statistics (see Figure 3.2 on page 119) allowed you to compare the central tendency, variability, and shape of the returns of the growth funds and the value funds. The mean indicated that the growth funds returned an average of 22.44, and the median indicated that half of the growth funds had returns of 22.32 or more. The value funds' central tendencies were lower than those of the growth funds—they had a mean of 20.42, and half the funds had three-year annualized returns above 19.46. The growth funds showed slightly more variability than the value funds, with a standard deviation of 6.6408 as compared to 5.6783. While both the growth funds and the value funds showed right- or positive skewness, the growth funds were much more skewed. The kurtosis of growth funds was very positive, indicating a distribution that was much more peaked than a normal distribution. Although past performance is no assurance of future performance, the growth funds outperformed the value funds from 2009 through 2011. (You can examine other variables in Retirement Funds to see if the growth funds outperformed the value funds in 2011, for the 5-year period 2007–2011 and for the 10-year period 2002–2011.)

SUMMARY

In this chapter and the previous chapter, you studied descriptive statistics—how you can organize data through tables, visualize data through charts, and how you can use various statistics to help analyze the data and reach conclusions. In Chapter 2, you organized data by constructing summary tables and visualized data by constructing bar and pie charts, histograms, and other charts. In this chapter, you learned how descriptive statistics such as the mean, median, quartiles, range, and standard deviation describe the characteristics of central tendency, variability, and shape. In addition, you constructed boxplots to visualize the distribution of the data. You also learned how the coefficient of correlation describes the relationship between two numerical variables. All the methods of this chapter are summarized in Table 3.9.

You also learned a number of concepts about variation in data that will prove useful in later chapters. These concepts are:

- The greater the spread or dispersion of the data, the larger the range, variance, and standard deviation.
- The smaller the spread or dispersion of the data, the smaller the range, variance, and standard deviation.
- If the values are all the same (so that there is no variation in the data), the range, variance, and standard deviation will all equal zero.
- None of the measures of variation (the range, variance, and standard deviation) can ever be negative.

In the next chapter, the basic principles of probability are presented in order to bridge the gap between the subject of descriptive statistics and the subject of inferential statistics.

TABLE 3.9
Chapter 3 Descriptive Statistics Methods

Type of Analysis	Methods
Central tendency	Mean, median, mode (Section 3.1)
Variation and shape	Quartiles, range, interquartile range, variance, standard deviation, coefficient of variation, *Z* scores, boxplot (Sections 3.2 through 3.4)
Describing the relationship between two numerical variables	Covariance, coefficient of correlation (Section 3.5)

REFERENCES

1. Booker, J., and L Ticknor. "A Brief Overview of Kurtosis." **www.osti.gov/bridge/purl.cover.jsp?purl=/677174-zdulqk/webviewable/677174.pdf**.
2. Kendall, M. G., A. Stuart, and J. K. Ord. *Kendall's Advanced Theory of Statistics, Volume 1: Distribution Theory*, 6th ed. New York: Oxford University Press, 1994.
3. *Microsoft Excel 2010*. Redmond, WA: Microsoft Corporation, 2010.
4. Taleb, N. *The Black Swan*, 2nd ed. New York: Random House, 2010.

KEY EQUATIONS

Sample Mean

$$\bar{X} = \frac{\sum_{i=1}^{n} X_i}{n} \quad \textbf{(3.1)}$$

Median

$$\text{Median} = \frac{n+1}{2} \text{ ranked value} \quad \textbf{(3.2)}$$

Geometric Mean

$$\bar{X}_G = (X_1 \times X_2 \times \cdots \times X_n)^{1/n} \quad \textbf{(3.3)}$$

Geometric Mean Rate of Return

$$\bar{R}_G = [(1 + R_1) \times (1 + R_2) \times \cdots \times (1 + R_n)]^{1/n} - 1 \quad \textbf{(3.4)}$$

Range

$$\text{Range} = X_{\text{largest}} - X_{\text{smallest}} \quad (3.5)$$

Sample Variance

$$S^2 = \frac{\sum_{i=1}^{n}(X_i - \bar{X})^2}{n-1} \quad (3.6)$$

Sample Standard Deviation

$$S = \sqrt{S^2} = \sqrt{\frac{\sum_{i=1}^{n}(X_i - \bar{X})^2}{n-1}} \quad (3.7)$$

Coefficient of Variation

$$CV = \left(\frac{S}{\bar{X}}\right)100\% \quad (3.8)$$

Z Score

$$Z = \frac{X - \bar{X}}{S} \quad (3.9)$$

First Quartile, Q_1

$$Q_1 = \frac{n+1}{4} \text{ ranked value} \quad (3.10)$$

Third Quartile, Q_3

$$Q_3 = \frac{3(n+1)}{4} \text{ ranked value} \quad (3.11)$$

Interquartile Range

$$\text{Interquartile range} = Q_3 - Q_1 \quad (3.12)$$

Population Mean

$$\mu = \frac{\sum_{i=1}^{N} X_i}{N} \quad (3.13)$$

Population Variance

$$\sigma^2 = \frac{\sum_{i=1}^{N}(X_i - \mu)^2}{N} \quad (3.14)$$

Population Standard Deviation

$$\sigma = \sqrt{\frac{\sum_{i=1}^{N}(X_i - \mu)^2}{N}} \quad (3.15)$$

Sample Covariance

$$\text{cov}(X, Y) = \frac{\sum_{i=1}^{n}(X_i - \bar{X})(Y_i - \bar{Y})}{n-1} \quad (3.16)$$

Sample Coefficient of Correlation

$$r = \frac{\text{cov}(X, Y)}{S_X S_Y} \quad (3.17)$$

KEY TERMS

arithmetic mean (mean) 106
boxplot 128
central tendency 106
Chebyshev rule 134
coefficient of correlation 137
coefficient of variation (CV) 116
covariance 136
dispersion (spread) 111
empirical rule 133
five-number summary 126
geometric mean 110
interquartile range (midspread) 125
kurtosis 119
left-skewed 118
lepokurtic 119
mean (arithmetic mean) 106
median 108
midspread (interquartile range) 125
mode 109
outliers 117
platykurtic 119
population mean 131
population standard deviation 132
population variance 132
Q_1: first quartile 124
Q_2: second quartile 124
Q_3: third quartile 124
quartiles 124
range 111
resistant measure 126
right-skewed 118
sample coefficient of correlation (r) 138
sample covariance 136
sample mean 106
sample standard deviation (S) 112
sample variance (S^2) 112
shape 118
skewed 118
skewness 118
spread (dispersion) 111
standard deviation 112
sum of squares (SS) 112
symmetrical 118
variance 112
variation 106
Z score 117

CHECKING YOUR UNDERSTANDING

3.50 What are the properties of a set of numerical data?

3.51 What is meant by *the property of central tendency*?

3.52 What are the differences among the mean, median, and mode, and what are the advantages and disadvantages of each?

3.53 How do you interpret the first quartile, median, and third quartile?

3.54 What is meant by the property of variation?

3.55 What does the *Z* score measure?

3.56 What are the differences among the various measures of variation, such as the range, interquartile range, variance, standard deviation, and coefficient of variation, and what are the advantages and disadvantages of each?

3.57 How does the empirical rule help explain the ways in which the values in a set of numerical data cluster and distribute?

3.58 How do the empirical rule and the Chebyshev rule differ?

3.59 What is meant by the property of shape?

3.60 What is the difference between the arithmetic mean and the geometric mean?

3.61 What is the difference between skewness and kurtosis?

3.62 How do the covariance and the coefficient of correlation differ?

CHAPTER REVIEW PROBLEMS

3.63 The American Society for Quality (ASQ) conducted a salary survey of all its members. ASQ members work in all areas of manufacturing and service-related institutions, with a common theme of an interest in quality. For the survey, emails were sent to 57,029 members, and 7,036 valid responses were received. The two most common job titles were manager and quality engineer. Another title is Master Black Belt, a person who takes a leadership role as the keeper of the Six Sigma process (see Section 18.6). An additional title is Green Belt, someone who works on Six Sigma projects part time. Descriptive statistics concerning salaries for these four titles are given in the following table:

Title	Sample Size	Minimum	Maximum	Standard Deviation	Mean	Median
Green Belt	26	34,000	135,525	25,911	64,794	59,700
Manager	1,710	10,400	700,000	30,004	90,950	89,500
Quality Engineer	947	10,400	690,008	33,191	78,819	75,000
Master Black Belt	105	10,000	216,000	31,064	116,706	117,078

Source: Data extracted from M. Hansen, N. Wilde, and E. Kinch, "Slow and Steady," *Quality Progress*, December 2011, p. 33.

Compare the salaries of Green Belts, managers, quality engineers, and Master Black Belts.

3.64 In certain states, savings banks are permitted to sell life insurance. The approval process consists of underwriting, which includes a review of the application, a medical information bureau check, possible requests for additional medical information and medical exams, and a policy compilation stage, in which the policy pages are generated and sent to the bank for delivery. The ability to deliver approved policies to customers in a timely manner is critical to the profitability of this service to the bank. Using the Define, Collect, Organize, Visualize, and Analyze steps first discussed in Chapter 2, you define the variable of interest as the total processing time in days. You collect the data by selecting a random sample of 27 approved policies during a period of one month. You organize the data collected in a worksheet and store them in **Insurance**:

73 19 16 64 28 28 31 90 60 56 31 56 22 18

45 48 17 17 17 91 92 63 50 51 69 16 17

a. Compute the mean, median, first quartile, and third quartile.

b. Compute the range, interquartile range, variance, standard deviation, and coefficient of variation.

c. Construct a boxplot. Are the data skewed? If so, how?

d. What would you tell a customer who enters the bank to purchase this type of insurance policy and asks how long the approval process takes?

3.65 One of the major measures of the quality of service provided by an organization is the speed with which it responds to customer complaints. A large family-held department store selling furniture and flooring, including carpet, had undergone a major expansion in the past several years. In particular, the flooring department had expanded from 2 installation crews to an installation supervisor, a measurer, and 15 installation crews. The business objective of the company was to reduce the time between when a complaint is received and when it is resolved. During a recent year, the company received 50 complaints concerning carpet installation. The data from the 50 complaints, organized in **Furniture**, represent the number of days between the receipt of a complaint and the resolution of the complaint:

54	5	35	137	31	27	152	2	123	81	74	27	11
19	126	110	110	29	61	35	94	31	26	5	12	4
165	32	29	28	29	26	25	1	14	13	13	10	5
27	4	52	30	22	36	26	20	23	33	68		

a. Compute the mean, median, first quartile, and third quartile.
b. Compute the range, interquartile range, variance, standard deviation, and coefficient of variation.
c. Construct a boxplot. Are the data skewed? If so, how?
d. On the basis of the results of (a) through (c), if you had to tell the president of the company how long a customer should expect to wait to have a complaint resolved, what would you say? Explain.

3.66 A manufacturing company produces steel housings for electrical equipment. The main component part of the housing is a steel trough that is made of a 14-gauge steel coil. It is produced using a 250-ton progressive punch press with a wipe-down operation and two 90-degree forms placed in the flat steel to make the trough. The distance from one side of the form to the other is critical because of weatherproofing in outdoor applications. The company requires that the width of the trough be between 8.31 inches and 8.61 inches. Data are collected from a sample of 49 troughs and stored in **Trough**, which contains these widths of the troughs, in inches:

8.312	8.343	8.317	8.383	8.348	8.410	8.351	8.373	8.481	8.422
8.476	8.382	8.484	8.403	8.414	8.419	8.385	8.465	8.498	8.447
8.436	8.413	8.489	8.414	8.481	8.415	8.479	8.429	8.458	8.462
8.460	8.444	8.429	8.460	8.412	8.420	8.410	8.405	8.323	8.420
8.396	8.447	8.405	8.439	8.411	8.427	8.420	8.498	8.409	

a. Compute the mean, median, range, and standard deviation for the width. Interpret these measures of central tendency and variability.
b. List the five-number summary.
c. Construct a boxplot and describe its shape.
d. What can you conclude about the number of troughs that will meet the company's requirement of troughs being between 8.31 and 8.61 inches wide?

3.67 The manufacturing company in Problem 3.66 also produces electric insulators. If the insulators break when in use, a short circuit is likely to occur. To test the strength of the insulators, destructive testing is carried out to determine how much force is required to break the insulators. Force is measured by observing how many pounds must be applied to an insulator before it breaks. Data are collected from a sample of 30 insulators. The file **Force** contains the strengths, as follows:

1,870	1,728	1,656	1,610	1,634	1,784	1,522	1,696	1,592	1,662
1,866	1,764	1,734	1,662	1,734	1,774	1,550	1,756	1,762	1,866
1,820	1,744	1,788	1,688	1,810	1,752	1,680	1,810	1,652	1,736

a. Compute the mean, median, range, and standard deviation for the force needed to break the insulators.
b. Interpret the measures of central tendency and variability in (a).
c. Construct a boxplot and describe its shape.
d. What can you conclude about the strength of the insulators if the company requires a force of at least 1,500 pounds before breakage?

3.68 Data were collected on the typical cost of dining at American-cuisine restaurants within a 1-mile walking distance of a hotel located in a large city. The file **Bundle** contains the typical cost (a per transaction cost in $) as well as a Bundle score, a measure of overall popularity and customer loyalty, for each of 40 selected restaurants. (Data extracted from www.bundle.com via the link **on-msn.com/MnlBxo**.)
a. For each variable, compute the mean, median, first quartile, and third quartile.
b. For each variable, compute the range, interquartile range, variance, standard deviation, and coefficient of variation.
c. For each variable, construct a boxplot. Are the data skewed? If so, how?
d. Compute the coefficient of correlation between Bundle score and typical cost.
e. What conclusions can you reach concerning Bundle score and typical cost?

3.69 A quality characteristic of interest for a tea-bag-filling process is the weight of the tea in the individual bags. If the bags are underfilled, two problems arise. First, customers may not be able to brew the tea to be as strong as they wish. Second, the company may be in violation of the truth-in-labeling laws. For this product, the label weight on the package indicates that, on average, there are 5.5 grams of tea in a bag. If the mean amount of tea in a bag exceeds the label weight, the company is giving away product. Getting an exact amount of tea in a bag is problematic because of variation in the temperature and humidity inside the factory, differences in the density of the tea, and the extremely fast filling operation of the machine (approximately 170 bags per minute). The file **Teabags** contains these weights, in grams, of a sample of 50 tea bags produced in one hour by a single machine:

5.65	5.44	5.42	5.40	5.53	5.34	5.54	5.45	5.52	5.41
5.57	5.40	5.53	5.54	5.55	5.62	5.56	5.46	5.44	5.51
5.47	5.40	5.47	5.61	5.53	5.32	5.67	5.29	5.49	5.55
5.77	5.57	5.42	5.58	5.58	5.50	5.32	5.50	5.53	5.58
5.61	5.45	5.44	5.25	5.56	5.63	5.50	5.57	5.67	5.36

a. Compute the mean, median, first quartile, and third quartile.
b. Compute the range, interquartile range, variance, standard deviation, and coefficient of variation.
c. Interpret the measures of central tendency and variation within the context of this problem. Why should the company producing the tea bags be concerned about the central tendency and variation?
d. Construct a boxplot. Are the data skewed? If so, how?
e. Is the company meeting the requirement set forth on the label that, on average, there are 5.5 grams of tea in a bag? If you were in charge of this process, what changes, if any, would you try to make concerning the distribution of weights in the individual bags?

3.70 The manufacturer of Boston and Vermont asphalt shingles provides its customers with a 20-year warranty on most of its products. To determine whether a shingle will last as long as the warranty period, accelerated-life testing is conducted at the manufacturing plant. Accelerated-life testing exposes a shingle to the stresses it would be subject to in a lifetime of normal use via an experiment in a laboratory setting that takes only a few minutes to conduct. In this test, a shingle is repeatedly scraped with a brush for a short period of time, and the shingle granules removed by the brushing are weighed (in grams). Shingles that experience low amounts of granule loss are expected to last longer in normal use than shingles that experience high amounts of granule loss. In this situation, a shingle should experience no more than 0.8 gram of granule loss if it is expected to last the length of the warranty period. The file Granule contains a sample of 170 measurements made on the company's Boston shingles and 140 measurements made on Vermont shingles.
a. List the five-number summaries for the Boston shingles and for the Vermont shingles.
b. Construct side-by-side boxplots for the two brands of shingles and describe the shapes of the distributions.
c. Comment on the ability of each type of shingle to achieve a granule loss of 0.8 gram or less.

3.71 The file Restaurants contains the cost per meal and the ratings of 50 city and 50 suburban restaurants on their food, décor, and service (and their summated ratings). Complete the following for the urban and suburban restaurants:

Source: Data extracted from *Zagat Survey 2012 New York City Restaurants* and *Zagat Survey 2011–2012 Long Island Restaurants*.

a. Construct the five-number summary of the cost of a meal.
b. Construct a boxplot of the cost of a meal. What is the shape of the distribution?
c. Compute and interpret the correlation coefficient of the summated rating and the cost of a meal.

3.72 The file Protein contains calories, protein, and cholesterol of popular protein foods (fresh red meats, poultry, and fish).

Source: U.S. Department of Agriculture.

a. Compute the correlation coefficient between calories and protein.
b. Compute the correlation coefficient between calories and cholesterol.
c. Compute the correlation coefficient between protein and cholesterol.
d. Based on the results of (a) through (c), what conclusions can you reach concerning calories, protein, and cholesterol?

3.73 The file HotelPrices contains the prices in English pounds (about US\$1.56 as of January 2012) of a room at two-star, three-star, and four-star hotels in cities around the world in 2011. (Data extracted from **press.hotels.com/en-gb/files/2012/03/HPI_2011_UK.pdf**.) Complete the following for two-star, three-star, and four-star hotels:
a. Compute the mean, median, first quartile, and third quartile.
b. Compute the range, interquartile range, variance, standard deviation, and coefficient of variation.
c. Interpret the measures of central tendency and variation within the context of this problem.
d. Construct a boxplot. Are the data skewed? If so, how?
e. Compute the covariance between the average price at two-star and three-star hotels, between two-star and four-star hotels, and between three-star and four-star hotels.
f. Compute the coefficient of correlation between the average price at two-star and three-star hotels, between two-star and four-star hotels, and between three-star and four-star hotels.
g. Which do you think is more valuable in expressing the relationship between the average price of a room at two-star, three-star, and four-star hotels—the covariance or the coefficient of correlation? Explain.
h. Based on (f), what conclusions can you reach about the relationship between the average price of a room at two-star, three-star, and four-star hotels?

3.74 The file PropertyTaxes contains the property taxes per capita for the 50 states and the District of Columbia.
a. Compute the mean, median, first quartile, and third quartile.
b. Compute the range, interquartile range, variance, standard deviation, and coefficient of variation.
c. Construct a boxplot. Are the data skewed? If so, how?
d. Based on the results of (a) through (c), what conclusions can you reach concerning property taxes per capita (in \$thousands) for each state and the District of Columbia?

3.75 The file CEO-Compensation includes the total compensation (in $millions) of CEOs of 194 large public companies and the investment return in 2011.

Source: Data extracted from **nytimes.com/2012/06/17/business/executive-pay-still-climbing-despite-a-shareholder-din.html**.

a. Compute the mean, median, first quartile, and third quartile.

b. Compute the range, interquartile range, variance, standard deviation, and coefficient of variation.

c. Construct a boxplot. Are the data skewed? If so, how?

d. Based on the results of (a) through (c), what conclusions can you reach concerning the total compensation (in $millions) of CEOs?

e. Compute the correlation coefficient between compensation and the investment return in 2011.

f. What conclusions can you reach from the results of (e)?

3.76 You are planning to study for your statistics examination with a group of classmates, one of whom you particularly want to impress. This individual has volunteered to use Microsoft Excel to generate the needed summary information, tables, and charts for a data set that contains several numerical and categorical variables assigned by the instructor for study purposes. This person comes over to you with the printout and exclaims, "I've got it all—the means, the medians, the standard deviations, the boxplots, the pie charts—for all our variables. The problem is, some of the output looks weird—like the boxplots for gender and for major and the pie charts for grade point average and for height. Also, I can't understand why Professor Szabat said we can't get the descriptive stats for some of the variables; I got them for everything! See, the mean for height is 68.23, the mean for grade point average is 2.76, the mean for gender is 1.50, the mean for major is 4.33." What is your reply?

REPORT WRITING EXERCISES

3.77 The file DomesticBeer contains the percentage alcohol, number of calories per 12 ounces, and number of carbohydrates (in grams) per 12 ounces for 150 of the best-selling domestic beers in the United States. (Data extracted from **www.beer100.com/beercalories.htm**, June 1, 2012.) Write a report that includes a complete descriptive evaluation of each of the numerical variables—percentage of alcohol, number of calories per 12 ounces, and number of carbohydrates (in grams) per 12 ounces. Append to your report all appropriate tables, charts, and numerical descriptive measures.

CASES FOR CHAPTER 3

Managing Ashland MultiComm Services

For what variable in the Chapter 2 "Managing Ashland MultiComm Services" case (see page 90) are numerical descriptive measures needed?

1. For the variable you identify, compute the appropriate numerical descriptive measures and construct a boxplot.
2. For the variable you identify, construct a graphical display. What conclusions can you reach from this other plot that cannot be made from the boxplot?
3. Summarize your findings in a report that can be included with the task force's study.

Digital Case

Apply your knowledge about the proper use of numerical descriptive measures in this continuing Digital Case from Chapter 2.

Open **EndRunGuide.pdf**, the EndRun Financial Services "Guide to Investing." Reexamine EndRun's supporting data for the "More Winners Than Losers" and "The Big Eight Difference" and then answer the following:

1. Can descriptive measures be computed for any variables? How would such summary statistics support EndRun's claims? How would those summary statistics affect your perception of EndRun's record?
2. Evaluate the methods EndRun used to summarize the results presented on the "Customer Survey Results" page. Is there anything you would do differently to summarize these results?
3. Note that the last question of the survey has fewer responses than the other questions. What factors may have limited the number of responses to that question?

CardioGood Fitness

Return to the CardioGood Fitness case first presented on page 91. Using the data stored in CardioGoodFitness:

1. Compute descriptive statistics to create a customer profile for each CardioGood Fitness treadmill product line.
2. Write a report to be presented to the management of CardioGood Fitness, detailing your findings.

More Descriptive Choices Follow-up

Follow up the Using Statistics Revisited section on page 142 by computing descriptive statistics to analyze the differences in 1-year return percentages, 5-year return percentages, and 10-year return percentages for the sample of 318 retirement funds stored in Retirement Funds. In your analysis, examine differences between the growth and value funds as well as the differences among the small, mid-cap, and large market cap funds.

Clear Mountain State Student Surveys

1. The student news service at Clear Mountain State University (CMSU) has decided to gather data about the undergraduate students who attend CMSU. They create and distribute a survey of 14 questions and receive responses from 62 undergraduates (stored in UndergradSurvey). For each numerical variable asked in the survey, compute all the appropriate descriptive statistics and write a report summarizing your conclusions.
2. The dean of students at CMSU has learned about the undergraduate survey and has decided to undertake a similar survey for graduate students at CMSU. She creates and distributes a survey of 14 questions and receives responses from 44 graduate students (stored in GradSurvey). For each numerical variable in the survey, compute all the appropriate descriptive statistics and write a report summarizing your conclusions.

CHAPTER 3 EXCEL GUIDE

EG3.1 CENTRAL TENDENCY

The Mean, Median, and Mode

Key Technique Use the following Excel functions to compute these measures.

AVERAGE(*variable cell range*)

MEDIAN(*variable cell range*)

MODE(*variable cell range*)

Example Compute the mean, median, and mode for the sample of getting-ready times introduced in Section 3.1.

PHStat Use **Descriptive Summary.**
For the example, open to the **DATA worksheet** of the **Times workbook.** Select **PHStat → Descriptive Statistics → Descriptive Summary**. In the procedure's dialog box (shown below):

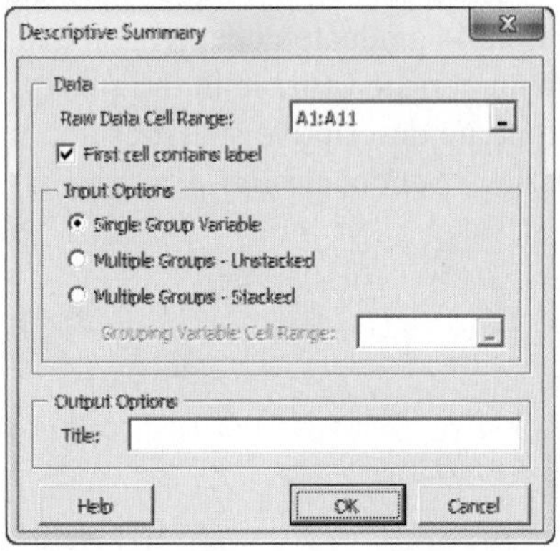

1. Enter **A1:A11** as the **Raw Data Cell Range** and check **First cell contains label.**
2. Click **Single Group Variable.**
3. Enter a **Title** and click **OK.**

PHStat inserts a new worksheet that contains various measures of central tendency, variation, and shape discussed in Sections 3.1 and 3.2. This worksheet is similar to the CompleteStatistics worksheet of the Descriptive workbook.

In-Depth Excel Use the **CentralTendency worksheet** of the **Descriptive workbook** as a model.
For the example, open to the **DATA worksheet** of the **Times workbook.** Insert a new worksheet (see Section EG.7 on page 14). Enter a title in cell **A1**, **Get-Ready Times** in cell **B3**, **Mean** in cell **A4**, **Median** in cell **A5**, and **Mode** in cell **A6**. Enter the formula **=AVERAGE(DATA!A:A)** in cell **B4**, the formula **=MEDIAN(DATA!A:A)** in cell **B5**, and the formula **=MODE(DATA!A:A)** in cell **B6**. Note that for these functions, the *variable cell range* includes the name of the DATA worksheet because the data being summarized appears on the separate DATA worksheet.

Analysis ToolPak Use **Descriptive Statistics.**
For the example, open to the **DATA worksheet** of the **Times workbook** and:

1. Select **Data → Data Analysis.**
2. In the Data Analysis dialog box, select **Descriptive Statistics** from the **Analysis Tools** list and then click **OK.**

In the Descriptive Statistics dialog box (shown below):

3. Enter **A1:A11** as the **Input Range**. Click **Columns** and check **Labels in First Row.**
4. Click **New Worksheet Ply** and check **Summary statistics, Kth Largest**, and **Kth Smallest.**
5. Click **OK.**

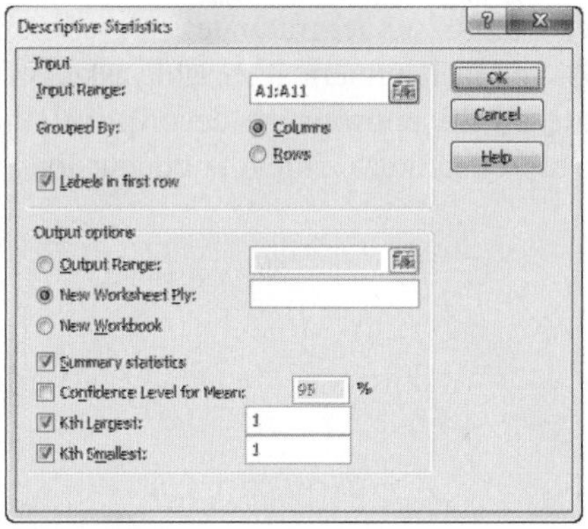

The ToolPak inserts a new worksheet that contains various measures of central tendency, variation, and shape discussed in Sections 3.1 and 3.2. This worksheet is comparable to the CompleteStatistics worksheet of the Descriptive workbook (used throughout the *In-Depth Excel* instructions of this Excel Guide) and the worksheet generated by the PHStat Descriptive Summary procedure.

The Geometric Mean

Key Technique Use the **GEOMEAN((1 + (*R1*)), (1 + (*R2*)), ...(1 + (*Rn*))) – 1** function to compute the geometric mean rate of return.

Example Compute the geometric mean rate of return in the Russell 2000 Index for the two years as shown in Example 3.4 on page 111.

In-Depth Excel Enter the formula **=GEOMEAN((1 + (0.253)), (1 + (-0.055))) – 1** in any cell.

EG3.2 VARIATION and SHAPE

The Range

Key Technique Use the **MIN(*variable cell range*)** and **MAX(*variable cell range*)** functions to help compute the range.

Example Compute the range for the sample of getting-ready times first introduced in Section 3.1.

PHStat Use **Descriptive Summary** (see Section EG3.1).

In-Depth Excel Use the **Range worksheet** of the **Descriptive workbook** as a model.
For the example, open the worksheet implemented for the example in the *In-Depth Excel* "The Mean, Median, and Mode" instructions (or open to the **DATA worksheet** of the **Times workbook** and insert a new worksheet).

Enter **Minimum** in cell **A7**, **Maximum** in cell **A8**, and **Range** in cell **A9**. Enter the formula **=MIN(DATA!A:A)** in cell **B7**, the formula **=MAX(DATA!A:A)** in cell **B8**, and the formula **=B8 – B7** in cell **B9**.

The Variance, Standard Deviation, Coefficient of Variation, and *Z* Scores

Key Technique Use the following Excel functions to compute these measures:

VAR.S(*variable cell range*) for the sample variance

STDEV.S(*variable cell range*) for the sample standard deviation

AVERAGE(see Section EG3.1) and **STDEV** for the coefficient of variation

STANDARDIZE(*value, mean, standard deviation*) for the Z scores

Example Compute the variance, standard deviation, coefficient of variation, and *Z* scores for the sample of getting-ready times first introduced in Section 3.1.

PHStat Use **Descriptive Summary** (see Section EG3.1).

In-Depth Excel Use the **Variation** and **ZScores worksheets** of the **Descriptive workbook** as models.
For the example, open to the worksheet implemented for the earlier examples (or open to the **DATA worksheet** of the **Times workbook** and insert a new worksheet). Enter **Variance** in cell **A10**, **Standard Deviation** in cell **A11**, and **Coeff. of Variation** in cell **A12**. Enter the formula **=VAR(DATA!A:A)** in cell **B10**, the formula **=STDEV(DATA!A:A)** in cell **B11**, and the formula **=B11/AVERAGE(DATA!A:A)** in cell **B12**. If you previously entered the formula for the mean in cell A4 using the Section EG3.1 *In-Depth Excel* instructions, enter the simpler formula **=B11/B4** in cell **B12**. Right-click cell **B12** and click **Format Cells** in the shortcut menu. In the **Number** tab of the Format Cells dialog box, click **Percentage** in the **Category** list, enter **2** as the **Decimal places**, and click **OK**. (To enhance the formatting of other column B values, see Appendix Section F.1.)

To compute the *Z* scores, copy the DATA worksheet. In the new, copied worksheet, enter **Z Score** in cell **B1**. Enter the formula **=STANDARDIZE(A2, Variation!$B$4, Variation!$B$11)** in cell **B2** and copy the formula down through row **11**.

Analysis ToolPak Use **Descriptive Statistics** (see Section EG3.1). This procedure does not compute *Z* scores.

Shape: Skewness and Kurtosis

Key Technique Use the following Excel functions to compute these measures:

SKEW(*variable cell range*) for the skewness

KURT(*variable cell range*) for the kurtosis

Example Compute the skewness and kurtosis for the sample of getting-ready times first introduced in Section 3.1.

PHStat Use **Descriptive Summary** (see Section EG3.1).

In-Depth Excel Use the **Shape worksheet** of the **Descriptive workbook** as a model.
For the example, open to the worksheet implemented for the earlier examples (or open to the **DATA worksheet** of the **Times workbook** and insert a new worksheet). Enter **Skewness** in cell **A13** and **Kurtosis** in cell **A14**. Enter the formula **=SKEW(DATA!A:A)** in cell **B13** and the formula **=KURT(DATA!A:A)** in cell **B14**. Then format cells B13 and B14 for four decimal places.

Analysis ToolPak Use **Descriptive Statistics** (see Section EG3.1).

EG3.3 EXPLORING NUMERICAL DATA

Quartiles

Key Technique Use the MEDIAN, COUNT, SMALL, INT, FLOOR, and CEILING functions in combination with the IF decision-making function to compute the quartiles. To apply the rules of Section 3.3, avoid using the QUARTILE function (or the newer QUARTILE.EXC function discussed in Appendix Section F.3 to compute the first and third quartiles.

Example Compute the quartiles for the sample of getting-ready times first introduced in Section 3.1.

PHStat Use **Boxplot** (discussed later on page 152).

In-Depth Excel Use the **COMPUTE worksheet** of the **Quartiles workbook** as a model.
For the example, the COMPUTE worksheet already computes the quartiles for the getting-ready times. To compute the quartiles for another set of data, paste the data into **column A** of the **DATA worksheet**, overwriting the existing getting-ready times.

Open to the **COMPUTE_FORMULAS worksheet** to examine the formulas and read the SHORT TAKES for Chapter 3 for an extended discussion of the formulas in the worksheet.

The workbook uses the older **QUARTILE(*variable cell range, quartile number*)** function and avoids using the newer QUARTILE.EXC function for reasons explained in Appendix Section F.3. Both the older and newer quartile functions use rules that differ from the Section 3.3 rules to compute quartiles. To compare the results using these newer functions, open to the **COMPARE worksheet**.

The Interquartile Range

Key Technique Use a formula to subtract the first quartile from the third quartile.

Example Compute the interquartile range for the sample of getting-ready times first introduced in Section 3.1.

In-Depth Excel Use the **COMPUTE worksheet** of the **Quartiles workbook** (introduced in the previous section) as a model.
For the example, the interquartile range is already computed in cell B19 using the formula =B18 – B16.

The Five-Number Summary and the Boxplot

Key Technique Plot a series of line segments on the same chart to create a boxplot. (Excel chart types do not include boxplots.)

Example Compute the five-number summary and boxplots for the growth and value funds from the sample of 318 retirement funds shown in Example 3.13 on page 128.

PHStat Use **Boxplot**.
For the example, open to the **DATA worksheet** of the **Retirement Funds workbook**. Select **PHStat → Descriptive Statistics → Boxplot**. In the procedure's dialog box (shown in next column):

1. Enter **J1:J319** as the **Raw Data Cell Range** and check **First cell contains label**.
2. Click **Multiple Groups - Stacked** and enter **C1:C319** as the **Grouping Variable Cell Range**.
3. Enter a **Title**, check **Five-Number Summary**, and click **OK**.

The boxplot appears on its own chart sheet, separate from the worksheet that contains the five-number summary.

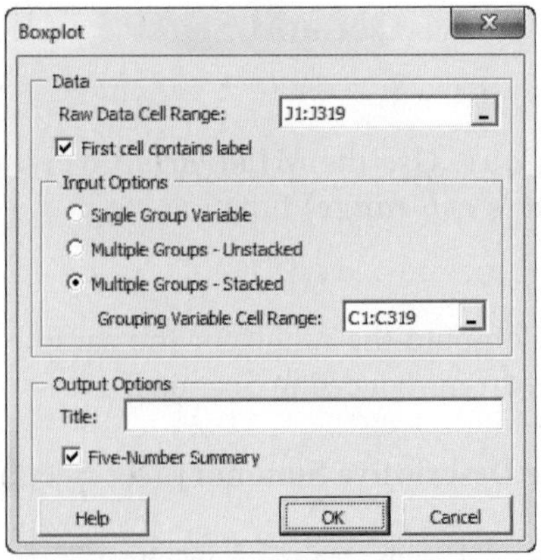

In-Depth Excel Use the worksheets of the **Boxplot workbook** as templates.
For the example, use the **PLOT_DATA worksheet** which already shows the five-number summary and boxplot for the value funds. To compute the five-number summary and construct a boxplot for the growth funds, copy the growth funds from **column A** of the **UNSTACKED worksheet** of the **Retirement Funds workbook** and paste into **column A** of the **DATA worksheet** of the **Boxplot workbook**.

For other problems, use the **PLOT_SUMMARY worksheet** as the template if the five-number summary has already been determined; otherwise, paste your unsummarized data into column A of the DATA worksheet and use the PLOT_DATA worksheet as was done for the example.

The template worksheets creatively "misuse" Excel line charting features to construct a boxplot. Read the SHORT TAKES for Chapter 3 for an extended discussion of this "misuse," including a discussion of the formulas you can review by opening to the **PLOT_FORMULAS worksheet**.

EG3.4 NUMERICAL DESCRIPTIVE MEASURES for a POPULATION

The Population Mean, Population Variance, and Population Standard Deviation

Key Technique Use **AVERAGE(*variable cell range*)**, **VAR.P(*variable cell range*)**, and **STDEV.P(*variable cell range*)** to compute these measures.

Example Compute the population mean, population variance, and population standard deviation for the "Dow Dogs" population data of Table 3.6 on page 131.

In-Depth Excel Use the **Parameters workbook** as a model.
For the example, the **COMPUTE worksheet** of the **Parameters workbook** already computes the three population parameters for the "Dow Dogs." (If you use an Excel version older than Excel 2010, use the COMPUTE_OLDER worksheet instead of the COMPUTE worksheet.)

The Empirical Rule and the Chebyshev Rule

Use the **COMPUTE worksheet** of the **VE-Variability workbook** to explore the effects of changing the mean and standard deviation on the ranges associated with ± 1 standard deviation, ± 2 standard deviations, and ± 3 standard deviations from the mean. Change the mean in cell **B4** and the standard deviation in cell **B5** and then note the updated results in rows 9 through 11.

EG3.5 The COVARIANCE and the COEFFICIENT of CORRELATION

The Covariance

Key Technique Use the **COVARIANCE.S(*variable 1 cell range, variable 2 cell range*)** function to compute this measure.

Example Compute the sample covariance for the NBA team revenue and value data of Example 3.16 on page 136.

In-Depth Excel Use the **Covariance workbook** as a model.

For the example, the revenue and value have already been placed in columns A and B of the DATA worksheet and the COMPUTE worksheet displays the computed covariance in cell B9. For other problems, paste the data for two variables into columns A and B of the DATA worksheet, overwriting the revenue and value data.

Read the SHORT TAKES for Chapter 3 for an explanation of the formulas found in the DATA and COMPUTE worksheets.

If you use an Excel version older than Excel 2010, use the COMPUTE_OLDER worksheet instead of the COMPUTE worksheet. Appendix Section F.3 explains the need for using alternatives such as COMPUTE_OLDER.)

The Coefficient of Correlation

Key Technique Use the **CORREL(*variable 1 cell range, variable 2 cell range*)** function to compute this measure.

Example Compute the coefficient of correlation for the NBA team revenue and value data of Example 3.16 on page 136.

In-Depth Excel Use the **Correlation workbook** as a model.

For the example, the revenue and value have already been placed in columns A and B of the DATA worksheet and the COMPUTE worksheet displays the coefficient of correlation in cell B14. For other problems, paste the data for two variables into columns A and B of the DATA worksheet, overwriting the revenue and value data.

The COMPUTE worksheet that uses the COVARIANCE.S function to compute the covariance (see the previous section) and also uses the DEVSQ, COUNT, and SUMPRODUCT functions discussed in Appendix Section F.4. Open to the **COMPUTE_FORMULAS worksheet** to examine the use of all these functions.

CHAPTER

4

Basic Probability

Learning Objectives

In this chapter, you learn:

- Basic probability concepts
- Conditional probability
- Bayes' theorem to revise probabilities

USING STATISTICS

Yuri Arcurs / Shutterstock

Possibilities at M&R Electronics World

As the marketing manager for M&R Electronics World, you are analyzing the survey results of an intent-to-purchase study. This study asked the heads of 1,000 households about their intentions to purchase a large-screen HDTV (one that is high definition with a screen size of at least 50 inches) sometime during the next 12 months. As a follow-up, you plan to survey the same people 12 months later to see whether they purchased televisions. In addition, for households that purchase a large-screen HDTV, you would like to know whether the television they purchased had a faster refresh rate (240 Hz or higher) or a standard refresh rate (60 or 120 Hz), whether they also purchased a streaming media box in the past 12 months, and whether they were satisfied with their purchase of the large-screen HDTV.

You are expected to use the results of this survey to plan a new marketing strategy that will enhance sales and better target those households likely to purchase multiple or more expensive products. What questions can you ask in this survey? How can you express the relationships among the various intent-to-purchase responses of individual households?

In previous chapters, you learned descriptive methods to summarize categorical and numerical variables. In this chapter, you will learn about probability to answer questions such as the following:

- What is the probability that a household is planning to purchase a large-screen HDTV in the next year?
- What is the probability that a household will actually purchase a large-screen HDTV?
- What is the probability that a household is planning to purchase a large-screen HDTV and actually purchases the television?
- Given that the household is planning to purchase a large-screen HDTV, what is the probability that the purchase is made?
- Does knowledge of whether a household *plans* to purchase the television change the likelihood of predicting whether the household *will* purchase the television?
- What is the probability that a household that purchases a large-screen HDTV will purchase a television with a faster refresh rate?
- What is the probability that a household that purchases a large-screen HDTV with a faster refresh rate will also purchase a streaming media box?
- What is the probability that a household that purchases a large-screen HDTV will be satisfied with the purchase?

Ljupco Smokovski / Shutterstock

With answers to questions such as these, you can begin to make decisions about your marketing strategy. Should your strategy for selling more large-screen HDTVs target households that have indicated an intent to purchase? Should you concentrate on selling televisions that have faster refresh rates? Is it likely that households that purchase large-screen HDTVs with faster refresh rates can be easily persuaded to also purchase streaming media boxes?

The principles of probability help bridge the worlds of descriptive statistics and inferential statistics. Reading this chapter will help you learn about different types of probabilities, how to compute probabilities, and how to revise probabilities in light of new information. Probability principles are the foundation for the probability distribution, the concept of mathematical expectation, and the binomial, Poisson, and hypergeometric distributions, topics that are discussed in Chapter 5.

4.1 Basic Probability Concepts

Student Tip
Remember, a probability cannot be negative or greater than 1.

What is meant by the word *probability*? A **probability** is the numerical value representing the chance, likelihood, or possibility that a particular event will occur, such as the price of a stock increasing, a rainy day, a defective product, or the outcome five dots in a single toss of a die. In all these instances, the probability involved is a proportion or fraction whose value ranges between 0 and 1, inclusive. An event that has no chance of occurring (the **impossible event**) has a probability of 0. An event that is sure to occur (the **certain event**) has a probability of 1.

There are three types of probability:

- *A priori*
- Empirical
- Subjective

In the simplest case, where each outcome is equally likely, the chance of occurrence of the event is defined in Equation (4.1).

PROBABILITY OF OCCURRENCE

$$\text{Probability of occurrence} = \frac{X}{T} \tag{4.1}$$

where

X = number of ways in which the event occurs
T = total number of possible outcomes

In ***a priori* probability**, the probability of an occurrence is based on prior knowledge of the process involved. Consider a standard deck of cards that has 26 red cards and 26 black cards. The probability of selecting a black card is $26/52 = 0.50$ because there are $X = 26$ black cards and $T = 52$ total cards. What does this probability mean? If each card is replaced after it is selected, does it mean that 1 out of the next 2 cards selected will be black? No, because you cannot say for certain what will happen on the next several selections. However, you can say that in the long run, if this selection process is continually repeated, the proportion of black cards selected will approach 0.50. Example 4.1 shows another example of computing an *a priori* probability.

EXAMPLE 4.1

Finding *A Priori* Probabilities

A standard six-sided die has six faces. Each face of the die contains either one, two, three, four, five, or six dots. If you roll a die, what is the probability that you will get a face with five dots?

SOLUTION Each face is equally likely to occur. Because there are six faces, the probability of getting a face with five dots is 1/6.

The preceding examples use the *a priori* probability approach because the number of ways the event occurs and the total number of possible outcomes are known from the composition of the deck of cards or the faces of the die.

In the **empirical probability** approach, the probabilities are based on observed data, not on prior knowledge of a process. Surveys are often used to generate empirical probabilities. Examples of this type of probability are the proportion of individuals in the Using Statistics scenario who actually purchase large-screen HDTVs, the proportion of registered voters who prefer a certain political candidate, and the proportion of students who have part-time jobs. For example, if you take a survey of students, and 60% state that they have part-time jobs, then there is a 0.60 probability that an individual student has a part-time job.

The third approach to probability, **subjective probability**, differs from the other two approaches because subjective probability differs from person to person. For example, the development team for a new product may assign a probability of 0.60 to the chance of success for the product, while the president of the company may be less optimistic and assign a probability of 0.30. The assignment of subjective probabilities to various outcomes is usually based on a combination of an individual's past experience, personal opinion, and analysis of a particular situation. Subjective probability is especially useful in making decisions in situations in which you cannot use *a priori* probability or empirical probability.

Events and Sample Spaces

The basic elements of probability theory are the individual outcomes of a variable under study. You need the following definitions to understand probabilities.

Student Tip
Events are represented by letters of the alphabet.

EVENT

Each possible outcome of a variable is referred to as an **event**.
A **simple event** is described by a single characteristic.

For example, when you toss a coin, the two possible outcomes are heads and tails. Each of these represents a simple event. When you roll a standard six-sided die in which the six faces of the die contain either one, two, three, four, five, or six dots, there are six possible simple events. An event can be any one of these simple events, a set of them, or a subset of all of them. For example, the event of an *even number of dots* consists of three simple events (i.e., two, four, or six dots).

Student Tip
The key word when describing a joint event is *and*.

JOINT EVENT

A **joint event** is an event that has two or more characteristics.

Getting two heads when you toss a coin twice is an example of a joint event because it consists of heads on the first toss and heads on the second toss.

COMPLEMENT

The **complement** of event A (represented by the symbol A') includes all events that are not part of A.

The complement of a head is a tail because that is the only event that is not a head. The complement of five dots on a die is not getting five dots. Not getting five dots consists of getting one, two, three, four, or six dots.

SAMPLE SPACE

The collection of all the possible events is called the **sample space**.

The sample space for tossing a coin consists of heads and tails. The sample space when rolling a die consists of one, two, three, four, five, and six dots. Example 4.2 demonstrates events and sample spaces.

EXAMPLE 4.2
Events and Sample Spaces

The Using Statistics scenario on page 155 concerns M&R Electronics World. Table 4.1 presents the results of the sample of 1,000 households in terms of purchase behavior for large-screen HDTVs.

TABLE 4.1
Purchase Behavior for Large-screen HDTVs

PLANNED TO PURCHASE	ACTUALLY PURCHASED Yes	No	Total
Yes	200	50	250
No	100	650	750
Total	300	700	1,000

What is the sample space? Give examples of simple events and joint events.

SOLUTION The sample space consists of the 1,000 respondents. Simple events are "planned to purchase," "did not plan to purchase," "purchased," and "did not purchase." The complement of the event "planned to purchase" is "did not plan to purchase." The event "planned to purchase and actually purchased" is a joint event because in this joint event, the respondent must plan to purchase the television *and* actually purchase it.

Contingency Tables

There are several ways in which you can view a particular sample space. The method used in this book involves using a **contingency table** (see Section 2.1) such as the one displayed in Table 4.1. You get the values in the cells of the table by subdividing the sample space of 1,000 households according to whether someone planned to purchase and actually purchased a large-screen HDTV. For example, 200 of the respondents planned to purchase a large-screen HDTV and subsequently did purchase the large-screen HDTV.

Simple Probability

Now you can answer some of the questions posed in the Using Statistics scenario. Because the results are based on data collected in a survey (refer to Table 4.1), you can use the empirical probability approach.

As stated previously, the most fundamental rule for probabilities is that they range in value from 0 to 1. An impossible event has a probability of 0, and an event that is certain to occur has a probability of 1.

Simple probability refers to the probability of occurrence of a simple event, $P(A)$. A simple probability in the Using Statistics scenario is the probability of planning to purchase a large-screen HDTV. How can you determine the probability of selecting a household that planned to purchase a large-screen HDTV? Using Equation (4.1) on page 156:

$$\text{Probability of occurrence} = \frac{X}{T}$$

$$P(\text{Planned to purchase}) = \frac{\text{Number who planned to purchase}}{\text{Total number of households}}$$

$$= \frac{250}{1{,}000} = 0.25$$

Thus, there is a 0.25 (or 25%) chance that a household planned to purchase a large-screen HDTV.

Example 4.3 illustrates another application of simple probability.

EXAMPLE 4.3

Computing the Probability That the Large-Screen HDTV Purchased Had a Faster Refresh Rate

In the Using Statistics follow-up survey, additional questions were asked of the 300 households that actually purchased large-screen HDTVs. Table 4.2 indicates the consumers' responses to whether the television purchased had a faster refresh rate and whether they also purchased a streaming media box in the past 12 months.

Find the probability that if a household that purchased a large-screen HDTV is randomly selected, the television purchased had a faster refresh rate.

TABLE 4.2

Purchase Behavior Regarding Purchasing a Faster Refresh Rate Television and a Streaming Media Box

REFRESH RATE OF TELEVISION PURCHASED	STREAMING MEDIA BOX		
	Yes	No	Total
Faster	38	42	80
Standard	70	150	220
Total	108	192	300

SOLUTION Using the following definitions:

$$
\begin{aligned}
A &= \text{purchased a television with a faster refresh rate} \\
A' &= \text{purchased a television with a standard refresh rate} \\
B &= \text{purchased a streaming media box} \\
B' &= \text{did not purchase a streaming media box}
\end{aligned}
$$

$$
\begin{aligned}
P(\text{Faster refresh rate}) &= \frac{\text{Number of faster refresh rate televisions}}{\text{Total number of televisions}} \\
&= \frac{80}{300} = 0.267
\end{aligned}
$$

There is a 26.7% chance that a randomly selected large-screen HDTV purchased has a faster refresh rate.

Joint Probability

Whereas simple probability refers to the probability of occurrence of simple events, **joint probability** refers to the probability of an occurrence involving two or more events. An example of joint probability is the probability that you will get heads on the first toss of a coin and heads on the second toss of a coin.

In Table 4.1 on page 158, the group of individuals who planned to purchase and actually purchased a large-screen HDTV consist only of the outcomes in the single cell "yes—planned to purchase *and* yes—actually purchased." Because this group consists of 200 households, the probability of picking a household that planned to purchase *and* actually purchased a large-screen HDTV is

$$
\begin{aligned}
P(\text{Planned to purchase } \textit{and} \text{ actually purchased}) &= \frac{\text{Planned to purchase } \textit{and} \text{ actually purchased}}{\text{Total number of respondents}} \\
&= \frac{200}{1{,}000} = 0.20
\end{aligned}
$$

Example 4.4 also demonstrates how to determine joint probability.

EXAMPLE 4.4

Determining the Joint Probability That a Household Purchased a Large-Screen HDTV with a Faster Refresh Rate and Purchased a Streaming Media Box

In Table 4.2 on page 159, the purchases are cross-classified as having a faster refresh rate or having a standard refresh rate and whether the household purchased a streaming media box. Find the probability that a randomly selected household that purchased a large-screen HDTV also purchased a television that had a faster refresh rate and purchased a streaming media box.

SOLUTION Using Equation (4.1) on page 156,

$$P(\text{Television with a faster refresh rate } \textit{and} \text{ streaming media box}) = \frac{\text{Number that purchased a television with a faster refresh rate } \textit{and} \text{ purchased a streaming media box}}{\text{Total number of large-screen HDTV purchasers}}$$

$$= \frac{38}{300} = 0.127$$

Therefore, there is a 12.7% chance that a randomly selected household that purchased a large-screen HDTV purchased a television that had a faster refresh rate and purchased a streaming media box.

Marginal Probability

The **marginal probability** of an event consists of a set of joint probabilities. You can determine the marginal probability of a particular event by using the concept of joint probability just discussed. For example, if B consists of two events, B_1 and B_2, then $P(A)$, the probability of event A, consists of the joint probability of event A occurring with event B_1 and the joint probability of event A occurring with event B_2. You use Equation (4.2) to compute marginal probabilities.

MARGINAL PROBABILITY

$$P(A) = P(A \textit{ and } B_1) + P(A \textit{ and } B_2) + \cdots + P(A \textit{ and } B_k) \quad \textbf{(4.2)}$$

where $B_1, B_2, \ldots, B_k$ are k mutually exclusive and collectively exhaustive events, defined as follows:

Two events are **mutually exclusive** if both the events cannot occur simultaneously.
A set of events is **collectively exhaustive** if one of the events must occur.

Heads and tails in a coin toss are mutually exclusive events. The result of a coin toss cannot simultaneously be a head and a tail. Heads and tails in a coin toss are also collectively exhaustive events. One of them must occur. If heads does not occur, tails must occur. If tails does not occur, heads must occur. Being male and being female are mutually exclusive and collectively exhaustive events. No person is both (the two are mutually exclusive), and everyone is one or the other (the two are collectively exhaustive).

You can use Equation (4.2) to compute the marginal probability of "planned to purchase" a large-screen HDTV:

$$\begin{aligned} P(\text{Planned to purchase}) &= P(\text{Planned to purchase } \textit{and} \text{ purchased}) \\ &\quad + P(\text{Planned to purchase } \textit{and} \text{ did not purchase}) \\ &= \frac{200}{1{,}000} + \frac{50}{1{,}000} \\ &= \frac{250}{1{,}000} = 0.25 \end{aligned}$$

You get the same result if you add the number of outcomes that make up the simple event "planned to purchase."

Student Tip
The key word when using the addition rule is *or*.

General Addition Rule

How do you find the probability of event "*A or B*"? You need to consider the occurrence of either event *A* or event *B* or both *A* and *B*. For example, how can you determine the probability that a household planned to purchase *or* actually purchased a large-screen HDTV?

The event "planned to purchase *or* actually purchased" includes all households that planned to purchase and all households that actually purchased a large-screen HDTV. You examine each cell of the contingency table (Table 4.1 on page 158) to determine whether it is part of this event. From Table 4.1, the cell "planned to purchase *and* did not actually purchase" is part of the event because it includes respondents who planned to purchase. The cell "did not plan to purchase *and* actually purchased" is included because it contains respondents who actually purchased. Finally, the cell "planned to purchase *and* actually purchased" has both characteristics of interest. Therefore, one way to calculate the probability of "planned to purchase *or* actually purchased" is

$$\begin{aligned} P(\text{Planned to purchase } or \text{ actually purchased}) &= P(\text{Planned to purchase } and \text{ did not actually purchase}) + P(\text{Did not plan to purchase } and \text{ actually purchased}) + P(\text{Planned to purchase } and \text{ actually purchased}) \\ &= \frac{50}{1{,}000} + \frac{100}{1{,}000} + \frac{200}{1{,}000} \\ &= \frac{350}{1{,}000} = 0.35 \end{aligned}$$

Often, it is easier to determine *P*(*A or B*), the probability of the event *A or B*, by using the **general addition rule**, defined in Equation (4.3).

GENERAL ADDITION RULE

The probability of *A or B* is equal to the probability of *A* plus the probability of *B* minus the probability of *A and B*.

$$P(A \text{ or } B) = P(A) + P(B) - P(A \text{ and } B) \qquad \textbf{(4.3)}$$

Applying Equation (4.3) to the previous example produces the following result:

$$\begin{aligned} P(\text{Planned to purchase } or \text{ actually purchased}) &= P(\text{Planned to purchase}) + P(\text{Actually purchased}) - P(\text{Planned to purchase } and \text{ actually purchased}) \\ &= \frac{250}{1{,}000} + \frac{300}{1{,}000} - \frac{200}{1{,}000} \\ &= \frac{350}{1{,}000} = 0.35 \end{aligned}$$

The general addition rule consists of taking the probability of *A* and adding it to the probability of *B* and then subtracting the probability of the joint event *A and B* from this total because the joint event has already been included in computing both the probability of *A* and the probability of *B*. Referring to Table 4.1 on page 158, if the outcomes of the event "planned to purchase" are added to those of the event "actually purchased," the joint event "planned to purchase *and* actually purchased" has been included in each of these simple events. Therefore, because this joint event has been included twice, you must subtract it to provide the correct result. Example 4.5 illustrates another application of the general addition rule.

EXAMPLE 4.5
Using the General Addition Rule for the Households That Purchased Large-Screen HDTVs

In Example 4.3 on page 159, the purchases were cross-classified in Table 4.2 as televisions that had a faster refresh rate or televisions that had a standard refresh rate and whether the household purchased a streaming media box. Find the probability that among households that purchased a large-screen HDTV, they purchased a television that had a faster refresh rate or purchased a streaming media box.

SOLUTION Using Equation (4.3),

$$\begin{aligned} &P(\text{Television had a faster refresh rate } \textit{or} \text{ purchased a streaming media box}) \\ &= P(\text{Television had a faster refresh rate}) + P(\text{purchased a streaming media box}) \\ &\quad - P(\text{Television had a faster refresh rate } \textit{and} \text{ purchased a streaming media box}) \\ &= \frac{80}{300} + \frac{108}{300} - \frac{38}{300} \\ &= \frac{150}{300} = 0.50 \end{aligned}$$

Therefore, of households that purchased a large-screen HDTV, there is a 50% chance that a randomly selected household purchased a television that had a faster refresh rate or purchased a streaming media box.

Problems for Section 4.1

LEARNING THE BASICS

4.1 Two coins are tossed.
a. Give an example of a simple event.
b. Give an example of a joint event.
c. What is the complement of a head on the first toss?
d. What does the sample space consist of?

4.2 An urn contains 12 red balls and 8 white balls. One ball is to be selected from the urn.
a. Give an example of a simple event.
b. What is the complement of a red ball?
c. What does the sample space consist of?

4.3 Consider the following contingency table:

	B	B'
A	10	20
A'	20	40

What is the probability of event
a. A?
b. A'?
c. A *and* B?
d. A *or* B?

4.4 Consider the following contingency table:

	B	B'
A	10	30
A'	25	35

What is the probability of event
a. A'?
b. A *and* B?
c. A' *and* B'?
d. A' *or* B'?

APPLYING THE CONCEPTS

4.5 For each of the following, indicate whether the type of probability involved is an example of *a priori* probability, empirical probability, or subjective probability.
a. The next toss of a fair coin will land on heads.
b. Italy will win soccer's World Cup the next time the competition is held.
c. The sum of the faces of two dice will be seven.
d. The train taking a commuter to work will be more than 10 minutes late.

4.6 For each of the following, state whether the events created are mutually exclusive and whether they are collectively exhaustive.

a. Undergraduate business students were asked whether they were sophomores or juniors.

b. Each respondent was classified by the type of car he or she drives: sedan, SUV, American, European, Asian, or none.

c. People were asked, "Do you currently live in (i) an apartment or (ii) a house?"

d. A product was classified as defective or not defective.

4.7 Which of the following events occur with a probability of zero? For each, state why or why not.

a. A company is listed on the New York Stock Exchange and NASDAQ.

b. A consumer owns a smartphone and a tablet.

c. A cellphone is a Motorola and a Samsung.

d. An automobile is a Toyota and was manufactured in the United States.

4.8 Does it take more time to be removed from an email list than it used to take? A study of 100 large online retailers revealed the following:

	NEED THREE OR MORE CLICKS TO BE REMOVED	
YEAR	**Yes**	**No**
2009	39	61
2008	7	93

Source: Data extracted from "More Clicks to Escape an Email List," *The New York Times*, March 29, 2010, p. B2.

a. Give an example of a simple event.

b. Give an example of a joint event.

c. What is the complement of "Needs three or more clicks to be removed from an email list"?

d. Why is "Needs three or more clicks to be removed from an email list in 2009" a joint event?

4.9 Referring to the contingency table in Problem 4.8, if a large online retailer is selected at random, what is the probability that

a. you needed three or more clicks to be removed from an email list?

b. you needed three or more clicks to be removed from an email list in 2009?

c. you needed three or more clicks to be removed from an email list or were a large online retailer surveyed in 2009?

d. Explain the difference in the results in (b) and (c).

4.10 How will marketers change their social media use in the near future? A survey by Social Media Examiner reported that 76% of B2B marketers (marketers that focus primarily on attracting businesses) plan to increase their use of LinkedIn, as compared to 55% of B2C marketers (marketers that primarily target consumers). The survey was based on 1,945 B2B marketers and 1,868 B2C marketers. The following table summarizes the results:

	BUSINESS FOCUS		
INCREASE USE OF LINKEDIN?	**B2B**	**B2C**	**Total**
Yes	1,478	1,027	2,505
No	467	841	1,308
Total	1,945	1,868	3,813

Source: Data extracted from "2012 Social Media Marketing Industry Report," April 2012, p. 27, **bit.ly/HaWwDu**.

a. Give an example of a simple event.

b. Give an example of a joint event.

c. What is the complement of a marketer who plans to increase use of LinkedIn?

d. Why is a marketer who plans to increase use of LinkedIn and is a B2C marketer a joint event?

4.11 Referring to the contingency table in Problem 4.10, if a marketer is selected at random, what is the probability that

a. he or she plans to increase use of LinkedIn?

b. he or she is a B2C marketer?

c. he or she plans to increase use of LinkedIn *or* is a B2C marketer?

d. Explain the difference in the results in (b) and (c).

SELF Test **4.12** What business and technical skills are critical for today's business intelligence/analytics and information management professionals? As part of InformationWeek's 2012 U.S. IT Salary Survey, business intelligence/analytics and information management professionals, both staff and managers, were asked to indicate what business and technical skills are critical to their job. The list of business and technical skills included *Analyzing Data*. The following table summarizes the responses to this skill:

	PROFESSIONAL POSITION		
ANALYZING DATA	**Staff**	**Management**	**Total**
Critical	296	216	512
Not critical	83	65	148
Total	379	281	660

Source: Data extracted from "Big Data Widens Analytic Talent Gap," *InformationWeek Reports*, April 2012, p. 24, **bit.ly/GSIdDL**.

If a professional is selected at random, what is the probability that he or she

a. indicates analyzing data as critical to his or her job?

b. is a manager?

c. indicates analyzing data as critical to his or her job *or* is a manager?

d. Explain the difference in the results in (b) and (c).

4.13 What is the preferred way for people to order fast food? A survey was conducted in 2009, but the sample sizes were not reported. Suppose the results, based on a sample of 100 males and 100 females, were as follows:

	GENDER		
DINING PREFERENCE	Male	Female	Total
Dine inside	21	12	33
Order inside to go	19	10	29
Order at the drive-through	60	78	138
Total	100	100	200

Source: Data extracted from **bit.ly/JDB1s**.

If a respondent is selected at random, what is the probability that he or she

a. prefers to order at the drive-through?
b. is a male *and* prefers to order at the drive-through?
c. is a male *or* prefers to order at the drive-through?
d. Explain the difference in the results in (b) and (c).

4.14 A survey of 1,085 adults asked, "Do you enjoy shopping for clothing for yourself?" The results (data extracted from "Split Decision on Clothes Shopping," *USA Today*, January 28, 2011, p. 1B) indicated that 51% of the females enjoyed shopping for clothing for themselves as compared to 44% of the males. The sample sizes of males and females were not provided. Suppose that the results indicated that of 542 males, 238 answered yes. Of 543 females, 276 answered yes. Construct a contingency table to evaluate the probabilities. What is the probability that a respondent chosen at random

a. enjoys shopping for clothing for himself or herself?
b. is a female *and* enjoys shopping for clothing for herself?
c. is a female *or* is a person who enjoys shopping for clothing?
d. is a male *or* a female?

4.15 Each year, ratings are compiled concerning the performance of new cars during the first 90 days of use. Suppose that the cars have been categorized according to whether a car needs warranty-related repair (yes or no) and the country in which the company manufacturing a car is based (United States or not United States). Based on the data collected, the probability that the new car needs a warranty repair is 0.04, the probability that the car was manufactured by a U.S.-based company is 0.60, and the probability that the new car needs a warranty repair *and* was manufactured by a U.S.-based company is 0.025. Construct a contingency table to evaluate the probabilities of a warranty-related repair. What is the probability that a new car selected at random

a. needs a warranty repair?
b. needs a warranty repair *and* was manufactured by a U.S.-based company?
c. needs a warranty repair *or* was manufactured by a U.S.-based company?
d. needs a warranty repair *or* was not manufactured by a U.S.-based company?

4.2 Conditional Probability

Each example in Section 4.1 involves finding the probability of an event when sampling from the entire sample space. How do you determine the probability of an event if you know certain information about the events involved?

Computing Conditional Probabilities

Conditional probability refers to the probability of event *A*, given information about the occurrence of another event, *B*.

CONDITIONAL PROBABILITY

The probability of *A* given *B* is equal to the probability of *A and B* divided by the probability of *B*.

$$P(A|B) = \frac{P(A \text{ and } B)}{P(B)} \quad \textbf{(4.4a)}$$

The probability of *B* given *A* is equal to the probability of *A and B* divided by the probability of *A*.

$$P(B|A) = \frac{P(A \text{ and } B)}{P(A)} \quad \textbf{(4.4b)}$$

where

$P(A \text{ and } B)$ = joint probability of *A and B*
$P(A)$ = marginal probability of *A*
$P(B)$ = marginal probability of *B*

Student Tip
The variable that is *given* goes in the denominator of Equation (4.4). Since you were given planned to purchase, planned to purchase is in the denominator.

Referring to the Using Statistics scenario involving the purchase of large-screen HDTVs, suppose you were told that a household planned to purchase a large-screen HDTV. Now, what is the probability that the household actually purchased the television?

In this example, the objective is to find $P(\text{Actually purchased} \mid \text{Planned to purchase})$. Here you are given the information that the household planned to purchase the large-screen HDTV. Therefore, the sample space does not consist of all 1,000 households in the survey. It consists of only those households that planned to purchase the large-screen HDTV. Of 250 such households, 200 actually purchased the large-screen HDTV. Therefore, based on Table 4.1 on page 158, the probability that a household actually purchased the large-screen HDTV given that they planned to purchase is

$$P(\text{Actually purchased} \mid \text{Planned to purchase}) = \frac{\text{Planned to purchase } \textit{and} \text{ actually purchased}}{\text{Planned to purchase}} = \frac{200}{250} = 0.80$$

You can also use Equation (4.4b) to compute this result:

$$P(B \mid A) = \frac{P(A \text{ and } B)}{P(A)}$$

where

A = planned to purchase
B = actually purchased

then

$$P(\text{Actually purchased} \mid \text{Planned to purchase}) = \frac{200/1{,}000}{250/1{,}000} = \frac{200}{250} = 0.80$$

Example 4.6 further illustrates conditional probability.

EXAMPLE 4.6
Finding the Conditional Probability of Purchasing a Streaming Media Box

Table 4.2 on page 159 is a contingency table for whether a household purchased a television with a faster refresh rate and whether the household purchased a streaming media box. If a household purchased a television with a faster refresh rate, what is the probability that it also purchased a streaming media box?

SOLUTION Because you know that the household purchased a television with a faster refresh rate, the sample space is reduced to 80 households. Of these 80 households, 38 also purchased a streaming media box. Therefore, the probability that a household purchased a streaming media box, given that the household purchased a television with a faster refresh rate, is

$$P(\text{Purchased streaming media box} \mid \text{Purchased television with faster refresh rate}) = \frac{\text{Number purchasing television with faster refresh rate } \textit{and} \text{ streaming media box}}{\text{Number purchasing television with faster refresh rate}} = \frac{38}{80} = 0.475$$

If you use Equation (4.4b) on page 164:

A = purchased a television with a faster refresh rate
B = purchased a streaming media box

then

$$P(B \mid A) = \frac{P(A \text{ and } B)}{P(A)} = \frac{38/300}{80/300} = 0.475$$

Therefore, given that the household purchased a television with a faster refresh rate, there is a 47.5% chance that the household also purchased a streaming media box. You can compare this conditional probability to the marginal probability of purchasing a streaming media box, which is $108/300 = 0.36$, or 36%. These results tell you that households that purchased televisions with a faster refresh rate are more likely to purchase a streaming media box than are households that purchased large-screen HDTVs that have a standard refresh rate.

Decision Trees

In Table 4.1 on page 158, households are classified according to whether they planned to purchase and whether they actually purchased large-screen HDTVs. A **decision tree** is an alternative to the contingency table. Figure 4.1 represents the decision tree for this example.

FIGURE 4.1

Decision tree for planned to purchase and actually purchased

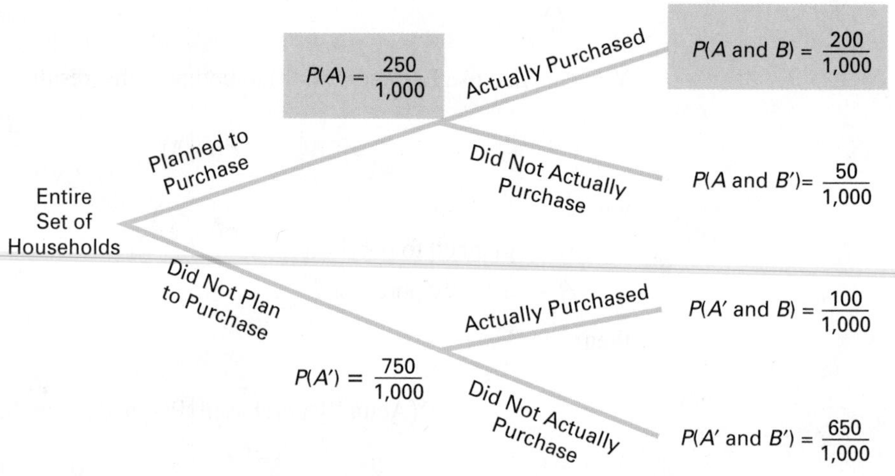

In Figure 4.1, beginning at the left with the entire set of households, there are two "branches" for whether or not the household planned to purchase a large-screen HDTV. Each of these branches has two subbranches, corresponding to whether the household actually purchased or did not actually purchase the large-screen HDTV. The probabilities at the end of the initial branches represent the marginal probabilities of A and A'. The probabilities at the end of each of the four subbranches represent the joint probability for each combination of events A and B. You compute the conditional probability by dividing the joint probability by the appropriate marginal probability.

For example, to compute the probability that the household actually purchased, given that the household planned to purchase the large-screen HDTV, you take P(Planned to purchase *and* actually purchased) and divide by P(Planned to purchase). From Figure 4.1,

$$P(\text{Actually purchased} \mid \text{Planned to purchase}) = \frac{200/1{,}000}{250/1{,}000} = \frac{200}{250} = 0.80$$

Example 4.7 illustrates how to construct a decision tree.

EXAMPLE 4.7

Constructing the Decision Tree for the Households That Purchased Large-Screen HDTVs

Using the cross-classified data in Table 4.2 on page 159, construct the decision tree. Use the decision tree to find the probability that a household purchased a streaming media box, given that the household purchased a television with a faster refresh rate.

SOLUTION The decision tree for purchased a streaming media box and a television with a faster refresh rate is displayed in Figure 4.2 on page 167.

FIGURE 4.2
Decision tree for purchased a television with a faster refresh rate and a streaming media box

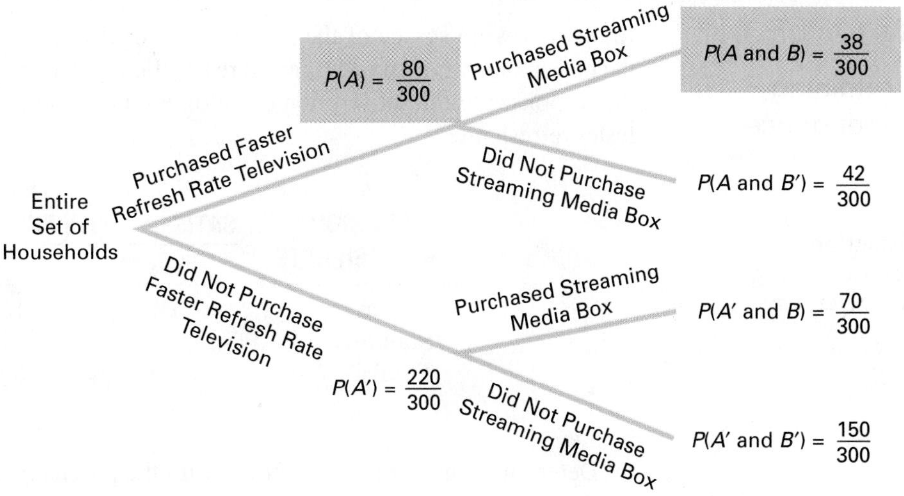

Using Equation (4.4b) on page 164 and the following definitions,

A = purchased a television with a faster refresh rate

B = purchased a streaming media box

$$P(B|A) = \frac{P(A \text{ and } B)}{P(A)} = \frac{38/300}{80/300} = 0.475$$

Independence

In the example concerning the purchase of large-screen HDTVs, the conditional probability is $200/250 = 0.80$ that the selected household actually purchased the large-screen HDTV, given that the household planned to purchase. The simple probability of selecting a household that actually purchased is $300/1{,}000 = 0.30$. This result shows that the prior knowledge that the household planned to purchase affected the probability that the household actually purchased the television. In other words, the outcome of one event is *dependent* on the outcome of a second event.

When the outcome of one event does *not* affect the probability of occurrence of another event, the events are said to be independent. **Independence** can be determined by using Equation (4.5).

INDEPENDENCE

Two events, A and B, are independent if and only if

$$P(A|B) = P(A) \tag{4.5}$$

where

$P(A|B)$ = conditional probability of A given B

$P(A)$ = marginal probability of A

Example 4.8 demonstrates the use of Equation (4.5).

EXAMPLE 4.8

Determining Independence

In the follow-up survey of the 300 households that actually purchased large-screen HDTVs, the households were asked if they were satisfied with their purchases. Table 4.3 cross-classifies the responses to the satisfaction question with the responses to whether the television had a faster refresh rate.

TABLE 4.3

Satisfaction with Purchase of Large-Screen HDTVs

TELEVISION REFRESH RATE	SATISFIED WITH PURCHASE?		
	Yes	No	Total
Faster	64	16	80
Standard	176	44	220
Total	240	60	300

Determine whether being satisfied with the purchase and the refresh rate of the television purchased are independent.

SOLUTION For these data,

$$P(\text{Satisfied} \mid \text{Faster refresh rate}) = \frac{64/300}{80/300} = \frac{64}{80} = 0.80$$

which is equal to

$$P(\text{Satisfied}) = \frac{240}{300} = 0.80$$

Thus, being satisfied with the purchase and the refresh rate of the television purchased are independent. Knowledge of one event does not affect the probability of the other event.

Multiplication Rules

The **general multiplication rule** is derived using Equation (4.4a) on page 164:

$$P(A \mid B) = \frac{P(A \text{ and } B)}{P(B)}$$

and solving for the joint probability $P(A \text{ and } B)$.

GENERAL MULTIPLICATION RULE

The probability of *A* and *B* is equal to the probability of *A* given *B* times the probability of *B*.

$$P(A \text{ and } B) = P(A \mid B)P(B) \qquad \textbf{(4.6)}$$

Example 4.9 demonstrates the use of the general multiplication rule.

EXAMPLE 4.9

Using the General Multiplication Rule

Consider the 80 households that purchased televisions that had a faster refresh rate. In Table 4.3 above, you see that 64 households are satisfied with their purchase, and 16 households are dissatisfied. Suppose 2 households are randomly selected from the 80 households. Find the probability that both households are satisfied with their purchase.

SOLUTION Here you can use the multiplication rule in the following way. If

A = second household selected is satisfied

B = first household selected is satisfied

then, using Equation (4.6),

$$P(A \text{ and } B) = P(A \mid B)P(B)$$

The probability that the first household is satisfied with the purchase is 64/80. However, the probability that the second household is also satisfied with the purchase depends on the result of the first selection. If the first household is not returned to the sample after the satisfaction level is determined (i.e., sampling without replacement), the number of households remaining is 79. If the first household is satisfied, the probability that the second is also satisfied is 63/79 because 63 satisfied households remain in the sample. Therefore,

$$P(A \text{ and } B) = \left(\frac{63}{79}\right)\left(\frac{64}{80}\right) = 0.6380$$

There is a 63.80% chance that both of the households sampled will be satisfied with their purchase.

The **multiplication rule for independent events** is derived by substituting $P(A)$ for $P(A|B)$ in Equation (4.6).

MULTIPLICATION RULE FOR INDEPENDENT EVENTS

If A and B are independent, the probability of A *and* B is equal to the probability of A times the probability of B.

$$P(A \text{ and } B) = P(A)P(B) \quad \textbf{(4.7)}$$

If this rule holds for two events, A and B, then A and B are independent. Therefore, there are two ways to determine independence:

1. Events A and B are independent if, and only if, $P(A|B) = P(A)$.
2. Events A and B are independent if, and only if, $P(A \text{ and } B) = P(A)P(B)$.

Marginal Probability Using the General Multiplication Rule

In Section 4.1, marginal probability was defined using Equation (4.2) on page 160. You can state the equation for marginal probability by using the general multiplication rule. If

$$P(A) = P(A \text{ and } B_1) + P(A \text{ and } B_2) + \cdots + P(A \text{ and } B_k)$$

then, using the general multiplication rule, Equation (4.8) defines the marginal probability.

MARGINAL PROBABILITY USING THE GENERAL MULTIPLICATION RULE

$$P(A) = P(A|B_1)P(B_1) + P(A|B_2)P(B_2) + \cdots + P(A|B_k)P(B_k) \quad \textbf{(4.8)}$$

where $B_1, B_2, \ldots, B_k$ are k mutually exclusive and collectively exhaustive events.

To illustrate Equation (4.8), refer to Table 4.1 on page 158. Let

$P(A)$ = probability of "planned to purchase"
$P(B_1)$ = probability of "actually purchased"
$P(B_2)$ = probability of "did not actually purchase"

Then, using Equation (4.8), the probability of planned to purchase is

$$\begin{aligned} P(A) &= P(A|B_1)P(B_1) + P(A|B_2)P(B_2) \\ &= \left(\frac{200}{300}\right)\left(\frac{300}{1{,}000}\right) + \left(\frac{50}{700}\right)\left(\frac{700}{1{,}000}\right) \\ &= \frac{200}{1{,}000} + \frac{50}{1{,}000} = \frac{250}{1{,}000} = 0.25 \end{aligned}$$

Problems for Section 4.2

LEARNING THE BASICS

4.16 Consider the following contingency table:

	B	*B'*
A	10	20
A'	20	40

What is the probability of

a. $A|B$?
b. $A|B'$?
c. $A'|B'$?
d. Are events *A* and *B* independent?

4.17 Consider the following contingency table:

	B	*B'*
A	10	30
A'	25	35

What is the probability of

a. $A|B$?
b. $A'|B'$?
c. $A|B'$?
d. Are events *A* and *B* independent?

4.18 If $P(A\ and\ B) = 0.4$ and $P(B) = 0.8$, find $P(A|B)$.

4.19 If $P(A) = 0.7$, $P(B) = 0.6$, and *A* and *B* are independent, find *P*(*A and B*).

4.20 If $P(A) = 0.3$, $P(B) = 0.4$, and $P(A\ and\ B) = 0.2$, are *A* and *B* independent?

APPLYING THE CONCEPTS

4.21 Does it take more time to be removed from an email list than it used to take? A study of 100 large online retailers revealed the following:

	NEED THREE OR MORE CLICKS TO BE REMOVED	
YEAR	**Yes**	**No**
2009	39	61
2008	7	93

Source: Data extracted from "More Clicks to Escape an Email List," *The New York Times*, March 29, 2010, p. B2.

a. Given that three or more clicks are needed to be removed from an email list, what is the probability that this occurred in 2009?
b. Given that the year 2009 is involved, what is the probability that three or more clicks are needed to be removed from an email list?
c. Explain the difference in the results in (a) and (b).
d. Are needing three or more clicks to be removed from an email list and the year independent?

4.22 How will marketers change their social media use in the near future? A survey by Social Media Examiner reported that 76% of B2B marketers (marketers that focus primarily on attracting businesses) plan to increase their use of LinkedIn, as compared to 55% of B2C marketers (marketers that primarily target consumers). The survey was based on 1,945 B2B marketers and 1,868 B2C marketers. The following table summarizes the results:

INCREASE USE OF LINKEDIN?	BUSINESS FOCUS		
	B2B	**B2C**	**Total**
Yes	1,478	1,027	2,505
No	467	841	1,308
Total	1,945	1,868	3,813

Source: Data extracted from "2012 Social Media Marketing Industry Report," April 2012, p. 27, **bit.ly/HaWwDu**.

a. Suppose you know that the marketer is a B2B marketer. What is the probability that he or she plans to increase use of LinkedIn?
b. Suppose you know that the marketer is a B2C marketer. What is the probability that he or she plans to increase use of LinkedIn?
c. Are the two events, increase use of LinkedIn and business focus, independent? Explain.

4.23 What is the preferred way for people to order fast food? A survey was conducted in 2009, but the sample sizes were not reported. Suppose the results, based on a sample of 100 males and 100 females, were as follows:

	GENDER		
DINING PREFERENCE	**Male**	**Female**	**Total**
Dine inside	21	12	33
Order inside to go	19	10	29
Order at the drive-through	60	78	138
Total	100	100	200

Source: Data extracted from **bit.ly/JDB1s**.

a. Given that a respondent is a male, what is the probability that he prefers to order at the drive-through?
b. Given that a respondent is a female, what is the probability that she prefers to order at the drive-through?
c. Is dining preference independent of gender? Explain.

SELF Test **4.24** What business and technical skills are critical for today's business intelligence/analytics and information management professionals? As part of InformationWeek's 2012 U.S. IT Salary Survey, business intelligence/analytics and information management professionals, both staff and managers, were asked to indicate what business and technical skills are critical to their job. The list of business and technical skills included *Analyzing Data*. The following table summarizes the responses to this skill:

	PROFESSIONAL POSITION		
ANALYZING DATA	Staff	Management	Total
Critical	296	216	512
Not Critical	83	65	148
Total	379	281	660

Source: Data extracted from "Big Data Widens Analytic Talent Gap," *InformationWeek Reports*, April 2012, p. 24 **bit.ly/GSIdDL**.

a. Given that a professional is staff, what is the probability that the professional indicates analyzing data as critical to his or her job?
b. Given that a professional is staff, what is the probability that the professional does not indicate analyzing data as critical to his or her job?
c. Given that a professional is a manager, what is the probability that the professional indicates analyzing data as critical to his or her job?
d. Given that a professional is a manager, what is the probability that the professional does not indicate analyzing data as critical to his or her job?

4.25 A survey of 1,085 adults asked, "Do you enjoy shopping for clothing for yourself?" The results (data extracted from "Split Decision on Clothes Shopping," *USA Today*, January 28, 2011, p. 1B) indicated that 51% of the females enjoyed shopping for clothing for themselves as compared to 44% of the males. The sample sizes of males and females were not provided. Suppose that the results were as shown in the following table:

ENJOYS SHOPPING FOR CLOTHING	GENDER		
	Male	Female	Total
Yes	238	276	514
No	304	267	571
Total	542	543	1,085

a. Suppose that the respondent chosen is a female. What is the probability that she does not enjoy shopping for clothing?
b. Suppose that the respondent chosen enjoys shopping for clothing. What is the probability that the individual is a male?
c. Are enjoying shopping for clothing and the gender of the individual independent? Explain.

4.26 Each year, ratings are compiled concerning the performance of new cars during the first 90 days of use. Suppose that the cars have been categorized according to whether a car needs warranty-related repair (yes or no) and the country in which the company manufacturing a car is based (United States or not United States). Based on the data collected, the probability that the new car needs a warranty repair is 0.04, the probability that the car is manufactured by a U.S.-based company is 0.60, and the probability that the new car needs a warranty repair *and* was manufactured by a U.S.-based company is 0.025.

a. Suppose you know that a company based in the United States manufactured a particular car. What is the probability that the car needs a warranty repair?
b. Suppose you know that a company based in the United States did not manufacture a particular car. What is the probability that the car needs a warranty repair?
c. Are need for a warranty repair and location of the company manufacturing the car independent?

4.27 In 39 of the 61 years from 1950 through 2010 (in 2011 there was virtually no change), the S&P 500 finished higher after the first five days of trading. In 34 of those 39 years, the S&P 500 finished higher for the year. Is a good first week a good omen for the upcoming year? The following table gives the first-week and annual performance over this 61-year period:

	S&P 500'S ANNUAL PERFORMANCE	
FIRST WEEK	Higher	Lower
Higher	34	5
Lower	11	11

a. If a year is selected at random, what is the probability that the S&P 500 finished higher for the year?
b. Given that the S&P 500 finished higher after the first five days of trading, what is the probability that it finished higher for the year?
c. Are the two events "first-week performance" and "annual performance" independent? Explain.
d. Look up the performance after the first five days of 2012 and the 2012 annual performance of the S&P 500 at **finance.yahoo.com**. Comment on the results.

4.28 A standard deck of cards is being used to play a game. There are four suits (hearts, diamonds, clubs, and spades), each having 13 faces (ace, 2, 3, 4, 5, 6, 7, 8, 9, 10, jack, queen, and king), making a total of 52 cards. This complete deck is thoroughly mixed, and you will receive the first 2 cards from the deck, without replacement (the first card is not returned to the deck after it is selected).

a. What is the probability that both cards are queens?
b. What is the probability that the first card is a 10 and the second card is a 5 or 6?

c. If you were sampling with replacement (the first card is returned to the deck after it is selected), what would be the answer in (a)?

d. In the game of blackjack, the face cards (jack, queen, king) count as 10 points, and the ace counts as either 1 or 11 points. All other cards are counted at their face value. Blackjack is achieved if 2 cards total 21 points. What is the probability of getting blackjack in this problem?

4.29 A box of nine gloves contains two left-handed gloves and seven right-handed gloves.

a. If two gloves are randomly selected from the box, without replacement (the first glove is not returned to the box after it is selected), what is the probability that both gloves selected will be right-handed?

b. If two gloves are randomly selected from the box, without replacement (the first glove is not returned to the box after it is selected), what is the probability that there will be one right-handed glove and one left-handed glove selected?

c. If three gloves are selected, with replacement (the gloves are returned to the box after they are selected), what is the probability that all three will be left-handed?

d. If you were sampling with replacement (the first glove is returned to the box after it is selected), what would be the answers to (a) and (b)?

4.3 Bayes' Theorem

Bayes' theorem is used to revise previously calculated probabilities based on new information. Developed by Thomas Bayes in the eighteenth century (see references 1, 2, and 6), Bayes' theorem is an extension of what you previously learned about conditional probability.

You can apply Bayes' theorem to the situation in which M&R Electronics World is considering marketing a new model of televisions. In the past, 40% of the new-model televisions have been successful, and 60% have been unsuccessful. Before introducing the new model television, the marketing research department conducts an extensive study and releases a report, either favorable or unfavorable. In the past, 80% of the successful new-model television(s) had received favorable market research reports, and 30% of the unsuccessful new-model television(s) had received favorable reports. For the new model of television under consideration, the marketing research department has issued a favorable report. What is the probability that the television will be successful?

Bayes' theorem is developed from the definition of conditional probability. To find the conditional probability of B given A, consider Equation (4.4b) (originally presented on page 164 and shown again below):

$$P(B|A) = \frac{P(A \text{ and } B)}{P(A)} = \frac{P(A|B)P(B)}{P(A)}$$

Bayes' theorem is derived by substituting Equation (4.8) on page 169 for $P(A)$ in the denominator of Equation (4.4b).

BAYES' THEOREM

$$P(B_i|A) = \frac{P(A|B_i)P(B_i)}{P(A|B_1)P(B_1) + P(A|B_2)P(B_2) + \cdots + P(A|B_k)P(B_k)} \quad \textbf{(4.9)}$$

where B_i is the ith event out of k mutually exclusive and collectively exhaustive events.

To use Equation (4.9) for the television-marketing example, let

event S = successful television   event F = favorable report
event S' = unsuccessful television   event F' = unfavorable report

and

$$P(S) = 0.40 \quad P(F|S) = 0.80$$
$$P(S') = 0.60 \quad P(F|S') = 0.30$$

Then, using Equation (4.9),

$$P(S|F) = \frac{P(F|S)P(S)}{P(F|S)P(S) + P(F|S')P(S')}$$
$$= \frac{(0.80)(0.40)}{(0.80)(0.40) + (0.30)(0.60)}$$
$$= \frac{0.32}{0.32 + 0.18} = \frac{0.32}{0.50}$$
$$= 0.64$$

The probability of a successful television, given that a favorable report was received, is 0.64. Thus, the probability of an unsuccessful television, given that a favorable report was received, is $1 - 0.64 = 0.36$.

Table 4.4 summarizes the computation of the probabilities, and Figure 4.3 presents the decision tree. Example 4.10 applies Bayes' theorem to a medical diagnosis problem.

TABLE 4.4
Bayes' Theorem Computations for the Television-Marketing Example

Event S_i	Prior Probability $P(S_i)$	Conditional Probability $P(F\|S_i)$	Joint Probability $P(F\|S_i)P(S_i)$	Revised Probability $P(S_i\|F)$
S = successful television	0.40	0.80	0.32	$P(S\|F) = 0.32/0.50 = 0.64$
S' = unsuccessful television	0.60	0.30	0.18	$P(S'\|F) = 0.18/0.50 = 0.36$
			0.50	

FIGURE 4.3
Decision tree for marketing a new television

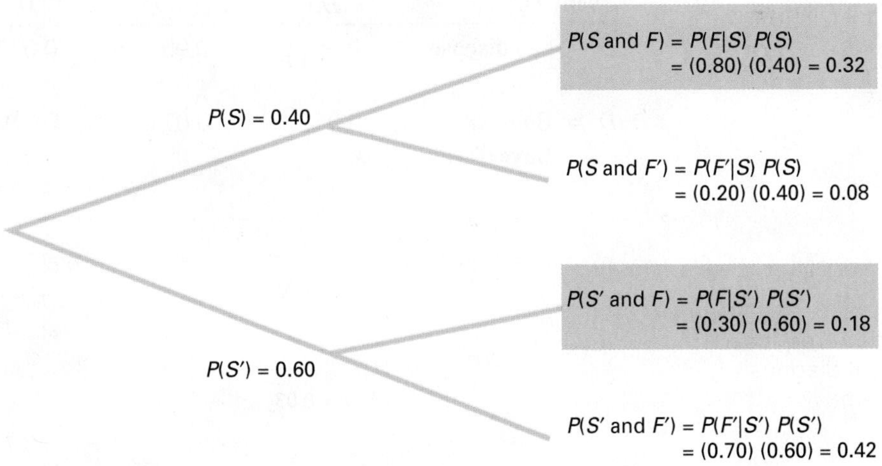

EXAMPLE 4.10
Using Bayes' Theorem in a Medical Diagnosis Problem

The probability that a person has a certain disease is 0.03. Medical diagnostic tests are available to determine whether the person actually has the disease. If the disease is actually present, the probability that the medical diagnostic test will give a positive result (indicating that the disease is present) is 0.90. If the disease is not actually present, the probability of a positive test result (indicating that the disease is present) is 0.02. Suppose that the medical diagnostic test has given a positive result (indicating that the disease is present). What is the probability that the disease is actually present? What is the probability of a positive test result?

SOLUTION Let

$$\text{event } D = \text{has disease} \qquad \text{event } T = \text{test is positive}$$
$$\text{event } D' = \text{does not have disease} \qquad \text{event } T' = \text{test is negative}$$

and

$$P(D) = 0.03 \quad P(T|D) = 0.90$$
$$P(D') = 0.97 \quad P(T|D') = 0.02$$

Using Equation (4.9) on page 172,

$$\begin{aligned} P(D|T) &= \frac{P(T|D)P(D)}{P(T|D)P(D) + P(T|D')P(D')} \\ &= \frac{(0.90)(0.03)}{(0.90)(0.03) + (0.02)(0.97)} \\ &= \frac{0.0270}{0.0270 + 0.0194} = \frac{0.0270}{0.0464} \\ &= 0.582 \end{aligned}$$

The probability that the disease is actually present, given that a positive result has occurred (indicating that the disease is present), is 0.582. Table 4.5 summarizes the computation of the probabilities, and Figure 4.4 presents the decision tree. The denominator in Bayes' theorem represents $P(T)$, the probability of a positive test result, which in this case is 0.0464, or 4.64%.

TABLE 4.5

Bayes' Theorem Computations for the Medical Diagnosis Problem

Event D_i	Prior Probability $P(D_i)$	Conditional Probability $P(T\|D_i)$	Joint Probability $P(T\|D_i)P(D_i)$	Revised Probability $P(D_i\|T)$
D = has disease	0.03	0.90	0.0270	$P(D\|T) = 0.0270/0.0464 = 0.582$
D' = does not have disease	0.97	0.02	0.0194	$P(D'\|T) = 0.0194/0.0464 = 0.418$
			0.0464	

FIGURE 4.4

Decision tree for a medical diagnosis problem

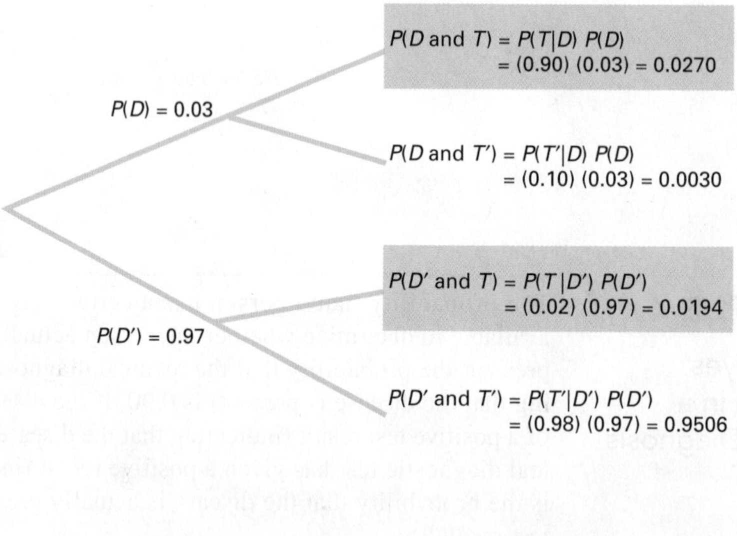

THINK ABOUT THIS Divine Providence and Spam

Would you ever guess that the essays *Divine Benevolence: Or, An Attempt to Prove That the Principal End of the Divine Providence and Government Is the Happiness of His Creatures* and *An Essay Towards Solving a Problem in the Doctrine of Chances* were written by the same person? Probably not, and in doing so, you illustrate a modern-day application of Bayesian statistics: spam, or junk mail filters.

In not guessing correctly, you probably looked at the words in the titles of the essays and concluded that they were talking about two different things. An implicit rule you used was that word frequencies vary by subject matter. A statistics essay would very likely contain the word *statistics* as well as words such as *chance*, *problem*, and *solving*. An eighteenth-century essay about theology and religion would be more likely to contain the uppercase forms of *Divine* and *Providence*.

Likewise, there are words you would guess to be very unlikely to appear in either book, such as technical terms from finance, and words that are most likely to appear in both—common words such as *a*, *and*, and *the*. That words would either be likely or unlikely suggests an application of probability theory. Of course, likely and unlikely are fuzzy concepts, and we might occasionally misclassify an essay if we kept things too simple, such as relying solely on the occurrence of the words *Divine* and *Providence*.

For example, a profile of the late Harris Milstead, better known as *Divine*, the star of *Hairspray* and other films, visiting Providence (Rhode Island), would most certainly not be an essay about theology. But if we widened the number of words we examined and found such words as *movie* or the name John Waters (Divine's director in many films), we probably would quickly realize the essay had something to do with twentieth-century cinema and little to do with theology and religion.

We can use a similar process to try to classify a new email message in your in-box as either spam or a legitimate message (called "ham," in this context). We would first need to add to your email program a "spam filter" that has the ability to track word frequencies associated with spam and ham messages as you identify them on a day-to-day basis. This would allow the filter to constantly update the prior probabilities necessary to use Bayes' theorem. With these probabilities, the filter can ask, "What is the probability that an email is spam, given the presence of a certain word?"

Applying the terms of Equation (4.9) on page 172, such a Bayesian spam filter would multiply the probability of finding the word in a spam email, $P(A|B)$, by the probability that the email is spam, $P(B)$, and then divide by the probability of finding the word in an email, the denominator in Equation (4.9). Bayesian spam filters also use shortcuts by focusing on a small set of words that have a high probability of being found in a spam message as well as on a small set of other words that have a low probability of being found in a spam message.

As spammers (people who send junk email) learned of such new filters, they tried to outfox them. Having learned that Bayesian filters might be assigning a high $P(A|B)$ value to words commonly found in spam, such as Viagra, spammers thought they could fool the filter by misspelling the word as Vi@gr@ or V1agra. What they overlooked was that the misspelled variants were even *more likely* to be found in a spam message than the original word. Thus, the misspelled variants made the job of spotting spam *easier* for the Bayesian filters.

Other spammers tried to fool the filters by adding "good" words, words that would have a low probability of being found in a spam message, or "rare" words, words not frequently encountered in any message. But these spammers overlooked the fact that the conditional probabilities are constantly updated and that words once considered "good" would be soon discarded from the good list by the filter as their $P(A|B)$ value increased. Likewise, as "rare" words grew more common in spam and yet stayed rare in ham, such words acted like the misspelled variants that others had tried earlier.

Even then, and perhaps after reading about Bayesian statistics, spammers thought that they could "break" Bayesian filters by inserting random words in their messages. Those random words would affect the filter by causing it to see many words whose $P(A|B)$ value would be low. The Bayesian filter would begin to label many spam messages as ham and end up being of no practical use. Spammers again overlooked that conditional probabilities are constantly updated.

Other spammers decided to eliminate all or most of the words in their messages and replace them with graphics so that Bayesian filters would have very few words with which to form conditional probabilities. But this approach failed, too, as Bayesian filters were rewritten to consider things other than words in a message. After all, Bayes' theorem concerns *events*, and "graphics present with no text" is as valid an event as "some word, *X*, present in a message." Other future tricks will ultimately fail for the same reason. (By the way, spam filters use non-Bayesian techniques as well, which makes spammers' lives even more difficult.)

Bayesian spam filters are an example of the unexpected way that applications of statistics can show up in your daily life. You will discover more examples as you read the rest of this book. By the way, the author of the two essays mentioned earlier was Thomas Bayes, who is a lot more famous for the second essay than the first essay, a failed attempt to use mathematics and logic to prove the existence of God.

Problems for Section 4.3

LEARNING THE BASICS

4.30 If $P(B) = 0.05$, $P(A|B) = 0.80$, $P(B') = 0.95$, and $P(A|B') = 0.40$, find $P(B|A)$.

4.31 If $P(B) = 0.30$, $P(A|B) = 0.60$, $P(B') = 0.70$, and and $P(A|B') = 0.50$, find $P(B|A)$.

APPLYING THE CONCEPTS

4.32 In Example 4.10 on page 173, suppose that the probability that a medical diagnostic test will give a positive result if the disease is not present is reduced from 0.02 to 0.01.

a. If the medical diagnostic test has given a positive result (indicating that the disease is present), what is the probability that the disease is actually present?

b. If the medical diagnostic test has given a negative result (indicating that the disease is not present), what is the probability that the disease is not present?

4.33 An advertising executive is studying television viewing habits of married men and women during prime-time hours. Based on past viewing records, the executive has determined that during prime time, husbands are watching television 60% of the time. When the husband is watching television, 40% of the time the wife is also watching. When the husband is not watching television, 30% of the time the wife is watching television.

a. Find the probability that if the wife is watching television, the husband is also watching television.

b. Find the probability that the wife is watching television during prime time.

SELF Test **4.34** Olive Construction Company is determining whether it should submit a bid for a new shopping center. In the past, Olive's main competitor, Base Construction Company, has submitted bids 70% of the time. If Base Construction Company does not bid on a job, the probability that Olive Construction Company will get the job is 0.50. If Base Construction Company bids on a job, the probability that Olive Construction Company will get the job is 0.25.

a. If Olive Construction Company gets the job, what is the probability that Base Construction Company did not bid?

b. What is the probability that Olive Construction Company will get the job?

4.35 Laid-off workers who become entrepreneurs because they cannot find meaningful employment with another company are known as *entrepreneurs by necessity. The Wall Street Journal* reported that these entrepreneurs by necessity are less likely to grow into large businesses than are *entrepreneurs by choice* (J. Bailey, "Desire—More Than Need—Builds a Business," *The Wall Street Journal*, May 21, 2001, p. B4). This article states that 89% of the entrepreneurs in the United States are entrepreneurs by choice and 11% are entrepreneurs by necessity. Only 2% of entrepreneurs by necessity expect their new business to employ 20 or more people within five years, whereas 14% of entrepreneurs by choice expect to employ at least 20 people within five years.

a. If an entrepreneur is selected at random and that individual expects that his or her new business will employ 20 or more people within five years, what is the probability that this individual is an entrepreneur by choice?

b. Discuss several possible reasons why entrepreneurs by choice are more likely than entrepreneurs by necessity to believe that they will grow their businesses.

4.36 The editor of a textbook publishing company is trying to decide whether to publish a proposed business statistics textbook. Information on previous textbooks published indicates that 10% are huge successes, 20% are modest successes, 40% break even, and 30% are losers. However, before a publishing decision is made, the book will be reviewed. In the past, 99% of the huge successes received favorable reviews, 70% of the moderate successes received favorable reviews, 40% of the break-even books received favorable reviews, and 20% of the losers received favorable reviews.

a. If the proposed textbook receives a favorable review, how should the editor revise the probabilities of the various outcomes to take this information into account?

b. What proportion of textbooks receives favorable reviews?

4.37 A municipal bond service has three rating categories (*A*, *B*, and *C*). Suppose that in the past year, of the municipal bonds issued throughout the United States, 70% were rated *A*, 20% were rated *B*, and 10% were rated *C*. Of the municipal bonds rated *A*, 50% were issued by cities, 40% by suburbs, and 10% by rural areas. Of the municipal bonds rated *B*, 60% were issued by cities, 20% by suburbs, and 20% by rural areas. Of the municipal bonds rated *C*, 90% were issued by cities, 5% by suburbs, and 5% by rural areas.

a. If a new municipal bond is to be issued by a city, what is the probability that it will receive an *A* rating?

b. What proportion of municipal bonds are issued by cities?

c. What proportion of municipal bonds are issued by suburbs?

4.4 Ethical Issues and Probability

Ethical issues can arise when any statements related to probability are presented to the public, particularly when these statements are part of an advertising campaign for a product or service. Unfortunately, many people are not comfortable with numerical concepts (see reference 4) and tend to misinterpret the meaning of the probability. In some instances, the misinterpretation is not intentional, but in other cases, advertisements may unethically try to mislead potential customers.

One example of a potentially unethical application of probability relates to advertisements for state lotteries. When purchasing a lottery ticket, the customer selects a set of numbers (such as 6) from a larger list of numbers (such as 54). Although virtually all participants know that they are unlikely to win the lottery, they also have very little idea of how unlikely it is for them to select all 6 winning numbers from the list of 54 numbers. They have even less of an idea of the probability of not selecting any winning numbers.

Given this background, you might consider a recent commercial for a state lottery that stated, "We won't stop until we have made everyone a millionaire" to be deceptive and possibly unethical. Do you think the state has any intention of ever stopping the lottery, given the fact that the state relies on it to bring millions of dollars into its treasury? Is it possible that the lottery can make everyone a millionaire? Is it ethical to suggest that the purpose of the lottery is to make everyone a millionaire?

Another example of a potentially unethical application of probability relates to an investment newsletter promising a 90% probability of a 20% annual return on investment. To make the claim in the newsletter an ethical one, the investment service needs to (a) explain the basis on which this probability estimate rests, (b) provide the probability statement in another format, such as 9 chances in 10, and (c) explain what happens to the investment in the 10% of the cases in which a 20% return is not achieved (e.g., is the entire investment lost?).

These are serious ethical issues. If you were going to write an advertisement for the state lottery that ethically describes the probability of winning a certain prize, what would you say? If you were going to write an advertisement for the investment newsletter that ethically states the probability of a 20% return on an investment, what would you say?

4.5 Counting Rules (*online*)

LEARN MORE

Learn more about counting rules in a Chapter 4 eBook bonus section (See Appendix C to learn how to access this bonus section.).

In many cases, there are a large number of possible outcomes, and determining the exact number of outcomes can be difficult. In these situations, rules have been developed for counting the exact number of possible outcomes.

USING STATISTICS Possibilities at M&R Electronics World, Revisited

Yuri Arcurs / Shutterstock

As the marketing manager for M&R Electronics World, you analyzed the survey results of an intent-to-purchase study. This study asked the heads of 1,000 households about their intentions to purchase a large-screen HDTV sometime during the next 12 months, and as a follow-up, M&R surveyed the same people 12 months later to see whether such a television was purchased. In addition, for households purchasing large-screen HDTVs, the survey asked whether the television they purchased had a faster refresh rate, whether they also purchased a streaming media box in the past 12 months, and whether they were satisfied with their purchase of the large-screen HDTV.

By analyzing the results of these surveys, you were able to uncover many pieces of valuable information that will help you plan a marketing strategy to enhance sales and better target those households likely to purchase multiple or more expensive products. Whereas only 30% of the households actually purchased a large-screen HDTV, if a household indicated that it planned to purchase a large-screen HDTV in the next 12 months, there was an 80% chance that the household actually made the purchase. Thus the marketing strategy should target those households that have indicated an intention to purchase.

You determined that for households that purchased a television that had a faster refresh rate, there was a 47.5% chance that the household also purchased a streaming media box. You then compared this conditional probability to the marginal probability of purchasing a streaming media box, which was 36%. Thus, households that purchased televisions that had a faster refresh rate are more likely to purchase a streaming media box than are households that purchased large-screen HDTVs that have a standard refresh rate.

You were also able to apply Bayes' theorem to M&R Electronics World's market research reports. The reports investigate a potential new television model prior to its scheduled release. If a favorable report was received, then there was a 64% chance that the new television model would be successful. However, if an unfavorable report was received, there is only a 16% chance that the model would be successful. Therefore, the marketing strategy of M&R needs to pay close attention to whether a report's conclusion is favorable or unfavorable.

SUMMARY

This chapter began by developing the basic concepts of probability. You learned that probability is a numeric value from 0 to 1 that represents the chance, likelihood, or possibility that a particular event will occur. In addition to simple probability, you learned about conditional probabilities and independent events. Bayes' theorem was used to revise previously calculated probabilities based on new information. Throughout the chapter, contingency tables and decision trees were used to display information. In the next chapter, important discrete probability distributions such as the binomial, Poisson, and hypergeometric distributions are developed.

REFERENCES

1. Bellhouse, D. R. "The Reverend Thomas Bayes, FRS: A Biography to Celebrate the Tercentenary of His Birth." *Statistical Science*, 19 (2004), 3–43.
2. Lowd, D., and C. Meek. "Good Word Attacks on Statistical Spam Filters." Presented at the Second Conference on Email and Anti-Spam, 2005.
3. Microsoft Excel 2010. Redmond, WA: Microsoft Corp., 2010.
4. Paulos, J. A. *Innumeracy*. New York: Hill and Wang, 1988.
5. Silberman, S. "The Quest for Meaning," *Wired 8.02*, February 2000.
6. Zeller, T. "The Fight Against V1@gra (and Other Spam)." *The New York Times*, May 21, 2006, pp. B1, B6.

KEY EQUATIONS

Probability of Occurrence

$$\text{Probability of occurrence} = \frac{X}{T} \tag{4.1}$$

Marginal Probability

$$P(A) = P(A \text{ and } B_1) + P(A \text{ and } B_2) + \cdots + P(A \text{ and } B_k) \tag{4.2}$$

General Addition Rule

$$P(A \text{ or } B) = P(A) + P(B) - P(A \text{ and } B) \tag{4.3}$$

Conditional Probability

$$P(A|B) = \frac{P(A \text{ and } B)}{P(B)} \tag{4.4a}$$

$$P(B|A) = \frac{P(A \text{ and } B)}{P(A)} \tag{4.4b}$$

Independence

$$P(A|B) = P(A) \tag{4.5}$$

General Multiplication Rule

$$P(A \text{ and } B) = P(A|B)P(B) \tag{4.6}$$

Multiplication Rule for Independent Events

$$P(A \text{ and } B) = P(A)P(B) \tag{4.7}$$

Marginal Probability Using the General Multiplication Rule

$$P(A) = P(A|B_1)P(B_1) + P(A|B_2)P(B_2) + \cdots + P(A|B_k)P(B_k) \tag{4.8}$$

Bayes' Theorem

$$P(B_i|A) = \frac{P(A|B_i)P(B_i)}{P(A|B_1)P(B_1) + P(A|B_2)P(B_2) + \cdots + P(A|B_k)P(B_k)} \tag{4.9}$$

KEY TERMS

a priori probability 156
Bayes' theorem 172
certain event 156
collectively exhaustive 160
complement 157
conditional probability 164
contingency table 158
decision tree 166
empirical probability 157
event 157
general addition rule 161
general multiplication rule 168
impossible event 156
independence 167
joint event 157
joint probability 159
marginal probability 160
multiplication rule for independent events 169
mutually exclusive 160
probability 156
sample space 157
simple event 157
simple probability 158
subjective probability 157

CHECKING YOUR UNDERSTANDING

4.38 What are the differences between *a priori* probability, empirical probability, and subjective probability?

4.39 What is the difference between a simple event and a joint event?

4.40 How can you use the general addition rule to find the probability of occurrence of event *A* or *B*?

4.41 What is the difference between mutually exclusive and collectively exhaustive events?

4.42 How does conditional probability relate to the concept of independence?

4.43 How does the multiplication rule differ for events that are and are not independent?

4.44 How can you use Bayes' theorem to revise probabilities in light of new information?

4.45 In Bayes' theorem, how does the prior probability differ from the revised probability?

CHAPTER REVIEW PROBLEMS

4.46 A survey by the Health Research Institute at PricewaterhouseCoopers LLP indicated that 80% of "young invincibles" (those aged 18 to 24) are likely to share health information through social media, as compared to 45% of "baby boomers" (those aged 45 to 64).

Source: Data extracted from "Social Media 'Likes' Healthcare: From Marketing to Social Business," Health Research Institute, April 2012, p. 8, **pwchealth.com/cgi-local/hregister.cgi/reg/health-care-social-media-report.pdf**.

Suppose that the survey was based on 500 respondents from each of the two groups.

a. Construct a contingency table.
b. Give an example of a simple event and a joint event.
c. What is the probability that a randomly selected respondent is likely to share health information through social media?
d. What is the probability that a randomly selected respondent is likely to share health information through social media *and* is in the 45-to-64-year-old group?
e. Are the events "age group" and "likely to share health information through social media" independent? Explain.

4.47 The owner of a restaurant serving Continental-style entrées was interested in studying ordering patterns of patrons for the Friday-to-Sunday weekend time period. Records were maintained that indicated the demand for dessert during the same time period. The owner decided to study two other variables, along with whether a dessert was ordered: the gender of the individual and whether a beef entrée was ordered. The results are as follows:

DESSERT ORDERED	GENDER		
	Male	Female	Total
Yes	96	40	136
No	224	240	464
Total	320	280	600

DESSERT ORDERED	BEEF ENTRÉE		
	Yes	No	Total
Yes	71	65	136
No	116	348	464
Total	187	413	600

A waiter approaches a table to take an order for dessert. What is the probability that the first customer to order at the table

a. orders a dessert?
b. orders a dessert *or* has ordered a beef entrée?
c. is a female *and* does not order a dessert?
d. is a female *or* does not order a dessert?
e. Suppose the first person from whom the waiter takes the dessert order is a female. What is the probability that she does not order dessert?
f. Are gender and ordering dessert independent?
g. Is ordering a beef entrée independent of whether the person orders dessert?

4.48 The 2012 Restaurant Industry Forecast takes a closer look at today's consumers. Based on a 2011 National Restaurant Association survey, consumers are divided into three segments (optimistic, cautious, and hunkered-down) based on their financial situation, current spending behavior, and economic outlook. Suppose the results, based on a sample of 100 males and 100 females, were as follows:

CONSUMER SEGMENT	GENDER		
	Male	Female	Total
Optimistic	26	16	42
Cautious	41	43	84
Hunkered-down	33	41	74
Total	100	100	200

Source: Data extracted from "The 2012 Restaurant Industry Forecast," National Restaurant Association, 2012, p. 12. **restaurant.org/research/forecast**.

If a consumer is selected at random, what is the probability that he or she

a. is classified as cautious?
b. is classified as optimistic or cautious?
c. is a male *or* is classified as hunkered-down?
d. is a male *and* is classified as hunkered-down?
e. Given that the consumer selected is a female, what is the probability that she is classified as optimistic?

4.49 According to a Gallup poll, companies with employees who are engaged with their workplace have greater innovation, productivity, and profitability, as well as less employee turnover. A survey of 1,895 workers in Germany found that 13% of the workers were engaged, 67% were not engaged, and 20% were actively disengaged. The survey also noted that 48% of engaged workers strongly agreed with the statement "My current job brings out my most creative ideas." Only 20% of the not engaged workers and 3% of the actively disengaged workers agreed with this statement (data extracted from M. Nink, "Employee Disengagement Plagues Germany," *Gallup Management Journal*, gmj.gallup.com, April 9, 2009). If a worker is known to strongly agree with the statement "My current job brings out my most creative ideas," what is the probability that the worker is engaged?

4.50 Sport utility vehicles (SUVs), vans, and pickups are generally considered to be more prone to roll over than cars. In 1997, 24.0% of all highway fatalities involved rollovers; 15.8% of all fatalities in 1997 involved SUVs, vans, and pickups, given that the fatality involved a rollover. Given that a rollover was not involved, 5.6% of all fatalities involved SUVs, vans, and pickups (data extracted from A. Wilde Mathews, "Ford Ranger, Chevy Tracker Tilt in Test," *The Wall Street Journal*, July 14, 1999, p. A2). Consider the following definitions:

A = fatality involved an SUV, van, or pickup
B = fatality involved a rollover

a. Use Bayes' theorem to find the probability that a fatality involved a rollover, given that the fatality involved an SUV, a van, or a pickup.
b. Compare the result in (a) to the probability that a fatality involved a rollover and comment on whether SUVs, vans, and pickups are generally more prone to rollover accidents than other vehicles.

4.51 Enzyme-linked immunosorbent assay (ELISA) is the most common type of screening test for detecting the HIV virus. A positive result from an ELISA indicates that the HIV virus is present. For most populations, ELISA has a high degree of sensitivity (to detect infection) and specificity (to detect noninfection). (See "HIV InSite Gateway to HIV and AIDS Knowledge" at **HIVInsite.ucsf.edu**.) Suppose the probability that a person is infected with the HIV virus for a certain population is 0.015. If the HIV virus is actually present, the probability that the ELISA test will give a positive result is 0.995. If the HIV virus is not actually present, the probability of a positive result from an ELISA is 0.01. If the ELISA has given a positive result, use Bayes' theorem to find the probability that the HIV virus is actually present.

CASES FOR CHAPTER 4

Digital Case

Apply your knowledge about contingency tables and the proper application of simple and joint probabilities in this continuing Digital Case from Chapter 3.

Open **EndRunGuide.pdf**, the EndRun Financial Services "Guide to Investing," and read the information about the Guaranteed Investment Package (GIP). Read the claims and examine the supporting data. Then answer the following questions:

1. How accurate is the claim of the probability of success for EndRun's GIP? In what ways is the claim misleading? How would you calculate and state the probability of having an annual rate of return not less than 15%?
2. Using the table found under the "Show Me the Winning Probabilities" subhead, compute the proper probabilities for the group of investors. What mistake was made in reporting the 7% probability claim?
3. Are there any probability calculations that would be appropriate for rating an investment service? Why or why not?

CardioGood Fitness

1. For each CardioGood Fitness treadmill product line (see the CardioGoodFitness file), construct two-way contingency tables of gender, education in years, relationship status, and self-rated fitness. (There will be a total of 8 tables for each treadmill product.)
2. For each table you construct, compute all conditional and marginal probabilities.
3. Write a report detailing your findings to be presented to the management of CardioGood Fitness.

The Choice *Is* Yours Follow-up

1. Follow up the "Using Statistics: The Choice *Is* Yours, Revisited" on page 83 by constructing contingency tables of market cap and type, market cap and risk, market cap and rating, type and risk, type and rating, and risk and rating for the sample of 318 retirement funds stored in Retirement Funds.
2. For each table you construct, compute all conditional and marginal probabilities.
3. Write a report summarizing your conclusions.

Clear Mountain State Student Surveys

The Student News Service at Clear Mountain State University (CMSU) has decided to gather data about the undergraduate students that attend CMSU. CMSU creates and distributes a survey of 14 questions and receive responses from 62 undergraduates (stored in UndergradSurvey).

1. For these data, construct contingency tables of gender and major, gender and graduate school intention, gender and employment status, gender and computer preference, class and graduate school intention, class and employment status, major and graduate school intention, major and employment status, and major and computer preference.

   a. For each of these contingency tables, compute all the conditional and marginal probabilities.

   b. Write a report summarizing your conclusions.

2. The Dean of Students at Clear Mountain State University has learned about the undergraduate survey and has decided to undertake a similar survey for graduate students at Clear Mountain State. She creates and distributes a survey of 14 questions and receives responses from 44 graduate students (stored in GradSurvey). Construct contingency tables of gender and graduate major, gender and undergraduate major, gender and employment status, gender and computer preference, graduate major and undergraduate major, graduate major and employment status, and graduate major and computer preference.

a. For each of these contingency tables, compute all the conditional and marginal probabilities.
b. Write a report summarizing your conclusions.

CHAPTER 4 EXCEL GUIDE

EG4.1 BASIC PROBABILITY CONCEPTS

Simple and Joint Probability and the General Addition Rule

Key Technique Use Excel arithmetic formulas.

Example Compute simple and joint probabilities for the Table 4.1 purchase behavior data on page 158.

PHStat2 Use **Simple & Joint Probabilities.**
For the example, select **PHStat → Probability & Prob. Distributions → Simple & Joint Probabilities.** In the new worksheet template, similar to Figure EG4.1 below, fill in the **Sample Space** area with your data.

In-Depth Excel Use the **COMPUTE worksheet** of the **Probabilities workbook** as a template.
The worksheet (shown in Figure EG4.1) already contains the Table 4.1 purchase behavior data. For other problems, change the sample space table entries in the cell ranges **C3:D4** and **A5:D6.**

Read the SHORT TAKES for Chapter 4 for an explanation of the formulas found in the COMPUTE worksheet (shown in the **COMPUTE_FORMULAS worksheet**).

EG4.2 CONDITIONAL PROBABILITY

There is no Excel material for this section.

FIGURE EG4.1 COMPUTE worksheet of the Probabilities workbook

	A	B	C	D	E
1	**Probabilities**				
2					
3	**Sample Space**		**ACTUALLY PURCHASED**		
4			Yes	No	Totals
5	**PLANNED TO PURCHASE**	Yes	200	50	250
6		No	100	650	750
7		Totals	300	700	1000
8					
9	**Simple Probabilities**				
10	P(Yes)	0.25			
11	P(No)	0.75			
12	P(Yes)	0.30			
13	P(No)	0.70			
14					
15	**Joint Probabilities**				
16	P(Yes and Yes)	0.20			
17	P(Yes and No)	0.05			
18	P(No and Yes)	0.10			
19	P(No and No)	0.65			
20					
21	**Addition Rule**				
22	P(Yes or Yes)	0.35			
23	P(Yes or No)	0.90			
24	P(No or Yes)	0.95			
25	P(No or No)	0.80			

Simple Probabilities	
="P(" & B5 & ")"	=E5/E7
="P(" & B6 & ")"	=E6/E7
="P(" & C4 & ")"	=C7/E7
="P(" & D4 & ")"	=D7/E7
Joint Probabilities	
="P(" & B5 & " and " & C4 & ")"	=C5/E7
="P(" & B5 & " and " & D4 & ")"	=D5/E7
="P(" & B6 & " and " & C4 & ")"	=C6/E7
="P(" & B6 & " and " & D4 & ")"	=D6/E7
Addition Rule	
="P(" & B5 & " or " & C4 & ")"	=H16 + H18 - H22
="P(" & B5 & " or " & D4 & ")"	=H16 + H19 - H23
="P(" & B6 & " or " & C4 & ")"	=H17 + H18 - H24
="P(" & B6 & " or " & D4 & ")"	=H17 + H19 - H25

EG4.3 BAYES' THEOREM

Key Technique Use Excel arithmetic formulas.

Example Apply Bayes' theorem to the television marketing example in Section 4.3.

In-Depth Excel Use the **COMPUTE worksheet** of the **Bayes workbook** as a template.

The worksheet (shown below) already contains the probabilities for the Section 4.3 example. For other problems, change those probabilities in the cell range **B5:C6.**

Open to the **COMPUTE_FORMULAS worksheet** to examine the arithmetic formulas that compute the probabilities, which are also shown as an inset to the worksheet.

	A	B	C	D	E
1	**Bayes' Theorem Computations**				
2					
3		**Probabilities**			
4	**Event**	Prior	Conditional	Joint	Revised
5	**S**	0.4	0.8	0.32	0.64
6	**S'**	0.6	0.3	0.18	0.36
7			**Total:**	0.5	

Joint	**Revised**
=B5 * C5	=D5/$D$7
=B6 * C6	=D6/$D$7
=D5 + D6	

CHAPTER

5 Discrete Probability Distributions

Learning Objectives

In this chapter, you learn:

- The properties of a probability distribution
- To compute the expected value and variance of a probability distribution
- To calculate the covariance and understand its use in finance
- To compute probabilities from the binomial, Poisson, and hypergeometric distributions
- How the binomial, Poisson, and hypergeometric distributions can be used to solve business problems

USING STATISTICS

Monkey Business Images / Shutterstock

Events of Interest at Ricknel Home Centers

Like most other large businesses, Ricknel Home Centers, LLC, a regional home improvement chain, uses an accounting information system (AIS) to manage its accounting and financial data. The Ricknel AIS collects, organizes, stores, analyzes, and distributes financial information to decision makers both inside and outside the firm.

One important function of the Ricknel AIS is to continuously audit accounting information, looking for errors or incomplete or improbable information. For example, when customers submit orders online, the Ricknel AIS reviews the orders for possible mistakes. Any questionable invoices are tagged and included in a daily *exceptions report*. Recent data collected by the company show that the likelihood is 0.10 that an order form will be tagged.

As a member of the AIS team, you have been asked by Ricknel management to determine the likelihood of finding a certain number of tagged forms in a sample of a specific size. For example, what would be the likelihood that none of the order forms are tagged in a sample of four forms? That one of the order forms is tagged?

How could you determine the solution to this type of probability problem? One way is to use a model, or small-scale representation, that approximates the process. By using such an approximation, you could make inferences about the actual order process. In this case, you can use a *probability distribution*, a mathematical model suited for solving the type of probability problems that Ricknel managers have posed.

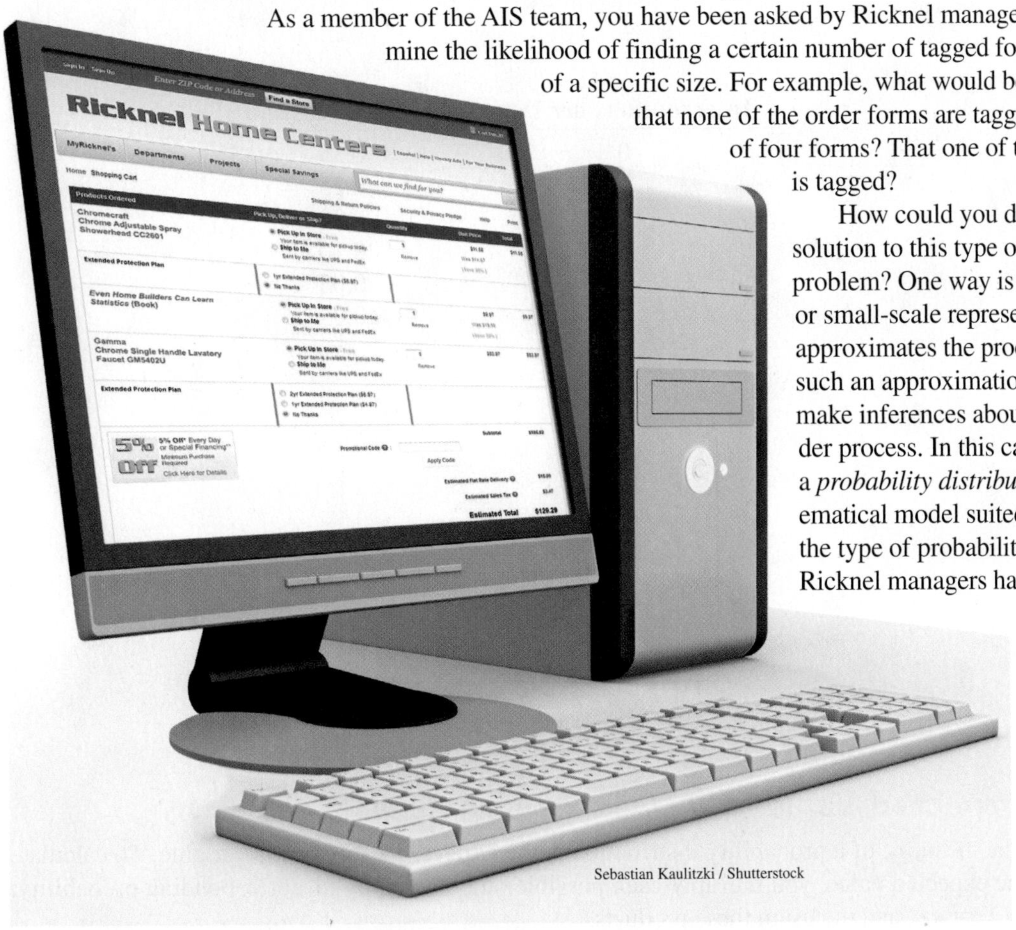

Sebastian Kaulitzki / Shutterstock

This chapter introduces you to the concept and characteristics of probability distributions. You will learn how the knowledge about a probability distribution can help you choose between alternative investment strategies. You will also learn how the binomial, Poisson, and hypergeometric distributions can be applied to help solve business problems.

5.1 The Probability Distribution for a Discrete Variable

Recall from Section 1.1 that *numerical* variables are variables that have values that represent quantities, such as the three-year return percentage for a retirement fund or the number of social media sites to which you belong. Some numerical variables are *discrete*, having numerical values that arise from a counting process, while others are *continuous*, having numerical values that arise from a measuring process (e.g., the three-year returns of growth and value funds that were the subject of the Using Statistics scenario in Chapters 2 and 3). This chapter deals with probability distributions that represent a discrete numerical variable, such as the number of social media sites to which you belong.

PROBABILITY DISTRIBUTION FOR A DISCRETE VARIABLE

A **probability distribution for a discrete variable** is a mutually exclusive list of all the possible numerical outcomes along with the probability of occurrence of each outcome.

For example, Table 5.1 gives the distribution of the number of interruptions per day in a large computer network. The list in Table 5.1 is collectively exhaustive because all possible outcomes are included. Thus, the probabilities sum to 1. Figure 5.1 is a graphical representation of Table 5.1.

TABLE 5.1

Probability Distribution of the Number of Interruptions per Day

Interruptions per Day	Probability
0	0.35
1	0.25
2	0.20
3	0.10
4	0.05
5	0.05

FIGURE 5.1

Probability distribution of the number of interruptions per day

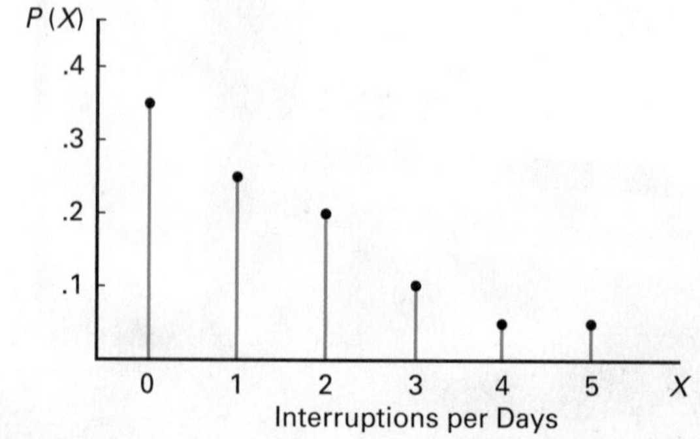

Student Tip

Remember, *expected value* is just another word for *mean.*

Expected Value of a Discrete Variable

The mean, μ, of a probability distribution is the **expected value** of the variable. To calculate the expected value, you multiply each possible outcome, x, by its corresponding probability, $P(X = x_i)$, and then sum these products.

EXPECTED VALUE, μ, OF A DISCRETE VARIABLE

$$\mu = E(X) = \sum_{i=1}^{N} x_i P(X = x_i) \tag{5.1}$$

where

x_i = the ith outcome of the discrete variable X

$P(X = x_i)$ = probability of occurrence of the ith outcome of X

For the probability distribution of the number of interruptions per day in a large computer network (Table 5.1), the expected value is computed as follows, using Equation (5.1), and is also shown in Table 5.2:

$$\begin{aligned}\mu = E(X) &= \sum_{i=1}^{N} x_i P(X = x_i)\\ &= (0)(0.35) + (1)(0.25) + (2)(0.20) + (3)(0.10) + (4)(0.05) + (5)(0.05)\\ &= 0 + 0.25 + 0.40 + 0.30 + 0.20 + 0.25\\ &= 1.40\end{aligned}$$

TABLE 5.2

Computing the Expected Value of the Number of Interruptions per Day

Interruptions per Day (x_i)	$P(X = x_i)$	$x_i P(X = x_i)$
0	0.35	$(0)(0.35) = 0.00$
1	0.25	$(1)(0.25) = 0.25$
2	0.20	$(2)(0.20) = 0.40$
3	0.10	$(3)(0.10) = 0.30$
4	0.05	$(4)(0.05) = 0.20$
5	0.05	$(5)(0.05) = 0.25$
	1.00	$\mu = E(X) = 1.40$

The expected value is 1.40. The expected value of 1.40 for the number of interruptions per day is not a possible outcome because the actual number of interruptions in a given day must be an integer value. The expected value represents the *mean* number of interruptions in a given day.

Variance and Standard Deviation of a Discrete Variable

You compute the variance of a probability distribution by multiplying each possible squared difference $[x_i - E(X)]^2$ by its corresponding probability, $P(X = x_i)$, and then summing the resulting products. Equation (5.2) defines the **variance of a discrete variable**, and Equation (5.3) defines the **standard deviation of a discrete variable**.

VARIANCE OF A DISCRETE VARIABLE

$$\sigma^2 = \sum_{i=1}^{N} [x_i - E(X)]^2 P(X = x_i) \tag{5.2}$$

where

x_i = the ith outcome of the discrete variable X

$P(X = x_i)$ = probability of occurrence of the ith outcome of X

Use the Section EG5.1 instructions to compute the variance and standard deviation of a discrete variable.

STANDARD DEVIATION OF A DISCRETE VARIABLE

$$\sigma = \sqrt{\sigma^2} = \sqrt{\sum_{i=1}^{N}[x_i - E(X)]^2 P(X = x_i)} \tag{5.3}$$

The variance and the standard deviation of the number of interruptions per day are computed as follows and in Table 5.3, using Equations (5.2) and (5.3):

$$\begin{aligned}\sigma^2 &= \sum_{i=1}^{N}[x_i - E(X)]^2 P(X = x_i)\\ &= (0 - 1.4)^2(0.35) + (1 - 1.4)^2(0.25) + (2 - 1.4)^2(0.20) + (3 - 1.4)^2(0.10)\\ &\quad + (4 - 1.4)^2(0.05) + (5 - 1.4)^2(0.05)\\ &= 0.686 + 0.040 + 0.072 + 0.256 + 0.338 + 0.648\\ &= 2.04\end{aligned}$$

and

$$\sigma = \sqrt{\sigma^2} = \sqrt{2.04} = 1.4283$$

TABLE 5.3

Computing the Variance and Standard Deviation of the Number of Interruptions per Day

Interruptions per Day (x_i)	$P(X = x_i)$	$x_iP(X = x_i)$	$[x_i - E(X)]^2$	$[x_i - E(X)]^2 P(X = x_i)$
0	0.35	0.00	$(0 - 1.4)^2 = 1.96$	$(1.96)(0.35) = 0.686$
1	0.25	0.25	$(1 - 1.4)^2 = 0.96$	$(0.96)(0.25) = 0.040$
2	0.20	0.40	$(2 - 1.4)^2 = 0.36$	$(0.36)(0.20) = 0.072$
3	0.10	0.30	$(3 - 1.4)^2 = 2.56$	$(2.56)(0.10) = 0.256$
4	0.05	0.20	$(4 - 1.4)^2 = 6.76$	$(6.76)(0.05) = 0.338$
5	0.05	0.25	$(5 - 1.4)^2 = 12.96$	$(12.96)(0.05) = 0.648$
	1.00	$\mu = E(X) = 1.40$		$\sigma^2 = 2.04$
				and $\sigma = \sqrt{\sigma^2} = \sqrt{2.04} = 1.4283$

Thus, the mean number of interruptions per day is 1.4, the variance is 2.04, and the standard deviation is approximately 1.43 interruptions per day.

Problems for Section 5.1

LEARNING THE BASICS

5.1 Given the following probability distributions:

Distribution *A*		Distribution *B*	
X	$P(X = x_i)$	X	$P(X = x_i)$
0	0.50	0	0.05
1	0.20	1	0.10
2	0.15	2	0.15
3	0.10	3	0.20
4	0.05	4	0.50

a. Compute the expected value for each distribution.
b. Compute the standard deviation for each distribution.
c. Compare the results of distributions *A* and *B*.

APPLYING THE CONCEPTS

SELF Test **5.2** The following table contains the probability distribution for the number of traffic accidents daily in a small city:

Number of Accidents Daily (X)	$P(X = x_i)$
0	0.10
1	0.20
2	0.45
3	0.15
4	0.05
5	0.05

a. Compute the mean number of accidents per day.
b. Compute the standard deviation.

5.3 Recently, a regional automobile dealership sent out fliers to perspective customers, indicating that they had already won one of three different prizes: a Kia Optima valued at $15,000, a $500 gas card, or a $5 Walmart shopping card. To claim his or her prize, a prospective customer needed to present the flier at the dealership's showroom. The fine print on the back of the flier listed the probabilities of winning. The chance of winning the car was 1 out of 31,478, the chance of winning the gas card was 1 out of 31,478, and the chance of winning the shopping card was 31,476 out 31,478.

a. How many fliers do you think the automobile dealership sent out?

b. Using your answer to (a) and the probabilities listed on the flier, what is the expected value of the prize won by a prospective customer receiving a flier?

c. Using your answer to (a) and the probabilities listed on the flier, what is the standard deviation of the value of the prize won by a prospective customer receiving a flier?

d. Do you think this is an effective promotion? Why or why not?

5.4 In the carnival game Under-or-Over-Seven, a pair of fair dice is rolled once, and the resulting sum determines whether the player wins or loses his or her bet. For example, the player can bet $1 that the sum will be under 7—that is, 2, 3, 4, 5, or 6. For this bet, the player wins $1 if the result is under 7 and loses $1 if the outcome equals or is greater than 7. Similarly, the player can bet $1 that the sum will be over 7—that is, 8, 9, 10, 11, or 12. Here, the player wins $1 if the result is over 7 but loses $1 if the result is 7 or under. A third method of play is to bet $1 on the outcome 7. For this bet, the player wins $4 if the result of the roll is 7 and loses $1 otherwise.

a. Construct the probability distribution representing the different outcomes that are possible for a $1 bet on under 7.

b. Construct the probability distribution representing the different outcomes that are possible for a $1 bet on over 7.

c. Construct the probability distribution representing the different outcomes that are possible for a $1 bet on 7.

d. Show that the expected long-run profit (or loss) to the player is the same, no matter which method of play is used.

5.5 The number of arrivals per minute at a bank located in the central business district of a large city was recorded over a period of 200 minutes, with the following results:

Arrivals	Frequency
0	14
1	31
2	47
3	41
4	29
5	21
6	10
7	5
8	2

a. Compute the expected number of arrivals per minute.

b. Compute the standard deviation.

5.6 The manager of the commercial mortgage department of a large bank has collected data during the past two years concerning the number of commercial mortgages approved per week. The results from these two years (104 weeks) are as follows:

Number of Commercial Mortgages Approved	Frequency
0	13
1	25
2	32
3	17
4	9
5	6
6	1
7	1

a. Compute the expected number of mortgages approved per week.

b. Compute the standard deviation.

5.2 Covariance of a Probability Distribution and Its Application in Finance

Section 5.1 defined the expected value, variance, and standard deviation for a single discrete variable. In this section, the covariance between two variables is introduced and applied to portfolio management, a topic of great interest to financial analysts.

Covariance

The **covariance of a probability distribution** (σ_{XY}) measures the strength of the relationship between two numerical variables, *X* and *Y*. A positive covariance indicates a positive relationship. A negative covariance indicates a negative relationship. A covariance of 0 indicates that the two variables are independent. Equation (5.4) defines the covariance for a discrete probability distribution.

COVARIANCE

$$\sigma_{XY} = \sum_{i=1}^{N}[x_i - E(X)][y_i - E(Y)]P(x_i y_i) \quad \textbf{(5.4)}$$

where

X = discrete variable X

x_i = ith outcome of X

Y = discrete variable Y

y_i = ith outcome of Y

$P(x_i y_i)$ = probability of occurrence of the ith outcome of X and the ith outcome of Y

$i = 1, 2, \ldots, N$ for X and Y

To illustrate the covariance, suppose that you are deciding between two different investments for the coming year. The first investment is a mutual fund that consists of the stocks that comprise the Dow Jones Industrial Average. The second investment is a mutual fund that is expected to perform best when economic conditions are weak. Table 5.4 summarizes your estimate of the returns (per \$1,000 investment) under three economic conditions, each with a given probability of occurrence.

TABLE 5.4
Estimated Returns for Each Investment Under Three Economic Conditions

$P(x_i y_i)$	Economic Condition	Investment: Dow Jones Fund	Investment: Weak-Economy Fund
0.2	Recession	−\$300	+\$200
0.5	Stable economy	+100	+50
0.3	Expanding economy	+250	−100

The expected value and standard deviation for each investment and the covariance of the two investments are computed as follows:

Student Tip
The covariance discussed in this section measures the strength of the linear relationship between the *probability distributions* of two variables, while the *sample* covariance discussed in Chapter 3 measures the strength of the linear relationship between two numerical variables.

Let X = Dow Jones fund and Y = weak-economy fund

$$E(X) = \mu_X = (-300)(0.2) + (100)(0.5) + (250)(0.3) = \$65$$

$$E(Y) = \mu_Y = (+200)(0.2) + (50)(0.5) + (-100)(0.3) = \$35$$

$$Var(X) = \sigma_X^2 = (-300 - 65)^2(0.2) + (100 - 65)^2(0.5) + (250 - 65)^2(0.3)$$

$$= 37{,}525$$

$$\sigma_X = \$193.71$$

$$Var(Y) = \sigma_Y^2 = (200 - 35)^2(0.2) + (50 - 35)^2(0.5) + (-100 - 35)^2(0.3)$$

$$= 11{,}025$$

$$\sigma_Y = \$105.00$$

$$\sigma_{XY} = (-300 - 65)(200 - 35)(0.2) + (100 - 65)(50 - 35)(0.5)$$

$$+ (250 - 65)(-100 - 35)(0.3)$$

$$= -12{,}045 + 262.5 - 7{,}492.5$$

$$= -19{,}275$$

Thus, the Dow Jones fund has a higher expected value (i.e., larger expected return) than the weak-economy fund but also has a higher standard deviation (i.e., more risk). The covariance of −19,275 between the two investments indicates a negative relationship in which the two investments are varying in the *opposite* direction. Therefore, when the return on one investment is high, typically, the return on the other investment is low.

Expected Value, Variance, and Standard Deviation of the Sum of Two Variables

Equations (5.1) through (5.3) define the expected value, variance, and standard deviation of a probability distribution, and Equation (5.4) defines the covariance between two variables, X and Y. The **expected value of the sum of two variables** is equal to the sum of the expected values. The **variance of the sum of two variables** is equal to the sum of the variances plus twice the covariance. The **standard deviation of the sum of two variables** is the square root of the variance of the sum of two variables.

EXPECTED VALUE OF THE SUM OF TWO VARIABLES

$$E(X+Y) = E(X) + E(Y) \quad \textbf{(5.5)}$$

VARIANCE OF THE SUM OF TWO VARIABLES

$$Var(X+Y) = \sigma_{X+Y}^2 = \sigma_X^2 + \sigma_Y^2 + 2\sigma_{XY} \quad \textbf{(5.6)}$$

STANDARD DEVIATION OF THE SUM OF TWO VARIABLES

$$\sigma_{X+Y} = \sqrt{\sigma_{X+Y}^2} \quad \textbf{(5.7)}$$

To illustrate the expected value, variance, and standard deviation of the sum of two variables, consider the two investments previously discussed. If X = Dow Jones fund and Y = weak-economy fund, using Equations (5.5), (5.6), and (5.7),

$$E(X+Y) = E(X) + E(Y) = 65 + 35 = \$100$$

$$\begin{aligned}\sigma_{X+Y}^2 &= \sigma_X^2 + \sigma_Y^2 + 2\sigma_{XY}\\ &= 37{,}525 + 11{,}025 + (2)(-19{,}275)\\ &= 10{,}000\\ \sigma_{X+Y} &= \$100\end{aligned}$$

The expected value of the sum of the Dow Jones fund and the weak-economy fund is \$100, with a standard deviation of \$100. The standard deviation of the sum of the two investments is less than the standard deviation of either single investment because there is a large negative covariance between the investments.

Portfolio Expected Return and Portfolio Risk

The covariance and the expected value and standard deviation of the sum of two random variables can be applied to analyzing **portfolios**, or groupings of assets made for investment purposes. Investors combine assets into portfolios to reduce their risk (see references 1 and 2). Often, the objective is to maximize the return while minimizing the risk. For such portfolios, rather than study the sum of two random variables, the investor weights each investment by the proportion of assets assigned to that investment. Equations (5.8) and (5.9) define the **portfolio expected return** and **portfolio risk**.

PORTFOLIO EXPECTED RETURN

The portfolio expected return for a two-asset investment is equal to the weight assigned to asset *X* multiplied by the expected return of asset *X* plus the weight assigned to asset *Y* multiplied by the expected return of asset *Y*.

$$E(P) = wE(X) + (1 - w)E(Y) \quad \textbf{(5.8)}$$

where

$E(P)$ = portfolio expected return

w = portion of the portfolio value assigned to asset *X*

$(1 - w)$ = portion of the portfolio value assigned to asset *Y*

$E(X)$ = expected return of asset *X*

$E(Y)$ = expected return of asset *Y*

PORTFOLIO RISK

The portfolio risk for a two-asset investment is equal to the square root of the sum of these three products: w^2 multiplied by the variance of *X*, $(1 - w)^2$ multiplied by the variance of *Y*, and 2 multiplied by w multiplied by $(1 - w)$ multiplied by the covariance.

$$\sigma_p = \sqrt{w^2\sigma_X^2 + (1 - w)^2\sigma_Y^2 + 2w(1 - w)\sigma_{XY}} \quad \textbf{(5.9)}$$

In the previous section, you evaluated the expected return and risk of two different investments, a Dow Jones fund and a weak-economy fund. You also computed the covariance of the two investments. Now, suppose that you want to form a portfolio of these two investments that consists of an equal investment in each of these two funds. To compute the portfolio expected return and the portfolio risk, using Equations (5.8) and (5.9), with $w = 0.50$, $E(X) = \$65$, $E(Y) = \$35$, $\sigma_X^2 = 37{,}525$, $\sigma_Y^2 = 11{,}025$, and $\sigma_{XY} = -19{,}275$,

$$E(P) = (0.5)(65) + (1 - 0.5)(35) = \$50$$

$$\sigma_p = \sqrt{(0.5)^2(37{,}525) + (1 - 0.5)^2(11{,}025) + 2(0.5)(1 - 0.5)(-19{,}275)}$$

$$= \sqrt{2{,}500} = \$50$$

Thus, the portfolio has an expected return of \$50 for each \$1,000 invested (a return of 5%) and a portfolio risk of \$50. The portfolio risk here is smaller than the standard deviation of either investment because there is a large negative covariance between the two investments. The fact that each investment performs best under different circumstances reduces the overall risk of the portfolio.

Collapses in the financial marketplace that have occurred in the recent past have caused some investors to consider the effect of outcomes that have a only small chance of occurring but that could produce extremely negative results. (Some, including the author of reference 5, have labeled these outcomes "black swans.") Example 5.1 considers such an outcome by examining the expected return, the standard deviation of the return, and the covariance of two investment strategies—one that invests in a fund that does well when there is an extreme recession and the other that invests in a fund that does well under positive economic conditions.

EXAMPLE 5.1

Computing the Expected Return, the Standard Deviation of the Return, and the Covariance of Two Investment Strategies

You plan to invest $1,000 in one of two funds. Table 5.5 shows the annual return (per $1,000) of each of these investments under different economic conditions, along with the probability that each of these economic conditions will occur.

TABLE 5.5

Estimated Returns of Two Funds

Probability	Economic Condition	"Black Swan" Fund	Good Times Fund
0.01	Extreme recession	400	−200
0.09	Recession	−30	−100
0.15	Stagnation	30	50
0.35	Slow growth	50	90
0.30	Moderate growth	100	250
0.10	High growth	100	225

For the Black Swan fund and the Good Times fund, compute the expected return and standard deviation of the return for each fund, and the covariance between the two funds. Would you invest in the Black Swan fund or the Good Times fund? Explain.

SOLUTION Let $X =$ Black Swan fund and $Y =$ Good Times fund.

$$E(X) = \mu_X = (400)(0.01) + (-30)(0.09) + (30)(0.15) + (50)(0.35) + (100)(0.30) + (100)(0.1) = \$63.30$$

$$E(Y) = \mu_Y = (-200)(0.01) + (-100)(0.09) + (50)(0.15) + (90)(0.35) (250)(0.30) + (225)(0.10) = \$125.50$$

$$Var(X) = \sigma_X^2 = (400 - 63.30)^2(0.01) + (-30 - 63.30)^2(0.09) + (30 - 63.30)^2(0.15) (50 - 63.30)^2(0.35) + (100 - 63.30)^2(0.3) + (100 - 63.30)^2(0.1) = 2{,}684.11$$

$$\sigma_X = \$51.81$$

$$Var(Y) = \sigma_Y^2 = (-200 - 125.50)^2(0.01) + (-100 - 125.50)^2(0.09) + (50 - 125.50)^2(0.15) + (90 - 125.50)^2(0.35) + (250 - 125.50)^2(0.3) + (225 - 125.50)^2(0.1) = 12{,}572.25$$

$$\sigma_Y = \$112.13$$

$$\sigma_{XY} = (400 - 63.30)(-200 - 125.50)(0.01) + (-30 - 63.30)(-100 - 125.50)(0.09) + (30 - 63.30)(50 - 125.50)(0.15) + (50 - 63.30)(90 - 125.50)(0.35) + (100 - 63.30)(250 - 125.50)(0.3) + (100 - 63.30)(225 - 125.50)(0.1)$$

$$\sigma_{xy} = \$3{,}075.85$$

Thus, the Good Times fund has a much higher expected value (i.e., larger expected return) than the Black Swan fund ($125.50 as compared to $63.30 per $1,000) but also has a much higher standard deviation ($112.13 vs. $51.81). Deciding which fund to invest in is a matter of how much risk you are willing to tolerate. Although the Good Times fund has a much higher expected return, many people would be reluctant to invest in a fund where there is a chance of a substantial loss.

The covariance of $3,075.85 between the two investments indicates a positive relationship in which the two investments are varying in the *same* direction. Therefore, when the return on one investment is high, typically, the return on the other is also high. However, from Table 5.5, you can see that the magnitude of the return varies, depending on the economic condition that actually occurs. Therefore, you might decide to include both funds in your portfolio. The percentage allocated to each fund would be based on your tolerance of risk balanced by your desire for maximum return (see Problem 5.15).

Problems for Section 5.2

LEARNING THE BASICS

5.7 Given the following probability distributions for variables X and Y:

$P(X_i Y_i)$	X	Y
0.4	100	200
0.6	200	100

Compute

a. $E(X)$ and $E(Y)$.

b. σ_X and σ_Y.

c. σ_{XY}.

d. $E(X + Y)$.

5.8 Given the following probability distributions for variables X and Y:

$P(X_i Y_i)$	X	Y
0.2	−100	50
0.4	50	30
0.3	200	20
0.1	300	20

Compute

a. $E(X)$ and $E(Y)$.

b. σ_X and σ_Y.

c. σ_{XY}.

d. $E(X + Y)$.

5.9 Two investments, X and Y, have the following characteristics:

$$E(X) = \$50, E(Y) = \$100, \sigma_X^2 = 9{,}000,$$

$$\sigma_Y^2 = 15{,}000, \text{ and } \sigma_{XY} = 7{,}500.$$

If the weight of portfolio assets assigned to investment X is 0.4, compute the

a. portfolio expected return.

b. portfolio risk.

APPLYING THE CONCEPTS

5.10 The process of being served at a bank consists of two independent parts—the time waiting in line and the time it takes to be served by the teller. Suppose that the time waiting in line has an expected value of 4 minutes, with a standard deviation of 1.2 minutes, and the time it takes to be served by the teller has an expected value of 5.5 minutes, with a standard deviation of 1.5 minutes. Compute the

a. expected value of the total time it takes to be served at the bank.

b. standard deviation of the total time it takes to be served at the bank.

5.11 In the portfolio example in this section (see page 192), half the portfolio assets are invested in the Dow Jones fund and half in a weak-economy fund. Recalculate the portfolio expected return and the portfolio risk if

a. 30% of the portfolio assets are invested in the Dow Jones fund and 70% in a weak-economy fund.

b. 70% of the portfolio assets are invested in the Dow Jones fund and 30% in a weak-economy fund.

c. Which of the three investment strategies (30%, 50%, or 70% in the Dow Jones fund) would you recommend? Why?

SELF Test **5.12** You are trying to develop a strategy for investing in two different stocks. The anticipated annual return for a \$1,000 investment in each stock under four different economic conditions has the following probability distribution:

		Returns	
Probability	**Economic Condition**	**Stock X**	**Stock Y**
0.1	Recession	−100	50
0.3	Slow growth	0	150
0.3	Moderate growth	80	−20
0.3	Fast growth	150	−100

Compute the

a. expected return for stock X and for stock Y.

b. standard deviation for stock X and for stock Y.

c. covariance of stock X and stock Y.

d. Would you invest in stock X or stock Y? Explain.

5.13 Suppose that in Problem 5.12 you wanted to create a portfolio that consists of stock X and stock Y. Compute the portfolio expected return and portfolio risk for each of the following percentages invested in stock X:

a. 30%

b. 50%

c. 70%

d. On the basis of the results of (a) through (c), which portfolio would you recommend? Explain.

5.14 You are trying to develop a strategy for investing in two different stocks. The anticipated annual return for a \$1,000 investment in each stock under four different economic conditions has the following probability distribution:

		Returns	
Probability	**Economic Condition**	**Stock X**	**Stock Y**
0.1	Recession	−50	−100
0.3	Slow growth	20	50
0.4	Moderate growth	100	130
0.2	Fast growth	150	200

Compute the

a. expected return for stock X and for stock Y.
b. standard deviation for stock X and for stock Y.
c. covariance of stock X and stock Y.
d. Would you invest in stock X or stock Y? Explain.

5.15 Suppose that in Example 5.1 on page 193, you wanted to create a portfolio that consists of the Black Swan fund and the Good Times fund. Compute the portfolio expected return and portfolio risk for each of the following percentages invested in the Black Swan fund:

a. 30%
b. 50%
c. 70%
d. On the basis of the results of (a) through (c), which portfolio would you recommend? Explain.

5.16 You plan to invest $1,000 in a corporate bond fund or in a common stock fund. The following table presents the annual return (per $1,000) of each of these investments under various economic conditions and the probability that each of those economic conditions will occur.

Probability	Economic Condition	Corporate Bond Fund	Common Stock Fund
0.01	Extreme recession	−200	−999
0.09	Recession	−70	−300
0.15	Stagnation	30	−100
0.35	Slow growth	80	100
0.30	Moderate growth	100	150
0.10	High growth	120	350

Compute the

a. expected return for the corporate bond fund and for the common stock fund.
b. standard deviation for the corporate bond fund and for the common stock fund.
c. covariance of the corporate bond fund and the common stock fund.
d. Would you invest in the corporate bond fund or the common stock fund? Explain.
e. If you chose to invest in the common stock fund in (d), what do you think about the possibility of losing $999 of every $1,000 invested if there is an extreme recession?

5.17 Suppose that in Problem 5.16 you wanted to create a portfolio that consists of the corporate bond fund and the common stock fund. Compute the portfolio expected return and portfolio risk for each of the following situations:

a. $300 in the corporate bond fund and $700 in the common stock fund.
b. $500 in each fund.
c. $700 in the corporate bond fund and $300 in the common stock fund.
d. On the basis of the results of (a) through (c), which portfolio would you recommend? Explain.

5.3 Binomial Distribution

This is the first of three sections that considers mathematical models. A **mathematical model** is a mathematical expression that represents a variable of interest. When a mathematical model exists, you can compute the exact probability of occurrence of any particular outcome of the variable. For discrete random variables, the mathematical model is a **probability distribution function.**

The **binomial distribution** is an important mathematical model used in many business situations. You use the binomial distribution when the discrete variable is the number of events of interest in a sample of n observations. The binomial distribution has four important properties.

Student Tip

Do not confuse this use of the Greek letter pi, π, to represent the probability of an event of interest with the mathematical constant that is the ratio of the circumference to a diameter of a circle—approximately 3.14159—which is also known by the same Greek letter.

PROPERTIES OF THE BINOMIAL DISTRIBUTION

- The sample consists of a fixed number of observations, n.
- Each observation is classified into one of two mutually exclusive and collectively exhaustive categories.
- The probability of an observation being classified as the event of interest, π, is constant from observation to observation. Thus, the probability of an observation being classified as not being the event of interest, $1 - \pi$, is constant over all observations.
- The outcome of any observation is independent of the outcome of any other observation.

Returning to the Ricknel Home Improvement scenario presented on page 185 concerning the accounting information system, suppose the event of interest is defined as a tagged order form. You want to determine the number of tagged order forms in a given sample of orders.

What results can occur? If the sample contains four orders, there could be none, one, two, three, or four tagged order forms. No other value can occur because the number of tagged order forms cannot be more than the sample size, *n*, and cannot be less than zero. Therefore, the range of the binomial random variable is from 0 to *n*.

Suppose that you observe the following result in a sample of four orders:

First Order	Second Order	Third Order	Fourth Order
Tagged	Tagged	Not tagged	Tagged

What is the probability of having three tagged order forms in a sample of four orders in this particular sequence? Because the historical probability of a tagged order is 0.10, the probability that each order occurs in the sequence is

First Order	Second Order	Third Order	Fourth Order
$\pi = 0.10$	$\pi = 0.10$	$1 - \pi = 0.90$	$\pi = 0.10$

Each outcome is independent of the others because the order forms were selected from an extremely large or practically infinite population and each order form could only be selected once. Therefore, the probability of having this particular sequence is

$$\begin{aligned}\pi\pi(1 - \pi)\pi &= \pi^3(1 - \pi)^1 \\ &= (0.10)^3(0.90)^1 \\ &= (0.10)(0.10)(0.10)(0.90) \\ &= 0.0009\end{aligned}$$

This result indicates only the probability of three tagged order forms (events of interest) from a sample of four order forms in a *specific sequence*. To find the number of ways of selecting *x* objects from *n* objects, *irrespective of sequence*, you use the **rule of combinations**[1] given in Equation (5.10).

[1]Refer to Section 4.5 in the Chapter 4 eBook for further discussion of counting rules.

COMBINATIONS

The number of combinations of selecting *x* objects[2] out of *n* objects is given by

$$_nC_x = \frac{n!}{x!(n - x)!} \tag{5.10}$$

where

$n! = (n)(n - 1) \cdots (1)$ is called *n* factorial. By definition, $0! = 1$.

[2]On many scientific calculators, there is a button labeled $_nC_r$ that allows you to compute the number of combinations. On these calculators, the symbol *r* is used instead of *x*.

With $n = 4$ and $x = 3$, there are

$$_nC_x = \frac{n!}{x!(n - x)!} = \frac{4!}{3!(4 - 3)!} = \frac{4 \times 3 \times 2 \times 1}{(3 \times 2 \times 1)(1)} = 4$$

such sequences. The four possible sequences are

Sequence 1 = *tagged, tagged, tagged, not tagged*, with probability

$$\pi\pi\pi(1 - \pi) = \pi^3(1 - \pi)^1 = 0.0009$$

Sequence 2 = *tagged, tagged, not tagged, tagged*, with probability

$$\pi\pi(1 - \pi)\pi = \pi^3(1 - \pi)^1 = 0.0009$$

Sequence 3 = *tagged, not tagged, tagged, tagged*, with probability

$$\pi(1 - \pi)\pi\pi = \pi^3(1 - \pi)^1 = 0.0009$$

Sequence 4 = *not tagged, tagged, tagged, tagged*, with probability

$$(1 - \pi)\pi\pi\pi = \pi^3(1 - \pi)^1 = 0.0009$$

Therefore, the probability of three tagged order forms is equal to

$$(\text{number of possible sequences}) \times (\text{probability of a particular sequence})$$
$$= (4) \times (0.0009) = 0.0036$$

You can make a similar, intuitive derivation for the other possible outcomes of the random variable—zero, one, two, and four tagged order forms. However, as n, the sample size, gets large, the computations involved in using this intuitive approach become time-consuming. Equation (5.11) is the mathematical model that provides a general formula for computing any probability from the binomial distribution with the number of events of interest, x, given n and π.

BINOMIAL DISTRIBUTION

$$P(X = x \mid n, \pi) = \frac{n!}{x!(n - x)!}\pi^x(1 - \pi)^{n-x} \qquad \textbf{(5.11)}$$

where

$P(X = x \mid n, \pi)$ = probability that $X = x$ events of interest, given n and π

n = number of observations

π = probability of an event of interest

$1 - \pi$ = probability of not having an event of interest

x = number of events of interest in the sample $(X = 0, 1, 2, \cdots, n)$

$\frac{n!}{x!(n - x)!}$ = number of combinations of x events of interest out of n observations

Equation (5.11) restates what was intuitively derived previously. The binomial variable X can have any integer value x from 0 through n. In Equation (5.11), the product

$$\pi^x(1 - \pi)^{n-x}$$

represents the probability of exactly x events of interest from n observations in a *particular sequence*.

The term

$$\frac{n!}{x!(n - x)!}$$

is the number of *combinations* of the x events of interest from the n observations possible. Hence, given the number of observations, n, and the probability of an event of interest, π, the probability of x events of interest is

$$P(X = x \mid n, \pi) = (\text{number of combinations}) \times (\text{probability of a particular combination})$$
$$= \frac{n!}{x!(n - x)!}\pi^x(1 - \pi)^{n-x}$$

Example 5.2 illustrates the use of Equation (5.11). Examples 5.3 and 5.4 show the computations for other values of X.

EXAMPLE 5.2

Determining $P(X = 3)$, Given $n = 4$ and $\pi = 0.1$

If the likelihood of a tagged order form is 0.1, what is the probability that there are three tagged order forms in the sample of four?

SOLUTION Using Equation (5.11), the probability of three tagged orders from a sample of four is

$$P(X = 3 \mid n = 4, \pi = 0.1) = \frac{4!}{3!(4-3)!}(0.1)^3(1-0.1)^{4-3}$$

$$= \frac{4!}{3!(1)!}(0.1)^3(0.9)^1$$

$$= 4(0.1)(0.1)(0.1)(0.9) = 0.0036$$

EXAMPLE 5.3

Determining $P(X \geq 3)$, Given $n = 4$ and $\pi = 0.1$

If the likelihood of a tagged order form is 0.1, what is the probability that there are three or more (i.e., at least three) tagged order forms in the sample of four?

SOLUTION In Example 5.2, you found that the probability of *exactly* three tagged order forms from a sample of four is 0.0036. To compute the probability of *at least* three tagged order forms, you need to add the probability of three tagged order forms to the probability of four tagged order forms. The probability of four tagged order forms is

Student Tip
Another way of saying "three or more" is "at least three."

$$P(X = 4 \mid n = 4, \pi = 0.1) = \frac{4!}{4!(4-4)!}(0.1)^4(1-0.1)^{4-4}$$

$$= \frac{4!}{4!(0)!}(0.1)^4(0.9)^0$$

$$= 1(0.1)(0.1)(0.1)(0.1)(1) = 0.0001$$

Thus, the probability of at least three tagged order forms is

$$P(X \geq 3) = P(X = 3) + P(X = 4)$$

$$= 0.0036 + 0.0001$$

$$= 0.0037$$

There is a 0.37% chance that there will be at least three tagged order forms in a sample of four.

EXAMPLE 5.4

Determining $P(X < 3)$, Given $n = 4$ and $\pi = 0.1$

If the likelihood of a tagged order form is 0.1, what is the probability that there are less than three tagged order forms in the sample of four?

SOLUTION The probability that there are less than three tagged order forms is

$$P(X < 3) = P(X = 0) + P(X = 1) + P(X = 2)$$

Using Equation (5.11) on page 197, these probabilities are

$$P(X = 0 \mid n = 4, \pi = 0.1) = \frac{4!}{0!(4-0)!}(0.1)^0(1-0.1)^{4-0} = 0.6561$$

$$P(X = 1 \mid n = 4, \pi = 0.1) = \frac{4!}{1!(4-1)!}(0.1)^1(1-0.1)^{4-1} = 0.2916$$

$$P(X = 2 \mid n = 4, \pi = 0.1) = \frac{4!}{2!(4-2)!}(0.1)^2(1-0.1)^{4-2} = 0.0486$$

Therefore, $P(X < 3) = 0.6561 + 0.2916 + 0.0486 = 0.9963$. $P(X < 3)$ could also be calculated from its complement, $P(X \geq 3)$, as follows:

$$\begin{aligned} P(X < 3) &= 1 - P(X \geq 3) \\ &= 1 - 0.0037 = 0.9963 \end{aligned}$$

LEARN MORE

A table of binomial probabilities and instructions for its use appears in a Chapter 5 eBook bonus section.

Computing binomial probabilities become tedious as n gets large. Figure 5.2 shows how the worksheet BINOM.DIST function can compute binomial probabilities for you. You can also look up binomial probabilities in a table of probabilities.

FIGURE 5.2

Worksheet for computing binomial probabilities with $n = 4$ and $\pi = 0.1$

*Figure 5.2 displays the **COMPUTE worksheet** of **Binomial workbook** that the Section EG5.3 instructions use.*

	A	B	
1	Binomial Probabilities		
2			
3	Data		
4	Sample size	4	
5	Probability of an event of interest	0.1	
6			
7	Statistics		
8	Mean	0.4	=B4 * B5
9	Variance	0.36	=B8 * (1 - B5)
10	Standard deviation	0.6	=SQRT(B9)
11			
12	Binomial Probabilities Table		
13	X	P(X)	
14	0	0.6561	=BINOM.DIST(A14, $B$4, $B$5, FALSE)
15	1	0.2916	=BINOM.DIST(A15, $B$4, $B$5, FALSE)
16	2	0.0486	=BINOM.DIST(A16, $B$4, $B$5, FALSE)
17	3	0.0036	=BINOM.DIST(A17, $B$4, $B$5, FALSE)
18	4	0.0001	=BINOM.DIST(A18, $B$4, $B$5, FALSE)

The shape of a binomial probability distribution depends on the values of n and π. Whenever $\pi = 0.5$, the binomial distribution is symmetrical, regardless of how large or small the value of n. When $\pi \neq 0.5$, the distribution is skewed. The closer π is to 0.5 and the larger the number of observations, n, the less skewed the distribution becomes. For example, the distribution of the number of tagged order forms is highly right skewed because $\pi = 0.1$ and $n = 4$ (see Figure 5.3).

FIGURE 5.3

Histogram of the binomial probability with $n = 4$ and $\pi = 0.1$

Use the Appendix Section B.9 instructions to construct binomial probability histograms.

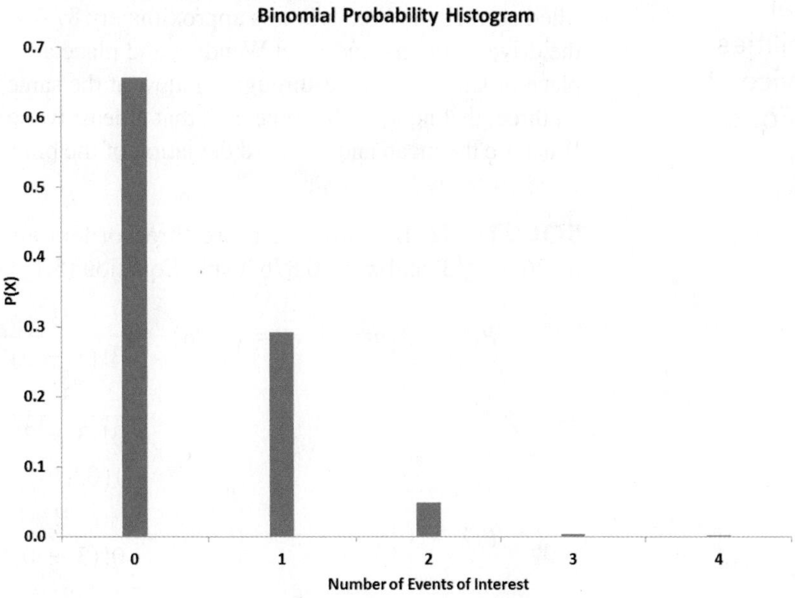

Observe from Figure 5.3 that unlike in the histogram for continuous variables in Section 2.4, the bars for the values are very thin, and there is a large gap between each pair of values. That is because the histogram represents a discrete variable. (Theoretically, the bars should have no width. They should be vertical lines.)

The mean (or expected value) of the binomial distribution is equal to the product of n and π. Instead of using Equation (5.1) on page 187 to compute the mean of the probability distribution, you can use Equation (5.12) to compute the mean for variables that follow the binomial distribution.

MEAN OF THE BINOMIAL DISTRIBUTION

The mean, μ, of the binomial distribution is equal to the sample size, n, multiplied by the probability of an event of interest, π.

$$\mu = E(X) = n\pi \tag{5.12}$$

On the average, over the long run, you theoretically expect $\mu = E(X) = n\pi = (4)(0.1) = 0.4$ tagged order form in a sample of four orders.

The standard deviation of the binomial distribution can be calculated using Equation (5.13).

STANDARD DEVIATION OF THE BINOMIAL DISTRIBUTION

$$\sigma = \sqrt{\sigma^2} = \sqrt{Var(X)} = \sqrt{n\pi(1 - \pi)} \tag{5.13}$$

The standard deviation of the number of tagged order forms is

$$\sigma = \sqrt{4(0.1)(0.9)} = 0.60$$

You get the same result if you use Equation (5.3) on page 188.

Example 5.5 applies the binomial distribution to service at a fast-food restaurant.

EXAMPLE 5.5

Computing Binomial Probabilities for Service at a Fast-Food Restaurant

Accuracy in taking orders at a drive-through window is important for fast-food chains. Periodically, *QSR Magazine* publishes the results of a survey that measures accuracy, defined as the percentage of orders that are filled correctly. In a recent year, the percentage of orders filled correctly at Wendy's was approximately 87.6% (**bit.ly/NELUyi**). Suppose that you go to the drive-through window at Wendy's and place an order. Two friends of yours independently place orders at the drive-through window at the same Wendy's. What are the probabilities that all three, that none of the three, and that at least two of the three orders will be filled correctly? What are the mean and standard deviation of the binomial distribution for the number of orders filled correctly?

SOLUTION Because there are three orders and the probability of a correct order is 0.876, $n = 3$, and $\pi = 0.876$, using Equation (5.11) on page 197,

$$\begin{aligned}
P(X = 3 \mid n = 3, \pi = 0.876) &= \frac{3!}{3!(3-3)!}(0.876)^3(1 - 0.876)^{3-3} \\
&= \frac{3!}{3!(3-3)!}(0.876)^3(0.124)^0 \\
&= 1(0.876)(0.876)(0.876)(1) = 0.6722 \\
P(X = 0 \mid n = 3, \pi = 0.876) &= \frac{3!}{0!(3-0)!}(0.876)^0(1 - 0.876)^{3-0} \\
&= \frac{3!}{0!(3-0)!}(0.876)^0(0.124)^3 \\
&= 1(1)(0.124)(0.124)(0.124) = 0.0019
\end{aligned}$$

$$P(X = 2|n = 3, \pi = 0.876) = \frac{3!}{2!(3-2)!}(0.876)^2(1-0.876)^{3-2}$$
$$= \frac{3!}{2!(3-2)!}(0.876)^2(0.124)^1$$
$$= 3(0.876)(0.876)(0.124) = 0.2855$$
$$P(X \geq 2) = P(X = 2) + P(X = 3)$$
$$= 0.2855 + 0.6722$$
$$= 0.9577$$

Using Equations (5.12) and (5.13),

$$\mu = E(X) = n\pi = 3(0.876) = 2.628$$
$$\sigma = \sqrt{\sigma^2} = \sqrt{Var(X)} = \sqrt{n\pi(1-\pi)}$$
$$= \sqrt{3(0.876)(0.124)}$$
$$= \sqrt{0.3259} = 0.5709$$

The mean number of orders filled correctly in a sample of three orders is 2.628, and the standard deviation is 0.5709. The probability that all three orders are filled correctly is 0.6722, or 67.22%. The probability that none of the orders are filled correctly is 0.0019, or 0.19%. The probability that at least two orders are filled correctly is 0.9577, or 95.77%.

Problems for Section 5.3

LEARNING THE BASICS

5.18 Determine the following:

a. For $n = 4$ and $\pi = 0.12$, what is $P(X = 0)$?
b. For $n = 10$ and $\pi = 0.40$, what is $P(X = 9)$?
c. For $n = 10$ and $\pi = 0.50$, what is $P(X = 8)$?
d. For $n = 6$ and $\pi = 0.83$, what is $P(X = 5)$?

5.19 If $n = 5$ and $\pi = 0.40$, what is the probability that

a. $X = 4$?
b. $X \leq 3$?
c. $X < 2$?
d. $X > 1$?

5.20 Determine the mean and standard deviation of the variable X in each of the following binomial distributions:

a. $n = 4$ and $\pi = 0.10$
b. $n = 4$ and $\pi = 0.40$
c. $n = 5$ and $\pi = 0.80$
d. $n = 3$ and $\pi = 0.50$

APPLYING THE CONCEPTS

5.21 The increase or decrease in the price of a stock between the beginning and the end of a trading day is assumed to be an equally likely random event. What is the probability that a stock will show an increase in its closing price on five consecutive days?

5.22 A recent survey reported that 22% of adults 55 and older own a smartphone. (Data extracted from "Who Owns a Smartphone?" *USA Today*, March 5, 2012, p. 1A.) Using the binomial distribution, what is the probability that in the next six adults 55 and older surveyed,

a. four will own a smartphone?
b. all six will own a smartphone?
c. at least four will own a smartphone?
d. What are the mean and standard deviation of the number of adults 55 and older who will own a smartphone in a survey of six?
e. What assumptions do you need to make in (a) through (c)?

5.23 A student is taking a multiple-choice exam in which each question has four choices. Assume that the student has no knowledge of the correct answers to any of the questions. She has decided on a strategy in which she will place four balls (marked *A*, *B*, *C*, and *D*) into a box. She randomly selects one ball for each question and replaces the ball in the box. The marking on the ball will determine her answer to the question. There are five multiple-choice questions on the exam. What is the probability that she will get

a. five questions correct?
b. at least four questions correct?
c. no questions correct?
d. no more than two questions correct?

5.24 A manufacturing company regularly conducts quality control checks at specified periods on the products it manufactures. Historically, the failure rate for LED light bulbs that the company manufactures is 5%. Suppose a random sample of 10 LED light bulbs is selected. What is the probability that

a. none of the LED light bulbs are defective?
b. exactly one of the LED light bulbs is defective?
c. two or fewer of the LED light bulbs are defective?
d. three or more of the LED light bulbs are defective?

5.25 When a customer places an order with Rudy's On-Line Office Supplies, a computerized accounting information system (AIS) automatically checks to see if the customer has exceeded his or her credit limit. Past records indicate that the probability of customers exceeding their credit limit is 0.05. Suppose that, on a given day, 20 customers place orders. Assume that the number of customers that the AIS detects as having exceeded their credit limit is distributed as a binomial random variable.

a. What are the mean and standard deviation of the number of customers exceeding their credit limits?
b. What is the probability that zero customers will exceed their limits?
c. What is the probability that one customer will exceed his or her limit?
d. What is the probability that two or more customers will exceed their limits?

SELF Test **5.26** In Example 5.5 on page 200, you and two friends decided to go to Wendy's. Now, suppose that instead you go to Burger King, which last year filled approximately 89.7% of orders correctly. What is the probability that

a. all three orders will be filled correctly?
b. none of the three will be filled correctly?
c. at least two of the three will be filled correctly?
d. What are the mean and standard deviation of the binomial distribution used in (a) through (c)? Interpret these values.

5.27 In Example 5.5 on page 200, you and two friends decided to go to Wendy's. Now, suppose that instead you go to McDonald's, which last month filled approximately 89% of the orders correctly. What is the probability that

a. all three orders will be filled correctly?
b. none of the three will be filled correctly?
c. at least two of the three will be filled correctly?
d. What are the mean and standard deviation of the binomial distribution used in (a) through (c)? Interpret these values.
e. Compare the result of (a) through (d) with those of Burger King in Problem 5.26 and Wendy's in Example 5.5 on page 200.

5.4 Poisson Distribution

Many studies are based on counts of the times a particular event occurs in a given *area of opportunity*. An **area of opportunity** is a continuous unit or interval of time, volume, or any physical area in which there can be more than one occurrence of an event. The Poisson distribution can be used to compute probabilities in such situations. Examples of variables that follow the Poisson distribution are the surface defects on a new refrigerator, the number of network failures in a day, the number of people arriving at a bank, and the number of fleas on the body of a dog. You can use the **Poisson distribution** to calculate probabilities in situations such as these if the following properties hold:

- You are interested in counting the number of times a particular event occurs in a given area of opportunity. The area of opportunity is defined by time, length, surface area, and so forth.
- The probability that an event occurs in a given area of opportunity is the same for all the areas of opportunity.
- The number of events that occur in one area of opportunity is independent of the number of events that occur in any other area of opportunity.
- The probability that two or more events will occur in an area of opportunity approaches zero as the area of opportunity becomes smaller.

Consider the number of customers arriving during the lunch hour at a bank located in the central business district in a large city. You are interested in the number of customers who arrive each minute. Does this situation match the four properties of the Poisson distribution given earlier?

First, the *event* of interest is a customer arriving, and the *given area of opportunity* is defined as a one-minute interval. Will zero customers arrive, one customer arrive, two customers arrive, and so on? Second, it is reasonable to assume that the probability that a customer arrives during a particular one-minute interval is the same as the probability for all the other one-minute intervals. Third, the arrival of one customer in any one-minute interval has no effect on (i.e., is independent of) the arrival of any other customer in any other one-minute interval. Finally, the probability that two or more customers will arrive in a given time period approaches zero as the time interval becomes small. For example, the probability is virtually zero that two customers will arrive in a time interval of 0.01 second. Thus, you can use the Poisson distribution to determine probabilities involving the number of customers arriving at the bank in a one-minute time interval during the lunch hour.

The Poisson distribution has one characteristic, called λ (the Greek lowercase letter *lambda*), which is the mean or expected number of events per unit. The variance of a Poisson distribution is also equal to λ, and the standard deviation is equal to $\sqrt{\lambda}$. The number of events, X, of the Poisson random variable ranges from 0 to infinity (∞).

Equation (5.14) is the mathematical expression for the Poisson distribution for computing the probability of $X = x$ events, given that λ events are expected.

POISSON DISTRIBUTION

$$P(X = x \mid \lambda) = \frac{e^{-\lambda}\lambda^x}{x!} \quad \textbf{(5.14)}$$

where

$P(X = x \mid \lambda)$ = probability that $X = x$ events in an area of opportunity given λ

λ = expected number of events

e = mathematical constant approximated by 2.71828

x = number of events $(x = 0, 1, 2, \ldots, \infty)$

To illustrate an application of the Poisson distribution, suppose that the mean number of customers who arrive per minute at the bank during the noon-to-1 P.M. hour is equal to 3.0. What is the probability that in a given minute, exactly two customers will arrive? And what is the probability that more than two customers will arrive in a given minute?

Using Equation (5.14) and $\lambda = 3$, the probability that in a given minute exactly two customers will arrive is

$$P(X = 2 \mid \lambda = 3) = \frac{e^{-3.0}(3.0)^2}{2!} = \frac{9}{(2.71828)^3(2)} = 0.2240$$

To determine the probability that in any given minute more than two customers will arrive,

$$P(X > 2) = P(X = 3) + P(X = 4) + \cdots + P(X = \infty)$$

Because in a probability distribution, all the probabilities must sum to 1, the terms on the right side of the equation $P(X > 2)$ also represent the complement of the probability that X is less than or equal to 2 [i.e., $1 - P(X \le 2)$]. Thus,

$$P(X > 2) = 1 - P(X \le 2) = 1 - [P(X = 0) + P(X = 1) + P(X = 2)]$$

Now, using Equation (5.14),

$$
\begin{aligned}
P(X > 2) &= 1 - \left[\frac{e^{-3.0}(3.0)^0}{0!} + \frac{e^{-3.0}(3.0)^1}{1!} + \frac{e^{-3.0}(3.0)^2}{2!}\right] \\
&= 1 - [0.0498 + 0.1494 + 0.2240] \\
&= 1 - 0.4232 = 0.5768
\end{aligned}
$$

Thus, there is a 57.68% chance that more than two customers will arrive in the same minute.

Computing Poisson probabilities can be tedious. Figure 5.4 shows how the worksheet POISSON.DIST function can compute Poisson probabilities for you. You can also look up Poisson probabilities in a table of probabilities.

FIGURE 5.4

Worksheet for computing Poisson probabilities with $\lambda = 3$

	A	B	C	D	E
1	**Poisson Probabilities**				
2					
3		**Data**			
4	Mean/Expected number of events of interest:				3
5					
6	**Poisson Probabilities Table**				
7	*X*	*P(X)*			
8	0	0.0498	=POISSON.DIST(A8, $E$4, FALSE)		
9	1	0.1494	=POISSON.DIST(A9, $E$4, FALSE)		
10	2	0.2240	=POISSON.DIST(A10, $E$4, FALSE)		
11	3	0.2240	=POISSON.DIST(A11, $E$4, FALSE)		
12	4	0.1680	=POISSON.DIST(A12, $E$4, FALSE)		
13	5	0.1008	=POISSON.DIST(A13, $E$4, FALSE)		
14	6	0.0504	=POISSON.DIST(A14, $E$4, FALSE)		
15	7	0.0216	=POISSON.DIST(A15, $E$4, FALSE)		
16	8	0.0081	=POISSON.DIST(A16, $E$4, FALSE)		
17	9	0.0027	=POISSON.DIST(A17, $E$4, FALSE)		
18	10	0.0008	=POISSON.DIST(A18, $E$4, FALSE)		
19	11	0.0002	=POISSON.DIST(A19, $E$4, FALSE)		
20	12	0.0001	=POISSON.DIST(A20, $E$4, FALSE)		
21	13	0.0000	=POISSON.DIST(A21, $E$4, FALSE)		
22	14	0.0000	=POISSON.DIST(A22, $E$4, FALSE)		
23	15	0.0000	=POISSON.DIST(A23, $E$4, FALSE)		

LEARN MORE

A table of Poisson probabilities and instructions for its use appears in a Chapter 5 bonus eBook bonus section.

*Figure 5.4 displays the **COMPUTE worksheet** of **Poisson workbook** that the Section EG5.4 instructions use.*

EXAMPLE 5.6

Computing Poisson Probabilities

The number of work-related injuries per month in a manufacturing plant is known to follow a Poisson distribution, with a mean of 2.5 work-related injuries a month. What is the probability that in a given month, no work-related injuries occur? That at least one work-related injury occurs?

SOLUTION Using Equation (5.14) on page 203 with $\lambda = 2.5$ (or Excel or a Poisson table lookup), the probability that in a given month no work-related injuries occur is

$$P(X = 0 \mid \lambda = 2.5) = \frac{e^{-2.5}(2.5)^0}{0!} = \frac{1}{(2.71828)^{2.5}(1)} = 0.0821$$

The probability that there will be no work-related injuries in a given month is 0.0821, or 8.21%. Thus,

$$
\begin{aligned}
P(X \geq 1) &= 1 - P(X = 0) \\
&= 1 - 0.0821 \\
&= 0.9179
\end{aligned}
$$

The probability that there will be at least one work-related injury is 0.9179, or 91.79%.

Problems for Section 5.4

LEARNING THE BASICS

5.28 Assume a Poisson distribution.

a. If $\lambda = 2.5$, find $P(X = 2)$.
b. If $\lambda = 8.0$, find $P(X = 8)$.
c. If $\lambda = 0.5$, find $P(X = 1)$.
d. If $\lambda = 3.7$, find $P(X = 0)$.

5.29 Assume a Poisson distribution.

a. If $\lambda = 2.0$, find $P(X \geq 2)$.
b. If $\lambda = 8.0$, find $P(X \geq 3)$.
c. If $\lambda = 0.5$, find $P(X \leq 1)$.
d. If $\lambda = 4.0$, find $P(X \geq 1)$.
e. If $\lambda = 5.0$, find $P(X \leq 3)$.

5.30 Assume a Poisson distribution with $\lambda = 5.0$. What is the probability that

a. $X = 1$?
b. $X < 1$?
c. $X > 1$?
d. $X \leq 1$?

APPLYING THE CONCEPTS

5.31 Assume that the number of network errors experienced in a day on a local area network (LAN) is distributed as a Poisson variable. The mean number of network errors experienced in a day is 2.4. What is the probability that in any given day

a. zero network errors will occur?
b. exactly one network error will occur?
c. two or more network errors will occur?
d. fewer than three network errors will occur?

SELF Test **5.32** The quality control manager of Marilyn's Cookies is inspecting a batch of chocolate-chip cookies that has just been baked. If the production process is in control, the mean number of chocolate-chip parts per cookie is 6.0. What is the probability that in any particular cookie being inspected

a. fewer than five chocolate-chip parts will be found?
b. exactly five chocolate-chip parts will be found?
c. five or more chocolate-chip parts will be found?
d. either four or five chocolate-chip parts will be found?

5.33 Refer to Problem 5.32. How many cookies in a batch of 100 should the manager expect to discard if company policy requires that all chocolate-chip cookies sold have at least four chocolate-chip parts?

5.34 The U.S. Department of Transportation maintains statistics for mishandled bags per 1,000 airline passengers. In May 2012, Delta mishandled 1.93 bags per 1,000 passengers. What is the probability that in the next 1,000 passengers, Delta will have

a. no mishandled bags?
b. at least one mishandled bag?
c. at least two mishandled bags?

5.35 The U.S. Department of Transportation maintains statistics for involuntary denial of boarding. In May 2012, the American Airlines rate of involuntarily denying boarding was 0.81 per 10,000 passengers. What is the probability that in the next 10,000 passengers, there will be

a. no one involuntarily denied boarding?
b. at least one person involuntarily denied boarding?
c. at least two persons involuntarily denied boarding?

5.36 Based on past experience, it is assumed that the number of flaws per foot in rolls of grade 2 wallpaper follows a Poisson distribution with a mean of 1 flaw per 5 feet of wallpaper (i.e., 0.2 flaw per foot). What is the probability that in a

a. 1-foot roll, there will be at least 2 flaws?
b. 12-foot roll, there will be at least 1 flaw?
c. 50-foot roll, there will be more than or equal to 5 flaws and fewer than or equal to 15 flaws?

5.37 J.D. Power and Associates calculates and publishes various statistics concerning car quality. The initial quality score measures the number of problems per new car sold. For 2012 model cars, Ford had 1.18 problems per car, and Toyota had 0.88 problem per car. (Data extracted from J.D. Power and Associates 2012 Initial Quality Study, June 27, 2012, **autos.jdpower.com/ratings/quality-press-release.htm**.) Let *X* be equal to the number of problems with a newly purchased 2012 Ford.

a. What assumptions must be made in order for *X* to be distributed as a Poisson random variable? Are these assumptions reasonable?

Making the assumptions as in (a), if you purchased a 2012 Ford, what is the probability that the new car will have

b. zero problems?
c. two or fewer problems?
d. Give an operational definition for *problem*. Why is the operational definition important in interpreting the initial quality score?

5.38 Refer to Problem 5.37. If you purchased a 2012 Toyota, what is the probability that the new car will have

a. zero problems?
b. two or fewer problems?
c. Compare your answers in (a) and (b) to those for the 2012 Ford in Problem 5.37 (b) and (c).

5.39 Refer to Problem 5.37. Another article reported that in 2011, Ford had 1.16 problems per car and Toyota had 1.01 problems per car. (Data extracted from M. Ramsey, "Ford Drops in Quality Survey," *The Wall Street Journal*, June 24, 2011, p. B4.) If you purchased a 2011 Ford, what is the probability that the new car will have

a. zero problems?
b. two or fewer problems?
c. Compare your answers in (a) and (b) to those for the 2012 Ford in Problem 5.37 (b) and (c).

5.40 Refer to Problem 5.39. If you purchased a 2011 Toyota, what is the probability that the new car will have

a. zero problems?

b. two or fewer problems?

c. Compare your answers in (a) and (b) to those for the 2012 Toyota in Problem 5.38 (a) and (b).

5.41 A toll-free phone number is available from 9 A.M. to 9 P.M. for your customers to register complaints about a product purchased from your company. Past history indicates that an average of 0.8 calls is received per minute.

a. What properties must be true about the situation described here in order to use the Poisson distribution to calculate probabilities concerning the number of phone calls received in a one-minute period?

Assuming that this situation matches the properties discussed in (a), what is the probability that during a one-minute period

b. zero phone calls will be received?

c. three or more phone calls will be received?

d. What is the maximum number of phone calls that will be received in a one-minute period 99.99% of the time?

5.5 Hypergeometric Distribution

Both the binomial distribution and the **hypergeometric distribution** use the number of events of interest in a sample containing n observations. One of the differences in these two probability distributions is in the way the samples are selected. For the binomial distribution, the sample data are selected *with* replacement from a *finite* population or *without* replacement from an *infinite* population. Thus, the probability of an event of interest, π, is constant over all observations, and the outcome of any particular observation is independent of any other. For the hypergeometric distribution, the sample data are selected *without* replacement from a *finite* population. Thus, the outcome of one observation is dependent on the outcomes of the previous observations.

Consider a population of size N. Let A represent the total number of events of interest in the population. The hypergeometric distribution is then used to find the probability of X events of interest in a sample of size n, selected without replacement. Equation (5.15) represents the mathematical expression of the hypergeometric distribution for finding x events of interest, given a knowledge of n, N, and A.

HYPERGEOMETRIC DISTRIBUTION

$$P(X = x \mid n, N, A) = \frac{\binom{A}{x}\binom{N-A}{n-x}}{\binom{N}{n}} \quad \textbf{(5.15)}$$

where

$P(X = x \mid n, N, A)$ = probability of x events of interest, given knowledge of n, N, and A

n = sample size

N = population size

A = number of events of interest in the population

$N - A$ = number of events that are not of interest in the population

x = number of events of interest in the sample

$\binom{A}{x} = {}_AC_x$ = number of combinations [see Equation (5.10) on page 196]

$x \leq A$

$x \leq n$

Because the number of events of interest in the sample, represented by x, cannot be greater than the number of events of interest in the population, A, nor can x be greater than the sample size, n, the range of the hypergeometric random variable is limited to the sample size or to the number of events of interest in the population, whichever is smaller.

Equation (5.16) defines the mean of the hypergeometric distribution, and Equation (5.17) defines the standard deviation.

MEAN OF THE HYPERGEOMETRIC DISTRIBUTION

$$\mu = E(X) = \frac{nA}{N} \quad \textbf{(5.16)}$$

STANDARD DEVIATION OF THE HYPERGEOMETRIC DISTRIBUTION

$$\sigma = \sqrt{\frac{nA(N - A)}{N^2}}\sqrt{\frac{N - n}{N - 1}} \quad \textbf{(5.17)}$$

In Equation (5.17), the expression $\sqrt{\frac{N-n}{N-1}}$ is a **finite population correction factor** that results from sampling without replacement from a finite population.

To illustrate the hypergeometric distribution, suppose that you are forming a team of 8 managers from different departments within your company. Your company has a total of 30 managers, and 10 of these managers are from the finance department. If you are to randomly select members of the team, what is the probability that the team will contain 2 managers from the finance department? Here, the population of $N = 30$ managers within the company is finite. In addition, $A = 10$ are from the finance department. A team of $n = 8$ members is to be selected.

Using Equation (5.15),

$$P(X = 2 | n = 8, N = 30, A = 10) = \frac{\binom{10}{2}\binom{20}{6}}{\binom{30}{8}}$$

$$= \frac{\left(\frac{10!}{2!(8)!}\right)\left(\frac{(20)!}{(6)!(14)!}\right)}{\left(\frac{30!}{8!(22)!}\right)}$$

$$= 0.298$$

Thus, the probability that the team will contain two members from the finance department is 0.298, or 29.8%.

Computing hypergeometric probabilities can be tedious, especially as N gets large. Figure 5.5 shows how the worksheet HYPGEOM.DIST function can compute hypergeometric probabilities for the team formation example.

FIGURE 5.5
Worksheet for computing hypergeometric probabilities for the team formation problem

Figure 5.5 displays the ***COMPUTE worksheet*** *of* ***Hypergeometric workbook*** *that the Section EG5.5 instructions use.*

	A	B	
1	**Hypergeometric Probabilities**		
2			
3	**Data**		
4	Sample size	8	
5	No. of events of interest in population	10	
6	Population size	30	
7			
8	**Hypergeometric Probabilities Table**		
9	***X***	***P(X)***	
10	0	0.0215	=HYPGEOM.DIST(A10, $B$4, $B$5, $B$6, FALSE)
11	1	0.1324	=HYPGEOM.DIST(A11, $B$4, $B$5, $B$6, FALSE)
12	2	0.2980	=HYPGEOM.DIST(A12, $B$4, $B$5, $B$6, FALSE)
13	3	0.3179	=HYPGEOM.DIST(A13, $B$4, $B$5, $B$6, FALSE)
14	4	0.1738	=HYPGEOM.DIST(A14, $B$4, $B$5, $B$6, FALSE)
15	5	0.0491	=HYPGEOM.DIST(A15, $B$4, $B$5, $B$6, FALSE)
16	6	0.0068	=HYPGEOM.DIST(A16, $B$4, $B$5, $B$6, FALSE)
17	7	0.0004	=HYPGEOM.DIST(A17, $B$4, $B$5, $B$6, FALSE)
18	8	0.0000	=HYPGEOM.DIST(A18, $B$4, $B$5, $B$6, FALSE)

Example 5.7 shows an application of the hypergeometric distribution in portfolio selection.

EXAMPLE 5.7

Computing Hypergeometric Probabilities

You are a financial analyst facing the task of selecting mutual funds to purchase for a client's portfolio. You have narrowed the funds to be selected to 10 different funds. In order to diversify your client's portfolio, you will recommend the purchase of 4 different funds. Six of the funds are growth funds. What is the probability that of the 4 funds selected, 3 are growth funds?

SOLUTION Using Equation (5.15) with $X = 3$, $n = 4$, $N = 10$, and $A = 6$,

$$P(X = 3 \mid n = 4, N = 10, A = 6) = \frac{\binom{6}{3}\binom{4}{1}}{\binom{10}{4}}$$

$$= \frac{\left(\frac{6!}{3!(3)!}\right)\left(\frac{(4)!}{(1)!(3)!}\right)}{\left(\frac{10!}{4!(6)!}\right)}$$

$$= 0.3810$$

The probability that of the 4 funds selected, 3 are growth funds, is 0.3810, or 38.10%.

Problems for Section 5.5

LEARNING THE BASICS

5.42 Determine the following:

a. If $n = 4$, $N = 10$, and $A = 5$, find $P(X = 3)$.
b. If $n = 4$, $N = 6$, and $A = 3$, find $P(X = 1)$.
c. If $n = 5$, $N = 12$, and $A = 3$, find $P(X = 0)$.
d. If $n = 3$, $N = 10$, and $A = 3$, find $P(X = 3)$.

5.43 Referring to Problem 5.42, compute the mean and standard deviation for the hypergeometric distributions described in (a) through (d).

APPLYING THE CONCEPTS

SELF Test **5.44** An auditor for the Internal Revenue Service is selecting a sample of 6 tax returns for an audit. If 2 or more of these returns are "improper," the entire population of 100 tax returns will be audited. What is the probability that the entire population will be audited if the true number of improper returns in the population is

a. 25?
b. 30?
c. 5?
d. 10?
e. Discuss the differences in your results, depending on the true number of improper returns in the population.

5.45 KSDLDS-Pros, an IT project management consulting firm, is forming an IT project management team of 5 professionals. In the firm of 50 professionals, 8 are considered to be data analytics specialists. If the professionals are selected at random, what is the probability that the team will include

a. no data analytics specialist?
b. at least one data analytics specialist?
c. no more than two data analytics specialists?
d. What is your answer to (a) if the team consists of 7 members?

5.46 From an inventory of 30 cars being shipped to a local automobile dealer, 4 are SUVs. What is the probability that if 4 cars arrive at a particular dealership,

a. all 4 are SUVs?
b. none are SUVs?
c. at least 1 is an SUV?
d. What are your answers to (a) through (c) if 6 cars being shipped are SUVs?

5.47 As a quality control manager, you are responsible for checking the quality level of AC adapters for tablet PCs that your company manufactures. You must reject a shipment if you find 4 defective units. Suppose a shipment of 40 AC adapters has 8 defective units and 32 nondefective units. If you sample 12 AC adapters, what's the probability that

a. there will be no defective units in the shipment?

b. there will be at least 1 defective unit in the shipment?

c. there will be 4 defective units in the shipment?

d. the shipment will be accepted?

5.48 In Example 5.7 on page 208, a financial analyst was facing the task of selecting mutual funds to purchase for a client's portfolio. Suppose that the number of funds had been narrowed to 12 funds instead of the 10 funds (still with 6 growth funds) in Example 5.7. What is the probability that of the 4 funds selected,

a. exactly 1 is a growth fund?

b. at least 1 is a growth fund?

c. 3 are growth fund?

d. Compare the result of (c) to the result of Example 5.7.

USING STATISTICS Events of Interest at Ricknel Home Centers, Revisited

Monkey Business Images / Shutterstock

In the Ricknel Home Improvement scenario at the beginning of this chapter, you were an accountant for the Ricknel Home Improvement Company. The company's accounting information system automatically reviews order forms from online customers for possible mistakes. Any questionable invoices are tagged and included in a daily exceptions report. Knowing that the probability that an order will be tagged is 0.10, you were able to use the binomial distribution to determine the chance of finding a certain number of tagged forms in a sample of size four. There was a 65.6% chance that none of the forms would be tagged, a 29.2% chance that one would be tagged, and a 5.2% chance that two or more would be tagged. You were also able to determine that, on average, you would expect 0.4 forms to be tagged, and the standard deviation of the number of tagged order forms would be 0.6. Now that you have learned the mechanics of using the binomial distribution for a known probability of 0.10 and a sample size of four, you will be able to apply the same approach to any given probability and sample size. Thus, you will be able to make inferences about the online ordering process and, more importantly, evaluate any changes or proposed changes to the process.

SUMMARY

In this chapter, you have studied the probability distribution for a discrete variable, the covariance and its application in finance, and three important discrete probability distributions: the binomial, Poisson, and hypergeometric distributions. In the next chapter, you will study several important continuous distributions, including the normal distribution.

To help decide which discrete probability distribution to use for a particular situation, you need to ask the following questions:

- Is there a fixed number of observations, n, each of which is classified as an event of interest or not an event of interest? Is there an area of opportunity? If there is a fixed number of observations, n, each of which is classified as an event of interest or not an event of interest, you use the binomial or hypergeometric distribution. If there is an area of opportunity, you use the Poisson distribution.
- In deciding whether to use the binomial or hypergeometric distribution, is the probability of an event of interest constant over all trials? If yes, you can use the binomial distribution. If no, you can use the hypergeometric distribution.

REFERENCES

1. Bernstein, P. L. *Against the Gods: The Remarkable Story of Risk*. New York: Wiley, 1996.
2. Emery, D. R., J. D. Finnerty, and J. D. Stowe. *Corporate Financial Management*, 3rd ed. Upper Saddle River, NJ: Prentice Hall, 2007.
3. Levine, D. M., P. Ramsey, and R. Smidt. *Applied Statistics for Engineers and Scientists Using Microsoft Excel and Minitab*. Upper Saddle River, NJ: Prentice Hall, 2001.
4. *Microsoft Excel 2010*. Redmond, WA: Microsoft Corp., 2010.
5. Taleb, N. *The Black Swan*, 2nd ed. New York: Random House, 2010.

KEY EQUATIONS

Expected Value, μ, of a Discrete Variable

$$\mu = E(X) = \sum_{i=1}^{N} x_i P(X = x_i) \quad (5.1)$$

Variance of a Discrete Variable

$$\sigma^2 = \sum_{i=1}^{N} [x_i - E(X)]^2 P(X = x_i) \quad (5.2)$$

Standard Deviation of a Discrete Variable

$$\sigma = \sqrt{\sigma^2} = \sqrt{\sum_{i=1}^{N} [x_i - E(X)]^2 P(X = x_i)} \quad (5.3)$$

Covariance

$$\sigma_{XY} = \sum_{i=1}^{N} [x_i - E(X)][y_i - E(Y)] P(x_i y_i) \quad (5.4)$$

Expected Value of the Sum of Two Variables

$$E(X + Y) = E(X) + E(Y) \quad (5.5)$$

Variance of the Sum of Two Variables

$$Var(X + Y) = \sigma^2_{X+Y} = \sigma^2_X + \sigma^2_Y + 2\sigma_{XY} \quad (5.6)$$

Standard Deviation of the Sum of Two Variables

$$\sigma_{X+Y} = \sqrt{\sigma^2_{X+Y}} \quad (5.7)$$

Portfolio Expected Return

$$E(P) = wE(X) + (1 - w)E(Y) \quad (5.8)$$

Portfolio Risk

$$\sigma_p = \sqrt{w^2\sigma^2_X + (1 - w)^2\sigma^2_Y + 2w(1 - w)\sigma_{XY}} \quad (5.9)$$

Combinations

$$_nC_x = \frac{n!}{x!(n - x)!} \quad (5.10)$$

Binomial Distribution

$$P(X = x|n, \pi) = \frac{n!}{x!(n - x)!}\pi^x(1 - \pi)^{n-x} \quad (5.11)$$

Mean of the Binomial Distribution

$$\mu = E(X) = n\pi \quad (5.12)$$

Standard Deviation of the Binomial Distribution

$$\sigma = \sqrt{\sigma^2} = \sqrt{Var(X)} = \sqrt{n\pi(1 - \pi)} \quad (5.13)$$

Poisson Distribution

$$P(X = x|\lambda) = \frac{e^{-\lambda}\lambda^x}{x!} \quad (5.14)$$

Hypergeometric Distribution

$$P(X = x|n, N, A) = \frac{\binom{A}{x}\binom{N - A}{n - x}}{\binom{N}{n}} \quad (5.15)$$

Mean of the Hypergeometric Distribution

$$\mu = E(X) = \frac{nA}{N} \quad (5.16)$$

Standard Deviation of the Hypergeometric Distribution

$$\sigma = \sqrt{\frac{nA(N - A)}{N^2}}\sqrt{\frac{N - n}{N - 1}} \quad (5.17)$$

KEY TERMS

CHECKING YOUR UNDERSTANDING

5.49 What is the meaning of the expected value of a probability distribution?

5.50 What are the four properties that must be present in order to use the binomial distribution?

5.51 What are the four properties that must be present in order to use the Poisson distribution?

5.52 When do you use the hypergeometric distribution instead of the binomial distribution?

CHAPTER REVIEW PROBLEMS

5.53 Darwin Head, a 35-year-old sawmill worker, won \$1 million and a Chevrolet Malibu Hybrid by scoring 15 goals within 24 seconds at the Vancouver Canucks National Hockey League game (B. Ziemer, "Darwin Evolves into an Instant Millionaire," *Vancouver Sun*, February 28, 2008, p. 1). Head said he would use the money to pay off his mortgage and provide for his children, and he had no plans to quit his job. The contest was part of the Chevrolet Malibu Million Dollar Shootout, sponsored by General Motors Canadian Division. Did GM-Canada risk the \$1 million? No! GM-Canada purchased event insurance from a company specializing in promotions at sporting events such as a half-court basketball shot or a hole-in-one giveaway at the local charity golf outing. The event insurance company estimates the probability of a contestant winning the contest, and for a modest charge, insures the event. The promoters pay the insurance premium but take on no added risk as the insurance company will make the large payout in the unlikely event that a contestant wins. To see how it works, suppose that the insurance company estimates that the probability a contestant would win a Million Dollar Shootout is 0.001, and that the insurance company charges \$4,000.

a. Calculate the expected value of the profit made by the insurance company.

b. Many call this kind of situation a win–win opportunity for the insurance company and the promoter. Do you agree? Explain.

5.54 Between 1896 when the Dow Jones Index was created and 2009, the index rose in 64% of the years. (Data extracted from M. Hulbert, "What the Past Can't Tell Investors," *The New York Times*, January 3, 2010, p. BU2.) Based on this information, and assuming a binomial distribution, what do you think is the probability that the stock market will rise

a. next year?

b. the year after next?

c. in four of the next five years?

d. in none of the next five years?

e. For this situation, what assumption of the binomial distribution might not be valid?

5.55 In early 2012, it was reported that 38% of U.S. adult cellphone owners called a friend for advice about a purchase while in a store. (Data extracted from "Mobile Advice, Sunday Stats" *The Palm Beach Post*, February 19, 2012, p. 1F,) If a sample of 10 U.S. adult cellphone owners is selected, what is the probability that

a. 6 called a friend for advice about a purchase while in a store?

b. at least 6 called a friend for advice about a purchase while in a store?

c. all 10 called a friend for advice about a purchase while in a store?

d. If you selected the sample in a particular geographical area and found that none of the 10 respondents called a friend for advice about a purchase while in a store, what conclusion might you reach about whether the percentage of adult cellphone owners who called a friend for advice about a purchase while in a store in this area was 38%?

5.56 One theory concerning the Dow Jones Industrial Average is that it is likely to increase during U.S. presidential election years. From 1964 through 2008, the Dow Jones Industrial Average increased in 9 of the 12 U.S. presidential election years. Assuming that this indicator is a random event with no predictive value, you would expect that the indicator would be correct 50% of the time.

a. What is the probability of the Dow Jones Industrial Average increasing in 9 or more of the 12 U.S. presidential election years if the probability of an increase in the Dow Jones Industrial Average is 0.50?

b. What is the probability that the Dow Jones Industrial Average will increase in 9 or more of the 12 U.S. presidential election years if the probability of an increase in the Dow Jones Industrial Average in any year is 0.75?

5.57 Medical billing errors and fraud are on the rise. According to Medical Billing Advocates of America, 8 out of 10 times, the medical bills that you get are not right. (Data extracted from "Services Diagnose, Treat Medical Billing Errors," *USA Today*, June 20, 2012.) If a sample of 10 medical bills is selected, what is the probability that

a. 0 medical bills will contain errors?

b. exactly 5 medical bills will contain errors?

c. more than 5 medical bills will contain errors?

d. What are the mean and standard deviation of the probability distribution?

5.58 Refer to Problem 5.57. Suppose that a quality improvement initiative has reduced the percentage of medical bills containing errors to 40%. If a sample of 10 medical bills is selected, what is the probability that

a. 0 medical bills will contain errors?
b. exactly 5 medical bills will contain errors?
c. more than 5 medical bills contain errors?
d. What are the mean and standard deviation of the probability distribution?
e. Compare the results of (a) through (c) to those of Problem 5.57 (a) through (c).

5.59 Social log-ins involve recommending or sharing an article that you read online. According to Janrain ("T. Wayne, One Log-In Catches on for Many Sites," *The New York Times*, May 2, 2011, p. B2), in the first quarter of 2011, 35% signed in via Facebook compared with 31% for Google.

If a sample of 10 social log-ins is selected, what is the probability that

a. more than 4 signed in using Facebook?
b. more than 4 signed in using Google?
c. none signed in using Facebook?
d. What assumptions did you have to make to answer (a) through (c)?

5.60 One of the biggest frustrations for the consumer electronics industry is that customers are accustomed to returning goods for any reason (C. Lawton, "The War on Returns," *The Wall Street Journal*, May 8, 2008, pp. D1, D6). Recently, it was reported that returns for "no trouble found" were 68% of all the returns. Consider a sample of 20 customers who returned consumer electronics purchases. Use the binomial model to answer the following questions:

a. What is the expected value, or mean, of the binomial distribution?
b. What is the standard deviation of the binomial distribution?
c. What is the probability that 15 of the 20 customers made a return for "no trouble found"?
d. What is the probability that no more than 10 of the customers made a return for "no trouble found"?
e. What is the probability that 10 or more of the customers made a return for "no trouble found"?

5.61 Refer to Problem 5.60. In the same time period, 27% of the returns were for "buyer's remorse."

a. What is the expected value, or mean, of the binomial distribution?
b. What is the standard deviation of the binomial distribution?
c. What is the probability that none of the 20 customers made a return for "buyer's remorse"?
d. What is the probability that no more than 2 of the customers made a return for "buyer's remorse"?
e. What is the probability that 3 or more of the customers made a return for "buyer's remorse"?

5.62 One theory concerning the S&P 500 Index is that if it increases during the first five trading days of the year, it is likely to increase during the entire year. From 1950 through 2010, the S&P 500 Index had these early gains in 39 years. In 34 of these 39 years, the S&P 500 Index increased for the entire year. Assuming that this indicator is a random event with no predictive value, you would expect that the indicator would be correct 50% of the time. What is the probability of the S&P 500 Index increasing in 34 or more years if the true probability of an increase in the S&P 500 Index is

a. 0.50?
b. 0.70?
c. 0.90?
d. Based on the results of (a) through (c), what do you think is the probability that the S&P 500 Index will increase if there is an early gain in the first five trading days of the year? Explain.

5.63 *Spurious correlation* refers to the apparent relationship between variables that either have no true relationship or are related to other variables that have not been measured. One widely publicized stock market indicator in the United States that is an example of spurious correlation is the relationship between the winner of the National Football League Super Bowl and the performance of the Dow Jones Industrial Average in that year. The "indicator" states that when a team that existed before the National Football League merged with the American Football League wins the Super Bowl, the Dow Jones Industrial Average will increase in that year. (Of course, any correlation between these is spurious as one thing has absolutely nothing to do with the other!) Since the first Super Bowl was held in 1967 through 2011, the indicator has been correct 36 out of 45 times. Assuming that this indicator is a random event with no predictive value, you would expect that the indicator would be correct 50% of the time.

a. What is the probability that the indicator would be correct 36 or more times in 45 years?
b. What does this tell you about the usefulness of this indicator?

5.64 In a recent year, it was reported that approximately 300 million golf balls were lost in the United States. Assume that the number of golf balls lost in an 18-hole round is distributed as a Poisson random variable with a mean of 5 balls.

a. What assumptions need to be made so that the number of golf balls lost in an 18-hole round is distributed as a Poisson random variable?

Making the assumptions given in (a), what is the probability that

b. 0 balls will be lost in an 18-hole round?
c. 5 or fewer balls will be lost in an 18-hole round?
d. 6 or more balls will be lost in an 18-hole round?

5.65 In the Florida lottery Lotto game, you select six numbers from a pool of numbers from 1 to 53 (see **flalottery.com**).

Each wager costs $1. You win the jackpot if you match all six numbers that you have selected.

Find the probability of

a. winning the jackpot.
b. matching five numbers.
c. matching four numbers.
d. matching three numbers.
e. matching two numbers.
f. matching one number.
g. matching none of the numbers.
h. If you match zero, one, or two numbers, you do not win anything. What is the probability that you will not win anything?
i. The Lotto ticket gives complete game rules and probabilities of matching zero through six numbers. The lottery ticket has the saying "A Win for Education" on the back of the ticket. Do you think Florida's slogan and the printed complete game rules and probabilities of matching zero through six numbers is an ethical approach to running the lottery game?

CASES FOR CHAPTER 5

Managing Ashland MultiComm Services

The Ashland MultiComm Services (AMS) marketing department wants to increase subscriptions for its *3-For-All* telephone, cable, and Internet combined service. AMS marketing has been conducting an aggressive direct-marketing campaign that includes postal and electronic mailings and telephone solicitations. Feedback from these efforts indicates that including premium channels in this combined service is a very important factor for both current and prospective subscribers. After several brainstorming sessions, the marketing department has decided to add premium cable channels as a no-cost benefit of subscribing to the *3-For-All* service.

The research director, Mona Fields, is planning to conduct a survey among prospective customers to determine how many premium channels need to be added to the *3-For-All* service in order to generate a subscription to the service. Based on past campaigns and on industry-wide data, she estimates the following:

Number of Free Premium Channels	Probability of Subscriptions
0	0.02
1	0.04
2	0.06
3	0.07
4	0.08
5	0.085

1. If a sample of 50 prospective customers is selected and no free premium channels are included in the *3-For-All* service offer, given past results, what is the probability that

a. fewer than 3 customers will subscribe to the *3-For-All* service offer?
b. 0 customers or 1 customer will subscribe to the *3-For- All* service offer?
c. more than 4 customers will subscribe to the *3-For-All* service offer?
d. Suppose that in the actual survey of 50 prospective customers, 4 customers subscribe to the *3-For-All* service offer. What does this tell you about the previous estimate of the proportion of customers who would subscribe to the *3-For-All* service offer?

2. Instead of offering no premium free channels as in Problem 1, suppose that two free premium channels are included in the *3-For-All* service offer. Given past results, what is the probability that

a. fewer than 3 customers will subscribe to the *3-For-All* service offer?
b. 0 customers or 1 customer will subscribe to the *3-For-All* service offer?
c. more than 4 customers will subscribe to the *3-For-All* service offer?
d. Compare the results of (a) through (c) to those of **1**.
e. Suppose that in the actual survey of 50 prospective customers, 6 customers subscribe to the *3-For-All* service offer. What does this tell you about the previous estimate of the proportion of customers who would subscribe to the *3-For-All* service offer?
f. What do the results in (e) tell you about the effect of offering free premium channels on the likelihood of obtaining subscriptions to the *3-For-All* service?

3. Suppose that additional surveys of 50 prospective customers were conducted in which the number of free premium channels was varied. The results were as follows:

Number of Free Premium Channels	Number of Subscriptions
1	5
3	6
4	6
5	7

How many free premium channels should the research director recommend for inclusion in the *3-For-All* service? Explain.

Digital Case

Apply your knowledge about expected value and the covariance in this continuing Digital Case from Chapters 3 and 4.

Open **BullsAndBears.pdf**, a marketing brochure from EndRun Financial Services. Read the claims and examine the supporting data. Then answer the following:

1. Are there any "catches" about the claims the brochure makes for the rate of return of Happy Bull and Worried Bear funds?

2. What subjective data influence the rate-of-return analyses of these funds? Could EndRun be accused of making false and misleading statements? Why or why not?

3. The expected-return analysis seems to show that the Worried Bear fund has a greater expected return than the Happy Bull fund. Should a rational investor never invest in the Happy Bull fund? Why or why not?

CHAPTER 5 EXCEL GUIDE

EG5.1 The PROBABILITY DISTRIBUTION for a DISCRETE VARIABLE

Key Technique Use the **SUMPRODUCT(*cell range 1, cell range 2*)** function (see Appendix Section F.4) to compute the expected value and variance.

Example Compute the expected value, variance, and standard deviation for the data of Table 5.1 number of interruptions per day on page 186.

In-Depth Excel Use the **Discrete Variable workbook** as a model.

For the example, open to the **DATA worksheet** of the **Discrete Variable workbook**. The worksheet already contains the entries needed to compute the expected value, variance, and standard deviation (shown in the COMPUTE worksheet) for the example.

For other problems, modify the DATA worksheet. Enter the probability distribution data into columns **A** and **B** and, if necessary, extend columns C through E, first selecting cell range **C7:E7** and then copying that cell range down as many rows as necessary. If the probability distribution has fewer than six outcomes, select the rows that contain the extra, unwanted outcomes, right-click, and then click **Delete** in the shortcut menu.

Read the SHORT TAKES for Chapter 5 for an explanation of the formulas found in the DATA and COMPUTE worksheets and to see illustrations of these worksheets.

EG5.2 COVARIANCE of a PROBABILITY DISTRIBUTION and ITS APPLICATION in FINANCE

Key Technique Use the **SQRT** and **SUMPRODUCT** functions (see Appendix Section F.4) to help compute the portfolio analysis statistics.

Example Perform the portfolio analysis for the Section 5.2 investment example.

PHStat Use **Covariance and Portfolio Analysis**

For the example, select **PHStat → Decision-Making → Covariance and Portfolio Analysis**. In the procedure's dialog box (shown at top right):

1. Enter **5** as the **Number of Outcomes**.
2. Enter a **Title**, check **Portfolio Management Analysis**, and click **OK**.

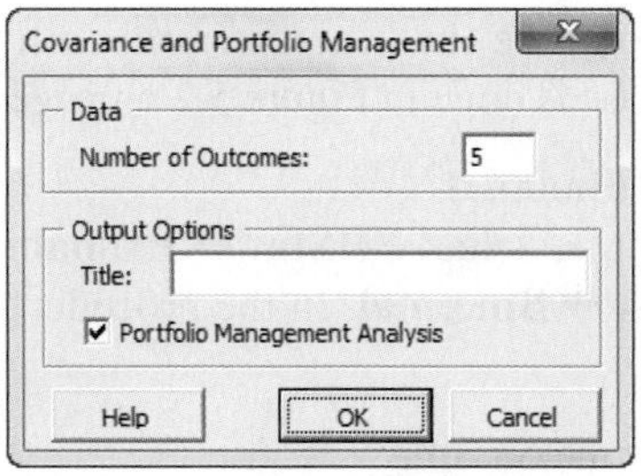

In the new worksheet (shown in Figure EG5.1):

3. Enter the probabilities and outcomes in the table that begins in cell B3.
4. Enter **0.5** as the **Weight assigned to X**.

In-Depth Excel Use the **COMPUTE worksheet** of the **Portfolio workbook** as a template.

The worksheet (shown in Figure EG5.1) already contains the data for the example. Overwrite the *X* and *P*(*X*) values and the weight assigned to the *X* value when you enter data for other problems. If a problem has more or fewer than three outcomes, first select row **5**, right-click, and click **Insert** (or **Delete**) in the shortcut menu to insert (or delete) rows one at a time. If you insert rows, select the cell range **B4:J4** and copy the contents of this range down through the new table rows.

FIGURE EG5.1

Portfolio analysis worksheet

	A	B	C	D	
1	Portfolio Expected Return and Risk				
2					
3	Probabilities & Outcomes:	P	X	Y	
4		0.2	-300	200	
5		0.5	100	50	
6		0.3	250	-100	
7					
8	Weight Assigned to X	0.5			
9					
10	Statistics				
11	E(X)	65			=SUMPRODUCT(B4:B6, C4:C6)
12	E(Y)	35			=SUMPRODUCT(B4:B6, D4:D6)
13	Variance(X)	37525			=SUMPRODUCT(B4:B6, H4:H6)
14	Standard Deviation(X)	193.71			=SQRT(B13)
15	Variance(Y)	11025			=SUMPRODUCT(B4:B6, I4:I6)
16	Standard Deviation(Y)	105			=SQRT(B15)
17	Covariance(XY)	-19275			=SUMPRODUCT(B4:B6, J4:J6)
18	Variance(X+Y)	10000			=B13 + B15 + 2 * B17
19	Standard Deviation(X+Y)	100			=SQRT(B18)
20					
21	Portfolio Management				
22	Weight Assigned to X	0.5			=B8
23	Weight Assigned to Y	0.5			=1-B22
24	Portfolio Expected Return	50			=B22 * B11 + B23 * B12
25	Portfolio Risk	50			=SQRT(B22^2 * B13 + B23^2 * B15 + 2 * B22 * B23 * B17)

The worksheet also contains a Calculations Area that contains various intermediate calculations. Open the **COMPUTE_FORMULAS worksheet** to examine all the formulas used in this area.

EG5.3 BINOMIAL DISTRIBUTION

Key Technique Use the **BINOM.DIST(*number of events of interest, sample size, probability of an event of interest,* FALSE)**.

Example Compute the binomial probabilities for $n = 4$ and $\pi = 0.1$, as is done in Figure 5.2 on page 199.

PHStat Use **Binomial**.
For the example, select **PHStat ➔ Probability & Prob. Distributions ➔ Binomial**. In the procedure's dialog box (shown below):

1. Enter **4** as the **Sample Size**.
2. Enter **0.1** as the **Prob. of an Event of Interest**.
3. Enter **0** as the **Outcomes From** value and enter **4** as the (Outcomes) **To** value.
4. Enter a **Title**, check **Histogram**, and click **OK**.

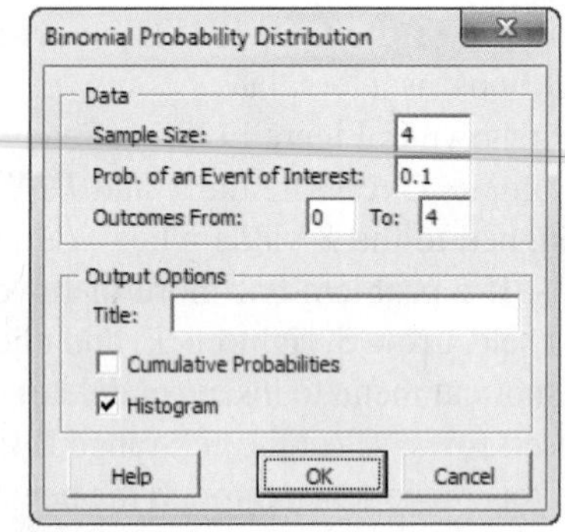

Check **Cumulative Probabilities** before clicking **OK** in step 4 to have the procedure include columns for $P(\leq X)$, $P(< X)$, $P(> X)$, and $P(\geq X)$ in the binomial probabilities table.

In-Depth Excel Use the **Binomial workbook** as a template and model.
For the example, open to the **COMPUTE worksheet** of the **Binomial workbook**, shown in Figure 5.2 on page 199. The worksheet already contains the entries needed for the example. For other problems, change the sample size in cell **B4** and the probability of an event of interest in cell **B5**. If necessary, extend the binomial probabilities table by first selecting cell range **A18:B18** and then copying that cell range down as many rows as necessary. To construct a histogram of the probability distribution, use the Appendix Section B.9 instructions.

Read the SHORT TAKES for Chapter 5 for an explanation of the formulas found in the CUMULATIVE worksheet, which demonstrates the use of the BINOM.DIST function to compute cumulative probabilities. If you use an Excel version older than Excel 2010, use the CUMULATIVE_OLDER worksheet instead of the COMPUTE or CUMULATIVE worksheets.

EG5.4 POISSON DISTRIBUTION

Key Technique Use the **POISSON.DIST(*number of events of interest, the average or expected number of events of interest,* FALSE)**.

Example Compute the Poisson probabilities for the customer arrival problem in which $\lambda = 3$, as is done in Figure 5.4 on page 204.

PHStat2 Use **Poisson**.
For the example, select **PHStat ➔ Probability & Prob. Distributions ➔ Poisson**. In this procedure's dialog box (shown below):

1. Enter **3** as the **Mean/Expected No. of Events of Interest**.
2. Enter a **Title** and click **OK**.

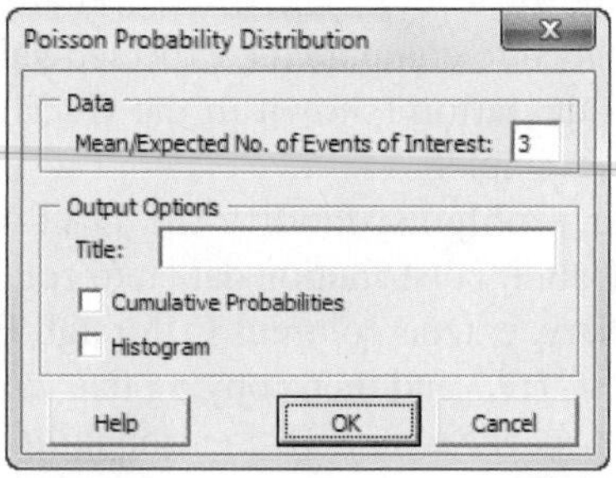

Check **Cumulative Probabilities** before clicking **OK** in step 2 to have the procedure include columns for $P(\leq X)$, $P(< X)$, $P(> X)$, and $P(\geq X)$ in the Poisson probabilities table. You can also check **Histogram** to produce a histogram of the Poisson probability distribution.

In-Depth Excel Use the **Poisson workbook** as a template.
For the example, open to the **COMPUTE worksheet** of the **Poisson workbook**, shown in Figure 5.4 on page 204. The worksheet already contains the entries for the example. For other problems, change the mean or expected number of events of interest in cell **E4**. To construct a histogram of the probability distribution, use the Appendix Section B.9 instructions.

Read the SHORT TAKES for Chapter 5 for an explanation of the formulas found in the CUMULATIVE worksheet, which demonstrates the use of the POISSON.DIST function to compute cumulative probabilities. If you use an Excel version older than Excel 2010, use the CUMULATIVE_OLDER worksheet instead of the COMPUTE or CUMULATIVE worksheets.

EG5.5 HYPGEOMETRIC DISTRIBUTION

Key Technique Use the **HYPERGEOM.DIST(*X, sample size, number of events of interest in the population, population size*, FALSE)**.

Example Compute the hypergeometric probabilities for the team formation problem as is done in Figure 5.5 on page 207.

PHStat Use **Hypergeometric**.

For the example, select **PHStat ➔ Probability & Prob. Distributions ➔ Hypergeometric**. In this procedure's dialog box (shown below):

1. Enter **8** as the **Sample Size**.
2. Enter **10** as the **No. of Events of Interest in Pop**.
3. Enter **30** as the **Population Size**.
4. Enter a **Title** and click **OK**.

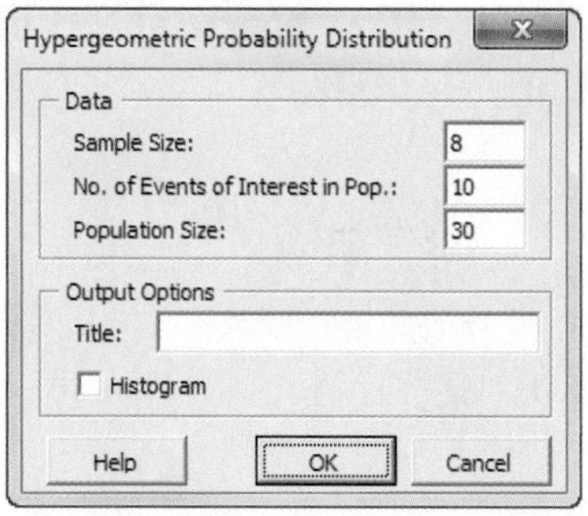

Check **Histogram** to produce a histogram of the probability distribution.

In-Depth Excel Use the **Hypergeometric workbook** as a template.

For the example, open to the **COMPUTE worksheet** of the **Hypergeometric workbook**, shown in Figure 5.5 on page 207. The worksheet already contains the entries for the example. For other problems, change the sample size in cell **B4**, the number of events of interest in the population in cell **B5**, and the population size in cell **B6**. To construct a histogram of the probability distribution, use the Appendix Section B.9 instructions.

Read the SHORT TAKES for Chapter 5 an explanation of the formulas found in the CUMULATIVE worksheet, which demonstrates the use of the HYPERGEOM.DIST function to compute cumulative probabilities. If you use an Excel version older than Excel 2010, use the CUMULATIVE_OLDER worksheet instead of the COMPUTE or CUMULATIVE worksheets.

CHAPTER 6

The Normal Distribution and Other Continuous Distributions

Learning Objectives

In this chapter, you learn:

- To compute probabilities from the normal distribution
- How to use the normal distribution to solve business problems
- To use the normal probability plot to determine whether a set of data is approximately normally distributed
- To compute probabilities from the uniform distribution
- To compute probabilities from the exponential distribution

USING STATISTICS

Angela Waye / Shutterstock

Normal Downloading at MyTVLab

You are a project manager for the MyTVLab website, an online service that streams movies and episodes from broadcast and cable TV series and that allows users to upload and share original videos. To attract and retain visitors to the website, you need to ensure that users can quickly download the exclusive-content daily videos.

To check how fast a video downloads, you open a web browser on a computer at the corporate offices of MyTVLab, load the MyTVLab home page, download the first website-exclusive video, and measure the download time. Download time—the amount of time in seconds, that passes from first clicking a download link until the video is ready to play—is a function of both the streaming media technology used and the number of simultaneous users of the website. Past data indicate that the mean download time is 7 seconds and that the standard deviation is 2 seconds. Approximately two-thirds of the download times are between 5 and 9 seconds, and about 95% of the download times are between 3 and 11 seconds. In other words, the download times are distributed as a bell-shaped curve, with a clustering around the mean of 7 seconds. How could you use this information to answer questions about the download times of the first video?

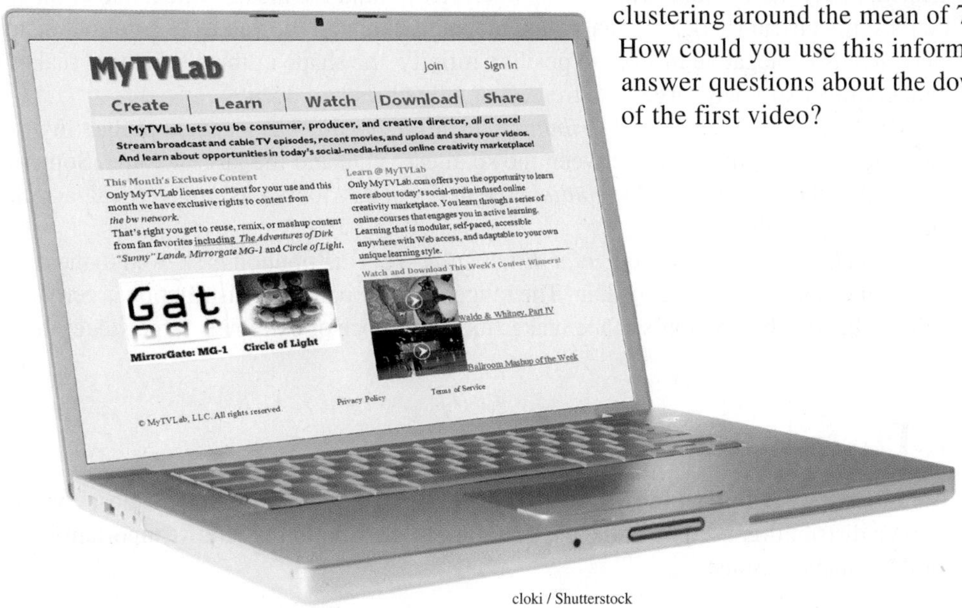

cloki / Shutterstock

In Chapter 5, accounting managers at Ricknel Home Centers wanted to be able to answer questions about the number of tagged items in a given sample size. As a MyTVLab project manager, you face a different task—one that involves a continuous measurement because a download time could be any value and not just a whole number. How can you answer questions, such as the following, about this *continuous numerical variable*:

- What proportion of the video downloads take more than 9 seconds?
- How many seconds elapse before 10% of the downloads are complete?
- How many seconds elapse before 99% of the downloads are complete?
- How would enhancing the streaming media technology used affect the answers to these questions?

As in Chapter 5, you can use a probability distribution as a model. Reading this chapter will help you learn about characteristics of continuous probability distributions and how to use the normal distribution to solve business problems.

6.1 Continuous Probability Distributions

A **probability density function** is a mathematical expression that defines the distribution of the values for a continuous variable. Figure 6.1 graphically displays three probability density functions.

FIGURE 6.1
Three continuous probability distributions

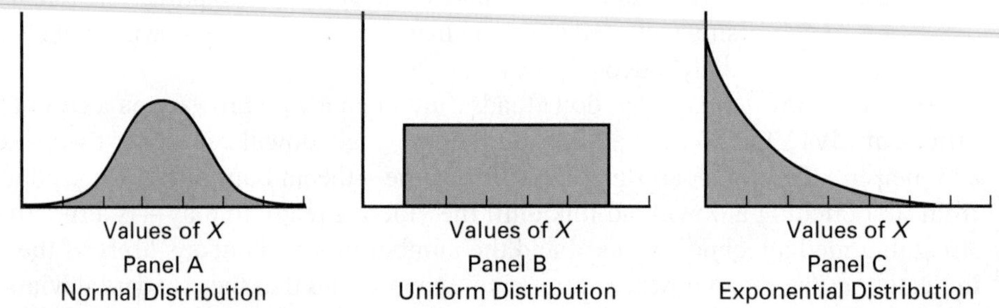

Panel A depicts a *normal* distribution. The normal distribution is symmetrical and bell-shaped, implying that most values tend to cluster around the mean, which, due to the distribution's symmetrical shape, is equal to the median. Although the values in a normal distribution can range from negative infinity to positive infinity, the shape of the distribution makes it very unlikely that extremely large or extremely small values will occur.

Panel B shows a *uniform distribution* where each value has an equal probability of occurrence anywhere in the range between the smallest value and the largest value. Sometimes referred to as the *rectangular distribution*, the uniform distribution is symmetrical, and therefore the mean equals the median.

Panel C illustrates an *exponential distribution.* This distribution is skewed to the right, making the mean larger than the median. The range for an exponential distribution is zero to positive infinity, but the distribution's shape makes the occurrence of extremely large values unlikely.

6.2 The Normal Distribution

The **normal distribution** (also known as the *Gaussian distribution*) is the most common continuous distribution used in statistics. The normal distribution is vitally important in statistics for three main reasons:

- Numerous continuous variables common in business have distributions that closely resemble the normal distribution.
- The normal distribution can be used to approximate various discrete probability distributions.
- The normal distribution provides the basis for *classical statistical inference* because of its relationship to the *Central Limit Theorem* (which is discussed in Section 7.2).

The normal distribution is represented by the classic bell shape shown in Panel A of Figure 6.1. In the normal distribution, you can calculate the probability that values occur within certain ranges or intervals. However, because probability for continuous variables is measured as an area under the curve, the *exact* probability of a *particular value* from a continuous distribution such as the normal distribution is zero. As an example, time (in seconds) is measured and not counted. Therefore, you can determine the probability that the download time for a video on a web browser is between 7 and 10 seconds, or the probability that the download time is between 8 and 9 seconds, or the probability that the download time is between 7.99 and 8.01 seconds. However, the probability that the download time is *exactly* 8 seconds is zero.

The normal distribution has several important theoretical properties:

- It is symmetrical, and its mean and median are therefore equal.
- It is bell-shaped in appearance.
- Its interquartile range is equal to 1.33 standard deviations. Thus, the middle 50% of the values are contained within an interval of two-thirds of a standard deviation below the mean and two-thirds of a standard deviation above the mean.
- It has an infinite range ($-\infty < X < \infty$).

In practice, many variables have distributions that closely resemble the theoretical properties of the normal distribution. The data in Table 6.1 represent the amount of soft drink in 10,000 1-liter bottles filled on a recent day. The continuous variable of interest, the amount of soft drink filled, can be approximated by the normal distribution. The measurements of the amount of soft drink in the 10,000 bottles cluster in the interval 1.05 to 1.055 liters and distribute symmetrically around that grouping, forming a bell-shaped pattern.

TABLE 6.1

Amount of Fill in 10,000 Bottles of a Soft Drink

Amount of Fill (liters)	Relative Frequency
< 1.025	48/10,000 = 0.0048
1.025 < 1.030	122/10,000 = 0.0122
1.030 < 1.035	325/10,000 = 0.0325
1.035 < 1.040	695/10,000 = 0.0695
1.040 < 1.045	1,198/10,000 = 0.1198
1.045 < 1.050	1,664/10,000 = 0.1664
1.050 < 1.055	1,896/10,000 = 0.1896
1.055 < 1.060	1,664/10,000 = 0.1664
1.060 < 1.065	1,198/10,000 = 0.1198
1.065 < 1.070	695/10,000 = 0.0695
1.070 < 1.075	325/10,000 = 0.0325
1.075 < 1.080	122/10,000 = 0.0122
1.080 or above	48/10,000 = 0.0048
Total	1.0000

Figure 6.2 shows the relative frequency histogram and polygon for the distribution of the amount filled in 10,000 bottles.

FIGURE 6.2

Relative frequency histogram and polygon of the amount filled in 10,000 bottles of a soft drink

Source: Data are taken from Table 6.1.

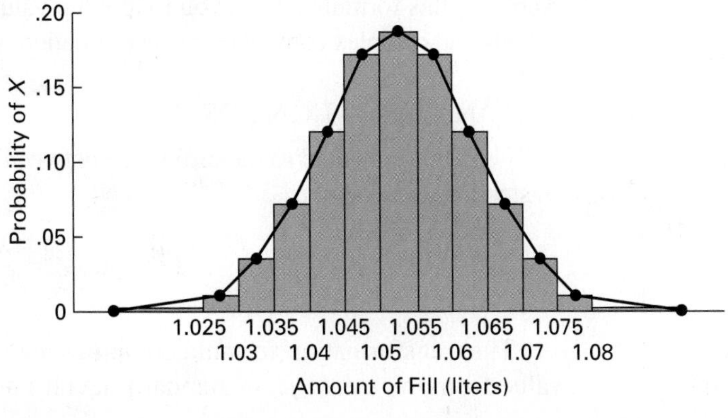

For these data, the first three theoretical properties of the normal distribution are approximately satisfied. However, the fourth one, having an infinite range, is not. The amount filled in a bottle cannot possibly be zero or below, nor can a bottle be filled beyond its capacity. From Table 6.1, you see that only 48 out of every 10,000 bottles filled are expected to contain 1.08 liters or more, and an equal number are expected to contain less than 1.025 liters.

The symbol $f(X)$ is used to represent a probability density function. The **probability density function for the normal distribution** is given in Equation (6.1).

NORMAL PROBABILITY DENSITY FUNCTION

$$f(X) = \frac{1}{\sqrt{2\pi}\sigma}e^{-(1/2)[(X-\mu)/\sigma]^2} \qquad \textbf{(6.1)}$$

where

e = mathematical constant approximated by 2.71828
π = mathematical constant approximated by 3.14159
μ = mean
σ = standard deviation
X = any value of the continuous variable, where $-\infty < X < \infty$

Although Equation (6.1) may look complicated, because e and π are mathematical constants, the probabilities of the random variable X are dependent only on the two parameters of the normal distribution—the mean, μ, and the standard deviation, σ. Every time you specify particular values of μ and σ, a *different* normal probability distribution is generated. Figure 6.3 illustrates this principle. The distributions labeled A and B have the same mean (μ) but have different standard deviations. Distributions A and C have the same standard deviation (σ) but have different means. Distributions B and C have different values for both μ and σ.

FIGURE 6.3
Three normal distributions

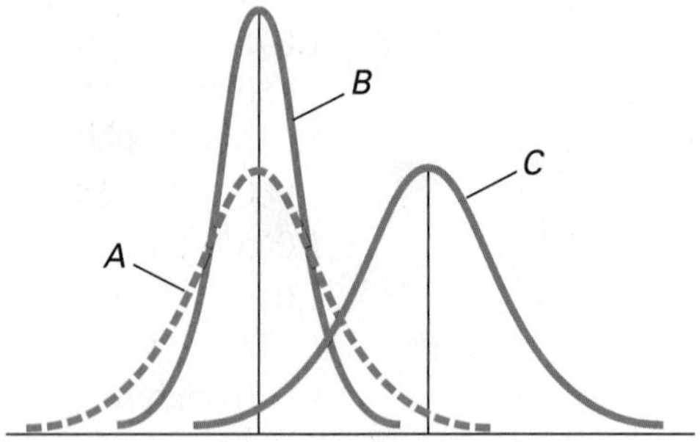

Student Tip
There is a different normal distribution for each combination of the mean, μ, and the standard deviation, σ.

Computing Normal Probabilities

To compute normal probabilities, you first convert a normally distributed variable, X, to a **standardized normal variable**, Z, using the **transformation formula**, shown in Equation (6.2). Applying this formula allows you to look up values in a normal probability table and avoid the tedious and complex computations that Equation (6.1) would otherwise require.

TRANSFORMATION FORMULA

The Z value is equal to the difference between X and the mean, μ, divided by the standard deviation, σ.

$$Z = \frac{X - \mu}{\sigma} \qquad \textbf{(6.2)}$$

The transformation formula computes a Z value that expresses the difference of the X value from the mean, μ, in standard deviation units (see Section 3.2 on page 117) called *standardized units*. While a variable, X, has mean, μ, and standard deviation, σ, the standardized variable, Z, always has mean $\mu = 0$ and standard deviation $\sigma = 1$.

Then you can determine the probabilities by using Table E.2, the **cumulative standardized normal distribution**. For example, recall from the Using Statistics scenario on page 219 that past data indicate that the time to download a video is normally distributed, with a mean $\mu = 7$ seconds and a standard deviation $\sigma = 2$ seconds. From Figure 6.4, you see that every measurement X has a corresponding standardized measurement Z, computed from Equation (6.2), the transformation formula.

FIGURE 6.4
Transformation of scales

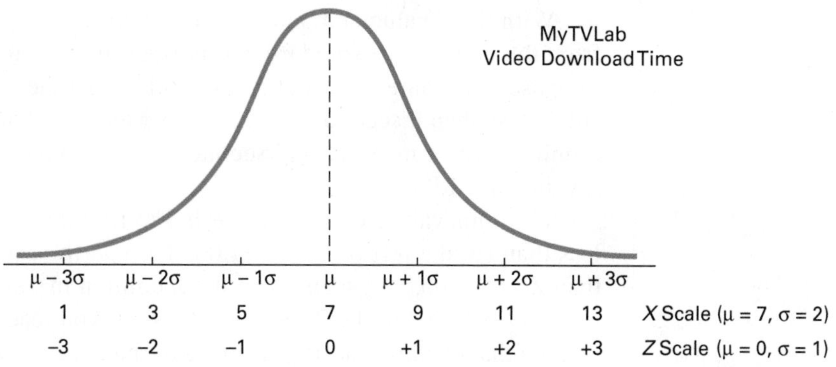

Therefore, a download time of 9 seconds is equivalent to 1 standardized unit (1 standard deviation) above the mean because

$$Z = \frac{9 - 7}{2} = +1$$

A download time of 1 second is equivalent to -3 standardized units (3 standard deviations) below the mean because

$$Z = \frac{1 - 7}{2} = -3$$

In Figure 6.4, the standard deviation is the unit of measurement. In other words, a time of 9 seconds is 2 seconds (1 standard deviation) higher, or *slower*, than the mean time of 7 seconds. Similarly, a time of 1 second is 6 seconds (3 standard deviations) lower, or *faster*, than the mean time.

To further illustrate the transformation formula, suppose that another website has a download time for a video that is normally distributed, with a mean $\mu = 4$ seconds and a standard deviation $\sigma = 1$ second. Figure 6.5 shows this distribution.

FIGURE 6.5
A different transformation of scales

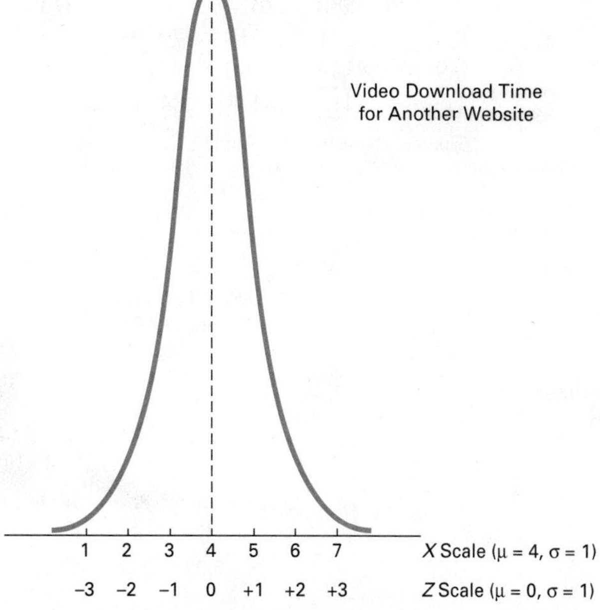

Comparing these results with those of the MyTVLab website, you see that a download time of 5 seconds is 1 standard deviation above the mean download time because

$$Z = \frac{5 - 4}{1} = +1$$

A time of 1 second is 3 standard deviations below the mean download time because

$$Z = \frac{1 - 4}{1} = -3$$

With the Z value computed, you look up the normal probability using a table of values from the cumulative standardized normal distribution, such as Table E.2 in Appendix E. Suppose you wanted to find the probability that the download time for the MyTVLab website is less than 9 seconds. Recall from page 223 that transforming $X = 9$ to standardized Z units, given a mean $\mu = 7$ seconds and a standard deviation $\sigma = 2$ seconds, leads to a Z value of $+1.00$.

Student Tip
Remember that when dealing with a continuous distribution such as the normal, the word *area* has the same meaning as *probability*.

With this value, you use Table E.2 to find the cumulative area under the normal curve less than (to the left of) $Z = +1.00$. To read the probability or area under the curve less than $Z = +1.00$, you scan down the Z column in Table E.2 until you locate the Z value of interest (in 10ths) in the Z row for 1.0. Next, you read across this row until you intersect the column that contains the 100ths place of the Z value. Therefore, in the body of the table, the probability for $Z = 1.00$ corresponds to the intersection of the row $Z = 1.0$ with the column $Z = .00$. Table 6.2, which reproduces a portion of Table E.2, shows this intersection. The probability listed at the intersection is 0.8413, which means that there is an 84.13% chance that the download time will be less than 9 seconds. Figure 6.6 graphically shows this probability.

TABLE 6.2

Finding a Cumulative Area Under the Normal Curve

	Cumulative Probabilities									
Z	.00	.01	.02	.03	.04	.05	.06	.07	.08	.09
0.0	.5000	.5040	.5080	.5120	.5160	.5199	.5239	.5279	.5319	.5359
0.1	.5398	.5438	.5478	.5517	.5557	.5596	.5636	.5675	.5714	.5753
0.2	.5793	.5832	.5871	.5910	.5948	.5987	.6026	.6064	.6103	.6141
0.3	.6179	.6217	.6255	.6293	.6331	.6368	.6406	.6443	.6480	.6517
0.4	.6554	.6591	.6628	.6664	.6700	.6736	.6772	.6808	.6844	.6879
0.5	.6915	.6950	.6985	.7019	.7054	.7088	.7123	.7157	.7190	.7224
0.6	.7257	.7291	.7324	.7357	.7389	.7422	.7454	.7486	.7518	.7549
0.7	.7580	.7612	.7642	.7673	.7704	.7734	.7764	.7794	.7823	.7852
0.8	.7881	.7910	.7939	.7967	.7995	.8023	.8051	.8078	.8106	.8133
0.9	.8159	.8186	.8212	.8238	.8264	.8289	.8315	.8340	.8365	.8389
1.0 →	.8413	.8438	.8461	.8485	.8508	.8531	.8554	.8577	.8599	.8621

Source: Extracted from Table E.2.

FIGURE 6.6

Determining the area less than Z from a cumulative standardized normal distribution

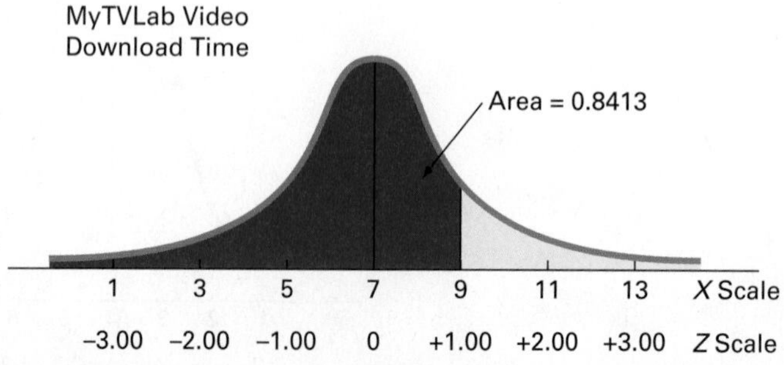

However, for the other website, you see that a time of 5 seconds is 1 standardized unit above the mean time of 4 seconds. Thus, the probability that the download time will be less than 5 seconds is also 0.8413. Figure 6.7 shows that regardless of the value of the mean, μ, and standard deviation, σ, of a normally distributed variable, Equation (6.2) can transform the X value to a Z value.

FIGURE 6.7
Demonstrating a transformation of scales for corresponding cumulative portions under two normal curves

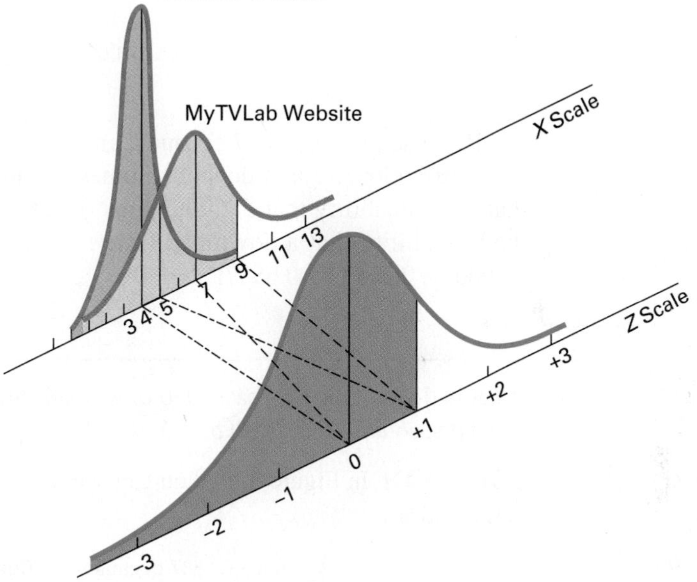

Student Tip
You will find it very helpful when computing probabilities under the normal curve if you draw a normal curve and then enter the values for the mean and X below the curve and shade the desired area to be determined under the curve.

Now that you have learned to use Table E.2 with Equation (6.2), you can answer many questions related to the MyTVLab video download, using the normal distribution.

EXAMPLE 6.1
Finding $P(X > 9)$

What is the probability that the video download time for the MyTVLab website will be more than 9 seconds?

SOLUTION The probability that the download time will be less than 9 seconds is 0.8413 (see Figure 6.6 on page 224). Thus, the probability that the download time will be more than 9 seconds is the *complement* of less than 9 seconds, $1 - 0.8413 = 0.1587$. Figure 6.8 illustrates this result.

FIGURE 6.8
Finding $P(X > 9)$

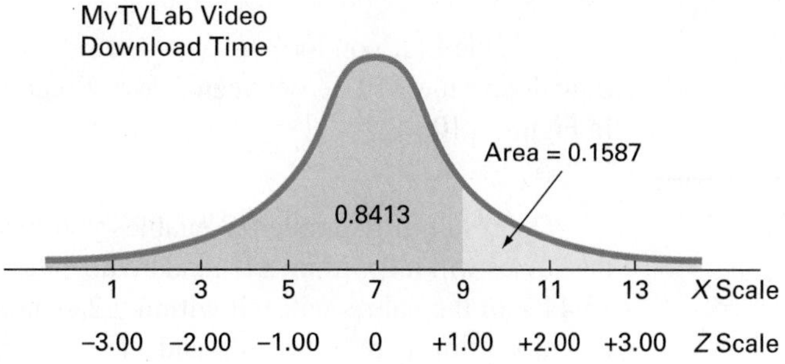

EXAMPLE 6.2
Finding $P(X < 7$ or $X > 9)$

What is the probability that the video download time for the MyTVLab website will be less than 7 seconds or more than 9 seconds?

SOLUTION To find this probability, you separately calculate the probability of a download time less than 7 seconds and the probability of a download time greater than 9 seconds and then add these two probabilities together. Figure 6.9 illustrates this result.

FIGURE 6.9
Finding $P(X < 7$ or $X > 9)$

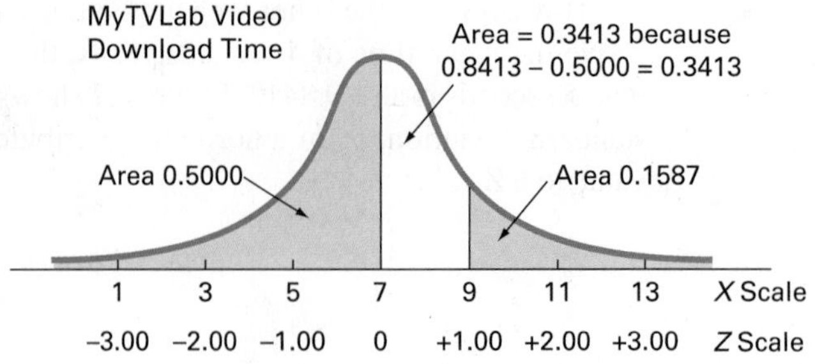

Because the mean is 7 seconds, and because the mean is equal to the median in a normal distribution, 50% of download times are under 7 seconds. From Example 6.1, you know that the probability that the download time is greater than 9 seconds is 0.1587. Therefore, the probability that a download time is under 7 or over 9 seconds, $P(X < 7 \text{ or } X > 9)$, is $0.5000 + 0.1587 = 0.6587$.

EXAMPLE 6.3

Finding $P(5 < X < 9)$

What is the probability that video download time for the MyTVLab website will be between 5 and 9 seconds—that is, $P(5 < X < 9)$?

SOLUTION In Figure 6.10, you can see that the area of interest is located between two values, 5 and 9.

FIGURE 6.10
Finding $P(5 < X < 9)$

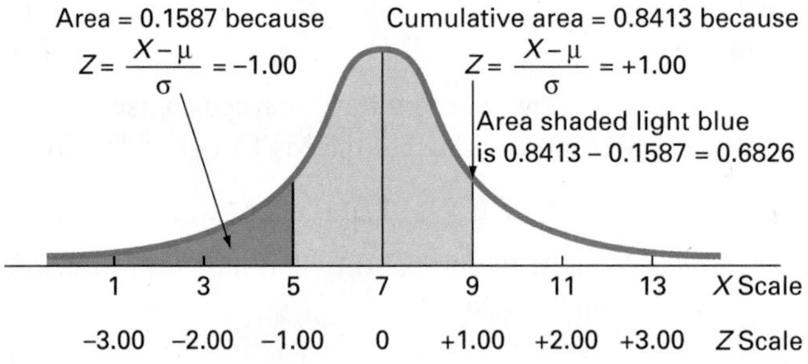

In Example 6.1 on page 225, you already found that the area under the normal curve less than 9 seconds is 0.8413. To find the area under the normal curve less than 5 seconds,

$$Z = \frac{5 - 7}{2} = -1.00$$

Using Table E.2, you look up $Z = -1.00$ and find 0.1587. Therefore, the probability that the download time will be between 5 and 9 seconds is $0.8413 - 0.1587 = 0.6826$, as displayed in Figure 6.10.

The result of Example 6.3 enables you to state that for any normal distribution, 68.26% of the values will fall within ± 1 standard deviation of the mean. From Figure 6.11, you can see that 95.44% of the values will fall within ± 2 standard deviations of the mean. Thus, 95.44% of the download times are between 3 and 11 seconds. From Figure 6.12, you can see that 99.73% of the values are within ± 3 standard deviations above or below the mean.

FIGURE 6.11
Finding $P(3 < X < 11)$

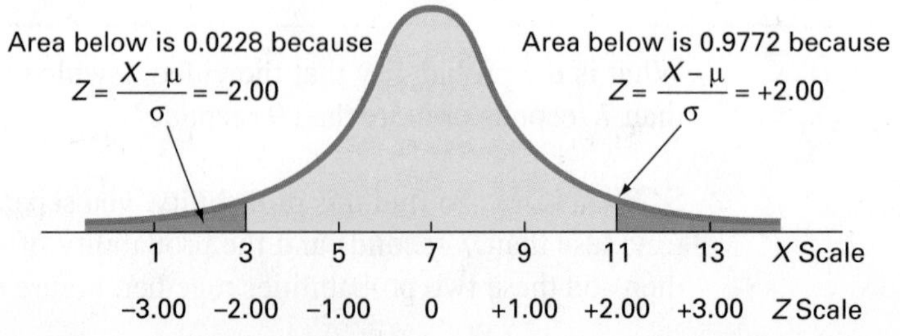

FIGURE 6.12
Finding $P(1 < X < 13)$

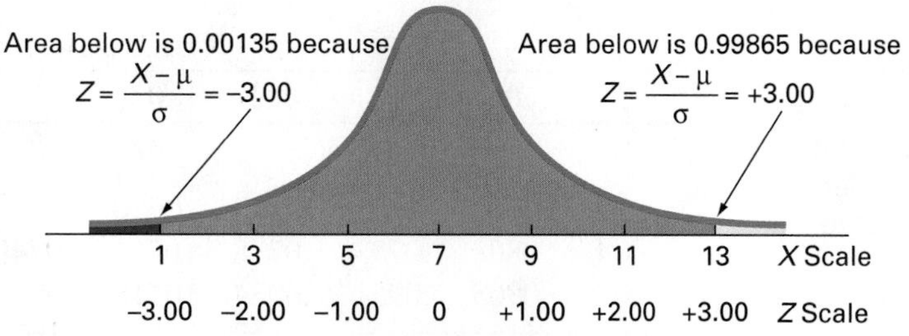

Thus, 99.73% of the download times are between 1 and 13 seconds. Therefore, it is unlikely (0.0027, or only 27 in 10,000) that a download time will be so fast or so slow that it will take under 1 second or more than 13 seconds. In general, you can use 6σ (i.e., 3 standard deviations below the mean to 3 standard deviations above the mean) as a practical approximation of the range for normally distributed data.

Figures 6.10, 6.11, and 6.12 illustrate that for any normal distribution,

- Approximately 68.26% of the values fall within ± 1 standard deviation of the mean
- Approximately 95.44% of the values fall within ± 2 standard deviations of the mean
- Approximately 99.73% of the values fall within ± 3 standard deviations of the mean

This result is the justification for the empirical rule presented on page 133. The accuracy of the empirical rule improves as a data set follows the normal distribution more closely.

Finding X Values

Examples 6.1 through 6.3 require you to use the normal distribution Table E.2 to find an area under the normal curve that corresponds to a specific X value. For other situations, you may need to do the reverse: Find the X value that corresponds to a specific area. In general, you use Equation (6.3) for finding an X value.

FINDING AN X VALUE ASSOCIATED WITH A KNOWN PROBABILITY

The X value is equal to the mean, μ, plus the product of the Z value and the standard deviation, σ.

$$X = \mu + Z\sigma \quad \textbf{(6.3)}$$

To find a *particular* value associated with a known probability, follow these steps:

- Sketch the normal curve and then place the values for the mean and X on the X and Z scales.
- Find the cumulative area less than X.
- Shade the area of interest.
- Using Table E.2, determine the Z value corresponding to the area under the normal curve less than X.
- Using Equation (6.3), solve for X:

$$X = \mu + Z\sigma$$

Examples 6.4 and 6.5 illustrate this technique.

EXAMPLE 6.4

Finding the X Value for a Cumulative Probability of 0.10

How much time (in seconds) will elapse before the fastest 10% of the downloads of a MyTVLab video are complete?

SOLUTION Because 10% of the videos are expected to download in under X seconds, the area under the normal curve less than this value is 0.1000. Using the body of Table E.2, you search for the area or probability of 0.1000. The closest result is 0.1003, as shown in Table 6.3 (which is extracted from Table E.2).

TABLE 6.3

Finding a Z Value Corresponding to a Particular Cumulative Area (0.10) Under the Normal Curve

	Cumulative Probabilities									
Z	.00	.01	.02	.03	.04	.05	.06	.07	.08	.09
⋮	⋮	⋮	⋮	⋮	⋮	⋮	⋮	⋮	⋮	⋮
−1.5	.0668	.0655	.0643	.0630	.0618	.0606	.0594	.0582	.0571	.0559
−1.4	.0808	.0793	.0778	.0764	.0749	.0735	.0721	.0708	.0694	.0681
−1.3	.0968	.0951	.0934	.0918	.0901	.0885	.0869	.0853	.0838	.0823
−1.2	.1151	.1131	.1112	.1093	.1075	.0156	.0138	.1020	.1003	.0985

Source: Extracted from Table E.2.

Working from this area to the margins of the table, you find that the Z value corresponding to the particular Z row (-1.2) and Z column (.08) is -1.28 (see Figure 6.13).

FIGURE 6.13

Finding Z to determine X

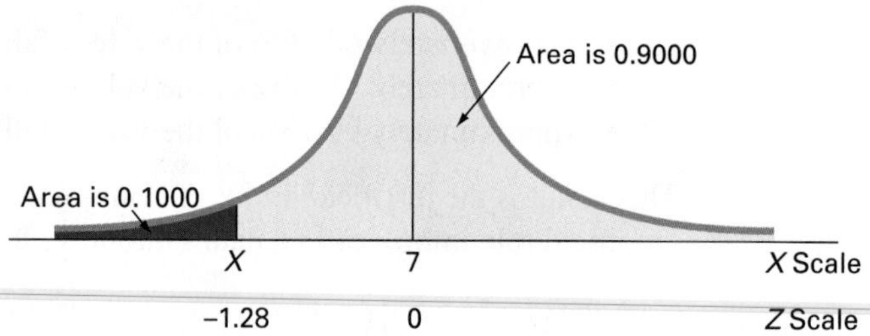

Once you find Z, you use Equation (6.3) on page 227 to determine the X value. Substituting $\mu = 7$, $\sigma = 2$, and $Z = -1.28$,

$$X = \mu + Z\sigma$$

$$X = 7 + (-1.28)(2) = 4.44 \text{ seconds}$$

Thus, 10% of the download times are 4.44 seconds or less.

EXAMPLE 6.5

Finding the X Values That Include 95% of the Download Times

What are the lower and upper values of X, symmetrically distributed around the mean, that include 95% of the download times for a video at the MyTVLab website?

SOLUTION First, you need to find the lower value of X (called X_L). Then, you find the upper value of X (called X_U). Because 95% of the values are between X_L and X_U, and because X_L and X_U are equally distant from the mean, 2.5% of the values are below X_L (see Figure 6.14).

FIGURE 6.14

Finding Z to determine X_L

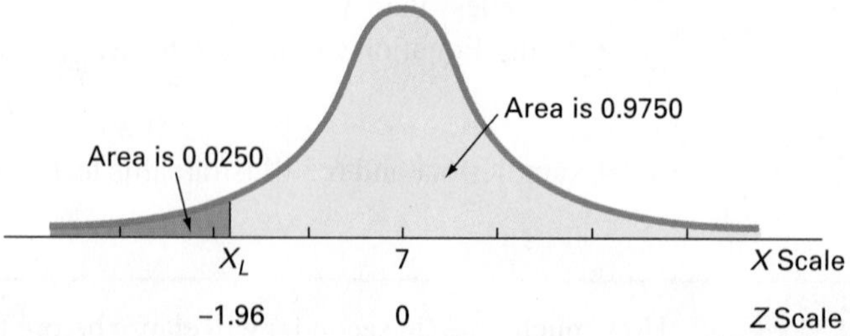

Although X_L is not known, you can find the corresponding Z value because the area under the normal curve less than this Z is 0.0250. Using the body of Table 6.4, you search for the probability 0.0250.

TABLE 6.4
Finding a Z Value Corresponding to a Cumulative Area of 0.025 Under the Normal Curve

	Cumulative Area									
Z	.00	.01	.02	.03	.04	.05	.06	.07	.08	.09
⋮	⋮	⋮	⋮	⋮	⋮	⋮	⋮	⋮	⋮	⋮
−2.0	.0228	.0222	.0217	.0212	.0207	.0202	.0197	.0192	.0188	.0183
−1.9	.0287	.0281	.0274	.0268	.0262	.0256	.0250	.0244	.0239	.0233
−1.8	.0359	.0351	.0344	.0336	.0329	.0232	.0314	.0307	.0301	.0294

Source: Extracted from Table E.2.

Working from the body of the table to the margins of the table, you see that the Z value corresponding to the particular Z row (-1.9) and Z column (.06) is -1.96.

Once you find Z, the final step is to use Equation (6.3) on page 227 as follows:

$$\begin{aligned} X &= \mu + Z\sigma \\ &= 7 + (-1.96)(2) \\ &= 7 - 3.92 \\ &= 3.08 \text{ seconds} \end{aligned}$$

You use a similar process to find X_U. Because only 2.5% of the video downloads take longer than X_U seconds, 97.5% of the video downloads take less than X_U seconds. From the symmetry of the normal distribution, you find that the desired Z value, as shown in Figure 6.15, is $+1.96$ (because Z lies to the right of the standardized mean of 0). You can also extract this Z value from Table 6.5. You can see that 0.975 is the area under the normal curve less than the Z value of $+1.96$.

FIGURE 6.15
Finding Z to determine X_U

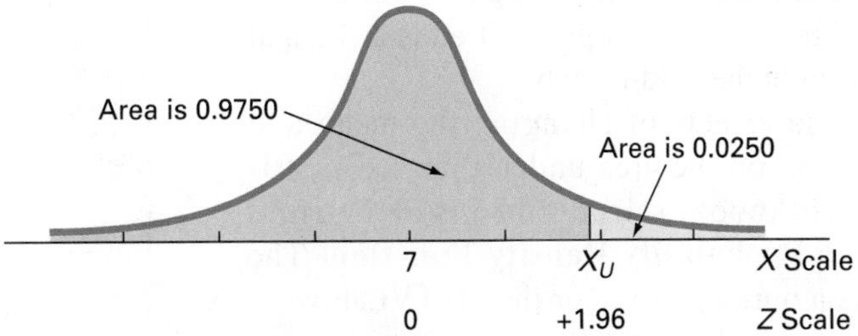

TABLE 6.5
Finding a Z Value Corresponding to a Cumulative Area of 0.975 Under the Normal Curve

	Cumulative Area									
Z	.00	.01	.02	.03	.04	.05	.06	.07	.08	.09
⋮	⋮	⋮	⋮	⋮	⋮	⋮	⋮	⋮	⋮	⋮
+1.8	.9641	.9649	.9656	.9664	.9671	.9678	.9686	.9693	.9699	.9706
+1.9	.9713	.9719	.9726	.9732	.9738	.9744	.9750	.9756	.9761	.9767
+2.0	.9772	.9778	.9783	.9788	.9793	.9798	.9803	.9808	.9812	.9817

Source: Extracted from Table E.2.

Using Equation (6.3) on page 227,

$$\begin{aligned} X &= \mu + Z\sigma \\ &= 7 + (+1.96)(2) \\ &= 7 + 3.92 \\ &= 10.92 \text{ seconds} \end{aligned}$$

Therefore, 95% of the download times are between 3.08 and 10.92 seconds.

Instead of looking up cumulative probabilities in a table, you can use Excel to compute normal probabilities. Figure 6.16 displays a worksheet that computes normal probabilities and finds *X* values for problems similar to Examples 6.1 through 6.5.

FIGURE 6.16

Worksheet for computing normal probabilities and finding *X* values (shown in two parts)

*Figure 6.16 displays the **COMPUTE worksheet** of **Normal workbook** that the Section EG6.2 instructions use.*

	A	B	
1	Normal Probabilities		
2			
3	Common Data		
4	Mean	7	
5	Standard Deviation	2	
6			
7	Probability for X <=		
8	X Value	7	
9	Z Value	0	=STANDARDIZE(B8, B4, B5)
10	P(X<=7)	0.5000	=NORM.DIST(B8, B4, B5, TRUE)
11			
12	Probability for X >		
13	X Value	9	
14	Z Value	1	=STANDARDIZE(B13, B4, B5)
15	P(X>9)	0.1587	=1 - NORM.DIST(B13, B4, B5, TRUE)
16			
17	Probability for X<7 or X>9		
18	P(X<7 or X>9)	0.6587	=B10 + B15
19			

	A	B	
20	Probability for a Range		
21	From X Value	5	
22	To X Value	9	
23	Z Value for 5	-1	=STANDARDIZE(B21, B4, B5)
24	Z Value for 9	1	=STANDARDIZE(B22, B4, B5)
25	P(X<=5)	0.1587	=NORM.DIST(B21, B4, B5, TRUE)
26	P(X<=9)	0.8413	=NORM.DIST(B22, B4, B5, TRUE)
27	P(5<=X<=9)	0.6827	=ABS(B26 - B25)
28			
29	Find X and Z Given a Cum. Pctage.		
30	Cumulative Percentage	10.00%	
31	Z Value	-1.28	=NORM.S.INV(B30)
32	X Value	4.44	=NORM.INV(B30, B4, B5)
33			
34	Find X Values Given a Percentage		
35	Percentage	95.00%	
36	Z Value	-1.96	=NORM.S.INV((1 - B35)/2)
37	Lower X Value	3.08	=B4 + (B36 * B5)
38	Upper X Value	10.92	=B4 - (B36 * B5)

VISUAL EXPLORATIONS Exploring the Normal Distribution

Open the **VE-Normal Distribution add-in workbook** to explore the normal distribution. (See Appendix C to learn how you can download a copy of this workbook and Appendix Section D.5 before using this workbook.) When this workbook opens properly, it adds a Normal Distribution menu in the Add-ins tab.

To explore the effects of changing the mean and standard deviation on the area under a normal distribution curve workbook, select **Add-ins → Normal Distribution → Probability Density Function**. The add-in displays a normal curve for the MyTVLab website download example and a floating control panel (show at top right). Use the control panel spinner buttons to change the values for the mean, standard deviation, and *X* value and then note the effects of these changes on the probability of *X* < value and the corresponding shaded area under the curve. To see the normal curve labeled with *Z* values, click **Z Values**. Click the **Reset** button to reset the control panel values. Click **Finish** to finish exploring.

To create shaded areas under the curve for problems similar to Examples 6.2 and 6.3, select **Add-ins → Normal Distribution → Areas**. In the Areas dialog box (show at bottom right), enter values, select an Area Option, and click **OK**. The add-in creates a normal distribution curve with areas that are shaded according to the values you entered.

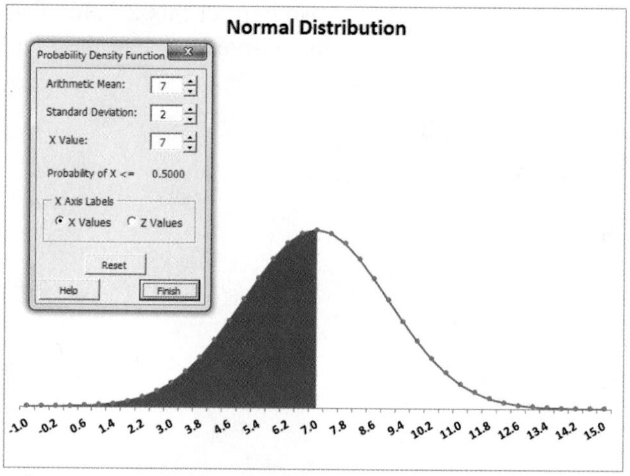

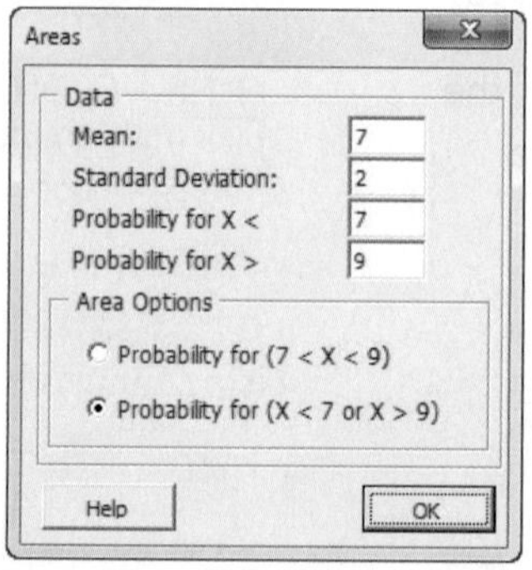

THINK ABOUT THIS What Is Normal?

Ironically, the statistician who popularized the use of "normal" to describe the distribution discussed in Section 6.2 was someone who saw the distribution as anything but the everyday, anticipated occurrence that the adjective *normal* usually suggests.

Starting with an 1894 paper, Karl Pearson argued that measurements of phenomena do not naturally, or "normally," conform to the classic bell shape. While this principle underlies statistics today, Pearson's point of view was radical to contemporaries who saw the world as standardized and normal. Pearson changed minds by showing that some populations are naturally *skewed* (coining that term in passing), and he helped put to rest the notion that the normal distribution underlies all phenomena.

Today, unfortunately, people still make the type of mistake that Pearson refuted. As a student, you are probably familiar with discussions about grade inflation, a real phenomenon at many schools. But, have you ever realized that a "proof" of this inflation—that there are "too few" low grades because grades are skewed toward A's and B's—wrongly implies that grades should be "normally" distributed. By the time you finish reading this book, you may realize that because college students represent small nonrandom samples, there are plenty of reasons to suspect that the distribution of grades would not be "normal."

Misunderstandings about the normal distribution have occurred both in business and in the public sector through the years. These misunderstandings have caused a number of business blunders and have sparked several public policy debates, including the causes of the collapse of large financial institutions in 2008. According to one theory, the investment banking industry's application of the normal distribution to assess risk may have contributed to the global collapse (see "A Finer Formula for Assessing Risks," *The New York Times*, May 11, 2010, p. B2 and reference 7). Using the normal distribution led these banks to overestimate the probability of having stable market conditions and underestimate the chance of unusually large market losses. According to this theory, the use of other distributions that have less area in the middle of their curves, and, therefore, more in the "tails" that represent unusual market outcomes, may have led to less serious losses.

As you study this chapter, make sure you understand the assumptions that must hold for the proper use of the "normal" distribution, assumptions that were not explicitly verified by the investment bankers. And, most importantly, always remember that the name *normal distribution* does not mean normal in the everyday sense of the word.

Problems for Section 6.2

LEARNING THE BASICS

6.1 Given a standardized normal distribution (with a mean of 0 and a standard deviation of 1, as in Table E.2), what is the probability that

a. Z is less than 1.57?
b. Z is greater than 1.84?
c. Z is between 1.57 and 1.84?
d. Z is less than 1.57 or greater than 1.84?

6.2 Given a standardized normal distribution (with a mean of 0 and a standard deviation of 1, as in Table E.2), what is the probability that

a. Z is between -1.57 and 1.84?
b. Z is less than -1.57 or greater than 1.84?
c. What is the value of Z if only 2.5% of all possible Z values are larger?
d. Between what two values of Z (symmetrically distributed around the mean) will 68.26% of all possible Z values be contained?

6.3 Given a standardized normal distribution (with a mean of 0 and a standard deviation of 1, as in Table E.2), what is the probability that

a. Z is less than 1.08?
b. Z is greater than -0.21?
c. Z is less than -0.21 or greater than the mean?
d. Z is less than -0.21 or greater than 1.08?

6.4 Given a standardized normal distribution (with a mean of 0 and a standard deviation of 1, as in Table E.2), determine the following probabilities:

a. $P(Z > 1.08)$
b. $P(Z < -0.21)$
c. $P(-1.96 < Z < -0.21)$
d. What is the value of Z if only 15.87% of all possible Z values are larger?

6.5 Given a normal distribution with $\mu = 100$ and $\sigma = 10$, what is the probability that

a. $X > 75$?
b. $X < 70$?
c. $X < 80$ or $X > 110$?
d. Between what two X values (symmetrically distributed around the mean) are 80% of the values?

6.6 Given a normal distribution with $\mu = 50$ and $\sigma = 4$, what is the probability that

a. $X > 43$?
b. $X < 42$?
c. 5% of the values are less than what X value?
d. Between what two X values (symmetrically distributed around the mean) are 60% of the values?

APPLYING THE CONCEPTS

6.7 In 2011, the per capita consumption of coffee in the United States was reported to be 4.16 kg, or 9.152 pounds. (Data extracted from **www.ico.org**.) Assume that the per capita consumption of coffee in the United States is approximately normally distributed with a mean of 9.152 pounds and a standard deviation of 3 pounds.

a. What is the probability that someone in the United States consumed more than 10 pounds of coffee in 2011?

b. What is the probability that someone in the United States consumed between 3 and 5 pounds of coffee in 2011?

c. What is the probability that someone in the United States consumed less than 5 pounds of coffee in 2011?

d. 99% of the people in the United States consumed less than how many pounds of coffee?

SELF Test **6.8** Toby's Trucking Company determined that the distance traveled per truck per year is normally distributed, with a mean of 50 thousand miles and a standard deviation of 12 thousand miles.

a. What proportion of trucks can be expected to travel between 34 and 50 thousand miles in a year?

b. What percentage of trucks can be expected to travel either below 30 or above 60 thousand miles in a year?

c. How many miles will be traveled by at least 80% of the trucks?

d. What are your answers to (a) through (c) if the standard deviation is 10 thousand miles?

6.9 Consumers spend an average of $21 per week in cash without being aware of where it goes. (Data extracted from "A Hole in Our Pockets," *USA Today*, January 18, 2010, p. 1A.) Assume that the amount of cash spent without being aware of where it goes is normally distributed and that the standard deviation is $5.

a. What is the probability that a randomly selected person will spend more than $25?

b. What is the probability that a randomly selected person will spend between $10 and $20?

c. Between what two values will the middle 95% of the amounts of cash spent fall?

6.10 A set of final examination grades in an introductory statistics course is normally distributed, with a mean of 73 and a standard deviation of 8.

a. What is the probability that a student scored below 91 on this exam?

b. What is the probability that a student scored between 65 and 89?

c. The probability is 5% that a student taking the test scores higher than what grade?

d. If the professor grades on a curve (i.e., gives A's to the top 10% of the class, regardless of the score), are you better off with a grade of 81 on this exam or a grade of 68 on a different exam, where the mean is 62 and the standard deviation is 3? Show your answer statistically and explain.

6.11 A Nielsen study indicates that mobile subscribers between 18 and 24 years of age spend a substantial amount of time watching video on their devices, reporting a mean of 325 minutes per month. (Data extracted from **bit.ly/NfLzE9**.) Assume that the amount of time watching video on a mobile device per month is normally distributed and that the standard deviation is 50 minutes.

a. What is the probability that an 18- to 24-year-old mobile subscriber spends less than 250 minutes watching video on his or her mobile device per month?

b. What is the probability that an 18- to 24-year-old mobile subscriber spends between 250 minutes and 400 minutes watching video on his or her mobile device per month?

c. What is the probability that an 18- to 24-year-old mobile subscriber spends more than 400 minutes watching video on his or her mobile device per month?

d. 1% of all 18- to 24-year-old mobile subscribers will spend less than how many minutes watching video on his or her mobile device per month?

6.12 In 2011, the per capita consumption of coffee in Sweden was reported to be 7.27 kg, or 15.994 pounds. (Data extracted from **www.ico.org**.) Assume that the per capita consumption of coffee in Sweden in 2011 is approximately normally distributed with a mean of 15.994 pounds and a standard deviation of 5 pounds.

a. What is the probability that someone in Sweden consumed more than 10 pounds of coffee in 2011?

b. What is the probability that someone in Sweden consumed between 3 and 5 pounds of coffee in 2011?

c. What is the probability that someone in Sweden consumed less than 5 pounds of coffee in 2011?

d. 99% of the people in Sweden consumed less than how many pounds of coffee in 2011?

6.13 Many manufacturing problems involve the matching of machine parts, such as shafts that fit into a valve hole. A particular design requires a shaft with a diameter of 22.000 mm, but shafts with diameters between 21.990 mm and 22.010 mm are acceptable. Suppose that the manufacturing process yields shafts with diameters normally distributed, with a mean of 22.002 mm and a standard deviation of 0.005 mm. For this process, what is

a. the proportion of shafts with a diameter between 21.99 mm and 22.00 mm?

b. the probability that a shaft is acceptable?

c. the diameter that will be exceeded by only 2% of the shafts?

d. What would be your answers in (a) through (c) if the standard deviation of the shaft diameters were 0.004 mm?

6.3 Evaluating Normality

As first stated in Section 6.2, the normal distribution has several important theoretical properties:

- It is symmetrical; thus, the mean and median are equal.
- It is bell-shaped; thus, the empirical rule applies.
- The interquartile range equals 1.33 standard deviations.
- The range is approximately equal to 6 standard deviations.

As Section 6.2 notes, many continuous variables used in business closely follow a normal distribution. To determine whether a set of data can be approximated by the normal distribution, you either compare the characteristics of the data with the theoretical properties of the normal distribution or construct a normal probability plot.

Comparing Data Characteristics to Theoretical Properties

Many continuous variables have characteristics that approximate theoretical properties. However, other continuous variables are often neither normally distributed nor approximately normally distributed. For such variables, the descriptive characteristics of the data are inconsistent with the properties of a normal distribution. One approach you can use to determine whether a variable follows a normal distribution is to compare the observed characteristics of the variable with what would be expected if the variable followed a normal distribution. To do so, you can

- Construct charts and observe their appearance. For small- or moderate-sized data sets, create a stem-and-leaf display or a boxplot. For large data sets, in addition, plot a histogram or polygon.
- Compute descriptive statistics and compare these statistics with the theoretical properties of the normal distribution. Compare the mean and median. Is the interquartile range approximately 1.33 times the standard deviation? Is the range approximately 6 times the standard deviation?
- Evaluate how the values are distributed. Determine whether approximately two-thirds of the values lie between the mean and ± 1 standard deviation. Determine whether approximately four-fifths of the values lie between the mean and ± 1.28 standard deviations. Determine whether approximately 19 out of every 20 values lie between the mean and ± 2 standard deviations.

For example, you can use these techniques to determine whether the three-year returns discussed in Chapters 2 and 3 (stored in **Retirement Funds**) follow a normal distribution. Figure 6.17 displays relevant Excel results for these data, using techniques discussed in the Chapter 2 Excel Guide.

FIGURE 6.17
Descriptive statistics, five-number summary, and boxplot for the three-year return percentages

Use the instructions from Sections EG3.1 through EG3.3 to compute descriptive statistics, a five-number summary, and to construct a boxplot.

	3YrReturn%
Mean	21.84
Median	21.65
Mode	21.74
Minimum	3.39
Maximum	62.91
Range	59.52
Variance	41.2968
Standard Deviation	6.4263
Coeff. of Variation	29.43%
Skewness	1.6976
Kurtosis	8.4670
Count	318
Standard Error	0.3604

Five-Number Summary	
Minimum	3.39
First quartile	17.76
Median	21.65
Third quartile	24.74
Maximum	62.91

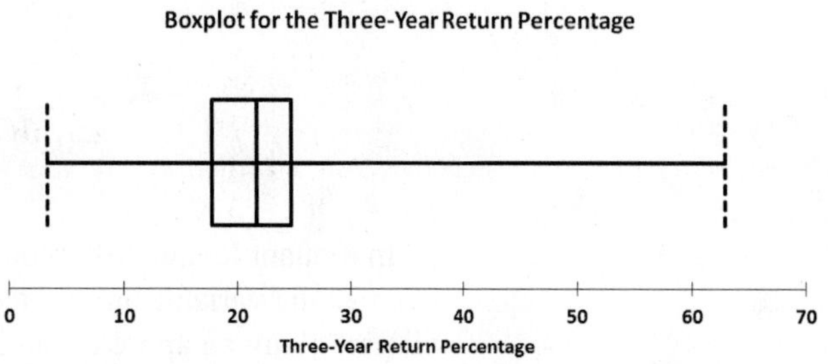

From Figure 6.17 and from an ordered array of the returns (not shown here), you can make the following statements about the three-year returns:

- The mean of 21.84 is approximately the same as the median of 21.65. (In a normal distribution, the mean and median are equal.)
- The boxplot is very right-skewed, with a long tail on the right. (The normal distribution is symmetrical.)
- The interquartile range of 6.98 is approximately 1.09 standard deviations. (In a normal distribution, the interquartile range is 1.33 standard deviations.)
- The range of 59.52 is equal to 9.26 standard deviations. (In a normal distribution, the range is approximately 6 standard deviations.)
- 77.04% of the returns are within ±1 standard deviation of the mean. (In a normal distribution, 68.26% of the values lie within ±1 standard deviation of the mean.)
- 86.79% of the returns are within ±1.28 standard deviations of the mean. (In a normal distribution, 80% of the values lie within ±1.28 standard deviations of the mean.)
- 96.86% of the returns are within ±2 standard deviations of the mean. (In a normal distribution, 95.44% of the values lie within ±2 standard deviations of the mean.)
- The skewness statistic is 1.698 and the kurtosis statistic is 8.467. (In a normal distribution, each of these statistics equals zero.)

Based on these statements and the criteria given on page 233, you can conclude that the three-year returns are highly right-skewed and have somewhat more values within ±1 standard deviation of the mean than expected. The range is higher than what would be expected in a normal distribution, but this is mostly due to the single outlier at 62.91. The skewness is highly positive, and the kurtosis indicates a distribution that is much more peaked than a normal distribution. Thus, you can conclude that the data characteristics of the three-year returns differ from the theoretical properties of a normal distribution.

Constructing the Normal Probability Plot

A **normal probability plot** is a visual display that helps you evaluate whether the data are normally distributed. One common plot is called the **quantile–quantile plot**. To create this plot, you first transform each ordered value to a Z value. For example, if you have a sample of $n = 19$, the Z value for the smallest value corresponds to a cumulative area of

$$\frac{1}{n+1} = \frac{1}{19+1} = \frac{1}{20} = 0.05$$

The Z value for a cumulative area of 0.05 (from Table E.2) is -1.65. Table 6.6 illustrates the entire set of Z values for a sample of $n = 19$.

TABLE 6.6

Ordered Values and Corresponding Z Values for a Sample of $n = 19$

Ordered Value	Z Value	Ordered Value	Z Value	Ordered Value	Z Value
1	−1.65	8	−0.25	14	0.52
2	−1.28	9	−0.13	15	0.67
3	−1.04	10	−0.00	16	0.84
4	−0.84	11	0.13	17	1.04
5	−0.67	12	0.25	18	1.28
6	−0.52	13	0.39	19	1.65
7	−0.39				

In a quantile–quantile plot, the Z values are plotted on the X axis, and the corresponding values of the variable are plotted on the Y axis. If the data are normally distributed, the values will plot along an approximately straight line. Figure 6.18 illustrates the typical shape of the quantile–quantile normal probability plot for a left-skewed distribution (Panel A), a normal distribution (Panel B), and a right-skewed distribution (Panel C). If the data are left-skewed, the curve will rise more rapidly at first and then level off. If the data are normally distributed, the points will plot along an approximately straight line. If the data are right-skewed, the data will rise more slowly at first and then rise at a faster rate for higher values of the variable being plotted.

FIGURE 6.18
Normal probability plots for a left-skewed distribution, a normal distribution, and a right-skewed distribution

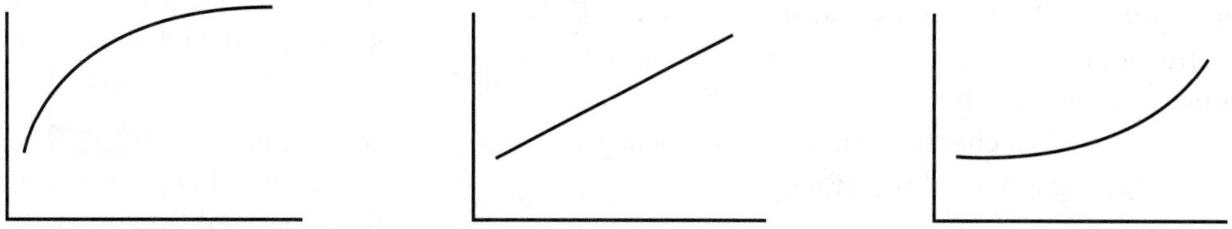

Figure 6.19 shows a normal probability plot for the three-year returns, as created using Excel. The Excel quantile–quantile plot shows that the three-year returns rise slowly at first and then rise more rapidly. Therefore, you can conclude that the three-year returns are right-skewed.

FIGURE 6.19
Excel (quantile–quantile) normal probability plot for the three-year returns

Use the Section EG6.3 instructions to construct a normal probability plot.

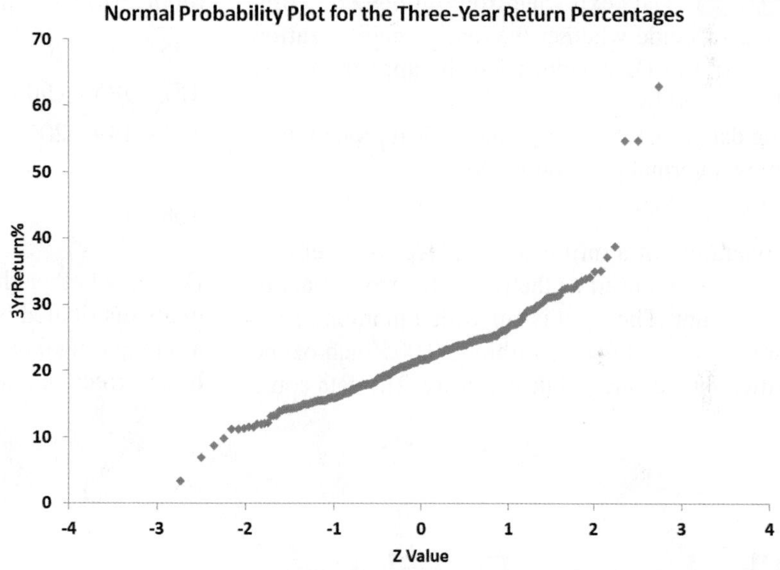

Problems for Section 6.3

LEARNING THE BASICS

6.14 Show that for a sample of $n = 39$, the smallest and largest Z values are -1.96 and $+1.96$, and the middle (i.e., 20th) Z value is 0.00.

6.15 For a sample of $n = 6$, list the six Z values.

APPLYING THE CONCEPTS

SELF Test **6.16** The file SUV contains the overall miles per gallon (MPG) of 2012 small SUVs ($n = 18$):

20 22 23 22 23 22 22 21 19 22 22 26
23 24 19 21 22 16

Source: Data extracted from "Ratings," *Consumer Reports*, April 2012, pp. 35–36.

Decide whether the data appear to be approximately normally distributed by

a. comparing data characteristics to theoretical properties.
b. constructing a normal probability plot.

6.17 As player salaries have increased, the cost of attending baseball games has increased dramatically. The file BBCost2011 contains the cost of four tickets, two beers, four soft drinks, four hot dogs, two game programs, two baseball caps, and the parking fee for one car for each of the 30 Major League Baseball teams in 2011:

174, 339, 259, 171, 207, 160, 130, 213, 338, 178, 184, 140, 159, 212, 121, 169, 306, 162, 161, 160, 221, 226, 160, 242, 241, 128, 223, 126, 208, 196

Source: Data extracted from **seamheads.com/2012/01/29/mlb-fan-cost-index/**.

Decide whether the data appear to be approximately normally distributed by

a. comparing data characteristics to theoretical properties.
b. constructing a normal probability plot.

6.18 The file Property Taxes contains the property taxes per capita for the 50 states and the District of Columbia. Decide whether the data appear to be approximately normally distributed by

a. comparing data characteristics to theoretical properties.
b. constructing a normal probability plot.

6.19 Thirty companies comprise the DJIA. How big are these companies? One common method for measuring the size of a company is to use its market capitalization, which is computed by multiplying the number of stock shares by the price of a share of stock. On June 27, 2012, the market capitalization of these companies ranged from Alcoa's $8.9 billion to ExxonMobil's $379.9 billion. The entire population of market capitalization values is stored in DowMarketCap. (Data extracted from **money.cnn.com**, June 27, 2012.) Decide whether the market capitalization of companies in the DJIA appears to be approximately normally distributed by

a. comparing data characteristics to theoretical properties.
b. constructing a normal probability plot.
c. constructing a histogram.

6.20 One operation of a mill is to cut pieces of steel into parts that will later be used as the frame for front seats in an automotive plant. The steel is cut with a diamond saw, and the resulting parts must be within ±0.005 inch of the length specified by the automobile company. The data come from a sample of 100 steel parts and are stored in Steel. The measurement reported is the difference, in inches, between the actual length of the steel part, as measured by a laser measurement device, and the specified length of the steel part. Determine whether the data appear to be approximately normally distributed by

a. comparing data characteristics to theoretical properties.
b. constructing a normal probability plot.

6.21 The file CD Rate contains the yields for a one-year certificate of deposit (CD) and a five-year CD for 24 banks in the United States, as of June 21, 2012. (Data extracted from **www.Bankrate.com**, June 21, 2012.) For each type of investment, decide whether the data appear to be approximately normally distributed by

a. comparing data characteristics to theoretical properties.
b. constructing a normal probability plot.

6.22 The file Utility contains the electricity costs, in dollars, during July 2012 for a random sample of 50 one-bedroom apartments in a large city:

96	171	202	178	147	102	153	197	127	82
157	185	90	116	172	111	148	213	130	165
141	149	206	175	123	128	144	168	109	167
95	163	150	154	130	143	187	166	139	149
108	119	183	151	114	135	191	137	129	158

Decide whether the data appear to be approximately normally distributed by

a. comparing data characteristics to theoretical properties.
b. constructing a normal probability plot.

6.4 The Uniform Distribution

In the **uniform distribution**, a value has the same probability of occurrence anywhere in the range between the smallest value, *a*, and the largest value, *b*. Because of its shape, the uniform distribution is sometimes called the **rectangular distribution** (see Panel B of Figure 6.1 on page 220). Equation (6.4) defines the probability density function for the uniform distribution.

UNIFORM PROBABILITY DENSITY FUNCTION

$$f(X) = \frac{1}{b - a} \text{ if } a \le X \le b \text{ and 0 elsewhere} \quad (6.4)$$

where

a = minimum value of X
b = maximum value of X

Equation (6.5) defines the mean of the uniform distribution, and Equation (6.6) defines the variance and standard deviation of the uniform distribution.

MEAN OF THE UNIFORM DISTRIBUTION

$$\mu = \frac{a + b}{2} \tag{6.5}$$

VARIANCE AND STANDARD DEVIATION OF THE UNIFORM DISTRIBUTION

$$\sigma^2 = \frac{(b - a)^2}{12} \tag{6.6a}$$

$$\sigma = \sqrt{\frac{(b - a)^2}{12}} \tag{6.6b}$$

One of the most common uses of the uniform distribution is in the selection of random numbers. When you use simple random sampling (see Section 1.4), you assume that each random number comes from a uniform distribution that has a minimum value of 0 and a maximum value of 1.

Figure 6.20 illustrates the uniform distribution with $a = 0$ and $b = 1$. The total area inside the rectangle is equal to the base (1.0) times the height (1.0). Thus, the resulting area of 1.0 satisfies the requirement that the area under any probability density function equals 1.0.

FIGURE 6.20
Probability density function for a uniform distribution with $a = 0$ and $b = 1$

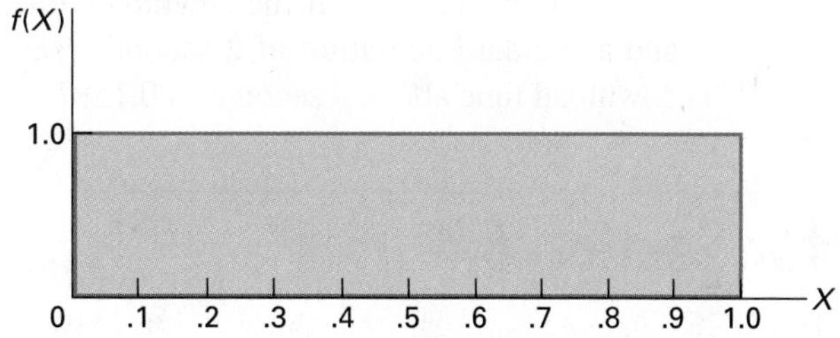

In this uniform distribution, what is the probability of getting a random number between 0.10 and 0.30? The area between 0.10 and 0.30, depicted in Figure 6.21, is equal to the base (which is $0.30 - 0.10 = 0.20$) times the height (1.0). Therefore,

$$P(0.10 < X < 0.30) = (\text{Base})(\text{Height}) = (0.20)(1.0) = 0.20$$

FIGURE 6.21
Finding $P(0.10 < X < 0.30)$ for a uniform distribution with $a = 0$ and $b = 1$

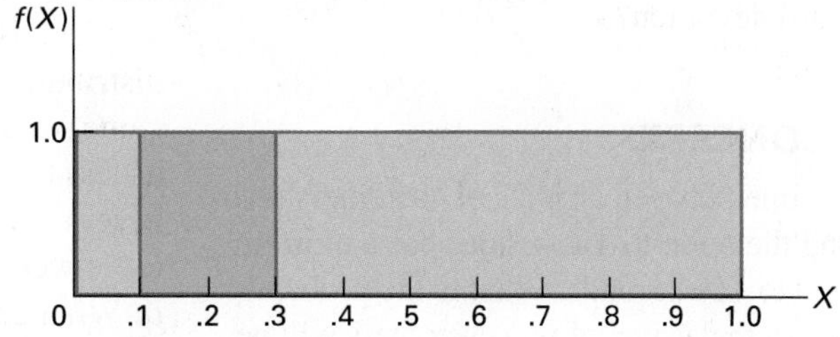

From Equations (6.5) and (6.6), the mean and standard deviation of the uniform distribution for $a = 0$ and $b = 1$ are computed as follows:

$$\mu = \frac{a + b}{2}$$

$$= \frac{0 + 1}{2} = 0.5$$

and

$$\sigma^2 = \frac{(b - a)^2}{12} = \frac{(1 - 0)^2}{12} = \frac{1}{12} = 0.0833$$

$$\sigma = \sqrt{0.0833} = 0.2887$$

Thus, the mean is 0.5, and the standard deviation is 0.2887.

Example 6.6 provides another application of the uniform distribution.

EXAMPLE 6.6

Computing Uniform Probabilities

In the Normal Downloading at MyTVLab scenario on page 219, the download time of videos was assumed to be normally distributed with a mean of 7 seconds. Suppose that the download time follows a uniform (instead of a normal) distribution between 4.5 and 9.5 seconds. What is the probability that a download time will take more than 9 seconds?

SOLUTION The download time is uniformly distributed from 4.5 to 9.5 seconds. The area between 9 and 9.5 seconds is equal to 0.5 seconds, and the total area in the distribution is $9.5 - 4.5 = 5$ seconds. Therefore, the probability of a download time between 9 and 9.5 seconds is the portion of the area greater than 9, which is equal to $0.5/5.0 = 0.10$. Because 9.5 is the maximum value in this distribution, the probability of a download time above 9 seconds is 0.10. In comparison, if the download time is normally distributed with a mean of 7 seconds and a standard deviation of 2 seconds (see Example 6.1 on page 225), the probability of a download time above 9 seconds is 0.1587.

Problems for Section 6.4

LEARNING THE BASICS

6.23 Suppose you select one value from a uniform distribution with $a = 0$ and $b = 10$. What is the probability that the value will be

a. between 5 and 7?

b. between 2 and 3?

c. What is the mean?

d. What is the standard deviation?

APPLYING THE CONCEPTS

SELF Test **6.24** The time between arrivals of customers at a bank during the noon-to-1 P.M. hour has a uniform distribution between 0 to 120 seconds. What is the probability that the time between the arrival of two customers will be

a. less than 20 seconds?

b. between 10 and 30 seconds?

c. more than 35 seconds?

d. What are the mean and standard deviation of the time between arrivals?

6.25 A study of the time spent shopping in a supermarket for a market basket of 20 specific items showed an approximately uniform distribution between 20 minutes and 40 minutes. What is the probability that the shopping time will be

a. between 25 and 30 minutes?

b. less than 35 minutes?

c. What are the mean and standard deviation of the shopping time?

6.26 How long does it take to download a game for your iPod? According to Apple's technical support site, **support.apple.com/kb/ht1577**, downloading an iPod game using a 5 Mbit/s broadband connection should take 30 to 70 seconds. Assume that the download times are uniformly distributed between 30 and 70 seconds. If you download a game, what is the probability that the download time will be

a. less than 34 seconds?

b. less than 40 seconds?

c. between 40 and 50 seconds?

d. What are the mean and standard deviation of the download times?

6.27 The scheduled commuting time on the Long Island Railroad from Glen Cove to New York City is 65 minutes. Suppose that the actual commuting time is uniformly distributed between 64 and 74 minutes. What is the probability that the commuting time will be

a. less than 70 minutes?

b. between 65 and 70 minutes?

c. greater than 65 minutes?

d. What are the mean and standard deviation of the commuting time?

6.5 The Exponential Distribution

The **exponential distribution** is a continuous distribution that is right-skewed and ranges from zero to positive infinity (see Panel C of Figure 6.1 on page 220). The exponential distribution is widely used in waiting-line (i.e., queuing) theory to model the length of time between arrivals in processes such as customers arriving at a bank's ATM, patients entering a hospital emergency room, and hits on a website.

The exponential distribution is defined by a single parameter, λ, the mean number of arrivals per unit of time. The probability density function for the length of time between arrivals is given by Equation (6.7).

EXPONENTIAL PROBABILITY DENSITY FUNCTION

$$f(X) = \lambda e^{-\lambda x} \text{ for } X > 0 \tag{6.7}$$

where

e = mathematical constant approximated by 2.71828
λ = mean number of arrivals per unit
X = any value of the continuous variable where $0 < X < \infty$

The mean time between arrivals, μ, is given by Equation (6.8), and the standard deviation of the time between arrivals, σ, is given by Equation (6.9).

MEAN TIME BETWEEN ARRIVALS

$$\mu = \frac{1}{\lambda} \tag{6.8}$$

STANDARD DEVIATION OF THE TIME BETWEEN ARRIVALS

$$\sigma = \frac{1}{\lambda} \tag{6.9}$$

The value $1/\lambda$ is equal to the mean time between arrivals. For example, if the mean number of arrivals in a minute is $\lambda = 4$, then the mean time between arrivals is $1/\lambda = 0.25$ minute, or 15 seconds. Equation (6.10) defines the cumulative probability that the length of time before the next arrival is less than or equal to X.

CUMULATIVE EXPONENTIAL PROBABILITY

$$P(\text{arrival time} \le X) = 1 - e^{-\lambda x} \tag{6.10}$$

To illustrate the exponential distribution, suppose that customers arrive at a bank's ATM at a rate of 20 per hour. If a customer has just arrived, what is the probability that the next customer will arrive within 6 minutes (i.e., 0.1 hour)? For this example, $\lambda = 20$ and $X = 0.1$. Using Equation (6.10),

$$\begin{aligned} P(\text{arrival time} \le 0.1) &= 1 - e^{-20(0.1)} \\ &= 1 - e^{-2} \\ &= 1 - 0.1353 = 0.8647 \end{aligned}$$

Thus, the probability that a customer will arrive within 6 minutes is 0.8647, or 86.47%. Figure 6.22 shows this probability as computed by Excel.

FIGURE 6.22

Worksheet for computing exponential probability that a customer will arrive within six minutes

*Figure 6.22 displays the **COMPUTE worksheet** of **the Exponential workbook** that the Section EG6.5 instructions use.*

	A	B	
1	Exponential Probability		
2			
3	Data		
4	Mean	20	
5	X Value	0.1	
6			
7	Results		
8	P(<=X)	0.8647	=EXPON.DIST(B5, B4, TRUE)

Example 6.7 illustrates the effect on the exponential probability of changing the time between arrivals.

EXAMPLE 6.7

Computing Exponential Probabilities

In the ATM example, what is the probability that the next customer will arrive within 3 minutes (i.e., 0.05 hour)?

SOLUTION For this example, $\lambda = 20$ and $X = 0.05$. Using Equation (6.10),

$$\begin{aligned} P(\text{arrival time} \leq 0.05) &= 1 - e^{-20(0.05)} \\ &= 1 - e^{-1} \\ &= 1 - 0.3679 = 0.6321 \end{aligned}$$

Thus, the probability that a customer will arrive within 3 minutes is 0.6321, or 63.21%.

Problems for Section 6.5

LEARNING THE BASICS

6.28 Given an exponential distribution with $\lambda = 10$, what is the probability that the arrival time is

a. less than $X = 0.1$?
b. greater than $X = 0.1$?
c. between $X = 0.1$ and $X = 0.2$?
d. less than $X = 0.1$ or greater than $X = 0.2$?

6.29 Given an exponential distribution with $\lambda = 30$, what is the probability that the arrival time is

a. less than $X = 0.1$?
b. greater than $X = 0.1$?
c. between $X = 0.1$ and $X = 0.2$?
d. less than $X = 0.1$ or greater than $X = 0.2$?

6.30 Given an exponential distribution with $\lambda = 5$, what is the probability that the arrival time is

a. less than $X = 0.3$?
b. greater than $X = 0.3$?
c. between $X = 0.3$ and $X = 0.5$?
d. less than $X = 0.3$ or greater than $X = 0.5$?

APPLYING THE CONCEPTS

6.31 Autos arrive at a toll plaza located at the entrance to a bridge at a rate of 50 per minute during the 5:00-to-6:00 P.M. hour. If an auto has just arrived,

a. what is the probability that the next auto will arrive within 3 seconds (0.05 minute)?
b. what is the probability that the next auto will arrive within 1 second (0.0167 minute)?
c. What are your answers to (a) and (b) if the rate of arrival of autos is 60 per minute?
d. What are your answers to (a) and (b) if the rate of arrival of autos is 30 per minute?

SELF Test **6.32** Customers arrive at the drive-up window of a fast-food restaurant at a rate of 2 per minute during the lunch hour.

a. What is the probability that the next customer will arrive within 1 minute?
b. What is the probability that the next customer will arrive within 5 minutes?
c. During the dinner time period, the arrival rate is 1 per minute. What are your answers to (a) and (b) for this period?

6.33 Telephone calls arrive at the information desk of a large computer software company at a rate of 15 per hour.

a. What is the probability that the next call will arrive within 3 minutes (0.05 hour)?
b. What is the probability that the next call will arrive within 15 minutes (0.25 hour)?
c. Suppose the company has just introduced an updated version of one of its software programs, and telephone calls are now arriving at a rate of 25 per hour. Given this information, what are your answers to (a) and (b)?

6.34 An on-the-job injury occurs once every 10 days on average at an automobile plant. What is the probability that the next on-the-job injury will occur within

a. 10 days?
b. 5 days?
c. 1 day?

6.35 The time between unplanned shutdowns of a power plant has an exponential distribution with a mean of 20 days. Find the probability that the time between two unplanned shutdowns is

a. less than 14 days.
b. more than 21 days.
c. less than 7 days.

6.36 Golfers arrive at the starter's booth of a public golf course at a rate of 8 per hour during the Monday-to-Friday midweek period. If a golfer has just arrived,

a. what is the probability that the next golfer will arrive within 15 minutes (0.25 hour)?
b. what is the probability that the next golfer will arrive within 3 minutes (0.05 hour)?
c. The actual arrival rate on Fridays is 15 per hour. What are your answers to (a) and (b) for Fridays?

6.37 Some Internet companies sell a service that will boost a website's traffic by delivering additional unique visitors. Assume that one such company claims it can deliver 1,000 visitors a day. If this amount of website traffic is experienced, then the time between visitors has a mean of 1.44 minutes (or 0.6944 per minute). Assume that your website gets 1,000 visitors a day and that the time between visitors has an exponential distribution. What is the probability that the time between two visitors is

a. less than 1 minute?
b. less than 2 minutes?
c. more than 3 minutes?
d. Do you think it is reasonable to assume that the time between visitors has an exponential distribution?

6.6 The Normal Approximation to the Binomial Distribution (*online*)

LEARN MORE

Learn more about this application of the normal distribution in a Chapter 6 eBook bonus section.

In many circumstances, you can use the normal distribution to approximate the binomial distribution that is discussed in Section 5.3.

USING STATISTICS Normal Downloading at MyTVLab, Revisited

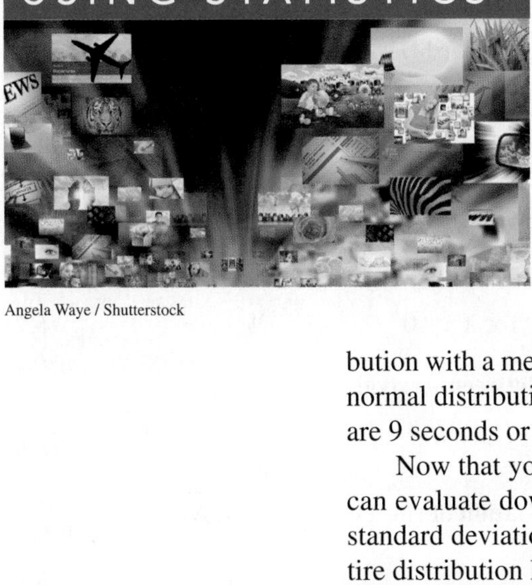

Angela Waye / Shutterstock

In the Normal Downloading at MyTVLab scenario, you were a project manager for an online social media and video website. You sought to ensure that a video could be downloaded quickly by visitors to the website. By running experiments in the corporate offices, you determined that the amount of time, in seconds, that passes from clicking a download link until a video is fully displayed is a bell-shaped distribution with a mean download time of 7 seconds and standard deviation of 2 seconds. Using the normal distribution, you were able to calculate that approximately 84% of the download times are 9 seconds or less, and 95% of the download times are between 3.08 and 10.92 seconds.

Now that you understand how to compute probabilities from the normal distribution, you can evaluate download times of a video using different website designs. For example, if the standard deviation remained at 2 seconds, lowering the mean to 6 seconds would shift the entire distribution lower by 1 second. Thus, approximately 84% of the download times would be 8 seconds or less, and 95% of the download times would be between 2.08 and 9.92 seconds. Another change that could reduce long download times would be reducing the variation. For example, consider the case where the mean remained at the original 7 seconds but the standard deviation was reduced to 1 second. Again, approximately 84% of the download times would be 8 seconds or less, and 95% of the download times would be between 5.04 and 8.96 seconds.

SUMMARY

In this and the previous chapter, you have learned about mathematical models called probability distributions and how they can be used to solve business problems. In Chapter 5, you used discrete probability distributions in situations where the outcomes come from a counting process such as the number of courses you are enrolled in or the number of tagged order forms in a report generated by an accounting information system. In this chapter, you learned about continuous probability distributions where the outcomes come from a measuring process such as your height or the download time of a video.

Continuous probability distributions come in various shapes, but the most common and most important in business is the normal distribution. The normal distribution is symmetrical; thus, its mean and median are equal. It is also bell-shaped, and approximately 68.26% of its observations are within ± 1 standard deviation of the mean, approximately 95.44% of its observations are within ± 2 standard deviations of the mean, and approximately 99.73% of its observations are within ± 3 standard deviations of the mean. Although many data sets in business are closely approximated by the normal distribution, do not think that all data can be approximated using the normal distribution.

In Section 6.3, you learned about various methods for evaluating normality in order to determine whether the normal distribution is a reasonable mathematical model to use in specific situations. In Sections 6.4 and 6.5, you studied continuous distributions that were not normally distributed—in particular, the uniform and exponential distributions. Chapter 7 uses the normal distribution to develop the subject of statistical inference.

REFERENCES

1. Gunter, B. "Q-Q Plots." *Quality Progress* (February 1994): 81–86.
2. Levine, D. M., P. Ramsey, and R. Smidt. *Applied Statistics for Engineers and Scientists Using Microsoft Excel and Minitab.* Upper Saddle River, NJ: Prentice Hall, 2001.
3. *Microsoft Excel 2010.* Redmond, WA: Microsoft Corp., 2010.
4. Miller, J. "Earliest Known Uses of Some of the Words of Mathematics." **jeff560.tripod.com/mathword.html**.
5. Pearl, R. "Karl Pearson, 1857–1936." *Journal of the American Statistical Association*, 31 (1936): 653–664.
6. Pearson, E. S. "Some Incidents in the Early History of Biometry and Statistics, 1890–94." *Biometrika* 52 (1965): 3–18.
7. Taleb, N. *The Black Swan*, 2nd ed. New York: Random House, 2010.
8. Walker, H. "The Contributions of Karl Pearson." *Journal of the American Statistical Association* 53 (1958): 11–22.

KEY EQUATIONS

Normal Probability Density Function

$$f(X) = \frac{1}{\sqrt{2\pi}\sigma} e^{-(1/2)[(X-\mu)/\sigma]^2} \quad (6.1)$$

Transformation Formula

$$Z = \frac{X - \mu}{\sigma} \quad (6.2)$$

Finding an X Value Associated with a Known Probability

$$X = \mu + Z\sigma \quad (6.3)$$

Uniform Probability Density Function

$$f(X) = \frac{1}{b - a} \quad (6.4)$$

Mean of the Uniform Distribution

$$\mu = \frac{a + b}{2} \quad (6.5)$$

Variance and Standard Deviation of the Uniform Distribution

$$\sigma^2 = \frac{(b - a)^2}{12} \quad (6.6a)$$

$$\sigma = \sqrt{\frac{(b - a)^2}{12}} \quad (6.6b)$$

Exponential Probability Density Function

$$f(X) = \lambda e^{-\lambda x} \text{ for } X > 0 \quad (6.7)$$

Mean Time Between Arrivals

$$\mu = \frac{1}{\lambda} \quad (6.8)$$

Standard Deviation of the Time Between Arrivals

$$\sigma = \frac{1}{\lambda} \quad (6.9)$$

Cumulative Exponential Probability

$$P(\text{arrival time} \leq X) = 1 - e^{-\lambda x} \quad (6.10)$$

KEY TERMS

CHECKING YOUR UNDERSTANDING

6.38 Why is only one normal distribution table such as Table E.2 needed to find any probability under the normal curve?

6.39 How do you find the area between two values under the normal curve?

6.40 How do you find the X value that corresponds to a given percentile of the normal distribution?

6.41 What are some of the distinguishing properties of a normal distribution?

6.42 How does the shape of the normal distribution differ from the shapes of the uniform and exponential distributions?

6.43 How can you use the normal probability plot to evaluate whether a set of data is normally distributed?

6.44 Under what circumstances can you use the exponential distribution?

CHAPTER REVIEW PROBLEMS

6.45 An industrial sewing machine uses ball bearings that are targeted to have a diameter of 0.75 inch. The lower and upper specification limits under which the ball bearings can operate are 0.74 inch and 0.76 inch, respectively. Past experience has indicated that the actual diameter of the ball bearings is approximately normally distributed, with a mean of 0.753 inch and a standard deviation of 0.004 inch. What is the probability that a ball bearing is

a. between the target and the actual mean?
b. between the lower specification limit and the target?
c. above the upper specification limit?
d. below the lower specification limit?
e. Of all the ball bearings, 93% of the diameters are greater than what value?

6.46 The fill amount in 2-liter soft drink bottles is normally distributed, with a mean of 2.0 liters and a standard deviation of 0.05 liter. If bottles contain less than 95% of the listed net content (1.90 liters, in this case), the manufacturer may be subject to penalty by the state office of consumer affairs. Bottles that have a net content above 2.10 liters may cause excess spillage upon opening. What proportion of the bottles will contain

a. between 1.90 and 2.0 liters?
b. between 1.90 and 2.10 liters?
c. below 1.90 liters or above 2.10 liters?
d. At least how much soft drink is contained in 99% of the bottles?
e. 99% of the bottles contain an amount that is between which two values (symmetrically distributed) around the mean?

6.47 In an effort to reduce the number of bottles that contain less than 1.90 liters, the bottler in Problem 6.46 sets the filling machine so that the mean is 2.02 liters. Under these circumstances, what are your answers in Problem 6.46 (a) through (e)?

6.48 An orange juice producer buys all his oranges from a large orange grove. The amount of juice squeezed from each of these oranges is approximately normally distributed, with a mean of 4.70 ounces and a standard deviation of 0.40 ounce.

a. What is the probability that a randomly selected orange will contain between 4.70 and 5.00 ounces of juice?
b. What is the probability that a randomly selected orange will contain between 5.00 and 5.50 ounces of juice?
c. At least how many ounces of juice will 77% of the oranges contain?
d. 80% of the oranges contain between what two values (in ounces of juice), symmetrically distributed around the population mean?

6.49 The file **DomesticBeer** contains the percentage alcohol, number of calories per 12 ounces, and number of carbohydrates (in grams) per 12 ounces for 150 of the best-selling domestic beers in the United States. For each of the three variables, decide whether the data appear to be approximately normally distributed. Support your decision through the use of appropriate statistics and graphs. (Data extracted from **www.Beer100.com**, June 1, 2012.)

6.50 The evening manager of a restaurant was very concerned about the length of time some customers were waiting in line to be seated. She also had some concern about the seating times—that is, the length of time between when a customer is seated and the time he or she leaves the restaurant. Over the course of one week, 100 customers (no more than 1 per party) were randomly selected, and their waiting and seating times (in minutes) were recorded in **Wait**.

a. Think about your favorite restaurant. Do you think waiting times more closely resemble a uniform, an exponential, or a normal distribution?
b. Again, think about your favorite restaurant. Do you think seating times more closely resemble a uniform, an exponential, or a normal distribution?
c. Construct a histogram and a normal probability plot of the waiting times. Do you think these waiting times more closely resemble a uniform, an exponential, or a normal distribution?
d. Construct a histogram and a normal probability plot of the seating times. Do you think these seating times more closely resemble a uniform, an exponential, or a normal distribution?

6.51 The major stock market indexes had mixed results in 2011. The mean one-year return for stocks in the S&P 500, a group of 500 very large companies, was 0.00%. The mean one-year return for the NASDAQ, a group of 3,200 small and medium-sized companies, was −1.8%. Historically, the one-year returns are approximately normally distributed, the standard deviation in the S&P 500 is approximately 20%, and the standard deviation in the NASDAQ is approximately 30%.

a. What is the probability that a stock in the S&P 500 gained value in 2011?
b. What is the probability that a stock in the S&P 500 gained 10% or more in 2011?
c. What is the probability that a stock in the S&P 500 lost 20% or more in 2011?
d. What is the probability that a stock in the S&P 500 lost 40% or more in 2011?
e. Repeat (a) through (d) for a stock in the NASDAQ.
f. Write a short summary on your findings. Be sure to include a discussion of the risks associated with a large standard deviation.

6.52 The speed at which you can log into a website through a smartphone is an important quality characteristic of that website. In a recent test, the mean time to log into the JetBlue Airways website through a smartphone was 4.237 seconds. (Data extracted from N. Trejos, "Travelers Have No Patience for Slow Mobile Sites," *USA Today*, April 4, 2012, p. 3B.) Suppose that the download time is normally distributed, with a standard deviation of 1.3 seconds. What is the probability that a download time is

a. less than 2 seconds?
b. between 1.5 and 2.5 seconds?
c. above 1.8 seconds?
d. 99% of the download times are slower (higher) than how many seconds?
e. 95% of the download times are between what two values, symmetrically distributed around the mean?
f. Suppose that the download times are uniformly distributed between 1 and 9 seconds. What are your answers to (a) through (c)?

6.53 The speed at which you can log into a website through a smartphone is an important quality characteristic of that website. In a recent test, the mean time to log into the Hertz website through a smartphone was 7.524 seconds. (Data extracted from N. Trejos, "Travelers Have No Patience for Slow Mobile Sites," *USA Today*, April 4, 2012, p. 3B.) Suppose that the download time is normally distributed, with a standard deviation of 1.7 seconds. What is the probability that a download time is

a. less than 2 seconds?
b. between 1.5 and 2.5 seconds?
c. above 1.8 seconds?
d. 99% of the download times are slower (higher) than how many seconds ?
e. 95% of the download times are between what two values, symmetrically distributed around the mean?
f. Suppose that the download times are uniformly distributed between 1 and 14 seconds. What are your answers to (a) through (d)?
g. Compare the results for the JetBlue Airways site computed in Problem 6.52 to those of the Hertz website.

6.54 (Class Project) One theory about the daily changes in the closing price of stock is that these changes follow a *random walk*—that is, these daily events are independent of each other and move upward or downward in a random manner—and can be approximated by a normal distribution. To test this theory, use either a newspaper or the Internet to select one company traded on the NYSE, one company traded on the American Stock Exchange, and one company traded on the NASDAQ and then do the following:

1. Record the daily closing stock price of each of these companies for six consecutive weeks (so that you have 30 values per company).
2. Compute the daily changes in the closing stock price of each of these companies for six consecutive weeks (so that you have 30 values per company).

Note: *The random-walk theory pertains to the daily changes in the closing stock price, not the daily closing stock price.*

For each of your six data sets, decide whether the data are approximately normally distributed by

a. constructing the stem-and-leaf display, histogram or polygon, and boxplot.
b. comparing data characteristics to theoretical properties.
c. constructing a normal probability plot.
d. Discuss the results of (a) through (c). What can you say about your three stocks with respect to daily closing prices and daily changes in closing prices? Which, if any, of the data sets are approximately normally distributed?

CASES FOR CHAPTER 6

Managing Ashland MultiComm Services

The AMS technical services department has embarked on a quality improvement effort. Its first project relates to maintaining the target upload speed for its Internet service subscribers. Upload speeds are measured on a standard scale in which the target value is 1.0. Data collected over the past year indicate that the upload speed is approximately normally distributed, with a mean of 1.005 and a standard deviation of 0.10. Each day, one upload speed is measured.

The upload speed is considered acceptable if the measurement on the standard scale is between 0.95 and 1.05.

1. Assuming that the distribution has not changed from what it was in the past year, what is the probability that the upload speed is
   a. less than 1.0?
   b. between 0.95 and 1.0?
   c. between 1.0 and 1.05?
   d. less than 0.95 or greater than 1.05?
2. The objective of the operations team is to reduce the probability that the upload speed is below 1.0. Should the team focus on process improvement that increases the mean upload speed to 1.05 or on process improvement that reduces the standard deviation of the upload speed to 0.075? Explain.

Digital Case

Apply your knowledge about the normal distribution in this Digital Case, which extends the Using Statistics scenario from this chapter.

To satisfy concerns of potential customers, the management of MyTVLab has undertaken a research project to learn how much time it takes users to load a complex video features page. The research team has collected data and has made some claims based on the assertion that the data follow a normal distribution.

Open **MTL_QRTStudy.pdf**, which documents the work of a quality response team at MyTVLab. Read the internal report that documents the work of the team and their conclusions. Then answer the following:

1. Can the collected data be approximated by the normal distribution?
2. Review and evaluate the conclusions made by the MyTVLab research team. Which conclusions are correct? Which ones are incorrect?
3. If MyTVLab could improve the mean time by five seconds, how would the probabilities change?

CardioGood Fitness

Return to the CardioGood Fitness case (stored in CardioGood Fitness) first presented on page 33.

1. For each CardioGood Fitness treadmill product line, determine whether the age, income, usage, and the number of miles the customer expects to walk/run each week can be approximated by the normal distribution.
2. Write a report to be presented to the management of CardioGood Fitness, detailing your findings.

More Descriptive Choices Follow-up

Follow up the More Descriptive Choices Revisited Using Statistics scenario on page 149 by constructing normal probability plots for the 1-year return percentages, 5-year return percentages, and 10-year return percentages for the sample of 318 retirement funds stored in Retirement Funds. In your analysis, examine differences between the growth and value funds as well as the differences among the small, mid-cap, and large market cap funds.

Clear Mountain State Student Surveys

1. The Student News Service at Clear Mountain State University (CMSU) has decided to gather data about the undergraduate students who attend CMSU. They create and distribute a survey of 14 questions and receive responses from 62 undergraduates (stored in UndergradSurvey). For each numerical variable in the survey, decide whether the variable is approximately normally distributed by
   a. comparing data characteristics to theoretical properties.
   b. constructing a normal probability plot.
   c. writing a report summarizing your conclusions.
2. The dean of students at CMSU has learned about the undergraduate survey and has decided to undertake a similar survey for graduate students at CMSU. She creates and distributes a survey of 14 questions and receives responses from 44 graduate students (stored in GradSurvey). For each numerical variable in the survey, decide whether the variable is approximately normally distributed by
   a. comparing data characteristics to theoretical properties.
   b. constructing a normal probability plot.
   c. writing a report summarizing your conclusions.

CHAPTER 6 EXCEL GUIDE

EG6.1 CONTINUOUS PROBABILITY DISTRIBUTIONS

There are no Excel Guide instructions for this section.

EG6.2 The NORMAL DISTRIBUTION

Key Technique Use the **NORM.DIST(*X value*, *mean*, *standard deviation*, True)** function to compute normal probabilities and use the **NORM.S.INV(*percentage*)** function and the STANDARDIZE function (see Section EG3.2) to compute the *Z* value.

Example Compute the normal probabilities for Examples 6.1 through 6.3 on pages 225 and 226 and the *X* and Z values for Examples 6.4 and 6.5 on pages 227 and 228.

PHStat Use **Normal**.
For the example, select **PHStat → Probability & Prob. Distributions → Normal**. In this procedure's dialog box (shown below):

1. Enter **7** as the **Mean** and **2** as the **Standard Deviation**.
2. Check **Probability for: X <=** and enter **7** in its box.
3. Check **Probability for: X >** and enter **9** in its box.
4. Check **Probability for range** and enter **5** in the first box and **9** in the second box.
5. Check **X for Cumulative Percentage** and enter **10** in its box.
6. Check **X Values for Percentage** and enter **95** in its box.
7. Enter a **Title** and click **OK**.

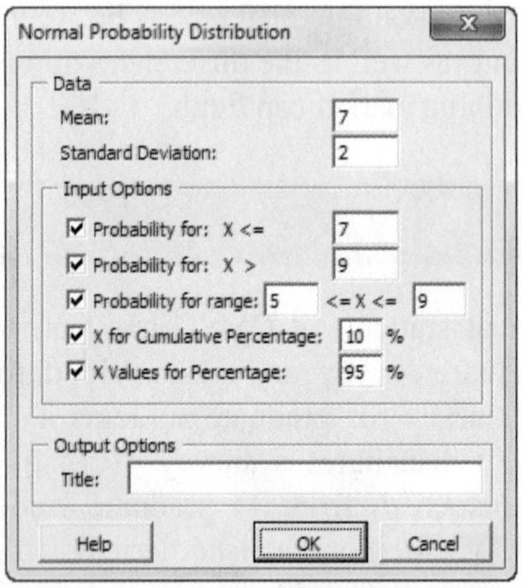

In-Depth Excel Use the **COMPUTE worksheet** of the **Normal workbook** as a template.

The worksheet already contains the data for solving the problems in Examples 6.1 through 6.5. For other problems, change the values for the **Mean**, **Standard Deviation**, **X Value**, **From X Value**, **To X Value**, **Cumulative Percentage**, and/or **Percentage**.

Read the SHORT TAKES for Chapter 6 for an explanation of the formulas found in the COMPUTE worksheet (shown in the **COMPUTE_FORMULAS worksheet**). If you use an Excel version older than Excel 2010, use the COMPUTE_OLDER worksheet instead of the COMPUTE worksheet.

EG6.3 EVALUATING NORMALITY

Comparing Data Characteristics to Theoretical Properties

Use the Sections EG3.1 through EG3.3 instructions to compare data characteristics to theoretical properties.

Constructing the Normal Probability Plot

Key Technique Use an Excel XY (scatter) chart with *Z* values computed using the NORM.S.INV function.

Example Construct the normal probability plot for the three-year return percentages for the sample of 318 retirement funds that is shown in Figure 6.19 on page 235.

PHStat Use **Normal Probability Plot**.
For the example, open to the **DATA worksheet** of the **Retirement Funds workbook**. Select **PHStat → Probability & Prob. Distributions → Normal Probability Plot**. In the procedure's dialog box (shown below):

1. Enter **J1:J319** as the **Variable Cell Range**.
2. Check **First cell contains label**.
3. Enter a **Title** and click **OK**.

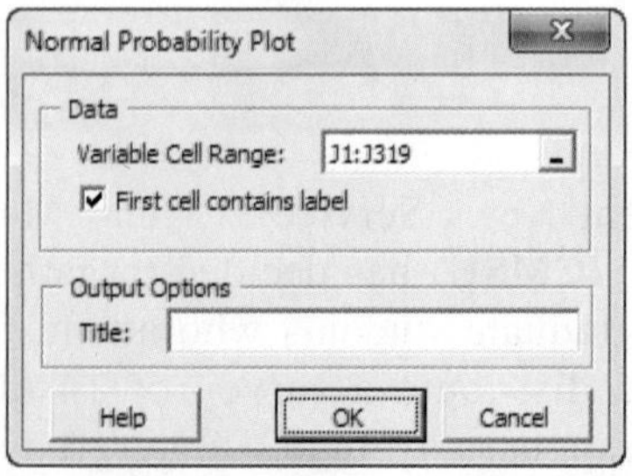

In addition to the chart sheet containing the normal probability plot, the procedure creates a plot data worksheet identical to the PlotData worksheet discussed in the *In-Depth Excel* instructions.

In-Depth Excel Use the worksheets of the **NPP workbook** as templates.

The **NORMAL_PLOT chart sheet** displays a normal probability plot using the rank, the proportion, the *Z* value, and the variable data found in the **PLOT_DATA worksheet**. The PLOT_DATA worksheet already contains the three-year return percentages for the example. To construct plots for other variables, paste *sorted* variable data in **column D** of the **PLOT_DATA worksheet** and adjust the number of ranks in **column A** and the formulas in **columns B and C** in that worksheet. Column B formulas divide the column A cell by the quantity $n + 1$ (319 for the example) to compute cumulative percentages, and column C formulas use the NORM.S.INV function to compute the *Z* values for those cumulative percentages.

If you have fewer than 318 values, delete rows from the bottom up. If you have more than 318 values, insert rows from somewhere inside the body of the table to ensure that the normal probability plot is properly updated. To create your own normal probability plot for the 3YrReturn% variable, open to the PLOT_DATA worksheet and select the cell range **C1:D319**. Then select **Insert ➔ Scatter** and select the **first Scatter** gallery item (**Scatter with only Markers**). Relocate the chart to a chart sheet, turn off the chart legend and gridlines, add axis titles, and modify the chart title by using the instructions in Appendix Section B.6.

Open to the **PLOT_FORMULAS worksheet** in the same workbook to examine these formulas. If you use an Excel version older than Excel 2010, use the PLOT_OLDER worksheet and the NORMAL_PLOT_OLDER chart sheet instead of the PLOT_DATA and NORMAL_PLOT sheets.

EG6.4 The UNIFORM DISTRIBUTION

There are no Excel Guide instructions for this section.

EG6.5 The EXPONENTIAL DISTRIBUTION

Key Technique Use the **EXPON.DIST(*X value, mean,* True)** function.

Example Compute the exponential probability for the bank ATM customer arrival example on page 239.

PHStat Use **Exponential**.
For the example, select **PHStat ➔ Probability & Prob. Distributions ➔ Exponential**. In the procedure's dialog box (shown below):

1. Enter **20** as the **Mean per unit (Lambda)** and **0.1** as the **X Value**.
2. Enter a **Title** and click **OK**.

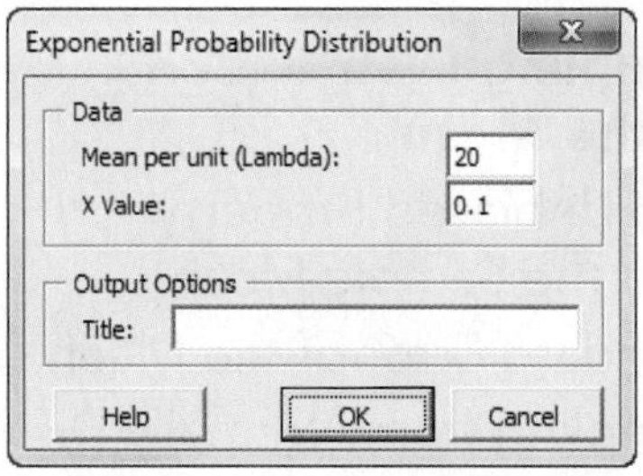

In-Depth Excel Use the **COMPUTE worksheet** of the **Exponential workbook** as a template.
The worksheet already contains the data for the example. For other problems, change the **Mean** and **X Value** in cells **B4** and **B5**. If you use an Excel version older than Excel 2010, use the COMPUTE_OLDER worksheet instead of the COMPUTE worksheet.

CHAPTER

7 Sampling Distributions

Learning Objectives

In this chapter, you learn:

- The concept of the sampling distribution
- To compute probabilities related to the sample mean and the sample proportion
- The importance of the Central Limit Theorem

© Corbis / Corbis Images

USING STATISTICS

Sampling Oxford Cereals

The automated production line at the Oxford Cereals main plant fills thousands of boxes of cereal during each shift. As the plant operations manager, you are responsible for monitoring the amount of cereal placed in each box. To be consistent with package labeling, boxes should contain a mean of 368 grams of cereal. Because of the speed of the process, the cereal weight varies from box to box, causing some boxes to be underfilled and others to be overfilled. If the automated process fails to work as intended, the mean weight in the boxes could vary too much from the label weight of 368 grams to be acceptable.

Because weighing every single box is too time-consuming, costly, and inefficient, you must take a sample of boxes. For each sample you select, you plan to weigh the individual boxes and calculate a sample mean. You need to determine the probability that such a sample mean could have been randomly selected from a population whose mean is 368 grams. Based on your analysis, you will have to decide whether to maintain, alter, or shut down the cereal-filling process.

R. MACKAY PHOTOGRAPHY, LLC / Shutterstock

In Chapter 6, you used the normal distribution to study the distribution of video download times from the MyTVLab website. In this chapter, you need to make a decision about a cereal-filling process, based on the weights of a sample of cereal boxes packaged at Oxford Cereals. You will learn about sampling distributions and how to use them to solve business problems.

7.1 Sampling Distributions

In many applications, you want to make inferences that are based on statistics calculated from samples to estimate the values of population parameters. In the next two sections, you will learn about how the sample mean (a statistic) is used to estimate the population mean (a parameter) and how the sample proportion (a statistic) is used to estimate the population proportion (a parameter). Your main concern when making a statistical inference is reaching conclusions about a population, *not* about a sample. For example, a political pollster is interested in the sample results only as a way of estimating the actual proportion of the votes that each candidate will receive from the population of voters. Likewise, as plant operations manager for Oxford Cereals, you are only interested in using the mean weight calculated from a sample of cereal boxes for estimating the mean weight of a population of boxes.

In practice, you select a single random sample of a predetermined size from the population. Hypothetically, to use the sample statistic to estimate the population parameter, you could examine *every* possible sample of a given size that could occur. A **sampling distribution** is the distribution of the results if you actually selected all possible samples. The single result you obtain in practice is just one of the results in the sampling distribution.

7.2 Sampling Distribution of the Mean

In Chapter 3, several measures of central tendency, including the mean, median, and mode, were discussed. For several reasons, the mean is the most widely used measure of central tendency and the sample mean is often used to estimate the population mean. The **sampling distribution of the mean** is the distribution of all possible sample means if you select all possible samples of a given size.

The Unbiased Property of the Sample Mean

The sample mean is **unbiased** because the mean of all the possible sample means (of a given sample size, n) is equal to the population mean, μ. A simple example concerning a population of four administrative assistants demonstrates this property. Each assistant is asked to apply the same set of updates to a human resources database. Table 7.1 presents the number of errors made by each of the administrative assistants. This population distribution is shown in Figure 7.1.

TABLE 7.1

Number of Errors Made by Each of Four Administrative Assistants

Administrative Assistant	Number of Errors
Ann	$X_1 = 3$
Bob	$X_2 = 2$
Carla	$X_3 = 1$
Dave	$X_4 = 4$

FIGURE 7.1

Number of errors made by a population of four administrative assistants

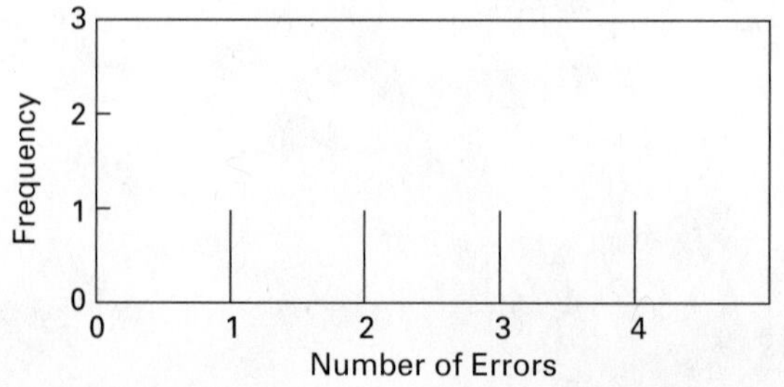

When you have data from a population, you compute the mean by using Equation (7.1), and you compute the population standard deviation, σ, by using Equation (7.2).

POPULATION MEAN

The population mean is the sum of the values in the population divided by the population size, N.

$$\mu = \frac{\sum_{i=1}^{N} X_i}{N} \tag{7.1}$$

POPULATION STANDARD DEVIATION

$$\sigma = \sqrt{\frac{\sum_{i=1}^{N}(X_i - \mu)^2}{N}} \tag{7.2}$$

For the data of Table 7.1,

$$\mu = \frac{3 + 2 + 1 + 4}{4} = 2.5 \text{ errors}$$

and

$$\sigma = \sqrt{\frac{(3 - 2.5)^2 + (2 - 2.5)^2 + (1 - 2.5)^2 + (4 - 2.5)^2}{4}} = 1.12 \text{ errors}$$

If you select samples of two administrative assistants *with* replacement from this population, there are 16 possible samples ($N^n = 4^2 = 16$). Table 7.2 lists the 16 possible sample outcomes. If you average all 16 of these sample means, the mean of these values is equal to 2.5, which is also the mean of the population, μ,

TABLE 7.2

All 16 Samples of $n = 2$ Administrative Assistants from a Population of $N = 4$ Administrative Assistants When Sampling with Replacement

Sample	Administrative Assistants	Sample Outcomes	Sample Mean
1	Ann, Ann	3, 3	$\bar{X}_1 = 3$
2	Ann, Bob	3, 2	$\bar{X}_2 = 2.5$
3	Ann, Carla	3, 1	$\bar{X}_3 = 2$
4	Ann, Dave	3, 4	$\bar{X}_4 = 3.5$
5	Bob, Ann	2, 3	$\bar{X}_5 = 2.5$
6	Bob, Bob	2, 2	$\bar{X}_6 = 2$
7	Bob, Carla	2, 1	$\bar{X}_7 = 1.5$
8	Bob, Dave	2, 4	$\bar{X}_8 = 3$
9	Carla, Ann	1, 3	$\bar{X}_9 = 2$
10	Carla, Bob	1, 2	$\bar{X}_{10} = 1.5$
11	Carla, Carla	1, 1	$\bar{X}_{11} = 1$
12	Carla, Dave	1, 4	$\bar{X}_{12} = 2.5$
13	Dave, Ann	4, 3	$\bar{X}_{13} = 3.5$
14	Dave, Bob	4, 2	$\bar{X}_{14} = 3$
15	Dave, Carla	4, 1	$\bar{X}_{15} = 2.5$
16	Dave, Dave	4, 4	$\bar{X}_{16} = 4$
			$\mu_{\bar{X}} = 2.5$

LEARN MORE

Read the SHORT TAKES for Chapter 7 to learn more about the unbiasedness property.

Because the mean of the 16 sample means is equal to the population mean, the sample mean is an unbiased estimator of the population mean. Therefore, although you do not know how close the sample mean of any particular sample selected comes to the population mean, you are assured that the mean of all the possible sample means that could have been selected is equal to the population mean.

Standard Error of the Mean

Figure 7.2 illustrates the variation in the sample means when selecting all 16 possible samples.

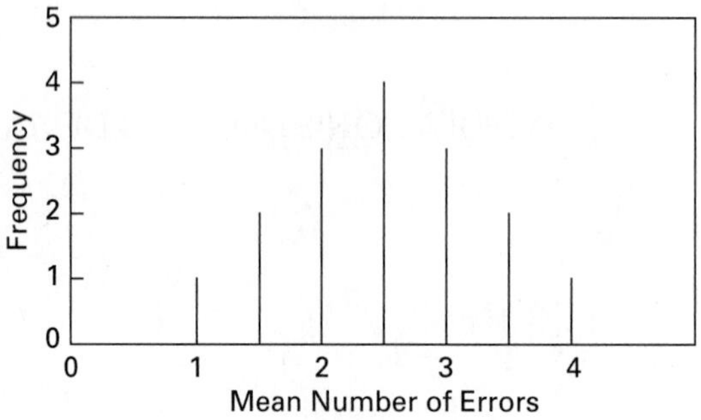

FIGURE 7.2
Sampling distribution of the mean, based on all possible samples containing two administrative assistants

Source: Data are from Table 7.2.

In this small example, although the sample means vary from sample to sample, depending on which two administrative assistants are selected, the sample means do not vary as much as the individual values in the population. That the sample means are less variable than the individual values in the population follows directly from the fact that each sample mean averages together all the values in the sample. A population consists of individual outcomes that can take on a wide range of values, from extremely small to extremely large. However, if a sample contains an extreme value, although this value will have an effect on the sample mean, the effect is reduced because the value is averaged with all the other values in the sample. As the sample size increases, the effect of a single extreme value becomes smaller because it is averaged with more values.

The value of the standard deviation of all possible sample means, called the **standard error of the mean**, expresses how the sample means vary from sample to sample. As the sample size increases, the standard error of the mean decreases by a factor equal to the square root of the sample size. Equation (7.3) defines the standard error of the mean when sampling *with* replacement or sampling *without* replacement from large or infinite populations.

Student Tip
Remember, the standard error of the mean measures variation among the means not the individual values.

STANDARD ERROR OF THE MEAN

The standard error of the mean, $\sigma_{\overline{X}}$, is equal to the standard deviation in the population, σ, divided by the square root of the sample size, n.

$$\sigma_{\overline{X}} = \frac{\sigma}{\sqrt{n}} \quad \textbf{(7.3)}$$

Example 7.1 computes the standard error of the mean when the sample selected without replacement contains less than 5% of the entire population.

EXAMPLE 7.1
Computing the Standard Error of the Mean

Returning to the cereal-filling process described in the Using Statistics scenario on page 249, if you randomly select a sample of 25 boxes without replacement from the thousands of boxes filled during a shift, the sample contains much less than 5% of the population. Given that the standard deviation of the cereal-filling process is 15 grams, compute the standard error of the mean.

SOLUTION Using Equation (7.3) with $n = 25$ and $\sigma = 15$ the standard error of the mean is

$$\sigma_{\overline{X}} = \frac{\sigma}{\sqrt{n}} = \frac{15}{\sqrt{25}} = \frac{15}{5} = 3$$

The variation in the sample means for samples of $n = 25$ is much less than the variation in the individual boxes of cereal (i.e., $\sigma_{\overline{X}} = 3$, while $\sigma = 15$).

Sampling from Normally Distributed Populations

Now that the concept of a sampling distribution has been introduced and the standard error of the mean has been defined, what distribution will the sample mean, $\overline{X}$, follow? If you are sampling from a population that is normally distributed with mean μ and standard deviation σ, then regardless of the sample size, n, the sampling distribution of the mean is normally distributed, with mean $\mu_{\overline{X}} = \mu$, and standard error of the mean $\sigma_{\overline{X}} = \sigma/\sqrt{n}$.

In the simplest case, if you take samples of size $n = 1$, each possible sample mean is a single value from the population because

$$\overline{X} = \frac{\sum_{i=1}^{n} X_i}{n} = \frac{X_1}{1} = X_1$$

Therefore, if the population is normally distributed, with mean μ and standard deviation σ, the sampling distribution $\overline{X}$ for samples of $n = 1$ must also follow the normal distribution, with mean $\mu_{\overline{X}} = \mu$ and standard error of the mean $\sigma_{\overline{X}} = \sigma/\sqrt{1} = \sigma$. In addition, as the sample size increases, the sampling distribution of the mean still follows a normal distribution, with $\mu_{\overline{X}} = \mu$, but the standard error of the mean decreases so that a larger proportion of sample means are closer to the population mean. Figure 7.3 illustrates this reduction in variability. Note that 500 samples of size 1, 2, 4, 8, 16, and 32 were randomly selected from a normally distributed population. From the polygons in Figure 7.3, you can see that, although the sampling distribution of the mean is approximately[1] normal for each sample size, the sample means are distributed more tightly around the population mean as the sample size increases.

[1]Remember that "only" 500 samples out of an infinite number of samples have been selected, so that the sampling distributions shown are only approximations of the population distributions.

FIGURE 7.3

Sampling distributions of the mean from 500 samples of sizes $n = 1, 2, 4, 8, 16$, and 32 selected from a normal population

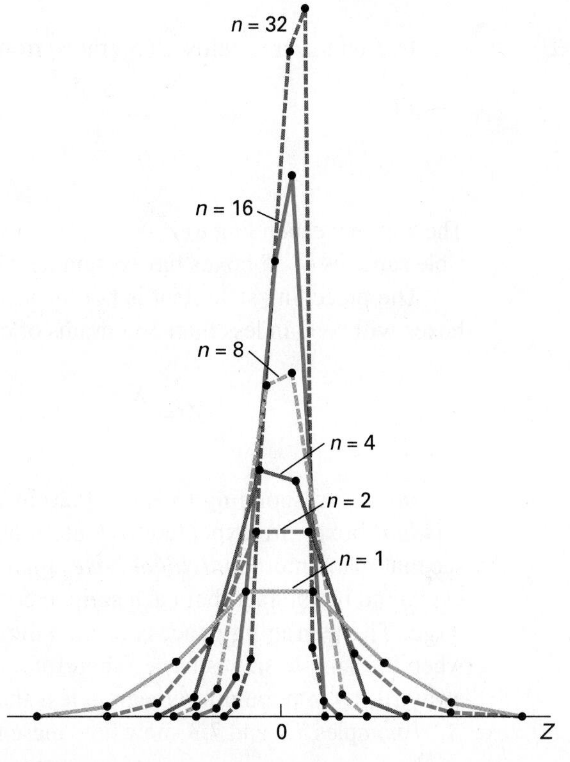

To further examine the concept of the sampling distribution of the mean, consider the Using Statistics scenario described on page 249. The packaging equipment that is filling 368-gram boxes of cereal is set so that the amount of cereal in a box is normally distributed, with a mean of 368 grams. From past experience, you know the population standard deviation for this filling process is 15 grams.

If you randomly select a sample of 25 boxes from the many thousands that are filled in a day and the mean weight is computed for this sample, what type of result could you expect? For example, do you think that the sample mean could be 368 grams? 200 grams? 365 grams?

The sample acts as a miniature representation of the population, so if the values in the population are normally distributed, the values in the sample should be approximately normally distributed. Thus, if the population mean is 368 grams, the sample mean has a good chance of being close to 368 grams.

How can you determine the probability that the sample of 25 boxes will have a mean below 365 grams? From the normal distribution (Section 6.2), you know that you can find the area below any value X by converting to standardized Z values:

$$Z = \frac{X - \mu}{\sigma}$$

In the examples in Section 6.2, you studied how any single value, X, differs from the population mean. Now, in this example, you want to study how a sample mean, $\overline{X}$, differs from the population mean. Substituting $\overline{X}$ for X, $\mu_{\overline{X}}$ for μ, and $\sigma_{\overline{X}}$ for σ in the equation above results in Equation (7.4).

FINDING Z FOR THE SAMPLING DISTRIBUTION OF THE MEAN

The Z value is equal to the difference between the sample mean, $\overline{X}$, and the population mean, μ, divided by the standard error of the mean, $\sigma_{\overline{X}}$.

$$Z = \frac{\overline{X} - \mu_{\overline{X}}}{\sigma_{\overline{X}}} = \frac{\overline{X} - \mu}{\dfrac{\sigma}{\sqrt{n}}} \tag{7.4}$$

To find the area below 365 grams, from Equation (7.4),

$$Z = \frac{\overline{X} - \mu_{\overline{X}}}{\sigma_{\overline{X}}} = \frac{365 - 368}{\dfrac{15}{\sqrt{25}}} = \frac{-3}{3} = -1.00$$

The area corresponding to $Z = -1.00$ in Table E.2 is 0.1587. Therefore, 15.87% of all the possible samples of 25 boxes have a sample mean below 365 grams.

The preceding statement is not the same as saying that a certain percentage of *individual* boxes will contain less than 365 grams of cereal. You compute that percentage as follows:

$$Z = \frac{X - \mu}{\sigma} = \frac{365 - 368}{15} = \frac{-3}{15} = -0.20$$

The area corresponding to $Z = -0.20$ in Table E.2 is 0.4207. Therefore, 42.07% of the *individual* boxes are expected to contain less than 365 grams. Comparing these results, you see that many more *individual boxes* than *sample means* are below 365 grams. This result is explained by the fact that each sample consists of 25 different values, some small and some large. The averaging process dilutes the importance of any individual value, particularly when the sample size is large. Therefore, the chance that the sample mean of 25 boxes is far away from the population mean is less than the chance that a *single* box is far away.

Examples 7.2 and 7.3 show how these results are affected by using different sample sizes.

EXAMPLE 7.2

The Effect of Sample Size, *n*, on the Computation of $\sigma_{\overline{X}}$

How is the standard error of the mean affected by increasing the sample size from 25 to 100 boxes?

SOLUTION If $n = 100$ boxes, then using Equation (7.3) on page 252:

$$\sigma_{\overline{X}} = \frac{\sigma}{\sqrt{n}} = \frac{15}{\sqrt{100}} = \frac{15}{10} = 1.5$$

The fourfold increase in the sample size from 25 to 100 reduces the standard error of the mean by half—from 3 grams to 1.5 grams. This demonstrates that taking a larger sample results in less variability in the sample means from sample to sample.

EXAMPLE 7.3

The Effect of Sample Size, *n*, on the Clustering of Means in the Sampling Distribution

If you select a sample of 100 boxes, what is the probability that the sample mean is below 365 grams?

SOLUTION Using Equation (7.4) on page 254,

$$Z = \frac{\overline{X} - \mu_{\overline{X}}}{\sigma_{\overline{X}}} = \frac{365 - 368}{\frac{15}{\sqrt{100}}} = \frac{-3}{1.5} = -2.00$$

From Table E.2, the area less than $Z = -2.00$ is 0.0228. Therefore, 2.28% of the samples of 100 boxes have means below 365 grams, as compared with 15.87% for samples of 25 boxes.

Sometimes you need to find the interval that contains a specific proportion of the sample means. To do so, determine a distance below and above the population mean containing a specific area of the normal curve. From Equation (7.4) on page 254,

$$Z = \frac{\overline{X} - \mu}{\frac{\sigma}{\sqrt{n}}}$$

Solving for $\overline{X}$ results in Equation (7.5).

FINDING $\overline{X}$ FOR THE SAMPLING DISTRIBUTION OF THE MEAN

$$\overline{X} = \mu + Z\frac{\sigma}{\sqrt{n}} \quad \textbf{(7.5)}$$

Example 7.4 illustrates the use of Equation (7.5).

EXAMPLE 7.4

Determining the Interval That Includes a Fixed Proportion of the Sample Means

In the cereal-filling example, find an interval symmetrically distributed around the population mean that will include 95% of the sample means, based on samples of 25 boxes.

SOLUTION If 95% of the sample means are in the interval, then 5% are outside the interval. Divide the 5% into two equal parts of 2.5%. The value of Z in Table E.2 corresponding to an area of 0.0250 in the lower tail of the normal curve is -1.96, and the value of Z corresponding to a cumulative area of 0.9750 (i.e., 0.0250 in the upper tail of the normal curve) is $+1.96$.

The lower value of $\overline{X}$ (called $\overline{X}_L$) and the upper value of $\overline{X}$ (called $\overline{X}_U$) are found by using Equation (7.5):

$$\overline{X}_L = 368 + (-1.96)\frac{15}{\sqrt{25}} = 368 - 5.88 = 362.12$$

$$\overline{X}_U = 368 + (1.96)\frac{15}{\sqrt{25}} = 368 + 5.88 = 373.88$$

Therefore, 95% of all sample means, based on samples of 25 boxes, are between 362.12 and 373.88 grams.

Sampling from Non-normally Distributed Populations—The Central Limit Theorem

So far in this section, only the sampling distribution of the mean for a normally distributed population has been considered. However, for many analyses, you will either be able to know that the population is not normally distributed or conclude that it would be unrealistic to assume that the population is normally distributed. An important theorem in statistics, the **Central Limit Theorem**, deals with these situations.

THE CENTRAL LIMIT THEOREM

As the sample size (the number of values in each sample) gets *large enough*, the sampling distribution of the mean is approximately normally distributed. This is true regardless of the shape of the distribution of the individual values in the population.

What sample size is *large enough*? A great deal of statistical research has gone into this issue. As a general rule, statisticians have found that for many population distributions, when the sample size is at least 30, the sampling distribution of the mean is approximately normal. However, you can apply the Central Limit Theorem for even smaller sample sizes if the population distribution is approximately bell-shaped. In the case in which the distribution of a variable is extremely skewed or has more than one mode, you may need sample sizes larger than 30 to ensure normality in the sampling distribution of the mean.

Figure 7.4 shows the sampling distributions from three different continuous distributions (normal, uniform, and exponential) for varying sample sizes ($n = 2$, 5, and 30) and illustrates the application of the Central Limit Theorem to these different populations. In each of the panels, because the sample mean is an unbiased estimator of the population mean, the mean of any sampling distribution is always equal to the mean of the population.

Figure 7.4 Panel A shows the sampling distribution of the mean selected from a normal population. As mentioned earlier in this section, when the population is normally distributed, the sampling distribution of the mean is normally distributed for *any* sample size. [You can measure the variability by using the standard error of the mean, Equation (7.3), on page 252.]

Figure 7.4 Panel B depicts the sampling distribution from a population with a uniform (or rectangular) distribution (see Section 6.4). When samples of size $n = 2$ are selected, there is a peaking, or *central limiting*, effect already working. For $n = 5$, the sampling distribution is bell-shaped and approximately normal. When $n = 30$, the sampling distribution looks very similar to a normal distribution. In general, the larger the sample size, the more closely the sampling distribution will follow a normal distribution. As with all other cases, the mean of

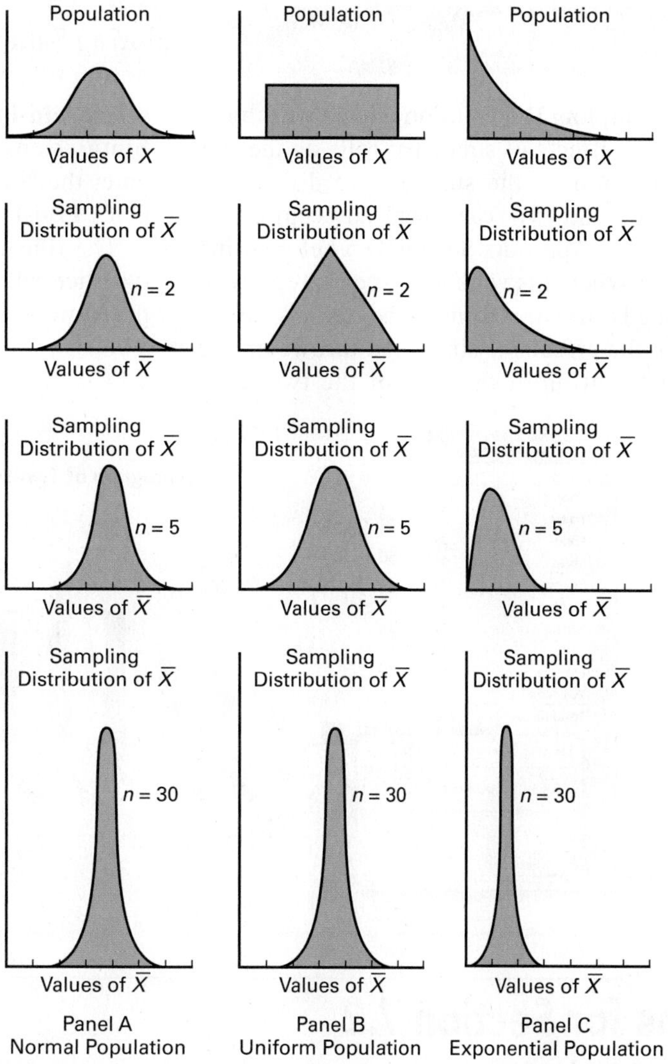

FIGURE 7.4
Sampling distribution of the mean for different populations for samples of ($n = 2, 5, 30$) and 30

each sampling distribution is equal to the mean of the population, and the variability decreases as the sample size increases.

Figure 7.4 Panel C presents an exponential distribution (see Section 6.5). This population is extremely right-skewed. When $n = 2$, the sampling distribution is still highly right-skewed but less so than the distribution of the population. For $n = 5$, the sampling distribution is slightly right-skewed. When $n = 30$, the sampling distribution looks approximately normal. Again, the mean of each sampling distribution is equal to the mean of the population, and the variability decreases as the sample size increases.

Using the results from the normal, uniform, and exponential distributions, you can reach the following conclusions regarding the Central Limit Theorem:

- For most distributions, regardless of shape of the population, the sampling distribution of the mean is approximately normally distributed if samples of at least size 30 are selected.
- If the distribution of the population is fairly symmetrical, the sampling distribution of the mean is approximately normal for samples as small as size 5.
- If the population is normally distributed, the sampling distribution of the mean is normally distributed, regardless of the sample size.

The Central Limit Theorem is of crucial importance in using statistical inference to reach conclusions about a population. It allows you to make inferences about the population mean without having to know the specific shape of the population distribution.

VISUAL EXPLORATIONS Exploring Sampling Distributions

Open the **VE-Sampling Distribution add-in workbook** to to observe the effects of simulated rolls on the frequency distribution of the sum of two dice. (See Appendix C to learn how you can download a copy of this workbook and read Appendix Section D.5 before using this workbook.) When this workbook opens properly, it adds a Sampling Distribution menu in the Add-ins tab.

To observe the effects of simulated throws on the frequency distribution of the sum of the two dice, select **Add-ins → Sampling Distribution → Two Dice Simulation**. In the Two Dice Simulation dialog box, enter the **Number of rolls per tally** and click **Tally**. Click **Finish** when done.

The illustration below shows the histogram of the two-dice rolls after Tally has been clicked 5 times to set the **Number of throws per tally** to **50**.

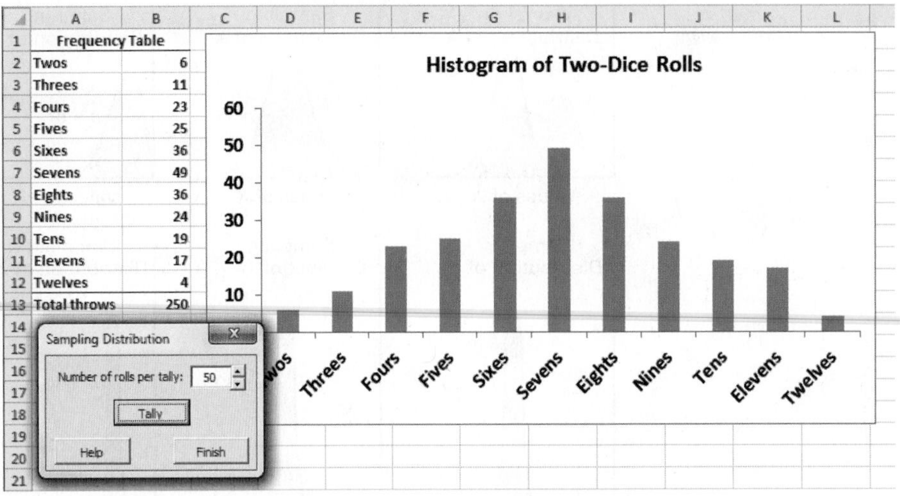

Problems for Section 7.2

LEARNING THE BASICS

7.1 Given a normal distribution with $\mu = 100$ and $\sigma = 10$, if you select a sample of $n = 25$, what is the probability that $\overline{X}$ is

a. less than 95?

b. between 95 and 97.5?

c. above 102.2?

d. There is a 65% chance that $\overline{X}$ is above what value?

7.2 Given a normal distribution with $\mu = 50$ and $\sigma = 5$, if you select a sample of $n = 100$, what is the probability that $\overline{X}$ is

a. less than 47?

b. between 47 and 49.5?

c. above 51.1?

d. There is a 35% chance that $\overline{X}$ is above what value?

APPLYING THE CONCEPTS

7.3 For each of the following three populations, indicate what the sampling distribution for samples of 25 would consist of:

a. Travel expense vouchers for a university in an academic year

b. Absentee records (days absent per year) in 2012 for employees of a large manufacturing company

c. Yearly sales (in gallons) of gasoline at service stations located in a particular state

7.4 The following data represent the number of days absent per year in a population of six employees of a small company:

1 3 6 7 9 10

a. Assuming that you sample without replacement, select all possible samples of $n = 2$ and construct the sampling distribution of the mean. Compute the mean of all the sample means and also compute the population mean. Are they equal? What is this property called?

b. Repeat (a) for all possible samples of $n = 3$.

c. Compare the shape of the sampling distribution of the mean in (a) and (b). Which sampling distribution has less variability? Why?

d. Assuming that you sample with replacement, repeat (a) through (c) and compare the results. Which sampling distributions have the least variability—those in (a) or (b)? Why?

7.5 The diameter of a brand of tennis balls is approximately normally distributed, with a mean of 2.63 inches and a standard deviation of 0.03 inch. If you select a random sample of 9 tennis balls,

a. what is the sampling distribution of the mean?

b. what is the probability that the sample mean is less than 2.61 inches?

c. what is the probability that the sample mean is between 2.62 and 2.64 inches?

d. The probability is 60% that the sample mean will be between what two values symmetrically distributed around the population mean?

7.6 The U.S. Census Bureau announced that the median sales price of new houses sold in 2011 was $227,200, and the mean sales price was $267,900 (**www.census.gov/newhomesales**, April 1, 2012). Assume that the standard deviation of the prices is $90,000.

a. If you select samples of $n = 2$, describe the shape of the sampling distribution of $\overline{X}$.

b. If you select samples of $n = 100$, describe the shape of the sampling distribution of $\overline{X}$.

c. If you select a random sample of $n = 100$, what is the probability that the sample mean will be less than $300,000?

d. If you select a random sample of $n = 100$, what is the probability that the sample mean will be between $275,000 and $290,000?

7.7 Time spent using email per session is normally distributed, with $\mu = 8$ minutes and $\sigma = 2$ minutes. If you select a random sample of 25 sessions,

a. what is the probability that the sample mean is between 7.8 and 8.2 minutes?

b. what is the probability that the sample mean is between 7.5 and 8 minutes?

c. If you select a random sample of 100 sessions, what is the probability that the sample mean is between 7.8 and 8.2 minutes?

d. Explain the difference in the results of (a) and (c).

SELF Test **7.8** The amount of time a bank teller spends with each customer has a population mean of $\mu = 3.10$ minutes and a standard deviation of $\sigma = 0.40$ minute. If you select a random sample of 16 customers,

a. what is the probability that the mean time spent per customer is at least 3 minutes?

b. there is an 85% chance that the sample mean is less than how many minutes?

c. What assumption must you make in order to solve (a) and (b)?

d. If you select a random sample of 64 customers, there is an 85% chance that the sample mean is less than how many minutes?

7.3 Sampling Distribution of the Proportion

Student Tip
Do not confuse this use of the Greek letter pi, π, to represent the population proportion with the mathematical constant that is the ratio of the circumference to a diameter of a circle—approximately 3.14159—which is also known by the same Greek letter.

Consider a categorical variable that has only two categories, such as the customer prefers your brand or the customer prefers the competitor's brand. You are interested in the proportion of items belonging to one of the categories—for example, the proportion of customers that prefer your brand. The population proportion, represented by π, is the proportion of items in the entire population with the characteristic of interest. The sample proportion, represented by p, is the proportion of items in the sample with the characteristic of interest. The sample proportion, a statistic, is used to estimate the population proportion, a parameter. To calculate the sample proportion, you assign one of two possible values, 1 or 0, to represent the presence or absence of the characteristic. You then sum all the 1 and 0 values and divide by n, the sample size. For example, if, in a sample of five customers, three preferred your brand and two did not, you have three 1s and two 0s. Summing the three 1s and two 0s and dividing by the sample size of 5 results in a sample proportion of 0.60.

SAMPLE PROPORTION

$$p = \frac{X}{n} = \frac{\text{Number of items having the characteristic of interest}}{\text{Sample size}} \quad (7.6)$$

Student Tip
Remember that the sample proportion cannot be negative and also cannot be greater than 1.0.

The sample proportion, p, will be between 0 and 1. If all items have the characteristic, you assign each a score of 1, and p is equal to 1. If half the items have the characteristic, you assign half a score of 1 and assign the other half a score of 0, and p is equal to 0.5. If none of the items have the characteristic, you assign each a score of 0, and p is equal to 0.

In Section 7.2, you learned that the sample mean, $\overline{X}$, is an unbiased estimator of the population mean, μ. Similarly, the statistic p is an unbiased estimator of the population proportion, π.

By analogy to the sampling distribution of the mean, whose standard error is $\sigma_{\overline{X}} = \dfrac{\sigma}{\sqrt{n}}$, the **standard error of the proportion**, σ_p, is given in Equation (7.7).

STANDARD ERROR OF THE PROPORTION

$$\sigma_p = \sqrt{\frac{\pi(1 - \pi)}{n}} \tag{7.7}$$

The **sampling distribution of the proportion** follows the binomial distribution, as discussed in Section 5.3, when sampling with replacement (or without replacement from extremely large populations). However, you can use the normal distribution to approximate the binomial distribution when $n\pi$ and $n(1 - \pi)$ are each at least 5. In most cases in which inferences are made about the population proportion, the sample size is substantial enough to meet the conditions for using the normal approximation (see reference 1). Therefore, in many instances, you can use the normal distribution to estimate the sampling distribution of the proportion.

Substituting p for $\overline{X}$, π for μ, and $\sqrt{\dfrac{\pi(1 - \pi)}{n}}$ for $\dfrac{\sigma}{\sqrt{n}}$ in Equation (7.4) on page 254 results in Equation (7.8).

FINDING Z FOR THE SAMPLING DISTRIBUTION OF THE PROPORTION

$$Z = \frac{p - \pi}{\sqrt{\dfrac{\pi(1 - \pi)}{n}}} \tag{7.8}$$

To illustrate the sampling distribution of the proportion, a recent survey ("Wired Vacationers," *USA Today Snapshots*, June 4, 2010, p. 1A) reported that 77% of adults want to have access to the Internet while on vacation in order to access their personal email. Suppose that you select a random sample of 200 travelers who have booked tours from a certain tour company, and you want to determine the probability that more than 80% of the travelers want to have access to the Internet while on vacation in order to access their personal email. Because $n\pi = 200(0.77) = 154 > 5$ and $n(1 - \pi) = 200(1 - 0.77) = 46 > 5$, the sample size is large enough to assume that the sampling distribution of the proportion is approximately normally distributed. Then, using the survey percentage of 77% as the population proportion, you can calculate the probability that more than 80% of the travelers want access to the Internet while on vacation in order to access their personal email by using Equation (7.8):

$$\begin{aligned} Z &= \frac{p - \pi}{\sqrt{\dfrac{\pi(1 - \pi)}{n}}} \\ &= \frac{0.80 - 0.77}{\sqrt{\dfrac{(0.77)(0.23)}{200}}} = \frac{0.03}{\sqrt{\dfrac{0.1771}{200}}} = \frac{0.03}{0.0298} \\ &= 1.01 \end{aligned}$$

Using Table E.2, the area under the normal curve greater than 1.01 is 0.1562. Therefore, if the population proportion is 0.77, the probability is 15.62% that more than 80% of the 200 travelers in the sample want to have access to the Internet while on vacation in order to access their personal email.

Problems for Section 7.3

LEARNING THE BASICS

7.9 In a random sample of 64 people, 48 are classified as "successful."

a. Determine the sample proportion, p, of "successful" people.

b. If the population proportion is 0.70, determine the standard error of the proportion.

7.10 A random sample of 50 households was selected for a phone (landline and cellphone) survey. The key question asked was, "Do you or any member of your household own an Apple product (iPhone, iPod, iPad, or Mac computer)?" Of the 50 respondents, 20 said yes and 30 said no.

a. Determine the sample proportion, p, of households that own an Apple product.

b. If the population proportion is 0.45, determine the standard error of the proportion.

7.11 The following data represent the responses (Y for yes and N for no) from a sample of 40 college students to the question "Do you currently own shares in any stocks?"

N N Y N N Y N Y N Y N N Y N Y Y N N N Y
N Y N N N N Y N N Y Y N N N Y N N Y N N

a. Determine the sample proportion, p, of college students who own shares of stock.

b. If the population proportion is 0.30, determine the standard error of the proportion.

APPLYING THE CONCEPTS

SELF Test **7.12** A political pollster is conducting an analysis of sample results in order to make predictions on election night. Assuming a two-candidate election, if a specific candidate receives at least 55% of the vote in the sample, that candidate will be forecast as the winner of the election. If you select a random sample of 100 voters, what is the probability that a candidate will be forecast as the winner when

a. the population percentage of her vote is 50.1%?

b. the population percentage of her vote is 60%?

c. the population percentage of her vote is 49% (and she will actually lose the election)?

d. If the sample size is increased to 400, what are your answers to (a) through (c)? Discuss.

7.13 You plan to conduct a marketing experiment in which students are to taste one of two different brands of soft drink. Their task is to correctly identify the brand tasted. You select a random sample of 200 students and assume that the students have no ability to distinguish between the two brands. (Hint: If an individual has no ability to distinguish between the two soft drinks, then the two brands are equally likely to be selected.)

a. What is the probability that the sample will have between 50% and 60% of the identifications correct?

b. The probability is 90% that the sample percentage is contained within what symmetrical limits of the population percentage?

c. What is the probability that the sample percentage of correct identifications is greater than 65%?

d. Which is more likely to occur—more than 60% correct identifications in the sample of 200 or more than 55% correct identifications in a sample of 1,000? Explain.

7.14 In a recent survey of full-time female workers ages 22 to 35 years, 46% said that they would rather give up some of their salary for more personal time. (Data extracted from "I'd Rather Give Up," *USA Today*, March 4, 2010, p. 1B.) Suppose you select a sample of 100 full-time female workers 22 to 35 years old.

a. What is the probability that in the sample fewer than 50% would rather give up some of their salary for more personal time?

b. What is the probability that in the sample between 40% and 50% would rather give up some of their salary for more personal time?

c. What is the probability that in the sample more than 40% would rather give up some of their salary for more personal time?

d. If a sample of 400 is taken, how does this change your answers to (a) through (c)?

7.15 Nielsen's Global Corporate Citizenship survey indicates that 35% of North American consumers are willing to spend extra for products and services from socially responsible companies. (Data extracted from **bit.ly/HdfOHL**.) Nielsen defines these consumers as socially conscious consumers. According to the vice president of Nielsen Cares, Nielsen's global corporate social responsibility program, marketers need to know who these consumers are if they want to maximize the social and business return of their cause-marketing efforts. Suppose you select a sample of 100 North American consumers.

a. What is the probability that in the sample fewer than 35% are willing to spend extra for products and services from socially responsible companies?

b. What is the probability that in the sample between 30% and 40% are willing to spend extra for products and services from socially responsible companies?

c. What is the probability that in the sample more than 30% are willing to spend extra for products and services from socially responsible companies?

d. If a sample of 400 is taken, how does this change your answers to (a) through (c)?

7.16 According to the GMI Ratings 2012 Women on Boards Report, the percentage of women on U.S. boards increased only marginally in 2009 to 2011, and it now stands at 12.6%, well below the figures for Nordic countries, Canada, Australia, and France. A number of initiatives are under way to increase female representation on boards. For example, a network of investors, corporate leaders, and other advocates, known as the 30% Coalition, is seeking to raise the proportion of female directors to that number (30%) by 2015. This study also reports that only 10% of U.S. companies have three or more female board directors. (Data extracted from **bit.ly/zBAnYv**.) If you select a random sample of 200 U.S. companies,

a. what is the probability that the sample will have between 8% and 12% U.S. companies that have three or more female board directors?
b. the probability is 90% that the sample percentage will be contained within what symmetrical limits of the population percentage?
c. the probability is 95% that the sample percentage will be contained within what symmetrical limits of the population percentage?

7.17 UK-based Chartered Institute of Management Accountants (CIMA) reports that 57% of its member organizations provide training on ethical standards at work. (Data extracted from **bit.ly/M1tO8H**.) Suppose that you select a sample of 100 CIMA member organizations.

a. What is the probability that the sample percentage providing training on ethical standards at work will be between 55% and 60%?
b. The probability is 90% that the sample percentage will be contained within what symmetrical limits of the population percentage?
c. The probability is 95% that the sample percentage will be contained within what symmetrical limits of the population percentage?
d. Suppose you selected a sample of 400 CIMA member organizations. How does this change your answers in (a) through (c)?

7.18 A survey of 2,250 American adults reported that 59% got news both online and offline in a typical day. (Data extracted from "How Americans Get News in a Typical Day," *USA Today*, March 10, 2010, p. 1A.)

a. Suppose that you take a sample of 100 American adults. If the population proportion of American adults who get news both online and offline in a typical day is 0.59, what is the probability that fewer than half in your sample will get news both online and offline in a typical day?
b. Suppose that you take a sample of 500 American adults. If the population proportion of American adults who get news both online and offline in a typical day is 0.59, what is the probability that fewer than half in your sample will get news both online and offline in a typical day?
c. Discuss the effect of sample size on the sampling distribution of the proportion in general and the effect on the probabilities in (a) and (b).

7.4 Sampling from Finite Populations (*online*)

Learn more about sampling from finite populations in a Chapter 7 eBook bonus section. (See Appendix C to learn how to access this bonus section.)

USING STATISTICS Sampling Oxford Cereals, Revisited

© Corbis / Corbis Images

As the plant operations manager for Oxford Cereals, you were responsible for monitoring the amount of cereal placed in each box. To be consistent with package labeling, boxes should contain a mean of 368 grams of cereal. Thousands of boxes are produced during a shift, and weighing every single box was determined to be too time-consuming, costly, and inefficient. Instead, a sample of boxes was selected. Based on your analysis of the sample, you had to decide whether to maintain, alter, or shut down the process.

Using the concept of the sampling distribution of the mean, you were able to determine probabilities that such a sample mean could have been randomly selected from a population with a mean of 368 grams. Specifically, if a sample of size $n = 25$ is selected from a population with a mean of 368 and standard deviation of 15, you calculated the probability of selecting a sample with a mean of 365 grams or less to be 15.87%. If a larger sample size is selected, the sample mean should be closer to the population mean. This result was illustrated when you calculated the probability if the sample size were increased to $n = 100$. Using the larger sample size, you determined the probability of selecting a sample with a mean of 365 grams or less to be 2.28%.

SUMMARY

You studied the sampling distribution of the sample mean and the sampling distribution of the sample proportion and their relationship to the Central Limit Theorem. You learned that the sample mean is an unbiased estimator of the population mean, and the sample proportion is an unbiased estimator of the population proportion. In the next five chapters, the techniques of confidence intervals and tests of hypotheses commonly used for statistical inference are discussed.

REFERENCES

1. Cochran, W. G. *Sampling Techniques*, 3rd ed. New York: Wiley, 1977.
2. *Microsoft Excel 2010*. Redmond, WA: Microsoft Corp., 2010.

KEY EQUATIONS

Population Mean

$$\mu = \frac{\sum_{i=1}^{N} X_i}{N} \tag{7.1}$$

Population Standard Deviation

$$\sigma = \sqrt{\frac{\sum_{i=1}^{N}(X_i - \mu)^2}{N}} \tag{7.2}$$

Standard Error of the Mean

$$\sigma_{\overline{X}} = \frac{\sigma}{\sqrt{n}} \tag{7.3}$$

Finding *Z* for the Sampling Distribution of the Mean

$$Z = \frac{\overline{X} - \mu_{\overline{X}}}{\sigma_{\overline{X}}} = \frac{\overline{X} - \mu}{\frac{\sigma}{\sqrt{n}}} \tag{7.4}$$

Finding $\overline{X}$ for the Sampling Distribution of the Mean

$$\overline{X} = \mu + Z\frac{\sigma}{\sqrt{n}} \tag{7.5}$$

Sample Proportion

$$p = \frac{X}{n} \tag{7.6}$$

Standard Error of the Proportion

$$\sigma_p = \sqrt{\frac{\pi(1 - \pi)}{n}} \tag{7.7}$$

Finding *Z* for the Sampling Distribution of the Proportion

$$Z = \frac{p - \pi}{\sqrt{\frac{\pi(1 - \pi)}{n}}} \tag{7.8}$$

KEY TERMS

CHECKING YOUR UNDERSTANDING

7.19 Why is the sample mean an unbiased estimator of the population mean?

7.20 Why does the standard error of the mean decrease as the sample size, *n*, increases?

7.21 Why does the sampling distribution of the mean follow a normal distribution for a large enough sample size, even though the population may not be normally distributed?

7.22 What is the difference between a population distribution and a sampling distribution?

7.23 Under what circumstances does the sampling distribution of the proportion approximately follow the normal distribution?

CHAPTER REVIEW PROBLEMS

7.24 An industrial sewing machine uses ball bearings that are targeted to have a diameter of 0.75 inch. The lower and upper specification limits under which the ball bearing can operate are 0.74 inch (lower) and 0.76 inch (upper). Past experience has indicated that the actual diameter of the ball bearings is approximately normally distributed, with a mean of 0.753 inch and a standard deviation of 0.004 inch. If you select a random sample of 25 ball bearings, what is the probability that the sample mean is

a. between the target and the population mean of 0.753?
b. between the lower specification limit and the target?
c. greater than the upper specification limit?
d. less than the lower specification limit?
e. The probability is 93% that the sample mean diameter will be greater than what value?

7.25 The fill amount of bottles of a soft drink is normally distributed, with a mean of 2.0 liters and a standard deviation of 0.05 liter. If you select a random sample of 25 bottles, what is the probability that the sample mean will be

a. between 1.99 and 2.0 liters?
b. below 1.98 liters?
c. greater than 2.01 liters?
d. The probability is 99% that the sample mean amount of soft drink will be at least how much?
e. The probability is 99% that the sample mean amount of soft drink will be between which two values (symmetrically distributed around the mean)?

7.26 An orange juice producer buys oranges from a large orange grove that has one variety of orange. The amount of juice squeezed from these oranges is approximately normally distributed, with a mean of 4.70 ounces and a standard deviation of 0.40 ounce. Suppose that you select a sample of 25 oranges.

a. What is the probability that the sample mean amount of juice will be at least 4.60 ounces?
b. The probability is 70% that the sample mean amount of juice will be contained between what two values symmetrically distributed around the population mean?
c. The probability is 77% that the sample mean amount of juice will be greater than what value?

7.27 In Problem 7.26, suppose that the mean amount of juice squeezed is 5.0 ounces.

a. What is the probability that the sample mean amount of juice will be at least 4.60 ounces?
b. The probability is 70% that the sample mean amount of juice will be contained between what two values symmetrically distributed around the population mean?
c. The probability is 77% that the sample mean amount of juice will be greater than what value?

7.28 The stock market in Mexico reported weak returns in 2011. The population of stocks earned a mean return of −3.8% in 2011. (Data extracted from *USA Today*, January 3, 2012, p. 2B.) Assume that the returns for stocks on the Mexican stock market were distributed as a normal random variable, with a mean of −3.8 and a standard deviation of 20. If you selected a random sample of 16 stocks from this population, what is the probability that the sample would have a mean return

a. less than 0?
b. between −10 and 10?
c. greater than 10?

7.29 The article mentioned in Problem 7.28 reported that the stock market in France had a mean return of −17.0% in 2011. Assume that the returns for stocks on the French stock market were distributed as a normal random variable, with a mean of −17.0 and a standard deviation of 10. If you select an individual stock from this population, what is the probability that it would have a return

a. less than 0 (i.e., a loss)?
b. between −10 and −20?
c. greater than −5?

If you selected a random sample of four stocks from this population, what is the probability that the sample would have a mean return

d. less than 0—that is, a loss?
e. between −10 and −20?
f. greater than −5?
g. Compare your results in parts (d) through (f) to those in (a) through (c).

7.30 (Class Project) The table of random numbers is an example of a uniform distribution because each digit is equally likely to occur. Starting in the row corresponding to the day of the month in which you were born, use a table of random numbers (Table E.1) to take one digit at a time.

Select five different samples each of $n = 2, n = 5$, and $n = 10$. Compute the sample mean of each sample. Develop a frequency distribution of the sample means for the results of the entire class, based on samples of sizes $n = 2, n = 5$, and $n = 10$.

What can be said about the shape of the sampling distribution for each of these sample sizes?

7.31 (Class Project) Toss a coin 10 times and record the number of heads. If each student performs this experiment five times, a frequency distribution of the number of heads can be developed from the results of the entire class. Does this distribution seem to approximate the normal distribution?

7.32 (Class Project) The number of cars waiting in line at a car wash is distributed as follows:

Number of Cars	Probability
0	0.25
1	0.40
2	0.20
3	0.10
4	0.04
5	0.01

You can use a table of random numbers (Table E.1) to select samples from this distribution by assigning numbers as follows:

1. Start in the row corresponding to the day of the month in which you were born.
2. Select a two-digit random number.
3. If you select a random number from 00 to 24, record a length of 0; if from 25 to 64, record a length of 1; if from 65 to 84, record a length of 2; if from 85 to 94, record a length of 3; if from 95 to 98, record a length of 4; if 99, record a length of 5.

Select samples of $n = 2$, $n = 5$, and $n = 10$. Compute the mean for each sample. For example, if a sample of size 2 results in the random numbers 18 and 46, these would correspond to lengths 0 and 1, respectively, producing a sample mean of 0.5. If each student selects five different samples for each sample size, a frequency distribution of the sample means (for each sample size) can be developed from the results of the entire class. What conclusions can you reach concerning the sampling distribution of the mean as the sample size is increased?

7.33 (Class Project) Using a table of random numbers (Table E.1), simulate the selection of different-colored balls from a bowl, as follows:

1. Start in the row corresponding to the day of the month in which you were born.
2. Select one-digit numbers.
3. If a random digit between 0 and 6 is selected, consider the ball white; if a random digit is a 7, 8, or 9, consider the ball red.

Select samples of $n = 10$, $n = 25$, and $n = 50$ digits. In each sample, count the number of white balls and compute the proportion of white balls in the sample. If each student in the class selects five different samples for each sample size, a frequency distribution of the proportion of white balls (for each sample size) can be developed from the results of the entire class. What conclusions can you reach about the sampling distribution of the proportion as the sample size is increased?

7.34 (Class Project) Suppose that step 3 of Problem 7.33 uses the following rule: "If a random digit between 0 and 8 is selected, consider the ball to be white; if a random digit of 9 is selected, consider the ball to be red." Compare and contrast the results in this problem and those in Problem 7.33.

CASES FOR CHAPTER 7

Managing Ashland MultiComm Services

Continuing the quality improvement effort first described in the Chapter 6 Managing Ashland MultiComm Services case, the target upload speed for AMS Internet service subscribers has been monitored. As before, upload speeds are measured on a standard scale in which the target value is 1.0. Data collected over the past year indicate that the upload speeds are approximately normally distributed, with a mean of 1.005 and a standard deviation of 0.10.

1. Each day, at 25 random times, the upload speed is measured. Assuming that the distribution has not changed from what it was in the past year, what is the probability that the upload speed is
   a. less than 1.0?
   b. between 0.95 and 1.0?
   c. between 1.0 and 1.05?
   d. less than 0.95 or greater than 1.05?
   e. Suppose that the mean upload speed of today's sample of 25 is 0.952. What conclusion can you reach about the upload speed today based on this result? Explain.
2. Compare the results of AMS Problem 1 (a) through (d) to those of AMS Problem 1 in Chapter 6 on page 245. What conclusions can you reach concerning the differences?

Digital Case

Apply your knowledge about sampling distributions in this Digital Case, which reconsiders the Oxford Cereals Using Statistics scenario.

The advocacy group Consumers Concerned About Cereal Cheaters (CCACC) suspects that cereal companies, including Oxford Cereals, are cheating consumers by packaging cereals at less than labeled weights. Recently, the group investigated the package weights of two popular Oxford brand cereals. Open **CCACC.pdf** to examine the group's claims and supporting data, and then answer the following questions:

1. Are the data collection procedures that the CCACC uses to form its conclusions flawed? What procedures could the group follow to make its analysis more rigorous?
2. Assume that the two samples of five cereal boxes (one sample for each of two cereal varieties) listed on the CCACC website were collected randomly by organization members. For each sample,
   a. calculate the sample mean.
   b. assuming that the standard deviation of the process is 15 grams and the population mean is 368 grams, calculate the percentage of all samples for each process that have a sample mean less than the value you calculated in (a).
   c. assuming that the standard deviation is 15 grams, calculate the percentage of individual boxes of cereal that have a weight less than the value you calculated in (a).
3. What, if any, conclusions can you form by using your calculations about the filling processes for the two different cereals?
4. A representative from Oxford Cereals has asked that the CCACC take down its page discussing shortages in Oxford Cereals boxes. Is this request reasonable? Why or why not?
5. Can the techniques discussed in this chapter be used to prove cheating in the manner alleged by the CCACC? Why or why not?

CHAPTER 7 EXCEL GUIDE

EG7.1 SAMPLING DISTRIBUTIONS

There are no Excel Guide instructions for this section.

EG7.2 SAMPLING DISTRIBUTION of the MEAN

Key Technique Use an add-in procedure to create a simulated sampling distribution and use the **RAND()** function to create lists of random numbers.

Example Create a simulated sampling distribution that consists of 100 samples of $n = 30$ from a uniformly distributed population.

PHStat Use **Sampling Distributions Simulation.**
For the example, select **PHStat ➔ Sampling ➔ Sampling Distributions Simulation**. In the procedure's dialog box (shown below):

1. Enter **100** as the **Number of Samples**.
2. Enter **30** as the **Sample Size**.
3. Click **Uniform**.
4. Enter a **Title** and click **OK**.

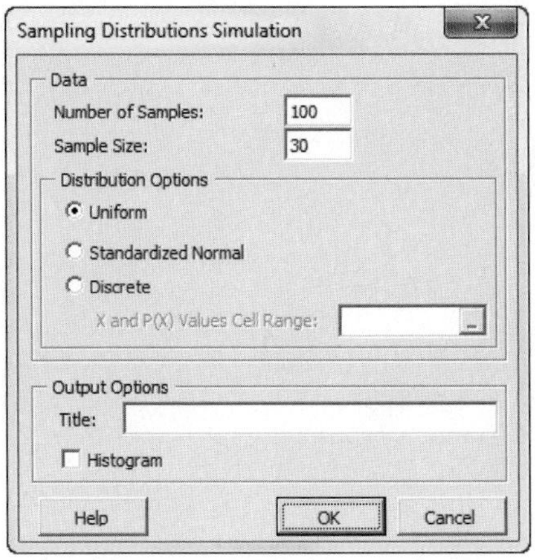

The procedure inserts a new worksheet in which the sample means, overall mean, and standard error of the mean can be found starting in row 34.

In-Depth Excel Use the **SDS worksheet** of the **SDS workbook** as a model.
For the example, in a new worksheet, first enter a title in cell A1. Then enter the formula **=RAND()** in cell **A2** and then copy the formula down **30 rows** and across **100 columns** (through **column CV**). Then select this cell range (**A2:CV31**) and use **copy and paste values** as discussed in Appendix Section B.4.

Use the formulas that appear in rows 33 through 37 in the **SDS_FORMULAS worksheet** of the **SDS workbook** as models if you want to compute sample means, the overall mean, and the standard error of the mean.

Analysis ToolPak Use **Random Number Generation**.
For the example, select **Data ➔ Data Analysis.** In the Data Analysis dialog box, select **Random Number Generation** from the **Analysis Tools** list and then click **OK**. In the procedure's dialog box (shown below):

1. Enter **100** as the **Number of Variables**.
2. Enter **30** as the **Number of Random Numbers**.
3. Select **Uniform** from the **Distribution** drop-down list.
4. Keep the **Parameters** values as is.
5. Click **New Worksheet Ply** and then click **OK**.

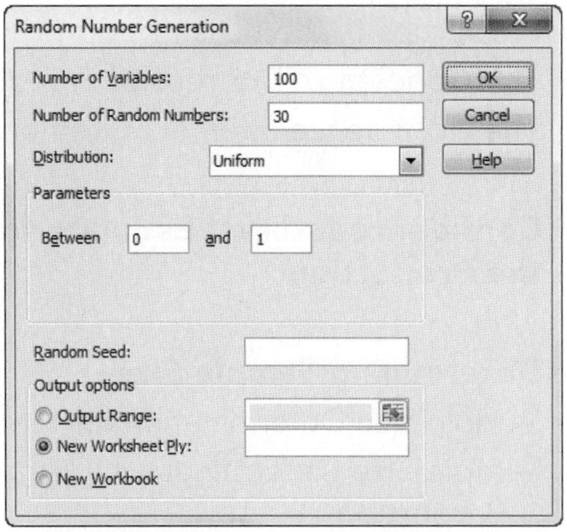

If, for other problems, you select **Discrete** in step 3, you must be open to a worksheet that contains a cell range of X and $P(X)$ values. Enter this cell range as the **Value and Probability Input Range** (not shown when **Uniform** has been selected) in the **Parameters** section of the dialog box.

Use the formulas that appear in rows 33 through 37 in the **SDS_FORMULAS worksheet** of the **SDS workbook** as models if you want to compute sample means, the overall mean, and the standard error of the mean.

EG7.3 SAMPLING DISTRIBUTION of the PROPORTION

There are no Excel Guide instructions for this section.

CHAPTER

8 Confidence Interval Estimation

Learning Objectives

In this chapter, you learn:

- To construct and interpret confidence interval estimates for the mean and the proportion
- How to determine the sample size necessary to develop a confidence interval estimate for the mean or proportion

mangostock / Shutterstock

USING STATISTICS

Getting Estimates at Ricknel Home Centers

As a member of the AIS team at Ricknel Home Centers (see page 185), you have already examined the probability of discovering questionable, or "tagged," invoices. Now you have been assigned the task of auditing the accuracy of the integrated inventory management and point of sale component of the firm's retail management system.

You could review the contents of each and every inventory and transactional record to check the accuracy of this system, but such a detailed review would be time-consuming and costly. Could you use statistical inference techniques to reach conclusions about the population of all records from a relatively small sample collected during an audit? At the end of each month, you could select a sample of the sales invoices to estimate population parameters such as

- The mean dollar amount listed on the sales invoices for the month
- The proportion of invoices that contain errors that violate the internal control policy of the warehouse

If you used the sampling technique, how accurate would the results from the sample be? How would you use the results you generate? How could you be certain that the sample size is large enough to give you the information you need?

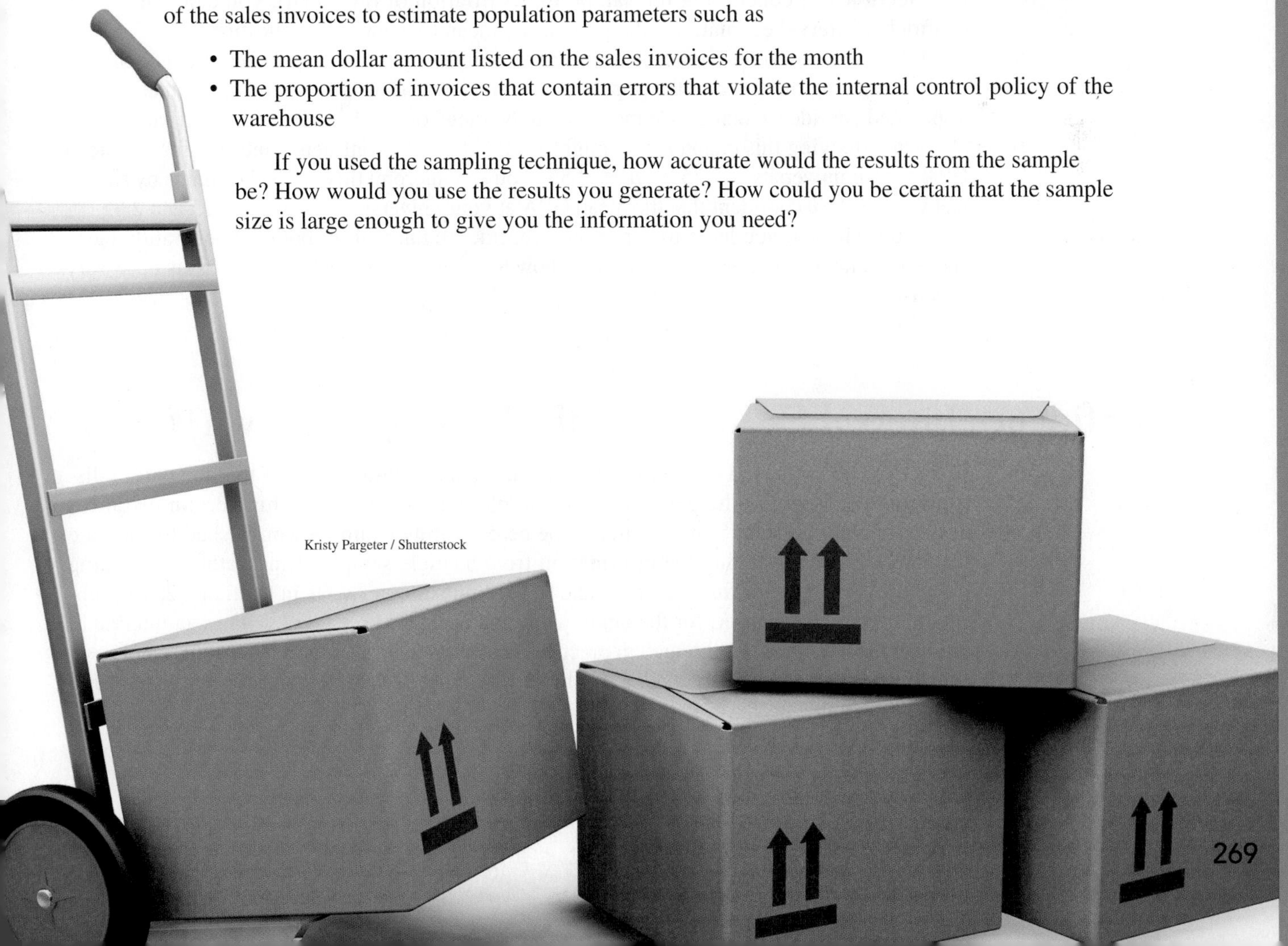

Kristy Pargeter / Shutterstock

In Section 7.2, you used the Central Limit Theorem and knowledge of the population distribution to determine the percentage of sample means that are within certain distances of the population mean. For instance, in the cereal-filling example used throughout Chapter 7 (see Example 7.4 on page 255), you can conclude that 95% of all sample means are between 362.12 and 373.88 grams. This is an example of *deductive* reasoning because the conclusion is based on taking something that is true in general (for the population) and applying it to something specific (the sample means).

Getting the results that Ricknel Home Centers needs requires *inductive* reasoning. Inductive reasoning lets you use some specifics to make broader generalizations. You cannot guarantee that the broader generalizations are absolutely correct, but with a careful choice of the specifics and a rigorous methodology, you can get useful conclusions. As a Ricknel accountant, you need to use inferential statistics, which uses sample results (the "some specifics") to *estimate* (the making of "broader generalizations") unknown population parameters such as a population mean or a population proportion. Note that statisticians use the word *estimate* in the same sense of the everyday usage: something you are reasonably certain about but cannot flatly say is absolutely correct.

You estimate population parameters by using either point estimates or interval estimates. A **point estimate** is the value of a single sample statistic, such as a sample mean. A **confidence interval estimate** is a range of numbers, called an *interval*, constructed around the point estimate. The confidence interval is constructed such that the probability that the interval includes the population parameter is known.

Suppose you want to estimate the mean GPA of all the students at your university. The mean GPA for all the students is an unknown population mean, denoted by μ. You select a sample of students and compute the sample mean, denoted by $\bar{X}$, to be 2.80. As a *point estimate* of the population mean, μ, you ask how accurate is the 2.80 value as an estimate of the population mean, μ? By taking into account the variability from sample to sample (see Section 7.2, concerning the sampling distribution of the mean), you can construct a confidence interval estimate for the population mean to answer this question.

When you construct a confidence interval estimate, you indicate the confidence of correctly estimating the value of the population parameter, μ. This allows you to say that there is a specified confidence that μ is somewhere in the range of numbers defined by the interval.

After studying this chapter, you might find that a 95% confidence interval for the mean GPA at your university is $2.75 \le \mu \le 2.85$. You can interpret this interval estimate by stating that you are 95% confident that the mean GPA at your university is between 2.75 and 2.85.

In this chapter, you learn to construct a confidence interval for both the population mean and population proportion. You also learn how to determine the sample size that is necessary to construct a confidence interval of a desired width.

8.1 Confidence Interval Estimate for the Mean (σ Known)

In Section 7.2, you used the Central Limit Theorem and knowledge of the population distribution to determine the percentage of sample means that are within certain distances of the population mean. Suppose that in the cereal-filling example, you wished to estimate the population mean, using the information from a single sample. Thus, rather than taking $\mu \pm (1.96)(\sigma/\sqrt{n})$ to find the upper and lower limits around μ, as in Section 7.2, you substitute the sample mean, $\bar{X}$, for the unknown μ and use $\bar{X} \pm (1.96)(\sigma/\sqrt{n})$ as an interval to estimate the unknown μ. Although in practice, you select a single sample of n values and compute the mean, $\bar{X}$, in order to understand the full meaning of the interval estimate, you need to examine a hypothetical set of all possible samples of n values.

Student Tip
Remember, the confidence interval is for the population mean not the sample mean.

Suppose that a sample of $n = 25$ cereal boxes has a mean of 362.3 grams and a standard deviation of 15 grams. The interval developed to estimate μ is $362.3 \pm (1.96)(15)/(\sqrt{25})$, or 362.3 ± 5.88. The estimate of μ is

$$356.42 \le \mu \le 368.18$$

Because the population mean, μ (equal to 368), is included within the interval, this sample results in a correct statement about μ (see Figure 8.1).

FIGURE 8.1

Confidence interval estimates for five different samples of $n = 25$ taken from a population where $\mu = 368$ and $\sigma = 15$

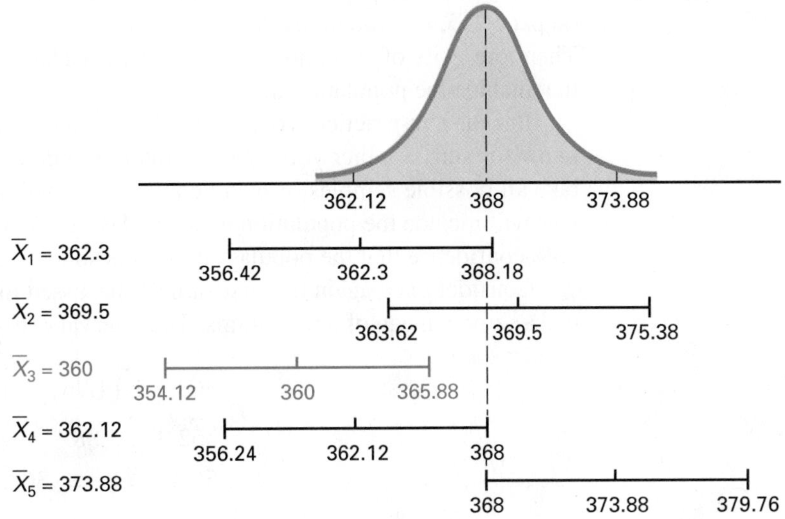

To continue this hypothetical example, suppose that for a different sample of $n = 25$ boxes, the mean is 369.5. The interval developed from this sample is

$$369.5 \pm (1.96)(15)/(\sqrt{25})$$

or 369.5 ± 5.88. The estimate is

$$363.62 \leq \mu \leq 375.38$$

Because the population mean, μ (equal to 368), is also included within this interval, this statement about μ is correct.

Now, before you begin to think that correct statements about μ are always made by developing a confidence interval estimate, suppose a third hypothetical sample of $n = 25$ boxes is selected and the sample mean is equal to 360 grams. The interval developed here is $360 \pm (1.96)(15)/(\sqrt{25})$, or 360 ± 5.88. In this case, the estimate of μ is

$$354.12 \leq \mu \leq 365.88$$

This estimate is *not* a correct statement because the population mean, μ, is not included in the interval developed from this sample (see Figure 8.1). Thus, for some samples, the interval estimate for μ is correct, but for others it is incorrect. In practice, only one sample is selected, and because the population mean is unknown, you cannot determine whether the interval estimate is correct. To resolve this, you need to determine the proportion of samples producing intervals that result in correct statements about the population mean, μ. To do this, consider two other hypothetical samples: the case in which $\bar{X} = 362.12$ grams and the case in which $\bar{X} = 373.88$ grams. If $\bar{X} = 362.12$, the interval is $362.12 \pm (1.96)(15)/(\sqrt{25})$, or 362.12 ± 5.88. This leads to the following interval:

$$356.24 \leq \mu \leq 368.00$$

Because the population mean of 368 is at the upper limit of the interval, the statement is correct (see Figure 8.1).

When $\bar{X} = 373.88$, the interval is $373.88 \pm (1.96)(15)/(\sqrt{25})$, or 373.88 ± 5.88. The interval estimate for the mean is

$$368.00 \leq \mu \leq 379.76$$

In this case, because the population mean of 368 is included at the lower limit of the interval, the statement is correct.

In Figure 8.1, you see that when the sample mean falls somewhere between 362.12 and 373.88 grams, the population mean is included *somewhere* within the interval. In Example 7.4 on page 255, you found that 95% of the sample means are between 362.12 and 373.88 grams. Therefore, 95% of all samples of $n = 25$ boxes have sample means that will result in intervals that include the population mean.

Because, in practice, you select only one sample of size n, and μ is unknown, you never know for sure whether your specific interval includes the population mean. However, if you take all possible samples of n and compute their 95% confidence intervals, 95% of the intervals will include the population mean, and only 5% of them will not. In other words, you have 95% confidence that the population mean is somewhere in your interval.

Consider once again the first sample discussed in this section. A sample of $n = 25$ boxes had a sample mean of 362.3 grams. The interval constructed to estimate μ is

$$362.3 \pm (1.96)(15)/(\sqrt{25})$$

$$362.3 \pm 5.88$$

$$356.42 \leq \mu \leq 368.18$$

The interval from 356.42 to 368.18 is referred to as a *95% confidence interval.* The following contains an interpretation of the interval that most business professionals will understand. (For a technical discussion of different ways to interpret confidence intervals, see reference 4.)

"I am 95% confident that the mean amount of cereal in the population of boxes is somewhere between 356.42 and 368.18 grams."

To help you understand the meaning of the confidence interval, consider the order-filling process at a website. Filling orders consists of several steps, including receiving an order, picking the parts of the order, checking the order, packing, and shipping the order. The file **Order** contains the time, in minutes, to fill orders for a population of $N = 200$ orders on a recent day. Although in practice the population characteristics are rarely known, for this population of orders, the mean, μ, is known to be equal to 69.637 minutes; the standard deviation, σ, is known to be equal to 10.411 minutes; and the population is normally distributed. To illustrate how the sample mean and sample standard deviation can vary from one sample to another, 20 different samples of $n = 10$ were selected from the population of 200 orders, and the sample mean and sample standard deviation (and other statistics) were calculated for each sample. Figure 8.2 shows these results.

FIGURE 8.2

Sample statistics and 95% confidence intervals for 20 samples of $n = 10$ randomly selected from the population of $N = 200$ orders

Variable	Count	Mean	StDev	Minimum	Median	Maximum	Range	95% CI
Sample 1	10	74.15	13.39	56.10	76.85	97.70	41.60	(67.6973, 80.6027)
Sample 2	10	61.10	10.60	46.80	61.35	79.50	32.70	(54.6473, 67.5527)
Sample 3	10	74.36	6.50	62.50	74.50	84.00	21.50	(67.9073, 80.8127)
Sample 4	10	70.40	12.80	47.20	70.95	84.00	36.80	(63.9473, 76.8527)
Sample 5	10	62.18	10.85	47.10	59.70	84.00	36.90	(55.7273, 68.6327)
Sample 6	10	67.03	9.68	51.10	69.60	83.30	32.20	(60.5773, 73.4827)
Sample 7	10	69.03	8.81	56.60	68.85	83.70	27.10	(62.5773, 75.4827)
Sample 8	10	72.30	11.52	54.20	71.35	87.00	32.80	(65.8473, 78.7527)
Sample 9	10	68.18	14.10	50.10	69.95	86.20	36.10	(61.7273, 74.6327)
Sample 10	10	66.67	9.08	57.10	64.65	86.10	29.00	(60.2173, 73.1227)
Sample 11	10	72.42	9.76	59.60	74.65	86.10	26.50	(65.9673, 78.8727)
Sample 12	10	76.26	11.69	50.10	80.60	87.00	36.90	(69.8073, 82.7127)
Sample 13	10	65.74	12.11	47.10	62.15	86.10	39.00	(59.2873, 72.1927)
Sample 14	10	69.99	10.97	51.00	73.40	84.60	33.60	(63.5373, 76.4427)
Sample 15	10	75.76	8.60	61.10	75.05	87.80	26.70	(69.3073, 82.2127)
Sample 16	10	67.94	9.19	56.70	67.70	87.80	31.10	(61.4873, 74.3927)
Sample 17	10	71.05	10.48	50.10	71.15	86.20	36.10	(64.5973, 77.5027)
Sample 18	10	71.68	7.96	55.60	72.35	82.60	27.00	(65.2273, 78.1327)
Sample 19	10	70.97	9.83	54.40	70.05	84.60	30.20	(64.5173, 77.4227)
Sample 20	10	74.48	8.80	62.00	76.25	85.70	23.70	(68.0273, 80.9327)

From Figure 8.2, you can see the following:

- The sample statistics differ from sample to sample. The sample means vary from 61.10 to 76.26 minutes, the sample standard deviations vary from 6.50 to 14.10 minutes, the sample medians vary from 59.70 to 80.60 minutes, and the sample ranges vary from 21.50 to 41.60 minutes.
- Some of the sample means are greater than the population mean of 69.637 minutes, and some of the sample means are less than the population mean.
- Some of the sample standard deviations are greater than the population standard deviation of 10.411 minutes, and some of the sample standard deviations are less than the population standard deviation.
- The variation in the sample ranges is much more than the variation in the sample standard deviations.

The variation of sample statistics from sample to sample is called *sampling error*. **Sampling error** is the variation that occurs due to selecting a single sample from the population. The size of the sampling error is primarily based on the amount of variation in the population and on the sample size. Large samples have less sampling error than small samples, but large samples cost more to select.

The last column of Figure 8.2 contains 95% confidence interval estimates of the population mean order-filling time, based on the results of those 20 samples of $n = 10$. Begin by examining the first sample selected. The sample mean is 74.15 minutes, and the interval estimate for the population mean is 67.6973 to 80.6027 minutes. In a typical study, you would not know for sure whether this interval estimate is correct because you rarely know the value of the population mean. However, for this example *concerning the order-filling times*, the population mean is known to be 69.637 minutes. If you examine the interval 67.6973 to 80.6027 minutes, you see that the population mean of 69.637 minutes is located *between* these lower and upper limits. Thus, the first sample provides a correct estimate of the population mean in the form of an interval estimate. Looking over the other 19 samples, you see that similar results occur for all the other samples *except* for samples 2, 5, and 12. For each of the intervals generated (other than samples 2, 5, and 12), the population mean of 69.637 minutes is located *somewhere* within the interval.

For sample 2, the sample mean is 61.10 minutes, and the interval is 54.6473 to 67.5527 minutes; for sample 5, the sample mean is 62.18, and the interval is between 55.7273 and 68.6327; for sample 12, the sample mean is 76.26, and the interval is between 69.8073 and 82.7127 minutes. The population mean of 69.637 minutes is *not* located within any of these intervals, and the estimate of the population mean made using these intervals is incorrect. Although 3 of the 20 intervals did not include the population mean, if you had selected all the possible samples of $n = 10$ from a population of $N = 200$, 95% of the intervals would include the population mean.

In some situations, you might want a higher degree of confidence of including the population mean within the interval (such as 99%). In other cases, you might accept less confidence (such as 90%) of correctly estimating the population mean. In general, the **level of confidence** is symbolized by $(1 - \alpha) \times 100\%$, where α is the proportion in the tails of the distribution that is outside the confidence interval. The proportion in the upper tail of the distribution is $\alpha/2$, and the proportion in the lower tail of the distribution is $\alpha/2$. You use Equation (8.1) to construct a $(1 - \alpha) \times 100\%$ confidence interval estimate for the mean with σ known.

CONFIDENCE INTERVAL FOR THE MEAN (σ KNOWN)

$$\bar{X} \pm Z_{\alpha/2}\frac{\sigma}{\sqrt{n}}$$

or

$$\bar{X} - Z_{\alpha/2}\frac{\sigma}{\sqrt{n}} \le \mu \le \bar{X} + Z_{\alpha/2}\frac{\sigma}{\sqrt{n}} \quad \textbf{(8.1)}$$

where $Z_{\alpha/2}$ is the value corresponding to an upper-tail probability of $\alpha/2$ from the standardized normal distribution (i.e., a cumulative area of $1 - \alpha/2$).

The value of $Z_{\alpha/2}$ needed for constructing a confidence interval is called the **critical value** for the distribution. 95% confidence corresponds to an α value of 0.05. The critical Z value corresponding to a cumulative area of 0.975 is 1.96 because there is 0.025 in the upper tail of the distribution, and the cumulative area less than $Z = 1.96$ is 0.975.

There is a different critical value for each level of confidence, $1 - \alpha$. A level of confidence of 95% leads to a Z value of 1.96 (see Figure 8.3). 99% confidence corresponds to an α value of 0.01. The Z value is approximately 2.58 because the upper-tail area is 0.005 and the cumulative area less than $Z = 2.58$ is 0.995 (see Figure 8.4).

FIGURE 8.3

Normal curve for determining the Z value needed for 95% confidence

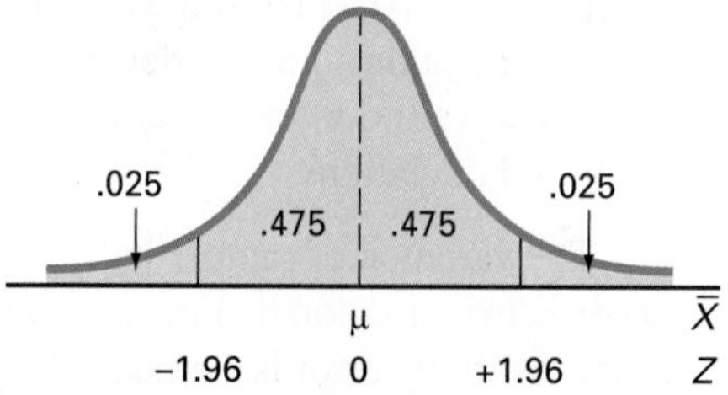

FIGURE 8.4

Normal curve for determining the Z value needed for 99% confidence

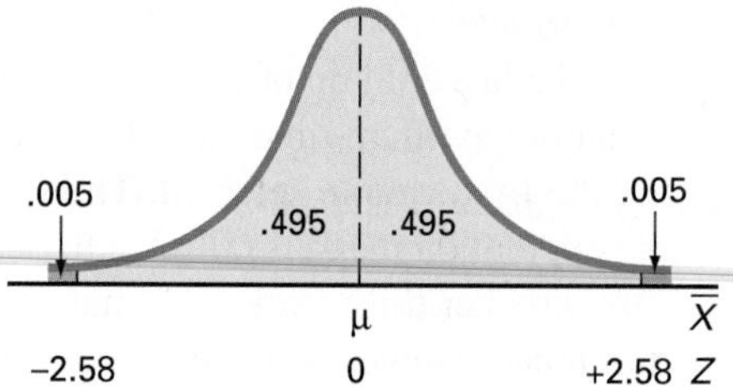

Now that various levels of confidence have been considered, why not make the confidence level as close to 100% as possible? Before doing so, you need to realize that any increase in the level of confidence is achieved only by widening (and making less precise) the confidence interval. There is no "free lunch" here. You would have more confidence that the population mean is within a broader range of values; however, this might make the interpretation of the confidence interval less useful. The trade-off between the width of the confidence interval and the level of confidence is discussed in greater depth in the context of determining the sample size in Section 8.4. Example 8.1 illustrates the application of the confidence interval estimate.

EXAMPLE 8.1

Estimating the Mean Paper Length with 95% Confidence

A paper manufacturer has a production process that operates continuously throughout an entire production shift. The paper is expected to have a mean length of 11 inches, and the standard deviation of the length is 0.02 inch. At periodic intervals, a sample is selected to determine whether the mean paper length is still equal to 11 inches or whether something has gone wrong in the production process to change the length of the paper produced. You select a random sample of 100 sheets, and the mean paper length is 10.998 inches. Construct a 95% confidence interval estimate for the population mean paper length.

SOLUTION Using Equation (8.1) on page 273, with $Z_{\alpha/2} = 1.96$ for 95% confidence,

$$\overline{X} \pm Z_{\alpha/2}\frac{\alpha}{\sqrt{n}} = 10.998 \pm (1.96)\frac{0.02}{\sqrt{100}}$$

$$= 10.998 \pm 0.0039$$

$$10.9941 \leq \mu \leq 11.0019$$

Thus, with 95% confidence, you conclude that the population mean is between 10.9941 and 11.0019 inches. Because the interval includes 11, the value indicating that the production process is working properly, you have no reason to believe that anything is wrong with the production process.

Example 8.2 illustrates the effect of using a 99% confidence interval.

EXAMPLE 8.2

Estimating the Mean Paper Length with 99% Confidence

Construct a 99% confidence interval estimate for the population mean paper length.

SOLUTION Using Equation (8.1) on page 273, with $Z_{\alpha/2} = 2.58$ for 99% confidence,

$$\bar{X} \pm Z_{\alpha/2}\frac{\sigma}{\sqrt{n}} = 10.998 \pm (2.58)\frac{0.02}{\sqrt{100}}$$

$$= 10.998 \pm 0.00516$$

$$10.9928 \le \mu \le 11.0032$$

Once again, because 11 is included within this wider interval, you have no reason to believe that anything is wrong with the production process.

As discussed in Section 7.2, the sampling distribution of the sample mean, $\bar{X}$, is normally distributed if the population for your characteristic of interest, X, follows a normal distribution. And if the population of X does not follow a normal distribution, the Central Limit Theorem almost always ensures that $\bar{X}$ is approximately normally distributed when n is large. However, when dealing with a small sample size and a population that does not follow a normal distribution, the sampling distribution of $\bar{X}$ is not normally distributed, and therefore the confidence interval discussed in this section is inappropriate. In practice, however, as long as the sample size is large enough and the population is not very skewed, you can use the confidence interval defined in Equation (8.1) to estimate the population mean when σ is known. To assess the assumption of normality, you can evaluate the shape of the sample data by constructing a histogram, stem-and-leaf display, boxplot, or normal probability plot.

Student Tip
Because understanding the confidence interval concept is very important when reading the rest of this book, review this section carefully to understand the underlying concept—even if you never have a practical reason to use the confidence interval estimate of the mean (σ known) method.

Can You Ever Know the Population Standard Deviation?

To solve Equation (8.1), you must know the value for σ, the population standard deviation. To know σ implies that you know all the values in the entire population. (How else would you know the value of this population parameter?) If you knew all the values in the entire population, you could directly compute the population mean. There would be no need to use the *inductive* reasoning of inferential statistics to *estimate* the population mean. In other words, if you know σ, you really do not have a need to use Equation (8.1) to construct a confidence interval estimate of the mean (σ known).

More significantly, in virtually all real-world business situations, you would never know the standard deviation of the population. In business situations, populations are often too large to examine all the values. So why study the confidence interval estimate of the mean (σ known) at all? This method serves as an important introduction to the concept of a confidence interval because it uses the normal distribution, which has already been thoroughly discussed in Chapters 6 and 7. In the next section, you will see that constructing a confidence interval estimate when σ is not known requires another distribution (the t distribution) not previously mentioned in this book.

Problems for Section 8.1

LEARNING THE BASICS

8.1 If $\bar{X} = 85$, $\sigma = 8$, and $n = 64$, construct a 95% confidence interval estimate for the population mean, μ.

8.2 If $\bar{X} = 125$, $\sigma = 24$, and $n = 36$, construct a 99% confidence interval estimate for the population mean, μ.

8.3 Why is it not possible in Example 8.1 on page 274 to have 100% confidence? Explain.

8.4 Is it true in Example 8.1 on page 274 that you do not know for sure whether the population mean is between 10.9941 and 11.0019 inches? Explain.

APPLYING THE CONCEPTS

8.5 A market researcher selects a simple random sample of $n = 100$ Twitter users from a population of over 100 million Twitter registered users. After analyzing the sample, she states that she has 95% confidence that the mean time spent on the site per day is between 15 and 57 minutes. Explain the meaning of this statement.

8.6 Suppose that you are going to collect a set of data, either from an entire population or from a random sample taken from that population.

a. Which statistical measure would you compute first: the mean or the standard deviation? Explain.

b. What does your answer to (a) tell you about the "practicality" of using the confidence interval estimate formula given in Equation (8.1)?

8.7 Consider the confidence interval estimate discussed in Problem 8.5. Suppose the population mean time spent on the site is 36 minutes a day. Is the confidence interval estimate stated in Problem 8.5 correct? Explain.

8.8 You are working as an assistant to the dean of institutional research at your university. The dean wants to survey members of the alumni association who obtained their baccalaureate degrees five years ago to learn what their starting salaries were in their first full-time job after receiving their degrees. A sample of 100 alumni is to be randomly selected from the list of 2,500 graduates in that class. If the dean's goal is to construct a 95% confidence interval estimate for the population mean starting salary, why is it not possible that you will be able to use Equation (8.1) on page 273 for this purpose? Explain.

8.9 The manager of a paint supply store wants to estimate the amount of paint contained in 1-gallon cans purchased from a nationally known manufacturer. The manufacturer's specifications state that the standard deviation of the amount of paint is equal to 0.02 gallon. A random sample of 50 cans is selected, and the sample mean amount of paint per 1-gallon can is 0.995 gallon.

a. Construct a 99% confidence interval estimate for the population mean amount of paint included in a 1-gallon can.

b. On the basis of these results, do you think that the manager has a right to complain to the manufacturer? Why?

c. Must you assume that the population amount of paint per can is normally distributed here? Explain.

d. Construct a 95% confidence interval estimate. How does this change your answer to (b)?

SELF Test **8.10** The quality control manager at a light bulb factory needs to estimate the mean life of a large shipment of light bulbs. The manufacturer's specifications are that the standard deviation is 100 hours. A random sample of 64 light bulbs indicated a sample mean life of 350 hours.

a. Construct a 95% confidence interval estimate for the population mean life of light bulbs in this shipment.

b. Do you think that the manufacturer has the right to state that the light bulbs have a mean life of 400 hours? Explain.

c. Must you assume that the population light bulb life is normally distributed? Explain.

d. Suppose that the standard deviation changes to 80 hours. What are your answers in (a) and (b)?

8.2 Confidence Interval Estimate for the Mean (σ Unknown)

In the previous section, you learned that in most business situations, you do not know σ, the population standard deviation. This section discusses a method of constructing a confidence interval estimate of μ that uses the sample statistic S as an estimate of the population parameter σ.

Student's t Distribution

At the start of the twentieth century, William S. Gosset was working at Guinness in Ireland, trying to help brew better beer less expensively (see reference 5). As he had only small samples to study, he needed to find a way to make inferences about means without having to know σ. Writing under the pen name "Student,"[1] Gosset solved this problem by developing what today is known as the **Student's *t* distribution**, or the *t* distribution.

If the random variable X is normally distributed, then the following statistic:

$$t = \frac{\overline{X} - \mu}{\dfrac{S}{\sqrt{n}}}$$

has a t distribution with $n - 1$ **degrees of freedom**. This expression has the same form as the Z statistic in Equation (7.4) on page 254, except that S is used to estimate the unknown σ.

[1]Guinness considered all research conducted to be proprietary and a trade secret. The firm prohibited its employees from publishing their results. Gosset circumvented this ban by using the pen name "Student" to publish his findings.

Properties of the t Distribution

The *t* distribution is very similar in appearance to the standardized normal distribution. Both distributions are symmetrical and bell-shaped, with the mean and the median equal to zero. However, because *S* is used to estimate the unknown σ, the values of *t* are more variable than those for *Z*. Therefore, the *t* distribution has more area in the tails and less in the center than does the standardized normal distribution (see Figure 8.5).

FIGURE 8.5
Standardized normal distribution and *t* distribution for 5 degrees of freedom

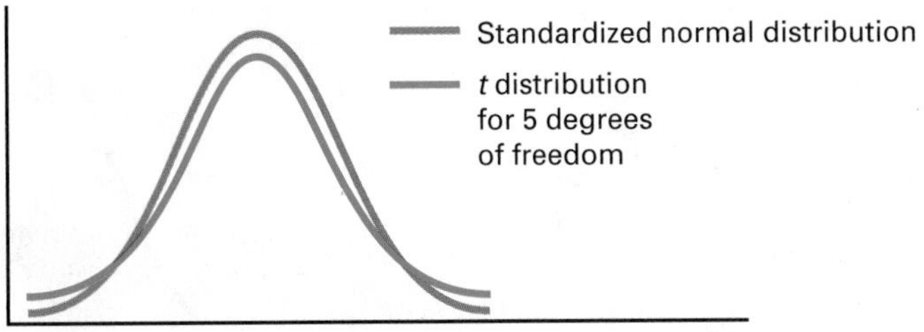

The degrees of freedom, $n - 1$, are directly related to the sample size, *n*. The concept of *degrees of freedom* is discussed further on page 278. As the sample size and degrees of freedom increase, *S* becomes a better estimate of σ, and the *t* distribution gradually approaches the standardized normal distribution, until the two are virtually identical. With a sample size of about 120 or more, *S* estimates σ closely enough so that there is little difference between the *t* and *Z* distributions.

As stated earlier, the *t* distribution assumes that the random variable *X* is normally distributed. In practice, however, when the sample size is large enough and the population is not very skewed, in most cases you can use the *t* distribution to estimate the population mean when σ is unknown. When dealing with a small sample size and a skewed population distribution, the confidence interval estimate may not provide a valid estimate of the population mean. To assess the assumption of normality, you can evaluate the shape of the sample data by constructing a histogram, stem-and-leaf display, boxplot, or normal probability plot. However, the ability of any of these graphs to help you evaluate normality is limited when you have a small sample size.

You find the critical values of *t* for the appropriate degrees of freedom from the table of the *t* distribution (see Table E.3). The columns of the table present the most commonly used cumulative probabilities and corresponding upper-tail areas. The rows of the table represent the degrees of freedom. The critical *t* values are found in the cells of the table. For example, with 99 degrees of freedom, if you want 95% confidence, you find the appropriate value of *t*, as shown in Table 8.1. The 95% confidence level means that 2.5% of the values (an area

TABLE 8.1
Determining the Critical Value from the *t* Table for an Area of 0.025 in Each Tail with 99 Degrees of Freedom

	Cumulative Probabilities					
	.75	.90	.95	.975	.99	.995
	Upper-Tail Areas					
Degrees of Freedom	.25	.10	.05	.025	.01	.005
1	1.0000	3.0777	6.3138	12.7062	31.8207	63.6574
2	0.8165	1.8856	2.9200	4.3027	6.9646	9.9248
3	0.7649	1.6377	2.3534	3.1824	4.5407	5.8409
4	0.7407	1.5332	2.1318	2.7764	3.7469	4.6041
5	0.7267	1.4759	2.0150	2.5706	3.3649	4.0322
⋮	⋮	⋮	⋮	⋮	⋮	⋮
96	0.6771	1.2904	1.6609	1.9850	2.3658	2.6280
97	0.6770	1.2903	1.6607	1.9847	2.3654	2.6275
98	0.6770	1.2902	1.6606	1.9845	2.3650	2.6269
99	0.6770	1.2902	1.6604	1.9842	2.3646	2.6264
100	0.6770	1.2901	1.6602	1.9840	2.3642	2.6259

Source: Extracted from Table E.3.

of 0.025) are in each tail of the distribution. Looking in the column for a cumulative probability of 0.975 and an upper-tail area of 0.025 in the row corresponding to 99 degrees of freedom gives you a critical value for t of 1.9842 (see Figure 8.6). Because t is a symmetrical distribution with a mean of 0, if the upper-tail value is +1.9842, the value for the lower-tail area (lower 0.025) is −1.9842. A t value of −1.9842 means that the probability that t is less than −1.9842 is 0.025, or 2.5%.

FIGURE 8.6
t distribution with 99 degrees of freedom

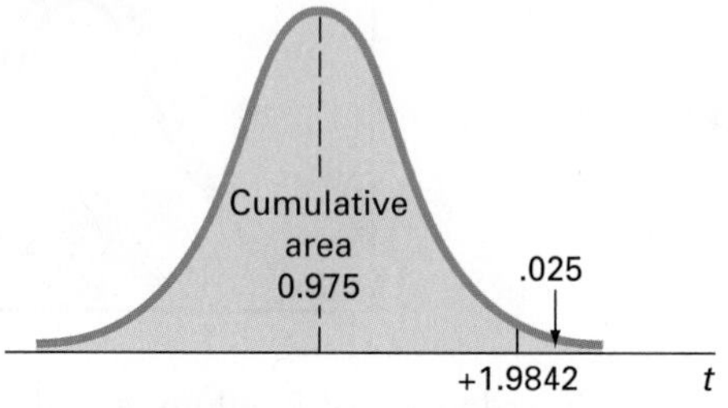

Note that for a 95% confidence interval, you will always have a cumulative probability of 0.975 and an upper-tail area of 0.025. Similarly, for a 99% confidence interval, you will have 0.995 and 0.005, and for a 90% confidence interval you will have 0.95 and 0.05.

The Concept of Degrees of Freedom

In Chapter 3, you learned that the numerator of sample variance, S^2 [see Equation (3.6) on page 113], requires the computation of the sum of squares around the sample mean:

$$\sum_{i=1}^{n}(X_i - \overline{X})^2$$

In order to compute S^2, you first need to know $\overline{X}$. Therefore, only $n-1$ of the sample values are free to vary. This means that you have $n - 1$ degrees of freedom. For example, suppose a sample of five values has a mean of 20. How many values do you need to know before you can determine the remainder of the values? The fact that $n = 5$ and $\overline{X} = 20$ also tells you that

$$\sum_{i=1}^{n} X_i = 100$$

because

$$\frac{\sum_{i=1}^{n} X_i}{n} = \overline{X}$$

Thus, when you know four of the values, the fifth one is *not* free to vary because the sum must be 100. For example, if four of the values are 18, 24, 19, and 16, the fifth value must be 23, so that the sum is 100.

The Confidence Interval Statement

Equation (8.2) defines the $(1 - \alpha) \times 100\%$ confidence interval estimate for the mean with σ unknown.

> **CONFIDENCE INTERVAL FOR THE MEAN (σ UNKNOWN)**
>
> $$\bar{X} \pm t_{\alpha/2}\frac{S}{\sqrt{n}}$$
>
> or
>
> $$\bar{X} - t_{\alpha/2}\frac{S}{\sqrt{n}} \le \mu \le \bar{X} + t_{\alpha/2}\frac{S}{\sqrt{n}} \quad \textbf{(8.2)}$$
>
> where $t_{\alpha/2}$ is the critical value corresponding to an upper-tail probability of $\alpha/2$ (i.e., a cumulative area of $1 - \alpha/2$) from the t distribution with $n - 1$ degrees of freedom.

To illustrate the application of the confidence interval estimate for the mean when the standard deviation is unknown, recall the Ricknel Home Centers scenario presented on page 269. Using the DCOVA steps first discussed on page 4, you define the variable of interest as the dollar amount listed on the sales invoices for the month. Your business objective is to estimate the mean dollar amount. Then you collect the data by selecting a sample of 100 sales invoices from the population of sales invoices during the month. Once you have collected the data, you organize the data in a worksheet. You can construct various graphs (not shown here) to better visualize the distribution of the dollar amounts. To analyze the data, you compute the sample mean of the 100 sales invoices to be equal to \$110.27 and the sample standard deviation to be equal to \$28.95. For 95% confidence, the critical value from the t distribution (as shown in Table 8.1 on page 277) is 1.9842. Using Equation (8.2),

$$\begin{aligned}
\bar{X} &\pm t_{\alpha/2}\frac{S}{\sqrt{n}} \\
&= 110.27 \pm (1.9842)\frac{28.95}{\sqrt{100}} \\
&= 110.27 \pm 5.74 \\
104.53 &\le \mu \le 116.01
\end{aligned}$$

Figure 8.7 shows a worksheet that computes this confidence interval estimate of the mean dollar amount.

FIGURE 8.7

Confidence interval estimate for the mean sales invoice amount worksheet for the Ricknel Home Centers example

*Figure 8.7 displays the **COMPUTE worksheet** of the **CIE sigma unknown workbook** that the Section EG8.2 instructions use.*

	A	B	
1	**Estimate for the Mean Sales Invoice Amount**		
2			
3	**Data**		
4	Sample Standard Deviation	28.95	
5	Sample Mean	110.27	
6	Sample Size	100	
7	Confidence Level	95%	
8			
9	Intermediate Calculations		
10	Standard Error of the Mean	2.8950	=B4/SQRT(B6)
11	Degrees of Freedom	99	=B6-1
12	*t* Value	1.9842	=T.INV.2T(1 - B7, B11)
13	Interval Half Width	5.7443	=B12 * B10
14			
15	**Confidence Interval**		
16	Interval Lower Limit	104.53	=B5 - B13
17	Interval Upper Limit	116.01	=B5 + B13

Thus, with 95% confidence, you conclude that the mean amount of all the sales invoices is between \$104.53 and \$116.01. The 95% confidence level indicates that if you selected all possible samples of 100 (something that is never done in practice), 95% of the intervals developed would include the population mean somewhere within the interval. The validity of this confidence interval estimate depends on the assumption of normality for the distribution of the amount of the sales invoices. With a sample of 100, the normality assumption is not overly restrictive (see the Central Limit Theorem on page 256), and the use of the t distribution is likely appropriate. Example 8.3 further illustrates how you construct the confidence interval for a mean when the population standard deviation is unknown.

EXAMPLE 8.3

Estimating the Mean Processing Time of Life Insurance Applications

An insurance company has the business objective of reducing the amount of time it takes to approve applications for life insurance. The approval process consists of underwriting, which includes a review of the application, a medical information bureau check, possible requests for additional medical information and medical exams, and a policy compilation stage in which the policy pages are generated and sent for delivery. Using the DCOVA steps first discussed on page 4, you define the variable of interest as the total processing time in days. You collect the data by selecting a random sample of 27 approved policies during a period of one month. You organize the data collected in a worksheet. Table 8.2 lists the total processing time, in days, which are stored in **Insurance**. To analyze the data, you need to construct a 95% confidence interval estimate for the population mean processing time.

TABLE 8.2
Processing Time for Life Insurance Applications

73	19	16	64	28	28	31	90	60	56	31	56	22	18
45	48	17	17	17	91	92	63	50	51	69	16	17	

SOLUTION To visualize the data, you construct a boxplot of the processing time, as displayed in Figure 8.8, and a normal probability plot, as shown in Figure 8.9. To analyze the data, you construct the confidence interval estimate shown in Figure 8.10.

FIGURE 8.8
Boxplot for the processing time for life insurance applications

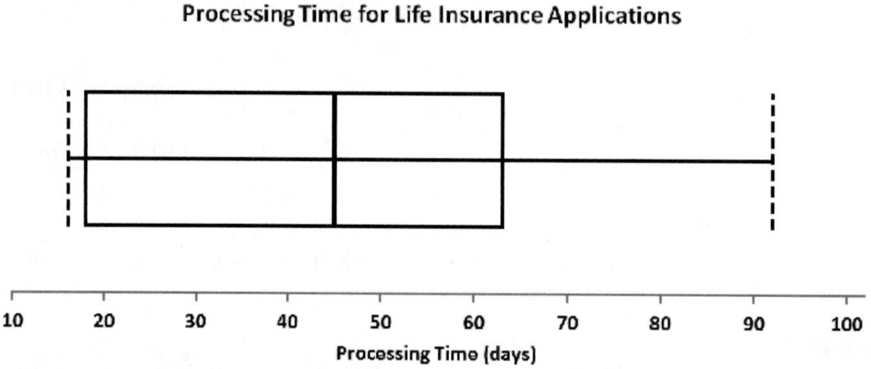

FIGURE 8.9
Normal probability plot for the processing time for life insurance applications

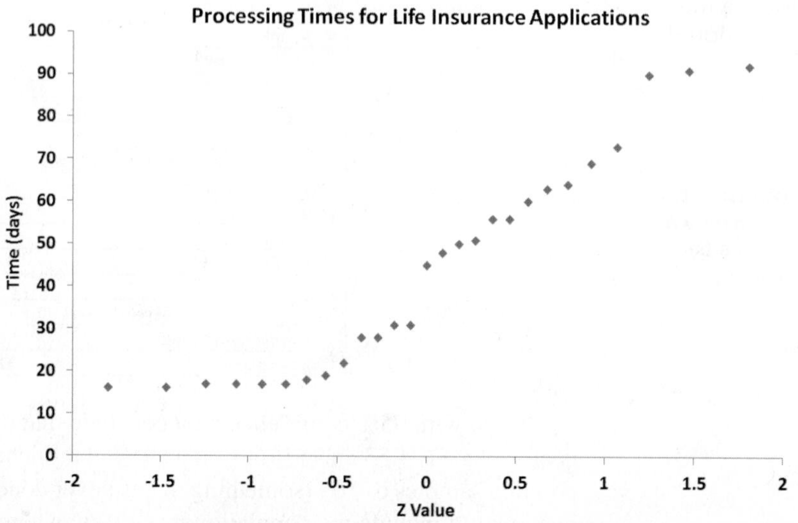

FIGURE 8.10
Confidence interval estimate for the mean processing time worksheet for life insurance applications

Use the Section EG8.2 instructions to construct this worksheet.

	A	B	
1	**Processing Time for Life Insurance Applications**		
2			
3	**Data**		
4	Sample Standard Deviation	25.28	
5	Sample Mean	43.89	
6	Sample Size	27	
7	Confidence Level	95%	
8			
9	Intermediate Calculations		
10	Standard Error of the Mean	4.8651	=B4/SQRT(B6)
11	Degrees of Freedom	26	=B6-1
12	*t* Value	2.0555	=T.INV.2T(1 - B7, B11)
13	Interval Half Width	10.0004	=B12 * B10
14			
15	**Confidence Interval**		
16	Interval Lower Limit	33.89	=B5 - B13
17	Interval Upper Limit	53.89	=B5 + B13

Figure 8.10 shows that the sample mean is $\overline{X} = 43.89$ days and the sample standard deviation is $S = 25.28$ days. Using Equation (8.2) on page 279 to construct the confidence interval, you need to determine the critical value from the t table, using the row for 26 degrees of freedom. For 95% confidence, you use the column corresponding to an upper-tail area of 0.025 and a cumulative probability of 0.975. From Table E.3, you see that $t_{\alpha/2} = 2.0555$. Thus, using $\overline{X} = 43.89$, $S = 25.28$, $n = 27$, and $t_{\alpha/2} = 2.0555$,

$$\overline{X} \pm t_{\alpha/2}\frac{S}{\sqrt{n}}$$

$$= 43.89 \pm (2.0555)\frac{25.28}{\sqrt{27}}$$

$$= 43.89 \pm 10.00$$

$$33.89 \le \mu \le 53.89$$

You conclude with 95% confidence that the mean processing time for the population of life insurance applications is between 33.89 and 53.89 days. The validity of this confidence interval estimate depends on the assumption that the processing time is normally distributed. From the boxplot displayed in Figure 8.8 and the normal probability plot shown in Figure 8.9, the processing time appears right-skewed. Thus, although the sample size is close to 30, you would have some concern about the validity of this confidence interval in estimating the population mean processing time. The concern is that a 95% confidence interval based on a small sample from a skewed distribution will contain the population mean less than 95% of the time in repeated sampling. In the case of small sample sizes and skewed distributions, you might consider the sample median as an estimate of central tendency and construct a confidence interval for the population median (see reference 2).

The interpretation of the confidence interval when σ is unknown is the same as when σ is known. To illustrate the fact that the confidence interval for the mean varies more when σ is unknown, return to the example concerning the order-filling times discussed in Section 8.1 on pages 272 and 273. Suppose that, in this case, you do *not* know the population standard deviation and instead use the sample standard deviation to construct the confidence interval estimate of the mean. Figure 8.11 shows the results for each of 20 samples of $n = 10$ orders.

In Figure 8.11, observe that the standard deviation of the samples varies from 6.25 (sample 17) to 14.83 (sample 3). Thus, the width of the confidence interval developed varies from 8.94 in sample 17 to 21.22 in sample 3. Because you know that the population mean order time $\mu = 69.637$ minutes, you can see that the interval for sample 8 ($69.68 - 85.48$) and the

FIGURE 8.11

Confidence interval estimates of the mean for 20 samples of $n = 10$ randomly selected from the population of $N = 200$ orders with σ unknown

Variable	n	Mean	Std Dev	SE Mean	95% CI
Sample 1	10	71.64	7.58	2.40	(66.22, 77.06)
Sample 2	10	67.22	10.95	3.46	(59.39, 75.05)
Sample 3	10	67.97	14.83	4.69	(57.36, 78.58)
Sample 4	10	73.90	10.59	3.35	(66.33, 81.47)
Sample 5	10	67.11	11.12	3.52	(59.15, 75.07)
Sample 6	10	68.12	10.83	3.43	(60.37, 75.87)
Sample 7	10	65.80	10.85	3.43	(58.03, 73.57)
Sample 8	10	77.58	11.04	3.49	(69.68, 85.48)
Sample 9	10	66.69	11.45	3.62	(58.50, 74.88)
Sample 10	10	62.55	8.58	2.71	(56.41, 68.69)
Sample 11	10	71.12	12.82	4.05	(61.95, 80.29)
Sample 12	10	70.55	10.52	3.33	(63.02, 78.08)
Sample 13	10	65.51	8.16	2.58	(59.67, 71.35)
Sample 14	10	64.90	7.55	2.39	(59.50, 70.30)
Sample 15	10	66.22	11.21	3.54	(58.20, 74.24)
Sample 16	10	70.43	10.21	3.23	(63.12, 77.74)
Sample 17	10	72.04	6.25	1.96	(67.57, 76.51)
Sample 18	10	73.91	11.29	3.57	(65.83, 81.99)
Sample 19	10	71.49	9.76	3.09	(64.51, 78.47)
Sample 20	10	70.15	10.84	3.43	(62.39, 77.91)

interval for sample 10 (56.41 − 68.69) do not correctly estimate the population mean. All the other intervals correctly estimate the population mean. Once again, remember that in practice you select only one sample, and you are unable to know for sure whether your one sample provides a confidence interval that includes the population mean.

Problems for Section 8.2

LEARNING THE BASICS

8.11 If $\bar{X} = 75$, $S = 24$, and $n = 36$, and assuming that the population is normally distributed, construct a 95% confidence interval estimate for the population mean, μ.

8.12 Determine the critical value of t in each of the following circumstances:

a. $1 - \alpha = 0.95, n = 10$
b. $1 - \alpha = 0.99, n = 10$
c. $1 - \alpha = 0.95, n = 32$
d. $1 - \alpha = 0.95, n = 65$
e. $1 - \alpha = 0.90, n = 16$

8.13 Assuming that the population is normally distributed, construct a 95% confidence interval estimate for the population mean for each of the following samples:

Sample A: 1 1 1 1 8 8 8 8

Sample B: 1 2 3 4 5 6 7 8

Explain why these two samples produce different confidence intervals even though they have the same mean and range.

8.14 Assuming that the population is normally distributed, construct a 95% confidence interval for the population mean, based on the following sample of size $n = 7$:

1 2 3 4 5 6 20

Change the number 20 to 7 and recalculate the confidence interval. Using these results, describe the effect of an outlier (i.e., an extreme value) on the confidence interval.

APPLYING THE CONCEPTS

8.15 A stationery store wants to estimate the mean retail value of greeting cards that it has in its inventory. A random sample of 100 greeting cards indicates a mean value of \$2.55 and a standard deviation of \$0.44.

a. Assuming a normal distribution, construct a 95% confidence interval estimate for the mean value of all greeting cards in the store's inventory.
b. Suppose there are 2,500 greeting cards in the store's inventory. How are the results in (a) useful in assisting the store owner to estimate the total value of the inventory?

SELF Test **8.16** A survey of nonprofit organizations showed that online fundraising has increased in the past year. Based on a random sample of 60 nonprofits, the mean one-time gift donation in the past year was \$62, with a standard deviation of \$9.

a. Construct a 95% confidence interval estimate for the population mean one-time gift donation.
b. Interpret the interval constructed in (a).

8.17 The U.S. Department of Transportation requires tire manufacturers to provide tire performance information on the sidewall of a tire to better inform prospective customers as they make purchasing decisions. One very important measure of tire performance is the tread wear index, which indicates the tire's resistance to tread wear compared with a tire graded with a base of 100. A tire with a grade of 200 should last twice as long, on average, as a tire graded with a base of 100. A consumer organization wants to estimate the actual tread wear index of a brand name of tires that claims "graded 200" on the sidewall of the tire. A random sample of $n = 18$ indicates a sample mean tread wear index of 195.3 and a sample standard deviation of 21.4.

a. Assuming that the population of tread wear indexes is normally distributed, construct a 95% confidence interval estimate for the population mean tread wear index for tires produced by this manufacturer under this brand name.
b. Do you think that the consumer organization should accuse the manufacturer of producing tires that do not meet the performance information provided on the sidewall of the tire? Explain.
c. Explain why an observed tread wear index of 210 for a particular tire is not unusual, even though it is outside the confidence interval developed in (a).

8.18 The file FastFood contains the amount that a sample of fifteen customers spent for lunch (\$) at a fast-food restaurant:

7.42 6.29 5.83 6.50 8.34 9.51 7.10 6.80 5.90
4.89 6.50 5.52 7.90 8.30 9.60

a. Construct a 95% confidence interval estimate for the population mean amount spent for lunch (\$) at a fast-food restaurant, assuming a normal distribution.
b. Interpret the interval constructed in (a).

8.19 The file Sedans contains the overall miles per gallon (MPG) of 2012 family sedans:

38 24 26 21 25 22 24 34 23 20 37 22 20 33 22 21

Source: Data extracted from "Ratings," *Consumer Reports*, April 2012, pp. 31.

a. Construct a 95% confidence interval estimate for the population mean MPG of 2012 family sedans, assuming a normal distribution.
b. Interpret the interval constructed in (a).
c. Compare the results in (a) to those in Problem 8.20(a).

8.20 The file SUV contains the overall miles per gallon (MPG) of 2012 small SUVs:

20 22 23 22 23 22 22 21 19
22 22 26 23 24 19 21 22 16

Source: Data extracted from "Ratings," *Consumer Reports*, April 2012, pp. 35–36.

a. Construct a 95% confidence interval estimate for the population mean MPG of 2012 small SUVs, assuming a normal distribution.
b. Interpret the interval constructed in (a).
c. Compare the results in (a) to those in Problem 8.19(a).

8.21 Is there a difference in the yields of different types of investments? The file CDRate contains the yields for a one-year certificate of deposit (CD) and a five-year CD for 24 banks in the United States as of June 21, 2011. (Data extracted from **www.Bankrate.com**, June 21, 2011.)

a. Construct a 95% confidence interval estimate for the mean yield of one-year CDs.
b. Construct a 95% confidence interval estimate for the mean yield of five-year CDs.
c. Compare the results of (a) and (b).

8.22 One of the major measures of the quality of service provided by any organization is the speed with which the organization responds to customer complaints. A large family-held department store selling furniture and flooring, including carpet, had undergone a major expansion in the past several years. In particular, the flooring department had expanded from 2 installation crews to an installation supervisor, a measurer, and 15 installation crews. The store had the business objective of improving its response to complaints. The variable of interest was defined as the number of days between when the complaint was made and when it was resolved. Data were collected from 50 complaints that were made in the past year. The data, stored in Furniture, are as follows:

54	5	35	137	31	27	152	2	123	81	74	27
11	19	126	110	110	29	61	35	94	31	26	5
12	4	165	32	29	28	29	26	25	1	14	13
13	10	5	27	4	52	30	22	36	26	20	23
33	68										

a. Construct a 95% confidence interval estimate for the population mean number of days between the receipt of a complaint and the resolution of the complaint.
b. What assumption must you make about the population distribution in order to construct the confidence interval estimate in (a)?
c. Do you think that the assumption needed in order to construct the confidence interval estimate in (a) is valid? Explain.
d. What effect might your conclusion in (c) have on the validity of the results in (a)?

8.23 A manufacturing company produces electric insulators. You define the variable of interest as the strength of the insulators. If the insulators break when in use, a short circuit is likely. To test the strength of the insulators, you carry out destructive testing to determine how much force is required to break the insulators. You measure force by observing how many pounds are applied to the insulator before it breaks. You collect the force data for 30 insulators selected for the experiment and organize and store these data in **Force**:

1,870	1,728	1,656	1,610	1,634	1,784	1,522	1,696
1,592	1,662	1,866	1,764	1,734	1,662	1,734	1,774
1,550	1,756	1,762	1,866	1,820	1,744	1,788	1,688
1,810	1,752	1,680	1,810	1,652	1,736		

a. Construct a 95% confidence interval estimate for the population mean force.

b. What assumption must you make about the population distribution in order to construct the confidence interval estimate in (a)?

c. Do you think that the assumption needed in order to construct the confidence interval estimate in (a) is valid? Explain.

8.24 The file **MarketPenetration** contains Facebook penetration values (the percentage of a country's population that are Facebook users) for 15 countries:

50.19	25.45	4.25	18.04	31.66	49.14	39.99	28.29
37.52	28.87	37.73	46.04	52.24	38.06	34.91	

Source: Data extracted from **www.socialbakers.com/facebook-statistics/**.

a. Construct a 95% confidence interval estimate for the population mean Facebook penetration.

b. What assumption do you need to make about the population to construct the interval in (a)?

c. Given the data presented, do you think the assumption needed in (a) is valid? Explain.

8.25 One operation of a mill is to cut pieces of steel into parts that are used in the frame for front seats in an automobile. The steel is cut with a diamond saw, and the resulting parts must be cut to be within ±0.005 inch of the length specified by the automobile company. The measurement reported from a sample of 100 steel parts (stored in **Steel**) is the difference, in inches, between the actual length of the steel part, as measured by a laser measurement device, and the specified length of the steel part. For example, the first observation, −0.002, represents a steel part that is 0.002 inch shorter than the specified length.

a. Construct a 95% confidence interval estimate for the population mean difference between the actual length of the steel part and the specified length of the steel part.

b. What assumption must you make about the population distribution in order to construct the confidence interval estimate in (a)?

c. Do you think that the assumption needed in order to construct the confidence interval estimate in (a) is valid? Explain.

d. Compare the conclusions reached in (a) with those of Problem 2.39 on page 68.

8.3 Confidence Interval Estimate for the Proportion

> **Student Tip**
> As noted in Chapter 7, do not confuse this use of the Greek letter pi, π, to represent the population proportion with the mathematical constant that is the ratio of the circumference to a diameter of a circle—approximately 3.14159—which is also known by the same Greek letter.

The concept of a confidence interval also applies to categorical data. With categorical data, you want to estimate the proportion of items in a population having a certain characteristic of interest. The unknown population proportion is represented by the Greek letter π. The point estimate for π is the sample proportion, $p = X/n$, where n is the sample size and X is the number of items in the sample having the characteristic of interest. Equation (8.3) defines the confidence interval estimate for the population proportion.

CONFIDENCE INTERVAL ESTIMATE FOR THE PROPORTION

$$p \pm Z_{\alpha/2}\sqrt{\frac{p(1-p)}{n}}$$

or

$$p - Z_{\alpha/2}\sqrt{\frac{p(1-p)}{n}} \le \pi \le p + Z_{\alpha/2}\sqrt{\frac{p(1-p)}{n}} \quad \textbf{(8.3)}$$

Student Tip
Remember, the sample proportion, p, must be between 0 and 1.

where

$$p = \text{sample proportion} = \frac{X}{n} = \frac{\text{Number of items having the characteristic}}{\text{sample size}}$$

$$\pi = \text{population proportion}$$

$$Z_{\alpha/2} = \text{critical value from the standardized normal distribution}$$

$$n = \text{sample size}$$

Note: To use this equation for the confidence interval, the sample size n must be large enough to ensure that both X and $n - X$ are greater than 5.

You can use the confidence interval estimate for the proportion defined in Equation (8.3) to estimate the proportion of sales invoices that contain errors (see the Ricknel Home Centers scenario on page 269). Using the DCOVA steps, you define the variable of interest as whether the invoice contains errors (yes or no). Then, you collect the data from a sample of 100 sales invoices. The results, which you organize and store in a worksheet, show that 10 invoices contain errors. To analyze the data, you compute, for these data, $p = X/n = 10/100 = 0.10$. Since both X and $n - X$ are > 5, using Equation (8.3) and $Z_{\alpha/2} = 1.96$, for 95% confidence,

$$p \pm Z_{\alpha/2}\sqrt{\frac{p(1-p)}{n}}$$

$$= 0.10 \pm (1.96)\sqrt{\frac{(0.10)(0.90)}{100}}$$

$$= 0.10 \pm (1.96)(0.03)$$

$$= 0.10 \pm 0.0588$$

$$0.0412 \le \pi \le 0.1588$$

Therefore, you have 95% confidence that the population proportion of all sales invoices containing errors is between 0.0412 and 0.1588. This means that between 4.12% and 15.88% of all the sales invoices contain errors. Figure 8.12 shows a confidence interval estimate for this example.

FIGURE 8.12
Confidence interval estimate for the proportion of sales invoices that contain errors worksheet

Figure 8.12 displays the ***COMPUTE worksheet*** *of the* ***CIE Proportion workbook*** *that the Section EG8.3 instructions use.*

	A	B	
1	**Proportion of In-Error Sales Invoices**		
2			
3	Data		
4	Sample Size	100	
5	Number of Successes	10	
6	Confidence Level	95%	
7			
8	Intermediate Calculations		
9	Sample Proportion	0.1	=B5/B4
10	Z Value	-1.9600	=NORM.S.INV((1 - B6)/2)
11	Standard Error of the Proportion	0.03	=SQRT(B9 * (1 - B9)/B4)
12	Interval Half Width	0.0588	=ABS(B10 * B11)
13			
14	**Confidence Interval**		
15	Interval Lower Limit	0.0412	=B9 - B12
16	Interval Upper Limit	0.1588	=B9 + B12

Example 8.4 illustrates another application of a confidence interval estimate for the proportion.

EXAMPLE 8.4

Estimating the Proportion of Nonconforming Newspapers Printed

The operations manager at a large newspaper wants to estimate the proportion of newspapers printed that have a nonconforming attribute. Using the DCOVA steps, you define the variable of interest as whether the newspaper has excessive ruboff, improper page setup, missing pages, or duplicate pages. You collect the data by selecting a random sample of $n = 200$ newspapers from all the newspapers printed during a single day. You organize the results in a worksheet which shows that 35 newspapers contain some type of nonconformance. To analyze the data, you need to construct and interpret a 90% confidence interval estimate for the proportion of newspapers printed during the day that have a nonconforming attribute.

SOLUTION Using Equation (8.3),

$$p = \frac{X}{n} = \frac{35}{200} = 0.175, \text{ and with a 90\% level of confidence } Z_{\alpha/2} = 1.645$$

$$\begin{aligned} & p \pm Z_{\alpha/2}\sqrt{\frac{p(1-p)}{n}} \\ &= 0.175 \pm (1.645)\sqrt{\frac{(0.175)(0.825)}{200}} \\ &= 0.175 \pm (1.645)(0.0269) \\ &= 0.175 \pm 0.0442 \\ & 0.1308 \le \pi \le 0.2192 \end{aligned}$$

You conclude with 90% confidence that the population proportion of all newspapers printed that day with nonconformities is between 0.1308 and 0.2192. This means that between 13.08% and 21.92% of the newspapers printed on that day have some type of nonconformance.

Equation (8.3) contains a Z statistic because you can use the normal distribution to approximate the binomial distribution when the sample size is sufficiently large. In Example 8.4, the confidence interval using Z provides an excellent approximation for the population proportion because both X and $n - X$ are greater than 5. However, if you do not have a sufficiently large sample size, you should use the binomial distribution rather than Equation (8.3) (see references 1, 3, and 8). The exact confidence intervals for various sample sizes and proportions of successes have been tabulated by Fisher and Yates (reference 3).

Problems for Section 8.3

LEARNING THE BASICS

8.26 If $n = 200$ and $X = 50$, construct a 95% confidence interval estimate for the population proportion.

8.27 If $n = 400$ and $X = 25$, construct a 99% confidence interval estimate for the population proportion.

APPLYING THE CONCEPTS

SELF Test **8.28** A cellphone provider has the business objective of wanting to estimate the proportion of subscribers who would upgrade to a new cellphone with improved features if it were made available at a substantially reduced cost. Data are collected from a random sample of 500 subscribers. The results indicate that 135 of the subscribers would upgrade to a new cellphone at a reduced cost.

a. Construct a 99% confidence interval estimate for the population proportion of subscribers that would upgrade to a new cellphone at a reduced cost.

b. How would the manager in charge of promotional programs use the results in (a)?

8.29 In a survey of 1,200 social media users, 76% said it is okay to friend co-workers, but 56% said it is not okay to friend your boss. (Data extracted from "Facebook Etiquette at Work," *USA Today*, March 24, 2010, p. 1B.)

a. Construct a 95% confidence interval estimate for the population proportion of social media users who would say it is okay to friend co-workers.

b. Construct a 95% confidence interval estimate for the population proportion of social media users who would say it is not okay to friend their boss.

c. Write a short summary of the information derived from (a) and (b).

8.30 Are you more likely to purchase a brand mentioned by an athlete on a social media site? According to a Catalyst Digital Fan Engagement survey, 53% of social media sports fans would make such a purchase. (Data extracted from "Survey: Social Media Continues to Fuel Fans," *Sports Business Journal*, July 16, 2012, p. 24.)

a. Suppose that the survey had a sample size of $n = 500$. Construct a 95% confidence interval estimate for the population proportion of social media sports fans that would more likely purchase a brand mentioned by an athlete on a social media site.

b. Based on (a), can you claim that more than half of all social media sports fans would more likely purchase a brand mentioned by an athlete on a social media site?

c. Repeat parts (a) and (b), assuming that the survey had a sample size of $n = 5{,}000$.

d. Discuss the effect of sample size on confidence interval estimation.

8.31 In a survey of 280 qualified readers of *Logistics Management*, 62 responded that the "cloud" and Software as a Service (SaaS) is not an option for their firms, citing issues such as security and privacy concerns, system reliability and system performance, data integrity, and lack of control as the biggest concerns. (Data extracted from "2012 Supply Chain Software Users Survey: Spending Stabilizers," *Logistics Management*, May 2012, p. 38.) Construct a 95% confidence interval estimate for the population proportion of logistics firms for which the cloud and SaaS is not an option.

8.32 In a survey of 1,954 cellphone owners, adults aged 18 and over, 743 reported that they use their phone to keep themselves occupied during commercials or breaks in something they were watching on television, while 430 used their phone to check whether something they heard on television is true. (Data extracted from "The Rise of the Connected Viewer," Pew Research Center's Internet & American Life Project, July 17, 2012, **pewinternet.org/~/media//Files/Reports/2012/PIP_Connected_Viewers.pdf**.)

a. Construct a 95% confidence interval estimate for the population proportion of adult cellphone owners who report that they use their phone to keep themselves occupied during commercials or breaks in something they were watching on television.

b. Construct a 95% confidence interval estimate for the population proportion of adult cellphone owners who report that they use their phone to check whether something they heard on television was true.

c. Compare the results of (a) and (b).

8.33 What are the factors that influence technology (tech) CEOs' anticipated need to change strategy? In a survey by PricewaterhouseCoopers (PwC), 94 of 115 tech CEOs around the globe responded that customer demand is one of the reasons they are making strategic changes at their organization, and 40 responded that availability of talent is one of the reasons. (Data extracted from "Delivering Results: Key Findings in the Technology Sector," 15th Annual PwC Global CEO Survey, 2012.)

a. Construct a 95% confidence interval estimate for the population proportion of tech CEOs who indicate customer demand as one of the reasons for making strategic change.

b. Construct a 95% confidence interval estimate for the population proportion of tech CEOs who indicate availability of talent as one of the reasons for making strategic change.

c. Interpret the intervals in (a) and (b).

8.4 Determining Sample Size

In each confidence interval developed so far in this chapter, the sample size was reported along with the results, with little discussion of the width of the resulting confidence interval. In the business world, sample sizes are determined prior to data collection to ensure that the confidence interval is narrow enough to be useful in making decisions. Determining the proper sample size is a complicated procedure, subject to the constraints of budget, time, and the amount of acceptable sampling error. In the Ricknel Home Centers scenario, if you want to estimate the mean dollar amount of the sales invoices, you must determine in advance how large a sampling error to allow in estimating the population mean. You must also determine, in advance, the level of confidence (i.e., 90%, 95%, or 99%) to use in estimating the population parameter.

Sample Size Determination for the Mean

To develop an equation for determining the appropriate sample size needed when constructing a confidence interval estimate for the mean, recall Equation (8.1) on page 273:

$$\overline{X} \pm Z_{\alpha/2}\frac{\sigma}{\sqrt{n}}$$

The amount added to or subtracted from $\overline{X}$ is equal to half the width of the interval. This quantity represents the amount of imprecision in the estimate that results from sampling error.[2] The sampling error, e, is defined as

$$e = Z_{\alpha/2}\frac{\sigma}{\sqrt{n}}$$

[2]In this context, some statisticians refer to e as the **margin of error**.

Solving for n gives the sample size needed to construct the appropriate confidence interval estimate for the mean. "Appropriate" means that the resulting interval will have an acceptable amount of sampling error.

SAMPLE SIZE DETERMINATION FOR THE MEAN

The sample size, n, is equal to the product of the $Z_{\alpha/2}$ value squared and the standard deviation, σ, squared, divided by the square of the sampling error, e.

$$n = \frac{Z_{\alpha/2}^2 \sigma^2}{e^2} \quad \textbf{(8.4)}$$

To compute the sample size, you must know three quantities:

- The desired confidence level, which determines the value of $Z_{\alpha/2}$, the critical value from the standardized normal distribution[3]
- The acceptable sampling error, e
- The standard deviation, σ

[3]You use Z instead of t because, to determine the critical value of t, you need to know the sample size, but you do not know it yet. For most studies, the sample size needed is large enough that the standardized normal distribution is a good approximation of the t distribution.

In some business-to-business relationships that require estimation of important parameters, legal contracts specify acceptable levels of sampling error and the confidence level required. For companies in the food and drug sectors, government regulations often specify sampling errors and confidence levels. In general, however, it is usually not easy to specify the three quantities needed to determine the sample size. How can you determine the level of confidence and sampling error? Typically, these questions are answered only by a subject matter expert (i.e., an individual very familiar with the variables under study). Although 95% is the most common confidence level used, if more confidence is desired, then 99% might be more appropriate; if less confidence is deemed acceptable, then 90% might be used. For the sampling error, you should think not of how much sampling error you would like to have (you really do not want any error) but of how much you can tolerate when reaching conclusions from the confidence interval.

In addition to specifying the confidence level and the sampling error, you need an estimate of the standard deviation. Unfortunately, you rarely know the population standard deviation, σ. In some instances, you can estimate the standard deviation from past data. In other situations, you can make an educated guess by taking into account the range and distribution of the variable. For example, if you assume a normal distribution, the range is approximately equal to 6σ (i.e., $\pm 3\sigma$ around the mean) so that you estimate σ as the range divided by 6. If you cannot estimate σ in this way, you can conduct a small-scale study and estimate the standard deviation from the resulting data.

To explore how to determine the sample size needed for estimating the population mean, consider again the audit at Ricknel Home Centers. In Section 8.2, you selected a sample of 100 sales invoices and constructed a 95% confidence interval estimate for the population mean sales invoice amount. How was this sample size determined? Should you have selected a different sample size?

Suppose that, after consulting with company officials, you determine that a sampling error of no more than $\pm\$5$ is desired, along with 95% confidence. Past data indicate that the standard deviation of the sales amount is approximately \$25. Thus, $e = \$5$, $\sigma = \$25$, and $Z_{\alpha/2} = 1.96$ (for 95% confidence). Using Equation (8.4),

$$\begin{aligned} n &= \frac{Z_{\alpha/2}^2 \sigma^2}{e^2} = \frac{(1.96)^2(25)^2}{(5)^2} \\ &= 96.04 \end{aligned}$$

Because the general rule is to slightly oversatisfy the criteria by rounding the sample size up to the next whole integer, you should select a sample of size 97. Thus, the sample of size $n = 100$ used on page 279 is slightly more than what is necessary to satisfy the needs of the company, based on the estimated standard deviation, desired confidence level, and sampling error. Because the calculated sample standard deviation is slightly higher than expected, \$28.95 compared to \$25.00, the confidence interval is slightly wider than desired. Figure 8.13 shows a worksheet for determining the sample size.

FIGURE 8.13

Worksheet for determining the sample size for estimating the mean sales invoice amount for the Ricknel Home Centers example

*Figure 8.13 displays the **COMPUTE worksheet** of the **Sample Size Mean workbook** that the Section EG8.4 instructions use.*

	A	B	
1	**For the Mean Sales Invoice Amount**		
2			
3	**Data**		
4	Population Standard Deviation	25	
5	Sampling Error	5	
6	Confidence Level	95%	
7			
8	Intemediate Calculations		
9	Z Value	-1.9600	=NORM.S.INV((1 - B6)/2)
10	Calculated Sample Size	96.0365	=((B9 * B4)/B5)^2
11			
12	**Result**		
13	Sample Size Needed	97	=ROUNDUP(B10, 0)

Example 8.5 illustrates another application of determining the sample size needed to develop a confidence interval estimate for the mean.

EXAMPLE 8.5

Determining the Sample Size for the Mean

Returning to Example 8.3 on page 280, suppose you want to estimate, with 95% confidence, the population mean processing time to within ±4 days. On the basis of a study conducted the previous year, you believe that the standard deviation is 25 days. Determine the sample size needed.

SOLUTION Using Equation (8.4) on page 288 and $e = 5$, $\sigma = 25$, and $Z_{\alpha/2} = 1.96$ for 95% confidence,

$$n = \frac{Z_{\alpha/2}^2 \sigma^2}{e^2} = \frac{(1.96)^2(25)^2}{(4)^2}$$
$$= 150.06$$

Therefore, you should select a sample of 151 applications because the general rule for determining sample size is to always round up to the next integer value in order to slightly oversatisfy the criteria desired. An actual sampling error slightly larger than 4 will result if the sample standard deviation calculated in this sample of 151 is greater than 25 and slightly smaller if the sample standard deviation is less than 25.

Sample Size Determination for the Proportion

So far in this section, you have learned how to determine the sample size needed for estimating the population mean. Now suppose that you want to determine the sample size necessary for estimating a population proportion.

To determine the sample size needed to estimate a population proportion, π, you use a method similar to the method for a population mean. Recall that in developing the sample size for a confidence interval for the mean, the sampling error is defined by

$$e = Z_{\alpha/2}\frac{\sigma}{\sqrt{n}}$$

When estimating a proportion, you replace σ with $\sqrt{\pi(1 - \pi)}$. Thus, the sampling error is

$$e = Z_{\alpha/2}\sqrt{\frac{\pi(1 - \pi)}{n}}$$

Solving for n, you have the sample size necessary to develop a confidence interval estimate for a proportion.

SAMPLE SIZE DETERMINATION FOR THE PROPORTION

The sample size n is equal to the product of $Z_{\alpha/2}$ squared, the population proportion, π, and 1 minus the population proportion, π, divided by the square of the sampling error, e.

$$n = \frac{Z_{\alpha/2}^2 \pi(1 - \pi)}{e^2} \quad \textbf{(8.5)}$$

To determine the sample size, you must know three quantities:

- The desired confidence level, which determines the value of $Z_{\alpha/2}$, the critical value from the standardized normal distribution
- The acceptable sampling error (or margin of error), e
- The population proportion, π

In practice, selecting these quantities requires some planning. Once you determine the desired level of confidence, you can find the appropriate $Z_{\alpha/2}$ value from the standardized normal distribution. The sampling error, e, indicates the amount of error that you are willing to tolerate in estimating the population proportion. The third quantity, π, is actually the population parameter that you want to estimate! Thus, how do you state a value for what you are trying to determine?

Here you have two alternatives. In many situations, you may have past information or relevant experience that provides an educated estimate of π. If you do not have past information or relevant experience, you can try to provide a value for π that would never *underestimate* the sample size needed. Referring to Equation (8.5), you can see that the quantity $\pi(1 - \pi)$ appears in the numerator. Thus, you need to determine the value of π that will make the quantity $\pi(1 - \pi)$ as large as possible. When $\pi = 0.5$, the product $\pi(1 - \pi)$ achieves its maximum value. To show this result, consider the following values of π, along with the accompanying products of $\pi(1 - \pi)$:

When $\pi = 0.9$, then $\pi(1 - \pi) = (0.9)(0.1) = 0.09$.

When $\pi = 0.7$, then $\pi(1 - \pi) = (0.7)(0.3) = 0.21$.

When $\pi = 0.5$, then $\pi(1 - \pi) = (0.5)(0.5) = 0.25$.

When $\pi = 0.3$, then $\pi(1 - \pi) = (0.3)(0.7) = 0.21$.

When $\pi = 0.1$, then $\pi(1 - \pi) = (0.1)(0.9) = 0.09$.

Therefore, when you have no prior knowledge or estimate for the population proportion, π, you should use $\pi = 0.5$ for determining the sample size. Using $\pi = 0.5$ produces the largest possible sample size and results in the narrowest and most precise confidence interval. This increased precision comes at the cost of spending more time and money for an increased sample size. Also, note that if you use $\pi = 0.5$ and the proportion is different from 0.5, you will overestimate the sample size needed, because you will get a confidence interval narrower than originally intended.

Returning to the Ricknel Home Centers scenario on page 269, suppose that the auditing procedures require you to have 95% confidence in estimating the population proportion of sales invoices with errors to within ±0.07. The results from past months indicate that the largest proportion has been no more than 0.15. Thus, using Equation (8.5) with $e = 0.07$, $\pi = 0.15$, and $Z_{\alpha/2} = 1.96$ for 95% confidence,

$$n = \frac{Z_{\alpha/2}^2 \pi(1 - \pi)}{e^2}$$

$$= \frac{(1.96)^2(0.15)(0.85)}{(0.07)^2}$$

$$= 99.96$$

Because the general rule is to round the sample size up to the next whole integer to slightly oversatisfy the criteria, a sample size of 100 is needed. Thus, the sample size needed to satisfy the requirements of the company, based on the estimated proportion, desired confidence level, and sampling error, is equal to the sample size taken on page 279. The actual confidence interval is narrower than required because the sample proportion is 0.10, whereas 0.15 was used for π in Equation (8.5). Figure 8.14 shows a worksheet for determining the sample size.

FIGURE 8.14
Worksheet for determining sample size for estimating the proportion of in-error sales invoices for Ricknel Home Centers

Figure 8.14 displays the ***COMPUTE worksheet*** *of the* ***Sample Size Proportion workbook*** *that the Section EG8.4 instructions use.*

	A	B	
1	For the Proportion of In-Error Sales Invoices		
2			
3	Data		
4	Estimate of True Proportion	0.15	
5	Sampling Error	0.07	
6	Confidence Level	95%	
7			
8	Intermediate Calculations		
9	Z Value	-1.9600	=NORM.S.INV((1 - B6) / 2)
10	Calculated Sample Size	99.9563	=(B9^2 * B4 * (1 - B4)) / B5^2
11			
12	Result		
13	Sample Size Needed	100	=ROUNDUP(B10, 0)

Example 8.6 provides another application of determining the sample size for estimating the population proportion.

EXAMPLE 8.6

Determining the Sample Size for the Population Proportion

You want to have 90% confidence of estimating the proportion of office workers who respond to email within an hour to within ±0.05. Because you have not previously undertaken such a study, there is no information available from past data. Determine the sample size needed.

SOLUTION Because no information is available from past data, assume that $\pi = 0.50$. Using Equation (8.5) on page 290 and $e = 0.05$, $\pi = 0.50$, and $Z_{\alpha/2} = 1.645$ for 90% confidence,

$$n = \frac{Z_{\alpha/2}^2\, \pi(1 - \pi)}{e^2}$$

$$= \frac{(1.645)^2(0.50)(0.50)}{(0.05)^2}$$

$$= 270.6$$

Therefore, you need a sample of 271 office workers to estimate the population proportion to within ±0.05 with 90% confidence.

Problems for Section 8.4

LEARNING THE BASICS

8.34 If you want to be 95% confident of estimating the population mean to within a sampling error of ±5 and the standard deviation is assumed to be 15, what sample size is required?

8.35 If you want to be 99% confident of estimating the population mean to within a sampling error of ±20 and the standard deviation is assumed to be 100, what sample size is required?

8.36 If you want to be 99% confident of estimating the population proportion to within a sampling error of ±0.04, what sample size is needed?

8.37 If you want to be 95% confident of estimating the population proportion to within a sampling error of ±0.02 and there is historical evidence that the population proportion is approximately 0.40, what sample size is needed?

APPLYING THE CONCEPTS

SELF Test **8.38** A survey is planned to determine the mean annual family medical expenses of employees of a large company. The management of the company wishes to be 95% confident that the sample mean is correct to within ±\$50 of the population mean annual family medical expenses. A previous study indicates that the standard deviation is approximately \$400.

a. How large a sample is necessary?
b. If management wants to be correct to within ±\$25, how many employees need to be selected?

8.39 If the manager of a paint supply store wants to estimate, with 95% confidence, the mean amount of paint in a 1-gallon can to within ±0.004 gallon and also assumes that the standard deviation is 0.02 gallon, what sample size is needed?

8.40 If a quality control manager wants to estimate, with 95% confidence, the mean life of light bulbs to within ±20 hours and also assumes that the population standard deviation is 100 hours, how many light bulbs need to be selected?

8.41 If the inspection division of a county weights and measures department wants to estimate the mean amount of soft-drink fill in 2-liter bottles to within ±0.01 liter with 95% confidence and also assumes that the standard deviation is 0.05 liter, what sample size is needed?

8.42 A consumer group wants to estimate the mean electric bill for the month of July for single-family homes in a large city. Based on studies conducted in other cities, the standard deviation is assumed to be \$25. The group wants to estimate, with 99% confidence, the mean bill for July to within ±\$5.

a. What sample size is needed?
b. If 95% confidence is desired, how many homes need to be selected?

8.43 An advertising agency that serves a major radio station wants to estimate the mean amount of time that the station's audience spends listening to the radio daily. From past studies, the standard deviation is estimated as 45 minutes.

a. What sample size is needed if the agency wants to be 90% confident of being correct to within ±5 minutes?
b. If 99% confidence is desired, how many listeners need to be selected?

8.44 A growing niche in the restaurant business is gourmet-casual breakfast, lunch, and brunch. Chains in this group include EggSpectation and Panera Bread. Suppose that the mean per-person check for EggSpectation is approximately \$14.50, and the mean per-person check for Panera Bread is \$8.50.

a. Assuming a standard deviation of \$2.00, what sample size is needed to estimate, with 95% confidence, the mean per-person check for EggSpectation to within ±\$0.25?
b. Assuming a standard deviation of \$2.50, what sample size is needed to estimate, with 95% confidence, the mean per-person check for EggSpectation to within ±\$0.25?
c. Assuming a standard deviation of \$3.00, what sample size is needed to estimate, with 95% confidence, the mean per-person check for EggSpectation to within ±\$0.25?
d. Discuss the effect of variation on the sample size needed.

8.45 What advertising medium is most influential in making a purchase decision? According to a TVB survey, 37.2% of American adults point to TV. (Data extracted from "TV Seen Most Influential Ad Medium for Purchase Decisions," *MC Marketing Charts*, June 18, 2012.)

a. To conduct a follow-up study that would provide 95% confidence that the point estimate is correct to within ±0.04 of the population proportion, how large a sample size is required?
b. To conduct a follow-up study that would provide 99% confidence that the point estimate is correct to within ±0.04 of the population proportion, how many people need to be sampled?
c. To conduct a follow-up study that would provide 95% confidence that the point estimate is correct to within ±0.02 of the population proportion, how large a sample size is required?
d. To conduct a follow-up study that would provide 99% confidence that the point estimate is correct to within ±0.02 of the population proportion, how many people need to be sampled?
e. Discuss the effects on sample size requirements of changing the desired confidence level and the acceptable sampling error.

8.46 A survey of 300 U.S. online shoppers was conducted. In response to the question of what would influence the shopper to spend more money online in 2012, 18% said free shipping, 13% said offered discounts while shopping, and 9% said product reviews. (Data extracted from "2012 Consumer Shopping Trends and Insights," Steelhouse, Inc., 2012.) Construct a 95% confidence interval estimate of the population proportion of online shoppers who would be influenced to spend more money online in 2012 with

a. free shipping.
b. offered discounts while shopping.
c. product reviews.
d. You have been asked to update the results of this study. Determine the sample size necessary to estimate, with 95% confidence, the population proportions in (a) through (c) to within ± 0.02.

8.47 In a study of 368 San Francisco Bay Area nonprofits, 224 reported that they are collaborating with other organizations to provide services, a necessity as nonprofit agencies are called upon to do more with less. (Data extracted from "2012 Nonprofit Pulse Survey," United Way of the Bay Area, 2012, **bit.ly/MkGINA**.)

a. Construct a 95% confidence interval for the proportion of San Francisco Bay Area nonprofits that collaborated with other organizations to provide services.
b. Interpret the interval constructed in (a).
c. If you wanted to conduct a follow-up study to estimate the population proportion of San Francisco Bay Area nonprofits that collaborated with other organizations to provide service to within ± 0.01 with 95% confidence, how may Bay Area nonprofits would you survey?

8.48 According to a new study released by Infosys, a global leader in consulting, outsourcing and technology, more than three-quarters (77%) of U.S. consumers say that banking on their mobile device is convenient. (Data extracted from "Infosys Survey Finds Mobile Banking Customers Love Ease and Convenience, Yet Reliability and Security Concerns Remain," *PR Newswire*, 2012, **bit.ly/Ip9RUF**.)

a. If you conduct a follow-up study to estimate the population proportion of U.S. consumers who say that banking on their mobile device is convenient, would you use a π of 0.77 or 0.50 in the sample size formula?
b. Using you answer in part (a), find the sample size necessary to estimate, with 95% confidence, the population proportion to within ± 0.03.

8.49 Do you use the same password for all your social networking sites? A recent survey (*USA Today*, July 22, 2010, p. 1B) found that 32% of social network users use the same password for all their social networking sites.

a. To conduct a follow-up study that would provide 99% confidence that the point estimate is correct to within ± 0.03 of the population proportion, how many people need to be sampled?
b. To conduct a follow-up study that would provide 99% confidence that the point estimate is correct to within ± 0.05 of the population proportion, how many people need to be sampled?
c. Compare the results of (a) and (b).

8.5 Confidence Interval Estimation and Ethical Issues

The selection of samples and the inferences that accompany them raise several ethical issues. The major ethical issue concerns whether confidence interval estimates accompany point estimates. Failure to include a confidence interval estimate might mislead the user of the results into thinking that the point estimate is all that is needed to predict the population characteristic with certainty. Confidence interval limits (typically set at 95%), the sample size used, and an interpretation of the meaning of the confidence interval in terms that a person untrained in statistics can understand should always accompany point estimates.

When media outlets publicize the results of a political poll, they often overlook including this type of information. Sometimes, the results of a poll include the sampling error, but the sampling error is often presented in fine print or as an afterthought to the story being reported. A fully ethical presentation of poll results would give equal prominence to the confidence levels, sample size, sampling error, and confidence limits of the poll.

When you prepare your own point estimates, always state the interval estimate in a *prominent* place and include a brief explanation of the meaning of the confidence interval. In addition, make sure you highlight the sample size and sampling error.

8.6 Application of Confidence Interval Estimation in Auditing (*online*)

LEARN MORE

Learn more about this in a Chapter 8 eBook bonus section.

Auditing is an area that makes widespread use of probability sampling methods in order to develop confidence interval estimates.

8.7 Estimation and Sample Size Estimation for Finite Populations (*online*)

LEARN MORE

Learn more about this in a Chapter 8 eBook bonus section.

In some situations, confidence intervals need to be constructed and sample sizes need to be determined when sampling without replacement from a finite population.

USING STATISTICS

mangostock / Shutterstock

Getting Estimates at Ricknel Home Centers, Revisited

In the Ricknel Home Centers scenario, you were an accountant for a distributor of home improvement supplies in the northeastern United States. You were responsible for the accuracy of the integrated inventory management and sales information system. You used confidence interval estimation techniques to draw conclusions about the population of all records from a relatively small sample collected during an audit.

At the end of the month, you collected a random sample of 100 sales invoices and made the following inferences:

- With 95% confidence, you concluded that the mean amount of all the sales invoices is between \$104.53 and \$116.01.
- With 95% confidence, you concluded that between 4.12% and 15.88% of all the sales invoices contain errors.

These estimates provide an interval of values that you believe contain the true population parameters. If these intervals are too wide (i.e., the sampling error is too large) for the types of decisions Ricknel Home Centers needs to make, you will need to take a larger sample. You can use the sample size formulas in Section 8.4 to determine the number of sales invoices to sample to ensure that the size of the sampling error is acceptable.

SUMMARY

This chapter discusses confidence intervals for estimating the characteristics of a population, along with how you can determine the necessary sample size. You learned how to apply these methods to numerical and categorical data. Table 8.3 provides a list of topics covered in this chapter.

To determine what equation to use for a particular situation, you need to answer these questions:

- Are you constructing a confidence interval, or are you determining sample size?
- Do you have a numerical variable, or do you have a categorical variable?

The next four chapters develop a hypothesis-testing approach to making decisions about population parameters.

TABLE 8.3

Summary of Topics in Chapter 8

	Type of Data	
Type of Analysis	**Numerical**	**Categorical**
Confidence interval for a population parameter	Confidence interval estimate for the mean (Sections 8.1 and 8.2)	Confidence interval estimate for the proportion (Section 8.3)
Determining sample size	Sample size determination for the mean (Section 8.4)	Sample size determination for the proportion (Section 8.4)

REFERENCES

1. Cochran, W. G. *Sampling Techniques*, 3rd ed. New York: Wiley, 1977.
2. Daniel, W. W. *Applied Nonparametric Statistics*, 2nd ed. Boston: PWS Kent, 1990.
3. Fisher, R. A., and F. Yates. *Statistical Tables for Biological, Agricultural and Medical Research*, 5th ed. Edinburgh: Oliver & Boyd, 1957.
4. Hahn, G., and W. Meeker. *Statistical Intervals: A Guide for Practitioners*. New York: John Wiley and Sons, Inc., 1991.
5. Kirk, R. E., ed. *Statistical Issues: A Reader for the Behavioral Sciences*. Belmont, CA: Wadsworth, 1972.
6. Larsen, R. L., and M. L. Marx. *An Introduction to Mathematical Statistics and Its Applications*, 4th ed. Upper Saddle River, NJ: Prentice Hall, 2006.
7. *Microsoft Excel 2010*. Redmond, WA: Microsoft Corp., 2010.
8. Snedecor, G. W., and W. G. Cochran. *Statistical Methods*, 7th ed. Ames, IA: Iowa State University Press, 1980.

KEY EQUATIONS

Confidence Interval for the Mean (σ Known)

$$\bar{X} \pm Z_{\alpha/2}\frac{\sigma}{\sqrt{n}}$$

or

$$\bar{X} - Z_{\alpha/2}\frac{\sigma}{\sqrt{n}} \le \mu \le \bar{X} + Z_{\alpha/2}\frac{\sigma}{\sqrt{n}} \quad \textbf{(8.1)}$$

Confidence Interval for the Mean (σ Unknown)

$$\bar{X} \pm t_{\alpha/2}\frac{S}{\sqrt{n}}$$

or

$$\bar{X} - t_{\alpha/2}\frac{S}{\sqrt{n}} \le \mu \le \bar{X} + t_{\alpha/2}\frac{S}{\sqrt{n}} \quad \textbf{(8.2)}$$

Confidence Interval Estimate for the Proportion

$$p \pm Z_{\alpha/2}\sqrt{\frac{p(1-p)}{n}}$$

or

$$p - Z_{\alpha/2}\sqrt{\frac{p(1-p)}{n}} \le \pi \le p + Z_{\alpha/2}\sqrt{\frac{p(1-p)}{n}} \quad \textbf{(8.3)}$$

Sample Size Determination for the Mean

$$n = \frac{Z_{\alpha/2}^2\sigma^2}{e^2} \quad \textbf{(8.4)}$$

Sample Size Determination for the Proportion

$$n = \frac{Z_{\alpha/2}^2\pi(1-\pi)}{e^2} \quad \textbf{(8.5)}$$

KEY TERMS

confidence interval estimate 270
critical value 274
degrees of freedom 276
level of confidence 273
margin of error 287
point estimate 270
sampling error 273
Student's t distribution 276

CHECKING YOUR UNDERSTANDING

8.50 Why can you never really have 100% confidence of correctly estimating the population characteristic of interest?

8.51 When should you use the t distribution to develop the confidence interval estimate for the mean?

8.52 Why is it true that for a given sample size, n, an increase in confidence is achieved by widening (and making less precise) the confidence interval?

8.53 Why is the sample size needed to determine the proportion smaller when the population proportion is 0.20 than when the population proportion is 0.50?

CHAPTER REVIEW PROBLEMS

8.54 The Pew Internet Project survey of 2,253 American adults (data extracted from **pewinternet.org/Commentary/2012/February/Pew-Internet-Mobile**) found the following:

1,983 have a cellphone
1,307 have a desktop computer
1,374 have a laptop computer
406 have an ebook reader
406 have a tablet computer

a. Construct 95% confidence interval estimates for the population proportion of the electronic devices adults own.
b. What conclusions can you reach concerning what electronic devices adults have?

8.55 What do Americans do to conserve energy? The Associated Press-NORC Center for Public Affairs Research conducted a survey of 897 adults who had personally done something to try to save energy in the last year (data extracted from "Energy Efficiency and Independence: How the Public Understands, Learns, and Acts," **bit.ly/Maw5hd**), and found the following percentages:

Turn off lights: 39%
Turn down heat: 26%
Install more energy-saving appliances: 23%
Drive less/walk more/bicycle more: 18%
Unplug things: 16%

a. Construct a 95% confidence interval estimate for the population proportion of what adults do to conserve energy.
b. What conclusions can you reach concerning what adults do to conserve energy?

8.56 A market researcher for a consumer electronics company wants to study the television viewing habits of residents of a particular area. A random sample of 40 respondents is selected, and each respondent is instructed to keep a detailed record of all television viewing in a particular week. The results are as follows:

- Viewing time per week: $\overline{X} = 15.3$ hours, $S = 3.8$ hours.
- 27 respondents watch the evening news on at least three weeknights.

a. Construct a 95% confidence interval estimate for the mean amount of television watched per week in this area.
b. Construct a 95% confidence interval estimate for the population proportion who watch the evening news on at least three weeknights per week.

Suppose that the market researcher wants to take another survey in a different location. Answer these questions:

c. What sample size is required to be 95% confident of estimating the population mean viewing time to within ± 2 hours assuming that the population standard deviation is equal to five hours?
d. How many respondents need to be selected to be 95% confident of being within ± 0.035 of the population proportion who watch the evening news on at least three weeknights if no previous estimate is available?
e. Based on (c) and (d), how many respondents should the market researcher select if a single survey is being conducted?

8.57 The real estate assessor for a county government wants to study various characteristics of single-family houses in the county. A random sample of 70 houses reveals the following:

- Heated area of the houses (in square feet): $\overline{X} = 1{,}759$, $S = 380$.
- 42 houses have central air-conditioning.

a. Construct a 99% confidence interval estimate for the population mean heated area of the houses.
b. Construct a 95% confidence interval estimate for the population proportion of houses that have central air-conditioning.

8.58 The personnel director of a large corporation wishes to study absenteeism among clerical workers at the corporation's central office during the year. A random sample of 25 clerical workers reveals the following:

- Absenteeism: $\overline{X} = 9.7$ days, $S = 4.0$ days.
- 12 clerical workers were absent more than 10 days.

a. Construct a 95% confidence interval estimate for the mean number of absences for clerical workers during the year.
b. Construct a 95% confidence interval estimate for the population proportion of clerical workers absent more than 10 days during the year.

Suppose that the personnel director also wishes to take a survey in a branch office. Answer these questions:

c. What sample size is needed to have 95% confidence in estimating the population mean absenteeism to within ± 1.5 days if the population standard deviation is estimated to be 4.5 days?
d. How many clerical workers need to be selected to have 90% confidence in estimating the population proportion to within ± 0.075 if no previous estimate is available?
e. Based on (c) and (d), what sample size is needed if a single survey is being conducted?

8.59 A national association devoted to human resource (HR) and workplace programs, practices, and training wants to study HR department practices and employee turnover of its member organizations. HR professionals and organization executives focus on turnover not only because it has significant cost implications but also because it affects overall business performance. A survey is designed to estimate the proportion of member organizations that have both talent and development programs in place to drive human-capital management as well as the member organizations' mean annual employee turnover rate (the ratio of the number of employees that left an organization in a given time period to the average number of employees in the organization during the given time period). A previous survey found that the standard deviation of member organizations' annual employee turnover rates is approximately 5%.

a. What sample size is needed to have 99% confidence of estimating the population mean annual employee turnover rate to within ±1.5%?

b. How many member organizations need to be selected to have 90% confidence of estimating the population proportion of organizations that have both talent and development programs in place to drive human-capital management to within ±.045?

8.60 The financial impact of IT systems downtime is a concern of plant operations management today. A survey of manufacturers examined the satisfaction level with the reliability and availability of their manufacturing IT applications. The variables of focus are: whether the manufacturer experienced downtime in the past year that affected one or more manufacturing IT applications, the number of downtime incidents that occurred in the past year, and the approximate cost of a typical downtime incident. The results from a sample of 200 manufacturers are as follows:

- 62 experienced downtime this year that affected one or more manufacturing applications.
- Number of downtime incidents: $\overline{X} = 3.5, S = 2.0$
- Cost of downtime incidents: $\overline{X} = \$18{,}000, S = \$3{,}000$.

a. Construct a 90% confidence interval estimate for the population proportion of manufacturers who experienced downtime in the past year that affected one or more manufacturing IT applications.

b. Construct a 95% confidence interval estimate for the population mean number of downtime incidents experienced by manufacturers in the past year.

c. Construct a 95% confidence interval estimate for the population mean cost of downtime incidents.

8.61 The branch manager of an outlet (Store 1) of a nationwide chain of pet supply stores wants to study characteristics of her customers. In particular, she decides to focus on two variables: the amount of money spent by customers and whether the customers own only one dog, only one cat, or more than one dog and/or cat. The results from a sample of 70 customers are as follows:

- Amount of money spent: $\overline{X} = \$21.34, S = \$9.22$.
- 37 customers own only a dog.
- 26 customers own only a cat.
- 7 customers own more than one dog and/or cat.

a. Construct a 95% confidence interval estimate for the population mean amount spent in the pet supply store.

b. Construct a 90% confidence interval estimate for the population proportion of customers who own only a cat.

The branch manager of another outlet (Store 2) wishes to conduct a similar survey in his store. The manager does not have access to the information generated by the manager of Store 1. Answer the following questions:

c. What sample size is needed to have 95% confidence of estimating the population mean amount spent in this store to within ±\$1.50 if the standard deviation is estimated to be \$10?

d. How many customers need to be selected to have 90% confidence of estimating the population proportion of customers who own only a cat to within ±0.045?

e. Based on your answers to (c) and (d), how large a sample should the manager take?

8.62 Scarlett and Heather, the owners of an upscale restaurant in Dayton, Ohio, want to study the dining characteristics of their customers. They decide to focus on two variables: the amount of money spent by customers and whether customers order dessert. The results from a sample of 60 customers are as follows:

- Amount spent: $\overline{X} = \$38.54, S = \$7.26$.
- 18 customers purchased dessert.

a. Construct a 95% confidence interval estimate for the population mean amount spent per customer in the restaurant.

b. Construct a 90% confidence interval estimate for the population proportion of customers who purchase dessert.

Jeanine, the owner of a competing restaurant, wants to conduct a similar survey in her restaurant. Jeanine does not have access to the information that Scarlett and Heather have obtained from the survey they conducted. Answer the following questions:

c. What sample size is needed to have 95% confidence of estimating the population mean amount spent in her restaurant to within ±\$1.50, assuming that the standard deviation is estimated to be \$8?

d. How many customers need to be selected to have 90% confidence of estimating the population proportion of customers who purchase dessert to within ±0.04?

e. Based on your answers to (c) and (d), how large a sample should Jeanine take?

8.63 The manufacturer of Ice Melt claims that its product will melt snow and ice at temperatures as low as 0° Fahrenheit. A representative for a large chain of hardware stores is interested in testing this claim. The chain purchases a large shipment of 5-pound bags for distribution. The representative wants to know, with 95% confidence and within ±0.05, what proportion of bags of Ice Melt perform the job as claimed by the manufacturer.

a. How many bags does the representative need to test? What assumption should be made concerning the population proportion? (This is called *destructive testing*; i.e., the product being tested is destroyed by the test and is then unavailable to be sold.)

b. Suppose that the representative tests 50 bags, and 42 of them do the job as claimed. Construct a 95% confidence interval estimate for the population proportion that will do the job as claimed.

c. How can the representative use the results of (b) to determine whether to sell the Ice Melt product?

8.64 Claims fraud (illegitimate claims) and buildup (exaggerated loss amounts) continue to be major issues of concern among automobile insurance companies. Fraud is defined as specific material misrepresentation of the facts of a loss; buildup is defined as the inflation of an otherwise legitimate claim. A recent study examined auto injury claims closed with payment under private passenger coverages. Detailed data on injury, medical treatment, claimed losses, and total payments, as well as claim-handling techniques, were collected. In addition, auditors were asked to review the claim files to indicate whether specific elements of fraud or buildup appeared in the claim and, in the case of buildup, to specify the amount of excess payment. The file InsuranceClaims contains data for 90 randomly selected auto injury claims. The following variables are included: CLAIM—Claim ID; BUILDUP—1 if buildup indicated, 0 if not; and EXCESSPAYMENT—excess payment amount, in dollars.

a. Construct a 95% confidence interval for the population proportion of all auto injury files that have exaggerated loss amounts.

b. Construct a 95% confidence interval for the population mean dollar excess payment amount.

8.65 A quality characteristic of interest for a teabag-filling process is the weight of the tea in the individual bags. In this example, the label weight on the package indicates that the mean amount is 5.5 grams of tea in a bag. If the bags are underfilled, two problems arise. First, customers may not be able to brew the tea to be as strong as they wish. Second, the company may be in violation of the truth-in-labeling laws. On the other hand, if the mean amount of tea in a bag exceeds the label weight, the company is giving away product. Getting an exact amount of tea in a bag is problematic because of variation in the temperature and humidity inside the factory, differences in the density of the tea, and the extremely fast filling operation of the machine (approximately 170 bags per minute). The following data (stored in Teabags) are the weights, in grams, of a sample of 50 tea bags produced in one hour by a single machine:

5.65	5.44	5.42	5.40	5.53	5.34	5.54	5.45	5.52	5.41
5.57	5.40	5.53	5.54	5.55	5.62	5.56	5.46	5.44	5.51
5.47	5.40	5.47	5.61	5.53	5.32	5.67	5.29	5.49	5.55
5.77	5.57	5.42	5.58	5.58	5.50	5.32	5.50	5.53	5.58
5.61	5.45	5.44	5.25	5.56	5.63	5.50	5.57	5.67	5.36

a. Construct a 99% confidence interval estimate for the population mean weight of the tea bags.

b. Is the company meeting the requirement set forth on the label that the mean amount of tea in a bag is 5.5 grams?

c. Do you think the assumption needed to construct the confidence interval estimate in (a) is valid?

8.66 A manufacturing company produces steel housings for electrical equipment. The main component part of the housing is a steel trough that is made from a 14-gauge steel coil. It is produced using a 250-ton progressive punch press with a wipe-down operation that puts two 90-degree forms in the flat steel to make the trough. The distance from one side of the form to the other is critical because of weatherproofing in outdoor applications. The widths (in inches), shown below and stored in Trough, are from a sample of 49 troughs:

8.312	8.343	8.317	8.383	8.348	8.410	8.351	8.373	8.481
8.422	8.476	8.382	8.484	8.403	8.414	8.419	8.385	8.465
8.498	8.447	8.436	8.413	8.489	8.414	8.481	8.415	8.479
8.429	8.458	8.462	8.460	8.444	8.429	8.460	8.412	8.420
8.410	8.405	8.323	8.420	8.396	8.447	8.405	8.439	8.411
8.427	8.420	8.498	8.409					

a. Construct a 95% confidence interval estimate for the mean width of the troughs.

b. Interpret the interval developed in (a).

c. Do you think the assumption needed to construct the confidence interval estimate in (a) in valid?

8.67 The manufacturer of Boston and Vermont asphalt shingles knows that product weight is a major factor in a customer's perception of quality. The last stage of the assembly line packages the shingles before they are placed on wooden pallets. Once a pallet is full (a pallet for most brands holds 16 squares of shingles), it is weighed, and the measurement is recorded. The file Pallet contains the weight (in pounds) from a sample of 368 pallets of Boston shingles and 330 pallets of Vermont shingles.

a. For the Boston shingles, construct a 95% confidence interval estimate for the mean weight.

b. For the Vermont shingles, construct a 95% confidence interval estimate for the mean weight.

c. Do you think the assumption needed to construct the confidence interval estimates in (a) and (b) is valid?

d. Based on the results of (a) and (b), what conclusions can you reach concerning the mean weight of the Boston and Vermont shingles?

8.68 The manufacturer of Boston and Vermont asphalt shingles provides its customers with a 20-year warranty on most of its products. To determine whether a shingle will last the entire warranty period, accelerated-life testing is conducted at the manufacturing plant. Accelerated-life testing exposes the shingle to the stresses it would be subject to in a lifetime of normal use via a laboratory experiment that takes only a few minutes to conduct. In this test, a shingle is repeatedly scraped with a brush for a short period of time, and the shingle granules removed by the brushing are weighed (in grams). Shingles that experience low amounts of granule loss are expected to last longer in normal use than shingles that experience high amounts of granule loss. In this situation, a shingle should experience no more than 0.8 grams of granule loss if it is expected to last the length of the warranty period. The file **Granule** contains a sample of 170 measurements made on the company's Boston shingles and 140 measurements made on Vermont shingles.

a. For the Boston shingles, construct a 95% confidence interval estimate for the mean granule loss.

b. For the Vermont shingles, construct a 95% confidence interval estimate for the mean granule loss.

c. Do you think the assumption needed to construct the confidence interval estimates in (a) and (b) is valid?

d. Based on the results of (a) and (b), what conclusions can you reach concerning the mean granule loss of the Boston and Vermont shingles?

REPORT WRITING EXERCISE

8.69 Referring to the results in Problem 8.66 concerning the width of a steel trough, write a report that summarizes your conclusions.

CASES FOR CHAPTER 8

Managing Ashland MultiComm Services

The marketing department has been considering ways to increase the number of new subscriptions to the *3-For-All* cable/phone/Internet service. Following the suggestion of Assistant Manager Lauren Adler, the department staff designed a survey to help determine various characteristics of households who subscribe to cable television service from Ashland. The survey consists of the following 10 questions:

1. Does your household subscribe to telephone service from Ashland?
   (1) Yes (2) No
2. Does your household subscribe to Internet service from Ashland?
   (1) Yes (2) No
3. What type of cable television service do you have?
   (1) Basic (2) Enhanced
   (If Basic, skip to question 5.)
4. How often do you watch the cable television stations that are only available with enhanced service?
   (1) Every day (2) Most days
   (3) Occasionally or never
5. How often do you watch premium or on-demand services that require an extra fee?
   (1) Almost every day (3) Rarely
   (2) Several times a week (4) Never
6. Which method did you use to obtain your current AMS subscription?
   (1) AMS toll-free phone number
   (2) AMS website
   (3) Direct mail reply card
   (4) Good Tunes & More promotion
   (5) Other
7. Would you consider subscribing to the *3-For-All* cable/phone/Internet service for a trial period if a discount were offered?
   (1) Yes (2) No
   (If no, skip to question 9.)
8. If purchased separately, cable, Internet, and phone services would currently cost $24.99 per week. How much would you be willing to pay per week for the *3-For-All* cable/phone/Internet service?
9. Does your household use another provider of telephone service?
   (1) Yes (2) No
10. AMS may distribute Ashland Gold Cards that would provide discounts at selected Ashland-area restaurants for subscribers who agree to a two-year subscription contract to the *3-For-All* service. Would being eligible to receive a Gold Card cause you to agree to the two-year term?
    (1) Yes (2) No

Of the 500 households selected that subscribe to cable television service from Ashland, 82 households either refused to participate, could not be contacted after repeated attempts, or had telephone numbers that were not in service. The summary results for the 418 households that were contacted are as follows:

Household Has AMS Telephone Service	Frequency
Yes	83
No	335

Household Has AMS Internet Service	Frequency
Yes	262
No	156

Type of Cable Service	Frequency
Basic	164
Enhanced	254

Watches Enhanced Programming	Frequency
Every day	50
Most days	144
Occasionally or never	60

Watches Premium or On-Demand Services	Frequency
Almost every day	14
Several times a week	35
Almost never	313
Never	56

Method Used to Obtain Current AMS Subscription	Frequency
Toll-free phone number	230
AMS website	106
Direct mail	46
Good Tunes & More	10
Other	26

Would Consider Discounted Trial Offer	Frequency
Yes	40
No	378

Trial Weekly Rate ($) Willing to Pay (stored in AMS8)

23.00	20.00	22.75	20.00	20.00	24.50	17.50	22.25	18.00	21.00
18.25	21.00	18.50	20.75	21.25	22.25	22.75	21.75	19.50	20.75
16.75	19.00	22.25	21.00	16.75	19.00	22.25	21.00	19.50	22.75
23.50	19.50	21.75	22.00	24.00	23.25	19.50	20.75	18.25	21.50

Uses Another Phone Service Provider	Frequency
Yes	354
No	64

Gold Card Leads to Two-Year Agreement	Frequency
Yes	38
No	380

11. Analyze the results of the survey of Ashland households that receive AMS cable television service. Write a report that discusses the marketing implications of the survey results for Ashland MultiComm Services.

Digital Case

Apply your knowledge about confidence interval estimation in this Digital Case, which extends the MyTVLab Digital Case from Chapter 6.

Among its other features, the MyTVLab website allows customers to purchase MyTVLab LifeStyles merchandise online. To handle payment processing, the management of MyTVLab has contracted with the following firms:

- **PayAFriend (PAF)**—This is an online payment system with which customers and businesses such as MyTVLab register in order to exchange payments in a secure and convenient manner, without the need for a credit card.
- **Continental Banking Company (Conbanco)**—This processing services provider allows MyTVLab customers to pay for merchandise using nationally recognized credit cards issued by a financial institution.

To reduce costs, management is considering eliminating one of these two payment systems. However, Lorraine Hildick of the sales department suspects that customers use the two forms of payment in unequal numbers and that customers display different buying behaviors when using the two forms of payment. Therefore, she would like to first determine the following:

- The proportion of customers using PAF and the proportion of customers using a credit card to pay for their purchases.
- The mean purchase amount when using PAF and the mean purchase amount when using a credit card.

Assist Ms. Hildick by preparing an appropriate analysis. Open **PaymentsSample.pdf**, read Ms. Hildick's comments, and use her random sample of 50 transactions as the basis for your analysis. Summarize your findings to determine whether Ms. Hildick's conjectures about MyTVLab LifeStyle customer purchasing behaviors are correct. If you want the sampling error to be no more than $3 when estimating the mean purchase amount, is Ms. Hildick's sample large enough to perform a valid analysis?

Sure Value Convenience Stores

You work in the corporate office for a nationwide convenience store franchise that operates nearly 10,000 stores. The per-store daily customer count has been steady, at 900, for some time (i.e., the mean number of customers in a store in one day is 900). To increase the customer count, the franchise is considering cutting coffee prices. The 12-ounce size will now be \$0.59 instead of \$0.99, and the 16-ounce size will be \$0.69 instead of \$1.19. Even with this reduction in price, the franchise will have a 40% gross margin on coffee. To test the new initiative, the franchise has reduced coffee prices in a sample of 34 stores, where customer counts have been running almost exactly at the national average of 900. After four weeks, the sample stores stabilize at a mean customer count of 974 and a standard deviation of 96. This increase seems like a substantial amount to you, but it also seems like a pretty small sample. Is there some way to get a feel for what the mean per-store count in all the stores will be if you cut coffee prices nationwide? Do you think reducing coffee prices is a good strategy for increasing the mean customer count?

CardioGood Fitness

Return to the CardioGood Fitness case first presented on page 33. Using the data stored in **CardioGood Fitness**:

1. Construct 95% confidence interval estimates to create a customer profile for each CardioGood Fitness treadmill product line.
2. Write a report to be presented to the management of CardioGood Fitness detailing your findings.

More Descriptive Choices Follow-up

Follow up the More Descriptive Choices, Revisited Using Statistics scenario on page 142 by constructing 95% confidence intervals estimates of the 1-year return percentages, 5-year return percentages, and 10-year return percentages for the sample of growth and value funds and for the small, mid-cap, and large market cap funds (stored in **Retirement Funds**). In your analysis, examine differences between the growth and value funds as well as the differences among the small, mid-cap, and large market cap funds.

Clear Mountain State Student Surveys

1. The Student News Service at Clear Mountain State University (CMSU) has decided to gather data about the undergraduate students that attend CMSU. They create and distribute a survey of 14 questions and receive responses from 62 undergraduates (stored in **UndergradSurvey**). For each variable included in the survey, construct a 95% confidence interval estimate for the population characteristic and write a report summarizing your conclusions.
2. The Dean of Students at CMSU has learned about the undergraduate survey and has decided to undertake a similar survey for graduate students at CMSU. She creates and distributes a survey of 14 questions and receives responses from 44 graduate students (stored in **GradSurvey**). For each variable included in the survey, construct a 95% confidence interval estimate for the population characteristic and write a report summarizing your conclusions.

CHAPTER 8 EXCEL GUIDE

EG8.1 CONFIDENCE INTERVAL ESTIMATE for the MEAN (σ KNOWN)

Key Technique Use the **NORM.S.INV(*cumulative percentage*)** to compute the Z value for one-half of the $(1 - \alpha)$ value and use the **CONFIDENCE(1 − *confidence level*, *population standard deviation*, *sample size*)** function to compute the half-width of a confidence interval.

Example Compute the confidence interval estimate for the mean for the first cereal-filling example on page 272.

PHStat Use **Estimate for the Mean, sigma known.**
For the example, select **PHStat ➔ Confidence Intervals ➔ Estimate for the Mean, sigma known.** In the procedure's dialog box (shown below):

1. Enter **15** as the **Population Standard Deviation**.
2. Enter **95** as the **Confidence Level** percentage.
3. Click **Sample Statistics Known** and enter **25** as the **Sample Size** and **362.3** as the **Sample Mean**.
4. Enter a **Title** and click **OK**.

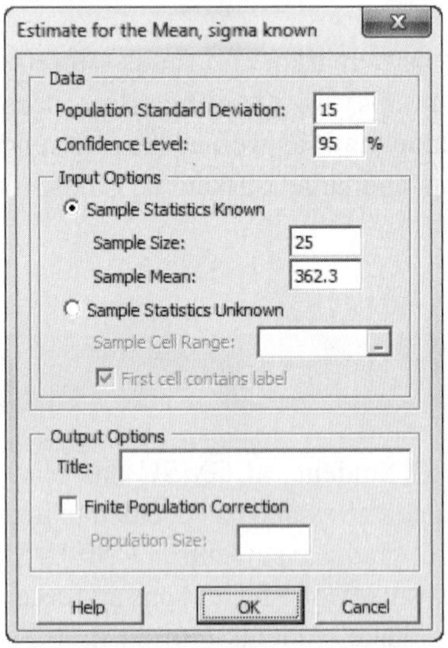

For problems that use unsummarized data, click **Sample Statistics Unknown** and enter the **Sample Cell Range** in step 3.

In-Depth Excel Use the **COMPUTE worksheet** of the **CIE sigma known workbook** as a template.
The worksheet already contains the data for the example. For other problems, change the **Population Standard Deviation, Sample Mean, Sample Size**, and **Confidence Level** values in cells B4 through B7. Open to the **COMPUTE_FORMULAS worksheet** to examine all the formulas in the worksheet.

EG8.2 CONFIDENCE INTERVAL ESTIMATE for the MEAN (σ UNKNOWN)

Key Technique Use the **T.INV.2T(1 − *confidence level*, *degrees of freedom*)** function to determine the critical value from the *t* distribution.

Example Compute the confidence interval estimate for the mean sales invoice amount that is shown in Figure 8.7 on page 279.

PHStat Use **Estimate for the Mean, sigma unknown.**
For the example, select **PHStat ➔ Confidence Intervals ➔ Estimate for the Mean, sigma unknown.** In the procedure's dialog box (shown below):

1. Enter **95** as the **Confidence Level** percentage.
2. Click **Sample Statistics Known** and enter **100** as the **Sample Size**, **110.27** as the **Sample Mean**, and **28.95** as the **Sample Std. Deviation**.
3. Enter a **Title** and click **OK**.

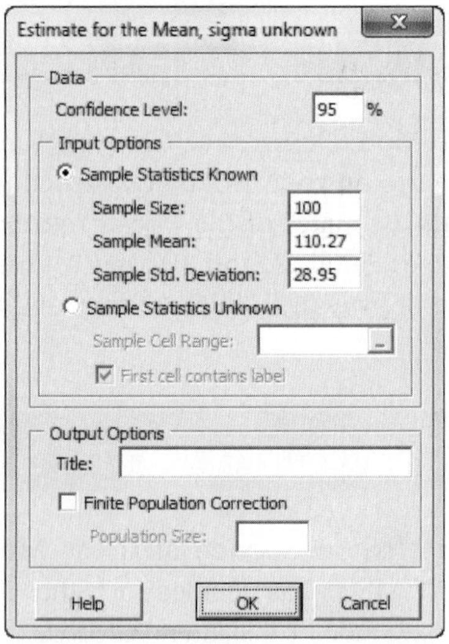

For problems that use unsummarized data, click **Sample Statistics Unknown** and enter the **Sample Cell Range** in step 2.

In-Depth Excel Use the **COMPUTE worksheet** of the **CIE sigma unknown workbook** as a template.
The worksheet already contains the data for solving the example. For other problems, change the **Sample Standard Deviation**, **Sample Mean**, **Sample Size**, and **Confidence Level** values in cells B4 through B7.

EG8.3 CONFIDENCE INTERVAL ESTIMATE for the PROPORTION

Key Technique Use the **NORM.S.INV((1 − *confidence level*)/2)** function to compute the Z value.

Example Compute the confidence interval estimate for the proportion of in-error sales invoices that is shown in Figure 8.12 on page 285.

PHStat Use **Estimate for the Proportion.**
For the example, select **PHStat → Confidence Intervals → Estimate for the Proportion.** In the procedure's dialog box (shown below):

1. Enter **100** as the **Sample Size.**
2. Enter **10** as the **Number of Successes.**
3. Enter **95** as the **Confidence Level** percentage.
4. Enter a **Title** and click **OK.**

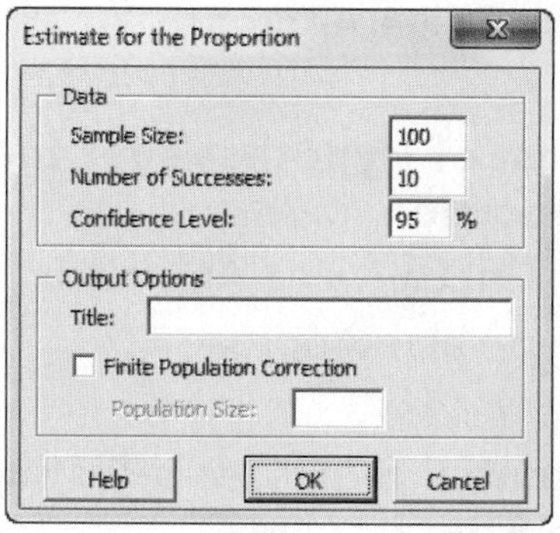

In-Depth Excel Use the **COMPUTE worksheet** of the **CIE Proportion workbook** as a template.

The worksheet contains the data for the example. Note that the formula **=SQRT(*sample proportion* * (1 – *sample proportion*)/*sample size*)** computes the standard error of the proportion in cell B11.

To compute confidence interval estimates for other problems, change the **Sample Size, Number of Successes,** and **Confidence Level** values in cells B4 through B6.

EG8.4 DETERMINING SAMPLE SIZE

Sample Size Determination for the Mean

Key Technique Use the **NORM.S.INV((1 – *confidence level*)/2)** function to compute the *Z* value and use the **ROUNDUP(*calculated sample size*, 0)** function to round up the computed sample size to the next higher integer.

Example Determine the sample size for the mean sales invoice amount example that is shown in Figure 8.13 on page 289.

PHStat Use **Determination for the Mean.**
For the example, select **PHStat → Sample Size → Determination for the Mean.** In the procedure's dialog box (shown at top right):

1. Enter **25** as the **Population Standard Deviation.**
2. Enter **5** as the **Sampling Error.**
3. Enter **95** as the **Confidence Level** percentage.
4. Enter a **Title** and click **OK.**

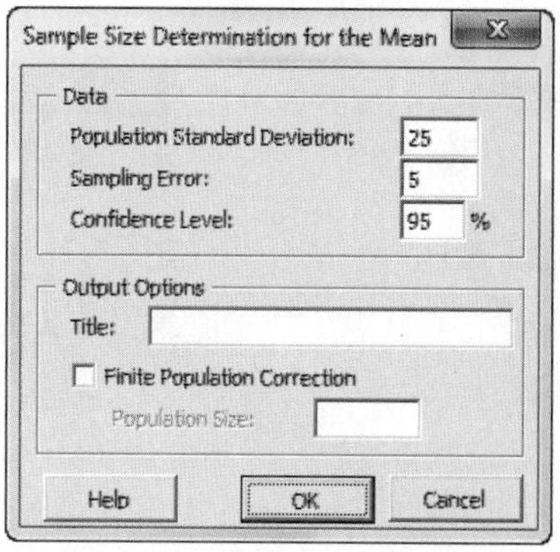

In-Depth Excel Use the **COMPUTE worksheet** of the **Sample Size Mean workbook** as a template.
The worksheet already contains the data for the example. For other problems, change the **Population Standard Deviation, Sampling Error,** and **Confidence Level** values in cells B4 through B6.

Sample Size Determination for the Proportion

Key Technique Use the **NORM.S.INV** and **ROUNDUP** functions (see previous section) to help determine the sample size needed for estimating the proportion.

Example Determine the sample size for the proportion of in-error sales invoices example that is shown in Figure 8.14 on page 291.

PHStat Use **Determination for the Proportion.**
For the example, select **PHStat → Sample Size → Determination for the Proportion.** In the procedure's dialog box (shown below):

1. Enter **0.15** as the **Estimate of True Proportion.**
2. Enter **0.07** as the **Sampling Error.**
3. Enter **95** as the **Confidence Level** percentage.
4. Enter a **Title** and click **OK.**

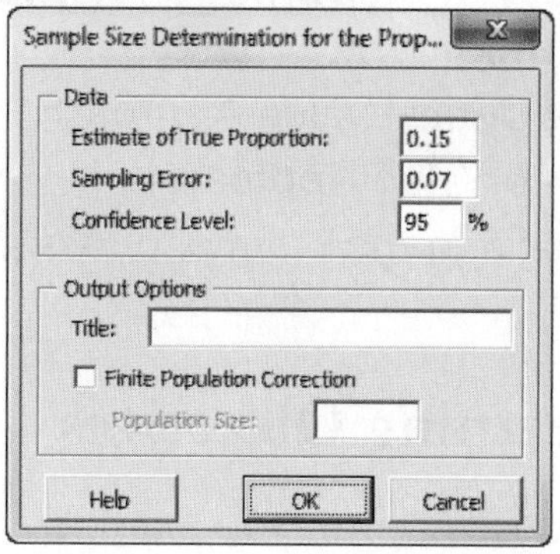

In-Depth Excel Use the **COMPUTE worksheet** of the **Sample Size Proportion workbook** as a template.
The worksheet already contains the data for the example. To compute confidence interval estimates for other problems, change the **Estimate of True Proportion, Sampling Error,** and **Confidence Level** in cells B4 through B6.

CHAPTER 9

Fundamentals of Hypothesis Testing: One-Sample Tests

Learning Objectives

In this chapter, you learn:

- The basic principles of hypothesis testing
- How to use hypothesis testing to test a mean or proportion
- The assumptions of each hypothesis-testing procedure, how to evaluate them, and the consequences if they are seriously violated
- Pitfalls and ethical issues involved in hypothesis testing
- How to avoid the pitfalls involved in hypothesis testing

USING STATISTICS

Maja Schon / Shutterstock

Significant Testing at Oxford Cereals

As in Chapter 7, you again find yourself as plant operations manager for Oxford Cereals. Among other responsibilities, you are responsible for monitoring the amount in each cereal box filled. Company specifications require a mean weight of 368 grams per box. You must adjust the cereal-filling process when the mean fill weight in the population of boxes differs from 368 grams. Adjusting the process requires shutting down the cereal production line temporarily, so you do not want to make unnecessary adjustments.

What decision-making method can you use to decide if the cereal-filling process needs to be adjusted? You decide to begin by selecting a random sample of 25 cereal boxes and weighing each box. From the weights collected, you compute a sample mean. How could that sample mean be used to help decide whether adjustment is necessary?

Peter Close / Shutterstock

In Chapter 7, you learned methods to determine whether the value of a sample mean is consistent with a known population mean. In this Oxford Cereals scenario, you seek to use a sample mean to validate a claim about the population mean, a somewhat different problem. For this type of situation, you use the inferential method known as **hypothesis testing**. Hypothesis testing requires that you state a claim unambiguously. In this scenario, the claim is that the population mean is 368 grams. You examine a sample statistic to see if it better supports the stated claim, called the *null hypothesis*, or the mutually exclusive alternative hypothesis (for this scenario, that the population mean is not 368 grams).

In this chapter, you will learn several applications of hypothesis testing. You will learn how to make inferences about a population parameter by *analyzing differences* between the results observed, the sample statistic, and the results you would expect to get if an underlying hypothesis were actually true. For the Oxford Cereals scenario, hypothesis testing allows you to infer one of the following:

- The mean weight of the cereal boxes in the sample is a value consistent with what you would expect if the mean of the entire population of cereal boxes were 368 grams.
- The population mean is not equal to 368 grams because the sample mean is significantly different from 368 grams.

9.1 Fundamentals of Hypothesis-Testing Methodology

Hypothesis testing typically begins with a theory, a claim, or an assertion about a particular parameter of a population. For example, your initial hypothesis in the cereal example is that the process is working properly, so the mean fill is 368 grams, and no corrective action is needed.

The Null and Alternative Hypotheses

The hypothesis that the population parameter is equal to the company specification is referred to as the null hypothesis. A **null hypothesis** is often one of status quo and is identified by the symbol H_0. Here the null hypothesis is that the filling process is working properly, and therefore the mean fill is the 368-gram specification provided by Oxford Cereals. This is stated as

$$H_0 : \mu = 368$$

Student Tip
Remember, hypothesis testing reaches conclusions about parameters not statistics.

Even though information is available only from the sample, the null hypothesis is stated in terms of the population parameter because your focus is on the population of all cereal boxes. You use the sample statistic to make inferences about the entire filling process. One inference may be that the results observed from the sample data indicate that the null hypothesis is false. If the null hypothesis is considered false, something else must be true.

Whenever a null hypothesis is specified, an alternative hypothesis is also specified, and it must be true if the null hypothesis is false. The **alternative hypothesis, H_1,** is the opposite of the null hypothesis, H_0. This is stated in the cereal example as

$$H_1 : \mu \neq 368$$

The alternative hypothesis represents the conclusion reached by rejecting the null hypothesis. The null hypothesis is rejected when there is sufficient evidence from the sample data that the null hypothesis is false. In the cereal example, if the weights of the sampled boxes are sufficiently above or below the expected 368-gram mean specified by Oxford Cereals, you reject the null hypothesis in favor of the alternative hypothesis that the mean fill is different from 368 grams. You stop production and take whatever action is necessary to correct the problem. If the null hypothesis is not rejected, you should continue to believe that the process is working correctly and that therefore no corrective action is necessary. In this second circumstance, you have not proven that the process is working correctly. Rather, you have failed to prove that it is working incorrectly, and therefore you continue your belief (although unproven) in the null hypothesis.

In hypothesis testing, you reject the null hypothesis when the sample evidence suggests that it is far more likely that the alternative hypothesis is true. However, failure to reject the null hypothesis is not proof that it is true. You can never prove that the null hypothesis is correct because the decision is based only on the sample information, not on the entire population. Therefore, if you fail to reject the null hypothesis, you can only conclude that there is insufficient evidence to warrant its rejection. The following key points summarize the null and alternative hypotheses:

- The null hypothesis, H_0, represents the current belief in a situation.
- The alternative hypothesis, H_1, is the opposite of the null hypothesis and represents a research claim or specific inference you would like to prove.
- If you reject the null hypothesis, you have statistical proof that the alternative hypothesis is correct.
- If you do not reject the null hypothesis, you have failed to prove the alternative hypothesis. The failure to prove the alternative hypothesis, however, does not mean that you have proven the null hypothesis.
- The null hypothesis, H_0, always refers to a specified value of the population parameter (such as μ), not a sample statistic (such as $\overline{X}$).
- The statement of the null hypothesis always contains an equal sign regarding the specified value of the population parameter (e.g., $H_0 : \mu = 368$ grams).
- The statement of the alternative hypothesis never contains an equal sign regarding the specified value of the population parameter (e.g., $H_1 : \mu \neq 368$ grams).

EXAMPLE 9.1

The Null and Alternative Hypotheses

You are the manager of a fast-food restaurant. You want to determine whether the waiting time to place an order has changed in the past month from its previous population mean value of 4.5 minutes. State the null and alternative hypotheses.

SOLUTION The null hypothesis is that the population mean has not changed from its previous value of 4.5 minutes. This is stated as

$$H_0 : \mu = 4.5$$

The alternative hypothesis is the opposite of the null hypothesis. Because the null hypothesis is that the population mean is 4.5 minutes, the alternative hypothesis is that the population mean is not 4.5 minutes. This is stated as

$$H_1 : \mu \neq 4.5$$

The Critical Value of the Test Statistic

The logic of hypothesis testing involves determining how likely the null hypothesis is to be true by considering the data collected in a sample. In the Oxford Cereal Company scenario, the null hypothesis is that the mean amount of cereal per box in the entire filling process is 368 grams (the population parameter specified by the company). You select a sample of boxes from the filling process, weigh each box, and compute the sample mean. This statistic is an estimate of the corresponding parameter (the population mean, μ). Even if the null hypothesis is true, the statistic (the sample mean, $\overline{X}$) is likely to differ from the value of the parameter (the population mean, μ) because of variation due to sampling. However, you expect the sample statistic to be close to the population parameter if the null hypothesis is true. If the sample statistic is close to the population parameter, you have insufficient evidence to reject the null hypothesis. For example, if the sample mean is 367.9 grams, you might conclude that the population mean has not changed (i.e., $\mu = 368$) because a sample mean of 367.9 grams is very close to the hypothesized value of 368 grams. Intuitively, you think that it is likely that you could get a sample mean of 367.9 grams from a population whose mean is 368.

However, if there is a large difference between the value of the statistic and the hypothesized value of the population parameter, you might conclude that the null hypothesis is false. For example, if the sample mean is 320 grams, you might conclude that the population mean is not 368 grams (i.e., $\mu \neq 368$) because the sample mean is very far from the hypothesized value of 368 grams. In such a case, you conclude that it is very unlikely to get a sample mean of 320 grams if the population mean is really 368 grams. Therefore, it is more logical to conclude that the population mean is not equal to 368 grams. Here you reject the null hypothesis.

However, the decision-making process is not always so clear-cut. Determining what is "very close" and what is "very different" is arbitrary without clear definitions. Hypothesis-testing methodology provides clear definitions for evaluating differences. Furthermore, it enables you to quantify the decision-making process by computing the probability of getting a certain sample result if the null hypothesis is true. You calculate this probability by determining the sampling distribution for the sample statistic of interest (e.g., the sample mean) and then computing the particular **test statistic** based on the given sample result. Because the sampling distribution for the test statistic often follows a well-known statistical distribution, such as the standardized normal distribution or *t* distribution, you can use these distributions to help determine whether the null hypothesis is true.

Regions of Rejection and Nonrejection

The sampling distribution of the test statistic is divided into two regions, a **region of rejection** (sometimes called the critical region) and a **region of nonrejection** (see Figure 9.1). If the test statistic falls into the region of nonrejection, you do not reject the null hypothesis. In the Oxford Cereals scenario, you conclude that there is insufficient evidence that the population mean fill is different from 368 grams. If the test statistic falls into the rejection region, you reject the null hypothesis. In this case, you conclude that the population mean is not 368 grams.

FIGURE 9.1
Regions of rejection and nonrejection in hypothesis testing

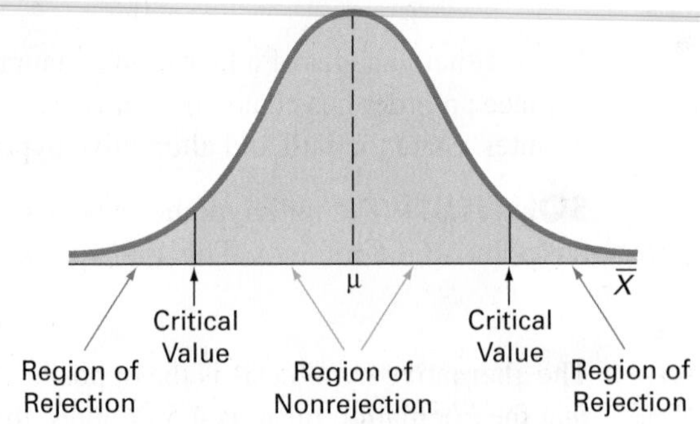

The region of rejection consists of the values of the test statistic that are unlikely to occur if the null hypothesis is true. These values are much more likely to occur if the null hypothesis is false. Therefore, if a value of the test statistic falls into this rejection region, you reject the null hypothesis because that value is unlikely if the null hypothesis is true.

To make a decision concerning the null hypothesis, you first determine the **critical value** of the test statistic. The critical value divides the nonrejection region from the rejection region. Determining the critical value depends on the size of the rejection region. The size of the rejection region is directly related to the risks involved in using only sample evidence to make decisions about a population parameter.

Risks in Decision Making Using Hypothesis Testing

Using hypothesis testing involves the risk of reaching an incorrect conclusion. You might wrongly reject a true null hypothesis, H_0, or, conversely, you might wrongly *not* reject a false null hypothesis, H_0. These types of risk are called Type I and Type II errors.

TYPE I AND TYPE II ERRORS

A **Type I error** occurs if you reject the null hypothesis, H_0, when it is true and should not be rejected. A Type I error is a "false alarm." The probability of a Type I error occurring is α.

A **Type II error** occurs if you do not reject the null hypothesis, H_0, when it is false and should be rejected. A Type II error represents a "missed opportunity" to take some corrective action. The probability of a Type II error occurring is β.

In the Oxford Cereals scenario, you would make a Type I error if you concluded that the population mean fill is *not* 368 grams when it *is* 368 grams. This error causes you to needlessly adjust the filling process (the "false alarm") even though the process is working properly. In the same scenario, you would make a Type II error if you concluded that the population mean fill *is* 368 grams when it is *not* 368 grams. In this case, you would allow the process to continue without adjustment, even though an adjustment is needed (the "missed opportunity").

Traditionally, you control the Type I error by determining the risk level, α (the lowercase Greek letter *alpha*), that you are willing to have of rejecting the null hypothesis when it is true. This risk, or probability, of committing a Type I error is called the *level of significance* (α). Because you specify the level of significance before you perform the hypothesis test, you directly control the risk of committing a Type I error. Traditionally, you select a level of 0.01, 0.05, or 0.10. The choice of a particular risk level for making a Type I error depends on the cost of making a Type I error. After you specify the value for α, you can then determine the critical values that divide the rejection and nonrejection regions. You know the size of the rejection region because α is the probability of rejection when the null hypothesis is true. From this, you can then determine the critical value or values that divide the rejection and nonrejection regions.

The probability of committing a Type II error is called the *β risk*. Unlike with a Type I error, which you control through the selection of α, the probability of making a Type II error depends on the difference between the hypothesized and actual values of the population parameter. Because large differences are easier to find than small ones, if the difference between the hypothesized and actual values of the population parameter is large, β is small. For example, if the population mean is 330 grams, there is a small chance (β) that you will conclude that the mean has not changed from 368 grams. However, if the difference between the hypothesized and actual values of the parameter is small, β is large. For example, if the population mean is actually 367 grams, there is a large chance (β) that you will conclude that the mean is still 368 grams.

PROBABILITY OF TYPE I AND TYPE II ERRORS

The **level of significance** ($\boldsymbol{\alpha}$) of a statistical test is the probability of committing a Type I error.

The **$\boldsymbol{\beta}$ risk** is the probability of committing a Type II error.

The complement of the probability of a Type I error, $(1 - \alpha)$, is called the *confidence coefficient*. The confidence coefficient is the probability that you will not reject the null hypothesis, H_0, when it is true and should not be rejected. In the Oxford Cereals scenario, the confidence coefficient measures the probability of concluding that the population mean fill is 368 grams when it is actually 368 grams.

The complement of the probability of a Type II error, $(1 - \beta)$, is called the *power of a statistical test*. The power of a statistical test is the probability that you will reject the null hypothesis when it is false and should be rejected. In the Oxford Cereals scenario, the power of the test is the probability that you will correctly conclude that the mean fill amount is not 368 grams when it actually is not 368 grams.

COMPLEMENTS OF TYPE I AND TYPE II ERRORS

The **confidence coefficient**, $(1 - \alpha)$, is the probability that you will not reject the null hypothesis, H_0, when it is true and should not be rejected.

The **power of a statistical test**, $(1 - \beta)$, is the probability that you will reject the null hypothesis when it is false and should be rejected.

Table 9.1 illustrates the results of the two possible decisions (do not reject H_0 or reject H_0) that you can make in any hypothesis test. You can make a correct decision or make one of two types of errors.

TABLE 9.1
Hypothesis Testing and Decision Making

	Actual Situation	
Statistical Decision	**H_0 True**	**H_0 False**
Do not reject H_0	Correct decision Confidence $= (1 - \alpha)$	Type II error $P(\text{Type II error}) = \beta$
Reject H_0	Type I error $P(\text{Type I error}) = \alpha$	Correct decision Power $= (1 - \beta)$

One way to reduce the probability of making a Type II error is by increasing the sample size. Large samples generally permit you to detect even very small differences between the hypothesized values and the actual population parameters. For a given level of α, increasing the sample size decreases β and therefore increases the power of the statistical test to detect that the null hypothesis, H_0, is false.

However, there is always a limit to your resources, and this affects the decision of how large a sample you can select. For any given sample size, you must consider the trade-offs between the two possible types of errors. Because you can directly control the risk of Type I error, you can reduce this risk by selecting a smaller value for α. For example, if the negative consequences associated with making a Type I error are substantial, you could select $\alpha = 0.01$ instead of 0.05. However, when you decrease α, you increase β, so reducing the risk of a Type I error results in an increased risk of a Type II error. However, to reduce β, you could select a larger value for α. Therefore, if it is important to try to avoid a Type II error, you can select α of 0.05 or 0.10 instead of 0.01.

In the Oxford Cereals scenario, the risk of a Type I error occurring involves concluding that the mean fill amount has changed from the hypothesized 368 grams when it actually has not changed. The risk of a Type II error occurring involves concluding that the mean fill amount has not changed from the hypothesized 368 grams when it actually has changed. The choice of reasonable values for α and β depends on the costs inherent in each type of error. For example, if it is very costly to change the cereal-filling process, you would want to be very confident that a change is needed before making any changes. In this case, the risk of a Type I error occurring is more important, and you would choose a small α. However, if you want to be very certain of detecting changes from a mean of 368 grams, the risk of a Type II error occurring is more important, and you would choose a higher level of α.

Now that you have been introduced to hypothesis testing, recall that in the Oxford Cereals scenario on page 305, the business problem facing Oxford Cereals is to determine if the mean fill weight in the population of boxes in the cereal-filling process differs from 368 grams. To make this determination, you select a random sample of 25 boxes, weigh each box, compute the sample mean, $\overline{X}$, and then evaluate the difference between this sample statistic and the hypothesized population parameter by comparing the sample mean weight (in grams) to the expected population mean of 368 grams specified by the company. The null and alternative hypotheses are:

$$H_0: \mu = 368$$
$$H_1: \mu \neq 368$$

Z Test for the Mean (σ Known)

When the standard deviation, σ, is known (which rarely occurs), you use the **Z test for the mean** if the population is normally distributed. If the population is not normally distributed, you can still use the Z test if the sample size is large enough for the Central Limit Theorem to take effect (see Section 7.2). Equation (9.1) defines the Z_{STAT} test statistic for determining the difference between the sample mean, $\overline{X}$, and the population mean, μ, when the standard deviation, σ, is known.

Z TEST FOR THE MEAN (σ KNOWN)

$$Z_{STAT} = \frac{\overline{X} - \mu}{\dfrac{\sigma}{\sqrt{n}}} \qquad \textbf{(9.1)}$$

Student Tip
You use the Z test because σ is known.

In Equation (9.1), the numerator measures the difference between the observed sample mean, $\bar{X}$, and the hypothesized mean, μ. The denominator is the standard error of the mean, so Z_{STAT} represents the difference between $\bar{X}$ and μ in standard error units.

Hypothesis Testing Using the Critical Value Approach

The critical value approach compares the value of the computed Z_{STAT} test statistic from Equation (9.1) to critical values that divide the normal distribution into regions of rejection and nonrejection. The critical values are expressed as standardized Z values that are determined by the level of significance.

Student Tip
Remember, first you determine the level of significance. This enables you to then determine the critical value. A different level of significance leads to a different critical value.

For example, if you use a level of significance of 0.05, the size of the rejection region is 0.05. Because the null hypothesis contains an equal sign and the alternative hypothesis contains a not equal sign, you have a **two-tail test** in which the rejection region is divided into the two tails of the distribution, with two equal parts of 0.025 in each tail. For this two-tail test, a rejection region of 0.025 in each tail of the normal distribution results in a cumulative area of 0.025 below the lower critical value and a cumulative area of 0.975 $(1 - 0.025)$ below the upper critical value (which leaves an area of 0.025 in the upper tail). According to the cumulative standardized normal distribution table (Table E.2), the critical values that divide the rejection and nonrejection regions are -1.96 and $+1.96$. Figure 9.2 illustrates that if the mean is actually 368 grams, as H_0 claims, the values of the Z_{STAT} test statistic have a standardized normal distribution centered at $Z = 0$ (which corresponds to an $\bar{X}$ value of 368 grams). Values of Z_{STAT} greater than $+1.96$ and less than -1.96 indicate that $\bar{X}$ is sufficiently different from the hypothesized $\mu = 368$ that it is unlikely that such an $\bar{X}$ value would occur if H_0 were true.

FIGURE 9.2
Testing a hypothesis about the mean (σ known) at the 0.05 level of significance

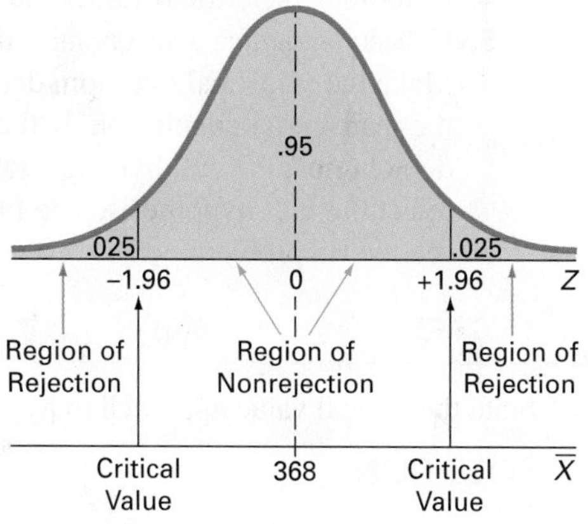

Therefore, the decision rule is

$$\text{Reject } H_0 \text{ if } Z_{STAT} > +1.96$$
$$\text{or if } Z_{STAT} < -1.96;$$
$$\text{otherwise, do not reject } H_0.$$

Student Tip
In a two-tail test, there is a rejection region in each tail of the distribution.

Suppose that the sample of 25 cereal boxes indicates a sample mean, $\bar{X}$, of 372.5 grams, and the population standard deviation, σ, is 15 grams. Using Equation (9.1) on page 310,

$$Z_{STAT} = \frac{\bar{X} - \mu}{\frac{\sigma}{\sqrt{n}}} = \frac{372.5 - 368}{\frac{15}{\sqrt{25}}} = +1.50$$

Student Tip
Remember, the decision always concerns H_0. Either you reject H_0 or you do not reject H_0.

Because $Z_{STAT} = +1.50$ is greater than -1.96 and less than $+1.96$, you do not reject H_0 (see Figure 9.3).

You continue to believe that the mean fill amount is 368 grams. To take into account the possibility of a Type II error, you state the conclusion as "there is insufficient evidence that the mean fill is different from 368 grams."

FIGURE 9.3

Testing a hypothesis about the mean cereal weight (σ known) at the 0.05 level of significance

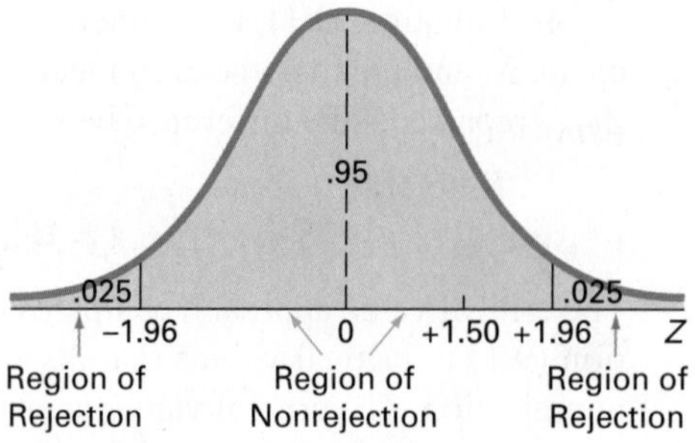

Exhibit 9.1 summarizes the critical value approach to hypothesis testing. Steps 1 and 2 are part of the Define task, step 5 combines the Collect and Organize tasks, and steps 3, 4, and 6 involve the Visualize and Analyze tasks of the DCOVA business problem-solving methodology first introduced on page 4. Examples 9.2 and 9.3 apply the critical value approach to hypothesis testing to Oxford Cereals and to a fast food restaurant.

EXHIBIT 9.1 THE CRITICAL VALUE APPROACH TO HYPOTHESIS TESTING

1. State the null hypothesis, H_0, and the alternative hypothesis, H_1.
2. Choose the level of significance, α, and the sample size, n. The level of significance is based on the relative importance of the risks of committing Type I and Type II errors in the problem.
3. Determine the appropriate test statistic and sampling distribution.
4. Determine the critical values that divide the rejection and nonrejection regions.
5. Collect the sample data, organize the results, and compute the value of the test statistic.
6. Make the statistical decision, determine whether the assumptions are valid, and state the managerial conclusion. If the test statistic falls into the nonrejection region, you do not reject the null hypothesis. If the test statistic falls into the rejection region, you reject the null hypothesis. The managerial conclusion is written in the context of the real-world problem.

EXAMPLE 9.2

Applying the Critical Value Approach to Hypothesis Testing at Oxford Cereals

State the critical value approach to hypothesis testing at Oxford Cereals.

SOLUTION

Step 1 State the null and alternative hypotheses. The null hypothesis, H_0, is always stated as a mathematical expression, using population parameters. In testing whether the mean fill is 368 grams, the null hypothesis states that μ equals 368. The alternative hypothesis, H_1, is also stated as a mathematical expression, using population parameters. Therefore, the alternative hypothesis states that μ is not equal to 368 grams.

Step 2 Choose the level of significance and the sample size. You choose the level of significance, α, according to the relative importance of the risks of committing Type I and Type II errors in the problem. The smaller the value of α, the less risk there is of making a Type I error. In this example, making a Type I error means that you conclude that the population mean is not 368 grams when it is 368 grams. Thus, you will take corrective action on the filling process even though the process is working properly. Here, $\alpha = 0.05$ is selected. The sample size, n, is 25.

Step 3 Select the appropriate test statistic. Because σ is known from information about the filling process, you use the normal distribution and the Z_{STAT} test statistic.

Step 4 Determine the rejection region. Critical values for the appropriate test statistic are selected so that the rejection region contains a total area of α when H_0 is true and the nonrejection region contains a total area of $1 - \alpha$ when H_0 is true. Because $\alpha = 0.05$ in the cereal example, the critical values of the Z_{STAT} test statistic are -1.96 and $+1.96$. The rejection region is therefore $Z_{STAT} < -1.96$ or $Z_{STAT} > +1.96$. The nonrejection region is $-1.96 \le Z_{STAT} \le +1.96$.

Step 5 Collect the sample data and compute the value of the test statistic. In the cereal example, $\bar{X} = 372.5$, and the value of the test statistic is $Z_{STAT} = +1.50$.

Step 6 State the statistical decision and the managerial conclusion. First, determine whether the test statistic has fallen into the rejection region or the nonrejection region. For the cereal example, $Z_{STAT} = +1.50$ is in the region of nonrejection because $-1.96 \le Z_{STAT} = +1.50 \le +1.96$. Because the test statistic falls into the nonrejection region, the statistical decision is to not reject the null hypothesis, H_0. The managerial conclusion is that insufficient evidence exists to prove that the mean fill is different from 368 grams. No corrective action on the filling process is needed.

EXAMPLE 9.3

Testing and Rejecting a Null Hypothesis

You are the manager of a fast-food restaurant. The business problem is to determine whether the population mean waiting time to place an order has changed in the past month from its previous population mean value of 4.5 minutes. From past experience, you can assume that the population is normally distributed, with a population standard deviation of 1.2 minutes. You select a sample of 25 orders during a one-hour period. The sample mean is 5.1 minutes. Use the six-step approach listed in Exhibit 9.1 on page 312 to determine whether there is evidence at the 0.05 level of significance that the population mean waiting time to place an order has changed in the past month from its previous population mean value of 4.5 minutes.

SOLUTION

Step 1 The null hypothesis is that the population mean has not changed from its previous value of 4.5 minutes:

$$H_0: \mu = 4.5$$

The alternative hypothesis is the opposite of the null hypothesis. Because the null hypothesis is that the population mean is 4.5 minutes, the alternative hypothesis is that the population mean is not 4.5 minutes:

$$H_1: \mu \neq 4.5$$

Step 2 You have selected a sample of $n = 25$. The level of significance is 0.05 (i.e., $\alpha = 0.05$).

Step 3 Because σ is assumed to be known, you use the normal distribution and the Z_{STAT} test statistic.

Step 4 Because $\alpha = 0.05$, the critical values of the Z_{STAT} test statistic are -1.96 and $+1.96$. The rejection region is $Z_{STAT} < -1.96$ or $Z_{STAT} > +1.96$. The nonrejection region is $-1.96 \le Z_{STAT} \le +1.96$

Step 5 You collect the sample data and compute $\bar{X} = 5.1$. Using Equation (9.1) on page 310, you compute the test statistic:

$$Z_{STAT} = \frac{\bar{X} - \mu}{\frac{\sigma}{\sqrt{n}}} = \frac{5.1 - 4.5}{\frac{1.2}{\sqrt{25}}} = +2.50$$

Step 6 Because $Z_{STAT} = +2.50 > +1.96$, you reject the null hypothesis. You conclude that there is evidence that the population mean waiting time to place an order has changed from its previous value of 4.5 minutes. The mean waiting time for customers is longer now than it was last month. As the manager, you would now want to determine how waiting time could be reduced to improve service.

Hypothesis Testing Using the *p*-Value Approach

The ***p*-value** is the probability of getting a test statistic equal to or more extreme than the sample result, given that the null hypothesis, H_0, is true. The *p*-value is also known as the *observed level of significance*. Using the *p*-value to determine rejection and nonrejection is another approach to hypothesis testing.

The decision rules for rejecting H_0 in the p-value approach are

- If the p-value is greater than or equal to α, do not reject the null hypothesis.
- If the p-value is less than α, reject the null hypothesis.

Many people confuse these rules, mistakenly believing that a high p-value is reason for rejection. You can avoid this confusion by remembering the following:

If the p-value is low, then H_0 must go.

Student Tip
A small (or low) p-value means a small probability that H_0 is true. A big or large p-value means a large probability that H_0 is true.

To understand the p-value approach, consider the Oxford Cereals scenario. You tested whether the mean fill was equal to 368 grams. The test statistic resulted in a Z_{STAT} value of $+1.50$ and you did not reject the null hypothesis because $+1.50$ was less than the upper critical value of $+1.96$ and greater than the lower critical value of -1.96.

To use the p-value approach for the *two-tail test*, you find the probability that the test statistic Z_{STAT} is equal to or *more extreme than* 1.50 standard error units from the center of a standardized normal distribution. In other words, you need to compute the probability that the Z_{STAT} value is greater than $+1.50$ along with the probability that the Z_{STAT} value is less than -1.50. Table E.2 shows that the probability of a Z_{STAT} value below -1.50 is 0.0668. The probability of a value below $+1.50$ is 0.9332, and the probability of a value above $+1.50$ is $1 - 0.9332 = 0.0668$. Therefore, the p-value for this two-tail test is $0.0668 + 0.0668 = 0.1336$ (see Figure 9.4). Thus, the probability of a test statistic equal to or more extreme than the sample result is 0.1336. Because 0.1336 is greater than $\alpha = 0.05$, you do not reject the null hypothesis.

FIGURE 9.4
Finding a p-value for a two-tail test

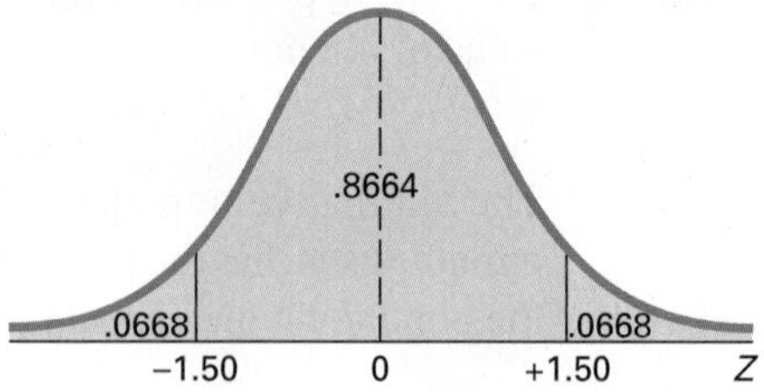

In this example, the observed sample mean is 372.5 grams, 4.5 grams above the hypothesized value, and the p-value is 0.1336. Thus, if the population mean is 368 grams, there is a 13.36% chance that the sample mean differs from 368 grams by at least 4.5 grams (i.e., is ≥ 372.5 grams or ≤ 363.5 grams). Therefore, even though 372.5 grams is above the hypothesized value of 368 grams, a result as extreme as or more extreme than 372.5 grams is not highly unlikely when the population mean is 368 grams.

Unless you are dealing with a test statistic that follows the normal distribution, you will only be able to approximate the p-value from the tables of the distribution. However, Excel can compute the p-value for any hypothesis test, and this allows you to substitute the p-value approach for the critical value approach when you conduct hypothesis testing.

Figure 9.5 shows a worksheet solution for the cereal-filling example discussed beginning on page 311. Although the worksheet in cell A18 uses the p-value approach to determine rejection or nonrejection, the worksheet results include the Z_{STAT} test statistic and the critical values.

FIGURE 9.5
Worksheet for the Z test for the mean (σ known) for the cereal-filling example

Figure 9.5 displays the **COMPUTE worksheet** *of the* **Z Mean workbook** *that the Section EG9.1 instructions use.*

	A	B	
1	**Z Test for the Mean**		
2			
3	**Data**		
4	Null Hypothesis μ =	368	
5	Level of Significance	0.05	
6	Population Standard Deviation	15	
7	Sample Size	25	
8	Sample Mean	372.5	
9			
10	Intermediate Calculations		
11	Standard Error of the Mean	3	=B6/SQRT(B7)
12	Z Test Statistic	1.5	=(B8 - B4)/B11
13			
14	**Two-Tail Test**		
15	Lower Critical Value	-1.9600	=NORM.S.INV(B5/2)
16	Upper Critical Value	1.9600	=NORM.S.INV(1 - B5/2)
17	*p*-Value	0.1336	=2 * (1 - NORM.S.DIST(ABS(B12), TRUE))
18	Do not reject the null hypothesis		=IF(B17 < B5,"Reject the null hypothesis", "Do not reject the null hypothesis")

Exhibit 9.2 summarizes the p-value approach to hypothesis testing. Example 9.4 applies the p-value approach to the fast food restaurant example.

EXHIBIT 9.2 THE p-VALUE APPROACH TO HYPOTHESIS TESTING

1. State the null hypothesis, H_0, and the alternative hypothesis, H_1.
2. Choose the level of significance, α, and the sample size, n. The level of significance is based on the relative importance of the risks of committing Type I and Type II errors in the problem.
3. Determine the appropriate test statistic and the sampling distribution.
4. Collect the sample data, compute the value of the test statistic, and compute the p-value.
5. Make the statistical decision and state the managerial conclusion. If the p-value is greater than or equal to α, do not reject the null hypothesis. If the p-value is less than α, reject the null hypothesis. The managerial conclusion is written in the context of the real-world problem.

EXAMPLE 9.4

Testing and Rejecting a Null Hypothesis Using the p-Value Approach

You are the manager of a fast-food restaurant. The business problem is to determine whether the population mean waiting time to place an order has changed in the past month from its previous value of 4.5 minutes. From past experience, you can assume that the population standard deviation is 1.2 minutes and the population waiting time is normally distributed. You select a sample of 25 orders during a one-hour period. The sample mean is 5.1 minutes. Use the five-step p-value approach of Exhibit 9.2 to determine whether there is evidence that the population mean waiting time to place an order has changed in the past month from its previous population mean value of 4.5 minutes.

SOLUTION

Step 1 The null hypothesis is that the population mean has not changed from its previous value of 4.5 minutes:

$$H_0: \mu = 4.5$$

The alternative hypothesis is the opposite of the null hypothesis. Because the null hypothesis is that the population mean is 4.5 minutes, the alternative hypothesis is that the population mean is not 4.5 minutes:

$$H_1: \mu \neq 4.5$$

Step 2 You have selected a sample of $n = 25$ and you have chosen a 0.05 level of significance (i.e., $\alpha = 0.05$).

Step 3 Select the appropriate test statistic. Because σ is assumed known, you use the normal distribution and the Z_{STAT} test statistic.

Step 4 You collect the sample data and compute $\overline{X} = 5.1$. Using Equation (9.1) on page 310, you compute the test statistic as follows:

$$Z_{STAT} = \frac{\overline{X} - \mu}{\dfrac{\sigma}{\sqrt{n}}} = \frac{5.1 - 4.5}{\dfrac{1.2}{\sqrt{25}}} = +2.50$$

To find the probability of getting a Z_{STAT} test statistic that is equal to or more extreme than 2.50 standard error units from the center of a standardized normal distribution, you compute the probability of a Z_{STAT} value greater than $+2.50$ along with the probability of a Z_{STAT} value less than -2.50. From Table E.2, the probability of a Z_{STAT} value below -2.50 is 0.0062. The probability of a value below $+2.50$ is 0.9938. Therefore, the probability of a value above $+2.50$ is $1 - 0.9938 = 0.0062$. Thus, the p-value for this two-tail test is $0.0062 + 0.0062 = 0.0124$.

Step 5 Because the p-value $= 0.0124 < \alpha = 0.05$, you reject the null hypothesis. You conclude that there is evidence that the population mean waiting time to place an order has changed from its previous population mean value of 4.5 minutes. The mean waiting time for customers is longer now than it was last month.

A Connection Between Confidence Interval Estimation and Hypothesis Testing

This chapter and Chapter 8 discuss confidence interval estimation and hypothesis testing, the two major elements of statistical inference. Although confidence interval estimation and hypothesis testing share the same conceptual foundation, they are used for different purposes. In Chapter 8, confidence intervals estimated parameters. In this chapter, hypothesis testing makes decisions about specified values of population parameters. Hypothesis tests are used when trying to determine whether a parameter is less than, more than, or not equal to a specified value. Proper interpretation of a confidence interval, however, can also indicate whether a parameter is less than, more than, or not equal to a specified value. For example, in this section, you tested whether the population mean fill amount was different from 368 grams by using Equation (9.1) on page 310:

$$Z_{STAT} = \frac{\overline{X} - \mu}{\frac{\sigma}{\sqrt{n}}}$$

Instead of testing the null hypothesis that $\mu = 368$ grams, you can reach the same conclusion by constructing a confidence interval estimate of μ. If the hypothesized value of $\mu = 368$ is contained within the interval, you do not reject the null hypothesis because 368 would not be considered an unusual value. However, if the hypothesized value does not fall into the interval, you reject the null hypothesis because $\mu = 368$ grams is then considered an unusual value. Using Equation (8.1) on page 273 and the following data:

$$n = 25,\ \overline{X} = 372.5 \text{ grams},\ \sigma = 15 \text{ grams}$$

for a confidence level of 95% (i.e., $\alpha = 0.05$),

$$\overline{X} \pm Z_{\alpha/2}\frac{\sigma}{\sqrt{n}}$$

$$372.5 \pm (1.96)\frac{15}{\sqrt{25}}$$

$$372.5 \pm 5.88$$

so that

$$366.62 \le \mu \le 378.38$$

Because the interval includes the hypothesized value of 368 grams, you do not reject the null hypothesis. There is insufficient evidence that the mean fill amount for the entire filling process is not 368 grams. You reached the same decision by using a two-tail hypothesis test.

Can You Ever Know the Population Standard Deviation?

The end of Section 8.1 on page 275 discussed how learning a confidence interval estimation method that required knowing σ, the population standard deviation, served as an effective introduction to the concept of a confidence interval. That section then revealed that you would be unlikely to use that procedure for most practical applications for several reasons.

Likewise, for most practical applications, you are unlikely to use a hypothesis-testing method that requires knowing σ. If you knew the population standard deviation, you would also know the population mean and would not need to form a hypothesis about the mean and then test that hypothesis. So why study a hypothesis testing of the mean that requires that σ is known? Using such a test makes it much easier to explain the fundamentals of hypothesis testing. With a known population standard deviation, you can use the normal distribution and compute *p*-values using the tables of the normal distribution.

Because it is important that you understand the concept of hypothesis testing when reading the rest of this book, review this section carefully—even if you anticipate never having a practical reason to use the test represented in Equation (9.1).

Problems for Section 9.1

LEARNING THE BASICS

9.1 If you use a 0.05 level of significance in a two-tail hypothesis test, what decision will you make if $Z_{STAT} = -0.76$?

9.2 If you use a 0.05 level of significance in a two-tail hypothesis test, what decision will you make if $Z_{STAT} = +2.21$?

9.3 If you use a 0.10 level of significance in a two-tail hypothesis test, what is your decision rule for rejecting a null hypothesis that the population mean is 500 if you use the *Z* test?

9.4 If you use a 0.01 level of significance in a two-tail hypothesis test, what is your decision rule for rejecting $H_0: \mu = 12.5$ if you use the *Z* test?

9.5 What is your decision in Problem 9.4 if $Z_{STAT} = -2.61$?

9.6 What is the *p*-value if, in a two-tail hypothesis test, $Z_{STAT} = +2.00$?

9.7 In Problem 9.6, what is your statistical decision if you test the null hypothesis at the 0.10 level of significance?

9.8 What is the *p*-value if, in a two-tail hypothesis test, $Z_{STAT} = -1.38$?

APPLYING THE CONCEPTS

9.9 In the U.S. legal system, a defendant is presumed innocent until proven guilty. Consider a null hypothesis, H_0, that a defendant is innocent, and an alternative hypothesis, H_1, that the defendant is guilty. A jury has two possible decisions: Convict the defendant (i.e., reject the null hypothesis) or do not convict the defendant (i.e., do not reject the null hypothesis). Explain the meaning of the risks of committing either a Type I or Type II error in this example.

9.10 Suppose the defendant in Problem 9.9 is presumed guilty until proven innocent. How do the null and alternative hypotheses differ from those in Problem 9.9? What are the meanings of the risks of committing either a Type I or Type II error here?

9.11 Many consumer groups feel that the U.S. Food and Drug Administration (FDA) drug approval process is too easy and, as a result, too many drugs are approved that are later found to be unsafe. On the other hand, a number of industry lobbyists have pushed for a more lenient approval process so that pharmaceutical companies can get new drugs approved more easily and quickly. Consider a null hypothesis that a new, unapproved drug is unsafe and an alternative hypothesis that a new, unapproved drug is safe.

a. Explain the risks of committing a Type I or Type II error.
b. Which type of error are the consumer groups trying to avoid? Explain.
c. Which type of error are the industry lobbyists trying to avoid? Explain.
d. How would it be possible to lower the chances of both Type I and Type II errors?

9.12 As a result of complaints from both students and faculty about lateness, the registrar at a large university is ready to undertake a study to determine whether the scheduled break between classes should be changed. Until now, the registrar has believed that there should be 20 minutes between scheduled classes. State the null hypothesis, H_0, and the alternative hypothesis, H_1.

9.13 Do marketing majors at your school study more than, less than, or about the same as marketing majors at other schools? *The Washington Post* reported the results of the National Survey of Student Engagement that found marketing majors studied an average of 12.1 hours per week. (Data extracted from "Is College Too Easy? As Study Time Falls, Debate Rises," *The Washington Post*, May 21, 2012.) Set up a hypothesis test to try to prove that the mean number of hours studied by marketing majors at your school is different from the 12.1-hour-per-week benchmark reported by *The Washington Post*.

a. State the null and alternative hypothesis.
b. What is a Type I error for your test?
c. What is a Type II error for your test?

SELF Test **9.14** The quality-control manager at a light bulb factory needs to determine whether the mean life of a large shipment of light bulbs is equal to 375 hours. The population standard deviation is 100 hours. A random sample of 64 light bulbs indicates a sample mean life of 350 hours.

a. At the 0.05 level of significance, is there evidence that the mean life is different from 375 hours?
b. Compute the *p*-value and interpret its meaning.
c. Construct a 95% confidence interval estimate of the population mean life of the light bulbs.
d. Compare the results of (a) and (c). What conclusions do you reach?

9.15 Suppose that in Problem 9.14, the standard deviation is 120 hours.

a. Repeat (a) through (d) of Problem 9.14, assuming a standard deviation of 120 hours.
b. Compare the results of (a) to those of Problem 9.14.

9.16 The manager of a paint supply store wants to determine whether the mean amount of paint contained in 1-gallon cans purchased from a nationally known manufacturer is actually 1 gallon. You know from the manufacturer's specifications that the standard deviation of the amount of paint is 0.02 gallon. You select a random sample of 50 cans, and the mean amount of paint per 1-gallon can is 0.995 gallon.

a. Is there evidence that the mean amount is different from 1.0 gallon? (Use $\alpha = 0.01$.)

b. Compute the p-value and interpret its meaning.
c. Construct a 99% confidence interval estimate of the population mean amount of paint.
d. Compare the results of (a) and (c). What conclusions do you reach?

9.17 Suppose that in Problem 9.16, the standard deviation is 0.012 gallon.
a. Repeat (a) through (d) of Problem 9.16, assuming a standard deviation of 0.012 gallon.
b. Compare the results of (a) to those of Problem 9.16.

9.2 *t* Test of Hypothesis for the Mean (σ Unknown)

In virtually all hypothesis-testing situations concerning the population mean, μ, you do not know the population standard deviation, σ. Instead, you use the sample standard deviation, S. If you assume that the population is normally distributed, the sampling distribution of the mean follows a t distribution with $n - 1$ degrees of freedom, and you use the ***t* test for the mean**. If the population is not normally distributed, you can still use the t test if the sample size is large enough for the Central Limit Theorem to take effect (see Section 7.2). Equation (9.2) defines the test statistic for determining the difference between the sample mean, $\bar{X}$, and the population mean, μ, when using the sample standard deviation, S.

t TEST FOR THE MEAN (σ UNKNOWN)

$$t_{STAT} = \frac{\bar{X} - \mu}{\frac{S}{\sqrt{n}}} \tag{9.2}$$

where the t_{STAT} test statistic follows a t distribution having $n - 1$ degrees of freedom.

To illustrate the use of the t test for the mean, return to the Chapter 8 Ricknel Home Centers scenario on page 269. The business objective is to determine whether the mean amount per sales invoice is unchanged from the $120 of the past five years. As an accountant for the company, you need to determine whether this amount changes. In other words, the hypothesis test is used to try to determine whether the mean amount per sales invoice is increasing or decreasing.

The Critical Value Approach

To perform this two-tail hypothesis test, you use the six-step method listed in Exhibit 9.1 on page 312.

Student Tip
Remember, the null hypothesis uses an equal sign and the alternative hypothesis *never* uses an equal sign.

Step 1 You define the following hypotheses:

$$H_0 : \mu = 120$$
$$H_1 : \mu \neq 120$$

The alternative hypothesis contains the statement you are trying to prove. If the null hypothesis is rejected, then there is statistical evidence that the population mean amount per sales invoice is no longer $120. If the statistical conclusion is "do not reject H_0," then you will conclude that there is insufficient evidence to prove that the mean amount differs from the long-term mean of $120.

Step 2 You collect the data from a sample of $n = 12$ sales invoices. You decide to use $\alpha = 0.05$.

Step 3 Because σ is unknown, you use the t distribution and the t_{STAT} test statistic. You must assume that the population of sales invoices is normally distributed because the sample size of 12 is too small for the Central Limit Theorem to take effect. This assumption is discussed on page 320.

Step 4 For a given sample size, n, the test statistic t_{STAT} follows a t distribution with $n - 1$ degrees of freedom. The critical values of the t distribution with $12 - 1 = 11$ degrees of freedom are found in Table E.3, as illustrated in Table 9.2 and Figure 9.6. The alternative hypothesis, $H_1 : \mu \neq 120$, has two tails. The area in the rejection region of

> **Student Tip**
> Since this is a two-tail test, the level of significance, $\alpha = 0.05$, is divided into two equal 0.025 parts, in each of the two tails of the distribution.

the t distribution's left (lower) tail is 0.025, and the area in the rejection region of the t distribution's right (upper) tail is also 0.025.

From the t table as given in Table E.3, a portion of which is shown in Table 9.2, the critical values are ± 2.2010. The decision rule is

$$\text{Reject } H_0 \text{ if } t_{STAT} < -2.2010$$

$$\text{or if } t_{STAT} > +2.2010;$$

$$\text{otherwise, do not reject } H_0.$$

TABLE 9.2

Determining the Critical Value from the t Table for an Area of 0.025 in Each Tail, with 11 Degrees of Freedom

	Cumulative Probabilities					
	.75	.90	.95	.975	.99	.995
	Upper-Tail Areas					
Degrees of Freedom	.25	.10	.05	.025	.01	.005
1	1.0000	3.0777	6.3138	12.7062	31.8207	63.6574
2	0.8165	1.8856	2.9200	4.3027	6.9646	9.9248
3	0.7649	1.6377	2.3534	3.1824	4.5407	5.8409
4	0.7407	1.5332	2.1318	2.7764	3.7469	4.6041
5	0.7267	1.4759	2.0150	2.5706	3.3649	4.0322
6	0.7176	1.4398	1.9432	2.4469	3.1427	3.7074
7	0.7111	1.4149	1.8946	2.3646	2.9980	3.4995
8	0.7064	1.3968	1.8595	2.3060	2.8965	3.3554
9	0.7027	1.3830	1.8331	2.2622	2.8214	3.2498
10	0.6998	1.3722	1.8125	2.2281	2.7638	3.1693
11	0.6974	1.3634	1.7959	2.2010	2.7181	3.1058

Source: Extracted from Table E.3.

FIGURE 9.6

Testing a hypothesis about the mean (σ unknown) at the 0.05 level of significance with 11 degrees of freedom

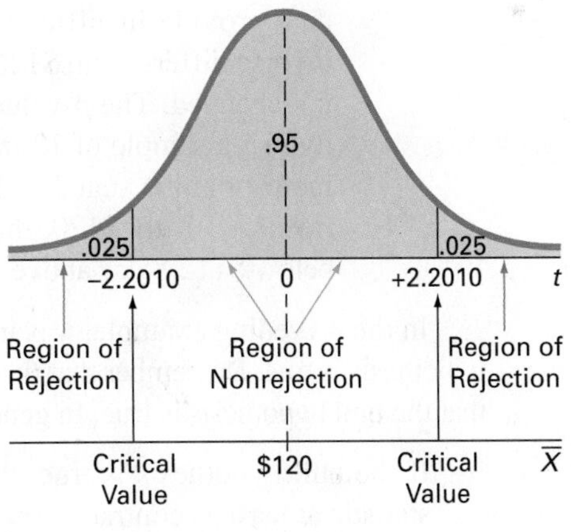

Step 5 You organize and store the data from a random sample of 12 sales invoices in **Invoices**:

108.98 152.22 111.45 110.59 127.46 107.26
93.32 91.97 111.56 75.71 128.58 135.11

Using Equations (3.1) and (3.7) on pages 106 and 113,

$$\bar{X} = \$112.85 \text{ and } S = \$20.80$$

From Equation (9.2) on page 318,

$$t_{STAT} = \frac{\bar{X} - \mu}{\frac{S}{\sqrt{n}}} = \frac{112.85 - 120}{\frac{20.80}{\sqrt{12}}} = -1.1908$$

Figure 9.7 shows a worksheet solution for this test of hypothesis.

FIGURE 9.7

Excel results for the t test of sales invoices

Figure 9.7 displays the **COMPUTE worksheet** *of the* **T Mean workbook** *that the Section EG9.2 instructions use.*

	A	B	
1	**t Test for the Hypothesis of the Mean**		
2			
3	**Data**		
4	Null Hypothesis μ=	120	
5	Level of Significance	0.05	
6	Sample Size	12	
7	Sample Mean	112.85	
8	Sample Standard Deviation	20.8	
9			
10	Intermediate Calculations		
11	Standard Error of the Mean	6.0044	=B8/SQRT(B6)
12	Degrees of Freedom	11	=B6 - 1
13	*t* Test Statistic	-1.1908	=(B7 - B4)/B11
14			
15	**Two-Tail Test**		
16	Lower Critical Value	-2.2010	=-T.INV.2T(B5, B12)
17	Upper Critical Value	2.2010	=T.INV.2T(B5, B12)
18	*p*-Value	0.2588	=T.DIST.2T(ABS(B13), B12)
19	Do not reject the null hypothesis		=IF(B18 < B5,"Reject the null hypothesis", "Do not reject the null hypothesis")

Step 6 Because $-2.2010 < t_{STAT} = -1.1908 < 2.2010$, you do not reject H_0. You have insufficient evidence to conclude that the mean amount per sales invoice differs from \$120. The audit suggests that the mean amount per invoice has not changed.

The *p*-Value Approach

To perform this two-tail hypothesis test, you use the five-step method listed in Exhibit 9.2 on page 315.

Step 1–3 These steps are the same as in the critical value approach.

Step 4 From the Figure 9.7 results, $t_{STAT} = -1.19$ and the p-value $= 0.2588$

Step 5 Because the p-value of 0.2588 is greater than $\alpha = 0.05$, you do not reject H_0. The data provide insufficient evidence to conclude that the mean amount per sales invoice differs from \$120. The audit suggests that the mean amount per invoice has not changed. The p-value indicates that if the null hypothesis is true, the probability that a sample of 12 invoices could have a sample mean that differs by \$7.15 or more from the stated \$120 is 0.2588. In other words, if the mean amount per sales invoice is truly \$120, then there is a 25.88% chance of observing a sample mean below \$112.85 or above \$127.15.

In the preceding example, it is incorrect to state that there is a 25.88% chance that the null hypothesis is true. Remember that the p-value is a conditional probability, calculated by *assuming* that the null hypothesis is true. In general, it is proper to state the following:

If the null hypothesis is true, there is a (p-value) $\times$ 100% chance of observing a test statistic at least as contradictory to the null hypothesis as the sample result.

Checking the Normality Assumption

You use the t test when the population standard deviation, σ, is not known and is estimated using the sample standard deviation, S. To use the t test, you assume that the data represent a random sample from a population that is normally distributed. In practice, as long as the sample size is not very small and the population is not very skewed, the t distribution provides a good approximation of the sampling distribution of the mean when σ is unknown.

There are several ways to evaluate the normality assumption necessary for using the t test. You can examine how closely the sample statistics match the normal distribution's theoretical properties. You can also construct a histogram, stem-and-leaf display, boxplot, or normal probability plot to visualize the distribution of the sales invoice amounts. For details on evaluating normality, see Section 6.3 on pages 233–235.

Figures 9.8 and 9.9 show the descriptive statistics, boxplot, and normal probability plot for the sales invoice data.

FIGURE 9.8

Descriptive statistics worksheet and boxplot for the sales invoice data

Use the instructions in Sections EG3.2 and EG3.3 to compute descriptive statistics and construct a boxplot.

	Invoice Amount
Mean	112.8508
Median	111.02
Mode	#N/A
Minimum	75.71
Maximum	152.22
Range	76.51
Variance	432.5565
Standard Deviation	20.7980
Coeff. of Variation	18.43%
Skewness	0.1336
Kurtosis	0.1727
Count	12
Standard Error	6.0039

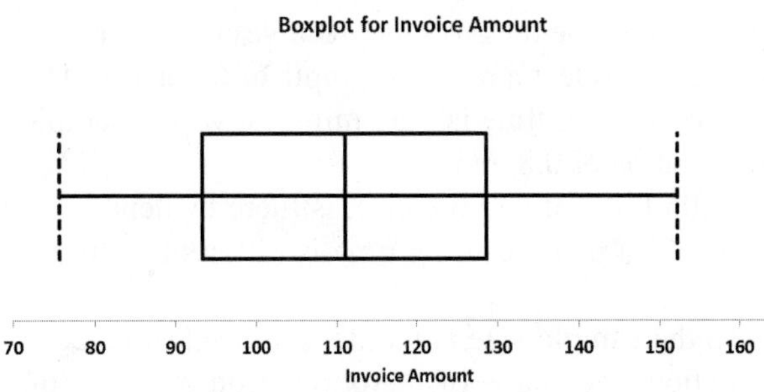

FIGURE 9.9

Normal probability plot for the sales invoice data

Use the Section EG6.3 instructions to construct a normal probability plot.

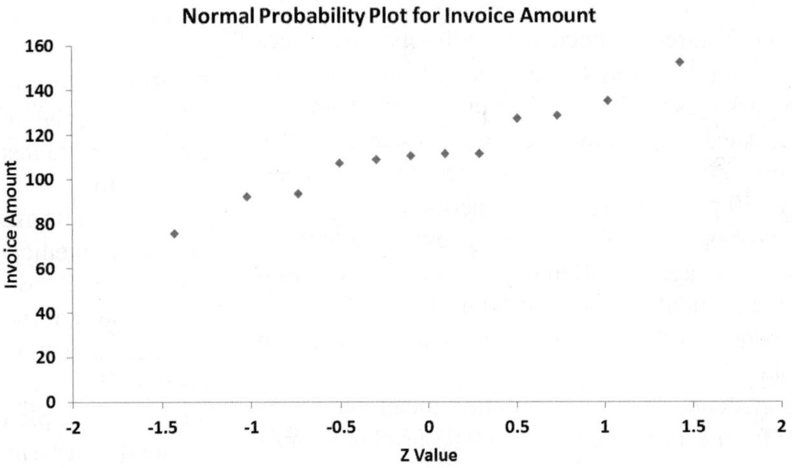

The mean is very close to the median, and the points on the normal probability appear to be increasing approximately in a straight line. The boxplot appears to be approximately symmetrical. Thus, you can assume that the population of sales invoices is approximately normally distributed. The normality assumption is valid, and therefore the auditor's results are valid.

The t test is a **robust** test. A robust test does not lose power if the shape of the population departs somewhat from a normal distribution, particularly when the sample size is large enough to enable the test statistic t to be influenced by the Central Limit Theorem (see Section 7.2). However, you can reach erroneous conclusions and can lose statistical power if you use the t test incorrectly. If the sample size, n, is small (i.e., less than 30) and you cannot easily make the assumption that the underlying population is at least approximately normally distributed, then *nonparametric* testing procedures are more appropriate (see references 2 and 3).

Problems for Section 9.2

LEARNING THE BASICS

9.18 If, in a sample of $n = 16$ selected from a normal population, $\bar{X} = 56$ and $S = 12$, what is the value of t_{STAT} if you are testing the null hypothesis $H_0: \mu = 50$?

9.19 In Problem 9.18, how many degrees of freedom does the t test have?

9.20 In Problems 9.18 and 9.19, what are the critical values of t if the level of significance, α, is 0.05 and the alternative hypothesis, H_1, is $\mu \neq 50$?

9.21 In Problems 9.18, 9.19, and 9.20, what is your statistical decision if the alternative hypothesis, H_1, is $\mu \neq 50$?

9.22 If, in a sample of $n = 16$ selected from a left-skewed population, $\bar{X} = 65$, and $S = 21$, would you use the t test to test the null hypothesis $H_0: \mu = 60$? Discuss.

9.23 If, in a sample of $n = 160$ selected from a left-skewed population, $\bar{X} = 65$, and $S = 21$, would you use the t test to test the null hypothesis $H_0: \mu = 60$? Discuss.

APPLYING THE CONCEPTS

SELF Test **9.24** You are the manager of a restaurant for a fast-food franchise. Last month, the mean waiting time at the drive-through window for branches in your geographic region, as measured from the time a customer places an order until the time the customer receives the order, was 3.7 minutes. You select a random sample of 64 orders. The sample mean waiting time is 3.57 minutes, with a sample standard deviation of 0.8 minute.

a. At the 0.05 level of significance, is there evidence that the population mean waiting time is different from 3.7 minutes?

b. Because the sample size is 64, do you need to be concerned about the shape of the population distribution when conducting the *t* test in (a)? Explain.

9.25 A manufacturer of chocolate candies uses machines to package candies as they move along a filling line. Although the packages are labeled as 8 ounces, the company wants the packages to contain a mean of 8.17 ounces so that virtually none of the packages contain less than 8 ounces. A sample of 50 packages is selected periodically, and the packaging process is stopped if there is evidence that the mean amount packaged is different from 8.17 ounces. Suppose that in a particular sample of 50 packages, the mean amount dispensed is 8.159 ounces, with a sample standard deviation of 0.051 ounce.

a. Is there evidence that the population mean amount is different from 8.17 ounces? (Use a 0.05 level of significance.)

b. Determine the *p*-value and interpret its meaning.

9.26 A stationery store wants to estimate the mean retail value of greeting cards that it has in its inventory. A random sample of 100 greeting cards indicates a mean value of \$2.55 and a standard deviation of \$0.44.

a. Is there evidence that the population mean retail value of the greeting cards is different from \$2.50? (Use a 0.05 level of significance.)

b. Determine the *p*-value and interpret its meaning.

9.27 The U.S. Department of Transportation requires tire manufacturers to provide performance information on tire sidewalls to help prospective buyers make their purchasing decisions. One very important piece of information is the tread wear index, which indicates the tire's resistance to tread wear. A tire with a grade of 200 should last twice as long, on average, as a tire with a grade of 100.

A consumer organization wants to test the actual tread wear index of a brand name of tires that claims "graded 200" on the sidewall of the tire. A random sample of $n = 18$ indicates a sample mean tread wear index of 195.3 and a sample standard deviation of 21.4.

a. Is there evidence that the population mean tread wear index is different from 200? (Use a 0.05 level of significance.)

b. Determine the *p*-value and interpret its meaning.

9.28 The file FastFood contains the amount that a sample of fifteen customers spent for lunch (\$) at a fast-food restaurant:

7.42	6.29	5.83	6.50	8.34	9.51	7.10	6.80	5.90
4.89	6.50	5.52	7.90	8.30	9.60			

a. At the 0.05 level of significance, is there evidence that the mean amount spent for lunch is different from \$6.50?

b. Determine the *p*-value in (a) and interpret its meaning.

c. What assumption must you make about the population distribution in order to conduct the *t* test in (a) and (b)?

d. Because the sample size is 15, do you need to be concerned about the shape of the population distribution when conducting the *t* test in (a)? Explain.

9.29 An insurance company has the business objective of reducing the amount of time it takes to approve applications for life insurance. The approval process consists of underwriting, which includes a review of the application, a medical information bureau check, possible requests for additional medical information and medical exams, and a policy compilation stage in which the policy pages are generated and sent for delivery. The ability to deliver approved policies to customers in a timely manner is critical to the profitability of this service. During a period of one month, a random sample of 27 approved policies is selected, and the total processing time, in days, is collected. These data, stored in Insurance, are:

73 19 16 64 28 28 31 90 60 56 31 56 22 18 45 48
17 17 17 91 92 63 50 51 69 16 17

a. In the past, the mean processing time was 45 days. At the 0.05 level of significance, is there evidence that the mean processing time has changed from 45 days?

b. What assumption about the population distribution is needed in order to conduct the *t* test in (a)?

c. Construct a boxplot or a normal probability plot to evaluate the assumption made in (b).

d. Do you think that the assumption needed in order to conduct the *t* test in (a) is valid? Explain.

9.30 The following data (in Drink) represent the amount of soft drink filled in a sample of 50 consecutive 2-liter bottles. The results, listed horizontally in the order of being filled, were:

2.109	2.086	2.066	2.075	2.065	2.057	2.052	2.044
2.036	2.038	2.031	2.029	2.025	2.029	2.023	2.020
2.015	2.014	2.013	2.014	2.012	2.012	2.012	2.010
2.005	2.003	1.999	1.996	1.997	1.992	1.994	1.986
1.984	1.981	1.973	1.975	1.971	1.969	1.966	1.967
1.963	1.957	1.951	1.951	1.947	1.941	1.941	1.938
1.908	1.894						

a. At the 0.05 level of significance, is there evidence that the mean amount of soft drink filled is different from 2.0 liters?
b. Determine the p-value in (a) and interpret its meaning.
c. In (a), you assumed that the distribution of the amount of soft drink filled was normally distributed. Evaluate this assumption by constructing a boxplot or a normal probability plot.
d. Do you think that the assumption needed in order to conduct the t test in (a) is valid? Explain.
e. Examine the values of the 50 bottles in their sequential order, as given in the problem. Does there appear to be a pattern to the results? If so, what impact might this pattern have on the validity of the results in (a)?

9.31 One of the major measures of the quality of service provided by any organization is the speed with which it responds to customer complaints. A large family-held department store selling furniture and flooring, including carpet, had undergone a major expansion in the past several years. In particular, the flooring department had expanded from 2 installation crews to an installation supervisor, a measurer, and 15 installation crews. The store had the business objective of improving its response to complaints. The variable of interest was defined as the number of days between when the complaint was made and when it was resolved. Data were collected from 50 complaints that were made in the past year. These data, stored in **Furniture**, are:

54	5	35	137	31	27	152	2	123	81	74	27
11	19	126	110	110	29	61	35	94	31	26	5
12	4	165	32	29	28	29	26	25	1	14	13
13	10	5	27	4	52	30	22	36	26	20	23
33	68										

a. The installation supervisor claims that the mean number of days between the receipt of a complaint and the resolution of the complaint is 20 days. At the 0.05 level of significance, is there evidence that the claim is not true (i.e., that the mean number of days is different from 20)?
b. What assumption about the population distribution is needed in order to conduct the t test in (a)?
c. Construct a boxplot or a normal probability plot to evaluate the assumption made in (b).
d. Do you think that the assumption needed in order to conduct the t test in (a) is valid? Explain.

9.32 A manufacturing company produces steel housings for electrical equipment. The main component part of the housing is a steel trough that is made out of a 14-gauge steel coil. It is produced using a 250-ton progressive punch press with a wipe-down operation that puts two 90-degree forms in the flat steel to make the trough. The distance from one side of the form to the other is critical because of weatherproofing in outdoor applications. The company requires that the width of the trough be between 8.31 inches and 8.61 inches. The file **Trough** contains the widths of the troughs, in inches, for a sample of $n = 49$:

8.312	8.343	8.317	8.383	8.348	8.410	8.351	8.373	8.481	8.422
8.476	8.382	8.484	8.403	8.414	8.419	8.385	8.465	8.498	8.447
8.436	8.413	8.489	8.414	8.481	8.415	8.479	8.429	8.458	8.462
8.460	8.444	8.429	8.460	8.412	8.420	8.410	8.405	8.323	8.420
8.396	8.447	8.405	8.439	8.411	8.427	8.420	8.498	8.409	

a. At the 0.05 level of significance, is there evidence that the mean width of the troughs is different from 8.46 inches?
b. What assumption about the population distribution is needed in order to conduct the t test in (a)?
c. Evaluate the assumption made in (b).
d. Do you think that the assumption needed in order to conduct the t test in (a) is valid? Explain.

9.33 One operation of a steel mill is to cut pieces of steel into parts that are used in the frame for front seats in an automobile. The steel is cut with a diamond saw and requires the resulting parts must be cut to be within ± 0.005 inch of the length specified by the automobile company. The file **Steel** contains a sample of 100 steel parts. The measurement reported is the difference, in inches, between the actual length of the steel part, as measured by a laser measurement device, and the specified length of the steel part. For example, a value of -0.002 represents a steel part that is 0.002 inch shorter than the specified length.
a. At the 0.05 level of significance, is there evidence that the mean difference is not equal to 0.0 inches?
b. Construct a 95% confidence interval estimate of the population mean. Interpret this interval.
c. Compare the conclusions reached in (a) and (b).
d. Because $n = 100$, do you have to be concerned about the normality assumption needed for the t test and t interval?

9.34 In Problem 3.69 on page 146, you were introduced to a tea-bag-filling operation. An important quality characteristic of interest for this process is the weight of the tea in the individual bags. The file **Teabags** contains an ordered array of the weight, in grams, of a sample of 50 tea bags produced during an eight-hour shift.
a. Is there evidence that the mean amount of tea per bag is different from 5.5 grams? (Use $\alpha = 0.01$.)
b. Construct a 99% confidence interval estimate of the population mean amount of tea per bag. Interpret this interval.
c. Compare the conclusions reached in (a) and (b).

9.35 An article appearing in *The Exponent*, an independent college newspaper published by the Purdue Student Publishing Foundation, reported that the average American college student spends one hour (60 minutes) on Facebook daily. (Data extracted from **bit.ly/QqQHow**.) In order to test the validity of this statement, you select a sample of 30 Facebook users at your college. The results for the time spent on Facebook per day (in minutes) are stored in **FacebookTime**.

a. Is there evidence that the population mean time Facebook time is different from 60 minutes? Use the *p*-value approach and a level of significance of 0.05.

b. What assumption about the population distribution is needed in order to conduct the *t* test in (a)?

c. Make a list of the various ways you could evaluate the assumption noted in (b).

d. Evaluate the assumption noted in (b) and determine whether the test in (a) is valid.

9.3 One-Tail Tests

In Section 9.1, hypothesis testing was used to examine the question of whether the population mean amount of cereal filled is 368 grams. The alternative hypothesis $(H_1 : \mu \neq 368)$ contains two possibilities: Either the mean is less than 368 grams or the mean is more than 368 grams. For this reason, the rejection region is divided into the two tails of the sampling distribution of the mean. In Section 9.2, a two-tail test was used to determine whether the mean amount per invoice had changed from $120.

In contrast to these two examples, many situations require an alternative hypothesis that focuses on a *particular direction*. For example, the population mean is *less than* a specified value. One such situation involves the business problem concerning the service time at the drive-through window of a fast-food restaurant. The speed with which customers are served is of critical importance to the success of the service (see **www.qsrmagazine.com/reports/qsr-drive-thru-performance-study**). In one past study, an audit of McDonald's drive-throughs had a mean service time of 184.2 seconds, which was slower than the drive-throughs of six other fast-food chains. Suppose that McDonald's began a quality improvement effort to reduce the service time by deploying an improved drive-through service process in a sample of 25 stores. Because McDonald's would want to institute the new process in all of its stores only if the test sample saw a *decreased* drive-through time, the entire rejection region is located in the lower tail of the distribution.

The Critical Value Approach

You wish to determine whether the new drive-through process has a mean that is less than 184.2 seconds. To perform this one-tail hypothesis test, you use the six-step method listed in Exhibit 9.1 on page 312:

Student Tip
The rejection region matches the direction of the alternative hypothesis. If the alternative hypothesis contains a $<$ sign, the rejection region is in the lower tail. If the alternative hypothesis contains a $>$ sign, the rejection region is in the upper tail.

Step 1 You define the null and alternative hypotheses:

$$H_0 : \mu \geq 184.2$$
$$H_1 : \mu < 184.2$$

The alternative hypothesis contains the statement for which you are trying to find evidence. If the conclusion of the test is "reject H_0," there is statistical evidence that the mean drive-through time is less than the drive-through time in the old process. This would be reason to change the drive-through process for the entire population of stores. If the conclusion of the test is "do not reject H_0," then there is insufficient evidence that the mean drive-through time in the new process is significantly less than the drive-through time in the old process. If this occurs, there would be insufficient reason to institute the new drive-through process in the population of stores.

Step 2 You collect the data by selecting a sample of $n = 25$ stores. You decide to use $\alpha = 0.05$.

Step 3 Because σ is unknown, you use the *t* distribution and the t_{STAT} test statistic. You need to assume that the drive-through time is normally distributed because only a sample of 25 drive-through times is selected.

Step 4 The rejection region is entirely contained in the lower tail of the sampling distribution of the mean because you want to reject H_0 only when the sample mean is significantly less than 184.2 seconds. When the entire rejection region is contained in one tail of the sampling distribution of the test statistic, the test is called a **one-tail test**, or **directional test**. If the alternative hypothesis includes the *less than* sign, the critical value of *t* is negative. As shown in Table 9.3 and Figure 9.10, because the entire rejection region is in the lower tail of the t distribution and contains an area of 0.05, due to the symmetry of the t distribution, the critical value of the t test statistic with $25 - 1 = 24$ degrees of freedom is -1.7109.

The decision rule is

$$\text{Reject } H_0 \text{ if } t_{STAT} < -1.7109;$$

$$\text{otherwise, do not reject } H_0.$$

TABLE 9.3

Determining the Critical Value from the t Table for an Area of 0.05 in the Lower Tail, with 24 Degrees of Freedom

	Cumulative Probabilities					
	.75	.90	.95	.975	.99	.995
	Upper-Tail Areas					
Degrees of Freedom	.25	.10	.05	.025	.01	.005
1	1.0000	3.0777	6.3138	12.7062	31.8207	63.6574
2	0.8165	1.8856	2.9200	4.3027	6.9646	9.9248
3	0.7649	1.6377	2.3534	3.1824	4.5407	5.8409
⋮	⋮	⋮	⋮	⋮	⋮	⋮
23	0.6853	1.3195	1.7139	2.0687	2.4999	2.8073
24	0.6848	1.3178	1.7109	2.0639	2.4922	2.7969
25	0.6844	1.3163	1.7081	2.0595	2.4851	2.7874

Source: Extracted from Table E.3.

FIGURE 9.10

One-tail test of hypothesis for a mean (σ unknown) at the 0.05 level of significance

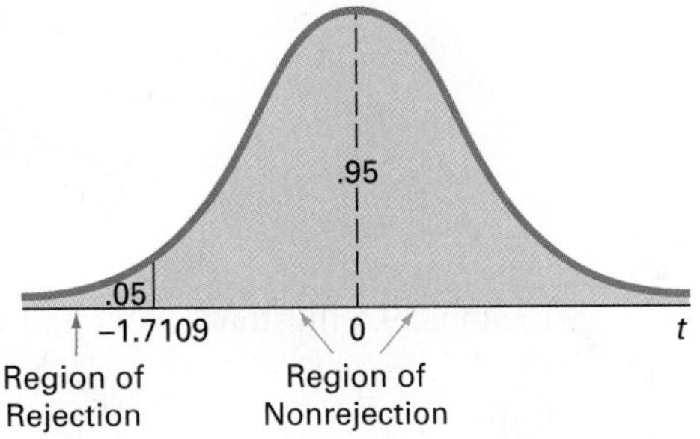

Step 5 From the sample of 25 stores you selected, you find that the sample mean service time at the drive-through equals 170.8 seconds and the sample standard deviation equals 21.3 seconds. Using $n = 25$, $\bar{X} = 170.8$, $S = 21.3$, and Equation (9.2) on page 318,

$$t_{STAT} = \frac{\bar{X} - \mu}{\dfrac{S}{\sqrt{n}}} = \frac{170.8 - 184.2}{\dfrac{21.3}{\sqrt{25}}} = -3.1455$$

Step 6 Because $t_{STAT} = -3.1455 < -1.7109$, you reject the null hypothesis (see Figure 9.10). You conclude that the mean service time at the drive-through is less than 184.2 seconds. There is sufficient evidence to change the drive-through process for the entire population of stores.

The *p*-Value Approach

Use the five steps listed in Exhibit 9.2 on page 315 to illustrate the t test for the drive-through time study using the p-value approach:

Step 1–3 These steps are the same as was used in the critical value approach on page 324.

Step 4 $t_{STAT} = -3.1455$ (see step 5 of the critical value approach). Because the alternative hypothesis indicates a rejection region entirely in the lower tail of the sampling distribution, to compute the p-value, you need to find the probability that the t_{STAT} test statistic will be less than –3.1455. Figure 9.11 shows that the p-value is 0.0022.

FIGURE 9.11

t test worksheet for the drive-through time study

Figure 9.11 displays the **COMPUTE_LOWER worksheet** *of the* **T Mean workbook** *that Section EG9.3 discusses.*

	A	B	
1	t Test for the Hypothesis of the Mean		
2			
3	Data		
4	Null Hypothesis μ=	184.2	
5	Level of Significance	0.05	
6	Sample Size	25	
7	Sample Mean	170.8	
8	Sample Standard Deviation	21.3	
9			
10	Intermediate Calculations		
11	Standard Error of the Mean	4.2600	=B8/SQRT(B6)
12	Degrees of Freedom	24	=B6 - 1
13	*t* Test Statistic	-3.1455	=(B7 - B4)/B11
14			
15	Lower-Tail Test		
16	Lower Critical Value	-1.7109	=-T.INV.2T(2 * B5, B12)
17	*p*-Value	0.0022	=IF(B13 < 0, E11, E12)
18	Reject the null hypothesis		=IF(B17 < B5,"Reject the null hypothesis", "Do not reject the null hypothesis")

	D	E	
10	One-Tail Calculations		
11	T.DIST.RT value	0.0022	=T.DIST.RT(ABS(B13), B12)
12	1-T.DIST.RT value	0.9978	=1 - E11

Step 5 The *p*-value of 0.0022 is less than $\alpha = 0.05$ (see Figure 9.12). You reject H_0 and conclude that the mean service time at the drive-through is less than 184.2 seconds. There is sufficient evidence to change the drive-through process for the entire population of stores.

FIGURE 9.12

Determining the *p*-value for a one-tail test

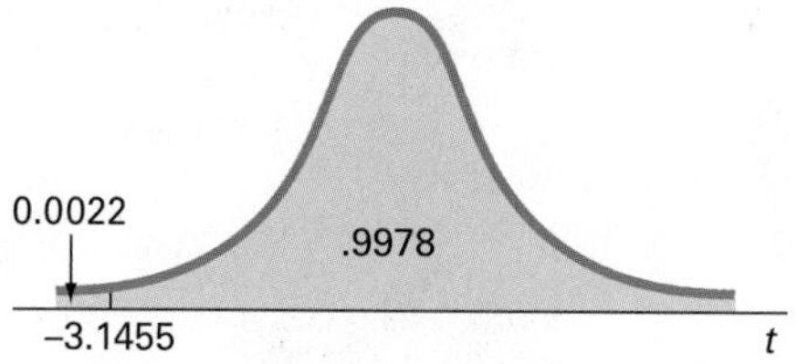

Example 9.5 illustrates a one-tail test in which the rejection region is in the upper tail.

EXAMPLE 9.5

A One-Tail Test for the Mean

A company that manufactures chocolate bars is particularly concerned that the mean weight of a chocolate bar is not greater than 6.03 ounces. A sample of 50 chocolate bars is selected; the sample mean is 6.034 ounces, and the sample standard deviation is 0.02 ounce. Using the $\alpha = 0.01$ level of significance, is there evidence that the population mean weight of the chocolate bars is greater than 6.03 ounces?

SOLUTION Using the critical value approach, listed in Exhibit 9.1 on page 312,

Step 1 First, you define your hypotheses:

$$H_0: \mu \leq 6.03$$

$$H_1: \mu > 6.03$$

Step 2 You collect the data from a sample of $n = 50$. You decide to use $\alpha = 0.01$.

Step 3 Because σ is unknown, you use the t distribution and the t_{STAT} test statistic.

Step 4 The rejection region is entirely contained in the upper tail of the sampling distribution of the mean because you want to reject H_0 only when the sample mean is significantly greater than 6.03 ounces. Because the entire rejection region is in the upper tail of the t distribution and contains an area of 0.01, the critical value of the t distribution with $50 - 1 = 49$ degrees of freedom is 2.4049 (see Table E.3).

The decision rule is

$$\text{Reject } H_0 \text{ if } t_{STAT} > 2.4049;$$

$$\text{otherwise, do not reject } H_0.$$

Step 5 From your sample of 50 chocolate bars, you find that the sample mean weight is 6.034 ounces, and the sample standard deviation is 0.02 ounces. Using $n = 50$, $\bar{X} = 6.034$, $S = 0.02$, and Equation (9.2) on page 318,

$$t_{STAT} = \frac{\bar{X} - \mu}{\frac{S}{\sqrt{n}}} = \frac{6.034 - 6.03}{\frac{0.02}{\sqrt{50}}} = 1.414$$

Step 6 Because $t_{STAT} = 1.414 < 2.4049$ or the p-value is $0.0818 > 0.01$, you do not reject the null hypothesis. There is insufficient evidence to conclude that the population mean weight is greater than 6.03 ounces.

To perform one-tail tests of hypotheses, you must properly formulate H_0 and H_1. A summary of the null and alternative hypotheses for one-tail tests is as follows:

- The null hypothesis, H_0, represents the status quo or the current belief in a situation.
- The alternative hypothesis, H_1, is the opposite of the null hypothesis and represents a research claim or specific inference you would like to prove.
- If you reject the null hypothesis, you have statistical proof that the alternative hypothesis is correct.
- If you do not reject the null hypothesis, you have failed to prove the alternative hypothesis. The failure to prove the alternative hypothesis, however, does not mean that you have proven the null hypothesis.
- The null hypothesis always refers to a specified value of the *population parameter* (such as μ), not to a *sample statistic* (such as $\bar{X}$).
- The statement of the null hypothesis *always* contains an equal sign regarding the specified value of the parameter (e.g., $H_0: \mu \geq 184.2$).
- The statement of the alternative hypothesis *never* contains an equal sign regarding the specified value of the parameter (e.g., $H_1: \mu < 184.2$).

Problems for Section 9.3

LEARNING THE BASICS

9.36 In a one-tail hypothesis test where you reject H_0 only in the *upper* tail, what is the p-value if $Z_{STAT} = +2.00$?

9.37 In Problem 9.36, what is your statistical decision if you test the null hypothesis at the 0.05 level of significance?

9.38 In a one-tail hypothesis test where you reject H_0 only in the *lower* tail, what is the p-value if $Z_{STAT} = -1.38$?

9.39 In Problem 9.38, what is your statistical decision if you test the null hypothesis at the 0.01 level of significance?

9.40 In a one-tail hypothesis test where you reject H_0 only in the *lower* tail, what is the p-value if $Z_{STAT} = +1.38$?

9.41 In Problem 9.40, what is the statistical decision if you test the null hypothesis at the 0.01 level of significance?

9.42 In a one-tail hypothesis test where you reject H_0 only in the *upper* tail, what is the critical value of the t-test statistic with 10 degrees of freedom at the 0.01 level of significance?

9.43 In Problem 9.42, what is your statistical decision if $t_{STAT} = +2.39$?

9.44 In a one-tail hypothesis test where you reject H_0 only in the *lower* tail, what is the critical value of the t_{STAT} test statistic with 20 degrees of freedom at the 0.01 level of significance?

9.45 In Problem 9.44, what is your statistical decision if $t_{STAT} = -1.15$?

APPLYING THE CONCEPTS

9.46 In a recent year, the Federal Communications Commission reported that the mean wait for repairs for Verizon customers was 36.5 hours. In an effort to improve this service, suppose that a new repair service process was developed. This new process, used for a sample of 100 repairs, resulted in a sample mean of 34.5 hours and a sample standard deviation of 11.7 hours.

a. Is there evidence that the population mean amount is less than 36.5 hours? (Use a 0.05 level of significance.)

b. Determine the p-value and interpret its meaning.

9.47 In a recent year, the Federal Communications Commission reported that the mean wait for repairs for AT&T customers was 25.3 hours. In an effort to improve this service, suppose that a new repair service process was developed. This new process, used for a sample of 100 repairs, resulted in a sample mean of 22.3 hours and a sample standard deviation of 8.3 hours.

a. Is there evidence that the population mean amount is less than 25.3 hours? (Use a 0.05 level of significance.)

b. Determine the p-value and interpret its meaning.

SELF Test **9.48** Southside Hospital in Bay Shore, New York, commonly conducts stress tests to study the heart muscle after a person has a heart attack. Members of the diagnostic imaging department conducted a quality improvement project with the objective of reducing the turnaround time for stress tests. Turnaround time is defined as the time from when a test is ordered to when the radiologist signs off on the test results. Initially, the mean turnaround time for a stress test was 68 hours. After incorporating changes into the stress-test process, the quality improvement team collected a sample of 50 turnaround times. In this sample, the mean turnaround time was 32 hours, with a standard deviation of 9 hours. (Data extracted from E. Godin, D. Raven, C. Sweetapple, and F. R. Del Guidice, "Faster Test Results," *Quality Progress*, January 2004, 37(1), pp. 33–39.)

a. If you test the null hypothesis at the 0.01 level of significance, is there evidence that the new process has reduced turnaround time?

b. Interpret the meaning of the p-value in this problem.

9.49 You are the manager of a restaurant that delivers pizza to college dormitory rooms. You have just changed your delivery process in an effort to reduce the mean time between the order and completion of delivery from the current 25 minutes. A sample of 36 orders using the new delivery process yields a sample mean of 22.4 minutes and a sample standard deviation of 6 minutes.

a. Using the six-step critical value approach, at the 0.05 level of significance, is there evidence that the population mean delivery time has been reduced below the previous population mean value of 25 minutes?

b. At the 0.05 level of significance, use the five-step p-value approach.

c. Interpret the meaning of the p-value in (b).

d. Compare your conclusions in (a) and (b).

9.50 A survey of nonprofit organizations showed that online fundraising has increased in the past year. Based on a random sample of 50 nonprofit organizations, the mean one-time gift donation in the past year was \$62, with a standard deviation of \$9.

a. If you test the null hypothesis at the 0.01 level of significance, is there evidence that the mean one-time gift donation is greater than \$60?

b. Interpret the meaning of the p-value in this problem.

9.51 The population mean waiting time to check out of a supermarket has been 10.73 minutes. Recently, in an effort to reduce the waiting time, the supermarket has experimented with a system in which there is a single waiting line with multiple checkout servers. A sample of 100 customers was selected, and their mean waiting time to check out was 9.52 minutes, with a sample standard deviation of 5.8 minutes.

a. At the 0.05 level of significance, using the critical value approach to hypothesis testing, is there evidence that the population mean waiting time to check out is less than 10.73 minutes?

b. At the 0.05 level of significance, using the p-value approach to hypothesis testing, is there evidence that the population mean waiting time to check out is less than 10.73 minutes?

c. Interpret the meaning of the p-value in this problem.

d. Compare your conclusions in (a) and (b).

9.4 *Z* Test of Hypothesis for the Proportion

In some situations, you want to test a hypothesis about the proportion of events of interest in the population, π, rather than test the population mean. To begin, you select a random sample and compute the **sample proportion**, $p = X/n$. You then compare the value of this statistic to the hypothesized value of the parameter, π, in order to decide whether to reject the null hypothesis.

> **Student Tip**
> Do not confuse this use of the Greek letter pi, π, to represent the population proportion with the mathematical constant that is the ratio of the circumference to a diameter of a circle—approximately 3.14159—which is also known by the same Greek letter.

If the number of events of interest (X) and the number of events that are not of interest ($n - X$) are each at least five, the sampling distribution of a proportion approximately follows a normal distribution, and you can use the ***Z* test for the proportion**. Equation (9.3) defines this hypothesis test for the difference between the sample proportion, p, and the hypothesized population proportion, π.

Z TEST FOR THE PROPORTION

$$Z_{STAT} = \frac{p - \pi}{\sqrt{\dfrac{\pi(1 - \pi)}{n}}} \qquad \textbf{(9.3)}$$

where

$$p = \text{sample proportion} = \frac{X}{n} = \frac{\text{number of events of interest in the sample}}{\text{sample size}}$$

$$\pi = \text{hypothesized proportion of events of interest in the population}$$

The Z_{STAT} test statistic approximately follows a standardized normal distribution when X and $(n - X)$ are each at least 5.

Alternatively, by multiplying the numerator and denominator by n, you can write the Z_{STAT} test statistic in terms of the number of events of interest, X, as shown in Equation (9.4).

Z TEST FOR THE PROPORTION IN TERMS OF THE NUMBER OF EVENTS OF INTEREST

$$Z_{STAT} = \frac{X - n\pi}{\sqrt{n\pi(1 - \pi)}} \tag{9.4}$$

The Critical Value Approach

To illustrate the Z test for a proportion, consider a survey conducted for American Express that sought to determine the reasons adults wanted Internet access while on vacation. (Data extracted from "Wired Vacationers," *USA Today*, June 4, 2010, p. 1A.) Of 2,000 adults, 1,540 said that they wanted Internet access so they could check personal email while on vacation. A survey conducted in the previous year indicated that 75% of adults wanted Internet access so they could check personal email while on vacation. Is there evidence that the percentage of adults who wanted Internet access to check personal email while on vacation has changed from the previous year? To investigate this question, the null and alternative hypotheses are follows:

$H_0 : \pi = 0.75$ (i.e., the proportion of adults who want Internet access to check personal email while on vacation has not changed from the previous year)

$H_1 : \pi \neq 0.75$ (i.e., the proportion of adults who want Internet access to check personal email while on vacation has changed from the previous year)

Because you are interested in determining whether the population proportion of adults who want Internet access to check personal email while on vacation has changed from 0.75 in the previous year, you use a two-tail test. If you select the $\alpha = 0.05$ level of significance, the rejection and nonrejection regions are set up as in Figure 9.13, and the decision rule is

$$\text{Reject } H_0 \text{ if } Z_{STAT} < -1.96 \text{ or if } Z_{STAT} > +1.96;$$
$$\text{otherwise, do not reject } H_0.$$

FIGURE 9.13
Two-tail test of hypothesis for the proportion at the 0.05 level of significance

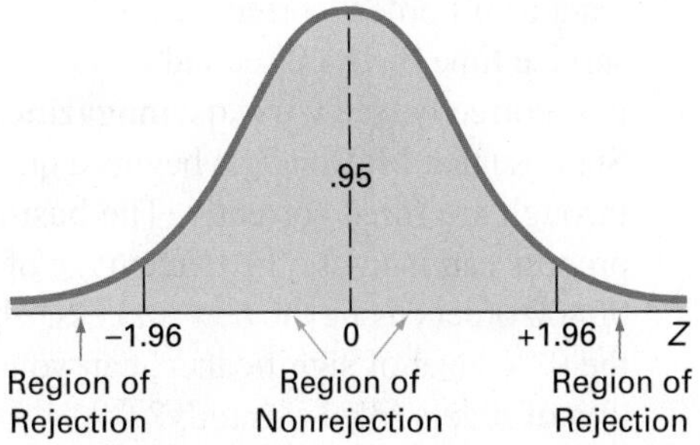

Because 1,540 of the 2,000 adults stated that they wanted Internet access to check personal email while on vacation,

$$p = \frac{1{,}540}{2{,}000} = 0.77$$

Since $X = 1{,}540$ and $n\text{-}X = 460$, each >5, using Equation (9.3),

$$Z_{STAT} = \frac{p - \pi}{\sqrt{\dfrac{\pi(1 - \pi)}{n}}} = \frac{0.77 - 0.75}{\sqrt{\dfrac{0.75(1 - 0.75)}{2{,}000}}} = \frac{0.02}{0.0097} = 2.0656$$

or, using Equation (9.4),

$$Z_{STAT} = \frac{X - n\pi}{\sqrt{n\pi(1 - \pi)}} = \frac{1{,}540 - (2{,}000)(0.75)}{\sqrt{2{,}000(0.75)(0.25)}} = \frac{40}{19.3649} = 2.0656$$

Because $Z_{STAT} = 2.0656 > 1.96$, you reject H_0. There is evidence that the population proportion of all adults who want Internet access to check personal email while on vacation has changed from 0.75 in the previous year. Figure 9.14 presents the worksheet results for these data.

FIGURE 9.14

Worksheet for the Z test for whether the proportion of adults who want Internet access to check personal email while on vacation has changed from the previous year

Figure 9.14 displays the ***COMPUTE worksheet*** *of the* ***Z Proportion workbook*** *that the Section EG9.4 instructions use.*

	A	B	
1	Z Test of Hypothesis for the Proportion		
2			
3	Data		
4	Null Hypothesis π=	0.75	
5	Level of Significance	0.05	
6	Number of Items of Interest	1540	
7	Sample Size	2000	
8			
9	Intermediate Calculations		
10	Sample Proportion	0.7700	=B6/B7
11	Standard Error	0.0097	=SQRT(B4 * (1 - B4)/B7)
12	Z Test Statistic	2.0656	=(B10 - B4)/B11
13			
14	Two-Tail Test		
15	Lower Critical Value	-1.9600	=NORM.S.INV(B5/2)
16	Upper Critical value	1.9600	=NORM.S.INV(1 - B5/2)
17	p-Value	0.0389	=2 * (1 - NORM.S.DIST(ABS(B12), TRUE))
18	Reject the null hypothesis		=IF(B17 < B5,"Reject the null hypothesis", "Do not reject the null hypothesis")

The *p*-Value Approach

As an alternative to the critical value approach, you can compute the *p*-value. For this two-tail test in which the rejection region is located in the lower tail and the upper tail, you need to find the area below a Z value of -2.0656 and above a Z value of $+2.0656$. Figure 9.14 reports a *p*-value of 0.0389. Because this value is less than the selected level of significance ($\alpha = 0.05$), you reject the null hypothesis.

Example 9.6 illustrates a one-tail test for a proportion.

EXAMPLE 9.6

Testing a Hypothesis for a Proportion

In addition to the business problem of the speed of service at the drive-through, fast-food chains want to fill orders correctly. The same audit that reported that McDonald's had a drive-through service time of 184.2 seconds also reported that McDonald's filled 89% of its drive-through orders correctly (see **www.qsrmagazine.com/reports/drive-thru_time_study-order-accuracy**). Suppose that McDonald's begins a quality improvement effort to ensure that orders at the drive-through are filled correctly. The business problem is defined as determining whether the new process can increase the percentage of orders filled correctly. Data are collected from a sample of 400 orders using the new process. The results indicate that 374 orders were filled correctly. At the 0.01 level of significance, can you conclude that the new process has increased the proportion of orders filled correctly?

SOLUTION The null and alternative hypotheses are

$H_0: \pi \le 0.89$ (i.e., the population proportion of orders filled correctly using the new process is less than or equal to 0.89)

$H_1: \pi > 0.89$ (*i.e.*, the population proportion of orders filled correctly using the new process is greater than 0.89)

Since $X = 374$ and $n - X = 26$, both >5, using Equation (9.3) on page 328,

$$p = \frac{X}{n} = \frac{374}{400} = 0.935$$

$$Z_{STAT} = \frac{p - \pi}{\sqrt{\dfrac{\pi(1 - \pi)}{n}}} = \frac{0.935 - 0.89}{\sqrt{\dfrac{0.89(1 - 0.89)}{400}}} = \frac{0.045}{0.0156} = 2.88$$

The p-value for $Z_{STAT} > 2.88$ is 0.0020.

Using the critical value approach, you reject H_0 if $Z_{STAT} > 2.33$. Using the p-value approach, you reject H_0 if p-value <0.01. Because $Z_{STAT} = 2.88 > 2.33$ or the *p-value* $=0.0020 < 0.01$, you reject H_0. You have evidence that the new process has increased the proportion of correct orders above 0.89 or 89%.

Problems for Section 9.4

LEARNING THE BASICS

9.52 If, in a random sample of 400 items, 88 are defective, what is the sample proportion of defective items?

9.53 In Problem 9.52, if the null hypothesis is that 20% of the items in the population are defective, what is the value of Z_{STAT}?

9.54 In Problems 9.52 and 9.53, suppose you are testing the null hypothesis $H_0: \pi = 0.20$ against the two-tail alternative hypothesis $H_1: \pi \ne 0.20$ and you choose the level of significance $\alpha = 0.05$. What is your statistical decision?

APPLYING THE CONCEPTS

9.55 The U.S. Department of Education reports that 40% of full-time college students are employed while attending college. (Data extracted from National Center for Education Statistics, *The Condition of Education 2012*, **nces.ed.gov/pubs2012/2012045.pdf**.) A recent survey of 60 full-time students at a university found that 25 were employed.

a. Use the five-step p-value approach to hypothesis testing and a 0.05 level of significance to determine whether the proportion of full-time students at the university is different from the national norm of 0.40.

b. Assume that the study found that 32 of the 60 full-time students were employed and repeat (a). Are the conclusions the same?

9.56 The worldwide market share for the Mozilla Firefox web browser was 18.35% in a recent month. (Data extracted from **bit.ly/NXxo1v**.) Suppose that you decide to select a sample of 100 students at your university and you find that 24 use the Mozilla Firefox web browser.

a. Use the five-step p-value approach to try to determine whether there is evidence that the market share for the Mozilla Firefox web browser at your university is greater than the worldwide market share of 18.35%. (Use the 0.05 level of significance.)

b. Suppose that the sample size is $n = 400$, and you find that 24% of the sample of students at your university (96 out of 400) use the Mozilla Firefox web browser. Use the five-step p-value approach to try to determine whether there is evidence that the market share for the Mozilla Firefox web browser at your university is greater than the worldwide market share of 18.35%. (Use the 0.05 level of significance.)

c. Discuss the effect that sample size has on hypothesis testing.

d. What do you think are your chances of rejecting any null hypothesis concerning a population proportion if a sample size of $n = 20$ is used?

9.57 One of the issues facing organizations is increasing diversity throughout an organization. One of the ways to evaluate an organization's success at increasing diversity is to compare the percentage of employees in the organization in a particular position with a specific background to the percentage in a particular position with that specific background in the general workforce. Recently, a large academic medical center determined that 9 of 17 employees in a particular position were female, whereas 55% of the employees for this position in the general workforce were female. At the 0.05 level of significance, is there evidence that the proportion of females in this position at this medical center is different from what would be expected in the general workforce?

SELF Test **9.58** Of 801 surveyed active LinkedIn members, 328 reported that they are planning to spend at least $1,000 on consumer electronics in the coming year. (Data extracted from **bit.ly/RITfFU**.) At the 0.05 level of significance, is there evidence that the proportion of all LinkedIn members who plan to spend at least $1,000 on consumer electronics in the coming year is different from 35%?

9.59 A cellphone provider has the business objective of wanting to estimate the proportion of subscribers who would upgrade to a new cellphone with improved features if it were made available at a substantially reduced cost. Data are collected from a random sample of 500 subscribers. The results indicate that 135 of the subscribers would upgrade to a new cellphone at a reduced cost.

a. At the 0.05 level of significance, is there evidence that more than 20% of the customers would upgrade to a new cellphone at a reduced cost?

b. How would the manager in charge of promotional programs concerning residential customers use the results in (a)?

9.60 Actuation Consulting and Enterprise Agility recently conducted a global survey of product teams with the goal of better understanding the dynamics of product team performance and uncovering the practices that make these teams successful. One question posed was "In which of the following ways does your organization support aligning members of a core product team?" Global respondents were offered five choices. (Data extracted from **www.actuationconsultingllc.com/blog/?p=285**.) The most common response (31%) was "shared organizational goals and objectives linking the team." Suppose another study is conducted to check the validity of this result, with the goal of proving that the percentage is less than 31%.

a. State the null and research hypotheses.

b. A sample of 100 organizations is selected, and results indicate that 28 organizations respond that "shared organizational goals and objectives linking the team" is the supported driver of alignment. Use either the six-step critical value hypothesis-testing approach or the five-step p-value approach to determine at the 0.05 level of significance whether there is evidence that the percentage is less than 31%.

9.5 Potential Hypothesis-Testing Pitfalls and Ethical Issues

To this point, you have studied the fundamental concepts of hypothesis testing. You have used hypothesis testing to analyze differences between sample statistics and hypothesized population parameters in order to make business decisions concerning the underlying population characteristics. You have also learned how to evaluate the risks involved in making these decisions.

When planning to carry out a hypothesis test based on a survey, research study, or designed experiment, you must ask several questions to ensure that you use proper methodology. You need to raise and answer questions such as the following in the planning stage:

- What is the goal of the survey, study, or experiment? How can you translate the goal into a null hypothesis and an alternative hypothesis?
- Is the hypothesis test a two-tail test or one-tail test?
- Can you select a random sample from the underlying population of interest?
- What types of data will you collect in the sample? Are the variables numerical or categorical?
- At what level of significance should you conduct the hypothesis test?
- Is the intended sample size large enough to achieve the desired power of the test for the level of significance chosen?
- What statistical test procedure should you use and why?
- What conclusions and interpretations can you reach from the results of the hypothesis test?

Failing to consider these questions early in the planning process can lead to biased or incomplete results. Proper planning can help ensure that the statistical study will provide objective information needed to make good business decisions.

Statistical Significance Versus Practical Significance

You need to make a distinction between the existence of a statistically significant result and its practical significance in a field of application. Sometimes, due to a very large sample size, you may get a result that is statistically significant but has little practical significance.

For example, suppose that prior to a national marketing campaign focusing on a series of expensive television commercials, you believe that the proportion of people who recognize your brand is 0.30. At the completion of the campaign, a survey of 20,000 people indicates that 6,168 recognized your brand. A one-tail test trying to prove that the proportion is now greater than 0.30 results in a p-value of 0.0047, and the correct statistical conclusion is that the proportion of consumers recognizing your brand name has now increased. Was the campaign successful? The result of the hypothesis test indicates a statistically significant increase in brand awareness, but is this increase practically important? The population proportion is now estimated at $6{,}168/20{,}000 = 0.3084 = 0.3084$ or 30.84%. This increase is less than 1% more than the hypothesized value of 30%. Did the large expenses associated with the marketing campaign produce a result with a meaningful increase in brand awareness? Because of the minimal real-world impact that an increase of less than 1% has on the overall marketing strategy and the huge expenses associated with the marketing campaign, you should conclude that the campaign was not successful. On the other hand, if the campaign increased brand awareness from 30% to 50%, you would be inclined to conclude that the campaign was successful.

Statistical *Insignificance* Versus Importance

In contrast to the issue of the practical significance of a statistically significant result is the situation in which an important result may not be statistically significant. In a recent case (see reference 1), the U.S. Supreme Court ruled that companies cannot rely solely on whether the result of a study is significant when determining what they communicate to investors. In some situations (see reference 5), the lack of a large enough sample size may result in a nonsignificant result when in fact an important difference does exist. A study that compared male and female entrepreneurship rates globally and within Massachusetts found a significant difference globally but not within Massachusetts, even though the entrepreneurship rates for females and for males in the two geographic areas were similar (8.8% for males in Massachusetts as compared to 8.4% globally; 5% for females in both geographic areas). The difference was due to the fact that the global sample size was 20 times larger than the Massachusetts sample size.

Reporting of Findings

In conducting research, you should document both good and bad results. You should not just report the results of hypothesis tests that show statistical significance but omit those for which there is insufficient evidence in the findings. In instances in which there is insufficient evidence to reject H_0, you must make it clear that this does not prove that the null hypothesis is true. What the result indicates is that with the sample size used, there is not enough information to *disprove* the null hypothesis.

Ethical Issues

You need to distinguish between poor research methodology and unethical behavior. Ethical considerations arise when the hypothesis-testing process is manipulated. Some of the areas where ethical issues can arise include the use of human subjects in experiments, the data collection method, the type of test (one-tail or two-tail test), the choice of the level of significance, the cleansing and discarding of data, and the failure to report pertinent findings.

9.6 Power of a Test (*online*)

The power of a test is affected by the level of significance, the sample size, and whether the test is one-tail or two-tail. Learn more about these concepts in a Chapter 9 eBook bonus section.

USING STATISTICS

Maja Schon / Shutterstock

Significant Testing at Oxford Cereals, Revisited

As the plant operations manager for Oxford Cereals, you were responsible for the cereal-filling process. It was your responsibility to adjust the process when the mean fill weight in the population of boxes deviated from the company specification of 368 grams. You chose to conduct a hypothesis test.

You determined that the null hypothesis should be that the population mean fill was 368 grams. If the mean weight of the sampled boxes was sufficiently above or below the expected 368-gram mean specified by Oxford Cereals, you would reject the null hypothesis in favor of the alternative hypothesis that the mean fill was different from 368 grams. If this happened, you would stop production and take whatever action was necessary to correct the problem. If the null hypothesis was not rejected, you would continue to believe in the status quo—that the process was working correctly—and therefore take no corrective action.

Before proceeding, you considered the risks involved with hypothesis tests. If you rejected a true null hypothesis, you would make a Type I error and conclude that the population mean fill was not 368 when it actually was 368 grams. This error would result in adjusting the filling process even though the process was working properly. If you did not reject a false null hypothesis, you would make a Type II error and conclude that the population mean fill was 368 grams when it actually was not 368 grams. Here, you would allow the process to continue without adjustment even though the process was not working properly.

After collecting a random sample of 25 cereal boxes, you used the six-step critical value approach to hypothesis testing. Because the test statistic fell into the nonrejection region, you did not reject the null hypothesis. You concluded that there was insufficient evidence to prove that the mean fill differed from 368 grams. No corrective action on the filling process was needed.

SUMMARY

This chapter presented the foundation of hypothesis testing. You learned how to perform tests on the population mean and on the population proportion. The chapter developed both the critical value approach and the *p*-value approach to hypothesis testing.

In deciding which test to use, you should ask the following question: Does the test involve a numerical variable or a categorical variable? If the test involves a numerical variable, you use the *t* test for the mean. If the test involves a categorical variable, you use the *Z* test for the proportion. Table 9.4 lists the hypothesis tests covered in the chapter.

TABLE 9.4

Summary of Topics in Chapter 9

	Type of Data	
Type of Analysis	**Numerical**	**Categorical**
Hypothesis test concerning a single parameter	*Z* test of hypothesis for the mean (Section 9.1) *t* test of hypothesis for the mean (Section 9.2)	*Z* test of hypothesis for the proportion (Section 9.4)

REFERENCES

1. Bialik, C. "Making a Stat Less Significant." *The Wall Street Journal*, April 2, 2011, A5.
2. Bradley, J. V. *Distribution-Free Statistical Tests*. Upper Saddle River, NJ: Prentice Hall, 1968.
3. Daniel, W. *Applied Nonparametric Statistics*, 2nd ed. Boston: Houghton Mifflin, 1990.
4. *Microsoft Excel 2010*. Redmond, WA: Microsoft Corp., 2007.
5. Seaman, J., and E. Allen. "Not Significant, But Important?" *Quality Progress*, August 2011, 57–59.

KEY EQUATIONS

Z Test for the Mean (σ Known)

$$Z_{STAT} = \frac{\overline{X} - \mu}{\dfrac{\sigma}{\sqrt{n}}} \quad (9.1)$$

t Test for the Mean (σ Unknown)

$$t_{STAT} = \frac{\overline{X} - \mu}{\dfrac{S}{\sqrt{n}}} \quad (9.2)$$

Z Test for the Proportion

$$Z_{STAT} = \frac{p - \pi}{\sqrt{\dfrac{\pi(1 - \pi)}{n}}} \quad (9.3)$$

Z Test for the Proportion in Terms of the Number of Events of Interest

$$Z_{STAT} = \frac{X - n\pi}{\sqrt{n\pi(1 - \pi)}} \quad (9.4)$$

KEY TERMS

CHECKING YOUR UNDERSTANDING

9.61 What is the difference between a null hypothesis, H_0, and an alternative hypothesis, H_1?

9.62 What is the difference between a Type I error and a Type II error?

9.63 What is meant by the power of a test?

9.64 What is the difference between a one-tail test and a two-tail test?

9.65 What is meant by a *p*-value?

9.66 How can a confidence interval estimate for the population mean provide conclusions for the corresponding two-tail hypothesis test for the population mean?

9.67 What is the six-step critical value approach to hypothesis testing?

9.68 What is the five-step *p*-value approach to hypothesis testing?

CHAPTER REVIEW PROBLEMS

9.69 In hypothesis testing, the common level of significance is $\alpha = 0.05$. Some might argue for a level of significance greater than 0.05. Suppose that web designers tested the proportion of potential web page visitors with a preference for a new web design over the existing web design. The null hypothesis was that the population proportion of web page visitors preferring the new design was 0.50, and the alternative hypothesis was that it was not equal to 0.50. The *p*-value for the test was 0.20.

a. State, in statistical terms, the null and alternative hypotheses for this example.

b. Explain the risks associated with Type I and Type II errors in this case.

c. What would be the consequences if you rejected the null hypothesis for a p-value of 0.20?
d. What might be an argument for raising the value of α?
e. What would you do in this situation?
f. What is your answer in (e) if the p-value equals 0.12? What if it equals 0.06?

9.70 Financial institutions utilize prediction models to predict bankruptcy. One such model is the Altman Z-score model, which uses multiple corporate income and balance sheet values to measure the financial health of a company. If the model predicts a low Z-score value, the firm is in financial stress and is predicted to go bankrupt within the next two years. If the model predicts a moderate or high Z-score value, the firm is financially healthy and is predicted to be a non-bankrupt firm (see **pages.stern.nyu.edu/~ealtman/Zscores.pdf**). This decision-making procedure can be expressed in the hypothesis-testing framework. The null hypothesis is that a firm is predicted to be a non-bankrupt firm. The alternative hypothesis is that the firm is predicted to be a bankrupt firm.
a. Explain the risks associated with committing a Type I error in this case.
b. Explain the risks associated with committing a Type II error in this case.
c. Which type of error do you think executives want to avoid? Explain.
d. How would changes in the model affect the probabilities of committing Type I and Type II errors?

9.71 The Pew Research Center conducted a survey of adults, aged 18 years and older, that included 1,954 cellphone owners. The survey found that 1,016 of adult cellphone owners use their phone while watching TV. (Data extracted from "The Rise of the Connected Viewer," *Pew Internet & American Life Project Report*, July 17, 2012, **bit.ly/Q27WND**). The authors of the article imply that the survey proves that more than half of all adult cellphone users use their phone while watching TV.
a. Use the five-step p-value approach to hypothesis testing and a 0.05 level of significance to try to prove that more than half of all adult cellphone users use their phone while watching TV.
b. Based on your result in (a), is the claim implied by the authors valid?
c. Suppose the survey found that 1,000 of adult cellphone owners use their phone while watching TV. Repeat parts (a) and (b).
d. Compare the results of (b) and (c).

9.72 The owner of a gasoline station wants to study gasoline purchasing habits of motorists at his station. He selects a random sample of 60 motorists during a certain week, with the following results:
- The amount purchased was $\bar{X} = 11.3$ gallons, $S = 3.1$ gallons.
- Eleven motorists purchased premium-grade gasoline.

a. At the 0.05 level of significance, is there evidence that the population mean purchase was different from 10 gallons?
b. Determine the p-value in (a).
c. At the 0.05 level of significance, is there evidence that less than 20% of all the motorists at the station purchased premium-grade gasoline?
d. What is your answer to (a) if the sample mean equals 10.3 gallons?
e. What is your answer to (c) if 7 motorists purchased premium-grade gasoline?

9.73 An auditor for a government agency was assigned the task of evaluating reimbursement for office visits to physicians paid by Medicare. The audit was conducted on a sample of 75 of the reimbursements, with the following results:
- In 12 of the office visits, there was an incorrect amount of reimbursement.
- The amount of reimbursement was $\bar{X} = \$93.70$, $S = \$34.55$.

a. At the 0.05 level of significance, is there evidence that the population mean reimbursement was less than $100?
b. At the 0.05 level of significance, is there evidence that the proportion of incorrect reimbursements in the population was greater than 0.10?
c. Discuss the underlying assumptions of the test used in (a).
d. What is your answer to (a) if the sample mean equals $90?
e. What is your answer to (b) if 15 office visits had incorrect reimbursements?

9.74 A bank branch located in a commercial district of a city has the business objective of improving the process for serving customers during the noon-to-1:00 P.M. lunch period. The waiting time (defined as the time the customer enters the line until he or she reaches the teller window) of a random sample of 15 customers is collected, and the results are organized and stored in **Bank1**. These data are:

4.21	5.55	3.02	5.13	4.77	2.34	3.54	3.20
4.50	6.10	0.38	5.12	6.46	6.19	3.79	

a. At the 0.05 level of significance, is there evidence that the population mean waiting time is less than 5 minutes?
b. What assumption about the population distribution is needed in order to conduct the t test in (a)?
c. Construct a boxplot or a normal probability plot to evaluate the assumption made in (b).
d. Do you think that the assumption needed in order to conduct the t test in (a) is valid? Explain.
e. As a customer walks into the branch office during the lunch hour, she asks the branch manager how long she can expect to wait. The branch manager replies, "Almost certainly not longer than 5 minutes." On the basis of the results of (a), evaluate this statement.

9.75 A manufacturing company produces electrical insulators. If the insulators break when in use, a short circuit is likely to occur. To test the strength of the insulators, destructive testing is carried out to determine how much force is required to break the insulators. Force is measured by observing the number of pounds of force applied to the insulator before it breaks. The following data (stored in **Force**) are from 30 insulators subjected to this testing:

1,870	1,728	1,656	1,610	1,634	1,784	1,522	1,696	1,592	1,662
1,866	1,764	1,734	1,662	1,734	1,774	1,550	1,756	1,762	1,866
1,820	1,744	1,788	1,688	1,810	1,752	1,680	1,810	1,652	1,736

a. At the 0.05 level of significance, is there evidence that the population mean force required to break the insulator is greater than 1,500 pounds?
b. What assumption about the population distribution is needed in order to conduct the t test in (a)?
c. Construct a histogram, boxplot, or normal probability plot to evaluate the assumption made in (b).
d. Do you think that the assumption needed in order to conduct the t test in (a) is valid? Explain.

9.76 An important quality characteristic used by the manufacturer of Boston and Vermont asphalt shingles is the amount of moisture the shingles contain when they are packaged. Customers may feel that they have purchased a product lacking in quality if they find moisture and wet shingles inside the packaging. In some cases, excessive moisture can cause the granules attached to the shingles for texture and coloring purposes to fall off the shingles, resulting in appearance problems. To monitor the amount of moisture present, the company conducts moisture tests. A shingle is weighed and then dried. The shingle is then reweighed, and, based on the amount of moisture taken out of the product, the pounds of moisture per 100 square feet are calculated. The company would like to show that the mean moisture content is less than 0.35 pound per 100 square feet. The file **Moisture** includes 36 measurements (in pounds per 100 square feet) for Boston shingles and 31 for Vermont shingles.
a. For the Boston shingles, is there evidence at the 0.05 level of significance that the population mean moisture content is less than 0.35 pound per 100 square feet?
b. Interpret the meaning of the p-value in (a).
c. For the Vermont shingles, is there evidence at the 0.05 level of significance that the population mean moisture content is less than 0.35 pound per 100 square feet?
d. Interpret the meaning of the p-value in (c).
e. What assumption about the population distribution is needed in order to conduct the t tests in (a) and (c)?
f. Construct histograms, boxplots, or normal probability plots to evaluate the assumption made in (a) and (c).
g. Do you think that the assumption needed in order to conduct the t tests in (a) and (c) is valid? Explain.

9.77 Studies conducted by the manufacturer of Boston and Vermont asphalt shingles have shown product weight to be a major factor in the customer's perception of quality. Moreover, the weight represents the amount of raw materials being used and is therefore very important to the company from a cost standpoint. The last stage of the assembly line packages the shingles before the packages are placed on wooden pallets. Once a pallet is full (a pallet for most brands holds 16 squares of shingles), it is weighed, and the measurement is recorded. The file **Pallet** contains the weight (in pounds) from a sample of 368 pallets of Boston shingles and 330 pallets of Vermont shingles.
a. For the Boston shingles, is there evidence at the 0.05 level of significance that the population mean weight is different from 3,150 pounds?
b. Interpret the meaning of the p-value in (a).
c. For the Vermont shingles, is there evidence at the 0.05 level of significance that the population mean weight is different from 3,700 pounds?
d. Interpret the meaning of the p-value in (c).
e. In (a) through (d), do you have to be concerned with the normality assumption? Explain.

9.78 The manufacturer of Boston and Vermont asphalt shingles provides its customers with a 20-year warranty on most of its products. To determine whether a shingle will last through the warranty period, accelerated-life testing is conducted at the manufacturing plant. Accelerated-life testing exposes the shingle to the stresses it would be subject to in a lifetime of normal use in a laboratory setting via an experiment that takes only a few minutes to conduct. In this test, a shingle is repeatedly scraped with a brush for a short period of time, and the shingle granules removed by the brushing are weighed (in grams). Shingles that experience low amounts of granule loss are expected to last longer in normal use than shingles that experience high amounts of granule loss. The file **Granule** contains a sample of 170 measurements made on the company's Boston shingles and 140 measurements made on Vermont shingles.
a. For the Boston shingles, is there evidence at the 0.05 level of significance that the population mean granule loss is different from 0.30 grams?
b. Interpret the meaning of the p-value in (a).
c. For the Vermont shingles, is there evidence at the 0.05 level of significance that the population mean granule loss is different from 0.30 grams?
d. Interpret the meaning of the p-value in (c).
e. In (a) through (d), do you have to be concerned with the normality assumption? Explain.

REPORT WRITING EXERCISE

9.79 Referring to the results of Problems 9.76 through 9.78 concerning Boston and Vermont shingles, write a report that evaluates the moisture level, weight, and granule loss of the two types of shingles.

CASES FOR CHAPTER 9

Managing Ashland MultiComm Services

Continuing its monitoring of the upload speed first described in the Chapter 6 Managing Ashland MultiComm Services case on page 244, the technical operations department wants to ensure that the mean target upload speed for all Internet service subscribers is at least 0.97 on a standard scale in which the target value is 1.0. Each day, upload speed was measured 50 times, with the following results (stored in AMS9).

0.854	1.023	1.005	1.030	1.219	0.977	1.044	0.778	1.122	1.114
1.091	1.086	1.141	0.931	0.723	0.934	1.060	1.047	0.800	0.889
1.012	0.695	0.869	0.734	1.131	0.993	0.762	0.814	1.108	0.805
1.223	1.024	0.884	0.799	0.870	0.898	0.621	0.818	1.113	1.286
1.052	0.678	1.162	0.808	1.012	0.859	0.951	1.112	1.003	0.972

1. Compute the sample statistics and determine whether there is evidence that the population mean upload speed is less than 0.97.
2. Write a memo to management that summarizes your conclusions.

Digital Case

Apply your knowledge about hypothesis testing in this Digital Case, which continues the cereal-fill-packaging dispute first discussed in the Digital Case from Chapter 7.

In response to the negative statements made by the Concerned Consumers About Cereal Cheaters (CCACC) in the Chapter 7 Digital Case, Oxford Cereals recently conducted an experiment concerning cereal packaging. The company claims that the results of the experiment refute the CCACC allegations that Oxford Cereals has been cheating consumers by packaging cereals at less than labeled weights.

Open **OxfordCurrentNews.pdf**, a portfolio of current news releases from Oxford Cereals. Review the relevant press releases and supporting documents. Then answer the following questions:

1. Are the results of the experiment valid? Why or why not? If you were conducting the experiment, is there anything you would change?
2. Do the results support the claim that Oxford Cereals is not cheating its customers?
3. Is the claim of the Oxford Cereals CEO that many cereal boxes contain *more* than 368 grams surprising? Is it true?
4. Could there ever be a circumstance in which the results of the Oxford Cereals experiment *and* the CCACC's results are both correct? Explain.

Sure Value Convenience Stores

You work in the corporate office for a nationwide convenience store franchise that operates nearly 10,000 stores. The per-store daily customer count (i.e., the mean number of customers in a store in one day) has been steady, at 900, for some time. To increase the customer count, the chain is considering cutting prices for coffee beverages. The small size will now be $0.59 instead of $0.99, and the medium size will be $0.69 instead of $1.19. Even with this reduction in price, the chain will have a 40% gross margin on coffee. To test the new initiative, the chain has reduced coffee prices in a sample of 34 stores, where customer counts have been running almost exactly at the national average of 900. After four weeks, the sample stores stabilize at a mean customer count of 974 and a standard deviation of 96. This increase seems like a substantial amount to you, but it also seems like a pretty small sample. Is there statistical evidence that reducing coffee prices is a good strategy for increasing the mean customer count? Be prepared to explain your conclusion.

CHAPTER 9 EXCEL GUIDE

EG9.1 FUNDAMENTALS of HYPOTHESIS-TESTING METHODOLOGY

Key Technique Use the **NORM.S.INV** function to compute the lower and upper critical values and use **NORM.S.DIST** (***absolute value of the Z test statistic*, True**) as part of a formula to compute the p-value. Use an **IF** function (see Appendix Section F.4) to determine whether to display a rejection or nonrejection message.

Example Perform the two-tail Z test for the mean for the cereal-filling example that is shown in Figure 9.5 on page 314.

PHStat Use **Z Test for the Mean, sigma known.**
For the example, select **PHStat → One-Sample Tests → Z Test for the Mean, sigma known**. In the procedure's dialog box (shown below):

1. Enter **368** as the **Null Hypothesis**.
2. Enter **0.05** as the **Level of Significance**.
3. Enter **15** as the **Population Standard Deviation**.
4. Click **Sample Statistics Known** and enter **25** as the **Sample Size** and **372.5** as the **Sample Mean**.
5. Click **Two-Tail Test**.
6. Enter a **Title** and click **OK**.

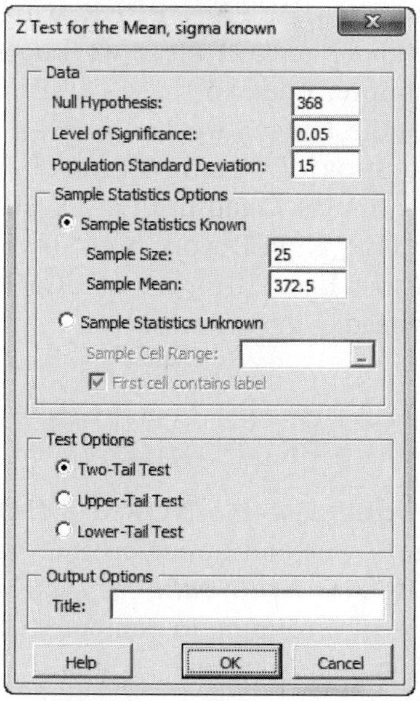

For problems that use unsummarized data, click **Sample Statistics Unknown** in step 4 and enter the cell range of the unsummarized data as the **Sample Cell Range**.

In-Depth Excel Use the **COMPUTE worksheet** of the **Z Mean workbook** as a template.
The worksheet already contains the data for the example. For other problems, change the null hypothesis, level of significance, population standard deviation, sample size, and sample mean values in cells B4 through B8 as necessary.

Read the SHORT TAKES for Chapter 9 for an explanation of the formulas found in the COMPUTE worksheet (shown in the **COMPUTE_ALL_FORMULAS worksheet**). If you use an Excel version older than Excel 2010, use the COMPUTE_OLDER worksheet instead of the COMPUTE worksheet.

EG9.2 t TEST of HYPOTHESIS for the MEAN (σ UNKNOWN)

Key Technique Use the **T.INV.2T**(***level of significance*, *degrees of freedom***) function to compute the lower and upper critical values and use **T.DIST.2T**(***absolute value of the t test statistic*, *degrees of freedom***) to compute the p-value. Use an **IF** function (see Appendix Section F.4) to determine whether to display a rejection or nonrejection message.

Example Perform the two-tail t test for the mean for the sales invoices example that is shown in Figure 9.7 on page 320.

PHStat Use ***t* Test for the Mean, sigma unknown.**
For the example, select **PHStat → One-Sample Tests → t Test for the Mean, sigma unknown**. In the procedure's dialog box (shown at top on page 340):

1. Enter **120** as the **Null Hypothesis**.
2. Enter **0.05** as the **Level of Significance**.
3. Click **Sample Statistics Known** and enter **12** as the **Sample Size**, **112.85** as the **Sample Mean**, and **20.8** as the **Sample Standard Deviation**.
4. Click **Two-Tail Test**.
5. Enter a **Title** and click **OK**.

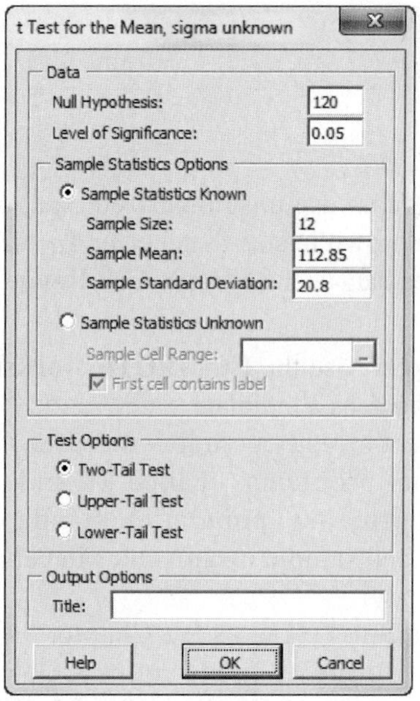

For problems that use unsummarized data, click **Sample Statistics Unknown** in step 3 and enter the cell range of the unsummarized data as the **Sample Cell Range**.

In-Depth Excel Use the **COMPUTE worksheet** of the **T mean workbook**, as a template.
The worksheet already contains the data for the example. For other problems, change the values in cells B4 through B8 as necessary.

Read the Short Takes for Chapter 9 for an explanation of the formulas found in the COMPUTE worksheet (shown in the **COMPUTE_ALL_FORMULAS worksheet**). If you use an Excel version older than Excel 2010, use the COMPUTE_OLDER worksheet instead of the COMPUTE worksheet.

EG9.3 ONE-TAIL TESTS

Key Technique Use the functions discussed in Section EG9.1 and EG9.2 to perform one-tail tests. For the *t* test of the mean, use **T.DIST.RT(*absolute value of the t test statistic*, *degrees of freedom*)** to help compute *p*-values. (See Appendix Section F.4.)

Example Perform the lower-tail *t* test for the mean for the drive-through time study example that is shown in Figure 9.11 on page 326.

PHStat Click either **Lower-Tail Test** or **Upper-Tail Test** in the procedure dialog boxes discussed in Sections EG9.1 and EG9.2 to perform a one-tail test.

For the example, select **PHStat → One-Sample Tests → t Test for the Mean, sigma unknown**. In the procedure's dialog box (shown below):

1. Enter **184.2** as the **Null Hypothesis**.
2. Enter **0.05** as the **Level of Significance**.
3. Click **Sample Statistics Known** and enter **25** as the **Sample Size**, **170.8** as the **Sample Mean**, and **21.3** as the **Sample Standard Deviation**.
4. Click **Lower-Tail Test**.
5. Enter a **Title** and click **OK**.

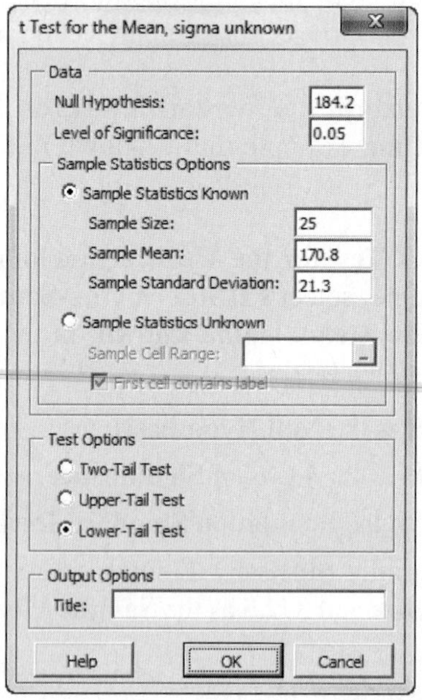

In-Depth Excel Use the **COMPUTE_LOWER worksheet** or the **COMPUTE_UPPER worksheet** of the **Z Mean workbook** or the **T mean workbook** as templates. For the example, open to the **COMPUTE_LOWER worksheet** of the **T mean workbook**.

Read the Short Takes for Chapter 9 for an explanation of the formulas found in the COMPUTE_LOWER and COMPUTER_UPPER worksheets. If you use an Excel version older than Excel 2010, use the COMPUTE_OLDER worksheet instead of those worksheets.

EG9.4 Z TEST of HYPOTHESIS for the PROPORTION

Key Technique Use the **NORM.S.INV** function to compute the lower and upper critical values and use **NORM.S.DIST(*absolute value of the Z test statistic*), True)** as part of a formula to compute the *p*-value. Use an **IF** function (see Appendix Section F.4) to determine whether to display a rejection or nonrejection message.

Example Perform the two-tail *Z* test for the proportion for the vacation Internet access example that is shown in Figure 9.14 on page 330.

PHStat Use **Z Test for the Proportion.**
For the example, select **PHStat → One-Sample Tests → Z Test for the Proportion**. In the procedure's dialog box (shown below):

1. Enter **0.75** as the **Null Hypothesis.**
2. Enter **0.05** as the **Level of Significance.**
3. Enter **1540** as the **Number of Items of Interest.**
4. Enter **2000** as the **Sample Size.**
5. Click **Two-Tail Test.**
6. Enter a **Title** and click **OK.**

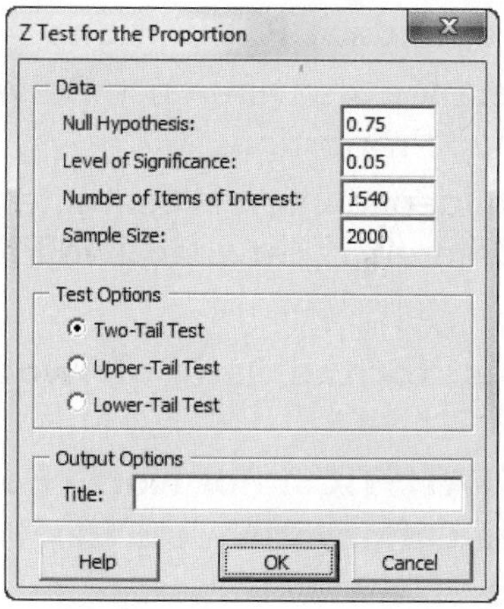

In-Depth Excel Use the **COMPUTE worksheet** of the **Z Proportion workbook** as a template.
The worksheet already contains the data for the example. For other problems, change the null hypothesis, level of significance, population standard deviation, sample size, and sample mean values in cells B4 through B7 as necessary.

Read the SHORT TAKES for Chapter 9 for an explanation of the formulas found in the COMPUTE worksheet (shown in the **COMPUTE_ALL_FORMULAS worksheet**). Use the **COMPUTE_LOWER** or **COMPUTE_UPPER worksheets** as templates for performing one-tail tests. If you use an Excel version older than Excel 2010, use the COMPUTE_OLDER worksheet as a template for both the two-tail and one-tail tests.

CHAPTER 10 Two-Sample Tests

Learning Objectives

In this chapter, you learn how to use hypothesis testing for comparing the difference between:

- The means of two independent populations
- The means of two related populations
- The proportions of two independent populations
- The variances of two independent populations

USING STATISTICS

Michael Bradley / Staff / Getty Images

For North Fork, Are There Different Means to the Ends?

To what extent does the location of products affect sales in a supermarket? As a regional sales manager for North Fork Beverages, you are negotiating with the management of FoodPlace Supermarkets for the location of displays of your new All-Natural Brain-Boost Cola. FoodPlace Supermarkets has offered you two different end-aisle display areas to feature your new cola: one near the produce department and the other at the front of the aisle that contains other beverage products. These ends of aisle, or end-caps, have different costs, and you would like to compare the effectiveness of the produce end-cap to the beverage end-cap.

To test the comparative effectiveness of the two end-caps, FoodPlace agrees to a pilot study. You will be able to select 20 stores from the supermarket chain that experience similar storewide sales volumes. You then randomly assign 10 of the 20 stores to sample 1 and 10 other stores to sample 2. In the sample 1 stores, you will place the new cola in the beverage end-cap, while in the sample 2 stores you will place the new cola in the produce end-cap. At the end of one week, the sales of the new cola will be recorded. How can you determine whether the sales of the new cola using beverage end-caps are the same as the sales of the new cola using produce end-caps? How can you decide if the variability in new cola sales from store to store is the same for the two types of displays? How could you use the answers to these questions to improve sales of your new All-Natural Brain-Boost Cola?

Travis Manley / Shutterstock

Hypothesis testing provides a *confirmatory* approach to data analysis. In Chapter 9, you learned a variety of commonly used hypothesis-testing procedures for a single sample of data selected from a single population. In this chapter, you learn how to extend hypothesis testing to **two-sample tests** that compare statistics from samples of data selected from two populations. One such test in the North Fork Beverages scenario would be "Are the mean weekly sales of the new cola when using the beverage end-cap location (one population) equal to the mean weekly sales of the new cola when using the produce end-cap location (a second population)?"

10.1 Comparing the Means of Two Independent Populations

In Sections 8.1 and 9.1, you learned that in almost all cases, you would not know the population standard deviation of the population under study. Likewise, when you take a random sample from each of two independent populations, you almost always do not know the standard deviation of either population. However, you also need to know whether you can assume that the variances in the two populations are equal because the method you use to compare the means of each population depends on whether you can assume that the variances of the two populations are equal.

Pooled-Variance t Test for the Difference Between Two Means

If you assume that the random samples are independently selected from two populations and that the populations are normally distributed and have equal variances, you can use a **pooled-variance *t* test** to determine whether there is a significant difference between the means of the two populations. If the populations are not normally distributed, the pooled-variance *t* test can still be used if the sample sizes are large enough (typically ≥ 30 for each sample)[1].

Using subscripts to distinguish between the population mean of the first population, μ_1, and the population mean of the second population, μ_2, the null hypothesis of no difference in the means of two independent populations can be stated as

$$H_0: \mu_1 = \mu_2 \quad \text{or} \quad \mu_1 - \mu_2 = 0$$

and the alternative hypothesis, that the means are not the same, can be stated as

$$H_1: \mu_1 \neq \mu_2 \quad \text{or} \quad \mu_1 - \mu_2 \neq 0$$

To test the null hypothesis, you use the pooled-variance *t* test statistic t_{STAT} shown in Equation (10.1). The pooled-variance *t* test gets its name from the fact that the test statistic pools, or combines, the two sample variances S_1^2 and S_2^2 to compute S_p^2, the best estimate of the variance common to both populations, under the assumption that the two population variances are equal.[2]

[1]Review the Section 7.2 discussion about the Central Limit Theorem on page 256 to understand more about "large enough" sample sizes.

[2]When the two sample sizes are equal (i.e., $n_1 = n_2$), the equation for the pooled variance can be simplified to

$$S_p^2 = \frac{S_1^2 + S_2^2}{2}$$

Student Tip
Whichever population is defined as population 1 in the null and alternative hypotheses must be defined as population 1 in Equation (10.1). Whichever population is defined as population 2 in the null and alternative hypotheses must be defined as population 2 in Equation (10.1).

POOLED-VARIANCE *t* TEST FOR THE DIFFERENCE BETWEEN TWO MEANS

$$t_{STAT} = \frac{(\bar{X}_1 - \bar{X}_2) - (\mu_1 - \mu_2)}{\sqrt{S_p^2\left(\frac{1}{n_1} + \frac{1}{n_2}\right)}} \tag{10.1}$$

where

$$S_p^2 = \frac{(n_1 - 1)S_1^2 + (n_2 - 1)S_2^2}{(n_1 - 1) + (n_2 - 1)}$$

and

S_p^2 = pooled variance
$\bar{X}_1$ = mean of the sample taken from population 1

S_1^2 = variance of the sample taken from population 1
n_1 = size of the sample taken from population 1
$\bar{X}_2$ = mean of the sample taken from population 2
S_2^2 = variance of the sample taken from population 2
n_2 = size of the sample taken from population 2

The t_{STAT} test statistic follows a t distribution with $n_1 + n_2 - 2$ degrees of freedom.

For a given level of significance, α, in a two-tail test, you reject the null hypothesis if the computed t_{STAT} test statistic is greater than the upper-tail critical value from the t distribution or if the computed t_{STAT} test statistic is less than the lower-tail critical value from the t distribution. Figure 10.1 displays the regions of rejection.

FIGURE 10.1
Regions of rejection and nonrejection for the pooled-variance t test for the difference between the means (two-tail test)

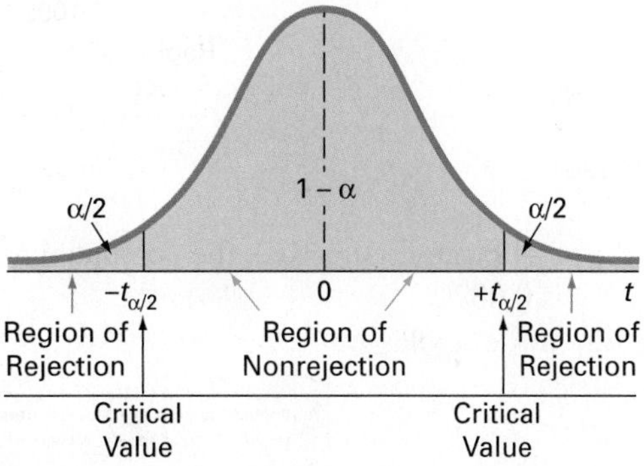

In a one-tail test in which the rejection region is in the lower tail, you reject the null hypothesis if the computed t_{STAT} test statistic is less than the lower-tail critical value from the t distribution. In a one-tail test in which the rejection region is in the upper tail, you reject the null hypothesis if the computed t_{STAT} test statistic is greater than the upper-tail critical value from the t distribution.

Student Tip
When *lower* or *less than* is used in an example, you have a lower-tail test. When *upper* or *more than* is used in an example, you have an upper-tail test. When different or the same as is used in an example, you have a two-tail test.

To demonstrate the pooled-variance t test, return to the North Fork Beverages scenario on page 343. Using the DCOVA problem-solving approach, you define the business objective as determining whether the mean weekly sales of the new cola are the same when using the beverage end-cap location and when using the produce end-cap location. There are two populations of interest. The first population is the set of all possible weekly sales of the new cola if all the FoodPlace Supermarkets used the beverage end-cap location. The second population is the set of all possible weekly sales of the new cola if all the FoodPlace Supermarkets used the produce end-cap location. You collect the data from a sample of 10 FoodPlace Supermarkets that have been assigned a beverage end-cap location and another sample of 10 FoodPlace Supermarkets that have been assigned a produce end-cap location. You organize and store the results in Cola. Table 10.1 contains the new cola sales (in number of cases) for the two samples.

TABLE 10.1
Comparing New Cola Weekly Sales from Two Different End-Cap Locations (in number of cases)

Display Location									
Beverage End-Cap					Produce End-Cap				
22	34	52	62	30	52	71	76	54	67
40	64	84	56	59	83	66	90	77	84

The null and alternative hypotheses are

$$H_0: \mu_1 = \mu_2 \quad \text{or} \quad \mu_1 - \mu_2 = 0$$
$$H_1: \mu_1 \neq \mu_2 \quad \text{or} \quad \mu_1 - \mu_2 \neq 0$$

Assuming that the samples are from normal populations having equal variances, you can use the pooled-variance t test. The t_{STAT} test statistic follows a t distribution with

$10 + 10 - 2 = 18$ degrees of freedom. Using an $\alpha = 0.05$ level of significance, you divide the rejection region into the two tails for this two-tail test (i.e., two equal parts of 0.025 each). Table E.3 shows that the critical values for this two-tail test are +2.1009 and −2.1009. As shown in Figure 10.2, the decision rule is

$$\text{Reject } H_0 \text{ if } t_{STAT} > +2.1009$$
$$\text{or if } t_{STAT} < -2.1009;$$
$$\text{otherwise, do not reject } H_0.$$

FIGURE 10.2
Two-tail test of hypothesis for the difference between the means at the 0.05 level of significance with 18 degrees of freedom

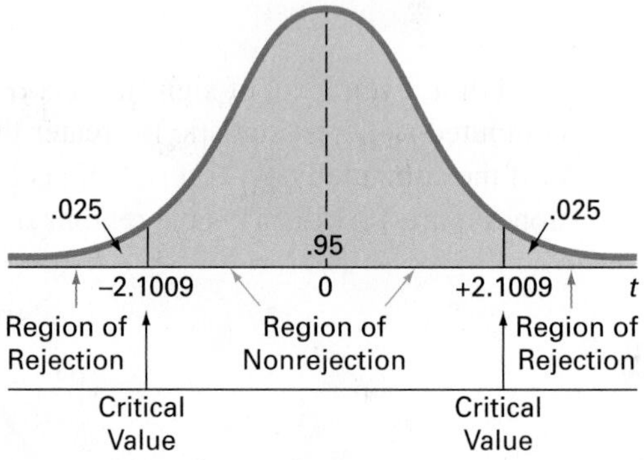

From Figure 10.3, the computed t_{STAT} test statistic for this test is −3.0446 and the p-value is 0.0070.

FIGURE 10.3
Pooled-variance t test worksheet for the two end-cap locations data

Figure 10.3 displays the **COMPUTE worksheet** *of the* **Pooled-Variance T workbook** *that the Section EG10.1 instructions use. (The Analysis ToolPak creates a different but equivalent worksheet.)*

	A	B	
1	Pooled-Variance t Test for Differences in Two Means		
2	(assumes equal population variances)		
3	Data		
4	Hypothesized Difference	0	
5	Level of Significance	0.05	
6	Population 1 Sample		
7	Sample Size	10	=COUNT(DATACOPY!$A:$A)
8	Sample Mean	50.3	=AVERAGE(DATACOPY!$A:$A)
9	Sample Standard Deviation	18.7264	=STDEV.S(DATACOPY!$A:$A)
10	Population 2 Sample		
11	Sample Size	10	=COUNT(DATACOPY!$B:$B)
12	Sample Mean	72	=AVERAGE(DATACOPY!$B:$B)
13	Sample Standard Deviation	12.5433	=STDEV.S(DATACOPY!$B:$B)
14			
15	Intermediate Calculations		
16	Population 1 Sample Degrees of Freedom	9	=B7 - 1
17	Population 2 Sample Degrees of Freedom	9	=B11 - 1
18	Total Degrees of Freedom	18	=B16 + B17
19	Pooled Variance	254.0056	=((B16 * B9^2) + (B17 * B13^2))/B18
20	Standard Error	7.1275	=SQRT(B19 * (1/B7 + 1/B11))
21	Difference in Sample Means	-21.7	=B8 - B12
22	*t* Test Statistic	-3.0446	=(B21 - B4)/B20
23			
24	Two-Tail Test		
25	Lower Critical Value	-2.1009	=-(T.INV.2T(B5, B18))
26	Upper Critical Value	2.1009	=T.INV.2T(B5, B18)
27	*p*-Value	0.0070	=T.DIST.2T(ABS(B22), B18)
28	Reject the null hypothesis		=IF(B27 < B5, "Reject the null hypothesis", "Do not reject the null hypothesis")

Using Equation (10.1) on page 344 and the descriptive statistics provided in Figure 10.3,

$$t_{STAT} = \frac{(\overline{X}_1 - \overline{X}_2) - (\mu_1 - \mu_2)}{\sqrt{S_p^2\left(\frac{1}{n_1} + \frac{1}{n_2}\right)}}$$

where

$$S_p^2 = \frac{(n_1 - 1)S_1^2 + (n_2 - 1)S_2^2}{(n_1 - 1) + (n_2 - 1)}$$

$$= \frac{9(18.7264)^2 + 9(12.5433)^2}{9 + 9} = 254.0056$$

Therefore,

$$t_{STAT} = \frac{(50.3 - 72.0) - 0.0}{\sqrt{254.0056\left(\frac{1}{10} + \frac{1}{10}\right)}} = \frac{-21.7}{\sqrt{50.801}} = -3.0446$$

You reject the null hypothesis because $t_{STAT} = -3.0446 < -2.1009$ and the p-value is 0.0070. In other words, the probability that $t_{STAT} > 3.0446$ or $t_{STAT} < -3.0446$ is equal to 0.0070. This p-value indicates that if the population means are equal, the probability of observing a difference this large or larger in the two sample means is only 0.0070. Because the p-value is less than $\alpha = 0.05$, there is sufficient evidence to reject the null hypothesis. You can conclude that the mean sales are different for the beverage end-cap and produce end-cap locations. Based on these results, the sales are lower for the beverage end-cap location (and, therefore, higher for the produce end-cap location).

In testing for the difference between the means, you assume that the populations are normally distributed, with equal variances. For situations in which the two populations have equal variances, the pooled-variance t test is **robust** (i.e., not sensitive) to moderate departures from the assumption of normality, provided that the sample sizes are large. In such situations, you can use the pooled-variance t test without serious effects on its power. However, if you cannot assume that both populations are normally distributed, you have two choices. You can use a nonparametric procedure, such as the Wilcoxon rank sum test (see Section 12.4), that does not depend on the assumption of normality for the two populations, or you can use a normalizing transformation (see reference 5) on each of the outcomes and then use the pooled-variance t test.

To check the assumption of normality in each of the two populations, you can construct a boxplot of the sales for the two display locations shown in Figure 10.4. For these two small samples, there appears to be only moderate departure from normality, so the assumption of normality needed for the t test is not seriously violated.

FIGURE 10.4

Boxplots for beverage and produce end-cap sales

Use the Section EG3.3 instructions to construct boxplots.

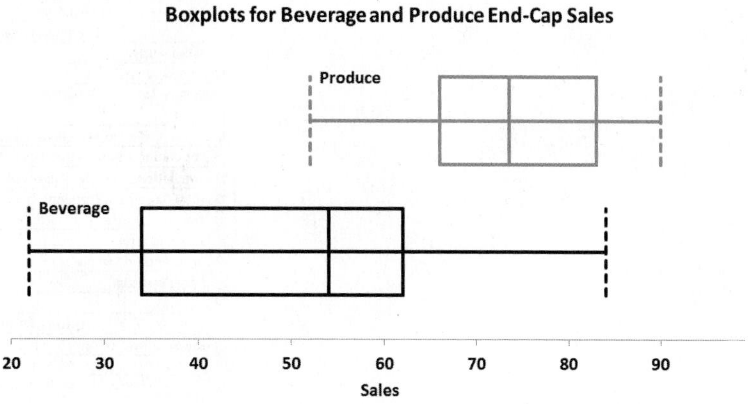

Example 10.1 provides another application of the pooled-variance t test.

EXAMPLE 10.1

Testing for the Difference in the Mean Delivery Times

You and some friends have decided to test the validity of an advertisement by a local pizza restaurant, which says it delivers to the dormitories faster than a local branch of a national chain. Both the local pizza restaurant and national chain are located across the street from your college campus. You define the variable of interest as the delivery time, in minutes, from the time the pizza is ordered to when it is delivered. You collect the data by ordering 10 pizzas from the local pizza restaurant and 10 pizzas from the national chain at different times. You organize and store the data in **PizzaTime**. Table 10.2 shows the delivery times.

TABLE 10.2

Delivery Times (in minutes) for a Local Pizza Restaurant and a National Pizza Chain

Local		Chain	
16.8	18.1	22.0	19.5
11.7	14.1	15.2	17.0
15.6	21.8	18.7	19.5
16.7	13.9	15.6	16.5
17.5	20.8	20.8	24.0

At the 0.05 level of significance, is there evidence that the mean delivery time for the local pizza restaurant is less than the mean delivery time for the national pizza chain?

SOLUTION Because you want to know whether the mean is *lower* for the local pizza restaurant than for the national pizza chain, you have a one-tail test with the following null and alternative hypotheses:

$H_0: \mu_1 \geq \mu_2$ (The mean delivery time for the local pizza restaurant is equal to or greater than the mean delivery time for the national pizza chain.)

$H_1: \mu_1 < \mu_2$ (The mean delivery time for the local pizza restaurant is less than the mean delivery time for the national pizza chain.)

Figure 10.5 displays the results for the pooled-variance *t* test for these data.

FIGURE 10.5

Pooled-variance *t* test worksheet for the pizza delivery time data

	A	B
1	Pooled-Variance t Test for Differences in Two Means	
2	(assumes equal population variances)	
3	Data	
4	Hypothesized Difference	0
5	Level of Significance	0.05
6	Population 1 Sample	
7	Sample Size	10
8	Sample Mean	16.7
9	Sample Standard Deviation	3.0955
10	Population 2 Sample	
11	Sample Size	10
12	Sample Mean	18.88
13	Sample Standard Deviation	2.8662
14		
15	Intermediate Calculations	
16	Population 1 Sample Degrees of Freedom	9
17	Population 2 Sample Degrees of Freedom	9
18	Total Degrees of Freedom	18
19	Pooled Variance	8.8986
20	Standard Error	1.3341
21	Difference in Sample Means	-2.18
22	*t* Test Statistic	-1.6341
23		
24	Lower-Tail Test	
25	Lower Critical Value	-1.7341
26	*p*-Value	0.0598
27	Do not reject the null hypothesis	

To illustrate the computations, using Equation (10.1) on page 344,

$$t_{STAT} = \frac{(\bar{X}_1 - \bar{X}_2) - (\mu_1 - \mu_2)}{\sqrt{S_p^2\left(\frac{1}{n_1} + \frac{1}{n_2}\right)}}$$

where

$$S_p^2 = \frac{(n_1 - 1)S_1^2 + (n_2 - 1)S_2^2}{(n_1 - 1) + (n_2 - 1)}$$

$$= \frac{9(3.0955)^2 + 9(2.8662)^2}{9 + 9} = 8.8986$$

Therefore,

$$t_{STAT} = \frac{(16.7 - 18.88) - 0.0}{\sqrt{8.8986\left(\frac{1}{10} + \frac{1}{10}\right)}} = \frac{-2.18}{\sqrt{1.7797}} = -1.6341$$

You do not reject the null hypothesis because $t_{STAT} = -1.6341 > -1.7341$. The p-value (as computed in Figure 10.5) is 0.0598. This p-value indicates that the probability that $t_{STAT} < -1.6341$ is equal to 0.0598. In other words, if the population means are equal, the probability that the sample mean delivery time for the local pizza restaurant is at least 2.18 minutes faster than the national chain is 0.0598. Because the p-value is greater than $\alpha = 0.05$, there is insufficient evidence to reject the null hypothesis. Based on these results, there is insufficient evidence for the local pizza restaurant to make the advertising claim that it has a faster delivery time.

Confidence Interval Estimate for the Difference Between Two Means

Instead of, or in addition to, testing for the difference between the means of two independent populations, you can use Equation (10.2) to develop a confidence interval estimate of the difference in the means.

CONFIDENCE INTERVAL ESTIMATE FOR THE DIFFERENCE BETWEEN THE MEANS OF TWO INDEPENDENT POPULATIONS

$$(\bar{X}_1 - \bar{X}_2) \pm t_{\alpha/2}\sqrt{S_p^2\left(\frac{1}{n_1} + \frac{1}{n_2}\right)}$$

or

$$(\bar{X}_1 - \bar{X}_2) - t_{\alpha/2}\sqrt{S_p^2\left(\frac{1}{n_1} + \frac{1}{n_2}\right)} \le \mu_1 - \mu_2 \le (\bar{X}_1 - \bar{X})_2 + t_{\alpha/2}\sqrt{S_p^2\left(\frac{1}{n_1} + \frac{1}{n_2}\right)} \quad \textbf{(10.2)}$$

where $t_{\alpha/2}$ is the critical value of the t distribution, with $n_1 + n_2 - 2$ degrees of freedom, for an area of $\alpha/2$ in the upper tail.

For the sample statistics pertaining to the two end-cap locations reported in Figure 10.3 on page 346, using 95% confidence, and Equation (10.2),

$$\bar{X}_1 = 50.3, n_1 = 10, \bar{X}_2 = 72.0, n_2 = 10, S_p^2 = 254.0056, \text{ and with } 10 + 10 - 2$$

$$= 18 \text{ degrees of freedom}, t_{0.025} = 2.1009$$

$$(50.3 - 72.0) \pm (2.1009)\sqrt{254.0056\left(\frac{1}{10} + \frac{1}{10}\right)}$$

$$-21.7 \pm (2.1009)(7.1275)$$

$$-21.7 \pm 14.97$$

$$-36.67 \le \mu_1 - \mu_2 \le -6.73$$

Therefore, you are 95% confident that the difference in mean sales between the beverage and produce end-cap locations is between −36.67 cases of cola and −6.73 cases of cola. In other words, the produce end-cap location sells, on average, 6.73 to 36.67 cases more than the beverage end-cap location. From a hypothesis-testing perspective, because the interval does not include zero, you reject the null hypothesis of no difference between the means of the two populations.

t Test for the Difference Between Two Means, Assuming Unequal Variances

If you cannot make the assumption that the two independent populations have equal variances, you cannot pool the two sample variances into the common estimate S_p^2 and therefore cannot use the pooled-variance t test. Instead, you use the **separate-variance t test** developed by Satterthwaite (see reference 4). Equation (10.3) defines the test statistic for the separate-variance t test.

SEPARATE-VARIANCE t TEST FOR THE DIFFERENCE BETWEEN TWO MEANS

$$t_{STAT} = \frac{(\overline{X}_1 - \overline{X}_2) - (\mu_1 - \mu_2)}{\sqrt{\dfrac{S_1^2}{n_1} + \dfrac{S_2^2}{n_2}}} \tag{10.3}$$

where

$\overline{X}_1$ = mean of the sample taken from population 1
S_1^2 = variance of the sample taken from population 1
n_1 = size of the sample taken from population 1
$\overline{X}_2$ = mean of the sample taken from population 2
S_2^2 = variance of the sample taken from population 2
n_2 = size of the sample taken from population 2

The separate-variance t test statistic approximately follows a t distribution with degrees of freedom V equal to the integer portion of the following computation.

COMPUTING DEGREES OF FREEDOM IN THE SEPARATE-VARIANCE t TEST

$$V = \frac{\left(\dfrac{S_1^2}{n_1} + \dfrac{S_2^2}{n_2}\right)^2}{\dfrac{\left(\dfrac{S_1^2}{n_1}\right)^2}{n_1 - 1} + \dfrac{\left(\dfrac{S_2^2}{n_2}\right)^2}{n_2 - 1}} \tag{10.4}$$

For a given level of significance α, you reject the null hypothesis if the computed t test statistic is greater than the upper-tail critical value $t_{\alpha/2}$ from the t distribution with V degrees of freedom or if the computed test statistic is less than the lower-tail critical value $-t_{\alpha/2}$ from the t distribution with V degrees of freedom. Thus, the decision rule is

Reject H_0 if $t > t_{\alpha/2}$
or if $t < -t_{\alpha/2}$;
otherwise, do not reject H_0.

Return to the North Fork Beverages scenario concerning the two end-cap display locations. Using Equation (10.4), the separate-variance t test statistic t_{STAT} is approximated by a t distribution with $V = 15$ degrees of freedom, the integer portion of the following computation:

$$V = \frac{\left(\dfrac{S_1^2}{n_1} + \dfrac{S_2^2}{n_2}\right)^2}{\dfrac{\left(\dfrac{S_1^2}{n_1}\right)^2}{n_1 - 1} + \dfrac{\left(\dfrac{S_2^2}{n_2}\right)^2}{n_2 - 1}}$$

$$= \frac{\left(\dfrac{350.6778}{10} + \dfrac{157.3333}{10}\right)^2}{\dfrac{\left(\dfrac{350.6778}{10}\right)^2}{9} + \dfrac{\left(\dfrac{157.3333}{10}\right)^2}{9}} = 15.72$$

Using $\alpha = 0.05$, the upper and lower critical values for this two-tail test found in Table E.3 are +2.1315 and −2.1315. As depicted in Figure 10.6, the decision rule is

Reject H_0 if $t_{STAT} > +2.1315$

or if $t_{STAT} < -2.1315$;

otherwise, do not reject H_0.

FIGURE 10.6

Two-tail test of hypothesis for the difference between the means at the 0.05 level of significance with 15 degrees of freedom

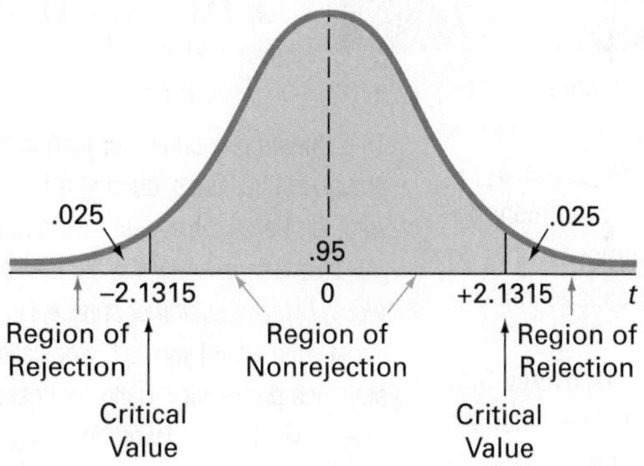

Using Equation (10.3) on page 350 and the descriptive statistics provided in Figure 10.3,

$$t_{STAT} = \frac{(\bar{X}_1 - \bar{X}_2) - (\mu_1 - \mu_2)}{\sqrt{\dfrac{S_1^2}{n_1} + \dfrac{S_2^2}{n_2}}}$$

$$= \frac{50.3 - 72}{\sqrt{\left(\dfrac{350.6778}{10} + \dfrac{157.3333}{10}\right)}} = \frac{-21.7}{\sqrt{50.801}} = -3.04$$

Using a 0.05 level of significance, you reject the null hypothesis because $t = -3.04 < -2.1315$.

Figure 10.7 displays the separate-variance t test results for the end-cap display location data.

From Figure 10.7, observe that the test statistic $t_{STAT} = -3.0446$ and the p-value is $0.0082 < 0.05$. Thus, the results for the separate-variance t test are almost exactly the same as those of the pooled-variance t test. The assumption of equality of population variances had no appreciable effect on the results. Sometimes, however, the results from the pooled-variance and separate-variance t tests conflict because the assumption of equal variances is violated. Therefore, it is important that you evaluate the assumptions and use those results as a guide in selecting a test procedure. In Section 10.4, the F test for the ratio of two variances is used to

FIGURE 10.7

Separate-variance *t* test worksheet (shown in two parts) for the sales data for the two end-caps

	A	B	
1	**Separate-Variances *t* Test**		
2	(assumes unequal population variances)		
3	**Data**		
4	Hypothesized Difference	0	
5	Level of Significance	0.05	
6	**Population 1 Sample**		
7	Sample Size	10	=COUNT(DATACOPY!$A:$A)
8	Sample Mean	50.3	=AVERAGE(DATACOPY!$A:$A)
9	Sample Standard Deviation	18.7264	=STDEV.S(DATACOPY!$A:$A)
10	**Population 2 Sample**		
11	Sample Size	10	=COUNT(DATACOPY!$B:$B)
12	Sample Mean	72	=AVERAGE(DATACOPY!$B:$B)
13	Sample Standard Deviation	12.5433	=STDEV.S(DATACOPY!$B:$B)
14			

	A	B	
15	Intermediate Calculations		
16	Pop. 1 Sample Variance	350.6778	=B9^2
17	Pop. 2 Sample Variance	157.3333	=B13^2
18	Pop. 1 Sample Var./Sample Size	35.0678	=B16/B7
19	Pop. 2 Sample Var./Sample Size	15.7333	=B17/B11
20	Numerator of Degrees of Freedom	2580.7529	=(B18 + B19)^2
21	Denominator of Degrees of Freedom	164.1430	=(B18^2)/(B7 - 1) + (B19^2)/(B11 - 1)
22	Total Degrees of Freedom	15.7226	=B20/B21
23	Degrees of Freedom	15	=INT(B22)
24	Separate Variance Denominator	7.1275	=SQRT(B18 + B19)
25	Difference in Sample Means	-21.7	=B8 - B12
26	*t* Test Statistic	-3.0446	=(B25 - B4)/B24
27			
28	**Two-Tail Test**		
29	Lower Critical Value	-2.1314	=-(T.INV.2T(B5, B23))
30	Upper Critical Value	2.1314	=T.INV.2T(B5, B23)
31	*p*-Value	0.0082	=T.DIST.2T(ABS(B26),B23) - B4
32	Reject the null hypothesis		=IF(B31 < B5,"Reject the null hypothesis", "Do not reject the null hypothesis")

Figure 10.7 displays the **COMPUTE worksheet** *of the* **Separate-Variance T workbook** *that the Section EG10.1 instructions use. (The Analysis ToolPak creates a different but equivalent worksheet.)*

determine whether there is evidence of a difference in the two population variances. The results of that test can help you decide which of the *t* tests—pooled-variance or separate-variance—is more appropriate.

THINK ABOUT THIS "This Call May Be Monitored ..."

When talking with a customer service representative by phone, you may have heard a "This call may be monitored" message. Typically, the message explains that the monitoring is for "quality assurance purposes," but do companies really monitor your calls to improve quality?

From one student, we've discovered that at least one large company really does monitor the quality of calls. This student was asked to develop an improved training program for a call center that was hiring people to answer phone calls customers make about outstanding loans. For feedback and evaluation, she planned to randomly select phone calls received by each new employee and rate the employee on 10 aspects of the call, including whether the employee maintained a pleasant tone with the customer.

Who You Gonna Call?

This student presented her plan to her boss for approval, but her boss, quoting a famous statistician, said, "In God we trust; all others must bring data." *Her boss wanted proof that her new training program would improve customer service.* Faced with this request, who would you call? She called her business statistics professor. "Hello, Professor, you'll never believe why I called. I work for a large company, and in the project I am currently working on, I have to put some of the statistics you taught us to work! Can you help?" Together they formulated this test:

- Randomly assign the 60 most recent hires to two training programs. Assign half to the preexisting training program and the other half to the new training program.
- At the end of the first month, compare the mean score for the 30 employees in the new training program against the mean score for the 30 employees in the preexisting training program.

She listened as her professor explained, "What you are trying to show is that the mean score from the new training program is higher than the mean score from the current program. You can make the null hypothesis that the means are equal and see if you can reject it in favor of the alternative that the mean score from the new program is higher."

"Or, as you used to say, 'if the *p*-value is low, H_0 must go!'—yes, I do remember!" she replied. Her professor chuckled and added, "If you can reject H_0 you will have the evidence to present to your boss." She thanked him for his help and got back to work, with the newfound confidence that she would be able to successfully apply the *t* test that compares the means of two independent populations.

Problems for Section 10.1

LEARNING THE BASICS

10.1 If you have samples of $n_1 = 12$ and $n_2 = 15$, in performing the pooled-variance *t* test, how many degrees of freedom do you have?

10.2 Assume that you have a sample of $n_1 = 8$, with the sample mean $\overline{X}_1 = 42$, and a sample standard deviation $S_1 = 4$, and you have an independent sample of $n_2 = 15$ from another population with a sample mean of $\overline{X}_2 = 34$ and a sample standard deviation $S_2 = 5$.

a. What is the value of the pooled-variance t_{STAT} test statistic for testing $H_0: \mu_1 = \mu_2$?

b. In finding the critical value, how many degrees of freedom are there?

c. Using the level of significance $\alpha = 0.01$, what is the critical value for a one-tail test of the hypothesis $H_0: \mu_1 \leq \mu_2$ against the alternative, $H_1: \mu_1 > \mu_2$?

d. What is your statistical decision?

10.3 What assumptions about the two populations are necessary in Problem 10.2?

10.4 Referring to Problem 10.2, construct a 95% confidence interval estimate of the population mean difference between μ_1 and μ_2.

10.5 Referring to Problem 10.2, if $n_1 = 5$ and $n_2 = 4$, how many degrees of freedom do you have?

10.6 Referring to Problem 10.2, if $n_1 = 5$ and $n_2 = 4$, at the 0.01 level of significance, is there evidence that $\mu_1 > \mu_2$?

APPLYING THE CONCEPTS

10.7 When people make estimates, they are influenced by anchors to their estimates. A study was conducted in which students were asked to estimate the number of calories in a cheeseburger. One group was asked to do this after thinking about a calorie-laden cheesecake. A second group was asked to do this after thinking about an organic fruit salad. The mean number of calories estimated in a cheeseburger was 780 for the group that thought about the cheesecake and 1,041 for the group that thought about the organic fruit salad. (Data extracted from "Drilling Down, Sizing Up a Cheeseburger's Caloric Heft," *The New York Times*, October 4, 2010, p. B2.) Suppose that the study was based on a sample of 20 people who thought about the cheesecake first and 20 people who thought about the organic fruit salad first, and the standard deviation of the number of calories in the cheeseburger was 128 for the people who thought about the cheesecake first and 140 for the people who thought about the organic fruit salad first.

a. State the null and alternative hypotheses if you want to determine whether the mean estimated number of calories in the cheeseburger is lower for the people who thought about the cheesecake first than for the people who thought about the organic fruit salad first.

b. In the context of this study, what is the meaning of the Type I error?

c. In the context of this study, what is the meaning of the Type II error?

d. At the 0.01 level of significance, is there evidence that the mean estimated number of calories in the cheeseburger is lower for the people who thought about the cheesecake first than for the people who thought about the organic fruit salad first?

10.8 A recent study ("Snack Ads Spur Children to Eat More," *The New York Times*, July 20, 2009, p. B3) found that children who watched a cartoon with food advertising ate, on average, 28.5 grams of Goldfish crackers as compared to an average of 19.7 grams of Goldfish crackers for children who watched a cartoon without food advertising. Although there were 118 children in the study, neither the sample size in each group nor the sample standard deviations were reported. Suppose that there were 59 children in each group, and the sample standard deviation for those children who watched the food ad was 8.6 grams and the sample standard deviation for those children who did not watch the food ad was 7.9 grams.

a. Assuming that the population variances are equal and $\alpha = 0.05$, is there evidence that the mean amount of Goldfish crackers eaten was significantly higher for the children who watched food ads?

b. Assuming that the population variances are equal, construct a 95% confidence interval estimate of the difference between the mean amount of Goldfish crackers eaten by the children who watched and did not watch the food ad.

c. Compare the results of (a) and (b) and discuss.

10.9 A problem with a phone line that prevents a customer from receiving or making calls is upsetting to both the customer and the telecommunications company. The file Phone contains samples of 20 problems reported to two different offices of a telecommunications company and the time to clear these problems (in minutes) from the customers' lines:

Central Office I Time to Clear Problems (minutes)

1.48 1.75 0.78 2.85 0.52 1.60 4.15 3.97 1.48 3.10
1.02 0.53 0.93 1.60 0.80 1.05 6.32 3.93 5.45 0.97

Central Office II Time to Clear Problems (minutes)

7.55 3.75 0.10 1.10 0.60 0.52 3.30 2.10 0.58 4.02
3.75 0.65 1.92 0.60 1.53 4.23 0.08 1.48 1.65 0.72

a. Assuming that the population variances from both offices are equal, is there evidence of a difference in the mean waiting time between the two offices? (Use $\alpha = 0.05$.)

b. Find the p-value in (a) and interpret its meaning.

c. What other assumption is necessary in (a)?

d. Assuming that the population variances from both offices are equal, construct and interpret a 95% confidence interval estimate of the difference between the population means in the two offices.

SELF Test **10.10** *Accounting Today* identified the top accounting firms in 10 geographic regions across the United States. Even though all 10 regions reported growth in 2011, the Southeast and Gulf Coast regions reported the highest combined growths, with 18% and 19%, respectively. A characteristic description of the accounting firms in the Southeast and Gulf Coast regions included the number of partners in the firm. The file AccountingPartners2 contains the number of partners. (Data extracted from **www.accountingtoday.com/gallery/Top-100-Accounting-Firms-Data-62569-1.html**).

a. At the 0.05 level of significance, is there evidence of a difference between Southeast region accounting firms and Gulf Coast accounting firms with respect to the mean number of partners?

b. Determine the p-value and interpret its meaning.
c. What assumptions do you have to make about the two populations in order to justify the use of the t test?

10.11 An important feature of digital cameras is battery life—the number of shots that can be taken before the battery needs to be recharged. The file Cameras contains the battery life of 11 subcompact cameras and 7 compact cameras. (Data extracted from "Cameras," *Consumer Reports*, July 2012, pp. 42–44.)

a. Assuming that the population variances from both types of digital cameras are equal, is there evidence of a difference in the mean battery life between the two types of digital cameras ($\alpha = 0.05$)?
b. Determine the p-value in (a) and interpret its meaning.
c. Assuming that the population variances from both types of digital cameras are equal, construct and interpret a 95% confidence interval estimate of the difference between the population mean battery life of the two types of digital cameras.

10.12 A bank with a branch located in a commercial district of a city has the business objective of developing an improved process for serving customers during the noon-to-1 P.M. lunch period. Management decides to first study the waiting time in the current process. The waiting time is defined as the number of minutes that elapses from when the customer enters the line until he or she reaches the teller window. Data are collected from a random sample of 15 customers and stored in Bank1. These data are:

4.21	5.55	3.02	5.13	4.77	2.34	3.54	3.20
4.50	6.10	0.38	5.12	6.46	6.19	3.79	

Suppose that another branch, located in a residential area, is also concerned with improving the process of serving customers in the noon-to-1 P.M. lunch period. Data are collected from a random sample of 15 customers and stored in Bank2. These data are:

9.66	5.90	8.02	5.79	8.73	3.82	8.01	8.35
10.49	6.68	5.64	4.08	6.17	9.91	5.47	

a. Assuming that the population variances from both banks are equal, is there evidence of a difference in the mean waiting time between the two branches? (Use $\alpha = 0.05$.)
b. Determine the p-value in (a) and interpret its meaning.
c. In addition to equal variances, what other assumption is necessary in (a)?
d. Construct and interpret a 95% confidence interval estimate of the difference between the population means in the two branches.

10.13 Repeat Problem 10.12 (a), assuming that the population variances in the two branches are not equal. Compare these results with those of Problem 10.12 (a).

10.14 In intaglio printing, a design or figure is carved beneath the surface of hard metal or stone. The business objective of an intaglio printing company is to determine whether there are differences in the mean surface hardness of steel plates, based on two different surface conditions—untreated and treated by lightly polishing with emery paper. An experiment is designed in which 40 steel plates are randomly assigned—20 plates are untreated and 20 plates are treated. The results of the experiment, stored in Intaglio, are as follows:

Untreated		Treated	
164.368	177.135	158.239	150.226
159.018	163.903	138.216	155.620
153.871	167.802	168.006	151.233
165.096	160.818	149.654	158.653
157.184	167.433	145.456	151.204
154.496	163.538	168.178	150.869
160.920	164.525	154.321	161.657
164.917	171.230	162.763	157.016
169.091	174.964	161.020	156.670
175.276	166.311	167.706	147.920

a. Assuming that the population variances from both conditions are equal, is there evidence of a difference in the mean surface hardness between untreated and treated steel plates? (Use $\alpha = 0.05$.)
b. Determine the p-value in (a) and interpret its meaning.
c. In addition to equal variances, what other assumption is necessary in (a)?
d. Construct and interpret a 95% confidence interval estimate of the difference between the population means from treated and untreated steel plates.

10.15 Repeat Problem 10.14 (a), assuming that the population variances from untreated and treated steel plates are not equal. Compare these results with those of Problem 10.14 (a).

10.16 An article appearing in *The Exponent*, an independent college newspaper published by the Purdue Student Publishing Foundation, reported that the average American college student spends one hour (60 minutes) on Facebook daily. (Data extracted from **bit.ly/NQRCJQ**.) But you wonder if there is a difference between males and females. You select a sample of 60 Facebook users (30 males and 30 females) at your college. The time spent on Facebook per day (in minutes) for these 60 users is stored in FacebookTime2.

a. Assuming that the variances in the population of times spent on Facebook per day are equal, is there evidence of a difference in the mean time spent on Facebook per day between males and females? (Use a 0.05 level of significance.)
b. In addition to equal variances, what other assumption is necessary in (a)?

10.17 Brand valuations are critical to CEOs, financial and marketing executives, security analysts, institutional investors, and others who depend on well-researched, reliable information needed for assessments, and comparisons in decision making. Millward Brown Optimor has developed the BrandZ Top 100 Most Valuable Global Brands for WPP, the world's largest communications services group. Unlike other studies, the BrandZ Top 100 Most Valuable Global Brands fuses consumer measures of brand equity with financial measures to place a financial value on brands. The file **BrandZTechFin** contains the brand values for two sectors in the BrandZ Top 100 Most Valuable Global Brands for 2011: the technology sector and the financial institutions sector. (Data extracted from **bit.ly/kNL8rx**.)

a. Assuming that the population variances are equal, is there evidence of a difference between the technology sector and the financial institutions sector with respect to mean brand value? (Use $\alpha = .05$.)

b. Repeat (a), assuming that the population variances are not equal.

c. Compare the results of (a) and (b).

10.2 Comparing the Means of Two Related Populations

The hypothesis-testing procedures presented in Section 10.1 enable you to examine differences between the means of two *independent* populations. In this section, you will learn about a procedure for analyzing the difference between the means of two populations when you collect sample data from populations that are related—that is, when results of the first population are *not* independent of the results of the second population.

There are two situations that involve related data. Either you take repeated measurements from the same set of items or individuals or you match items or individuals according to some characteristic. In either situation, you are interested in the *difference between the two related values* rather than the *individual values* themselves.

When you take **repeated measurements** on the same items or individuals, you assume that the same items or individuals will behave alike if treated alike. Your objective is to show that any differences between two measurements of the same items or individuals are due to different treatments that have been applied to the items or individuals. For example, when performing a taste-testing experiment comparing two beverages, you can use each person in the sample as his or her own control so that you can have *repeated measurements* on the same individual.

Another example of repeated measurements involves the pricing of the same goods from two different vendors. For example, have you ever wondered whether new textbook prices at a local college bookstore are different from the prices offered at a major online retailer? You could take two independent samples—that is, select two different sets of textbooks—and then use the hypothesis tests discussed in Section 10.1.

However, by random chance, the first sample may have many large-format hardcover textbooks and the second sample may have many small trade paperback books. This would imply that the first set of textbooks will always be more expensive than the second set of textbooks, regardless of where they are purchased. This observation means that using the Section 10.1 tests would not be a good choice. The better choice would be to use two related samples—that is, to determine the price of the *same* sample of textbooks at both the local bookstore and the online retailer.

The second situation that involves related data between populations is when you have **matched samples**. Here items or individuals are paired together according to some characteristic of interest. For example, in test marketing a product in two different advertising campaigns, a sample of test markets can be *matched* on the basis of the test market population size and/or demographic variables. By accounting for the differences in test market population size and/or demographic variables, you are better able to measure the effects of the two different advertising campaigns.

Regardless of whether you have matched samples or repeated measurements, the objective is to study the difference between two measurements by reducing the effect of the variability that is due to the items or individuals themselves. Table 10.3 shows the differences between the individual values for two related populations. To read this table, let $X_{11}, X_{12}, \ldots, X_{1n}$ represent the n values from a sample. And let $X_{21}, X_{22}, \ldots, X_{2n}$ represent either the corresponding n

matched values from a second sample or the corresponding n repeated measurements from the initial sample. Then $D_1, D_2, \ldots, D_n$ will represent the corresponding set of n difference *scores* such that

$$D_1 = X_{11} - X_{21}, D_2 = X_{12} - X_{22}, \ldots, \text{and } D_n = X_{1n} - X_{2n}.$$

To test for the mean difference between two related populations, you treat the difference scores, each D_i, as values from a single sample.

TABLE 10.3
Determining the Difference Between Two Related Samples

Value	Sample 1	Sample 2	Difference
1	X_{11}	X_{21}	$D_1 = X_{11} - X_{21}$
2	X_{12}	X_{22}	$D_2 = X_{12} - X_{22}$
⋮	⋮	⋮	⋮
i	X_{1i}	X_{2i}	$D_i = X_{1i} - X_{2i}$
⋮	⋮	⋮	⋮
n	X_{1n}	X_{2n}	$D_n = X_{1n} - X_{2n}$

Student Tip
Which sample you define as group 1 will determine whether you will be doing a lower-tail test or an upper-tail test if you are conducting a one-tail test.

Paired t Test

If you assume that the difference scores are randomly and independently selected from a population that is normally distributed, you can use the **paired *t* test for the mean difference** in related populations to determine whether there is a significant population mean difference. As with the one-sample *t* test developed in Section 9.2 [see Equation (9.2) on page 318], the paired *t* test statistic follows the *t* distribution with $n - 1$ degrees of freedom. Although the paired *t* test assumes that the population is normally distributed, you can use this test as long as the sample size is not very small and the population is not highly skewed.

To test the null hypothesis that there is no difference in the means of two related populations:

$$H_0: \mu_D = 0 \text{ (where } \mu_D = \mu_1 - \mu_2)$$

against the alternative that the means are not the same:

$$H_1: \mu_D \neq 0$$

you compute the t_{STAT} test statistic using Equation (10.5).

PAIRED *t* TEST FOR THE MEAN DIFFERENCE

$$t_{STAT} = \frac{\overline{D} - \mu_D}{\dfrac{S_D}{\sqrt{n}}} \quad \textbf{(10.5)}$$

where

$$\mu_D = \text{hypothesized mean difference}$$

$$\overline{D} = \frac{\sum_{i=1}^{n} D_i}{n}$$

$$S_D = \sqrt{\frac{\sum_{i=1}^{n}(D_i - \overline{D})^2}{n - 1}}$$

The t_{STAT} test statistic follows a *t* distribution with $n - 1$ degrees of freedom.

For a two-tail test with a given level of significance, α, you reject the null hypothesis if the computed t_{STAT} test statistic is greater than the upper-tail critical value $t_{\alpha/2}$ from the t distribution, or, if the computed t_{STAT} test statistic is less than the lower-tail critical value $-t_{\alpha/2}$, from the t distribution. The decision rule is

Reject H_0 if $t_{STAT} > t_{\alpha/2}$

or if $t_{STAT} < -t_{\alpha/2}$;

otherwise, do not reject H_0.

You can use the paired t test for the mean difference to investigate a question raised earlier in this section: Are new textbook prices at a local college bookstore different from the prices offered at a major online retailer?

In this repeated-measurements experiment, you use one set of textbooks. For each textbook, you determine the price at the local bookstore and the price at the online retailer. By determining the two prices for the same textbooks, you can reduce the variability in the prices compared with what would occur if you used two independent sets of textbooks. This approach focuses on the differences between the prices of the same textbooks offered by the two retailers.

You collect data by conducting an experiment from a sample of $n = 16$ textbooks used primarily in business school courses during the summer 2012 semester at a local college. You determine the college bookstore price and the online price (which includes shipping costs, if any). You organize and store the data in **BookPrices**. Table 10.4 shows the results.

TABLE 10.4

Prices of Textbooks at the College Bookstore and at the Online Retailer

Author	Title	Bookstore	Online
Bade	*Foundations of Micreconomics* 5/e	136.25	160.86
Baumol	*Macroeconomics* 12/e	223.25	195.80
Brigham	*Financial Management* 13/e	295.50	203.24
Foner	*Give Me Liberty!* Vol. 2 3/e	111.75	89.30
Grewal	*Marketing* 3/e	184.00	133.71
Landy	*Work in the Twenty First Century* 3/e	102.25	111.05
Mankiw	*Principles of Macroeconomics* 6/e	223.25	219.80
Meyer	*Matrix Analysis*	100.00	71.14
Mitchell	*Public Affairs in the Nation and New York*	55.95	102.99
Nickels	*Understanding Business* 10/e	227.75	157.46
Parsons	*Microsoft Excel 2010: Comprehensive*	150.00	102.69
Pindyck	*Microeconomics* 8/e	221.25	197.30
Robbins	*Organizational Behavior* 15/e	225.25	184.30
Ross	*Fundamentals of Corporate Finance* 9/e	251.25	200.01
Spiceland	*Intermediate Accounting* 6/e	230.50	234.58
Wilson	*American Government: The Essentials* 12/e	160.50	133.26

Your objective is to determine whether there is any difference between the mean textbook price at the college bookstore and at the online retailer. In other words, is there evidence that the mean price is different between the two textbook sellers? Thus, the null and alternative hypotheses are

H_0: $\mu_D = 0$ (There is no difference in the mean price between the college bookstore and the online retailer.)

H_1: $\mu_D \neq 0$ (There is a difference in the mean price between the college bookstore and the online retailer.)

Choosing the level of significance $\alpha = 0.05$ and assuming that the differences are normally distributed, you use the paired t test [Equation (10.5)]. For a sample of $n = 16$ textbooks, there are $n - 1 = 15$ degrees of freedom. Using Table E.3, the decision rule is

Reject H_0 if $t_{STAT} > 2.1314$

or if $t_{STAT} < -2.1314$;

otherwise, do not reject H_0.

For the $n = 16$ differences (see Table 10.4), the sample mean difference is

$$\bar{D} = \frac{\sum_{i=1}^{n} D_i}{n} = \frac{401.21}{16} = 25.0756$$

and

$$S_D = \sqrt{\frac{\sum_{i=1}^{n}(D_i - \bar{D})^2}{n-1}} = 35.3951$$

From Equation (10.5) on page 356,

$$t_{STAT} = \frac{\bar{D} - \mu_D}{\frac{S_D}{\sqrt{n}}} = \frac{25.0756 - 0}{\frac{35.3951}{\sqrt{16}}} = 2.8338$$

Because $t_{STAT} = 2.8338 > 2.1314$, you reject the null hypothesis, H_0 (see Figure 10.8). There is evidence of a difference in the mean price of textbooks purchased at the college bookstore and the online retailer. You can conclude that the mean price is higher at the college bookstore than at the online retailer.

FIGURE 10.8
Two-tail paired t test at the 0.05 level of significance with 15 degrees of freedom

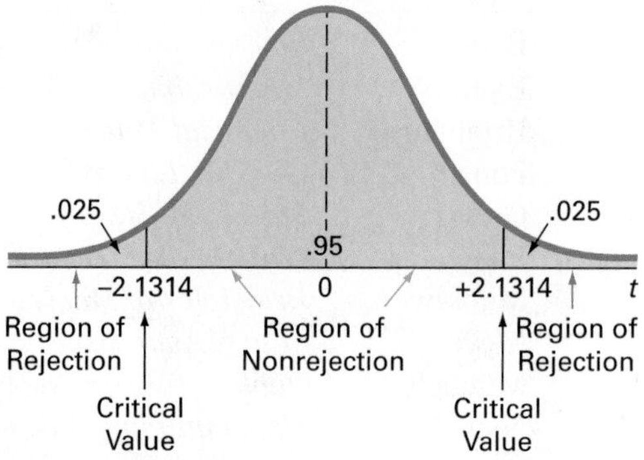

Figure 10.9 presents the results for this example, computing both the t test statistic and the p-value. Because the p-value $= 0.0126 < \alpha = 0.05$, you reject H_0. The p-value indicates that if the two sources for textbooks have the same population mean price, the probability that one source would have a sample mean \$25.08 more than the other is 0.0126. Because this probability is less than $\alpha = 0.05$, you conclude that there is evidence to reject the null hypothesis.

FIGURE 10.9
Paired t test worksheet for the textbook price data

Figure 10.9 displays the ***COMPUTE worksheet*** *of the* ***Paired T workbook*** *that the Section EG10.2 instructions use. (The Analysis ToolPak creates a different but equivalent worksheet.)*

	A	B	
1	**Paired *t* Test**		
2			
3	**Data**		
4	Hypothesized Mean Diff.	0	
5	Level of Significance	0.05	
6			
7	Intermediate Calculations		
8	Sample Size	16	=COUNT(PtCalcs!$A:$A)
9	DBar	25.0756	=AVERAGE(PtCalcs!$C:$C)
10	degrees of freedom	15	=B8 - 1
11	S_D	35.3951	=SQRT(DEVSQ(PtCalcs!C:C)/B10)
12	Standard Error	8.8488	=B11/SQRT(B8)
13	*t* Test Statistic	2.8338	=(B9 - B4)/B12
14			
15	**Two-Tailed Test**		
16	Lower Critical Value	-2.1314	=-T.INV.2T(B5, B10)
17	Upper Critical Value	2.1314	=T.INV.2T(B5, B10)
18	*p*-Value	0.0126	=T.DIST.2T(ABS(B13), B10)
19	Reject the null hypothesis		=IF(B18 < B5, "Reject the null hypothesis", "Do not reject the null hypothesis")

To evaluate the validity of the assumption of normality, you construct a boxplot of the differences, as shown in Figure 10.10.

FIGURE 10.10

Boxplot for the textbook price differences between the college bookstore and the online retailer

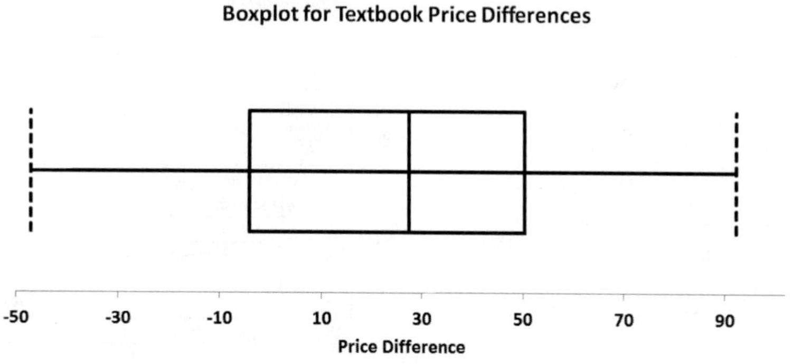

The Figure 10.10 boxplot shows approximate symmetry and looks similar to the boxplot for the normal distribution displayed in Figure 3.5 on page 129. Thus, the textbook price differences data do not greatly contradict the underlying assumption of normality. If a boxplot, histogram, or normal probability plot reveals that the assumption of underlying normality in the population is severely violated, then the t test may be inappropriate, especially if the sample size is small. If you believe that the t test is inappropriate, you can use either a *nonparametric* procedure that does not make the assumption of underlying normality (see references 1 and 2) or make a data transformation (see reference 5) and then recheck the assumptions to determine whether you should use the t test.

EXAMPLE 10.2

Paired t Test of Pizza Delivery Times

Recall from Example 10.1 on page 347 that a local pizza restaurant situated across the street from your college campus advertises that it delivers to the dormitories faster than the local branch of a national pizza chain. In order to determine whether this advertisement is valid, you and some friends decided to order 10 pizzas from the local pizza restaurant and 10 pizzas from the national chain. In fact, each time you ordered a pizza from the local pizza restaurant, at the same time, your friends ordered a pizza from the national pizza chain. Thus, you have matched samples. For each of the 10 times that pizzas were ordered, you have one measurement from the local pizza restaurant and one from the national chain. At the 0.05 level of significance, is the mean delivery time for the local pizza restaurant less than the mean delivery time for the national pizza chain?

SOLUTION Use the paired t test to analyze the Table 10.5 data (stored in **PizzaTime**). Figure 10.11 shows the paired t test results for the pizza delivery data.

TABLE 10.5

Delivery Times for Local Pizza Restaurant and National Pizza Chain

Time	Local	Chain	Difference
1	16.8	22.0	−5.2
2	11.7	15.2	−3.5
3	15.6	18.7	−3.1
4	16.7	15.6	1.1
5	17.5	20.8	−3.3
6	18.1	19.5	−1.4
7	14.1	17.0	−2.9
8	21.8	19.5	2.3
9	13.9	16.5	−2.6
10	20.8	24.0	−3.2
			−21.8

FIGURE 10.11

Paired *t* test worksheet for the pizza delivery data

Figure 10.11 displays the **COMPUTE_LOWER worksheet** *of the* **Paired T workbook** *that the Section EG10.2 instructions use. For this figure, the pizza delivery time data was pasted into the supporting PtCalcs worksheet (see the Section EG10.2 In-Depth Excel instructions).*

	A	B	C	D	E
1	**Paired *t* Test**				
2					
3	**Data**				
4	Hypothesized Mean Diff.	0			
5	Level of significance	0.05			
6					
7	Intermediate Calculations				
8	Sample Size	10			
9	DBar	-2.1800			
10	degrees of freedom	9			
11	S_D	2.2641			
12	Standard Error	0.7160			
13	*t* Test Statistic	-3.0448			
14					
15	**Lower-Tail Test**			One-Tail Calculations	
16	Lower Critical Value	-1.8331		T.DIST.RT	0.0070
17	*p*-Value	0.0070		1 - T.DIST.RT	0.9930
18	Reject the null hypothesis				

The null and alternative hypotheses are

H_0: $\mu_D \geq 0$ (Mean delivery time for the local pizza restaurant is greater than or equal to the mean delivery time for the national pizza chain.)

H_1: $\mu_D < 0$ (Mean delivery time for the local pizza restaurant is less than the mean delivery time for the national pizza chain.)

Choosing the level of significance $\alpha = 0.05$ and assuming that the differences are normally distributed, you use the paired *t* test [Equation (10.5) on page 356]. For a sample of $n = 10$ delivery times, there are $n - 1 = 9$ degrees of freedom. Using Table E.3, the decision rule is

$$\text{Reject } H_0 \text{ if } t_{STAT} < -t_{0.05} = -1.8331;$$

$$\text{otherwise, do not reject } H_0.$$

To illustrate the computations, for $n = 10$ differences (see Table 10.5), the sample mean difference is

$$\overline{D} = \frac{\sum_{i=1}^{n} D_i}{n} = \frac{-21.8}{10} = -2.18$$

and the sample standard deviation of the difference is

$$S_D = \sqrt{\frac{\sum_{i=1}^{n}(D_i - \overline{D})^2}{n-1}} = 2.2641$$

From Equation (10.5) on page 356,

$$t_{STAT} = \frac{\overline{D} - \mu_D}{\frac{S_D}{\sqrt{n}}} = \frac{-2.18 - 0}{\frac{2.2641}{\sqrt{10}}} = -3.0448$$

Because $t_{STAT} = -3.0448$ is less than -1.8331, you reject the null hypothesis, H_0 (the *p*-value is $0.0070 < 0.05$). There is evidence that the mean delivery time is lower for the local pizza restaurant than for the national pizza chain.

This conclusion differs from the conclusion you made on page 349 for Example 10.1 when you used the pooled-variance *t* test for these data. By pairing the delivery times, you are able to focus on the differences between the two pizza delivery services and not the variability created by ordering pizzas at different times of day. The paired *t* test is a more powerful statistical procedure that is better able to detect the difference between the two pizza delivery services because you are controlling for the time of day they were ordered.

Confidence Interval Estimate for the Mean Difference

Instead of or in addition to testing for the difference between the means of two related populations, you can use Equation (10.6) to construct a confidence interval estimate for the mean difference.

CONFIDENCE INTERVAL ESTIMATE FOR THE MEAN DIFFERENCE

$$\bar{D} \pm t_{\alpha/2}\frac{S_D}{\sqrt{n}}$$

or

$$\bar{D} - t_{\alpha/2}\frac{S_D}{\sqrt{n}} \le \mu_D \le \bar{D} + t_{\alpha/2}\frac{S_D}{\sqrt{n}} \qquad \textbf{(10.6)}$$

where $t_{\alpha/2}$ is the critical value of the t distribution, with $n - 1$ degrees of freedom, for an area of $\alpha/2$ in the upper tail.

Recall the example comparing textbook prices on page 357. Using Equation (10.6), $\bar{D} = 25.0756$, $S_D = 35.3951$, $n = 16$, and $t_{\alpha/2} = 2.1314$ (for 95% confidence and $n - 1 = 15$ degrees of freedom),

$$25.0756 \pm (2.1314)\frac{35.3951}{\sqrt{16}}$$

$$25.0756 \pm 18.8603$$

$$6.2153 \le \mu_D \le 43.9359$$

Thus, with 95% confidence, the mean difference in textbook prices between the college bookstore and the online retailer is between \$6.22 and \$43.94. Because the interval estimate does not contain zero, you can conclude that there is evidence of a difference in the population means. There is evidence of a difference in the mean prices of textbooks at the college bookstore and the online retailer. Since both the lower and upper limits of the confidence interval are above 0, you can conclude that the mean price is higher at the college bookstore than the online retailer.

Problems for Section 10.2

LEARNING THE BASICS

10.18 An experimental design for a paired t test has 20 pairs of identical twins. How many degrees of freedom are there in this t test?

10.19 Fifteen volunteers are recruited to participate in an experiment. A measurement is made (such as blood pressure) before each volunteer is asked to read a particularly upsetting passage from a book and after each volunteer reads the passage from the book. In the analysis of the data collected from this experiment, how many degrees of freedom are there in the test?

APPLYING THE CONCEPTS

SELF Test **10.20** Nine experts rated two brands of Colombian coffee in a taste-testing experiment. A rating on a 7-point scale (1 = extremely unpleasing, 7 = extremely pleasing) is given for each of four characteristics: taste, aroma, richness, and acidity. The following data stored in **Coffee** contain the ratings accumulated over all four characteristics:

	Brand	
Expert	**A**	**B**
C.C.	24	26
S.E.	27	27
E.G.	19	22
B.L.	24	27
C.M.	22	25
C.N.	26	27
G.N.	27	26
R.M.	25	27
P.V.	22	23

a. At the 0.05 level of significance, is there evidence of a difference in the mean ratings between the two brands?
b. What assumption is necessary about the population distribution in order to perform this test?
c. Determine the p-value in (a) and interpret its meaning.
d. Construct and interpret a 95% confidence interval estimate of the difference in the mean ratings between the two brands.

10.21 How does cellphone service compare between different cities? The data stored in **CellService** represent the rating of Verizon and AT&T in 22 different cities. (Data extracted from "Best Phones and Service," *Consumer Reports*, January 2012, p. 28, 37.)
a. At the 0.05 level of significance, is there evidence of a difference in the mean cellphone service rating between Verizon and AT&T?
b. What assumption is necessary about the population distribution in order to perform this test?
c. Use a graphical method to evaluate the validity of the assumption in (a).
d. Construct and interpret a 95% confidence interval estimate of the difference in the mean cellphone service rating between Verizon and AT&T.

10.22 Target versus Walmart: Who has the lowest prices? Given Walmart's slogan "Save Money—Live Better," you suspect that Walmart does. In order to test your suspicion, you identify 20 items (all brand-name items) currently on your household shopping list. You visit both Target and Walmart, price each item, and organize and store these data in **TargetWalmart**.
a. At the 0.05 level of significance, is there evidence that the mean price of items is higher at Target than at Walmart?
b. What assumption is necessary about the population distribution in order to perform this test?
c. Find the p-value in (a) and interpret its meaning.

10.23 What motivates employees? The Great Place to Work Institute evaluated nonfinancial factors both globally and in the United States. (Data extracted from L. Petrecca, "Tech Companies Top List of 'Great Workplaces,'" *USA Today*, October 31, 2011, p. 7B.) The results, which indicate the importance rating of each factor, are stored in **Motivation**.
a. At the 0.05 level of significance, is there evidence of a difference in the mean rating between global and U.S. employees?
b. What assumption is necessary about the population distribution in order to perform this test?
c. Use a graphical method to evaluate the validity of the assumption in (b).

10.24 Multiple myeloma, or blood plasma cancer, is characterized by increased blood vessel formulation (angiogenesis) in the bone marrow that is a predictive factor in survival. One treatment approach used for multiple myeloma is stem cell transplantation with the patient's own stem cells. The data stored in **Myeloma**, and shown below, represent the bone marrow microvessel density for patients who had a complete response to the stem cell transplant (as measured by blood and urine tests). The measurements were taken immediately prior to the stem cell transplant and at the time the complete response was determined.

Patient	Before	After
1	158	284
2	189	214
3	202	101
4	353	227
5	416	290
6	426	176
7	441	290

Data extracted from S. V. Rajkumar, R. Fonseca, T. E. Witzig, M. A. Gertz, and P. R. Greipp, "Bone Marrow Angiogenesis in Patients Achieving Complete Response After Stem Cell Transplantation for Multiple Myeloma," *Leukemia* 13 (1999): 469–472.

a. At the 0.05 level of significance, is there evidence that the mean bone marrow microvessel density is higher before the stem cell transplant than after the stem cell transplant?
b. Interpret the meaning of the p-value in (a).
c. Construct and interpret a 95% confidence interval estimate of the mean difference in bone marrow microvessel density before and after the stem cell transplant.
d. What assumption is necessary about the population distribution in order to perform the test in (a)?

10.25 Over the past year, the vice president for human resources at a large medical center has run a series of three-month workshops aimed at increasing worker motivation and performance. To check the effectiveness of the workshops, she selected a random sample of 35 employees from the personnel files. She collected the employee performance ratings recorded before and after workshop attendance and stored the paired ratings in **Perform**. Compute descriptive statistics and perform a paired t test. State your findings and conclusions in a report to the vice president for human resources.

10.26 The data in **Concrete1** represent the compressive strength, in thousands of pounds per square inch (psi), of 40 samples of concrete taken two and seven days after pouring. (Data extracted from O. Carrillo-Gamboa and R. F. Gunst, "Measurement-Error-Model Collinearities," *Technometrics*, 34(1992): 454–464.)
a. At the 0.01 level of significance, is there evidence that the mean strength is lower at two days than at seven days?
b. What assumption is necessary about the population distribution in order to perform this test?
c. Find the p-value in (a) and interpret its meaning.

10.3 Comparing the Proportions of Two Independent Populations

Often, you need to make comparisons and analyze differences between two population proportions. You can perform a test for the difference between two proportions selected from independent populations by using two different methods. This section presents a procedure whose test statistic, Z_{STAT}, is approximated by a standardized normal distribution. In Section 12.1, a procedure whose test statistic, χ^2_{STAT}, is approximated by a chi-square distribution is used. As you will see when you read that section, the results from these two tests are equivalent.

Z Test for the Difference Between Two Proportions

In evaluating differences between two population proportions, you can use a **Z test for the difference between two proportions**. The Z_{STAT} test statistic is based on the difference between two sample proportions $(p_1 - p_2)$. This test statistic, given in Equation (10.7), approximately follows a standardized normal distribution for large enough sample sizes.

Z TEST FOR THE DIFFERENCE BETWEEN TWO PROPORTIONS

$$Z_{STAT} = \frac{(p_1 - p_2) - (\pi_1 - \pi_2)}{\sqrt{\bar{p}(1 - \bar{p})\left(\frac{1}{n_1} + \frac{1}{n_2}\right)}} \quad \textbf{(10.7)}$$

with

$$\bar{p} = \frac{X_1 + X_2}{n_1 + n_2} \qquad p_1 = \frac{X_1}{n_1} \qquad p_2 = \frac{X_2}{n_2}$$

where

p_1 = proportion of items of interest in sample 1
X_1 = number of items of interest in sample 1
n_1 = sample size of sample 1
π_1 = proportion of items of interest in population 1
p_2 = proportion of items of interest in sample 2
X_2 = number of items of interest in sample 2
n_2 = sample size of sample 2
π_2 = proportion of items of interest in population 2
$\bar{p}$ = pooled estimate of the population proportion of items of interest

The Z_{STAT} test statistic approximately follows a standardized normal distribution.

Student Tip
Do not confuse this use of the Greek letter pi, π, to represent the population proportion with the mathematical constant that is the ratio of the circumference to a diameter of a circle—approximately 3.14159—which is also known by the same Greek letter.

Under the null hypothesis in the Z test for the difference between two proportions, you assume that the two population proportions are equal $(\pi_1 = \pi_2)$. Because the pooled estimate for the population proportion is based on the null hypothesis, you combine, or pool, the two sample proportions to compute $\bar{p}$, an overall estimate of the common population proportion. This estimate is equal to the number of items of interest in the two samples combined $(X_1 + X_2)$ divided by the total sample size from the two samples combined $(n_1 + n_2)$.

As shown in the following table, you can use this Z test for the difference between population proportions to determine whether there is a difference in the proportion of items of interest in the two populations (two-tail test) or whether one population has a higher proportion of items of interest than the other population (one-tail test):

Two-Tail Test	One-Tail Test	One-Tail Test
$H_0: \pi_1 = \pi_2$	$H_0: \pi_1 \geq \pi_2$	$H_0: \pi_1 \leq \pi_2$
$H_1: \pi_1 \neq \pi_2$	$H_1: \pi_1 < \pi_2$	$H_1: \pi_1 > \pi_2$

where

$$\pi_1 = \text{proportion of items of interest in population 1}$$

$$\pi_2 = \text{proportion of items of interest in population 2}$$

To test the null hypothesis that there is no difference between the proportions of two independent populations:

$$H_0: \pi_1 = \pi_2$$

against the alternative that the two population proportions are not the same:

$$H_1: \pi_1 \neq \pi_2$$

you use the Z_{STAT} test statistic, given by Equation (10.7). For a given level of significance, α, you reject the null hypothesis if the computed Z_{STAT} test statistic is greater than the upper-tail critical value from the standardized normal distribution or if the computed Z_{STAT} test statistic is less than the lower-tail critical value from the standardized normal distribution.

To illustrate the use of the Z test for the equality of two proportions, suppose that you are the manager of T.C. Resort Properties, a collection of five upscale resort hotels located on two tropical islands. On one of the islands, T.C. Resort Properties has two hotels, the Beachcomber and the Windsurfer. Using the DCOVA problem solving approach, you have defined the business objective as improving the return rate of guests at the Beachcomber and the Windsurfer hotels. On the survey completed by hotel guests upon or after their departure, one question asked is whether the guest is likely to return to the hotel. Responses to this and other questions were collected from 227 guests at the Beachcomber and 262 guests at the Windsurfer. The results for this question indicated that 163 of 227 guests at the Beachcomber responded yes, they were likely to return to the hotel and 154 of 262 guests at the Windsurfer responded yes, they were likely to return to the hotel. At the 0.05 level of significance, is there evidence of a significant difference in guest satisfaction (as measured by the likelihood to return to the hotel) between the two hotels?

The null and alternative hypotheses are

$$H_0: \pi_1 = \pi_2 \quad \text{or} \quad \pi_1 - \pi_2 = 0$$

$$H_1: \pi_1 \neq \pi_2 \quad \text{or} \quad \pi_1 - \pi_2 \neq 0$$

Using the 0.05 level of significance, the critical values are -1.96 and $+1.96$ (see Figure 10.12), and the decision rule is

$$\text{Reject } H_0 \text{ if } Z_{STAT} < -1.96$$
$$\text{or if } Z_{STAT} > +1.96;$$
$$\text{otherwise, do not reject } H_0.$$

FIGURE 10.12
Regions of rejection and nonrejection when testing a hypothesis for the difference between two proportions at the 0.05 level of significance

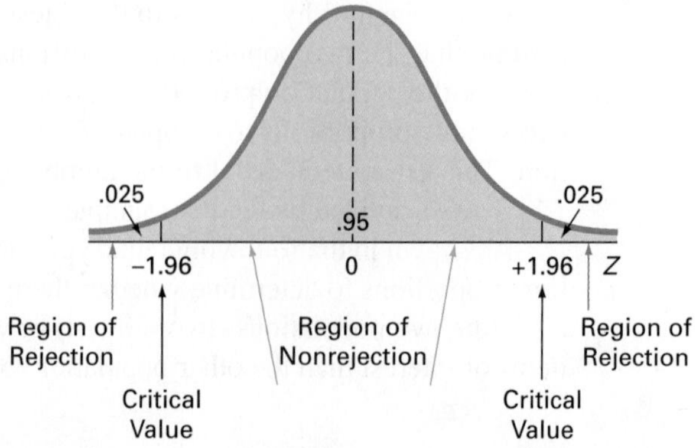

Using Equation (10.7) on page 363,

$$Z_{STAT} = \frac{(p_1 - p_2) - (\pi_1 - \pi_2)}{\sqrt{\bar{p}(1 - \bar{p})\left(\dfrac{1}{n_1} + \dfrac{1}{n_2}\right)}}$$

where

$$p_1 = \frac{X_1}{n_1} = \frac{163}{227} = 0.7181 \; p_2 = \frac{X_2}{n_2} = \frac{154}{262} = 0.5878$$

and

$$\bar{p} = \frac{X_1 + X_2}{n_1 + n_2} = \frac{163 + 154}{227 + 262} = \frac{317}{489} = 0.6483$$

so that

$$Z_{STAT} = \frac{(0.7181 - 0.5878) - (0)}{\sqrt{0.6483(1 - 0.6483)\left(\dfrac{1}{227} + \dfrac{1}{262}\right)}}$$

$$= \frac{0.1303}{\sqrt{(0.228)(0.0082)}}$$

$$= \frac{0.1303}{\sqrt{0.00187}}$$

$$= \frac{0.1303}{0.0432} = +3.0088$$

Using the 0.05 level of significance, you reject the null hypothesis because $Z_{STAT} = +3.0088 > +1.96$. The p-value is 0.0026 (computed using Table E.2 or from Figure 10.13) and indicates that if the null hypothesis is true, the probability that a Z_{STAT} test statistic is less than -3.0088 is 0.0013, and, similarly, the probability that a Z_{STAT} test statistic is greater than +3.0088 is 0.0013. Thus, for this two-tail test, the p-value is $0.0013 + 0.0013 = 0.0026$. Because $0.0026 < \alpha = 0.05$, you reject the null hypothesis. There is evidence to conclude that the two hotels are significantly different with respect to guest satisfaction; a greater proportion of guests are willing to return to the Beachcomber than to the Windsurfer.

FIGURE 10.13

Z test for the difference between two proportions worksheet for the hotel guest satisfaction problem

Figure 10.13 displays the **COMPUTE worksheet** *of the* **Z Two Proportions workbook** *that the Section EG10.3 instructions use.*

	A	B	
1	**Z Test for Differences in Two Proportions**		
2			
3	**Data**		
4	Hypothesized Difference	0	
5	Level of Significance	0.05	
6	**Group 1**		
7	Number of Successes	163	
8	Sample Size	227	
9	**Group 2**		
10	Number of Successes	154	
11	Sample Size	262	
12			
13	Intermediate Calculations		
14	Group 1 Proportion	0.7181	**=B7/B8**
15	Group 2 Proportion	0.5878	**=B10/B11**
16	Difference in Two Proportions	0.1303	**=B14 - B15**
17	Average Proportion	0.6483	**=(B7 + B10)/(B8 + B11)**
18	*Z* Test Statistic	3.0088	**=(B16 - B4)/SQRT(B17 * (1 - B17) * (1/B8 + 1/B11))**
19			
20	**Two-Tail Test**		
21	Lower Critical Value	-1.9600	**=NORM.S.INV(B5/2)**
22	Upper Critical Value	1.9600	**=NORM.S.INV(1 - B5/2)**
23	*p*-Value	0.0026	**=2 * (1 - NORM.S.DIST(ABS(B18), TRUE))**
24	Reject the null hypothesis		**=IF(B23 < B5, "Reject the null hypothesis",) "Do not reject the null hypothesis")**

EXAMPLE 10.3

Testing for the Difference Between Two Proportions

Are men less likely than women to shop for bargains? A survey reported that when going shopping, 24% of men (181 of 756 sampled) and 34% of women (275 of 809 sampled) go for bargains. (Data extracted from "Brands More Critical for Dads," *USA Today*, July 21, 2011, p. 1C.) At the 0.05 level of significance, is the proportion of men who shop for bargains less than the proportion of women who shop for bargains?

SOLUTION Because you want to know whether there is evidence that the proportion of men who shop for bargains is *less* than the proportion of women who shop for bargains, you have a one-tail test. The null and alternative hypotheses are

$H_0: \pi_1 \geq \pi_2$ (The proportion of men who shop for bargains is greater than or equal to the proportion of women who shop for bargains.)

$H_1: \pi_1 < \pi_2$ (The proportion of men who shop for bargains is less than the proportion of women who shop for bargains.)

Using the 0.05 level of significance, for the one-tail test in the lower tail, the critical value is +1.645. The decision rule is

$$\text{Reject } H_0 \text{ if } Z_{STAT} < -1.645;$$

$$\text{otherwise, do not reject } H_0.$$

Using Equation (10.7) on page 363,

$$Z_{STAT} = \frac{(p_1 - p_2) - (\pi_1 - \pi_2)}{\sqrt{\bar{p}(1 - \bar{p})\left(\frac{1}{n_1} + \frac{1}{n_2}\right)}}$$

where

$$p_1 = \frac{X_1}{n_1} = \frac{181}{756} = 0.2394 \quad p_2 = \frac{X_2}{n_2} = \frac{275}{809} = 0.3399$$

and

$$\bar{p} = \frac{X_1 + X_2}{n_1 + n_2} = \frac{181 + 275}{756 + 809} = \frac{456}{1565} = 0.2914$$

so that

$$Z_{STAT} = \frac{(0.2394 - 0.3399) - (0)}{\sqrt{0.2914(1 - 0.2914)\left(\frac{1}{756} + \frac{1}{809}\right)}}$$

$$= \frac{-0.1005}{\sqrt{(0.2065)(0.00256)}}$$

$$= \frac{-0.1005}{\sqrt{0.00053}}$$

$$= \frac{-0.1005}{0.0230} = -4.37$$

Using the 0.05 level of significance, you reject the null hypothesis because $Z_{STAT} = -4.37 < -1.645$. The *p*-value is approximately 0.0000. Therefore, if the null hypothesis is true, the probability that a Z_{STAT} test statistic is less than −4.37 is approximately 0.0000 (which is less than $\alpha = 0.05$). You conclude that there is evidence that the proportion of men who shop for bargains is less than the proportion of women who shop for bargains.

Confidence Interval Estimate for the Difference Between Two Proportions

Instead of or in addition to testing for the difference between the proportions of two independent populations, you can construct a confidence interval estimate for the difference between the two proportions using Equation (10.8).

CONFIDENCE INTERVAL ESTIMATE FOR THE DIFFERENCE BETWEEN TWO PROPORTIONS

$$(p_1 - p_2) \pm Z_{\alpha/2}\sqrt{\frac{p_1(1-p_1)}{n_1} + \frac{p_2(1-p_2)}{n_2}}$$

or

$$(p_1 - p_2) - Z_{\alpha/2}\sqrt{\frac{p_1(1-p_1)}{n_1} + \frac{p_2(1-p_2)}{n_2}} \le (\pi_1 - \pi_2)$$

$$\le (p_1 - p_2) + Z_{\alpha/2}\sqrt{\frac{p_1(1-p_1)}{n_1} + \frac{p_2(1-p_2)}{n_2}} \qquad \textbf{(10.8)}$$

To construct a 95% confidence interval estimate for the population difference between the proportion of guests who would return to the Beachcomber and who would return to the Windsurfer, you use the results on page 365 or from Figure 10.13 on page 365:

$$p_1 = \frac{X_1}{n_1} = \frac{163}{227} = 0.7181 \quad p_2 = \frac{X_2}{n_2} = \frac{154}{262} = 0.5878$$

Using Equation (10.8),

$$(0.7181 - 0.5878) \pm (1.96)\sqrt{\frac{0.7181(1 - 0.7181)}{227} + \frac{0.5878(1 - 0.5878)}{262}}$$

$$0.1303 \pm (1.96)(0.0426)$$

$$0.1303 \pm 0.0835$$

$$0.0468 \le (\pi_1 - \pi_2) \le 0.2138$$

Thus, you have 95% confidence that the difference between the population proportion of guests who would return to the Beachcomber and the Windsurfer is between 0.0468 and 0.2138. In percentages, the difference is between 4.68% and 21.38%. Guest satisfaction is higher at the Beachcomber than at the Windsurfer.

Problems for Section 10.3

LEARNING THE BASICS

10.27 Let $n_1 = 100, X_1 = 50, n_2 = 100$, and $X_2 = 30$.

a. At the 0.05 level of significance, is there evidence of a significant difference between the two population proportions?

b. Construct a 95% confidence interval estimate for the difference between the two population proportions.

10.28 Let $n_1 = 100, X_1 = 45, n_2 = 50$, and $X_2 = 25$.

a. At the 0.01 level of significance, is there evidence of a significant difference between the two population proportions?

b. Construct a 99% confidence interval estimate for the difference between the two population proportions.

APPLYING THE CONCEPTS

10.29 A survey of 1,085 adults asked, "Do you enjoy shopping for clothing for yourself?" The results indicated that 51% of the females enjoyed shopping for clothing for themselves as compared to 44% of the males. (Data extracted from "Split Decision on Clothes Shopping," *USA Today*, January 28, 2011, p. 1B.) The sample sizes of males and females were not provided. Suppose that of 542 males,

238 said that they enjoyed shopping for clothing for themselves while of 543 females, 276 said that they enjoyed shopping for clothing for themselves.

a. Is there evidence of a difference between males and females in the proportion who enjoy shopping for clothing for themselves at the 0.01 level of significance?

b. Find the p-value in (a) and interpret its meaning.

c. Construct and interpret a 99% confidence interval estimate for the difference between the proportion of males and females who enjoy shopping for clothing for themselves.

d. What are your answers to (a) through (c) if 218 males enjoyed shopping for clothing for themselves?

10.30 Do social recommendations increase ad effectiveness? A study of online video viewers compared viewers who arrived at an advertising video for a particular brand by following a social media recommendation link to viewers who arrived at the same video by web browsing. Data were collected on whether the viewer could correctly recall the brand being advertised after seeing the video. The results were:

	Correctly Recalled the Brand	
Arrival Method	**Yes**	**No**
Recommendation	407	150
Browsing	193	91

Source: Data extracted from "Social Ad Effectiveness: An Unruly White Paper," **www.unrulymedia.com**, January 2012, p.3.

a. Set up the null and alternative hypotheses to try to determine whether brand recall is higher following a social media recommendation than with only web browsing.

b. Conduct the hypothesis test defined in (a), using the 0.05 level of significance.

c. Does the result of your test in (b) make it appropriate to claim that brand recall is higher following a social media recommendation than by web browsing?

10.31 A/B testing is a testing method that businesses use to test different designs and formats of a web page to determine whether a new web page is more effective than a current web page. Web designers at TravelTips.com tested a new call to action button on its web page. Every visitor to the web page was randomly shown either the original call to action button (the control) or the new call to action button. The metric used to measure success was the download rate: the number of people who downloaded the file divided by the number of people who saw that particular call to action button. The experiment yielded the following results:

Variations	Downloads	Visitors
Original call to action button	351	3,642
New call to action button	485	3,556

a. What is the proportion (download rate) of visitors who saw the original call to action button and downloaded the file?

b. What is the proportion (download rate) of visitors who saw the new call to action button and downloaded the file?

c. At the 0.05 level of significance, is there evidence that the new call to action button is more effective than the original?

SELF Test **10.32** The consumer research firm Scarborough analyzed the 10% of American adults that are either "Superbanked" or "Unbanked." Superbanked consumers are defined as U.S. adults who live in a household that has multiple asset accounts at financial institutions, as well as some additional investments; Unbanked consumers are U.S. adults who live in a household that does not use a bank or credit union. By finding the 5% of Americans that are Superbanked, Scarborough identifies financially savvy consumers who might be open to diversifying their financial portfolios; by identifying the Unbanked, Scarborough provides insight into the ultimate prospective client for banks and financial institutions. As part of its analysis, Scarborough reported that 93% of Superbanked consumers use credit cards in the past three months as compared to 23% of Unbanked consumers. (Data extracted from **bit.ly/QlABwO**.) Suppose that these results were based on 1,000 Superbanked consumers and 1,000 Unbanked consumers.

a. At the 0.01 level of significance, is there evidence of a significant difference between the Superbanked and the Unbanked with respect to the proportion that use credit cards?

b. Find the p-value in (a) and interpret is meaning.

c. Construct and interpret a 99% confidence interval estimate for the difference between the Superbanked and the Unbanked with respect to the proportion that use credit cards.

10.33 A survey was conducted of 665 consumer magazines on the practices of their websites. Of these, 273 magazines reported that online-only content is copy-edited as rigorously as print content; 379 reported that online-only content is fact-checked as rigorously as print content. (Data extracted from S. Clifford, "Columbia Survey Finds a Slack Editing Process of Magazine Web Sites," *The New York Times*, March 1, 2010, p. B6.) Suppose that a sample of 500 newspapers revealed that 252 reported that online-only content is copy-edited as rigorously as print content and 296 reported that online-only content is fact-checked as rigorously as print content.

a. At the 0.05 level of significance, is there evidence of a difference between consumer magazines and newspapers in the proportion of online-only content that is copy-edited as rigorously as print content?

b. Find the p-value in (a) and interpret its meaning.

c. At the 0.05 level of significance, is there evidence of a difference between consumer magazines and newspapers in the proportion of online-only content that is fact-checked as rigorously as print content?

10.34 How do Americans feel about ads on websites? A survey of 1,000 adult Internet users found that 670 opposed ads on websites. (Data extracted from S. Clifford, "Tacked for Ads? Many Americans Say No Thanks," *The New York Times*, September 30, 2009, p. B3.) Suppose that a survey of 1,000 Internet users age 12–17 found that 510 opposed ads on websites.

a. At the 0.05 level of significance, is there evidence of a difference between adult Internet users and Internet users age 12–17 in the proportion who oppose ads?

b. Find the p-value in (a) and interpret its meaning.

10.35 Where people turn for news is different for various age groups. (Data extracted from "Cellphone Users Who Access News on Their Phones," *USA Today*, March 1, 2010, p. 1A.) A study was conducted on the use of cellphones for accessing news. The study reported that 47% of users under age 50 and 15% of users age 50 and over accessed news on their cellphones. Suppose that the survey consisted of 1,000 users under age 50, of whom 470 accessed news on their cellphones, and 891 users age 50 and over, of whom 134 accessed news on their cellphones.

a. Is there evidence of a significant difference in the proportion of users under age 50 and users 50 years and older that accessed the news on their cellphones? (Use $\alpha = 0.05$.)

b. Determine the p-value in (a) and interpret its meaning.

c. Construct and interpret a 95% confidence interval estimate for the difference between the population proportion of users under 50 years old and those 50 years or older who access the news on their cellphones.

10.4 *F* Test for the Ratio of Two Variances

Often you need to determine whether two independent populations have the same variability. By testing variances, you can detect differences in the variability in two independent populations. One important reason to test for the difference between the variances of two populations is to determine whether to use the pooled-variance t test (which assumes equal variances) or the separate-variance t test (which does not assume equal variances) when comparing the means of two independent populations.

The test for the difference between the variances of two independent populations is based on the ratio of the two sample variances. If you assume that each population is normally distributed, then the ratio S_1^2/S_2^2 follows the F distribution (see Table E.5). The critical values of the ***F* distribution** in Table E.5 depend on the degrees of freedom in the two samples. The degrees of freedom in the numerator of the ratio are for the first sample, and the degrees of freedom in the denominator are for the second sample. The first sample taken from the first population is defined as the sample that has the *larger* sample variance. The second sample taken from the second population is the sample with the *smaller* sample variance. Equation (10.9) defines the ***F* test for the ratio of two variances**.

F TEST STATISTIC FOR TESTING THE RATIO OF TWO VARIANCES

The F_{STAT} test statistic is equal to the variance of sample 1 (the larger sample variance) divided by the variance of sample 2 (the smaller sample variance).

$$F_{STAT} = \frac{S_1^2}{S_2^2} \tag{10.9}$$

where

S_1^2 = variance of sample 1 (the larger sample variance)

S_2^2 = variance of sample 2 (the smaller sample variance)

Student Tip
Since the numerator of Equation (10.9) contains the larger variance, the F_{STAT} statistic is always greater than or equal to 1.0.

n_1 = sample size selected from population 1

n_2 = sample size selected from population 2

$n_1 - 1$ = degrees of freedom from sample 1 (i.e., the numerator degrees of freedom)

$n_2 - 1$ = degrees of freedom from sample 2 (i.e., the denominator degrees of freedom)

The F_{STAT} test statistic follows an F distribution with $n_1 - 1$ and $n_2 - 1$ degrees of freedom.

For a given level of significance, α, to test the null hypothesis of equality of population variances:

$$H_0: \sigma_1^2 = \sigma_2^2$$

against the alternative hypothesis that the two population variances are not equal:

$$H_1: \sigma_1^2 \neq \sigma_2^2$$

you reject the null hypothesis if the computed F_{STAT} test statistic is greater than the upper-tail critical value, $F_{\alpha/2}$, from the F distribution, with $n_1 - 1$ degrees of freedom in the numerator and $n_2 - 1$ degrees of freedom in the denominator. Thus, the decision rule is

$$\text{Reject } H_0 \text{ if } F_{STAT} > F_{\alpha/2};$$

$$\text{otherwise, do not reject } H_0.$$

To illustrate how to use the F test to determine whether the two variances are equal, return to the North Fork Beverages scenario on page 343 concerning the sales of the new cola in two different end-cap locations. To determine whether to use the pooled-variance t test or the separate-variance t test in Section 10.1, you can test the equality of the two population variances. The null and alternative hypotheses are

$$H_0: \sigma_1^2 = \sigma_2^2$$
$$H_1: \sigma_1^2 \neq \sigma_2^2$$

Because you are defining sample 1 as the group with the larger sample variance, the rejection region in the upper tail of the F distribution contains $\alpha/2$. Using the level of significance $\alpha = 0.05$, the rejection region in the upper tail contains 0.025 of the distribution.

Because there are samples of 10 stores for each of the two end-cap locations, there are $10 - 1 = 9$ degrees of freedom in the numerator (the sample with the larger variance) and also in the denominator (the sample with the smaller variance). $F_{\alpha/2}$, the upper-tail critical value of the F distribution, is found directly from Table E.5, a portion of which is presented in Table 10.6. Because there are 9 degrees of freedom in the numerator and 9 degrees of freedom in the denominator, you find the upper-tail critical value, $F_{\alpha/2}$, by looking in the column labeled 9 and the row labeled 9. Thus, the upper-tail critical value of this F distribution is 4.03. Therefore, the decision rule is

$$\text{Reject } H_0 \text{ if } F_{STAT} > F_{0.025} = 4.03;$$

$$\text{otherwise, do not reject } H_0.$$

TABLE 10.6

Finding the Upper-Tail Critical Value of F with 9 and 9 Degrees of Freedom for an Upper-Tail Area of 0.025

	Cumulative Probabilities = 0.975 Upper-Tail Area = 0.025 Numerator df_1						
Denominator df_2	**1**	**2**	**3**	**. . .**	**7**	**8**	**[9]**
1	647.80	799.50	864.20	. . .	948.20	956.70	963.30
2	38.51	39.00	39.17	. . .	39.36	39.37	39.39
3	17.44	16.04	15.44	. . .	14.62	14.54	14.47
⋮	⋮	⋮	⋮	⋮	⋮	⋮	⋮
7	8.07	6.54	5.89	. . .	4.99	4.90	4.82
8	7.57	6.06	5.42	. . .	4.53	4.43	4.36
[9]	7.21	5.71	5.08	. . .	4.20	4.10	[4.03]

Source: Extracted from Table E.5.

Using Equation (10.9) on page 369 and the cola sales data (see Table 10.1 on page 345),

$$S_1^2 = (18.7264)^2 = 350.6778 \quad S_2^2 = (12.5433)^2 = 157.3333$$

so that

$$F_{STAT} = \frac{S_1^2}{S_2^2} = \frac{350.6778}{157.3333} = 2.2289$$

Because $F_{STAT} = 2.2289 < 4.03$, you do not reject H_0. Figure 10.14 shows the results for this test, including the *p*-value, 0.2482. Because $0.2482 > 0.05$, you conclude that there is no evidence of a significant difference in the variability of the sales of the new cola for the two end-cap locations.

FIGURE 10.14

F test results worksheet for the two end-cap locations data

	A	B	
1	**F Test for Differences in Two Variances**		
2			
3	**Data**		
4	Level of Significance	0.05	
5	**Larger-Variance Sample**		
6	Sample Size	10	**=COUNT(DATACOPY!$A:$A)**
7	Sample Variance	350.6778	**=VAR.S(DATACOPY!$A:$A)**
8	**Smaller-Variance Sample**		
9	Sample Size	10	**=COUNT(DATACOPY!$B:$B)**
10	Sample Variance	157.3333	**=VAR.S(DATACOPY!$B:$B)**
11			
12	Intermediate Calculations		
13	*F* Test Statistic	2.2289	**=B7/B10**
14	Population 1 Sample Degrees of Freedom	9	**=B6 - 1**
15	Population 2 Sample Degrees of Freedom	9	**=B9 - 1**
16			
17	**Two-Tail Test**		
18	Upper Critical Value	4.0260	**=F.INV.RT(B4/2, B14, B15)**
19	*p*-Value	0.2482	**=2 * F.DIST.RT(B13, B14, B15)**
20	Do not reject the null hypothesis		**=IF(B19 < B4, "Reject the null hypothesis", "Do not reject the null hypothesis")**

Figure 10.14 displays the **COMPUTE worksheet** *of the* **F Two Variances workbook** *that the Section EG10.4 instructions use. (The Analysis ToolPak creates a different but equivalent worksheet.)*

In testing for a difference between two variances using the *F* test described in this section, you assume that each of the two populations is normally distributed. The *F* test is very sensitive to the normality assumption. If boxplots or normal probability plots suggest even a mild departure from normality for either of the two populations, you should not use the *F* test.

If this happens, you should use the Levene test (see Section 11.1) or a nonparametric approach (see references 1 and 2).

In testing for the equality of variances as part of assessing the validity of the pooled-variance t test procedure, the F test is a two-tail test with $\alpha/2$ in the upper tail. However, when you are interested in examining the variability in situations other than the pooled-variance t test, the F test is often a one-tail test. Example 10.4 illustrates a one-tail test.

EXAMPLE 10.4

A One-Tail Test for the Difference Between Two Variances

Waiting time is a critical issue at fast-food chains, which not only want to minimize the mean service time but also want to minimize the variation in the service time from customer to customer. One fast-food chain carried out a study to measure the variability in the waiting time (defined as the time in minutes from when an order was completed to when it was delivered to the customer) at lunch and breakfast at one of the chain's stores. The results were as follows:

$$\text{Lunch: } n_1 = 25 \; S_1^2 = 4.4$$

$$\text{Breakfast: } n_2 = 21 \; S_2^2 = 1.9$$

At the 0.05 level of significance, is there evidence that there is more variability in the service time at lunch than at breakfast? Assume that the population service times are normally distributed.

SOLUTION The null and alternative hypotheses are

$$H_0: \sigma_L^2 \le \sigma_B^2$$

$$H_1: \sigma_L^2 > \sigma_B^2$$

The F_{STAT} test statistic is given by Equation (10.9) on page 369:

$$F_{STAT} = \frac{S_1^2}{S_2^2}$$

You use Table E.5 to find the upper critical value of the F distribution. With $n_1 - 1 = 25 - 1 = 24$ degrees of freedom in the numerator, $n_2 - 1 = 21 - 1 = 20$ degrees of freedom in the denominator, and $\alpha = 0.05$, the upper-tail critical value, $F_{0.05}$, is 2.08. The decision rule is

$$\text{Reject } H_0 \text{ if } F_{STAT} > 2.08;$$

$$\text{otherwise, do not reject } H_0.$$

From Equation (10.9) on page 369,

$$F_{STAT} = \frac{S_1^2}{S_2^2} = \frac{4.4}{1.9} = 2.3158$$

Because $F_{STAT} = 2.3158 > 2.08$, you reject H_0. Using a 0.05 level of significance, you conclude that there is evidence that there is more variability in the service time at lunch than at breakfast.

Problems for Section 10.4

LEARNING THE BASICS

10.36 Determine the upper-tail critical values of F in each of the following two-tail tests.

a. $\alpha = 0.10, n_1 = 16, n_2 = 21$

b. $\alpha = 0.05, n_1 = 16, n_2 = 21$

c. $\alpha = 0.01, n_1 = 16, n_2 = 21$

10.37 Determine the upper-tail critical value of F in each of the following one-tail tests.

a. $\alpha = 0.05, n_1 = 16, n_2 = 21$

b. $\alpha = 0.01, n_1 = 16, n_2 = 21$

10.38 The following information is available for two samples selected from independent normally distributed populations:

Population A: $n_1 = 25 \; S_1^2 = 16$

Population B: $n_2 = 25 \; S_2^2 = 25$

a. Which sample variance do you place in the numerator of F_{STAT}?
b. What is the value of F_{STAT}?

10.39 The following information is available for two samples selected from independent normally distributed populations:

Population A: $n_1 = 25 \quad S_1^2 = 161.9$

Population B: $n_2 = 25 \quad S_2^2 = 133.7$

What is the value of F_{STAT} if you are testing the null hypothesis $H_0: \sigma_1^2 = \sigma_2^2$?

10.40 In Problem 10.39, how many degrees of freedom are there in the numerator and denominator of the F test?

10.41 In Problems 10.39 and 10.40, what is the upper-tail critical value for F if the level of significance, α, is 0.05 and the alternative hypothesis is $H_1: \sigma_1^2 \neq \sigma_2^2$?

10.42 In Problems 10.39 through 10.41, what is your statistical decision?

10.43 The following information is available for two samples selected from independent but very right-skewed populations:

Population A: $n_1 = 16 \quad S_1^2 = 47.3$

Population B: $n_2 = 13 \quad S_2^2 = 36.4$

Should you use the F test to test the null hypothesis of equality of variances? Discuss.

10.44 In Problem 10.43, assume that two samples are selected from independent normally distributed populations.
a. At the 0.05 level of significance, is there evidence of a difference between σ_1^2 and σ_2^2?
b. Suppose that you want to perform a one-tail test. At the 0.05 level of significance, what is the upper-tail critical value of F to determine whether there is evidence that $\sigma_1^2 > \sigma_2^2$? What is your statistical decision?

APPLYING THE CONCEPTS

10.45 A problem with a telephone line that prevents a customer from receiving or making calls is upsetting to both the customer and the telecommunications company. The file **Phone** contains samples of 20 problems reported to two different offices of a telecommunications company and the time to clear these problems (in minutes) from the customers' lines.
a. At the 0.05 level of significance, is there evidence of a difference in the variability of the time to clear problems between the two central offices?
b. Interpret the p-value.
c. What assumption do you need to make in (a) about the two populations in order to justify your use of the F test?
d. Based on the results of (a) and (b), which t test defined in Section 10.1 should you use to compare the mean time to clear problems in the two central offices?

SELF Test **10.46** *Accounting Today* identified the top accounting firms in 10 geographic regions across the United States. Even though all 10 regions reported growth in 2011, the Southeast and Gulf Coast regions reported the highest combined growths, with 18% and 19%, respectively. A characteristic description of the accounting firms in the Southeast and Gulf Coast regions included the number of partners in the firm. The file **AccountingPartners2** contains the number of partners. (Data extracted from **bit.ly/KKeokV**.)
a. At the 0.05 level of significance, is there evidence of a difference in the variability in numbers of partners for Southeast region accounting firms and Gulf Coast accounting firms?
b. Interpret the p-value.
c. What assumption do you have to make about the two populations in order to justify the use of the F test?
d. Based on (a) and (b), which t test defined in Section 10.1 should you use to test whether there is a significant difference in the mean number of partners for Southeast region accounting firms and Gulf Coast accounting firms?

10.47 A bank with a branch located in a commercial district of a city has the business objective of improving the process for serving customers during the noon-to-1 P.M. lunch period. To do so, the waiting time (defined as the number of minutes that elapses from when the customer enters the line until he or she reaches the teller window) needs to be shortened to increase customer satisfaction. A random sample of 15 customers is selected and the waiting times are collected and stored in **Bank1**. These data are:

4.21	5.55	3.02	5.13	4.77	2.34	3.54	3.20
4.50	6.10	0.38	5.12	6.46	6.19	3.79	

Suppose that another branch, located in a residential area, is also concerned with the noon-to-1 P.M. lunch period. A random sample of 15 customers is selected and the waiting times are collected and stored in **Bank2**. These data are:

9.66	5.90	8.02	5.79	8.73	3.82	8.01	8.35
10.49	6.68	5.64	4.08	6.17	9.91	5.47	

a. Is there evidence of a difference in the variability of the waiting time between the two branches? (Use $\alpha = 0.05$.)
b. Determine the p-value in (a) and interpret its meaning.
c. What assumption about the population distribution of each bank is necessary in (a)? Is the assumption valid for these data?
d. Based on the results of (a), is it appropriate to use the pooled-variance t test to compare the means of the two branches?

10.48 An important feature of digital cameras is battery life, the number of shots that can be taken before the battery needs to be recharged. The file **Cameras** contains the battery life of 11 subcompact cameras and 7 compact cameras. (Data extracted from "Cameras," *Consumer Reports*, July 2012, pp. 42–44.)

a. Is there evidence of a difference in the variability of the battery life between the two types of digital cameras? (Use $\alpha = 0.05$.)
b. Determine the p-value in (a) and interpret its meaning.
c. What assumption about the population distribution of the two types of cameras is necessary in (a)? Is the assumption valid for these data?
d. Based on the results of (a), which t test defined in Section 10.1 should you use to compare the mean battery life of the two types of cameras?

10.49 An article appearing in *The Exponent*, an independent college newspaper published by the Purdue Student Publishing Foundation, reported that the average American college student spends one hour (60 minutes) on Facebook daily. (Data extracted from **bit.ly/NQRCJQ**.) You wonder if there is a difference between males and females. You select a sample of 60 Facebook users (30 males and 30 females) at your college and collect data about the time spent on Facebook per day (in minutes) and store these data in **FacebookTime2**.

a. Using a 0.05 level of significance, is there evidence of a difference in the variances of time spent on Facebook per day between males and females?
b. On the basis of the results in part (a), which t test defined in Section 10.1 should you use to compare the means of males and females? Discuss.

10.50 Is there a difference in the variation of the yield of five-year certificates of deposit (CDs) in different cities? The file **FiveYearCDRate** contains the yields for a five-year CD for nine banks in New York and nine banks in Los Angeles, as of August 6, 2012. (Data extracted from **www.Bankrate.com**, August 6, 2012.) At the 0.05 level of significance, is there evidence of a difference in the variance of the yield of five-year CDs in the two cities? Assume that the population yields are normally distributed.

USING STATISTICS

For North Fork, Are There Different Means to the Ends? Revisited

Michael Bradley / Staff / Getty Images

In the North Fork Beverages scenario, you were a regional sales manager for North Fork Beverages. You compared the sales volume of your new All-Natural Brain-Boost Cola when the product was featured in the beverage aisle end-cap to the sales volume when the product was featured in the end-cap by the produce department. An experiment was performed in which 10 stores used the beverage end-cap location and 10 stores used the produce end-cap location. Using a t test for the difference between two means, you were able to conclude that the mean sales using the produce end-cap location are higher than the mean sales for the beverage end-cap location. A confidence interval allowed you to infer with 95% confidence that the produce end-cap location sells, on average, 6.73 to 36.67 cases more than the beverage end-cap location. You also performed the F test for the difference between two variances to see if the store-to-store variability in sales in stores using the produce end-cap location differed from the store-to-store variability in sales in stores using the beverage end-cap location. You concluded that there was no significant difference in the variability of the sales of cola for the two display locations. As a regional sales manager, you decide to lease the produce end-cap location in all FoodPlace Supermarkets during your next sales promotional period.

SUMMARY

In this chapter, you were introduced to a variety of tests for two samples. For situations in which the samples are independent, you learned statistical test procedures for analyzing possible differences between means, variances, and proportions. In addition, you learned a test procedure that is frequently used when analyzing differences between the means of two related samples. Remember that you need to select the test that is most appropriate for a given set of conditions and to critically investigate the validity of the assumptions underlying each of the hypothesis-testing procedures.

Table 10.7 provides a list of topics covered in this chapter. The roadmap in Figure 10.15 illustrates the steps needed in determining which two-sample test of hypothesis to use. The following are the questions you need to consider:

1. What type of data do you have? If you are dealing with categorical variables, use the Z test for the difference between two proportions. (This test assumes independent samples.)
2. If you have a numerical variable, determine whether you have independent samples or related samples. If you have related samples, and you can assume approximate normality, use the paired t test.
3. If you have independent samples, is your focus on variability or central tendency? If the focus is on variability, and you can assume approximate normality, use the F test.
4. If your focus is central tendency and you can assume approximate normality, determine whether you can assume that the variances of the two populations are equal. (This assumption can be tested using the F test.)
5. If you can assume that the two populations have equal variances, use the pooled-variance t test. If you cannot assume that the two populations have equal variances, use the separate-variance t test.

TABLE 10.7

Summary of Topics in Chapter 10

	Types of Data	
Type of Analysis	**Numerical**	**Categorical**
Comparing two populations	t tests for the difference in the means of two independent populations (Section 10.1) Paired t test (Section 10.2) F test for the difference between two variances (Section 10.4)	Z test for the difference between two proportions (Section 10.3)

FIGURE 10.15

Roadmap for selecting a test of hypothesis for two samples

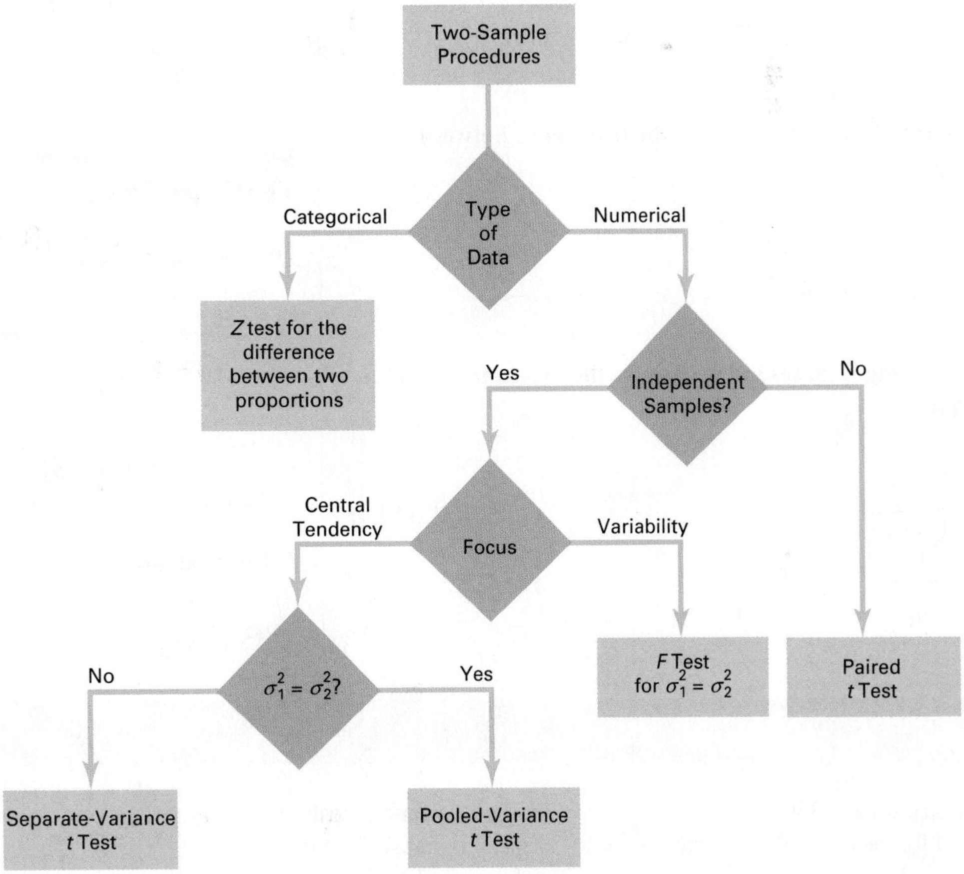

REFERENCES

1. Conover, W. J. *Practical Nonparametric Statistics*, 3rd ed. New York: Wiley, 2000.
2. Daniel, W. *Applied Nonparametric Statistics*, 2nd ed. Boston: Houghton Mifflin, 1990.
3. *Microsoft Excel 2010*. Redmond, WA: Microsoft Corp., 2010.
4. Satterthwaite, F. E. "An Approximate Distribution of Estimates of Variance Components." *Biometrics Bulletin*, 2(1946): 110–114.
5. Snedecor, G. W., and W. G. Cochran. *Statistical Methods*, 8th ed. Ames, IA: Iowa State University Press, 1989.

KEY EQUATIONS

Pooled-Variance t Test for the Difference Between Two Means

$$t_{STAT} = \frac{(\overline{X}_1 - \overline{X}_2) - (\mu_1 - \mu_2)}{\sqrt{S_p^2\left(\frac{1}{n_1} + \frac{1}{n_2}\right)}} \quad \textbf{(10.1)}$$

Confidence Interval Estimate for the Difference Between the Means of Two Independent Populations

$$(\overline{X}_1 - \overline{X}_2) \pm t_{\alpha/2}\sqrt{S_p^2\left(\frac{1}{n_1} + \frac{1}{n_2}\right)} \quad \textbf{(10.2)}$$

or

$$(\overline{X}_1 - \overline{X}_2) - t_{\alpha/2}\sqrt{S_p^2\left(\frac{1}{n_1} + \frac{1}{n_2}\right)} \le \mu_1 - \mu_2 \le (\overline{X}_1 - \overline{X}_2) + t_{\alpha/2}\sqrt{S_p^2\left(\frac{1}{n_1} + \frac{1}{n_2}\right)}$$

Separate-Variance t Test for the Difference Between Two Means

$$t_{STAT} = \frac{(\overline{X}_1 - \overline{X}_2) - (\mu_1 - \mu_2)}{\sqrt{\frac{S_1^2}{n_1} + \frac{S_2^2}{n_2}}} \quad \textbf{(10.3)}$$

Computing Degrees of Freedom in the Separate-Variance t Test

$$V = \frac{\left(\frac{S_1^2}{n_1} + \frac{S_2^2}{n_2}\right)^2}{\frac{\left(\frac{S_1^2}{n_1}\right)^2}{n_1 - 1} + \frac{\left(\frac{S_2^2}{n_2}\right)^2}{n_2 - 1}} \quad \textbf{(10.4)}$$

Paired t Test for the Mean Difference

$$t_{STAT} = \frac{\overline{D} - \mu_D}{\frac{S_D}{\sqrt{n}}} \quad \textbf{(10.5)}$$

Confidence Interval Estimate for the Mean Difference

$$\overline{D} \pm t_{\alpha/2}\frac{S_D}{\sqrt{n}} \quad \textbf{(10.6)}$$

or

$$\overline{D} - t_{\alpha/2}\frac{S_D}{\sqrt{n}} \le \mu_D \le \overline{D} + t_{\alpha/2}\frac{S_D}{\sqrt{n}}$$

Z Test for the Difference Between Two Proportions

$$Z_{STAT} = \frac{(p_1 - p_2) - (\pi_1 - \pi_2)}{\sqrt{\overline{p}(1 - \overline{p})\left(\frac{1}{n_1} + \frac{1}{n_2}\right)}} \quad \textbf{(10.7)}$$

Confidence Interval Estimate for the Difference Between Two Proportions

$$(p_1 - p_2) \pm Z_{\alpha/2}\sqrt{\left(\frac{p_1(1 - p_1)}{n_1} + \frac{p_2(1 - p_2)}{n_2}\right)} \quad \textbf{(10.8)}$$

or

$$(p_1 - p_2) - Z_{\alpha/2}\sqrt{\frac{p_1(1 - p_1)}{n_1} + \frac{p_2(1 - p_2)}{n_2}} \le (\pi_1 - \pi_2) \le (p_1 - p_2) + Z_{\alpha/2}\sqrt{\frac{p_1(1 - p_1)}{n_1} + \frac{p_2(1 - p_2)}{n_2}}$$

F Test Statistic for Testing the Ratio of Two Variances

$$F_{STAT} = \frac{S_1^2}{S_2^2} \quad \textbf{(10.9)}$$

KEY TERMS

F distribution 369
F test for the ratio of two variances 369
matched samples 355
paired t test for the mean difference 356
pooled-variance t test 344
repeated measurements 355
robust 347
separate-variance t test 350
two-sample tests 344
Z test for the difference between two proportions 363

CHECKING YOUR UNDERSTANDING

10.51 What are some of the criteria used in the selection of a particular hypothesis-testing procedure?

10.52 Under what conditions should you use the pooled-variance t test to examine possible differences in the means of two independent populations?

10.53 Under what conditions should you use the F test to examine possible differences in the variances of two independent populations?

10.54 What is the distinction between two independent populations and two related populations?

10.55 What is the distinction between repeated measurements and matched items?

10.56 When you have two independent populations, explain the similarities and differences between the test of hypothesis for the difference between the means and the confidence interval estimate for the difference between the means.

10.57 Under what conditions should you use the paired t test for the mean difference between two related populations?

CHAPTER REVIEW PROBLEMS

10.58 The American Society for Quality (ASQ) conducted a salary survey of all its members. ASQ members work in all areas of manufacturing and service-related institutions, with a common theme of an interest in quality. Two job titles are black belt and green belt. (See Section 18.6 for a description of these titles in a Six Sigma quality improvement initiative.) Descriptive statistics concerning salaries for these two job titles are given in the following table:

Job Title	Sample Size	Mean	Standard Deviation
Black belt	141	88,945	21,791
Green belt	26	64,794	25,911

Source: Data extracted from "QP Salary Survey," *Quality Progress*, December 2011, p. 33.

a. Using a 0.05 level of significance, is there a difference in the variability of salaries between black belts and green belts?

b. Based on the result of (a), which t test defined in Section 10.1 is appropriate for comparing mean salaries?

c. Using a 0.05 level of significance, is the mean salary of black belts greater than the mean salary of green belts?

10.59 Do male and female students study the same amount per week? In a recent year, 58 sophomore business students were surveyed at a large university that has more than 1,000 sophomore business students each year. The file **StudyTime** contains the gender and the number of hours spent studying in a typical week for the sampled students.

a. At the 0.05 level of significance, is there a difference in the variance of the study time for male students and female students?

b. Using the results of (a), which t test is appropriate for comparing the mean study time for male and female students?

c. At the 0.05 level of significance, conduct the test selected in (b).

d. Write a short summary of your findings.

10.60 Do males and females differ in the amount of time they talk on the phone and the number of text messages they send? A study reported that women spent a mean of 818 minutes per month talking as compared to 716 minutes per month for men. (Data extracted from "Women Talk and Text More," *USA Today*, February 1, 2011, p. 1A.) The sample sizes were not reported. Suppose that the sample sizes were 100 each for women and men and that the standard deviation for women was 125 minutes per month as compared to 100 minutes per month for men.

a. Using a 0.01 level of significance, is there evidence of a difference in the variances of the amount of time spent talking between women and men?

b. To test for a difference in the mean talking time of women and men, is it most appropriate to use the pooled-variance t test or the separate-variance t test? Use the most appropriate test to determine if there is a difference in the amount of time spent talking between women and men.

The article also reported that women sent a mean of 716 text messages per month compared to 555 per month for men. Suppose that the standard deviation for women was 150 text messages per month compared to 125 text messages per month for men.

c. Using a 0.01 level of significance, is there evidence of a difference in the variances of the number of text messages sent per month by women and men?

d. Based on the results of (c), use the most appropriate test to determine, at the 0.01 level of significance, whether there is evidence of a difference in the mean number of text messages sent per month by women and men.

10.61 The file **Restaurants** contains the ratings for food, décor, service, and the price per person for a sample of 50 restaurants located in a city and 50 restaurants located in a suburb. Completely analyze the differences between city and suburban restaurants for the variables food rating, décor rating, service rating, and cost per person, using $\alpha = 0.05$.

Source: Data extracted from *Zagat Survey 2012: New York City Restaurants* and *Zagat Survey 2011–2012: Long Island Restaurants.*

10.62 A computer information systems professor is interested in studying the amount of time it takes students enrolled in the Introduction to Computers course to write a program in Visual Basic. The professor hires you to analyze the following results (in minutes), stored in VB, from a random sample of nine students:

10 13 9 15 12 13 11 13 12

a. At the 0.05 level of significance, is there evidence that the population mean time is greater than 10 minutes? What will you tell the professor?

b. Suppose that the professor, when checking her results, realizes that the fourth student needed 51 minutes rather than the recorded 15 minutes to write the Visual Basic program. At the 0.05 level of significance, reanalyze the question posed in (a), using the revised data. What will you tell the professor now?

c. The professor is perplexed by these paradoxical results and requests an explanation from you regarding the justification for the difference in your findings in (a) and (b). Discuss.

d. A few days later, the professor calls to tell you that the dilemma is completely resolved. The original number 15 (the fourth data value) was correct, and therefore your findings in (a) are being used in the article she is writing for a computer journal. Now she wants to hire you to compare the results from that group of Introduction to Computers students against those from a sample of 11 computer majors in order to determine whether there is evidence that computer majors can write a Visual Basic program in less time than introductory students. For the computer majors, the sample mean is 8.5 minutes, and the sample standard deviation is 2.0 minutes. At the 0.05 level of significance, completely analyze these data. What will you tell the professor?

e. A few days later, the professor calls again to tell you that a reviewer of her article wants her to include the *p*-value for the "correct" result in (a). In addition, the professor inquires about an unequal-variances problem, which the reviewer wants her to discuss in her article. In your own words, discuss the concept of *p*-value and also describe the unequal-variances problem. Then, determine the *p*-value in (a) and discuss whether the unequal-variances problem had any meaning in the professor's study.

10.63 Do men and women differ in the number of online friends that they have? A study of 3,011 people reported that men had a mean of 180 friends and women had a mean of 140 friends. Suppose that the study consisted of 1,511 men and 1,500 women and that the standard deviation of the number of friends was 130 for men and 120 for women. Assume a level of significance of 0.05.

a. Is there evidence of a difference in the variances of the number of online friends between men and women?

b. Is there evidence of a difference in the mean number of online friends between men and women?

c. Construct and interpret a 95% confidence interval estimate for the difference in the mean number of online friends between men and women.

10.64 The lengths of life (in hours) of a sample of 40 100-watt light bulbs produced by manufacturer A and a sample of 40 100-watt light bulbs produced by manufacturer B are stored in Bulbs. Completely analyze the differences between the lengths of life of the bulbs produced by the two manufacturers. (Use $\alpha = 0.05$.)

10.65 A hotel manager looks to enhance the initial impressions that hotel guests have when they check in. Contributing to initial impressions is the time it takes to deliver a guest's luggage to the room after check-in. A random sample of 20 deliveries on a particular day were selected in Wing A of the hotel, and a random sample of 20 deliveries were selected in Wing B. The results are stored in Luggage. Analyze the data and determine whether there is a difference between the mean delivery times in the two wings of the hotel. (Use $\alpha = 0.05$.)

10.66 The owner of a restaurant that serves Continental-style entrées has the business objective of learning more about the patterns of patron demand during the Friday-to-Sunday weekend time period. She decided to study the demand for dessert during this time period. In addition to studying whether a dessert was ordered, she will study the gender of the individual and whether a beef entrée was ordered. Data were collected from 600 customers and organized in the following contingency tables:

	Gender		
Dessert Ordered	**Male**	**Female**	**Total**
Yes	40	96	136
No	240	224	464
Total	280	320	600

	Beef Entrée		
Dessert Ordered	**Yes**	**No**	**Total**
Yes	71	65	136
No	116	348	464
Total	187	413	600

a. At the 0.05 level of significance, is there evidence of a difference between males and females in the proportion who order dessert?

b. At the 0.05 level of significance, is there evidence of a difference in the proportion who order dessert based on whether a beef entrée has been ordered?

10.67 The manufacturer of Boston and Vermont asphalt shingles knows that product weight is a major factor in the customer's perception of quality. Moreover, the weight represents the amount of raw materials being used and is therefore very important to the company from a cost standpoint.

The last stage of the assembly line packages the shingles before they are placed on wooden pallets. Once a pallet is full (a pallet for most brands holds 16 squares of shingles), it is weighed, and the measurement is recorded. The file **Pallet** contains the weight (in pounds) from a sample of 368 pallets of Boston shingles and 330 pallets of Vermont shingles. Completely analyze the differences in the weights of the Boston and Vermont shingles, using $\alpha = 0.05$.

10.68 The manufacturer of Boston and Vermont asphalt shingles provides its customers with a 20-year warranty on most of its products. To determine whether a shingle will last as long as the warranty period, the manufacturer conducts accelerated-life testing. Accelerated-life testing exposes the shingle to the stresses it would be subject to in a lifetime of normal use in a laboratory setting via an experiment that takes only a few minutes to conduct. In this test, a shingle is repeatedly scraped with a brush for a short period of time, and the shingle granules removed by the brushing are weighed (in grams). Shingles that experience low amounts of granule loss are expected to last longer in normal use than shingles that experience high amounts of granule loss. In this situation, a shingle should experience no more than 0.8 grams of granule loss if it is expected to last the length of the warranty period. The file **Granule** contains a sample of 170 measurements made on the company's Boston shingles and 140 measurements made on Vermont shingles. Completely analyze the differences in the granule loss of the Boston and Vermont shingles, using $\alpha = 0.05$.

10.69 There are a very large number of mutual funds from which an investor can choose. Each mutual fund has its own mix of different types of investments. The data in **BestFunds1** present the one-year return and the three-year annualized return for the 10 best mutual funds, according to the *U.S. News & World Report* score for short-term bond funds and long-term bond funds. (Data extracted from **money.usnews.com/mutual-funds/rankings**.) Analyze the data and determine whether any differences exist between short-term and long-term bond funds. (Use the 0.05 level of significance.)

REPORT WRITING EXERCISE

10.70 Referring to the results of Problems 10.67 and 10.68 concerning the weight and granule loss of Boston and Vermont shingles, write a report that summarizes your conclusions.

CASES FOR CHAPTER 10

Managing Ashland MultiComm Services

AMS communicates with customers who subscribe to cable television services through a special secured email system that sends messages about service changes, new features, and billing information to in-home digital set-top boxes for later display. To enhance customer service, the operations department established the business objective of reducing the amount of time to fully update each subscriber's set of messages. The department selected two candidate messaging systems and conducted an experiment in which 30 randomly chosen cable subscribers were assigned one of the two systems (15 assigned to each system). Update times were measured, and the results are organized in Table AMS10.1 and stored in **AMS10**.

TABLE AMS10.1

Update Times (in seconds) for Two Different Email Interfaces

Email Interface 1	Email Interface 2
4.13	3.71
3.75	3.89
3.93	4.22
3.74	4.57
3.36	4.24
3.85	3.90
3.26	4.09
3.73	4.05
4.06	4.07
3.33	3.80
3.96	4.36
3.57	4.38
3.13	3.49
3.68	3.57
3.63	4.74

1. Analyze the data in Table AMS10.1 and write a report to the computer operations department that indicates your findings. Include an appendix in which you discuss the reason you selected a particular statistical test to compare the two independent groups of callers.
2. Suppose that instead of the research design described in the case, there were only 15 subscribers sampled, and the update process for each subscriber email was measured for each of the two messaging systems. Suppose that the results were organized in Table AMS10.1—making each row in the table a pair of values for an individual subscriber. Using these suppositions, reanalyze the Table AMS10.1 data and write a report for presentation to the team that indicates your findings.

Digital Case

Apply your knowledge about hypothesis testing in this Digital Case, which continues the cereal-fill packaging dispute Digital Case from Chapters 7 and 9.

Even after the recent public experiment about cereal box weights, Consumers Concerned About Cereal Cheaters (CCACC) remains convinced that Oxford Cereals has misled the public. The group has created and circulated **MoreCheating.pdf**, a document in which it claims that cereal boxes produced at Plant Number 2 in Springville weigh less than the claimed mean of 368 grams. Review this document and then answer the following questions:

1. Do the CCACC's results prove that there is a statistically significant difference in the mean weights of cereal boxes produced at Plant Numbers 1 and 2?
2. Perform the appropriate analysis to test the CCACC's hypothesis. What conclusions can you reach based on the data?

Sure Value Convenience Stores

You work in the corporate office for a nationwide convenience store franchise that operates nearly 10,000 stores. The per-store daily customer count (i.e., the mean number of customers in a store in one day) has been steady, at 900, for some time. To increase the customer count, the chain is considering cutting prices for coffee beverages. The small size will now be either \$0.59 or \$0.79 instead of \$0.99. Even with this reduction in price, the chain will have a 40% gross margin on coffee.

The question to be determined is how much to cut prices to increase the daily customer count without reducing the gross margin on coffee sales too much. The chain decides to carry out an experiment in a sample of 30 stores where customer counts have been running almost exactly at the national average of 900. In 15 of the stores, the price of a small coffee will now be \$0.59 instead of \$0.99, and in 15 other stores, the price of a small coffee will now be \$0.79. After four weeks, the 15 stores that priced the small coffee at \$0.59 had a mean daily customer count of 964 and a standard deviation of 88, and the 15 stores that priced the small coffee at \$0.79 had a mean daily customer count of 941 and a standard deviation of 76. Analyze these data (using the 0.05 level of significance) and answer the following questions.

a. Does reducing the price of a small coffee to either \$0.59 or \$0.79 increase the mean per-store daily customer count?
b. If reducing the price of a small coffee to either \$0.59 or \$0.79 increases the mean per-store daily customer count, is there any difference in the mean per-store daily customer count between stores in which a small coffee was priced at \$0.59 and stores in which a small coffee was priced at \$0.79?
c. What price do you recommend for a small coffee?

CardioGood Fitness

Return to the CardioGood Fitness case first presented on page 33. Using the data stored in **CardioGood Fitness**:

1. Determine whether differences exist between males and females in their age in years, education in years, annual household income (\$), mean number of times the customer plans to use the treadmill each week, and mean number of miles the customer expects to walk/run each week.
2. Write a report to be presented to the management of CardioGood Fitness detailing your findings.

More Descriptive Choices Follow-up

Follow up the Using Statistics scenario "More Descriptive Choices, Revisited" on page 149 by determining whether there is a difference in the 1-year return percentages, 5-year return percentages, and 10-year return percentages of the growth and value funds (stored in Retirement Funds).

Clear Mountain State Student Surveys

1. The Student News Service at Clear Mountain State University (CMSU) has decided to gather data about the undergraduate students that attend CMSU. It creates and distributes a survey of 14 questions and receives responses from 62 undergraduates (stored in UndergradSurvey).

a. At the 0.05 level of significance, is there evidence of a difference between males and females in grade point average, expected starting salary, number of social networking sites registered for, age, spending on textbooks and supplies, text messages sent in a week, and the wealth needed to feel rich?

b. At the 0.05 level of significance, is there evidence of a difference between students who plan to go to graduate school and those who do not plan to go to graduate school in grade point average, expected starting salary, number of social networking sites registered for, age, spending on textbooks and supplies, text messages sent in a week, and the wealth needed to feel rich?

2. The dean of students at Clear Mountain State University has learned about the undergraduate survey and has decided to undertake a similar survey for graduate students at Clear Mountain State. She creates and distributes a survey of fourteen questions and receives responses from 44 graduate students (stored in GradSurvey). For these data, at the 0.05 level of significance, is there evidence of a difference between males and females in age, undergraduate grade point average, graduate grade point average, expected salary upon graduation, spending on textbooks and supplies, text messages sent in a week, and the wealth needed to feel rich?

CHAPTER 10 EXCEL GUIDE

EG10.1 COMPARING the MEANS of TWO INDEPENDENT POPULATIONS

Pooled-Variance *t* Test for the Difference Between Two Means

Key Technique Use the **T.INV.2T(*level of significance, degrees of freedom*)** function to compute the lower and upper critical values and use the **T.DIST.2T(*absolute value of the t test statistic, degrees of freedom*)** to compute the *p*-value.

Example Perform the pooled-variance *t* test for the two end-cap locations data that is shown in Figure 10.3 on page 346.

PHStat Use **Pooled-Variance t Test.**
For the example, open to the **DATA worksheet** of the **Cola workbook**. Select **PHStat → Two-Sample Tests (Unsummarized Data) → Pooled-Variance t Test**. In the procedure's dialog box (shown below):

1. Enter **0** as the **Hypothesized Difference**.
2. Enter **0.05** as the **Level of Significance**.
3. Enter **A1:A11** as the **Population 1 Sample Cell Range**.
4. Enter **B1:B11** as the **Population 2 Sample Cell Range**.
5. Check **First cells in both ranges contain label**.
6. Click **Two-Tail Test**.
7. Enter a **Title** and click **OK**.

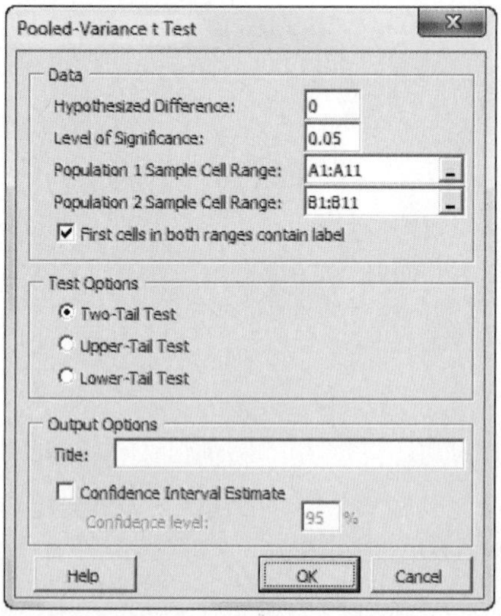

For problems that use summarized data, select **PHStat → Two-Sample Tests (Summarized Data) → Pooled-Variance t Test**. In that procedure's dialog box, enter the hypothesized difference and level of significance, as well as the sample size, sample mean, and sample standard deviation for each sample.

In-Depth Excel Use the **COMPUTE worksheet** of the **Pooled-Variance T workbook** as a template.
The worksheet already contains the data and formulas to use the unsummarized data for the example. For other problems, use the COMPUTE worksheet with either unsummarized or summarized data. For unsummarized data, paste the data in columns A and B in the **DATACOPY worksheet** and keep the COMPUTE worksheet formulas that compute the sample size, sample mean, and sample standard deviation in the cell range B7:B13. For summarized data, replace the formulas in the cell range B7:B13 with the sample statistics and ignore the DATACOPY worksheet.

Use the similar **COMPUTE_LOWER** or **COMPUTE_UPPER worksheets** in the same workbook as templates for performing one-tail pooled-variance *t* tests with either unsummarized or summarized data. If you use an Excel version older than Excel 2010, use the COMPUTE_OLDER worksheet as a template for both the two-tail and one-tail tests.

Analysis ToolPak Use **t-Test: Two-Sample Assuming Equal Variances.**
For the example, open to the **DATA worksheet** of the **Cola workbook** and:

1. Select **Data → Data Analysis**.
2. In the Data Analysis dialog box, select **t-Test: Two-Sample Assuming Equal Variances** from the **Analysis Tools** list and then click **OK**.

In the procedure's dialog box (shown at top on page 383):

3. Enter **A1:A11** as the **Variable 1 Range**
4. Enter **B1:B11** as the **Variable 2 Range**.
5. Enter **0** as the **Hypothesized Mean Difference**.
6. Check **Labels** and enter **0.05** as **Alpha**.
7. Click **New Worksheet Ply**.
8. Click **OK**.

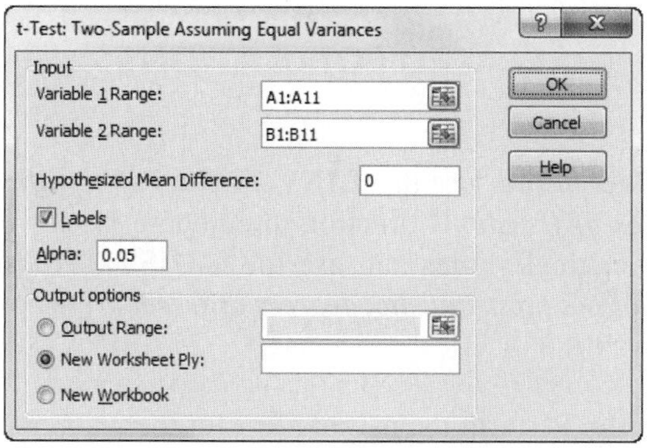

Results (shown below) appear in a new worksheet that contains both two-tail and one-tail test critical values and *p*-values. Unlike the results shown in Figure 10.3 worksheet, only the positive (upper) critical value is listed for the two-tail test.

	A	B	C
1	**t-Test: Two-Sample Assuming Equal Variances**		
2			
3		***Beverage***	***Produce***
4	**Mean**	**50.3**	**72**
5	**Variance**	**350.6778**	**157.3333**
6	**Observations**	**10**	**10**
7	**Pooled Variance**	**254.0056**	
8	**Hypothesized Mean Difference**	**0**	
9	**df**	**18**	
10	**t Stat**	**-3.0446**	
11	**P(T<=t) one-tail**	**0.0035**	
12	**t Critical one-tail**	**1.7341**	
13	**P(T<=t) two-tail**	**0.0070**	
14	**t Critical two-tail**	**2.1009**	

Confidence Interval Estimate for the Difference Between Two Means

PHStat Modify the *PHStat* instructions for the pooled-variance *t* test. In step 7, check **Confidence Interval Estimate** and enter a **Confidence Level** in its box, in addition to entering a **Title** and clicking **OK**.

In-Depth Excel Use the *In-Depth Excel* instructions for the pooled-variance *t* test. The worksheets in the **Pooled-Variance T workbook** include a confidence interval estimate for the difference between two means in the cell range D3:D16.

t Test for the Difference Between Two Means, Assuming Unequal Variances

Key Technique Use the **T.INV.2T(*level of significance, degrees of freedom*)** function to compute the lower and upper critical values and use the **T.DIST.2T(*absolute value of the t test statistic, degrees of freedom*)** to compute the *p*-value.

Example Perform the separate-variance *t* test for the two end-cap locations data that is shown in Figure 10.7 on page 352.

PHStat Use **Separate-Variance t Test.**
For the example, open to the **DATA worksheet** of the **Cola workbook**. Select **PHStat → Two-Sample Tests (Unsummarized Data) → Separate-Variance t Test**. In the procedure's dialog box (shown below):

1. Enter **0** as the **Hypothesized Difference**.
2. Enter **0.05** as the **Level of Significance**.
3. Enter **A1:A11** as the **Population 1 Sample Cell Range**.
4. Enter **B1:B11** as the **Population 2 Sample Cell Range**.
5. Check **First cells in both ranges contain label**.
6. Click **Two-Tail Test**.
7. Enter a **Title** and click **OK**.

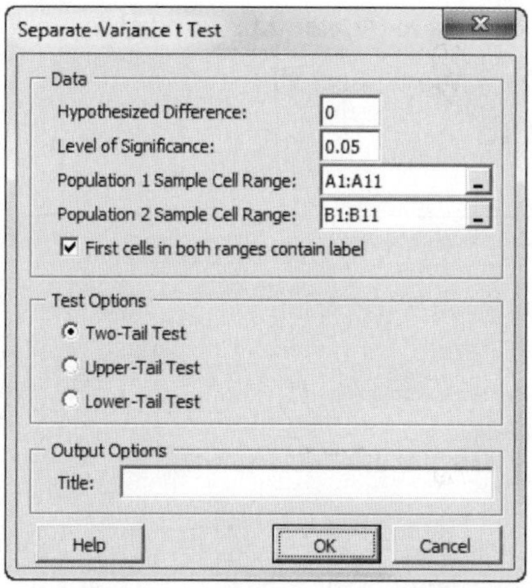

For problems that use summarized data, select **PHStat → Two-Sample Tests (Summarized Data) → Separate-Variance t Test**. In that procedure's dialog box, enter the hypothesized difference and the level of significance, as well as the sample size, sample mean, and sample standard deviation for each group.

In-Depth Excel Use the **COMPUTE worksheet** of the **Separate-Variance T workbook** as a template.
The worksheet already contains the data and formulas to use the unsummarized data for the example. For other problems, use the COMPUTE worksheet with either unsummarized or summarized data. For unsummarized data, paste the data in columns A and B in the **DATACOPY worksheet** and keep the COMPUTE worksheet formulas that compute the sample size, sample mean, and sample standard deviation in the cell range B7:B13. For summarized data, replace those formulas in the cell range B7:B13 with the sample statistics and ignore the DATACOPY worksheet.

Use the similar **COMPUTE_LOWER** or **COMPUTE_UPPER worksheets** in the same workbook as templates for performing one-tail pooled-variance t tests with either unsummarized or summarized data. If you use an Excel version older than Excel 2010, use the COMPUTE_OLDER worksheet as a template for both the two-tail and one-tail tests.

Analysis ToolPak Use **t-Test: Two-Sample Assuming Unequal Variances.**
For the example, open to the **DATA worksheet** of the **Cola workbook** and:

1. Select **Data → Data Analysis.**
2. In the Data Analysis dialog box, select **t-Test: Two-Sample Assuming Unequal Variances** from the **Analysis Tools** list and then click **OK.**

In the procedure's dialog box (shown below):

3. Enter **A1:A11** as the **Variable 1 Range.**
4. Enter **B1:B11** as the **Variable 2 Range.**
5. Enter **0** as the **Hypothesized Mean Difference.**
6. Check **Labels** and enter **0.05** as **Alpha.**
7. Click **New Worksheet Ply.**
8. Click **OK.**

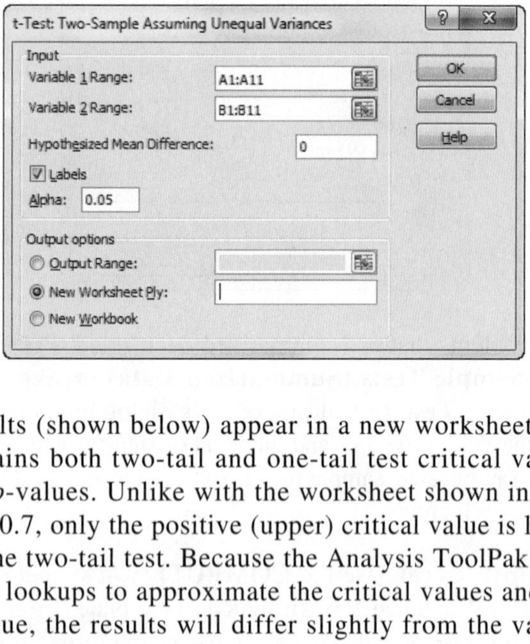

Results (shown below) appear in a new worksheet that contains both two-tail and one-tail test critical values and p-values. Unlike with the worksheet shown in Figure 10.7, only the positive (upper) critical value is listed for the two-tail test. Because the Analysis ToolPak uses table lookups to approximate the critical values and the p-value, the results will differ slightly from the values shown in Figure 10.7.

	A	B	C
1	t-Test: Two-Sample Assuming Unequal Variances		
2			
3		*Beverage*	*Produce*
4	Mean	50.3	72
5	Variance	350.6778	157.3333
6	Observations	10	10
7	Hypothesized Mean Difference	0	
8	df	16	
9	t Stat	-3.04455	
10	P(T<=t) one-tail	0.003863	
11	t Critical one-tail	1.745884	
12	P(T<=t) two-tail	0.007726	
13	t Critical two-tail	2.119905	

EG10.2 COMPARING the MEANS of TWO RELATED POPULATIONS

Paired t Test

Key Technique Use the **T.INV.2T(*level of significance, degrees of freedom*)** function to compute the lower and upper critical values and use the **T.DIST.2T(*absolute value of the t test statistic, degrees of freedom*)** to compute the p-value.

Example Perform the paired t test for the textbook price data that is shown in Figure 10.9 on page 358.

PHStat Use **Paired t Test.**
For the example, open to the **DATA worksheet** of the **BookPrices workbook**. Select **PHStat → Two-Sample Tests (Unsummarized Data) → Paired t Test.** In the procedure's dialog box (shown below):

1. Enter **0** as the **Hypothesized Mean Difference.**
2. Enter **0.05** as the **Level of Significance.**
3. Enter **C1:C17** as the **Population 1 Sample Cell Range.**
4. Enter **D1:D17** as the **Population 2 Sample Cell Range.**
5. Check **First cells in both ranges contain label.**
6. Click **Two-Tail Test.**
7. Enter a **Title** and click **OK.**

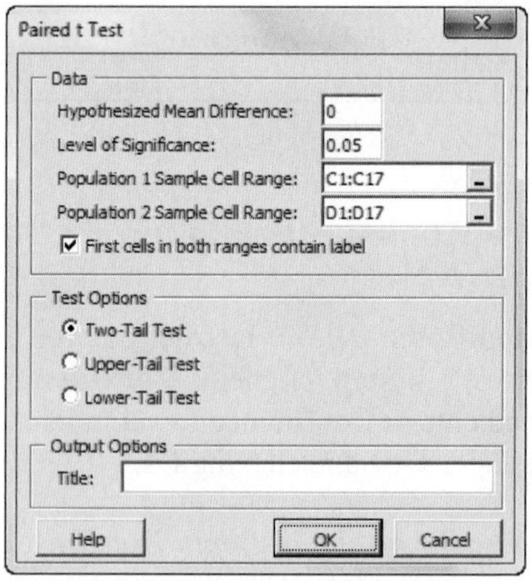

The procedure creates two worksheets, one of which is similar to the PtCalcs worksheet discussed in the following *In-Depth Excel* section. For problems that use summarized data, select **PHStat → Two-Sample Tests (Summarized Data) → Paired t Test.** In that procedure's dialog box, enter the hypothesized mean difference and the level of significance, as well as the sample size, sample mean, and sample standard deviation for each sample.

In-Depth Excel Use the **COMPUTE** and **PtCalcs worksheets** of the **Paired T workbook** as a template.

The COMPUTE and supporting PtCalcs worksheets already contain the textbook price data for the example. The PtCalcs worksheet also computes the differences that allow the COMPUTE worksheet to compute the S_D in cell B11.

For other problems, paste the unsummarized data into columns A and B of the PtCalcs worksheet. For sample sizes greater than 16, select cell C17 and copy the formula in that cell down through the last data row. For sample sizes less than 16, delete the column C formulas for which there are no column A and B values. If you know the sample size, $\overline{D}$, and S_D values, you can ignore the PtCalcs worksheet and enter the values in cells B8, B9, and B11 of the COMPUTE worksheet, overwriting the formulas that those cells contain.

Use the similar **COMPUTE_LOWER** and **COMPUTE_UPPER worksheets** in the same workbook as templates for performing one-tail tests. If you use an Excel version older than Excel 2010, use the COMPUTE_OLDER worksheet as a template for both the two-tail and one-tail tests.

Analysis ToolPak Use **t-Test: Paired Two Sample for Means**.

For the example, open to the **DATA worksheet** of the **BookPrices workbook** and:

1. Select **Data ➔ Data Analysis**.
2. In the Data Analysis dialog box, select **t-Test: Paired Two Sample for Means** from the **Analysis Tools** list and then click **OK**.

In the procedure's dialog box (shown in right column):

3. Enter **C1:C17** as the **Variable 1 Range**.
4. Enter **D1:D17** as the **Variable 2 Range**.
5. Enter **0** as the **Hypothesized Mean Difference**.
6. Check **Labels** and enter **0.05** as **Alpha**.
7. Click **New Worksheet Ply**.
8. Click **OK**.

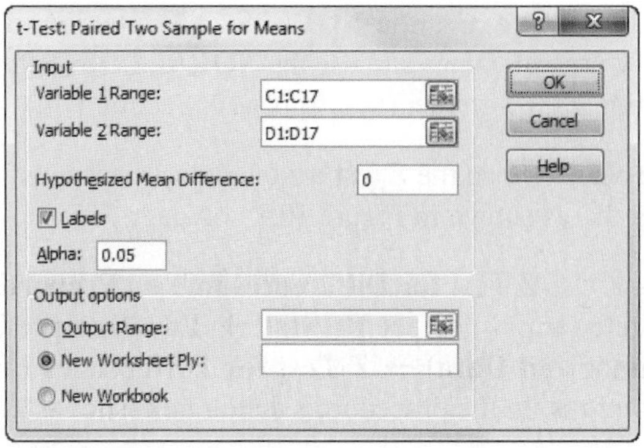

Results (shown below) appear in a new worksheet that contains both two-tail and one-tail test critical values and p-values. Unlike in Figure 10.9, only the positive (upper) critical value is listed for the two-tail test.

	A	B	C
1	**t-Test: Paired Two Sample for Means**		
2			
3		*Bookstore*	*Online*
4	Mean	181.1688	156.0931
5	Variance	4427.8240	2591.1044
6	Observations	16	16
7	Pearson Correlation	0.8512	
8	Hypothesized Mean Difference	0	
9	df	15	
10	t Stat	2.8338	
11	P(T<=t) one-tail	0.0063	
12	t Critical one-tail	1.7531	
13	P(T<=t) two-tail	0.0126	
14	t Critical two-tail	2.1314	

EG10.3 COMPARING the PROPORTIONS of TWO INDEPENDENT POPULATIONS

Z Test for the Difference Between Two Proportions

Key Technique Use the **NORM.S.INV** function to compute the critical values and use the **NORM.S.DIST** function to compute the *p*-value. (See Appendix Section F.4.)

Example Perform the *Z* test for the hotel guest satisfaction survey that is shown in Figure 10.13 on page 365.

PHStat Use ***Z* Test for Differences in Two Proportions**. For the example, select **PHStat → Two-Sample Tests (Summarized Data) → *Z* Test for Differences in Two Proportions**. In the procedure's dialog box (shown below):

1. Enter **0** as the **Hypothesized Difference**.
2. Enter **0.05** as the **Level of Significance**.
3. For the Population 1 Sample, enter **163** as the **Number of Items of Interest** and **227** as the **Sample Size**.
4. For the Population 2 Sample, enter **154** as the **Number of Items of Interest** and **262** as the **Sample Size**.
5. Click **Two-Tail Test**.
6. Enter a **Title** and click **OK**.

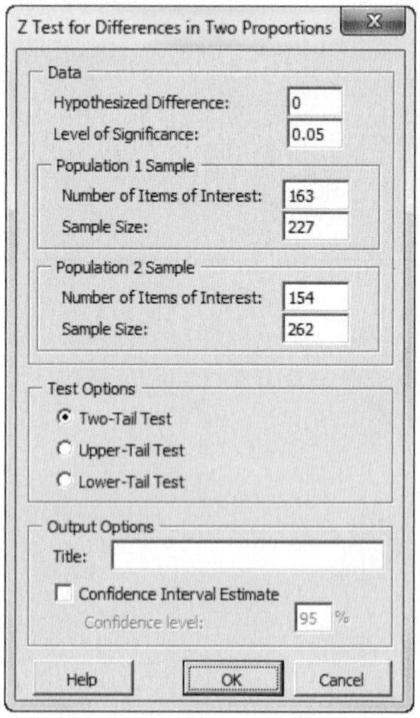

In-Depth Excel Use the **COMPUTE worksheet** of the **Z Two Proportions workbook** as a template.

The worksheet already contains data for the hotel guest satisfaction survey. For other problems, change the hypothesized difference, the level of significance, and the number of successes and sample size for each group in the cell range B4:B11.

Use the similar **COMPUTE_LOWER** and **COMPUTE_UPPER worksheets** in the same workbook as templates for performing one-tail separate-variance *t* tests. If you use an Excel version older than Excel 2010, use the COMPUTE_OLDER worksheet as a template for both the two-tail and one-tail tests.

Confidence Interval Estimate for the Difference Between Two Proportions

PHStat Modify the *PHStat* instructions for the *Z* test for the difference between two proportions. In step 6, also check **Confidence Interval Estimate** and enter a **Confidence Level** in its box, in addition to entering a **Title** and clicking **OK**.

In-Depth Excel Use the *In-Depth Excel* instructions for the *Z* test for the difference between two proportions. The worksheets in the **Z Two Proportions workbook** include a confidence interval estimate for the difference between two means in the cell range D3:E16.

EG10.4 *F* TEST for the RATIO of TWO VARIANCES

Key Technique Use the **F.INV.RT(*level of significance* / 2, *population 1 sample degrees of freedom*, *population 2 sample degrees of freedom*)** function to compute the upper critical value and use the **F.DIST.RT(*F test statistic*, *population 1 sample degrees of freedom*, *population 2 sample degrees of freedom*)** function to compute the *p*-values.

Example Perform the *F* test for the ratio of two variances for the two end-cap locations data that is shown in Figure 10.14 on page 371.

PHStat Use **F Test for Differences in Two Variances.** For the example, open to the **DATA worksheet** of the **Cola workbook**. Select **PHStat ➔ Two-Sample Tests (Unsummarized Data) ➔ F Test for Differences in Two Variances.** In the procedure's dialog box (shown below):

1. Enter **0.05** as the **Level of Significance.**
2. Enter **A1:A11** as the **Population 1 Sample Cell Range.**
3. Enter **B1:B11** as the **Population 2 Sample Cell Range.**
4. Check **First cells in both ranges contain label.**
5. Click **Two-Tail Test.**
6. Enter a **Title** and click **OK.**

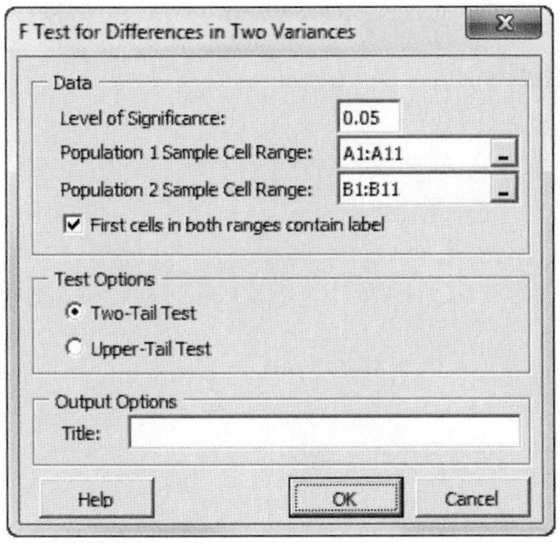

For problems that use summarized data, select **PHStat ➔ Two-Sample Tests (Summarized Data) ➔ F Test for Differences in Two Variances.** In that procedure's dialog box, enter the level of significance and the sample size and sample variance for each sample.

In-Depth Excel Use the **COMPUTE worksheet** of the **F Two Variances workbook** as a template.

The worksheet already contains the data and formulas for using the unsummarized data for the example. For unsummarized data, paste the data in columns A and B in the **DATACOPY worksheet** and keep the COMPUTE worksheet formulas that compute the sample size and sample variance for the two samples in cell range B4:B10. For summarized data, replace the COMPUTE worksheet formulas in cell ranges B4:B10 with the sample statistics and ignore the DATACOPY worksheet.

Use the similar **COMPUTE_UPPER worksheet** in the same workbook as a template for performing the upper-tail test. If you use an Excel version older than Excel 2010, use the COMPUTE_OLDER worksheet as a template for both the two-tail and upper-tail tests.

Analysis ToolPak Use **F-Test Two-Sample for Variances.** For the example, open to the **DATA worksheet** of the **Cola workbook** and:

1. Select **Data ➔ Data Analysis.**
2. In the Data Analysis dialog box, select **F-Test Two-Sample for Variances** from the **Analysis Tools** list and then click **OK.**

In the procedure's dialog box (shown below):

3. Enter **A1:A11** as the **Variable 1 Range** and enter **B1:B11** as the **Variable 2 Range.**
4. Check **Labels** and enter **0.05** as **Alpha.**
5. Click **New Worksheet Ply.**
6. Click **OK.**

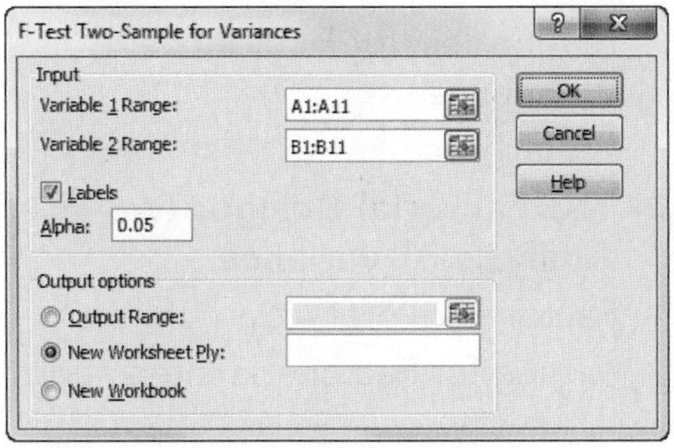

Results (shown below) appear in a new worksheet and include only the one-tail test *p*-value (0.1241), which must be doubled for the two-tail test shown in Figure 10.14 on page 371.

	A	B	C
1	F-Test Two-Sample for Variances		
2			
3		*Beverage*	*Produce*
4	Mean	50.3	72
5	Variance	350.6778	157.3333
6	Observations	10	10
7	df	9	9
8	F	2.2289	
9	P(F<=f) one-tail	0.1241	
10	F Critical one-tail	3.1789	

CHAPTER

11 Analysis of Variance

Learning Objectives

In this chapter, you learn:

- The basic concepts of experimental design
- How to use the one-way analysis of variance to test for differences among the means of several groups
- How to use the two-way analysis of variance and interpret the interaction effect
- How to perform multiple comparisons in a one-way analysis of variance and a two-way analysis of variance

Joggie Botma / Shutterstock

USING STATISTICS

Are There Looming Differences at Perfect Parachutes?

You are the production manager at the Perfect Parachutes Company. Parachutes are woven in your factory using a synthetic fiber purchased from one of four different suppliers. Strength of these fibers is an important characteristic that ensures quality parachutes. You need to decide whether the synthetic fibers from each of your four suppliers result in parachutes of equal strength. Furthermore, to produce parachutes, your factory uses two types of looms, the Jetta and the Turk. You need to establish that the parachutes woven on both types of looms are equally strong. You also want to know if any differences in the strength of the parachute that can be attributed to the four suppliers are dependent on the type of loom used. How would you go about finding this information?

Alexey U / Shutterstock

In Chapter 10, you used hypothesis testing to reach conclusions about possible differences between two populations. As a manager at Perfect Parachutes, you need to design an experiment to test the strength of parachutes woven from the synthetic fibers from the *four* suppliers. That is, you need to evaluate differences among *more than two* populations, or groups. (Populations are called *groups* in this chapter.)

This chapter begins by examining a *completely randomized design* that has one *factor* (which supplier to use) and several groups (the four suppliers). Then the completely randomized design is extended to the *factorial design*, in which more than one factor is simultaneously studied in a single experiment. For example, an experiment incorporating the four suppliers and the two types of looms would help you determine which supplier and type of loom to use in order to manufacture the strongest parachutes. Throughout the chapter, emphasis is placed on the assumptions behind the use of the various testing procedures.

11.1 The Completely Randomized Design: One-Way Analysis of Variance

In many situations, you need to examine differences among more than two **groups**. The groups involved are classified according to **levels** of a **factor** of interest. For example, a factor such as the price for which a product is sold may have several groups defined by *numerical levels* such as \$0.59, \$0.79, and \$0.99, and a factor such as preferred supplier for a parachute manufacturer may have several groups defined by *categorical levels* such as Supplier 1, Supplier 2, Supplier 3, and Supplier 4. When there is only one factor, the experimental design is called a **completely randomized design**.

One-Way ANOVA *F* Test for Differences Among More Than Two Means

Organize multiple-sample data as unstacked data, one column per group, in order to use the Excel Guide instructions for this chapter. For more information about unstacked (and stacked) data, see Section 2.2.

When you are analyzing a numerical variable and certain assumptions are met, you use the **analysis of variance (ANOVA)** to compare the means of the groups. The ANOVA procedure used for the completely randomized design is referred to as the **one-way ANOVA**, and it is an extension of the pooled variance t test for the difference between two means discussed in Section 10.1. Although ANOVA is an acronym for *analysis of variance*, the term is misleading because the objective in ANOVA is to analyze differences among the group means, *not* the variances. However, by analyzing the variation among and within the groups, you can reach conclusions about possible differences in group means. In ANOVA, the total variation is subdivided into variation that is due to differences *among* the groups and variation that is due to differences *within* the groups (see Figure 11.1). **Within-group variation** measures random variation. **Among-group variation** measures differences from group to group. The symbol c is used to indicate the number of groups.

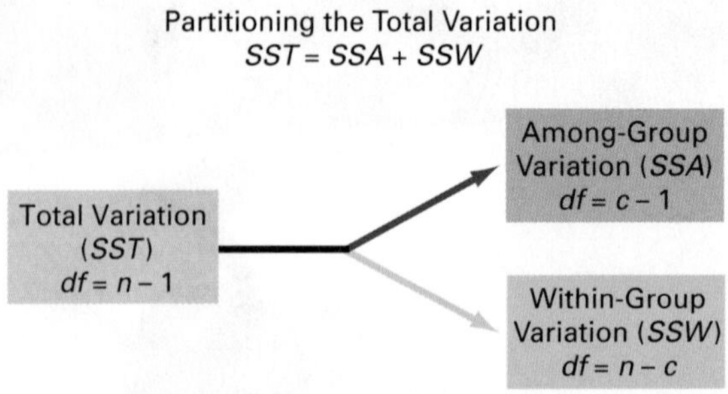

FIGURE 11.1
Partitioning the total variation in a completely randomized design

Student Tip
Another way of stating the alternative hypothesis, H_1, is that at least one population mean is different from the others.

Assuming that the c groups represent populations whose values are randomly and independently selected, follow a normal distribution, and have equal variances, the null hypothesis of no differences in the population means:

$$H_0: \mu_1 = \mu_2 = \cdots = \mu_c$$

is tested against the alternative that not all the c population means are equal:

$$H_1: \text{Not all } \mu_j \text{ are equal (where } j = 1, 2, \ldots, c).$$

To perform an ANOVA test of equality of population means, you subdivide the total variation in the values into two parts—that which is due to variation among the groups and that which is due to variation within the groups. The **total variation** is represented by the **sum of squares total (*SST*)**. Because the population means of the *c* groups are assumed to be equal under the null hypothesis, you compute the total variation among all the values by summing the squared differences between each individual value and the **grand mean, $\bar{\bar{X}}$**. The grand mean is the mean of all the values in all the groups combined. Equation (11.1) shows the computation of the total variation.

Student Tip
Remember that a sum of squares (SS) cannot be negative.

TOTAL VARIATION IN ONE-WAY ANOVA

$$SST = \sum_{j=1}^{c} \sum_{i=1}^{n_j} (X_{ij} - \bar{\bar{X}})^2 \tag{11.1}$$

where

$$\bar{\bar{X}} = \frac{\sum_{j=1}^{c} \sum_{i=1}^{n_j} X_{ij}}{n} = \text{Grand mean}$$

X_{ij} = *i*th value in group *j*

n_j = number of values in group *j*

n = total number of values in all groups combined (that is, $n = n_1 + n_2 + \cdots + n_c$)

c = number of groups

You compute the among-group variation, usually called the **sum of squares among groups (*SSA*)**, by summing the squared differences between the sample mean of each group, $\bar{X}_j$, and the grand mean, $\bar{\bar{X}}$, weighted by the sample size, n_j, in each group. Equation (11.2) shows the computation of the among-group variation.

AMONG-GROUP VARIATION IN ONE-WAY ANOVA

$$SSA = \sum_{j=1}^{c} n_j (\bar{X}_j - \bar{\bar{X}})^2 \tag{11.2}$$

where

c = number of groups

n_j = number of values in group *j*

$\bar{X}_j$ = sample mean of group *j*

$\bar{\bar{X}}$ = grand mean

The within-group variation, usually called the **sum of squares within groups (*SSW*)**, measures the difference between each value and the mean of its own group and sums the squares of these differences over all groups. Equation (11.3) shows the computation of the within-group variation.

WITHIN-GROUP VARIATION IN ONE-WAY ANOVA

$$SSW = \sum_{j=1}^{c} \sum_{i=1}^{n_j} (X_{ij} - \bar{X}_j)^2 \tag{11.3}$$

where

$$X_{ij} = i\text{th value in group } j$$
$$\overline{X}_j = \text{sample mean of group } j$$

Because you are comparing c groups, there are $c - 1$ degrees of freedom associated with the sum of squares among groups. Because each of the c groups contributes $n_j - 1$ degrees of freedom, there are $n - c$ degrees of freedom associated with the sum of squares within groups. In addition, there are $n - 1$ degrees of freedom associated with the sum of squares total because you are comparing each value, X_{ij}, to the grand mean, $\overline{\overline{X}}$, based on all n values.

If you divide each of these sums of squares by its respective degrees of freedom, you have three variances, which in ANOVA are called **mean square** terms: *MSA* (mean square among), *MSW* (mean square within), and *MST* (mean square total).

Student Tip
Remember, *mean square* is just another term for *variance* that is used in the Analysis of Variance. Also, since the mean square is equal to the sum of squares divided by the degrees of freedom, a mean square can never be negative.

MEAN SQUARES IN ONE-WAY ANOVA

$$MSA = \frac{SSA}{c - 1} \quad \textbf{(11.4a)}$$

$$MSW = \frac{SSW}{n - c} \quad \textbf{(11.4b)}$$

$$MST = \frac{SST}{n - 1} \quad \textbf{(11.4c)}$$

Although you want to compare the means of the c groups to determine whether a difference exists among them, the name ANOVA comes from the fact that you are comparing variances. If the null hypothesis is true and there are no differences in the c group means, all three mean squares (or *variances*)—*MSA*, *MSW*, and *MST*—provide estimates of the overall variance in the data. Thus, to test the null hypothesis:

$$H_0: \mu_1 = \mu_2 = \cdots = \mu_c$$

against the alternative:

$$H_1: \text{Not all } \mu_j \text{ are equal (where } j = 1, 2, \ldots, c)$$

you compute the one-way ANOVA F_{STAT} test statistic as the ratio of *MSA* to *MSW*, as in Equation (11.5).

ONE-WAY ANOVA F_{STAT} TEST STATISTIC

$$F_{STAT} = \frac{MSA}{MSW} \quad \textbf{(11.5)}$$

The F_{STAT} test statistic follows an ***F* distribution**, with $c - 1$ degrees of freedom in the numerator and $n - c$ degrees of freedom in the denominator.

For a given level of significance, α, you reject the null hypothesis if the F_{STAT} test statistic computed in Equation (11.5) is greater than the upper-tail critical value, F_α, from the F distribution

Student Tip
Because the *F* statistic is the ratio of two mean squares, it can never be negative.

with $c - 1$ degrees of freedom in the numerator and $n - c$ in the denominator (see Table E.5). Thus, as shown in Figure 11.2, the decision rule is

$$\text{Reject } H_0 \text{ if } F_{STAT} > F_\alpha;$$

$$\text{otherwise, do not reject } H_0.$$

FIGURE 11.2
Regions of rejection and nonrejection when using ANOVA

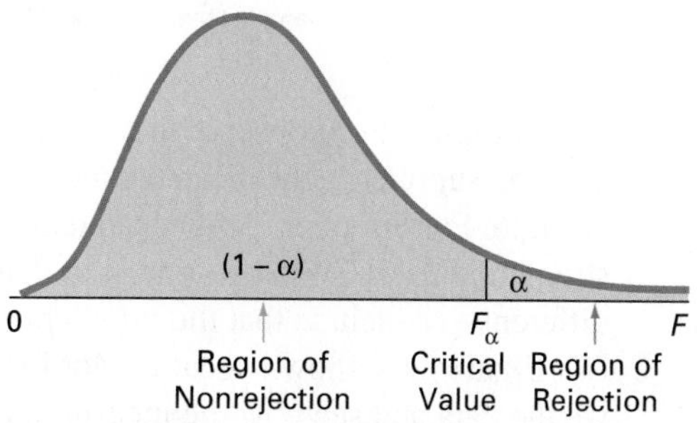

If the null hypothesis is true, the computed F_{STAT} test statistic is expected to be approximately equal to 1 because both the numerator and denominator mean square terms are estimating the overall variance in the data. If H_0 is false (and there are differences in the group means), the computed F_{STAT} test statistic is expected to be larger than 1 because the numerator, *MSA*, is estimating the differences among groups in addition to the overall variability in the values, while the denominator, *MSW*, is measuring only the overall variability in the values. Thus, when you use the ANOVA procedure, you reject the null hypothesis at a selected level of significance, α, only if the computed F_{STAT} test statistic is *greater than* F_α, the upper-tail critical value of the *F* distribution having $c - 1$ and $n - c$ degrees of freedom, as illustrated in Figure 11.2.

The results of an analysis of variance are usually displayed in an **ANOVA summary table**, as shown in Table 11.1. The entries in this table include the sources of variation (i.e., among-groups, within-groups, and total), the degrees of freedom, the sums of squares, the mean squares (i.e., the variances), and the computed F_{STAT} test statistic. The *p*-value, the probability of having an F_{STAT} value as large as or larger than the one computed, given that the null hypothesis is true, usually appears also. The *p*-value allows you to reach conclusions about the null hypothesis without needing to refer to a table of critical values of the *F* distribution. If the *p*-value is less than the chosen level of significance, α, you reject the null hypothesis.

TABLE 11.1
Analysis-of-Variance Summary Table

Source	Degrees of Freedom	Sum of Squares	Mean Square (Variance)	*F*
Among groups	$c - 1$	*SSA*	$MSA = \frac{SSA}{c - 1}$	$F_{STAT} = \frac{MSA}{MSW}$
Within groups	$n - c$	*SSW*	$MSW = \frac{SSW}{n - c}$	
Total	$n - 1$	*SST*		

To illustrate the one-way ANOVA *F* test, return to the Perfect Parachutes scenario (see page 389). You define the business problem as whether significant differences exist in the strength of parachutes woven using synthetic fiber purchased from each of the four suppliers. The strength of the parachutes is measured by placing them in a testing device that pulls on both ends of a parachute until it tears apart. The amount of force required to tear the parachute is measured on a tensile-strength scale, where the larger the value, the stronger the parachute.

Five parachutes are woven using the fiber supplied by each group—Supplier 1, Supplier 2, Supplier 3, and Supplier 4. You perform the experiment of testing the strength of each of the 20 parachutes by collecting the tensile strength measurement of each parachute. Results are organized by group and stored in **Parachute**. Those results, along with the sample mean and the sample standard deviation of each group, are shown in Figure 11.3.

FIGURE 11.3

Tensile strength for parachutes woven with synthetic fibers from four different suppliers, along with the sample mean and sample standard deviation

	Supplier 1	Supplier 2	Supplier 3	Supplier 4
	18.5	26.3	20.6	25.4
	24.0	25.3	25.2	19.9
	17.2	24.0	20.8	22.6
	19.9	21.2	24.7	17.5
	18.0	24.5	22.9	20.4
Sample Mean	19.52	24.26	22.84	21.16
Sample Standard Deviation	2.69	1.92	2.13	2.98

In Figure 11.3, observe that there are differences in the sample means for the four suppliers. For Supplier 1, the mean tensile strength is 19.52. For Supplier 2, the mean tensile strength is 24.26. For Supplier 3, the mean tensile strength is 22.84, and for Supplier 4, the mean tensile strength is 21.16. What you need to determine is whether these sample results are sufficiently different to conclude that the *population* means are not all equal.

Figure 11.4 shows a scatter plot for the four suppliers. A scatter plot enables you to visualize the data and see how the measurements of tensile strength distribute. You can also observe differences among the groups as well as within groups. If the sample sizes in each group were larger, you could construct stem-and-leaf displays, boxplots, and normal probability plots.

FIGURE 11.4

Scatter plot of tensile strengths for four different suppliers

Use the Section EG2.5 instructions to construct scatter plots.

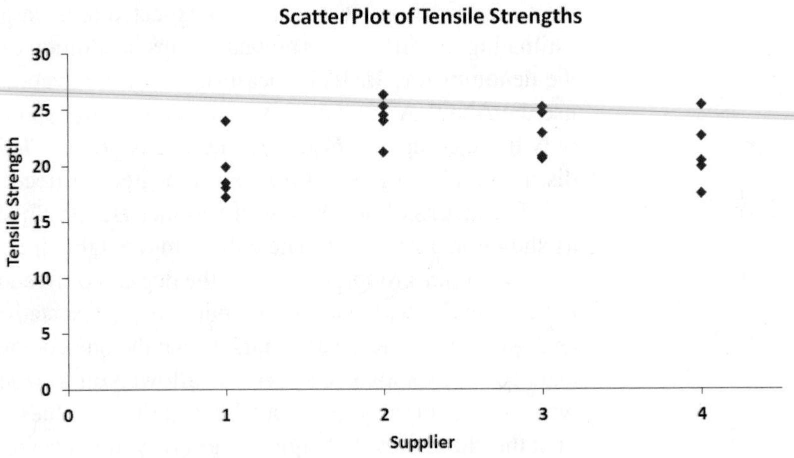

The null hypothesis states that there is no difference in mean tensile strength among the four suppliers:

$$H_0: \mu_1 = \mu_2 = \mu_3 = \mu_4$$

The alternative hypothesis states that at least one of the suppliers differs with respect to the mean tensile strength:

$$H_1: \text{Not all the means are equal.}$$

To construct the ANOVA summary table, you first compute the sample means in each group (see Figure 11.3 above). Then you compute the grand mean by summing all 20 values and dividing by the total number of values:

$$\bar{\bar{X}} = \frac{\sum_{j=1}^{c}\sum_{i=1}^{n_j} X_{ij}}{n} = \frac{438.9}{20} = 21.945$$

Then, using Equations (11.1) through (11.3) on page 391, you compute the sum of squares:

$$SSA = \sum_{j=1}^{c} n_j(\bar{X}_j - \bar{\bar{X}})^2 = (5)(19.52 - 21.945)^2 + (5)(24.26 - 21.945)^2$$
$$+ (5)(22.84 - 21.945)^2 + (5)(21.16 - 21.945)^2$$
$$= 63.2855$$

$$SSW = \sum_{j=1}^{c}\sum_{i=1}^{n_j}(X_{ij} - \bar{X}_j)^2$$

$$= (18.5 - 19.52)^2 + \cdots + (18 - 19.52)^2 + (26.3 - 24.26)^2 + \cdots + (24.5 - 24.26)^2$$
$$+ (20.6 - 22.84)^2 + \cdots + (22.9 - 22.84)^2 + (25.4 - 21.16)^2 + \cdots + (20.4 - 21.16)^2$$
$$= 97.5040$$

$$SST = \sum_{j=1}^{c}\sum_{i=1}^{n_j}(X_{ij} - \bar{\bar{X}})^2$$

$$= (18.5 - 21.945)^2 + (24 - 21.945)^2 + \cdots + (20.4 - 21.945)^2$$
$$= 160.7895$$

You compute the mean squares by dividing the sum of squares by the corresponding degrees of freedom [see Equation (11.4) on page 392]. Because $c = 4$ and $n = 20$,

$$MSA = \frac{SSA}{c - 1} = \frac{63.2855}{4 - 1} = 21.0952$$

$$MSW = \frac{SSW}{n - c} = \frac{97.5040}{20 - 4} = 6.0940$$

so that using Equation (11.5) on page 392,

$$F_{STAT} = \frac{MSA}{MSW} = \frac{21.0952}{6.0940} = 3.4616$$

For a selected level of significance, α, you find the upper-tail critical value, F_α, from the F distribution using Table E.5. A portion of Table E.5 is presented in Table 11.2. In the parachute supplier example, there are 3 degrees of freedom in the numerator and 16 degrees of freedom in the denominator. F_α, the upper-tail critical value at the 0.05 level of significance, is 3.24.

TABLE 11.2

Finding the Critical Value of F with 3 and 16 Degrees of Freedom at the 0.05 Level of Significance

	Cumulative Probabilities = 0.95 Upper-Tail Area = 0.05 Numerator df_1								
Denominator df_2	**1**	**2**	**3**	**4**	**5**	**6**	**7**	**8**	**9**
⋮	⋮	⋮	⋮	⋮	⋮	⋮	⋮	⋮	⋮
11	4.84	3.98	3.59	3.36	3.20	3.09	3.01	2.95	2.90
12	4.75	3.89	3.49	3.26	3.11	3.00	2.91	2.85	2.80
13	4.67	3.81	3.41	3.18	3.03	2.92	2.83	2.77	2.71
14	4.60	3.74	3.34	3.11	2.96	2.85	2.76	2.70	2.65
15	4.54	3.68	3.29	3.06	2.90	2.79	2.71	2.64	2.59
16	4.49	3.63	3.24	3.01	2.85	2.74	2.66	2.59	2.54

Source: Extracted from Table E.5.

Because $F_{STAT} = 3.4616$ is greater than $F_\alpha = 3.24$, you reject the null hypothesis (see Figure 11.5). You conclude that there is a significant difference in the mean tensile strength among the four suppliers.

FIGURE 11.5

Regions of rejection and nonrejection for the one-way ANOVA at the 0.05 level of significance, with 3 and 16 degrees of freedom

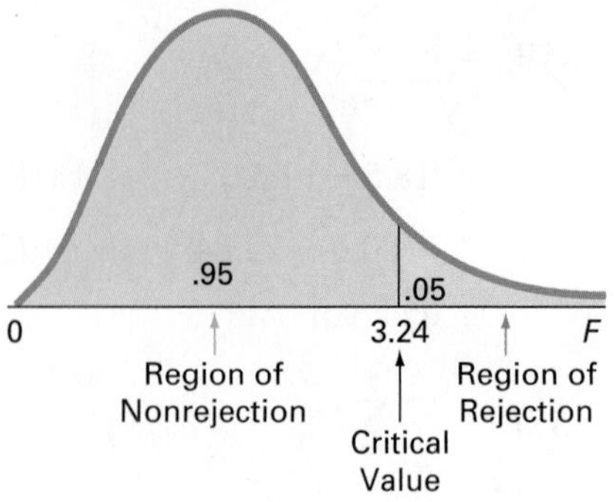

Figure 11.6 shows the ANOVA results for the parachute experiment, including the p-value. In Figure 11.6, what Table 11.1 (see page 393) labels Among Groups is labeled Between Groups in the worksheet.

FIGURE 11.6

ANOVA worksheet for the parachute experiment (formulas for rows 13 through 16 are shown in the inset)

	A	B	C	D	E	F	G	H	I	J
1	ANOVA: Single Factor								Calculations	
2									c	4
3	SUMMARY								n	20
4	*Groups*	*Count*	*Sum*	*Average*	*Variance*					
5	Supplier 1	5	97.6	19.52	7.237					
6	Supplier 2	5	121.3	24.26	3.683					
7	Supplier 3	5	114.2	22.84	4.553					
8	Supplier 4	5	105.8	21.16	8.903					
9										
10										
11	ANOVA									
12	*Source of Variation*	*SS*	*df*	*MS*	*F*	*P-value*	*F crit*			
13	Between Groups	63.2855	3	21.0952	3.4616	0.0414	3.2389			
14	Within Groups	97.504	16	6.0940						
15										
16	Total	160.7895	19							
17					*Level of significance*		0.05			

ANOVA						
Source of Variation	*SS*	*df*	*MS*	*F*	*P - value*	*F crit*
Between Groups	=B16 - DEVSQ(ASFData!A:A) - DEVSQ(ASFData!B:B) - DEVSQ(ASFData!C:C) - DEVSQ(ASFData!D:D)	=J2 - 1	=B13/C13	=D13/D14	=F.DIST.RT(E13, C13, C14)	=F.INV.RT(G17, C13, C14)
Within Groups	=B16 - B13	=J3 - J2	=B14/C14			
Total	=DEVSQ(ASFData!A1:D6)	=C13 + C14				

Figure 11.6 displays the ***COMPUTE worksheet*** *of the* ***One-Way ANOVA workbook*** *that the Section EG11.1 instructions use. (The Analysis ToolPak creates a worksheet that does not display formulas.)*

The p-value, or probability of getting a computed F_{STAT} statistic of 3.4616 or larger when the null hypothesis is true, is 0.0414. Because this p-value is less than the specified α of 0.05, you reject the null hypothesis. The p-value of 0.0414 indicates that there is a 4.14% chance of observing differences this large or larger if the population means for the four suppliers are all equal. After performing the one-way ANOVA and finding a significant difference among the suppliers, you still do not know *which* suppliers differ. All you know is that there is sufficient evidence to state that the population means are not all the same. In other words, one or more population means are significantly different. To determine which suppliers differ, you can use a multiple comparisons procedure such as the Tukey-Kramer procedure.

Multiple Comparisons: The Tukey-Kramer Procedure

Student Tip

You have an α level of risk in the entire set of comparisons not just a single comparison.

In the Perfect Parachutes scenario on page 389, you used the one-way ANOVA F test to determine that there was a difference among the suppliers. The next step is to construct **multiple comparisons** to determine which suppliers are different.

Although many procedures are available (see references 5, 6, and 9), this text uses the **Tukey-Kramer multiple comparisons procedure for one-way ANOVA** to determine which of the c means are significantly different. This procedure enables you to simultaneously make comparisons between *all* pairs of groups. The procedure consists of the following four steps:

1. Compute the absolute mean differences, $|\bar{X}_j - \bar{X}_{j'}|$ (where $j \neq j'$), among all $c(c - 1)/2$ pairs of sample means.
2. Compute the **critical range** for the Tukey-Kramer procedure, using Equation (11.6). If the sample sizes differ, compute a critical range for each pairwise comparison of sample means.

CRITICAL RANGE FOR THE TUKEY-KRAMER PROCEDURE

$$\text{Critical range} = Q_{\alpha}\sqrt{\frac{MSW}{2}\left(\frac{1}{n_j} + \frac{1}{n_{j'}}\right)} \quad \textbf{(11.6)}$$

where Q_{α} is the upper-tail critical value from a **Studentized range distribution** having c degrees of freedom in the numerator and $n - c$ degrees of freedom in the denominator. (Values for the Studentized range distribution are found in Table E.7.)

3. Compare each of the $c(c - 1)/2$ pairs of means against its corresponding critical range. Declare a specific pair significantly different if the absolute difference in the sample means, $|\bar{X}_j - \bar{X}_{j'}|$, is greater than the critical range.
4. Interpret the results.

In the parachute example, there are four suppliers. Thus, there are $4(4 - 1)/2 = 6$ pairwise comparisons. To apply the Tukey-Kramer multiple comparisons procedure, you first compute the absolute mean differences for all six pairwise comparisons:

1. $|\bar{X}_1 - \bar{X}_2| = |19.52 - 24.26| = 4.74$
2. $|\bar{X}_1 - \bar{X}_3| = |19.52 - 22.84| = 3.32$
3. $|\bar{X}_1 - \bar{X}_4| = |19.52 - 21.16| = 1.64$
4. $|\bar{X}_2 - \bar{X}_3| = |24.26 - 22.84| = 1.42$
5. $|\bar{X}_2 - \bar{X}_4| = |24.26 - 21.16| = 3.10$
6. $|\bar{X}_3 - \bar{X}_4| = |22.84 - 21.16| = 1.68$

You need to compute only one critical range because the sample sizes in the four groups are equal. From the ANOVA summary table (Figure 11.6 on page 396), $MSW = 6.094$ and $n_j = n_{j'} = 5$. From Table E.7, for $\alpha = 0.05$, $c = 4$, and $n - c = 20 - 4 = 16$, Q_{α}, the upper-tail critical value of the test statistic, is 4.05 (see Table 11.3).

TABLE 11.3

Finding the Studentized Range, Q_{α}, Statistic for $\alpha = 0.05$, with 4 and 16 Degrees of Freedom

	Cumulative Probabilities = 0.95 Upper-Tail Area = 0.05 Numerator df_1							
Denominator df_2	**2**	**3**	**4**	**5**	**6**	**7**	**8**	**9**
⋮	⋮	⋮	⋮	⋮	⋮	⋮	⋮	⋮
11	3.11	3.82	4.26	4.57	4.82	5.03	5.20	5.35
12	3.08	3.77	4.20	4.51	4.75	4.95	5.12	5.27
13	3.06	3.73	4.15	4.45	4.69	4.88	5.05	5.19
14	3.03	3.70	4.11	4.41	4.64	4.83	4.99	5.13
15	3.01	3.67	4.08	4.37	4.60	4.78	4.94	5.08
16	3.00	3.65	4.05	4.33	4.56	4.74	4.90	5.03

Source: Extracted from Table E.7.

From Equation (11.6),

$$\text{Critical range} = 4.05\sqrt{\left(\frac{6.094}{2}\right)\left(\frac{1}{5} + \frac{1}{5}\right)} = 4.4712$$

Because 4.74 > 4.4712, there is a significant difference between the means of Suppliers 1 and 2. All other pairwise differences are less than 4.4712. With 95% confidence, you can conclude that parachutes woven using fiber from Supplier 1 have a lower mean tensile strength than those from Supplier 2, but there are no statistically significant differences between Suppliers 1 and 3, Suppliers 1 and 4, Suppliers 2 and 3, Suppliers 2 and 4, and Suppliers 3 and 4. Note that by using $\alpha = 0.05$, you are able to make all six of the comparisons with an overall error rate of only 5%. These results are shown in Figure 11.7.

FIGURE 11.7
Tukey-Kramer procedure worksheet for the parachute experiment

Figure 11.7 displays the ***TK4 worksheet*** *of the* ***One-Way ANOVA workbook*** *that the Section EG11.1 instructions use.*

	A	B	C	D	E	F	G	H	I
1	Tukey Kramer Multiple Comparisons								
2									
3		Sample	Sample			Absolute	Std. Error	Critical	
4	Group	Mean	Size		Comparison	Difference	of Difference	Range	Results
5	1: Supplier 1	19.52	5		Group 1 to Group 2	4.74	1.103992754	4.4712	Means are different
6	2: Supplier 2	24.26	5		Group 1 to Group 3	3.32	1.103992754	4.4712	Means are not different
7	3: Supplier 3	22.84	5		Group 1 to Group 4	1.64	1.103992754	4.4712	Means are not different
8	4: Supplier 4	21.16	5		Group 2 to Group 3	1.42	1.103992754	4.4712	Means are not different
9					Group 2 to Group 4	3.1	1.103992754	4.4712	Means are not different
10	Other Data				Group 3 to Group 4	1.68	1.103992754	4.4712	Means are not different
11	Level of significance	0.05							
12	Numerator d.f.	4							
13	Denominator d.f.	16							
14	MSW	6.094							
15	Q Statistic	4.05							

The Figure 11.7 worksheet results follow the steps used on pages 396–397 for evaluating the comparisons. Each mean is computed, and the absolute differences are determined, the critical range is computed, and then each comparison is declared significant (means are different) or not significant (means are not different).

The Analysis of Means (ANOM) (*online*)

LEARN MORE

Learn more about this in a Chapter 11 eBook bonus section.

The analysis of means (ANOM) provides an alternative approach that allows you to determine which, if any, of the c groups has a mean significantly different from the overall mean of all the group means combined.

ANOVA Assumptions

In Chapters 9 and 10, you learned about the assumptions required in order to use each hypothesis-testing procedure and the consequences of departures from these assumptions. To use the one-way ANOVA F test, you must make the following assumptions about the populations:

- Randomness and independence
- Normality
- Homogeneity of variance

The first assumption, **randomness and independence**, is critically important. The validity of any experiment depends on random sampling and/or the randomization process. To avoid biases in the outcomes, you need to select random samples from the c groups or use the randomization process to randomly assign the items to the c levels of the factor. Selecting a random sample or randomly assigning the levels ensures that a value from one group is independent of any other value in the experiment. Departures from this assumption can seriously affect inferences from the ANOVA. These problems are discussed more thoroughly in references 5 and 9.

The second assumption, **normality**, states that the sample values in each group are from a normally distributed population. Just as in the case of the t test, the one-way ANOVA F test is fairly robust against departures from the normal distribution. As long as the distributions are not extremely different from a normal distribution, the level of significance of the ANOVA F test is usually not greatly affected, particularly for large samples. You can assess the normality of each of the c samples by constructing a normal probability plot or a boxplot.

The third assumption, **homogeneity of variance**, states that the variances of the c groups are equal (i.e., $\sigma_1^2 = \sigma_2^2 = \cdots = \sigma_c^2$). If you have equal sample sizes in each group, inferences based on the F distribution are not seriously affected by unequal variances. However, if you have unequal sample sizes, unequal variances can have a serious effect on inferences from the ANOVA procedure. Thus, when possible, you should have equal sample sizes in all groups. You can use the Levene test for homogeneity of variance to test whether the variances of the c groups are equal.

When only the normality assumption is violated, you can use the Kruskal-Wallis rank test, a nonparametric procedure discussed in Section 12.5. When only the homogeneity-of-variance assumption is violated, you can use procedures similar to those used in the separate-variance t test of Section 10.1(see references 1 and 2). When both the normality and homogeneity-of-variance assumptions have been violated, you need to use an appropriate data transformation that both normalizes the data and reduces the differences in variances (see reference 6) or use a more general nonparametric procedure (see references 2 and 3).

Levene Test for Homogeneity of Variance

Although the one-way ANOVA F test is relatively robust with respect to the assumption of equal group variances, large differences in the group variances can seriously affect the level of significance and the power of the F test. One powerful yet simple procedure for testing the equality of the variances is the modified **Levene test** (see references 1 and 7). To test for the homogeneity of variance, you use the following null hypothesis:

$$H_0: \sigma_1^2 = \sigma_2^2 = \cdots = \sigma_c^2$$

against the alternative hypothesis:

$$H_1: \text{Not all } \sigma_j^2 \text{ are equal } (j = 1, 2, 3, \ldots, c)$$

Student Tip
Remember when performing the Levene test that you are conducting a one-way ANOVA on the absolute differences from the median in each group, not on the actual values themselves.

To test the null hypothesis of equal variances, you first compute the absolute value of the difference between each value and the median of the group. Then you perform a one-way ANOVA on these *absolute differences*. Most statisticians suggest using a level of significance of $\alpha = 0.05$ when performing the ANOVA. To illustrate the modified Levene test, return to the Perfect Parachutes scenario concerning the tensile strength of parachutes first presented in Figure 11.3 on page 394. Table 11.4 summarizes the absolute differences from the median of each supplier.

TABLE 11.4
Absolute Differences from the Median Tensile Strength for Four Suppliers

Supplier 1 (Median = 18.5)	Supplier 2 (Median = 24.5)	Supplier 3 (Median = 22.9)	Supplier 4 (Median = 20.4)
$\lvert 18.5 - 18.5 \rvert = 0.0$	$\lvert 26.3 - 24.5 \rvert = 1.8$	$\lvert 20.6 - 22.9 \rvert = 2.3$	$\lvert 25.4 - 20.4 \rvert = 5.0$
$\lvert 24.0 - 18.5 \rvert = 5.5$	$\lvert 25.3 - 24.5 \rvert = 0.8$	$\lvert 25.2 - 22.9 \rvert = 2.3$	$\lvert 19.9 - 20.4 \rvert = 0.5$
$\lvert 17.2 - 18.5 \rvert = 1.3$	$\lvert 24.0 - 24.5 \rvert = 0.5$	$\lvert 20.8 - 22.9 \rvert = 2.1$	$\lvert 22.6 - 20.4 \rvert = 2.2$
$\lvert 19.9 - 18.5 \rvert = 1.4$	$\lvert 21.2 - 24.5 \rvert = 3.3$	$\lvert 24.7 - 22.9 \rvert = 1.8$	$\lvert 17.5 - 20.4 \rvert = 2.9$
$\lvert 18.0 - 18.5 \rvert = 0.5$	$\lvert 24.5 - 24.5 \rvert = 0.0$	$\lvert 22.9 - 22.9 \rvert = 0.0$	$\lvert 20.4 - 20.4 \rvert = 0.0$

Using the absolute differences given in Table 11.4, you perform a one-way ANOVA (see Figure 11.8).

FIGURE 11.8
Levene test worksheet for the absolute differences for the parachute experiment

	A	B	C	D	E	F	G	H	I	J
1	ANOVA: Levene Test								Calculations	
2									c	4
3	SUMMARY								n	20
4	Groups	Count	Sum	Average	Variance					
5	Supplier 1	5	8.7	1.74	4.753					
6	Supplier 2	5	6.4	1.28	1.707					
7	Supplier 3	5	8.5	1.7	0.945					
8	Supplier 4	5	10.6	2.12	4.007					
9										
10										
11	ANOVA									
12	Source of Variation	SS	df	MS	F	P-value	F crit			
13	Between Groups	1.77	3	0.5900	0.2068	0.8902	3.2389			
14	Within Groups	45.648	16	2.8530						
15										
16	Total	47.418	19							
17					Level of significance		0.05			

Figure 11.8 displays the ***COMPUTE worksheet*** *of the* ***Levene workbook*** *that the Section EG11.1 instructions use. This COMPUTE worksheet shares the identical design to the COMPUTE worksheet in the One-Way ANOVA workbook.*

From the Figure 11.8 results, observe that $F_{STAT} = 0.2068$. (The worksheet labels this value F.) Because $F_{STAT} = 0.2068 < 3.2389$ (or the p-value $= 0.8902 > 0.05$), you do not reject H_0. There is no evidence of a significant difference among the four variances. In other words, it is reasonable to assume that the materials from the four suppliers produce parachutes with an equal amount of variability. Therefore, the homogeneity-of-variance assumption for the ANOVA procedure is justified.

Example 11.1 illustrates another example of the one-way ANOVA.

EXAMPLE 11.1

ANOVA of the Speed of Drive-Through Service at Fast-Food Chains

For fast-food restaurants, the drive-through window is an increasing source of revenue. The chain that offers the fastest service is likely to attract additional customers. Each year *QSR Magazine*, **www.qsrmagazine.com**, publishes its results of a survey of drive-through service times (from menu board to departure) at fast-food chains. In a recent year, the mean time was 145.5 seconds for Wendy's, 146.7 seconds for Taco Bell, 171.1 seconds for Burger King, 184.2 seconds for McDonald's, and 178.9 seconds for Chick-fil-A. Suppose the study was based on 20 customers for each fast-food chain. At the 0.05 level of significance, is there evidence of a difference in the mean drive-through service times of the five chains?

Table 11.5 contains the ANOVA table for this problem.

TABLE 11.5

ANOVA Summary Table of Drive-Through Service Times at Fast-Food Chains

Source	Degrees of Freedom	Sum of Squares	Mean Squares	F	p-value
Among chains	4	26,276.16	6,569.04	50.2989	0.0000
Within chains	95	12,407.00	130.60		

SOLUTION

H_0: $\mu_1 = \mu_2 = \mu_3 = \mu_4 = \mu_5$ where 1 = Wendy's, 2 = Taco Bell, 3 = Burger King, 4 = McDonald's, 5 = Chick-fil-A

H_1: Not all μ_j are equal, where $j = 1, 2, 3, 4, 5$

Decision rule: If p-value < 0.05, reject H_0. Because the p-value is virtually 0, which is less than $\alpha = 0.05$, reject H_0. You have sufficient evidence to conclude that the mean drive-through times of the five chains are not all equal.

To determine which of the means are significantly different from one another, use the Tukey-Kramer procedure [Equation (11.6) on page 397] to establish the critical range:

$$\text{Critical value of } Q \text{ with 5 and 95 degrees of freedom} \approx 3.92$$

$$\text{Critical range} = Q_\alpha \sqrt{\left(\frac{MSW}{2}\right)\left(\frac{1}{n_j} + \frac{1}{n_{j'}}\right)} = (3.92)\sqrt{\left(\frac{130.6}{2}\right)\left(\frac{1}{20} + \frac{1}{20}\right)}$$
$$= 10.02$$

Any observed difference greater than 10.02 is considered significant. The mean drive-through service times are different between Wendy's (mean of 145.5 seconds) and Burger King, McDonald's, and Chick-fil-A and also between Taco Bell (mean of 146.7) and Burger King, McDonald's, and Chick-fil-A. In addition, the mean drive-through service time is different between Burger King and McDonald's. Thus, with 95% confidence, you can conclude that the mean drive-through service time for Wendy's and for Taco Bell is faster than those of Burger King, McDonald's, and Chick-fil-A. In addition, the mean drive-through service time for McDonald's is slower than for Burger King.

Problems for Section 11.1

LEARNING THE BASICS

11.1 An experiment has a single factor with five groups and seven values in each group.

a. How many degrees of freedom are there in determining the among-group variation?

b. How many degrees of freedom are there in determining the within-group variation?

c. How many degrees of freedom are there in determining the total variation?

11.2 You are working with the same experiment as in Problem 11.1.

a. If $SSA = 60$ and $SST = 210$, what is SSW?

b. What is MSA?

c. What is MSW?

d. What is the value of F_{STAT}?

11.3 You are working with the same experiment as in Problems 11.1 and 11.2.

a. Construct the ANOVA summary table and fill in all values in the table.

b. At the 0.05 level of significance, what is the upper-tail critical value from the *F* distribution?

c. State the decision rule for testing the null hypothesis that all five groups have equal population means.

d. What is your statistical decision?

11.4 Consider an experiment with three groups, with seven values in each.

a. How many degrees of freedom are there in determining the among-group variation?

b. How many degrees of freedom are there in determining the within-group variation?

c. How many degrees of freedom are there in determining the total variation?

11.5 Consider an experiment with four groups, with eight values in each. For the ANOVA summary table below, fill in all the missing results:

Source	Degrees of Freedom	Sum of Squares	Mean Square (Variance)	F
Among groups	$c - 1 = ?$	$SSA = ?$	$MSA = 80$	$F_{STAT} = ?$
Within groups	$n - c = ?$	$SSW = 560$	$MSW = ?$	
Total	$n - 1 = ?$	$SST = ?$		

11.6 You are working with the same experiment as in Problem 11.5.

a. At the 0.05 level of significance, state the decision rule for testing the null hypothesis that all four groups have equal population means.

b. What is your statistical decision?

c. At the 0.05 level of significance, what is the upper-tail critical value from the Studentized range distribution?

d. To perform the Tukey-Kramer procedure, what is the critical range?

APPLYING THE CONCEPTS

11.7 *Accounting Today* identified the top accounting firms in 10 geographic regions across the United States. Even though all 10 regions reported growth in 2011, the Capital, Great Lakes, Mid-Atlantic, and Northeast regions reported relatively similar combined growths, of 4.97%, 6.04%, 6.55%, and 5.20%, respectively. A characteristic description of the accounting firms in the Capital, Great Lakes, Mid-Atlantic, and Northeast regions included the number of partners in the firm. The file AccountingPartners4 contains the number of partners. (Data extracted from **bit.ly/KKeokV**.)

a. At the 0.05 level of significance, is there evidence of a difference among the Capital, Great Lakes, Mid-Atlantic, and Northeast region accounting firms with respect to the mean number of partners?

b. If the results in (a) indicate that it is appropriate to do so, use the Tukey-Kramer procedure to determine which regions differ in the mean number of partners. Discuss your findings.

SELF Test **11.8** Students in a business statistics course performed a completely randomized design to test the strength of four brands of trash bags. One-pound weights were placed into a bag, one at a time, until the bag broke. A total of 40 bags, 10 for each brand, were used. The data in Trashbags give the weight (in pounds) required to break the trash bags.

a. At the 0.05 level of significance, is there evidence of a difference in the mean strength of the four brands of trash bags?

b. If appropriate, determine which brands differ in mean strength.

c. At the 0.05 level of significance, is there evidence of a difference in the variation in strength among the four brands of trash bags?

d. Which brand(s) should you buy, and which brand(s) should you avoid? Explain.

11.9 A hospital conducted a study of the waiting time in its emergency room. The hospital has a main campus and three satellite locations. Management had a business objective of reducing waiting time for emergency room cases that did not require immediate attention. To study this, a random sample of 15 emergency room cases that did not require immediate attention at each location were selected on a particular day, and the waiting times (measured from check-in to when the patient was called into the clinic area) were collected and stored in **ERWaiting**.

a. At the 0.05 level of significance, is there evidence of a difference in the mean waiting times in the four locations?
b. If appropriate, determine which locations differ in mean waiting time.
c. At the 0.05 level of significance, is there evidence of a difference in the variation in waiting time among the four locations?

11.10 A manufacturer of pens has hired an advertising agency to develop an advertising campaign for the upcoming holiday season. To prepare for this project, the research director decides to initiate a study of the effect of advertising on product perception. An experiment is designed to compare five different advertisements. Advertisement *A* greatly undersells the pen's characteristics. Advertisement *B* slightly undersells the pen's characteristics. Advertisement *C* slightly oversells the pen's characteristics. Advertisement *D* greatly oversells the pen's characteristics. Advertisement *E* attempts to correctly state the pen's characteristics. A sample of 30 adult respondents, taken from a larger focus group, is randomly assigned to the five advertisements (so that there are 6 respondents to each advertisement). After reading the advertisement and developing a sense of "product expectation," all respondents unknowingly receive the same pen to evaluate. The respondents are permitted to test the pen and the plausibility of the advertising copy. The respondents are then asked to rate the pen from 1 to 7 (lowest to highest) on the product characteristic scales of appearance, durability, and writing performance. The *combined* scores of three ratings (appearance, durability, and writing performance) for the 30 respondents, stored in **Pen**, are as follows:

A	B	C	D	E
15	16	8	5	12
18	17	7	6	19
17	21	10	13	18
19	16	15	11	12
19	19	14	9	17
20	17	14	10	14

a. At the 0.05 level of significance, is there evidence of a difference in the mean rating of the pens following exposure to five advertisements?
b. If appropriate, determine which advertisements differ in mean ratings.
c. At the 0.05 level of significance, is there evidence of a difference in the variation in ratings among the five advertisements?
d. Which advertisement(s) should you use, and which advertisement(s) should you avoid? Explain.

11.11 *QSR* has been reporting on the largest quick-serve and fast-casual brands in the United States for nearly 15 years. The file **QSR** contains the food segment (burger, chicken, pizza, or sandwich) and U.S. average sales per unit ($thousands) for each of 58 quick-service brands. (Data extracted from **bit.ly/Oj6EcY**.)

a. At the 0.05 level of significance, is there evidence of a difference in the mean U.S. average sales per unit ($ thousands) among the food segments?
b. At the 0.05 level of significance, is there a difference in the variation in U.S. average sales per unit ($thousands) among the food segments?
c. What effect does your result in (b) have on the validity of the results in (a)?

11.12 Researchers conducted a study to determine whether graduates with an academic background in the discipline of leadership studies were better equipped with essential soft skills required to be successful in contemporary organizations than students with no leadership education and/or students with a certificate in leadership. The Teams Skills Questionnaire was used to capture students' self-reported ratings of their soft skills. The researchers found the following:

Source	Degrees of Freedom	Sum of Squares	Mean Squares	*F*
Among groups	2	1.879		
Within groups	297	31.865		
Total	299	33.744		

Group	*N*	Mean
No coursework in leadership	109	3.290
Certificate in leadership	90	3.362
Degree in leadership	102	3.471

Source: Data Extracted from C. Brungardt, "The Intersection Between Soft Skill Development and Leadership Education," *Journal of Leadership Education*, 10 (Winter 2011): 1–22.

a. Complete the ANOVA summary table.
b. At the 0.05 level of significance, is there evidence of a difference in the mean soft-skill score reported by different groups?
c. If the results in (b) indicate that it is appropriate, use the Tukey-Kramer procedure to determine which groups differ in mean soft-skill score. Discuss your findings.

11.13 A pet food company has a business objective of expanding its product line beyond its current kidney- and shrimp-based cat foods. The company developed two new products, one based on chicken liver and the other based on salmon. The company conducted an experiment to compare the two new products with its two existing ones, as well as a generic beef-based product sold in a supermarket chain.

For the experiment, a sample of 50 cats from the population at a local animal shelter was selected. Ten cats were randomly assigned to each of the five products being tested. Each of the cats was then presented with 3 ounces of the selected food in a dish at feeding time. The researchers defined the variable to be measured as the number of ounces of food that the cat consumed within a 10-minute time interval that began when the filled dish was presented. The results for this experiment are summarized in the following table and stored in CatFood:

Kidney	Shrimp	Chicken Liver	Salmon	Beef
2.37	2.26	2.29	1.79	2.09
2.62	2.69	2.23	2.33	1.87
2.31	2.25	2.41	1.96	1.67
2.47	2.45	2.68	2.05	1.64
2.59	2.34	2.25	2.26	2.16
2.62	2.37	2.17	2.24	1.75
2.34	2.22	2.37	1.96	1.18
2.47	2.56	2.26	1.58	1.92
2.45	2.36	2.45	2.18	1.32
2.32	2.59	2.57	1.93	1.94

a. At the 0.05 level of significance, is there evidence of a difference in the mean amount of food eaten among the various products?

b. If appropriate, determine which products appear to differ significantly in the mean amount of food eaten.

c. At the 0.05 level of significance, is there evidence of a difference in the variation in the amount of food eaten among the various products?

d. What should the pet food company conclude? Fully describe the pet food company's options with respect to the products.

11.14 A sporting goods manufacturing company wanted to compare the distance traveled by golf balls produced using four different designs. Ten balls were manufactured with each design and were brought to the local golf course for the club professional to test. The order in which the balls were hit with the same club from the first tee was randomized so that the pro did not know which type of ball was being hit. All 40 balls were hit in a short period of time, during which the environmental conditions were essentially the same. The results (distance traveled in yards) for the four designs are stored in Golfball and shown in the following table:

Design 1	Design 2	Design 3	Design 4
206.32	217.08	226.77	230.55
207.94	221.43	224.79	227.95
206.19	218.04	229.75	231.84
204.45	224.13	228.51	224.87
209.65	211.82	221.44	229.49
203.81	213.90	223.85	231.10
206.75	221.28	223.97	221.53
205.68	229.43	234.30	235.45
204.49	213.54	219.50	228.35
210.86	214.51	233.00	225.09

a. At the 0.05 level of significance, is there evidence of a difference in the mean distances traveled by the golf balls with different designs?

b. If the results in (a) indicate that it is appropriate to do so, use the Tukey-Kramer procedure to determine which designs differ in mean distances.

c. What assumptions are necessary in (a)?

d. At the 0.05 level of significance, is there evidence of a difference in the variation of the distances traveled by the golf balls with different designs?

e. What golf ball design should the manufacturing manager choose? Explain.

11.2 The Factorial Design: Two-Way Analysis of Variance

In Section 11.1, you learned about the completely randomized design. In this section, the single-factor completely randomized design is extended to the **two-factor factorial design**, in which two factors are simultaneously evaluated. Each factor is evaluated at two or more levels. For example, in the Perfect Parachutes scenario on page 389, the company faces the business problem of simultaneously evaluating four suppliers and two types of looms to determine which supplier and which loom produce the strongest parachutes. Although this section uses only two factors, you can extend factorial designs to three or more factors (see references 4, 5, 6, 7, and 9).

To analyze data from a two-factor factorial design, you use **two-way ANOVA**. The following definitions are needed to develop the two-way ANOVA procedure:

r = number of levels of factor A

c = number of levels of factor B

n' = number of values (replicates) for each cell (combination of a particular level of factor A and a particular level of factor B)

n = number of values in the entire experiment (where $n = rcn'$)

X_{ijk} = value of the kth observation for level i of factor A and level j of factor B

$$\bar{\bar{X}} = \frac{\sum_{i=1}^{r}\sum_{j=1}^{c}\sum_{k=1}^{n'} X_{ijk}}{rcn'} = \text{grand mean}$$

$$\bar{X}_{i..} = \frac{\sum_{j=1}^{c}\sum_{k=1}^{n'} X_{ijk}}{cn'} = \text{mean of the } i\text{th level of factor } A \text{ (where } i = 1, 2, \ldots, r)$$

$$\bar{X}_{.j.} = \frac{\sum_{i=1}^{r}\sum_{k=1}^{n'} X_{ijk}}{rn'} = \text{mean of the } j\text{th level of factor } B \text{ (where } i = 1, 2, \ldots, c)$$

$$\bar{X}_{ij.} = \frac{\sum_{k=1}^{n'} X_{ijk}}{n'} = \text{mean of the cell } ij\text{, the combination of the } i\text{th level of factor } A \text{ and the } j\text{th level of factor } B$$

Because of the complexity of these computations, you should only use computerized methods when performing this analysis. However, to help explain the two-way ANOVA, the decomposition of the total variation is illustrated. In this discussion, only cases in which there are an equal number of **replicates** (sample sizes n') for each combination of the levels of factor A with those of factor B are considered. (See references 1 and 6 for a discussion of two-factor factorial designs with unequal sample sizes.)

Factor and Interaction Effects

There is an **interaction** between factors A and B if the effect of factor A is dependent on the level of factor B. Thus, when dividing the total variation into different sources of variation, you need to account for a possible interaction effect, as well as for factor A, factor B, and random error. To accomplish this, the total variation (SST) is subdivided into sum of squares due to factor A (or SSA), sum of squares due to factor B (or SSB), sum of squares due to the interaction effect of A and B (or $SSAB$), and sum of squares due to random variation (or SSE). This decomposition of the total variation (SST) is displayed in Figure 11.9.

FIGURE 11.9
Partitioning the total variation in a two-factor factorial design

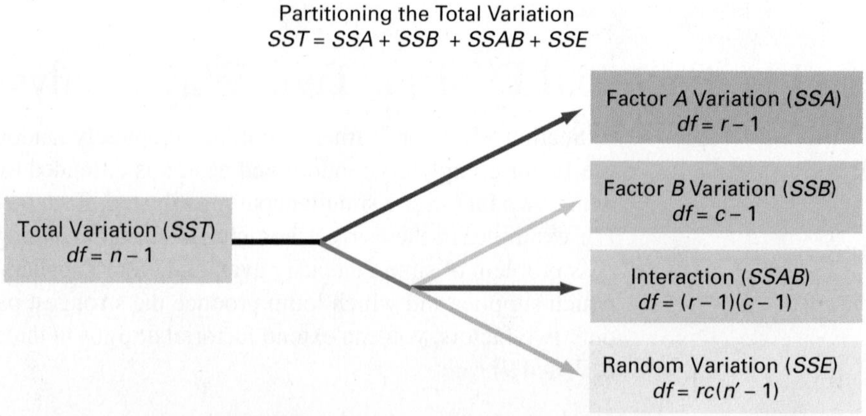

The sum of squares total (*SST*) represents the total variation among all the values around the grand mean. Equation (11.7) shows the computation for total variation.

TOTAL VARIATION IN TWO-WAY ANOVA

$$SST = \sum_{i=1}^{r}\sum_{j=1}^{c}\sum_{k=1}^{n'}(X_{ijk} - \overline{\overline{X}})^2 \tag{11.7}$$

The **sum of squares due to factor *A* (*SSA*)** represents the differences among the various levels of factor *A* and the grand mean. Equation (11.8) shows the computation for factor *A* variation.

FACTOR *A* VARIATION

$$SSA = cn'\sum_{i=1}^{r}(\overline{X}_{i..} - \overline{\overline{X}})^2 \tag{11.8}$$

The **sum of squares due to factor *B* (*SSB*)** represents the differences among the various levels of factor *B* and the grand mean. Equation (11.9) shows the computation for factor *B* variation.

FACTOR *B* VARIATION

$$SSB = rn'\sum_{j=1}^{c}(\overline{X}_{.j.} - \overline{\overline{X}})^2 \tag{11.9}$$

The **sum of squares due to interaction (*SSAB*)** represents the interacting effect of specific combinations of factor *A* and factor *B*. Equation (11.10) shows the computation for interaction variation.

INTERACTION VARIATION

$$SSAB = n'\sum_{i=1}^{r}\sum_{j=1}^{c}(\overline{X}_{ij.} - \overline{X}_{i..} - \overline{X}_{.j.} + \overline{\overline{X}})^2 \tag{11.10}$$

The **sum of squares error (*SSE*)** represents random variation—that is, the differences among the values within each cell and the corresponding cell mean. Equation (11.11) shows the computation for random variation.

RANDOM VARIATION IN TWO-WAY ANOVA

$$SSE = \sum_{i=1}^{r}\sum_{j=1}^{c}\sum_{k=1}^{n'}(X_{ijk} - \overline{X}_{ij.})^2 \tag{11.11}$$

Because there are r levels of factor A, there are $r - 1$ degrees of freedom associated with SSA. Similarly, because there are c levels of factor B, there are $c - 1$ degrees of freedom associated with SSB. Because there are n' replicates in each of the rc cells, there are $rc(n'-1)$ degrees of freedom associated with the SSE term. Carrying this further, there are $n - 1$ degrees of freedom associated with the sum of squares total (SST) because you are comparing each value, X_{ijk}, to the grand mean, $\bar{\bar{X}}$, based on all n values. Therefore, because the degrees of freedom for each of the sources of variation must add to the degrees of freedom for the total variation (SST), you can calculate the degrees of freedom for the interaction component ($SSAB$) by subtraction. The degrees of freedom for interaction are $(r - 1)(c - 1)$.

If you divide each sum of squares by its associated degrees of freedom, you have the four variances or mean square terms (MSA, MSB, $MSAB$, and MSE). Equations (11.12a–d) give the mean square terms needed for the two-way ANOVA table.

Student Tip
Remember, *mean square* is another term for *variance.*

MEAN SQUARES IN TWO-WAY ANOVA

$$MSA = \frac{SSA}{r - 1} \qquad \textbf{(11.12a)}$$

$$MSB = \frac{SSB}{c - 1} \qquad \textbf{(11.12b)}$$

$$MSAB = \frac{SSAB}{(r - 1)(c - 1)} \qquad \textbf{(11.12c)}$$

$$MSE = \frac{SSE}{rc(n'-1)} \qquad \textbf{(11.12d)}$$

Testing for Factor and Interaction Effects

There are three different tests to perform in a two-way ANOVA:

- A test of the hypothesis of no difference due to factor A
- A test of the hypothesis of no difference due to factor B
- A test of the hypothesis of no interaction of factors A and B

To test the hypothesis of no difference due to factor A:

$$H_0: \mu_{1..} = \mu_{2..} = \cdots = \mu_{r..}$$

against the alternative:

$$H_1: \text{Not all } \mu_{i..} \text{ are equal}$$

you use the F_{STAT} test statistic in Equation (11.13).

F TEST FOR FACTOR A EFFECT

$$F_{STAT} = \frac{MSA}{MSE} \qquad \textbf{(11.13)}$$

You reject the null hypothesis at the α level of significance if

$$F_{STAT} = \frac{MSA}{MSE} > F_{\alpha}$$

where F_α is the upper-tail critical value from an F distribution with $r - 1$ and $rc(n'-1)$ degrees of freedom.

To test the hypothesis of no difference due to factor B:

$$H_0: \mu_{.1.} = \mu_{.2.} = \cdots = \mu_{.c.}$$

against the alternative:

$$H_1: \text{Not all } \mu_{.j.} \text{ are equal}$$

you use the F_{STAT} test statistic in Equation (11.14).

F TEST FOR FACTOR B EFFECT

$$F_{STAT} = \frac{MSB}{MSE} \quad \textbf{(11.14)}$$

You reject the null hypothesis at the α level of significance if

$$F_{STAT} = \frac{MSB}{MSE} > F_\alpha$$

where F_α is the upper-tail critical value from an F distribution with $c - 1$ and $rc(n'-1)$ degrees of freedom.

To test the hypothesis of no interaction of factors A and B:

$$H_0: \text{The interaction of } A \text{ and } B \text{ is equal to zero}$$

against the alternative:

$$H_1: \text{The interaction of } A \text{ and } B \text{ is not equal to zero}$$

you use the F_{STAT} test statistic in Equation (11.15).

F TEST FOR INTERACTION EFFECT

$$F_{STAT} = \frac{MSAB}{MSE} \quad \textbf{(11.15)}$$

You reject the null hypothesis at the α level of significance if

$$F_{STAT} = \frac{MSAB}{MSE} > F_\alpha$$

Student Tip
In each of the F tests, the denominator of the F_{STAT} statistic is MSE.

where F_α is the upper-tail critical value from an F distribution with $(r - 1)(c - 1)$ and $rc(n'-1)$ degrees of freedom.

Table 11.6 presents the entire two-way ANOVA table.

To illustrate a two-way ANOVA, return to the Perfect Parachutes scenario on page 389. As production manager at Perfect Parachutes, the business problem you decided to examine involved not just the different suppliers but also whether parachutes woven on the Jetta looms are as strong as those woven on the Turk looms. In addition, you need to determine whether any differences among the four suppliers in the strength of the parachutes are dependent on the type of loom being used. Thus, you have decided to collect the data by performing an experiment in which five different parachutes from each supplier are manufactured on each of the two different looms. The results are organized in Table 11.7 and stored in **Parachute2**.

TABLE 11.6

Analysis of Variance Table for the Two-Factor Factorial Design

Source	Degrees of Freedom	Sum of Squares	Mean Square (Variance)	F
A	$r - 1$	SSA	$MSA = \frac{SSA}{r-1}$	$F_{STAT} = \frac{MSA}{MSE}$
B	$c - 1$	SSB	$MSB = \frac{SSB}{c-1}$	$F_{STAT} = \frac{MSB}{MSE}$
AB	$(r - 1)(c - 1)$	$SSAB$	$MSAB = \frac{SSAB}{(r-1)(c-1)}$	$F_{STAT} = \frac{MSAB}{MSE}$
Error	$rc(n'-1)$	SSE	$MSE = \frac{SSE}{rc(n'-1)}$	
Total	$n - 1$	SST		

TABLE 11.7

Tensile Strengths of Parachutes Woven by Two Types of Looms, Using Synthetic Fibers from Four Suppliers

	Supplier			
Loom	**1**	**2**	**3**	**4**
Jetta	20.6	22.6	27.7	21.5
Jetta	18.0	24.6	18.6	20.0
Jetta	19.0	19.6	20.8	21.1
Jetta	21.3	23.8	25.1	23.9
Jetta	13.2	27.1	17.7	16.0
Turk	18.5	26.3	20.6	25.4
Turk	24.0	25.3	25.2	19.9
Turk	17.2	24.0	20.8	22.6
Turk	19.9	21.2	24.7	17.5
Turk	18.0	24.5	22.9	20.4

Figure 11.10 presents the worksheet results for this example. In this worksheet, the *A*, *B*, and Error sources of variation in Table 11.6 above are labeled in the ANOVA table Sample, Columns, and Within, respectively.

FIGURE 11.10

Two-way ANOVA worksheet for the parachute loom and supplier experiment (ANOVA table formulas for columns B and C are shown in the inset)

	A	B	C	D	E	F	G
1	ANOVA: Two - Factor With Replication						
2							
3	SUMMARY	Supplier 1	Supplier 2	Supplier 3	Supplier 4	Total	
4	*Jetta*						
5	Count	5	5	5	5	20	
6	Sum	92.1	117.7	109.9	102.5	422.2	
7	Average	18.42	23.54	21.98	20.5	21.11	
8	Variance	10.2020	7.5680	18.3970	8.3550	13.1283	
9							
10	*Turk*						
11	Count	5	5	5	5	20	
12	Sum	97.6	121.3	114.2	105.8	438.9	
13	Average	19.52	24.26	22.84	21.16	21.945	
14	Variance	7.2370	3.6830	4.5530	8.9030	8.4626	
15							
16	*Total*						
17	Count	10	10	10	10		
18	Sum	189.7	239	224.1	208.3		
19	Average	18.97	23.9	22.41	20.83		
20	Variance	8.0868	5.1444	10.4054	7.7912		
21							
22							
23	ANOVA						
24	*Source of Variation*	*SS*	*df*	*MS*	*F*	*P - value*	*F crit*
25	Sample	6.9722	1	6.9722	0.8096	0.3750	4.1491
26	Columns	134.3488	3	44.7829	5.1999	0.0049	2.9011
27	Interaction	0.2868	3	0.0956	0.0111	0.9984	2.9011
28	Within	275.5920	32	8.6123			
29							
30	Total	417.1998	39				
31					Level of significance		0.05

ANOVA		
Source of Variation	*SS*	*df*
Sample	=B30 - DEVSQ(ATFData!B2:E6) - DEVSQ(ATFData!B7:E11)	=INT(COUNTA(ATFData!A:A) / COUNTIF(ATFData!A:A, ATFData!A2)) - 1
Columns	=B30 - DEVSQ(ATFData!B:B) - DEVSQ(ATFData!C:C) - DEVSQ(ATFData!D:D) - DEVSQ(ATFData!E:E)	=COUNTA(3:3) - 3
Interaction	=B30 - B25 - B26 - B28	=C25 * C26
Within	=DEVSQ(ATFData!B2:B6) + DEVSQ(ATFData!B7:B11) + DEVSQ(ATFData!C2:C6) + DEVSQ(ATFData!C7:C11) + DEVSQ(ATFData!D2:D6) + DEVSQ(ATFData!D7:D11) + DEVSQ(ATFData!E2:E6) + DEVSQ(ATFData!E7:E11)	=(C25 + 1) * (C26 + 1) * (B5 - 1)
Total	=DEVSQ(ATFData!B2:E11)	=SUM(C25:C28)

Figure 11.10 displays the ***COMPUTE worksheet*** *of the* ***Two-Way ANOVA workbook*** *that the Section EG11.2 instructions use. (The Analysis ToolPak creates a worksheet that does not contain formulas and is missing the level of significance in row 31.)*

To interpret the results, you start by testing whether there is an interaction effect between factor *A* (loom) and factor *B* (supplier). If the interaction effect is significant, further analysis will focus on this interaction. If the interaction effect is not significant, you can focus on the **main effects**—potential differences in looms (factor *A*) and potential differences in suppliers (factor *B*).

Using the 0.05 level of significance, to determine whether there is evidence of an interaction effect, you reject the null hypothesis of no interaction between loom and supplier if the computed F_{STAT} statistic is greater than 2.9011, the upper-tail critical value from the *F* distribution, with 3 and 32 degrees of freedom (see Figures 11.10 and 11.11).[1]

[1]Table E.5 does not provide the upper-tail critical values from the *F* distribution with 32 degrees of freedom in the denominator. When the desired degrees of freedom are not provided in the table, use the *p*-value computed by Excel.

FIGURE 11.11

Regions of rejection and nonrejection at the 0.05 level of significance, with 3 and 32 degrees of freedom

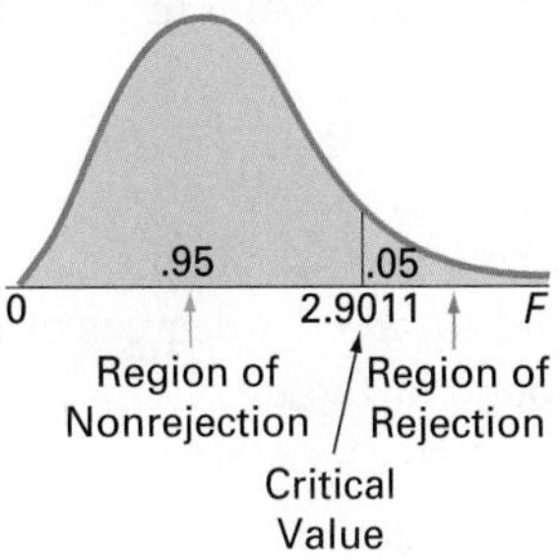

Because $F_{STAT} = 0.0111 < 2.9011$ or the p-value $= 0.9984 > 0.05$, you do not reject H_0. You conclude that there is insufficient evidence of an interaction effect between loom and supplier. You can now focus on the main effects.

Using the 0.05 level of significance and testing for a difference between the two looms (factor *A*), you reject the null hypothesis if the computed F_{STAT} test statistic is greater than 4.1491, the upper-tail critical value from the *F* distribution with 1 and 32 degrees of freedom (see Figures 11.10 and 11.12). Because $F_{STAT} = 0.8096 < 4.1491$ or the p-value $= 0.3750 > 0.05$, you do not reject H_0. You conclude that there is insufficient evidence of a difference in the mean tensile strengths of the parachutes manufactured between the two looms.

FIGURE 11.12

Regions of rejection and nonrejection at the 0.05 level of significance, with 1 and 32 degrees of freedom

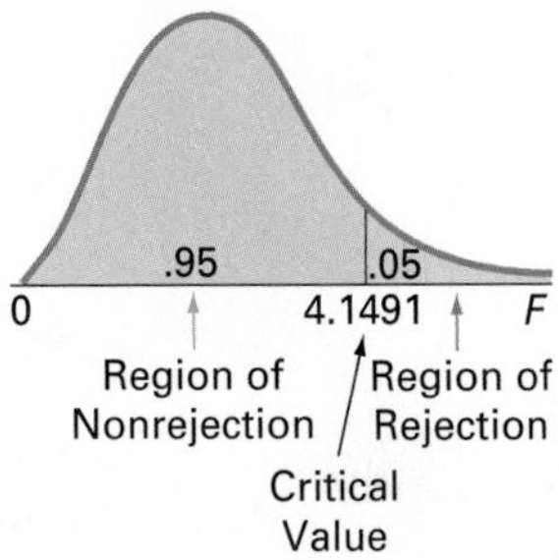

Using the 0.05 level of significance and testing for a difference among the suppliers (factor B), you reject the null hypothesis of no difference if the computed F_{STAT} test statistic is greater than 2.9011, the upper-tail critical value from the F distribution with 3 degrees of freedom in the numerator and 32 degrees of freedom in the denominator (see Figures 11.10 and 11.11). Because $F_{STAT} = 5.1999 > 2.9011$ or the p-value $= 0.0049 < 0.05$, you reject H_0. You conclude that there is evidence of a difference in the mean tensile strength of the parachutes among the suppliers.

Multiple Comparisons: The Tukey Procedure

If one or both of the factor effects are significant and there is no significant interaction effect, when there are more than two levels of a factor, you can determine the particular levels that are significantly different by using the **Tukey multiple comparisons procedure for two-way ANOVA** (see references 6 and 9). Equation (11.16) gives the critical range for factor A.

CRITICAL RANGE FOR FACTOR *A*

$$\text{Critical range} = Q_{\alpha}\sqrt{\frac{MSE}{cn'}} \tag{11.16}$$

where Q_{α} is the upper-tail critical value from a Studentized range distribution having r and $rc(n' - 1)$ degrees of freedom. (Values for the Studentized range distribution are found in Table E.7.)

Equation (11.17) gives the critical range for factor B.

CRITICAL RANGE FOR FACTOR *B*

$$\text{Critical range} = Q_{\alpha}\sqrt{\frac{MSE}{rn'}} \tag{11.17}$$

where Q_{α} is the upper-tail critical value from a Studentized range distribution having c and $rc(n'-1)$ degrees of freedom. (Values for the Studentized range distribution are found in Table E.7.)

To use the Tukey procedure, return to the parachute manufacturing data of Table 11.7 on page 408. In the ANOVA summary table in Figure 11.10 on page 409, the interaction effect is not significant. Using $\alpha = 0.05$, there is no evidence of a significant difference between the two looms (Jetta and Turk) that comprise factor A, but there is evidence of a significant difference among the four suppliers that comprise factor B. Thus, you can use the Tukey multiple comparisons procedure to determine which of the four suppliers differ.

Because there are four suppliers, there are $4(4 - 1)/2 = 6$ pairwise comparisons. Using the calculations presented in Figure 11.10, the absolute mean differences are as follows:

1. $|\overline{X}_{.1.} - \overline{X}_{.2.}| = |18.97 - 23.90| = 4.93$
2. $|\overline{X}_{.1.} - \overline{X}_{.3.}| = |18.97 - 22.41| = 3.44$
3. $|\overline{X}_{.1.} - \overline{X}_{.4.}| = |18.97 - 20.83| = 1.86$
4. $|\overline{X}_{.2.} - \overline{X}_{.3.}| = |23.90 - 22.41| = 1.49$
5. $|\overline{X}_{.2.} - \overline{X}_{.4.}| = |23.90 - 20.83| = 3.07$
6. $|\overline{X}_{.3.} - \overline{X}_{.4.}| = |22.41 - 20.83| = 1.58$

To determine the critical range, refer to Figure 11.10 to find $MSE = 8.6123$, $r = 2$, $c = 4$, and $n' = 5$. From Table E.7 [for $\alpha = 0.05$, $c = 4$, and $rc(n'-1) = 32$], Q_α, the upper-tail critical value of the Studentized range distribution with 4 and 32 degrees of freedom is approximately 3.84. Using Equation (11.17),

$$\text{Critical range} = 3.84\sqrt{\frac{8.6123}{10}} = 3.56$$

Because $4.93 > 3.56$, only the means of Suppliers 1 and 2 are different. You can conclude that the mean tensile strength is lower for Supplier 1 than for Supplier 2, but there are no statistically significant differences between Suppliers 1 and 3, Suppliers 1 and 4, Suppliers 2 and 3, Suppliers 2 and 4, and Suppliers 3 and 4. Note that by using $\alpha = 0.05$, you are able to make all six comparisons with an overall error rate of only 5%.

Visualizing Interaction Effects: The Cell Means Plot

You can get a better understanding of the interaction effect by plotting the **cell means**, the means of all possible factor-level combinations. Figure 11.13 presents a cell means plot that uses the cell means for the loom/supplier combinations shown in Figure 11.10 on page 409. From the plot of the mean tensile strength for each combination of loom and supplier, observe that the two lines (representing the two looms) are roughly parallel. This indicates that the *difference* between the mean tensile strengths of the two looms is virtually the same for the four suppliers. In other words, there is no *interaction* between these two factors, as was indicated by the *F* test.

FIGURE 11.13
Cell means plot of tensile strength based on loom and supplier

Use the Section EG11.2 instructions to construct a cell means plot.

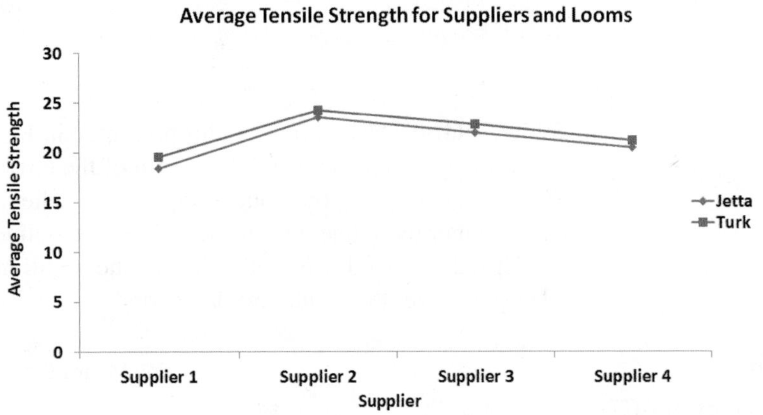

Interpreting Interaction Effects

How do you interpret an interaction? When there is an interaction, some levels of factor *A* respond better with certain levels of factor *B*. For example, with respect to tensile strength, suppose that some suppliers were better for the Jetta loom and other suppliers were better for the Turk loom. If this were true, the lines of Figure 11.13 would not be nearly as parallel, and the interaction effect might be statistically significant. In such a situation, the difference between the looms is no longer the same for all suppliers. Such an outcome would also complicate the interpretation of the *main effects* because differences in one factor (the loom) would not be consistent across the other factor (the supplier).

Example 11.2 illustrates a situation with a significant interaction effect.

EXAMPLE 11.2

Interpreting Significant Interaction Effects

A nationwide company specializing in preparing students for college and graduate school entrance exams, such as the SAT, ACT, and LSAT, had the business objective of improving its ACT preparatory course. Two factors of interest to the company are the length of the course (a condensed 10-day period or a regular 30-day period) and the type of course (traditional classroom or online distance learning). The company collected data by randomly assigning 10 clients to each of the four cells that represent a combination of length of the course and type of course. The results are organized in the file ACT and presented in Table 11.8.

What are the effects of the type of course and the length of the course on ACT scores?

TABLE 11.8

ACT Scores for Different Types and Lengths of Courses

	Length of Course			
Type of Course	**Condensed**		**Regular**	
Traditional	26	18	34	28
Traditional	27	24	24	21
Traditional	25	19	35	23
Traditional	21	20	31	29
Traditional	21	18	28	26
Online	27	21	24	21
Online	29	32	16	19
Online	30	20	22	19
Online	24	28	20	24
Online	30	29	23	25

SOLUTION The cell means plot presented in Figure 11.14 shows a strong interaction between the type of course and the length of the course. The nonparallel lines indicate that the effect of condensing the course depends on whether the course is taught in the traditional classroom or by online distance learning. The online mean score is higher when the course is condensed to a 10-day period, whereas the traditional mean score is higher when the course takes place over the regular 30-day period.

FIGURE 11.14

Cell means plot of ACT scores

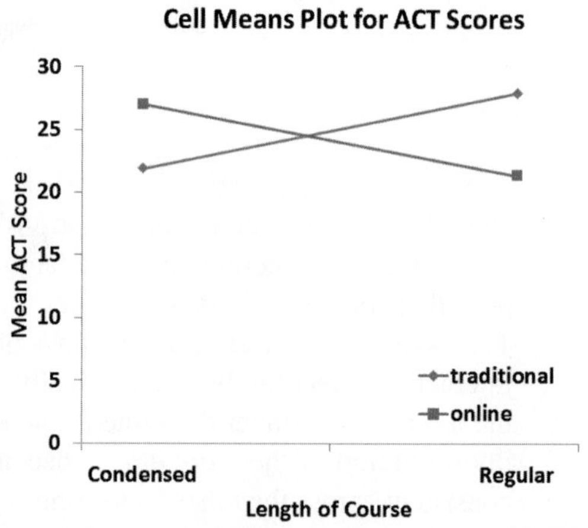

To verify the visual analysis provided by interpreting the cell means plot, you begin by testing whether there is a statistically significant interaction between factor A (length of course) and factor B (type of course). Using a 0.05 level of significance, you reject the null hypothesis because $F_{STAT} = 24.2569 > 4.1132$ or the p-value equals $0.000 < 0.05$ (see Figure 11.15). Thus, the hypothesis test confirms the interaction evident in the cell means plot.

FIGURE 11.15

Two-way ANOVA worksheet (in two parts) for the ACT scores

	A	B	C	D
1	ANOVA: Two-Factor With Replication			
2				
3	SUMMARY	Condensed	Regular	Total
4	*traditional*			
5	Count	10	10	20
6	Sum	219	279	498
7	Average	21.9	27.9	24.9
8	Variance	11.2111	20.9889	24.7263
9				
10	*online*			
11	Count	10	10	20
12	Sum	270	213	483
13	Average	27	21.3	24.15
14	Variance	16.2222	8.0111	20.0289
15				
16	*Total*			
17	Count	20	20	
18	Sum	489	492	
19	Average	24.45	24.6	
20	Variance	19.8395	25.2000	

	A	B	C	D	E	F	G
23	ANOVA						
24	*Source of Variation*	*SS*	*df*	*MS*	*F*	*P-value*	*F crit*
25	Sample	5.6250	1	5.6250	0.3987	0.5318	4.1132
26	Columns	0.2250	1	0.2250	0.0159	0.9002	4.1132
27	Interaction	342.2250	1	342.2250	24.2569	0.0000	4.1132
28	Within	507.9000	36	14.1083			
29							
30	Total	855.9750	39				
31						*Level of significance*	0.05

The existence of this significant interaction effect complicates the interpretation of the hypothesis tests concerning the two main effects. You cannot directly conclude that there is no effect with respect to length of course and type of course, even though both have p-values > 0.05.

Given that the interaction is significant, you can reanalyze the data with the two factors collapsed into four groups of a single factor rather than a two-way ANOVA with two levels of each of the two factors. You can reorganize the data as follows: Group 1 is traditional condensed, Group 2 is traditional regular, Group 3 is online condensed, and Group 4 is online regular. Figure 11.16 shows the results for these data, stored in **ACT-OneWay**.

FIGURE 11.16

One-way ANOVA and Tukey-Kramer worksheets for the ACT scores

	A	B	C	D	E	F	G
1	ANOVA: Single Factor						
2							
3	SUMMARY						
4	*Groups*	*Count*	*Sum*	*Average*	*Variance*		
5	Supplier 1	10	219	21.9	11.21111		
6	Supplier 2	10	279	27.9	20.98889		
7	Supplier 3	10	270	27	16.22222		
8	Supplier 4	10	213	21.3	8.011111		
9							
10							
11	ANOVA						
12	*Source of Variation*	*SS*	*df*	*MS*	*F*	*P-value*	*F crit*
13	Between Groups	348.075	3	116.0250	8.2239	0.0003	2.8663
14	Within Groups	507.9	36	14.1083			
15							
16	Total	855.975	39				
17					*Level of significance*		0.05

	A	B	C	D	E	F	G	H	I
1	Tukey Kramer Multiple Comparisons								
2									
3		Sample	Sample			Absolute	Std. Error	Critical	
4	Group	Mean	Size		Comparison	Difference	of Difference	Range	Results
5	1: Supplier 1	21.9	10		Group 1 to Group 2	6	1.1878	4.8105	Means are different
6	2: Supplier 2	27.9	10		Group 1 to Group 3	5.1	1.1878	4.8105	Means are different
7	3: Supplier 3	27	10		Group 1 to Group 4	0.6	1.1878	4.8105	Means are not different
8	4: Supplier 4	21.3	10		Group 2 to Group 3	0.9	1.1878	4.8105	Means are not different
9					Group 2 to Group 4	6.6	1.1878	4.8105	Means are different
10	Other Data				Group 3 to Group 4	5.7	1.1878	4.8105	Means are different
11	Level of significance	0.05							
12	Numerator d.f.	4							
13	Denominator d.f.	36							
14	MSW	14.10833							
15	Q Statistic	4.05							

From Figure 11.16, because $F_{STAT} = 8.2239 > 2.8663$ or p-value $= 0.0003 < 0.05$, there is evidence of a significant difference in the four groups (traditional condensed, traditional regular, online condensed, and online regular). Traditional condensed is different from traditional regular and from online condensed. Traditional regular is also different from online regular, and online condensed is also different from online regular. Thus, whether condensing a course is a good idea depends on whether the course is offered in a traditional classroom or as an online distance learning course. To ensure the highest mean ACT scores, the company should use the traditional approach for courses that are given over a 30-day period but use the online approach for courses that are condensed into a 10-day period.

Problems for Section 11.2

LEARNING THE BASICS

11.15 Consider a two-factor factorial design with three levels for factor A, three levels for factor B, and four replicates in each of the nine cells.

a. How many degrees of freedom are there in determining the factor A variation and the factor B variation?

b. How many degrees of freedom are there in determining the interaction variation?

c. How many degrees of freedom are there in determining the random variation?

d. How many degrees of freedom are there in determining the total variation?

11.16 Assume that you are working with the results from Problem 11.15, and $SSA = 120$, $SSB = 110$, $SSE = 270$, and $SST = 540$.

a. What is $SSAB$?

b. What are MSA and MSB?

c. What is $MSAB$?

d. What is MSE?

11.17 Assume that you are working with the results from Problems 11.15 and 11.16.

a. What is the value of the F_{STAT} test statistic for the interaction effect?

b. What is the value of the F_{STAT} test statistic for the factor A effect?

c. What is the value of the F_{STAT} test statistic for the factor B effect?

d. Form the ANOVA summary table and fill in all values in the body of the table.

11.18 Given the results from Problems 11.15 through 11.17,

a. at the 0.05 level of significance, is there an effect due to factor A?

b. at the 0.05 level of significance, is there an effect due to factor B?

c. at the 0.05 level of significance, is there an interaction effect?

11.19 Given a two-way ANOVA with two levels for factor A, five levels for factor B, and four replicates in each of the 10 cells, with $SSA = 18$, $SSB = 64$, $SSE = 60$, and $SST = 150$,

a. form the ANOVA summary table and fill in all values in the body of the table.

b. at the 0.05 level of significance, is there an effect due to factor A?

c. at the 0.05 level of significance, is there an effect due to factor B?

d. at the 0.05 level of significance, is there an interaction effect?

11.20 Given a two-factor factorial experiment and the ANOVA summary table that follows, fill in all the missing results:

Source	Degrees of Freedom	Sum of Squares	Mean Square (Variance)	F
A	$r - 1 = 2$	$SSA = ?$	$MSA = 80$	$F_{STAT} = ?$
B	$c - 1 = ?$	$SSB = 220$	$MSB = ?$	$F_{STAT} = 11.0$
AB	$(r - 1)(c - 1) = 8$	$SSAB = ?$	$MSAB = 10$	$F_{STAT} = ?$
Error	$rc(n'-1) = 30$	$SSE = ?$	$MSE = ?$	
Total	$n - 1 = ?$	$SST = ?$		

11.21 Given the results from Problem 11.20,

a. at the 0.05 level of significance, is there an effect due to factor A?

b. at the 0.05 level of significance, is there an effect due to factor B?

c. at the 0.05 level of significance, is there an interaction effect?

APPLYING THE CONCEPTS

11.22 The effects of developer strength (factor A) and development time (factor B) on the density of photographic plate film were being studied. Two strengths and two development times were used, and four replicates in each of the four cells were evaluated. The results (with larger being best) are stored in **Photo** and shown in the following table:

Developer Strength	Development Time (minutes) 10	14
1	0	1
1	5	4
1	2	3
1	4	2
2	4	6
2	7	7
2	6	8
2	5	7

At the 0.05 level of significance,

a. is there an interaction between developer strength and development time?

b. is there an effect due to developer strength?

c. is there an effect due to development time?

d. Plot the mean density for each developer strength for each development time.

e. What can you conclude about the effect of developer strength and development time on density?

11.23 A chef in a restaurant that specializes in pasta dishes was experiencing difficulty in getting brands of pasta to be *al dente*—that is, cooked enough so as not to feel starchy or hard but still feel firm when bitten into. She decided to conduct an experiment in which two brands of pasta, one American and one Italian, were cooked for either 4 or 8 minutes. The variable of interest was weight of the pasta because cooking the pasta enables it to absorb water. A pasta with a faster rate of water absorption may provide a shorter interval in which the pasta is *al dente*, thereby increasing the chance that it might be overcooked. The experiment was conducted by using 150 grams of uncooked pasta. Each trial began by bringing a pot containing 6 quarts of cold, unsalted water to a moderate boil. The 150 grams of uncooked pasta was added and then weighed after a given period of time by lifting the pasta from the pot via a built-in strainer. The results (in terms of weight in grams) for two replicates of each type of pasta and cooking time are stored in **Pasta** and are as follows:

	Cooking Time (minutes)	
Type of Pasta	**4**	**8**
American	265	310
American	270	320
Italian	250	300
Italian	245	305

At the 0.05 level of significance,

a. is there an interaction between type of pasta and cooking time?

b. is there an effect due to type of pasta?

c. is there an effect due to cooking time?

d. Plot the mean weight for each type of pasta for each cooking time.

e. What conclusions can you reach concerning the importance of each of these two factors on the weight of the pasta?

SELF Test **11.24** A student team in a business statistics course performed a factorial experiment to investigate the time required for pain-relief tablets to dissolve in a glass of water. The two factors of interest were brand name (Equate, Kroger, or Alka-Seltzer) and water temperature (hot or cold). The experiment consisted of four replicates for each of the six factor combinations. The following data, stored in **PainRelief**, show the time a tablet took to dissolve (in seconds) for the 24 tablets used in the experiment:

	Pain-Relief Tablet Brand		
Water	**Equate**	**Kroger**	**Alka-Seltzer**
Cold	85.87	75.98	100.11
Cold	78.69	87.66	99.65
Cold	76.42	85.71	100.83
Cold	74.43	86.31	94.16
Hot	21.53	24.10	23.80
Hot	26.26	25.83	21.29
Hot	24.95	26.32	20.82
Hot	21.52	22.91	23.21

At the 0.05 level of significance,

a. is there an interaction between brand of pain reliever and water temperature?

b. is there an effect due to brand?

c. is there an effect due to water temperature?

d. Plot the mean dissolving time for each brand for each water temperature.

e. Discuss the results of (a) through (d).

11.25 A metallurgy company wanted to investigate the effect of the percentage of ammonium and the stir rate on the density of the powder produced. The results (stored in **Density**) are as follows:

	Stir Rate	
Ammonium (%)	**100**	**150**
2	10.95	7.54
2	14.68	6.66
2	17.68	8.03
2	15.18	8.84
30	12.65	12.46
30	15.12	14.96
30	17.48	14.96
30	15.96	12.62

Source: Extracted from L. Johnson and K. McNeilly, "Results May Not Vary," *Quality Progress*, May 2011, pp. 41–48.

At the 0.05 level of significance,

a. is there an interaction between the percentage of ammonium and the stir rate?

b. is there an effect due to the percentage of ammonium?

c. is there an effect due to the stir rate?

d. Plot the mean density for each percentage of ammonium and the stir rate.

e. Discuss the results of (a) through (d).

11.26 An experiment was conducted to try to resolve a problem of brake discs overheating at high speed on construction equipment. Five different brake discs were measured by two different temperature gauges. The temperature of each brake disc and gauge combination was measured at eight different times and the results stored in **Brakes**.

Source: Data extracted from M. Awad, T. P. Erdmann, V. Shansal, and B. Barth, "A Measurement System Analysis Approach for Hard-to-Repeat Events," *Quality Engineering* 21 (2009): 300–305.

At the 0.05 level of significance,

a. is there an interaction between the brake discs and the gauges?

b. is there an effect due to brake discs?

c. is there an effect due to the gauges?

d. Plot the mean temperature for each brake disc for each gauge.

e. Discuss the results of (a) through (d).

11.3 The Randomized Block Design (*online*)

LEARN MORE

Learn more about randomized block designs in a Chapter 11 eBook bonus section.

Section 11.1 discussed how to use the one-way ANOVA *F* test to evaluate differences among the means of more than two independent groups. Section 10.2 discussed how to use the paired *t* test to evaluate the difference between the means of two groups when you had repeated measurements or matched samples. The randomized block design evaluates differences among more than two groups that contain matched samples or repeated measures that have been placed in blocks.

11.4 Fixed Effects, Random Effects, and Mixed Effects Models (*online*)

LEARN MORE

Learn more about this issue in a Chapter 11 eBook bonus section.

Sections 11.1 through 11.3 do not consider the distinction between how the levels of a factor were selected. The equation for the *F* test depends on whether the levels of a factor were specifically selected or randomly selected from a population.

USING STATISTICS Are There Looming Differences at Perfect Parachutes? Revisited

Joggie Botma / Shutterstock

In the Perfect Parachutes scenario, you were the production manager who needed to decide whether there were differences among the synthetic fibers from four different suppliers as well as establish that parachutes woven on two types of looms were equally strong.

Using the one-way ANOVA, you were able to determine that there was a difference in the mean strength of the parachutes from the different suppliers. You then were able to conclude that the mean strength of parachutes woven from synthetic fibers from Supplier 1 was less than for supplier 2. Using the two-way ANOVA, you determined that there was no interaction between the supplier and loom and there was no difference in mean strength between the looms. Your next step as production manager is to investigate reasons the mean strength of parachutes woven from synthetic fibers from supplier 1 was less than for supplier 2 and possibly reduce the number of suppliers.

SUMMARY

In this chapter, various statistical procedures were used to analyze the effect of one or two factors of interest. The assumptions required for using these procedures were discussed in detail. Remember that you need to critically investigate the validity of the assumptions underlying the hypothesis-testing procedures. Table 11.9 summarizes the topics covered in this chapter.

TABLE 11.9

Summary of Topics in Chapter 11

Type of Analysis (numerical data only)	Number of Factors
Comparing more than two groups	One-way analysis of variance (Section 11.1) Two-way analysis of variance (Section 11.2)

2 each, to the 16 detergent/washing cycle time combinations. The results, in pounds of dirt removed, are collected and stored in **Laundry**. These data are:

	Washing Cycle Time (minutes)			
Detergent Brand	**18**	**20**	**22**	**24**
A	0.11	0.13	0.17	0.17
A	0.09	0.13	0.19	0.18
B	0.12	0.14	0.17	0.19
B	0.10	0.15	0.18	0.17
C	0.08	0.16	0.18	0.20
C	0.09	0.13	0.17	0.16
D	0.11	0.12	0.16	0.15
D	0.13	0.13	0.17	0.17

At the 0.05 level of significance,

a. is there an interaction between detergent brand and washing cycle time?

b. is there an effect due to detergent brand?

c. is there an effect due to washing cycle time?

d. Plot the mean amount of dirt removed (in pounds) for each detergent brand for each washing cycle time.

e. If appropriate, use the Tukey procedure to determine differences between detergent brands and between washing cycle times.

f. What washing cycle time should be used for this type of household clothes washer?

g. Repeat the analysis, using washing cycle time as the only factor. Compare your results to those of (c), (e), and (f).

11.37 The quality control director for a clothing manufacturer wants to study the effect of operators and machines on the breaking strength (in pounds) of wool serge material. A batch of the material is cut into square-yard pieces, and these pieces are randomly assigned, 3 each, to each of the 12 combinations of 4 operators and 3 machines chosen specifically for the experiment. The results, stored in **Breakstw**, are as follows:

	Machine		
Operator	**I**	**II**	**III**
A	115	111	109
A	115	108	110
A	119	114	107
B	117	105	110
B	114	102	113
B	114	106	114
C	109	100	103
C	110	103	102
C	106	101	105
D	112	105	108
D	115	107	111
D	111	107	110

At the 0.05 level of significance,

a. is there an interaction between operator and machine?

b. is there an effect due to operator?

c. is there an effect due to machine?

d. Plot the mean breaking strength for each operator for each machine.

e. If appropriate, use the Tukey procedure to examine differences among operators and among machines.

f. What can you conclude about the effects of operators and machines on breaking strength? Explain.

g. Repeat the analysis, using machines as the only factor. Compare your results to those of (c), (e), and (f).

11.38 An operations manager wants to examine the effect of air-jet pressure (in pounds per square inch [psi]) on the breaking strength of yarn. Three different levels of air-jet pressure are to be considered: 30 psi, 40 psi, and 50 psi. A random sample of 18 yarns are selected from the same batch, and the yarns are randomly assigned, 6 each, to the 3 levels of air-jet pressure. The breaking strength scores are stored in **Yarn**.

a. Is there evidence of a significant difference in the variances of the breaking strengths for the three air-jet pressures? (Use $\alpha = 0.05$.)

b. At the 0.05 level of significance, is there evidence of a difference among mean breaking strengths for the three air-jet pressures?

c. If appropriate, use the Tukey-Kramer procedure to determine which air-jet pressures significantly differ with respect to mean breaking strength. (Use $\alpha = 0.05$.)

d. What should the operations manager conclude?

11.39 Suppose that, when setting up the experiment in Problem 11.38, the operations manager is able to study the effect of side-to-side aspect in addition to air-jet pressure. Thus, instead of the one-factor completely randomized design in Problem 11.38, a two-factor factorial design was used, with the first factor, side-to-side aspect, having two levels (nozzle and opposite) and the second factor, air-jet pressure, having three levels (30 psi, 40 psi, and 50 psi). A sample of 18 yarns is randomly assigned, 3 to each of the 6 side-to-side aspect and pressure level combinations. The breaking-strength scores, stored in **Yarn**, are as follows:

	Air-Jet Pressure		
Side-to-Side Aspect	**30 psi**	**40 psi**	**50 psi**
Nozzle	25.5	24.8	23.2
Nozzle	24.9	23.7	23.7
Nozzle	26.1	24.4	22.7
Opposite	24.7	23.6	22.6
Opposite	24.2	23.3	22.8
Opposite	23.6	21.4	**24.9**

At the 0.05 level of significance,

a. is there an interaction between side-to-side aspect and air-jet pressure?

b. is there an effect due to side-to-side aspect?

c. is there an effect due to air-jet pressure?
d. Plot the mean yarn breaking strength for each level of side-to-side aspect for each level of air-jet pressure.
e. If appropriate, use the Tukey procedure to study differences among the air-jet pressures.
f. On the basis of the results of (a) through (e), what conclusions can you reach concerning yarn breaking strength? Discuss.
g. Compare your results in (a) through (f) with those from the completely randomized design in Problem 11.38. Discuss fully.

11.40 A hotel wanted to develop a new system for delivering room service breakfasts. In the current system, an order form is left on the bed in each room. If the customer wishes to receive a room service breakfast, he or she places the order form on the doorknob before 11 P.M. The current system requires customers to select a 15-minute interval for desired delivery time (6:30–6:45 A.M., 6:45–7:00 A.M., etc.). The new system is designed to allow the customer to request a specific delivery time. The hotel wants to measure the difference (in minutes) between the actual delivery time and the requested delivery time of room service orders for breakfast. (A negative time means that the order was delivered before the requested time. A positive time means that the order was delivered after the requested time.) The factors included were the menu choice (American or Continental) and the desired time period in which the order was to be delivered (Early Time Period [6:30–8:00 A.M.] or Late Time Period [8:00–9:30 A.M.]). Ten orders for each combination of menu choice and desired time period were studied on a particular day. The data, stored in **Breakfast**, are as follows:

	Desired Time	
Type of Breakfast	**Early Time Period**	**Late Time Period**
Continental	1.2	−2.5
Continental	2.1	3.0
Continental	3.3	−0.2
Continental	4.4	1.2
Continental	3.4	1.2
Continental	5.3	0.7
Continental	2.2	−1.3
Continental	1.0	0.2
Continental	5.4	−0.5
Continental	1.4	3.8
American	4.4	6.0
American	1.1	2.3
American	4.8	4.2
American	7.1	3.8
American	6.7	5.5
American	5.6	1.8
American	9.5	5.1
American	4.1	4.2
American	7.9	4.9
American	9.4	4.0

At the 0.05 level of significance,
a. is there an interaction between type of breakfast and desired time?
b. is there an effect due to type of breakfast?
c. is there an effect due to desired time?
d. Plot the mean delivery time difference for each desired time for each type of breakfast.
e. On the basis of the results of (a) through (d), what conclusions can you reach concerning delivery time difference? Discuss.

11.41 Refer to the room service experiment in Problem 11.40. Now suppose that the results are as shown below and stored in **Breakfast2**. Repeat (a) through (e), using these data, and compare the results to those of (a) through (e) of Problem 11.40.

	Desired Time	
Type of Breakfast	**Early**	**Late**
Continental	1.2	−0.5
Continental	2.1	5.0
Continental	3.3	1.8
Continental	4.4	3.2
Continental	3.4	3.2
Continental	5.3	2.7
Continental	2.2	0.7
Continental	1.0	2.2
Continental	5.4	1.5
Continental	1.4	5.8
American	4.4	6.0
American	1.1	2.3
American	4.8	4.2
American	7.1	3.8
American	6.7	5.5
American	5.6	1.8
American	9.5	5.1
American	4.1	4.2
American	7.9	4.9
American	9.4	4.0

11.42 A pet food company has the business objective of having the weight of a can of cat food come as close to the specified weight as possible. Realizing that the size of the pieces of meat contained in a can and the can fill height could impact the weight of a can, a team studying the weight of canned cat food wondered whether the current larger chunk size produced higher can weight and more variability. The team decided to study the effect on weight of a cutting size that was finer than the current size. In addition, the team slightly lowered the target for the sensing mechanism that determines the fill height in order to determine the effect of the fill height on can weight.

Twenty cans were filled for each of the four combinations of piece size (fine and current) and fill height (low and current). The contents of each can were weighed, and the amount above or below the label weight of 3 ounces was recorded as the variable coded weight. For example, a can containing 2.90 ounces was given a coded weight of −0.10. Results were stored in CatFood2.

Analyze these data and write a report for presentation to the team. Indicate the importance of the piece size and the fill height on the weight of the canned cat food. Be sure to include a recommendation for the level of each factor that will come closest to meeting the target weight and the limitations of this experiment, along with recommendations for future experiments that might be undertaken.

11.43 Brand valuations are critical to CEOs, financial and marketing executives, security analysts, institutional investors, and others who depend on well-researched, reliable information needed for assessments and comparisons in decision making. Millward Brown Optimor has developed the BrandZ Top 100 Most Valuable Global Brands for WPP, the world's largest communications services group. Unlike other studies, the BrandZ Top 100 Most Valuable Global Brands fuses consumer measures of brand equity with financial measures to place a financial value on brands. The file BrandZTechFinTele contains the brand values for three sectors in the BrandZ Top 100 Most Valuable Global Brands for 2011: the technology sector, the financial institutions sector, and the telecom sector. (Data extracted from **bit.ly/kNL8rx**.)

a. At the 0.01 level of significance, is there evidence of a difference in mean brand value among the sectors?

b. What assumptions are necessary in order to complete (a)? Comment on the validity of these assumptions.

c. If appropriate, use the Tukey procedure to determine the sectors that differ in mean rating. (Use $\alpha = 0.01$.)

11.44 An investor can choose from a very large number of mutual funds. Each mutual fund has its own mix of different types of investments. The data in BestFunds2 present the one-year return and the three-year annualized return for the 10 best mutual funds, according to the *U.S. News & World Report* score for short-term bond, long-term bond, and world bond funds. (Data extracted from **money.usnews.com/mutual-funds/rankings**.) Analyze the data and determine whether any differences exist between short-term, long-term, and world bond funds. (Use the 0.05 level of significance.)

11.45 An investor can choose from a very large number of mutual funds. Each mutual fund has its own mix of different types of investments. The data in BestFunds3 present the one-year return and the three-year annualized return for the 10 best mutual funds, according to the *U.S. News & World Report* score for small cap growth, mid-cap growth, and large cap growth funds. (Data extracted from **money.usnews.com/mutual-funds/rankings**.) Analyze the data and determine whether any differences exist between small cap growth, mid-cap growth, and large cap growth funds. (Use the 0.05 level of significance.)

CASES FOR CHAPTER 11

Managing Ashland MultiComm Services

PHASE 1

The computer operations department had a business objective of reducing the amount of time to fully update each subscriber's set of messages in a special secured email system. An experiment was conducted in which 24 subscribers were selected and three different messaging systems were used. Eight subscribers were assigned to each system, and the update times were measured. The results, stored in AMS11-1, are presented in Table AMS11.1.

TABLE AMS11.1

Update Times (in seconds) for Three Different Systems

System 1	System 2	System 3
38.8	41.8	32.9
42.1	36.4	36.1
45.2	39.1	39.2
34.8	28.7	29.3
48.3	36.4	41.9
37.8	36.1	31.7
41.1	35.8	35.2
43.6	33.7	38.1

1. Analyze the data in Table AMS11.1 and write a report to the computer operations department that indicates your findings. Include an appendix in which you discuss the reason you selected a particular statistical test to compare the three email interfaces.

DO NOT CONTINUE UNTIL THE PHASE 1 EXERCISE HAS BEEN COMPLETED.

PHASE 2

After analyzing the data in Table AMS11.1, the computer operations department team decided to also study the effect of the connection media used (cable or fiber).

The team designed a study in which a total of 30 subscribers were chosen. The subscribers were randomly assigned to one of the three messaging systems so that there were five subscribers in each of the six combinations of the two factors—messaging system and media used. Measurements were taken on the updated time. Table AMS11.2 summarizes the results that are stored in AMS11-2.

TABLE AMS11.2

Update Times (in seconds), Based on Messaging System and Media Used

	Interface		
Media	**System 1**	**System 2**	**System 3**
Cable	4.56	4.17	3.53
	4.90	4.28	3.77
	4.18	4.00	4.10
	3.56	3.96	2.87
	4.34	3.60	3.18
Fiber	4.41	3.79	4.33
	4.08	4.11	4.00
	4.69	3.58	4.31
	5.18	4.53	3.96
	4.85	4.02	3.32

2. Completely analyze these data and write a report to the team that indicates the importance of each of the two factors and/or the interaction between them on the length of the call. Include recommendations for future experiments to perform.

Digital Case

Apply your knowledge about ANOVA in this Digital Case, which continues the cereal-fill packaging dispute Digital Case from Chapters 7, 9, and 10.

After reviewing CCACC's latest document (see the Digital Case for Chapter 10 on page 380), Oxford Cereals has released **SecondAnalysis.pdf**, a press kit that Oxford Cereals has assembled to refute the claim that it is guilty of using selective data. Review the Oxford Cereals press kit and then answer the following questions.

1. Does Oxford Cereals have a legitimate argument? Why or why not?

2. Assuming that the samples Oxford Cereals has posted were randomly selected, perform the appropriate analysis to resolve the ongoing weight dispute.

3. What conclusions can you reach from your results? If you were called as an expert witness, would you support the claims of the CCACC or the claims of Oxford Cereals? Explain.

Sure Value Convenience Stores

You work in the corporate office for a nationwide convenience store franchise that operates nearly 10,000 stores. The per-store daily customer count (i.e., the mean number of customers in a store in one day) has been steady, at 900, for some time. To increase the customer count, the chain is considering cutting prices for coffee beverages. The question to be determined is how much to cut prices to increase the daily customer count without reducing the gross margin on coffee sales too much. You decide to carry out an experiment in a sample of 24 stores where customer counts have been running almost exactly at the national average of 900. In 6 of the stores, the price of a small coffee will now be \$0.59, in 6 stores the price of a small coffee will now be \$0.69, in 6 stores, the price of a small coffee will now be \$0.79, and in 6 stores, the price of a small coffee will now be \$0.89. After four weeks of selling the coffee at the new price, the daily customer counts in the stores were recorded and stored in **CoffeeSales**.

1. Analyze the data and determine whether there is evidence of a difference in the daily customer count, based on the price of a small coffee.

2. If appropriate, determine which prices differ in daily customer counts.

3. What price do you recommend for a small coffee?

CardioGood Fitness

Return to the CardioGood Fitness case (stored in CardioGood Fitness) first presented on page 33.

1. Determine whether differences exist between customers based on the product purchased (TM195, TM498, TM798) in their age in years, education in years, annual household income ($), mean number of times the customer plans to use the treadmill each week, and mean number of miles the customer expects to walk/run each week.
2. Write a report to be presented to the management of CardioGood Fitness detailing your findings.

More Descriptive Choices Follow-up

Follow up the Using Statistics scenario "More Descriptive Choices, Revisited" on page 149 by determining whether there is a difference between the small, mid-cap, and large market cap funds in the 1-year return percentages, 5-year return percentages, and 10-year return percentages (stored in Retirement Funds).

Clear Mountain State Student Surveys

1. The Student News Service at Clear Mountain State University (CMSU) has decided to gather data about the undergraduate students who attend CMSU. They create and distribute a survey of 14 questions and receive responses from 62 undergraduates (stored in UndergradSurvey).
   a. At the 0.05 level of significance, is there evidence of a difference based on academic major in expected starting salary, number of social networking sites registered for, age, spending on textbooks and supplies, text messages sent in a week, and the wealth needed to feel rich?
   b. At the 0.05 level of significance, is there evidence of a difference based on graduate school intention in grade point average, expected starting salary, number of social networking sites registered for, age, spending on textbooks and supplies, text messages sent in a week, and the wealth needed to feel rich?
2. The dean of students at CMSU has learned about the undergraduate survey and has decided to undertake a similar survey for graduate students at Clear Mountain State. She creates and distributes a survey of 14 questions and receives responses from 44 graduate students (stored in GradSurvey). For these data, at the 0.05 level of significance,
   a. is there evidence of a difference based on undergraduate major in age, undergraduate grade point average, graduate grade point average, expected salary upon graduation, spending on textbooks and supplies, text messages sent in a week, and the wealth needed to feel rich?
   b. is there evidence of a difference based on graduate major in age, undergraduate grade point average, graduate grade point average, expected salary upon graduation, spending on textbooks and supplies, text messages sent in a week, and the wealth needed to feel rich?
   c. is there evidence of a difference based on employment status in age, undergraduate grade point average, graduate grade point average, expected salary upon graduation, spending on textbooks and supplies, text messages sent in a week, and the wealth needed to feel rich?

CHAPTER 11 EXCEL GUIDE

EG11.1 The COMPLETELY RANDOMIZED DESIGN: ONE-WAY ANALYSIS of VARIANCE

One-Way ANOVA *F* Test for Differences Among More Than Two Means

Key Technique Use the **DEVSQ (*cell range of data of all groups*)** function to compute *SST* and uses an expression in the form *SST* – **DEVSQ (*group 1 data cell range*)** – **DEVSQ (*group 2 data cell range*) ... – DEVSQ (*group n data cell range*)** to compute *SSA*.

Example Perform the one-way ANOVA for the parachute experiment that is shown in Figure 11.6 on page 396.

PHStat Use **One-Way ANOVA**.
For the example, open to the **DATA worksheet** of the **Parachute workbook**. Select **PHStat → Multiple-Sample Tests → One-Way ANOVA**. In the procedure's dialog box (shown below):

1. Enter **0.05** as the **Level of Significance**.
2. Enter **A1:D6** as the **Group Data Cell Range**.
3. Check **First cells contain label**.
4. Enter a **Title**, clear the **Tukey-Kramer Procedure** check box, and click **OK**.

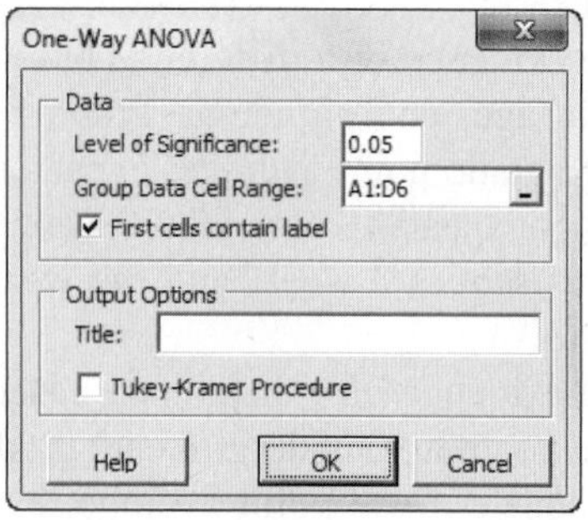

In addition to the worksheet shown in Figure 11.6, this procedure creates an **ASFData worksheet** to hold the data used for the test. See the following *In-Depth Excel* section for a complete description of this worksheet.

In-Depth Excel Use the **COMPUTE worksheet** of the **One-Way ANOVA workbook** as a template.
The COMPUTE worksheet, and the supporting ASFData worksheet, already contains the data for the example. Modifying the One-Way ANOVA workbook for use with other problems is a bit more difficult than modifications discussed in the Excel Guide in previous chapters, but it can be done using these steps:

1. Paste the data for the problem into the **ASFData worksheet**, overwriting the parachute experiment data.

In the COMPUTE worksheet (see Figure 11.6):

2. Edit the *SST* formula **=DEVSQ(ASFData!A1:D6)** in cell B16 to use the cell range of the new data just pasted into the ASFData worksheet.
3. Edit the cell B13 *SSA* formula so there are as many **DEVSQ(*group n data cell range*)** terms as there are groups.
4. Change the level of significance in cell G17, if necessary.
5. If the problem contains three groups, select **row 8**, right-click, and select **Delete** from the shortcut menu.
6. If the problem contains more than four groups, select **row 8**, right-click, and click **Insert** from the shortcut menu. Repeat this step as many times as necessary.
7. If the problem contains more than four groups, cut and paste the formulas in columns B through E of the new last row of the summary table to the cell range **B8:E8**. (These formulas were in row 8 before you inserted new rows.) For each new row inserted, enter formulas in columns B through E that refer to the next subsequent column in the ASFData worksheet.
8. Adjust table formatting as necessary.

Read the SHORT TAKES for Chapter 11 for an explanation of the formulas found in the COMPUTE worksheet (shown in the **COMPUTE_FORMULAS worksheet**). If you are using an older Excel version, use the COMPUTE_OLDER worksheet instead of the COMPUTE worksheet.

Analysis ToolPak Use **Anova: Single Factor**.
For the example, open to the **DATA worksheet** of the **Parachute workbook** and:

1. Select **Data → Data Analysis**.
2. In the Data Analysis dialog box, select **Anova: Single Factor** from the **Analysis Tools** list and then click **OK**.

In the procedure's dialog box (shown below):

3. Enter **A1:D6** as the **Input Range**.
4. Click **Columns**, check **Labels in First Row**, and enter **0.05** as **Alpha**.
5. Click **New Worksheet Ply**.
6. Click **OK**.

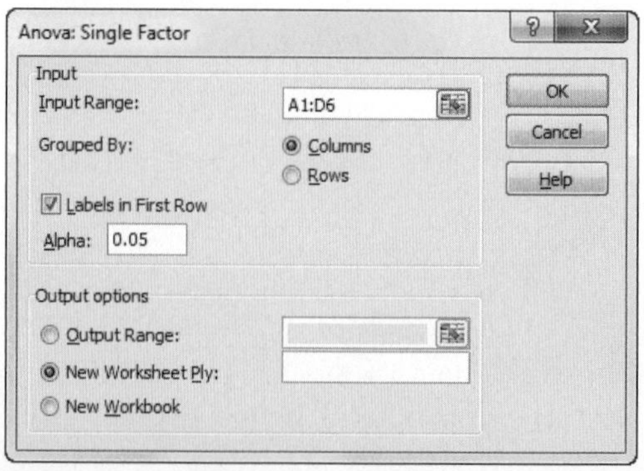

The Analysis ToolPak creates a worksheet that does not use formulas but is similar in layout to the worksheet shown in Figure 11.6 on page 396.

Multiple Comparisons: The Tukey-Kramer Procedure

Key Technique Use formulas to compute the absolute mean differences and use the **IF** function to compare pairs of means.

Example Perform the Tukey-Kramer procedure for the parachute experiment that is shown in Figure 11.7 on page 398.

PHStat Use the *PHStat* instructions for the one-way ANOVA *F* test to perform the Tukey-Kramer procedure, but in step 4, check **Tukey-Kramer Procedure** instead of clearing this check box. The procedure creates a worksheet identical to the one shown in Figure 11.7 on page 398 and discussed in the following *In-Depth Excel* section. To complete the worksheet, enter the **Studentized Range *Q* statistic** (use Table E.7 on pages 704–705) for the level of significance and the numerator and denominator degrees of freedom that are given in the worksheet.

In-Depth Excel To perform the Tukey-Kramer procedure, first use the *In-Depth Excel* instructions for the one-way ANOVA *F* test. Then open to the appropriate "**TK**" **worksheet** in the **One-Way ANOVA workbook** and enter the **Studentized Range *Q* statistic** (use Table E.7 on pages 704–705) for the level of significance and the numerator and denominator degrees of freedom that are given in the worksheet.

For the example, open to the **TK4 worksheet**. Enter the **Studentized Range *Q* statistic** (look up the value using Table E.7 on pages 704–705) in cell B15 for the level of significance and the numerator and denominator degrees of freedom that are given in cells B11 through B13.

Other TK worksheets can be used for problems using three (**TK3**), four (**TK4**), five (**TK5**), six (**TK6**), or seven (**TK7**) groups. When you use either the **TK5**, **TK6**, and **TK7** worksheets, you must also enter the name, sample mean, and sample size for the fifth and, if applicable, sixth and seventh groups.

Read the SHORT TAKES for Chapter 11 for an explanation of the formulas found in the COMPUTE worksheet (shown in the **COMPUTE_FORMULAS worksheet**). If you use an Excel version older than Excel 2010, use the TK4_OLDER worksheet instead of the TK4 worksheet for the example.

Analysis ToolPak Modify the previous *In-Depth Excel* instructions to perform the Tukey-Kramer procedure in conjunction with using the **Anova: Single Factor** procedure. Transfer selected values from the Analysis ToolPak results worksheet to one of the TK worksheets in the **One-Way ANOVA workbook.** For example, to perform the Figure 11.7 Tukey-Kramer procedure for the parachute experiment on page 398:

1. Use the **Anova: Single Factor** procedure, as described earlier in this section, to create a worksheet that contains ANOVA results for the parachute experiment.
2. Record the name, **sample size** (in the **Count** column), and **sample mean** (in the **Average** column) of each group. Also record the ***MSW*** value, found in the cell that is the intersection of the **MS** column and **Within Groups** row, and the **denominator degrees of freedom**, found in the cell that is the intersection of the **df** column and **Within Groups** row.
3. Open to the **TK4 worksheet** of the **One-Way ANOVA workbook**.

In the TK4 worksheet:

4. Overwrite the formulas in cell range A5:C8 by entering the name, sample mean, and sample size of each group into that range.
5. Enter **0.05** in cell B11 (the level of significance used in the Anova: Single Factor procedure).
6. Enter **4** in cell B12 as the **Numerator d.f.** (equal to the number of groups).
7. Enter **16** in cell B13 as the **Denominator d.f.**
8. Enter **6.094** in cell B14 as the **MSW**.
9. Enter **4.05** in cell B15 as the **Q Statistic**. (Look up the **Studentized Range *Q* statistic** using Table E.7 on pages 704–705.)

Levene Test for Homogeneity of Variance

Key Technique Use the techniques for performing a one-way ANOVA.

Example Perform the Levene test for the parachute experiment shown in Figure 11.8 on page 399.

PHStat Use **Levene Test**.
For the example, open to the **DATA worksheet** of the **Parachute workbook**. Select **PHStat → Multiple-Sample Tests → Levene Test**. In the procedure's dialog box (shown below):

1. Enter **0.05** as the **Level of Significance**.
2. Enter **A1:D6** as the **Sample Data Cell Range**.
3. Check **First cells contain label**.
4. Enter a **Title** and click **OK**.

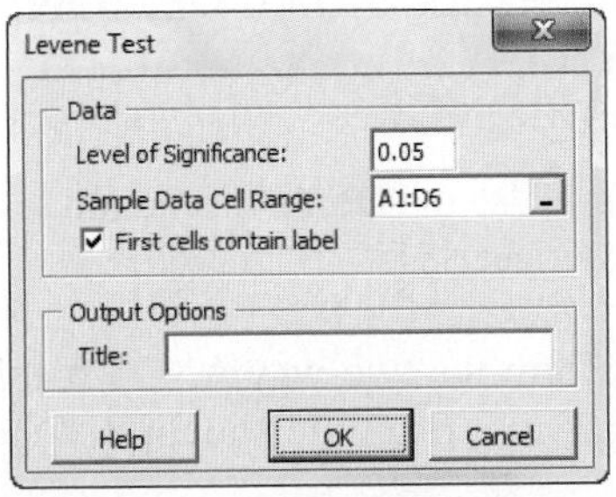

The procedure creates a worksheet that performs the Table 11.4 absolute differences computations (see page 399) as well as the worksheet shown in Figure 11.8 (see page 399). (See the following *In-Depth Excel* section for a description of these worksheets.)

In-Depth Excel Use the **COMPUTE worksheet** of the **Levene workbook** as a template.

The COMPUTE worksheet and the supporting AbsDiffs and DATA worksheets already contain the data for the example.

For other problems in which the absolute differences are already known, paste the absolute differences into the AbsDiffs worksheet. Otherwise, paste the problem data into the DATA worksheet, add formulas to compute the median for each group, and adjust the AbsDiffs worksheet as necessary. For example, for the parachute experiment data, the following steps 1 through 7 were done with the workbook open to the DATA worksheet:

1. Enter the label **Medians** in cell **A7**, the first empty cell in column A.
2. Enter the formula **=MEDIAN(A2:A6)** in cell **A8**. (Cell range A2:A6 contains the data for the first group, Supplier 1.)
3. Copy the **cell A8 formula** across through column **D**.
4. Open to the **AbsDiffs worksheet**.

In the AbsDiffs worksheet:

5. Enter row 1 column headings **AbsDiff1**, **AbsDiff2**, **AbsDiff3**, and **AbsDiff4** in columns A through D.
6. Enter the formula **=ABS(DATA!A2 – DATA!A8)** in cell A2. Copy this formula down through row 6. This formula computes the absolute difference of the first data value (DATA!A2) and the median of the Supplier 1 group data (DATA!A8).
7. Copy the formulas now in cell range A2:A6 across through column D. Absolute differences now appear in the cell range A2:D6.

If you use an Excel version older than Excel 2010, use the COMPUTE_OLDER worksheet instead of the COMPUTE worksheet.

Analysis ToolPak Use **Anova: Single Factor** with absolute difference data to perform the Levene test. If the absolute differences have not already been computed, use steps 1 through 7 of the preceding *In-Depth Excel* instructions to compute them.

EG11.2 The FACTORIAL DESIGN: TWO-WAY ANALYSIS of VARIANCE

Key Technique Use the **DEVSQ** function to compute *SSA*, *SSB*, *SSAB*, *SSE*, and *SST*.

Example Perform the two-way ANOVA for the supplier and loom parachute example shown in Figure 11.10 on page 409.

PHStat Use **Two-Way ANOVA with replication.**

For the example, open to the **DATA worksheet** of the **Parachute2 workbook**. Select **PHStat → Multiple-Sample Tests → Two-Way ANOVA**. In the procedure's dialog box (shown below):

1. Enter **0.05** as the **Level of Significance**.
2. Enter **A1:E11** as the **Sample Data Cell Range**.
3. Check **First cells contain label**.
4. Enter a **Title** and click **OK**.

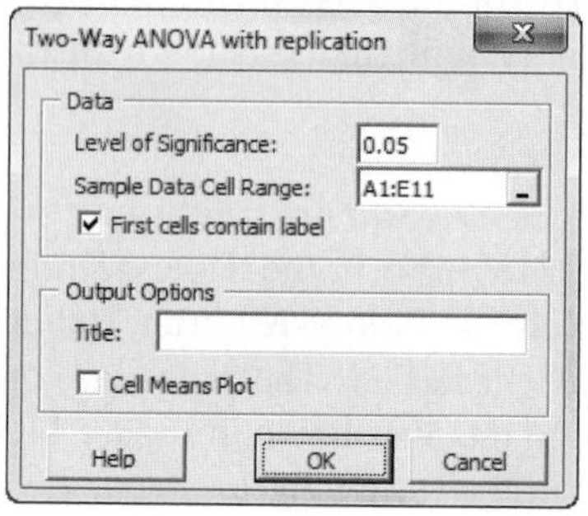

This procedure requires that the labels that identify factor *A* appear stacked in column A, followed by columns for factor *B*.

In-Depth Excel Use the **COMPUTE worksheet** of the **Two-Way ANOVA workbook** as a model.

For the example, the worksheet already uses the contents of the DATA worksheet to perform the test for the example.

Because of the complexity of the COMPUTE worksheet, consider using either PHStat or the Analysis ToolPak for other problems, especially ones that have a different mix of factors and levels. For problems similar to the supplier and loom parachute example of Section 11.2, use the following steps to modify the Two-Way ANOVA workbook:

1. Paste the data for the problem into the **ATFData worksheet**, overwriting the parachute experiment data.

In the COMPUTE worksheet (see Figure 11.10 on page 409):

2. Select the cell range **E1:E20** (the current Supplier 4 column).
3. For problems in which $c > 4$, right-click and select **Insert** from the shortcut menu. In the Insert dialog box, click **Shift cells right** and click **OK**. Repeat this step as many times as necessary.

   For problems in which $c < 4$, right-click and select **Delete** from the shortcut menu. In the Delete dialog box, click **Shift cells left** and click **OK**.

   For problems in which $c = 2$, select cell range **D1:D20**, right-click, and select **Delete** from the shortcut menu. In the Delete dialog box, again click **Shift cells left** and click **OK**.
4. For problems in which $r > 2$, select the cell range **A10:G15** (which includes the current Turk rows).

Right-click and select **Insert** from the shortcut menu. In the Insert dialog box, click **Shift cells down** and click **OK**. Repeat the previous sentence as many times as necessary. Enter new row labels in the new column A cells as necessary.

5. Edit the formulas in the top table area. Remember that each cell range in every formula in this area refers to a cell range on the ATFData worksheet that contains the range that hold the n' number of cells for a unique combination of a factor *A* level and a factor *B* level.
6. Edit the column B formulas for *SSA*, *SSB*, *SSE*, and *SST* that appear in the ANOVA summary table at the bottom of the worksheet. (The formula for *SSAB* does not need to be edited.) As noted earlier, this step becomes harder as the product of *r* and *c* increases.

Read the SHORT TAKES for Chapter 11 for an explanation of the formulas found in the COMPUTE worksheet (shown in the **COMPUTE_FORMULAS worksheet**). If you are using an older Excel version, use the COMPUTE_OLDER worksheet instead of the COMPUTE worksheet.

Analysis ToolPak Use **Anova: Two-Factor With Replication**.
For the example, open to the **DATA worksheet** of the **Parachute2 workbook** and:

1. Select **Data ➔ Data Analysis**.
2. In the Data Analysis dialog box, select **Anova: Two-Factor With Replication** from the **Analysis Tools** list and then click **OK**.

In the procedure's dialog box (shown below):

3. Enter **A1:E11** as the **Input Range**.
4. Enter **5** as the **Rows per sample**.
5. Enter **0.05** as **Alpha**.
6. Click **New Worksheet Ply**.
7. Click **OK**.

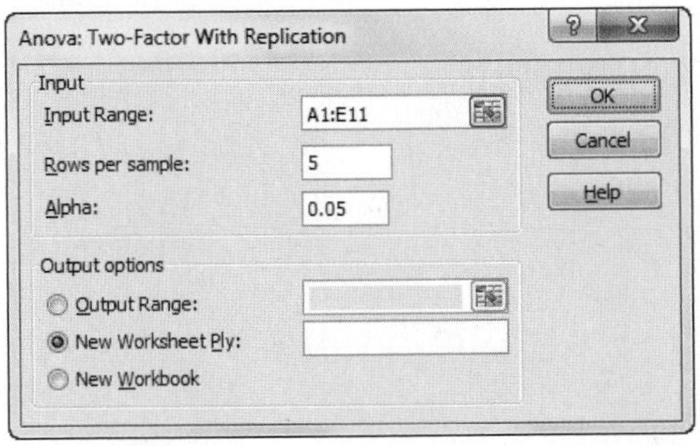

This procedure requires that the labels that identify factor *A* appear stacked in column A, followed by columns for factor *B*. The Analysis ToolPak creates a worksheet that does not use formulas but is similar in layout to the worksheet shown in Figure 11.10.

Visualizing Interaction Effects: The Cell Means Plot

Key Technique Use the **SUMPRODUCT(*cell range 1, cell range 2*)** function to compute the expected value and variance.

Example Construct the cell means plot for the mean tensile strength for suppliers and looms shown in Figure 11.13 on page 411.

PHStat Modify the *PHStat* instructions for the two-way ANOVA. In step 4, check **Cell Means Plot** before clicking **OK**.

In-Depth Excel Create a cell means plot from a two-way ANOVA COMPUTE worksheet.
For the example, open to the **COMPUTE worksheet** of the **Two-Way ANOVA** workbook and:

1. Insert a new worksheet.
2. Copy and paste the cell range **B3:E3** of the COMPUTE worksheet (the factor *B* level names) to cell **B1** of the new worksheet.
3. Copy the cell range **B7:E7** of the COMPUTE worksheet (the AVERAGE row for the *Jetta* level of Factor *A*) and paste to cell **B2** of the new worksheet, using the Paste Special **Values** option.
4. Copy the cell range **B13:E13** of the COMPUTE worksheet (the AVERAGE row for the *Turk* level of Factor *A*) and paste to cell **B3** of a new worksheet, using the Paste Special **Values** option.
5. Enter **Jetta** in cell **B3** and **Turk** in cell **A3** of the new worksheet as labels for the Factor *A* levels.
6. Select the cell range **A1:E3**.
7. Select **Insert ➔ Line** and select the **fourth 2-D Line gallery choice** (**Line with Markers**).
8. Relocate the chart to a chart sheet, add axis titles, and modify the chart title by using the instructions in Appendix Section B.6.

For other problems, insert a new worksheet and first copy and paste the Factor *B* level names to row 1 of the new worksheet and then copy and use Paste Special to transfer the values in the **Average** rows data for each Factor *B* level to the new worksheet. (See Appendix Section B.4 to learn more about the Paste Special command.)

Analysis ToolPak Use the *In-Depth Excel* instructions.

CHAPTER

12 Chi-Square and Nonparametric Tests

Learning Objectives

In this chapter, you learn:

- How and when to use the chi-square test for contingency tables
- How to use the Marascuilo procedure for determining pairwise differences when evaluating more than two proportions
- How and when to use nonparametric tests

ziggysofi / Shutterstock

USING STATISTICS

Not Resorting to Guesswork About Resort Guests

You are the manager of T.C. Resort Properties, a collection of five upscale hotels located on two tropical islands. Guests who are satisfied with the quality of services during their stay are more likely to return on a future vacation and to recommend the hotel to friends and relatives. You have defined the business objective as improving the percentage of guests who choose to return to the hotels later. To assess the quality of services being provided by your hotels, your staff encourages guests to complete a satisfaction survey when they check out or via email after they check out.

You need to analyze the data from these surveys to determine the overall satisfaction with the services provided, the likelihood that the guests will return to the hotel, and the reasons some guests indicate that they will not return. For example, on one island, T.C. Resort Properties operates the Beachcomber and Windsurfer hotels. Is the perceived quality at the Beachcomber Hotel the same as at the Windsurfer Hotel? If there is a difference, how can you use this information to improve the overall quality of service at T.C. Resort Properties? Furthermore, if guests indicate that they are not planning to return, what are the most common reasons cited for this decision? Are the reasons cited unique to a certain hotel or common to all hotels operated by T.C. Resort Properties?

maturos1812 / Shutterstock

In the preceding three chapters, you used hypothesis-testing procedures to analyze both numerical and categorical data. Chapter 9 presented some one-sample tests, Chapter 10 developed several two-sample tests, and Chapter 11 discussed the one-way and two-way analysis of variance (ANOVA). This chapter extends hypothesis testing to analyze differences between population proportions based on two or more samples and to test the hypothesis of *independence* in the joint responses to two categorical variables. The chapter concludes with nonparametric tests as alternatives to several hypothesis tests considered in Chapters 10 and 11.

12.1 Chi-Square Test for the Difference Between Two Proportions

In Section 10.3, you studied the Z test for the difference between two proportions. In this section, the data are examined from a different perspective. The hypothesis-testing procedure uses a test statistic that is approximated by a chi-square (χ^2) distribution. The results of this χ^2 test are equivalent to those of the Z test described in Section 10.3.

If you are interested in comparing the counts of categorical responses between two independent groups, you can develop a **two-way contingency table** to display the frequency of occurrence of items of interest and items not of interest for each group. (Contingency tables were first discussed in Section 2.1, and in Chapter 4, contingency tables were used to define and study probability.)

To illustrate the use of a contingency table, return to the Using Statistics scenario concerning T.C. Resort Properties. On one of the islands, T.C. Resort Properties has two hotels (the Beachcomber and the Windsurfer). You collect data from customer satisfaction surveys and focus on the responses to the single question "Are you likely to choose this hotel again?" You organize the results of the survey and determine that 163 of 227 guests at the Beachcomber responded yes to "Are you likely to choose this hotel again?" and 154 of 262 guests at the Windsurfer responded yes to "Are you likely to choose this hotel again?" You want to analyze the results to determine whether, at the 0.05 level of significance, there is evidence of a significant difference in guest satisfaction (as measured by likelihood to return to the hotel) between the two hotels.

The contingency table displayed in Table 12.1, which has two rows and two columns, is called a **2 × 2 contingency table**. The cells in the table indicate the frequency for each row-and-column combination.

TABLE 12.1

Layout of a 2 × 2 Contingency Table

	COLUMN VARIABLE (GROUP)		
ROW VARIABLE	**1**	**2**	**Totals**
Items of interest	X_1	X_2	X
Items not of interest	$n_1 - X_1$	$n_2 - X_2$	$n - X$
Totals	n_1	n_2	n

where

$$X_1 = \text{number of items of interest in group 1}$$
$$X_2 = \text{number of items of interest in group 2}$$
$$n_1 - X_1 = \text{number of items that are not of interest in group 1}$$
$$n_2 - X_2 = \text{number of items that are not of interest in group 2}$$
$$X = X_1 + X_2, \text{ the total number of items of interest}$$
$$n - X = (n_1 - X_1) + (n_2 - X_2), \text{ the total number of items that are not of interest}$$
$$n_1 = \text{sample size in group 1}$$
$$n_2 = \text{sample size in group 2}$$
$$n = n_1 + n_2 = \text{total sample size}$$

Table 12.2 contains the contingency table for the hotel guest satisfaction study. The contingency table has two rows, indicating whether the guests would return to the hotel or would not return to the hotel, and two columns, one for each hotel. The cells in the table indicate the frequency of each row-and-column combination. The row totals indicate the number of guests who would return to the hotel and the number of guests who would not return to the hotel. The column totals are the sample sizes for each hotel location.

TABLE 12.2

2 × 2 Contingency Table for the Hotel Guest Satisfaction Survey

	HOTEL		
CHOOSE HOTEL AGAIN?	Beachcomber	Windsurfer	Total
Yes	163	154	317
No	64	108	172
Total	227	262	489

Student Tip
Do not confuse this use of the Greek letter pi, π, to represent the population proportion with the mathematical constant that is the ratio of the circumference to a diameter of a circle—approximately 3.14159—which is also known by the same Greek letter.

To test whether the population proportion of guests who would return to the Beachcomber, π_1, is equal to the population proportion of guests who would return to the Windsurfer, π_2, you can use the **chi-square (χ^2) test for the difference between two proportions**. To test the null hypothesis that there is no difference between the two population proportions:

$$H_0: \pi_1 = \pi_2$$

against the alternative that the two population proportions are not the same:

$$H_1: \pi_1 \neq \pi_2$$

you use the χ^2_{STAT} test statistic, shown in Equation (12.1).

Student Tip
You are computing the squared difference between f_o and f_e. Therefore, unlike the Z_{STAT} and t_{STAT} statistics, the χ^2_{STAT} test statistic can never be negative.

χ^2 TEST FOR THE DIFFERENCE BETWEEN TWO PROPORTIONS

The χ^2_{STAT} test statistic is equal to the squared difference between the observed and expected frequencies, divided by the expected frequency in each cell of the table, summed over all cells of the table.

$$\chi^2_{STAT} = \sum_{\text{all cells}} \frac{(f_o - f_e)^2}{f_e} \qquad \textbf{(12.1)}$$

where

f_o = **observed frequency** in a particular cell of a contingency table
f_e = **expected frequency** in a particular cell if the null hypothesis is true

The χ^2_{STAT} test statistic approximately follows a chi-square distribution with 1 degree of freedom.[1]

[1]In general, the degrees of freedom in a contingency table are equal to (number of rows − 1) multiplied by (number of columns − 1).

To compute the expected frequency, f_e, in any cell, you need to understand that if the null hypothesis is true, the proportion of items of interest in the two populations will be equal. Then the sample proportions you compute from each of the two groups would differ from each other only by chance. Each would provide an estimate of the common population parameter, π. A statistic that combines these two separate estimates together into one overall estimate of the population parameter provides more information than either of the two separate estimates could provide by itself. This statistic, given by the symbol $\bar{p}$, represents the estimated overall proportion of items of interest for the two groups combined (i.e., the total number of items of interest divided by the total sample size). The complement of $\bar{p}$, $1 - \bar{p}$, represents the estimated overall proportion of items that are not of interest in the two groups. Using the notation presented in Table 12.1 on page 430, Equation (12.2) defines $\bar{p}$.

Student Tip
Remember, the sample proportion, p, must be between 0 and 1.

COMPUTING THE ESTIMATED OVERALL PROPORTION FOR TWO GROUPS

$$\bar{p} = \frac{X_1 + X_2}{n_1 + n_2} = \frac{X}{n} \quad (12.2)$$

To compute the expected frequency, f_e, for cells that involve items of interest (i.e., the cells in the first row in the contingency table), you multiply the sample size (or column total) for a group by $\bar{p}$. To compute the expected frequency, f_e, for cells that involve items that are not of interest (i.e., the cells in the second row in the contingency table), you multiply the sample size (or column total) for a group by $1 - \bar{p}$.

Student Tip
Remember that the rejection region for this test is only in the upper tail of the chi-square distribution.

The χ^2_{STAT} test statistic shown in Equation (12.1) on page 431 approximately follows a **chi-square (χ^2) distribution** (see Table E.4) with 1 degree of freedom. Using a level of significance α, you reject the null hypothesis if the computed χ^2_{STAT} test statistic is greater than χ^2_α, the upper-tail critical value from the χ^2 distribution with 1 degree of freedom. Thus, the decision rule is

Reject H_0 if $\chi^2_{STAT} > \chi^2_\alpha$;

otherwise, do not reject H_0.

Figure 12.1 illustrates the decision rule.

FIGURE 12.1
Regions of rejection and nonrejection when using the chi-square test for the difference between two proportions, with level of significance α

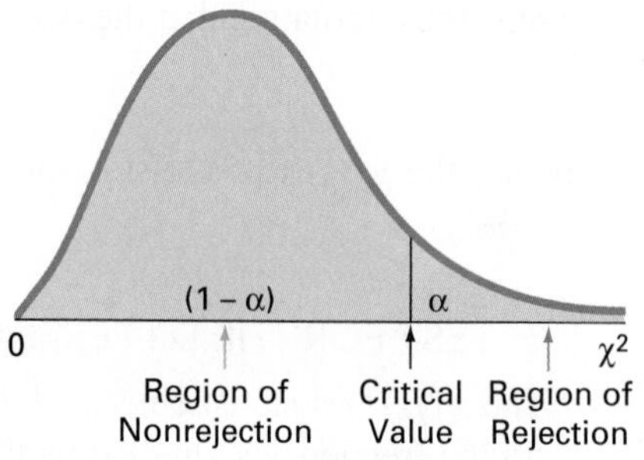

If the null hypothesis is true, the computed χ^2_{STAT} test statistic should be close to zero because the squared difference between what is actually observed in each cell, f_o, and what is theoretically expected, f_e, should be very small. If H_0 is false, then there are differences in the population proportions, and the computed χ^2_{STAT} test statistic is expected to be large. However, what is a large difference in a cell is relative. The same actual difference between f_o and f_e from a cell with a small number of expected frequencies contributes more to the χ^2_{STAT} test statistic than a cell with a large number of expected frequencies.

To illustrate the use of the chi-square test for the difference between two proportions, return to the Using Statistics scenario concerning T.C. Resort Properties on page 429 and the corresponding contingency table displayed in Table 12.2 on page 431. The null hypothesis (H_0: $\pi_1 = \pi_2$) states that there is no difference between the proportion of guests who are likely to choose either of these hotels again. To begin,

$$\bar{p} = \frac{X_1 + X_2}{n_1 + n_2} = \frac{163 + 154}{227 + 262} = \frac{317}{489} = 0.6483$$

$\bar{p}$ is the estimate of the common parameter π, the population proportion of guests who are likely to choose either of these hotels again if the null hypothesis is true. The estimated proportion of guests who are *not* likely to choose these hotels again is the complement of $\bar{p}$, $1 - 0.6483 = 0.3517$. Multiplying these two proportions by the sample size for the Beachcomber Hotel gives the number of guests expected to choose the Beachcomber again and the number not expected to choose this hotel again. In a similar manner, multiplying the two proportions by the Windsurfer Hotel's sample size yields the corresponding expected frequencies for that group.

EXAMPLE 12.1

Computing the Expected Frequencies

Compute the expected frequencies for each of the four cells of Table 12.2 on page 431.

SOLUTION

Yes—Beachcomber: $\bar{p} = 0.6483$ and $n_1 = 227$, so $f_e = 147.16$

Yes—Windsurfer: $\bar{p} = 0.6483$ and $n_2 = 262$, so $f_e = 169.84$

No—Beachcomber: $1 - \bar{p} = 0.3517$ and $n_1 = 227$, so $f_e = 79.84$

No—Windsurfer: $1 - \bar{p} = 0.3517$ and $n_2 = 262$, so $f_e = 92.16$

Table 12.3 presents these expected frequencies next to the corresponding observed frequencies.

TABLE 12.3

Comparing the Observed (f_o) and Expected (f_e) Frequencies

	HOTEL				
	Beachcomber		Windsurfer		
CHOOSE HOTEL AGAIN?	Observed	Expected	Observed	Expected	Total
Yes	163	147.16	154	169.84	317
No	64	79.84	108	92.16	172
Total	227	227.00	262	262.00	489

To test the null hypothesis that the population proportions are equal:

$$H_0: \pi_1 = \pi_2$$

against the alternative that the population proportions are not equal:

$$H_1: \pi_1 \neq \pi_2$$

you use the observed and expected frequencies from Table 12.3 to compute the χ^2_{STAT} test statistic given by Equation (12.1) on page 431. Table 12.4 presents these calculations.

TABLE 12.4

Computing the χ^2_{STAT} Test Statistic for the Hotel Guest Satisfaction Survey

f_o	f_e	$(f_o - f_e)$	$(f_o - f_e)^2$	$(f_o - f_e)^2/f_e$
163	147.16	15.84	250.91	1.71
154	169.84	−15.84	250.91	1.48
64	79.84	−15.84	250.91	3.14
108	92.16	15.84	250.91	2.72
				9.05

The chi-square (χ^2) distribution is a right-skewed distribution whose shape depends solely on the number of degrees of freedom. You find the critical value for the χ^2 test from Table E.4, a portion of which is presented in Table 12.5.

TABLE 12.5

Finding the Critical Value from the Chi-Square Distribution with 1 Degree of Freedom, Using the 0.05 Level of Significance

	Cumulative Probabilities						
	.005	.01	. . .	.95	.975	.99	.995
	Upper-Tail Area						
Degrees of Freedom	.995	.99	. . .	.05	.025	.01	.005
1			. . .	3.841	5.024	6.635	7.879
2	0.010	0.020	. . .	5.991	7.378	9.210	10.597
3	0.072	0.115	. . .	7.815	9.348	11.345	12.838
4	0.207	0.297	. . .	9.488	11.143	13.277	14.860
5	0.412	0.554	. . .	11.071	12.833	15.086	16.750

The values in Table 12.5 refer to selected upper-tail areas of the χ^2 distribution. A 2 $\times$ 2 contingency table has 1 degree of freedom because there are two rows and two columns. [The degrees of freedom are equal to the (number of rows $-$ 1)(number of columns $-$ 1).] Using $\alpha = 0.05$, with 1 degree of freedom, the critical value of χ^2 from Table 12.5 is 3.841. You reject H_0 if the computed χ^2_{STAT} test statistic is greater than 3.841 (see Figure 12.2). Because $\chi^2_{STAT} = 9.05 > 3.841$, you reject H_0. You conclude that the proportion of guests who would return to the Beachcomber is different from the proportion of guests who would return to the Windsurfer.

FIGURE 12.2

Regions of rejection and nonrejection when finding the χ^2 critical value with 1 degree of freedom, at the 0.05 level of significance

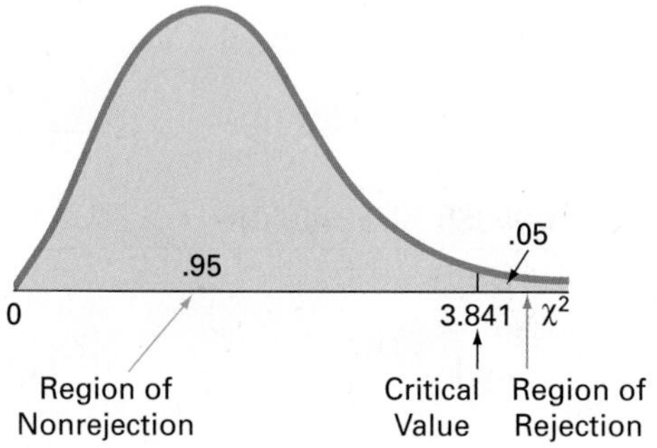

Figure 12.3 shows the results for the Table 12.2 guest satisfaction contingency table on page 431.

FIGURE 12.3

Chi-square test worksheet for the two-hotel guest satisfaction data

Figure 12.3 displays the ***COMPUTE worksheet*** *of the* ***Chi-Square workbook*** *that the Section EG12.1 instructions use.*

	A	B	C	D	E	F	G
1	**Chi-Square Test**						
2							
3	**Observed Frequencies**						
4		Hotel				Calculations	
5	Choose Again?	Beachcomber	Windsurfer	Total		fo-fe	
6	Yes	163	154	317		15.8446	-15.8446
7	No	64	108	172		-15.8446	15.8446
8	Total	227	262	489			
9							
10	Expected Frequencies						
11		Hotel					
12	Choose Again?	Beachcomber	Windsurfer	Total		(fo-fe)^2/fe	
13	Yes	147.1554	169.8446	317		1.7060	1.4781
14	No	79.8446	92.1554	172		3.1442	2.7242
15	Total	227	262	489			
16							
17	**Data**						
18	Level of Significance	0.05					
19	Number of Rows	2					
20	Number of Columns	2					
21	Degrees of Freedom	1	**=(B19 - 1) * (B20 - 1)**				
22							
23	**Results**						
24	Critical Value	3.8415	**=CHISQ.INV.RT(B18, B21)**				
25	Chi-Square Test Statistic	9.0526	**=SUM(F13:G14)**				
26	*p*-Value	0.0026	**=CHISQ.DIST.RT(B25, B21)**				
27	Reject the null hypothesis		**=IF(B26 < B18, "Reject the null hypothesis",**				
28			**"Do not reject the null hypothesis")**				
29	***Expected frequency assumption***						
30	***is met.***		**=IF(OR(B13 < 5, C13 < 5, B14 < 5, C14 < 5),**				
			" is violated.", " is met.")				

These results include the expected frequencies, χ^2_{STAT}, degrees of freedom, and p-value. The computed χ^2_{STAT} test statistic is 9.0526, which is greater than the critical value of 3.8415 (or the p-value $= 0.0026 < 0.05$), so you reject the null hypothesis that there is no difference in guest satisfaction between the two hotels. The p-value, equal to 0.0026, is the probability of observing sample proportions as different as or more different from the actual difference between the Beachcomber and Windsurfer ($0.718 - 0.588 = 0.13$) observed in the sample data, if the population proportions for the Beachcomber and Windsurfer hotels are equal. Thus, there is strong evidence to conclude that the two hotels are significantly different with respect to guest satisfaction, as measured by whether a guest is likely to return to the hotel again. From Table 12.3 on page 433 you can see that a greater proportion of guests are likely to return to the Beachcomber than to the Windsurfer.

For the χ^2 test to give accurate results for a 2 $\times$ 2 table, you must assume that each expected frequency is at least 5. If this assumption is not satisfied, you can use alternative procedures, such as Fisher's exact test (see references 1, 2, and 4).

In the hotel guest satisfaction survey, both the Z test based on the standardized normal distribution (see Section 10.3) and the χ^2 test based on the chi-square distribution lead to the same conclusion. You can explain this result by the interrelationship between the standardized normal distribution and a chi-square distribution with 1 degree of freedom. For such situations, the χ^2_{STAT} test statistic is the square of the Z_{STAT} test statistic. For instance, in the guest satisfaction study, the computed Z_{STAT} test statistic is +3.0088, and the computed χ^2_{STAT} test statistic is 9.0526. Except for rounding differences, this 9.0526 value is the square of +3.0088 [i.e., $(+3.0088)^2 \cong 9.0526$]. Also, if you compare the critical values of the test statistics from the two distributions, at the 0.05 level of significance, the χ^2 value of 3.841 with 1 degree of freedom is the square of the Z value of ± 1.96. Furthermore, the p-values for both tests are equal. Therefore, when testing the null hypothesis of equality of proportions:

$$H_0: \pi_1 = \pi_2$$

against the alternative that the population proportions are not equal:

$$H_1: \pi_1 \neq \pi_2$$

the Z test and the χ^2 test are equivalent.

If you are interested in determining whether there is evidence of a *directional* difference, such as $\pi_1 > \pi_2$, you must use the Z test, with the entire rejection region located in one tail of the standardized normal distribution.

In Section 12.2, the χ^2 test is extended to make comparisons and evaluate differences between the proportions among more than two groups. However, you cannot use the Z test if there are more than two groups.

Problems for Section 12.1

LEARNING THE BASICS

12.1 Determine the critical value of χ^2 with 1 degree of freedom in each of the following circumstances:

a. $\alpha = 0.01$
b. $\alpha = 0.005$
c. $\alpha = 0.10$

12.2 Determine the critical value of χ^2 with 1 degree of freedom in each of the following circumstances:

a. $\alpha = 0.05$
b. $\alpha = 0.025$
c. $\alpha = 0.01$

12.3 Use the following contingency table:

	A	B	Total
1	20	30	50
2	30	45	75
Total	50	75	125

a. Compute the expected frequency for each cell.
b. Compare the observed and expected frequencies for each cell.
c. Compute χ^2_{STAT}. Is it significant at $\alpha = 0.05$?

12.4 Use the following contingency table:

	A	B	Total
1	20	30	50
2	30	20	50
Total	50	50	100

a. Compute the expected frequency for each cell.
b. Compute χ^2_{STAT}. Is it significant at $\alpha = 0.05$?

APPLYING THE CONCEPTS

12.5 A survey of 1,085 adults asked, "Do you enjoy shopping for clothing for yourself?" The results indicated that 51% of the females enjoyed shopping for clothing for themselves as compared to 44% of the males. (Data extracted from "Split Decision on Clothes Shopping," *USA Today*, January 28, 2011, p. 1B.) The sample sizes of males and females were not provided. Suppose that the results were as shown in the following table:

Enjoy Shopping for Clothing	Gender		
	Male	Female	Total
Yes	238	276	514
No	304	267	571
Total	542	543	1,085

a. Is there evidence of a significant difference between the proportion of males and females who enjoy shopping for clothing for themselves at the 0.01 level of significance?
b. Determine the p-value in (a) and interpret its meaning.
c. What are your answers to (a) and (b) if 218 males enjoyed shopping for clothing and 324 did not?
d. Compare the results of (a) through (c) to those of Problem 10.29 (a), (b), and (d) on page 367.

12.6 Do social recommendations increase ad effectiveness? A study of online video viewers compared viewers who arrived at an advertising video for a particular brand by following a social media recommendation link to viewers who arrived at the same video by web browsing. Data were collected on whether the viewer could correctly recall the brand being advertised after seeing the video. The results were:

	Correctly Recalled the Brand	
Arrival Method	Yes	No
Recommendation	407	150
Browsing	193	91

Source: Data extracted from "Social Ad Effectiveness: An Unruly White Paper," **www.unrulymedia.com**, January 2012, p. 3.

a. Set up the null and alternative hypotheses to determine whether there is a difference in brand recall between viewers who arrived by following a social media recommendation and those who arrived by web browsing.
b. Conduct the hypothesis test defined in (a), using the 0.05 level of significance.
c. Compare the results of (a) and (b) to those of Problem 10.30 (a) and (b) on page 368.

12.7 A survey was conducted of 665 consumer magazines on the practices of their websites. Of these, 273 magazines reported that online-only content is copy-edited as rigorously as print content; 379 reported that online-only content is fact-checked as rigorously as print content. (Data extracted from S. Clifford, "Columbia Survey Finds a Slack Editing Process of Magazine Web Sites," *The New York Times*, March 1, 2010, p. B6.) Suppose that a sample of 500 newspapers revealed that 252 reported that online-only content is copy-edited as rigorously as print content and 296 reported that online-only content is fact-checked as rigorously as print content.

a. At the 0.05 level of significance, is there evidence of a difference between consumer magazines and newspapers in the proportion of online-only content that is copy-edited as rigorously as print content?
b. Determine the p-value in (a) and interpret its meaning.
c. At the 0.05 level of significance, is there evidence of a difference between consumer magazines and newspapers in the proportion of online-only content that is fact-checked as rigorously as print content?
d. Determine the p-value in (c) and interpret its meaning.

SELF Test **12.8** Consumer research firm Scarborough analyzed the 10% of American adults who are either "Superbanked" or "Unbanked." Superbanked consumers are defined as U.S. adults who live in a household that has multiple asset accounts at financial institutions, as well as some additional investments; Unbanked consumers are U.S. adults who live in a household that does not use a bank or credit union. By finding the 5% of Americans who are Superbanked, Scarborough identifies financially savvy consumers who might be open to diversifying their financial portfolios; by identifying the Unbanked, Scarborough provides insight into the ultimate prospective client for banks and financial institutions. As part of its analysis, Scarborough reported that 93% of Superbanked consumers use credit cards as compared to 23% of Unbanked consumers. (Data extracted from **bit.ly/Syi9kN**.) Suppose that these results were based on 1,000 Superbanked consumers and 1,000 Unbanked consumers.

a. At the 0.01 level of significance, is there evidence of a significant difference between the Superbanked and the Unbanked with respect to the proportion that use credit cards?
b. Determine the p-value in (a) and interpret is meaning.
c. Compare the results of (a) and (b) to those of Problem 10.32 on page 368.

12.9 Different age groups use different media sources for news. A study on this issue explored the use of cellphones for accessing news. The study reported that 47% of users under age 50 and 15% of users age 50 and over accessed news on their cellphones. (Data extracted from "Cellphone Users Who Access News on Their Phones," *USA Today*, March 1, 2010, p. 1A.) Suppose that the survey consisted of 1,000 users under age 50, of whom 470 accessed news on their cellphones, and 891 users age 50 and over, of whom 134 accessed news on their cellphones.

a. Construct a 2×2 contingency table.
b. Is there evidence of a significant difference in the proportion that accessed the news on their cellphones between users under age 50 and users 50 years and older? (Use $\alpha = 0.05$.)
c. Determine the p-value in (b) and interpret its meaning.
d. Compare the results of (b) and (c) to those of Problem 10.35 (a) and (b) on page 369.

12.10 How do Americans feel about ads on websites? A survey of 1,000 adult Internet users found that 670 opposed ads on websites. (Data extracted from S. Clifford, "Tracked for Ads? Many Americans Say No Thanks," *The New York Times*, September 30, 2009, p. B3.) Suppose that a survey of 1,000 Internet users age 12–17 found that 510 opposed ads on websites.

a. At the 0.05 level of significance, is there evidence of a difference between adult Internet users and Internet users age 12–17 in the proportion who oppose ads?
b. Determine the p-value in (a) and interpret its meaning.

12.2 Chi-Square Test for Differences Among More Than Two Proportions

In this section, the χ^2 test is extended to compare more than two independent populations. The letter c is used to represent the number of independent populations under consideration. Thus, the contingency table now has two rows and c columns. To test the null hypothesis that there are no differences among the c population proportions:

$$H_0: \pi_1 = \pi_2 = \cdots = \pi_c$$

against the alternative that not all the c population proportions are equal:

$$H_1: \text{Not all } \pi_j \text{ are equal (where } j = 1, 2, \ldots, c)$$

you use Equation (12.1) on page 431:

$$\chi^2_{STAT} = \sum_{\textit{all} \text{ cells}} \frac{(f_o - f_e)^2}{f_e}$$

where

f_o = observed frequency in a particular cell of a $2 \times c$ contingency table
f_e = expected frequency in a particular cell if the null hypothesis is true

If the null hypothesis is true and the proportions are equal across all c populations, the c sample proportions should differ only by chance. In such a situation, a statistic that combines these c separate estimates into one overall estimate of the population proportion, π, provides more information than any one of the c separate estimates alone. To expand on Equation (12.2) on page 432, the statistic $\bar{p}$ in Equation (12.3) represents the estimated overall proportion for all c groups combined.

COMPUTING THE ESTIMATED OVERALL PROPORTION FOR c GROUPS

$$\bar{p} = \frac{X_1 + X_2 + \cdots + X_c}{n_1 + n_2 + \cdots + n_c} = \frac{X}{n} \quad \textbf{(12.3)}$$

To compute the expected frequency, f_e, for each cell in the first row in the contingency table, multiply each sample size (or column total) by $\bar{p}$. To compute the expected frequency, f_e, for each cell in the second row in the contingency table, multiply each sample size (or column total) by $(1 - \bar{p})$. The test statistic shown in Equation (12.1) on page 431 approximately follows a chi-square distribution, with degrees of freedom equal to the number of rows in the contingency table minus 1, multiplied by the number of columns in the table minus 1. For a **$2 \times c$ contingency table**, there are $c - 1$ degrees of freedom:

$$\text{Degrees of freedom} = (2 - 1)(c - 1) = c - 1$$

Using the level of significance α, you reject the null hypothesis if the computed χ^2_{STAT} test statistic is greater than χ^2_α, the upper-tail critical value from a chi-square distribution with $c - 1$ degrees of freedom. Therefore, the decision rule is

$$\text{Reject } H_0 \text{ if } \chi^2_{STAT} > \chi^2_\alpha;$$

otherwise, do not reject H_0.

Figure 12.4 illustrates this decision rule.

FIGURE 12.4
Regions of rejection and nonrejection when testing for differences among c proportions using the χ^2 test

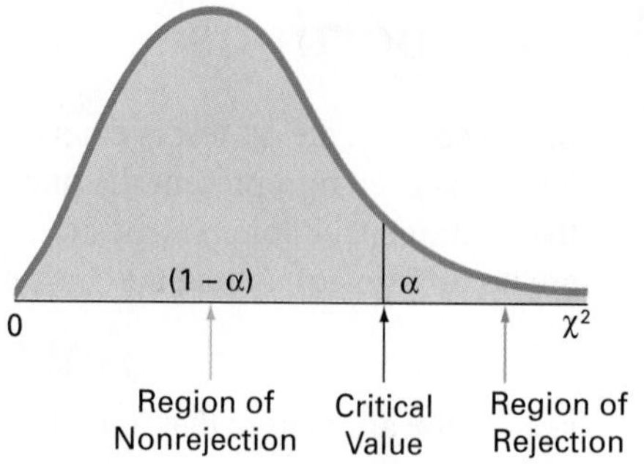

To illustrate the χ^2 test for equality of proportions when there are more than two groups, return to the Using Statistics scenario on page 429 concerning T.C. Resort Properties. Once again, you define the business objective as improving the quality of service, but this time, you are comparing three hotels located on a different island. Data are collected from customer satisfaction surveys at these three hotels. You organize the responses into the contingency table shown in Table 12.6.

TABLE 12.6
2 × 3 Contingency Table for Guest Satisfaction Survey

	HOTEL			
CHOOSE HOTEL AGAIN?	**Golden Palm**	**Palm Royale**	**Palm Princess**	**Total**
Yes	128	199	186	513
No	88	33	66	187
Total	216	232	252	700

Because the null hypothesis states that there are no differences among the three hotels in the proportion of guests who would likely return again, you use Equation (12.3) to calculate an estimate of π, the population proportion of guests who would likely return again:

$$\bar{p} = \frac{X_1 + X_2 + \cdots + X_c}{n_1 + n_2 + \cdots + n_c} = \frac{X}{n}$$
$$= \frac{(128 + 199 + 186)}{(216 + 232 + 252)} = \frac{513}{700}$$
$$= 0.733$$

The estimated overall proportion of guests who would *not* be likely to return again is the complement, $(1 - \bar{p})$, or 0.267. Multiplying these two proportions by the sample size for each hotel yields the expected number of guests who would and would not likely return.

EXAMPLE 12.2

Computing the Expected Frequencies

Compute the expected frequencies for each of the six cells in Table 12.6.

SOLUTION

Yes—Golden Palm: $\bar{p} = 0.733$ and $n_1 = 216$, so $f_e = 158.30$
Yes—Palm Royale: $\bar{p} = 0.733$ and $n_2 = 232$, so $f_e = 170.02$
Yes—Palm Princess: $\bar{p} = 0.733$ and $n_3 = 252$, so $f_e = 184.68$
No—Golden Palm: $1 - \bar{p} = 0.267$ and $n_1 = 216$, so $f_e = 57.70$
No—Palm Royale: $1 - \bar{p} = 0.267$ and $n_2 = 232$, so $f_e = 61.98$
No—Palm Princess: $1 - \bar{p} = 0.267$ and $n_3 = 252$, so $f_e = 67.32$

Table 12.7 presents these expected frequencies.

TABLE 12.7

Contingency Table of Expected Frequencies from a Guest Satisfaction Survey of Three Hotels

	HOTEL			
CHOOSE HOTEL AGAIN?	**Golden Palm**	**Palm Royale**	**Palm Princess**	**Total**
Yes	158.30	170.02	184.68	513
No	57.70	61.98	67.32	187
Total	216.00	232.00	252.00	700

To test the null hypothesis that the proportions are equal:

$$H_0: \pi_1 = \pi_2 = \pi_3$$

against the alternative that not all three proportions are equal:

$$H_1: \text{Not all } \pi_j \text{ are equal (where } j = 1, 2, 3)$$

you use the observed frequencies from Table 12.6 and the expected frequencies from Table 12.7 to compute the χ^2_{STAT} test statistic [given by Equation (12.1) on page 431]. Table 12.8 presents the calculations.

TABLE 12.8

Computing the χ^2_{STAT} Test Statistic for the Guest Satisfaction Survey of Three Hotels

f_o	f_e	$(f_o - f_e)$	$(f_o - f_e)^2$	$(f_o - f_e)^2/f_e$
128	158.30	−30.30	918.09	5.80
199	170.02	28.98	839.84	4.94
186	184.68	1.32	1.74	0.01
88	57.70	30.30	918.09	15.91
33	61.98	−28.98	839.84	13.55
66	67.32	−1.32	1.74	0.02
				40.23

You use Table E.4 to find the critical value of the χ^2 test statistic. In the guest satisfaction survey, because there are three hotels, there are $(2 - 1)(3 - 1) = 2$ degrees of freedom. Using $\alpha = 0.05$, the χ^2 critical value with 2 degrees of freedom is 5.991 (see Figure 12.5).

FIGURE 12.5

Regions of rejection and nonrejection when testing for differences in three proportions at the 0.05 level of significance, with 2 degrees of freedom

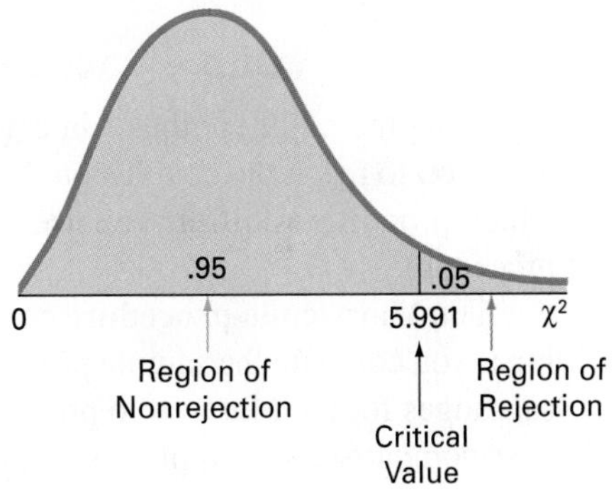

Because the computed χ^2_{STAT} test statistic is 40.23, which is greater than this critical value, you reject the null hypothesis. Figure 12.6 shows the worksheet solution for this problem. The worksheet results also report the p-value. Because the p-value is (approximately) 0.0000, less than $\alpha = 0.05$, you reject the null hypothesis. Further, this p-value indicates that there is virtually no chance that there will be differences this large or larger among the three sample proportions, if the population proportions for the three hotels are equal. Thus, there is sufficient evidence to conclude that the hotel properties are different with respect to the proportion of guests who are likely to return.

FIGURE 12.6

Chi-square test worksheet for the Table 12.6 guest satisfaction data

Figure 12.6 displays the ***ChiSquare2x3 worksheet*** *of the* ***Chi_Square Worksheets workbook*** *that the Section EG12.2 instructions use.*

	A	B	C	D	E	F	G	H	I
1	**Chi-Square Test**								
2									
3			**Observed Frequencies**						
4			Hotel				Calculations		
5	Choose Again?	Golden Palm	Palm Royale	Palm Princess	Total			fo - fe	
6	Yes	128	199	186	513		-30.2971	28.9771	1.32
7	No	88	33	66	187		30.2971	-28.9771	-1.32
8	Total	216	232	252	700				
9									
10			Expected Frequencies						
11			Hotel						
12	Choose Again?	Golden Palm	Palm Royale	Palm Princess	Total			(fo - fe)^2/fe	
13	Yes	158.2971	170.0229	184.68	513		5.7987	4.9386	0.0094
14	No	57.7029	61.9771	67.32	187		15.9077	13.5481	0.0259
15	Total	216	232	252	700				
16									
17	**Data**								
18	Level of Significance	0.05							
19	Number of Rows	2							
20	Number of Columns	3							
21	Degrees of Freedom	2	=(B19 - 1) * (B20 - 1)						
22									
23	**Results**								
24	Critical Value	5.9915	=CHISQ.INV.RT(B18, B21)						
25	Chi-Square Test Statistic	40.2284	=SUM(G13:I14)						
26	*p*-Value	0.0000	=CHISQ.DIST.RT(B25, B21)						
27	Reject the null hypothesis		=IF(B26 < B18, "Reject the null hypothesis",						
28			"Do not reject the null hypothesis")						
29	***Expected frequency assumption***								
30	***is met.***		=IF(OR(B13 < 1, C13 < 1, D13 < 1, B14 < 1, C14 < 1, D14 < 1), " is violated.", " is met.")						

For the χ^2 test to give accurate results when dealing with $2 \times c$ contingency tables, all expected frequencies must be large. The definition of "large" has led to research among statisticians. Some statisticians (see reference 5) have found that the test gives accurate results as long as all expected frequencies are at least 0.5. Other statisticians, more conservative in their approach, believe that no more than 20% of the cells should contain expected frequencies less than 5, and no cells should have expected frequencies less than 1 (see reference 3). As a reasonable compromise between these points of view, to ensure the validity of the test, you should make sure that each expected frequency is at least 1. To do this, you may need to collapse two or more low-expected-frequency categories into one category in the contingency table before performing the test. If combining categories is undesirable, you can use one of the available alternative procedures (see references 1, 2, and 7).

The Marascuilo Procedure

Rejecting the null hypothesis in a χ^2 test of equality of proportions in a $2 \times c$ table only allows you to reach the conclusion that not all c population proportions are equal. To determine which proportions differ, you use a multiple-comparisons procedure such as the Marascuilo procedure.

The **Marascuilo procedure** enables you to make comparisons between all pairs of groups. First, you compute the sample proportions. Then, you use Equation (12.4) to compute the critical ranges for the Marascuilo procedure. You compute a different critical range for each pairwise comparison of sample proportions.

Student Tip
You have an α level of risk in the entire set of comparisons not just a single comparison.

CRITICAL RANGE FOR THE MARASCUILO PROCEDURE

$$\text{Critical range} = \sqrt{\chi^2_{\alpha}}\sqrt{\frac{p_j(1 - p_j)}{n_j} + \frac{p_{j'}(1 - p_{j'})}{n_{j'}}} \quad \textbf{(12.4)}$$

Then, you compare each of the $c(c - 1)/2$ pairs of sample proportions against its corresponding critical range. You declare a specific pair significantly different if the absolute difference in the sample proportions, $|p_j - p_{j'}|$, is greater than its critical range.

To apply the Marascuilo procedure, return to the guest satisfaction survey. Using the χ^2 test, you concluded that there was evidence of a significant difference among the population proportions. From Table 12.6 on page 438, the three sample proportions are

$$p_1 = \frac{X_1}{n_1} = \frac{128}{216} = 0.5926$$

$$p_2 = \frac{X_2}{n_2} = \frac{199}{232} = 0.8578$$

$$p_3 = \frac{X_3}{n_3} = \frac{186}{252} = 0.7381$$

Next, you compute the absolute differences in sample proportions and their corresponding critical ranges. Because there are three hotels, there are $(3)(3 - 1)/2 = 3$ pairwise comparisons. Using Table E.4 and an overall level of significance of 0.05, the upper-tail critical value for a chi-square distribution having $(c - 1) = 2$ degrees of freedom is 5.991. Thus,

$$\sqrt{\chi^2_\alpha} = \sqrt{5.991} = 2.4477$$

The following displays the absolute differences and the critical ranges for each comparison.

Absolute Difference in Proportions	Critical Range
$\lvert p_j - p_{j'} \rvert$	$2.4477\sqrt{\frac{p_j(1 - p_j)}{n_j} + \frac{p_{j'}(1 - p_{j'})}{n_{j'}}}$
$\lvert p_1 - p_2 \rvert = \lvert 0.5926 - 0.8578 \rvert = 0.2652$	$2.4477\sqrt{\frac{(0.5926)(0.4074)}{216} + \frac{(0.8578)(0.1422)}{232}} = 0.0992$
$\lvert p_1 - p_3 \rvert = \lvert 0.5926 - 0.7381 \rvert = 0.1455$	$2.4477\sqrt{\frac{(0.5926)(0.4074)}{216} + \frac{(0.7381)(0.2619)}{252}} = 0.1063$
$\lvert p_2 - p_3 \rvert = \lvert 0.8578 - 0.7381 \rvert = 0.1197$	$2.4477\sqrt{\frac{(0.8578)(0.1422)}{232} + \frac{(0.7381)(0.2619)}{252}} = 0.0880$

Figure 12.7 shows a worksheet solution for this example.

FIGURE 12.7
Marascuilo procedure worksheet for the guest satisfaction survey

Figure 12.7 displays the ***Marascuilo2x3 worksheet*** *of the* ***Chi-Square Worksheets workbook*** *that the Section EG12.2 instructions use.*

<table>
<tr><th></th><th>A</th><th>B</th><th>C</th><th>D</th></tr>
<tr><td>1</td><td>Marascuilo Procedure for Guest Satisfaction Analysis</td><td></td><td></td><td></td></tr>
<tr><td>2</td><td></td><td></td><td></td><td></td></tr>
<tr><td>3</td><td>Level of Significance</td><td>0.05</td><td>=ChiSquare2x3!B18</td><td></td></tr>
<tr><td>4</td><td>Square Root of Critical Value</td><td>2.4477</td><td>=SQRT(ChiSquare2x3!B24)</td><td></td></tr>
<tr><td>5</td><td></td><td></td><td></td><td></td></tr>
<tr><td>6</td><td>Group Sample Proportions</td><td></td><td></td><td></td></tr>
<tr><td>7</td><td>1: Golden Palm</td><td>0.5926</td><td>=ChiSquare2x3!B6/ChiSquare2x3!B8</td><td></td></tr>
<tr><td>8</td><td>2: Palm Royale</td><td>0.8578</td><td>=ChiSquare2x3!C6/ChiSquare2x3!C8</td><td></td></tr>
<tr><td>9</td><td>3: Palm Princess</td><td>0.7381</td><td>=ChiSquare2x3!D6/ChiSquare2x3!D8</td><td></td></tr>
<tr><td>10</td><td></td><td></td><td></td><td></td></tr>
<tr><td>11</td><td>MARASCUILO TABLE</td><td></td><td></td><td></td></tr>
<tr><td>12</td><td>Proportions</td><td>Absolute Differences</td><td>Critical Range</td><td></td></tr>
<tr><td>13</td><td>| Group 1 - Group 2 |</td><td>0.2652</td><td>0.0992</td><td>Significant</td></tr>
<tr><td>14</td><td>| Group 1 - Group 3 |</td><td>0.1455</td><td>0.1063</td><td>Significant</td></tr>
<tr><td>15</td><td></td><td></td><td></td><td></td></tr>
<tr><td>16</td><td>| Group 2 - Group 3 |</td><td>0.1197</td><td>0.0880</td><td>Significant</td></tr>
</table>

As the final step, you compare the absolute differences to the critical ranges. If the absolute difference is greater than the critical range, the proportions are significantly different. At the 0.05 level of significance, you can conclude that guest satisfaction is higher at the Palm Royale ($p_2 = 0.858$) than at either the Golden Palm ($p_1 = 0.593$) or the Palm Princess ($p_3 = 0.738$) and that guest satisfaction is also higher at the Palm Princess than at the Golden Palm. These results clearly suggest that you should investigate possible reasons for these differences. In particular, you should try to determine why satisfaction is significantly lower at the Golden Palm than at the other two hotels.

LEARN MORE

Learn more about this method in a Chapter 12 eBook bonus section.

The Analysis of Proportions (ANOP) (*online*)

The ANOP method provides a confidence interval approach that allows you to determine which, if any, of the c groups has a proportion significantly different from the overall mean of all the group proportions combined.

Problems for Section 12.2

LEARNING THE BASICS

12.11 Consider a contingency table with two rows and five columns.

a. How many degrees of freedom are there in the contingency table?
b. Determine the critical value for $\alpha = 0.05$.
c. Determine the critical value for $\alpha = 0.01$.

12.12 Use the following contingency table:

	A	B	C	Total
1	10	30	50	90
2	40	45	50	135
Total	50	75	100	225

a. Compute the expected frequency for each cell.
b. Compute χ^2_{STAT}. Is it significant at $\alpha = 0.05$?

12.13 Use the following contingency table:

	A	B	C	Total
1	20	30	25	75
2	30	20	25	75
Total	50	50	50	150

a. Compute the expected frequency for each cell.
b. Compute χ^2_{STAT}. Is it significant at $\alpha = 0.05$?

APPLYING THE CONCEPTS

12.14 Do workers prefer to buy lunch rather than pack their own lunch? A survey of employed Americans found that 75% of the 18- to 24-year-olds, 77% of the 25- to 34-year-olds, 72% of the 35- to 44-year-olds, 58% of the 45- to 54-year-olds, 57% of the 54- to 64-year-olds, and 55% of the 65+-year-olds buy lunch throughout the work week. (Data extracted from **bit.ly/z99CeN**.) Suppose the survey was based on 200 employed Americans in each of six age groups: 18 to 24, 25 to 34, 35 to 44, 45 to 54, 55 to 64, and 65+.

a. At the 0.05 level of significance, is there evidence of a difference among the age groups in the preference for lunch?
b. Determine the p-value in (a) and interpret its meaning.
c. If appropriate, use the Marascuilo procedure and $\alpha = 0.05$ to determine which age groups differ.

12.15 What are travelers' technologies of choice? Tablets account for a growing share of the multiuse devices travelers are using. An observational study of passengers on air, bus, and train travel found that 8.4% of airline passengers, 5.9% of Amtrak passengers, 4.9% of commuter train passengers, and 3.7% of curbside bus passengers were observed using a tablet at some point during their travel. (Data extracted from **afterhours.e-strategy.com/passenger-tablet-use-by-transportation-mode-c**.) Suppose these results were based on 500 passengers in each of the four transportation modes: airline, Amtrak train, commuter train, and curbside bus.

a. At the 0.05 level of significance, is there evidence of a difference among the transportation modes with respect to use of tablets?
b. Compute the p-value and interpret its meaning.
c. If appropriate, use the Marascuilo procedure and $\alpha = 0.05$ to determine which transportation modes differ.

SELF Test **12.16** Social media users use a variety of devices to access social networking; mobile phones are increasingly popular. However, is there a difference in the various age groups in the proportion of social media users who use their mobile phone to access social networking? A study showed the following results for the different age groups:

USE MOBILE PHONE TO ACCESS SOCIAL NETWORKING?	AGE 18-34	35-64	65+
Yes	59%	36%	13%
No	41%	64%	87%

Source: Data extracted from "State of the Media: U.S. Digital Consumer Report Q3–Q4 2011," The Nielsen Company, 2012, p. 9.

Assume that 200 social media users for each age group were surveyed.

a. At the 0.05 level of significance, is there evidence of a difference among the age groups with respect to use of mobile phone for accessing social networking?
b. Determine the p-value in (a) and interpret its meaning.
c. If appropriate, use the Marascuilo procedure and $\alpha = 0.05$ to determine which age groups differ with respect to use of a mobile phone for accessing social networking.
d. Discuss the implications of (a) and (c). How can marketers use this information to improve their sales return on investment (ROI)?

12.17 Repeat (a) and (b) of Problem 12.16, assuming that only 50 social media users for each age group were surveyed. Discuss the implications of sample size on the χ^2 test for differences among more than two populations.

12.18 Who uses a cellphone while watching TV? The Pew Research Center's Internet and American Life Project measured the prevalence of multiscreen viewing experiences by asking American adults who are cellphone owners whether they had used their phone to engage in several activities while watching TV. The study reported that 171 of 316 (54%) of urban American cellphone owners sampled, 516 of 993 (52%) of suburban American cellphone owners sampled, and 251 of 557 (45%) of rural American cellphone owners used their phone to engage in several activities while watching TV. (Data extracted from "The Rise of the Connected Viewer," Pew Research Center's Internet & American Life Project, July 17, 2012.)

a. Is there evidence of a significant difference among the urban, suburban, and rural American cellphone owners with respect to the proportion who use their phone to engage in several activities while watching TV? (Use $\alpha = 0.05$).

b. Determine the p-value and interpret its meaning.

c. If appropriate, use the Marascuilo procedure and $\alpha = 0.05$ to determine which groups differ.

12.19 The GMI Ratings' 2012 Women on Boards Survey showed incremental improvements in most measures of female board representation in the past year. The study reported that 90 of 101 (89%) of French companies sampled, 136 of 197 (69%) of Australian companies sampled, 26 of 28 (93%) of Norwegian companies sampled, 27 of 53 (51%) of Singaporean companies, and 95 of 134 (71%) of Canadian companies sampled have at least one female director on their boards. (Data extracted from **bit.ly/zBAnYv**.)

a. Is there evidence of a significant difference among the countries with respect to the proportion of companies who have at least one female director on their boards? (Use $\alpha = 0.05$).

b. Determine the p-value and interpret its meaning.

c. If appropriate, use the Marascuilo procedure and $\alpha = 0.05$ to determine which countries differ.

12.3 Chi-Square Test of Independence

In Sections 12.1 and 12.2, you used the χ^2 test to evaluate potential differences among population proportions. For a contingency table that has r rows and c columns, you can generalize the χ^2 test as a *test of independence* for two categorical variables.

For a test of independence, the null and alternative hypotheses follow:

H_0: The two categorical variables are independent (i.e., there is no relationship between them).

H_1: The two categorical variables are dependent (i.e., there is a relationship between them).

Once again, you use Equation (12.1) on page 431 to compute the test statistic:

$$\chi^2_{STAT} = \sum_{\textit{all cells}} \frac{(f_o - f_e)^2}{f_e}$$

You reject the null hypothesis at the α level of significance if the computed value of the χ^2_{STAT} test statistic is greater than χ^2_α, the upper-tail critical value from a chi-square distribution with $(r - 1)(c - 1)$ degrees of freedom (see Figure 12.8).

FIGURE 12.8
Regions of rejection and nonrejection when testing for independence in an $r \times c$ contingency table, using the χ^2 test

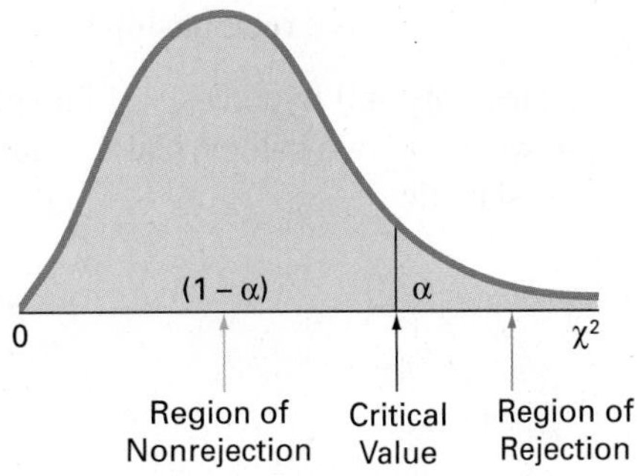

Thus, the decision rule is

Reject H_0 if $\chi^2_{STAT} > \chi^2_\alpha$;

otherwise, do not reject H_0.

Student Tip
Remember that *independence* means no relationship, so you do not reject the null hypothesis. *Dependence* means there is a relationship, so you reject the null hypothesis.

The **chi-square (χ^2) test of independence** is similar to the χ^2 test for equality of proportions. The test statistics and the decision rules are the same, but the null and alternative hypotheses and conclusions are different. For example, in the guest satisfaction survey of Sections 12.1 and 12.2, there is evidence of a significant difference between the hotels with respect to the proportion of guests who would return. From a different viewpoint, you could conclude that there is a significant relationship between the hotels and the likelihood that a guest would return. However, the two types of tests differ in how the samples are selected.

In a test for equality of proportions, there is one factor of interest, with two or more levels. These levels represent samples drawn from independent populations. The categorical responses in each group or level are classified into two categories, such as *an item of interest* and *not an item of interest*. The objective is to make comparisons and evaluate differences between the proportions of the *items of interest* among the various levels. However, in a test for independence, there are two factors of interest, each of which has two or more levels. You select one sample and tally the joint responses to the two categorical variables into the cells of a contingency table.

To illustrate the χ^2 test for independence, suppose that, in the survey on hotel guest satisfaction, respondents who stated that they were not likely to return also indicated the primary reason for their unwillingness to return to the hotel. Table 12.9 presents the resulting 4 × 3 contingency table.

TABLE 12.9

Contingency Table of Primary Reason for Not Returning and Hotel

PRIMARY REASON FOR	HOTEL			
NOT RETURNING	Golden Palm	Palm Royale	Palm Princess	Total
Price	23	7	37	67
Location	39	13	8	60
Room accommodation	13	5	13	31
Other	13	8	8	29
Total	88	33	66	187

In Table 12.9, observe that of the primary reasons for not planning to return to the hotel, 67 were due to price, 60 were due to location, 31 were due to room accommodation, and 29 were due to other reasons. In Table 12.6 on page 438, there were 88 guests at the Golden Palm, 33 guests at the Palm Royale, and 66 guests at the Palm Princess who were not planning to return. The observed frequencies in the cells of the 4 × 3 contingency table represent the joint tallies of the sampled guests with respect to primary reason for not returning and the hotel where they stayed. The null and alternative hypotheses are

H_0: There is no relationship between the primary reason for not returning and the hotel.

H_1: There is a relationship between the primary reason for not returning and the hotel.

To test this null hypothesis of independence against the alternative that there is a relationship between the two categorical variables, you use Equation (12.1) on page 431 to compute the test statistic:

$$\chi^2_{STAT} = \sum_{\text{all cells}} \frac{(f_o - f_e)^2}{f_e}$$

where

f_o = observed frequency in a particular cell of the $r \times c$ contingency table

f_e = expected frequency in a particular cell if the null hypothesis of independence is true

To compute the expected frequency, f_e, in any cell, you use the multiplication rule for independent events discussed on page 169 [see Equation (4.7)]. For example, under the null hypothesis of independence, the probability of responses expected in the upper-left-corner cell representing primary reason of price for the Golden Palm is the product of the two separate probabilities $P(\text{Price})$ and $P(\text{Golden Palm})$. Here, the proportion of reasons that are due to price, $P(\text{Price})$, is $67/187 = 0.3583$, and the proportion of all responses from the Golden Palm, $P(\text{Golden Palm})$, is $88/187 = 0.4706$. If the null hypothesis is true, then the primary reason for not returning and the hotel are independent:

$$\begin{aligned} P(\text{Price } \textit{and} \text{ Golden Palm}) &= P(\text{Price}) \times P(\text{Golden Palm}) \\ &= (0.3583) \times (0.4706) \\ &= 0.1686 \end{aligned}$$

The expected frequency is the product of the overall sample size, n, and this probability, $187 \times 0.1686 = 31.53$. The f_e values for the remaining cells are shown in Table 12.10.

TABLE 12.10

Contingency Table of Expected Frequencies of Primary Reason for Not Returning with Hotel

PRIMARY REASON FOR NOT RETURNING	HOTEL			
	Golden Palm	**Palm Royale**	**Palm Princess**	**Total**
Price	31.53	11.82	23.65	67
Location	28.24	10.59	21.18	60
Room accommodation	14.59	5.47	10.94	31
Other	13.65	5.12	10.24	29
Total	88.00	33.00	66.00	187

You can also compute the expected frequency by taking the product of the row total and column total for a cell and dividing this product by the overall sample size, as Equation (12.5) shows.

COMPUTING THE EXPECTED FREQUENCY

The expected frequency in a cell is the product of its row total and column total, divided by the overall sample size.

$$f_e = \frac{\text{row total} \times \text{column total}}{n} \tag{12.5}$$

where

$$\begin{aligned} \text{Row total} &= \text{sum of the frequencies in the row} \\ \text{Column total} &= \text{sum of the frequencies in the column} \\ n &= \text{overall sample size} \end{aligned}$$

This alternate method results in simpler computations. For example, using Equation (12.5) for the upper-left-corner cell (price for the Golden Palm),

$$f_e = \frac{\text{Row total} \times \text{Column total}}{n} = \frac{(67)(88)}{187} = 31.53$$

and for the lower-right-corner cell (other reason for the Palm Princess),

$$f_e = \frac{\text{Row total} \times \text{Column total}}{n} = \frac{(29)(66)}{187} = 10.24$$

To perform the test of independence, you use the χ^2_{STAT} test statistic shown in Equation (12.1) on page 431. The χ^2_{STAT} test statistic approximately follows a chi-square distribution, with degrees of freedom equal to the number of rows in the contingency table minus 1, multiplied by the number of columns in the table minus 1:

$$\begin{aligned} \text{Degrees of freedom} &= (r - 1)(c - 1) \\ &= (4 - 1)(3 - 1) = 6 \end{aligned}$$

Table 12.11 presents the computations for the χ^2_{STAT} test statistic.

TABLE 12.11

Computing the χ^2_{STAT} Test Statistic for the Test of Independence

Cell	f_o	f_e	$(f_o - f_e)$	$(f_o - f_e)^2$	$(f_o - f_e)^2/f_e$
Price/Golden Palm	23	31.53	−8.53	72.76	2.31
Price/Palm Royale	7	11.82	−4.82	23.23	1.97
Price/Palm Princess	37	23.65	13.35	178.22	7.54
Location/Golden Palm	39	28.24	10.76	115.78	4.10
Location/Palm Royale	13	10.59	2.41	5.81	0.55
Location/Palm Princess	8	21.18	−13.18	173.71	8.20
Room/Golden Palm	13	14.59	−1.59	2.53	0.17
Room/Palm Royale	5	5.47	−0.47	0.22	0.04
Room/Palm Princess	13	10.94	2.06	4.24	0.39
Other/Golden Palm	13	13.65	−0.65	0.42	0.03
Other/Palm Royale	8	5.12	2.88	8.29	1.62
Other/Palm Princess	8	10.24	−2.24	5.02	0.49
					27.41

Using the $\alpha = 0.05$ level of significance, the upper-tail critical value from the chi-square distribution with 6 degrees of freedom is 12.592 (see Table E.4). Because $\chi^2_{STAT} = 27.41 > 12.592$, you reject the null hypothesis of independence (see Figure 12.9).

FIGURE 12.9

Regions of rejection and nonrejection when testing for independence in the hotel guest satisfaction survey example at the 0.05 level of significance, with 6 degrees of freedom

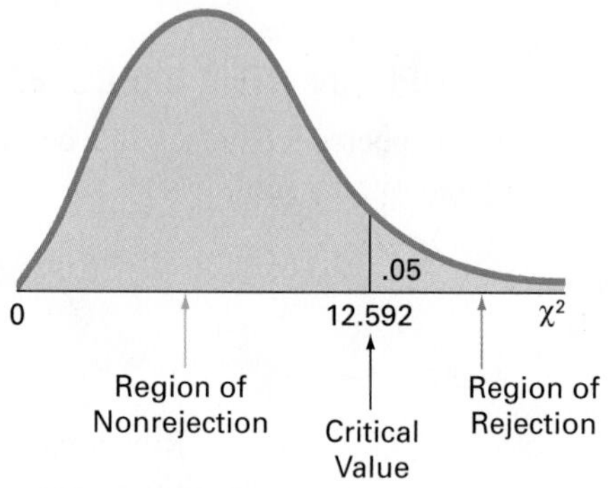

The worksheet results for this test, shown in Figure 12.10, include the p-value, 0.0001. Since $\chi^2_{STAT} = 27.4104 > 12.592$, you reject the null hypothesis of independence. Using the p-value approach, you reject the null hypothesis of independence because the p-value $= 0.0001 < 0.05$. The p-value indicates that there is virtually no chance of having a relationship this strong or stronger between the hotel and the primary reasons for not returning in a sample, if the primary reasons for not returning are independent of the specific hotels in the entire population. Thus, there is strong evidence of a relationship between the primary reason for not returning and the hotel.

Examination of the observed and expected frequencies (see Table 12.11 above) reveals that price is underrepresented as a reason for not returning to the Golden Palm (i.e., $f_o = 23$ and $f_e = 31.53$) but is overrepresented at the Palm Princess. Guests are more satisfied with the price at the Golden Palm than at the Palm Princess. Location is overrepresented as a reason for not returning to the Golden Palm but greatly underrepresented at the Palm Princess. Thus, guests are much more satisfied with the location of the Palm Princess than with that of the Golden Palm.

To ensure accurate results, all expected frequencies need to be large in order to use the χ^2 test when dealing with $r \times c$ contingency tables. As in the case of $2 \times c$ contingency tables

FIGURE 12.10
Chi-square test worksheet for the Table 12.9 primary reason for not returning to hotel data

*Figure 12.10 displays the **ChiSquare4x3 worksheet** of the **Chi-Square Worksheets workbook** that the Section EG12.3 instructions use.*

	A	B	C	D	E	F	G	H	I
1	**Chi-Square Test of Independence**								
2									
3		**Observed Frequencies**							
4		Hotel						Calculations	
5	Reason for Not Returning	Golden Palm	Palm Royale	Palm Princess	Total			fo - fe	
6	Price	23	7	37	67		-8.5294	-4.8235	13.3529
7	Location	39	13	8	60		10.7647	2.4118	-13.1765
8	Room accommodation	13	5	13	31		-1.5882	-0.4706	2.0588
9	Other	13	8	8	29		-0.6471	2.8824	-2.2353
10	Total	88	33	66	187				
11									
12		Expected Frequencies							
13		Hotel							
14	Reason for Not Returning	Golden Palm	Palm Royale	Palm Princess	Total			(fo - fe)^2/fe	
15	Price	31.5294	11.8235	23.6471	67		2.3074	1.9678	7.5401
16	Location	28.2353	10.5882	21.1765	60		4.1040	0.5493	8.1987
17	Room accommodation	14.5882	5.4706	10.9412	31		0.1729	0.0405	0.3874
18	Other	13.6471	5.1176	10.2353	29		0.0307	1.6234	0.4882
19	Total	88	33	66	187				
20									
21	**Data**								
22	Level of Significance	0.05							
23	Number of Rows	4							
24	Number of Columns	3							
25	Degrees of Freedom	6	**=(B23 - 1) * (B24 - 1)**						
26									
27	**Results**								
28	Critical Value	12.5916	**=CHISQ.INV.RT(B22, B25)**						
29	Chi-Square Test Statistic	27.4104	**=SUM(G15:I18)**						
30	*p*-Value	0.0001	**=CHISQ.DIST.RT(B29, B25)**						
31	Reject the null hypothesis		**=IF(B30 < B22, "Reject the null hypothesis",**						
32			**"Do not reject the null hypothesis")**						
33	***Expected frequency assumption***								
34	***is met.***		**=IF(OR(B15 < 1, C15 < 1, D15 < 1, B16 < 1, C16 < 1, D16 < 1, B17 < 1, C17 < 1, D17 < 1, B18 < 1, C18 < 1, D18 < 1), " is violated.", " is met.")**						

in Section 12.2, all expected frequencies should be at least 1. For contingency tables in which one or more expected frequencies are less than 1, you can use the chi-square test after collapsing two or more low-frequency rows into one row (or collapsing two or more low-frequency columns into one column). Merging rows or columns usually results in expected frequencies sufficiently large to ensure the accuracy of the χ^2 test.

Problems for Section 12.3

LEARNING THE BASICS

12.20 If a contingency table has three rows and four columns, how many degrees of freedom are there for the χ^2 test of independence?

12.21 When performing a χ^2 test of independence in a contingency table with r rows and c columns, determine the upper-tail critical value of the test statistic in each of the following circumstances:

a. $\alpha = 0.05, r = 4$ rows, $c = 5$ columns
b. $\alpha = 0.01, r = 4$ rows, $c = 5$ columns
c. $\alpha = 0.01, r = 4$ rows, $c = 6$ columns
d. $\alpha = 0.01, r = 3$ rows, $c = 6$ columns
e. $\alpha = 0.01, r = 6$ rows, $c = 3$ columns

APPLYING THE CONCEPTS

12.22 The owner of a restaurant serving Continental-style entrées has the business objective of learning more about the patterns of patron demand during the Friday-to-Sunday weekend time period. Data were collected from 630 customers on the type of entrée ordered and the type of dessert ordered and organized into the following table:

TYPE OF DESSERT	TYPE OF ENTRÉE				
	Beef	Poultry	Fish	Pasta	Total
Ice cream	13	8	12	14	47
Cake	98	12	29	6	145
Fruit	8	10	6	2	26
None	124	98	149	41	412
Total	243	128	196	63	630

At the 0.05 level of significance, is there evidence of a relationship between type of dessert and type of entrée?

12.23 Is there a generation gap in the type of music that people listen to? The following table represents the type of favorite music for a sample of 1,000 respondents classified according to their age group:

FAVORITE TYPE	AGE				
	16–29	30–49	50–64	65 and over	Total
Rock	71	62	51	27	211
Rap or hip-hop	40	21	7	3	71
Rhythm and blues	48	46	46	40	180
Country	43	53	59	79	234
Classical	22	28	33	46	129
Jazz	18	26	36	43	123
Salsa	8	14	18	12	52
Total	250	250	250	250	1000

At the 0.05 level of significance, is there evidence of a relationship between favorite type of music and age group?

SELF Test **12.24** A large corporation is interested in determining whether a relationship exists between the commuting time of its employees and the level of stress-related problems observed on the job. A study of 116 workers reveals the following:

COMMUTING TIME	STRESS LEVEL			
	High	Moderate	Low	Total
Under 15 min.	9	5	18	32
15–45 min.	17	8	28	53
Over 45 min.	18	6	7	31
Total	44	19	53	116

a. At the 0.01 level of significance, is there evidence of a significant relationship between commuting time and stress level?

b. What is your answer to (a) if you use the 0.05 level of significance?

12.25 Where people look for news is different for various age groups. A study indicated where different age groups primarily get their news:

MEDIA	AGE GROUP		
	Under 36	36–50	50+
Local TV	107	119	133
National TV	73	102	127
Radio	75	97	109
Local newspaper	52	79	107
Internet	95	83	76

At the 0.05 level of significance, is there evidence of a significant relationship between the age group and where people primarily get their news? If so, explain the relationship.

12.26 The 2012 Restaurant Industry Forecast takes a closer look at today's consumers. Based on a 2011 National Restaurant Association survey, American adults are categorized into one of three consumer segments (optimistic, cautious, and hunkered down) based on their financial situation, current spending behavior, and economic outlook, as well as the geographic region where they reside. Suppose the results, based on a sample 1,000 American adults, are as follows:

CONSUMER SEGMENT	GEOGRAPHIC REGION				
	Midwest	Northeast	South	West	Total
Optimistic	67	23	60	63	213
Cautious	101	57	127	133	418
Hunkered down	83	46	115	125	369
Total	251	126	302	321	1000

Source: Data extracted from "The 2012 Restaurant Industry Forecast," National Restaurant Association, 2012, p. 12.

At the 0.05 level of significance, is there evidence of a significant relationship between consumer segment and geographic region?

12.4 Wilcoxon Rank Sum Test: A Nonparametric Method for Two Independent Populations

In Section 10.1, you used the *t* test for the difference between the means of two independent populations. If sample sizes are small and you cannot assume that the data in each sample are from normally distributed populations, you have two choices:

- Use a *nonparametric* method that does not depend on the assumption of normality for the two populations.
- Use the pooled-variance *t* test, following a *normalizing transformation* on the data (see reference 9).

Nonparametric methods require few or no assumptions about the populations from which data are obtained (see reference 4). One such method is the Wilcoxon rank sum test for testing whether there is a difference between two *medians*. The **Wilcoxon rank sum test** is almost as powerful as the pooled-variance and separate-variance t tests discussed in Section 10.1 under conditions appropriate to these tests and is likely to be more powerful when the assumptions of those t tests are not met. In addition, you can use the Wilcoxon rank sum test when you have only ordinal data, as often happens in consumer behavior and marketing research.

Student Tip
Remember that you combine the two groups before you rank the values.

To perform the Wilcoxon rank sum test, you replace the values in the two samples of sizes n_1 and n_2 with their combined ranks (unless the data contained the ranks initially). You begin by defining $n = n_1 + n_2$ as the total sample size. Next, you assign the ranks so that rank 1 is given to the smallest of the n combined values, rank 2 is given to the second smallest, and so on, until rank n is given to the largest. If several values are tied, you assign each value the average of the ranks that otherwise would have been assigned had there been no ties.

Whenever the two sample sizes are unequal, n_1 represents the smaller sample and n_2 the larger sample. The Wilcoxon rank sum test statistic, T_1, is defined as the sum of the ranks assigned to the n_1 values in the smaller sample. (For equal-sized samples, either sample may be used for determining T_1.) For any integer value n, the sum of the first n consecutive integers is $n(n+1)/2$. Therefore, T_1 plus T_2, the sum of the ranks assigned to the n_2 items in the second sample, must equal $n(n+1)/2$. You can use Equation (12.6) to check the accuracy of your rankings.

CHECKING THE RANKINGS

$$T_1 + T_2 = \frac{n(n+1)}{2} \tag{12.6}$$

When n_1 and n_2 are each ≤ 10, you use Table E.6 to find the critical values of the test statistic T_1. For a two-tail test, you reject the null hypothesis (see Panel A of Figure 12.11) if the computed value of T_1 is greater than or equal to the upper critical value, or if T_1 is less than or equal to the lower critical value. For one-tail tests having the alternative hypothesis $H_1\text{: } M_1 < M_2$ [i.e., the median of population 1(M_1) is less than the median of population 2 (M_2)], you reject the null hypothesis if the observed value of T_1 is less than or equal to the lower critical value (see Panel B of Figure 12.11). For one-tail tests having the alternative hypothesis $H_1\text{: } M_1 > M_2$, you reject the null hypothesis if the observed value of T_1 equals or is greater than the upper critical value (see Panel C of Figure 12.11).

FIGURE 12.11
Regions of rejection and nonrejection using the Wilcoxon rank sum test

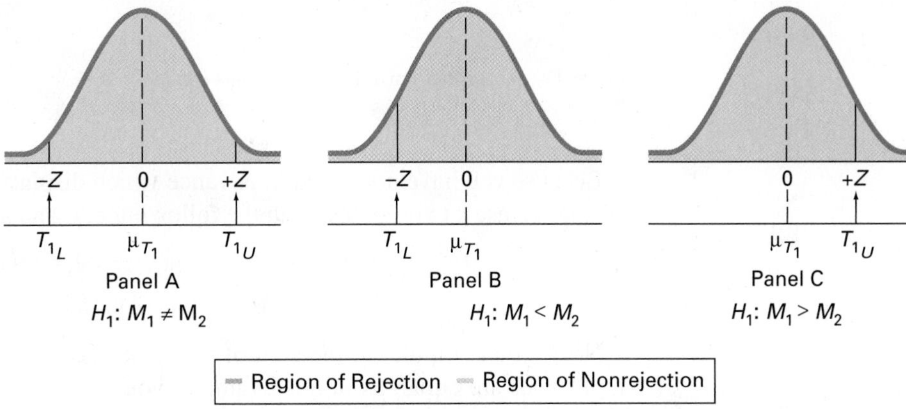

Student Tip
Remember that the group that is defined as group 1 when computing the test statistic T_1 must also must be defined as group 1 in the null and alternative hypotheses.

For large sample sizes, the test statistic T_1 is approximately normally distributed, with the mean, μ_{T_1}, equal to

$$\mu_{T_1} = \frac{n_1(n+1)}{2}$$

and the standard deviation, σ_{T_1}, equal to

$$\sigma_{T_1} = \sqrt{\frac{n_1 n_2 (n + 1)}{12}}$$

Therefore, Equation (12.7) defines the standardized Z test statistic.

LARGE-SAMPLE WILCOXON RANK SUM TEST

$$Z_{STAT} = \frac{T_1 - \dfrac{n_1(n + 1)}{2}}{\sqrt{\dfrac{n_1 n_2 (n + 1)}{12}}} \qquad \textbf{(12.7)}$$

where the test statistic Z_{STAT} approximately follows a standardized normal distribution.

You use Equation (12.7) when the sample sizes are outside the range of Table E.6. Based on α, the level of significance selected, you reject the null hypothesis if the Z_{STAT} test statistic falls in the rejection region.

To study an application of the Wilcoxon rank sum test, recall the Chapter 10 Using Statistics scenario concerning cola sales for two different end-cap display locations (stored in **Cola**). If you cannot assume that the populations are normally distributed, you can use the Wilcoxon rank sum test to evaluate possible differences in the median sales for the two display locations.[2] The cola sales data and the combined ranks are shown in Table 12.12.

[2]To test for differences in the median sales between the two locations, you must assume that the distributions of sales in both populations are identical except for differences in central tendency (i.e., the medians).

TABLE 12.12

Forming the Combined Rankings

Beverage End-cap ($n_1 = 10$)	Combined Ranking	Produce End-cap ($n_2 = 10$)	Combined Ranking
22	1.0	52	5.5
34	3.0	71	14.0
52	5.5	76	15.0
62	10.0	54	7.0
30	2.0	67	13.0
40	4.0	83	17.0
64	11.0	66	12.0
84	18.5	90	20.0
56	8.0	77	16.0
59	9.0	84	18.5

Source: Data are taken from Table 10.1 on page 345.

Because you have not stated in advance which display location is likely to have a higher median, you use a two-tail test with the following null and alternative hypotheses:

$$H_0: M_1 = M_2 \text{ (the median sales are equal)}$$
$$H_1: M_1 \neq M_2 \text{ (the median sales are not equal)}$$

Next, you compute T_1, the sum of the ranks assigned to the *smaller* sample. When the sample sizes are equal, as in this example, you can define either sample as the group from which to compute T_1. Choosing the beverage end-cap display as the first group,

$$T_1 = 1 + 3 + 5.5 + 10 + 2 + 4 + 11 + 18.5 + 8 + 9 = 72$$

As a check on the ranking procedure, you compute T_2 from

$$T_2 = 5.5 + 14 + 15 + 7 + 13 + 17 + 12 + 20 + 16 + 18.5 = 138$$

and then use Equation (12.6) on page 449 to show that the sum of the first $n = 20$ integers in the combined ranking is equal to $T_1 + T_2$:

$$T_1 + T_2 = \frac{n(n + 1)}{2}$$

$$72 + 138 = \frac{20(21)}{2} = 210$$

$$210 = 210$$

Next, you use Table E.6 to determine the lower- and upper-tail critical values for the test statistic T_1. From Table 12.13, a portion of Table E.6, observe that for a level of significance of 0.05, the critical values are 78 and 132. The decision rule is

$$\text{Reject } H_0 \text{ if } T_1 \le 78 \text{ or if } T_1 \ge 132;$$

$$\text{otherwise, do not reject } H_0.$$

TABLE 12.13

Finding the Lower- and Upper-Tail Critical Values for the Wilcoxon Rank Sum Test Statistic, T_1, Where $n_1 = 10$, $n_2 = 10$, and $\alpha = 0.05$

	α		n_1						
n_2	One-tail	Two-tail	4	5	6	7	8	9	10
						(Lower, Upper)			
	.05	.10	16,40	24,51	33,63	43,76	54,90	66,105	
9	.025	.05	14,42	22,53	31,65	40,79	51,93	62,109	
	.01	.02	13,43	20,55	28,68	37,82	47,97	59,112	
	.005	.01	11,45	18,57	26,70	35,84	45,99	56,115	
	.05	.10	17,43	26,54	35,67	45,81	56,96	69,111	82,128
10	.025	.05	15,45	23,57	32,70	42,84	53,99	65,115	78,132
	.01	.02	13,47	21,59	29,73	39,87	49,103	61,119	74,136
	.005	.01	12,48	19,61	27,75	37,89	47,105	58,122	71,139

Source: Extracted from Table E.6.

Because the test statistic $T_1 = 72 < 78$, you reject H_0. There is evidence of a significant difference in the median sales for the two display locations. Because the sum of the ranks is lower for the beverage end-cap display, you conclude that median sales are lower for the beverage end-cap display.

Figure 12.12 shows the Wilcoxon rank sum test worksheet results for the cola sales data. From these results, you reject the null hypothesis because the p-value is 0.0126, which is less than $\alpha = 0.05$. This p-value indicates that if the medians of the two populations are equal, the chance of finding a difference at least this large in the samples is only 0.0126.

FIGURE 12.12

Wilcoxon rank sum test results for the cola sales data for the two end-cap locations

Figure 12.12 displays the ***COMPUTE worksheet*** *of the* ***Wilcoxon workbook*** *that the Section EG12.4 instructions use. The COMPUTE worksheet uses the sorted ranks of the SortedRanks worksheet as explained in Section EG12.4.*

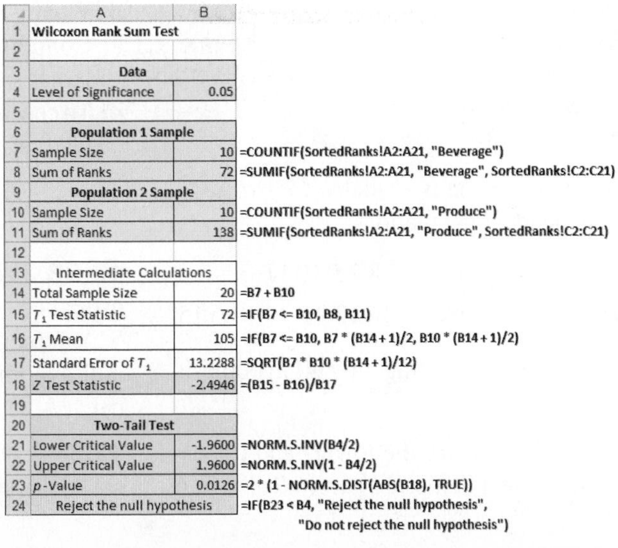

	A	B	
1	Wilcoxon Rank Sum Test		
2			
3	Data		
4	Level of Significance	0.05	
5			
6	Population 1 Sample		
7	Sample Size	10	=COUNTIF(SortedRanks!A2:A21, "Beverage")
8	Sum of Ranks	72	=SUMIF(SortedRanks!A2:A21, "Beverage", SortedRanks!C2:C21)
9	Population 2 Sample		
10	Sample Size	10	=COUNTIF(SortedRanks!A2:A21, "Produce")
11	Sum of Ranks	138	=SUMIF(SortedRanks!A2:A21, "Produce", SortedRanks!C2:C21)
12			
13	Intermediate Calculations		
14	Total Sample Size	20	=B7 + B10
15	T_1 Test Statistic	72	=IF(B7 <= B10, B8, B11)
16	T_1 Mean	105	=IF(B7 <= B10, B7 * (B14 + 1)/2, B10 * (B14 + 1)/2)
17	Standard Error of T_1	13.2288	=SQRT(B7 * B10 * (B14 + 1)/12)
18	Z Test Statistic	-2.4946	=(B15 - B16)/B17
19			
20	Two-Tail Test		
21	Lower Critical Value	-1.9600	=NORM.S.INV(B4/2)
22	Upper Critical Value	1.9600	=NORM.S.INV(1 - B4/2)
23	p-Value	0.0126	=2 * (1 - NORM.S.DIST(ABS(B18), TRUE))
24	Reject the null hypothesis		=IF(B23 < B4, "Reject the null hypothesis", "Do not reject the null hypothesis")

Table E.6 shows the lower and upper critical values of the Wilcoxon rank sum test statistic, T_1, but only for situations in which both n_1 and n_2 are less than or equal to 10. If either one or both of the sample sizes are greater than 10, you *must* use the large-sample Z approximation formula [Equation (12.7) on page 450]. However, you can also use this approximation formula for small sample sizes. To demonstrate the large-sample Z approximation formula, consider the cola sales data. Using Equation (12.7),

$$Z_{STAT} = \frac{T_1 - \frac{n_1(n+1)}{2}}{\sqrt{\frac{n_1 n_2(n+1)}{12}}}$$

$$= \frac{72 - \frac{(10)(21)}{2}}{\sqrt{\frac{(10)(10)(21)}{12}}}$$

$$= \frac{72 - 105}{13.2288} = -2.4946$$

Because $Z_{STAT} = -2.4946 < -1.96$, the critical value of Z at the 0.05 level of significance (or p-value $= 0.0126 < 0.05$), you reject H_0.

Problems for Section 12.4

LEARNING THE BASICS

12.27 Using Table E.6, determine the lower- and upper-tail critical values for the Wilcoxon rank sum test statistic, T_1, in each of the following two-tail tests:

a. $\alpha = 0.10, n_1 = 6, n_2 = 8$
b. $\alpha = 0.05, n_1 = 6, n_2 = 8$
c. $\alpha = 0.01, n_1 = 6, n_2 = 8$
d. Given the results in (a) through (c), what do you conclude regarding the width of the region of nonrejection as the selected level of significance, α, gets smaller?

12.28 Using Table E.6, determine the lower-tail critical value for the Wilcoxon rank sum test statistic, T_1, in each of the following one-tail tests:

a. $\alpha = 0.05, n_1 = 6, n_2 = 8$
b. $\alpha = 0.025, n_1 = 6, n_2 = 8$
c. $\alpha = 0.01, n_1 = 6, n_2 = 8$
d. $\alpha = 0.005, n_1 = 6, n_2 = 8$

12.29 The following information is available for two samples selected from independent populations:

Sample 1: $n_1 = 7$ Assigned ranks: 4 1 8 2 5 10 11
Sample 2: $n_2 = 9$ Assigned ranks: 7 16 12 9 3 14 13 6 15

What is the value of T_1 if you are testing the null hypothesis H_0: $M_1 = M_2$?

12.30 In Problem 12.29, what are the lower- and upper-tail critical values for the test statistic T_1 from Table E.6 if you use a 0.05 level of significance and the alternative hypothesis is H_1: $M_1 \neq M_2$?

12.31 In Problems 12.29 and 12.30, what is your statistical decision?

12.32 The following information is available for two samples selected from independent and similarly shaped right-skewed populations:

Sample 1: $n_1 = 5$ 1.1 2.3 2.9 3.6 14.7
Sample 2: $n_2 = 6$ 2.8 4.4 4.4 5.2 6.0 18.5

a. Replace the observed values with the corresponding ranks (where 1 = smallest value; $n = n_1 + n_2 = 11$ = largest value) in the combined samples.
b. What is the value of the test statistic T_1?
c. Compute the value of T_2, the sum of the ranks in the larger sample.
d. To check the accuracy of your rankings, use Equation (12.7) on page 450 to demonstrate that

$$T_1 + T_2 = \frac{n(n+1)}{2}$$

12.33 From Problem 12.32, at the 0.05 level of significance, determine the lower-tail critical value for the Wilcoxon rank sum test statistic, T_1, if you want to test the null hypothesis, H_0: $M_1 \geq M_2$, against the one-tail alternative, H_1: $M_1 < M_2$.

12.34 In Problems 12.32 and 12.33, what is your statistical decision?

APPLYING THE CONCEPTS

12.35 A vice president for marketing recruits 20 college graduates for management training. Each of the 20 individuals is randomly assigned, to one of two groups (10 in each group). A "traditional" method of training (*T*) is used in one group, and an "experimental" method (*E*) is used in the other. After the graduates spend six months on the job, the vice president ranks them on the basis of their performance, from 1 (worst) to 20 (best), with the following results (stored in the file TestRank):

T: 1 2 3 5 9 10 12 13 14 15

E: 4 6 7 8 11 16 17 18 19 20

Is there evidence of a difference in the median performance between the two methods? (Use $\alpha = 0.05$.)

12.36 Wine experts Gaiter and Brecher use a six-category scale when rating wines: Yech, OK, Good, Very Good, Delicious, and Delicious! Suppose Gaiter and Brecher tested wines from a random sample of eight inexpensive California Cabernets and a random sample of eight inexpensive Washington Cabernets, where *inexpensive* means wines with a U.S. suggested retail price of less than $20, and assigned the following ratings:

California—Good, Delicious, Yech, OK, OK, Very Good, Yech, OK

Washington—Very Good, OK, Delicious!, Very Good, Delicious, Good, Delicious, Delicious!

The ratings were then ranked and the ratings and the rankings stored in Cabernet. (Data extracted from D. Gaiter and J. Brecher, "A Good U.S. Cabernet Is Hard to Find," *The Wall Street Journal*, May 19, 2006, p. W7.)

a. Are the data collected by rating wines using this scale nominal, ordinal, interval, or ratio?

b. Why is the two-sample *t* test defined in Section 10.1 inappropriate to test the mean rating of California Cabernets versus Washington Cabernets?

c. Is there evidence of a significant difference in the median rating of California Cabernets and Washington Cabernets? (Use $\alpha = 0.05$.)

12.37 A problem with a telephone line that prevents a customer from receiving or making calls is upsetting to both the customer and the telephone company. The file Phone contains samples of 20 problems reported to two different offices of a telecommunications company and the time to clear these problems (in minutes) from the customers' lines:

Central Office I Time to Clear Problems (Minutes)

1.48 1.75 0.78 2.85 0.52 1.60 4.15 3.97 1.48 3.10

1.02 0.53 0.93 1.60 0.80 1.05 6.32 3.93 5.45 0.97

Central Office II Time to Clear Problems (Minutes)

7.55 3.75 0.10 1.10 0.60 0.52 3.30 2.10 0.58 4.02

3.75 0.65 1.92 0.60 1.53 4.23 0.08 1.48 1.65 0.72

a. Is there evidence of a difference in the median time to clear problems between offices? (Use $\alpha = 0.05$.)

b. What assumptions must you make in (a)?

c. Compare the results of (a) with those of Problem 10.9(a) on page 353.

SELF Test **12.38** The management of a hotel has the business objective of increasing the return rate for hotel guests. One aspect of first impressions by guests relates to the time it takes to deliver a guest's luggage to the room after check-in to the hotel. A random sample of 20 deliveries on a particular day were selected in Wing A of the hotel, and a random sample of 20 deliveries were selected in Wing B. Delivery times were collected and stored in Luggage.

a. Is there evidence of a difference in the median delivery times in the two wings of the hotel? (Use $\alpha = 0.05$.)

b. Compare the results of (a) with those of Problem 10.65 on page 378.

12.39 The lengths of life (in hours) of a sample of 40 100-watt light bulbs produced by Manufacturer A and a sample of 40 100-watt light bulbs produced by Manufacturer B are stored in Bulbs.

a. Using a 0.05 level of significance, is there evidence of a difference in the median life of bulbs produced by the two manufacturers?

b. What assumptions must you make in (a)?

c. Compare the results of (a) with those of Problem 10.64 on page 378. Discuss.

12.40 Brand valuations are critical to CEOs, financial and marketing executives, security analysts, institutional investors, and others who depend on well-researched, reliable information for assessments and comparisons in decision making. Millward Brown, Inc., has annually compiled its BrandZ Top 100 Most Valuable Global Brands since 1996. Unlike other studies, the BrandZ rankings combines consumer measures of brand equity with financial measures to establish a *brand value* for each brands. The file BrankZTechFin contains the brand values for two sectors in the BrandZ Top 100 Most Valuable Global Brands for 2011: the technology sector and the financial institutions sector. (Data extracted from "BrandZ Top 1000 Most Valuable Global Brands 2011," Millward Brown, Inc., retrieved from **bit.ly/kNL8rx**.)

a. Using a 0.05 level of significance, is there evidence of a difference in the median brand value between the two sectors?

b. What assumptions must you make in (a)?

c. Compare the results of (a) with those of Problem 10.17 on page 355. Discuss.

12.41 A bank with a branch located in a commercial district of a city has developed an improved process for serving customers during the noon-to-1 P.M. lunch period. The bank has the business objective of reducing the waiting time (defined as the number of minutes that elapse from when the customer enters the line until he or she reaches the teller window) to increase customer satisfaction. A random sample of 15 customers is selected and waiting times are collected and stored in Bank1. These waiting times (in minutes) are:

4.21 5.55 3.02 5.13 4.77 2.34 3.54 3.20

4.50 6.10 0.38 5.12 6.46 6.19 3.79

Another branch, located in a residential area, is also concerned with the noon-to-1 P.M. lunch period. A random sample of 15 customers is selected and waiting times are collected and stored in Bank2. These waiting times (in minutes) are:

9.66 5.90 8.02 5.79 8.73 3.82 8.01 8.35
10.49 6.68 5.64 4.08 6.17 9.91 5.47

a. Is there evidence of a difference in the median waiting time between the two branches? (Use $\alpha = 0.05$.)
b. What assumptions must you make in (a)?
c. Compare the results (a) with those of Problem 10.12 (a) on page 354. Discuss.

12.42 An important feature of digital cameras is battery life, the number of shots that can be taken before the battery needs to be recharged. The file Cameras contains the battery life of 11 subcompact cameras and 7 compact cameras. (Data extracted from "Cameras," *Consumer Reports*, July 2012, pp. 42–44.)
a. Is there evidence of a difference in the median battery life between subcompact cameras and compact cameras? (Use $\alpha = 0.05$.)
b. What assumptions must you make in (a)?
c. Compare the results of (a) with those of Problem 10.11 (a) on page 354. Discuss.

12.5 Kruskal-Wallis Rank Test: A Nonparametric Method for the One-Way ANOVA

If the normality assumption of the one-way ANOVA F test is violated, you can use the Kruskal-Wallis rank test. The **Kruskal-Wallis rank test** for differences among c medians (where $c > 2$) is an extension of the Wilcoxon rank sum test for two independent populations, discussed in Section 12.4. Thus, the Kruskal-Wallis test has the same power relative to the one-way ANOVA F test that the Wilcoxon rank sum test has relative to the t test.

You use the Kruskal-Wallis rank test to test whether c independent groups have equal medians. The null hypothesis is

$$H_0: M_1 = M_2 = \cdots = M_c$$

and the alternative hypothesis is

$$H_1: \text{Not all } M_j \text{ are equal (where } j = 1, 2, \ldots, c).$$

Student Tip
Remember that you combine the groups before you rank the values.

To use the Kruskal-Wallis rank test, you first replace the values in the c samples with their combined ranks (if necessary). Rank 1 is given to the smallest of the combined values and rank n to the largest of the combined values (where $n = n_1 + n_2 + \cdots + n_c$). If any values are tied, you assign each of them the mean of the ranks they would have otherwise been assigned if ties had not been present in the data.

The Kruskal-Wallis test is an alternative to the one-way ANOVA F test. Instead of comparing each of the c group means against the grand mean, the Kruskal-Wallis test compares the mean rank in each of the c groups against the overall mean rank, based on all n combined values. Equation (12.8) defines the Kruskal-Wallis test statistic, H.

KRUSKAL-WALLIS RANK TEST FOR DIFFERENCES AMONG *c* MEDIANS

$$H = \left[\frac{12}{n(n+1)} \sum_{j=1}^{c} \frac{T_j^2}{n_j}\right] - 3(n+1) \tag{12.8}$$

where

n = total number of values over the combined samples
n_j = number of values in the jth sample ($j = 1, 2, \ldots, c$)
T_j = sum of the ranks assigned to the jth sample
T_j^2 = square of the sum of the ranks assigned to the jth sample
c = number of groups

If there is a significant difference among the c groups, the mean rank differs considerably from group to group. In the process of squaring these differences, the test statistic H becomes large. If there are no differences present, the test statistic H is small because the mean of the ranks assigned in each group should be very similar from group to group.

As the sample sizes in each group get large (i.e., at least 5), you can approximate the test statistic, H, by using the chi-square distribution with $c - 1$ degrees of freedom. Thus, you reject the null hypothesis if the computed value of H is greater than the upper-tail critical value (see Figure 12.13). Therefore, the decision rule is

$$\text{Reject } H_0 \text{ if } H > \chi^2_\alpha;$$

otherwise, do not reject H_0.

FIGURE 12.13
Determining the rejection region for the Kruskal-Wallis test

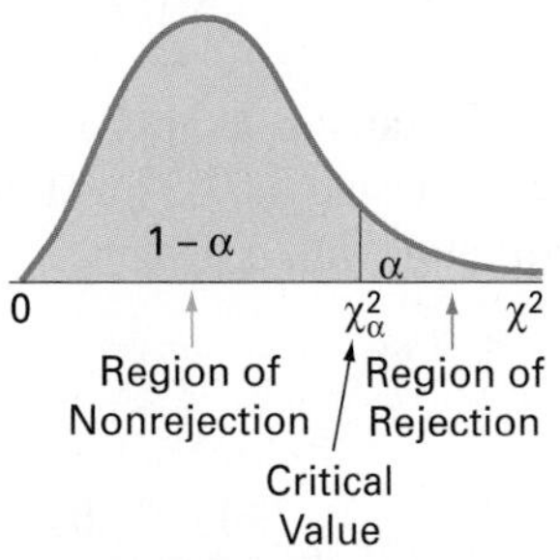

To illustrate the Kruskal-Wallis rank test for differences among c medians, recall the Chapter 11 Using Statistics scenario on page 389 about the strength of parachutes. If you cannot assume that the tensile strength of the parachutes is normally distributed in all c groups, you can use the Kruskal-Wallis rank test.

The null hypothesis is that the median tensile strengths of parachutes from the four suppliers are equal. The alternative hypothesis is that at least one of the suppliers differs from the others:

$$H_0: M_1 = M_2 = M_3 = M_4$$
$$H_1: \text{Not all } M_j \text{ are equal (where } j = 1, 2, 3, 4).$$

Table 12.14 presents the data (stored in **Parachute**), along with the corresponding ranks.

TABLE 12.14
Tensile Strength and Ranks of Parachutes Woven from Synthetic Fibers from Four Suppliers

Supplier 1		Supplier 2		Supplier 3		Supplier 4	
Amount	**Rank**	**Amount**	**Rank**	**Amount**	**Rank**	**Amount**	**Rank**
18.5	4	26.3	20	20.6	8	25.4	19
24.0	13.5	25.3	18	25.2	17	19.9	5.5
17.2	1	24.0	13.5	20.8	9	22.6	11
19.9	5.5	21.2	10	24.7	16	17.5	2
18.0	3	24.5	15	22.9	12	20.4	7

In converting the 20 tensile strengths to ranks, observe in Table 12.14 that the third parachute for Supplier 1 has the lowest tensile strength, 17.2. It is assigned a rank of 1. The fourth value for Supplier 1 and the second value for Supplier 4 each have a value of 19.9. Because they are tied for ranks 5 and 6, each is assigned the rank 5.5. Finally, the first value for Supplier 2 is the largest value, 26.3, and is assigned a rank of 20.

After all the ranks are assigned, you compute the sum of the ranks for each group:

$$\text{Rank sums: } T_1 = 27 \quad T_2 = 76.5 \quad T_3 = 62 \quad T_4 = 44.5$$

As a check on the rankings, recall from Equation (12.6) on page 449 that for any integer n, the sum of the first n consecutive integers is $n(n + 1)/2$. Therefore,

$$T_1 + T_2 + T_3 + T_4 = \frac{n(n + 1)}{2}$$
$$27 + 76.5 + 62 + 44.5 = \frac{(20)(21)}{2}$$
$$210 = 210$$

To test the null hypothesis of equal population medians, you calculate the test statistic H using Equation (12.8) on page 454:

$$H = \left[\frac{12}{n(n+1)}\sum_{j=1}^{c}\frac{T_j^2}{n_j}\right] - 3(n+1)$$

$$= \left\{\frac{12}{(20)(21)}\left[\frac{(27)^2}{5} + \frac{(76.5)^2}{5} + \frac{(62)^2}{5} + \frac{(44.5)^2}{5}\right]\right\} - 3(21)$$

$$= \left(\frac{12}{420}\right)(2,481.1) - 63 = 7.8886$$

The test statistic H approximately follows a chi-square distribution with $c - 1$ degrees of freedom. Using a 0.05 level of significance, χ^2_α, the upper-tail critical value of the chi-square distribution with $c - 1 = 3$ degrees of freedom, is 7.815 (see Table 12.15).

TABLE 12.15

Finding χ^2_α, the Upper-Tail Critical Value for the Kruskal-Wallis Rank Test, at the 0.05 Level of Significance with 3 Degrees of Freedom

	Cumulative Area									
	.005	.01	.025	.05	.10	.25	.75	.90	.95	.975
	Upper-Tail Area									
Degrees of Freedom	.995	.99	.975	.95	.90	.75	.25	.10	.05	.025
1	—	—	0.001	0.004	0.016	0.102	1.323	2.706	3.841	5.024
2	0.010	0.020	0.051	0.103	0.211	0.575	2.773	4.605	5.991	7.378
3	0.072	0.115	0.216	0.352	0.584	1.213	4.108	6.251	7.815	9.348
4	0.207	0.297	0.484	0.711	1.064	1.923	5.385	7.779	9.488	11.143
5	0.412	0.554	0.831	1.145	1.610	2.675	6.626	9.236	11.071	12.833

Source: Extracted from Table E.4.

Because the computed value of the test statistic $H = 7.8886$ is greater than the critical value of 7.815, you reject the null hypothesis and conclude that the median tensile strength is not the same for all the suppliers. You reach the same conclusion by using the p-value approach because, as shown in Figure 12.14, the p-value $= 0.0484 < 0.05$. At this point, you could simultaneously compare all pairs of suppliers to determine which ones differ (see reference 2).

FIGURE 12.14 Kruskal-Wallis rank test worksheet for the differences among the median tensile strengths of parachutes from the four suppliers (shown in two parts)

Figure 12.14 displays the ***KruskalWallis4 worksheet*** *of the* ***Kruskal-Wallis Worksheets workbook*** *that the Section EG12.5 instructions use.*

	A	B	
1	**Kruskal-Wallis Rank Test**		
2			
3	**Data**		
4	Level of Significance	0.05	
5			
6	Intermediate Calculations		
7	Sum of Squared Ranks/Sample Size	2481.1	=(G5 * F5) + (G6 * F6) + (G7 * F7) + (G8 * F8)
8	Sum of Sample Sizes	20	=SUM(E5:E8)
9	Number of Groups	4	
10			
11	**Test Result**		
12	*H* Test Statistic	7.8886	=(12/(B8 * (B8 + 1))) * B7 - (3 * (B8 + 1))
13	Critical Value	7.8147	=CHISQ.INV.RT(B4, B9 - 1)
14	*p*-Value	0.0484	=CHISQ.DIST.RT(B12, B9 - 1)
15	Reject the null hypothesis		=IF(B14 < B4,"Reject the null hypothesis", "Do not reject the null hypothesis")

	D	E	F	G				
1								
2								
3	Calculations				Calculations			
4	Group	Sample Size	Sum of Ranks	Mean Rank	Group	Sample Size	Sum of Ranks	Mean Rank
5	Supplier 1	5	27	5.4	=SortedRanks!E1	=COUNTIF(SortedRanks!A2:A21, D5)	=SUMIF(SortedRanks!A2:A21, D5, SortedRanks!C2:C21)	=F5/E5
6	Supplier 2	5	76.5	15.3	=SortedRanks!F1	=COUNTIF(SortedRanks!A2:A21, D6)	=SUMIF(SortedRanks!A2:A21, D6, SortedRanks!C2:C21)	=F6/E6
7	Supplier 3	5	62	12.4	=SortedRanks!G1	=COUNTIF(SortedRanks!A2:A21, D7)	=SUMIF(SortedRanks!A2:A21, D7, SortedRanks!C2:C21)	=F7/E7
8	Supplier 4	5	44.5	8.9	=SortedRanks!H1	=COUNTIF(SortedRanks!A2:A21, D8)	=SUMIF(SortedRanks!A2:A21, D8, SortedRanks!C2:C21)	=F8/E8

Assumptions

To use the Kruskal-Wallis rank test, the following assumptions must be met:

- The c samples are randomly and independently selected from their respective populations.
- The underlying variable is continuous.
- The data provide at least a set of ranks, both within and among the c samples.
- The c populations have the same variability.
- The c populations have the same shape.

The Kruskal-Wallis procedure makes less stringent assumptions than does the F test. If you ignore the last two assumptions (variability and shape), you can still use the Kruskal-Wallis rank test to determine whether at least one of the populations differs from the other populations in some characteristic—such as central tendency, variation, or shape.

To use the F test, you must assume that the c samples are from normal populations that have equal variances. When the more stringent assumptions of the F test hold, you should use the F test instead of the Kruskal-Wallis test because it has slightly more power to detect significant differences among groups. However, if the assumptions of the F test do not hold, you should use the Kruskal-Wallis test.

Problems for Section 12.5

LEARNING THE BASICS

12.43 What is the upper-tail critical value from the chi-square distribution if you use the Kruskal-Wallis rank test for comparing the medians in six populations at the 0.01 level of significance?

12.44 For this problem, use the results of Problem 12.43.

a. State the decision rule for testing the null hypothesis that all six groups have equal population medians.

b. What is your statistical decision if the computed value of the test statistic H is 13.77?

APPLYING THE CONCEPTS

12.45 A pet food company has the business objective of expanding its product line beyond its current kidney- and shrimp-based cat foods. The company developed two new products—one based on chicken livers and the other based on salmon. The company conducted an experiment to compare the two new products with its two existing ones, as well as a generic beef-based product sold in a supermarket chain.

For the experiment, a sample of 50 cats from the population at a local animal shelter was selected. Ten cats were randomly assigned to each of the five products being tested. Each of the cats was then presented with 3 ounces of the selected food in a dish at feeding time. The researchers defined the variable to be measured as the number of ounces of food that the cat consumed within a 10-minute time interval that began when the filled dish was presented.

The results for this experiment are summarized in the following table and stored in **CatFood**:

Kidney	Shrimp	Chicken Liver	Salmon	Beef
2.37	2.26	2.29	1.79	2.09
2.62	2.69	2.23	2.33	1.87
2.31	2.25	2.41	1.96	1.67
2.47	2.45	2.68	2.05	1.64
2.59	2.34	2.25	2.26	2.16
2.62	2.37	2.17	2.24	1.75
2.34	2.22	2.37	1.96	1.18
2.47	2.56	2.26	1.58	1.92
2.45	2.36	2.45	2.18	1.32
2.32	2.59	2.57	1.93	1.94

a. At the 0.05 level of significance, is there evidence of a significant difference in the median amount of food eaten among the various products?

b. Compare the results of (a) with those of Problem 11.13 (a) on page 403.

c. Which test is more appropriate for these data: the Kruskal-Wallis rank test or the one-way ANOVA F test? Explain.

SELF Test **12.46** A hospital conducted a study of the waiting time in its emergency room. The hospital has a main campus, along with three satellite locations. Management had a business objective of reducing waiting time for emergency room cases that did not require immediate attention. To study this, a random sample of 15 emergency room cases at each location were selected on a particular day, and the waiting time (recorded from check-in to when the patient was called into the clinic area) was measured. The results are stored in ERWaiting.

a. At the 0.05 level of significance, is there evidence of a difference in the median waiting times in the four locations?

b. Compare the results of (a) with those of Problem 11.9 (a) on page 402.

12.47 *QSR* magazine has been reporting on the largest quick-serve and fast-casual brands in the United States for nearly 15 years. The file QSR contains the food segment (burger, chicken, pizza, or sandwich) and U.S. average sales per unit ($thousands) for each of 58 quick-service brands. (Data extracted from **bit.ly/Oj6EcY**.)

a. At the 0.05 level of significance, is there evidence of a difference in the median U.S. average sales per unit ($thousands) among the food segments?

b. Compare the results of (a) with those of Problem 11.11 (a) on page 402.

12.48 An advertising agency has been hired by a manufacturer of pens to develop an advertising campaign for the upcoming holiday season. To prepare for this project, the research director decides to initiate a study of the effect of advertising on product perception. An experiment is designed to compare five different advertisements. Advertisement A greatly undersells the pen's characteristics. Advertisement B slightly undersells the pen's characteristics. Advertisement C slightly oversells the pen's characteristics. Advertisement D greatly oversells the pen's characteristics. Advertisement E attempts to correctly state the pen's characteristics.

A sample of 30 adult respondents, taken from a larger focus group, is randomly assigned to the five advertisements (so that there are six respondents to each). After reading the advertisement and developing a sense of product expectation, all respondents unknowingly receive the same pen to evaluate. The respondents are permitted to test the pen and the plausibility of the advertising copy. The respondents are then asked to rate the pen from 1 to 7 on the product characteristic scales of appearance, durability, and writing performance. The *combined* scores of three ratings (appearance, durability, and writing performance) for the 30 respondents are stored in Pen. These data are:

A	B	C	D	E
15	16	8	5	12
18	17	7	6	19
17	21	10	13	18
19	16	15	11	12
19	19	14	9	17
20	17	14	10	14

a. At the 0.05 level of significance, is there evidence of a difference in the median ratings of the five advertisements?

b. Compare the results of (a) with those of Problem 11.10 (a) on page 402.

c. Which test is more appropriate for these data: the Kruskal-Wallis rank test or the one-way ANOVA *F* test? Explain.

12.49 A sporting goods manufacturing company wanted to compare the distance traveled by golf balls produced using each of four different designs. Ten balls of each design were manufactured and brought to the local golf course for the club professional to test. The order in which the balls were hit with the same club from the first tee was randomized so that the pro did not know which type of ball was being hit. All 40 balls were hit in a short period of time, during which the environmental conditions were essentially the same. The results (distance traveled in yards) for the four designs are stored in Golfball.

a. At the 0.05 level of significance, is there evidence of a difference in the median distances traveled by the golf balls with different designs?

b. Compare the results of (a) with those of Problem 11.14 (a) on page 403.

12.50 Students in a business statistics course performed an experiment to test the strength of four brands of trash bags. One-pound weights were placed into a bag, one at a time, until the bag broke. A total of 40 bags were used (10 for each brand). The file Trashbags gives the weight (in pounds) required to break the trash bags.

a. At the 0.05 level of significance, is there evidence of a difference in the median strength of the four brands of trash bags?

b. Compare the results in (a) to those in Problem 11.8 (a) on page 401.

12.6 McNemar Test for the Difference Between Two Proportions (Related Samples) (*online*)

LEARN MORE

Learn more about this test in a Chapter 12 eBook bonus section.

Tests such as chi-square test for the difference between two proportions discussed in Section 12.1 require independent samples from each population. However, sometimes when you are testing differences between the proportion of items of interest, the data are collected from repeated measurements or matched samples.

To test whether there is evidence of a difference between the proportions when the data have been collected from two related samples, you can use the McNemar test.

12.7 Chi-Square Test for the Variance or Standard Deviation (*online*)

LEARN MORE

Learn more about this test in a Chapter 12 eBook bonus section.

When analyzing numerical data, sometimes you need to test a hypothesis about the population variance or standard deviation. Assuming that the data are normally distributed, you use the χ^2 test for the variance or standard deviation to test whether the population variance or standard deviation is equal to a specified value.

USING STATISTICS Not Resorting to Guesswork About Resort Guests, Revisited

ziggysofi / Shutterstock

In the Using Statistics scenario, you were the manager of T.C. Resort Properties, a collection of five upscale hotels located on two tropical islands. To assess the quality of services being provided by your hotels, guests are encouraged to complete a satisfaction survey when they check out or via email after they check out. You analyzed the data from these surveys to determine the overall satisfaction with the services provided, the likelihood that the guests will return to the hotel, and the reasons given by some guests for not wanting to return.

On one island, T.C. Resort Properties operates the Beachcomber and Windsurfer hotels. You performed a chi-square test for the difference in two proportions and concluded that a greater proportion of guests are willing to return to the Beachcomber Hotel than to the Windsurfer. On the other island, T.C. Resort Properties operates the Golden Palm, Palm Royale, and Palm Princess hotels. To see if guest satisfaction was the same among the three hotels, you performed a chi-square test for the differences among more than two proportions. The test confirmed that the three proportions are not equal, and guests seem to be most likely to return to the Palm Royale and least likely to return to the Golden Palm.

In addition, you investigated whether the reasons given for not returning to the Golden Palm, Palm Royale, and Palm Princess were unique to a certain hotel or common to all three hotels. By performing a chi-square test of independence, you determined that the reasons given for wanting to return or not depended on the hotel where the guests had been staying. By examining the observed and expected frequencies, you concluded that guests were more satisfied with the price at the Golden Palm and were much more satisfied with the location of the Palm Princess. Guest satisfaction with room accommodations was not significantly different among the three hotels.

SUMMARY

Figure 12.15 presents a roadmap for this chapter. First, you used hypothesis testing for analyzing categorical data from two independent samples and from more than two independent samples. In addition, the rules of probability from Section 4.2 were extended to the hypothesis of independence in the joint responses to two categorical variables. You also studied two nonparametric tests. You used the Wilcoxon rank sum test when the assumptions of the t test for two independent samples were violated and the Kruskal-Wallis test when the assumptions of the one-way ANOVA F test were violated.

FIGURE 12.15
Roadmap of Chapter 12

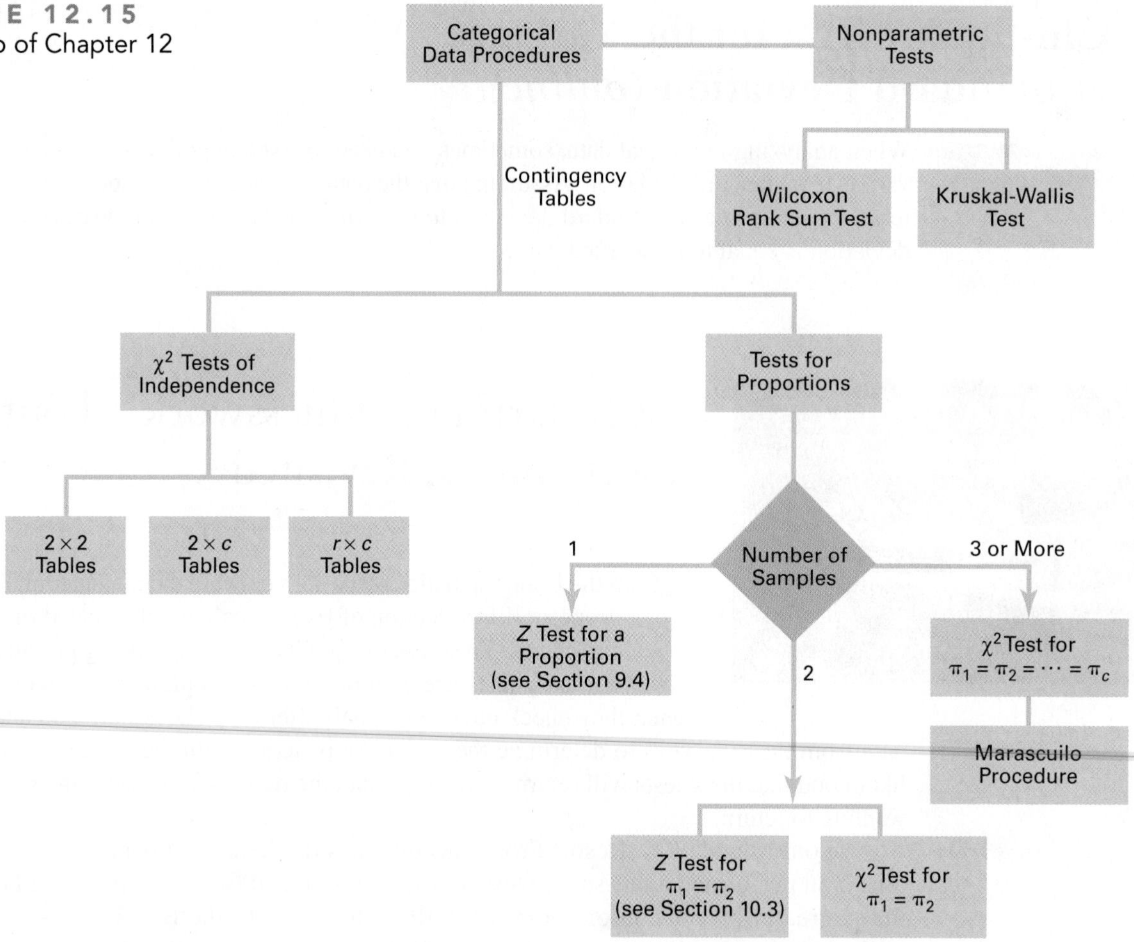

REFERENCES

1. Conover, W. J. *Practical Nonparametric Statistics*, 3rd ed. New York: Wiley, 2000).
2. Daniel, W. W. *Applied Nonparametric Statistics*, 2nd ed. Boston: PWS Kent, 1990.
3. Dixon, W. J., and F. J. Massey, Jr. *Introduction to Statistical Analysis*, 4th ed. New York: McGraw-Hill, 1983.
4. Hollander, M., and D. A. Wolfe. *Nonparametric Statistical Methods*, 2nd ed. New York: Wiley, 1999.
5. Lewontin, R. C., and J. Felsenstein. "Robustness of Homogeneity Tests in 2 × *n* Tables," *Biometrics*, 21(March 1965): 19–33.
6. Marascuilo, L. A. "Large-Sample Multiple Comparisons," *Psychological Bulletin*, 65(1966): 280–290.
7. Marascuilo, L. A., and M. McSweeney. *Nonparametric and Distribution-Free Methods for the Social Sciences*. Monterey, CA: Brooks/Cole, 1977.
8. *Microsoft Excel 2010*. Redmond, WA: Microsoft Corp., 2010.
9. Winer, B. J., D. R. Brown, and K. M. Michels. *Statistical Principles in Experimental Design*, 3rd ed. New York: McGraw-Hill, 1989.

KEY EQUATIONS

χ^2 Test for the Difference Between Two Proportions

$$\chi^2_{STAT} = \sum_{all\ cells} \frac{(f_o - f_e)^2}{f_e} \quad (12.1)$$

Computing the Estimated Overall Proportion for Two Groups

$$\bar{p} = \frac{X_1 + X_2}{n_1 + n_2} = \frac{X}{n} \quad (12.2)$$

Computing the Estimated Overall Proportion for c Groups

$$\bar{p} = \frac{X_1 + X_2 + \cdots + X_c}{n_1 + n_2 + \cdots + n_c} = \frac{X}{n} \quad (12.3)$$

Critical Range for the Marascuilo Procedure

$$\text{Critical range} = \sqrt{\chi^2_\alpha}\sqrt{\frac{p_j(1 - p_j)}{n_j} + \frac{p_{j'}(1 - p_{j'})}{n_{j'}}} \quad (12.4)$$

Computing the Expected Frequency

$$f_e = \frac{\text{Row total} \times \text{Column total}}{n} \quad (12.5)$$

Checking the Rankings

$$T_1 + T_2 = \frac{n(n + 1)}{2} \quad (12.6)$$

Large-Sample Wilcoxon Rank Sum Test

$$Z_{STAT} = \frac{T_1 - \frac{n_1(n + 1)}{2}}{\sqrt{\frac{n_1 n_2(n + 1)}{12}}} \quad (12.7)$$

Kruskal-Wallis Rank Test for Differences Among c Medians

$$H = \left[\frac{12}{n(n + 1)}\sum_{j=1}^{c}\frac{T_j^2}{n_j}\right] - 3(n + 1) \quad (12.8)$$

KEY TERMS

chi-square (χ^2) distribution 432
chi-square (χ^2) test for the difference between two proportions 431
chi-square (χ^2) test of independence 444
expected frequency (f_e) 431
Kruskal-Wallis rank test 454
Marascuilo procedure 440
nonparametric methods 449
observed frequency (f_o) 431
$2 \times c$ contingency table 437
2×2 contingency table 430
two-way contingency table 430
Wilcoxon rank sum test 449

CHECKING YOUR UNDERSTANDING

12.51 Under what conditions should you use the χ^2 test to determine whether there is a difference between the proportions of two independent populations?

12.52 Under what conditions should you use the χ^2 test to determine whether there is a difference among the proportions of more than two independent populations?

12.53 Under what conditions should you use the χ^2 test of independence?

12.54 Under what conditions should you use the Wilcoxon rank sum test instead of the t test for the difference between the means?

12.55 Under what conditions should you use the Kruskal-Wallis rank test instead of the one-way ANOVA?

CHAPTER REVIEW PROBLEMS

12.56 Undergraduate students at Miami University in Oxford, Ohio, were surveyed in order to evaluate the effect of gender and price on purchasing a pizza from Pizza Hut. Students were told to suppose that they were planning to have a large two-topping pizza delivered to their residence that evening. The students had to decide between ordering from Pizza Hut at a reduced price of \$8.49 (the regular price for a large two-topping pizza from the Oxford Pizza Hut at the time was \$11.49) and ordering a pizza from a different pizzeria. The results from this question are summarized in the following contingency table:

	PIZZERIA		
GENDER	**Pizza Hut**	**Other**	**Total**
Female	4	13	17
Male	6	12	18
Total	10	25	35

a. Using a 0.05 level of significance, is there evidence of a difference between males and females in their pizzeria selection?

b. What is your answer to (a) if nine of the male students selected Pizza Hut and nine selected another pizzeria?

A subsequent survey evaluated purchase decisions at other prices. These results are summarized in the following contingency table:

PIZZERIA	PRICE			
	\$8.49	**\$11.49**	**\$14.49**	**Total**
Pizza Hut	10	5	2	17
Other	25	23	27	75
Total	35	28	29	92

c. Using a 0.05 level of significance and using the data in the second contingency table, is there evidence of a difference in pizzeria selection based on price?

d. Determine the p-value in (c) and interpret its meaning.

12.57 What social media tools do marketers commonly use? The "2012 Social Media Marketing Industry Report" by Social Media Examiner (socialmediaexaminer.com) surveyed the percentage of marketers who commonly use an indicated social media tool. Surveyed were both B2B marketers, marketers that focus primarily on attracting businesses, and B2C marketers, marketers that primarily target consumers. Suppose the survey was based on 500 B2B marketers and 500 B2C marketers and yielded the results in the following table. (Data extracted from **bit.ly/QmMxPa**.)

SOCIAL MEDIA TOOL	BUSINESS FOCUS	
	B2B	**B2C**
Facebook	87%	96%
Twitter	84%	80%
LinkedIn	87%	59%
YouTube or other video	56%	59%

For *each social media tool*, at the 0.05 level of significance, determine whether there is a difference between B2B marketers and B2C marketers at the 0.05 level of significance.

12.58 A company is considering an organizational change involving the use of self-managed work teams. To assess the attitudes of employees of the company toward this change, a sample of 400 employees is selected and asked whether they favor the institution of self-managed work teams in the organization. Three responses are permitted: favor, neutral, or oppose. The results of the survey, cross-classified by type of job and attitude toward self-managed work teams, are summarized as follows:

TYPE OF JOB	SELF-MANAGED WORK TEAMS			
	Favor	**Neutral**	**Oppose**	**Total**
Hourly worker	108	46	71	225
Supervisor	18	12	30	60
Middle management	35	14	26	75
Upper management	24	7	9	40
Total	185	79	136	400

a. At the 0.05 level of significance, is there evidence of a relationship between attitude toward self-managed work teams and type of job?

The survey also asked respondents about their attitudes toward instituting a policy whereby an employee could take one additional vacation day per month without pay. The results, cross-classified by type of job, are as follows:

TYPE OF JOB	VACATION TIME WITHOUT PAY			
	Favor	**Neutral**	**Oppose**	**Total**
Hourly worker	135	23	67	225
Supervisor	39	7	14	60
Middle management	47	6	22	75
Upper management	26	6	8	40
Total	247	42	111	400

b. At the 0.05 level of significance, is there evidence of a relationship between attitude toward vacation time without pay and type of job?

12.59 A company that produces and markets continuing education programs on DVDs for the educational testing industry has traditionally mailed advertising to prospective customers. A market research study was undertaken to compare two approaches: mailing a sample DVD upon request that contained highlights of the full DVD and sending an email containing a link to a website from which sample material could be downloaded. Of those who responded to either the mailing or the email, the results were as follows in terms of purchase of the complete DVD:

PURCHASED	TYPE OF MEDIA USED		
	Mailing	**Email**	**Total**
Yes	26	11	37
No	227	247	474
Total	253	258	511

a. At the 0.05 level of significance, is there evidence of a difference in the proportion of DVDs purchased on the basis of the type of media used?

b. On the basis of the results of (a), which type of media should the company use in the future? Explain the rationale for your decision.

The company also wanted to determine which of three sales approaches should be used to generate sales among those who either requested the sample DVD by mail or downloaded the sample DVD but did not purchase the full DVD: (1) targeted email, (2) a DVD that contained additional features, or (3) a telephone call to prospective customers. The 474 respondents who did not initially purchase the full DVD were randomly assigned to one of the three sales approaches. The results, in terms of purchases of the full-program DVD, are as follows:

	SALES APPROACH			
ACTION	Targeted Email	More Complete DVD	Telephone Call	Total
Purchase	5	17	18	40
Don't purchase	153	141	140	434
Total	158	158	158	474

c. At the 0.05 level of significance, is there evidence of a difference in the proportion of DVDs purchased on the basis of the sales strategy used?

d. On the basis of the results of (c), which sales approach do you think the company should use in the future? Explain the rationale for your decision.

CASES FOR CHAPTER 12

Managing Ashland MultiComm Services

PHASE 1

Reviewing the results of its research, the marketing department team concluded that a segment of Ashland households might be interested in a discounted trial subscription to the AMS *3-For-All* cable/phone/Internet service. The team decided to test various discounts before determining the type of discount to offer during the trial period. It decided to conduct an experiment using three types of discounts plus a plan that offered no discount during the trial period:

1. No discount for the *3-For-All* cable/phone/Internet service. Subscribers would pay $24.99 per week for the *3-For-All* cable/phone/Internet service during the 90-day trial period.
2. Moderate discount for the *3-For-All* cable/phone/Internet service. Subscribers would pay $19.99 per week for the *3-For-All* cable/phone/Internet service during the 90-day trial period.
3. Substantial discount for the *3-For-All* cable/phone/Internet service. Subscribers would pay $14.99 per week for the *3-For-All* cable/phone/Internet service during the 90-day trial period.
4. Discount restaurant card. Subscribers would be given a Gold card providing a discount of 15% at selected restaurants in Ashland during the trial period.

Each participant in the experiment was randomly assigned to a discount plan. A random sample of 100 subscribers to each plan during the trial period was tracked to determine how many would continue to subscribe to the *3-For-All* service after the trial period. Table AMS12.1 summarizes the results.

TABLE AMS12.1

Number of Subscribers Who Continue Subscriptions After Trial Period with Four Discount Plans

CONTINUE SUBSCRIPTIONS AFTER TRIAL PERIOD	DISCOUNT PLANS				
	No Discount	Moderate Discount	Substantial Discount	Restaurant Card	Total
Yes	24	30	38	51	143
No	76	70	62	49	257
Total	100	100	100	100	400

1. Analyze the results of the experiment. Write a report to the team that includes your recommendation for which discount plan to use. Be prepared to discuss the limitations and assumptions of the experiment.

PHASE 2

The marketing department team discussed the results of the survey presented in Chapter 8, on pages 299–300. The team realized that the evaluation of individual questions was providing only limited information. In order to further understand the market for the *3-For-All* cable/phone/

Internet service, the data were organized in the following contingency tables:

HAS AMS TELEPHONE SERVICE	HAS AMS INTERNET SERVICE Yes	No	Total
Yes	55	28	83
No	207	128	335
Total	262	156	418

TYPE OF SERVICE	DISCOUNT TRIAL Yes	No	Total
Basic	8	156	164
Enhanced	32	222	254
Total	40	378	418

TYPE OF SERVICE	WATCHES PREMIUM OR ON-DEMAND SERVICES Almost Every Day	Several Times a Week	Almost Never	Never	Total
Basic	2	5	127	30	164
Enhanced	12	30	186	26	254
Total	14	35	313	56	418

DISCOUNT	WATCHES PREMIUM OR ON-DEMAND SERVICES Almost Every Day	Several Times a Week	Almost Never	Never	Total
Yes	4	5	27	4	40
No	10	30	286	52	378
Total	14	35	313	56	418

DISCOUNT	METHOD FOR CURRENT SUBSCRIPTION Toll-Free Phone	AMS Website	Direct Mail Reply Card	Good Tunes & More	Other	Total
Yes	11	21	5	1	2	40
No	219	85	41	9	24	378
Total	230	106	46	10	26	418

GOLD CARD	METHOD FOR CURRENT SUBSCRIPTION Toll-Free Phone	AMS Website	Direct Mail Reply Card	Good Tunes & More	Other	Total
Yes	10	20	5	1	2	38
No	220	86	41	9	24	380
Total	230	106	46	10	26	418

2. Analyze the results of the contingency tables. Write a report for the marketing department team, discussing the marketing implications of the results for Ashland MultiComm Services.

Digital Case

Apply your knowledge of testing for the difference between two proportions in this Digital Case, which extends the T.C. Resort Properties Using Statistics scenario of this chapter.

As T.C. Resort Properties seeks to improve its customer service, the company faces new competition from SunLow Resorts. SunLow has recently opened resort hotels on the islands where T.C. Resort Properties has its five hotels. SunLow is currently advertising that a random survey of 300 customers revealed that about 60% of the customers preferred its "Concierge Class" travel reward program over the T.C. Resorts "TCRewards Plus" program.

Open and review **ConciergeClass.pdf**, an electronic brochure that describes the Concierge Class program and compares it to the T.C. Resorts program. Then answer the following questions:

1. Are the claims made by SunLow valid?
2. What analyses of the survey data would lead to a more favorable impression about T.C. Resort Properties?
3. Perform one of the analyses identified in your answer to step 2.
4. Review the data about the T.C. Resort Properties customers presented in this chapter. Are there any other questions that you might include in a future survey of travel reward programs? Explain.

Sure Value Convenience Stores

You work in the corporate office for a nationwide convenience store franchise that operates nearly 10,000 stores. The per-store daily customer count (i.e., the mean number of customers in a store in one day) has been steady, at 900, for some time. To increase the customer count, the chain is considering cutting prices for coffee beverages. Management needs to determine how much prices can be cut in order to increase the daily customer count without reducing the gross margin on coffee sales too much. You decide to carry out an experiment in a sample of 24 stores where customer counts have been running almost exactly at the national average of 900. In 6 of the stores, a small coffee will be \$0.59, in another 6 stores the price will be \$0.69, in a third group of 6 stores, the price will be \$0.79, and in a fourth group of 6 stores, the price will now be \$0.89. After four weeks, the daily customer count in the stores is stored in **CoffeeSales**.

At the 0.05 level of significance, is there evidence of a difference in the median daily customer count based on the price of a small coffee? What price should the stores sell the coffee for?

CardioGood Fitness

Return to the CardioGood Fitness case first presented on page 33. The data for this case are stored in **CardioGood Fitness**.

1. Determine whether differences exist in the median age in years, education in years, annual household income (\$), number of times the customer plans to use the treadmill each week, and the number of miles the customer expects to walk/run each week based on the product purchased (TM195, TM498, TM798).
2. Determine whether differences exist in the relationship status (single or partnered), and the self-rated fitness based on the product purchased (TM195, TM498, TM798).
3. Write a report to be presented to the management of CardioGood Fitness, detailing your findings.

More Descriptive Choices Follow-up

Follow up the "Using Statistics: More Descriptive Choices, Revisited" on page 149 by using the data that are stored in **Retirement Funds** to:

1. Determine whether there is a difference between the growth and value funds in the median 1-year return percentages, 5-year return percentages, and 10-year return percentages.
2. Determine whether there is a difference between the small, mid-cap, and large market cap funds in the median 1-year return percentages, 5-year return percentages, and 10-year return percentages.
3. Determine whether there is a difference in risk based on market cap, a difference in rating based on market cap, a difference in risk based on type of fund, and a difference in rating based on type of fund.
4. Write a report summarizing your findings.

Clear Mountain State Student Surveys

1. The Student News Service at Clear Mountain State University (CMSU) has decided to gather data about the undergraduate students that attend CMSU. It creates and distributes a survey of 14 questions and receives responses from 62 undergraduates, which it stores in **UndergradSurvey**.

   a. Construct contingency tables using gender, major, plans to go to graduate school, and employment status. (You need to construct six tables, taking two variables at a time.) Analyze the data at the 0.05 level of significance to determine whether any significant relationships exist among these variables.

   b. At the 0.05 level of significance, is there evidence of a difference between males and females in median grade point average, expected starting salary, number of social networking sites registered for, age, spending on textbooks and supplies, text messages sent in a week, and the wealth needed to feel rich?

   c. At the 0.05 level of significance, is there evidence of a difference between students who plan to go to graduate school and those who do not plan to go to graduate school in median grade point average, expected starting salary, number of social networking sites registered for, age, spending on textbooks and supplies, text messages sent in a week, and the wealth needed to feel rich?

d. At the 0.05 level of significance, is there evidence of a difference based on academic major, in median expected starting salary, number of social networking sites registered for, age, spending on textbooks and supplies, text messages sent in a week, and the wealth needed to feel rich?

e. At the 0.05 level of significance, is there evidence of a difference based on graduate school intention in median grade point average, expected starting salary, number of social networking sites registered for, age, spending on textbooks and supplies, text messages sent in a week, and the wealth needed to feel rich?

2. The dean of students at CMSU has learned about the undergraduate survey and has decided to undertake a similar survey for graduate students at CMSU. She creates and distributes a survey of 14 questions and receives responses from 44 graduate students, which she stores them in GradSurvey. For these data, at the 0.05 level of significance:

a. Construct contingency tables using gender, undergraduate major, graduate major, and employment status. (You need to construct six tables, taking two variables at a time.) Analyze the data to determine whether any significant relationships exist among these variables.

b. Is there evidence of a difference between males and females in the median age, undergraduate grade point average, graduate grade point average, expected salary upon graduation, spending on textbooks and supplies, text messages sent in a week, and the wealth needed to feel rich?

c. Is there evidence of a difference based on undergraduate major in age, undergraduate grade point average, graduate grade point average, expected salary upon graduation, spending on textbooks and supplies, text messages sent in a week, and the wealth needed to feel rich?

d. Is there evidence of a difference based on graduate major in age, undergraduate grade point average, graduate grade point average, expected salary upon graduation, spending on textbooks and supplies, text messages sent in a week, and the wealth needed to feel rich?

e. Is there evidence of a difference based on employment status in age, undergraduate grade point average, graduate grade point average, expected salary upon graduation, spending on textbooks and supplies, text messages sent in a week, and the wealth needed to feel rich?

CHAPTER 12 EXCEL GUIDE

EG12.1 CHI-SQUARE TEST for the DIFFERENCE BETWEEN TWO PROPORTIONS

Key Technique Use the **CHISQ.INV.RT(*level of significance, degrees of freedom*)** function to compute the critical value and use the **CHISQ.DIST.RT(*chi-square test statistic, degrees of freedom*)** function to compute the p-value.

Example Perform this chi-square test for the two-hotel guest satisfaction data shown in Figure 12.3 on page 434.

PHStat Use **Chi-Square Test for Differences in Two Proportions.**
For the example, select **PHStat → Two-Sample Tests (Summarized Data) → Chi-Square Test for Differences in Two Proportions**. In the procedure's dialog box, enter **0.05** as the **Level of Significance**, enter a **Title**, and click **OK**. In the new worksheet:

1. Read the yellow note about entering values and then press the **Delete** key to delete the note.
2. Enter **Hotel** in cell **B4** and **Choose Again?** in cell **A5**.
3. Enter **Beachcomber** in cell **B5** and **Windsurfer** in cell **C5**.
4. Enter **Yes** in cell **A6** and **No** in cell **A7**.
5. Enter **163**, **64**, **154**, and **108** in cells **B6**, **B7**, **C6**, and **C7**, respectively.

In-Depth Excel Use the **COMPUTE worksheet** of the **Chi-Square workbook** as a template.
The worksheet already contains the Table 12.2 two-hotel guest satisfaction data. For other problems, change the **Observed Frequencies** cell counts and row and column labels in rows 4 through 7.

Read the SHORT TAKES for Chapter 12 for an explanation of the formulas found in the COMPUTE worksheet (shown in the **COMPUTE_FORMULAS worksheet**). If you are using an older Excel version, use the COMPUTE_OLDER worksheet instead of the COMPUTE worksheet.

EG12.2 CHI-SQUARE TEST for DIFFERENCES AMONG MORE THAN TWO PROPORTIONS

Key Technique Use the **CHISQ.INV.RT** and **CHISQ.DIST.RT** functions to compute the critical value and the p-value, respectively.

Example Perform this chi-square test for the three-hotel guest satisfaction data shown in Figure 12.6 on page 440.

PHStat Use **Chi-Square Test.**
For the example, select **PHStat → Multiple-Sample Tests → Chi-Square Test**. In the procedure's dialog box (shown below):

1. Enter **0.05** as the **Level of Significance**.
2. Enter **2** as the **Number of Rows**.
3. Enter **3** as the **Number of Columns**.
4. Enter a **Title** and click **OK**.

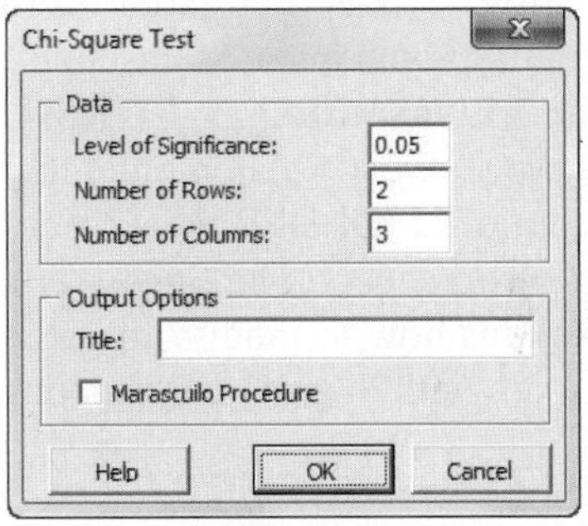

In the new worksheet:

5. Read the yellow note instructions about entering values and then press the **Delete** key to delete the note.
6. Enter the Table 12.6 data (see page 438), including row and column labels, in rows 4 through 7. The **#DIV/0!** error messages will disappear when you finish entering all the table data.

In-Depth Excel Use the **ChiSquare2x3 worksheet** of the **Chi-Square Worksheets workbook** as a model.
The worksheet already contains the data for Table 12.6 guest satisfaction data (see page 438). For other 2 × 3 problems, change the **Observed Frequencies** cell counts and row and column labels in rows 4 through 7. For 2 × 4 problems, use the **ChiSquare2x4 worksheet** and change the **Observed Frequencies** cell counts and row and column labels in that worksheet. For 2 × 5 problems, use the **ChiSquare2x5 worksheet** and change the **Observed Frequencies** cell counts and row and column labels in that worksheet.

The formulas that are found in the ChiSquare2x3 workbook (shown in the **ChiSquare2x3_FORMULAS worksheet**) are similar to the formulas found in the COMPUTE worksheet of the Chi-Square workbook (see the previous section). If you use an Excel version older than Excel 2010, use the ChiSquare2x3_OLDER worksheet instead of the ChiSquare2x3 worksheet. (The SHORT TAKES for Chapter 12 also explains how to modify the other ChiSquare worksheets for use with older Excel versions.)

The Marascuilo Procedure

Key Technique Use formulas to compute the absolute differences and the critical range.

Example Perform the **Marascuilo Procedure** for the guest satisfaction survey that is shown in Figure 12.7 on page 441.

PHStat Modify the *PHStat* instructions of the previous section. In step 4, check **Marascuilo Procedure** in addition to entering a **Title** and clicking **OK**.

In-Depth Excel Use the **Marascuilo2x3** of the **Chi-Square Worksheets workbook** as a template.

The worksheet requires no entries or changes to use. For 2×4 problems, use the **Marascuilo2x4 worksheet** and for 2×5 problems, use the **Marascuilo2x5 worksheet**.

Read the SHORT TAKES for Chapter 12 for an explanation of the formulas found in the Marascuilo2x3 worksheet (shown in the **Marascuilo2x3_FORMULAS worksheet**). If you use an Excel version older than Excel 2010, use the Marascuilo2x3_OLDER worksheet instead of the Marascuilo2x3 worksheet. (The SHORT TAKES for Chapter 12 also explains how to modify the other Marascuilo worksheets for use with older Excel versions.)

EG12.3 CHI-SQUARE TEST of INDEPENDENCE

Key Technique Use the **CHISQ.INV.RT** and **CHISQ.DIST.RT** functions to compute the critical value and the *p*-value, respectively.

Example Perform this chi-square test for the primary reason for not returning to hotel data that is shown in Figure 12.10 on page 447.

PHStat Use **Chi-Square Test**.

For the example, select **PHStat ➔ Multiple-Sample Tests ➔ Chi-Square Test**. In the procedure's dialog box (shown below):

1. Enter **0.05** as the **Level of Significance**.
2. Enter **4** as the **Number of Rows**.
3. Enter **3** as the **Number of Columns**.
4. Enter a **Title** and click **OK**.

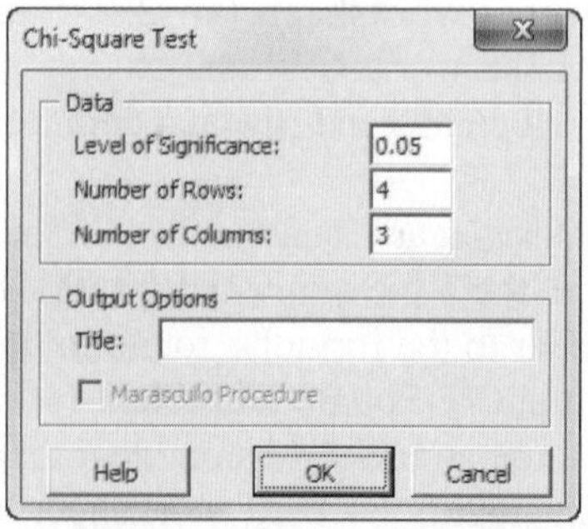

In the new worksheet:

5. Read the yellow note about entering values and then press the **Delete** key to delete the note.
6. Enter the Table 12.9 data on page 444, including row and column labels, in rows 4 through 9. The **#DIV/0!** error messages will disappear when you finish entering all of the table data.

In-Depth Excel Use the **ChiSquare4x3 worksheet** of the **Chi-Square Worksheets workbook** as a model.

The worksheet already contains the Table 12.9 primary reason for not returning to hotel data (see page 444). For other 4×3 problems, change the **Observed Frequencies** cell counts and row and column labels in rows 4 through 9. For 3×4 problems, use the **ChiSquare3x4 worksheet.** For 4×3 problems, use the **ChiSquare4x3 worksheet**. For 7×3 problems, use the **ChiSquare7x3 worksheet**. For 8×3 problems, use the **ChiSquare8x3 worksheet**. For each of these other worksheets, enter the contingency table data for the problem in the Observed Frequencies area.

If you use an Excel version older than Excel 2010, use the ChiSquare4x3_OLDER worksheet instead of the ChiSquare4x3 worksheet. The formulas used in these worksheets are similar to those in the other chi-square worksheets discussed in this Excel Guide.

EG12.4 WILCOXON RANK SUM TEST: a NONPARAMETRIC METHOD for TWO INDEPENDENT POPULATIONS

Key Technique Use the **NORM.S.INV(*level of significance*)** function to compute the upper and lower critical values and use **NORM.S.DIST(*absolute value of the Z test statistic*)** as part of a formula to compute the *p*-value. For unsummarized data, use the **COUNTIF** and **SUMIF** functions (see Appendix Section F.4) to compute the sample sizes and the sum of ranks for a sample, respectively.

PHStat Use **Wilcoxon Rank Sum Test**.

For the example, open to the **DATA worksheet** of the **Cola workbook**. Select **PHStat ➔ Two-Sample Tests (Unsummarized Data) ➔ Wilcoxon Rank Sum Test**. In the procedure's dialog box (shown on page 469):

1. Enter **0.05** as the **Level of Significance**.
2. Enter **A1:A11** as the **Population 1 Sample Cell Range**.
3. Enter **B1:B11** as the **Population 2 Sample Cell Range**.
4. Check **First cells in both ranges contain label**.
5. Click **Two-Tail Test**.
6. Enter a **Title** and click **OK**.

The procedure creates a SortedRanks worksheet that contains the sorted ranks in addition to the worksheet shown in Figure 12.12. Both of these worksheets are discussed in the following *In-Depth Excel* instructions.

In-Depth Excel Use the **COMPUTE worksheet** of the **Wilcoxon workbook** as a template.

The worksheet already contains data and formulas to use the unsummarized data for the example. For other problems that use unsummarized data, first open to the **SortedRanks worksheet** and enter the sorted values for both groups in stacked format. Use column A for the sample names and column B for the sorted values. Assign a rank for each value and enter the ranks in column C of the same worksheet. Then open to the COMPUTE worksheet (or the similar COMPUTE_ALL worksheet, if performing a one-tail test) and edit the formulas in cells B7, B8, B10, and B11.

For problems with summarized data, overwrite the formulas that compute the **Sample Size** and **Sum of Ranks** in the cell range **B7:B11**, with the values for these statistics.

Open to the **COMPUTE_ALL_ FORMULAS worksheet** to view all formulas in the COMPUTE_ALL worksheet. If you use an Excel version older than Excel 2010, use the COMPUTE_ALL_OLDER worksheet for all tests.

EG12.5 KRUSKAL-WALLIS RANK TEST: a NONPARAMETRIC METHOD for the ONE-WAY ANOVA

Key Technique Use the **CHISQ.INV.RT(*level of significance, number of groups* - 1)** function to compute the critical value and use the **CHISQ.DIST.RT(*H test statistic, number of groups* - 1)** function to compute the *p*-value. For unsummarized data, use the **COUNTIF** and **SUMIF** functions (see Appendix Section F.4) to compute the sample sizes and the sum of ranks for a sample, respectively.

Example Perform the Kruskal-Wallis rank test for differences among the four median tensile strengths of parachutes that is shown in Figure 12.14 on page 456.

PHStat Use **Kruskal-Wallis Rank Test**.

For the example, open to the **DATA worksheet** of the **Parachute workbook**. Select **PHStat → Multiple-Sample Tests → Kruskal-Wallis Rank Test**. In the procedure's dialog box (shown below):

1. Enter **0.05** as the **Level of Significance**.
2. Enter **A1:D6** as the **Sample Data Cell Range**.
3. Check **First cells contain label**.
4. Enter a **Title** and click **OK**.

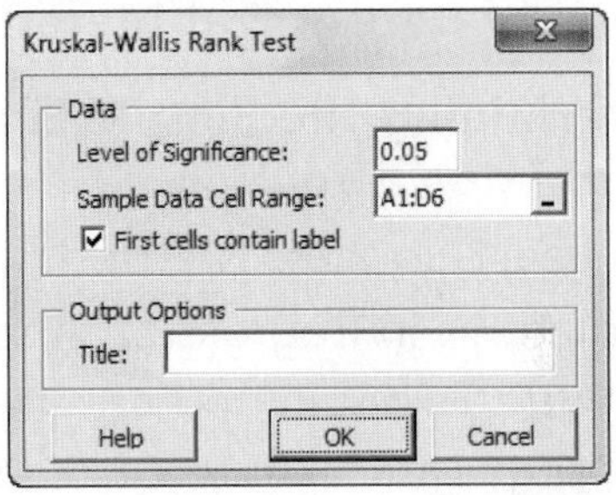

The procedure creates a SortedRanks worksheet that contains sorted ranks in addition to the worksheet shown in Figure 12.14 on page 456. Both of these worksheets are discussed in the following *In-Depth Excel* instructions.

In-Depth Excel Use the **KruskalWallis4 worksheet** of the **Kruskal-Wallis Worksheets workbook** as a template.

The worksheet already contains the data and formulas to use the unsummarized data for the example. For other problems with four groups and unsummarized data, first open to the **SortedRanks worksheet** and enter the sorted values for both groups in stacked format. Use column A for the sample names and column B for the sorted values. Assign ranks for each value and enter the ranks in column C of the same worksheet. Also paste your unsummarized stacked data in columns, starting with Column E. (The row 1 cells, starting with cell E1, are used to identify each group.) Then open to the KruskalWallis4 worksheet and edit the formulas in columns E and F.

For other problems with four groups and summarized data, open to the KruskalWallis4 worksheet and overwrite the formulas that display the group names and compute the **Sample Size** and **Sum of Ranks** in columns D, E, and F with the values for these statistics. For other problems with three groups, use the similar **KruskalWallis3 worksheet.**

Open to the **KruskalWallis4_FORMULAS worksheet** to view all formulas in the KruskalWallis4 worksheet. If you use an Excel version older than Excel 2010, use the KruskalWallis4_OLDER or KruskalWallis3_OLDER worksheets.

CHAPTER

13 Simple Linear Regression

Learning Objectives

In this chapter, you learn:

- How to use regression analysis to predict the value of a dependent variable based on the value of an independent variable
- The meaning of the regression coefficients b_0 and b_1
- How to evaluate the assumptions of regression analysis and know what to do if the assumptions are violated
- How to make inferences about the slope and correlation coefficient
- How to estimate mean values and predict individual values

Dmitriy Shironosov / Shutterstock

Knowing Customers at Sunflowers Apparel

Having survived recent economic slowdowns that have diminished their competitors, Sunflowers Apparel, a chain of upscale fashion stores for women, is in the midst of a companywide review that includes researching the factors that make their stores successful. Until recently, Sunflowers managers had no data analyses to support store location decisions, relying instead on subjective factors, such as the availability of an inexpensive lease or the perception that a particular location seemed ideal for one of their stores.

As the new director of planning, you have already consulted with marketing data firms that specialize in using business analytics (see page 6) to identify and classify groups of consumers. Based on such preliminary analyses, you have already tentatively discovered that the profile of Sunflowers shoppers may not only be the upper middle class long suspected of being the chain's clientele but may also include younger, aspirational families with young children, and, surprisingly, urban hipsters that set trends and are mostly single.

You seek to develop a systematic approach that will lead to making better decisions during the site-selection process. As a starting point, you have asked one marketing data firm to collect and organize data for the number of people in the identified categories who live within a fixed radius of each Sunflowers store. You believe that the greater numbers of profiled customers contribute to store sales, and you want to explore the possible use of this relationship in the decision-making process. How can you use statistics so that you can forecast the annual sales of a proposed store based on the number of profiled customers that reside within a fixed radius of a Sunflowers store?

crystalfoto / Shutterstock

In this chapter and the next two chapters, you learn how **regression analysis** enables you to develop a model to predict the values of a numerical variable, based on the value of other variables.

In regression analysis, the variable you wish to predict is called the **dependent variable**. The variables used to make the prediction are called **independent variables**. For example, as the director of planning, you might want to predict annual sales for a Sunflowers store based on the number of profiled customers. Other examples include predicting the monthly rent of an apartment based on its size and predicting the monthly sales of a product in a supermarket based on the amount of shelf space devoted to the product.

In addition to predicting values of the dependent variable, regression analysis allows you to identify the type of mathematical relationship that exists between a dependent variable and an independent variable, to quantify the effect that changes in the independent variable have on the dependent variable, and to identify unusual observations. This chapter discusses **simple linear regression**, in which a *single* numerical independent variable, *X*, is used to predict the numerical dependent variable *Y*, such as using the number of profiled customers to predict the annual sales of the store. Chapters 14 and 15 discuss *multiple regression models*, which use *several* independent variables to predict a dependent variable, *Y*. For example, you could use the amount of advertising expenditures, price, and the amount of shelf space devoted to a product to predict its monthly sales.

13.1 Types of Regression Models

Section 2.5 discussed using a **scatter plot** (also known as a **scatter diagram**) to examine the relationship between an *X* variable on the horizontal axis and a *Y* variable on the vertical axis. The nature of the relationship between two variables can take many forms, ranging from simple to extremely complicated mathematical functions. The simplest relationship consists of a straight-line relationship, or **linear relationship**. Figure 13.1 illustrates a straight-line relationship.

FIGURE 13.1
A straight-line relationship

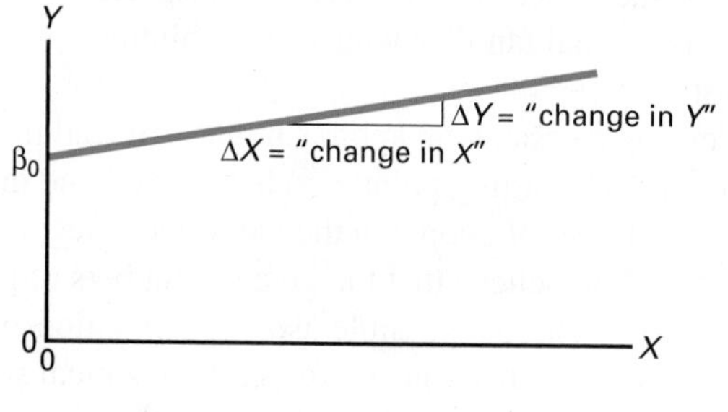

Equation (13.1) represents the straight-line (linear) model.

SIMPLE LINEAR REGRESSION MODEL

$$Y_i = \beta_0 + \beta_1 X_i + \varepsilon_i \quad (13.1)$$

where

β_0 = *Y* intercept for the population

β_1 = slope for the population

ε_i = random error in *Y* for observation *i*

Y_i = dependent variable (sometimes referred to as the **response variable**) for observation *i*

X_i = independent variable (sometimes referred to as the predictor, or **explanatory variable**) for observation *i*

The $Y_i = \beta_0 + \beta_1 X_i$ portion of the simple linear regression model expressed in Equation (13.1) is a straight line. The **slope** of the line, β_1, represents the expected change in Y per unit change in X. It represents the mean amount that Y changes (either positively or negatively) for a one-unit change in X. The ***Y* intercept**, β_0, represents the mean value of Y when X equals 0. The last component of the model, ε_i, represents the random error in Y for each observation, i. In other words, ε_i is the vertical distance of the actual value of Y_i above or below the expected value of Y_i on the line.

The selection of the proper mathematical model depends on the distribution of the X and Y values on the scatter plot. Figure 13.2 illustrates six different types of relationships.

FIGURE 13.2
Six types of relationships found in scatter plots

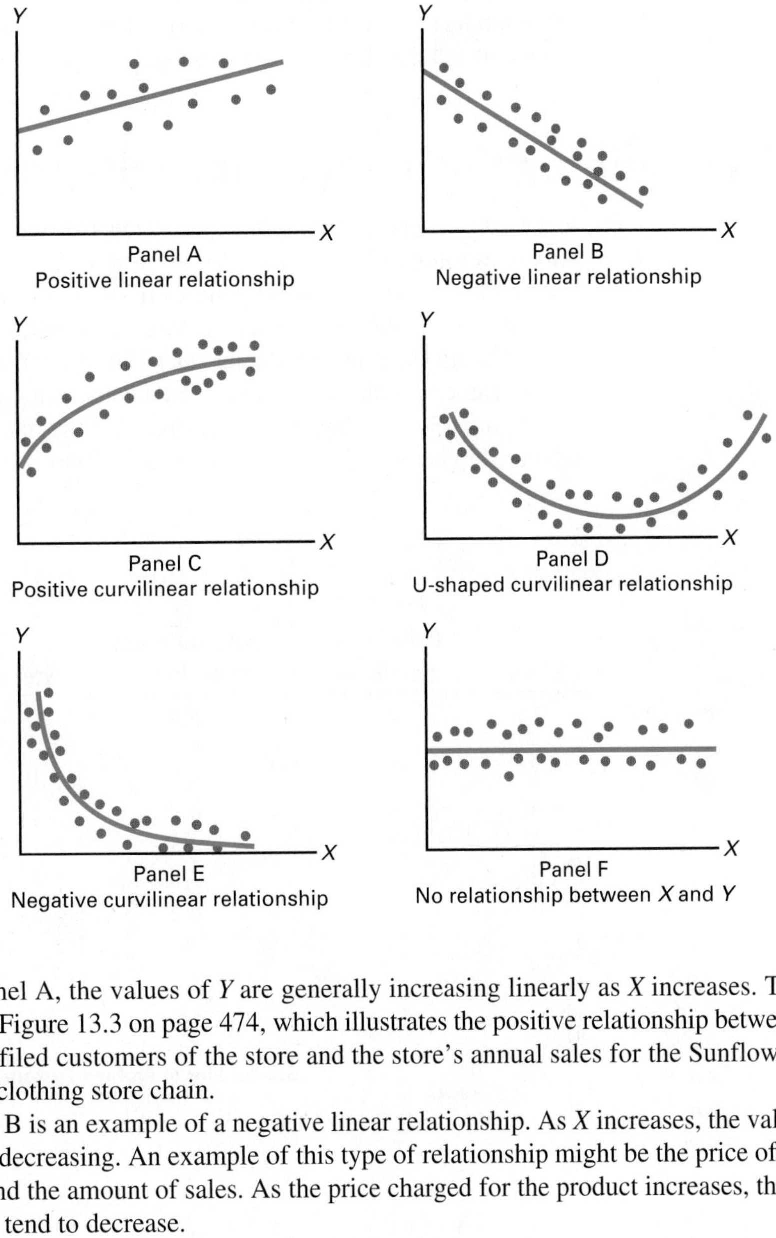

In Panel A, the values of Y are generally increasing linearly as X increases. This panel is similar to Figure 13.3 on page 474, which illustrates the positive relationship between the number of profiled customers of the store and the store's annual sales for the Sunflowers Apparel women's clothing store chain.

Panel B is an example of a negative linear relationship. As X increases, the values of Y are generally decreasing. An example of this type of relationship might be the price of a particular product and the amount of sales. As the price charged for the product increases, the amount of sales may tend to decrease.

Panel C shows a positive curvilinear relationship between X and Y. The values of Y increase as X increases, but this increase tapers off beyond certain values of X. An example of a positive curvilinear relationship might be the age and maintenance cost of a machine. As a machine gets older, the maintenance cost may rise rapidly at first but then level off beyond a certain number of years.

Panel D shows a U-shaped relationship between X and Y. As X increases, at first Y generally decreases; but as X continues to increase, Y not only stops decreasing but actually increases above its minimum value. An example of this type of relationship might be entrepreneurial activity and levels of economic development as measured by GDP per capita. Entrepreneurial activity occurs more in the least and most developed countries.

Panel E illustrates an exponential relationship between *X* and *Y*. In this case, *Y* decreases very rapidly as *X* first increases, but then it decreases much less rapidly as *X* increases further. An example of an exponential relationship could be the value of an automobile and its age. The value drops drastically from its original price in the first year, but it decreases much less rapidly in subsequent years.

Finally, Panel F shows a set of data in which there is very little or no relationship between *X* and *Y*. High and low values of *Y* appear at each value of *X*.

Although scatter plots are useful for visually displaying the mathematical form of a relationship, more sophisticated statistical procedures are available to determine the most appropriate model for a set of variables. The rest of this chapter discusses the model used when there is a *linear* relationship between variables.

13.2 Determining the Simple Linear Regression Equation

In the Sunflowers Apparel scenario on page 471, the business objective of the director of planning is to forecast annual sales for all new stores, based on the number of profiled customers who live no more than 30 minutes from a Sunflowers store. To examine the relationship between the number of profiled customers (in millions) who live within a fixed radius from a Sunflowers store and its annual sales ($millions), data were collected from a sample of 14 stores. Table 13.1 shows the organized data, which are stored in **SiteSelection**.

Figure 13.3 displays the scatter plot for the data in Table 13.1. Observe the increasing relationship between profiled customers (X) and annual sales (Y). As the number of profiled

TABLE 13.1

Number of Profiled Customers (in millions) and Annual Sales (in $millions) for a Sample of 14 Sunflowers Apparel Stores

Store	Profiled Customers (millions)	Annual Sales ($millions)	Store	Profiled Customers (millions)	Annual Sales ($millions)
1	3.7	5.7	8	3.1	4.7
2	3.6	5.9	9	3.2	6.1
3	2.8	6.7	10	3.5	4.9
4	5.6	9.5	11	5.2	10.7
5	3.3	5.4	12	4.6	7.6
6	2.2	3.5	13	5.8	11.8
7	3.3	6.2	14	3.0	4.1

FIGURE 13.3

Scatter plot for the Sunflowers Apparel data

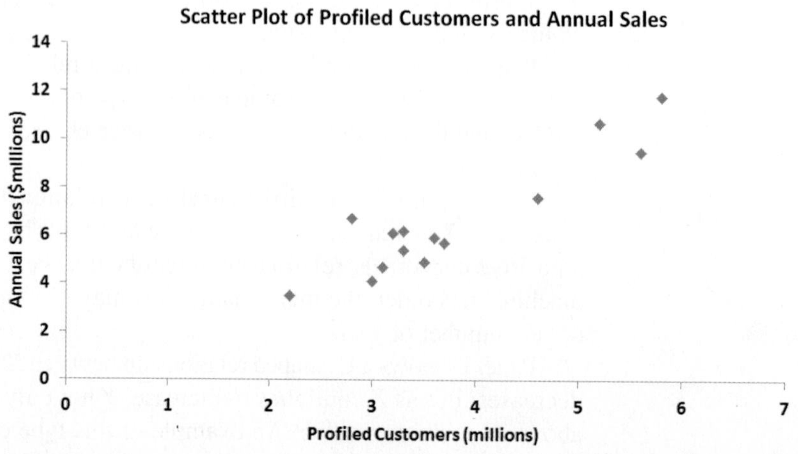

customers increases, annual sales increase approximately as a straight line. Thus, you can assume that a straight line provides a useful mathematical model of this relationship. Now you need to determine the specific straight line that is the *best* fit to these data.

The Least-Squares Method

In the preceding section, a statistical model is hypothesized to represent the relationship between two variables—number of profiled customers and sales—in the entire population of Sunflowers Apparel stores. However, as shown in Table 13.1, the data are collected from a random sample of stores. If certain assumptions are valid (see Section 13.4), you can use the sample Y intercept, b_0, and the sample slope, b_1, as estimates of the respective population parameters, β_0 and β_1. Equation (13.2) uses these estimates to form the **simple linear regression equation**. This straight line is often referred to as the **prediction line**.

Student Tip
In mathematics, the symbol b is often used for the Y intercept instead of b_0 and the symbol m is often used for the slope instead of b_1.

SIMPLE LINEAR REGRESSION EQUATION: THE PREDICTION LINE

The predicted value of Y equals the Y intercept plus the slope multiplied by the value of X.

$$\hat{Y}_i = b_0 + b_1X_i \tag{13.2}$$

where

$\hat{Y}_i$ = predicted value of Y for observation i

X_i = value of X for observation i

b_0 = sample Y intercept

b_1 = sample slope

Equation (13.2) requires you to determine two **regression coefficients**—b_0 (the sample Y intercept) and b_1 (the sample slope). The most common approach to finding b_0 and b_1 is using the least-squares method. This method minimizes the sum of the squared differences between the actual values (Y_i) and the predicted values $(\hat{Y}_i)$, using the simple linear regression equation [i.e., the prediction line; see Equation (13.2)]. This sum of squared differences is equal to

$$\sum_{i=1}^{n}(Y_i - \hat{Y}_i)^2$$

Student Tip
The equations used to compute these results are shown in Examples 13.3 and 13.4 on pages 478–480 and 485–486. You should use software to do these computations for large data sets, given the complex nature of the computations.

Because $\hat{Y}_i = b_0 + b_1X_i$,

$$\sum_{i=1}^{n}(Y_i - \hat{Y}_i)^2 = \sum_{i=1}^{n}[Y_i - (b_0 + b_1X_i)]^2$$

Because this equation has two unknowns, b_0 and b_1, the sum of squared differences depends on the sample Y intercept, b_0, and the sample slope, b_1. The **least-squares method** determines the values of b_0 and b_1 that minimize the sum of squared differences around the prediction line. Any values for b_0 and b_1 other than those determined by the least-squares method result in a greater sum of squared differences between the actual values (Y_i) and the predicted values $(\hat{Y}_i)$. Figure 13.4 presents the worksheet for the simple linear regression model for the Table 13.1 Sunflowers Apparel data.

FIGURE 13.4
Simple linear regression model worksheet for the Sunflowers Apparel data

Figure 13.4 displays the ***COMPUTE worksheet*** *of the* ***Simple Linear Regression workbook*** *that the Section EG13.2 instructions use. (The Analysis ToolPak creates a similar-looking worksheet that does not contain the formulas found in the COMPUTE worksheet.)*

If you use an Excel version that is older than Excel 2010, use the ***Simple Linear Regression 2007 workbook*** *for all the simple linear regression examples as is noted in Section EG13.2.*

	A	B	C	D	E	F	G
1	**Simple Linear Regression**						
2							
3	***Regression Statistics***						
4	Multiple R	0.9208					
5	R Square	0.8479					
6	Adjusted R Square	0.8352					
7	Standard Error	0.9993					
8	Observations	14					
9							
10	**ANOVA**						
11		*df*	*SS*	*MS*	*F*	*Significance F*	
12	Regression	1	66.7854	66.7854	66.8792	0.0000	
13	Residual	12	11.9832	0.9986			
14	Total	13	78.7686				
15							
16		*Coefficients*	*Standard Error*	*t Stat*	*P-value*	*Lower 95%*	*Upper 95%*
17	Intercept	-1.2088	0.9949	-1.2151	0.2477	-3.3765	0.9588
18	Profiled Customers	2.0742	0.2536	8.1780	0.0000	1.5216	2.6268

In Figure 13.4, observe that $b_0 = -1.2088$ and $b_1 = 2.0742$. Using Equation (13.2) on page 475, the prediction line for these data is

$$\hat{Y}_i = -1.2088 + 2.0742X_i$$

The slope, b_1, is $+2.0742$. This means that for each increase of 1 unit in X, the predicted value of Y is estimated to increase by 2.0742 units. In other words, for each increase of 1.0 million profiled customers within 30 minutes of the store, the predicted annual sales are estimated to increase by \$2.0742 million. Thus, the slope represents the portion of the annual sales that are estimated to vary according to the number of profiled customers.

The Y intercept, b_0, is -1.2088. The Y intercept represents the predicted value of Y when X equals 0. Because the number of profiled customers of the store cannot be 0, this Y intercept has little or no practical interpretation. Also, the Y intercept for this example is outside the range of the observed values of the X variable, and therefore interpretations of the value of b_0 should be made cautiously. Figure 13.5 displays the actual values and the prediction line.

To illustrate a situation in which there is a direct interpretation for the Y intercept, b_0, see Example 13.1.

Student Tip
Remember that a positive slope means that as X increases, Y is predicted to increase. A negative slope means that as X increases, Y is predicted to decrease.

FIGURE 13.5
Scatter plot and prediction line for Sunflowers Apparel data

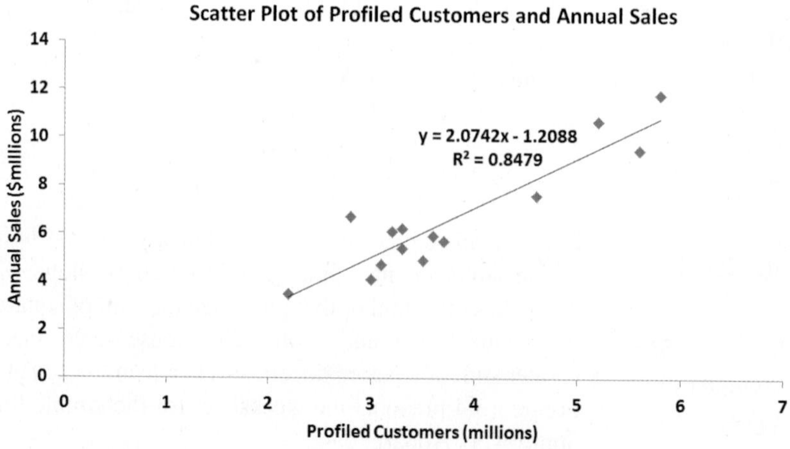

EXAMPLE 13.1

Interpreting the Y Intercept, b_0, and the Slope, b_1

A statistics professor wants to use the number of hours a student studies for a statistics final exam (X) to predict the final exam score (Y). A regression model is fit based on data collected from a class during the previous semester, with the following results:

$$\hat{Y}_i = 35.0 + 3X_i$$

What is the interpretation of the Y intercept, b_0, and the slope, b_1?

SOLUTION The Y intercept $b_0 = 35.0$ indicates that when the student does not study for the final exam, the predicted final exam score is 35.0. The slope $b_1 = 3$ indicates that for each increase of one hour in studying time, the predicted change in the final exam score is +3.0. In other words, the final exam score is predicted to increase by a mean of 3 points for each one-hour increase in studying time.

Return to the Sunflowers Apparel scenario on page 471. Example 13.2 illustrates how you use the prediction line to predict the annual sales.

EXAMPLE 13.2

Predicting Annual Sales Based on Number of Profiled Customers

Use the prediction line to predict the annual sales for a store with 4 million profiled customers.

SOLUTION You can determine the predicted value of annual sales by substituting $X = 4$ (millions of profiled customers) into the simple linear regression equation:

$$\hat{Y}_i = -1.2088 + 2.0742X_i$$

$$\hat{Y}_i = -1.2088 + 2.0742(4) = 7.0879 \text{ or } \$7{,}087{,}900$$

Thus, a store with 4 million profiled customers has predicted annual sales of $7,087,900.

Predictions in Regression Analysis: Interpolation Versus Extrapolation

When using a regression model for prediction purposes, you should consider only the **relevant range** of the independent variable in making predictions. This relevant range includes all values from the smallest to the largest X used in developing the regression model. Hence, when predicting Y for a given value of X, you can interpolate within this relevant range of the X values, but you should not extrapolate beyond the range of X values. When you use the number of profiled customers to predict annual sales, the number of profiled customers (in millions) varies from 2.2 to 5.8 (see Table 13.1 on page 474). Therefore, you should predict annual sales *only* for stores that have between 2.2 and 5.8 million profiled customers. Any prediction of annual sales for stores outside this range assumes that the observed relationship between sales and the number of profiled customers for stores that have between 2.2 and 5.8 million profiled customers is the same as for stores outside this range. For example, you cannot extrapolate the linear relationship beyond 5.8 million profiled customers in Example 13.2. It would be improper to use the prediction line to forecast the sales for a new store that has 8 million profiled customers because the relationship between sales and the number of profiled customers may have a point of diminishing returns. If that is true, as the number of profiled customers increases beyond 5.8 million, the effect on sales may become smaller and smaller.

Computing the Y Intercept, b_0 and the Slope, b_1

For small data sets, you can use a hand calculator to compute the least-squares regression coefficients. Equations (13.3) and (13.4) give the values of b_0 and b_1, which minimize

$$\sum_{i=1}^{n}(Y_i - \hat{Y}_i)^2 = \sum_{i=1}^{n}[Y_i - (b_0 + b_1X_i)]^2$$

COMPUTATIONAL FORMULA FOR THE SLOPE, b_1

$$b_1 = \frac{SSXY}{SSX} \tag{13.3}$$

where

$$SSXY = \sum_{i=1}^{n}(X_i - \bar{X})(Y_i - \bar{Y}) = \sum_{i=1}^{n}X_iY_i - \frac{\left(\sum_{i=1}^{n}X_i\right)\left(\sum_{i=1}^{n}Y_i\right)}{n}$$

$$SSX = \sum_{i=1}^{n}(X_i - \bar{X})^2 = \sum_{i=1}^{n}X_i^2 - \frac{\left(\sum_{i=1}^{n}X_i\right)^2}{n}$$

COMPUTATIONAL FORMULA FOR THE Y INTERCEPT, b_0

$$b_0 = \bar{Y} - b_1\bar{X} \tag{13.4}$$

where

$$\bar{Y} = \frac{\sum_{i=1}^{n}Y_i}{n}$$

$$\bar{X} = \frac{\sum_{i=1}^{n}X_i}{n}$$

EXAMPLE 13.3

Computing the Y Intercept, b_0, and the Slope, b_1

Compute the Y intercept, b_0, and the slope, b_1, for the Sunflowers Apparel data.

SOLUTION In Equations (13.3) and (13.4), five quantities need to be computed to determine b_1 and b_0. These are n, the sample size; $\sum_{i=1}^{n}X_i$, the sum of the X values; $\sum_{i=1}^{n}Y_i$, the sum of the Y values; $\sum_{i=1}^{n}X_i^2$, the sum of the squared X values; and $\sum_{i=1}^{n}X_iY_i$, the sum of the product of X and Y. For the Sunflowers Apparel data, the number of profiled customers (X) is used to predict the annual sales (Y) in a store. Table 13.2 presents the computations of the sums needed for the site selection problem. The table also includes $\sum_{i=1}^{n}Y_i^2$, the sum of the squared Y values that will be used to compute SST in Section 13.3.

TABLE 13.2

Computations for the Sunflowers Apparel Data

Store	Profiled Customers (X)	Annual Sales (Y)	X^2	Y^2	XY
1	3.7	5.7	13.69	32.49	21.09
2	3.6	5.9	12.96	34.81	21.24
3	2.8	6.7	7.84	44.89	18.76
4	5.6	9.5	31.36	90.25	53.20
5	3.3	5.4	10.89	29.16	17.82
6	2.2	3.5	4.84	12.25	7.70
7	3.3	6.2	10.89	38.44	20.46
8	3.1	4.7	9.61	22.09	14.57
9	3.2	6.1	10.24	37.21	19.52
10	3.5	4.9	12.25	24.01	17.15
11	5.2	10.7	27.04	114.49	55.64
12	4.6	7.6	21.16	57.76	34.96
13	5.8	11.8	33.64	139.24	68.44
14	3.0	4.1	9.00	16.81	12.30
Totals	52.9	92.8	215.41	693.90	382.85

Student Tip
If you use a hand calculator to compute the regression coefficients b_0 and b_1, your calculator results may not exactly match the results computed by Microsoft Excel because of rounding errors caused by the limited number of decimal places that your calculator may use.

Using Equations (13.3) and (13.4), you can compute b_0 and b_1:

$$SSXY = \sum_{i=1}^{n}(X_i - \overline{X})(Y_i - \overline{Y}) = \sum_{i=1}^{n}X_iY_i - \frac{\left(\sum_{i=1}^{n}X_i\right)\left(\sum_{i=1}^{n}Y_i\right)}{n}$$

$$SSXY = 382.85 - \frac{(52.9)(92.8)}{14}$$

$$= 382.85 - 350.65142$$

$$= 32.19858$$

$$SSX = \sum_{i=1}^{n}(X_i - \overline{X})^2 = \sum_{i=1}^{n}X_i^2 - \frac{\left(\sum_{i=1}^{n}X_i\right)^2}{n}$$

$$= 215.41 - \frac{(52.9)^2}{14}$$

$$= 215.41 - 199.88642$$

$$= 15.52358$$

With these values, compute b_1:

$$b_1 = \frac{SSXY}{SSX}$$

$$= \frac{32.19858}{15.52358}$$

$$= 2.07417$$

and:

$$\overline{Y} = \frac{\sum_{i=1}^{n}Y_i}{n} = \frac{92.8}{14} = 6.62857$$

$$\overline{X} = \frac{\sum_{i=1}^{n}X_i}{n} = \frac{52.9}{14} = 3.77857$$

With these values, compute b_0:

$$b_0 = \overline{Y} - b_1\overline{X}$$
$$= 6.62857 - 2.07417(3.77857)$$
$$= -1.2088265$$

VISUAL EXPLORATIONS Exploring Simple Linear Regression Coefficients

Open the **VE-Simple Linear Regression add-in workbook** to explore the coefficients. (See Appendix C to learn how you can download a copy of this workbook and Appendix Section D.5 before using this workbook.) When this workbook opens properly, it adds a **Simple Linear Regression** menu in either the Add-ins tab (Microsoft Windows) or the Apple menu bar (OS X).

To explore the effects of changing the simple linear coefficients, select **Simple Linear Regression → Explore Coefficients**. In the Explore Coefficients floating control panel (shown inset below), click for the spinner buttons for **b_1 slope** (the slope of the prediction line) and **b_0 intercept** (the Y intercept of the prediction line) to change the prediction line. Using the visual feedback of the chart, try to create a prediction line that is as close as possible to the prediction line defined by the least-squares estimates. In other words, try to make the **Difference from Target SSE** value as small as possible. (See page 484 for an explanation of SSE.)

At any time, click **Reset** to reset the b_1 and b_0 values or **Solution** to reveal the prediction line defined by the least-squares method. Click **Finish** when you are finished with this exercise.

Using Your Own Regression Data

Select **Simple Linear Regression using your worksheet data** from the **Simple Linear Regression** menu to explore the simple linear regression coefficients using data you supply from a worksheet. In the procedure's dialog box, enter the cell range of your Y variable as the **Y Variable Cell Range** and the cell range of your X variable as the **X Variable Cell Range**. Click **First cells in both ranges contain a label**, enter a **Title**, and click **OK**. After the scatter plot appears onscreen, continue with the Explore Coefficients floating control panel as described in the left column.

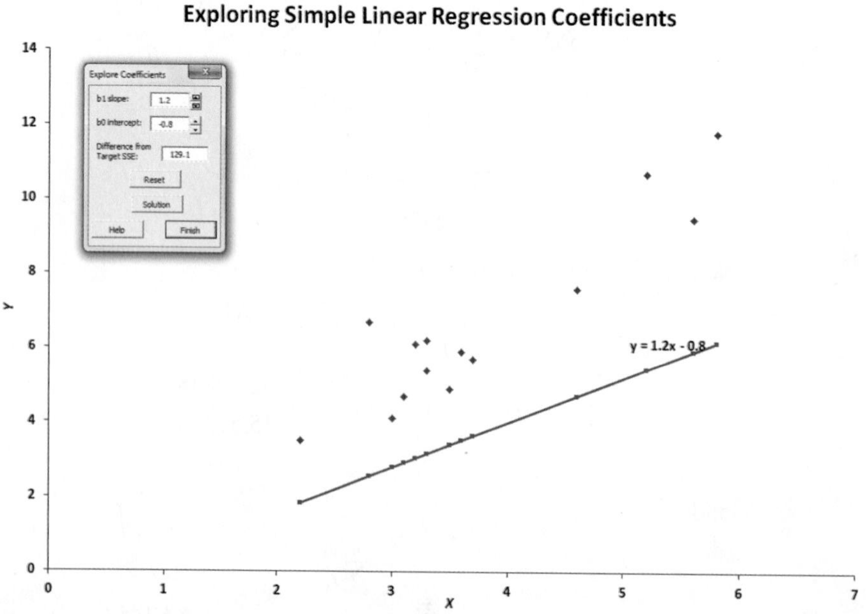

Problems for Section 13.2

LEARNING THE BASICS

13.1 Fitting a straight line to a set of data yields the following prediction line:

$$\hat{Y}_i = 2 + 5X_i$$

a. Interpret the meaning of the Y intercept, b_0.
b. Interpret the meaning of the slope, b_1.
c. Predict the value of Y for $X = 3$.

13.2 If the values of X in Problem 13.1 range from 2 to 25, should you use this model to predict the mean value of Y when X equals
a. 3?
b. −3?
c. 0?
d. 24?

13.3 Fitting a straight line to a set of data yields the following prediction line:

$$\hat{Y}_i = 16 - 0.5X_i$$

a. Interpret the meaning of the Y intercept, b_0.
b. Interpret the meaning of the slope, b_1.
c. Predict the value of Y for $X = 6$.

APPLYING THE CONCEPTS

SELF Test **13.4** The marketing manager of a large supermarket chain has the business objective of using shelf space most efficiently. Toward that goal, she would like to use shelf space to predict the sales of a specialty pet food. Data are collected from a random sample of 12 equal-sized stores, with the following results (stored in **PetFood**):

Store	Shelf Space (X)(square feet)	Weekly Sales (Y)($)
1	5	160
2	5	220
3	5	140
4	10	190
5	10	240
6	10	260
7	15	230
8	15	270
9	15	280
10	20	260
11	20	290
12	20	310

a. Construct a scatter plot.
For these data, $b_0 = 145$ and $b_1 = 7.4$.
b. Interpret the meaning of the slope, b_1, in this problem.
c. Predict the weekly sales of pet food for stores with 8 square feet of shelf space for pet food.

13.5 Zagat's publishes restaurant ratings for various locations in the United States. The file **Restaurants** contains the Zagat rating for food, décor, service, and the cost per person for a sample of 100 restaurants located in New York City and in a suburb of New York City. Develop a regression model to predict the cost per person, based on a variable that represents the sum of the ratings for food, décor, and service.

Sources: Extracted from *Zagat Survey 2012, New York City Restaurants*; and *Zagat Survey 2011–2012, Long Island Restaurants.*

a. Construct a scatter plot.
For these data, $b_0 = -43.1118$ and $b_1 = 1.4689$.
b. Assuming a linear relationship, use the least-squares method to compute the regression coefficients b_0 and b_1.
c. Interpret the meaning of the Y intercept, b_0, and the slope, b_1, in this problem.
d. Predict the cost per person for a restaurant with a summated rating of 50.

13.6 The owner of a moving company typically has his most experienced manager predict the total number of labor hours that will be required to complete an upcoming move. This approach has proved useful in the past, but the owner has the business objective of developing a more accurate method of predicting labor hours. In a preliminary effort to provide a more accurate method, the owner has decided to use the number of cubic feet moved as the independent variable and has collected data for 36 moves in which the origin and destination were within the borough of Manhattan in New York City and in which the travel time was an insignificant portion of the hours worked. The data are stored in **Moving**.
a. Construct a scatter plot.
b. Assuming a linear relationship, use the least-squares method to determine the regression coefficients b_0 and b_1.
c. Interpret the meaning of the slope, b_1, in this problem.
d. Predict the labor hours for moving 500 cubic feet.

13.7 Starbucks Coffee Co. uses a data-based approach to improving the quality and customer satisfaction of its products. When survey data indicated that Starbucks needed to improve its package-sealing process, an experiment was conducted to determine the factors in the bag-sealing equipment that might be affecting the ease of opening the bag without tearing the inner liner of the bag. (Data extracted from L. Johnson and S. Burrows, "For Starbucks, It's in the Bag," *Quality Progress*, March 2011, pp. 17–23.) One factor that could affect the rating of the ability of the bag to resist tears was the plate gap on the bag-sealing equipment. Data were collected on 19 bags in which the plate gap was varied. The results are stored in **Starbucks**.
a. Construct a scatter plot.
b. Assuming a linear relationship, use the least-squares method to determine the regression coefficients b_0 and b_1.
c. Interpret the meaning of the slope, b_1, in this problem.
d. Predict the tear rating when the plate gap is equal to 0.

13.8 The value of a sports franchise is directly related to the amount of revenue that a franchise can generate. The file **BBRevenue2012** represents the value in 2012 (in $millions) and the annual revenue (in $millions) for the 30 Major League Baseball franchises. (Data extracted from **www.forbes.com/mlb-valuations/list**.) Suppose you want to develop a simple linear regression model to predict franchise value based on annual revenue generated.

a. Construct a scatter plot.

b. Use the least-squares method to determine the regression coefficients b_0 and b_1.

c. Interpret the meaning of b_0 and b_1 in this problem.

d. Predict the value of a baseball franchise that generates $150 million of annual revenue.

13.9 An agent for a residential real estate company in a large city has the business objective of developing more accurate estimates of the monthly rental cost for apartments. Toward that goal, the agent would like to use the size of an apartment, as defined by square footage to predict the monthly rental cost. The agent selects a sample of 25 apartments in a particular residential neighborhood and collects the following data (stored in **Rent**):

Size (square feet)	Rent ($)
850	1,950
1,450	2,600
1,085	2,200
1,232	2,500
718	1,950
1,485	2,700
1,136	2,650
726	1,935
700	1,875
956	2,150
1,100	2,400
1,285	2,650
1,985	3,300
1,369	2,800
1,175	2,400
1,225	2,450
1,245	2,100
1,259	2,700
1,150	2,200
896	2,150
1,361	2,600
1,040	2,650
755	2,200
1,000	1,800
1,200	2,750

a. Construct a scatter plot.

b. Use the least-squares method to determine the regression coefficients b_0 and b_1.

c. Interpret the meaning of b_0 and b_1 in this problem.

d. Predict the monthly rent for an apartment that has 1,000 square feet.

e. Why would it not be appropriate to use the model to predict the monthly rent for apartments that have 500 square feet?

f. Your friends Jim and Jennifer are considering signing a lease for an apartment in this residential neighborhood. They are trying to decide between two apartments, one with 1,000 square feet for a monthly rent of $2,275 and the other with 1,200 square feet for a monthly rent of $2,425. Based on (a) through (d), which apartment do you think is a better deal?

13.10 A company that holds the DVD distribution rights to movies previously released only in theaters has the business objective of developing estimates of the sales revenue of DVDs. Toward this goal, a company analyst plans to use box office gross to predict DVD sales revenue. For 22 movies, the analyst collects the box office gross (in $millions) in the year that they were released and the DVD revenue (in $millions) in the following year. These data are stored in **Movie** and shown in the following table:

Title	Gross	DVD Revenue
Tangled	167.82	96.71
The Fighter	46.39	21.49
Social Network	93.22	21.85
Black Swan	47.81	18.40
Eat, Pray, Love	80.57	8.68
Toy Story 3	415.00	23.64
Twilight Saga: Eclipse	300.53	33.71
The King's Speech	22.93	31.57
The Tourist	54.63	16.91
Inception	292.57	32.19
The A Team	77.22	10.99
The Expendables	103.07	10.70
Harry Potter & the Deathly Hallows: Part 1	283.50	85.93
Despicable Me	251.20	49.89
Little Fockers	102.58	20.19
Unstoppable	79.47	27.02
Dinner for Schmucks	73.03	13.44
The Town	92.17	15.17
Letters to Juliet	53.03	7.19
How to Train Your Dragon	217.58	15.76
Salt	118.31	20.65
Tron: Legacy	131.30	24.42

Sources: Data extracted from **www.the-numbers.com/market/movies2010.php** and **www.the-numbers.com/dvd/charts/annual/2011.php**.

For these data,

a. Construct a scatter plot.

b. Assuming a linear relationship, use the least-squares method to determine the regression coefficients b_0 and b_1.

c. Interpret the meaning of the slope, b_1, in this problem.

d. Predict the sales revenue for a movie DVD that had a box office gross of $75 million.

13.3 Measures of Variation

When using the least-squares method to determine the regression coefficients for a set of data, you need to compute three measures of variation. The first measure, the **total sum of squares (*SST*)**, is a measure of variation of the Y_i values around their mean, $\bar{Y}$. The **total variation**, or total sum of squares, is subdivided into **explained variation** and **unexplained variation**. The explained variation, or **regression sum of squares (*SSR*)**, represents variation that is explained by the relationship between *X* and *Y*, and the unexplained variation, or **error sum of squares (*SSE*)**, represents variation due to factors other than the relationship between *X* and *Y*. Figure 13.6 shows the different measures of variation for a single Y_i value.

FIGURE 13.6
Measures of variation

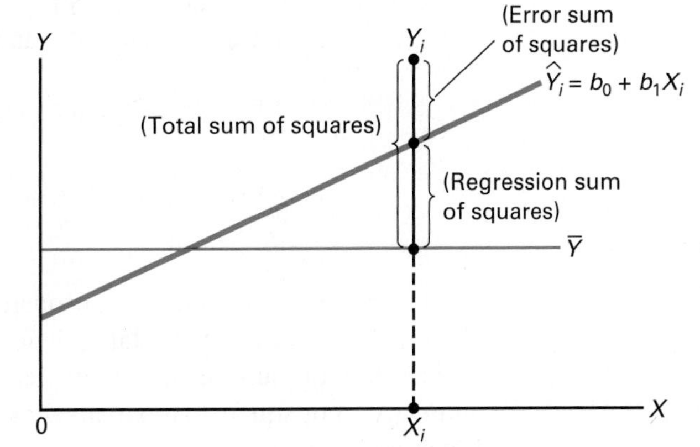

Computing the Sum of Squares

The regression sum of squares (*SSR*) is based on the difference between $\hat{Y}_i$ (the predicted value of *Y* from the prediction line) and $\bar{Y}$ (the mean value of *Y*). The error sum of squares (*SSE*) represents the part of the variation in *Y* that is not explained by the regression. It is based on the difference between Y_i and $\hat{Y}_i$. The total sum of squares (*SST*) is equal to the regression sum of squares (*SSR*) plus the error sum of squares (*SSE*). Equations (13.5), (13.6), (13.7), and (13.8) define these measures of variation and the total sum of squares (*SST*).

MEASURES OF VARIATION IN REGRESSION

The total sum of squares (*SST*) is equal to the regression sum of squares (*SSR*) plus the error sum of squares (*SSE*).

$$SST = SSR + SSE \quad \textbf{(13.5)}$$

TOTAL SUM OF SQUARES (*SST*)

The total sum of squares (*SST*) is equal to the sum of the squared differences between each observed value of *Y* and the mean value of *Y*.

$$SST = \text{Total sum of squares}$$
$$= \sum_{i=1}^{n}(Y_i - \bar{Y})^2 \quad \textbf{(13.6)}$$

REGRESSION SUM OF SQUARES (*SSR*)

The regression sum of squares (*SSR*) is equal to the sum of the squared differences between each predicted value of *Y* and the mean value of *Y*.

$$SSR = \text{Explained variation or regression sum of squares}$$
$$= \sum_{i=1}^{n}(\hat{Y}_i - \overline{Y})^2 \qquad \textbf{(13.7)}$$

ERROR SUM OF SQUARES (*SSE*)

The error sum of squares (*SSE*) is equal to the sum of the squared differences between each observed value of *Y* and the predicted value of *Y*.

$$SSE = \text{Unexplained variation or error sum of squares}$$
$$= \sum_{i=1}^{n}(Y_i - \hat{Y}_i)^2 \qquad \textbf{(13.8)}$$

Figure 13.7 shows the sum of squares portion of the Figure 13.4 results for the Sunflowers Apparel data. The total variation, *SST*, is equal to 78.7686. This amount is subdivided into the sum of squares explained by the regression (*SSR*), equal to 66.7854, and the sum of squares unexplained by the regression (*SSE*), equal to 11.9832. From Equation (13.5) on page 483:

$$SST = SSR + SSE$$
$$78.7686 = 66.7854 + 11.9832$$

FIGURE 13.7
Sum of squares portion for the Sunflowers Apparel data

	A	B	C	D	E	F
10	**ANOVA**					
11		*df*	*SS*	*MS*	*F*	*Significance F*
12	Regression	1	66.7854	66.7854	66.8792	0.0000
13	Residual	12	11.9832	0.9986		
14	Total	13	78.7686			

The Coefficient of Determination

By themselves, *SSR*, *SSE*, and *SST* provide little information. However, the ratio of the regression sum of squares (*SSR*) to the total sum of squares (*SST*) measures the proportion of variation in *Y* that is explained by the independent variable *X* in the regression model. This ratio, called the coefficient of determination, r^2, is defined in Equation (13.9).

COEFFICIENT OF DETERMINATION

The coefficient of determination is equal to the regression sum of squares (i.e., explained variation) divided by the total sum of squares (i.e., total variation).

$$r^2 = \frac{\text{regression sum of squares}}{\text{total sum of squares}} = \frac{SSR}{SST} \qquad \textbf{(13.9)}$$

Student Tip
r^2 must be a value between 0 and 1. It cannot be negative.

The **coefficient of determination** measures the proportion of variation in *Y* that is explained by the variation in the independent variable *X* in the regression model.

For the Sunflowers Apparel data, with $SSR = 66.7854$, $SSE = 11.9832$, and $SST = 78.7686$,

$$r^2 = \frac{66.7854}{78.7686} = 0.8479$$

Therefore, 84.79% of the variation in annual sales is explained by the variability in the number of profiled customers. This large r^2 indicates a strong linear relationship between these two variables because the regression model has explained 84.79% of the variability in predicting annual sales. Only 15.21% of the sample variability in annual sales is due to factors other than what is accounted for by the linear regression model that uses the number of profiled customers.

Figure 13.8 presents the regression statistics table portion of the Figure 13.4 results for the Sunflowers Apparel data. This table contains the coefficient of determination.

FIGURE 13.8
Regression statistics for the Sunflowers Apparel data

	A	B
3	*Regression Statistics*	
4	Multiple R	0.9208
5	R Square	0.8479
6	Adjusted R Square	0.8352
7	Standard Error	0.9993
8	Observations	14

EXAMPLE 13.4

Computing the Coefficient of Determination

Compute the coefficient of determination, r^2, for the Sunflowers Apparel data.

SOLUTION You can compute *SST*, *SSR*, and *SSE*, which are defined in Equations (13.6), (13.7), and (13.8) on pages 483 and 484, by using Equations (13.10), (13.11), and (13.12).

COMPUTATIONAL FORMULA FOR *SST*

$$SST = \sum_{i=1}^{n}(Y_i - \overline{Y})^2 = \sum_{i=1}^{n}Y_i^2 - \frac{\left(\sum_{i=1}^{n}Y_i\right)^2}{n} \tag{13.10}$$

COMPUTATIONAL FORMULA FOR *SSR*

$$SSR = \sum_{i=1}^{n}(\hat{Y}_i - \overline{Y})^2$$

$$= b_0\sum_{i=1}^{n}Y_i + b_1\sum_{i=1}^{n}X_iY_i - \frac{\left(\sum_{i=1}^{n}Y_i\right)^2}{n} \tag{13.11}$$

COMPUTATIONAL FORMULA FOR *SSE*

$$SSE = \sum_{i=1}^{n}(Y_i - \hat{Y}_i)^2 = \sum_{i=1}^{n}Y_i^2 - b_0\sum_{i=1}^{n}Y_i - b_1\sum_{i=1}^{n}X_iY_i \tag{13.12}$$

Using the summary results from Table 13.2 on page 479,

$$SST = \sum_{i=1}^{n}(Y_i - \overline{Y})^2 = \sum_{i=1}^{n}Y_i^2 - \frac{\left(\sum_{i=1}^{n}Y_i\right)^2}{n}$$

$$= 693.9 - \frac{(92.8)^2}{14}$$

$$= 693.9 - 615.13142$$

$$= 78.76858$$

$$SSR = \sum_{i=1}^{n}(\hat{Y}_i - \overline{Y})^2$$

$$= b_0\sum_{i=1}^{n}Y_i + b_1\sum_{i=1}^{n}X_iY_i - \frac{\left(\sum_{i=1}^{n}Y_i\right)^2}{n}$$

$$= (-1.2088265)(92.8) + (2.07417)(382.85) - \frac{(92.8)^2}{14}$$

$$= 66.7854$$

Student Tip

Any slight differences between the calculator solution and the Excel results are due to the limited accuracy of the calculator solution.

$$SSE = \sum_{i=1}^{n}(Y_i - \hat{Y}_i)^2$$

$$= \sum_{i=1}^{n}Y_i^2 - b_0\sum_{i=1}^{n}Y_i - b_1\sum_{i=1}^{n}X_iY_i$$

$$= 693.9 - (-1.2088265)(92.8) - (2.07417)(382.85)$$

$$= 11.9832$$

Therefore,

$$r^2 = \frac{66.7854}{78.7686} = 0.8479$$

Standard Error of the Estimate

Although the least-squares method produces the line that fits the data with the minimum amount of prediction error, unless all the observed data points fall on a straight line, the prediction line is not a perfect predictor. Just as all data values cannot be expected to be exactly equal to their mean, neither can all the values in a regression analysis be expected to fall exactly on the prediction line. Figure 13.5 on page 476 illustrates the variability around the prediction line for the Sunflowers Apparel data. Notice that many of the observed values of Y fall near the prediction line, but none of the values are exactly on the line.

The **standard error of the estimate** measures the variability of the observed Y values from the predicted Y values in the same way that the standard deviation in Chapter 3 measures the variability of each value around the sample mean. In other words, the standard error of the estimate is the standard deviation *around* the prediction line, whereas the standard deviation in Chapter 3 is the standard deviation *around* the sample mean. Equation (13.13) defines the standard error of the estimate, represented by the symbol S_{YX}.

STANDARD ERROR OF THE ESTIMATE

$$S_{YX} = \sqrt{\frac{SSE}{n-2}} = \sqrt{\frac{\sum_{i=1}^{n}(Y_i - \hat{Y}_i)^2}{n-2}} \quad \textbf{(13.13)}$$

where

Y_i = actual value of Y for a given X_i
$\hat{Y}_i$ = predicted value of Y for a given X_i
SSE = error sum of squares

From Equation (13.8) and Figure 13.4 or Figure 13.7 on pages 476 or 484, $SSE = 11.9832$. Thus,

$$S_{YX} = \sqrt{\frac{11.9832}{14-2}} = 0.9993$$

This standard error of the estimate, equal to 0.9993 millions of dollars (i.e., $999,300), is labeled Standard Error in the Figure 13.8 worksheet results. The standard error of the estimate represents a measure of the variation around the prediction line. It is measured in the same units as the dependent variable Y. The interpretation of the standard error of the estimate is similar to that of the standard deviation. Just as the standard deviation measures variability around the mean, the standard error of the estimate measures variability around the prediction line. For Sunflowers Apparel, the typical difference between actual annual sales at a store and the predicted annual sales using the regression equation is approximately $999,300.

Problems for Section 13.3

LEARNING THE BASICS

13.11 How do you interpret a coefficient of determination, r^2, equal to 0.80?

13.12 If $SSR = 36$ and $SSE = 4$, determine SST and then compute the coefficient of determination, r^2, and interpret its meaning.

13.13 If $SSR = 66$ and $SST = 88$, compute the coefficient of determination, r^2, and interpret its meaning.

13.14 If $SSE = 10$ and $SSR = 30$, compute the coefficient of determination, r^2, and interpret its meaning.

13.15 If $SSR = 120$, why is it impossible for SST to equal 110?

APPLYING THE CONCEPTS

SELF Test **13.16** In Problem 13.4 on page 481, the marketing manager used shelf space for pet food to predict weekly sales (stored in Petfood). For those data, $SSR = 20{,}535$ and $SST = 30{,}025$.

a. Determine the coefficient of determination, r^2, and interpret its meaning.
b. Determine the standard error of the estimate.
c. How useful do you think this regression model is for predicting sales?

13.17 In Problem 13.5 on page 481, you used the summated rating to predict the cost of a restaurant meal (stored in Restaurants). For those data, $SSR = 8{,}126.7714$ and $SST = 18{,}810.75$.

a. Determine the coefficient of determination, r^2, and interpret its meaning.
b. Determine the standard error of the estimate.
c. How useful do you think this regression model is for predicting the cost of a restaurant meal?

13.18 In Problem 13.6 on page 481, an owner of a moving company wanted to predict labor hours, based on the cubic feet moved (stored in Moving). Using the results of that problem,

a. determine the coefficient of determination, r^2, and interpret its meaning.
b. determine the standard error of the estimate.
c. How useful do you think this regression model is for predicting labor hours?

13.19 In Problem 13.7 on page 481, you used the plate gap on the bag-sealing equipment to predict the tear rating of a bag of coffee (stored in Starbucks). Using the results of that problem,

a. determine the coefficient of determination, r^2, and interpret its meaning.
b. determine the standard error of the estimate.
c. How useful do you think this regression model is for predicting the tear rating based on the plate gap in the bag-sealing equipment?

13.20 In Problem 13.8 on page 482, you used annual revenues to predict the value of a baseball franchise (stored in BBRevenue2012). Using the results of that problem,

a. determine the coefficient of determination, r^2, and interpret its meaning.
b. determine the standard error of the estimate.
c. How useful do you think this regression model is for predicting the value of a baseball franchise?

13.21 In Problem 13.9 on page 482, an agent for a real estate company wanted to predict the monthly rent for apartments, based on the size of the apartment (stored in Rent). Using the results of that problem,

a. determine the coefficient of determination, r^2, and interpret its meaning.
b. determine the standard error of the estimate.
c. How useful do you think this regression model is for predicting the monthly rent?
d. Can you think of other variables that might explain the variation in monthly rent?

13.22 In Problem 13.10 on page 482, you used box office gross to predict DVD revenue (stored in Movie). Using the results of that problem,

a. determine the coefficient of determination, r^2, and interpret its meaning.
b. determine the standard error of the estimate.
c. How useful do you think this regression model is for predicting DVD revenue?
d. Can you think of other variables that might explain the variation in DVD revenue?

13.4 Assumptions of Regression

When hypothesis testing and the analysis of variance were discussed in Chapters 9 through 12, the importance of the assumptions to the validity of any conclusions reached was emphasized. The assumptions necessary for regression are similar to those of the analysis of variance because both are part of the general category of *linear models* (reference 4).

The four **assumptions of regression** (known by the acronym LINE) are as follows:

- Linearity
- Independence of errors
- Normality of error
- Equal variance

The first assumption, **linearity**, states that the relationship between variables is linear. Relationships between variables that are not linear are discussed in Chapter 15.

The second assumption, **independence of errors**, requires that the errors (ε_i) be independent of one another. This assumption is particularly important when data are collected over a period of time. In such situations, the errors in a specific time period are sometimes correlated with those of the previous time period.

The third assumption, **normality**, requires that the errors (ε_i) be normally distributed at each value of X. Like the t test and the ANOVA F test, regression analysis is fairly robust against departures from the normality assumption. As long as the distribution of the errors at each level of X is not extremely different from a normal distribution, inferences about β_0 and β_1 are not seriously affected.

The fourth assumption, **equal variance**, or **homoscedasticity**, requires that the variance of the errors (ε_i) be constant for all values of X. In other words, the variability of Y values is the same when X is a low value as when X is a high value. The equal-variance assumption is important when making inferences about β_0 and β_1. If there are serious departures from this assumption, you can use either data transformations or weighted least-squares methods (see reference 4).

13.5 Residual Analysis

Sections 13.2 and 13.3 developed a regression model using the least-squares method for the Sunflowers Apparel data. Is this the correct model for these data? Are the assumptions presented in Section 13.4 valid? **Residual analysis** visually evaluates these assumptions and helps you determine whether the regression model that has been selected is appropriate.

The **residual**, or estimated error value, e_i, is the difference between the observed (Y_i) and predicted $(\hat{Y}_i)$ values of the dependent variable for a given value of X_i. A residual appears on a scatter plot as the vertical distance between an observed value of Y and the prediction line. Equation (13.14) defines the residual.

RESIDUAL

The residual is equal to the difference between the observed value of Y and the predicted value of Y.

$$e_i = Y_i - \hat{Y}_i \qquad (13.14)$$

Student Tip
Not seeing any apparent pattern in the residual plot means that when you look at the residual plot, it just looks like a random scattering of points. If there is a pattern, it usually can be seen clearly.

Evaluating the Assumptions

Recall from Section 13.4 that the four assumptions of regression (known by the acronym LINE) are linearity, independence, normality, and equal variance.

Linearity To evaluate linearity, you plot the residuals on the vertical axis against the corresponding X_i values of the independent variable on the horizontal axis. If the linear model is appropriate for the data, you will not see any apparent pattern in the plot. However, if the linear model is not appropriate, in the residual plot, there will be a relationship between the X_i values and the residuals, e_i.

You can see such a pattern in the residuals in Figure 13.9. Panel A shows a situation in which, although there is an increasing trend in Y as X increases, the relationship seems curvilinear because the upward trend decreases for increasing values of X. This quadratic effect is even more apparent in Panel B, where there is a clear relationship between X_i and e_i. By removing the linear trend of X with Y, the residual plot has exposed the lack of fit in the simple linear model more clearly than the scatter plot in Panel A. For these data, a quadratic model (see Section 15.1) is a better fit and should be used instead of the simple linear model.

FIGURE 13.9
Studying the appropriateness of the simple linear regression model

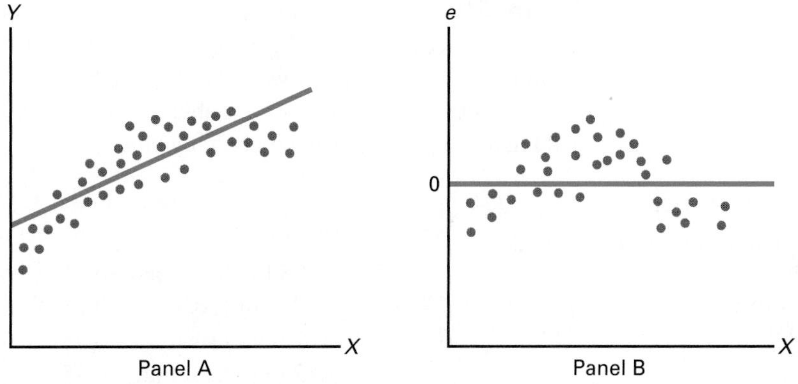

To determine whether the simple linear regression model for the Sunflowers Apparel data is appropriate, you need to determine the residuals. Figure 13.10 displays the predicted annual sales values and residuals for the Sunflowers Apparel data.

FIGURE 13.10
Table of residuals for the Sunflowers Apparel data

Figure 13.10 displays a slightly modified version of the ***RESIDUALS worksheet*** *of the* ***Simple Linear Regression workbook*** *that the Section EG13.5 instructions use. (The Analysis ToolPak adds a similar set of columns to the regression results worksheets.)*

	A	B	C	D	E
1	Observation	Profiled Customers	Predicted Annual Sales	Annual Sales	Residuals
2	1	3.7	6.4656	5.7	-0.7656
3	2	3.6	6.2582	5.9	-0.3582
4	3	2.8	4.5988	6.7	2.1012
5	4	5.6	10.4065	9.5	-0.9065
6	5	3.3	5.6359	5.4	-0.2359
7	6	2.2	3.3543	3.5	0.1457
8	7	3.3	5.6359	6.2	0.5641
9	8	3.1	5.2211	4.7	-0.5211
10	9	3.2	5.4285	6.1	0.6715
11	10	3.5	6.0508	4.9	-1.1508
12	11	5.2	9.5769	10.7	1.1231
13	12	4.6	8.3324	7.6	-0.7324
14	13	5.8	10.8214	11.8	0.9786
15	14	3	5.0137	4.1	-0.9137

To assess linearity, you plot the residuals against the independent variable (number of profiled customers, in millions) in Figure 13.11. Although there is widespread scatter in the residual plot, there is no clear pattern or relationship between the residuals and X_i. The residuals appear to be evenly spread above and below 0 for different values of X. You can conclude that the linear model is appropriate for the Sunflowers Apparel data.

FIGURE 13.11
Plot of residuals against the profiled customers of a store for the Sunflowers Apparel data

Use the Section EG2.5 instructions for constructing scatter plots to construct a plot of residuals.

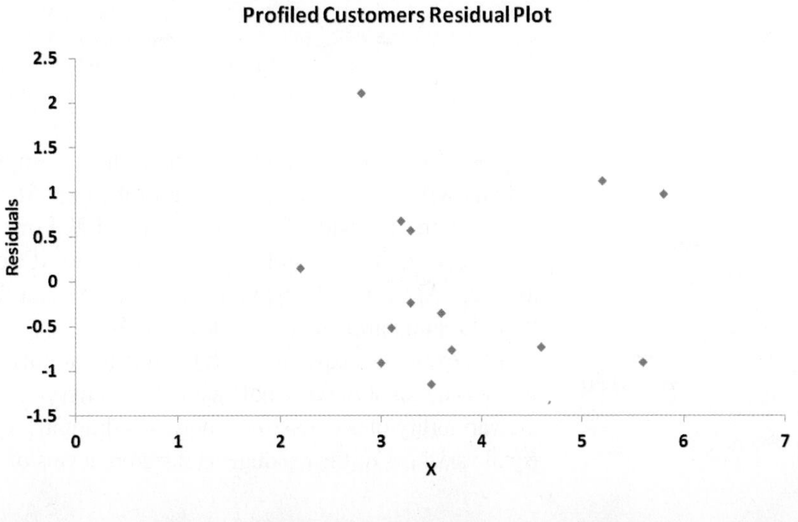

Independence You can evaluate the assumption of independence of the errors by plotting the residuals in the order or sequence in which the data were collected. If the values of Y are part of a time series (see Section 2.5), a residual may sometimes be related to the residual that precedes it. If this relationship exists between consecutive residuals (which violates the assumption of independence), the plot of the residuals versus the time in which the data were collected will often show a cyclical pattern. Because the Sunflowers Apparel data were collected during the same time period, you do not need to evaluate the independence assumption for these data.

Normality You can evaluate the assumption of normality in the errors by constructing a histogram (see Section 2.2), using a stem-and-leaf display (see Section 2.4), a boxplot (see Section 3.3), or a normal probability plot (see Section 6.3). To evaluate the normality assumption for the Sunflowers Apparel data, Table 13.3 organizes the residuals into a frequency distribution and Figure 13.12 is a normal probability plot.

TABLE 13.3
Frequency Distribution of 14 Residual Values for the Sunflowers Apparel Data

Residuals	Frequency
−1.25 but less than −0.75	4
−0.75 but less than −0.25	3
−0.25 but less than +0.25	2
+0.25 but less than +0.75	2
+0.75 but less than +1.25	2
+1.25 but less than +1.75	0
+1.75 but less than +2.25	1
	14

Although the small sample size makes it difficult to evaluate normality, from the normal probability plot of the residuals in Figure 13.12, the data do not appear to depart substantially from a normal distribution. The robustness of regression analysis with modest departures from normality enables you to conclude that you should not be overly concerned about departures from this normality assumption in the Sunflowers Apparel data.

FIGURE 13.12
Normal probability plot of the residuals for the Sunflowers Apparel data

Use the Section EG6.3 instructions to construct normal probability plots.

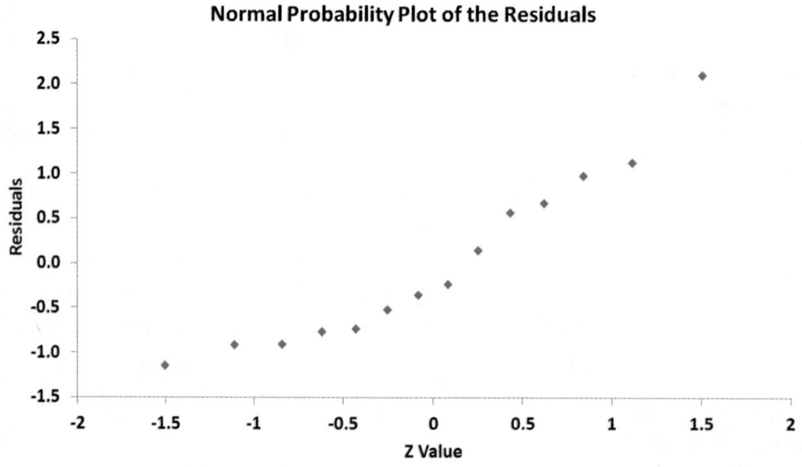

Equal Variance You can evaluate the assumption of equal variance from a plot of the residuals with X_i. You examine the plot to see if there is approximately the same amount of variation in the residuals at each value of X. For the Sunflowers Apparel data of Figure 13.11 on page 489, there do not appear to be major differences in the variability of the residuals for different X_i values. Thus, you can conclude that there is no apparent violation in the assumption of equal variance at each level of X.

To examine a case in which the equal-variance assumption is violated, observe Figure 13.13, which is a plot of the residuals with X_i for a hypothetical set of data. This plot is fan shaped because the variability of the residuals increases dramatically as X increases. Because this plot shows unequal variances of the residuals at different levels of X, the equal-variance assumption is invalid.

LEARN MORE

You can also test the assumption of equal variance by performing the White test (see reference 6). Learn more about this test in a Chapter 13 eBook bonus section.

FIGURE 13.13
Violation of equal variance

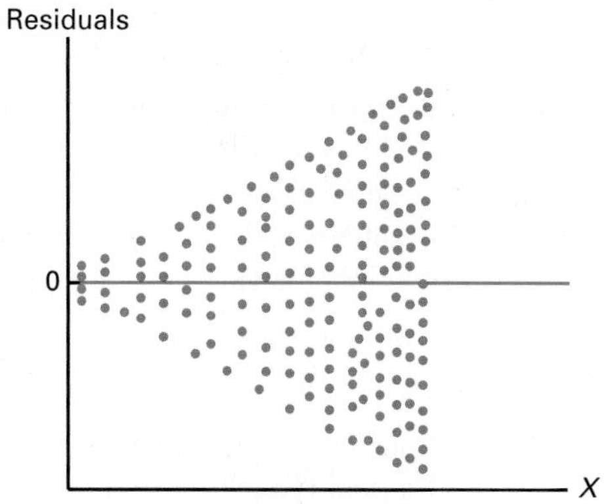

Problems for Section 13.5

LEARNING THE BASICS

13.23 The following results provide the X values, residuals, and a residual plot from a regression analysis:

X	Residuals
1	0.70
2	-0.78
3	1.03
4	0.33
5	2.39
6	-0.67
7	0.16
8	1.65
9	-1.19
10	0.84
11	0.29
12	-1.28
13	1.21
14	-0.37
15	1.02
16	-0.16
17	1.42
18	-0.71
19	-0.63
20	0.67

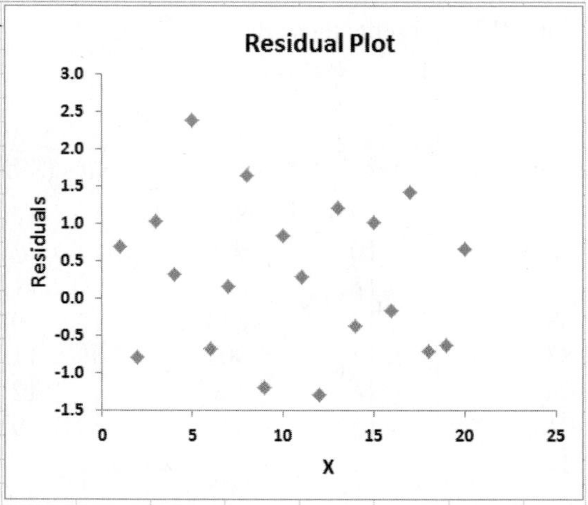

Is there any evidence of a pattern in the residuals? Explain.

13.24 The following results show the X values, residuals, and a residual plot from a regression analysis:

X	Residuals
1	0.70
2	1.58
3	1.03
4	0.33
5	-0.39
6	-0.67
7	-0.56
8	-0.65
9	-1.19
10	-0.84
11	-0.29
12	-1.28
13	-0.21
14	-0.37
15	0.22
16	-0.16
17	0.82

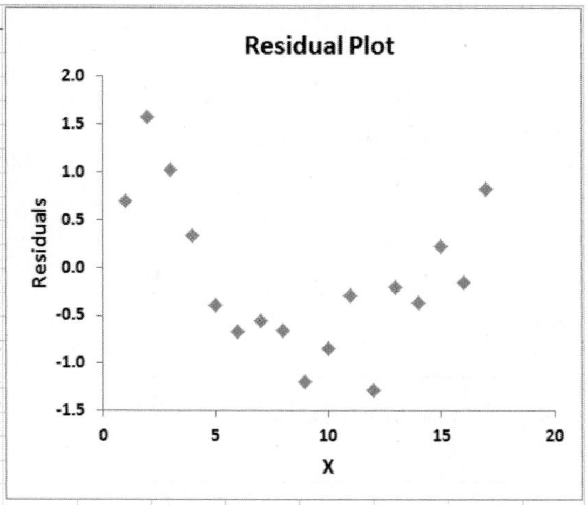

Is there any evidence of a pattern in the residuals? Explain.

APPLYING THE CONCEPTS

13.25 In Problem 13.5 on page 481, you used the summated rating to predict the cost of a restaurant meal. Perform a residual analysis for these data (stored in **Restaurants**). Evaluate whether the assumptions of regression have been seriously violated.

SELF Test **13.26** In Problem 13.4 on page 481, the marketing manager used shelf space for pet food to predict weekly sales. Perform a residual analysis for these data (stored in **Petfood**). Evaluate whether the assumptions of regression have been seriously violated.

13.27 In Problem 13.7 on page 481, you used the plate gap on the bag-sealing equipment to predict the tear rating of a bag of coffee. Perform a residual analysis for these data (stored in **Starbucks**). Based on these results, evaluate whether the assumptions of regression have been seriously violated.

13.28 In Problem 13.6 on page 481, the owner of a moving company wanted to predict labor hours based on the cubic feet moved. Perform a residual analysis for these data (stored in **Moving**). Based on these results, evaluate whether the assumptions of regression have been seriously violated.

13.29 In Problem 13.9 on page 482, an agent for a real estate company wanted to predict the monthly rent for apartments, based on the size of the apartments. Perform a residual analysis for these data (stored in **Rent**). Based on these results, evaluate whether the assumptions of regression have been seriously violated.

13.30 In Problem 13.8 on page 482, you used annual revenues to predict the value of a baseball franchise. Perform a residual analysis for these data (stored in **BBRevenue2012**). Based on these results, evaluate whether the assumptions of regression have been seriously violated.

13.31 In Problem 13.10 on page 482, you used box office gross to predict DVD revenue. Perform a residual analysis for these data (stored in **Movie**). Based on these results, evaluate whether the assumptions of regression have been seriously violated.

13.6 Measuring Autocorrelation: The Durbin-Watson Statistic

One of the basic assumptions of the regression model is the independence of the errors. This assumption is sometimes violated when data are collected over sequential time periods because a residual at any one time period sometimes is similar to residuals at adjacent time periods. This pattern in the residuals is called **autocorrelation**. When a set of data has substantial autocorrelation, the validity of a regression model is in serious doubt.

Residual Plots to Detect Autocorrelation

As mentioned in Section 13.5, one way to detect autocorrelation is to plot the residuals in time order. If a positive autocorrelation effect exists, there will be clusters of residuals with the same sign, and you will readily detect an apparent pattern. If negative autocorrelation exists, residuals will tend to jump back and forth from positive to negative to positive, and so on. Because negative autocorrelation is very rarely seen in regression analysis, the example in this section illustrates positive autocorrelation.

To illustrate positive autocorrelation, consider the case of a package delivery store manager who wants to be able to predict weekly sales. In approaching this problem, the manager has decided to develop a regression model to use the number of customers making purchases as an independent variable. She collects data for a period of 15 weeks and then organizes and stores these data in FifteenWeeks). Table 13.4 presents these data.

TABLE 13.4

Customers and Sales for a Period of 15 Consecutive Weeks

Week	Customers	Sales ($thousands)	Week	Customers	Sales ($thousands)
1	794	9.33	9	880	12.07
2	799	8.26	10	905	12.55
3	837	7.48	11	886	11.92
4	855	9.08	12	843	10.27
5	845	9.83	13	904	11.80
6	844	10.09	14	950	12.15
7	863	11.01	15	841	9.64
8	875	11.49			

Because the data are collected over a period of 15 consecutive weeks at the same store, you need to determine whether there is autocorrelation. First, you can develop the simple linear regression model you can use to predict sales based on the number of customers assuming there is no autocorrelation in the residuals. Figure 13.14 presents results for these data.

FIGURE 13.14

Regression results for the Table 13.4 package delivery store data

	A	B	C	D	E	F	G
1	**Package Delivery Store Sales Analysis**						
2							
3	*Regression Statistics*						
4	Multiple R	0.8108					
5	R Square	0.6574					
6	Adjusted R Square	0.6311					
7	Standard Error	0.9360					
8	Observations	15					
9							
10	**ANOVA**						
11		*df*	*SS*	*MS*	*F*	*Significance F*	
12	Regression	1	21.8604	21.8604	24.9501	0.0002	
13	Residual	13	11.3901	0.8762			
14	Total	14	33.2506				
15							
16		*Coefficients*	*Standard Error*	*t Stat*	*P-value*	*Lower 95%*	*Upper 95%*
17	Intercept	-16.0322	5.3102	-3.0192	0.0099	-27.5041	-4.5603
18	Customers	0.0308	0.0062	4.9950	0.0002	0.0175	0.0441

From Figure 13.14, observe that r^2 is 0.6574, indicating that 65.74% of the variation in sales is explained by variation in the number of customers. In addition, the Y intercept, b_0, is -16.0322 and the slope, b_1, is 0.0308. However, before using this model for prediction, you must perform a residual analysis. Because the data have been collected over a consecutive period of 15 weeks, in addition to checking the linearity, normality, and equal-variance assumptions, you must investigate the independence-of-errors assumption. To do this, you plot the residuals versus time in Figure 13.15 in order to examine whether a pattern in the residuals exists. In Figure 13.15, you can see that the residuals tend to fluctuate up and down in a cyclical pattern. This cyclical pattern provides strong cause for concern about the existence of autocorrelation in the residuals and, therefore, a violation of the independence-of-errors assumption.

FIGURE 13.15
Residual plot for the Table 13.4 package delivery store data

The Durbin-Watson Statistic

The **Durbin-Watson statistic** is used to measure autocorrelation. This statistic measures the correlation between each residual and the residual for the previous time period. Equation (13.15) defines the Durbin-Watson statistic.

DURBIN-WATSON STATISTIC

$$D = \frac{\sum_{i=2}^{n}(e_i - e_{i-1})^2}{\sum_{i=1}^{n} e_i^2} \tag{13.15}$$

where

e_i = residual at the time period i

In Equation (13.15), the numerator, $\sum_{i=2}^{n}(e_i - e_{i-1})^2$, represents the squared difference between two successive residuals, summed from the second value to the nth value and the denominator, $\sum_{i=1}^{n} e_i^2$, represents the sum of the squared residuals. This means that the value of the Durbin-Watson statistic, D, will approach 0 if successive residuals are positively autocorrelated. If the residuals are not correlated, the value of D will be close to 2. (If the residuals are negatively autocorrelated, D will be greater than 2 and could even approach its maximum value of 4.) For the package delivery store data, the Durbin-Watson statistic, D, is 0.8830. (See the Figure 13.16 Excel results.)

FIGURE 13.16

Excel Durbin-Watson statistic worksheet for the package delivery store data

	A	B	
1	Durbin-Watson Statistic		
2			
3	Sum of Squared Difference of Residuals	10.0575	=SUMXMY2(RESIDUALS!E3:E16, RESIDUALS!E2:E15)
4	Sum of Squared Residuals	11.3901	=SUMSQ(RESIDUALS!E2:E16)
5			
6	Durbin-Watson Statistic	0.8830	=B3/B4

Figure 13.16 displays the ***DURBIN_WATSON worksheet*** *of the* ***Package Delivery workbook*** *that the Section EG13.6 instructions use. (The DURBIN_WATSON worksheet is one of the template worksheets of the Simple Linear Regression workbook.)*

You need to determine when the autocorrelation is large enough to conclude that there is significant positive autocorrelation. After computing D, you compare it to the critical values of the Durbin-Watson statistic found in Table E.8, a portion of which is presented in Table 13.5. The critical values depend on α, the significance level chosen, n, the sample size, and k, the number of independent variables in the model (in simple linear regression, $k = 1$).

TABLE 13.5

Finding Critical Values of the Durbin-Watson Statistic

	$\alpha = .05$									
	$k = 1$		$k = 2$		$k = 3$		$k = 4$		$k = 5$	
n	d_L	d_U	d_L	d_U	d_L	d_U	d_L	d_U	d_L	d_U
15	1.08	1.36	.95	1.54	.82	1.75	.69	1.97	.56	2.21
16	1.10	1.37	.98	1.54	.86	1.73	.74	1.93	.62	2.15
17	1.13	1.38	1.02	1.54	.90	1.71	.78	1.90	.67	2.10
18	1.16	1.39	1.05	1.53	.93	1.69	.82	1.87	.71	2.06

In Table 13.5, two values are shown for each combination of α (level of significance), n (sample size), and k (number of independent variables in the model). The first value, d_L, represents the lower critical value. If D is below d_L, you conclude that there is evidence of positive autocorrelation among the residuals. If this occurs, the least-squares method used in this chapter is inappropriate, and you should use alternative methods (see reference 4). The second value, d_U, represents the upper critical value of D, above which you would conclude that there is no evidence of positive autocorrelation among the residuals. If D is between d_L and d_U, you are unable to arrive at a definite conclusion.

For the package delivery store data, with one independent variable ($k = 1$) and 15 values ($n = 15$), $d_L = 1.08$ and $d_U = 1.36$. Because $D = 0.8830 < 1.08$, you conclude that there is positive autocorrelation among the residuals. The least-squares regression analysis of the data shown in Figure 13.14 on page 492 is inappropriate because of the presence of significant positive autocorrelation among the residuals. In other words, the independence-of-errors assumption is invalid. You need to use alternative approaches, discussed in reference 4.

Problems for Section 13.6

LEARNING THE BASICS

13.32 The residuals for 10 consecutive time periods are as follows:

Time Period	Residual	Time Period	Residual
1	−5	6	+1
2	−4	7	+2
3	−3	8	+3
4	−2	9	+4
5	−1	10	+5

a. Plot the residuals over time. What conclusion can you reach about the pattern of the residuals over time?

b. Based on (a), what conclusion can you reach about the autocorrelation of the residuals?

13.33 The residuals for 15 consecutive time periods are as follows:

Time Period	Residual	Time Period	Residual
1	+4	9	+6
2	−6	10	−3
3	−1	11	+1
4	−5	12	+3
5	+2	13	0
6	+5	14	−4
7	−2	15	−7
8	+7		

a. Plot the residuals over time. What conclusion can you reach about the pattern of the residuals over time?
b. Compute the Durbin-Watson statistic. At the 0.05 level of significance, is there evidence of positive autocorrelation among the residuals?
c. Based on (a) and (b), what conclusion can you reach about the autocorrelation of the residuals?

APPLYING THE CONCEPTS

13.34 In Problem 13.4 on page 481 concerning pet food sales, the marketing manager used shelf space for pet food to predict weekly sales.
a. Is it necessary to compute the Durbin-Watson statistic in this case? Explain.
b. Under what circumstances is it necessary to compute the Durbin-Watson statistic before proceeding with the least-squares method of regression analysis?

13.35 What is the relationship between the price of crude oil and the price you pay at the pump for gasoline? The file Oil & Gasoline contains the price ($) for a barrel of crude oil (Cushing, Oklahoma, spot price) and a gallon of gasoline (U.S. average conventional spot price) for 189 weeks, ending August 13, 2012. (Data extracted from Energy Information Administration, U.S. Department of Energy, **www.eia.doe.gov**.)
a. Construct a scatter plot with the price of oil on the horizontal axis and the price of gasoline on the vertical axis.
b. Use the least-squares method to develop a simple linear regression equation to predict the price of a gallon of gasoline using the price of a barrel of crude oil as the independent variable.
c. Interpret the meaning of the slope, b_1, in this problem.
d. Plot the residuals versus the time period.
e. Compute the Durbin-Watson statistic.
f. At the 0.05 level of significance, is there evidence of positive autocorrelation among the residuals?
g. Based on the results of (d) through (f), is there reason to question the validity of the model?

SELF Test **13.36** A mail-order catalog business that sells personal computer supplies, software, and hardware maintains a centralized warehouse for the distribution of products ordered. Management is currently examining the process of distribution from the warehouse and has the business objective of determining the factors that affect warehouse distribution costs. Currently, a handling fee is added to the order, regardless of the amount of the order. Data that indicate the warehouse distribution costs and the number of orders received have been collected over the past 24 months and are stored in Warecost. The results are:

Months	Distribution Cost ($thousands)	Number of Orders
1	52.95	4,015
2	71.66	3,806
3	85.58	5,309
4	63.69	4,262
5	72.81	4,296
6	68.44	4,097
7	52.46	3,213
8	70.77	4,809
9	82.03	5,237
10	74.39	4,732
11	70.84	4,413
12	54.08	2,921
13	62.98	3,977
14	72.30	4,428
15	58.99	3,964
16	79.38	4,582
17	94.44	5,582
18	59.74	3,450
19	90.50	5,079
20	93.24	5,735
21	69.33	4,269
22	53.71	3,708
23	89.18	5,387
24	66.80	4,161

a. Assuming a linear relationship, use the least-squares method to find the regression coefficients b_0 and b_1.
b. Predict the monthly warehouse distribution costs when the number of orders is 4,500.
c. Plot the residuals versus the time period.
d. Compute the Durbin-Watson statistic. At the 0.05 level of significance, is there evidence of positive autocorrelation among the residuals?
e. Based on the results of (c) and (d), is there reason to question the validity of the model?

13.37 A freshly brewed shot of espresso has three distinct components: the heart, body, and crema. The separation of these three components typically lasts only 10 to 20 seconds. To use the espresso shot in making a latte, a cappuccino, or another drink, the shot must be poured into the beverage during the separation of the heart, body, and crema. If the shot is used after the separation occurs, the drink becomes excessively bitter and acidic, ruining the final drink. Thus, a longer separation time allows the drink-maker more time to pour the shot and ensure that the beverage will meet expectations. An employee at a coffee shop hypothesized that the harder the espresso grounds were tamped down into the portafilter before brewing, the longer the separation time would be. An experiment using 24 observations was conducted to test this relationship. The independent variable Tamp measures the distance, in inches, between the espresso grounds and the top of the portafilter (i.e., the harder the tamp, the greater the distance). The dependent variable Time is the number of seconds the heart, body, and crema are separated (i.e., the amount of time after the shot is poured before it must be used for the customer's beverage). The data are stored in **Espresso**.

a. Use the least-squares method to develop a simple regression equation with Time as the dependent variable and Tamp as the independent variable.
b. Predict the separation time for a tamp distance of 0.50 inch.
c. Plot the residuals versus the time order of experimentation. Are there any noticeable patterns?
d. Compute the Durbin-Watson statistic. At the 0.05 level of significance, is there evidence of positive autocorrelation among the residuals?
e. Based on the results of (c) and (d), is there reason to question the validity of the model?

13.38 The owners of a chain of ice cream stores have the business objective of improving the forecast of daily sales so that staffing shortages can be minimized during the summer season. As a starting point, the owners decide to develop a simple linear regression model to predict daily sales based on atmospheric temperature. They select a sample of 21 consecutive days and store the results in **IceCream**. (Hint: Determine which are the independent and dependent variables.)

a. Assuming a linear relationship, use the least-squares method to compute the regression coefficients b_0 and b_1.
b. Predict the sales for a day in which the temperature is 83°F.
c. Plot the residuals versus the time period.
d. Compute the Durbin-Watson statistic. At the 0.05 level of significance, is there evidence of positive autocorrelation among the residuals?
e. Based on the results of (c) and (d), is there reason to question the validity of the model?

13.7 Inferences About the Slope and Correlation Coefficient

In Sections 13.1 through 13.3, regression was used solely for descriptive purposes. You learned how to determine the regression coefficients using the least-squares method and how to predict Y for a given value of X. In addition, you learned how to compute and interpret the standard error of the estimate and the coefficient of determination.

When residual analysis, as discussed in Section 13.5, indicates that the assumptions of a least-squares regression model are not seriously violated and that the straight-line model is appropriate, you can make inferences about the linear relationship between the variables in the population.

t Test for the Slope

To determine the existence of a significant linear relationship between the X and Y variables, you test whether β_1 (the population slope) is equal to 0. The null and alternative hypotheses are as follows:

$$H_0: \beta_1 = 0 \text{ [There is no linear relationship (the slope is zero).]}$$
$$H_1: \beta_1 \neq 0 \text{ [There is a linear relationship (the slope is not zero).]}$$

If you reject the null hypothesis, you conclude that there is evidence of a linear relationship. Equation (13.16) defines the test statistic for the slope.

TESTING A HYPOTHESIS FOR A POPULATION SLOPE, β_1, USING THE *t* TEST

The t_{STAT} test statistic equals the difference between the sample slope and hypothesized value of the population slope divided by the standard error of the slope.

$$t_{STAT} = \frac{b_1 - \beta_1}{S_{b_1}} \quad \textbf{(13.16)}$$

where

$$S_{b_1} = \frac{S_{YX}}{\sqrt{SSX}}$$

$$SSX = \sum_{i=1}^{n}(X_i - \overline{X})^2$$

The t_{STAT} test statistic follows a t distribution with $n - 2$ degrees of freedom.

Return to the Sunflowers Apparel scenario on page 471. To test whether there is a significant linear relationship between the size of the store and the annual sales at the 0.05 level of significance, refer to the t test results shown in Figure 13.17.

FIGURE 13.17
t test results for the slope for the Sunflowers Apparel data

	A	B	C	D	E	F	G	H	I
16		Coefficients	Standard Error	t Stat	P-value	Lower 95%	Upper 95%	Lower 95%	Upper 95%
17	Intercept	-1.2088	0.9949	-1.2151	0.2477	-3.3765	0.9588	-3.3765	0.95881
18	Profiled Customers	2.0742	0.2536	8.1780	0.0000	1.5216	2.6268	1.5216	2.62678

From Figure 13.4 or Figure 13.17,

$$b_1 = +2.0742 \quad n = 14 \quad S_{b_1} = 0.2536$$

and

$$t_{STAT} = \frac{b_1 - \beta_1}{S_{b_1}}$$

$$= \frac{2.0742 - 0}{0.2536} = 8.178$$

Using the 0.05 level of significance, the critical value of t with $n - 2 = 12$ degrees of freedom is 2.1788. Because $t_{STAT} = 8.178 > 2.1788$ or because the p-value is approximately 0, which is less than $\alpha = 0.05$, you reject H_0 (see Figure 13.18). Hence, you can conclude that there is a significant linear relationship between mean annual sales and the number of profiled customers.

FIGURE 13.18
Testing a hypothesis about the population slope at the 0.05 level of significance, with 12 degrees of freedom

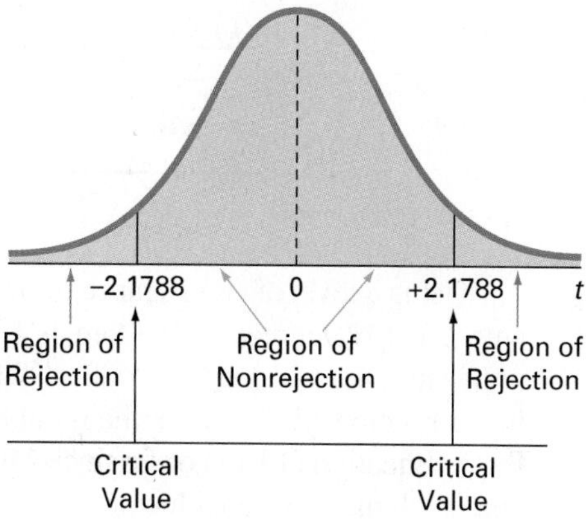

F Test for the Slope

As an alternative to the t test, in simple linear regression, you can use an F test to determine whether the slope is statistically significant. In Section 10.4, you used the F distribution to test the ratio of two variances. Equation (13.17) defines the F test for the slope as the ratio of the variance that is due to the regression (MSR) divided by the error variance ($MSE = S_{YX}^2$).

TESTING A HYPOTHESIS FOR A POPULATION SLOPE, β_1, USING THE F TEST

The F_{STAT} test statistic is equal to the regression mean square (MSR) divided by the mean square error (MSE).

$$F_{STAT} = \frac{MSR}{MSE} \tag{13.17}$$

where

$$MSR = \frac{SSR}{1} = SSR$$

$$MSE = \frac{SSE}{n - 2}$$

The F_{STAT} test statistic follows an F distribution with 1 and $n - 2$ degrees of freedom.

Using a level of significance α, the decision rule is

$$\text{Reject } H_0 \text{ if } F_{STAT} > F_\alpha;$$
$$\text{otherwise, do not reject } H_0.$$

Table 13.6 organizes the complete set of results into an analysis of variance (ANOVA) table.

TABLE 13.6

ANOVA Table for Testing the Significance of a Regression Coefficient

Source	df	Sum of Squares	Mean Square (variance)	F
Regression	1	SSR	$MSR = \frac{SSR}{1} = SSR$	$F_{STAT} = \frac{MSR}{MSE}$
Error	$n - 2$	SSE	$MSE = \frac{SSE}{n-2}$	
Total	$n - 1$	SST		

Figure 13.19, a completed ANOVA table for the Sunflowers sales data (extracted from Figure 13.4), shows that the computed F_{STAT} test statistic is 66.8792 and the p-value is approximately 0.

FIGURE 13.19

F test results for the Sunflowers Apparel data

	A	B	C	D	E	F
10	ANOVA					
11		df	SS	MS	F	Significance F
12	Regression	1	66.7854	66.7854	66.8792	0.0000
13	Residual	12	11.9832	0.9986		
14	Total	13	78.7686			

Using a level of significance of 0.05, from Table E.5, the critical value of the *F* distribution, with 1 and 12 degrees of freedom, is 4.75 (see Figure 13.20). Because $F_{STAT} = 66.8792 > 4.75$ or because the p-value $= 0.0000 < 0.05$, you reject H_0 and conclude that there is a significant linear relationship between the number of profiled customers and annual sales. Because the *F* test in Equation (13.17) on page 497 is equivalent to the *t* test in Equation (13.16) on page 496, you reach the same conclusion.

FIGURE 13.20

Regions of rejection and nonrejection when testing for the significance of the slope at the 0.05 level of significance, with 1 and 12 degrees of freedom

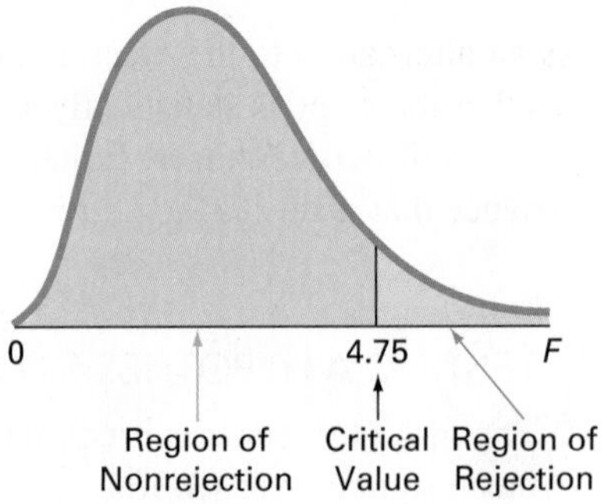

Confidence Interval Estimate for the Slope

As an alternative to testing for the existence of a linear relationship between the variables, you can construct a confidence interval estimate of β_1 using Equation (13.18).

CONFIDENCE INTERVAL ESTIMATE OF THE SLOPE, β_1

The confidence interval estimate for the population slope can be constructed by taking the sample slope, b_1, and adding and subtracting the critical t value multiplied by the standard error of the slope.

$$b_1 \pm t_{\alpha/2}S_{b_1}$$

$$b_1 - t_{\alpha/2}S_{b_1} \le \beta_1 \le b_1 + t_{\alpha/2}S_{b_1} \quad \textbf{(13.18)}$$

where

$t_{\alpha/2}$ = critical value corresponding to an upper-tail probability of $\alpha/2$ from the t distribution with $n - 2$ degrees of freedom (i.e., a cumulative area of $1 - \alpha/2$)

From the Figure 13.17 results on page 497,

$$b_1 = 2.0742 \quad n = 14 \quad S_{b_1} = 0.2536$$

To construct a 95% confidence interval estimate, $\alpha/2 = 0.025$, and from Table E.3, $t_{\alpha/2} = 2.1788$. Thus,

$$b_1 \pm t_{\alpha/2}S_{b_1} = 2.0742 \pm (2.1788)(0.2536)$$
$$= 2.0742 \pm 0.5526$$
$$1.5216 \le \beta_1 \le 2.6268$$

Therefore, you estimate with 95% confidence that the population slope is between 1.5216 and 2.6268. Because both of these values are above 0, you conclude that there is a significant linear relationship between annual sales and the number of profiled customers. Had the interval included 0, you would have concluded that no significant relationship exists between the variables. The confidence interval indicates that for each increase of one million profiled customers, predicted annual sales are estimated to increase by at least \$1,521,600 but no more than \$2,626,800.

t Test for the Correlation Coefficient

In Section 3.5 on page 138, the strength of the relationship between two numerical variables was measured using the **correlation coefficient**, r. The values of the coefficient of correlation range from -1 for a perfect negative correlation to $+1$ for a perfect positive correlation. You can use the correlation coefficient to determine whether there is a statistically significant linear relationship between X and Y. To do so, you hypothesize that the population correlation coefficient, ρ, is 0. Thus, the null and alternative hypotheses are

$$H_0: \rho = 0 \text{ (no correlation)}$$
$$H_1: \rho \ne 0 \text{ (correlation)}$$

Equation (13.19) defines the test statistic for determining the existence of a significant correlation.

TESTING FOR THE EXISTENCE OF CORRELATION

$$t_{STAT} = \frac{r - \rho}{\sqrt{\dfrac{1 - r^2}{n - 2}}} \quad \textbf{(13.19a)}$$

where

$$r = +\sqrt{r^2} \quad \text{if} \quad b_1 > 0$$
$$r = -\sqrt{r^2} \quad \text{if} \quad b_1 < 0$$

The t_{STAT} test statistic follows a t distribution with $n - 2$ degrees of freedom. r is calculated as in Equation (3.17) on page 497:

$$r = \frac{\text{cov}(X, Y)}{S_X S_Y} \qquad \textbf{(13.19b)}$$

where

$$\text{cov}(X, Y) = \frac{\sum_{i=1}^{n}(X_i - \overline{X})(Y_i - \overline{Y})}{n - 1}$$

$$S_X = \sqrt{\frac{\sum_{i=1}^{n}(X_i - \overline{X})^2}{n - 1}}$$

$$S_Y = \sqrt{\frac{\sum_{i=1}^{n}(Y_i - \overline{Y})^2}{n - 1}}$$

In the Sunflowers Apparel problem, $r^2 = 0.8479$ and $b_1 = +2.0742$ (see Figure 13.4 on page 476). Because $b_1 > 0$, the correlation coefficient for annual sales and store size is the positive square root of r^2—that is, $r = +\sqrt{0.8479} = +0.9208$. You use Equation (13.19a) to test the null hypothesis that there is no correlation between these two variables. This results in the following observed t statistic:

$$t_{STAT} = \frac{r - 0}{\sqrt{\frac{1 - r^2}{n - 2}}}$$

$$= \frac{0.9208 - 0}{\sqrt{\frac{1 - (0.9208)^2}{14 - 2}}} = 8.178$$

Using the 0.05 level of significance, because $t_{STAT} = 8.178 > 2.1788$, you reject the null hypothesis. You conclude that there is a significant association between annual sales and the number of profiled customers. This t_{STAT} test statistic is equivalent to the t_{STAT} test statistic found when testing whether the population slope, β_1, is equal to zero.

Problems for Section 13.7

LEARNING THE BASICS

13.39 You are testing the null hypothesis that there is no linear relationship between two variables, X and Y. From your sample of $n = 10$, you determine that $r = 0.80$.

a. What is the value of the t test statistic t_{STAT}?

b. At the $\alpha = 0.05$ level of significance, what are the critical values?

c. Based on your answers to (a) and (b), what statistical decision should you make?

13.40 You are testing the null hypothesis that there is no linear relationship between two variables, X and Y. From your sample of $n = 18$, you determine that $b_1 = +4.5$ and $S_{b_1} = 1.5$.

a. What is the value of t_{STAT}?

b. At the $\alpha = 0.05$ level of significance, what are the critical values?

c. Based on your answers to (a) and (b), what statistical decision should you make?

d. Construct a 95% confidence interval estimate of the population slope, β_1.

13.41 You are testing the null hypothesis that there is no linear relationship between two variables, X and Y. From your sample of $n = 20$, you determine that $SSR = 60$ and $SSE = 40$.

a. What is the value of F_{STAT}?

b. At the $\alpha = 0.05$ level of significance, what is the critical value?

c. Based on your answers to (a) and (b), what statistical decision should you make?

d. Compute the correlation coefficient by first computing r^2 and assuming that b_1 is negative.

e. At the 0.05 level of significance, is there a significant correlation between X and Y?

APPLYING THE CONCEPTS

SELF Test **13.42** In Problem 13.4 on page 481, the marketing manager used shelf space for pet food to predict weekly sales. The data are stored in Petfood. From the results of that problem, $b_1 = 7.4$ and $S_{b_1} = 1.59$.

a. At the 0.05 level of significance, is there evidence of a linear relationship between shelf space and sales?

b. Construct a 95% confidence interval estimate of the population slope, β_1.

13.43 In Problem 13.5 on page 481, you used the summated rating of a restaurant to predict the cost of a meal. The data are stored in Restaurants. Using the results of that problem, $b_1 = 1.4689$ and $S_{b_1} = 0.1701$.

a. At the 0.05 level of significance, is there evidence of a linear relationship between the summated rating of a restaurant and the cost of a meal?

b. Construct a 95% confidence interval estimate of the population slope, β_1.

13.44 In Problem 13.6 on page 481, the owner of a moving company wanted to predict labor hours, based on the number of cubic feet moved. The data are stored in Moving. Use the results of that problem.

a. At the 0.05 level of significance, is there evidence of a linear relationship between the number of cubic feet moved and labor hours?

b. Construct a 95% confidence interval estimate of the population slope, β_1.

13.45 In Problem 13.7 on page 481, you used the plate gap in the bag-sealing equipment to predict the tear rating of a bag of coffee. The data are stored in Starbucks. Use the results of that problem.

a. At the 0.05 level of significance, is there evidence of a linear relationship between the plate gap of the bag-sealing machine and the tear rating of a bag of coffee?

b. Construct a 95% confidence interval estimate of the population slope, β_1.

13.46 In Problem 13.8 on page 482, you used annual revenues to predict the value of a baseball franchise. The data are stored in BBRevenue2012. Use the results of that problem.

a. At the 0.05 level of significance, is there evidence of a linear relationship between annual revenue and franchise value?

b. Construct a 95% confidence interval estimate of the population slope, β_1.

13.47 In Problem 13.9 on page 482, an agent for a real estate company wanted to predict the monthly rent for apartments, based on the size of the apartment. The data are stored in Rent. Use the results of that problem.

a. At the 0.05 level of significance, is there evidence of a linear relationship between the size of the apartment and the monthly rent?

b. Construct a 95% confidence interval estimate of the population slope, β_1.

13.48 In Problem 13.10 on page 482, you used box office gross to predict DVD revenue. The data are stored in Movie. Use the results of that problem.

a. At the 0.05 level of significance, is there evidence of a linear relationship between box office gross and DVD revenue?

b. Construct a 95% confidence interval estimate of the population slope, β_1.

13.49 The volatility of a stock is often measured by its beta value. You can estimate the beta value of a stock by developing a simple linear regression model, using the percentage weekly change in the stock as the dependent variable and the percentage weekly change in a market index as the independent variable. The S&P 500 Index is a common index to use. For example, if you wanted to estimate the beta value for Disney, you could use the following model, which is sometimes referred to as a *market model*:

$$(\%\text{ weekly change in Disney}) = \beta_0 + \beta_1(\%\text{ weekly change in S \& P 500 index}) + \varepsilon$$

The least-squares regression estimate of the slope b_1 is the estimate of the beta value for Disney. A stock with a beta value of 1.0 tends to move the same as the overall market. A stock with a beta value of 1.5 tends to move 50% more than the overall market, and a stock with a beta value of 0.6 tends to move only 60% as much as the overall market. Stocks with negative beta values tend to move in the opposite direction of the overall market. The following table gives some beta values for some widely held stocks as of August 12, 2012:

Company	Ticker Symbol	Beta
Procter & Gamble	PG	0.27
AT&T	T	0.44
Disney	DIS	1.15
Apple	AAPL	0.87
eBay	EBAY	0.97
Ford	F	1.64

Source: Data extracted from finance.yahoo.com, August 12, 2012.

a. For each of the six companies, interpret the beta value.
b. How can investors use the beta value as a guide for investing?

13.50 Index funds are mutual funds that try to mimic the movement of leading indexes, such as the S&P 500 or the Russell 2000. The beta values (as described in Problem 13.49) for these funds are therefore approximately 1.0, and the estimated market models for these funds are approximately

$$(\%\text{ weekly change in index fund}) = 0.0 + 1.0(\%\text{ weekly change in the index})$$

Leveraged index funds are designed to magnify the movement of major indexes. Direxion Funds is a leading provider of leveraged index and other alternative-class mutual fund products for investment advisors and sophisticated investors. Two of the company's funds are shown in the following table:

Name	Ticker Symbol	Description
Daily Small Cap 3x Fund	TNA	300% of the Russell 2000 Index
Daily India Bull 2x Fund	INDL	200% of the Indus India Index

Source: Data extracted from **www.direxionfunds.com**.

The estimated market models for these funds are approximately

$$(\%\text{ weekly change in TNA}) = 0.0 + 3.0(\%\text{ weekly change in the Russell 2000})$$

$$(\%\text{ weekly change in INDL}) = 0.0 + 2.(\%\text{ weekly change in the Indus India Index})$$

Thus, if the Russell 2000 Index gains 10% over a period of time, the leveraged mutual fund TNA gains approximately 30%. On the downside, if the same index loses 20%, TNA loses approximately 60%.

a. The objective of the Direxion Funds Large Cap Bull 3x fund, BGU, is 300% of the performance of the Russell 1000 Index. What is its approximate market model?
b. If the Russell 1000 Index gains 10% in a year, what return do you expect BGU to have?
c. If the Russell 1000 Index loses 20% in a year, what return do you expect BGU to have?
d. What type of investors should be attracted to leveraged index funds? What type of investors should stay away from these funds?

13.51 The file Cereals contains the calories and sugar, in grams, in one serving of seven breakfast cereals:

Cereal	Calories	Sugar
Kellogg's All Bran	80	6
Kellogg's Corn Flakes	100	2
Wheaties	100	4
Nature's Path Organic Multigrain Flakes	110	4
Kellogg's Rice Krispies	130	4
Post Shredded Wheat Vanilla Almond	190	11
Kellogg's Mini Wheats	200	10

a. Compute and interpret the coefficient of correlation, r.
b. At the 0.05 level of significance, is there a significant linear relationship between calories and sugar?

13.52 Movie companies need to predict the gross receipts of an individual movie once the movie has debuted. The following results (stored in **PotterMovies**) are the first weekend gross, the U.S. gross, and the worldwide gross (in $millions) of the eight Harry Potter movies that debuted from 2001 to 2011:

Title	First Weekend	U.S. Gross	Worldwide Gross
Sorcerer's Stone	90.295	317.558	976.458
Chamber of Secrets	88.357	261.988	878.988
Prisoner of Azkaban	93.687	249.539	795.539
Goblet of Fire	102.335	290.013	896.013
Order of the Phoenix	77.108	292.005	938.469
Half-Blood Prince	77.836	301.460	934.601
Deathly Hallows: Part I	125.017	295.001	955.417
Deathly Hallows: Part II	169.189	381.001	1,328.11

Source: Data extracted from **www.the-numbers.com/interactive/comp-Harry-Potter.php**.

a. Compute the coefficient of correlation between first weekend gross and U.S. gross, first weekend gross and worldwide gross, and U.S. gross and worldwide gross.
b. At the 0.05 level of significance, is there a significant linear relationship between first weekend gross and U.S. gross, first weekend gross and worldwide gross, and U.S. gross and worldwide gross?

13.53 College basketball is big business, with coaches' salaries, revenues, and expenses in millions of dollars. The file **College Basketball** contains the coaches' salary and revenue for college basketball at 60 of the 65 schools that played in the 2009 NCAA men's basketball tournament. (Data extracted from "Compensation for Division I Men's Basketball Coaches," *USA Today*, April 2, 2010, p. 8C; and C. Isadore, "Nothing but Net: Basketball Dollars by School," **money.cnn.com/2010/03/18/news/companies/basketball_profits**.)
a. Compute and interpret the coefficient of correlation, r.
b. At the 0.05 level of significance, is there a significant linear relationship between a coach's salary and revenue?

13.54 A survey by the Pew Research Center found that social networking is popular in many nations around the world. The file **GlobalSocialMedia** contains the level of social media networking (measured as the percent of individuals polled who use social networking sites) and the GDP per capita based on purchasing power parity (PPP) for each of 25 selected countries. (Data extracted from "Global Digital Communication: Texting, Social Networking Popular Worldwide," The Pew Research Center, updated February 29, 2012, p.5.)
a. Compute and interpret the coefficient of correlation, r.
b. At the 0.05 level of significance, is there a significant linear relationship between GDP and social media usage?
c. What conclusions can you reach about the relationship between GDP and social media usage?

13.8 Estimation of Mean Values and Prediction of Individual Values

In Chapter 8, you studied the concept of the confidence interval estimate of the population mean. In Example 13.2 on page 477, you used the prediction line to predict the mean value of Y for a given X. The annual sales for stores that had 4 million profiled customers within a fixed radius was predicted to be 7.0879 millions of dollars ($7,087,900). This estimate, however, is a *point estimate* of the population mean. This section presents methods to develop a confidence interval estimate for the mean response for a given X and for developing a prediction interval for an individual response, Y, for a given value of X.

The Confidence Interval Estimate for the Mean Response

Equation (13.20) defines the **confidence interval estimate for the mean response** for a given X.

CONFIDENCE INTERVAL ESTIMATE FOR THE MEAN OF Y

$$\hat{Y}_i \pm t_{\alpha/2} S_{YX} \sqrt{h_i}$$

$$\hat{Y}_i - t_{\alpha/2} S_{YX} \sqrt{h_i} \leq \mu_{Y|X=X_i} \leq \hat{Y}_i + t_{\alpha/2} S_{YX} \sqrt{h_i} \quad \textbf{(13.20)}$$

where

$$h_i = \frac{1}{n} + \frac{(X_i - \overline{X})^2}{SSX}$$

$\hat{Y}_i$ = predicted value of Y; $\hat{Y}_i = b_0 + b_1 X_i$

S_{YX} = standard error of the estimate

n = sample size

X_i = given value of X

$\mu_{Y|X=X_i}$ = mean value of Y when $X = X_i$

$$SSX = \sum_{i=1}^{n} (X_i - \overline{X})^2$$

$t_{\alpha/2}$ = critical value corresponding to an upper-tail probability of $\alpha/2$ from the t distribution with $n - 2$ degrees of freedom (i.e., a cumulative area of $1 - \alpha/2$)

The width of the confidence interval in Equation (13.20) depends on several factors. Increased variation around the prediction line, as measured by the standard error of the estimate, results in a wider interval. As you would expect, increased sample size reduces the width of the interval. In addition, the width of the interval varies at different values of X. When you predict Y for values of X close to $\overline{X}$, the interval is narrower than for predictions for X values farther away from $\overline{X}$.

In the Sunflowers Apparel example, suppose you want to construct a 95% confidence interval estimate of the mean annual sales for the entire population of stores that have 4 million profiled customers $(X = 4)$. Using the simple linear regression equation,

$$\begin{aligned} \hat{Y}_i &= -1.2088 + 2.0742X_i \\ &= -1.2088 + 2.0742(4) = 7.0879 \text{ (millions of dollars)} \end{aligned}$$

Also, given the following:

$$\overline{X} = 3.7786 \quad S_{YX} = 0.9993$$

$$SSX = \sum_{i=1}^{n} (X_i - \overline{X})^2 = 15.5236$$

From Table E.3, $t_{\alpha/2} = 2.1788$. Thus,

$$\hat{Y}_i \pm t_{\alpha/2} S_{YX} \sqrt{h_i}$$

where

$$h_i = \frac{1}{n} + \frac{(X_i - \overline{X})^2}{SSX}$$

so that

$$\hat{Y}_i \pm t_{\alpha/2} S_{YX} \sqrt{\frac{1}{n} + \frac{(X_i - \overline{X})^2}{SSX}}$$

$$= 7.0879 \pm (2.1788)(0.9993)\sqrt{\frac{1}{14} + \frac{(4 - 3.7786)^2}{15.5236}}$$

$$= 7.0879 \pm 0.5946$$

so

$$6.4932 \le \mu_{Y/X=4} \le 7.6825$$

Therefore, the 95% confidence interval estimate is that the mean annual sales are between \$6,493,200 and \$7,682,500 for the population of stores with 4 million profiled customers.

The Prediction Interval for an Individual Response

In addition to constructing a confidence interval for the mean value of Y, you can also construct a prediction interval for an individual value of Y. Although the form of this interval is similar to that of the confidence interval estimate of Equation (13.20), the prediction interval is predicting an individual value, not estimating a mean. Equation (13.21) defines the **prediction interval for an individual response, Y**, at a given value, X_i, denoted by $Y_{X=X_i}$.

PREDICTION INTERVAL FOR AN INDIVIDUAL RESPONSE, Y

$$\hat{Y}_i \pm t_{\alpha/2} S_{YX} \sqrt{1 + h_i} \quad \textbf{(13.21)}$$

$$\hat{Y}_i - t_{\alpha/2} S_{YX} \sqrt{1 + h_i} \le Y_{X=X_i} \le \hat{Y}_i + t_{\alpha/2} S_{YX} \sqrt{1 + h_i}$$

where

$Y_{X=X_i}$ = future value of Y when $X = X_i$

$t_{\alpha/2}$ = critical value corresponding to an upper-tail probability of $\alpha/2$ from the t distribution with $n - 2$ degrees of freedom (i.e., a cumulative area of $1 - \alpha/2$)

In addition, h_i, $\hat{Y}_i$, S_{YX}, n, and X_i are defined as in Equation (13.20) on page 504.

To construct a 95% prediction interval of the annual sales for an individual store that has 4 million profiled customers ($X = 4$), you first compute $\hat{Y}_i$. Using the prediction line:

$$\hat{Y}_i = -1.2088 + 2.0742X_i$$
$$= -1.2088 + 2.0742(4)$$
$$= 7.0879 \text{ (millions of dollars)}$$

Also, given the following:

$$\bar{X} = 3.7786 \quad S_{YX} = 0.9993$$

$$SSX = \sum_{i=1}^{n}(X_i - \bar{X})^2 = 15.5236$$

From Table E.3, $t_{\alpha/2} = 2.1788$. Thus,

$$\hat{Y}_i \pm t_{\alpha/2} S_{YX} \sqrt{1 + h_i}$$

where

$$h_i = \frac{1}{n} + \frac{(X_i - \bar{X})^2}{\sum_{i=1}^{n}(X_i - \bar{X})^2}$$

so that

$$\hat{Y}_i \pm t_{\alpha/2} S_{YX} \sqrt{1 + \frac{1}{n} + \frac{(X_i - \overline{X})^2}{SSX}}$$

$$= 7.0879 \pm (2.1788)(0.9993)\sqrt{1 + \frac{1}{14} + \frac{(4 - 3.7786)^2}{15.5236}}$$

$$= 7.0879 \pm 2.2570$$

so

$$4.8308 \le Y_{X=4} \le 9.3449$$

Therefore, with 95% confidence, you predict that the annual sales for an individual store with 4 million profiled customers is between \$4,830,800 and \$9,344,900.

Figure 13.21 presents results for the confidence interval estimate and the prediction interval for the Sunflowers Apparel data. If you compare the results of the confidence interval estimate and the prediction interval, you see that the width of the prediction interval for an individual store is much wider than the confidence interval estimate for the mean. Remember that there is much more variation in predicting an individual value than in estimating a mean value.

FIGURE 13.21

Confidence interval estimate and prediction interval worksheet for the Sunflowers Apparel data

	A	B	
1	Confidence Interval Estimate and Prediction Interval		
2			
3	Data		
4	X Value	4	
5	Confidence Level	95%	
6			
7	Intermediate Calculations		
8	Sample Size	14	=COUNT(SLRData!A:A)
9	Degrees of Freedom	12	=B8 - 2
10	t Value	2.1788	=T.INV.2T(1 - B5, B9)
11	Sample Mean	3.7786	=AVERAGE(SLRData!A:A)
12	Sum of Squared Difference	15.5236	=DEVSQ(SLRData!A:A)
13	Standard Error of the Estimate	0.9993	=COMPUTE!B7
14	h Statistic	0.0746	=1/B8 + (B4 - B11)^2/B12
15	Predicted Y (YHat)	7.0879	=TREND(SLRData!B2:B15, SLRData!A2:A15, B4)
16			
17	For Average Y		
18	Interval Half Width	0.5946	=B10 * B13 * SQRT(B14)
19	Confidence Interval Lower Limit	6.4932	=B15 - B18
20	Confidence Interval Upper Limit	7.6825	=B15 + B18
21			
22	For Individual Response Y		
23	Interval Half Width	2.2570	=B10 * B13 * SQRT(1 + B14)
24	Prediction Interval Lower Limit	4.8308	=B15 - B23
25	Prediction Interval Upper Limit	9.3449	=B15 + B23

*Figure 13.21 displays the **CIEandPI worksheet** of the **Simple Linear Regression workbook** that the Section EG13.8 instructions use.*

Problems for Section 13.8

LEARNING THE BASICS

13.55 Based on a sample of $n = 20$, the least-squares method was used to develop the following prediction line: $\hat{Y}_i = 5 + 3X_i$. In addition,

$$S_{YX} = 1.0 \quad \overline{X} = 2 \quad \sum_{i=1}^{n}(X_i - \overline{X})^2 = 20$$

a. Construct a 95% confidence interval estimate of the population mean response for $X = 2$.

b. Construct a 95% prediction interval of an individual response for $X = 2$.

13.56 Based on a sample of $n = 20$, the least-squares method was used to develop the following prediction line: $\hat{Y}_i = 5 + 3X_i$. In addition,

$$S_{YX} = 1.0 \quad \overline{X} = 2 \quad \sum_{i=1}^{n}(X_i - \overline{X})^2 = 20$$

a. Construct a 95% confidence interval estimate of the population mean response for $X = 4$.

b. Construct a 95% prediction interval of an individual response for $X = 4$.

c. Compare the results of (a) and (b) with those of Problem 13.55 (a) and (b). Which intervals are wider? Why?

APPLYING THE CONCEPTS

13.57 In Problem 13.5 on page 481, you used the summated rating of a restaurant to predict the cost of a meal. The data are stored in **Restaurants**. For these data, $S_{YX} = 10.4413$ and $h_i = 0.046904$ when $X = 50$.

a. Construct a 95% confidence interval estimate of the mean cost of a meal for restaurants that have a summated rating of 50.

b. Construct a 95% prediction interval of the cost of a meal for an individual restaurant that has a summated rating of 50.

c. Explain the difference in the results in (a) and (b).

SELF Test **13.58** In Problem 13.4 on page 481, the marketing manager used shelf space for pet food to predict weekly sales. The data are stored in **Petfood**. For these data, $S_{YX} = 30.81$ and $h_i = 0.1373$ when $X = 8$.

a. Construct a 95% confidence interval estimate of the mean weekly sales for all stores that have 8 square feet of shelf space for pet food.

b. Construct a 95% prediction interval of the weekly sales of an individual store that has 8 square feet of shelf space for pet food.

c. Explain the difference in the results in (a) and (b).

13.59 In Problem 13.7 on page 481, you used the plate gap on the bag-sealing equipment to predict the tear rating of a bag of coffee. The data are stored in **Starbucks**.

a. Construct a 95% confidence interval estimate of the mean tear rating for all bags of coffee when the plate gap is 0.

b. Construct a 95% prediction interval of the tear rating for an individual bag of coffee when the plate gap is 0.

c. Why is the interval in (a) narrower than the interval in (b)?

13.60 In Problem 13.6 on page 481, the owner of a moving company wanted to predict labor hours based on the number of cubic feet moved. The data are stored in **Moving**.

a. Construct a 95% confidence interval estimate of the mean labor hours for all moves of 500 cubic feet.

b. Construct a 95% prediction interval of the labor hours of an individual move that has 500 cubic feet.

c. Why is the interval in (a) narrower than the interval in (b)?

13.61 In Problem 13.9 on page 482, an agent for a real estate company wanted to predict the monthly rent for apartments, based on the size of an apartment. The data are stored in **Rent**.

a. Construct a 95% confidence interval estimate of the mean monthly rental for all apartments that are 1,000 square feet in size.

b. Construct a 95% prediction interval of the monthly rental for an individual apartment that is 1,000 square feet in size.

c. Explain the difference in the results in (a) and (b).

13.62 In Problem 13.8 on page 482, you predicted the value of a baseball franchise, based on current revenue. The data are stored in **BBRevenue2012**.

a. Construct a 95% confidence interval estimate of the mean value of all baseball franchises that generate $150 million of annual revenue.

b. Construct a 95% prediction interval of the value of an individual baseball franchise that generates $150 million of annual revenue.

c. Explain the difference in the results in (a) and (b).

13.63 In Problem 13.10 on page 482, you used box office gross to predict DVD revenue. The data are stored in **Movie**. The company is about to release a movie on DVD that had a box office gross of $75 million.

a. What is the predicted DVD revenue?

b. Which interval is more useful here, the confidence interval estimate of the mean or the prediction interval for an individual response? Explain.

c. Construct and interpret the interval you selected in (b).

13.9 Pitfalls in Regression

Some of the pitfalls involved in using regression analysis are as follows:

- Lacking awareness of the assumptions of least-squares regression
- Not knowing how to evaluate the assumptions of least-squares regression
- Not knowing what the alternatives are to least-squares regression if a particular assumption is violated
- Using a regression model without knowledge of the subject matter
- Extrapolating outside the relevant range
- Concluding that a significant relationship identified in an observational study is due to a cause-and-effect relationship

The widespread availability of spreadsheet and statistical applications has made regression analysis much more feasible today than it once was. However, many users who have access to such applications do not understand how to use regression analysis properly. Someone who is not familiar with either the assumptions of regression or how to evaluate the assumptions cannot be expected to know what the alternatives to least-squares regression are if a particular assumption is violated.

The data in Table 13.7 (stored in **Anscombe**) illustrate the importance of using scatter plots and residual analysis to go beyond the basic number crunching of computing the Y intercept, the slope, and r^2.

TABLE 13.7

Four Sets of Artificial Data

Data Set A		Data Set B		Data Set C		Data Set D	
X_i	Y_i	X_i	Y_i	X_i	Y_i	X_i	Y_i
10	8.04	10	9.14	10	7.46	8	6.58
14	9.96	14	8.10	14	8.84	8	5.76
5	5.68	5	4.74	5	5.73	8	7.71
8	6.95	8	8.14	8	6.77	8	8.84
9	8.81	9	8.77	9	7.11	8	8.47
12	10.84	12	9.13	12	8.15	8	7.04
4	4.26	4	3.10	4	5.39	8	5.25
7	4.82	7	7.26	7	6.42	19	12.50
11	8.33	11	9.26	11	7.81	8	5.56
13	7.58	13	8.74	13	12.74	8	7.91
6	7.24	6	6.13	6	6.08	8	6.89

Source: Data extracted from F. J. Anscombe, "Graphs in Statistical Analysis," *The American Statistician*, 27 (1973), 17–21.

Anscombe (reference 1) showed that all four data sets given in Table 13.7 have the following identical results:

$$\hat{Y}_i = 3.0 + 0.5X_i$$
$$S_{YX} = 1.237$$
$$S_{b_1} = 0.118$$
$$r^2 = 0.667$$

$$SSR = \text{Explained variation} = \sum_{i=1}^{n}(\hat{Y}_i - \overline{Y})^2 = 27.51$$

$$SSE = \text{Unexplained variation} = \sum_{i=1}^{n}(Y_i - \hat{Y}_i)^2 = 13.76$$

$$SST = \text{Total variation} = \sum_{i=1}^{n}(Y_i - \overline{Y})^2 = 41.27$$

If you stopped the analysis at this point, you would fail to observe the important differences among the four data sets that scatter plots and residual plots can reveal.

From the scatter plots and the residual plots of Figure 13.22 on page 509, you see how different the data sets are. Each has a different relationship between X and Y. The only data set that seems to approximately follow a straight line is data set A. The residual plot for data set A does not show any obvious patterns or outlying residuals. This is certainly not true for data sets B, C, and D. The scatter plot for data set B shows that a curvilinear regression model is more appropriate. This conclusion is reinforced by the residual plot for data set B. The scatter plot and the residual plot for data set C clearly show an outlying observation. In this case, one approach used is to remove the outlier and reestimate the regression model (see reference 4).

The scatter plot for data set D represents a situation in which the model is heavily dependent on the outcome of a single data point ($X_8 = 19$ and $Y_8 = 12.50$). Any regression model with this characteristic should be used with caution.

FIGURE 13.22 Scatter plots and residual plots for four data sets

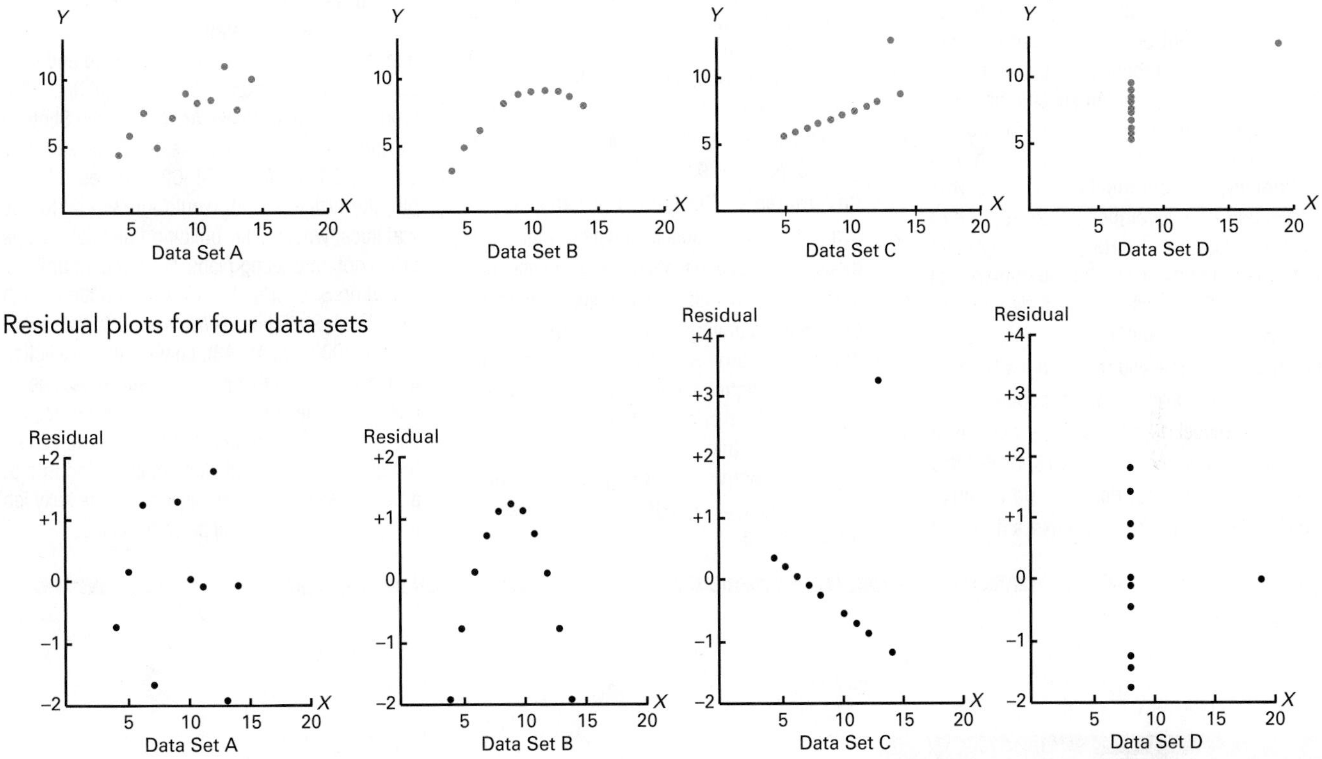

Strategy for Avoiding the Pitfalls

Scatter plots and residual plots play an important role in helping you to avoid the pitfalls of regression. They form part of a strategy that you can use every time you undertake a regression analysis. The complete strategy to avoid the pitfalls of regression is as follows:

1. Construct a scatter plot to observe the possible relationship between X and Y.
2. Check the assumptions of regression (linearity, independence, normality, equal variance) by performing a residual analysis that includes the following:
   a. Plot the residuals versus the independent variable to determine whether the linear model is appropriate and to check for equal variance.
   b. Construct a histogram, stem-and-leaf display, boxplot, or normal probability plot of the residuals to check for normality.
   c. Plot the residuals versus time to check for independence. (This step is necessary only if the data are collected over time.)
3. If there are violations of the assumptions, use alternative methods to least-squares regression or alternative least-squares models (see reference 4).
4. If there are no violations of the assumptions, carry out tests for the significance of the regression coefficients and develop confidence and prediction intervals.
5. Refrain from making predictions and forecasts outside the relevant range of the independent variable.
6. Remember that the relationships identified in observational studies may or may not be due to cause-and-effect relationships. And while causation implies correlation, correlation does not imply causation.

THINK ABOUT THIS By Any Other Name

You may not have frequently heard the phrase "regression model" outside a classroom, but the basic concepts of regression can be found under a variety of names in many sectors of the economy:

- **Advertising and marketing**—Managers use econometric models (in other words, regression models) to determine the effect of an advertisement on sales, based on a set of factors. In one recent example, the number of tweets that mention specific products was used to make accurate prediction of sales trends. (See H. Rui, A. Whinston, and E. Winkler, "Follow the Tweets," *The Wall Street Journal*, November 30, 2009, p. R4.) Also, managers use data mining to predict patterns of behavior of what customers will buy in the future, based on historic information about the consumer.
- **Finance**—Any time you read about a financial "model," you should assume that some type of regression model is being used. For example, a *New York Times* article on June 18, 2006, titled "An Old Formula That Points to New Worry" by Mark Hulbert (p. BU8), discusses a market timing model that predicts the returns of stocks in the next three to five years, based on the dividend yield of the stock market and the interest rate of 90-day Treasury bills.
- **Food and beverage**—Enologix, a California consulting company, has developed a "formula" (a regression model) that predicts a wine's quality index, based on a set of chemical compounds found in the wine. (See D. Darlington, "The Chemistry of a 90+ Wine," *The New York Times Magazine*, August 7, 2005, pp. 36–39.)
- **Government**—The Bureau of Labor Statistics uses hedonic models, a type of regression model, to adjust and manage its consumer price index. (See "Hedonic Quality Adjustment in the CPI," **stat.bls.gov/cpi/cpihqaitem.htm.**).
- **Transportation**—Bing Travel uses data mining and predictive technologies to objectively predict airfare pricing. (See "Bing Travel's Crean: 'We save the average couple $50 per trip,'" **www.elliott.org/first-person/bing-travel-we-save-the-average-couple-50-per-trip/.**)
- **Real estate**—Zillow.com uses information about the features contained in a home and its location to develop estimates about the market value of the home, using a "formula" built with a proprietary model.

In a famous 2006 cover story, *BusinessWeek* predicted that statistics and probability will become core skills for businesspeople and consumers. (See S. Baker, "Why Math Will Rock Your World: More Math Geeks Are Calling the Shots in Business. Is Your Industry Next?" *BusinessWeek*, January 23, 2006, pp. 54–62.) Successful people, the article noted, would know how to use statistics, whether for building financial models or making marketing plans. More recent articles, including S. Lohr's "For Today's Graduate, Just One Word: Statistics" (*The New York Times*, August 6, 2009, pp. A1, A3), confirm this prediction and discuss such things as how statistics is being used to "mine" large data sets to discover patterns, often using regression models. Hal Varian, the chief economist at Google, is quoted in that article as saying, "I keep saying that the sexy job in the next ten years will be statisticians."

USING STATISTICS Knowing Customers at Sunflowers Apparel, Revisited

Dmitriy Shironosov / Shutterstock

In the Knowing Customers at Sunflowers Apparel scenario, you were the director of planning for a chain of upscale clothing stores for women. Until now, Sunflowers managers selected sites based on factors such as the availability of a good lease or a subjective opinion that a location seemed like a good place for a store. To make more objective decisions, you used the more systematic DCOVA approach to identify and classify groups of consumers and developed a regression model to analyze the relationship between the number of profiled customers that live within a fixed radius of a Sunflowers store and the annual sales of the store. The model indicated that about 84.8% of the variation in sales was explained by the number of profiled customers that live within a fixed radius of a Sunflowers store. Furthermore, for each increase of one million profiled customers, mean annual sales were estimated to increase by $2.0742 million. You can now use your model to help make better decisions when selecting new sites for stores as well as to forecast sales for existing stores.

SUMMARY

As you can see from the chapter roadmap in Figure 13.23, this chapter develops the simple linear regression model and discusses the assumptions and how to evaluate them. Once you are assured that the model is appropriate, you can predict values by using the prediction line and test for the significance of the slope. In Chapters 14 and 15, regression analysis is extended to situations in which more than one independent variable is used to predict the value of a dependent variable.

FIGURE 13.23
Roadmap for simple linear regression

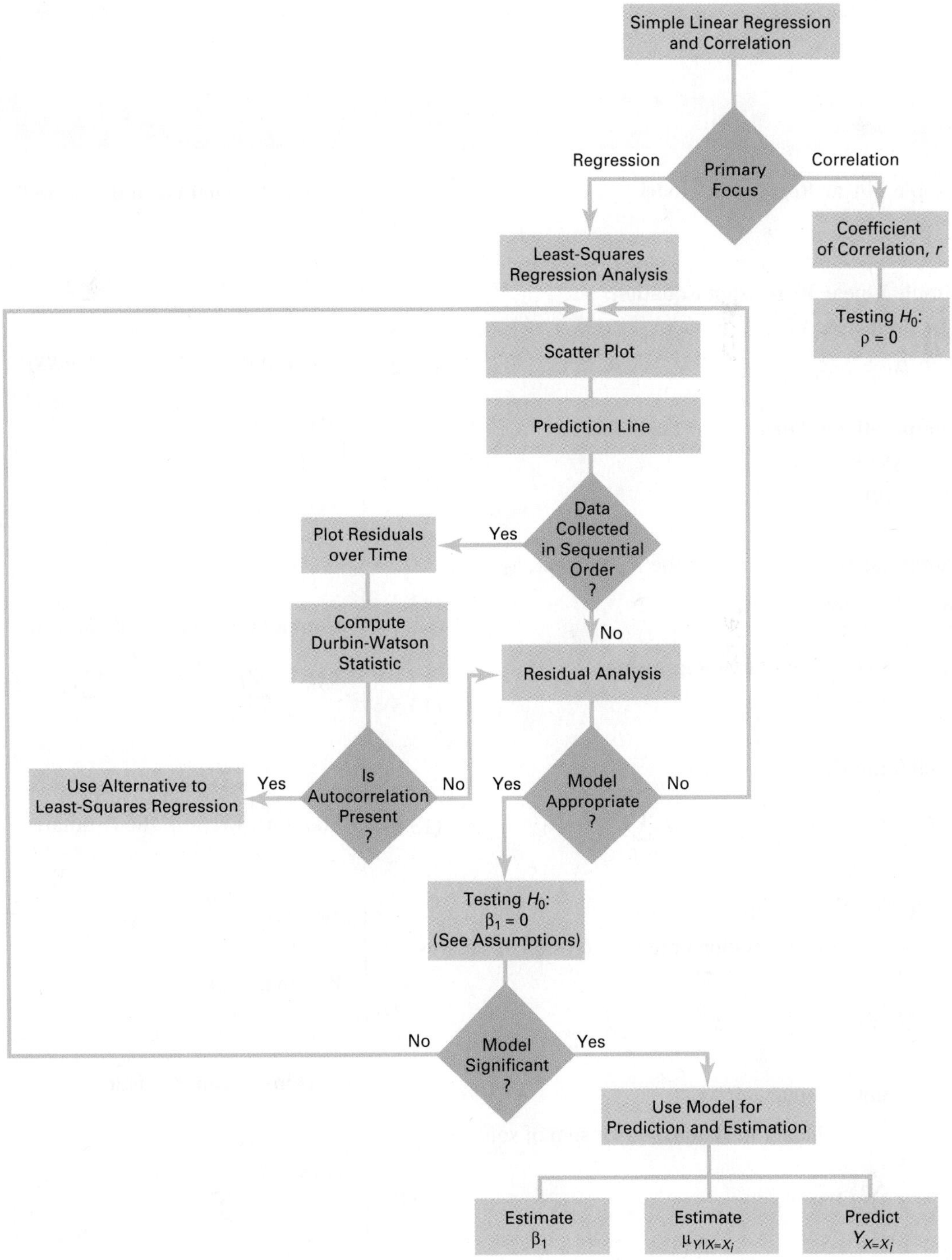

REFERENCES

1. Anscombe, F. J. "Graphs in Statistical Analysis." *The American Statistician*, 27(1973): 17–21.
2. Hoaglin, D. C., and R. Welsch. "The Hat Matrix in Regression and ANOVA." *The American Statistician*, 32(1978): 17–22.
3. Hocking, R. R. "Developments in Linear Regression Methodology: 1959–1982." *Technometrics*, 25(1983): 219–250.
4. Kutner, M. H., C. J. Nachtsheim, J. Neter, and W. Li. *Applied Linear Statistical Models*, 5th ed. New York: McGraw-Hill/Irwin, 2005.
5. *Microsoft Excel 2010*. Redmond, WA: Microsoft Corp., 2010.
6. White, H. "A Heteroscedasticity-Consistent Covariance Matrix Estimator and a Direct Test for Heteroscedasticity." *Econometrica*, 48(1980): 817–838.

KEY EQUATIONS

Simple Linear Regression Model

$$Y_i = \beta_0 + \beta_1 X_i + \varepsilon_i \quad (13.1)$$

Simple Linear Regression Equation: The Prediction Line

$$\hat{Y}_i = b_0 + b_1 X_i \quad (13.2)$$

Computational Formula for the Slope, b_1

$$b_1 = \frac{SSXY}{SSX} \quad (13.3)$$

Computational Formula for the Y Intercept, b_0

$$b_0 = \overline{Y} - b_1\overline{X} \quad (13.4)$$

Measures of Variation in Regression

$$SST = SSR + SSE \quad (13.5)$$

Total Sum of Squares (SST)

$$SST = \text{Total sum of squares} = \sum_{i=1}^{n}(Y_i - \overline{Y})^2 \quad (13.6)$$

Regression Sum of Squares (SSR)

$$SSR = \text{Explained variation or regression sum of squares}$$

$$= \sum_{i=1}^{n}(\hat{Y}_i - \overline{Y})^2 \quad (13.7)$$

Error Sum of Squares (SSE)

$$SSE = \text{Unexplained variation or error sum of squares}$$

$$= \sum_{i=1}^{n}(Y_i - \hat{Y}_i)^2 \quad (13.8)$$

Coefficient of Determination

$$r^2 = \frac{\text{Regression sum of squares}}{\text{Total sum of squares}} = \frac{SSR}{SST} \quad (13.9)$$

Computational Formula for SST

$$SST = \sum_{i=1}^{n}(Y_i - \overline{Y})^2 = \sum_{i=1}^{n}Y_i^2 - \frac{\left(\sum_{i=1}^{n}Y_i\right)^2}{n} \quad (13.10)$$

Computational Formula for SSR

$$SSR = \sum_{i=1}^{n}(\hat{Y}_i - \overline{Y})^2$$

$$= b_0\sum_{i=1}^{n}Y_i + b_1\sum_{i=1}^{n}X_iY_i - \frac{\left(\sum_{i=1}^{n}Y_i\right)^2}{n} \quad (13.11)$$

Computational Formula for SSE

$$SSE = \sum_{i=1}^{n}(Y_i - \hat{Y}_i)^2 = \sum_{i=1}^{n}Y_i^2 - b_0\sum_{i=1}^{n}Y_i - b_1\sum_{i=1}^{n}X_iY_i \quad (13.12)$$

Standard Error of the Estimate

$$S_{YX} = \sqrt{\frac{SSE}{n-2}} = \sqrt{\frac{\sum_{i=1}^{n}(Y_i - \hat{Y}_i)^2}{n-2}} \quad (13.13)$$

Residual

$$e_i = Y_i - \hat{Y}_i \quad (13.14)$$

Durbin-Watson Statistic

$$D = \frac{\sum_{i=2}^{n}(e_i - e_{i-1})^2}{\sum_{i=1}^{n}e_i^2} \quad (13.15)$$

Testing a Hypothesis for a Population Slope, β_1, Using the *t* Test

$$t_{STAT} = \frac{b_1 - \beta_1}{S_{b_1}} \quad (13.16)$$

Testing a Hypothesis for a Population Slope, β_1, Using the *F* Test

$$F_{STAT} = \frac{MSR}{MSE} \quad (13.17)$$

Confidence Interval Estimate of the Slope, β_1

$$b_1 \pm t_{\alpha/2} S_{b_1}$$

$$b_1 - t_{\alpha/2} S_{b_1} \le \beta_1 \le b_1 + t_{\alpha/2} S_{b_1} \quad (13.18)$$

Testing for the Existence of Correlation

$$t_{STAT} = \frac{r - \rho}{\sqrt{\dfrac{1 - r^2}{n - 2}}} \quad (13.19a)$$

$$r = \frac{\text{cov}(X, Y)}{S_X S_Y} \quad (13.19b)$$

Confidence Interval Estimate for the Mean of *Y*

$$\hat{Y}_i \pm t_{\alpha/2} S_{YX} \sqrt{h_i}$$

$$\hat{Y}_i - t_{\alpha/2} S_{YX} \sqrt{h_i} \le \mu_{Y|X=X_i} \le \hat{Y}_i + t_{\alpha/2} S_{YX} \sqrt{h_i} \quad (13.20)$$

Prediction Interval for an Individual Response, *Y*

$$\hat{Y}_i \pm t_{\alpha/2} S_{YX} \sqrt{1 + h_i}$$

$$\hat{Y}_i - t_{\alpha/2} S_{YX} \sqrt{1 + h_i} \le Y_{X=X_i} \le \hat{Y}_i + t_{\alpha/2} S_{YX} \sqrt{1 + h_i} \quad (13.21)$$

KEY TERMS

CHECKING YOUR UNDERSTANDING

13.64 What is the interpretation of the *Y* intercept and the slope in the simple linear regression equation?

13.65 What is the interpretation of the coefficient of determination?

13.66 When is the unexplained variation (i.e., error sum of squares) equal to 0?

13.67 When is the explained variation (i.e., regression sum of squares) equal to 0?

13.68 Why should you always carry out a residual analysis as part of a regression model?

13.69 What are the assumptions of regression analysis?

13.70 How do you evaluate the assumptions of regression analysis?

13.71 When and how do you use the Durbin-Watson statistic?

13.72 What is the difference between a confidence interval estimate of the mean response, $\mu_{Y|X=X_i}$, and a prediction interval of $Y_{X=X_i}$?

CHAPTER REVIEW PROBLEMS

13.73 Can you use Twitter activity to forecast box office receipts on the opening weekend? The following data (stored in **TwitterMovies**) indicate the Twitter activity ("want to see") and the receipts ($) per theater on the weekend a movie opened for seven movies:

Movie	Twitter Activity	Receipts ($)
The Devil Inside	219,509	14,763
The Dictator	6405	5,796
Paranormal Activity 3	165,128	15,829
The Hunger Games	579,288	36,871
Bridesmaids	6,564	8,995
Red Tails	11,104	7,477
Act of Valor	9,152	8,054

Source: R. Dodes, "Twitter Goes to the Movies," *The Wall Street Journal*, August 3, 2012, pp. D1–D12.

a. Use the least-squares method to compute the regression coefficients b_0 and b_1.
b. Interpret the meaning of b_0 and b_1 in this problem.
c. Predict the receipts for a movie that has a Twitter activity of 100,000.
d. Should you use the model to predict the receipts for a movie that has a Twitter activity of 1,000,000? Why or why not?
e. Determine the coefficient of determination, r^2, and explain its meaning in this problem.
f. Perform a residual analysis. Is there any evidence of a pattern in the residuals? Explain.
g. At the 0.05 level of significance, is there evidence of a linear relationship between Twitter activity and receipts?
h. Construct a 95% confidence interval estimate of the mean receipts for a movie that has a Twitter activity of 100,000 and a 95% prediction interval of the receipts for a single movie that has a Twitter activity of 100,000.
i. Based on the results of (a)–(h), do you think that Twitter activity is a useful predictor of receipts on the first weekend a movie opens? What issues about these data might make you hesitant to use Twitter activity to predict receipts?

13.74 Management of a soft-drink bottling company has the business objective of developing a method for allocating delivery costs to customers. Although one cost clearly relates to travel time within a particular route, another variable cost reflects the time required to unload the cases of soft drink at the delivery point. To begin, management decided to develop a regression model to predict delivery time based on the number of cases delivered. A sample of 20 deliveries within a territory was selected. The delivery times and the number of cases delivered were organized in the following table and stored in **Delivery**:

Customer	Number of Cases	Delivery Time (minutes)	Customer	Number of Cases	Delivery Time (minutes)
1	52	32.1	11	161	43.0
2	64	34.8	12	184	49.4
3	73	36.2	13	202	57.2
4	85	37.8	14	218	56.8
5	95	37.8	15	243	60.6
6	103	39.7	16	254	61.2
7	116	38.5	17	267	58.2
8	121	41.9	18	275	63.1
9	143	44.2	19	287	65.6
10	157	47.1	20	298	67.3

a. Use the least-squares method to compute the regression coefficients b_0 and b_1.
b. Interpret the meaning of b_0 and b_1 in this problem.
c. Predict the delivery time for 150 cases of soft drink.
d. Should you use the model to predict the delivery time for a customer who is receiving 500 cases of soft drink? Why or why not?
e. Determine the coefficient of determination, r^2, and explain its meaning in this problem.
f. Perform a residual analysis. Is there any evidence of a pattern in the residuals? Explain.
g. At the 0.05 level of significance, is there evidence of a linear relationship between delivery time and the number of cases delivered?
h. Construct a 95% confidence interval estimate of the mean delivery time for 150 cases of soft drink and a 95% prediction interval of the delivery time for a single delivery of 150 cases of soft drink.

13.75 Measuring the height of a California redwood tree is a very difficult undertaking because these trees grow to heights of over 300 feet. People familiar with these trees understand that the height of a California redwood tree is related to other characteristics of the tree, including the diameter of the tree at the breast height of a person. The data in **Redwood** represent the height (in feet) and diameter (in inches) at the breast height of a person for a sample of 21 California redwood trees.
a. Assuming a linear relationship, use the least-squares method to compute the regression coefficients b_0 and b_1. State the regression equation that predicts the height of a tree based on the tree's diameter at breast height of a person.
b. Interpret the meaning of the slope in this equation.

c. Predict the height for a tree that has a breast height diameter of 25 inches.
d. Interpret the meaning of the coefficient of determination in this problem.
e. Perform a residual analysis on the results and determine the adequacy of the model.
f. Determine whether there is a significant relationship between the height of redwood trees and the breast height diameter at the 0.05 level of significance.
g. Construct a 95% confidence interval estimate of the population slope between the height of the redwood trees and breast height diameter.

13.76 You want to develop a model to predict the selling price of homes based on assessed value. A sample of 30 recently sold single-family houses in a small city is selected to study the relationship between selling price (in \$thousands) and assessed value (in \$thousands). The houses in the city were reassessed at full value one year prior to the study. The results are in House1. (Hint: First determine which are the independent and dependent variables.)

a. Construct a scatter plot and, assuming a linear relationship, use the least-squares method to compute the regression coefficients b_0 and b_1.
b. Interpret the meaning of the Y intercept, b_0, and the slope, b_1, in this problem.
c. Use the prediction line developed in (a) to predict the selling price for a house whose assessed value is \$170,000.
d. Determine the coefficient of determination, r^2, and interpret its meaning in this problem.
e. Perform a residual analysis on your results and evaluate the regression assumptions.
f. At the 0.05 level of significance, is there evidence of a linear relationship between selling price and assessed value?
g. Construct a 95% confidence interval estimate of the population slope.

13.77 You want to develop a model to predict the assessed value of houses, based on heating area. A sample of 15 single-family houses in a city is selected. The assessed value (in \$thousands) and the heating area of the houses (in thousands of square feet) are recorded and stored in House2. (Hint: First determine which are the independent and dependent variables.)

a. Construct a scatter plot and, assuming a linear relationship, use the least-squares method to compute the regression coefficients b_0 and b_1.
b. Interpret the meaning of the Y intercept, b_0, and the slope, b_1, in this problem.
c. Use the prediction line developed in (a) to predict the assessed value for a house whose heating area is 1,750 square feet.
d. Determine the coefficient of determination, r^2, and interpret its meaning in this problem.
e. Perform a residual analysis on your results and evaluate the regression assumptions.
f. At the 0.05 level of significance, is there evidence of a linear relationship between assessed value and heating area?

13.78 The director of graduate studies at a large college of business has the objective of predicting the grade point average (GPA) of students in an MBA program. The director begins by using the Graduate Management Admission Test (GMAT) score. A sample of 20 students who have completed two years in the program is selected and stored in GPIGMAT.

a. Construct a scatter plot and, assuming a linear relationship, use the least-squares method to compute the regression coefficients b_0 and b_1.
b. Interpret the meaning of the Y intercept, b_0, and the slope, b_1, in this problem.
c. Use the prediction line developed in (a) to predict the GPA for a student with a GMAT score of 600.
d. Determine the coefficient of determination, r^2, and interpret its meaning in this problem.
e. Perform a residual analysis on your results and evaluate the regression assumptions.
f. At the 0.05 level of significance, is there evidence of a linear relationship between GMAT score and GPA?
g. Construct a 95% confidence interval estimate of the mean GPA of students with a GMAT score of 600 and a 95% prediction interval of the GPA for a particular student with a GMAT score of 600.
h. Construct a 95% confidence interval estimate of the population slope.

13.79 An accountant for a large department store has the business objective of developing a model to predict the amount of time it takes to process invoices. Data are collected from the past 32 working days, and the number of invoices processed and completion time (in hours) are stored in Invoice. (Hint: First determine which are the independent and dependent variables.)

a. Assuming a linear relationship, use the least-squares method to compute the regression coefficients b_0 and b_1.
b. Interpret the meaning of the Y intercept, b_0, and the slope, b_1, in this problem.
c. Use the prediction line developed in (a) to predict the amount of time it would take to process 150 invoices.
d. Determine the coefficient of determination, r^2, and interpret its meaning.
e. Plot the residuals against the number of invoices processed and also against time.
f. Based on the plots in (e), does the model seem appropriate?
g. Based on the results in (e) and (f), what conclusions can you reach about the validity of the prediction made in (c)?

13.80 On January 28, 1986, the space shuttle *Challenger* exploded, and seven astronauts were killed. Prior to the launch, the predicted atmospheric temperature was for freezing weather at the launch site. Engineers for Morton Thiokol (the manufacturer of the rocket motor) prepared charts to make the case that the launch should not take place due to the cold weather. These arguments were rejected, and the launch tragically took place. Upon investigation after the tragedy, experts agreed that the disaster occurred because of leaky rubber O-rings that did not seal properly due to the cold temperature. Data indicating the atmospheric temperature at the time of 23 previous launches and the O-ring damage index are stored in **O-Ring**.

Note: Data from flight 4 is omitted due to unknown O-ring condition.

Sources: Data extracted from *Report of the Presidential Commission on the Space Shuttle Challenger Accident*, Washington, DC, 1986, Vol. II (H1–H3) and Vol. IV (664); and *Post-Challenger Evaluation of Space Shuttle Risk Assessment and Management*, Washington, DC, 1988, pp. 135–136.

a. Construct a scatter plot for the seven flights in which there was O-ring damage (O-ring damage index $\neq 0$). What conclusions, if any, can you reach about the relationship between atmospheric temperature and O-ring damage?

b. Construct a scatter plot for all 23 flights.

c. Explain any differences in the interpretation of the relationship between atmospheric temperature and O-ring damage in (a) and (b).

d. Based on the scatter plot in (b), provide reasons why a prediction should not be made for an atmospheric temperature of 31°F, the temperature on the morning of the launch of the *Challenger*.

e. Although the assumption of a linear relationship may not be valid for the set of 23 flights, fit a simple linear regression model to predict O-ring damage, based on atmospheric temperature.

f. Include the prediction line found in (e) on the scatter plot developed in (b).

g. Based on the results in (f), do you think a linear model is appropriate for these data? Explain.

h. Perform a residual analysis. What conclusions do you reach?

13.81 A baseball analyst would like to study various team statistics for the 2011 baseball season to determine which variables might be useful in predicting the number of wins achieved by teams during the season. He begins by using a team's earned run average (ERA), a measure of pitching performance, to predict the number of wins. He collects the team ERA and team wins for each of the 30 Major League Baseball teams and stores these data in **BB2011**. (Hint: First determine which are the independent and dependent variables.)

a. Assuming a linear relationship, use the least-squares method to compute the regression coefficients b_0 and b_1.

b. Interpret the meaning of the Y intercept, b_0, and the slope, b_1, in this problem.

c. Use the prediction line developed in (a) to predict the number of wins for a team with an ERA of 4.50.

d. Compute the coefficient of determination, r^2, and interpret its meaning.

e. Perform a residual analysis on your results and determine the adequacy of the fit of the model.

f. At the 0.05 level of significance, is there evidence of a linear relationship between the number of wins and the ERA?

g. Construct a 95% confidence interval estimate of the mean number of wins expected for teams with an ERA of 4.50.

h. Construct a 95% prediction interval of the number of wins for an individual team that has an ERA of 4.50.

i. Construct a 95% confidence interval estimate of the population slope.

j. The 30 teams constitute a population. In order to use statistical inference, as in (f) through (i), the data must be assumed to represent a random sample. What "population" would this sample be drawing conclusions about?

k. What other independent variables might you consider for inclusion in the model?

13.82 Can you use the annual revenues generated by National Basketball Association (NBA) franchises to predict franchise values? Figure 2.14 on page 70 shows a scatter plot of revenue with franchise value, and Figure 3.9 on page 140, shows the correlation coefficient. Now, you want to develop a simple linear regression model to predict franchise values based on revenues. (Franchise values and revenues are stored in **NBAValues**.)

a. Assuming a linear relationship, use the least-squares method to compute the regression coefficients b_0 and b_1.

b. Interpret the meaning of the Y intercept, b_0, and the slope, b_1, in this problem.

c. Predict the value of an NBA franchise that generates $150 million of annual revenue.

d. Compute the coefficient of determination, r^2, and interpret its meaning.

e. Perform a residual analysis on your results and evaluate the regression assumptions.

f. At the 0.05 level of significance, is there evidence of a linear relationship between the annual revenues generated and the value of an NBA franchise?

g. Construct a 95% confidence interval estimate of the mean value of all NBA franchises that generate $150 million of annual revenue.

h. Construct a 95% prediction interval of the value of an individual NBA franchise that generates $150 million of annual revenue.

i. Compare the results of (a) through (h) to those of baseball franchises in Problems 13.8, 13.20, 13.30, 13.46, and 13.62 and European soccer teams in Problem 13.83.

13.83 In Problem 13.82 you used annual revenue to develop a model to predict the franchise value of National Basketball Association (NBA) teams. Can you also use the annual revenues generated by European soccer teams to predict franchise values? (European soccer team values and revenues are stored in **SoccerValues2012**.)

a. Repeat Problem 13.82 (a) through (h) for the European soccer teams.

b. Compare the results of (a) to those of baseball franchises in Problems 13.8, 13.20, 13.30, 13.46, and 13.62 and NBA franchises in Problem 13.82.

13.84 During the fall harvest season in the United States, pumpkins are sold in large quantities at farm stands. Often, instead of weighing the pumpkins prior to sale, the farm stand operator will just place the pumpkin in the appropriate circular cutout on the counter. When asked why this was done, one farmer replied, "I can tell the weight of the pumpkin from its circumference." To determine whether this was really true, the circumference and weight of each pumpkin from a sample of 23 pumpkins were determined and the results stored in **Pumpkin**.

a. Assuming a linear relationship, use the least-squares method to compute the regression coefficients b_0 and b_1.

b. Interpret the meaning of the slope, b_1, in this problem.

c. Predict the weight for a pumpkin that is 60 centimeters in circumference.

d. Do you think it is a good idea for the farmer to sell pumpkins by circumference instead of weight? Explain.

e. Determine the coefficient of determination, r^2, and interpret its meaning.

f. Perform a residual analysis for these data and evaluate the regression assumptions.

g. At the 0.05 level of significance, is there evidence of a linear relationship between the circumference and weight of a pumpkin?

h. Construct a 95% confidence interval estimate of the population slope, β_1.

13.85 Can demographic information be helpful in predicting sales at sporting goods stores? The file **Sporting** contains the monthly sales totals from a random sample of 38 stores in a large chain of nationwide sporting goods stores. All stores in the franchise, and thus within the sample, are approximately the same size and carry the same merchandise. The county or, in some cases, counties in which the store draws the majority of its customers is referred to here as the customer base. For each of the 38 stores, demographic information about the customer base is provided. The data are real, but the name of the franchise is not used, at the request of the company. The data set contains the following variables:

Sales—Latest one-month sales total (dollars)
Age—Median age of customer base (years)
HS—Percentage of customer base with a high school diploma
College—Percentage of customer base with a college diploma
Growth—Annual population growth rate of customer base over the past 10 years
Income—Median family income of customer base (dollars)

a. Construct a scatter plot, using sales as the dependent variable and median family income as the independent variable. Discuss the scatter plot.

b. Assuming a linear relationship, use the least-squares method to compute the regression coefficients b_0 and b_1.

c. Interpret the meaning of the Y intercept, b_0, and the slope, b_1, in this problem.

d. Compute the coefficient of determination, r^2, and interpret its meaning.

e. Perform a residual analysis on your results and determine the adequacy of the fit of the model.

f. At the 0.05 level of significance, is there evidence of a linear relationship between the independent variable and the dependent variable?

g. Construct a 95% confidence interval estimate of the population slope and interpret its meaning.

13.86 For the data of Problem 13.85, repeat (a) through (g), using Age as the independent variable.

13.87 For the data of Problem 13.85, repeat (a) through (g), using HS as the independent variable.

13.88 For the data of Problem 13.85, repeat (a) through (g), using College as the independent variable.

13.89 For the data of Problem 13.85, repeat (a) through (g), using Growth as the independent variable.

13.90 The file **CEO-Compensation** includes the total compensation (in $millions) for CEOs of 194 large public companies and the investment return in 2011. (Data extracted from **nytimes.com/2012/06/17/business/executive-pay-still-climbing-despite-a-shareholder-din.html**.)

a. Compute the correlation coefficient between compensation and the investment return in 2011.

b. At the 0.05 level of significance, is the correlation between compensation and the investment return in 2011 statistically significant?

c. Write a short summary of your findings in (a) and (b). Do the results surprise you?

13.91 Refer to the discussion of beta values and market models in Problem 13.49 on page 502. The S&P 500 Index tracks the overall movement of the stock market by considering the stock prices of 500 large corporations. The file **StockPrices2011** contains 2011 weekly data for the S&P 500 and three companies. The following variables are included:

WEEK—Week ending on date given
S&P—Weekly closing value for the S&P 500 Index
GE—Weekly closing stock price for General Electric
DISCA—Weekly closing stock price for Discovery Communications
GOOG—Weekly closing stock price for Google

Source: Data extracted from finance.yahoo.com, August 21, 2012.

a. Estimate the market model for GE. (Hint: Use the percentage change in the S&P 500 Index as the independent variable and the percentage change in GE's stock price as the dependent variable.)
b. Interpret the beta value for GE.
c. Repeat (a) and (b) for Discovery Communications.
d. Repeat (a) and (b) for Google.
e. Write a brief summary of your findings.

REPORT WRITING EXERCISE

13.92 In Problems 13.85 through 13.89, you developed regression models to predict monthly sales at a sporting goods store. Now, write a report based on the models you developed. Append to your report all appropriate charts and statistical information.

CASES FOR CHAPTER 13

Managing Ashland MultiComm Services

To ensure that as many trial subscriptions to the *3-For-All* service as possible are converted to regular subscriptions, the marketing department works closely with the customer support department to accomplish a smooth initial process for the trial subscription customers. To assist in this effort, the marketing department needs to accurately forecast the monthly total of new regular subscriptions.

A team consisting of managers from the marketing and customer support departments was convened to develop a better method of forecasting new subscriptions. Previously, after examining new subscription data for the prior three months, a group of three managers would develop a subjective forecast of the number of new subscriptions. Livia Salvador, who was recently hired by the company to provide expertise in quantitative forecasting methods, suggested that the department look for factors that might help in predicting new subscriptions.

Members of the team found that the forecasts in the past year had been particularly inaccurate because in some months, much more time was spent on telemarketing than in other months. Livia collected data (stored in AMS13) for the number of new subscriptions and hours spent on telemarketing for each month for the past two years.

1. What criticism can you make concerning the method of forecasting that involved taking the new subscriptions data for the prior three months as the basis for future projections?
2. What factors other than number of telemarketing hours spent might be useful in predicting the number of new subscriptions? Explain.
3. **a.** Analyze the data and develop a regression model to predict the number of new subscriptions for a month, based on the number of hours spent on telemarketing for new subscriptions.
   b. If you expect to spend 1,200 hours on telemarketing per month, estimate the number of new subscriptions for the month. Indicate the assumptions on which this prediction is based. Do you think these assumptions are valid? Explain.
   c. What would be the danger of predicting the number of new subscriptions for a month in which 2,000 hours were spent on telemarketing?

Digital Case

Apply your knowledge of simple linear regression in this Digital Case, which extends the Sunflowers Apparel Using Statistics scenario from this chapter.

Leasing agents from the Triangle Mall Management Corporation have suggested that Sunflowers consider several locations in some of Triangle's newly renovated lifestyle malls that cater to shoppers with higher-than-mean disposable income. Although the locations are smaller than the typical Sunflowers location, the leasing agents argue that higher-than-mean disposable income in the surrounding community is a better predictor than store size of higher sales. The leasing agents maintain that sample data from 14 Sunflowers stores prove that this is true.

Open **Triangle_Sunflower.pdf** and review the leasing agents' proposal and supporting documents. Then answer the following questions:

1. Should mean disposable income be used to predict sales based on the sample of 14 Sunflowers stores?
2. Should the management of Sunflowers accept the claims of Triangle's leasing agents? Why or why not?
3. Is it possible that the mean disposable income of the surrounding area is not an important factor in leasing new locations? Explain.
4. Are there any other factors not mentioned by the leasing agents that might be relevant to the store leasing decision?

Brynne Packaging

Brynne Packaging is a large packaging company, offering its customers the highest standards in innovative packaging solutions and reliable service. About 25% of the employees at Brynne Packaging are machine operators. The human resources department has suggested that the company consider using the Wesman Personnel Classification Test (WPCT), a measure of reasoning ability, to screen applicants for the machine operator job. In order to assess the WPCT as a predictor of future job performance, 25 recent applicants were tested using the WPCT; all were hired, regardless of their WPCT score. At a later time, supervisors were asked to rate the quality of the job performance of these 25 employees, using a 1-to-10 rating scale (where 1 = very low and 10 = very high). Factors considered in the ratings included the employee's output, defect rate, ability to implement continuous quality procedures, and contributions to team problem solving efforts. The file BrynnePackaging contains the WPCT scores (WPCT) and job performance ratings (Ratings) for the 25 employees.

1. Assess the significance and importance of WPCT score as a predictor of job performance. Defend your answer.
2. Predict the mean job performance rating for all employees with a WPCT score of 6. Give a point prediction as well as a 95% confidence interval. Do you have any concerns using the regression model for predicting mean job performance rating given the WPCT score of 6?
3. Evaluate whether the assumptions of regression have been seriously violated.

CHAPTER 13 EXCEL GUIDE

EG13.1 TYPES of REGRESSION MODELS

There are no Excel Guide instructions for this section.

EG13.2 DETERMINING the SIMPLE LINEAR REGRESSION EQUATION

Key Technique Use the **LINEST(*cell range of Y variable*, *cell range of X variable*, True, True)** array function to compute the b_1 and b_0 coefficients, the b_1 and b_0 standard errors, r^2 and the standard error of the estimate, the F test statistic and error *df*, and *SSR* and *SSE*.

Example Perform the Figure 13.4 analysis of the Sunflowers Apparel data on page 476.

PHStat Use **Simple Linear Regression.**

For the example, open to the **DATA worksheet** of the **SiteSelection workbook**. Select **PHStat → Regression → Simple Linear Regression**. In the procedure's dialog box (shown below):

1. Enter **C1:C15** as the **Y Variable Cell Range.**
2. Enter **B1:B15** as the **X Variable Cell Range.**
3. Check **First cells in both ranges contain label.**
4. Enter **95** as the **Confidence level for regression coefficients.**
5. Check **Regression Statistics Table** and **ANOVA and Coefficients Table.**
6. Enter a **Title** and click **OK.**

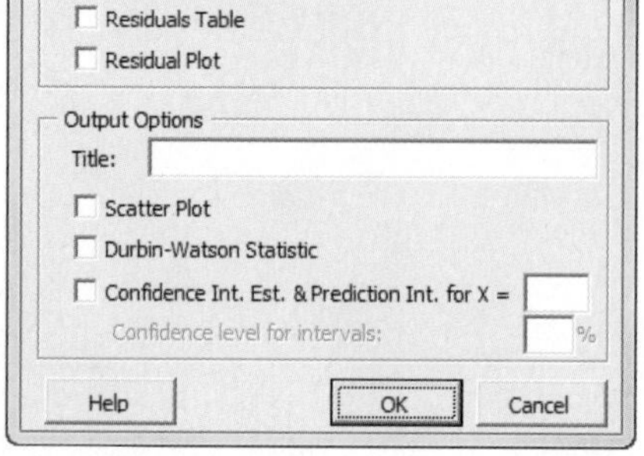

The procedure creates a worksheet that contains a copy of your data as well as the worksheet shown in Figure 13.4. For more information about these worksheets, read the following *In-Depth Excel* section.

To create a scatter plot that contains a prediction line and regression equation similar to Figure 13.5 on page 476, modify step 6 by checking **Scatter Plot** before clicking **OK.**

In-Depth Excel Use the **COMPUTE worksheet** of the **Simple Linear Regression workbook** as a template. (Use the **Simple Linear Regression 2007 workbook** instead if you use an Excel version that is older than Excel 2010.) The worksheet uses the regression data already in the **SLRDATA worksheet** to perform the regression analysis for the example.

Not shown in Figure 13.4 is the Calculations area in columns K through M. This area contains an array formula in the cell range L2:M6 that contains the expression **LINEST(*cell range of Y variable*, *cell range of X variable*, True, True)** to compute the b_1 and b_0 coefficients in cells L2 and M2, the b_1 and b_0 standard errors in cells L3 and M3, r^2 and the standard error of the estimate in cells L4 and M4, the F test statistic and error *df* in cells L5 and M5, and *SSR* and *SSE* in cells L6 and M6. In cell L9, the expression **T.INV.2T(1 – *confidence level*, *Error degrees of freedom*)** computes the critical value for the t test. Open the COMPUTE_FORMULAS worksheet to examine all the formulas in the worksheet, some of which are discussed in later sections in this Excel Guide.

To perform simple linear regression for other data, paste the regression data into the SLRDATA worksheet. Paste the values for the X variable into column A and the values for the Y variable into column B. Then, open to the COMPUTE worksheet. Enter the confidence level in cell L8 and edit the array formula in the cell range L2:M6. To edit the array formula, first select L2:M6, next make changes to the array formula, and then, while holding down the **Control** and **Shift** keys (or the **Command** key on a Mac), press the **Enter** key.

To create a scatter plot that contains a prediction line and regression equation similar to Figure 13.5 on page 476, first use the Section EG2.5 *In-Depth Excel* scatter plot instructions with the Table 13.1 Sunflowers Apparel data to create a scatter plot. Then select the chart and:

1. Select **Layout → Trendline → More Trendline Options.**

In the Format Trendline dialog box (shown below):

2. Click **Trendline Options** in the left pane. In the Trendline Options right pane, click **Linear**, check **Display Equation on chart**, check **Display R-squared value on chart**, and then click **Close**.

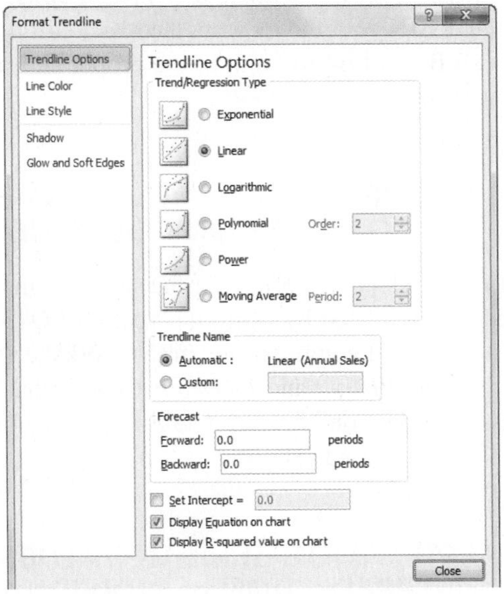

If you use Excel 2013, after selecting the chart:

1. Select **Design → Add Chart Element → Trendline → More Trendline Options**.

In the Format Trendline pane (similar to the Format Trendline dialog box):

2. Click **Linear**, check both **Display Equation on chart** and **Display R-squared value on chart**.

For scatter plots of other data, if the *X* axis does not appear at the bottom of the plot, right-click the ***Y* axis** and click **Format Axis** from the shortcut menu. In the Format Axis dialog box, click **Axis Options** in the left pane. In the **Axis Options** pane on the right, click **Axis value** and in its box enter the value shown in the dimmed **Minimum** box at the top of the pane. Then click **Close**.

Analysis ToolPak Use **Regression**.
For the example, open to the **DATA worksheet** of the **Site-Selection workbook** and:

1. Select **Data → Data Analysis.**
2. In the Data Analysis dialog box, select **Regression** from the **Analysis** Tools list and then click **OK**.

In the Regression dialog box (shown in next column):

3. Enter **C1:C15** as the **Input Y Range** and enter **B1:B15** as the **Input X Range**.
4. Check **Labels** and check **Confidence Level** and enter **95** in its box.
5. Click **New Worksheet Ply** and then click **OK**.

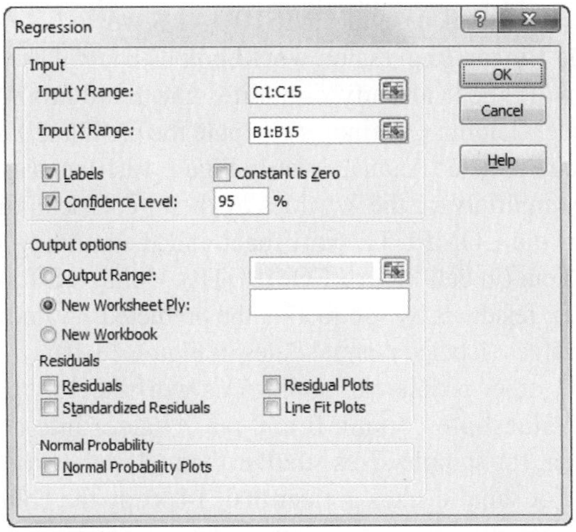

EG13.3 MEASURES of VARIATION

The measures of variation are computed as part of creating the simple linear regression worksheet using the Section EG13.2 instructions.

If you use either Section EG13.2 *PHStat* or *In-Depth Excel* instructions, formulas used to compute these measures are in the **COMPUTE worksheet** that is created. Formulas in cells B5, B7, B13, C12, C13, D12, and E12 copy values computed by the array formula in cell range L2:M6. In cell F12, the function **F.DIST.RT(*F test statistic*, *regression degrees of freedom*, *error degrees of freedom*)**, computes the *p*-value for the *F* test for the slope, discussed in Section 13.7. (The similar FDIST function computes the *p*-value in the COMPUTE worksheet of the Simple Linear Regression 2007 workbook.)

EG13.4 ASSUMPTIONS of REGRESSION

There are no Excel Guide instructions for this section.

EG13.5 RESIDUAL ANALYSIS

Key Technique Use arithmetic formulas to compute the residuals. To evaluate assumptions, use the Section EG2.5 scatter plot instructions for constructing residual plots and the Section EG6.3 instructions for constructing normal probability plots.

Example Compute the residuals for the Sunflowers Apparel data on page 474.

PHStat Use the Section EG13.2 *PHStat* instructions. Modify step 5 by checking **Residuals Table** and **Residual Plot** in addition to checking **Regression Statistics Table** and **ANOVA and Coefficients Table**. To construct a normal probability plot, follow the Section EG6.3 *PHStat* instructions using the cell range of the residuals as the **Variable Cell Range** in step 1.

In-Depth Excel Use the **RESIDUALS worksheet** of the **Simple Linear Regression workbook** as a template.
This worksheet already computes the residuals for the example. Column C formulas compute the predicted Y values (labeled Predicted Annual Sales in Figure 13.10 on page 489) by first multiplying the X values by the b_1 coefficient in cell B18 of the COMPUTE worksheet and then adding the b_0 coefficient (in cell B17 of COMPUTE). Column E formulas compute residuals by subtracting the predicted Y values from the Y values (labeled Annual Sales in Figure 13.10).

For other problems, modify this worksheet by pasting the X values into column B and the Y values into column D. Then, for sample sizes smaller than 14, delete the extra rows. For sample sizes greater than 14, copy the column C and E formulas down through the row containing the last pair and X and Y values and add the new observation numbers in column A.

To construct a residual plot similar to Figure 13.11 on page 489, use the original X variable and the residuals (plotted as the Y variable) as the chart data and follow the Section EG2.5 scatter plot instructions. To construct a normal probability plot, follow the Section EG6.3 *In-Depth Excel* instructions, using the residuals as the "variable data."

Analysis ToolPak Use the Section EG13.2 *Analysis ToolPak* instructions. Modify step 5 by checking **Residuals** and **Residual Plots** before clicking **New Worksheet Ply** and then **OK**.

To create a scatter plot or normal probability plot, use the *In-Depth Excel* instructions.

EG13.6 MEASURING AUTOCORRELATION: the DURBIN-WATSON STATISTIC

Key Technique Use the **SUMXMY2(*cell range of the second through last residual*, *cell range of the first through the second-to-last residual*)** function to compute the sum of squared difference of the residuals, the numerator in Equation (13.15) on page 493, and use the **SUMSQ(*cell range of the residuals*)** function to compute the sum of squared residuals, the denominator in Equation (13.15).

Example Compute the Durbin-Watson statistic for the Sunflowers Apparel data on page 474.

PHStat Use the *PHStat* instructions at the beginning of Section EG13.2. Modify step 6 by checking the **Durbin-Watson Statistic** output option before clicking **OK**.

In-Depth Excel Use the **DURBIN_WATSON worksheet** of the **Simple Linear Regression** workbook as a template.
The worksheet uses the SUMXMY2 function in cell B3 and the SUMSQ function in cell B4.

The **DURBIN_WATSON worksheet** of the **Package Delivery workbook** computes the statistic for the example. (This workbook also uses the COMPUTE and RESIDUALS worksheet templates from the Simple Linear Regression workbook.)

To compute the Durbin-Watson statistic for other problems, first create the simple linear regression model and the residuals for the problem, using the Sections EG13.2 and EG13.5 *In-Depth Excel* instructions. Then open the DURBIN_WATSON worksheet and edit the formulas in cell B3 and B4 to point to the proper cell ranges of the new residuals.

EG13.7 INFERENCES ABOUT the SLOPE and CORRELATION COEFFICIENT

The t test for the slope and F test for the slope are included in the worksheet created by using the Section EG13.2 instructions. The t test computations in the worksheets created by using the *PHStat* and *In-Depth Excel* instructions are discussed in Section EG13.2. The F test computations are discussed in Section EG13.3.

EG13.8 ESTIMATION of MEAN VALUES and PREDICTION of INDIVIDUAL VALUES

Key Technique Use the **TREND(*Y variable cell range*, *X variable cell range*, *X value*)** function to compute the predicted Y value for the X value and use the **DEVSQ(*X variable cell range*)** function to compute the SSX value.

Example Compute the confidence interval estimate and prediction interval for the Sunflowers Apparel data that is shown in Figure 13.21 on page 506.

PHStat Use the Section EG13.2 *PHStat* instructions but replace step 6 with these steps 6 and 7:

6. Check **Confidence Int. Est. & Prediction Int. for *X* =** and enter **4** in its box. Enter **95** as the percentage for **Confidence level for intervals**.
7. Enter a **Title** and click **OK**.

The additional worksheet created is discussed in the following *In-Depth Excel* instructions.

In-Depth Excel Use the **CIEandPI worksheet** of the **Simple Linear Regression workbook**, as a template.
The worksheet already contains the data and formulas for the example. The worksheet uses the **T.INV.2T (1 – *confidence level*, *degrees of freedom*)** function to compute the t critical value in cell B10 and the TREND function to compute the predicted Y value for the X value in cell B15. In cell B12, the function **DEVSQ(SLRData!A:A)** computes the SSX value that is used, in turn, to help compute the h statistic in cell B14.

To compute a confidence interval estimate and prediction interval for other problems:

1. Paste the regression data into the **SLRData worksheet**. Use column A for the *X* variable data and column B for the *Y* variable data.
2. Open to the **CIEandPI worksheet**.

In the CIEandPI worksheet:

3. Change values for the **X Value** and **Confidence Level**, as is necessary.
4. Edit the cell ranges used in the cell B15 formula that uses the TREND function to refer to the new cell ranges for the *Y* and *X* variables.

CHAPTER

14 Introduction to Multiple Regression

Learning Objectives

In this chapter, you learn:

- How to develop a multiple regression model
- How to interpret the regression coefficients
- How to determine which independent variables to include in the regression model
- How to determine which independent variables are most important in predicting a dependent variable
- How to use categorical independent variables in a regression model
- How to predict a categorical dependent variable using logistic regression

Igor Dutina / Shutterstock

USING STATISTICS

The Multiple Effects of OmniPower Bars

You are a marketing manager for OmniFoods, with oversight for nutrition bars and similar snack items. You seek to revive the sales of OmniPower, the company's primary product in this category. Originally marketed as a high-energy bar to runners, mountain climbers, and other athletes, OmniPower reached its greatest sales in an earlier time, when high-energy bars were most popular with consumers. Now, you seek to remarket the product as a nutrition bar to benefit from the booming market for such bars.

Because the marketplace already contains several successful nutrition bars, you need to develop an effective marketing strategy. In particular, you need to determine the effect that price and in-store promotions will have on sales of OmniPower. Before marketing the bar nationwide, you plan to conduct a test-market study of OmniPower sales, using a sample of 34 stores in a supermarket chain. How can you extend the linear regression methods discussed in Chapter 13 to incorporate the effects of price *and* promotion into the same model? How can you use this model to improve the success of the nationwide introduction of OmniPower?

Ariwasabi / Shutterstock

Chapter 13 focused on simple linear regression models that use *one* numerical independent variable, X, to predict the value of a numerical dependent variable, Y. Often you can make better predictions by using *more than one* independent variable. This chapter introduces you to multiple regression models that use two or more independent variables to predict the value of a dependent variable.

14.1 Developing a Multiple Regression Model

The business objective you face in the Using Statistics scenario is to develop a model to predict monthly OmniPower sales per store and to determine which variables influence sales. As a starting point, you consider the following two independent variables: the price of an OmniPower bar in cents (X_1) and the monthly budget for in-store promotional expenditures in dollars (X_2). (In-store promotional expenditures typically include signs and displays, in-store coupons, and free samples.)

To develop a **multiple regression model** that uses these two independent variables with the dependent variable, the number of OmniPower bars sold in a month (Y), you collect data from a sample of 34 stores in a supermarket chain selected for a test-market study of OmniPower. You choose stores in a way to ensure that they all have approximately the same monthly sales volume. You organize and store the data collected in OmniPower. Table 14.1 presents these data.

TABLE 14.1

Monthly OmniPower Sales, Price, and Promotional Expenditures

Store	Sales	Price	Promotion	Store	Sales	Price	Promotion
1	4,141	59	200	18	2,730	79	400
2	3,842	59	200	19	2,618	79	400
3	3,056	59	200	20	4,421	79	400
4	3,519	59	200	21	4,113	79	600
5	4,226	59	400	22	3,746	79	600
6	4,630	59	400	23	3,532	79	600
7	3,507	59	400	24	3,825	79	600
8	3,754	59	400	25	1,096	99	200
9	5,000	59	600	26	761	99	200
10	5,120	59	600	27	2,088	99	200
11	4,011	59	600	28	820	99	200
12	5,015	59	600	29	2,114	99	400
13	1,916	79	200	30	1,882	99	400
14	675	79	200	31	2,159	99	400
15	3,636	79	200	32	1,602	99	400
16	3,224	79	200	33	3,354	99	600
17	2,295	79	400	34	2,927	99	600

Interpreting the Regression Coefficients

When there are several independent variables, you can extend the simple linear regression model of Equation (13.1) on page 472 by assuming a linear relationship between each independent variable and the dependent variable. For example, with k independent variables, the multiple regression model is expressed in Equation (14.1).

MULTIPLE REGRESSION MODEL WITH k INDEPENDENT VARIABLES

$$Y_i = \beta_0 + \beta_1 X_{1i} + \beta_2 X_{2i} + \beta_3 X_{3i} + \cdots + \beta_k X_{ki} + \varepsilon_i \quad \textbf{(14.1)}$$

where

$\beta_0 = Y$ intercept
$\beta_1 =$ slope of Y with variable X_1, holding variables $X_2, X_3, \ldots, X_k$ constant
$\beta_2 =$ slope of Y with variable X_2, holding variables $X_1, X_3, \ldots, X_k$ constant
$\beta_3 =$ slope of Y with variable X_3, holding variables $X_1, X_2, \ldots, X_k$ constant
⋮
$\beta_k =$ slope of Y with variable X_k holding variables $X_1, X_2, X_3, \ldots, X_{k-1}$ constant
$\varepsilon_i =$ random error in Y for observation i

Equation (14.2) defines the multiple regression model with two independent variables.

MULTIPLE REGRESSION MODEL WITH TWO INDEPENDENT VARIABLES

$$Y_i = \beta_0 + \beta_1 X_{1i} + \beta_2 X_{2i} + \varepsilon_i \quad \textbf{(14.2)}$$

where

$\beta_0 =$ intercept
$\beta_1 =$ slope of Y with variable X_1, holding variable X_2 constant
$\beta_2 =$ slope of Y with variable X_2, holding variable X_1 constant
$\varepsilon_i =$ random error in Y for observation i

Compare the multiple regression model to the simple linear regression model [Equation (13.1) on page 472]:

$$Y_i = \beta_0 + \beta_1 X_i + \varepsilon_i$$

In the simple linear regression model, the slope, β_1, represents the change in the mean of Y per unit change in X and does not take into account any other variables. In the multiple regression model with two independent variables [Equation (14.2)], the slope, β_1, represents the change in the mean of Y per unit change in X_1, taking into account the effect of X_2.

As in the case of simple linear regression, you use the least-squares method to compute sample regression coefficients (b_0, b_1, and b_2) as estimates of the population parameters (β_0, β_1, and β_2). Equation (14.3) defines the regression equation for a multiple regression model with two independent variables.

Student Tip
Because multiple regression computations are more complex than computations for simple linear regression, always use a computerized method to obtain multiple regression results.

MULTIPLE REGRESSION EQUATION WITH TWO INDEPENDENT VARIABLES

$$\hat{Y}_i = b_0 + b_1 X_{1i} + b_2 X_{2i} \quad \textbf{(14.3)}$$

Figure 14.1 shows a regression results worksheet for the OmniPower sales data multiple regression model. The values for the three regression coefficients are contained in cells B17 through B19.

FIGURE 14.1

Partial regression results worksheet for the OmniPower sales multiple regression model

Figure 14.1 displays the ***COMPUTE worksheet*** *of the* ***Multiple Regression workbook*** *that the Section EG14.1 instructions use. To learn more about the formulas used in the worksheet, see the Section EG14.1 In-Depth Excel instructions. (The Analysis ToolPak creates a similar-looking worksheet that does not contain formulas.)*

	A	B	C	D	E	F	G
1	**Multiple Regression**						
2							
3	***Regression Statistics***						
4	Multiple R	0.8705					
5	R Square	0.7577					
6	Adjusted R Square	0.7421					
7	Standard Error	638.0653					
8	Observations	34					
9							
10	**ANOVA**						
11		*df*	*SS*	*MS*	*F*	*Significance F*	
12	Regression	2	39472730.7730	19736365.3865	48.4771	0.0000	
13	Residual	31	12620946.6682	407127.3119			
14	Total	33	52093677.4412				
15							
16		*Coefficients*	*Standard Error*	*t Stat*	*P - value*	*Lower 95%*	*Upper 95%*
17	Intercept	5837.5208	628.1502	9.2932	0.0000	4556.3999	7118.6416
18	Price	-53.2173	6.8522	-7.7664	0.0000	-67.1925	-39.2421
19	Promotion	3.6131	0.6852	5.2728	0.0000	2.2155	5.0106

From Figure 14.1, the computed values of the three regression coefficients are

$$b_0 = 5{,}837.5208 \quad b_1 = -53.2173 \quad b_2 = 3.6131$$

Therefore, the multiple regression equation is

$$\hat{Y}_i = 5{,}837.5208 - 53.2173X_{1i} + 3.6131X_{2i}$$

where

$$\hat{Y}_i = \text{predicted monthly sales of OmniPower bars for store } i$$
$$X_{1i} = \text{price of OmniPower bar (in cents) for store } i$$
$$X_{2i} = \text{monthly in-store promotional expenditures (in \$) for store } i$$

The sample Y intercept ($b_0 = 5{,}837.5208$) estimates the number of OmniPower bars sold in a month if the price is \$0.00 and the total amount spent on promotional expenditures is also \$0.00. Because these values of price and promotion are outside the range of price and promotion used in the test-market study, and because they make no sense in the context of the problem, the value of b_0 has little or no practical interpretation.

The slope of price with OmniPower sales ($b_1 = -53.2173$) indicates that, for a given amount of monthly promotional expenditures, the predicted sales of OmniPower are estimated to decrease by 53.2173 bars per month for each 1-cent increase in the price. The slope of monthly promotional expenditures with OmniPower sales ($b_2 = 3.6131$) indicates that, for a given price, the estimated sales of OmniPower are predicted to increase by 3.6131 bars for each additional \$1 spent on promotions. These estimates allow you to better understand the likely effect that price and promotion decisions will have in the marketplace. For example, a 10-cent decrease in price is predicted to increase sales by 532.173 bars, with a fixed amount of monthly promotional expenditures. A \$100 increase in promotional expenditures is predicted to increase sales by 361.31 bars for a given price.

Student Tip

Remember that in multiple regression, the regression coefficients are conditional on holding constant the other independent variables. The slope of b_1 holds constant the effect of variable X_2. The slope of b_2 holds constant the effect of variable X_1.

Regression coefficients in multiple regression are called **net regression coefficients**, and they estimate the predicted change in Y per unit change in a particular X, *holding constant the effect of the other X variables*. For example, in the study of OmniPower bar sales, for a store with a given amount of promotional expenditures, the estimated sales are predicted to decrease by 53.2173 bars per month for each 1-cent increase in the price of an OmniPower bar. Another way to interpret this "net effect" is to think of two stores with an equal amount of promotional expenditures. If the first store charges 1 cent more than the other store, the net effect of this difference is that the first store is predicted to sell 53.2173 fewer bars per month than the second store. To interpret the net effect of promotional expenditures, you can consider two stores that are charging the same price. If the first store spends \$1 more on promotional expenditures, the net effect of this difference is that the first store is predicted to sell 3.6131 more bars per month than the second store.

Predicting the Dependent Variable Y

You can use the multiple regression equation to predict values of the dependent variable. For example, what are the predicted sales for a store charging 79 cents during a month in which promotional expenditures are \$400? Using the multiple regression equation,

$$\hat{Y}_i = 5{,}837.5208 - 53.2173X_{1i} + 3.6131X_{2i}$$

with $X_{1i} = 79$ and $X_{2i} = 400$,

$$\hat{Y}_i = 5{,}837.5208 - 53.2173(79) + 3.6131(400)$$
$$= 3{,}078.57$$

> **Student Tip**
> The rule that you should only predict within the range of the values of all the independent variables, first mentioned in the discussion of simple linear regression, equally applies to multiple regression.

Thus, you predict that stores charging 79 cents and spending \$400 in promotional expenditures will sell 3,078.57 OmniPower bars per month.

After you have developed the regression equation, done a residual analysis (see Section 14.3), and determined the significance of the overall fitted model (see Section 14.2), you can construct a confidence interval estimate of the mean value and a prediction interval for an individual value. Figure 14.2 presents a confidence interval estimate and a prediction interval worksheet for the OmniPower sales data.

FIGURE 14.2
Confidence interval estimate and prediction interval worksheet for the OmniPower sales data

	A	B	C	D	
1	**Confidence Interval Estimate and Prediction Interval**				
2					
3	**Data**				
4	Confidence Level	95%			
5		1			
6	Price given value	79			
7	Promotion given value	400			
8					
9	X'X	34	2646	13200	**Array Formula:**
10		2646	214674	1018800	**{=MMULT(TRANSPOSE(MRArray!A2:C35), MRArray!A2:C35)}**
11		13200	1018800	6000000	
12					
13	Inverse of X'X	0.9692	-0.0094	-0.0005	**Array Formula:**
14		-0.0094	0.0001	0.0000	**{=MINVERSE(B9:D11)}**
15		-0.0005	0.0000	0.0000	
16					**Array Formula:**
17	X'G times Inverse of X'X	0.0121	0.0001	0.0000	**{=MMULT(TRANSPOSE(B5:B7), B13:D15)}**
18					
19	[X'G times Inverse of X'X] times XG	0.0298	**=MMULT(B17:D17, B5:B7)**		
20	*t* Statistic	2.0395	**=T.INV.2T(1 - B4, COMPUTE!B13)**		
21	Predicted Y (YHat)	3078.57	**{=MMULT(TRANSPOSE(B5:B7), COMPUTE!B17:B19)}**		
22					
23	**For Average Predicted Y (YHat)**				
24	Interval Half Width	224.50	**=B20 * SQRT(B19) * COMPUTE!B7**		
25	Confidence Interval Lower Limit	2854.07	**=B21 - B24**		
26	Confidence Interval Upper Limit	3303.08	**=B21 + B24**		
27					
28	**For Individual Response Y**				
29	Interval Half Width	1320.57	**=B20 * SQRT(1 + B19) * COMPUTE!B7**		
30	Prediction Interval Lower Limit	1758.01	**=B21 - B29**		
31	Prediction Interval Upper Limit	4399.14	**=B21 + B29**		

Figure 14.2 displays the ***CIEandPI worksheet*** *of the* ***Multiple Regression workbook*** *that the Section EG14.1 instructions use. Array formulas (see Appendix Section B.3) in cell ranges B8:D11, B13:D15, and B17:D17 and in cell B21 help to compute the results.*

The 95% confidence interval estimate of the mean OmniPower sales for all stores charging 79 cents and spending \$400 in promotional expenditures is 2,854.07 to 3,303.08 bars. The prediction interval for an individual store is 1,758.01 to 4,399.14 bars.

Problems for Section 14.1

LEARNING THE BASICS

14.1 For this problem, use the following multiple regression equation:

$$\hat{Y}_i = 10 + 5X_{1i} + 3X_{2i}$$

a. Interpret the meaning of the slopes.
b. Interpret the meaning of the *Y* intercept.

14.2 For this problem, use the following multiple regression equation:

$$\hat{Y}_i = 50 - 2X_{1i} + 7X_{2i}$$

a. Interpret the meaning of the slopes.
b. Interpret the meaning of the *Y* intercept.

APPLYING THE CONCEPTS

14.3 A shoe manufacturer is considering developing a new brand of running shoes. The business problem facing the marketing analyst is to determine which variables should be used to predict durability (i.e., the effect of long-term impact). Two independent variables under consideration are X_1 (FOREIMP), a measurement of the forefoot shock-absorbing capability, and X_2 (MIDSOLE), a measurement of the change in impact properties over time. The dependent variable Y is LTIMP, a measure of the shoe's durability after a repeated impact test. Data are collected from a random sample of 15 types of currently manufactured running shoes, with the following results:

Variable	Coefficients	Standard Error	*t* Statistic	*p*-Value
Intercept	−0.02686	0.06905	−0.39	0.7034
FOREIMP	0.79116	0.06295	12.57	0.0000
MIDSOLE	0.60484	0.07174	8.43	0.0000

a. State the multiple regression equation.
b. Interpret the meaning of the slopes, b_1 and b_2, in this problem.

SELF Test **14.4** A mail-order catalog business selling personal computer supplies, software, and hardware maintains a centralized warehouse. Management is currently examining the process of distribution from the warehouse. The business problem facing management relates to the factors that affect warehouse distribution costs. Currently, a handling fee is added to each order, regardless of the amount of the order. Data collected over the past 24 months (stored in WareCost) indicate the warehouse distribution costs (in $thousands), the sales (in $thousands), and the number of orders received.
a. State the multiple regression equation.
b. Interpret the meaning of the slopes, b_1 and b_2, in this problem.
c. Explain why the regression coefficient, b_0, has no practical meaning in the context of this problem.
d. Predict the monthly warehouse distribution cost when sales are $400,000 and the number of orders is 4,500.
e. Construct a 95% confidence interval estimate for the mean monthly warehouse distribution cost when sales are $400,000 and the number of orders is 4,500.
f. Construct a 95% prediction interval for the monthly warehouse distribution cost for a particular month when sales are $400,000 and the number of orders is 4,500.
g. Explain why the interval in (e) is narrower than the interval in (f).

14.5 How do horsepower and weight affect the mileage of family cars? Data from a sample of 16 2012 family cars were collected, organized, and stored in Auto2012. (Data extracted from "Top 2012 Cars," *Consumer Reports*, April 2012, pp. 40–73.) Develop a regression model to predict mileage (as measured by miles per gallon) based on the horsepower of the car's engine and the weight of the car (in pounds).
a. State the multiple regression equation.
b. Interpret the meaning of the slopes, b_1 and b_2, in this problem.
c. Explain why the regression coefficient, b_0, has no practical meaning in the context of this problem.
d. Predict the miles per gallon for cars that have 190 horsepower and weigh 3,500 pounds.
e. Construct a 95% confidence interval estimate for the mean miles per gallon for cars that have 190 horsepower and weigh 3,500 pounds.
f. Construct a 95% prediction interval for the miles per gallon for an individual car that has 190 horsepower and weighs 3,500 pounds.

14.6 The business problem facing a consumer products company is to measure the effectiveness of different types of advertising media in the promotion of its products. Specifically, the company is interested in the effectiveness of radio advertising and newspaper advertising (including the cost of discount coupons). During a one-month test period, data were collected from a sample of 22 cities with approximately equal populations. Each city is allocated a specific expenditure level for radio advertising and for newspaper advertising. The sales of the product (in $thousands) and also the levels of media expenditure (in $thousands) during the test month are recorded, with the following results shown below and stored in Advertise:

City	Sales ($thousands)	Radio Advertising ($thousands)	Newspaper Advertising ($thousands)
1	973	0	40
2	1,119	0	40
3	875	25	25
4	625	25	25
5	910	30	30
6	971	30	30
7	931	35	35
8	1,177	35	35
9	882	40	25
10	982	40	25
11	1,628	45	45
12	1,577	45	45
13	1,044	50	0
14	914	50	0
15	1,329	55	25
16	1,330	55	25
17	1,405	60	30
18	1,436	60	30
19	1,521	65	35
20	1,741	65	35
21	1,866	70	40
22	1,717	70	40

a. State the multiple regression equation.
b. Interpret the meaning of the slopes, b_1 and b_2, in this problem.
c. Interpret the meaning of the regression coefficient, b_0.
d. Which type of advertising is more effective? Explain.

14.7 The business problem facing the director of broadcasting operations for a television station was the issue of standby hours (i.e., hours in which unionized graphic artists at the station are paid but are not actually involved in any activity) and what factors were related to standby hours. The study included the following variables:

Standby hours (Y)—Total number of standby hours in a week
Total staff present (X_1)—Weekly total of people-days
Remote hours (X_2)—Total number of hours worked by employees at locations away from the central plant

Data were collected for 26 weeks; these data are organized and stored in Standby.
a. State the multiple regression equation.
b. Interpret the meaning of the slopes, b_1 and b_2, in this problem.
c. Explain why the regression coefficient, b_0, has no practical meaning in the context of this problem.
d. Predict the standby hours for a week in which the total staff present have 310 people-days and the remote hours are 400.
e. Construct a 95% confidence interval estimate for the mean standby hours for weeks in which the total staff present have 310 people-days and the remote hours are 400.
f. Construct a 95% prediction interval for the standby hours for a single week in which the total staff present have 310 people-days and the remote hours are 400.

14.8 Nassau County is located approximately 25 miles east of New York City. The data organized and stored in GlenCove include the appraised value, land area of the property in acres, and age, in years, for a sample of 30 single-family homes located in Glen Cove, a small city in Nassau County. Develop a multiple linear regression model to predict appraised value based on land area of the property and age, in years.
a. State the multiple regression equation.
b. Interpret the meaning of the slopes, b_1 and b_2, in this problem.
c. Explain why the regression coefficient, b_0, has no practical meaning in the context of this problem.
d. Predict the appraised value for a house that has a land area of 0.25 acre and is 45 years old.
e. Construct a 95% confidence interval estimate for the mean appraised value for houses that have a land area of 0.25 acre and are 45 years old.
f. Construct a 95% prediction interval estimate for the appraised value for an individual house that has a land area of 0.25 acre and is 45 years old.

14.2 r^2, Adjusted r^2, and the Overall F Test

This section discusses three methods you can use to evaluate the overall multiple regression model: the coefficient of multiple determination, r^2, the adjusted r^2, and the overall F test.

Coefficient of Multiple Determination

Recall from Section 13.3 that the coefficient of determination, r^2, measures the proportion of the variation in Y that is explained by the independent variable X in the simple linear regression model. In multiple regression, the **coefficient of multiple determination** represents the proportion of the variation in Y that is explained by the set of independent variables. Equation (14.4) defines the coefficient of multiple determination for a multiple regression model with two or more independent variables.

COEFFICIENT OF MULTIPLE DETERMINATION

The coefficient of multiple determination is equal to the regression sum of squares (SSR) divided by the total sum of squares (SST).

$$r^2 = \frac{\text{Regression sum of squares}}{\text{Total sum of squares}} = \frac{SSR}{SST} \quad (14.4)$$

In the OmniPower example, from Figure 14.1 on page 529, $SSR = 39{,}472{,}730.77$ and $SST = 52{,}093{,}677.44$. Thus,

$$r^2 = \frac{SSR}{SST} = \frac{39{,}472{,}730.77}{52{,}093{,}677.44} = 0.7577$$

Student Tip
Remember that r^2 in multiple regression represents the proportion of the variation in the dependent variable Y that is explained by all the independent X variables included in the model.

The coefficient of multiple determination ($r^2 = 0.7577$) indicates that 75.77% of the variation in sales is explained by the variation in the price and in the promotional expenditures. The coefficient of multiple determination also appears in cell B5 in the Figure 14.1 results on page 528, labeled R Square.

Adjusted r^2

When considering multiple regression models, some statisticians suggest that you should use the **adjusted r^2** to take into account both the number of independent variables in the model and the sample size. Reporting the adjusted r^2 is extremely important when you are comparing two or more regression models that predict the same dependent variable but have a different number of independent variables. Equation (14.5) defines the adjusted r^2.

ADJUSTED r^2

$$r^2_{adj} = 1 - \left[(1 - r^2)\frac{n-1}{n-k-1}\right] \tag{14.5}$$

where k is the number of independent variables in the regression equation.

Thus, for the OmniPower data, because $r^2 = 0.7577$, $n = 34$, and $k = 2$,

$$\begin{aligned} r^2_{adj} &= 1 - \left[(1 - 0.7577)\frac{34-1}{34-2-1}\right] \\ &= 1 - \left[(0.2423)\frac{33}{31}\right] \\ &= 1 - 0.2579 \\ &= 0.7421 \end{aligned}$$

Therefore, 74.21% of the variation in sales is explained by the multiple regression model—adjusted for the number of independent variables and sample size. The adjusted r^2 also appears in cell B6 in the Figure 14.1 results on page 528, labeled Adjusted R Square.

Test for the Significance of the Overall Multiple Regression Model

You use the **overall F test** to determine whether there is a significant relationship between the dependent variable and the entire set of independent variables (the overall multiple regression model). Because there is more than one independent variable, you use the following null and alternative hypotheses:

H_0: $\beta_1 = \beta_2 = \cdots = \beta_k = 0$ (There is no linear relationship between the dependent variable and the independent variables.)

H_1: At least one $\beta_j \neq 0, j = 1, 2, \ldots, k$ (There is a linear relationship between the dependent variable and at least one of the independent variables.)

Equation (14.6) defines the overall F test statistic. Table 14.2 presents the ANOVA summary table.

OVERALL F TEST

The F_{STAT} test statistic is equal to the regression mean square (MSR) divided by the mean square error (MSE).

$$F_{STAT} = \frac{MSR}{MSE} \tag{14.6}$$

where

k = number of independent variables in the regression model

The F_{STAT} test statistic follows an F distribution with k and $n - k - 1$ degrees of freedom.

TABLE 14.2

ANOVA Summary Table for the Overall F Test

Source	Degrees of Freedom	Sum of Squares	Mean Squares (Variance)	F
Regression	k	SSR	$MSR = \frac{SSR}{k}$	$F_{STAT} = \frac{MSR}{MSE}$
Error	$n - k - 1$	SSE	$MSE = \frac{SSE}{n - k - 1}$	
Total	$n - 1$	SST		

Student Tip

Remember that you are testing whether at least one independent variable has a linear relationship with the dependent variable. If you reject H_0, you are *not* concluding that all the independent variables have a linear relationship with the dependent variable, only that *at least one* independent variable does.

The decision rule is

Reject H_0 at the α level of significance if $F_{STAT} > F_\alpha$;

otherwise, do not reject H_0.

Using a 0.05 level of significance, the critical value of the F distribution with 2 and 31 degrees of freedom found in Table E.5 is approximately 3.32 (see Figure 14.3 below). From Figure 14.1 on page 528, the F_{STAT} test statistic given in the ANOVA summary table is 48.4771. Because $48.4771 > 3.32$, or because the p-value $= 0.000 < 0.05$, you reject H_0 and conclude that at least one of the independent variables (price and/or promotional expenditures) is related to sales.

FIGURE 14.3

Testing for the significance of a set of regression coefficients at the 0.05 level of significance, with 2 and 31 degrees of freedom

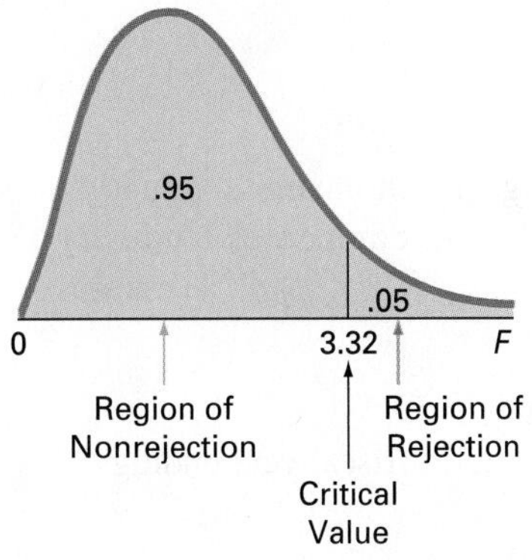

Problems for Section 14.2

LEARNING THE BASICS

14.9 The following ANOVA summary table is for a multiple regression model with two independent variables:

Source	Degrees of Freedom	Sum of Squares	Mean Squares	F
Regression	2	60		
Error	18	120		
Total	20	180		

a. Determine the regression mean square (*MSR*) and the mean square error (*MSE*).
b. Compute the overall F_{STAT} test statistic.
c. Determine whether there is a significant relationship between Y and the two independent variables at the 0.05 level of significance.
d. Compute the coefficient of multiple determination, r^2, and interpret its meaning.
e. Compute the adjusted r^2.

14.10 The following ANOVA summary table is for a multiple regression model with two independent variables:

Source	Degrees of Freedom	Sum of Squares	Mean Squares	F
Regression	2	30		
Error	10	120		
Total	12	150		

a. Determine the regression mean square (*MSR*) and the mean square error (*MSE*).
b. Compute the overall F_{STAT} test statistic.
c. Determine whether there is a significant relationship between Y and the two independent variables at the 0.05 level of significance.
d. Compute the coefficient of multiple determination, r^2, and interpret its meaning.
e. Compute the adjusted r^2.

APPLYING THE CONCEPTS

14.11 A financial analyst engaged in business valuation obtained financial data on 71 drug companies (Industry Group SIC 3 code: 283). The file BusinessValuation contains the following variables:

COMPANY—Drug Company name
PB fye—Price-to-book-value ratio (fiscal year ending)
ROE—Return on equity
SGROWTH—Growth (GS5)

a. Develop a regression model to predict price-to-book-value ratio based on return on equity.
b. Develop a regression model to predict price-to-book-value ratio based on growth.
c. Develop a regression model to predict price-to-book-value ratio based on return on equity and growth.
d. Compute and interpret the adjusted r^2 for each of the three models.
e. Which of these three models do you think is the best predictor of price-to-book-value ratio?

14.12 In Problem 14.3 on page 530, you predicted the durability of a brand of running shoe, based on the forefoot shock-absorbing capability and the change in impact properties over time. The regression analysis resulted in the following ANOVA summary table:

Source	Degrees of Freedom	Sum of Squares	Mean Squares	F	p-Value
Regression	2	12.61020	6.30510	97.69	0.0001
Error	12	0.77453	0.06454		
Total	14	13.38473			

a. Determine whether there is a significant relationship between durability and the two independent variables at the 0.05 level of significance.
b. Interpret the meaning of the p-value.
c. Compute the coefficient of multiple determination, r^2, and interpret its meaning.
d. Compute the adjusted r^2.

14.13 In Problem 14.5 on page 530, you used horsepower and weight to predict mileage (stored in Auto2012). Use the results from that problem to do the following:
a. Determine whether there is a significant relationship between mileage and the two independent variables (horsepower and weight) at the 0.05 level of significance.
b. Interpret the meaning of the p-value.
c. Compute the coefficient of multiple determination, r^2, and interpret its meaning.
d. Compute the adjusted r^2.

SELF Test **14.14** In Problem 14.4 on page 530, you used sales and number of orders to predict distribution costs at a mail-order catalog business (stored in WareCost). Using the results from that problem,
a. determine whether there is a significant relationship between distribution costs and the two independent variables (sales and number of orders) at the 0.05 level of significance.
b. interpret the meaning of the p-value.

c. compute the coefficient of multiple determination, r^2, and interpret its meaning.
d. compute the adjusted r^2.

14.15 In Problem 14.7 on page 531, you used the total staff present and remote hours to predict standby hours (stored in Standby). Using the results from that problem,
a. determine whether there is a significant relationship between standby hours and the two independent variables (total staff present and remote hours) at the 0.05 level of significance.
b. interpret the meaning of the *p*-value.
c. compute the coefficient of multiple determination, r^2, and interpret its meaning.
d. compute the adjusted r^2.

14.16 In Problem 14.6 on page 530, you used radio advertising and newspaper advertising to predict sales (stored in Advertise). Using the results from that problem,
a. determine whether there is a significant relationship between sales and the two independent variables (radio advertising and newspaper advertising) at the 0.05 level of significance.
b. interpret the meaning of the *p*-value.
c. compute the coefficient of multiple determination, r^2, and interpret its meaning.
d. compute the adjusted r^2.

14.17 In Problem 14.8 on page 531, you used the land area of a property and the age of a house to predict appraised value (stored in GlenCove). Using the results from that problem,
a. determine whether there is a significant relationship between appraised value and the two independent variables (land area of a property and age of a house) at the 0.05 level of significance.
b. interpret the meaning of the *p*-value.
c. compute the coefficient of multiple determination, r^2, and interpret its meaning.
d. compute the adjusted r^2.

14.3 Residual Analysis for the Multiple Regression Model

In Section 13.5, you used residual analysis to evaluate the fit of the simple linear regression model. For the multiple regression model with two independent variables, you need to construct and analyze the following residual plots:

- Residuals versus $\hat{Y}_i$
- Residuals versus X_{1i}
- Residuals versus X_{2i}
- Residuals versus time

> **Student Tip**
> As is the case with simple linear regression, a residual plot that does not contain any apparent patterns will look like a random scattering of points.

The first residual plot examines the pattern of residuals versus the predicted values of Y. If the residuals show a pattern for the predicted values of Y, there is evidence of a possible curvilinear effect (see Section 15.1) in at least one independent variable, a possible violation of the assumption of equal variance (see Figure 13.13 on page 491), and/or the need to transform the Y variable.

The second and third residual plots involve the independent variables. Patterns in the plot of the residuals versus an independent variable may indicate the existence of a curvilinear effect and, therefore, the need to add a curvilinear independent variable to the multiple regression model (see Section 15.1).

The fourth plot is used to investigate patterns in the residuals in order to validate the independence assumption when the data are collected in time order. Associated with this residual plot, as in Section 13.6, you can compute the Durbin-Watson statistic to determine the existence of positive autocorrelation among the residuals.

Figure 14.4 presents the residual plots for the OmniPower sales example. There is very little or no pattern in the relationship between the residuals and the predicted value of Y, the value of X_1 (price), or the value of X_2 (promotional expenditures). Thus, you can conclude that the multiple regression model is appropriate for predicting sales. There is no need to plot the residuals versus time because the data were not collected in time order.

FIGURE 14.4

Residual plots for the OmniPower sales data: residuals versus predicted Y, residuals versus price, and residuals versus promotional expenditures

Construct residual plots using the instructions in Section EG13.5.

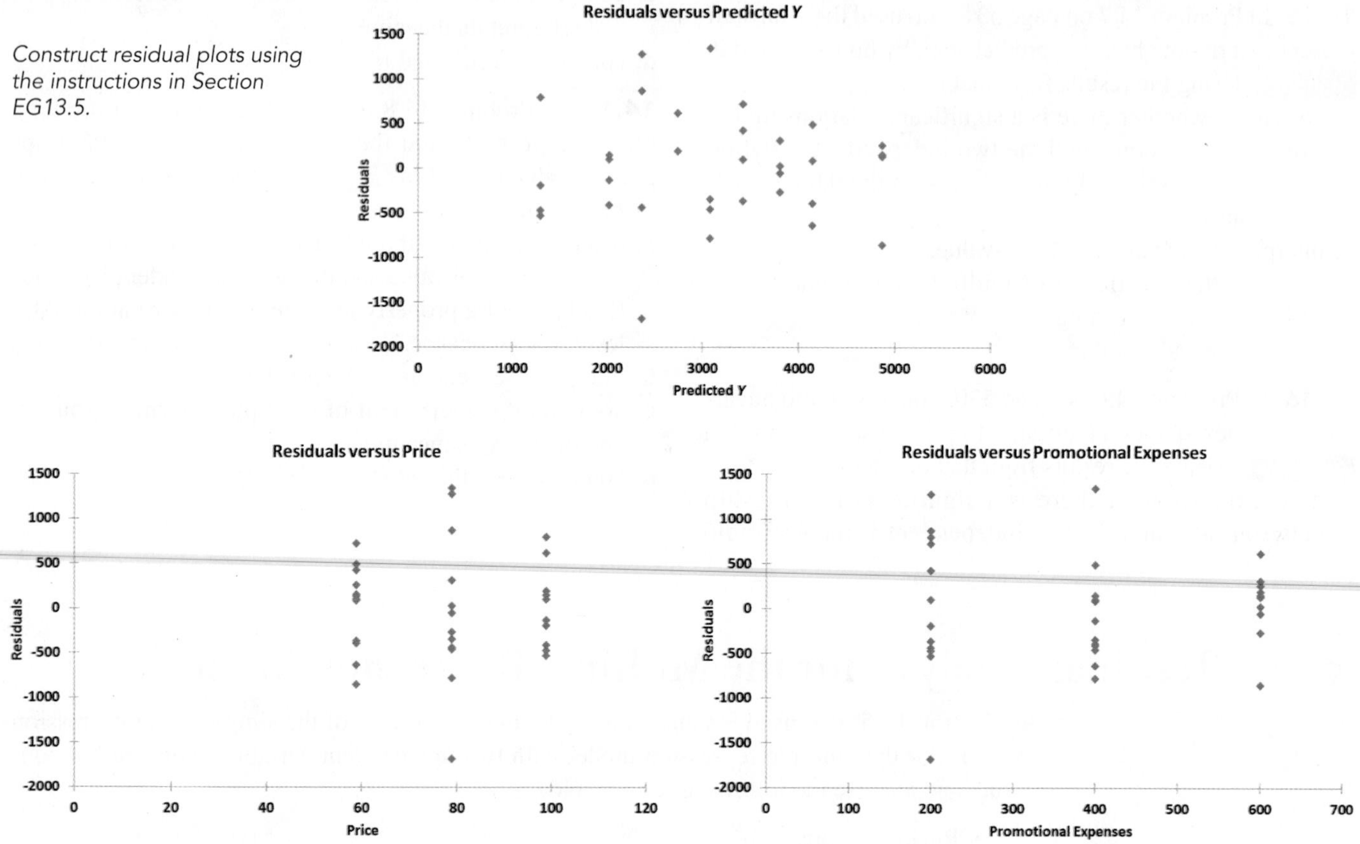

Problems for Section 14.3

APPLYING THE CONCEPTS

14.18 In Problem 14.4 on page 530, you used sales and number of orders to predict distribution costs at a mail-order catalog business (stored in **WareCost**).

a. Plot the residuals versus $\hat{Y}_i$.
b. Plot the residuals versus X_{1i}.
c. Plot the residuals versus X_{2i}.
d. Plot the residuals versus time.
e. In the residual plots created in (a) through (d), is there any evidence of a violation of the regression assumptions? Explain.
f. Determine the Durbin-Watson statistic.
g. At the 0.05 level of significance, is there evidence of positive autocorrelation in the residuals?

14.19 In Problem 14.5 on page 530, you used horsepower and weight to predict mileage (stored in **Auto2012**).

a. Plot the residuals versus $\hat{Y}_i$
b. Plot the residuals versus X_{1i}.
c. Plot the residuals versus X_{2i}.
d. In the residual plots created in (a) through (c), is there any evidence of a violation of the regression assumptions? Explain.
e. Should you compute the Durbin-Watson statistic for these data? Explain.

14.20 In Problem 14.6 on page 530, you used radio advertising and newspaper advertising to predict sales (stored in **Advertise**).

a. Perform a residual analysis on your results.
b. If appropriate, perform the Durbin-Watson test, using $\alpha = 0.05$.
c. Are the regression assumptions valid for these data?

14.21 In Problem 14.7 on page 531, you used the total staff present and remote hours to predict standby hours (stored in Standby).

a. Perform a residual analysis on your results.

b. If appropriate, perform the Durbin-Watson test, using $\alpha = 0.05$.

c. Are the regression assumptions valid for these data?

14.22 In Problem 14.8 on page 531, you used the land area of a property and the age of a house to predict appraised value (stored in GlenCove).

a. Perform a residual analysis on your results.

b. If appropriate, perform the Durbin-Watson test, using $\alpha = 0.05$.

c. Are the regression assumptions valid for these data?

14.4 Inferences Concerning the Population Regression Coefficients

In Section 13.7, you tested the slope in a simple linear regression model to determine the significance of the relationship between *X* and *Y*. In addition, you constructed a confidence interval estimate of the population slope. This section extends those procedures to multiple regression.

Tests of Hypothesis

In a simple linear regression model, to test a hypothesis concerning the population slope, β_1, you used Equation (13.16) on page 496:

$$t_{STAT} = \frac{b_1 - \beta_1}{S_{b_1}}$$

Equation (14.7) generalizes this equation for multiple regression.

TESTING FOR THE SLOPE IN MULTIPLE REGRESSION

$$t_{STAT} = \frac{b_j - \beta_j}{S_{b_j}} \quad \textbf{(14.7)}$$

where

b_j = slope of variable *j* with *Y*, holding constant the effects of all other independent variables

S_{b_j} = standard error of the regression coefficient b_j

k = number of independent variables in the regression equation

β_j = hypothesized value of the population slope for variable *j*, holding constant the effects of all other independent variables

t_{STAT} = test statistic for a *t* distribution with $n - k - 1$ degrees of freedom

To determine whether variable X_2 (amount of promotional expenditures) has a significant effect on sales, taking into account the price of OmniPower bars, the null and alternative hypotheses are

$$H_0: \beta_2 = 0$$
$$H_1: \beta_2 \neq 0$$

From Equation (14.7) and Figure 14.1 on page 528,

$$t_{STAT} = \frac{b_2 - \beta_2}{S_{b_2}}$$

$$= \frac{3.6131 - 0}{0.6852} = 5.2728$$

If you select a level of significance of 0.05, the critical values of t for 31 degrees of freedom from Table E.3 are -2.0395 and $+2.0395$ (see Figure 14.5).

FIGURE 14.5

Testing for significance of a regression coefficient at the 0.05 level of significance, with 31 degrees of freedom

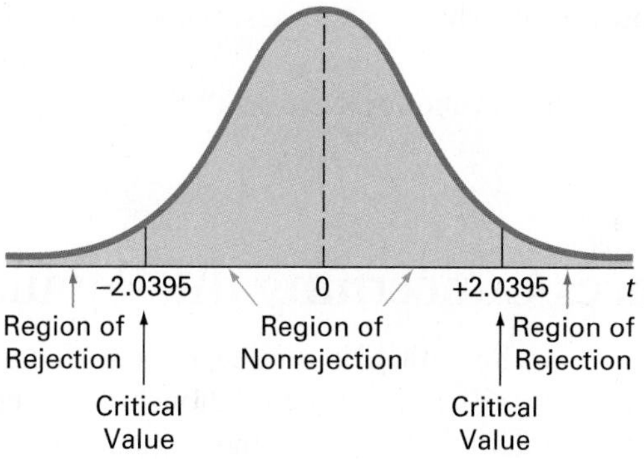

From Figure 14.1 on page 528, observe that the computed t_{STAT} test statistic is 5.2728. Because $t_{STAT} = 5.2728 > 2.0395$ or because the p-value is approximately zero, you reject H_0 and conclude that there is a significant relationship between the variable X_2 (promotional expenditures) and sales, taking into account the price, X_1. The extremely small p-value allows you to strongly reject the null hypothesis that there is no linear relationship between sales and promotional expenditures. Example 14.1 presents the test for the significance of β_1, the slope of sales with price.

EXAMPLE 14.1

Testing for the Significance of the Slope of Sales with Price

At the 0.05 level of significance, is there evidence that the slope of sales with price is different from zero?

SOLUTION From Figure 14.1 on page 528, $t_{STAT} = -7.7664 < -2.0395$ (the critical value for $\alpha = 0.05$) or the p-value $= 0.0000 < 0.05$. Thus, there is a significant relationship between price, X_1, and sales, taking into account the promotional expenditures, X_2.

As shown with these two independent variables, the test of significance for a specific regression coefficient in multiple regression is a test for the significance of adding that variable into a regression model, given that the other variable is included. In other words, the t test for the regression coefficient is actually a test for the contribution of each independent variable.

Confidence Interval Estimation

Instead of testing the significance of a population slope, you may want to estimate the value of a population slope. Equation (14.8) defines the confidence interval estimate for a population slope in multiple regression.

CONFIDENCE INTERVAL ESTIMATE FOR THE SLOPE

$$b_j \pm t_{\alpha/2} S_{b_j} \quad \textbf{(14.8)}$$

where

$t_{\alpha/2}$ = the critical value corresponding to an upper-tail probability of $\alpha/2$ from the t distribution with $n - k - 1$ degrees of freedom (i.e., a cumulative area of $1 - \alpha/2$)

k = the number of independent variables

To construct a 95% confidence interval estimate of the population slope, β_1 (the effect of price, X_1, on sales, Y, holding constant the effect of promotional expenditures, X_2), the critical value of t at the 95% confidence level with 31 degrees of freedom is 2.0395 (see Table E.3). Then, using Equation (14.8) and Figure 14.1 on page 528,

$$b_1 \pm t_{\alpha/2}S_{b_1}$$
$$-53.2173 \pm (2.0395)(6.8522)$$
$$-53.2173 \pm 13.9752$$
$$-67.1925 \leq \beta_1 \leq -39.2421$$

Taking into account the effect of promotional expenditures, the estimated effect of a 1-cent increase in price is to reduce mean sales by approximately 39.2 to 67.2 bars. You have 95% confidence that this interval correctly estimates the relationship between these variables. From a hypothesis-testing viewpoint, because this confidence interval does not include 0, you conclude that the regression coefficient, β_1, has a significant effect.

Example 14.2 constructs and interprets a confidence interval estimate for the slope of sales with promotional expenditures.

EXAMPLE 14.2

Constructing a Confidence Interval Estimate for the Slope of Sales with Promotional Expenditures

Construct a 95% confidence interval estimate of the population slope of sales with promotional expenditures.

SOLUTION The critical value of t at the 95% confidence level, with 31 degrees of freedom, is 2.0395 (see Table E.3). Using Equation (14.8) and Figure 14.1 on page 528,

$$b_2 \pm t_{\alpha/2}S_{b_2}$$
$$3.6131 \pm (2.0395)(0.6852)$$
$$3.6131 \pm 1.3975$$
$$2.2156 \leq \beta_2 \leq 5.0106$$

Thus, taking into account the effect of price, the estimated effect of each additional dollar of promotional expenditures is to increase mean sales by approximately 2.22 to 5.01 bars. You have 95% confidence that this interval correctly estimates the relationship between these variables. From a hypothesis-testing viewpoint, because this confidence interval does not include 0, you can conclude that the regression coefficient, β_2, has a significant effect.

Problems for Section 14.4

LEARNING THE BASICS

14.23 Use the following information from a multiple regression analysis:

$$n = 25 \quad b_1 = 5 \quad b_2 = 10 \quad S_{b_1} = 2 \quad S_{b_2} = 8$$

a. Which variable has the largest slope, in units of a t statistic?

b. Construct a 95% confidence interval estimate of the population slope, β_1.

c. At the 0.05 level of significance, determine whether each independent variable makes a significant contribution to the regression model. On the basis of these results, indicate the independent variables to include in this model.

14.24 Use the following information from a multiple regression analysis:

$$n = 20 \quad b_1 = 4 \quad b_2 = 3 \quad S_{b_1} = 1.2 \quad S_{b_2} = 0.8$$

a. Which variable has the largest slope, in units of a t statistic?

b. Construct a 95% confidence interval estimate of the population slope, β_1.

c. At the 0.05 level of significance, determine whether each independent variable makes a significant contribution to the regression model. On the basis of these results, indicate the independent variables to include in this model.

APPLYING THE CONCEPTS

14.25 In Problem 14.3 on page 530, you predicted the durability of a brand of running shoe, based on the forefoot shock-absorbing capability (FOREIMP) and the change in impact properties over time (MIDSOLE) for a sample of 15 pairs of shoes. Use the following results:

Variable	Coefficient	Standard Error	*t* Statistic	*p*-Value
Intercept	−0.02686	0.06905	−0.39	0.7034
FOREIMP	0.79116	0.06295	12.57	0.0000
MIDSOLE	0.60484	0.07174	8.43	0.0000

a. Construct a 95% confidence interval estimate of the population slope between durability and forefoot shock-absorbing capability.
b. At the 0.05 level of significance, determine whether each independent variable makes a significant contribution to the regression model. On the basis of these results, indicate the independent variables to include in this model.

SELF Test **14.26** In Problem 14.4 on page 530, you used sales and number of orders to predict distribution costs at a mail-order catalog business (stored in WareCost). Using the results from that problem,
a. construct a 95% confidence interval estimate of the population slope between distribution cost and sales.
b. at the 0.05 level of significance, determine whether each independent variable makes a significant contribution to the regression model. On the basis of these results, indicate the independent variables to include in this model.

14.27 In Problem 14.5 on page 530, you used horsepower and weight to predict mileage (stored in Auto2012). Using the results from that problem,
a. construct a 95% confidence interval estimate of the population slope between mileage and horsepower.
b. at the 0.05 level of significance, determine whether each independent variable makes a significant contribution to the regression model. On the basis of these results, indicate the independent variables to include in this model.

14.28 In Problem 14.6 on page 530, you used radio advertising and newspaper advertising to predict sales (stored in Advertise). Using the results from that problem,
a. construct a 95% confidence interval estimate of the population slope between sales and radio advertising.
b. at the 0.05 level of significance, determine whether each independent variable makes a significant contribution to the regression model. On the basis of these results, indicate the independent variables to include in this model.

14.29 In Problem 14.7 on page 531, you used the total number of staff present and remote hours to predict standby hours (stored in Standby). Using the results from that problem,
a. construct a 95% confidence interval estimate of the population slope between standby hours and total number of staff present.
b. at the 0.05 level of significance, determine whether each independent variable makes a significant contribution to the regression model. On the basis of these results, indicate the independent variables to include in this model.

14.30 In Problem 14.8 on page 531, you used land area of a property and age of a house to predict appraised value (stored in GlenCove). Using the results from that problem,
a. construct a 95% confidence interval estimate of the population slope between appraised value and land area of a property.
b. at the 0.05 level of significance, determine whether each independent variable makes a significant contribution to the regression model. On the basis of these results, indicate the independent variables to include in this model.

14.5 Testing Portions of the Multiple Regression Model

In developing a multiple regression model, you want to use only those independent variables that significantly reduce the error in predicting the value of a dependent variable. If an independent variable does not improve the prediction, you can delete it from the multiple regression model and use a model with fewer independent variables.

The **partial *F* test** is an alternative method to the *t* test discussed in Section 14.4 for determining the contribution of an independent variable. Using this method, you determine the contribution to the regression sum of squares made by each independent variable after all the other independent variables have been included in the model. The new independent variable is included only if it significantly improves the model.

To conduct partial *F* tests for the OmniPower sales example, you need to evaluate the contribution of promotional expenditures (X_2) after price (X_1) has been included in the model and also evaluate the contribution of price (X_1) after promotional expenditures (X_2) have been included in the model.

In general, if there are several independent variables, you determine the contribution of each independent variable by taking into account the regression sum of squares of a model that includes all independent variables except the one of interest, j. This regression sum of squares is denoted SSR (all Xs except j). Equation (14.9) determines the contribution of variable j, assuming that all other variables are already included.

DETERMINING THE CONTRIBUTION OF AN INDEPENDENT VARIABLE TO THE REGRESSION MODEL

$$SSR(X_j \mid \text{All } Xs \text{ except } j) = SSR(\text{All } Xs) - SSR(\text{All } Xs \text{ except } j) \quad \textbf{(14.9)}$$

If there are two independent variables, you use Equations (14.10a) and (14.10b) to determine the contribution of each variable.

CONTRIBUTION OF VARIABLE X_1, GIVEN THAT X_2 HAS BEEN INCLUDED

$$SSR(X_1 \mid X_2) = SSR(X_1 \text{ and } X_2) - SSR(X_2) \quad \textbf{(14.10a)}$$

CONTRIBUTION OF VARIABLE X_2, GIVEN THAT X_1 HAS BEEN INCLUDED

$$SSR(X_2 \mid X_1) = SSR(X_1 \text{ and } X_2) - SSR(X_1) \quad \textbf{(14.10b)}$$

The term $SSR(X_2)$ represents the sum of squares due to regression for a model that includes only the independent variable X_2 (promotional expenditures). Similarly, $SSR(X_1)$ represents the sum of squares due to regression for a model that includes only the independent variable X_1 (price). Figures 14.6 and 14.7 present results for these two models.

FIGURE 14.6

Regression results for a simple linear regression model of sales with promotional expenditures, $SSR(X_2)$

See Section EG13.2 for a discussion about simple linear regression worksheets.

	A	B	C	D	E	F	G
1	**Sales and Promotional Expenses Analysis**						
2							
3	*Regression Statistics*						
4	Multiple R	0.5351					
5	R Square	0.2863					
6	Adjusted R Square	0.2640					
7	Standard Error	1077.8721					
8	Observations	34					
9							
10	ANOVA						
11		*df*	*SS*	*MS*	*F*	*Significance F*	
12	Regression	1	14915814.1025	14915814.1025	12.8384	0.0011	
13	Residual	32	37177863.3387	1161808.2293			
14	Total	33	52093677.4412				
15							
16		*Coefficients*	*Standard Error*	*t Stat*	*P-value*	*Lower 95%*	*Upper 95%*
17	Intercept	1496.0161	483.9789	3.0911	0.0041	510.1843	2481.8480
18	Promotion	4.1281	1.1521	3.5831	0.0011	1.7813	6.4748

FIGURE 14.7

Regression results for a simple linear regression model of sales with price, $SSR(X_1)$

	A	B	C	D	E	F	G
1	**Sales and Price Analysis**						
2							
3	*Regression Statistics*						
4	Multiple R	0.7351					
5	R Square	0.5404					
6	Adjusted R Square	0.5261					
7	Standard Error	864.9457					
8	Observations	34					
9							
10	ANOVA						
11		*df*	*SS*	*MS*	*F*	*Significance F*	
12	Regression	1	28153486.1482	28153486.1482	37.6318	0.0000	
13	Residual	32	23940191.2930	748130.9779			
14	Total	33	52093677.4412				
15							
16		*Coefficients*	*Standard Error*	*t Stat*	*P-value*	*Lower 95%*	*Upper 95%*
17	Intercept	7512.3480	734.6189	10.2262	0.0000	6015.9796	9008.7164
18	Price	-56.7138	9.2451	-6.1345	0.0000	-75.5455	-37.8822

From Figure 14.6, $SSR(X_2) = 14{,}915{,}814.10$ and from Figure 14.1 on page 528, SSR (X_1 and X_2) $= 39{,}472{,}730.77$. Then, using Equation (14.10a),

$$\begin{aligned} SSR(X_1|X_2) &= SSR(X_1 \text{ and } X_2) - SSR(X_2) \\ &= 39{,}472{,}730.77 - 14{,}915{,}814.10 \\ &= 24{,}556{,}916.67 \end{aligned}$$

To determine whether X_1 significantly improves the model after X_2 has been included, you divide the regression sum of squares into two component parts, as shown in Table 14.3.

TABLE 14.3

ANOVA Table Dividing the Regression Sum of Squares into Components to Determine the Contribution of Variable X_1

Source	Degrees of Freedom	Sum of Squares	Mean Square (Variance)	F
Regression	2	39,472,730.77	19,736,365.39	
$\left\{\begin{matrix} X_2 \\ X_1 \mid X_2 \end{matrix}\right\}$	$\left\{\begin{matrix} 1 \\ 1 \end{matrix}\right\}$	$\left\{\begin{matrix} 14{,}915{,}814.10 \\ 24{,}556{,}916.67 \end{matrix}\right\}$	24,556,916.67	60.32
Error	31	12,620,946.67	407,127.31	
Total	33	52,093,677.44		

The null and alternative hypotheses to test for the contribution of X_1 to the model are

H_0: Variable X_1 does not significantly improve the model after variable X_2 has been included.

H_1: Variable X_1 significantly improves the model after variable X_2 has been included.

Equation (14.11) defines the partial F test statistic for testing the contribution of an independent variable.

PARTIAL F TEST STATISTIC

$$F_{STAT} = \frac{SSR(X_j|\text{All } Xs \text{ } except \text{ } j)}{MSE} \tag{14.11}$$

The partial F test statistic follows an F distribution with 1 and $n - k - 1$ degrees of freedom.

From Table 14.3,

$$F_{STAT} = \frac{24{,}556{,}916.67}{407{,}127.31} = 60.32$$

The partial F_{STAT} test statistic has 1 and $n - k - 1 = 34 - 2 - 1 = 31$ degrees of freedom. Using a level of significance of 0.05, the critical value from Table E.5 is approximately 4.17 (see Figure 14.8).

FIGURE 14.8

Testing for the contribution of a regression coefficient to a multiple regression model at the 0.05 level of significance, with 1 and 31 degrees of freedom

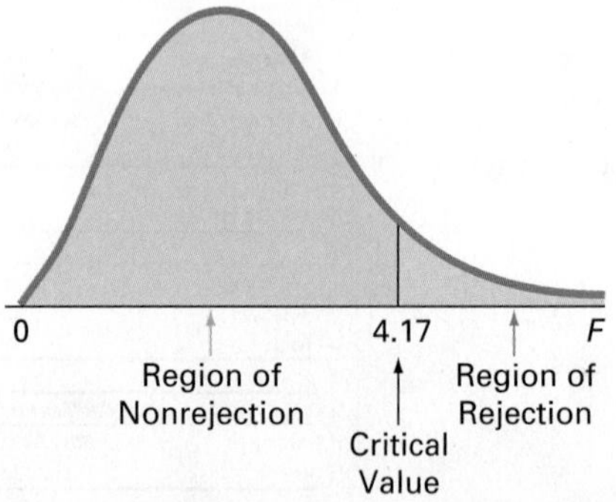

Because the computed partial F_{STAT} test statistic (60.32) is greater than this critical F value (4.17), you reject H_0. You conclude that the addition of variable X_1 (price) significantly improves a regression model that already contains variable X_2 (promotional expenditures).

To evaluate the contribution of variable X_2 (promotional expenditures) to a model in which variable X_1 (price) has been included, you need to use Equation (14.10b). First, from Figure 14.7 on page 541, observe that $SSR(X_1) = 28{,}153{,}486.15$. Second, from Table 14.3, observe that $SSR(X_1 \text{ and } X_2) = 39{,}472{,}730.77$. Then, using Equation (14.10b) on page 541,

$$SSR(X_2|X_1) = 39{,}472{,}730.77 - 28{,}153{,}486.15 = 11{,}319{,}244.62$$

To determine whether X_2 significantly improves a model after X_1 has been included, you can divide the regression sum of squares into two component parts, as shown in Table 14.4.

TABLE 14.4

ANOVA Table Dividing the Regression Sum of Squares into Components to Determine the Contribution of Variable X_2

Source	Degrees of Freedom	Sum of Squares	Mean Square (Variance)	F
Regression	2	39,472,730.77	19,736,365.39	
$\begin{Bmatrix} X_1 \\ X_2 \mid X_1 \end{Bmatrix}$	$\begin{Bmatrix} 1 \\ 1 \end{Bmatrix}$	$\begin{Bmatrix} 28{,}153{,}486.15 \\ 11{,}319{,}244.62 \end{Bmatrix}$	11,319,244.62	27.80
Error	31	12,620,946.67	407,127.31	
Total	33	52,093,677.44		

The null and alternative hypotheses to test for the contribution of X_2 to the model are

H_0: Variable X_2 does not significantly improve the model after variable X_1 has been included.

H_1: Variable X_2 significantly improves the model after variable X_1 has been included.

Using Equation (14.11) and Table 14.4,

$$F_{STAT} = \frac{11{,}319{,}244.62}{407{,}127.31} = 27.80$$

In Figure 14.8, you can see that, using a 0.05 level of significance, the critical value of F, with 1 and 31 degrees of freedom, is approximately 4.17. Because the computed partial F_{STAT} test statistic (27.80) is greater than this critical value (4.17), you reject H_0. You can conclude that the addition of variable X_2 (promotional expenditures) significantly improves the multiple regression model already containing X_1 (price).

Thus, by testing for the contribution of each independent variable after the other independent variable has been included in the model, you determine that each of the two independent variables significantly improves the model. Therefore, the multiple regression model should include both price, X_1, and promotional expenditures, X_2.

The partial F test statistic developed in this section and the t test statistic of Equation (14.7) on page 537 are both used to determine the contribution of an independent variable to a multiple regression model. The hypothesis tests associated with these two statistics always result in the same decision (i.e., the p-values are identical). The t_{STAT} test statistics for the OmniPower regression model are -7.7664 and $+5.2728$, and the corresponding F_{STAT} test statistics are 60.32 and 27.80. Equation (14.12) states this relationship between t and F.[1]

[1]This relationship holds only when the F_{STAT} statistic has 1 degree of freedom in the numerator.

RELATIONSHIP BETWEEN A t STATISTIC AND AN F STATISTIC

$$t_{STAT}^2 = F_{STAT} \qquad (14.12)$$

Student Tip
The coefficients of partial determination measure the proportion of the variation in the dependent variable explained by a specific independent variable, holding the other independent variables constant. They are different from the *coefficient of multiple* determination that measures the proportion of the variation in the dependent variable explained by the entire set of independent variables included in the model.

Coefficients of Partial Determination

Recall from Section 14.2 that the coefficient of multiple determination, r^2, measures the proportion of the variation in Y that is explained by variation in the independent variables. The **coefficients of partial determination** ($r^2_{Y1.2}$ and $r^2_{Y2.1}$) measure the proportion of the variation in the dependent variable that is explained by each independent variable while controlling for, or holding constant, the other independent variable. Equation (14.13) defines the coefficients of partial determination for a multiple regression model with two independent variables.

COEFFICIENTS OF PARTIAL DETERMINATION FOR A MULTIPLE REGRESSION MODEL CONTAINING TWO INDEPENDENT VARIABLES

$$r^2_{Y1.2} = \frac{SSR(X_1|X_2)}{SST - SSR(X_1 \text{ and } X_2) + SSR(X_1|X_2)} \quad \textbf{(14.13a)}$$

and

$$r^2_{Y2.1} = \frac{SSR(X_2|X_1)}{SST - SSR(X_1 \text{ and } X_2) + SSR(X_2|X_1)} \quad \textbf{(14.13b)}$$

where

$SSR(X_1|X_2)$ = sum of squares of the contribution of variable X_1 to the regression model, given that variable X_2 has been included in the model

SST = total sum of squares for Y

$SSR(X_1 \text{ and } X_2)$ = regression sum of squares when variables X_1 and X_2 are both included in the multiple regression model

$SSR(X_2|X_1)$ = sum of squares of the contribution of variable X_2 to the regression model, given that variable X_1 has been included in the model

For the OmniPower sales example,

$$r^2_{Y1.2} = \frac{24{,}556{,}916.67}{52{,}093{,}677.44 - 39{,}472{,}730.77 + 24{,}556{,}916.67} = 0.6605$$

$$r^2_{Y2.1} = \frac{11{,}319{,}244.62}{52{,}093{,}677.44 - 39{,}472{,}730.77 + 11{,}319{,}244.62} = 0.4728$$

The coefficient of partial determination, $r^2_{Y1.2}$, of variable Y with X_1 while holding X_2 constant is 0.6605. Thus, for a given (constant) amount of promotional expenditures, 66.05% of the variation in OmniPower sales is explained by the variation in the price. The coefficient of partial determination, $r^2_{Y2.1}$, of variable Y with X_2 while holding X_1 constant is 0.4728. Thus, for a given (constant) price, 47.28% of the variation in sales of OmniPower bars is explained by variation in the amount of promotional expenditures.

Equation (14.14) defines the coefficient of partial determination for the jth variable in a multiple regression model containing several (k) independent variables.

*The **CPD worksheets** of the **Multiple Regression workbook** compute the coefficients of partial determination. See Section EG14.5.*

COEFFICIENT OF PARTIAL DETERMINATION FOR A MULTIPLE REGRESSION MODEL CONTAINING *K* INDEPENDENT VARIABLES

$$r^2_{Yj.(\text{All variables } except\, j)} = \frac{SSR(X_j|\text{All Xs } except\, j)}{SST - SSR(All\, Xs) + SSR(X_j|\text{All Xs } except\, j)} \quad \textbf{(14.14)}$$

Problems for Section 14.5

LEARNING THE BASICS

14.31 The following is the ANOVA summary table for a multiple regression model with two independent variables:

Source	Degrees of Freedom	Sum of Squares	Mean Squares	F
Regression	2	60		
Error	18	120		
Total	20	180		

If $SSR(X_1) = 45$ and $SSR(X_2) = 25$,

a. determine whether there is a significant relationship between Y and each independent variable at the 0.05 level of significance.

b. compute the coefficients of partial determination, $r^2_{Y1.2}$ and $r^2_{Y2.1}$, and interpret their meaning.

14.32 The following is the ANOVA summary table for a multiple regression model with two independent variables:

Source	Degrees of Freedom	Sum of Squares	Mean Squares	F
Regression	2	30		
Error	10	120		
Total	12	150		

If $SSR(X_1) = 20$ and $SSR(X_2) = 15$,

a. determine whether there is a significant relationship between Y and each independent variable at the 0.05 level of significance.

b. compute the coefficients of partial determination, $r^2_{Y1.2}$ and $r^2_{Y2.1}$, and interpret their meaning.

APPLYING THE CONCEPTS

14.33 In Problem 14.5 on page 530, you used horsepower and weight to predict mileage (stored in Auto2012). Using the results from that problem,

a. at the 0.05 level of significance, determine whether each independent variable makes a significant contribution to the regression model. On the basis of these results, indicate the most appropriate regression model for this set of data.

b. compute the coefficients of partial determination, $r^2_{Y1.2}$ and $r^2_{Y2.1}$, and interpret their meaning.

SELF Test **14.34** In Problem 14.4 on page 530, you used sales and number of orders to predict distribution costs at a mail-order catalog business (stored in WareCost). Using the results from that problem,

a. at the 0.05 level of significance, determine whether each independent variable makes a significant contribution to the regression model. On the basis of these results, indicate the most appropriate regression model for this set of data.

b. compute the coefficients of partial determination, $r^2_{Y1.2}$ and $r^2_{Y2.1}$, and interpret their meaning.

14.35 In Problem 14.7 on page 531, you used the total staff present and remote hours to predict standby hours (stored in Standby). Using the results from that problem,

a. at the 0.05 level of significance, determine whether each independent variable makes a significant contribution to the regression model. On the basis of these results, indicate the most appropriate regression model for this set of data.

b. compute the coefficients of partial determination, $r^2_{Y1.2}$ and $r^2_{Y2.1}$, and interpret their meaning.

14.36 In Problem 14.6 on page 530, you used radio advertising and newspaper advertising to predict sales (stored in Advertise). Using the results from that problem,

a. at the 0.05 level of significance, determine whether each independent variable makes a significant contribution to the regression model. On the basis of these results, indicate the most appropriate regression model for this set of data.

b. compute the coefficients of partial determination, $r^2_{Y1.2}$ and $r^2_{Y2.1}$, and interpret their meaning.

14.37 In Problem 14.8 on page 531, you used land area of a property and age of a house to predict appraised value (stored in GlenCove). Using the results from that problem,

a. at the 0.05 level of significance, determine whether each independent variable makes a significant contribution to the regression model. On the basis of these results, indicate the most appropriate regression model for this set of data.

b. compute the coefficients of partial determination, $r^2_{Y1.2}$ and $r^2_{Y2.1}$, and interpret their meaning.

14.6 Using Dummy Variables and Interaction Terms in Regression Models

The multiple regression models discussed in Sections 14.1 through 14.5 assumed that each independent variable is a numerical variable. For example, in Section 14.1, you used price and promotional expenditures, two numerical independent variables, to predict the monthly sales of OmniPower nutrition bars. However, for some models, you need to include the effect of a categorical independent variable. For example, to predict the monthly sales of the OmniPower bars, you might include the categorical variable end-cap location in the model to explore the possible effect on sales caused by displaying the OmniPower bars in two different end-cap display locations: produce or beverage. (See the Chapter 10 Using Statistics scenario involving the sales of All-Natural Brain-Boost Cola.)

Dummy Variables

To include a categorical independent variable in a regression model, you use a **dummy variable**. A dummy variable recodes the categories of a categorical variable using the numeric values 0 and 1 to represent the absence (value 0) or presence of the characteristic (value 1). If a given categorical independent variable has only two categories, you can define one dummy variable, X_d, to represent the two categories. For example, for the categorical variable end-cap location, you can define the dummy variable, X_d, as

$$X_d = 0 \text{ if the observation is in first category (produce end-cap)}$$

$$X_d = 1 \text{ if the observation is in second category (beverage end-cap)}$$

To illustrate using dummy variables in regression, consider a business problem that involves developing a model for predicting the assessed value of houses ($thousands), based on the size of the house (in thousands of square feet) and whether the house has a fireplace. To include the categorical variable for the presence of a fireplace, the dummy variable X_2 is defined as

$$X_2 = 0 \text{ if the house does not have a fireplace}$$

$$X_2 = 1 \text{ if the house has a fireplace}$$

Data collected from a sample of 15 houses are organized and stored in House3. Table 14.5 presents the data. In the last column of Table 14.5, you can see how the categorical values are converted to numerical values.

TABLE 14.5

Predicting Assessed Value, Based on Size of House and Presence of a Fireplace

Assessed Value	Size	Fireplace	Fireplace Coded
234.4	2.00	Yes	1
227.4	1.71	No	0
225.7	1.45	No	0
235.9	1.76	Yes	1
229.1	1.93	No	0
220.4	1.20	Yes	1
225.8	1.55	Yes	1
235.9	1.93	Yes	1
228.5	1.59	Yes	1
229.2	1.50	Yes	1
236.7	1.90	Yes	1
229.3	1.39	Yes	1
224.5	1.54	No	0
233.8	1.89	Yes	1
226.8	1.59	No	0

Assuming that the slope of assessed value with the size of the house is the same for houses that have and do not have a fireplace, the multiple regression model is

$$Y_i = \beta_0 + \beta_1 X_{1i} + \beta_2 X_{2i} + \varepsilon_i$$

where

Y_i = assessed value, in thousands of dollars, for house i

β_0 = Y intercept

X_{1i} = size of the house, in thousands of square feet, for house i

β_1 = slope of assessed value with size of the house, holding constant the presence or absence of a fireplace

X_{2i} = dummy variable that represents the absence or presence of a fireplace for house i

β_2 = net effect of the presence of a fireplace on assessed value, holding constant the size of the house

ε_i = random error in Y for house i

Figure 14.9 presents the regression results for this model, in which FireplaceCoded is the dummy variable that represents the absence or presence of a fireplace for a house.

FIGURE 14.9

Regression results worksheet for the model that includes size of house and presence of fireplace

Create dummy variables using the Section EG14.6 instructions.

	A	B	C	D	E	F	G
1	**Assessed Value Analysis**						
2							
3	***Regression Statistics***						
4	Multiple R	0.9006					
5	R Square	0.8111					
6	Adjusted R Square	0.7796					
7	Standard Error	2.2626					
8	Observations	15					
9							
10	**ANOVA**						
11		*df*	*SS*	*MS*	*F*	*Significance F*	
12	Regression	2	263.7039	131.8520	25.7557	0.0000	
13	Residual	12	61.4321	5.1193			
14	Total	14	325.1360				
15							
16		*Coefficients*	*Standard Error*	*t Stat*	*P-value*	*Lower 95%*	*Upper 95%*
17	Intercept	200.0905	4.3517	45.9803	0.0000	190.6090	209.5719
18	Size	16.1858	2.5744	6.2871	0.0000	10.5766	21.7951
19	FireplaceCoded	3.8530	1.2412	3.1042	0.0091	1.1486	6.5574

From Figure 14.9, the regression equation is

$$\hat{Y}_i = 200.0905 + 16.1858X_{1i} + 3.8530X_{2i}$$

For houses without a fireplace, you substitute $X_2 = 0$ into the regression equation:

$$\begin{aligned}\hat{Y}_i &= 200.0905 + 16.1858X_{1i} + 3.8530X_{2i}\\ &= 200.0905 + 16.1858X_{1i} + 3.8530(0)\\ &= 200.0905 + 16.1858X_{1i}\end{aligned}$$

For houses with a fireplace, you substitute $X_2 = 1$ into the regression equation:

$$\begin{aligned}\hat{Y}_i &= 200.0905 + 16.1858X_{1i} + 3.8530X_{2i}\\ &= 200.0905 + 16.1858X_{1i} + 3.8530(1)\\ &= 203.9435 + 16.1858X_{1i}\end{aligned}$$

In this model, the regression coefficients are interpreted as follows:

- Holding constant whether a house has a fireplace, for each increase of 1.0 thousand square feet in the size of the house, the predicted assessed value is estimated to increase by 16.1858 thousand dollars (i.e., $16,185.80).
- Holding constant the size of the house, the presence of a fireplace is estimated to increase the predicted assessed value of the house by 3.8530 thousand dollars (i.e., $3,853).

In Figure 14.9, the t_{STAT} test statistic for the slope of the size of the house with assessed value is 6.2871, and the p-value is approximately 0.000; the t_{STAT} test statistic for presence of a fireplace is 3.1042, and the p-value is 0.0091. Thus, each of the two variables makes a significant contribution to the model at the 0.01 level of significance. In addition, the coefficient of multiple determination indicates that 81.11% of the variation in assessed value is explained by variation in the size of the house and whether the house has a fireplace.

In some situations, the categorical independent variable has more than two categories. When this occurs, two or more dummy variables are needed. Example 14.3 illustrates such a situation.

EXAMPLE 14.3

Modeling a Three-Level Categorical Variable

Define a multiple regression model using sales as the dependent variable and package design and price as independent variables. Package design is a three-level categorical variable with designs *A*, *B*, or *C*.

SOLUTION To model the three-level categorical variable package design, two dummy variables, X_1 and X_2, are needed:

$$X_{1i} = 1 \text{ if package design } A \text{ is used in observation } i\text{; 0 otherwise}$$

$$X_{2i} = 1 \text{ if package design } B \text{ is used in observation } i\text{; 0 otherwise}$$

Thus, if observation i uses package design A, then $X_{1i} = 1$ and $X_{2i} = 0$; if observation i uses package design B, then $X_{1i} = 0$ and $X_{2i} = 1$; and if observation i uses package design C, then $X_{1i} = X_{2i} = 0$. Thus, package design C becomes the baseline category to which the effect of package design A and package design B is compared. A third independent variable is used for price:

$$X_{3i} = \text{price for observation } i$$

Thus, the regression model for this example is

$$Y_i = \beta_0 + \beta_1 X_{1i} + \beta_2 X_{2i} + \beta_3 X_{3i} + \varepsilon_i$$

where

Y_i = sales for observation i

β_0 = Y intercept

β_1 = difference between the predicted sales of design A and the predicted sales of design C, holding price constant

β_2 = difference between the predicted sales of design B and the predicted sales of design C, holding price constant

β_3 = slope of sales with price, holding the package design constant

ε_i = random error in Y for observation i

Interactions

In all the regression models discussed so far, the effect an independent variable has on the dependent variable has been assumed to be independent of the other independent variables in the model. An **interaction** occurs if the effect of an independent variable on the dependent variable changes according to the *value* of a second independent variable. For example, it is possible for advertising to have a large effect on the sales of a product when the price of a product is low. However, if the price of the product is too high, increases in advertising will not dramatically change sales. In this case, price and advertising are said to interact. In other words, you cannot make general statements about the effect of advertising on sales. The effect that advertising has on sales is *dependent* on the price. You use an **interaction term** (sometimes referred to as a **cross-product term**) to model an interaction effect in a regression model.

To illustrate the concept of interaction and use of an interaction term, return to the example concerning the assessed values of homes discussed on pages 546–547. In the regression model, you assumed that the effect the size of the home has on the assessed value is independent of whether the house has a fireplace. In other words, you assumed that the slope of assessed value with size is the same for houses with fireplaces as it is for houses without fireplaces. If these two slopes are different, an interaction exists between the size of the home and the fireplace.

To evaluate whether an interaction exists, you first define an interaction term that is the product of the independent variable X_1 (size of house) and the dummy variable X_2 (FireplaceCoded). You then test whether this interaction variable makes a significant contribution to the regression model. If the interaction is significant, you cannot use the original model for prediction. For the data of Table 14.5 on page 546, you define the following:

$$X_3 = X_1 \times X_2$$

Figure 14.10 presents a regression results worksheet for this regression model, which includes the size of the house, X_1, the presence of a fireplace, X_2, and the interaction of X_1 and X_2 (defined as X_3 and labeled Size * FireplaceCoded in the worksheet).

FIGURE 14.10

Regression results for a model that includes size, presence of fireplace, and interaction of size and fireplace

	A	B	C	D	E	F	G
1	**Assessed Value Analysis**						
2							
3	***Regression Statistics***						
4	Multiple R	0.9179					
5	R Square	0.8426					
6	Adjusted R Square	0.7996					
7	Standard Error	2.1573					
8	Observations	15					
9							
10	**ANOVA**						
11		*df*	*SS*	*MS*	*F*	*Significance F*	
12	Regression	3	273.9441	91.3147	19.6215	0.0001	
13	Residual	11	51.1919	4.6538			
14	Total	14	325.1360				
15							
16		*Coefficients*	*Standard Error*	*t Stat*	*P-value*	*Lower 95%*	*Upper 95%*
17	Intercept	212.9522	9.6122	22.1544	0.0000	191.7959	234.1084
18	Size	8.3624	5.8173	1.4375	0.1784	-4.4414	21.1662
19	FireplaceCoded	-11.8404	10.6455	-1.1122	0.2898	-35.2710	11.5902
20	Size * FireplaceCoded	9.5180	6.4165	1.4834	0.1661	-4.6046	23.6406

To test for the existence of an interaction, you use the null hypothesis:

$$H_0: \beta_3 = 0$$

versus the alternative hypothesis:

$$H_1: \beta_3 \neq 0.$$

In Figure 14.10, the t_{STAT} test statistic for the interaction of size and fireplace is 1.4834. Because $t_{STAT} = 1.4834 < 2.201$ or the p-value $= 0.1661 > 0.05$, you do not reject the null hypothesis. Therefore, the interaction does not make a significant contribution to the model, given that size and presence of a fireplace are already included. You can conclude that the slope of assessed value with size is the same for houses with fireplaces and without fireplaces.

Regression models can have several numerical independent variables along with a dummy variable. Example 14.4 illustrates a regression model in which there are two numerical independent variables and a categorical independent variable.

EXAMPLE 14.4

Studying a Regression Model That Contains a Dummy Variable

The business problem facing a real estate developer involves predicting heating oil consumption in single-family houses. The independent variables considered are atmospheric temperature (°F), X_1, and the amount of attic insulation (inches), X_2. Data are collected from a sample of 15 single-family houses. Of the 15 houses selected, houses 1, 4, 6, 7, 8, 10, and 12 are ranch-style houses. The data are organized and stored in **HeatingOil**. Develop and analyze an appropriate regression model, using these three independent variables X_1, X_2, and X_3 (where X_3 is the dummy variable for ranch-style houses).

SOLUTION Define X_3, a dummy variable for ranch-style house, as follows:

$$X_3 = 0 \text{ if the style is not ranch}$$
$$X_3 = 1 \text{ if the style is ranch}$$

Assuming that the slope between heating oil consumption and atmospheric temperature, X_1, and between heating oil consumption and the amount of attic insulation, X_2, is the same for both styles of houses, the regression model is

$$Y_i = \beta_0 + \beta_1 X_{1i} + \beta_2 X_{2i} + \beta_3 X_{3i} + \varepsilon_i$$

where

Y_i = monthly heating oil consumption, in gallons, for house i

β_0 = Y intercept

β_1 = slope of heating oil consumption with atmospheric temperature, holding constant the effect of attic insulation and the style of the house

β_2 = slope of heating oil consumption with attic insulation, holding constant the effect of atmospheric temperature and the style of the house

β_3 = incremental effect of the presence of a ranch-style house, holding constant the effect of atmospheric temperature and attic insulation

ε_i = random error in Y for house i

Figure 14.11 presents results for this regression model.

FIGURE 14.11
Regression results for a model that includes temperature, insulation, and style for the heating oil data

	A	B	C	D	E	F	G
1	**Heating Oil Consumption Analysis**						
2							
3	*Regression Statistics*						
4	Multiple R	0.9942					
5	R Square	0.9884					
6	Adjusted R Square	0.9853					
7	Standard Error	15.7489					
8	Observations	15					
9							
10	ANOVA						
11		*df*	*SS*	*MS*	*F*	*Significance F*	
12	Regression	3	233406.9094	77802.3031	313.6822	0.0000	
13	Residual	11	2728.3200	248.0291			
14	Total	14	236135.2293				
15							
16		*Coefficients*	*Standard Error*	*t Stat*	*P-value*	*Lower 95%*	*Upper 95%*
17	Intercept	592.5401	14.3370	41.3295	0.0000	560.9846	624.0956
18	Temperature	-5.5251	0.2044	-27.0267	0.0000	-5.9751	-5.0752
19	Insulation	-21.3761	1.4480	-14.7623	0.0000	-24.5632	-18.1891
20	Ranch-style	-38.9727	8.3584	-4.6627	0.0007	-57.3695	-20.5759

From the results in Figure 14.11, the regression equation is

$$\hat{Y}_i = 592.5401 - 5.5251X_{1i} - 21.3761X_{2i} - 38.9727X_{3i}$$

For houses that are not ranch style, because $X_3 = 0$, the regression equation reduces to

$$\hat{Y}_i = 592.5401 - 5.5251X_{1i} - 21.3761X_{2i}$$

For houses that are ranch style, because $X_3 = 1$, the regression equation reduces to

$$\hat{Y}_i = 553.5674 - 5.5251X_{1i} - 21.3761X_{2i}$$

In this model, the regression coefficients are interpreted as follows:

- Holding constant the attic insulation and the house style, for each additional 1°F increase in atmospheric temperature, you estimate that the predicted heating oil consumption decreases by 5.5251 gallons.
- Holding constant the atmospheric temperature and the house style, for each additional 1-inch increase in attic insulation, you estimate that the predicted heating oil consumption decreases by 21.3761 gallons.

- b_3 measures the effect on oil consumption of having a ranch-style house ($X_3 = 1$) compared with having a house that is not ranch style ($X_3 = 0$). Thus, with atmospheric temperature and attic insulation held constant, you estimate that the predicted heating oil consumption is 38.9727 gallons less for a ranch-style house than for a house that is not ranch style.

The three t_{STAT} test statistics representing the slopes for temperature, insulation, and ranch style are -27.0267, -14.7623, and -4.6627. Each of the corresponding p-values is extremely small (less than 0.001). Thus, each of the three variables makes a significant contribution to the model. In addition, the coefficient of multiple determination indicates that 98.84% of the variation in oil usage is explained by variation in temperature, insulation, and whether the house is ranch style.

Before you can use the model in Example 14.4, you need to determine whether the independent variables interact with each other. In Example 14.5, three interaction terms are added to the model.

EXAMPLE 14.5

Evaluating a Regression Model with Several Interactions

For the data of Example 14.4, determine whether adding the interaction terms makes a significant contribution to the regression model.

SOLUTION To evaluate possible interactions between the independent variables, three interaction terms are constructed as follows: $X_4 = X_1 \times X_2$, $X_5 = X_1 \times X_3$, and $X_6 = X_2 \times X_3$. The regression model is now

$$Y_i = \beta_0 + \beta_1 X_{1i} + \beta_2 X_{2i} + \beta_3 X_{3i} + \beta_4 X_{4i} + \beta_5 X_{5i} + \beta_6 X_{6i} + \varepsilon_i$$

where X_1 is temperature, X_2 is insulation, X_3 is the dummy variable ranch style, X_4 is the interaction between temperature and insulation, X_5 is the interaction between temperature and ranch style, and X_6 is the interaction between insulation and ranch style. Figure 14.12 presents the results for this regression model.

FIGURE 14.12

Regression results worksheet for a model that includes temperature, X_1; insulation, X_2; the dummy variable ranch-style, X_3; the interaction of temperature and insulation, X_4; the interaction of temperature and ranch-style, X_5; and the interaction of insulation and ranch-style, X_6

	A	B	C	D	E	F	G
1	**Heating Oil Consumption Analysis**						
2							
3	***Regression Statistics***						
4	Multiple R	0.9966					
5	R Square	0.9931					
6	Adjusted R Square	0.9880					
7	Standard Error	14.2506					
8	Observations	15					
9							
10	**ANOVA**						
11		*df*	*SS*	*MS*	*F*	*Significance F*	
12	Regression	6	234510.5818	39085.0970	192.4607	0.0000	
13	Residual	8	1624.6475	203.0809			
14	Total	14	236135.2293				
15							
16		*Coefficients*	*Standard Error*	*t Stat*	*P-value*	*Lower 95%*	*Upper 95%*
17	Intercept	642.8867	26.7059	24.0728	0.0000	581.3027	704.4707
18	Temperature	-6.9263	0.7531	-9.1969	0.0000	-8.6629	-5.1896
19	Insulation	-27.8825	3.5801	-7.7882	0.0001	-36.1383	-19.6268
20	Style	-84.6088	29.9956	-2.8207	0.0225	-153.7788	-15.4389
21	Temperature * Insulation	0.1702	0.0886	1.9204	0.0911	-0.0342	0.3746
22	Temperature * Ranch-style	0.6596	0.4617	1.4286	0.1910	-0.4051	1.7242
23	Insulation * Ranch-style	4.9870	3.5137	1.4193	0.1936	-3.1156	13.0895

To test whether the three interactions significantly improve the regression model, you use the partial F test. The null and alternative hypotheses are

$$H_0: \beta_4 = \beta_5 = \beta_6 = 0 \text{ (There are no interactions among } X_1, X_2, \text{ and } X_3.)$$

$$H_1: \beta_4 \neq 0 \text{ and/or } \beta_5 \neq 0 \text{ and/or } \beta_6 \neq 0 (X_1 \text{ interacts with } X_2, \text{ and/or } X_1 \text{ interacts with } X_3, \text{ and/or } X_2 \text{ interacts with } X_3.)$$

From Figure 14.12,

$$SSR(X_1, X_2, X_3, X_4, X_5, X_6) = 234{,}510.5818 \text{ with 6 degrees of freedom}$$

and from Figure 14.11 on page 550, $SSR(X_1, X_2, X_3) = 233{,}406.9094$ with 3 degrees of freedom. Thus,

$$SSR(X_1, X_2, X_3, X_4, X_5, X_6) - SSR(X_1, X_2, X_3) = 234{,}510.5818 - 233{,}406.9094 = 1{,}103.6724$$

The difference in degrees of freedom is $6 - 3 = 3$.

To use the partial F test for the simultaneous contribution of three variables to a model, you use an extension of Equation (14.11) on page 542.[2] The partial F_{STAT} test statistic is

$$F_{STAT} = \frac{[SSR(X_1, X_2, X_3, X_4, X_5, X_6) - SSR(X_1, X_2, X_3)]/3}{MSE(X_1, X_2, X_3, X_4, X_5, X_6)} = \frac{1{,}103.6724/3}{203.0809} = 1.8115$$

You compare the computed F_{STAT} test statistic to the critical F value for 3 and 8 degrees of freedom. Using a level of significance of 0.05, the critical F value from Table E.5 is 4.07. Because $F_{STAT} = 1.8115 < 4.07$, you conclude that the interactions do not make a significant contribution to the model, given that the model already includes temperature, X_1; insulation, X_2; and whether the house is ranch style, X_3. Therefore, the multiple regression model using X_1, X_2, and X_3 but no interaction terms is the better model. If you rejected this null hypothesis, you would then test the contribution of each interaction separately in order to determine which interaction terms to include in the model.

[2] In general, if a model has several independent variables and you want to test whether additional independent variables contribute to the model, the numerator of the F test is SSR (for all independent variables) minus SSR (for the initial set of variables) divided by the number of independent variables whose contribution is being tested.

Problems for Section 14.6

LEARNING THE BASICS

14.38 Suppose X_1 is a numerical variable and X_2 is a dummy variable and the regression equation for a sample of $n = 20$ is

$$\hat{Y}_i = 6 + 4X_{1i} + 2X_{2i}$$

a. Interpret the regression coefficient associated with variable X_1.

b. Interpret the regression coefficient associated with variable X_2.

c. Suppose that the t_{STAT} test statistic for testing the contribution of variable X_2 is 3.27. At the 0.05 level of significance, is there evidence that variable X_2 makes a significant contribution to the model?

APPLYING THE CONCEPTS

14.39 The chair of the accounting department plans to develop a regression model to predict the grade point average in accounting for those students who are graduating and have completed the accounting major, based on a student's SAT score and whether the student received a grade of B or higher in the introductory statistics course ($0 =$ no and $1 =$ yes).

a. Explain the steps involved in developing a regression model for these data. Be sure to indicate the particular models you need to evaluate and compare.

b. Suppose the regression coefficient for the variable whether the student received a grade of B or higher in the introductory statistics course is $+0.30$. How do you interpret this result?

14.40 A real estate association in a suburban community would like to study the relationship between the size of a single-family house (as measured by the number of rooms) and the selling price of the house (in $thousands). Two different neighborhoods are included in the study, one on the east side of the community ($=0$) and the other on the west side ($=1$). A random sample of 20 houses was selected, with the results stored in **Neighbor**. For (a) through (k), do not include an interaction term.

a. State the multiple regression equation that predicts the selling price, based on the number of rooms and the neighborhood.

b. Interpret the regression coefficients in (a).

c. Predict the selling price for a house with nine rooms that is located in an east-side neighborhood. Construct a 95% confidence interval estimate and a 95% prediction interval.

d. Perform a residual analysis on the results and determine whether the regression assumptions are valid.
e. Is there a significant relationship between selling price and the two independent variables (rooms and neighborhood) at the 0.05 level of significance?
f. At the 0.05 level of significance, determine whether each independent variable makes a contribution to the regression model. Indicate the most appropriate regression model for this set of data.
g. Construct and interpret a 95% confidence interval estimate of the population slope for the relationship between selling price and number of rooms.
h. Construct and interpret a 95% confidence interval estimate of the population slope for the relationship between selling price and neighborhood.
i. Compute and interpret the adjusted r^2.
j. Compute the coefficients of partial determination and interpret their meaning.
k. What assumption do you need to make about the slope of selling price with number of rooms?
l. Add an interaction term to the model and, at the 0.05 level of significance, determine whether it makes a significant contribution to the model.
m. On the basis of the results of (f) and (l), which model is most appropriate? Explain.

14.41 The marketing manager of a large supermarket chain faced the business problem of determining the effect on the sales of specialty pet food of shelf space and whether the product was placed at the front (=1) or back (=0) of the aisle. Data are collected from a random sample of 12 equal-sized stores and organized and stored in **Petfood**. These data are:

Store	Shelf Space (square feet)	Location	Weekly Sales ($)
1	5	Back	160
2	5	Front	220
3	5	Back	140
4	10	Back	190
5	10	Back	240
6	10	Front	260
7	15	Back	230
8	15	Back	270
9	15	Front	280
10	20	Back	260
11	20	Back	290
12	20	Front	310

For (a) through (m), do not include an interaction term.
a. State the multiple regression equation that predicts weekly sales based on shelf space and location.
b. Interpret the regression coefficients in (a).
c. Predict the weekly sales of specialty pet food for a store with 8 square feet of shelf space situated at the back of the aisle. Construct a 95% confidence interval estimate and a 95% prediction interval.
d. Perform a residual analysis on the results and determine whether the regression assumptions are valid.
e. Is there a significant relationship between sales and the two independent variables (shelf space and aisle position) at the 0.05 level of significance?
f. At the 0.05 level of significance, determine whether each independent variable makes a contribution to the regression model. Indicate the most appropriate regression model for this set of data.
g. Construct and interpret 95% confidence interval estimates of the population slope for the relationship between sales and shelf space and between sales and aisle location.
h. Compare the slope in (b) with the slope for the simple linear regression model of Problem 13.4 on page 481. Explain the difference in the results.
i. Compute and interpret the meaning of the coefficient of multiple determination, r^2.
j. Compute and interpret the adjusted r^2.
k. Compare r^2 with the r^2 value computed in Problem 13.16 (a) on page 487.
l. Compute the coefficients of partial determination and interpret their meaning.
m. What assumption about the slope of shelf space with sales do you need to make in this problem?
n. Add an interaction term to the model and, at the 0.05 level of significance, determine whether it makes a significant contribution to the model.
o. On the basis of the results of (f) and (n), which model is most appropriate? Explain.

14.42 In mining engineering, holes are often drilled through rock, using drill bits. As a drill hole gets deeper, additional rods are added to the drill bit to enable additional drilling to take place. It is expected that drilling time increases with depth. This increased drilling time could be caused by several factors, including the mass of the drill rods that are strung together. The business problem relates to whether drilling is faster using dry drilling holes or wet drilling holes. Using dry drilling holes involves forcing compressed air down the drill rods to flush the cuttings and drive the hammer. Using wet drilling holes involves forcing water rather than air down the hole. Data have been collected from a sample of 50 drill holes that contains measurements of the time to drill each additional 5 feet (in minutes), the depth (in feet), and whether the hole was a dry drilling hole or a wet drilling hole. The data are organized and stored in **Drill**. (Data extracted from R. Penner and D. G. Watts, "Mining Information," *The American Statistician*, 45, 1991, pp. 4–9.) Develop a model to predict additional drilling time, based on depth and type of drilling hole (dry or wet). For (a) through (k) do not include an interaction term.
a. State the multiple regression equation.
b. Interpret the regression coefficients in (a).

c. Predict the additional drilling time for a dry drilling hole at a depth of 100 feet. Construct a 95% confidence interval estimate and a 95% prediction interval.
d. Perform a residual analysis on the results and determine whether the regression assumptions are valid.
e. Is there a significant relationship between additional drilling time and the two independent variables (depth and type of drilling hole) at the 0.05 level of significance?
f. At the 0.05 level of significance, determine whether each independent variable makes a contribution to the regression model. Indicate the most appropriate regression model for this set of data.
g. Construct a 95% confidence interval estimate of the population slope for the relationship between additional drilling time and depth.
h. Construct a 95% confidence interval estimate of the population slope for the relationship between additional drilling time and the type of hole drilled.
i. Compute and interpret the adjusted r^2.
j. Compute the coefficients of partial determination and interpret their meaning.
k. What assumption do you need to make about the slope of additional drilling time with depth?
l. Add an interaction term to the model and, at the 0.05 level of significance, determine whether it makes a significant contribution to the model.
m. On the basis of the results of (f) and (l), which model is most appropriate? Explain.

14.43 The owner of a moving company typically has his most experienced manager predict the total number of labor hours that will be required to complete an upcoming move. This approach has proved useful in the past, but the owner has the business objective of developing a more accurate method of predicting labor hours. In a preliminary effort to provide a more accurate method, the owner has decided to use the number of cubic feet moved and whether there is an elevator in the apartment building as the independent variables and has collected data for 36 moves in which the origin and destination were within the borough of Manhattan in New York City and the travel time was an insignificant portion of the hours worked. The data are organized and stored in **Moving**. For (a) through (k), do not include an interaction term.
a. State the multiple regression equation for predicting labor hours, using the number of cubic feet moved and whether there is an elevator.
b. Interpret the regression coefficients in (a).
c. Predict the labor hours for moving 500 cubic feet in an apartment building that has an elevator and construct a 95% confidence interval estimate and a 95% prediction interval.
d. Perform a residual analysis on the results and determine whether the regression assumptions are valid.
e. Is there a significant relationship between labor hours and the two independent variables (cubic feet moved and whether there is an elevator in the apartment building) at the 0.05 level of significance?
f. At the 0.05 level of significance, determine whether each independent variable makes a contribution to the regression model. Indicate the most appropriate regression model for this set of data.
g. Construct a 95% confidence interval estimate of the population slope for the relationship between labor hours and cubic feet moved.
h. Construct a 95% confidence interval estimate for the relationship between labor hours and the presence of an elevator.
i. Compute and interpret the adjusted r^2.
j. Compute the coefficients of partial determination and interpret their meaning.
k. What assumption do you need to make about the slope of labor hours with cubic feet moved?
l. Add an interaction term to the model and, at the 0.05 level of significance, determine whether it makes a significant contribution to the model.
m. On the basis of the results of (f) and (l), which model is most appropriate? Explain.

SELF Test **14.44** In Problem 14.4 on page 530, you used sales and orders to predict distribution cost (stored in **WareCost**). Develop a regression model to predict distribution cost that includes sales, orders, and the interaction of sales and orders.
a. At the 0.05 level of significance, is there evidence that the interaction term makes a significant contribution to the model?
b. Which regression model is more appropriate, the one used in (a) or the one used in Problem 14.4? Explain.

14.45 Zagat's publishes restaurant ratings for various locations in the United States. The file **Restaurants** contains the Zagat rating for food, décor, service, and cost per person for a sample of 50 restaurants located in a city and 50 restaurants located in a suburb. (Data extracted from *Zagat Survey 2012, New York City Restaurants*; and *Zagat Survey 2011–2012, Long Island Restaurants*.) Develop a regression model to predict the cost per person, based on a variable that represents the sum of the ratings for food, décor, and service and a dummy variable concerning location (city vs. suburban). For (a) through (m), do not include an interaction term.
a. State the multiple regression equation.
b. Interpret the regression coefficients in (a).
c. Predict the cost for a restaurant with a summated rating of 60 that is located in a city and construct a 95% confidence interval estimate and a 95% prediction interval.
d. Perform a residual analysis on the results and determine whether the regression assumptions are satisfied.
e. Is there a significant relationship between price and the two independent variables (summated rating and location) at the 0.05 level of significance?
f. At the 0.05 level of significance, determine whether each independent variable makes a contribution to the

regression model. Indicate the most appropriate regression model for this set of data.

g. Construct a 95% confidence interval estimate of the population slope for the relationship between cost and summated rating.

h. Compare the slope in (b) with the slope for the simple linear regression model of Problem 13.5 on page 481. Explain the difference in the results.

i. Compute and interpret the meaning of the coefficient of multiple determination.

j. Compute and interpret the adjusted r^2.

k. Compare r^2 with the r^2 value computed in Problem 13.17 (b) on page 487.

l. Compute the coefficients of partial determination and interpret their meaning.

m. What assumption about the slope of cost with summated rating do you need to make in this problem?

n. Add an interaction term to the model and, at the 0.05 level of significance, determine whether it makes a significant contribution to the model.

o. On the basis of the results of (f) and (n), which model is most appropriate? Explain.

14.46 In Problem 14.6 on page 530, you used radio advertising and newspaper advertising to predict sales (stored in Advertise). Develop a regression model to predict sales that includes radio advertising, newspaper advertising, and the interaction of radio advertising and newspaper advertising.

a. At the 0.05 level of significance, is there evidence that the interaction term makes a significant contribution to the model?

b. Which regression model is more appropriate, the one used in this problem or the one used in Problem 14.6? Explain.

14.47 In Problem 14.5 on page 530, horsepower and weight were used to predict miles per gallon (stored in Auto2012). Develop a regression model that includes horsepower, weight, and the interaction of horsepower and weight to predict miles per gallon.

a. At the 0.05 level of significance, is there evidence that the interaction term makes a significant contribution to the model?

b. Which regression model is more appropriate, the one used in this problem or the one used in Problem 14.5? Explain.

14.48 In Problem 14.7 on page 531, you used total staff present and remote hours to predict standby hours (stored in Standby). Develop a regression model to predict standby hours that includes total staff present, remote hours, and the interaction of total staff present and remote hours.

a. At the 0.05 level of significance, is there evidence that the interaction term makes a significant contribution to the model?

b. Which regression model is more appropriate, the one used in this problem or the one used in Problem 14.7? Explain.

14.49 The director of a training program for a large insurance company has the business objective of determining which training method is best for training underwriters. The three methods to be evaluated are classroom, online, and courseware app. The 30 trainees are divided into three randomly assigned groups of 10. Before the start of the training, each trainee is given a proficiency exam that measures mathematics and computer skills. At the end of the training, all students take the same end-of-training exam. The results are organized and stored in Underwriting.

Develop a multiple regression model to predict the score on the end-of-training exam, based on the score on the proficiency exam and the method of training used. For (a) through (k), do not include an interaction term.

a. State the multiple regression equation.

b. Interpret the regression coefficients in (a).

c. Predict the end-of-training exam score for a student with a proficiency exam score of 100 who had courseware app-based training.

d. Perform a residual analysis on your results and determine whether the regression assumptions are valid.

e. Is there a significant relationship between the end-of-training exam score and the independent variables (proficiency score and training method) at the 0.05 level of significance?

f. At the 0.05 level of significance, determine whether each independent variable makes a contribution to the regression model. Indicate the most appropriate regression model for this set of data.

g. Construct and interpret 95% confidence interval estimates of the population slope for the relationship between the end-of-training exam score and the proficiency exam score.

h. Construct and interpret a 95% confidence interval estimate of the population slope for the relationship between the end-of-training exam score and type of training method.

i. Compute and interpret the adjusted r^2.

j. Compute the coefficients of partial determination and interpret their meaning.

k. What assumption about the slope of proficiency score with end-of-training exam score do you need to make in this problem?

l. Add interaction terms to the model and, at the 0.05 level of significance, determine whether any interaction terms make a significant contribution to the model.

m. On the basis of the results of (f) and (l), which model is most appropriate? Explain.

14.7 Logistic Regression

The discussion of the simple linear regression model in Chapter 13 and the multiple regression models in Sections 14.1 through 14.6 only considered *numerical* dependent variables. However, in many applications, the dependent variable is a *categorical* variable that takes on one of only two possible values, such as a customer purchases a product or a customer does not purchase a product. Using a categorical dependent variable violates the normality assumption of the least-squares method and can also result in predicted Y values that are impossible.

An alternative approach to least-squares regression originally applied to survival data in the health sciences (see reference 1), **logistic regression**, enables you to use regression models to predict the probability of a particular categorical response for a given set of independent variables. The logistic regression model uses the **odds ratio**, which represents the probability of an event of interest compared with the probability of not having an event of interest. Equation (14.15) defines the odds ratio.

ODDS RATIO

$$\text{odds ratio} = \frac{\text{probability of an event of interest}}{1 - \text{probability of an event of interest}} \quad \textbf{(14.15)}$$

Using Equation (14.15), if the probability of an event of interest is 0.50, the odds ratio is

$$\text{odds ratio} = \frac{0.50}{1 - 0.50} = 1.0, \text{ or } 1 \text{ to } 1$$

If the probability of an event of interest is 0.75, the odds ratio is

$$\text{odds ratio} = \frac{0.75}{1 - 0.75} = 3.0, \text{ or } 3 \text{ to } 1$$

The logistic regression model is based on the natural logarithm of the odds ratio, ln(odds ratio).

Equation (14.16) defines the logistic regression model for k independent variables.

Student Tip
ln is the symbol used for natural logarithms, also known as base *e* logarithms. ln(x) is the logarithm of x having base e, where $e \cong 2.718282$.

LOGISTIC REGRESSION MODEL

$$\ln(\text{odds ratio}) = \beta_0 + \beta_1 X_{1i} + \beta_2 X_{2i} + \cdots + \beta_k X_{ki} + \varepsilon_i \quad \textbf{(14.16)}$$

where

k = number of independent variables in the model

ε_i = random error in observation i

In Sections 13.2 and 14.1, the method of least squares was used to develop a regression equation. In logistic regression, a mathematical method called *maximum likelihood estimation* is typically used to develop a regression equation to predict the natural logarithm of this odds ratio. Equation (14.17) defines the logistic regression equation.

LOGISTIC REGRESSION EQUATION

$$\ln(\text{Estimated odds ratio}) = b_0 + b_1 X_{1i} + b_2 X_{2i} + \cdots + b_k X_{ki} \quad \textbf{(14.17)}$$

Once you have determined the logistic regression equation, you use Equation (14.18) to compute the estimated odds ratio.

ESTIMATED ODDS RATIO

$$\text{Estimated odds ratio} = e^{\ln(\text{Estimated odds ratio})} \quad \textbf{(14.18)}$$

Once you have computed the estimated odds ratio, you use Equation (14.19) to compute the estimated probability of an event of interest.

ESTIMATED PROBABILITY OF AN EVENT OF INTEREST

$$\text{Estimated probability of an event of interest} = \frac{\text{estimated odds ratio}}{1 + \text{estimated odds ratio}} \quad \textbf{(14.19)}$$

To illustrate the use of logistic regression, consider the case of the sales and marketing manager for the credit card division of a major financial company. The manager wants to conduct a campaign to persuade existing holders of the bank's standard credit card to upgrade, for a nominal annual fee, to the bank's platinum card. The manager wonders "Which of the existing standard credit cardholders should we target for this campaign?"

The manager has access to the results from a sample of 30 cardholders who were targeted during a pilot campaign last year. These results have been organized as three variables and stored in **CardStudy**. The three variables are cardholder upgraded to a premium card (0 = no, 1 = yes), Y; and two independent variables: prior year's credit card purchases (in $thousands), X_1; and cardholder ordered additional credit cards for other authorized users (0 = no, 1 = yes), X_2. Figure 14.13 is a regression results worksheet for the logistic regression model using these data.

FIGURE 14.13
Logistic regression results worksheet for the credit card pilot study data

*Figure 14.13 displays the **COMPUTE worksheet** in the **Logistic Regression workbook** that the Section EG14.7 instructions use.*

	A	B	C	D	E
1	**Logistic Regression**				
2					
3	Predictor	Coefficients	SE Coef	*Z*	*p*-Value
4	Intercept	-6.9394	2.9471	-2.3547	0.0185
5	Purchases	0.1395	0.0681	2.0490	0.0405
6	Extra Cards:1	2.7743	1.1927	2.3261	0.0200
7					
8	Deviance	20.0769			

In this model, the regression coefficients are interpreted as follows:

- The regression constant, b_0, is –6.9394. This means that for a credit cardholder who did not charge any purchases last year and who does not have additional cards, the estimated natural logarithm of the odds ratio of purchasing the premium card is –6.9394.
- The regression coefficient, b_1, is 0.1395. This means that holding constant the effect of whether the credit cardholder has additional cards for members of the household, for each increase of $1,000 in annual credit card spending using the company's card, the estimated natural logarithm of the odds ratio of purchasing the premium card increases by 0.1395. Therefore, cardholders who charged more in the previous year are more likely to upgrade to a premium card.
- The regression coefficient, b_2, is 2.7743. This means that holding constant the annual credit card spending, the estimated natural logarithm of the odds ratio of purchasing the premium card increases by 2.7743 for a credit cardholder who has additional cards for members of the household compared with one who does not have additional cards. Therefore, cardholders possessing additional cards for other members of the household are much more likely to upgrade to a premium card.

The regression coefficients suggest that the credit card company should develop a marketing campaign that targets cardholders who tend to charge large amounts to their cards, and to households that possess more than one card.

As is the case with least-squares regression models, a main purpose of performing logistic regression analysis is to provide predictions of a dependent variable. For example, consider a cardholder who charged $36,000 last year and possesses additional cards for members of the household. What is the probability the cardholder will upgrade to the premium card during the marketing campaign? Using $X_1 = 36, X_2 = 1$, Equation (14.17) on page 556, and the results displayed in Figure 14.13 on page 557,

$$\begin{aligned}\ln(\text{estimated odds of purchasing versus not purchasing}) &= -6.9394 + (0.1395)(36) + (2.7743)(1)\\ &= 0.8569\end{aligned}$$

Then, using Equation (14.18) on page 557,

$$\text{estimated odds ratio} = e^{0.8569} = 2.3558$$

Therefore, the odds are 2.3558 to 1 that a credit cardholder who spent $36,000 last year and has additional cards will purchase the premium card during the campaign. Using Equation (14.19) on page 557, you can convert this odds ratio to a probability:

$$\begin{aligned}\text{estimated probability of purchasing premium card} &= \frac{2.3558}{1 + 2.3558}\\ &= 0.702\end{aligned}$$

Thus, the estimated probability is 0.702 that a credit cardholder who spent $36,000 last year and has additional cards will purchase the premium card during the campaign. In other words, you predict 70.2% of such individuals will purchase the premium card.

Now that you have used the logistic regression model for prediction, you need to determine whether or not the model is a good-fitting model. The **deviance statistic** is frequently used to determine whether the current model provides a good fit to the data. This statistic measures the fit of the current model compared with a model that has as many parameters as there are data points (what is called a *saturated* model). The deviance statistic follows a chi-square distribution with $n - k - 1$ degrees of freedom. The null and alternative hypotheses are

H_0: The model is a good-fitting model.

H_1: The model is not a good-fitting model.

When using the deviance statistic for logistic regression, the null hypothesis represents a good-fitting model, which is the opposite of the null hypothesis when using the overall F test for the multiple regression model (see Section 14.2). Using the α level of significance, the decision rule is

Reject H_0 if deviance $> \chi^2_\alpha$;

otherwise, do not reject H_o.

The critical value for a χ^2 statistic with $n - k - 1 = 30 - 2 - 1 = 27$ degrees of freedom is 40.113 (see Table E.4). From Figure 14.13 on page 557, the deviance $= 20.0769 < 40.113$. Thus, you do not reject H_0, and you conclude that the model is a good-fitting one.

Now that you have concluded that the model is a good-fitting one, you need to evaluate whether each of the independent variables makes a significant contribution to the model in the presence of the others. As is the case with linear regression in Sections 13.7 and 14.4, the test statistic is based on the ratio of the regression coefficient to the standard error of the regression coefficient. In logistic regression, this ratio is defined by the **Wald statistic**, which approximately follows the normal distribution. From Figure 14.13, the Wald statistic (labeled Z) is 2.049 for X_1 and 2.3261 for X_2. Each of these is greater than the critical value of +1.96 of the normal distribution at the 0.05 level of significance (the p-values are 0.0405 and 0.02). You can conclude that each of the two independent variables makes a contribution to the model in the presence of the other. Therefore, you should include both these independent variables in the model.

Problems for Section 14.7

LEARNING THE BASICS

14.50 Interpret the meaning of a slope coefficient equal to 2.2 in logistic regression.

14.51 Given an estimated odds ratio of 2.5, compute the estimated probability of an event of interest.

14.52 Given an estimated odds ratio of 0.75, compute the estimated probability of an event of interest.

14.53 Consider the following logistic regression equation:

$$\ln(\text{Estimated odds ratio}) = 0.1 + 0.5X_{1i} + 0.2X_{2i}$$

a. Interpret the meaning of the logistic regression coefficients.
b. If $X_1 = 2$ and $X_2 = 1.5$, compute the estimated odds ratio and interpret its meaning.
c. On the basis of the results of (b), compute the estimated probability of an event of interest.

APPLYING THE CONCEPTS

14.54 Refer to Figure 14.13 on page 557.
a. Predict the probability that a cardholder who charged \$36,000 last year and does not have any additional credit cards for members of the household will purchase the platinum card during the marketing campaign.
b. Compare the results in (a) with those for a person with additional credit cards.
c. Predict the probability that a cardholder who charged \$18,000 and does not have any additional credit cards for other authorized users will purchase the platinum card during the marketing campaign.
d. Compare the results of (a) and (c) and indicate what implications these results might have for the strategy for the marketing campaign.

14.55 Undergraduate students at Miami University in Oxford, Ohio, were surveyed in order to evaluate the effect of price on the purchase of a pizza from Pizza Hut. The students were asked to suppose that they were going to have a large two-topping pizza delivered to their residence. Then they were asked to select from either Pizza Hut or another pizzeria of their choice. The price they would have to pay to get a Pizza Hut pizza differed from survey to survey. For example, some surveys used the price \$11.49. Other prices investigated were \$8.49, \$9.49, \$10.49, \$12.49, \$13.49, and \$14.49. The dependent variable for this study is whether or not a student will select Pizza Hut. Possible independent variables are the price of a Pizza Hut pizza and the gender of the student. The file PizzaHut contains responses from 220 students and includes these three variables:

Gender—1 = male, 0 = female

Price—8.49, 9.49, 10.49, 11.49, 12.49, 13.49, or 14.49)

Purchase—1 = the student selected Pizza Hut, 0 = the student selected another pizzeria

a. Develop a logistic regression model to predict the probability that a student selects Pizza Hut based on the price of the pizza. Is price an important indicator of purchase selection?
b. Develop a logistic regression model to predict the probability that a student selects Pizza Hut based on the price of the pizza and the gender of the student. Is price an important indicator of purchase selection? Is gender an important indicator of purchase selection?
c. Compare the results from (a) and (b). Which model would you choose? Discuss.
d. Using the model selected in (c), predict the probability that a student will select Pizza Hut if the price is \$8.99.
e. Using the model selected in (c), predict the probability that a student will select Pizza Hut if the price is \$11.49.
f. Using the model selected in (c), predict the probability that a student will select Pizza Hut if the price is \$13.99.

14.56 The director of graduate studies at a college of business wants to predict the success of students in an MBA program using two independent variables, undergraduate grade point average (GPA) and GMAT score. Data from a random sample of 30 students, organized and stored in MBA, show that 20 successfully completed the program (coded as 1) and 10 did not (coded as 0):
a. Develop a logistic regression model to predict the probability of successful completion of the MBA program, based on undergraduate grade point average and GMAT score.

Success in MBA Program	Undergraduate GPA	GMAT Score	Success in MBA Program	Undergraduate GPA	GMAT Score
0	2.93	617	1	3.17	639
0	3.05	557	1	3.24	632
0	3.11	599	1	3.41	639
0	3.24	616	1	3.37	619
0	3.36	594	1	3.46	665
0	3.41	567	1	3.57	694
0	3.45	542	1	3.62	641
0	3.60	551	1	3.66	594
0	3.64	573	1	3.69	678
0	3.57	536	1	3.70	624
1	2.75	688	1	3.78	654
1	2.81	647	1	3.84	718
1	3.03	652	1	3.77	692
1	3.10	608	1	3.79	632
1	3.06	680	1	3.97	784

b. Explain the meaning of the regression coefficients for the model in (a).
c. Predict the probability of successful completion of the program for a student with an undergraduate grade point average of 3.25 and a GMAT score of 600.
d. At the 0.05 level of significance, is there evidence that a logistic regression model that uses undergraduate grade

point average and GMAT score to predict the probability of success in the MBA program is a good-fitting model?

e. At the 0.05 level of significance, is there evidence that undergraduate grade point average and GMAT score each make a significant contribution to the logistic regression model?

f. Develop a logistic regression model that includes only undergraduate grade point average to predict the probability of success in the MBA program.

g. Develop a logistic regression model that includes only GMAT score to predict the probability of success in the MBA program.

h. Compare the models in (a), (f), and (g). Evaluate the differences among the models.

14.57 A hotel has designed a new system for room service delivery of breakfast that allows the customer to select a specific delivery time. The difference between the actual and requested delivery times was recorded for 30 deliveries on a particular day along with whether the customer had previously stayed at the hotel. (A negative time means that the breakfast was delivered before the requested time.) These data are stored in **Satisfaction**.

a. Develop a logistic regression model to predict the probability that the customer will be satisfied (0 = unfavorable, 1 = favorable), based on the delivery time difference and whether the customer had previously stayed at the hotel.

b. Explain the meaning of the regression coefficients for the model in (a).

c. Predict the probability that the customer will be satisfied if the delivery time difference is +3 minutes and he or she did not previously stay at the hotel.

d. At the 0.05 level of significance, is there evidence that a logistic regression model that uses delivery time difference and whether the customer had previously stayed at the hotel is a good-fitting model?

e. At the 0.05 level of significance, is there evidence that both independent variables (delivery time difference and whether the customer had previously stayed at the hotel) make a significant contribution to the logistic regression model?

USING STATISTICS The Multiple Effects of OmniPower Bars, Revisited

Igor Dutina / Shutterstock

In the Using Statistics scenario, you were a marketing manager for OmniFoods, responsible for nutrition bars and similar snack items. You needed to determine the effect that price and in-store promotions would have on sales of OmniPower nutrition bars in order to develop an effective marketing strategy. A sample of 34 stores in a supermarket chain was selected for a test-market study. The stores charged between 59 and 99 cents per bar and were given an in-store promotion budget between $200 and $600.

At the end of the one-month test-market study, you performed a multiple regression analysis on the data. Two independent variables were considered: the price of an OmniPower bar and the monthly budget for in-store promotional expenditures. The dependent variable was the number of OmniPower bars sold in a month. The coefficient of determination indicated that 75.8% of the variation in sales was explained by knowing the price charged and the amount spent on in-store promotions. The model indicated that the predicted sales of OmniPower are estimated to decrease by 532 bars per month for each 10-cent increase in the price, and the predicted sales are estimated to increase by 361 bars for each additional $100 spent on promotions.

After studying the relative effects of price and promotion, OmniFoods needs to set price and promotion standards for a nationwide introduction (obviously, lower prices and higher promotion budgets lead to more sales, but they do so at a lower profit margin). You determined that if stores spend $400 a month for in-store promotions and charge 79 cents, the 95% confidence interval estimate of the mean monthly sales is 2,854 to 3,303 bars. OmniFoods can multiply the lower and upper bounds of this confidence interval by the number of stores included in the nationwide introduction to estimate total monthly sales. For example, if 1,000 stores are in the nationwide introduction, then total monthly sales should be between 2.854 million and 3.308 million bars.

SUMMARY

In this chapter, you learned how multiple regression models allow you to use two or more independent variables to predict the value of a dependent variable. You also learned how to include categorical independent variables and interaction terms in regression models. In addition, you used the logistic regression model to predict a categorical dependent variable. Figure 14.14 presents a roadmap of the chapter.

FIGURE 14.14
Roadmap for multiple regression

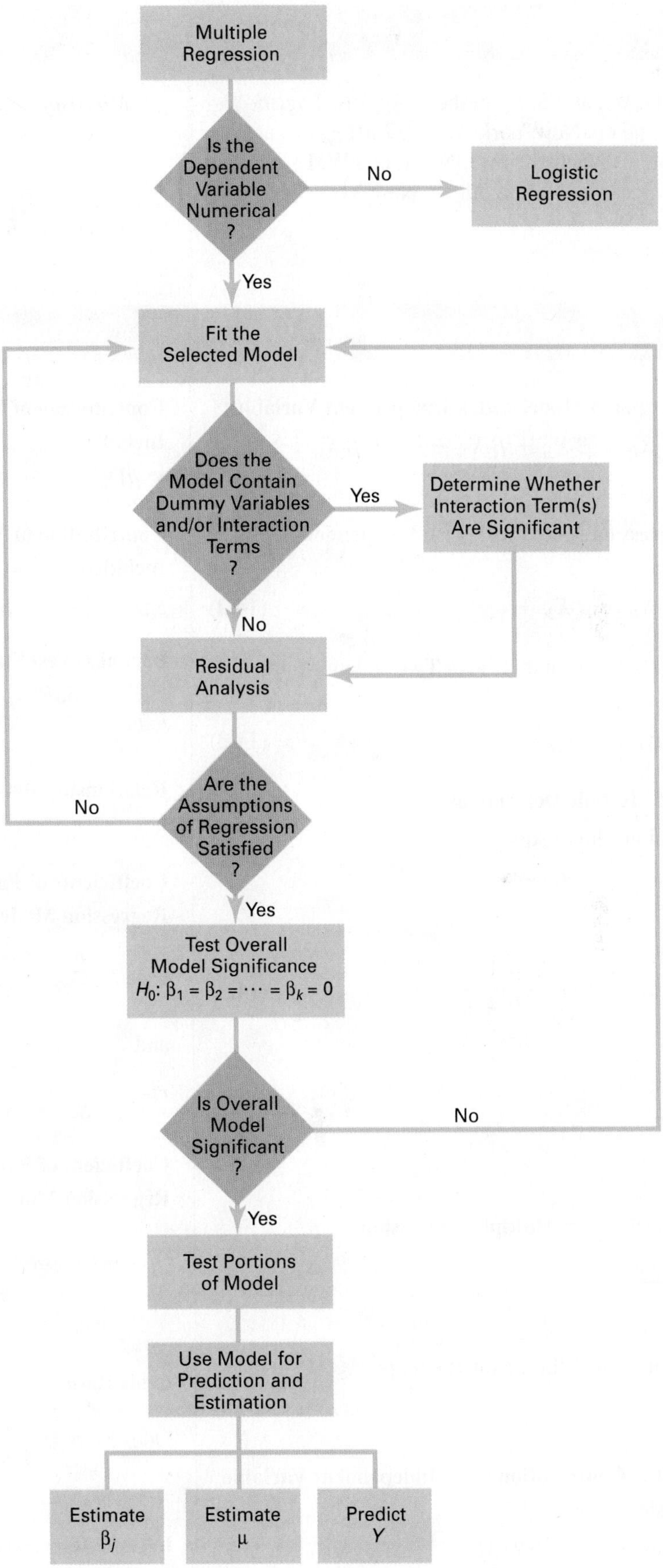

REFERENCES

1. Hosmer, D. W., and S. Lemeshow. *Applied Logistic Regression*, 2nd ed. New York: Wiley, 2001.
2. Kutner, M., C. Nachtsheim, J. Neter, and W. Li. *Applied Linear Statistical Models*, 5th ed. New York: McGraw-Hill/Irwin, 2005.
3. *Microsoft Excel 2010*. Redmond, WA: Microsoft Corp., 2010.

KEY EQUATIONS

Multiple Regression Model with *k* Independent Variables

$$Y_i = \beta_0 + \beta_1 X_{1i} + \beta_2 X_{2i} + \beta_3 X_{3i} + \cdots + \beta_k X_{ki} + \varepsilon_i \quad \textbf{(14.1)}$$

Multiple Regression Model with Two Independent Variables

$$Y_i = \beta_0 + \beta_1 X_{1i} + \beta_2 X_{2i} + \varepsilon_i \quad \textbf{(14.2)}$$

Multiple Regression Equation with Two Independent Variables

$$\hat{Y}_i = b_0 + b_1 X_{1i} + b_2 X_{2i} \quad \textbf{(14.3)}$$

Coefficient of Multiple Determination

$$r^2 = \frac{\text{Regression sum of squares}}{\text{Total sum of squares}} = \frac{SSR}{SST} \quad \textbf{(14.4)}$$

Adjusted r^2

$$r^2_{\text{adj}} = 1 - \left[(1 - r^2)\frac{n-1}{n-k-1}\right] \quad \textbf{(14.5)}$$

Overall *F* Test

$$F_{STAT} = \frac{MSR}{MSE} \quad \textbf{(14.6)}$$

Testing for the Slope in Multiple Regression

$$t_{STAT} = \frac{b_j - \beta_j}{S_{b_j}} \quad \textbf{(14.7)}$$

Confidence Interval Estimate for the Slope

$$b_j \pm t_{\alpha/2} S_{b_j} \quad \textbf{(14.8)}$$

Determining the Contribution of an Independent Variable to the Regression Model

$$SSR(X_j | \text{All } Xs \text{ except } j) = SSR\,(\text{All } Xs) - SSR\,(\text{All } Xs \text{ except } j) \quad \textbf{(14.9)}$$

Contribution of Variable X_1, Given That X_2 Has Been Included

$$SSR(X_1 | X_2) = SSR(X_1 \text{ and } X_2) - SSR(X_2) \quad \textbf{(14.10a)}$$

Contribution of Variable X_2, Given That X_1 Has Been Included

$$SSR(X_2 | X_1) = SSR(X_1 \text{ and } X_2) - SSR(X_1) \quad \textbf{(14.10b)}$$

Partial *F* Test Statistic

$$F_{STAT} = \frac{SSR(X_j | \text{All } Xs \text{ } except\ j)}{MSE} \quad \textbf{(14.11)}$$

Relationship Between a *t* Statistic and an *F* Statistic

$$t^2_{STAT} = F_{STAT} \quad \textbf{(14.12)}$$

Coefficients of Partial Determination for a Multiple Regression Model Containing Two Independent Variables

$$r^2_{Y1.2} = \frac{SSR(X_1 | X_2)}{SST - SSR(X_1\ and\ X_2) + SSR(X_1 | X_2)} \quad \textbf{(14.13a)}$$

and

$$r^2_{Y2.1} = \frac{SSR(X_2 | X_1)}{SST - SSR(X_1\ and\ X_2) + SSR(X_2 | X_1)} \quad \textbf{(14.13b)}$$

Coefficient of Partial Determination for a Multiple Regression Model Containing *k* Independent Variables

$$r^2_{Yj.(\text{All variables except } j)} = \frac{SSR(X_j | \text{All } Xs\ except\ j)}{SST - SSR(All\ Xs) + SSR(X_j | \text{All } Xs\ except\ j)} \quad \textbf{(14.14)}$$

Odds Ratio

$$\text{Odds ratio} = \frac{\text{probability of an event of interest}}{1 - \text{probability of an event of interest}} \quad \textbf{(14.15)}$$

Logistic Regression Model

$$\ln(\text{Odds ratio}) = \beta_0 + \beta_1 X_{1i} + \beta_2 X_{2i} + \cdots + \beta_k X_{ki} + \varepsilon_i \quad \textbf{(14.16)}$$

Logistic Regression Equation

$$\ln(\text{Estimated odds ratio}) = b_0 + b_1X_{1i} + b_2X_{2i} + \cdots + b_kX_{ki} \quad \textbf{(14.17)}$$

Estimated Odds Ratio

$$\text{Estimated odds ratio} = e^{\ln(\text{Estimated odds ratio})} \quad \textbf{(14.18)}$$

Estimated Probability of an Event of Interest

$$\text{Estimated probability of an event of interest} = \frac{\text{estimated odds ratio}}{1 + \text{estimated odds ratio}} \quad \textbf{(14.19)}$$

KEY TERMS

CHECKING YOUR UNDERSTANDING

14.58 What is the difference between r^2 and adjusted r^2?

14.59 How does the interpretation of the regression coefficients differ in multiple regression and simple linear regression?

14.60 How does testing the significance of the entire multiple regression model differ from testing the contribution of each independent variable?

14.61 How do the coefficients of partial determination differ from the coefficient of multiple determination?

14.62 Why and how do you use dummy variables?

14.63 How can you evaluate whether the slope of the dependent variable with an independent variable is the same for each level of the dummy variable?

14.64 Under what circumstances do you include an interaction term in a regression model?

14.65 When a dummy variable is included in a regression model that has one numerical independent variable, what assumption do you need to make concerning the slope between the dependent variable, Y, and the numerical independent variable, X?

14.66 When do you use logistic regression?

CHAPTER REVIEW PROBLEMS

14.67 Increasing customer satisfaction typically results in increased purchase behavior. For many products, there is more than one measure of customer satisfaction. In many, purchase behavior can increase dramatically with an increase in just one of the customer satisfaction measures. Gunst and Barry ("One Way to Moderate Ceiling Effects," *Quality Progress*, October 2003, pp. 83–85) consider a product with two satisfaction measures, X_1 and X_2, that range from the lowest level of satisfaction, 1, to the highest level of satisfaction, 7. The dependent variable, Y, is a measure of purchase behavior, with the highest value generating the most sales. Consider the regression equation:

$$\hat{Y}_i = -3.888 + 1.449X_{1i} + 1.462X_{2i} - 0.190X_{1i}X_{2i}$$

Suppose that X_1 is the perceived quality of the product and X_2 is the perceived value of the product. (Note: If the customer thinks the product is overpriced, he or she perceives it to be of low value and vice versa.)

a. What is the predicted purchase behavior when $X_1 = 2$ and $X_2 = 2$?
b. What is the predicted purchase behavior when $X_1 = 2$ and $X_2 = 7$?
c. What is the predicted purchase behavior when $X_1 = 7$ and $X_2 = 2$?
d. What is the predicted purchase behavior when $X_1 = 7$ and $X_2 = 7$?
e. What is the regression equation when $X_2 = 2$? What is the slope for X_1 now?
f. What is the regression equation when $X_2 = 7$? What is the slope for X_1 now?
g. What is the regression equation when $X_1 = 2$? What is the slope for X_2 now?
h. What is the regression equation when $X_1 = 7$? What is the slope for X_2 now?
i. Discuss the implications of (a) through (h) in the context of increasing sales for this product with two customer satisfaction measures.

14.68 The owner of a moving company typically has his most experienced manager predict the total number of labor hours that will be required to complete an upcoming move. This approach has proved useful in the past, but the owner has the business objective of developing a more accurate method of predicting labor hours. In a preliminary effort to provide a more accurate method, the owner has decided to use the number of cubic feet moved and the number of pieces of large furniture as the independent variables and has collected data for 36 moves in which the origin and destination were within the borough of Manhattan in New York City and the travel time was an insignificant portion of the hours worked. The data are organized and stored in **Moving**.

a. State the multiple regression equation.
b. Interpret the meaning of the slopes in this equation.
c. Predict the labor hours for moving 500 cubic feet with two large pieces of furniture.
d. Perform a residual analysis on your results and determine whether the regression assumptions are valid.
e. Determine whether there is a significant relationship between labor hours and the two independent variables (the number of cubic feet moved and the number of pieces of large furniture) at the 0.05 level of significance.
f. Determine the p-value in (e) and interpret its meaning.
g. Interpret the meaning of the coefficient of multiple determination in this problem.
h. Determine the adjusted r^2.
i. At the 0.05 level of significance, determine whether each independent variable makes a significant contribution to the regression model. Indicate the most appropriate regression model for this set of data.
j. Determine the p-values in (i) and interpret their meaning.
k. Construct a 95% confidence interval estimate of the population slope between labor hours and the number of cubic feet moved. How does the interpretation of the slope here differ from that in Problem 13.44 on page 501?
l. Compute and interpret the coefficients of partial determination.

14.69 Professional basketball has truly become a sport that generates interest among fans around the world. More and more players come from outside the United States to play in the National Basketball Association (NBA). You want to develop a regression model to predict the number of wins achieved by each NBA team, based on field goal (shots made) percentage for the team and for the opponent. The data are stored in **NBA2011**.

a. State the multiple regression equation.
b. Interpret the meaning of the slopes in this equation.
c. Predict the number of wins for a team that has a field goal percentage of 45% and an opponent field goal percentage of 44%.
d. Perform a residual analysis on your results and determine whether the regression assumptions are valid.
e. Is there a significant relationship between number of wins and the two independent variables (field goal percentage for the team and for the opponent) at the 0.05 level of significance?
f. Determine the p-value in (e) and interpret its meaning.
g. Interpret the meaning of the coefficient of multiple determination in this problem.
h. Determine the adjusted r^2.
i. At the 0.05 level of significance, determine whether each independent variable makes a significant contribution to the regression model. Indicate the most appropriate regression model for this set of data.
j. Determine the p-values in (i) and interpret their meaning.
k. Compute and interpret the coefficients of partial determination.

14.70 A sample of 30 recently sold single-family houses in a small city is selected. Develop a model to predict the selling price (in \$thousands), using the assessed value (in \$thousands) as well as time (in months since reassessment). The houses in the city had been reassessed at full value one year prior to the study. The results are stored in **House1**.

a. State the multiple regression equation.
b. Interpret the meaning of the slopes in this equation.
c. Predict the selling price for a house that has an assessed value of \$170,000 and was sold 12 months after reassessment.
d. Perform a residual analysis on your results and determine whether the regression assumptions are valid.
e. Determine whether there is a significant relationship between selling price and the two independent variables (assessed value and time period) at the 0.05 level of significance.
f. Determine the p-value in (e) and interpret its meaning.
g. Interpret the meaning of the coefficient of multiple determination in this problem.
h. Determine the adjusted r^2.
i. At the 0.05 level of significance, determine whether each independent variable makes a significant contribution to the regression model. Indicate the most appropriate regression model for this set of data.
j. Determine the p-values in (i) and interpret their meaning.
k. Construct a 95% confidence interval estimate of the population slope between selling price and assessed value. How does the interpretation of the slope here differ from that in Problem 13.76 on page 515?
l. Compute and interpret the coefficients of partial determination.

14.71 Measuring the height of a California redwood tree is very difficult because these trees grow to heights over 300 feet. People familiar with these trees understand that the height of a California redwood tree is related to other characteristics of the tree, including the diameter of the tree at the breast height of a person (in inches) and the thickness of the bark of the tree (in inches). The file **Redwood** contains the height, diameter at breast height of a person, and bark thickness for a sample of 21 California redwood trees.

a. State the multiple regression equation that predicts the height of a tree, based on the tree's diameter at breast height and the thickness of the bark.
b. Interpret the meaning of the slopes in this equation.
c. Predict the height for a tree that has a breast height diameter of 25 inches and a bark thickness of 2 inches.
d. Interpret the meaning of the coefficient of multiple determination in this problem.
e. Perform a residual analysis on the results and determine whether the regression assumptions are valid.
f. Determine whether there is a significant relationship between the height of redwood trees and the two independent variables (breast-height diameter and bark thickness) at the 0.05 level of significance.
g. Construct a 95% confidence interval estimate of the population slope between the height of redwood trees and breast-height diameter and between the height of redwood trees and the bark thickness.
h. At the 0.05 level of significance, determine whether each independent variable makes a significant contribution to the regression model. Indicate the independent variables to include in this model.
i. Construct a 95% confidence interval estimate of the mean height for trees that have a breast-height diameter of 25 inches and a bark thickness of 2 inches, along with a prediction interval for an individual tree.
j. Compute and interpret the coefficients of partial determination.

14.72 Develop a model to predict the assessed value of houses (in $thousands), using the size of the houses (in thousands of square feet) and the age of the houses (in years) from the following table (stored in **House2**):

House	Assessed Value ($thousands)	Size of House (thousands of square feet)	Age (years)
1	184.4	2.00	3.42
2	177.4	1.71	11.50
3	175.7	1.45	8.33
4	185.9	1.76	0.00
5	179.1	1.93	7.42
6	170.4	1.20	32.00
7	175.8	1.55	16.00
8	185.9	1.93	2.00
9	178.5	1.59	1.75
10	179.2	1.50	2.75
11	186.7	1.90	0.00
12	179.3	1.39	0.00
13	174.5	1.54	12.58
14	183.8	1.89	2.75
15	176.8	1.59	7.17

a. State the multiple regression equation.
b. Interpret the meaning of the slopes in this equation.
c. Predict the assessed value for a house that has a size of 1,750 square feet and is 10 years old.
d. Perform a residual analysis on the results and determine whether the regression assumptions are valid.
e. Determine whether there is a significant relationship between assessed value and the two independent variables (size and age) at the 0.05 level of significance.
f. Determine the p-value in (e) and interpret its meaning.
g. Interpret the meaning of the coefficient of multiple determination in this problem.
h. Determine the adjusted r^2.
i. At the 0.05 level of significance, determine whether each independent variable makes a significant contribution to the regression model. Indicate the most appropriate regression model for this set of data.
j. Determine the p-values in (i) and interpret their meaning.
k. Construct a 95% confidence interval estimate of the population slope between assessed value and size. How does the interpretation of the slope here differ from that of Problem 13.77 on page 515?
l. Compute and interpret the coefficients of partial determination.
m. The real estate assessor's office has been publicly quoted as saying that the age of a house has no bearing on its assessed value. Based on your answers to (a) through (l), do you agree with this statement? Explain.

14.73 A baseball analytics specialist wants to determine which variables are important in predicting a team's wins in a given season. He has collected data related to wins, earned run average (ERA), and runs scored for the 2011 season (stored in **BB2011**). Develop a model to predict the number of wins based on ERA and runs scored.

a. State the multiple regression equation.
b. Interpret the meaning of the slopes in this equation.
c. Predict the number of wins for a team that has an ERA of 4.50 and has scored 750 runs.
d. Perform a residual analysis on the results and determine whether the regression assumptions are valid.
e. Is there a significant relationship between number of wins and the two independent variables (ERA and runs scored) at the 0.05 level of significance?
f. Determine the p-value in (e) and interpret its meaning.
g. Interpret the meaning of the coefficient of multiple determination in this problem.
h. Determine the adjusted r^2.
i. At the 0.05 level of significance, determine whether each independent variable makes a significant contribution to the regression model. Indicate the most appropriate regression model for this set of data.
j. Determine the p-values in (i) and interpret their meaning.
k. Construct a 95% confidence interval estimate of the population slope between wins and ERA.

l. Compute and interpret the coefficients of partial determination.

m. Which is more important in predicting wins—pitching, as measured by ERA, or offense, as measured by runs scored? Explain.

14.74 Referring to Problem 14.73, suppose that in addition to using ERA to predict the number of wins, the analytics specialist wants to include the league (0 = American, 1 = National) as an independent variable. Develop a model to predict wins based on ERA and league. For (a) through (k), do not include an interaction term.

a. State the multiple regression equation.

b. Interpret the slopes in (a).

c. Predict the number of wins for a team with an ERA of 4.50 in the American League. Construct a 95% confidence interval estimate for all teams and a 95% prediction interval for an individual team.

d. Perform a residual analysis on the results and determine whether the regression assumptions are valid.

e. Is there a significant relationship between wins and the two independent variables (ERA and league) at the 0.05 level of significance?

f. At the 0.05 level of significance, determine whether each independent variable makes a contribution to the regression model. Indicate the most appropriate regression model for this set of data.

g. Construct a 95% confidence interval estimate of the population slope for the relationship between wins and ERA.

h. Construct a 95% confidence interval estimate of the population slope for the relationship between wins and league.

i. Compute and interpret the adjusted r^2.

j. Compute and interpret the coefficients of partial determination.

k. What assumption do you have to make about the slope of wins with ERA?

l. Add an interaction term to the model and, at the 0.05 level of significance, determine whether it makes a significant contribution to the model.

m. On the basis of the results of (f) and (l), which model is most appropriate? Explain.

14.75 You are a real estate broker who wants to compare property values in Glen Cove and Roslyn (which are located approximately 8 miles apart). In order to do so, you will analyze the data in GCRoslyn, a file that includes samples of houses from Glen Cove and Roslyn. Making sure to include the dummy variable for location (Glen Cove or Roslyn), develop a regression model to predict appraised value, based on the land area of a property, the age of a house, and location. Be sure to determine whether any interaction terms need to be included in the model.

14.76 A recent article discussed a metal deposition process in which a piece of metal is placed in an acid bath and an alloy is layered on top of it. The business objective of engineers working on the process was to reduce variation in the thickness of the alloy layer. To begin, the temperature and the pressure in the tank holding the acid bath are to be studied as independent variables. Data are collected from 50 samples. The results are organized and stored in Thickness. (Data extracted from J. Conklin, "It's a Marathon, Not a Sprint," *Quality Progress*, June 2009, pp. 46–49.)

Develop a multiple regression model that uses temperature and the pressure in the tank holding the acid bath to predict the thickness of the alloy layer. Be sure to perform a thorough residual analysis. The article suggests that there is a significant interaction between the pressure and the temperature in the tank. Do you agree?

14.77 Starbucks Coffee Co. uses a data-based approach to improving the quality and customer satisfaction of its products. When survey data indicated that Starbucks needed to improve its package sealing process, an experiment was conducted to determine the factors in the bag-sealing equipment that might be affecting the ease of opening the bag without tearing the inner liner of the bag. (Data extracted from L. Johnson and S. Burrows, "For Starbucks, It's in the Bag," *Quality Progress*, March 2011, pp. 17–23.) Among the factors that could affect the rating of the ability of the bag to resist tears were the viscosity, pressure, and plate gap on the bag-sealing equipment. Data were collected on 19 bags in which the plate gap was varied. The results are stored in Starbucks. Develop a multiple regression model that uses the viscosity, pressure, and plate gap on the bag-sealing equipment to predict the tear rating of the bag. Be sure to perform a thorough residual analysis. Do you think that you need to use all three independent variables in the model? Explain.

CASES FOR CHAPTER 14

Managing Ashland MultiComm Services

In its continuing study of the *3-For-All* subscription solicitation process, a marketing department team wants to test the effects of two types of structured sales presentations (personal formal and personal informal) and the number of hours spent on telemarketing on the number of new subscriptions. The staff has recorded these data for the past 24 weeks in AMS14.

Analyze these data and develop a multiple regression model to predict the number of new subscriptions for a week, based on the number of hours spent on telemarketing and the sales presentation type. Write a report, giving detailed findings concerning the regression model used.

Digital Case

Apply your knowledge of multiple regression models in this Digital Case, which extends the OmniFoods Using Statistics scenario from this chapter.

To ensure a successful test marketing of its OmniPower energy bars, the OmniFoods marketing department has contracted with In-Store Placements Group (ISPG), a merchandising consulting firm. ISPG will work with the grocery store chain that is conducting the test-market study. Using the same 34-store sample used in the test-market study, ISPG claims that the choice of shelf location and the presence of in-store OmniPower coupon dispensers both increase sales of the energy bars.

Open **Omni_ISPGMemo.pdf** to review the ISPG claims and supporting data. Then answer the following questions:

1. Are the supporting data consistent with ISPG's claims? Perform an appropriate statistical analysis to confirm (or discredit) the stated relationship between sales and the two independent variables of product shelf location and the presence of in-store OmniPower coupon dispensers.
2. If you were advising OmniFoods, would you recommend using a specific shelf location and in-store coupon dispensers to sell OmniPower bars?
3. What additional data would you advise collecting in order to determine the effectiveness of the sales promotion techniques used by ISPG?

CHAPTER 14 EXCEL GUIDE

EG14.1 DEVELOPING a MULTIPLE REGRESSION MODEL

Interpreting the Regression Coefficients

Key Technique Use the **LINEST(*cell range of Y variable, cell range of X variables,* True, True)** function to compute the regression coefficients and other values related to a multiple regression analysis.

Example Develop the multiple regression model for the OmniPower sales data that is shown in Figure 14.1 on page 528.

PHStat Use **Multiple Regression.**
For the example, open to the **DATA worksheet** of the **OmniPower workbook**. Select **PHStat → Regression → Multiple Regression**, and in the procedure's dialog box (shown below):

1. Enter **A1:A35** as the **Y Variable Cell Range**.
2. Enter **B1:C35** as the **X Variables Cell Range**.
3. Check **First cells in both ranges contain label**.
4. Enter **95** as the **Confidence level for regression coefficients**.
5. Check **Regression Statistics Table** and **ANOVA and Coefficients Table**.
6. Enter a **Title** and click **OK**.

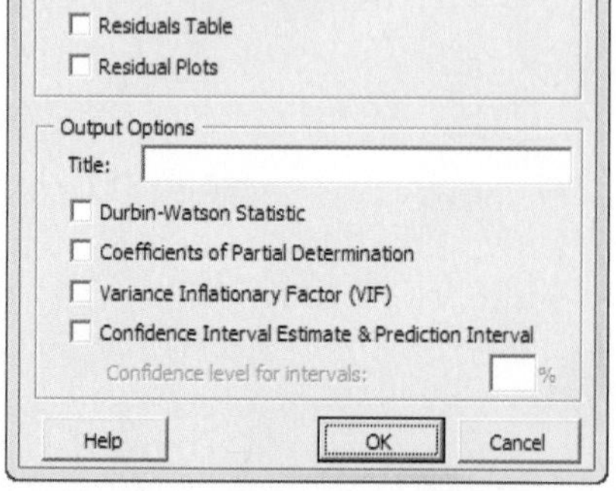

The procedure creates a worksheet that contains a copy of your data in addition to the regression results worksheet shown in Figure 14.1. For more information about these worksheets, read the following *In-Depth Excel* section.

In-Depth Excel Use the **COMPUTE worksheet** of the **Multiple Regression workbook** as a template. (Use the **Multiple Regression 2007 workbook** if you use an Excel version that is older than Excel 2010.)
The **MRData worksheet**, which the COMPUTE worksheet uses to perform the regression analysis, already contains the OmniPower sales data. To perform multiple regression analyses for other data, paste the regression data into the MRData worksheet. Paste the values for the *Y* variable into column A. Paste the values for the *X* variables into consecutive columns, starting with column B. Then, open to the COMPUTE worksheet. Enter the confidence level in cell L8 and edit the 5-row by-3-column array formula that starts with cell L2 (the cell range L2:N6). First adjust the cell range of the array formula, adding a column for each independent variable in excess of two. Then, edit the cell ranges in the array formula to reflect the data you pasted into the MRData worksheet.

Your edited cell ranges should start with row 2 so as to exclude the row 1 variable names (an exception to the usual practice in this book). Remember to press the **Enter** key while holding down the **Control** and **Shift** keys (or the **Command** key on a Mac) to enter the array formula as discussed in Appendix Section B.3.

Columns A through I of the COMPUTE worksheet duplicate the visual design of the Analysis Toolpak regression worksheet. Figure 14.1 does not show columns K through N, the area that contains the array formula, in the cell range L2:N6, and calculations for the *t* test for the slope (see Section 13.7 on page 497), in the cell range K8:L12.

Read the SHORT TAKES for Chapter 14 for an explanation of the formulas found in these areas and the rest of the COMPUTE worksheet (shown in the **COMPUTE_FORMULAS worksheet**).

Analysis ToolPak Use **Regression.**
For the example, open to the **DATA worksheet** of the **OmniPower workbook** and:

1. Select **Data → Data Analysis**.
2. In the Data Analysis dialog box, select **Regression** from the **Analysis Tools** list and then click **OK**.

In the Regression dialog box (shown on page 569):

3. Enter **A1:A35** as the **Input Y Range** and enter **B1:C35** as the **Input X Range**.
4. Check **Labels** and check **Confidence Level** and enter **95** in its box.

5. Click **New Worksheet Ply**.
6. Click **OK**.

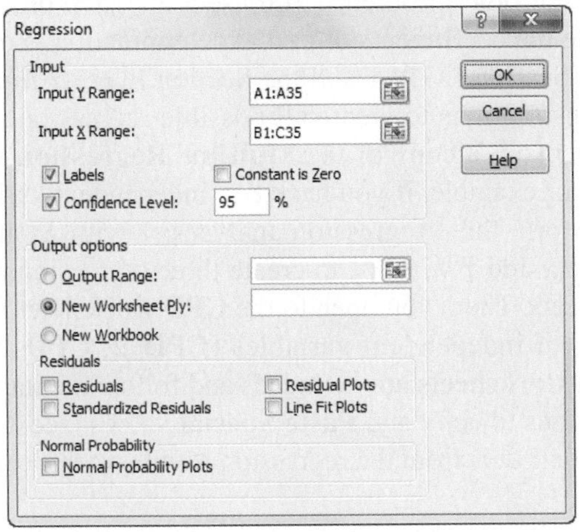

Predicting the Dependent Variable Y

Key Technique Use the **MMULT** array function and the **T.INV.2T** function to help compute intermediate values that determine the confidence interval estimate and prediction interval.

Example Compute the confidence interval estimate and prediction interval for the OmniPower sales data shown in Figure 14.2 on page 529.

PHStat Use the *PHStat* "Interpreting the Regression Coefficients" instructions but replace step 6 with the following steps 6 through 8:

6. Check **Confidence Interval Estimate & Prediction Interval** and enter **95** as the percentage for **Confidence level for intervals**.
7. Enter a **Title** and click **OK**.
8. In the new worksheet, enter **79** in cell **B6** and enter **400** in cell **B7**.

These steps create a new worksheet that is discussed in the following *In-Depth Excel* instructions.

In-Depth Excel Use the **CIEandPI worksheet** of the **Multiple Regression workbook** as a template.

The worksheet already contains the data and formulas for the OmniPower sales example shown in Figure 14.2. The worksheet uses the **MMULT** function (see Appendix Section F.4) in several array formulas that perform matrix operations to compute the matrix product X′ X (in cell range B9:D11), the inverse of the X′X matrix (in cell range B13:D15), the product of X′G multiplied by the inverse of X′X (in cell range B17:D17), and the predicted *Y* (in cell B21).

Modifying this worksheet for other models with more than two independent variables requires knowledge that is beyond the scope of this book. For other models with two independent variables, paste the data for those variables into columns B and C of the **MRArray worksheet** and adjust the number of entries in column A (all of which are **1**). Adjust the COMPUTE worksheet to reflect the new regression data, using the instructions in the *In-Depth Excel* "Interpreting the Regression Coefficients" instructions. Then open to the CIEandPI worksheet and edit the array formula in cell range B9:D11 and edit the labels in cells A6 and A7.

EG14.2 r^2, ADJUSTED r^2, and the OVERALL *F* TEST

The coefficient of multiple determination, r^2, the adjusted r^2, and the overall *F* test are all computed as part of creating the multiple regression results worksheet using the Section EG14.1 instructions. If you use either the *PHStat* or *In-Depth Excel* instructions, formulas are used to compute these results in the **COMPUTE worksheet**. Formulas in cells B5, B7, B13, C12, C13, D12, and E12 copy values computed by an array formula in cell range L2:N6 and in cell F12, the expression **F.DIST.RT(*F test statistic*, 1, *error degrees of freedom*)** computes the *p*-value for the overall *F* test.

EG14.3 RESIDUAL ANALYSIS for the MULTIPLE REGRESSION MODEL

Key Technique Use arithmetic formulas and some results from the multiple regression COMPUTE worksheet to compute residuals.

Example Perform the residual analysis for the OmniPower sales data discussed in Section 14.3, starting on page 535.

PHStat Use the Section EG14.1 "Interpreting the Regression Coefficients" *PHStat* instructions. Modify step 5 by checking **Residuals Table** and **Residual Plots** in addition to checking **Regression Statistics Table** and **ANOVA and Coefficients Table.**

In-Depth Excel Use the **RESIDUALS worksheet** of the **Multiple Regression workbook** as a template. Then construct residual plots for the residuals and the predicted value of *Y* and for the residuals and each of the independent variables.

The **MRData worksheet**, which the RESIDUALS worksheet uses to compute the residuals, already contains the OmniPower sales data for the example. For other problems, modify this worksheet as follows:

1. If the number of independent variables is greater than 2, select column D, right-click, and click **Insert** from the shortcut menu. Repeat this step as many times as necessary to create the additional columns to hold all the *X* variables.

2. Paste the data for the *X* variables into columns, starting with column B.
3. Paste *Y* values in column E (or in the second-to-last column if there are more than two *X* variables).
4. For sample sizes smaller than 34, delete the extra rows. For sample sizes greater than 34, copy the predicted *Y* and residuals formulas down through the row containing the last pair of *X* and *Y* values. Also, add the new observation numbers in column A.

To construct the residual plots, open to the RESIDUALS worksheet and select pairs of columns and then apply the Section EG2.5 *In-Depth Excel* "The Scatter Plot" instructions. (If you forgot to select the columns, Excel will construct a meaningless plot of all of the data in the RESIDUALS worksheet.) For example, to construct the residual plot for the residuals and the predicted value of *Y*, select columns D and F. (See Appendix Section B.7 for help in selecting a non-contiguous cell range.)

Read the SHORT TAKES for Chapter 14 for an explanation of the formulas found in the RESIDUALS worksheet (shown in the **RESIDUALS_FORMULAS worksheet**).

Analysis ToolPak Use the Section EG14.1 *Analysis ToolPak* instructions. Modify step 5 by checking **Residuals** and **Residual Plots** before clicking **New Worksheet Ply** and then **OK**. The **Residuals Plots** option constructs residual plots only for each independent variable. To construct for the residuals and the predicted value of *Y*, select the predicted and residuals cells (in the RESIDUAL OUTPUT area of the regression results worksheet) and then apply the Section EG2.5 *In-Depth Excel* "The Scatter Plot" instructions.

EG14.4 INFERENCES CONCERNING the POPULATION REGRESSION COEFFICIENTS

The regression results worksheets created by using the Section EG14.1 instructions include the information needed to make the inferences discussed in Section 14.4.

EG14.5 TESTING PORTIONS of the MULTIPLE REGRESSION MODEL

Key Technique Adapt the Section EG14.1 "Interpreting the Regression Coefficients" instructions and the Section EG13.2 instructions to develop the regression analyses needed.

Example Test portions of the multiple regression model for the OmniPower sales data as discussed in Section 14.5, starting on page 540.

PHStat Use the Section EG14.1 *PHStat* "Interpreting the Regression Coefficients" instructions but modify step 6 by checking **Coefficients of Partial Determination** before you click **OK**.

In-Depth Excel Use one of the **CPD worksheets** of the **Multiple Regression workbook** as a template.

The **CPD_2 worksheet** already contains the data to compute the coefficients of partial determination for the example. For other problems, you use a two-step process to compute the coefficients of partial determination. You first use the Section EG14.1 and the Section EG13.2 *In-Depth Excel* instructions to create all possible regression results worksheets in a copy of the **Multiple Regression workbook**. For example, if you have two independent variables, you perform three regression analyses: *Y* with X_1 and X_2, *Y* with X_1, and *Y* with X_2, to create three regression results worksheets. Then, you open to the **CPD worksheet** for the number of independent variables (**CPD_2**, **CPD_3**, and **CPD_4 worksheets** are included) and follow the italicized instructions to copy and **Paste Special** values (see Appendix Section B.4) from the regression results worksheets.

EG14.6 USING DUMMY VARIABLES and INTERACTION TERMS in REGRESSION MODELS

Dummy Variables

Key Technique Use **Find and Replace** to create a dummy variable from a two-level categorical variable. Before using **Find and Replace**, copy and paste the categorical values to another column in order to preserve the original values.

Example Create a dummy variable named FireplaceCoded from the two-level categorical variable Fireplace as shown in Table 14.5 on page 546.

In-Depth Excel For the example, open to the **DATA worksheet** of the **House3 workbook** and:

1. Copy and paste the **Fireplace** values in column **C** to column D (the first empty column).
2. Select column **D**.
3. Press **Ctrl+H** (the keyboard shortcut for **Find and Replace**).

In the Find and Replace dialog box:

4. Enter **Yes** in the **Find what** box and enter **1** in the **Replace with** box.
5. Click **Replace All**. If a message box to confirm the replacement appears, click **OK** to continue.
6. Enter **No** in the **Find what** box and enter **0** in the **Replace with** box.
7. Click **Replace All**. If a message box to confirm the replacement appears, click **OK** to continue.
8. Click **Close**.

Categorical variables that have more than two levels require the use of formulas in multiple columns. For example, to create the dummy variables for Example 14.3 on page 548, two columns are needed. Assume that the three-level categorical variable mentioned in the example is in Column D of the opened worksheet. A first new column that contains formulas in the form **=IF(*column D cell* = *first level*, 1, 0)** and a second new column that contains formulas in the form **=IF(*column D cell* = *second level*, 1, 0)** would properly create the two dummy variables that the example requires.

Interactions

To create an interaction term, add a column of formulas that multiply one independent variable by another. For example, if the first independent variable appeared in column B and the second independent variable appeared in column C, enter the formula **=B2 * C2** in the row 2 cell of an empty new column and then copy the formula down through all rows of data to create the interaction.

EG14.7 LOGISTIC REGRESSION

Key Technique Use an automated process that incorporates the use of the Solver add-in to develop a logistic regression analysis model.

Example Develop the logistic regression model for the credit card pilot study data that is shown in Figure 14.13 on page 557.

PHStat Use **Logistic Regression.**
For the example, open to the **DATA worksheet** of the **CardStudy workbook**. Select **PHStat Regression Logistic Regression**, and in the procedure's dialog box (shown below):

1. Enter **A1:A31** as the **Y Variable Cell Range**.
2. Enter **B1:C31** as the **X Variables Cell Range**.
3. Check **First cells in both ranges contain label**.
4. Enter a **Title** and click **OK**.

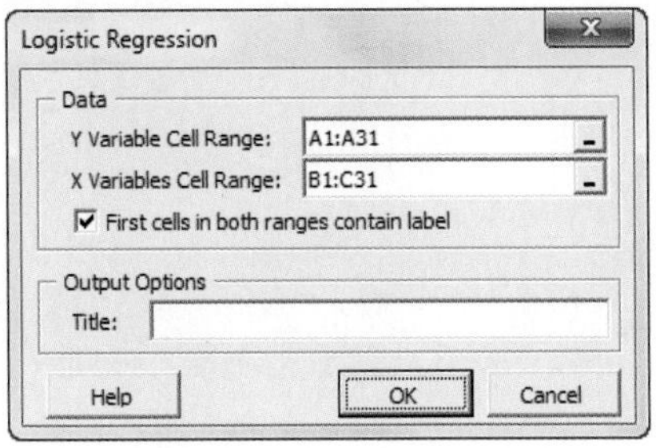

If the Solver add-in is not installed (see Appendix Section D.6), PHStat will display an error message instead of the Logistic Regression dialog box. The COMPUTE worksheet created contains a number of columns not shown in Figure 14.13 that contain supporting data.

In-Depth Excel Use the **Logistic Regression add-in workbook**. This workbook requires that the Solver add-in be installed (see Appendix Section D.6).
For the example, first open to the **DATA worksheet** of the **CardStudy workbook**. Then open the **Logistic Regression add-in workbook**. When this workbook opens properly, it adds a **Logistic Add-in** menu in either Add-ins tab (Microsoft Windows) or the Apple menu bar (OS X). Select **Logistic Add-in ➔ Logistic Regression** from either the Add-ins tab or the Apple menu bar. In the Logistic Regression dialog box (shown below):

1. Enter **A1:A31** as the **Y Variable Cell Range**.
2. Enter **B1:C31** as the **X Variables Cell Range**.
3. Check **First cells in both ranges contain label**.
4. Enter a **Title** and click **OK**.

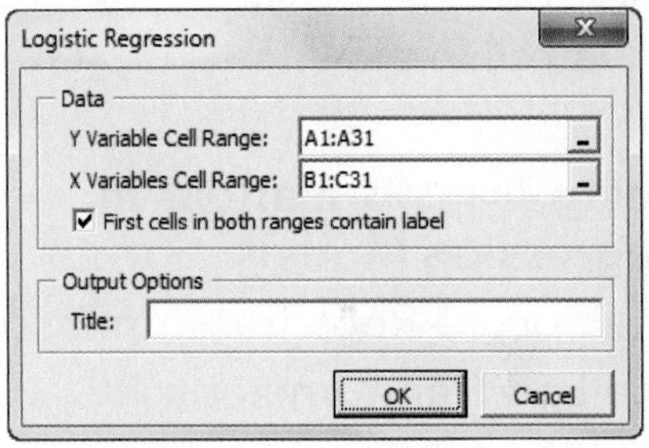

If the Solver add-in is not installed, you will see an error message in lieu of the Logistic Regression dialog box. This add-in workbook requires data workbooks to be in the **.xlsx** format and not the older **.xls** format.

CHAPTER

15 Multiple Regression Model Building

Learning Objectives

In this chapter, you learn:

- To use quadratic terms in a regression model
- To use transformed variables in a regression model
- To measure the correlation among independent variables
- To build a regression model using either the stepwise or best-subsets approach
- To avoid the pitfalls involved in developing a multiple regression model
- About the methods of data mining that are used in business analytics

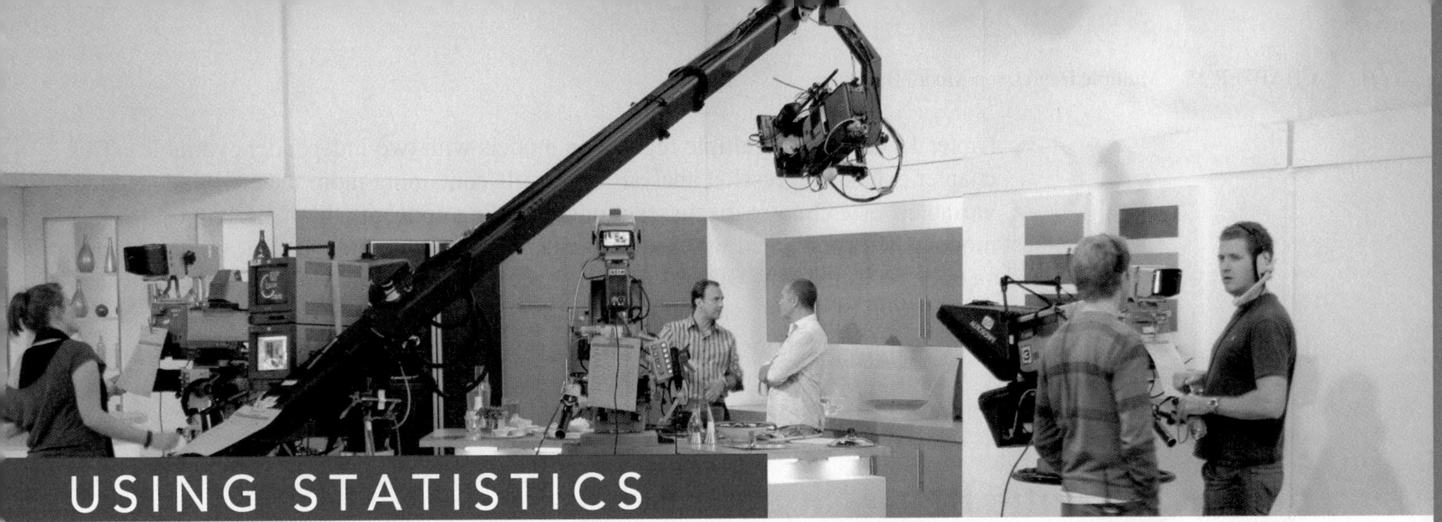

USING STATISTICS

Glyn Allan / Alamy

Valuing Parsimony at WHIT-DT

Your job as the broadcast operations manager at local station WHIT-DT has proven more challenging of late, as you adjust to changes caused by the recent acquisition of the station by the Berg Broadcasting Group. Now, the new general manager has announced the business objective of reducing expenses by 8% during the next fiscal year and has asked you to investigate ways to reduce unnecessary labor expenses associated with the staff of graphic artists employed by the station. Currently, these graphic artists receive hourly pay for a significant number of *standby hours*, hours for which they are present at the station but not assigned any specific task to do.

You believe that an appropriate model will help you to predict the number of future standby hours, identify the root causes of excessive numbers of standby hours, and allow you to reduce the total number of future standby hours. You plan to first collect weekly data for the number of standby hours and these four variables: the number of graphic artists present, the number of remote hours, the number of Dubner hours, and the total labor hours. Then, you seek to build a multiple regression model that will help determine which variables most heavily affect standby hours.

How do you build the model that has the most appropriate mix of independent variables? Are there statistical techniques that can help you identify a "best" model without having to consider all possible models?

Yurly Ponomarev / Shutterstock

Chapter 14 discussed multiple regression models with two independent variables. This chapter extends regression analysis to models containing more than two independent variables. The chapter discusses model-building concepts that will help to develop the best model when confronted with a set of data that has many independent variables, such as the data to be collected at WHIT-DT. These concepts include quadratic independent variables, transformations of the dependent or independent variables, stepwise regression, and best-subsets regression. The chapter concludes with a discussion of data mining methods that are used in business analytics when dealing with very large databases.

15.1 The Quadratic Regression Model

The simple regression model discussed in Chapter 13 and the multiple regression model discussed in Chapter 14 assume that the relationship between Y and each independent variable is linear. However, in Section 13.1, several different types of nonlinear relationships between variables were introduced. One of the most common nonlinear relationships is a quadratic, or curvilinear, relationship between two variables in which Y increases (or decreases) at a changing rate for various values of X (see Figure 13.2, Panels C through E, on page 473). You can use the quadratic regression model defined in Equation (15.1) to analyze this type of relationship between X and Y.

QUADRATIC REGRESSION MODEL

$$Y_i = \beta_0 + \beta_1 X_{1i} + \beta_2 X_{1i}^2 + \varepsilon_i \qquad \textbf{(15.1)}$$

where

β_0 = Y intercept

β_1 = coefficient of the linear effect on Y

β_2 = coefficient of the quadratic effect on Y

ε_i = random error in Y for observation i

This **quadratic regression model** is similar to the multiple regression model with two independent variables [see Equation (14.2) on page 527] except that the second independent variable, the **quadratic term**, is the square of the first independent variable. Once again, you use the least-squares method to compute sample regression coefficients (b_0, b_1, and b_2) as estimates of the population parameters (β_0, β_1, and β_2). Equation (15.2) defines the regression equation for the quadratic model with an independent variable (X_1) and a dependent variable (Y).

Student Tip
A quadratic regression model is a curvilinear model that has an X term and an X squared term. Other curvilinear models can have additional X terms that might involve X cubed, X raised to the fourth power, and so on.

QUADRATIC REGRESSION EQUATION

$$\hat{Y}_i = b_0 + b_1 X_{1i} + b_2 X_{1i}^2 \qquad \textbf{(15.2)}$$

In Equation (15.2), the first regression coefficient, b_0, represents the Y intercept; the second regression coefficient, b_1, represents the linear effect; and the third regression coefficient, b_2, represents the quadratic effect.

Finding the Regression Coefficients and Predicting Y

To illustrate the quadratic regression model, consider a study that examined the business problem facing a concrete supplier of how adding fly ash affects the strength of concrete. (Fly ash is an inexpensive industrial waste by-product that can be used as a substitute for Portland cement, a more expensive ingredient of concrete.) Batches of concrete were prepared in which the percentage of fly ash ranged from 0% to 60%. Data were collected from a sample of 18 batches and organized and stored in **FlyAsh**. Table 15.1 summarizes the results.

TABLE 15.1

Fly Ash Percentage and Strength of 18 Batches of 28-Day-Old Concrete

Fly Ash %	Strength (psi)	Fly Ash %	Strength (psi)
0	4,779	40	5,995
0	4,706	40	5,628
0	4,350	40	5,897
20	5,189	50	5,746
20	5,140	50	5,719
20	4,976	50	5,782
30	5,110	60	4,895
30	5,685	60	5,030
30	5,618	60	4,648

By creating the scatter plot in Figure 15.1 to visualize these data, you will be better able to select the proper model for expressing the relationship between fly ash percentage and strength.

FIGURE 15.1

Scatter plot of fly ash percentage (X) and strength (Y)

Use the Section EG2.5 instructions to construct scatter plots.

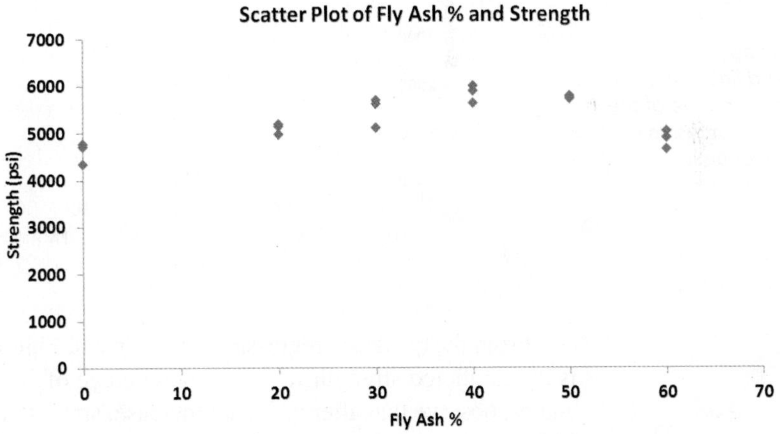

Figure 15.1 indicates an initial increase in the strength of the concrete as the percentage of fly ash increases. The strength appears to level off and then drop after achieving maximum strength at about 40% fly ash. Strength for 50% fly ash is slightly below strength at 40%, but strength at 60% fly ash is substantially below strength at 50%. Therefore, you should fit a quadratic model, not a linear model, to estimate strength based on fly ash percentage.

Figure 15.2 on page 576 shows regression results for these data.

From Figure 15.2,

$$b_0 = 4{,}486.3611 \quad b_1 = 63.0052 \quad b_2 = -0.8765$$

Therefore, the quadratic regression equation is

$$\hat{Y}_i = 4{,}486.3611 + 63.0052X_{1i} - 0.8765X_{1i}^2$$

where

$\hat{Y}_i$ = predicted strength for sample i

X_{1i} = percentage of fly ash for sample i

FIGURE 15.2

Regression results worksheet for the concrete strength data

	A	B	C	D	E	F	G
1	**Concrete Strength Analysis**						
2							
3	***Regression Statistics***						
4	Multiple R	0.8053					
5	R Square	0.6485					
6	Adjusted R Square	0.6016					
7	Standard Error	312.1129					
8	Observations	18					
9							
10	**ANOVA**						
11		*df*	*SS*	*MS*	*F*	*Significance F*	
12	Regression	2	2695473.4897	1347736.745	13.8351	0.0004	
13	Residual	15	1461217.0103	97414.4674			
14	Total	17	4156690.5000				
15							
16		*Coefficients*	*Standard Error*	*t Stat*	*P-value*	*Lower 95%*	*Upper 95%*
17	Intercept	4486.3611	174.7531	25.6726	0.0000	4113.8834	4858.8389
18	Fly Ash%	63.0052	12.3725	5.0923	0.0001	36.6338	89.3767
19	Fly Ash% ^2	-0.8765	0.1966	-4.4578	0.0005	-1.2955	-0.4574

Figure 15.3 is a scatter plot of this quadratic regression equation that shows the fit of the quadratic regression model to the original data.

FIGURE 15.3

Scatter plot showing the quadratic relationship between fly ash percentage and strength for the concrete data

Use the Section EG15.1 instructions to add a quadratic trend line. Note that Excel rounds some of the coefficients when it displays the regression equation.

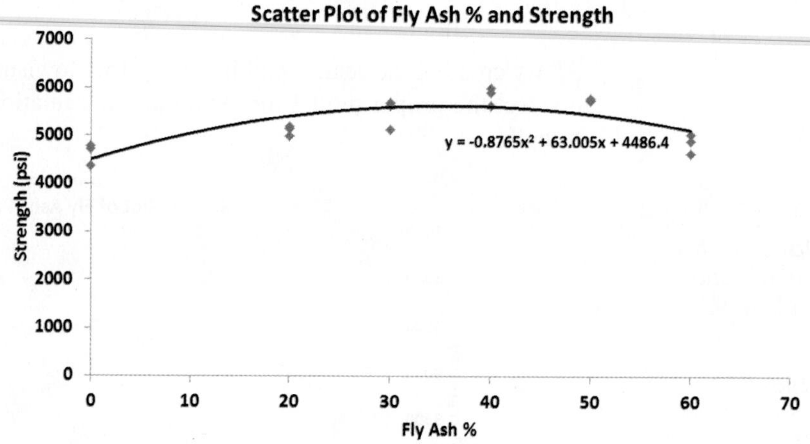

From the quadratic regression equation and Figure 15.3, the Y intercept ($b_0 = 4{,}486.3611$) is the predicted strength when the percentage of fly ash is 0. To interpret the coefficients b_1 and b_2, observe that after an initial increase, strength decreases as fly ash percentage increases. This nonlinear relationship is further demonstrated by predicting the strength for fly ash percentages of 20, 40, and 60. Using the quadratic regression equation,

$$\hat{Y}_i = 4{,}486.3611 + 63.0052X_{1i} - 0.8765X_{1i}^2$$

for $X_{1i} = 20$,

$$\hat{Y}_i = 4{,}486.3611 + 63.0052(20) - 0.8765(20)^2 = 5{,}395.865$$

for $X_{1i} = 40$,

$$\hat{Y}_i = 4{,}486.3611 + 63.0052(40) - 0.8765(40)^2 = 5{,}604.169$$

and for $X_{1i} = 60$,

$$\hat{Y}_i = 4{,}486.3611 + 63.0052(60) - 0.8765(60)^2 = 5{,}111.273$$

Thus, the predicted concrete strength for 40% fly ash is 208.304 psi above the predicted strength for 20% fly ash, but the predicted strength for 60% fly ash is 492.896 psi below the predicted strength for 40% fly ash. The concrete supplier should consider using a fly ash percentage of 40% and not using fly ash percentages of 20% or 60% because those percentages lead to reduced concrete strength.

Testing for the Significance of the Quadratic Model

After you calculate the quadratic regression equation, you can test whether there is a significant overall relationship between strength, Y, and fly ash percentage, X_1. The null and alternative hypotheses are as follows:

Student Tip
Remember that you are testing whether at least one independent variable has a linear relationship with the dependent variable. If you reject H_0, you are *not* concluding that all the independent variables have a linear relationship with the dependent variable, only that *at least one* independent variable does.

H_0: $\beta_1 = \beta_2 = 0$ (There is no overall relationship between X_1 and Y.)

H_1: β_1 and/or $\beta_2 \neq 0$ (There is an overall relationship between X_1 and Y.)

Equation (14.6) on page 533 defines the overall F_{STAT} test statistic used for this test:

$$F_{STAT} = \frac{MSR}{MSE}$$

From the Figure 15.2 results on page 576,

$$F_{STAT} = \frac{MSR}{MSE} = \frac{1{,}347{,}736.745}{97{,}414.4674} = 13.8351$$

If you choose a level of significance of 0.05, from Table E.5, the critical value of the F distribution, with 2 and $18 - 2 - 1 = 15$ degrees of freedom, is 3.68 (see Figure 15.4). Because $F_{STAT} = 13.8351 > 3.68$, or because the p-value $= 0.0004 < 0.05$, you reject the null hypothesis (H_0) and conclude that there is a significant overall relationship between strength and fly ash percentage.

FIGURE 15.4
Testing for the existence of the overall relationship at the 0.05 level of significance, with 2 and 15 degrees of freedom

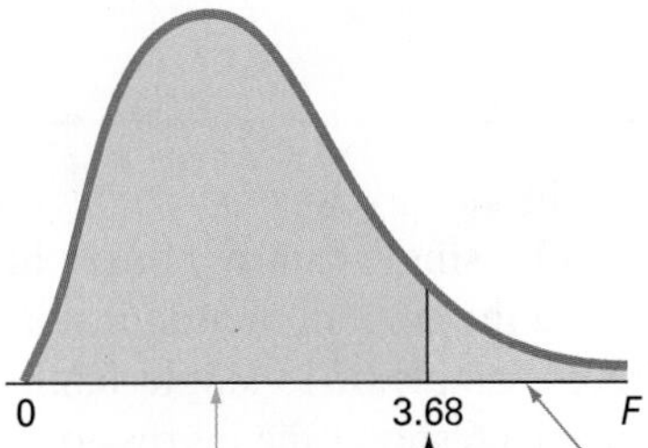

Testing the Quadratic Effect

In using a regression model to examine a relationship between two variables, you want to find not only the most accurate model but also the simplest model that expresses that relationship. Therefore, you need to examine whether there is a significant difference between the quadratic model:

$$Y_i = \beta_0 + \beta_1 X_{1i} + \beta_2 X_{1i}^2 + \varepsilon_i$$

and the linear model:

$$Y_i = \beta_0 + \beta_1 X_{1i} + \varepsilon_i$$

In Section 14.4, you used the t test to determine whether each independent variable makes a significant contribution to the regression model. To test the significance of the contribution of the quadratic effect, you use the following null and alternative hypotheses:

H_0: Including the quadratic effect does not significantly improve the model ($\beta_2 = 0$).

H_1: Including the quadratic effect significantly improves the model ($\beta_2 \neq 0$).

The standard error of each regression coefficient and its corresponding t_{STAT} test statistic are part of the regression results (see Figure 15.2 on page 576). Equation (14.7) on page 537 defines the t_{STAT} test statistic:

$$t_{STAT} = \frac{b_2 - \beta_2}{S_{b_2}}$$

$$= \frac{-0.8765 - 0}{0.1966} = -4.4578$$

If you select the 0.05 level of significance, then from Table E.3, the critical values for the t distribution with 15 degrees of freedom are -2.1315 and $+2.1315$ (see Figure 15.5).

FIGURE 15.5

Testing for the contribution of the quadratic effect to a regression model at the 0.05 level of significance, with 15 degrees of freedom

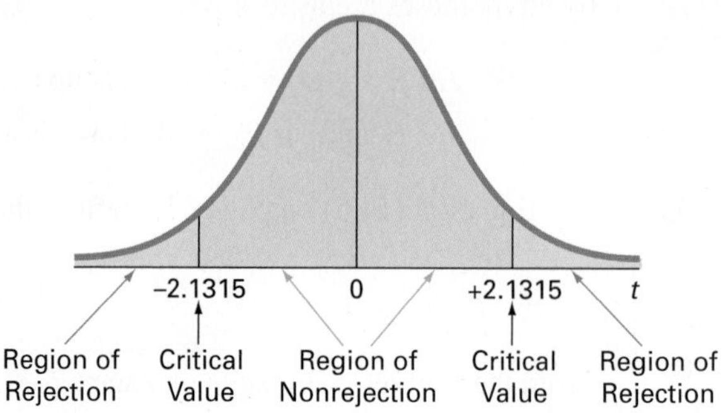

Because $t_{STAT} = -4.4578 < -2.1315$ or because the p-value $= 0.0005 < 0.05$, you reject H_0 and conclude that the quadratic model is significantly better than the linear model for representing the relationship between strength and fly ash percentage.

Example 15.1 provides an additional illustration of a possible quadratic effect.

EXAMPLE 15.1

Studying the Quadratic Effect in a Multiple Regression Model

A real estate developer studying the business problem of estimating the consumption of heating oil by single-family houses has decided to examine the effect of atmospheric temperature and the amount of attic insulation on heating oil consumption. Data are collected from a random sample of 15 single-family houses. The data are organized and stored in **HeatingOil**. Figure 15.6 shows the regression results for a multiple regression model using the two independent variables: atmospheric temperature and attic insulation.

FIGURE 15.6

Regression results worksheet for the multiple linear regression model predicting monthly consumption of heating oil

	A	B	C	D	E	F	G
1	**Heating Oil Consumption Analysis**						
2							
3	*Regression Statistics*						
4	Multiple R	0.9827					
5	R Square	0.9656					
6	Adjusted R Square	0.9599					
7	Standard Error	26.0138					
8	Observations	15					
9							
10	ANOVA						
11		*df*	*SS*	*MS*	*F*	*Significance F*	
12	Regression	2	228014.6263	114007.3132	168.4712	0.0000	
13	Residual	12	8120.6030	676.7169			
14	Total	14	236135.2293				
15							
16		*Coefficients*	*Standard Error*	*t Stat*	*P-value*	*Lower 95%*	*Upper 95%*
17	Intercept	562.1510	21.0931	26.6509	0.0000	516.1931	608.1089
18	Temperature	-5.4366	0.3362	-16.1699	0.0000	-6.1691	-4.7040
19	Insulation	-20.0123	2.3425	-8.5431	0.0000	-25.1162	-14.9084

The residual plot for attic insulation (not shown here) contained some evidence of a quadratic effect. Thus, the real estate developer reanalyzed the data by adding a quadratic term for attic insulation to the multiple regression model. At the 0.05 level of significance, is there evidence of a significant quadratic effect for attic insulation?

SOLUTION Figure 15.7 shows the results for this regression model.

FIGURE 15.7
Regression results worksheet for the multiple regression model with a quadratic term for attic insulation

	A	B	C	D	E	F	G
1	Quadratic Effect for Insulation Variable?						
2							
3	*Regression Statistics*						
4	Multiple R	0.9862					
5	R Square	0.9725					
6	Adjusted R Square	0.9650					
7	Standard Error	24.2938					
8	Observations	15					
9							
10	ANOVA						
11		*df*	*SS*	*MS*	*F*	*Significance F*	
12	Regression	3	229643.1645	76547.7215	129.7006	0.0000	
13	Residual	11	6492.0649	590.1877			
14	Total	14	236135.2293				
15							
16		*Coefficients*	*Standard Error*	*t Stat*	*P-value*	*Lower 95%*	*Upper 95%*
17	Intercept	624.5864	42.4352	14.7186	0.0000	531.1872	717.9856
18	Temperature	-5.3626	0.3171	-16.9099	0.0000	-6.0606	-4.6646
19	Insulation	-44.5868	14.9547	-2.9815	0.0125	-77.5019	-11.6717
20	Insulation ^2	1.8667	1.1238	1.6611	0.1249	-0.6067	4.3401

The multiple regression equation is

$$\hat{Y}_i = 624.5864 - 5.3626X_{1i} - 44.5868X_{2i} + 1.8667X_{2i}^2$$

To test for the significance of the quadratic effect:

H_0: Including the quadratic effect of insulation does not significantly improve the model ($\beta_3 = 0$).

H_1: Including the quadratic effect of insulation significantly improves the model ($\beta_3 \neq 0$).

From Figure 15.7 and Table E.3 with $15 - 3 - 1 = 11$ degrees of freedom, $-2.2010 < t_{STAT} = 1.6611 < 2.2010$ (or the p-value $= 0.1249 > 0.05$). Therefore, you do not reject the null hypothesis. You conclude that there is insufficient evidence that the quadratic effect for attic insulation is different from zero. In the interest of keeping the model as simple as possible, you should use the multiple regression equation shown in Figure 15.6:

$$\hat{Y}_i = 562.1510 - 5.4366X_{1i} - 20.0123X_{2i}$$

The Coefficient of Multiple Determination

In the multiple regression model, the coefficient of multiple determination, r^2 (see Section 14.2), represents the proportion of variation in Y that is explained by variation in the independent variables. Consider the quadratic regression model you used to predict the strength of concrete using fly ash and fly ash squared. You compute r^2 by using Equation (14.4) on page 531:

$$r^2 = \frac{SSR}{SST}$$

From Figure 15.2 on page 576,

$$SSR = 2{,}695{,}473.897 \qquad SST = 4{,}156{,}690.5$$

Thus,

$$r^2 = \frac{SSR}{SST} = \frac{2{,}695{,}473.897}{4{,}156{,}690.5} = 0.6485$$

Student Tip
Remember that r^2 in multiple regression represents the proportion of the variation in the dependent variable Y that is explained by *all* the independent X variables included in the model. So, in this case of quadratic regression, r^2 represents the proportion of the variation in the dependent variable Y that is explained by the linear term and the quadratic term.

This coefficient of multiple determination indicates that 64.85% of the variation in strength is explained by the quadratic relationship between strength and the percentage of fly ash. You should also compute r^2_{adj} to account for the number of independent variables and the sample size. In the quadratic regression model, $k = 2$ because there are two independent variables, X_1 and X_1^2. Thus, using Equation (14.5) on page 532,

$$\begin{aligned} r^2_{adj} &= 1 - \left[(1 - r^2)\frac{(n-1)}{(n-k-1)}\right] \\ &= 1 - \left[(1 - 0.6485)\frac{17}{15}\right] \\ &= 1 - 0.3984 \\ &= 0.6016 \end{aligned}$$

Problems for Section 15.1

LEARNING THE BASICS

15.1 The following is the quadratic regression equation for a sample of $n = 25$:

$$\hat{Y}_i = 5 + 3X_{1i} + 1.5X_{1i}^2$$

a. Predict Y for $X_1 = 2$.
b. Suppose that the computed t_{STAT} test statistic for the quadratic regression coefficient is 2.35. At the 0.05 level of significance, is there evidence that the quadratic model is better than the linear model?
c. Suppose that the computed t_{STAT} test statistic for the quadratic regression coefficient is 1.17. At the 0.05 level of significance, is there evidence that the quadratic model is better than the linear model?
d. Suppose the regression coefficient for the linear effect is -3.0. Predict Y for $X_1 = 2$.

APPLYING THE CONCEPTS

15.2 Businesses actively recruit business students with well-developed higher-order cognitive skills (HOCS) such as problem identification, analytical reasoning, and content integration skills. Researchers conducted a study to see if improvement in students' HOCS was related to the students' GPA. (Data extracted from R. V. Bradley, C. S. Sankar, H. R. Clayton, V. W. Mbarika, and P. K. Raju, "A Study on the Impact of GPA on Perceived Improvement of Higher-Order Cognitive Skills," *Decision Sciences Journal of Innovative Education*, January 2007, 5(1), pp. 151–168.) The researchers conducted a study in which business students were taught using the case study method. Using data collected from 300 business students, the following quadratic regression equation was derived:

$$\text{HOCS} = -3.48 + 4.53(\text{GPA}) - 0.68(\text{GPA})^2$$

where the dependent variable HOCS measured the improvement in higher-order cognitive skills, with 1 being the lowest improvement in HOCS and 5 being the highest improvement in HOCS.

a. Construct a table of predicted HOCS, using GPA equal to 2.0, 2.1, 2.2, . . . , 4.0.
b. Plot the values in the table constructed in (a), with GPA on the horizontal axis and predicted HOCS on the vertical axis.
c. Discuss the curvilinear relationship between students' GPA and their predicted improvement in HOCS.
d. The researchers reported that the model had an r^2 of 0.07 and an adjusted r^2 of 0.06. What does this tell you about the scatter of individual HOCS scores around the curvilinear relationship plotted in (b) and discussed in (c)?

15.3 A national chain of consumer electronics stores had the business objective of determining the effectiveness of newspaper advertising. To promote sales, the chain relies heavily on local newspaper advertising to support its modest exposure in nationwide television commercials. A sample of 20 cities with similar populations and monthly sales totals were assigned different newspaper advertising budgets for one month. The following table on page 581, stored in **Advertising**, summarizes the sales (in \$millions) and the newspaper advertising budgets (in \$thousands) observed during the study:

a. Construct a scatter plot for newspaper advertising and sales.
b. Fit a quadratic regression model and state the quadratic regression equation.
c. Predict the monthly sales for a city with newspaper advertising of \$20,000.
d. Perform a residual analysis on the results and determine whether the regression assumptions are valid.
e. At the 0.05 level of significance, is there a significant quadratic relationship between monthly sales and newspaper advertising?

Sales ($millions)	Newspaper Advertising ($thousands)	Sales ($millions)	Newspaper Advertising ($thousands)
6.14	5	6.84	15
6.04	5	6.66	15
6.21	5	6.95	20
6.32	5	6.65	20
6.42	10	6.83	20
6.56	10	6.81	20
6.67	10	7.03	25
6.35	10	6.88	25
6.76	15	6.84	25
6.79	15	6.99	25

f. At the 0.05 level of significance, determine whether the quadratic model is a better fit than the linear model.
g. Interpret the meaning of the coefficient of multiple determination.
h. Compute the adjusted r^2.

15.4 Is the number of calories in a beer related to the number of carbohydrates and/or the percentage of alcohol in the beer? Data concerning 150 of the best-selling domestic beers in the United States are stored in DomesticBeer. The values for three variables are included: the number of calories per 12 ounces, the alcohol percentage, and the number of carbohydrates (in grams) per 12 ounces. (Data extracted from **www.beer100.com/beercalories.htm**, June 1, 2012.)
a. Perform a multiple linear regression analysis, using calories as the dependent variable and percentage alcohol and number of carbohydrates as the independent variables.
b. Add quadratic terms for alcohol percentage and the number of carbohydrates.
c. Which model is better, the one in (a) or (b)?
d. Write a short summary concerning the relationship between the number of calories in a beer and the alcohol percentage and number of carbohydrates.

15.5 In the production of printed circuit boards, errors in the alignment of electrical connections are a source of scrap. The data in the file RegistrationError-HighCost contains the registration error and the temperature used in the production of circuit boards in an experiment in which higher cost material was used. (Data extracted from C. Nachtsheim and B. Jones, "A Powerful Analytical Tool," *Six Sigma Forum Magazine*, August 2003, pp. 30–33.)
a. Construct a scatter plot for temperature and registration error.
b. Fit a quadratic regression model to predict registration error and state the quadratic regression equation.
c. Perform a residual analysis on the results and determine whether the regression model is valid.
d. At the 0.05 level of significance, is there a significant quadratic relationship between temperature and registration error?
e. At the 0.05 level of significance, determine whether the quadratic model is a better fit than the linear model.
f. Interpret the meaning of the coefficient of multiple determination.
g. Compute the adjusted r^2.

SELF Test **15.6** A production manager wishes to examine the relationship between unit production (number of units produced) and associated costs (total cost). The file CostEstimation contains data for 10 months of production.
a. Construct a scatter plot for unit production and total cost.
b. Fit a quadratic regression model to predict total cost and state the quadratic regression equation.
c. Predict the total cost when production is 145 units.
d. Perform a residual analysis on the results and determine whether the regression model is valid.
e. At the 0.05 level of significance, is there a significant overall relationship between monthly unit production and total cost?
f. What is the p-value in (e)? Interpret its meaning.
g. At the 0.05 level of significance, determine whether there is a significant quadratic effect.
h. What is the p-value in (g)? Interpret its meaning.
i. Interpret the meaning of the coefficient of multiple determination.
j. Compute the adjusted r^2.

15.7 An auditor for a county government would like to develop a model to predict county taxes, based on the age of single-family houses. She selects a random sample of 19 single-family houses, and the results are stored in Taxes.
a. Construct a scatter plot of age and county taxes.
b. Fit a quadratic regression model and state the quadratic regression equation.
c. Predict the county taxes for a house that is 20 years old.
d. Perform a residual analysis on the results and determine whether the regression model is valid.
e. At the 0.05 level of significance, is there a significant overall relationship between age and county taxes?
f. What is the p-value in (e)? Interpret its meaning.
g. At the 0.05 level of significance, determine whether the quadratic model is superior to the linear model.
h. What is the p-value in (g)? Interpret its meaning.
i. Interpret the meaning of the coefficient of multiple determination.
j. Compute the adjusted r^2.

15.2 Using Transformations in Regression Models

This section introduces regression models in which the independent variable, the dependent variable, or both are transformed in order to either overcome violations of the assumptions of regression or to make a model whose form is not linear into a linear model. Among the many transformations available (see reference 3) are the square-root transformation and transformations involving the common logarithm (base 10) and the natural logarithm (base e).[1]

[1]For more information on logarithms, see Appendix Section A.3.

Student Tip

Log is the symbol used for base 10 logarithms. The log of a number is the power to which 10 needs to be raised to equal that number. *ln* is the symbol used for base *e* logarithms, commonly referred to as *natural logarithms*. *e* is Euler's number, and e ≅ 2.718282. The natural log of a number is the power to which *e* needs to be raised to equal that number.

The Square-Root Transformation

The **square-root transformation** is often used to overcome violations of the equal-variance assumption as well as to transform a model whose form is not linear into a linear model. Equation (15.3) shows a regression model that uses a square-root transformation of the independent variable.

REGRESSION MODEL WITH A SQUARE-ROOT TRANSFORMATION

$$Y_i = \beta_0 + \beta_1\sqrt{X_{1i}} + \varepsilon_i \quad (15.3)$$

Example 15.2 illustrates the use of a square-root transformation.

EXAMPLE 15.2 Using the Square-Root Transformation

Given the following values for Y and X, use a square-root transformation for the X variable:

Y	X	Y	X
42.7	1	100.4	3
50.4	1	104.7	4
69.1	2	112.3	4
79.8	2	113.6	5
90.0	3	123.9	5

Construct a scatter plot for X and Y and for the square root of X and Y.

SOLUTION Figure 15.8 displays both scatter plots.

FIGURE 15.8

Example 15.2 scatter plots of X and Y and the square root of X and Y

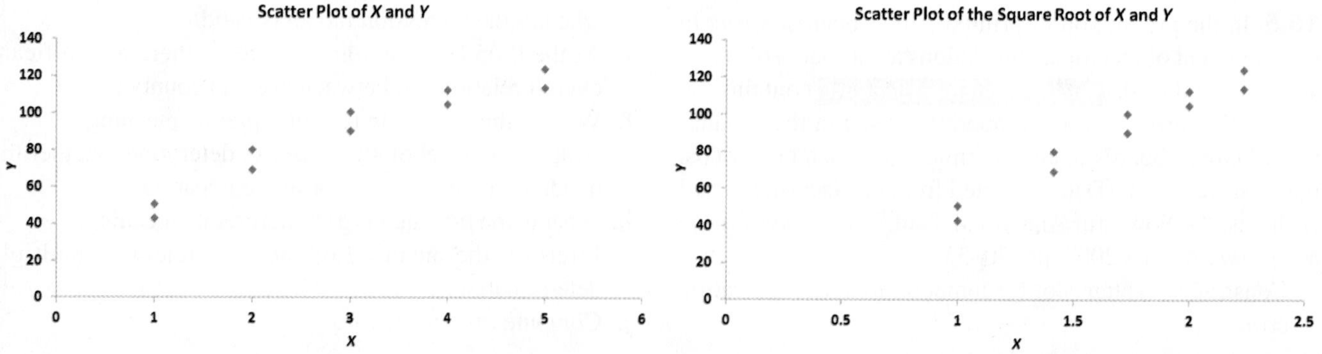

You can see that the square-root transformation has transformed a nonlinear relationship into a linear relationship.

To begin, refer to the WHIT-DT scenario introduced on page 573, in which four independent variables (total staff present, remote hours, Dubner hours, and total labor hours) are considered in the business problem that involves developing a regression model to predict standby hours of unionized graphic artists. Data are collected over a period of 26 weeks and organized and stored in Standby. Table 15.2 summarizes these data.

TABLE 15.2

Predicting Standby Hours Based on Total Staff Present, Remote Hours, Dubner Hours, and Total Labor Hours

Week	Standby Hours	Total Staff Present	Remote Hours	Dubner Hours	Total Labor Hours
1	245	338	414	323	2,001
2	177	333	598	340	2,030
3	271	358	656	340	2,226
4	211	372	631	352	2,154
5	196	339	528	380	2,078
6	135	289	409	339	2,080
7	195	334	382	331	2,073
8	118	293	399	311	1,758
9	116	325	343	328	1,624
10	147	311	338	353	1,889
11	154	304	353	518	1,988
12	146	312	289	440	2,049
13	115	283	388	276	1,796
14	161	307	402	207	1,720
15	274	322	151	287	2,056
16	245	335	228	290	1,890
17	201	350	271	355	2,187
18	183	339	440	300	2,032
19	237	327	475	284	1,856
20	175	328	347	337	2,068
21	152	319	449	279	1,813
22	188	325	336	244	1,808
23	188	322	267	253	1,834
24	197	317	235	272	1,973
25	261	315	164	223	1,839
26	232	331	270	272	1,935

To develop a model to predict the dependent variable, standby hours in the WHIT-DT scenario, you need to be guided by a general problem-solving strategy, or *heuristic*. One heuristic appropriate for building regression models uses the principle of parsimony.

Parsimony guides you to select the regression model with the fewest independent variables that can predict the dependent variable adequately. Regression models with fewer independent variables are easier to interpret, particularly because they are less likely to be affected by collinearity problems (described in Section 15.3).

Developing an appropriate model when many independent variables are under consideration involves complexities that are not present with a model that has only two independent variables. The evaluation of all possible regression models is more computationally complex. And, although you can quantitatively evaluate competing models, there may not be a *uniquely* best model but several *equally appropriate* models.

To begin analyzing the standby-hours data, you compute the variance inflationary factors [see Equation (15.8) on page 585] to measure the amount of collinearity among the independent variables. The values for the four *VIF*s for this model appear in Figure 15.10, along with the results for the model that uses the four independent variables.

FIGURE 15.10

Regression results worksheet for predicting standby hours based on four independent variables (with worksheets for Durbin-Watson statistic and *VIF*, inset)

	A	B	C	D	E	F	G
1	**Standby Hours Analysis**						
2							
3	*Regression Statistics*						
4	Multiple R	0.7894					
5	R Square	0.6231					
6	Adjusted R Square	0.5513					
7	Standard Error	31.8350					
8	Observations	26					
9							
10	**ANOVA**						
11		*df*	*SS*	*MS*	*F*	*Significance F*	
12	Regression	4	35181.7937	8795.4484	8.6786	0.0003	
13	Residual	21	21282.8217	1013.4677			
14	Total	25	56464.6154				
15							
16		*Coefficients*	*Standard Error*	*t Stat*	*P-value*	*Lower 95%*	*Upper 95%*
17	Intercept	-330.8318	110.8954	-2.9833	0.0071	-561.4514	-100.2123
18	Total Staff	1.2456	0.4121	3.0229	0.0065	0.3887	2.1026
19	Remote	-0.1184	0.0543	-2.1798	0.0408	-0.2314	-0.0054
20	Dubner	-0.2971	0.1179	-2.5189	0.0199	-0.5423	-0.0518
21	Total Labor	0.1305	0.0593	2.2004	0.0391	0.0072	0.2539

	A	B
1	**Durbin-Watson Calculations**	
2		
3	Sum of Squared Difference of Residuals	47241.6126
4	Sum of Squared Residuals	21282.8217
5		
6	Durbin-Watson Statistic	2.2197

	A	B	C	D	E
1	**Variance Inflationary Factor (*VIF*) Calculations**				
2		Regression Model			
3		Total Staff and all other X	Remote and all other X	Dubner and all other X	Total Labor and all other X
4	R Square	0.4143	0.1891	0.3147	0.4998
5	VIF	1.7074	1.2333	1.4592	1.9993

Observe that all the *VIF* values in Figure 15.10 are relatively small, ranging from a high of 1.9993 for the total labor hours to a low of 1.2333 for remote hours. Thus, on the basis of the criteria developed by Snee that all *VIF* values should be less than 5.0 (see reference 8), there is little evidence of collinearity among the set of independent variables.

The Stepwise Regression Approach to Model Building

You continue your analysis of the standby-hours data by attempting to determine whether a subset of all independent variables yields an adequate and appropriate model. The first approach described here is **stepwise regression**, which attempts to find the "best" regression model without examining all possible models.

The first step of stepwise regression is to find the best model that uses one independent variable. The next step is to find the best of the remaining independent variables to add to the model selected in the first step. An important feature of the stepwise approach is that an independent variable that has entered into the model at an early stage may subsequently be removed after other independent variables are considered. Thus, in stepwise regression, variables are either added to or deleted from the regression model at each step of the model-building process. The t test for the slope (see Section 14.4) or the partial F_{STAT} test statistic (see Section 14.5) is used to determine whether variables are added or deleted. The stepwise procedure terminates with the selection of a best-fitting model when no additional variables can be added to or deleted from the last model evaluated. Figure 15.11 on page 589 shows the stepwise regression results worksheet for the standby-hours data.

For this example, a significance level of 0.05 is used to enter a variable into the model or to delete a variable from the model. The first variable entered into the model is total staff, the variable that correlates most highly with the dependent variable standby hours. Because the p-value of 0.0011 is less than 0.05, total staff is included in the regression model.

The next step involves selecting a second independent variable for the model. The second variable chosen is one that makes the largest contribution to the model, given that the first variable has been selected. For this model, the second variable is remote hours. Because the p-value of 0.0269 for remote hours is less than 0.05, the remote hours variable is included in the regression model.

After the remote hours variable is entered into the model, the stepwise procedure determines whether total staff is still an important contributing variable or whether it can be eliminated from the model. Because the p-value of 0.0001 for total staff is less than 0.05, total staff remains in the regression model.

The next step involves selecting a third independent variable for the model. Because none of the other variables meets the 0.05 criterion for entry into the model, the stepwise procedure terminates with a model that includes total staff present and the number of remote hours.

FIGURE 15.11

Stepwise regression results worksheet for the standby-hours data

Figure 15.11 displays a worksheet that the Section EG15.4 instructions use. This worksheet can be created only by using PHStat.

Stepwise Analysis for Standby Hours

Table of Results for General Stepwise

Total Staff entered.

	df	*SS*	*MS*	*F*	*Significance F*	
Regression	1	20667.3980	20667.3980	13.8563	0.0011	
Residual	24	35797.2174	1491.5507			
Total	25	56464.6154				

	Coefficients	*Standard Error*	*t Stat*	*P-value*	*Lower 95%*	*Upper 95%*
Intercept	-272.3816	124.2402	-2.1924	0.0383	-528.8008	-15.9625
Total Staff	1.4241	0.3826	3.7224	0.0011	0.6345	2.2136

Remote entered.

	df	*SS*	*MS*	*F*	*Significance F*	
Regression	2	27662.5429	13831.2714	11.0450	0.0004	
Residual	23	28802.0725	1252.2640			
Total	25	56464.6154				

	Coefficients	*Standard Error*	*t Stat*	*P-value*	*Lower 95%*	*Upper 95%*
Intercept	-330.6748	116.4802	-2.8389	0.0093	-571.6322	-89.7175
Total Staff	1.7649	0.3790	4.6562	0.0001	0.9808	2.5490
Remote	-0.1390	0.0588	-2.3635	0.0269	-0.2606	-0.0173

No other variables could be entered into the model. Stepwise ends.

This stepwise regression approach to model building was originally developed more than four decades ago, when regression computations on computers were time-consuming and costly. Although stepwise regression limited the evaluation of alternative models, the method was deemed a good trade-off between evaluation and cost.

Given the ability of today's computers to perform regression computations at very low cost and high speed, stepwise regression has been superseded to some extent by the best-subsets approach, discussed next, which evaluates a larger set of alternative models. Stepwise regression is not obsolete, however. Today, many businesses use stepwise regression as part of data mining (see Section 15.6), which tries to identify significant statistical relationships in very large data sets that contain extremely large numbers of variables.

The Best-Subsets Approach to Model Building

The **best-subsets approach** evaluates all possible regression models for a given set of independent variables. Figure 15.12 presents best-subsets regression results of all possible regression models for the standby-hours data.

FIGURE 15.12

Best-subsets regression results worksheet for the standby-hours data

Figure 15.12 displays a worksheet that the Section EG15.4 instructions use. This worksheet can be created only by using PHStat.

Best-Subsets Analysis for Standby Hours

Intermediate Calculations	
R2T	0.6231
1 - *R2T*	0.3769
n	26
T	5
n - T	21

Model	Cp	k+1	R Square	Adj. R Square	Std. Error
X1	13.3215	2	0.3660	0.3396	38.6206
X1X2	8.4193	3	0.4899	0.4456	35.3873
X1X2X3	7.8418	4	0.5362	0.4729	34.5029
X1X2X3X4	5.0000	5	0.6231	0.5513	31.8350
X1X2X4	9.3449	4	0.5092	0.4423	35.4921
X1X3	10.6486	3	0.4499	0.4021	36.7490
X1X3X4	7.7517	4	0.5378	0.4748	34.4426
X1X4	14.7982	3	0.3754	0.3211	39.1579
X2	33.2078	2	0.0091	-0.0322	48.2836
X2X3	32.3067	3	0.0612	-0.0205	48.0087
X2X3X4	12.1381	4	0.4591	0.3853	37.2608
X2X4	23.2481	3	0.2238	0.1563	43.6540
X3	30.3884	2	0.0597	0.0205	47.0345
X3X4	11.8231	3	0.4288	0.3791	37.4466
X4	24.1846	2	0.1710	0.1365	44.1619

A criterion often used in model building is the adjusted r^2, which adjusts the r^2 of each model to account for the number of independent variables in the model as well as for the sample size (see Section 14.2). Because model building requires you to compare models with different numbers of independent variables, the adjusted r^2 is more appropriate than r^2. Referring to Figure 15.12, you see that the adjusted r^2 reaches a maximum value of 0.5513 when all four independent variables plus the intercept term (for a total of five estimated parameters) are included in the model.

A second criterion often used in the evaluation of competing models is the **C_p statistic** developed by Mallows (see reference 3). The C_p statistic, defined in Equation (15.9), measures the differences between a fitted regression model and a *true* model, along with random error.

C_p STATISTIC

$$C_p = \frac{(1 - R_k^2)(n - T)}{1 - R_T^2} - [n - 2(k + 1)] \quad \textbf{(15.9)}$$

where

k = number of independent variables included in a regression model

T = total number of parameters (including the intercept) to be estimated in the full regression model

R_k^2 = coefficient of multiple determination for a regression model that has k independent variables

R_T^2 = coefficient of multiple determination for a full regression model that contains all T estimated parameters

Using Equation (15.9) to compute C_p for the model containing total staff and remote hours,

$$n = 26 \qquad k = 2 \qquad T = 4 + 1 = 5 \qquad R_k^2 = 0.4899 \qquad R_T^2 = 0.6231$$

so that

$$C_p = \frac{(1 - 0.4899)(26 - 5)}{1 - 0.6231} - [26 - 2(2 + 1)]$$
$$= 8.4193$$

When a regression model with k independent variables contains only random differences from a *true* model, the mean value of C_p is $k + 1$, the number of parameters. Thus, in evaluating many alternative regression models, the goal is to find models whose C_p is close to or less than $k + 1$. In Figure 15.12, you see that only the model with all four independent variables considered contains a C_p value close to or below $k + 1$. Therefore, using the C_p criterion, you should choose that model.

Although it is not the case here, the C_p statistic often provides several alternative models for you to evaluate in greater depth. Moreover, the best model or models using the C_p criterion might differ from the model selected using the adjusted r^2 and/or the model selected using the stepwise procedure. (Note here that the model selected using stepwise regression has a C_p value of 8.4193, which is substantially above the suggested criterion of $k + 1 = 3$ for that model.) Remember that there may not be a uniquely best model, but there may be several equally appropriate models. Final model selection often involves using subjective criteria, such as parsimony, interpretability, and departure from model assumptions (as evaluated by residual analysis).

When you have finished selecting the independent variables to include in the model, you need to perform a residual analysis to evaluate the regression assumptions, and because the data were collected in time order, you also need to compute the Durbin-Watson statistic to determine whether there is autocorrelation in the residuals (see Section 13.6). From Figure 15.10

on page 588, you see that the Durbin-Watson statistic, D, is 2.2197. Because D is greater than 2.0, there is no indication of positive correlation in the residuals. Figure 15.13 presents the plots used in the residual analysis.

FIGURE 15.13
Residual plots for the standby-hours data

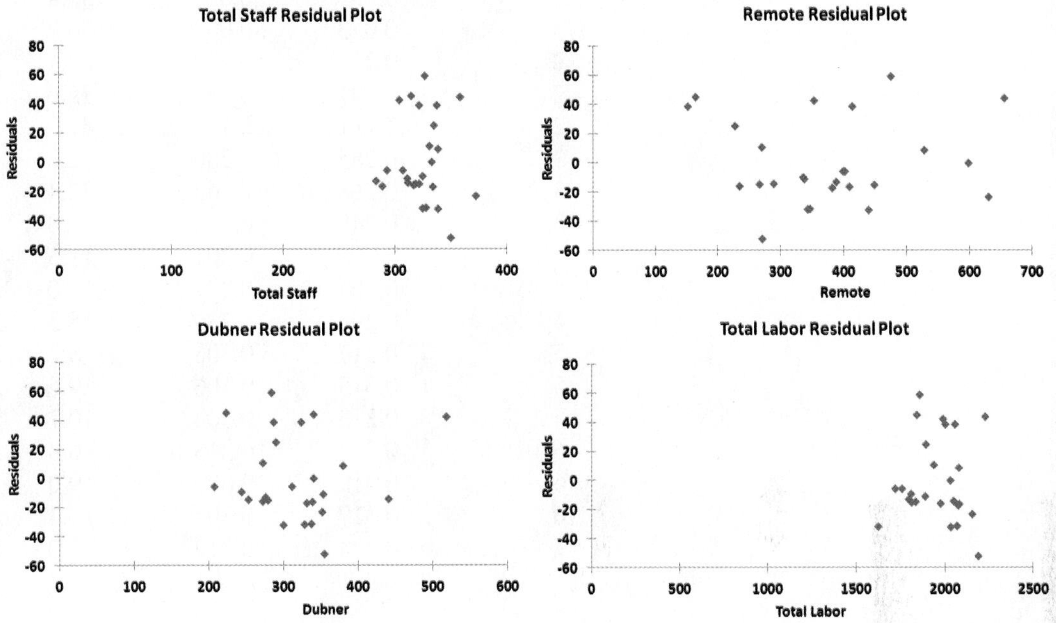

None of the residual plots versus the total staff, the remote hours, the Dubner hours, and the total labor hours reveal apparent patterns. In addition, a histogram of the residuals (not shown here) indicates only moderate departure from normality, and a plot of the residuals versus the predicted values of Y (also not shown here) does not show evidence of unequal variance. Thus, from Figure 15.10 on page 588, the regression equation is

$$\hat{Y}_i = -330.8318 + 1.2456X_{1i} - 0.1184X_{2i} - 0.2971X_{3i} + 0.1305X_{4i}$$

Example 15.4 presents a situation in which there are several alternative models in which the C_p statistic is close to or less than $k + 1$.

EXAMPLE 15.4
Choosing Among Alternative Regression Models

Table 15.3 on page 592 shows results from a best-subsets regression analysis of a regression model with seven independent variables. Determine which regression model you would choose as the *best* model.

SOLUTION From Table 15.3, you need to determine which models have C_p values that are less than or close to $k + 1$. Two models meet this criterion. The model with six independent variables $(X_1, X_2, X_3, X_4, X_5, X_6)$ has a C_p value of 6.8, which is less than $k + 1 = 6 + 1 = 7$, and the full model with seven independent variables $(X_1, X_2, X_3, X_4, X_5, X_6, X_7)$ has a C_p value of 8.0. One way you can choose among the two models is to select the model with the largest adjusted r^2—that is, the model with six independent variables. Another way to select a final model is to determine whether the models contain a subset of variables that are common. Then you test whether the contribution of the additional variables is significant. In this case, because the models differ only by the inclusion of variable X_7 in the full model, you test whether variable X_7 makes a significant contribution to the regression model, given that the variables X_1, X_2, X_3, X_4, X_5, and X_6 are already included in the model. If the contribution is statistically significant, then you should include variable X_7 in the regression model. If variable X_7 does not make a statistically significant contribution, you should not include it in the model.

TABLE 15.3

Partial Results from Best-Subsets Regression

Number of Variables	r^2	Adjusted r^2	C_p	Variables Included
1	0.121	0.119	113.9	X_4
1	0.093	0.090	130.4	X_1
1	0.083	0.080	136.2	X_3
2	0.214	0.210	62.1	X_3, X_4
2	0.191	0.186	75.6	X_1, X_3
2	0.181	0.177	81.0	X_1, X_4
3	0.285	0.280	22.6	X_1, X_3, X_4
3	0.268	0.263	32.4	X_3, X_4, X_5
3	0.240	0.234	49.0	X_2, X_3, X_4
4	0.308	0.301	11.3	X_1, X_2, X_3, X_4
4	0.304	0.297	14.0	X_1, X_3, X_4, X_6
4	0.296	0.289	18.3	X_1, X_3, X_4, X_5
5	0.317	0.308	8.2	X_1, X_2, X_3, X_4, X_5
5	0.315	0.306	9.6	X_1, X_2, X_3, X_4, X_6
5	0.313	0.304	10.7	X_1, X_3, X_4, X_5, X_6
6	0.323	0.313	6.8	$X_1, X_2, X_3, X_4, X_5, X_6$
6	0.319	0.309	9.0	$X_1, X_2, X_3, X_4, X_5, X_7$
6	0.317	0.306	10.4	$X_1, X_2, X_3, X_4, X_6, X_7$
7	0.324	0.312	8.0	$X_1, X_2, X_3, X_4, X_5, X_6, X_7$

Exhibit 15.1 summarizes the steps involved in model building.

EXHIBIT 15.1

Steps Involved in Model Building

1. Compile a list of all independent variables under consideration.
2. Fit a regression model that includes all the independent variables under consideration and determine the *VIF* for each independent variable. Three possible results can occur:
   a. None of the independent variables has a $VIF > 5$; in this case, proceed to step 3.
   b. One of the independent variables has a $VIF > 5$; in this case, eliminate that independent variable and proceed to step 3.
   c. More than one of the independent variables has a $VIF > 5$; in this case, eliminate the independent variable that has the highest *VIF* and repeat step 2.
3. Perform a best-subsets regression with the remaining independent variables and determine the C_p statistic and/or the adjusted r^2 for each model.
4. List all models that have C_p close to or less than $k + 1$ and/or a high adjusted r^2.
5. From the models listed in step 4, choose a best model.
6. Perform a complete analysis of the model chosen, including a residual analysis.
7. Depending on the results of the residual analysis, add quadratic and/or interaction terms, transform variables, and reanalyze the data.
8. Use the selected model for prediction and inference.

Figure 15.14 represents a roadmap for the steps involved in model building.

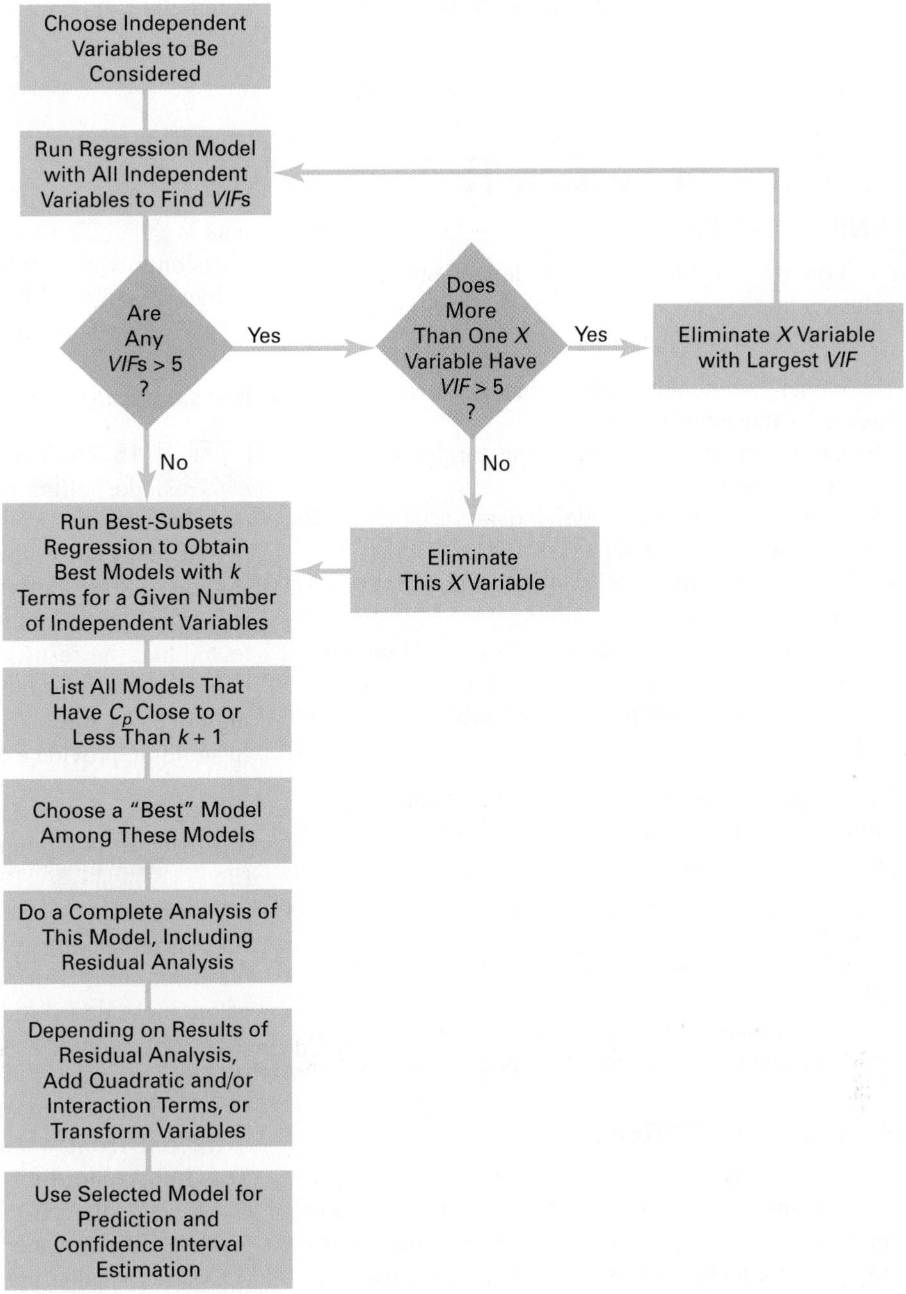

FIGURE 15.14
Roadmap for model building

Model Validation

The final step in the model-building process is to validate the selected regression model. This step involves checking the model against data that were not part of the sample analyzed. The following are several ways of validating a regression model:

- Collect new data and compare the results.
- Compare the results of the regression model to previous results.
- If the data set is large, split the data into two parts and cross-validate the results.

Perhaps the best way of validating a regression model is by collecting new data. If the results with new data are consistent with the selected regression model, you have strong reason to believe that the fitted regression model is applicable in a wide set of circumstances.

If it is not possible to collect new data, you can use one of the two other approaches. In one approach, you compare your regression coefficients and predictions to previous results.

If the data set is large, you can use **cross-validation**. First, you split the data into two parts. Then you use the first part of the data to develop the regression model. You then use the second part of the data to evaluate the predictive ability of the regression model.

Problems for Section 15.4

LEARNING THE BASICS

15.21 You are considering four independent variables for inclusion in a regression model. You select a sample of $n = 30$, with the following results:

1. The model that includes independent variables A and B has a C_p value equal to 4.6.
2. The model that includes independent variables A and C has a C_p value equal to 2.4.
3. The model that includes independent variables A, B, and C has a C_p value equal to 2.7.

a. Which models meet the criterion for further consideration? Explain.
b. How would you compare the model that contains independent variables A, B, and C to the model that contains independent variables A and B? Explain.

15.22 You are considering six independent variables for inclusion in a regression model. You select a sample of $n = 40$, with the following results:

$$k = 2 \quad T = 6 + 1 = 7 \quad R_k^2 = 0.274 \quad R_T^2 = 0.653$$

a. Compute the C_p value for this two-independent-variable model.
b. Based on your answer to (a), does this model meet the criterion for further consideration as the best model? Explain.

APPLYING THE CONCEPTS

15.23 In Problems 13.85 through 13.89 on page 517, you constructed simple linear regression models to investigate the relationship between demographic information and monthly sales for a chain of sporting goods stores using the data in Sporting. Develop the most appropriate multiple regression model to predict a store's monthly sales. Be sure to include a thorough residual analysis. In addition, provide a detailed explanation of the results, including a comparison of the most appropriate multiple regression model to the best simple linear regression model.

SELF Test **15.24** You need to develop a model to predict the selling price of houses in a small city, based on assessed value, time in months since the house was reassessed, and whether the house is new (0 = no, 1 = yes). A sample of 30 recently sold single-family houses that were reassessed at full value one year prior to the study is selected and the results are stored in House1. Develop the most appropriate multiple regression model to predict selling price. Be sure to perform a thorough residual analysis. In addition, provide a detailed explanation of the results.

15.25 *Accounting Today* identified top public accounting firms in ten geographic regions across the U.S. The file AccountingPartners6 contains data for public accounting firms in the Southeast, Gulf Coast, and Capital Regions. The variables are: revenue ($M), number of partners in the firm, number of professionals in the firm, proportion of business dedicated to management advisory services (MAS%), whether the firm is located in the Southeast Region (0 = no, 1 = yes), and whether the firm is located in the Gulf Coast Region (0 = no, 1 = yes). (Data extracted from **www.accountingtoday.com/gallery/Top-100-Accounting-Firms-Data-62569-1.html**.)

Develop the most appropriate multiple regression model to predict firm revenue. Be sure to perform a thorough residual analysis. In addition, provide a detailed explanation of the results.

15.5 Pitfalls in Multiple Regression and Ethical Issues

Pitfalls in Multiple Regression

Model building is an art as well as a science. Different individuals may not always agree on the best multiple regression model. To construct a good regression model, you should use the process described in Exhibit 15.1 on page 592. In doing so, you must avoid certain pitfalls that can interfere with the development of a useful model. Section 13.9 discussed pitfalls in simple linear regression and strategies for avoiding them. Now that you have studied a variety of multiple regression models, you need to take some additional precautions. To avoid pitfalls in multiple regression, you also need to

- Interpret the regression coefficient for a particular independent variable from a perspective in which the values of all other independent variables are held constant.
- Evaluate residual plots for each independent variable.
- Evaluate interaction and quadratic terms.
- Compute the *VIF* for each independent variable before determining which independent variables to include in the model.
- Examine several alternative models, using best-subsets regression.
- Validate the model before implementing it.

Ethical Issues

Ethical issues arise when a user who wants to make predictions manipulates the development process of the multiple regression model. The key here is intent. In addition to the situations discussed in Section 13.9, unethical behavior occurs when someone uses multiple regression analysis and *willfully fails* to remove from consideration independent variables that exhibit a high collinearity with other independent variables or *willfully fails* to use methods other than least-squares regression when the assumptions necessary for least-squares regression are seriously violated.

15.6 Predictive Analytics and Data Mining

Section LGS.3 (see page 6) introduced you to business analytics, the set of newer, interdisciplinary techniques that combine "traditional" statistical methods with methods from management science and information systems to better support fact-based management decision making. Section 2.8 (see page 82) discussed how Microsoft Excel can be used for *descriptive analytics*, the techniques that can summarize large amounts of past or current data. **Dashboards**, so called because of their similarity to an automotive dashboard, are examples of this type of business analytics. For example, The New York Jets football organization uses its "Command Center" application to help manage all activities in its stadium as they occur on game day. Using the Command Center, team managers can instantaneously track attendance and concession and merchandise sales and compare those statistics with historical averages or last-game values as well as determine such things as the elapsed time between when a fan first enters a parking lot and then first enters the stadium (see reference 7).

Other business analytics techniques extend the methods of predictive modeling discussed in this chapter and Chapters 13 and 14. Not surprisingly, these techniques are considered examples of **predictive analytics**. One such technique that has gained widespread use is *data mining*.

Data Mining

Data mining combines database technologies and statistical methods to enable the exploration and analysis of very large data sets that contain many, many variables, each with many, many values. While the regression methods discussed in this book are predictive, too, data mining differs from them in the following ways:

- Data mining examines a much greater number of variables at one time than regression techniques examine.
- Data mining is a semi-automated process that searches for possible independent variables from a much wider set of possible independent variables. Regression methods use a fixed list of previously-identified independent variables.
- Data mining makes extensive use of historical data sets.
- Data mining can increase the chance of encountering a pitfall in regression (see Sections 13.9 and 15.5) when used in an unknowing manner.

As with regression modeling, in order to validate any data mining analysis, where possible, you should split the data into a training sample that is used to develop models for analysis and a validation sample that is used to determine the validity of the models developed in the training sample.

Data Mining Examples

One recent application of data mining for predictive modeling was the consumer research that uncovered a correlation between the number of Web searches for a new feature film, new video game, or new song and the opening weekend revenue for a new film, the first-month sales for a new video game, and the rank of the new song on the Billboard Hot 100 chart (see reference 1). This research would not have been possible without the database technology that maintains the (Yahoo!) U.S. web search query logs that were used as the source of data for the analysis.

Predictive modeling applications of data mining are also used to assist in a wide variety of business decision-making processes. Some of these applications, by business field, are

- **Banking and financial services.** To predict which applicants will qualify for a specific type of mortgage and which applicants may default on their mortgage (mortgage acceptance and default), to predict which customers will not change their financial services company (retention)
- **Retailing and marketing.** To predict which customers will best respond to promotions (promotion planning), to predict which customers will remain loyal to a product or service (brand loyalty), to predict which customers are ready to purchase a product at a certain time (purchasing sequence), to predict which product a consumer will purchase given the previous purchase of another product (purchase association)
- **Quality and warranty management.** To predict the type of product that will fail during a warranty period (product failure analysis), to detect the type of individual who might be involved in fraudulent activities concerning the warranty of the product (warranty fraud)
- **Insurance.** To predict the characteristics of a claim and an individual that indicate a fraudulent claim (fraud detection), to predict the characteristics of an individual who will file a specific type of claim (claim submission)

Statistical Methods in Business Analytics

Besides the regression methods of Chapters 13 and 14 and this chapter, business analytics uses the following methods that are discussed in this book:

- Bar charts
- Pareto charts
- Multidimensional contingency tables
- Descriptive statistics such as the mean, median, and standard deviation
- Boxplots

Data mining also uses statistical methods that are beyond the scope of this book to fully discuss. Those methods include classification and regression trees (CART), chi-square automatic interaction detector (CHAID), neural nets, cluster analysis, and multidimensional scaling.

Classification and regression trees (CART) is an example of a decision tree (see Section 4.2) algorithm that splits the data set into groups based on the values of independent or explanatory (*X*) variables. The CART algorithm goes through a search process to optimize the split for each independent or explanatory (*X*) variable chosen. Often, the tree has many stages or nodes and a decision needs to be made as to how to prune (cut back) the tree.

Chi-square automatic interaction detector (CHAID) also uses a decision tree (see Section 4.2) algorithm that splits the data set into groups based on the values of independent or explanatory (X) variables. Unlike CART, CHAID allows a variable to be split into more than two categories at each node of the tree.

Neural nets have the advantage of using complex nonlinear regression functions to predict a response variable. Unfortunately, this method's use of a complex nonlinear function can make the results of a neural net difficult to interpret.

Cluster analysis is a dimension-free procedure that attempts to subdivide or partition a set of objects into relatively homogeneous groups. These homogenous groups are developed so that objects within a group are more like other objects in the group than they are to objects outside the group.

For more detailed discussion of the statistical methods that business analytics use, see references 2, 6, and 9.

Multidimensional scaling uses a measure of distance to develop a mapping of objects usually within a two-dimensional space so that the characteristics separating the objects can be interpreted. Typically, multidimensional scaling attempts to maximize the goodness of fit of the actual distance between objects with the fitted distances.

Data Mining Using Excel Add-ins

You can extend Microsoft Excel to help perform predictive analytic methods by using one of several add-in workbooks (see Appendix Section G.2). Microsoft offers as a separate, free download for certain Excel versions, the Data Mining Add-ins, that allow access to and analysis of data stored using Microsoft SQL Server technologies. Other add-ins, available from third parties, can bring small-scale predictive analytics into Excel and do not require the use of database technologies. One such add-in is the JMP add-in for Excel from the SAS Institute, Inc., which links Excel to the JMP data analytics program.

To illustrate using JMP for classification and regression tree (CART) analysis, return to the Section 14.7 example in which a logistic regression model was used to predict the proportion of credit cardholders who would upgrade to a premium card. Using JMP, it is possible to create the CART results shown in Figure 15.15.

FIGURE 15.15
Classification and regression tree (CART) results for predicting the proportion of credit card holders who would upgrade to a premium card

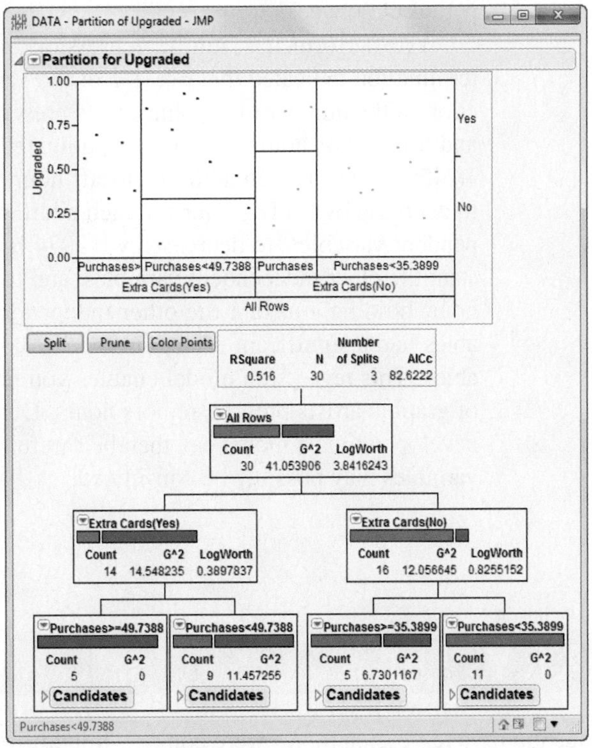

Observe from Figure 15.15 that the first split of the data is based on whether the cardholder has additional cards. Then, in the next row, the two categories "Extra Cards(Yes)" and "Extra Cards(No)" are split again, using the annual purchase amount as the basis of this second split. In the "Extra Cards(Yes)" category, the split is between those who charge more than $49,738.80

per year and those who charge less than $49,738.80 per year. In the "Extra Cards (No)" category, the split is between those who charge more than $35,389.90 per year and those who charge less than $35,389.90 per year.

These results show that customers who have extra cards and have charged over $49,738.80 per year are much more likely to upgrade to a premium card. (Least likely to upgrade to a premium card are customers who have only a single charge card and have charged less than $35,389.90.) Therefore, the credit card company might want to focus future premium-card upgrade marketing efforts on customers who have already have additional cards and charge more than $49,738.80 per year. The r^2 of 0.516 shown in the summary box below the plot means that 51.6% of the variation in whether a cardholder upgrades can be explained by the variation in whether the cardholder has additional cards and the amount the cardholder charges per year.

USING STATISTICS Valuing Parsimony at WHIT-DT, Revisited

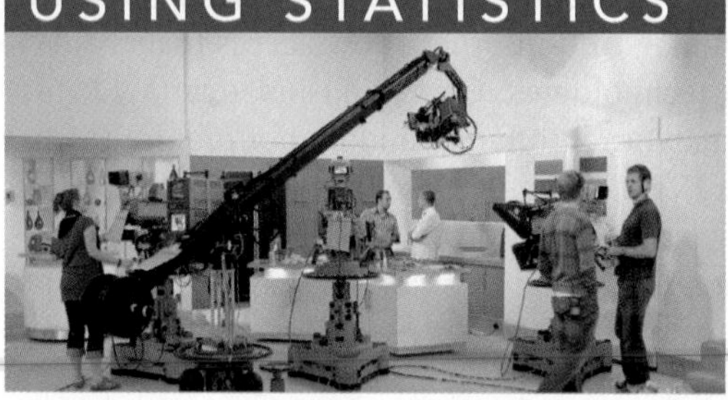

Glyn Allan / Alamy

In the Using Statistics scenario, you were the WHIT-DT broadcast operations manager, who had been asked to reduce labor expenses. You needed to determine which variables have an effect on standby hours, the time during which graphic artists employed by the station are idle but getting paid. You collected data concerning standby hours and the total number of staff present, remote hours, Dubner hours, and total labor hours over a period of 26 weeks.

You performed a multiple regression analysis on the data. The coefficient of multiple determination indicated that 62.31% of the variation in standby hours can be explained by variation in the number of graphic artists present and the number of remote hours, Dubner hours, and total labor hours. The model indicated that standby hours are estimated to increase by 1.2456 hours for each additional staff hour, holding constant the other independent variables; to decrease by 0.1184 hour for each additional remote hour, holding constant the other independent variables; to decrease by 0.2974 hour for each additional Dubner hour, holding constant the other independent variables; and to increase by 0.1305 hour for each additional labor hour, holding constant the other independent variables. Each of the four independent variables had a significant effect on standby hours, holding constant the other independent variables. This regression model enables you to predict standby hours based on the total number of graphic artists present, remote hours, Dubner hours, and total labor hours. Any predictions developed by the model can then be carefully monitored, new data can be collected, and other variables may possibly be considered.

SUMMARY

In this chapter, various multiple regression topics were considered (see Figure 15.16), including quadratic regression models, transformations, collinearity, and model building. In addition, the predictive analytics method of data mining was introduced and compared to predictive regression methods.

FIGURE 15.16

Roadmap for multiple regression

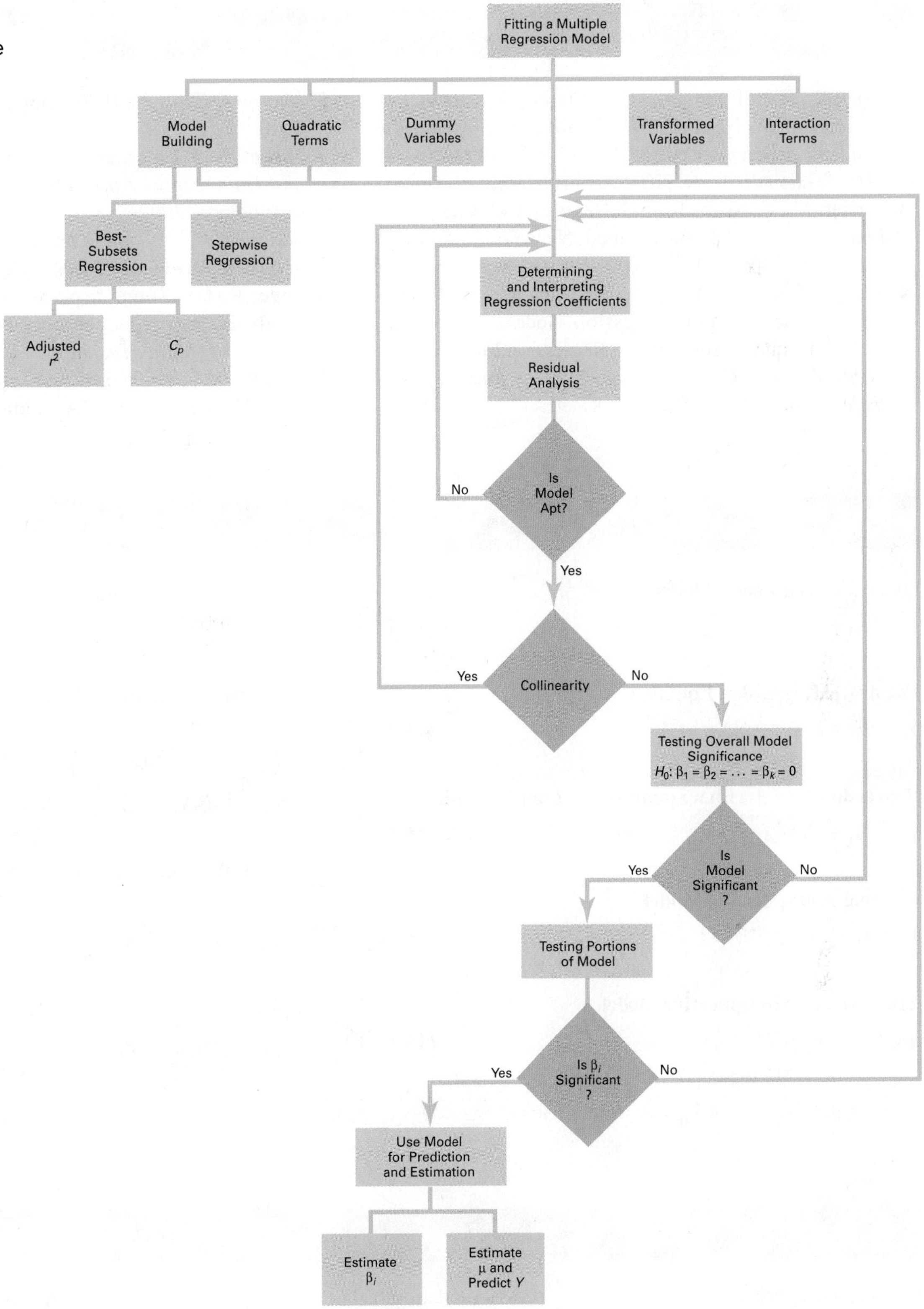

REFERENCES

1. Goel, S., J. Hofman, et al. "Predicting Consumer Behavior with Web Search." *Proceedings of the National Academy of Sciences* 107 (2010): 17486–17490.
2. *JMP Version 10*. Cary, NC: SAS Institute, Inc., 2012.
3. Kutner, M., C. Nachtsheim, J. Neter, and W. Li. *Applied Linear Statistical Models*, 5th ed. New York: McGraw-Hill/Irwin, 2005.
4. Marquardt, D. W. "You Should Standardize the Predictor Variables in Your Regression Models," discussion of "A Critique of Some Ridge Regression Methods," by G. Smith and F. Campbell, *Journal of the American Statistical Association*, 75 (1980): 87–91.
5. *Microsoft Excel 2010*. Redmond, WA: Microsoft Corp., 2010.
6. Nisbet, R, J. Elder, and G. Miner. *Statistical Analysis and Data Mining Applications*. Burlington, MA: Academic Press, 2009.
7. Serignese, K. "Business Intelligence Hits the Gridiron." *Software Development Times*, October 1, 2010, p. 3.
8. Snee, R. D. "Some Aspects of Nonorthogonal Data Analysis, Part I. Developing Prediction Equations." *Journal of Quality Technology* 5 (1973): 67–79.
9. Tan, P.-N., M. Steinbach, and V. Kumar. *Introduction to Data Mining*. Boston, MA: Addison-Wesley, 2006.

KEY EQUATIONS

Quadratic Regression Model

$$Y_i = \beta_0 + \beta_1 X_{1i} + \beta_2 X_{1i}^2 + \varepsilon_i \qquad \textbf{(15.1)}$$

Quadratic Regression Equation

$$\hat{Y}_i = b_0 + b_1 X_{1i} + b_2 X_{1i}^2 \qquad \textbf{(15.2)}$$

Regression Model with a Square-Root Transformation

$$Y_i = \beta_0 + \beta_1 \sqrt{X_{1i}} + \varepsilon_i \qquad \textbf{(15.3)}$$

Original Multiplicative Model

$$Y_i = \beta_0 X_{1i}^{\beta_1} X_{2i}^{\beta_2} \varepsilon_i \qquad \textbf{(15.4)}$$

Transformed Multiplicative Model

$$\begin{aligned} \log Y_i &= \log(\beta_0 X_{1i}^{\beta_1} X_{2i}^{\beta_2} \varepsilon_i) \qquad \textbf{(15.5)} \\ &= \log \beta_0 + \log(X_{1i}^{\beta_1}) + \log(X_{2i}^{\beta_2}) + \log \varepsilon_i \\ &= \log \beta_0 + \beta_1 \log X_{1i} + \beta_2 \log X_{2i} + \log \varepsilon_i \end{aligned}$$

Original Exponential Model

$$Y_i = e^{\beta_0 + \beta_1 X_{1i} + \beta_2 X_{2i}} \varepsilon_i \qquad \textbf{(15.6)}$$

Transformed Exponential Model

$$\begin{aligned} \ln Y_i &= \ln(e^{\beta_0 + \beta_1 X_{1i} + \beta_2 X_{2i}} \varepsilon_i) \qquad \textbf{(15.7)} \\ &= \ln(e^{\beta_0 + \beta_1 X_{1i} + \beta_2 X_{2i}}) + \ln \varepsilon_i \\ &= \beta_0 + \beta_1 X_{1i} + \beta_2 X_{2i} + \ln \varepsilon_i \end{aligned}$$

Variance Inflationary Factor

$$VIF_j = \frac{1}{1 - R_j^2} \qquad \textbf{(15.8)}$$

C_p Statistic

$$C_p = \frac{(1 - R_k^2)(n - T)}{1 - R_T^2} - [n - 2(k + 1)] \qquad \textbf{(15.9)}$$

KEY TERMS

best-subsets approach 589
C_p statistic 590
chi-square automatic interaction detector (CHAID) 596
classification and regression trees (CART) 596
cluster analysis 597
collinearity 585
cross-validation 594
dashboards 595
data mining 595
logarithmic transformation 583
multidimensional scaling 597
neural nets 597
parsimony 587
predictive analytics 595
quadratic regression model 574
quadratic term 574
square-root transformation 582
stepwise regression 588
variance inflationary factor (*VIF*) 585

CHECKING YOUR UNDERSTANDING

15.26 How can you evaluate whether collinearity exists in a multiple regression model?

15.27 What is the difference between stepwise regression and best-subsets regression?

15.28 How do you choose among models according to the C_p statistic in best-subsets regression?

CHAPTER REVIEW PROBLEMS

15.29 A specialist in baseball analytics has expanded his analysis, presented in Problem 14.73 on page 565, of which variables are important in predicting a team's wins in a given baseball season. He has collected data in BB2011 related to wins, ERA, saves, runs scored, hits allowed, walks allowed, and errors for the 2011 season.

a. Develop the most appropriate multiple regression model to predict a team's wins. Be sure to include a thorough residual analysis. In addition, provide a detailed explanation of the results.

b. Develop the most appropriate multiple regression model to predict a team's ERA on the basis of hits allowed, walks allowed, errors, and saves. Be sure to include a thorough residual analysis. In addition, provide a detailed explanation of the results.

15.30 In the production of printed circuit boards, errors in the alignment of electrical connections are a source of scrap. The file RegistrationError contains the registration error, the temperature, the pressure, and the cost of the material (low versus high) used in the production of circuit boards. (Data extracted from C. Nachtsheim and B. Jones, "A Powerful Analytical Tool," *Six Sigma Forum Magazine*, August 2003, pp. 30–33.) Develop the most appropriate multiple regression model to predict registration error.

15.31 Hemlock Farms is a community located in the Pocono Mountains area of eastern Pennsylvania. The file HemlockFarms contains information on homes that were recently for sale. The variables included were

List Price—Asking price of the house
Hot Tub—Whether the house has a hot tub, with 0 = No and 1 = Yes
Lake View—Whether the house has a lake view, with 0 = No and 1 = Yes
Bathrooms—Number of bathrooms
Bedrooms—Number of bedrooms
Loft/Den—Whether the house has a loft or den, with 0 = No and 1 = Yes
Finished basement—Whether the house has a finished basement, with 0 = No and 1 = Yes
Acres—Number of acres for the property

Develop the most appropriate multiple regression model to predict the asking price. Be sure to perform a thorough residual analysis. In addition, provide a detailed explanation of your results.

15.32 Nassau County is located approximately 25 miles east of New York City. The file GlenCove contains a sample of 30 single-family homes located in Glen Cove. Variables included are the appraised value, land area of the property (acres), interior size of the house (square feet), age (years), number of rooms, number of bathrooms, and number of cars that can be parked in the garage.

a. Develop the most appropriate multiple regression model to predict appraised value.

b. Compare the results in (a) with those of Problems 15.33(a) and 15.34 (a).

15.33 Data similar to those in Problem 15.32 are available for homes located in Roslyn (approximately 8 miles from Glen Cove) and are stored in Roslyn.

a. Perform an analysis similar to that of Problem 15.32.

b. Compare the results in (a) with those of Problems 15.32 (a) and 15.34 (a).

15.34 Data similar to Problem 15.32 are available for homes located in Freeport (located approximately 20 miles from Roslyn) and are stored in Freeport.

a. Perform an analysis similar to that of Problem 15.32.

b. Compare the results in (a) with those of Problems 15.32 (a) and 15.33 (a).

15.35 You are a real estate broker who wants to compare property values in Glen Cove and Roslyn (which are located approximately 8 miles apart). Use the data in GCRoslyn. Make sure to include the dummy variable for location (Glen Cove or Roslyn) in the regression model.

a. Develop the most appropriate multiple regression model to predict appraised value.

b. What conclusions can you reach concerning the differences in appraised value between Glen Cove and Roslyn?

15.36 You are a real estate broker who wants to compare property values in Glen Cove, Freeport, and Roslyn. Use the data in GCFreeRoslyn.

a. Develop the most appropriate multiple regression model to predict appraised value.

b. What conclusions can you reach concerning the differences in appraised value between Glen Cove, Freeport, and Roslyn?

15.37 Financial analysts engage in business valuation to determine a company's value. A standard approach uses the multiple of earnings method: You multiply a company's profits by a certain value (average or median) to arrive at a final value. More recently, regression analysis has been demonstrated to consistently deliver more accurate predictions. A valuator has been given the assignment of valuing a drug company. She obtained financial data on 71 drug companies (Industry Group Standard Industrial Classification [SIC] 3 code 283), which included pharmaceutical preparation firms (SIC 4 code 2834), in vitro and in vivo diagnostic substances firms (SIC 4 code 2835), and biological products firms (SIC 4 2836). The file **BusinessValuation2** contains the following variables:

COMPANY—Drug company name
TS—Ticker symbol
SIC 3—Standard Industrial Classification 3 code (industry group identifier)
SIC 4—Standard Industrial Classification 4 code (industry identifier)
PB fye—Price-to-book value ratio (fiscal year ending)
PE fye—Price-to-earnings ratio (fiscal year ending)
NL Assets—Natural log of assets (as a measure of size)
ROE—Return on equity
SGROWTH—Growth (GS5)
DEBT/EBITDA—Ratio of debt to earnings before interest, taxes, depreciation, and amortization
D2834—Dummy variable indicator of SIC 4 code 2834 (1 if 2834, 0 if not)
D2835—Dummy variable indicator of SIC 4 code 2835 (1 if 2835, 0 if not)

Develop the most appropriate multiple regression model to predict the price-to-book value ratio. Be sure to perform a thorough residual analysis. In addition, provide a detailed explanation of your results.

15.38 A recent article (J. Conklin, "It's a Marathon, Not a Sprint," *Quality Progress*, June 2009, pp. 46–49) discussed a metal deposition process in which a piece of metal is placed in an acid bath and an alloy is layered on top of it. The key quality characteristic is the thickness of the alloy layer. The file **Thickness** contains the following variables:

Thickness—Thickness of the alloy layer
Catalyst—Catalyst concentration in the acid bath
pH—pH level of the acid bath
Pressure—Pressure in the tank holding the acid bath
Temp—Temperature in the tank holding the acid bath
Voltage—Voltage applied to the tank holding the acid bath

Develop the most appropriate multiple regression model to predict the thickness of the alloy layer. Be sure to perform a thorough residual analysis. The article suggests that there is a significant interaction between the pressure and the temperature in the tank. Do you agree?

15.39 A molding machine that contains different cavities is used in producing plastic parts. The product characteristics of interest are the product length (in.) and weight (g). The mold cavities were filled with raw material powder and then vibrated during the experiment. The factors that were varied were the vibration time (seconds), the vibration pressure (psi), the vibration amplitude (%), the raw material density (g/mL), and the quantity of raw material (scoops). The experiment was conducted in two different cavities on the molding machine. The data are stored in **Molding**. (Data extracted from M. Lopez and M. McShane-Vaughn, "Maximizing Product, Minimizing Costs," *Six Sigma Forum Magazine*, February 2008, pp. 18–23.)

a. Develop the most appropriate multiple regression model to predict the product length in cavity 1. Be sure to perform a thorough residual analysis. In addition, provide a detailed explanation of your results.
b. Repeat (a) for cavity 2.
c. Compare the results for length in the two cavities.
d. Develop the most appropriate multiple regression model to predict the product weight in cavity 1. Be sure to perform a thorough residual analysis. In addition, provide a detailed explanation of your results.
e. Repeat (d) for cavity 2.
f. Compare the results for weight in the two cavities.

REPORT WRITING EXERCISE

15.40 In Problem 15.23 on page 594, you developed a multiple regression model to predict monthly sales at sporting goods stores for the data stored in **Sporting**. Now write a report based on the model you developed. Append all appropriate charts and statistical information to your report.

CASES FOR CHAPTER 15

The Mountain States Potato Company

Mountain States Potato Company sells a by-product of its potato-processing operation, called a filter cake, to area feedlots as cattle feed. The business problem faced by the feedlot owners is that the cattle are not gaining weight as quickly as they once were. The feedlot owners believe that the root cause of the problem is that the percentage of solids in the filter cake is too low.

Historically, the percentage of solids in the filter cakes ran slightly above 12%. Lately, however, the solids are running in the 11% range. What is actually affecting the solids is a mystery, but something has to be done quickly. Individuals involved in the process were asked to identify variables that might affect the percentage of solids. This review turned up the six variables (in addition to the percentage of solids) listed below. Data collected by monitoring the process several times daily for 20 days are stored in **Potato**.

Variable	Comments
SOLIDS	Percentage of solids in the filter cake.
PH	Acidity. This measure of acidity indicates bacterial action in the clarifier and is controlled by the amount of downtime in the system. As bacterial action progresses, organic acids are produced that can be measured using pH.
LOWER	Pressure of the vacuum line below the fluid line on the rotating drum.
UPPER	Pressure of the vacuum line above the fluid line on the rotating drum.
THICK	Filter cake thickness, measured on the drum.
VARIDRIV	Setting used to control the drum speed. May differ from DRUMSPD due to mechanical inefficiencies.
DRUMSPD	Speed at which the drum is rotating when collecting the filter cake. Measured with a stopwatch.

1. Thoroughly analyze the data and develop a regression model to predict the percentage of solids.
2. Write an executive summary concerning your findings to the president of the Mountain States Potato Company. Include specific recommendations on how to get the percentage of solids back above 12%.

Sure Value Convenience Stores

You work in the corporate office for a nationwide convenience store franchise that operates nearly 10,000 stores. The per-store daily customer count (i.e., the mean number of customers in a store in one day) has been steady, at 900, for some time. To increase the customer count, the chain is considering cutting prices for coffee beverages. The question to be determined is how much prices should be cut to increase the daily customer count without reducing the gross margin on coffee sales too much. You decide to carry out an experiment in a sample of 24 stores where customer counts have been running almost exactly at the national average of 900. In 6 of the stores, the price of a small coffee will now be \$0.59, in 6 stores the price of a small coffee will now be \$0.69, in 6 stores, the price of a small coffee will now be \$0.79, and in 6 stores, the price of a small coffee will now be \$0.89. After four weeks at the new prices, the daily customer count in the stores is determined and is stored in **CoffeeSales2**.

a. Construct a scatter plot for price and sales.

b. Fit a quadratic regression model and state the quadratic regression equation.

c. Predict the weekly sales for a small coffee priced at 79 cents.

d. Perform a residual analysis on the results and determine whether the regression model is valid.

e. At the 0.05 level of significance, is there a significant quadratic relationship between weekly sales and price?

f. At the 0.05 level of significance, determine whether the quadratic model is a better fit than the linear model.

g. Interpret the meaning of the coefficient of multiple determination.

h. Compute the adjusted r^2.

i. What price do you recommend the small coffee should be sold for?

Digital Case

Apply your knowledge of multiple regression model building in this Digital Case, which extends the Chapter 14 OmniPower Bars Using Statistics scenario.

Still concerned about ensuring a successful test marketing of its OmniPower bars, the marketing department of OmniFoods has contacted Connect2Coupons (C2C), another merchandising consultancy. C2C suggests that earlier analysis done by In-Store Placements Group (ISPG) was faulty because it did not use the correct type of data. C2C claims that its Internet-based viral marketing will have an even greater effect on OmniPower energy bar sales, as new data from the same 34-store sample will show. In response, ISPG says its earlier claims are valid and has reported to the OmniFoods marketing department that it can discern no simple relationship between C2C's viral marketing and increased OmniPower sales.

Open **OmniPowerForum15.pdf** to review all the claims made in a private online forum and chat hosted on the OmniFoods corporate website. Then answer the following:

1. Which of the claims are true? False? True but misleading? Support your answer by performing an appropriate statistical analysis.

2. If the grocery store chain allowed OmniFoods to use an unlimited number of sales techniques, which techniques should it use? Explain.

3. If the grocery store chain allowed OmniFoods to use only one sales technique, which technique should it use? Explain.

The Craybill Instrumentation Company Case

The Craybill Instrumentation Company produces highly technical industrial instrumentation devices. The human resources (HR) director has the business objective of improving recruiting decisions concerning sales managers. The company has 45 sales regions, each headed by a sales manager. Many of the sales managers have degrees in electrical engineering and, due to the technical nature of the product line, several company officials believe that only applicants with degrees in electrical engineering should be considered.

At the time of their application, candidates are asked to take the Strong-Campbell Interest Inventory Test and the Wonderlic Personnel Test. Due to the time and money involved with the testing, some discussion has taken place about dropping one or both of the tests. To start, the HR director gathered information on each of the 45 current sales managers, including years of selling experience, electrical engineering background, and the scores from both the Wonderlic and Strong-Campbell tests. The HR director has decided to use regression modeling to predict a dependent variable of "sales index" score, which is the ratio of the regions' actual sales divided by the target sales. The target values are constructed each year by upper management, in consultation with the sales managers, and are based on past performance and market potential within each region. The file **Managers** contains information on the 45 current sales managers. The following variables are included:

Sales—Ratio of yearly sales divided by the target sales value for that region; the target values were mutually agreed-upon "realistic expectations"

Wonder—Score from the Wonderlic Personnel Test; the higher the score, the higher the applicant's perceived ability to manage

SC—Score on the Strong-Campbell Interest Inventory Test; the higher the score, the higher the applicant's perceived interest in sales

Experience—Number of years of selling experience prior to becoming a sales manager

Engineer—Dummy variable that equals 1 if the sales manager has a degree in electrical engineering and 0 otherwise

a. Develop the most appropriate regression model to predict sales.

b. Do you think that the company should continue administering both the Wonderlic and Strong-Campbell tests? Explain.

c. Do the data support the argument that electrical engineers outperform the other sales managers? Would you support the idea to hire only electrical engineers? Explain.

d. How important is prior selling experience in this case? Explain.

e. Discuss in detail how the HR director should incorporate the regression model you developed into the recruiting process.

More Descriptive Choices Follow-up

Follow-up the Using Statistics scenario "More Descriptive Choices, Revisited" on page 149, by developing regression models to predict the 1-year return, the 3-year return, the 5-year return, and the 10-year return based on the assets, turnover ratio, expense ratio, beta, standard deviation, type of fund (growth versus value), and risk (stored in **Retirement Funds**. (For the purpose of this analysis, combine low and average risk into one category.) Be sure to perform a thorough residual analysis. Provide a summary report that explains your results in detail.

CHAPTER 15 EXCEL GUIDE

EG15.1 The QUADRATIC REGRESSION MODEL

Key Technique Use the exponential operator (^) in a column of formulas to create a quadratic term.

Example Create the quadratic term for the Section 15.1 fly ash percentage analysis and construct the scatter plot that shows the quadratic relationship between fly ash percentage and strength shown in Figure 15.3 on page 576.

PHStat/In-Depth Excel For the example, open to the **DATA worksheet** of the **FlyAsh workbook**. That worksheet contains the independent variable **FlyAsh%** in column A and the dependent variable **Strength** in column B. Select column B (**Strength**), right-click, and click **Insert** from the shortcut menu to add a new column B. (Strength becomes column C.) Enter the label **FlyAsh%^2** in cell B1 and then enter the formula **=A2^2** in cell **B2**. Copy this formula down the column through all the data rows.

Perform a regression analysis using this new variable using the appropriate Section EG14.1 instructions on page 568. Then use the Section EG2.5 instructions to construct a scatter plot. Select that chart. Then select **Layout → Trendline → More Trendline Options** and in the Format Trendline dialog box (shown below), click **Trendline Options** in the left pane and in the Trendline Options right pane, click **Polynomial**, check **Display Equation on chart**, and click **OK**. In Excel 2013, select **Design → Add Chart Element → Trendline → More Trendline Options** and click **Polynomial** and check **Display Equation on chart** in the Format Trendline pane.

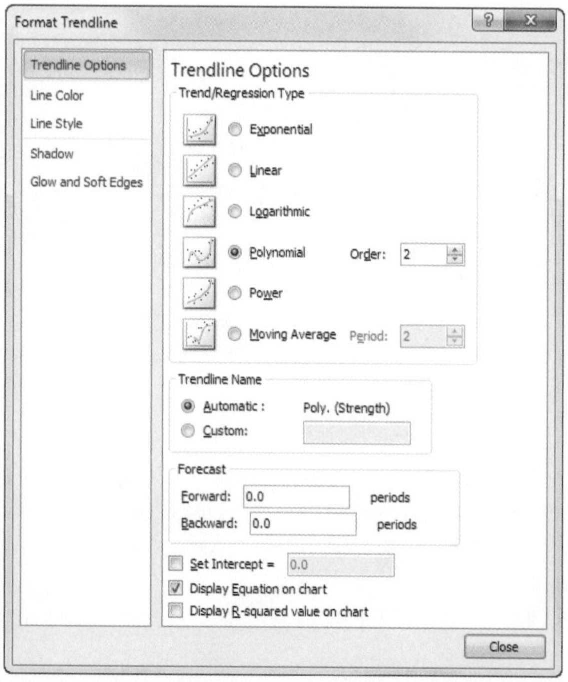

While the quadratic term **FlyAsh%^2** could be created in any column, placing independent variables in contiguous columns is a best practice and mandatory if you use the Analysis ToolPak Regression procedure.

EG15.2 USING TRANSFORMATIONS in REGRESSION MODELS

The Square-Root Transformation

To the worksheet that contains your regression data, add a new column of formulas that computes the square root of one of the independent variables to create a square-root transformation. For example, to create a square root transformation in a blank column D for an independent variable in a column C, enter the formula **=SQRT(C2)** in cell D2 of that worksheet and copy the formula down through all data rows. If the rightmost column in the worksheet contains the dependent variable, first select that column, right-click, and click **Insert** from the shortcut menu and place the transformation in that new column.

The Log Transformation

To the worksheet that contains your regression data, add a new column of formulas that computes the common (base 10) logarithm or natural logarithm (base *e*) of one of the independent variables to create a log transformation. For example, to create a common logarithm transformation in a blank column D for a variable in a column C, enter the formula **=LOG(C2)** in cell D2 of that worksheet and copy the formula down through all data rows. To create a natural logarithm transformation in a blank column D for a variable in a column C, enter the formula **=LN(C2)** in cell D2 of that worksheet and copy the formula down through all data rows.

If the dependent variable appears in a column to the immediate right of the independent variable being transformed, first select the dependent variable column, right-click, and click **Insert** from the shortcut menu and then place the transformation of the independent variable in that new column.

EG15.3 COLLINEARITY

PHStat To compute the variance inflationary factor (*VIF*), use the "Interpreting the Regression Coefficients" *PHStat* instructions in Section EG14.1 on page 568, but modify step 6 by checking **Variance Inflationary Factor** (*VIF*) before you click **OK**. The *VIF* will appear in cell B9 of the regression results worksheet, immediately following the Regression Statistics area.

In-Depth Excel To compute the variance inflationary factor, first use the "Interpreting the Regression Coefficients" *In-Depth Excel* instructions in Section EG14.1 on page 568 to create regression results worksheets for every combination of independent variables in which one serves as the dependent variable. Then, in each of the regression results worksheets, enter the label *VIF* in cell **A9** and enter the formula **=1/(1 − B5)** in cell **B9** to compute the *VIF*.

EG15.4 MODEL BUILDING

The Stepwise Regression Approach to Model Building

Key Technique Use PHStat to perform a stepwise analysis.

Example Perform the stepwise analysis for the standby-hours data that is shown in Figure 15.11 on page 589.

PHStat Use **Stepwise Regression.**
For the example, open to the **DATA worksheet** of the **Standby workbook**. Select **PHStat → Regression → Stepwise Regression**. In the procedure's dialog box (shown below):

1. Enter **A1:A27** as the **Y Variable Cell Range**.
2. Enter **B1:E27** as the **X Variables Cell Range**.
3. Check **First cells in both ranges contain label**.

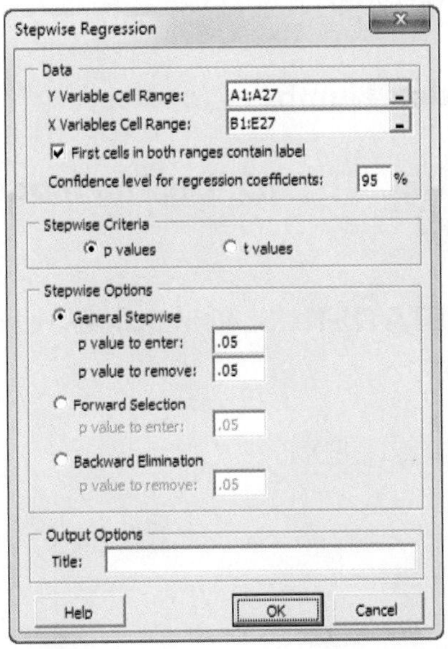

4. Enter **95** as the **Confidence level for regression coefficients**.
5. Click **p values** as the **Stepwise Criteria**.
6. Click **General Stepwise** and keep the pair of **.05** values as the **p value to enter** and the **p value to remove**.
7. Enter a **Title** and click **OK**.

This procedure may take more than a few seconds to construct its results. The procedure finishes when the statement "Stepwise ends" is added to the stepwise regression results worksheet (shown in row 29 in Figure 15.11 on page 589).

The Best-Subsets Approach to Model Building

Key Technique Use PHStat to perform a stepwise analysis.

Example Perform the best subsets analysis for the standby-hours data that is shown in Figure 15.12 on page 589.

PHStat Use **Best Subsets.**
For the example, open to the **DATA worksheet** of the **Standby workbook**. Select **PHStat → Regression → Best Subsets**. In the procedure's dialog box (shown below):

1. Enter **A1:A27** as the **Y Variable Cell Range**.
2. Enter **B1:E27** as the **X Variables Cell Range**.
3. Check **First cells in each range contains label**.
4. Enter **95** as the **Confidence level for regression coefficients**.
5. Enter a **Title** and click **OK**.

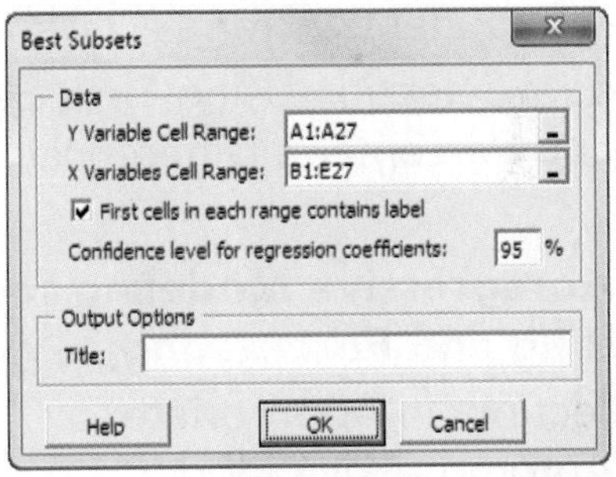

This procedure constructs many regression results worksheets (seen as a flickering in the Excel window) as it evaluates each subset of independent variables.

CHAPTER

16 Time-Series Forecasting

Learning Objectives

In this chapter, you learn:

- About different time-series forecasting models—moving averages, exponential smoothing, the linear trend, the quadratic trend, the exponential trend—and the autoregressive models and least-squares models for seasonal data
- To choose the most appropriate time-series forecasting model

USING STATISTICS

© Picture Contact BV / Alamy

Principled Forecasting

You are a financial analyst for The Principled, a large financial services company. You need to better evaluate investment opportunities for your clients. To assist in the forecasting, you have collected a time series for yearly movie attendance and the revenues of two large well-known companies, The Coca-Cola Company, and Wal-Mart Stores, Inc. Each time series has unique characteristics due to differences in business activities and growth patterns. You understand that you can choose among several different types of forecasting models. How do you decide which type of forecasting is best? How do you use the information gained from the forecasting models to evaluate investment opportunities for your clients?

Rudyanto Wijaya / iStock Photo

In Chapters 13 through 15, you used regression analysis as a tool for model building and prediction. In this chapter, regression analysis and other statistical methodologies are applied to time-series data. A **time series** is a set of numerical data collected over time. Due to differences in the features of data for various investments described in the Using Statistics scenario, you need to consider several different approaches to forecasting time-series data.

This chapter begins with an introduction to the importance of business forecasting (see Section 16.1) and a description of the components of time-series models (see Section 16.2). The coverage of forecasting models begins with annual time-series data. Section 16.3 presents moving averages and exponential smoothing methods for smoothing a series. This is followed by least-squares trend fitting and forecasting in Section 16.4 and autoregressive modeling in Section 16.5. Section 16.6 discusses how to choose among alternative forecasting models. Section 16.7 develops models for monthly and quarterly time series.

16.1 The Importance of Business Forecasting

Because economic and business conditions vary over time, managers must find ways to keep abreast of the effects that such changes will have on their organizations. One technique that can aid in planning for the future needs is *forecasting*. **Forecasting** involves monitoring changes that occur over time and predicting into the future. For example, marketing executives at a retailer might forecast product demand, sales revenues, consumer preferences, and inventory, among other things, in order to make decisions regarding product promotions and strategic planning. Government officials forecast unemployment, inflation, industrial production, and revenues from income taxes in order to formulate economic policies. And the administrators of a college must forecast student enrollment in order to plan for the construction of dormitories and academic facilities and plan for student and faculty recruitment.

Two common approaches to forecasting are *qualitative* and *quantitative* forecasting. **Qualitative forecasting methods** are especially important when historical data are unavailable. Qualitative forecasting methods are considered to be highly subjective and judgmental. **Quantitative forecasting methods** make use of historical data. The goal of these methods is to use past data to predict future values.

Quantitative forecasting methods are subdivided into two types: *time series* and *causal*. **Time-series forecasting methods** involve forecasting future values based entirely on the past and present values of a variable. For example, the daily closing prices of a particular stock on the New York Stock Exchange constitute a time series. Other examples of economic or business time series are the consumer price index (CPI), the quarterly gross domestic product (GDP), and the annual sales revenues of a particular company.

Causal forecasting methods involve the determination of factors that relate to the variable you are trying to forecast. These include multiple regression analysis with lagged variables, econometric modeling, leading indicator analysis, and other economic barometers that are beyond the scope of this text (see references 2–4). The emphasis in this chapter is on time-series forecasting methods.

16.2 Component Factors of Time-Series Models

Time-series forecasting assumes that the factors that have influenced activities in the past and present will continue to do so in approximately the same way in the future. Time-series forecasting seeks to identify and isolate these component factors in order to make predictions. Typically, the following four factors are examined in time-series models:

- Trend
- Cyclical effect
- Irregular or random effect
- Seasonal effect

A **trend** is an overall long-term upward or downward movement in a time series. Trend is not the only component factor that can influence data in a time series. The **cyclical effect** involves the up-and-down swings or movements through the series. Cyclical movements vary in length, usually lasting from 2 to 10 years. They differ in intensity and are often correlated with a business cycle. In some time periods, the values are higher than would be predicted by a trend line (i.e., they are at or near the peak of a cycle). In other time periods, the values are lower than would be predicted by a trend line (i.e., they are at or near the bottom of a cycle). Any data that do not follow the trend modified by the cyclical component are considered part of the **irregular effect**, or **random effect**. When you have monthly or quarterly data, an additional component, the **seasonal effect**, is considered, along with the trend, cyclical, and irregular effects.

Your first step in a time-series analysis is to visualize the data and observe whether any patterns exist over time. You must determine whether there is a long-term upward or downward movement in the series (i.e., a trend). If there is no obvious long-term upward or downward trend, then you can use moving averages or exponential smoothing to smooth the series (see Section 16.3). If a trend is present, you can consider several time-series forecasting methods. (See Sections 16.4 and 16.5 for forecasting annual data and Section 16.7 for forecasting monthly or quarterly time series.)

16.3 Smoothing an Annual Time Series

One of the investments considered in The Principled scenario is the entertainment industry. Table 16.1 gives the yearly movie attendance (in billions) from 2001 through 2011 (stored in Movie Attendance). Figure 16.1 presents the time-series plot.

TABLE 16.1

Movie Attendance from 2001 Through 2011

Year	Attendance (billions)	Year	Attendance (billions)	Year	Attendance (billions)
2001	1.44	2005	1.38	2009	1.42
2002	1.60	2006	1.40	2010	1.35
2003	1.52	2007	1.40	2011	1.30
2004	1.48	2008	1.36		

Source: Data extracted from Motion Picture Association of America, **www.mpaa.org**; and S. Bowles, "Ticket Sales Slump at 2010 Box Office," *USA Today*, January 3, 2011, p. 1D.

FIGURE 16.1

Time-series plot of movie attendance from 2001 through 2011

Use the Section EG2.5 instructions to construct time-series plots.

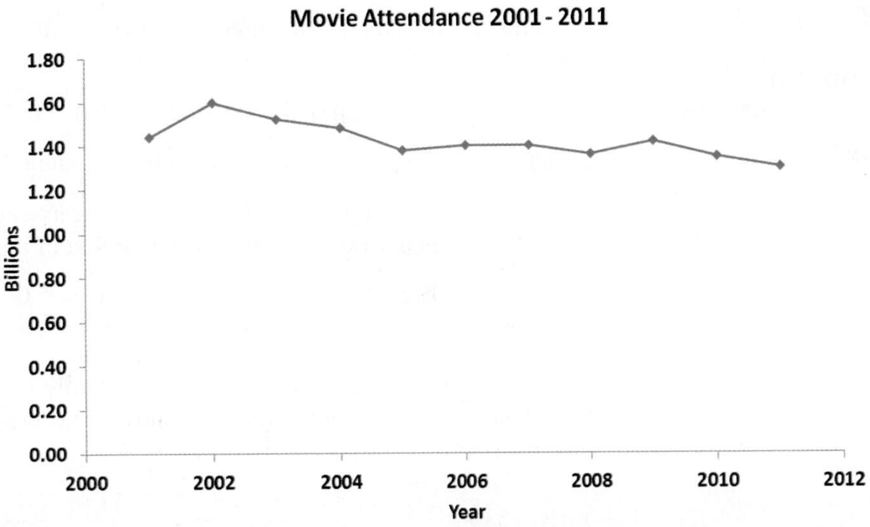

When you examine annual data such as in Figure 16.1, your visual impression of the long-term trend in the series is sometimes obscured by the amount of variation from year to year. Often, you cannot judge whether any long-term upward or downward trend exists in the series. To get a better overall impression of the pattern of movement in the data over time, you can use the methods of *moving averages* or *exponential smoothing*.

Moving Averages

Moving averages for a chosen period of length L consist of a series of means, each computed over time for a sequence of L observed values. Moving averages, represented by the symbol $MA(L)$, can be greatly affected by the value chosen for L, which should be an integer value that corresponds to, or is a multiple of, the estimated average length of a cycle in the time series.

To illustrate, suppose you want to compute five-year moving averages from a series that has $n = 11$ years. Because $L = 5$, the five-year moving averages consist of a series of means computed by averaging consecutive sequences of five values. You compute the first five-year moving average by summing the values for the first five years in the series and dividing by 5:

$$MA(5) = \frac{Y_1 + Y_2 + Y_3 + Y_4 + Y_5}{5}$$

You compute the second five-year moving average by summing the values of years 2 through 6 in the series and then dividing by 5:

$$MA(5) = \frac{Y_2 + Y_3 + Y_4 + Y_5 + Y_6}{5}$$

You continue this process until you have computed the last of these five-year moving averages by summing the values of the last 5 years in the series (i.e., years 7 through 11) and then dividing by 5:

$$MA(5) = \frac{Y_7 + Y_8 + Y_9 + Y_{10} + Y_{11}}{5}$$

Student Tip
Remember that you cannot compute moving averages at the beginning and at the end of the series.

When you have annual time-series data, L should be an *odd* number of years. By following this rule, you are unable to compute any moving averages for the first $(L - 1)/2$ years or the last $(L - 1)/2$ years of the series. Thus, for a five-year moving average, you cannot make computations for the first two years or the last two years of the series.

When plotting moving averages, you plot each of the computed values against the middle year of the sequence of years used to compute it. If $n = 11$ and $L = 5$, the first moving average is centered on the third year, the second moving average is centered on the fourth year, and the last moving average is centered on the ninth year. Example 16.1 illustrates the computation of five-year moving averages.

EXAMPLE 16.1 Computing Five-Year Moving Averages

The following data represent total revenues (in $millions) for a fast-food store over the 11-year period 2002 to 2012:

4.0 5.0 7.0 6.0 8.0 9.0 5.0 7.0 7.5 5.5 6.5

Compute the five-year moving averages for this annual time series.

SOLUTION To compute the five-year moving averages, you first compute the total for the five years and then divide this total by 5. The first of the five-year moving averages is

$$MA(5) = \frac{Y_1 + Y_2 + Y_3 + Y_4 + Y_5}{5} = \frac{4.0 + 5.0 + 7.0 + 6.0 + 8.0}{5} = \frac{30.0}{5} = 6.0$$

The moving average is centered on the middle value—the third year of this time series. To compute the second of the five-year moving averages, you compute the total of the second through sixth years and divide this total by 5:

$$MA(5) = \frac{Y_2 + Y_3 + Y_4 + Y_5 + Y_6}{5} = \frac{5.0 + 7.0 + 6.0 + 8.0 + 9.0}{5} = \frac{35.0}{5} = 7.0$$

This moving average is centered on the new middle value—the fourth year of the time series. The remaining moving averages are

$$MA(5) = \frac{Y_3 + Y_4 + Y_5 + Y_6 + Y_7}{5} = \frac{7.0 + 6.0 + 8.0 + 9.0 + 5.0}{5} = \frac{35.0}{5} = 7.0$$

$$MA(5) = \frac{Y_4 + Y_5 + Y_6 + Y_7 + Y_8}{5} = \frac{6.0 + 8.0 + 9.0 + 5.0 + 7.0}{5} = \frac{35.0}{5} = 7.0$$

$$MA(5) = \frac{Y_5 + Y_6 + Y_7 + Y_8 + Y_9}{5} = \frac{8.0 + 9.0 + 5.0 + 7.0 + 7.5}{5} = \frac{36.5}{5} = 7.3$$

$$MA(5) = \frac{Y_6 + Y_7 + Y_8 + Y_9 + Y_{10}}{5} = \frac{9.0 + 5.0 + 7.0 + 7.5 + 5.5}{5} = \frac{34.0}{5} = 6.8$$

$$MA(5) = \frac{Y_7 + Y_8 + Y_9 + Y_{10} + Y_{11}}{5} = \frac{5.0 + 7.0 + 7.5 + 5.5 + 6.5}{5} = \frac{31.5}{5} = 6.3$$

These moving averages are centered on their respective middle values—the fifth, sixth, seventh, eighth, and ninth years in the time series. When you use the five-year moving averages, you are unable to compute a moving average for the first two or last two values in the time series.

In practice, you can avoid the tedious computations by using Excel to compute moving averages. Figure 16.2 presents the annual movie attendance (in billions) from 2001 through 2011, the computations for three- and five-year moving averages, and a plot of the original data and the moving averages.

FIGURE 16.2

Three- and five-year moving averages worksheet and plot for the movie attendance data

Figure 16.2 displays the ***COMPUTE worksheet*** *and the* ***Moving AveragesPlot chart sheet*** *of the* ***Moving Averages workbook*** *that the Section EG16.3 instructions use.*

	A	B	C	D
1	Year	Attendance	MA 3-Yr	MA 5-Yr
2	2001	1.44	#N/A	#N/A
3	2002	1.60	1.52	#N/A
4	2003	1.52	1.53	1.48
5	2004	1.48	1.46	1.48
6	2005	1.38	1.42	1.44
7	2006	1.40	1.39	1.40
8	2007	1.40	1.39	1.39
9	2008	1.36	1.39	1.39
10	2009	1.42	1.38	1.37
11	2010	1.35	1.36	#N/A
12	2011	1.30	#N/A	#N/A

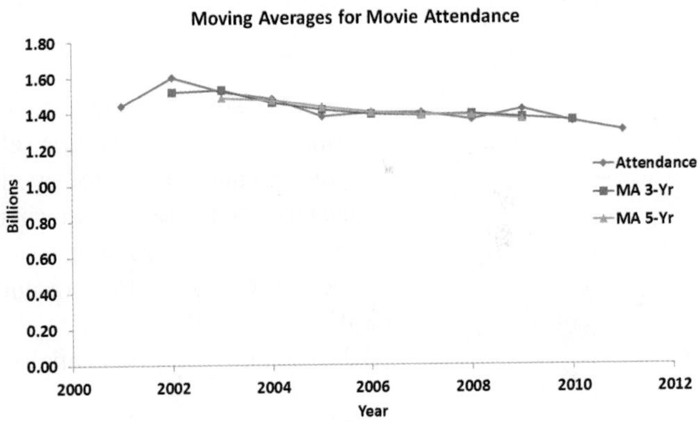

In Figure 16.2, there is no three-year moving average for the first year and the last year, and there is no five-year moving average for the first two years and last two years. Both the three-year and five-year moving averages have smoothed out the variation that exists in the movie attendance. The five-year moving average smooths the series more than the three-year moving average because the period is longer. However, the longer the period, the smaller the number of moving averages you can compute. Therefore, selecting moving averages that are longer than five or seven years is usually undesirable because too many moving average values are missing at the beginning and end of the series. The selection of L, the length of the period used for constructing the averages, is highly subjective. If cyclical fluctuations are present in the data, choose an integer value of L that corresponds to (or is a multiple of) the estimated length of a cycle in the series. For annual time-series data that has no obvious cyclical fluctuations, most people choose three years, five years, or seven years as the value of L, depending on the amount of smoothing desired and the amount of data available.

Exponential Smoothing

Exponential smoothing consists of a series of *exponentially weighted* moving averages. The weights assigned to the values change so that the most recent value receives the highest weight, the previous value receives the second-highest weight, and so on, with the first value receiving the lowest weight. Throughout the series, each exponentially smoothed value depends on all previous values, which is an advantage of exponential smoothing over the method of moving averages. Exponential smoothing also allows you to compute short-term (one period into the future) forecasts when the presence and type of long-term trend in a time series is difficult to determine.

The equation developed for exponentially smoothing a series in any time period, i, is based on only three terms—the current value in the time series, Y_i; the previously computed exponentially smoothed value, E_{i-1}; and an assigned weight or smoothing coefficient, W. You use Equation (16.1) to exponentially smooth a time series.

COMPUTING AN EXPONENTIALLY SMOOTHED VALUE IN TIME PERIOD *i*

$$E_1 = Y_1 \qquad \textbf{(16.1)}$$
$$E_i = WY_i + (1 - W)E_{i-1} \quad i = 2, 3, 4, \ldots$$

where

E_i = value of the exponentially smoothed series being computed in time period i

E_{i-1} = value of the exponentially smoothed series already computed in time period $i - 1$

Y_i = observed value of the time series in period i

W = subjectively assigned weight or smoothing coefficient (where $0 < W < 1$); although W can approach 1.0, in virtually all business applications, $W \le 0.5$

Choosing the weight or smoothing coefficient (i.e., W) that you assign to the time series is critical. Unfortunately, this selection is somewhat subjective. If your goal is to smooth a series by eliminating unwanted cyclical and irregular variations in order to see the overall long-term tendency of the series, you should select a small value for W (close to 0). If your goal is forecasting future short-term directions, you should choose a large value for W (close to 0.5). Figure 16.3 shows a worksheet that presents the exponentially smoothed values (with smoothing coefficients $W = 0.50$ and $W = 0.25$), the movie attendance from 2001 to 2011, and a plot of the original data and the two exponentially smoothed time series.

FIGURE 16.3

Exponentially smoothed series ($W = 0.50$ and $W = 0.25$) worksheet and plot for the movie attendance data

	A	B	C	D
1	Year	Attendance	ES(W=0.50)	ES(W=0.25)
2	2001	1.44	1.44	1.44
3	2002	1.60	1.52	1.48
4	2003	1.52	1.52	1.49
5	2004	1.48	1.50	1.49
6	2005	1.38	1.44	1.46
7	2006	1.40	1.42	1.45
8	2007	1.40	1.41	1.43
9	2008	1.36	1.39	1.42
10	2009	1.42	1.40	1.42
11	2010	1.35	1.38	1.40
12	2011	1.30	1.34	1.38

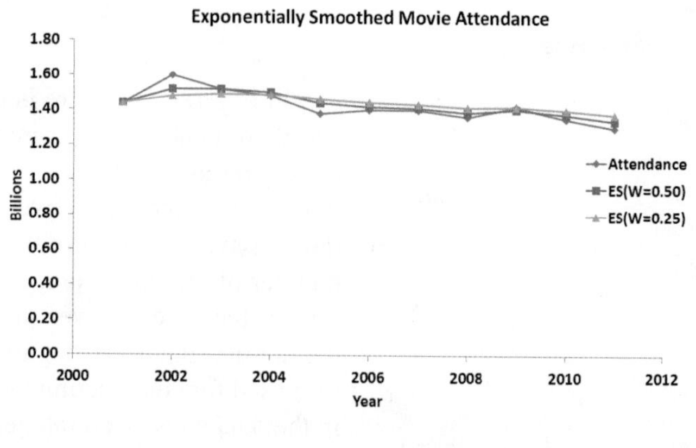

Figure 16.3 displays the ***COMPUTE worksheet*** *and the* ***ExpSmoothedPlot chart sheet*** *of the* ***Exponential Smoothed workbook*** *that the Section EG16.3 instructions use.*

To illustrate these exponential smoothing computations for a smoothing coefficient of $W = 0.25$, you begin with the initial value $Y_{2001} = 1.44$ as the first smoothed value ($E_{2001} = 1.44$). Then, using the value of the time series for 2002 ($Y_{2002} = 1.60$), you smooth the series for 2002 by computing

$$\begin{aligned} E_{2002} &= WY_{2002} + (1 - W)E_{2001} \\ &= (0.25)(1.60) + (0.75)(1.44) = 1.48 \end{aligned}$$

To smooth the series for 2003:

$$\begin{aligned} E_{2003} &= WY_{2003} + (1 - W)E_{2002} \\ &= (0.25)(1.52) + (0.75)(1.48) = 1.49 \end{aligned}$$

To smooth the series for 2004:

$$\begin{aligned} E_{2004} &= WY_{2004} + (1 - W)E_{2003} \\ &= (0.25)(1.48) + (0.75)(1.49) = 1.49 \end{aligned}$$

You continue this process until you have computed the exponentially smoothed values for all 11 years in the series, as shown in Figure 16.3.

In general, you compute the current smoothed value as follows:

$$\text{Current smoothed value} = (W)(\text{Current value}) + (1 - W)(\text{Previous smoothed value})$$

Remember that the smoothed value for the first year is the observed value in the first year.

To use exponential smoothing for forecasting, you use the smoothed value in the current time period as the forecast of the value in the following period ($\hat{Y}_{i+1}$).

FORECASTING TIME PERIOD $i + 1$

$$\hat{Y}_{i+1} = E_i \tag{16.2}$$

To forecast the movie attendance in 2012, using a smoothing coefficient of $W = 0.25$, you use the smoothed value for 2011 as its estimate. Figure 16.3 shows that this value is 1.38.

Problems for Section 16.3

LEARNING THE BASICS

16.1 If you are using exponential smoothing for forecasting an annual time series of revenues, what is your forecast for next year if the smoothed value for this year is \$32.4 million?

16.2 Consider a nine-year moving average used to smooth a time series that was first recorded in 1984.

a. Which year serves as the first centered value in the smoothed series?

b. How many years of values in the series are lost when computing all the nine-year moving averages?

16.3 You are using exponential smoothing on an annual time series concerning total revenues (in \$millions). You decide to use a smoothing coefficient of $W = 0.20$, and the exponentially smoothed value for 2012 is $E_{2012} = (0.20)(12.1) + (0.80)(9.4)$.

a. What is the smoothed value of this series in 2012?

b. What is the smoothed value of this series in 2013 if the value of the series in that year is \$11.5 million?

APPLYING THE CONCEPTS

SELF Test **16.4** The data on page 616 (stored in DriveThruSpeed) represent the average time (in seconds) it took to be served at the drive-through at McDonald's from 1998 to 2009:

a. Plot the time series.

b. Fit a three-year moving average to the data and plot the results.

c. Using a smoothing coefficient of $W = 0.50$, exponentially smooth the series and plot the results.

d. What is your exponentially smoothed forecast for 2010?

e. Repeat (c) and (d), using $W = 0.25$.

f. Compare the results of (d) and (e).

Year	Drive-Through Speed (seconds)
1998	177.59
1999	167.02
2000	169.88
2001	170.85
2002	162.72
2003	156.92
2004	152.52
2005	167.90
2006	163.90
2007	167.10
2008	158.77
2009	174.22

Source: Data extracted from **bit.ly/qhvP3Z.**

16.5 The following data, stored in **Spills** provide the number of oil spills in the Gulf of Mexico from 1996 to 2011:

Year	Number of Spills
1996	4
1997	3
1998	9
1999	5
2000	7
2001	9
2002	12
2003	12
2004	22
2005	49
2006	14
2007	4
2008	33
2009	11
2010	5
2011	3

Source: Data extracted from **www.bsee.gov/Inspection-and-Enforcement/Accidents-and-Incidents/Spills**

a. Plot the time series.
b. Fit a three-year moving average to the data and plot the results.
c. Using a smoothing coefficient of $W = 0.50$, exponentially smooth the series and plot the results.
d. What is your exponentially smoothed forecast for 2012?
e. Repeat (c) and (d), using $W = 0.25$.
f. Compare the results of (d) and (e).

16.6 How have stocks performed in the past? The following table presents the data stored in **Stock Performance**, which show the performance of a broad measure of stock performance (by percentage) for each decade from the 1830s through the 2000s:

Decade	Performance (%)	Decade	Performance (%)
1830s	2.8	1920s	13.3
1840s	12.8	1930s	−2.2
1850s	6.6	1940s	9.6
1860s	12.5	1950s	18.2
1870s	7.5	1960s	8.3
1880s	6.0	1970s	6.6
1890s	5.5	1980s	16.6
1900s	10.9	1990s	17.6
1910s	2.2	2000s*	−0.5

*Through December 15, 2009.

Source: T. Lauricella, "Investors Hope the '10s Beat the '00s," *The Wall Street Journal*, December 21, 2009, pp. C1, C2.

a. Plot the time series.
b. Fit a three-period moving average to the data and plot the results.
c. Using a smoothing coefficient of $W = 0.50$, exponentially smooth the series and plot the results.
d. What is your exponentially smoothed forecast for the 2010s?
e. Repeat (c) and (d), using $W = 0.25$.
f. Compare the results of (d) and (e).
g. What conclusions can you reach concerning how stocks have performed in the past?

16.7 The following data (stored in **CoffeePricesPortugal**) represent the retail price of coffee (in €/kg) in Portugal from 2004 to 2011:

Year	Retail Price (€/kg)
2004	8.60
2005	8.53
2006	8.32
2007	8.23
2008	8.58
2009	8.45
2010	8.31
2011	8.60

Source: International Coffee Organization, **www.ico.org.**

a. Plot the data.
b. Fit a three-year moving average to the data and plot the results.
c. Using a smoothing coefficient of $W = 0.50$, exponentially smooth the series and plot the results.
d. What is your exponentially smoothed forecast for 2012?
e. Repeat (c) and (d), using a smoothing coefficient of $W = 0.25$.
f. Compare the results of (d) and (e).

16.8 The file **Audits** contains the number of audits of corporations with assets of more than $250 million conducted by the Internal Revenue Service. (Data extracted from K. McCoy, "IRS Audits Big Firms Less Often," *USA Today*, April 15, 2010, p. 1B; and Internal Revenue Service, www.irs.gov.)
a. Plot the data.
b. Fit a three-year moving average to the data and plot the results.
c. Using a smoothing coefficient of $W = 0.50$, exponentially smooth the series and plot the results.
d. What is your exponentially smoothed forecast for 2012?
e. Repeat (c) and (d), using a smoothing coefficient of $W = 0.25$.
f. Compare the results of (d) and (e).

16.4 Least-Squares Trend Fitting and Forecasting

Trend is the component factor of a time series most often used to make intermediate and long-range forecasts. To get a visual impression of the overall long-term movements in a time series, you construct a time-series plot. If a straight-line trend adequately fits the data, you can use a linear trend model [see Equation (16.3) and Section 13.2]. If the time-series data indicate some long-run downward or upward quadratic movement, you can use a quadratic trend model [see Equation (16.4) and Section 15.1]. When the time-series data increase at a rate such that the percentage difference from value to value is constant, you can use an exponential trend model [see Equation (16.5)].

The Linear Trend Model

The **linear trend model**:

$$Y_i = \beta_0 + \beta_1 X_i + \varepsilon_i$$

is the simplest forecasting model. Equation (16.3) defines the linear trend forecasting equation.

LINEAR TREND FORECASTING EQUATION

$$\hat{Y}_i = b_0 + b_1 X_i \qquad \textbf{(16.3)}$$

Recall that in linear regression analysis, you use the method of least squares to compute the sample slope, b_1, and the sample Y intercept, b_0. You then substitute the values for X into Equation (16.3) to predict Y.

When using the least-squares method for fitting trends in a time series, you can simplify the interpretation of the coefficients by assigning coded values to the X (time) variable. You assign consecutively numbered integers, starting with 0, as the coded values for the time periods. For example, in time-series data that have been recorded annually for 17 years, you assign the coded value 0 to the first year, the coded value 1 to the second year, the coded value 2 to the third year, and so on, concluding by assigning 16 to the seventeenth year.

In The Principled scenario on page 609, one of the companies of interest is The Coca-Cola Company. Founded in 1886 and headquartered in Atlanta, Georgia, Coca-Cola manufactures, distributes, and markets more than 500 beverage brands in over 200 countries worldwide. Brands include Coca-Cola, Diet Coke, Fanta, and Sprite, four of the world's top five nonalcoholic sparkling beverage products. According to The Coca-Cola Company's website, revenues in 2011 topped $46 billion. Table 16.2 lists The Coca-Cola Company's gross revenues (in $billions) from 1995 to 2011 (stored in **Coca-Cola**).

TABLE 16.2

Revenues for The Coca-Cola Company (1995–2011)

Year	Revenues ($billions)	Year	Revenues ($billions)
1995	18.0	2004	21.9
1996	18.5	2005	23.1
1997	18.9	2006	24.1
1998	18.8	2007	28.9
1999	19.8	2008	31.9
2000	20.5	2009	31.0
2001	20.1	2010	35.1
2002	19.6	2011	46.5
2003	21.0		

Source: Data extracted from *Mergent's Handbook of Common Stocks*, 2006; and **www.thecoca-colacompany.com/investors/annual_other_reports.html.**

Figure 16.4 presents the regression results for the simple linear regression model that uses the consecutive coded values 0 through 16 as the X (coded year) variable.

FIGURE 16.4

Regression results worksheet for the linear trend model to forecast revenues (in $billions) for The Coca-Cola Company

Use the Section EG16.4 instructions to construct this worksheet.

	A	B	C	D	E	F	G
1	**Linear Trend Model for The Coca-Cola Company Revenues**						
2							
3	*Regression Statistics*						
4	Multiple R	0.8605					
5	R Square	0.7405					
6	Adjusted R Square	0.7232					
7	Standard Error	4.0697					
8	Observations	17					
9							
10	**ANOVA**						
11		*df*	*SS*	*MS*	*F*	*Significance F*	
12	Regression	1	708.8942	708.8942	42.8005	0.0000	
13	Residual	15	248.4411	16.5627			
14	Total	16	957.3353				
15							
16		*Coefficients*	*Standard Error*	*t Stat*	*P-value*	*Lower 95%*	*Upper 95%*
17	Intercept	14.0255	1.8901	7.4206	0.0000	9.9969	18.0541
18	Coded Year	1.3181	0.2015	6.5422	0.0000	0.8887	1.7476

These results produce the following linear trend forecasting equation:

$$\hat{Y}_i = 14.0255 + 1.3181X_i$$

where $X_1 = 0$ represents 1995.

You interpret the regression coefficients as follows:

- The Y intercept, $b_0 = 14.0255$, is the predicted revenues (in $billions) at The Coca-Cola Company during the origin, or base, year, 1995.
- The slope, $b_1 = 1.3181$, indicates that revenues are predicted to increase by $1.3181 billion per year.

To project the trend in the revenues at Coca-Cola to 2012, you substitute $X_{18} = 17$, the code for 2012, into the linear trend forecasting equation:

$$\hat{Y}_i = 14.0255 + 1.3181(17) = 36.4332 \text{ billions of dollars}$$

The trend line is plotted in Figure 16.5, along with the observed values of the time series. There is a strong upward linear trend, and r^2 is 0.7405, indicating that more than 74% of the variation in revenues is explained by the linear trend of the time series. However, you can observe that the revenue for the most recent year, 2011, is substantially above the trend line, that the early years are also slightly above the trend line, but the middle years are below the trend line. To investigate whether a different trend model might provide a better fit, a *quadratic* trend model and an *exponential* trend model can be fitted.

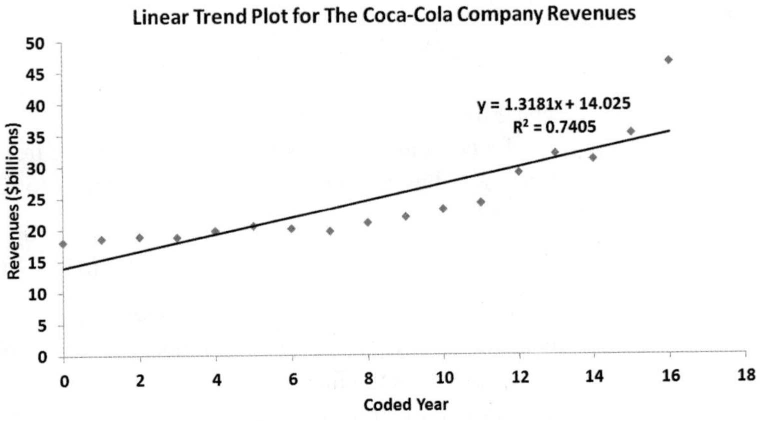

FIGURE 16.5
Plot of the linear trend forecasting equation for The Coca-Cola Company revenue data

Use the Section EG2.5 instructions to construct linear trend plots.

The Quadratic Trend Model

A **quadratic trend model**:

$$Y_i = \beta_0 + \beta_1 X_i + \beta_2 X_i^2 + \varepsilon_i$$

is a nonlinear model that contains a linear term and a curvilinear term in addition to a Y intercept. Using the least-squares method for a quadratic model described in Section 15.1, you can develop a quadratic trend forecasting equation, as presented in Equation (16.4).

QUADRATIC TREND FORECASTING EQUATION

$$\hat{Y}_i = b_0 + b_1 X_i + b_2 X_i^2 \tag{16.4}$$

where

b_0 = estimated Y intercept

b_1 = estimated *linear* effect on Y

b_2 = estimated *quadratic* effect on Y

Figure 16.6 presents the regression results for the quadratic trend model used to forecast revenues at The Coca-Cola Company.

FIGURE 16.6
Regression results worksheet for the quadratic trend model to forecast revenues (in $billions) for The Coca-Cola Company

Use the Section EG16.4 instructions to construct this worksheet.

	A	B	C	D	E	F	G
1	Quadratic Regression Model for The Coca-Cola Company Revenues						
2							
3	*Regression Statistics*						
4	Multiple R	0.9648					
5	R Square	0.9308					
6	Adjusted R Square	0.9209					
7	Standard Error	2.1755					
8	Observations	17					
9							
10	ANOVA						
11		*df*	*SS*	*MS*	*F*	*Significance F*	
12	Regression	2	891.0788	445.5394	94.1424	0.0000	
13	Residual	14	66.2565	4.7326			
14	Total	16	957.3353				
15							
16		*Coefficients*	*Standard Error*	*t Stat*	*P-value*	*Lower 95%*	*Upper 95%*
17	Intercept	20.1576	1.4134	14.2623	0.0000	17.1262	23.1889
18	Coded Year	-1.1347	0.4097	-2.7693	0.0151	-2.0135	-0.2559
19	Year Squared	0.1533	0.0247	6.2045	0.0000	0.1003	0.2063

In Figure 16.6,

$$\hat{Y}_i = 20.1576 - 1.1347X_i + 0.1533X_i^2$$

where the year coded 0 is 1995.

To compute a forecast using the quadratic trend equation, you substitute the appropriate coded X value into this equation. For example, to forecast the trend in revenues for 2012 (i.e., $X = 17$),

$$\hat{Y}_i = 20.1576 - 1.1347(17) + 0.1533(17)^2 = 45.1714$$

Figure 16.7 plots the quadratic trend forecasting equation along with the time series for the actual data. This quadratic trend model provides a better fit (adjusted $r^2 = 0.9209$) to the time series than does the linear trend model. The t_{STAT} test statistic for the contribution of the quadratic term to the model is 6.2045 (p-value = 0.0000).

FIGURE 16.7

Plot of the quadratic trend forecasting equation for The Coca-Cola Company revenue data

Use the Section EG15.1 instructions to construct quadratic trend plots.

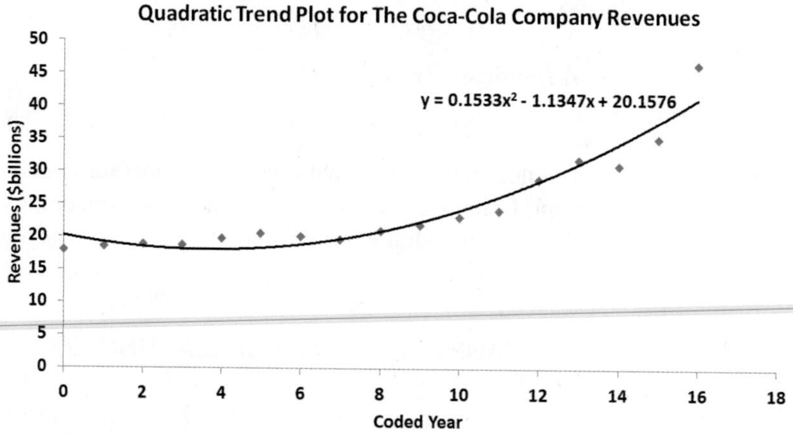

The Exponential Trend Model

When a time series increases at a rate such that the percentage difference from value to value is constant, an exponential trend is present. Equation (16.5) defines the **exponential trend model**.

EXPONENTIAL TREND MODEL

$$Y_i = \beta_0 \beta_1^{X_i} \varepsilon_i \tag{16.5}$$

where

$\beta_0 = Y$ intercept

$(\beta_1 - 1) \times 100\% =$ annual compound growth rate (in %)

The model in Equation (16.5) is not in the form of a linear regression model. To transform this nonlinear model to a linear model, you use a base 10 logarithm transformation.[1] Taking the logarithm of each side of Equation (16.5) results in Equation (16.6).

[1]Alternatively, you can use base e logarithms. For more information on logarithms, see Section A.3 in Appendix A.

TRANSFORMED EXPONENTIAL TREND MODEL

$$\begin{aligned} \log(Y_i) &= \log(\beta_0 \beta_1^{X_i} \varepsilon_i) \\ &= \log(\beta_0) + \log(\beta_1^{X_i}) + \log(\varepsilon_i) \\ &= \log(\beta_0) + X_i \log(\beta_1) + \log(\varepsilon_i) \end{aligned} \tag{16.6}$$

Student Tip
Log is the symbol used for base 10 logarithms. The log of a number is the power that 10 needs to be raised to equal that number.

Equation (16.6) is a linear model you can estimate using the least-squares method, with $\log(Y_i)$ as the dependent variable and X_i as the independent variable. This results in Equation (16.7).

EXPONENTIAL TREND FORECASTING EQUATION

$$\log(\hat{Y}_i) = b_0 + b_1X_i \quad \textbf{(16.7a)}$$

where

$$b_0 = \text{estimate of } \log(\beta_0) \text{ and thus } 10^{b_0} = \hat{\beta}_0$$
$$b_1 = \text{estimate of } \log(\beta_1) \text{ and thus } 10^{b_1} = \hat{\beta}_1$$

therefore,

$$\hat{Y}_i = \hat{\beta}_0\hat{\beta}_1^{X_i} \quad \textbf{(16.7b)}$$

where

$(\hat{\beta}_1 - 1) \times 100\%$ is the estimated annual compound growth rate (in %)

Figure 16.8 shows the regression results for an exponential trend model of revenues at The Coca-Cola Company.

FIGURE 16.8

Regression results worksheet for the exponential trend model to forecast revenues (in \$billions) for The Coca-Cola Company

Use the Section EG16.4 instructions to construct this worksheet.

	A	B	C	D	E	F	G
1	**Exponential Trend Model Model for The Coca-Cola Company Revenues**						
2							
3	*Regression Statistics*						
4	Multiple R	0.9117					
5	R Square	0.8312					
6	Adjusted R Square	0.8199					
7	Standard Error	0.0502					
8	Observations	17					
9							
10	ANOVA						
11		*df*	*SS*	*MS*	*F*	*Significance F*	
12	Regression	1	0.1863	0.1863	73.8590	0.0000	
13	Residual	15	0.0378	0.0025			
14	Total	16	0.2242				
15							
16		*Coefficients*	*Standard Error*	*t Stat*	*P-value*	*Lower 95%*	*Upper 95%*
17	Intercept	1.2028	0.0233	51.5664	0.0000	1.1531	1.2525
18	Coded Year	0.0214	0.0025	8.5941	0.0000	0.0161	0.0267

Using Equation (16.7a) and the results from Figure 16.8,

$$\log(\hat{Y}_i) = 1.2028 + 0.0214X_i$$

where the year coded 0 is 1995.

You compute the values for $\hat{\beta}_0$ and $\hat{\beta}_1$ by taking the antilog of the regression coefficients (b_0 and b_1):

$$\hat{\beta}_0 = \text{antilog}(b_0) = \text{antilog}(1.2028) = 10^{1.2028} = 15.9514$$
$$\hat{\beta}_1 = \text{antilog}(b_1) = \text{antilog}(0.0214) = 10^{0.0214} = 1.0505$$

Thus, using Equation (16.7b), the exponential trend forecasting equation is

$$\hat{Y}_i = (15.9514)(1.0505)^{X_i}$$

where the year coded 0 is 1995.

The Y intercept, $\hat{\beta}_0 = 15.9514$ billions of dollars, is the revenue forecast for the base year 1995. The value $(\hat{\beta}_1 - 1) \times 100\% = 5.05\%$ is the annual compound growth rate in revenues at The Coca-Cola Company.

For forecasting purposes, you substitute the appropriate coded X values into either Equation (16.7a) or Equation (16.7b). For example, to forecast revenues for 2012 (i.e., $X = 17$) using Equation (16.7a),

$$\log(\hat{Y}_i) = 1.2028 + 0.0214(17) = 1.5666$$
$$\hat{Y}_i = \text{antilog}(1.5666) = 10^{1.5666} = 36.8638 \text{ billions of dollars}$$

Figure 16.9 plots the exponential trend forecasting equation, along with the time-series data. The adjusted r^2 for the exponential trend model (0.8199) is greater than the adjusted r^2 for the linear trend model (0.7232) but less than for the quadratic model (0.9209).

FIGURE 16.9

Plot of the exponential trend forecasting equation for The Coca-Cola Company revenue data

Use the Section EG16.4 instructions to construct exponential trend plots.

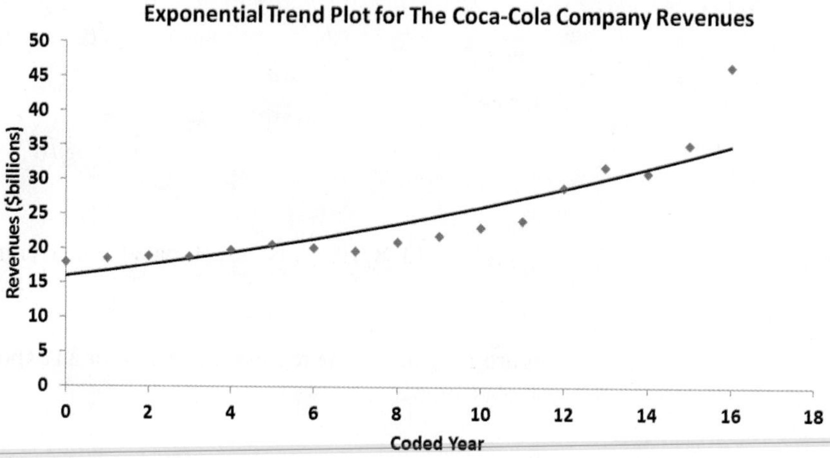

Model Selection Using First, Second, and Percentage Differences

You have used the linear, quadratic, and exponential models to forecast revenues for The Coca-Cola Company. How can you determine which of these models is the most appropriate model? In addition to visually inspecting time-series plots and comparing adjusted r^2 values, you can compute and examine first, second, and percentage differences. The identifying features of linear, quadratic, and exponential trend models are as follows:

- If a linear trend model provides a perfect fit to a time series, then the first differences are constant. Thus,

$$(Y_2 - Y_1) = (Y_3 - Y_2) = \ldots = (Y_n - Y_{n-1})$$

- If a quadratic trend model provides a perfect fit to a time series, then the second differences are constant. Thus,

$$[(Y_3 - Y_2) - (Y_2 - Y_1)] = [(Y_4 - Y_3) - (Y_3 - Y_2)] = \ldots = [(Y_n - Y_{n-1}) - (Y_{n-1} - Y_{n-2})]$$

- If an exponential trend model provides a perfect fit to a time series, then the percentage differences between consecutive values are constant. Thus,

$$\frac{Y_2 - Y_1}{Y_1} \times 100\% = \frac{Y_3 - Y_2}{Y_2} \times 100\% = \ldots = \frac{Y_n - Y_{n-1}}{Y_{n-1}} \times 100\%$$

Although you should not expect a perfectly fitting model for any particular set of time-series data, you can consider the first differences, second differences, and percentage differences as guides in choosing an appropriate model. Examples 16.2, 16.3, and 16.4 illustrate linear, quadratic, and exponential trend models that have perfect (or nearly perfect) fits to their respective data sets.

EXAMPLE 16.2

A Linear Trend Model with a Perfect Fit

The following time series represents the number of passengers per year (in millions) on ABC Airlines:

	Year									
	2003	**2004**	**2005**	**2006**	**2007**	**2008**	**2009**	**2010**	**2011**	**2012**
Passengers	30.0	33.0	36.0	39.0	42.0	45.0	48.0	51.0	54.0	57.0

Using first differences, show that the linear trend model provides a perfect fit to these data.

SOLUTION The following table shows the solution:

	Year									
	2003	**2004**	**2005**	**2006**	**2007**	**2008**	**2009**	**2009**	**2010**	**2012**
Passengers	30.0	33.0	36.0	39.0	42.0	45.0	48.0	51.0	54.0	57.0
First differences		3.0	3.0	3.0	3.0	3.0	3.0	3.0	3.0	3.0

The differences between consecutive values in the series are the same throughout. Thus, ABC Airlines shows a linear growth pattern. The number of passengers increases by 3 million per year.

EXAMPLE 16.3

A Quadratic Trend Model with a Perfect Fit

The following time series represents the number of passengers per year (in millions) on XYZ Airlines:

	Year									
	2003	**2004**	**2005**	**2006**	**2007**	**2008**	**2009**	**2010**	**2011**	**2012**
Passengers	30.0	31.0	33.5	37.5	43.0	50.0	58.5	68.5	80.0	93.0

Using second differences, show that the quadratic trend model provides a perfect fit to these data.

SOLUTION The following table shows the solution:

	Year									
	2003	**2004**	**2005**	**2006**	**2007**	**2008**	**2009**	**2010**	**2011**	**2012**
Passengers	30.0	31.0	33.5	37.5	43.0	50.0	58.5	68.5	80.0	93.0
First differences		1.0	2.5	4.0	5.5	7.0	8.5	10.0	11.5	13.0
Second differences			1.5	1.5	1.5	1.5	1.5	1.5	1.5	1.5

The second differences between consecutive pairs of values in the series are the same throughout. Thus, XYZ Airlines shows a quadratic growth pattern. Its rate of growth is accelerating over time.

EXAMPLE 16.4

An Exponential Trend Model with an Almost Perfect Fit

The following time series represents the number of passengers per year (in millions) for EXP Airlines:

	Year									
	2003	**2004**	**2005**	**2006**	**2007**	**2008**	**2009**	**2010**	**2011**	**2012**
Passengers	30.0	31.5	33.1	34.8	36.5	38.3	40.2	42.2	44.3	46.5

Using percentage differences, show that the exponential trend model provides almost a perfect fit to these data.

SOLUTION The following table shows the solution:

	Year									
	2003	**2004**	**2005**	**2006**	**2007**	**2008**	**2009**	**2010**	**2011**	**2012**
Passengers	30.0	31.5	33.1	34.8	36.5	38.3	40.2	42.2	44.3	46.5
First differences		1.5	1.6	1.7	1.7	1.8	1.9	2.0	2.1	2.2
Percentage differences		5.0	5.1	5.1	4.9	4.9	5.0	5.0	5.0	5.0

The percentage differences between consecutive values in the series are approximately the same throughout. Thus, EXP Airlines shows an exponential growth pattern. Its rate of growth is approximately 5% per year.

Figure 16.10 shows a worksheet that compares the first, second, and percentage differences for the revenues data at The Coca-Cola Company. Neither the first differences, second differences, nor percentage differences are constant across the series. Therefore, other models (including those considered in Section 16.5) may be more appropriate.

FIGURE 16.10

Worksheet that compares first, second, and percentage differences in revenues (in $billions) for The Coca-Cola Company

Figure 16.10 displays the ***COMPUTE worksheet of the Differences workbook*** *that is discussed in the Section EG16.4.*

	A	B	C	D	E
1	Year	Revenue	First Difference	Second Difference	Percentage Difference
2	1995	18.0	#N/A	#N/A	#N/A
3	1996	18.5	0.5	#N/A	2.78%
4	1997	18.9	0.4	-0.1	2.16%
5	1998	18.8	-0.1	-0.5	-0.53%
6	1999	19.8	1.0	1.1	5.32%
7	2000	20.5	0.7	-0.3	3.54%
8	2001	20.1	-0.4	-1.1	-1.95%
9	2002	19.6	-0.5	-0.1	-2.49%
10	2003	21.0	1.4	1.9	7.14%
11	2004	21.9	0.9	-0.5	4.29%
12	2005	23.1	1.2	0.3	5.48%
13	2006	24.1	1.0	-0.2	4.33%
14	2007	28.9	4.8	3.8	19.92%
15	2008	31.9	3.0	-1.8	10.38%
16	2009	31.0	-0.9	-3.9	-2.82%
17	2010	35.1	4.1	5.0	13.23%
18	2011	46.5	11.4	7.3	32.48%

Problems for Section 16.4

LEARNING THE BASICS

16.9 If you are using the method of least squares for fitting trends in an annual time series containing 25 consecutive yearly values,

a. what coded value do you assign to X for the first year in the series?

b. what coded value do you assign to X for the fifth year in the series?

c. what coded value do you assign to X for the most recent recorded year in the series?

d. what coded value do you assign to X if you want to project the trend and make a forecast five years beyond the last observed value?

16.10 The linear trend forecasting equation for an annual time series containing 22 values (from 1991 to 2012) on total revenues (in $millions) is

$$\hat{Y}_i = 4.0 + 1.5X_i$$

a. Interpret the Y intercept, b_0.

b. Interpret the slope, b_1.

c. What is the fitted trend value for the fifth year?

d. What is the fitted trend value for the most recent year?

e. What is the projected trend forecast three years after the last value?

16.11 The linear trend forecasting equation for an annual time series containing 42 values (from 1971 to 2012) on net sales (in $billions) is

$$\hat{Y}_i = 1.2 + 0.5X_i$$

a. Interpret the Y intercept, b_0.

b. Interpret the slope, b_1.

c. What is the fitted trend value for the tenth year?

d. What is the fitted trend value for the most recent year?

e. What is the projected trend forecast two years after the last value?

APPLYING THE CONCEPTS

SELF Test **16.12** Bed Bath & Beyond is a nationwide chain of retail stores that sell a wide assortment of merchandise, including domestics merchandise and home furnishings, as well as food, giftware, and health and beauty care items. The number of stores open at the end of the fiscal year from 1997 to 2012 is stored in Bed & Bath and shown in right column.

a. Plot the data.

b. Compute a linear trend forecasting equation and plot the results.

c. Compute a quadratic trend forecasting equation and plot the results.

d. Compute an exponential trend forecasting equation and plot the results.

e. Using the forecasting equations in (b) through (d), what are your annual forecasts of the number of stores open for 2013 and 2014?

f. How can you explain the differences in the three forecasts in (e)? What forecast do you think you should use? Why?

Year	Stores Opened	Year	Stores Opened
1997	108	2005	721
1998	141	2006	809
1999	186	2007	888
2000	241	2008	971
2001	311	2009	1,037
2002	396	2010	1,100
2003	519	2011	1,139
2004	629	2012	1,173

Source: Data extracted from *Bed Bath & Beyond Annual Report*, 2012.

16.13 Gross domestic product (GDP) is a major indicator of a nation's overall economic activity. It consists of personal consumption expenditures, gross domestic investment, net exports of goods and services, and government consumption expenditures. The file GDP contains the GDP (in billions of current dollars) for the United States from 1980 to 2011. (Data extracted from Bureau of Economic Analysis, U.S. Department of Commerce, www.bea.gov.)

a. Plot the data.

b. Compute a linear trend forecasting equation and plot the trend line.

c. What are your forecasts for 2012 and 2013?

d. What conclusions can you reach concerning the trend in GDP?

16.14 The data in FedReceipt represent federal receipts from 1978 through 2011, in billions of current dollars, from individual and corporate income tax, social insurance, excise tax, estate and gift tax, customs duties, and federal reserve deposits. (Data extracted from "Historical Federal Receipt and Outlay Summary," Tax Policy Center, **bit.ly/7dGCmz**)

a. Plot the series of data.

b. Compute a linear trend forecasting equation and plot the trend line.

c. What are your forecasts of the federal receipts for 2012 and 2013?

d. What conclusions can you reach concerning the trend in federal receipts?

16.15 The file ComputerSales contains the U.S. total computer and software sales (in $millions) from 1992 through 2011.

a. Plot the data.

b. Compute a linear trend forecasting equation and plot the trend line.

c. Compute a quadratic trend forecasting equation and plot the results.

d. Compute an exponential trend forecasting equation and plot the results.

e. Which model is the most appropriate?
f. Using the most appropriate model, forecast U.S. total computer and software sales, in millions, for 2012.

16.16 The data shown in the following table and stored in Solar Power represent the yearly amount of solar power generated by utilities (in millions of kWh) in the United States from 2002 through 2011:

Year	Solar Power Generated (millions of kWh)	Year	Solar Power Generated (millions of kWh)
2002	555	2007	612
2003	534	2008	864
2004	575	2009	891
2005	550	2010	1,212
2006	508	2011	1,814

Source: Data extracted from **en.wikipedia.org/wiki/Solar_power_in_the_United_States.**

a. Plot the data.
b. Compute a linear trend forecasting equation and plot the trend line.
c. Compute a quadratic trend forecasting equation and plot the results.
d. Compute an exponential trend forecasting equation and plot the results.
e. Using the models in (b) through (d), what are your annual trend forecasts of the yearly amount of solar power generated by utilities (in millions of kWh) in the United States in 2012 and 2013?

16.17 The file CarProduction) contains the number of passenger cars produced in the U.S. from 1999 to 2011. (Data extracted from www.statista.com.)
a. Plot the data.
b. Compute a linear trend forecasting equation and plot the trend line.
c. Compute a quadratic trend forecasting equation and plot the results.
d. Compute an exponential trend forecasting equation and plot the results.
e. Which model is the most appropriate?
f. Using the most appropriate model, forecast the U.S. car production for 2012.

16.18 The average salary of Major League Baseball players on opening day from 2000 to 2012 is stored in BBSalaries and shown in the right column.
a. Plot the data.
b. Compute a linear trend forecasting equation and plot the trend line.
c. Compute a quadratic trend forecasting equation and plot the results.
d. Compute an exponential trend forecasting equation and plot the results.
e. Which model is the most appropriate?
f. Using the most appropriate model, forecast the average salary for 2013.

Year	Salary ($millions)	Year	Salary ($millions)
2000	1.99	2007	2.92
2001	2.29	2008	3.13
2002	2.38	2009	3.26
2003	2.58	2010	3.27
2004	2.49	2011	3.32
2005	2.63	2012	3.38
2006	2.83		

Source: Data extracted from "Baseball Salaries," *USA Today*, April 6, 2009, p. 6C; and mlb.com.

16.19 The file Silver contains the following prices in London for an ounce of silver (in US$) on the last day of the year from 1999 to 2011:

Year	Price (US$/ounce)	Year	Price (US$/ounce)
1999	5.330	2006	12.900
2000	4.570	2007	14.760
2001	4.520	2008	10.790
2002	4.670	2009	16.990
2003	5.965	2010	30.630
2004	6.815	2011	28.180
2005	8.830		

Source: Data extracted from **bit.ly/1afifi.**

a. Plot the data.
b. Compute a linear trend forecasting equation and plot the trend line.
c. Compute a quadratic trend forecasting equation and plot the results.
d. Compute an exponential trend forecasting equation and plot the results.
e. Which model is the most appropriate?
f. Using the most appropriate model, forecast the price of silver at the end of 2012.

16.20 The data in CPI-U reflect the annual values of the consumer price index (CPI) in the United States over the 47-year period 1965 through 2011, using 1982 through 1984 as the base period. This index measures the average change in prices over time in a fixed "market basket" of goods and services purchased by all urban consumers, including urban wage earners (i.e., clerical, professional, managerial, and technical workers; self-employed individuals; and short-term workers), unemployed individuals, and retirees. (Data extracted from Bureau of Labor Statistics, U.S. Department of Labor, www.bls.gov.)

a. Plot the data.
b. Describe the movement in this time series over the 47-year period.
c. Compute a linear trend forecasting equation and plot the trend line.
d. Compute a quadratic trend forecasting equation and plot the results.
e. Compute an exponential trend forecasting equation and plot the results.
f. Which model is the most appropriate?
g. Using the most appropriate model, forecast the CPI for 2012 and 2013.

16.21 Although you should not expect a perfectly fitting model for any time-series data, you can consider the first differences, second differences, and percentage differences for a given series as guides in choosing an appropriate model.

Year	Series I	Series II	Series III
2000	10.0	30.0	60.0
2001	15.1	33.1	67.9
2002	24.0	36.4	76.1
2003	36.7	39.9	84.0
2004	53.8	43.9	92.2
2005	74.8	48.2	100.0
2006	100.0	53.2	108.0
2007	129.2	58.2	115.8
2008	162.4	64.5	124.1
2009	199.0	70.7	132.0
2010	239.3	77.1	140.0
2011	283.5	83.9	147.8

For this problem, use each of the time series presented in the table in the left column and stored in **Tsmodel1**:
a. Determine the most appropriate model.
b. Compute the forecasting equation.
c. Forecast the value for 2012.

16.22 A time-series plot often helps you determine the appropriate model to use. For this problem, use each of the time series presented in the following table and stored in **TsModel2**:

Year	Series I	Series II	Year	Series I	Series II
2000	100.0	100.0	2006	189.8	230.8
2001	115.2	115.2	2007	204.9	266.1
2002	130.1	131.7	2008	219.8	305.5
2003	144.9	150.8	2009	235.0	351.8
2004	160.0	174.1	2010	249.8	403
2005	175.0	200.0	2011	264.9	469.2

a. Plot the observed data (Y) over time (X) and plot the logarithm of the observed data ($\log Y$) over time (X) to determine whether a linear trend model or an exponential trend model is more appropriate. (Hint: If the plot of $\log Y$ vs. X appears to be linear, an exponential trend model provides an appropriate fit.)
b. Compute the appropriate forecasting equation.
c. Forecast the value for 2012.

16.5 Autoregressive Modeling for Trend Fitting and Forecasting

Frequently, the values of a time series at particular points in time are highly correlated with the values that precede and succeed them. This type of correlation is called *autocorrelation*. When the autocorrelation exists between values that are in consecutive periods in a time series, the time series displays **first-order autocorrelation**. When the autocorrelation exists between values that are two periods apart, the time series displays **second-order autocorrelation**. For the general case in which the autocorrelation exists between values that are p periods apart, the time series displays **pth-order autocorrelation**.

Autoregressive modeling is a technique used to forecast time series that display autocorrelation.[2] This type of modeling uses a set of *lagged predictor variables* to overcome the problems that autocorrelation causes with other models. A **lagged predictor variable** takes its value from the value of predictor variable for another time period. For the general case of pth-order autocorrelation, you create a set of p lagged predictor variables such that the first lagged predictor variable takes its value from the value of a predictor variable that is one time period away, the *lag*; that the second lagged predictor variable takes its value from the value of a predictor variable that is two time periods away; and so on until the last, or pth, lagged predictor variable that takes its value from the value of a predictor variable that is p time periods away.

[2]The exponential smoothing model described in Section 16.3 and the autoregressive models described in this section are special cases of autoregressive integrated moving average (ARIMA) models developed by Box and Jenkins (see reference 2).

Equation (16.8) defines the **pth-order autoregressive model**. In the equation, $A_0, A_1, \ldots, A_p$ represent the parameters and $a_0, a_1, \ldots, a_p$ represent the corresponding regression coefficients. This is similar to the multiple regression model, Equation (14.1) on page 527, in which $\beta_0, \beta_1, \ldots, \beta_k$, represent the regression parameters and $b_0, b_1, \ldots, b_k$ represent the corresponding regression coefficients.

pTH-ORDER AUTOREGRESSIVE MODELS

$$Y_i = A_0 + A_1 Y_{i-1} + A_2 Y_{i-2} + \cdots + A_p Y_{i-p} + \delta_i \qquad \textbf{(16.8)}$$

where

Y_i = observed value of the series at time i

Y_{i-1} = observed value of the series at time $i - 1$

Y_{i-2} = observed value of the series at time $i - 2$

Y_{i-p} = observed value of the series at time $i - p$

p = number of autoregression parameters (not including a Y intercept) to be estimated from least-squares regression analysis

$A_0, A_1, A_2, \ldots, A_p$ = autoregression parameters to be estimated from least-squares regression analysis

δ_i = a nonautocorrelated random error component (with mean = 0 and constant variance)

Equations (16.9) and (16.10) define two specific autoregressive models. Equation (16.9) defines the **first-order autoregressive model** and is similar in form to the simple linear regression model, Equation (13.1) on page 472. Equation (16.10) defines the **second-order autoregressive model** and is similar to the multiple regression model with two independent variables, Equation (14.2) on page 527.

FIRST-ORDER AUTOREGRESSIVE MODEL

$$Y_i = A_0 + A_1 Y_{i-1} + \delta_i \qquad \textbf{(16.9)}$$

SECOND-ORDER AUTOREGRESSIVE MODEL

$$Y_i = A_0 + A_1 Y_{i-1} + A_2 Y_{i-2} + \delta_i \qquad \textbf{(16.10)}$$

Selecting an Appropriate Autoregressive Model

Selecting an appropriate autoregressive model can be complicated. You must weigh the advantages of using a simpler model against the concern of not taking into account important autocorrelation in the data. You also must be concerned with selecting a higher-order model that requires estimates of numerous parameters, some of which may be unnecessary, especially if n, the number of values in the series, is small. The reason for this concern is that when computing an estimate of A_p, you lose p out of the n data values when comparing each data value with the data value p periods earlier. Examples 16.5 and 16.6 illustrate this loss of data values.

EXAMPLE 16.5

Comparison Schema for a First-Order Autoregressive Model

Consider the following series of $n = 7$ consecutive annual values:

	Year						
	1	**2**	**3**	**4**	**5**	**6**	**7**
Series	31	34	37	35	36	43	40

Show the comparisons needed for a first-order autoregressive model.

SOLUTION

Year i	First-Order Autoregressive Model (Y_i vs. Y_{i-1})
1	$31 \leftrightarrow \ldots$
2	$34 \leftrightarrow 31$
3	$37 \leftrightarrow 34$
4	$35 \leftrightarrow 37$
5	$36 \leftrightarrow 35$
6	$43 \leftrightarrow 36$
7	$40 \leftrightarrow 43$

Because Y_1 is the first value and there is no value prior to it, Y_1 is not used in the regression analysis. Therefore, the first-order autoregressive model would be based on six pairs of values.

EXAMPLE 16.6

Comparison Schema for a Second-Order Autoregressive Model

Consider the following series of $n = 7$ consecutive annual values:

	Year						
	1	**2**	**3**	**4**	**5**	**6**	**7**
Series	31	34	37	35	36	43	40

Show the comparisons needed for a second-order autoregressive model.

SOLUTION

Year i	Second-Order Autoregressive Model (Y_i vs. Y_{i-1} and Y_i vs. Y_{i-2})
1	$31 \leftrightarrow \ldots$ and $31 \leftrightarrow \ldots$
2	$34 \leftrightarrow 31$ and $34 \leftrightarrow \ldots$
3	$37 \leftrightarrow 34$ and $37 \leftrightarrow 31$
4	$35 \leftrightarrow 37$ and $35 \leftrightarrow 34$
5	$36 \leftrightarrow 35$ and $36 \leftrightarrow 37$
6	$43 \leftrightarrow 36$ and $43 \leftrightarrow 35$
7	$40 \leftrightarrow 43$ and $40 \leftrightarrow 36$

Because no value is recorded prior to Y_1, the first two comparisons, each of which requires a value prior to Y_1, cannot be used when performing regression analysis. Therefore, the second-order autoregressive model would be based on five pairs of values.

Determining the Appropriateness of a Selected Model

After selecting a model and using the least-squares method to compute the regression coefficients, you need to determine the appropriateness of the model. Either you can select a particular pth-order autoregressive model based on previous experiences with similar data or start with a model that contains several autoregressive parameters and then eliminate the higher-order parameters that do not significantly contribute to the model. In this latter approach, you use a t test for the significance of A_p, the highest-order autoregressive parameter in the current model under consideration. The null and alternative hypotheses are

$$H_0: A_p = 0$$
$$H_1: A_p \neq 0$$

Equation (16.11) defines the test statistic.

t TEST FOR SIGNIFICANCE OF THE HIGHEST-ORDER AUTOREGRESSIVE PARAMETER, A_p

$$t_{STAT} = \frac{a_p - A_p}{S_{a_p}} \quad \textbf{(16.11)}$$

where

A_p = hypothesized value of the highest-order parameter, A_p, in the autoregressive model

a_p = regression coefficient that estimates the highest-order parameter, A_p, in the autoregressive model

S_{a_p} = standard deviation of a_p

The t_{STAT} test statistic follows a t distribution with $n - 2p - 1$ degrees of freedom.[3]

[3]In addition to the degrees of freedom lost for each of the p population parameters you are estimating, p additional degrees of freedom are lost because there are p fewer comparisons to be made from the original n values in the time series.

For a given level of significance, α, you reject the null hypothesis if the t_{STAT} test statistic is greater than the upper-tail critical value from the t distribution or if the t_{STAT} test statistic is less than the lower-tail critical value from the t distribution. Thus, the decision rule is

Reject H_0 if $t_{STAT} < -t_{\alpha/2}$ or if $t_{STAT} > t_{\alpha/2}$;

otherwise, do not reject H_0.

Figure 16.11 illustrates the decision rule and regions of rejection and nonrejection.

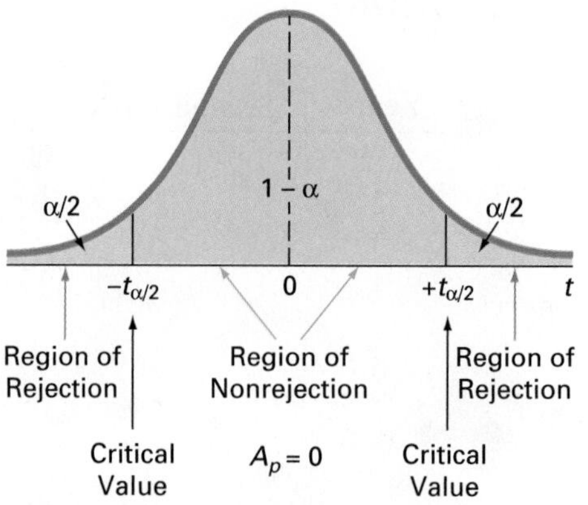

FIGURE 16.11
Rejection regions for a two-tail test for the significance of the highest-order autoregressive parameter A_p

If you do not reject the null hypothesis that $A_p = 0$, you conclude that the selected model contains too many estimated autoregressive parameters. You then discard the highest-order term and develop an autoregressive model of order $p - 1$, using the least-squares method.

You then repeat the test of the hypothesis that the new highest-order parameter is 0. This testing and modeling continues until you reject H_0. When this occurs, you can conclude that the remaining highest-order parameter is significant, and you can use that model for forecasting purposes.

Equation (16.12) defines the fitted pth-order autoregressive equation.

FITTED pTH-ORDER AUTOREGRESSIVE EQUATION

$$\hat{Y}_i = a_0 + a_1 Y_{i-1} + a_2 Y_{i-2} + \cdots + a_p Y_{i-p} \quad \textbf{(16.12)}$$

where

$\hat{Y}_i$ = fitted values of the series at time i

Y_{i-1} = observed value of the series at time $i - 1$

Y_{i-2} = observed value of the series at time $i - 2$

Y_{i-p} = observed value of the series at time $i - p$

p = number of autoregression parameters (not including a Y intercept) to be estimated from least-squares regression analysis

$a_0, a_1, a_2, \ldots, a_p$ = regression coefficients

You use Equation (16.13) to forecast j years into the future from the current nth time period.

pTH-ORDER AUTOREGRESSIVE FORECASTING EQUATION

$$\hat{Y}_{n+j} = a_0 + a_1 \hat{Y}_{n+j-1} + a_2 \hat{Y}_{n+j-2} + \cdots + a_p \hat{Y}_{n+j-p} \quad \textbf{(16.13)}$$

where

$a_0, a_1, a_2, \ldots, a_p$ = regression coefficients that estimate the parameters

p = number of autoregression parameters (not including a Y intercept) to be estimated from least-squares regression analysis

j = number of years into the future

$\hat{Y}_{n+j-p}$ = forecast of Y_{n+j-p} from the current year for $j - p > 0$

$\hat{Y}_{n+j-p}$ = observed value for Y_{n+j-p} for $j - p \leq 0$

Thus, to make forecasts j years into the future, using a third-order autoregressive model, you need only the most recent $p = 3$ values (Y_n, Y_{n-1}, and Y_{n-2}) and the regression estimates a_0, a_1, a_2, and a_3.

To forecast one year ahead, Equation (16.13) becomes

$$\hat{Y}_{n+1} = a_0 + a_1 Y_n + a_2 Y_{n-1} + a_3 Y_{n-2}$$

To forecast two years ahead, Equation (16.13) becomes

$$\hat{Y}_{n+2} = a_0 + a_1 \hat{Y}_{n+1} + a_2 Y_n + a_3 Y_{n-1}$$

To forecast three years ahead, Equation (16.13) becomes

$$\hat{Y}_{n+3} = a_0 + a_1 \hat{Y}_{n+2} + a_2 \hat{Y}_{n+1} + a_3 Y_n$$

and so on.

Autoregressive modeling is a powerful forecasting technique for time series that have autocorrelation. To summarize, you construct an autoregressive model by following these steps:

Use the Section EG15.6 instructions to construct autoregressive models.

1. Choose a value for p, the highest-order parameter in the autoregressive model to be evaluated, realizing that the t test for significance is based on $n - 2p - 1$ degrees of freedom.
2. Create a set of p lagged predictor variables. (See Figure 16.12 for an example.)
3. Perform a least-squares analysis of the multiple regression model containing all p lagged predictor variables using Excel.
4. Test for the significance of A_p, the highest-order autoregressive parameter in the model.
5. If you do not reject the null hypothesis, discard the pth variable and repeat steps 3 and 4. The test for the significance of the new highest-order parameter is based on a t distribution whose degrees of freedom are revised to correspond with the revised number of predictors.

   If you reject the null hypothesis, select the autoregressive model with all p predictors for fitting [see Equation (16.12)] and forecasting [see Equation (16.13)].

Student Tip
Remember that in an autoregressive model, the independent variable(s) are equal to the dependent variable lagged by a certain number of time periods.

To demonstrate the autoregressive modeling approach, return to the time series concerning the revenues for The Coca-Cola Company over the 17-year period 1995 through 2011. Figure 16.12 displays a worksheet that organizes the data for the first-order, second-order, and third-order autoregressive models. The worksheet contains the lagged predictor variables Lag1, Lag2, and Lag3 in columns C, D, and E. Use all three lagged predictors to fit the third-order autoregressive model. Use only Lag1 and Lag2 to fit the second-order autoregressive model, and use only Lag1 to fit the first-order autoregressive models. Thus, out of $n = 17$ values, $p = 1, 2,$ or 3 values out of $n = 17$ are lost in the comparisons needed for developing the first-order, second-order, and third-order autoregressive models.

FIGURE 16.12
Worksheet data for developing first-order, second-order, and third-order autoregressive models of the revenues for The Coca-Cola Company (1995–2011)

	A	B	C	D	E
1	Year	Revenue	Lag1	Lag2	Lag3
2	1995	18.0	#N/A	#N/A	#N/A
3	1996	18.5	18.0	#N/A	#N/A
4	1997	18.9	18.5	18.0	#N/A
5	1998	18.8	18.9	18.5	18.0
6	1999	19.8	18.8	18.9	18.5
7	2000	20.5	19.8	18.8	18.9
8	2001	20.1	20.5	19.8	18.8
9	2002	19.6	20.1	20.5	19.8
10	2003	21.0	19.6	20.1	20.5
11	2004	21.9	21.0	19.6	20.1
12	2005	23.1	21.9	21.0	19.6
13	2006	24.1	23.1	21.9	21.0
14	2007	28.9	24.1	23.1	21.9
15	2008	31.9	28.9	24.1	23.1
16	2009	31.0	31.9	28.9	24.1
17	2010	35.1	31.0	31.9	28.9
18	2011	46.5	35.1	31.0	31.9

Selecting an autoregressive model that best fits the annual time series begins with the third-order autoregressive model shown in Figure 16.13.

FIGURE 16.13
Regression results worksheets for a third-order autoregressive model for The Coca-Cola Company revenues

Use the Section EG16.5 instructions to construct autoregressive models.

	A	B	C	D	E	F	G
1	Third-Order Autoregressive Model for The Coca-Cola Company Revenues						
2							
3	*Regression Statistics*						
4	Multiple R	0.9897					
5	R Square	0.9795					
6	Adjusted R Square	0.9734					
7	Standard Error	1.2971					
8	Observations	14					
9							
10	ANOVA						
11		*df*	*SS*	*MS*	*F*	*Significance F*	
12	Regression	3	804.3797	268.1266	159.3727	0.0000	
13	Residual	10	16.8239	1.6824			
14	Total	13	821.2036				
15							
16		*Coefficients*	*Standard Error*	*t Stat*	*P-value*	*Lower 95%*	*Upper 95%*
17	Intercept	-12.0863	2.0603	-5.8662	0.0002	-16.6770	-7.4956
18	X Variable 1	1.1338	0.2354	4.8162	0.0007	0.6093	1.6584
19	X Variable 2	-1.1364	0.3321	-3.4222	0.0065	-1.8763	-0.3965
20	X Variable 3	1.6830	0.2858	5.8888	0.0002	1.0462	2.3198

From Figure 16.13, the fitted third-order autoregressive equation is

$$\hat{Y}_i = -12.0863 + 1.1338Y_{i-1} - 1.1364Y_{i-2} + 1.6830Y_{i-3}$$

where the first year in the series is 1998.

Next, you test for the significance of A_3, the highest-order parameter. The highest-order regression coefficient, a_3, for the fitted third-order autoregressive model is 1.683, with a standard error of 0.2858.

Student Tip
In many cases, the third-order autoregressive coefficient will not be significant. For such cases, you need to eliminate the third-order term and fit a second-order autoregressive model. If the second-order autoregressive coefficient is not significant, you eliminate the second-order term and fit a first-order autoregressive model.

To test the null hypothesis:

$$H_0: A_3 = 0$$

against the alternative hypothesis:

$$H_1: A_3 \neq 0$$

using Equation (16.11) on page 630 and the worksheet results given in Figure 16.13,

$$t_{STAT} = \frac{a_3 - A_3}{S_{a_3}} = \frac{1.683 - 0}{0.2858} = 5.8888$$

Using a 0.05 level of significance, the two-tail t test with $14 - 3 - 1 = 10$ degrees of freedom has critical values of ± 2.2281. Because $t_{STAT} = 5.8888 > +2.2281$ or because the p-value $= 0.0002 < 0.05$, you reject H_0. You conclude that the third-order parameter of the autoregressive model is significant and should remain in the model.

The model-building approach has led to the selection of the third-order autoregressive model as the most appropriate for the given data. Using the estimates $a_0 = -12.0863$, $a_1 = 1.1338$, $a_2 = -1.1364$, and $a_3 = 1.6830$, as well as the most recent data value $Y_{16} = 46.5$, the forecasts of revenues from Equation (16.13) on page 631 at The Coca-Cola Company for 2012 and 2013 are

$$\hat{Y}_{n+j} = -12.0863 + 1.1338\,\hat{Y}_{n+j-1} - 1.1364\hat{Y}_{n+j-2} + 1.6830\hat{Y}_{n+j-3}$$

Therefore, for 2012, one year ahead:

$$\hat{Y}_{17} = -12.0863 + 1.1338(46.5) - 1.1364(35.1) + 1.6830(31.0) = 52.9208 \text{ billions of dollars}$$

and for 2013, two years ahead:

$$\hat{Y}_{17} = -12.0863 + 1.1338(52.9208) - 1.1364(46.5) + 1.6830(35.1) = 54.146 \text{ billions of dollars}$$

Figure 16.14 displays the actual and predicted Y values from the third-order autoregressive model.

FIGURE 16.14
Plot of actual and predicted revenues from a third-order autoregressive model for The Coca-Cola Company

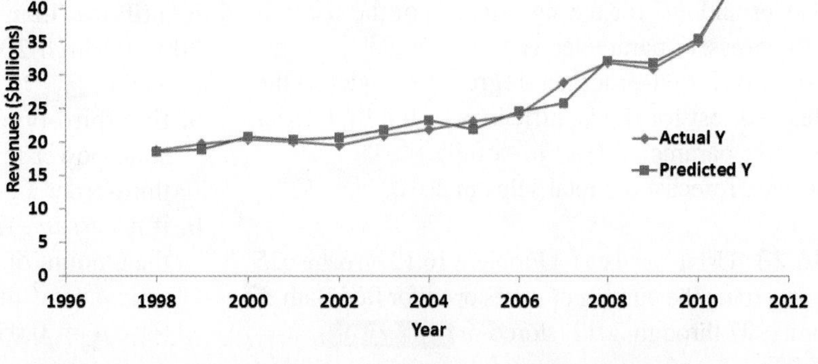

Problems for Section 16.5

LEARNING THE BASICS

16.23 You are given an annual time series with 40 consecutive values and asked to fit a fifth-order autoregressive model.

a. How many comparisons are lost in developing the autoregressive model?
b. How many parameters do you need to estimate?
c. Which of the original 40 values do you need for forecasting?
d. State the fifth-order autoregressive model.
e. Write an equation to indicate how you would forecast *j* years into the future.

16.24 A third-order autoregressive model is fitted to an annual time series with 17 values and has the following estimated parameters and standard errors:

$$a_0 = 4.50 \quad a_1 = 1.80 \quad a_2 = 0.80 \quad a_3 = 0.24$$

$$S_{a_1} = 0.50 \quad S_{a_2} = 0.30 \quad S_{a_3} = 0.10$$

At the 0.05 level of significance, test the appropriateness of the fitted model.

16.25 Refer to Problem 16.24. The three most recent values are

$$Y_{15} = 23 \quad Y_{16} = 28 \quad Y_{17} = 34$$

Forecast the values for the next year and the following year.

16.26 Refer to Problem 16.24. Suppose, when testing for the appropriateness of the fitted model, the standard errors are

$$S_{a_1} = 0.45 \quad S_{a_2} = 0.35 \quad S_{a_3} = 0.15$$

a. What conclusions can you reach?
b. Discuss how to proceed if forecasting is still your main objective.

APPLYING THE CONCEPTS

16.27 Using the data for Problem 16.15 on page 625 that represent U.S. total computer and software sales (in $millions) from 1992 through 2011 (stored in **ComputerSales**),

a. fit a third-order autoregressive model to the total sales and test for the significance of the third-order autoregressive parameter. (Use $\alpha = 0.05$.)
b. if necessary, fit a second-order autoregressive model to the total sales and test for the significance of the second-order autoregressive parameter. (Use $\alpha = 0.05$.)
c. if necessary, fit a first-order autoregressive model to the total sales and test for the significance of the first-order autoregressive parameter. (Use $\alpha = 0.05$.)
d. if appropriate, forecast the total sales in 2012.

SELF Test **16.28** Using the data for Problem 16.12 on page 625 concerning the number of stores open for Bed Bath & Beyond from 1997 through 2012 (stored in **Bed & Bath**),

a. fit a third-order autoregressive model to the number of stores and test for the significance of the third-order autoregressive parameter. (Use $\alpha = 0.05$.)
b. if necessary, fit a second-order autoregressive model to the number of stores and test for the significance of the second-order autoregressive parameter. (Use $\alpha = 0.05$.)
c. if necessary, fit a first-order autoregressive model to the number of stores and test for the significance of the first-order autoregressive parameter. (Use $\alpha = 0.05$.)
d. if appropriate, forecast the number of stores open in 2013 and 2014.

16.29 Using the data for Problem 16.17 on page 626 concerning the number of passenger cars produced in the United States from 1999 to 2011 (stored in **CarProduction**),

a. fit a third-order autoregressive model to the number of passenger cars produced in the United States and test for the significance of the third-order autoregressive parameter. (Use $\alpha = 0.05$.)
b. if necessary, fit a second-order autoregressive model to the number of passenger cars produced in the United States and test for the significance of the second-order autoregressive parameter. (Use $\alpha = 0.05$.)
c. if necessary, fit a first-order autoregressive model to the number of passenger cars produced in the United States and test for the significance of the first-order autoregressive parameter. (Use $\alpha = 0.05$.)
d. forecast the U.S. car production for 2012.

16.30 Using the average baseball salary from 2000 through 2012 data for Problem 16.18 on page 626 (stored in **BBSalaries**),

a. fit a third-order autoregressive model to the average baseball salary and test for the significance of the third-order autoregressive parameter. (Use $\alpha = 0.05$.)
b. if necessary, fit a second-order autoregressive model to the average baseball salary and test for the significance of the second-order autoregressive parameter. (Use $\alpha = 0.05$.)
c. if necessary, fit a first-order autoregressive model to the average baseball salary and test for the significance of the first-order autoregressive parameter. (Use $\alpha = 0.05$.)
d. forecast the average baseball salary for 2013.

16.31 Using the yearly amount of solar power generated by utilities (in millions of kWh) in the United States from 2002 through 2011 data for Problem 16.16 on page 626 (stored in **SolarPower**),

a. fit a third-order autoregressive model to the amount of solar power installed and test for the significance of the third-order autoregressive parameter. (Use $\alpha = 0.05$.)
b. if necessary, fit a second-order autoregressive model to the amount of solar power installed and test for the significance of the second-order autoregressive parameter. (Use $\alpha = 0.05$.)

c. if necessary, fit a first-order autoregressive model to the amount of solar power installed and test for the significance of the first-order autoregressive parameter. (Use $\alpha = 0.05$.)

d. forecast the yearly amount of solar power generated by utilities (in millions of kWh) in the United States in 2012 and 2013.

16.6 Choosing an Appropriate Forecasting Model

In Sections 16.4 and 16.5, you studied six time-series methods for forecasting: the linear trend model, the quadratic trend model, and the exponential trend model in Section 16.4; and the first-order, second-order, and *p*th-order autoregressive models in Section 16.5. Is there a *best* model? Among these models, which one should you select for forecasting? The following guidelines are provided for determining the adequacy of a particular forecasting model. These guidelines are based on a judgment of how well the model fits the data and assume that you can use past data to predict future values of the time series:

- Perform a residual analysis.
- Measure the magnitude of the residuals through squared differences.
- Measure the magnitude of the residuals through absolute differences.
- Use the principle of parsimony.

A discussion of these guidelines follows.

Performing a Residual Analysis

Recall from Sections 13.5 and 14.3 that residuals are the differences between observed and predicted values. After fitting a particular model to a time series, you plot the residuals over the n time periods. As shown in Figure 16.15 Panel A, if the particular model fits adequately, the residuals represent the irregular component of the time series. Therefore, they should be randomly distributed throughout the series. However, as illustrated in the three remaining panels of Figure 16.15, if the particular model does not fit adequately, the residuals may show a systematic pattern, such as a failure to account for trend (Panel B), a failure to account for cyclical variation (Panel C), or, with monthly or quarterly data, a failure to account for seasonal variation (Panel D).

FIGURE 16.15
Residual analysis for studying patterns of errors in regression models

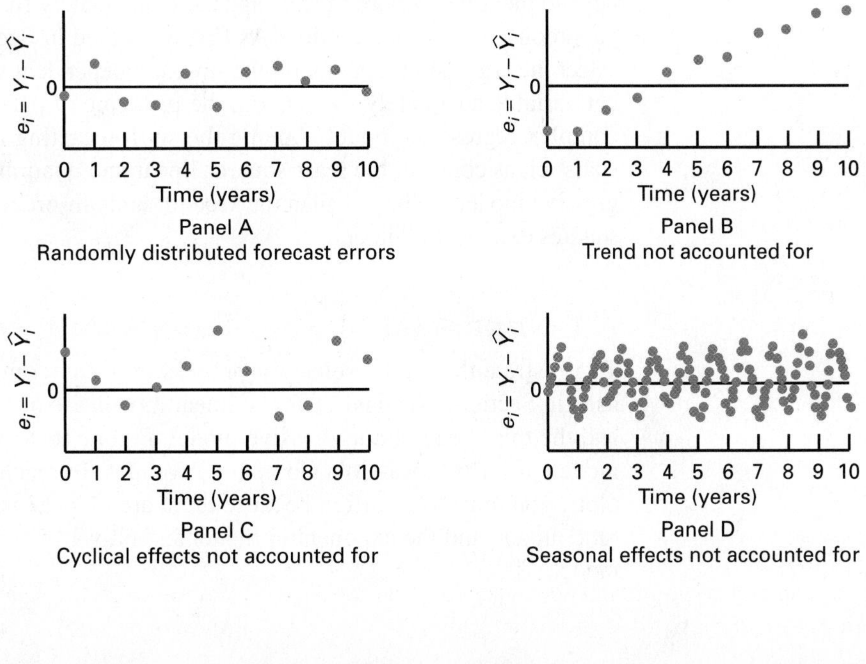

Measuring the Magnitude of the Residuals Through Squared or Absolute Differences

If, after performing a residual analysis, you still believe that two or more models appear to fit the data adequately, you can use additional methods for model selection. Numerous measures based on the residuals are available (see references 1 and 4).

In regression analysis (see Section 13.3), you have already used the standard error of the estimate S_{YX} as a measure of variation around the predicted values. For a particular model, this measure is based on the sum of squared differences between the actual and predicted values in a time series. If a model fits the time-series data perfectly, then the standard error of the estimate is zero. If a model fits the time-series data poorly, then S_{YX} is large. Thus, when comparing the adequacy of two or more forecasting models, you can select the model with the smallest S_{YX} as most appropriate.

However, a major drawback to using S_{YX} when comparing forecasting models is that whenever there is a large difference between even a single Y_i and $\hat{Y}_i$, the value of S_{YX} becomes overly inflated because the differences between Y_i and $\hat{Y}_i$ are squared. For this reason, many statisticians prefer the **mean absolute deviation (*MAD*)**. Equation (16.14) defines the *MAD* as the mean of the absolute differences between the actual and predicted values in a time series.

MEAN ABSOLUTE DEVIATION

$$MAD = \frac{\sum_{i=1}^{n} |Y_i - \hat{Y}_i|}{n} \tag{16.14}$$

If a model fits the time-series data perfectly, the *MAD* is zero. If a model fits the time-series data poorly, the *MAD* is large. When comparing two or more forecasting models, you can select the one with the smallest *MAD* as the most appropriate model.

Using the Principle of Parsimony

If, after performing a residual analysis and comparing the S_{YX} and *MAD* measures, you still believe that two or more models appear to adequately fit the data, you can use the principle of parsimony for model selection. As first explained in Section 15.4, **parsimony** guides you to select the regression model with the fewest independent variables that can predict the dependent variable adequately. In general, the principle of parsimony guides you to select the least complex regression model. Among the six forecasting models studied in this chapter, most statisticians consider the least-squares linear and quadratic models and the first-order autoregressive model as simpler than the second- and *p*th-order autoregressive models and the least-squares exponential model.

A Comparison of Four Forecasting Methods

To illustrate the model selection process, you can compare four of the forecasting models used in Sections 16.4 and 16.5: the linear model, the quadratic model, the exponential model, and the third-order autoregressive model. Figure 16.16 shows the residual plots for the four models for The Coca-Cola Company revenues. In reaching conclusions from these residual plots, you must use caution because there are only 17 values for the linear model, the quadratic model, and the exponential model and only 14 values for the third-order autoregressive model.

FIGURE 16.16
Residual plots for four forecasting models

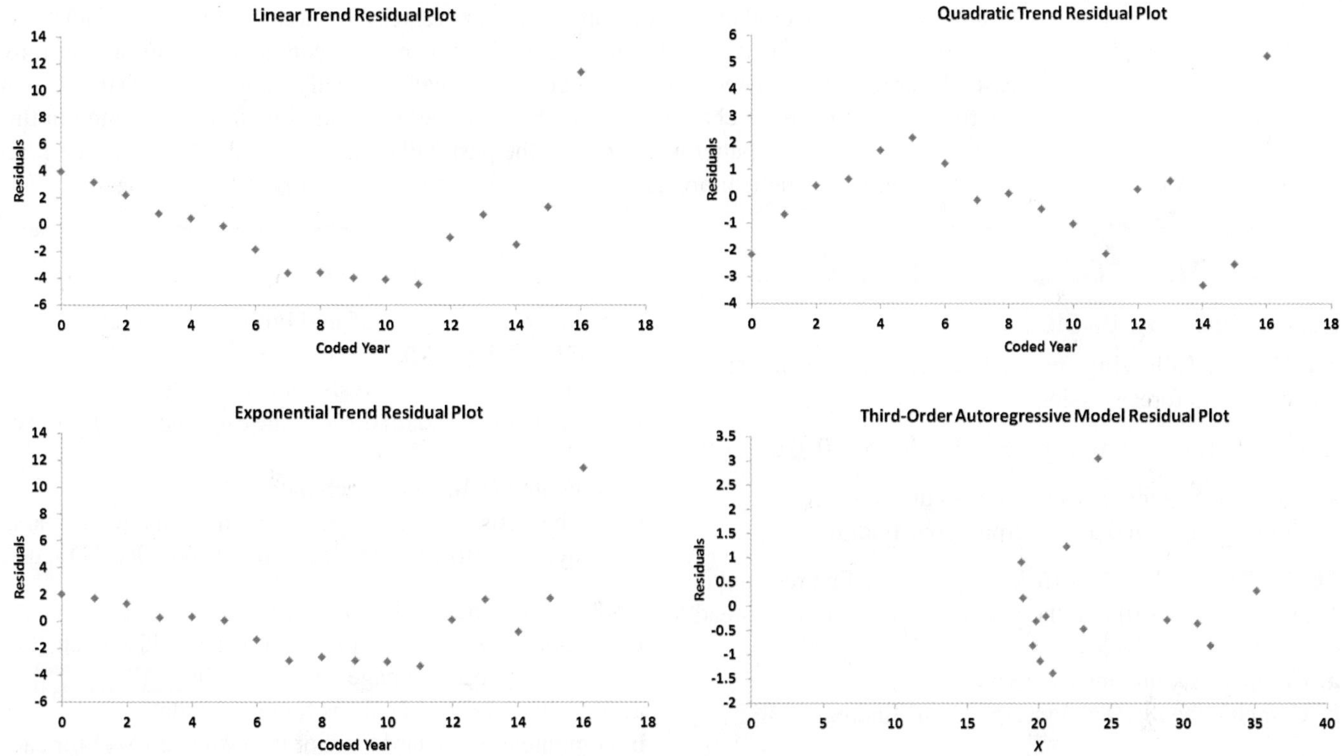

In Figure 16.16, observe that the residuals in the linear model, quadratic model, and exponential model are positive for the early years, negative for the intermediate years, and positive again for the latest years. For the autoregressive model, the residuals do not exhibit any systematic pattern.

To summarize, on the basis of the residual analysis of all four forecasting models, it appears that the third-order autoregressive model is the most appropriate, and the linear, quadratic, and exponential models are not appropriate. For further verification, you can compare the magnitude of the residuals in the four models. Figure 16.17 shows the actual values (Y_i) along with the predicted values $\hat{Y}_i$, the residuals (e_i), the error sum of squares (SSE), the standard error of the estimate (S_{YX}), and the mean absolute deviation (MAD) for each of the four models.

FIGURE 16.17
Comparison of four forecasting models using SSE, S_{YX}, and MAD

Use the Section EG16.6 instructions to construct model comparison worksheets.

	A	B	C	D	E	F	G	H	I	J
1			Linear		Quadratic		Exponential		Third-Order	
2	Year	Revenues	Predicted	Residual	Predicted	Residual	Predicted	Residual	Predicted	Residual
3	1995	18.0	14.0255	3.9745	20.1576	-2.1576	15.9519	2.0481	#N/A	#N/A
4	1996	18.5	15.3436	3.1564	19.1762	-0.6762	16.7564	1.7436	#N/A	#N/A
5	1997	18.9	16.6618	2.2382	18.5014	0.3986	17.6015	1.2985	#N/A	#N/A
6	1998	18.8	17.9799	0.8201	18.1332	0.6668	18.4893	0.3107	18.6149	0.1851
7	1999	19.8	19.2980	0.5020	18.0716	1.7284	19.4218	0.3782	18.8885	0.9115
8	2000	20.5	20.6162	-0.1162	18.3166	2.1834	20.4013	0.0987	20.8092	-0.3092
9	2001	20.1	21.9343	-1.8343	18.8683	1.2317	21.4303	-1.3303	20.2982	-0.1982
10	2002	19.6	23.2525	-3.6525	19.7265	-0.1265	22.5111	-2.9111	20.7322	-1.1322
11	2003	21.0	24.5706	-3.5706	20.8913	0.1087	23.6465	-2.6465	21.7980	-0.7980
12	2004	21.9	25.8887	-3.9887	22.3628	-0.4628	24.8391	-2.9391	23.2803	-1.3803
13	2005	23.1	27.2069	-4.1069	24.1408	-1.0408	26.0919	-2.9919	21.8683	1.2317
14	2006	24.1	28.5250	-4.4250	26.2255	-2.1255	27.4079	-3.3079	24.5624	-0.4624
15	2007	28.9	29.8431	-0.9431	28.6167	0.2833	28.7902	0.1098	25.8474	3.0526
16	2008	31.9	31.1613	0.7387	31.3146	0.5854	30.2422	1.6578	32.1731	-0.2731
17	2009	31.0	32.4794	-1.4794	34.3190	-3.3190	31.7675	-0.7675	31.8030	-0.8030
18	2010	35.1	33.7975	1.3025	37.6301	-2.5301	33.3697	1.7303	35.4519	-0.3519
19	2011	46.5	35.1157	11.3843	41.2478	5.2522	35.0527	11.4473	46.1726	0.3274
20			*SSE*	248.4411	*SSE*	66.2565	*SSE*	192.3338	*SSE*	16.8239
21			S_{YX}	4.0697	S_{YX}	2.1755	S_{YX}	3.5808	S_{YX}	1.2971
22			*MAD*	2.8373	*MAD*	1.4633	*MAD*	2.2187	*MAD*	0.8155

For this time series, S_{YX} and *MAD* provide fairly similar results. A comparison of the S_{YX} and *MAD* clearly indicates that the linear model provides the poorest fit followed by the exponential model and then the quadratic model. The third-order autoregressive model provides the best fit. Thus, you should choose the third-order autoregressive model as the best model.

After you select a particular forecasting model, you need to continually monitor your forecasts. If large errors between forecasted and actual values occur, the underlying structure of the time series may have changed. Remember that the forecasting methods presented in this chapter assume that the patterns inherent in the past will continue into the future. Large forecasting errors are an indication that this assumption may no longer be true.

Problems for Section 16.6

LEARNING THE BASICS

16.32 The following residuals are from a linear trend model used to forecast sales:

2.0 −0.5 1.5 1.0 0.0 1.0 −3.0 1.5 −4.5 2.0 0.0 −1.0

a. Compute S_{YX} and interpret your findings.
b. Compute the *MAD* and interpret your findings.

16.33 Refer to Problem 16.32. Suppose the first residual is 12.0 (instead of 2.0) and the last residual is −11.0 (instead of −1.0).
a. Compute S_{YX} and interpret your findings
b. Compute the *MAD* and interpret your findings.

APPLYING THE CONCEPTS

16.34 Using the yearly amount of solar power generated by utilities (in millions of kWh) in the United States from 2002 through 2011 data for Problem 16.16 on page 626 and Problem 16.31 on page 634 (stored in SolarPower),
a. perform a residual analysis.
b. compute the standard error of the estimate (S_{YX}).
c. compute the *MAD*.
d. On the basis of (a) through (c), and the principle of parsimony, which forecasting model would you select? Discuss.

16.35 Using the U.S. total computer and software sales data for Problem 16.15 on page 625 and Problem 16.27 on page 634 (stored in ComputerSales),
a. perform a residual analysis for each model.
b. compute the standard error of the estimate (S_{YX}) for each model.
c. compute the *MAD* for each model.
d. On the basis of (a) through (c) and the principle of parsimony, which forecasting model would you select? Discuss.

SELF Test **16.36** Using the number of stores open for Bed Bath & Beyond from 1997 through 2012 data for Problem 16.12 on page 625 and Problem 16.28 on page 634 (stored in Bed & Bath),
a. perform a residual analysis for each model.
b. compute the standard error of the estimate (S_{YX}) for each model.
c. compute the *MAD* for each model.
d. On the basis of (a) through (c) and the principle of parsimony, which forecasting model would you select? Discuss.

16.37 Using the number of passenger cars produced in the U.S. from 1999 to 2011 data for Problem 16.17 on page 626 and Problem 16.29 on page 634 (stored in CarProduction),
a. perform a residual analysis for each model.
b. compute the standard error of the estimate (S_{YX}) for each model.
c. compute the *MAD* for each model.
d. On the basis of (a) through (c) and the principle of parsimony, which forecasting model would you select? Discuss.

16.38 Using the average baseball salary from 2000 through 2012 data for Problem 16.18 on page 626 and Problem 16.30 on page 634 (stored in BBSalaries),
a. perform a residual analysis for each model.
b. compute the standard error of the estimate (S_{YX}) for each model.
c. compute the *MAD* for each model.
d. On the basis of (a) through (c) and the principle of parsimony, which forecasting model would you select? Discuss.

16.39 Refer to the results for Problem 16.13 on page 625 that used the file GDP,
a. perform a residual analysis.
b. compute the standard error of the estimate (S_{YX}).
c. compute the *MAD*.
d. On the basis of (a) through (c), are you satisfied with your linear trend forecasts in Problem 16.13? Discuss.

16.7 Time-Series Forecasting of Seasonal Data

So far, this chapter has focused on forecasting annual data. However, many time series are collected quarterly or monthly, and others are collected weekly, daily, and even hourly. When a time series is collected quarterly or monthly, you must consider the impact of seasonal effects. In this section, regression model building is used to forecast monthly or quarterly data.

One of the companies of interest in the Using Statistics scenario is Wal-Mart Stores, Inc. In 2012, according to the company's website, Wal-Mart Stores, Inc., operated more than 10,000 retail units in 27 countries and had revenues that exceeded $400 billion. Wal-Mart revenues are highly seasonal, and therefore you need to analyze quarterly revenues. The fiscal year for the company ends January 31. Thus, the fourth quarter of 2012 includes November and December 2011 as well as January 2012. Table 16.3 lists the quarterly revenues (in $billions) from 2007 to 2012 that are stored in Walmart. Figure 16.18 displays the time series.

TABLE 16.3
Quarterly Revenues (in $billions) for Wal-Mart Stores, Inc., 2007–2012

	Year					
Quarter	2007	2008	2009	2010	2011	2012
1	79.6	86.4	95.3	93.5	99.1	103.4
2	84.5	93.0	102.7	100.9	103.0	108.6
3	83.5	91.9	98.6	99.4	101.2	109.5
4	98.1	107.3	107.9	113.7	115.6	122.3

Source: Data extracted from Wal-Mart Stores, Inc., **walmartstores.com**.

FIGURE 16.18
Plot of quarterly revenues ($billions) for Wal-Mart Stores, Inc., 2007–2012

Use the Section EG2.5 instructions to construct time-series plots.

Least-Squares Forecasting with Monthly or Quarterly Data

To develop a least-squares regression model that includes a seasonal component, the least-squares exponential trend fitting method used in Section 16.4 is combined with dummy variables (see Section 14.6) to model the seasonal component.

Equation (16.15) defines the exponential trend model for quarterly data.

EXPONENTIAL MODEL WITH QUARTERLY DATA

$$Y_i = \beta_0 \beta_1^{X_i} \beta_2^{Q_1} \beta_3^{Q_2} \beta_4^{Q_3} \varepsilon_i \tag{16.15}$$

where

X_i = coded quarterly value, $i = 0, 1, 2, \ldots$
Q_1 = 1 if first quarter, 0 if not first quarter
Q_2 = 1 if second quarter, 0 if not second quarter
Q_3 = 1 if third quarter, 0 if not third quarter
β_0 = Y intercept
$(\beta_1 - 1) \times 100\%$ = quarterly compound growth rate (in %)
β_2 = multiplier for first quarter relative to fourth quarter
β_3 = multiplier for second quarter relative to fourth quarter
β_4 = multiplier for third quarter relative to fourth quarter
ε_i = value of the irregular component for time period i

[4]Alternatively, you can use base e logarithms. For more information on logarithms, see Section A.3 in Appendix A.

The model in Equation (16.15) is not in the form of a linear regression model. To transform this nonlinear model to a linear model, you use a base 10 logarithmic transformation.[4] Taking the logarithm of each side of Equation (16.15) results in Equation (16.16).

TRANSFORMED EXPONENTIAL MODEL WITH QUARTERLY DATA

$$\begin{aligned}\log(Y_i) &= \log(\beta_0\beta_1^{X_i}\beta_2^{Q_1}\beta_3^{Q_2}\beta_4^{Q_3}\varepsilon_i) \qquad (16.16)\\ &= \log(\beta_0) + \log(\beta_1^{X_i}) + \log(\beta_2^{Q_1}) + \log(\beta_3^{Q_2}) + \log(\beta_4^{Q_3}) + \log(\varepsilon_i)\\ &= \log(\beta_0) + X_i\log(\beta_1) + Q_1\log(\beta_2) + Q_2\log(\beta_3) + Q_3\log(\beta_4) + \log(\varepsilon_i)\end{aligned}$$

Equation (16.16) is a linear model that you can estimate using least-squares regression. Performing the regression analysis using $\log(Y_i)$ as the dependent variable and X_i, Q_1, Q_2, and Q_3 as the independent variables results in Equation (16.17).

EXPONENTIAL GROWTH WITH QUARTERLY DATA FORECASTING EQUATION

$$\log(\hat{Y}_i) = b_0 + b_1X_i + b_2Q_1 + b_3Q_2 + b_4Q_3 \qquad (16.17)$$

where

$$\begin{aligned} b_0 &= \text{estimate of } \log(\beta_0) \text{ and thus } 10^{b_0} = \hat{\beta}_0\\ b_1 &= \text{estimate of } \log(\beta_1) \text{ and thus } 10^{b_1} = \hat{\beta}_1\\ b_2 &= \text{estimate of } \log(\beta_2) \text{ and thus } 10^{b_2} = \hat{\beta}_2\\ b_3 &= \text{estimate of } \log(\beta_3) \text{ and thus } 10^{b_3} = \hat{\beta}_3\\ b_4 &= \text{estimate of } \log(\beta_4) \text{ and thus } 10^{b_4} = \hat{\beta}_4\end{aligned}$$

Equation (16.18) is used for monthly data.

EXPONENTIAL MODEL WITH MONTHLY DATA

$$Y_i = \beta_0\beta_1^{X_i}\beta_2^{M_1}\beta_3^{M_2}\beta_4^{M_3}\beta_5^{M_4}\beta_6^{M_5}\beta_7^{M_6}\beta_8^{M_7}\beta_9^{M_8}\beta_{10}^{M_9}\beta_{11}^{M_{10}}\beta_{12}^{M_{11}}\varepsilon_i \qquad (16.18)$$

where

$$\begin{aligned} X_i &= \text{coded monthly value, } i = 0, 1, 2, \ldots\\ M_1 &= 1 \text{ if January, 0 if not January}\\ M_2 &= 1 \text{ if February, 0 if not February}\\ M_3 &= 1 \text{ if March, 0 if not March}\\ &\vdots\\ M_{11} &= 1 \text{ if November, 0 if not November}\\ \beta_0 &= Y \text{ intercept}\\ (\beta_1 - 1) \times 100\% &= \text{monthly compound growth rate (in \%)}\\ \beta_2 &= \text{multiplier for January relative to December}\\ \beta_3 &= \text{multiplier for February relative to December}\\ \beta_4 &= \text{multiplier for March relative to December}\\ &\vdots\\ \beta_{12} &= \text{multiplier for November relative to December}\\ \varepsilon_i &= \text{value of the irregular component for time period } i\end{aligned}$$

The model in Equation (16.18) is not in the form of a linear regression model. To transform this nonlinear model into a linear model, you can use a base 10 logarithm transformation. Taking the logarithm of each side of Equation (16.18) results in Equation (16.19).

TRANSFORMED EXPONENTIAL MODEL WITH MONTHLY DATA

$$\begin{aligned}\log(Y_i) &= \log(\beta_0 \beta_1^{X_i} \beta_2^{M_1} \beta_3^{M_2} \beta_4^{M_3} \beta_5^{M_4} \beta_6^{M_5} \beta_7^{M_6} \beta_8^{M_7} \beta_9^{M_8} \beta_{10}^{M_9} \beta_{11}^{M_{10}} \beta_{12}^{M_{11}} \varepsilon_i) \\ &= \log(\beta_0) + X_i \log(\beta_1) + M_1 \log(\beta_2) + M_2 \log(\beta_3) \\ &\quad + M_3 \log(\beta_4) + M_4 \log(\beta_5) + M_5 \log(\beta_6) + M_6 \log(\beta_7) \\ &\quad + M_7 \log(\beta_8) + M_8 \log(\beta_9) + M_9 \log(\beta_{10}) + M_{10} \log(\beta_{11}) \\ &\quad + M_{11} \log(\beta_{12}) + \log(\varepsilon_i)\end{aligned} \quad \textbf{(16.19)}$$

Equation (16.19) is a linear model that you can estimate using the least-squares method. Performing the regression analysis using $\log(Y_i)$ as the dependent variable and $X_i, M_1, M_2, \ldots,$ and M_{11} as the independent variables results in Equation (16.20).

EXPONENTIAL GROWTH WITH MONTHLY DATA FORECASTING EQUATION

$$\begin{aligned}\log(\hat{Y}_i) &= b_0 + b_1 X_i + b_2 M_1 + b_3 M_2 + b_4 M_3 + b_5 M_4 + b_6 M_5 + b_7 M_6 \\ &\quad + b_8 M_7 + b_9 M_8 + b_{10} M_9 + b_{11} M_{10} + b_{12} M_{11}\end{aligned} \quad \textbf{(16.20)}$$

where

b_0 = estimate of $\log(\beta_0)$ and thus $10^{b_0} = \hat{\beta}_0$
b_1 = estimate of $\log(\beta_1)$ and thus $10^{b_1} = \hat{\beta}_1$
b_2 = estimate of $\log(\beta_2)$ and thus $10^{b_2} = \hat{\beta}_2$
b_3 = estimate of $\log(\beta_3)$ and thus $10^{b_3} = \hat{\beta}_3$
⋮
b_{12} = estimate of $\log(\beta_{12})$ and thus $10^{b_{12}} = \hat{\beta}_{12}$

Q_1, Q_2, and Q_3 are the three dummy variables needed to represent the four quarter periods in a quarterly time series. $M_1, M_2, M_3, \ldots, M_{11}$ are the 11 dummy variables needed to represent the 12 months in a monthly time series. In building the model, you use $\log(Y_i)$ instead of Y_i values and then find the regression coefficients by taking the antilog of the regression coefficients developed from Equations (16.17) and (16.20).

Although at first glance these regression models look imposing, when fitting or forecasting for any one time period, the values of all or all but one of the dummy variables in the model are equal to zero, and the equations simplify dramatically. In establishing the dummy variables for quarterly time-series data, the fourth quarter is the base period and has a coded value of zero for each dummy variable. With a quarterly time series, Equation (16.17) reduces as follows:

For any first quarter: $\log(\hat{Y}_i) = b_0 + b_1 X_i + b_2$
For any second quarter: $\log(\hat{Y}_i) = b_0 + b_1 X_i + b_3$
For any third quarter: $\log(\hat{Y}_i) = b_0 + b_1 X_i + b_4$
For any fourth quarter: $\log(\hat{Y}_i) = b_0 + b_1 X_i$

When establishing the dummy variables for each month, December serves as the base period and has a coded value of 0 for each dummy variable. For example, with a monthly time series, Equation (16.20) reduces as follows:

For any January: $\log(\hat{Y}_i) = b_0 + b_1X_i + b_2$

For any February: $\log(\hat{Y}_i) = b_0 + b_1X_i + b_3$

$\vdots$

For any November: $\log(\hat{Y}_i) = b_0 + b_1X_i + b_{12}$

For any December: $\log(\hat{Y}_i) = b_0 + b_1X_i$

To demonstrate the process of model building and least-squares forecasting with a quarterly time series, return to the Wal-Mart Stores, Inc., revenue data (in billions of dollars) originally displayed in Table 16.3 on page 639. The data are from the first quarter of 2007 through the last quarter of 2012. Figure 16.19 shows the regression results for the quarterly exponential trend model.

FIGURE 16.19
Regression results worksheet for the quarterly revenue data for Wal-Mart Stores, Inc.

	A	B	C	D	E	F	G
1	Quarterly Revenue Model for Wal-Mart Stores						
2							
3	Regression Statistics						
4	Multiple R	0.9670					
5	R Square	0.9351					
6	Adjusted R Square	0.9214					
7	Standard Error	0.0129					
8	Observations	24					
9							
10	ANOVA						
11		df	SS	MS	F	Significance F	
12	Regression	4	0.0459	0.0115	68.4206	0.0000	
13	Residual	19	0.0032	0.0002			
14	Total	23	0.0491				
15							
16		Coefficients	Standard Error	t Stat	P-value	Lower 95%	Upper 95%
17	Intercept	1.9803	0.0073	271.4032	0.0000	1.9650	1.9956
18	Coded Quarter	0.0049	0.0004	12.5772	0.0000	0.0041	0.0057
19	Q1	-0.0627	0.0076	-8.2818	0.0000	-0.0785	-0.0468
20	Q2	-0.0406	0.0075	-5.4015	0.0000	-0.0563	-0.0249
21	Q3	-0.0519	0.0075	-6.9328	0.0000	-0.0676	-0.0362

From Figure 16.19, the model fits the data very well. The coefficient of determination $r^2 = 0.9351$, the adjusted $r^2 = 0.9214$, and the overall F test results in an F_{STAT} test statistic of 68.4206 (p-value $= 0.000$). At the 0.05 level of significance, each regression coefficient is highly statistically significant and contributes to the model. The following summary includes the antilogs of all the regression coefficients:

Regression Coefficient	$b_i = \log \hat{\beta}_i$	$\hat{\beta}_i = \text{antilog}(b_i) = 10^{b_i}$
b_0: Y intercept	1.9803	95.5652
b_1: coded quarter	0.0049	1.0113
b_2: first quarter	−0.0627	0.8656
b_3: second quarter	−0.0406	0.9108
b_4: third quarter	−0.0519	0.8874

The interpretations for $\hat{\beta}_0$, $\hat{\beta}_1$, $\hat{\beta}_2$, $\hat{\beta}_3$, and $\hat{\beta}_4$ are as follows:

- The Y intercept, $\hat{\beta}_0 = 95.5652$ (in \$billions), is the *unadjusted* forecast for quarterly revenues in the first quarter of 2007, the initial quarter in the time series. *Unadjusted* means that the seasonal component is not incorporated in the forecast.

- The value $(\hat{\beta}_1 - 1) \times 100\% = 0.0113$, or 1.13%, is the estimated *quarterly compound growth rate* in revenues, after adjusting for the seasonal component.
- $\hat{\beta}_2 = 0.8656$ is the seasonal multiplier for the first quarter relative to the fourth quarter; it indicates that there is 13.44% less revenue for the first quarter than for the fourth quarter.
- $\hat{\beta}_3 = 0.9108$ is the seasonal multiplier for the second quarter relative to the fourth quarter; it indicates that there is 8.92% less revenue for the second quarter than for the fourth quarter.
- $\hat{\beta}_4 = 0.8874$ is the seasonal multiplier for the third quarter relative to the fourth quarter; it indicates that there is 11.26% less revenue for the third quarter than for the fourth quarter. Thus, the fourth quarter, which includes the holiday shopping season, has the strongest sales.

Using the regression coefficients b_0, b_1, b_2, b_3, and b_4, and Equation (16.17) on page 640, you can make forecasts for selected quarters. As an example, to predict revenues for the fourth quarter of 2012 ($X_i = 23$),

$$\begin{aligned}\log(\hat{Y}_i) &= b_0 + b_1X_i \\ &= 1.9803 + (0.0049)(23) \\ &= 2.093\end{aligned}$$

Thus,

$$\log(\hat{Y}_i) = 10^{2.093} = 123.8797$$

The predicted revenue for the fourth quarter of fiscal 2012 is \$123.8797 billion. To make a forecast for a future time period, such as the first quarter of fiscal 2013 ($X_i = 24$, $Q_1 = 1$),

$$\begin{aligned}\log(\hat{Y}_i) &= b_0 + b_1X_i + b_2Q_1 \\ &= 1.9803 + (0.0049)(24) + (-0.0627)(1) \\ &= 2.0352\end{aligned}$$

Thus,

$$\hat{Y}_i = 10^{2.0352} = 108.4426$$

The predicted revenue for the first quarter of fiscal 2013 is \$108.4426 billion.

Problems for Section 16.7

LEARNING THE BASICS

16.40 In forecasting a monthly time series over a five-year period from January 2008 to December 2012, the exponential trend forecasting equation for January is

$$\log \hat{Y}_i = 2.0 + 0.01X_i + 0.10(\text{January})$$

Take the antilog of the appropriate coefficient from this equation and interpret the

a. *Y* intercept, $\hat{b}_0$.
b. monthly compound growth rate.
c. January multiplier.

16.41 In forecasting daily time-series data, how many dummy variables are needed to account for the seasonal component day of the week?

16.42 In forecasting a quarterly time series over the five-year period from the first quarter of 2008 through the fourth quarter of 2012, the exponential trend forecasting equation is given by

$$\log \hat{Y}_i = 3.0 + 0.10X_i - 0.25Q_1 + 0.20Q_2 + 0.15Q_3$$

where quarter zero is the first quarter of 2008. Take the antilog of the appropriate coefficient from this equation and interpret the

a. *Y* intercept, $\hat{b}_0$.
b. quarterly compound growth rate.
c. second-quarter multiplier.

16.43 Refer to the exponential model given in Problem 16.42.

a. What is the fitted value of the series in the fourth quarter of 2010?

b. What is the fitted value of the series in the first quarter of 2010?

c. What is the forecast in the fourth quarter of 2012?

d. What is the forecast in the first quarter of 2013?

APPLYING THE CONCEPTS

SELF Test **16.44** The data in Toys R Us are quarterly revenues (in $millions) for Toys R Us from 1996-Q1 through 2012-Q2. (Data extracted from *Standard & Poor's Stock Reports*, November 1995, November 1998, and April 2002, and Toys R Us, Inc., **www.toysrus.com**.)

a. Do you think that the revenues for Toys R Us are subject to seasonal variation? Explain.

b. Plot the data. Does this chart support your answer in (a)?

c. Develop an exponential trend forecasting equation with quarterly components.

d. Interpret the quarterly compound growth rate.

e. Interpret the quarterly multipliers.

f. What are the forecasts for 2012-Q3, 2012-Q4, and all four quarters of 2013?

16.45 Are gasoline prices higher during the height of the summer vacation season than at other times? The file GasPrices contains the mean monthly prices (in $/gallon) for unleaded gasoline in the United States from January 2006 to July 2012. (Data extracted from U.S. Energy Information Administration, **www.eia.doe.gov/petroleum/data.ctm**.)

a. Construct a time-series plot.

b. Develop an exponential trend forecasting equation with monthly components.

c. Interpret the monthly compound growth rate.

d. Interpret the monthly multipliers.

e. Write a short summary of your findings.

16.46 The data in Travel show the average traffic on Google recorded at the beginning of each month from January 2004 to August 2012 for searches from the United States concerning travel (scaled to the average traffic for the entire time period based on a fixed point at the beginning of the time period). (Data retrieved from Google Trends, **www.google.com/trends**, August 13, 2012.)

a. Plot the time-series data.

b. Develop an exponential trend forecasting equation with monthly components.

c. What is the fitted value in August 2012?

d. What are the forecasts for the last four months of 2012?

e. Interpret the monthly compound growth rate.

f. Interpret the July multiplier.

16.47 The file CallCenter contains the monthly call volume for an existing product. (Data extracted from S. Madadevan and J. Overstreet, "Use of Warranty and Reliability Data to Inform Call Center Staffing," *Quality Engineering* 24 (2012): 386–399.)

a. Construct the time-series plot.

b. Describe the monthly pattern in the data.

c. In general, would you say that the overall call volume is increasing or decreasing? Explain.

d. Develop an exponential trend forecasting equation with monthly components.

e. Interpret the monthly compound growth rate.

f. Interpret the January multiplier.

g. What is the predicted call volume for month 60?

h. What is the predicted call volume for month 61?

i. How can this type of time-series forecasting benefit the call center?

16.48 The file Silver-Q contains the price in London for an ounce of silver (in US$) at the end of each quarter from 2004 through 2011. (Data extracted from **bit.ly/1afifi**.)

a. Plot the data.

b. Develop an exponential trend forecasting equation with quarterly components.

c. Interpret the quarterly compound growth rate.

d. Interpret the first quarter multiplier.

e. What is the fitted value for the last quarter of 2011?

f. What are the forecasts for all four quarters of 2012?

g. Are the forecasts in (f) accurate? Explain.

16.49 The file Gold contains the price in London for an ounce of gold (in US$) at the end of each quarter from 2004 through 2011. (Data extracted from **bit.ly/1afifi**.)

a. Plot the data.

b. Develop an exponential trend forecasting equation with quarterly components.

c. Interpret the quarterly compound growth rate.

d. Interpret the first quarter multiplier.

e. What is the fitted value for the last quarter of 2011?

f. What are the forecasts for all four quarters of 2012?

g. Are the forecasts in (f) accurate? Explain.

16.8 Index Numbers (*online*)

LEARN MORE

Learn more about this in a Chapter 16 eBook bonus section.

An index number measures the value of an item (or group of items) at a particular point in time as a percentage of the value of an item (or group of items) at another point in time.

THINK ABOUT THIS Let the Model User Beware

When you use a model, you must always review the assumptions built into the model and must always reflect how novel or changing circumstances may render the model less useful. No model can completely remove the risk involved in making a decision.

Implicit in the time-series models developed in this chapter is that past data can be used to help predict the future. While using past data in this way is a legitimate application of time-series models, every so often, a crisis in financial markets illustrates that using models that rely on the past to predict the future is not without risk.

For example, during August 2007, many hedge funds suffered unprecedented losses. Apparently, many hedge fund managers used models that based their investment strategy on trading patterns over long time periods. These models did not—and could not—reflect trading patterns contrary to historical patterns (G. Morgenson, "A Week When Risk Came Home to Roost," *The New York Times*, August 12, 2007, pp. B1, B7). When fund managers in early August 2007 needed to sell stocks due to losses in their fixed income portfolios, stocks that were previously stronger became weaker, and weaker ones became stronger—the reverse of what the models expected. Making matters worse was the fact that many fund managers were using similar models and rigidly made investment decisions solely based on what those models said. These similar actions multiplied the effect of the selling pressure, an effect that the models had not considered and that therefore could not be seen in the models' results.

This example illustrates that using models does not absolve you of the responsibility of being a thoughtful decision maker. Go ahead and use models—when appropriately used, they will enhance your decision making—but don't use them mindlessly, for, in the words of a famous public service announcement, "a mind is a terrible thing to waste."

USING STATISTICS Principled Forecasting, Revisited

In the Using Statistics scenario, you were the financial analyst for The Principled, a large financial services company. You needed to forecast movie attendance, revenues for Coca-Cola, and for Wal-Mart to better evaluate investment opportunities for your clients.

For movie attendance, you used moving averages and exponential smoothing methods to develop forecasts. You predicted that the movie attendance in 2012 would be 1.38 billion.

For The Coca-Cola Company, you used least-squares linear, quadratic, and exponential models and autoregressive models to develop forecasts. You evaluated these alternative models and determined that the third-order autoregressive model gave the best forecast, according to several criteria. You predicted that the revenue of The Coca-Cola Company would be $52.9208 billion in 2012 and $54.146 billion in 2013.

For Wal-Mart Stores, Inc., you used a least-squares regression model with seasonal components to develop forecasts. You predicted that Wal-Mart Stores would have revenues of $108.4426 billion in the first quarter of fiscal 2013.

Given these forecasts, you now need to determine whether your clients should invest, and if so, how much they should invest in the movie industry or in The Coca-Cola Company or in Wal-Mart Stores, Inc.

SUMMARY

In this chapter, you studied smoothing techniques, least-squares trend fitting, autoregressive models, and forecasting of seasonal data. Figure 16.20 on page 646 provides a summary chart for the time-series methods discussed in this chapter.

When using time-series forecasting, you need to plot the time series and answer the following question: Is there a trend in the data? If there is a trend, then you can use the autoregressive model or the linear, quadratic, or exponential trend models. If there is no obvious trend in the time-series plot, then you should use moving averages or exponential smoothing to smooth out the effect of random effects and possible cyclical effects. After smoothing the data, if a trend is still not present, then you can use exponential smoothing to forecast short-term future values. If smoothing the data reveals a trend, then you can use the autoregressive model, or the linear, quadratic, or exponential trend models.

FIGURE 16.20
Summary chart of time-series forecasting methods

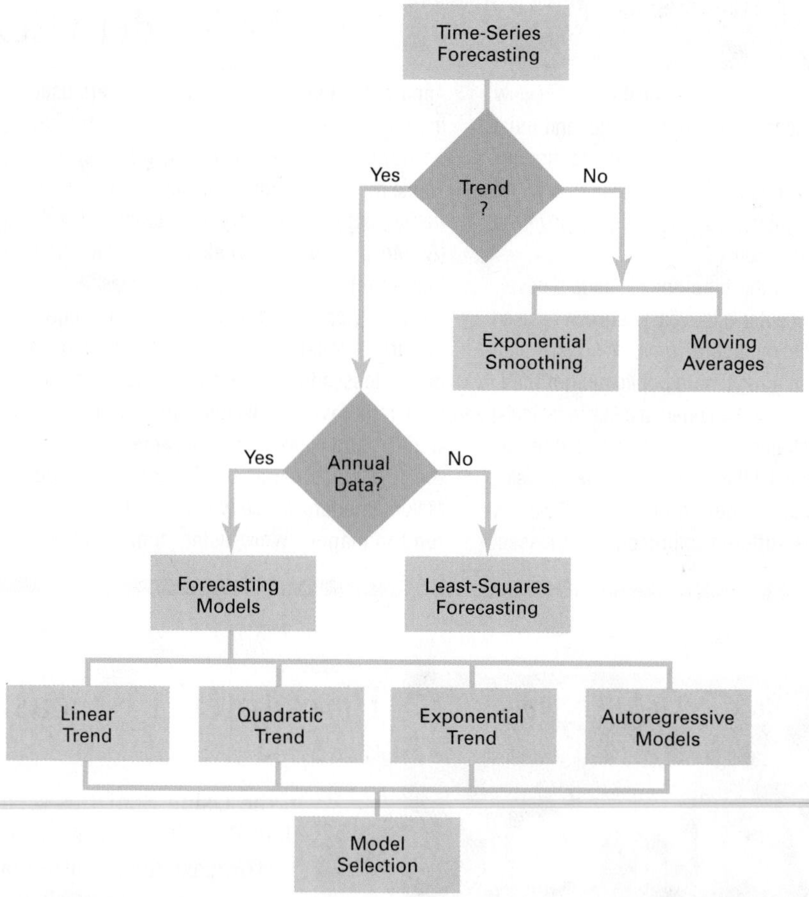

REFERENCES

1. Bowerman, B. L., R. T. O'Connell, and A. Koehler. *Forecasting, Time Series, and Regression*, 4th ed. Belmont, CA: Duxbury Press, 2005.
2. Box, G. E. P., G. M. Jenkins, and G. C. Reinsel. *Time Series Analysis: Forecasting and Control*, 3rd ed. Upper Saddle River, NJ: Prentice Hall, 1994.
3. Frees, E. W. *Data Analysis Using Regression Models: The Business Perspective*. Upper Saddle River, NJ: Prentice Hall, 1996.
4. Hanke, J. E., D. W. Wichern, and A. G. Reitsch. *Business Forecasting*, 7th ed. Upper Saddle River, NJ: Prentice Hall, 2001.
5. *Microsoft Excel 2010*. Redmond, WA: Microsoft Corp., 2010.

KEY EQUATIONS

Computing an Exponentially Smoothed Value in Time Period i

$$E_1 = Y_1 \qquad (16.1)$$
$$E_i = WY_i + (1 - W)E_{i-1} \quad i = 2, 3, 4, \ldots$$

Forecasting Time Period $i + 1$

$$\hat{Y}_{i+1} = E_i \qquad (16.2)$$

Linear Trend Forecasting Equation

$$\hat{Y}_i = b_0 + b_1X_i \qquad (16.3)$$

Quadratic Trend Forecasting Equation

$$\hat{Y}_i = b_0 + b_1X_i + b_2X_i^2 \qquad (16.4)$$

Exponential Trend Model

$$Y_i = \beta_0\beta_1^{X_i}\varepsilon_i \qquad (16.5)$$

Transformed Exponential Trend Model

$$\begin{aligned}\log(Y_i) &= \log(\beta_0\beta_1^{X_i}\varepsilon_i)\\ &= \log(\beta_0) + \log(\beta_1^{X_i}) + \log(\varepsilon_i)\\ &= \log(\beta_0) + X_i\log(\beta_1) + \log(\varepsilon_i)\end{aligned} \qquad (16.6)$$

Exponential Trend Forecasting Equation

$$\log(\hat{Y}_i) = b_0 + b_1X_i \quad (16.7a)$$

$$\hat{Y}_i = \hat{\beta}_0 \hat{\beta}_1^{X_i} \quad (16.7b)$$

***p*th-Order Autoregressive Models**

$$Y_i = A_0 + A_1Y_{i-1} + A_2Y_{i-2} + \cdots + A_pY_{i-p} + \delta_i \quad (16.8)$$

First-Order Autoregressive Model

$$Y_i = A_0 + A_1Y_{i-1} + \delta_i \quad (16.9)$$

Second-Order Autoregressive Model

$$Y_i = A_0 + A_1Y_{i-1} + A_2Y_{i-2} + \delta_i \quad (16.10)$$

***t* Test for Significance of the Highest-Order Autoregressive Parameter, A_p**

$$t_{STAT} = \frac{a_p - A_p}{S_{a_p}} \quad (16.11)$$

Fitted *p*th-Order Autoregressive Equation

$$\hat{Y}_i = a_0 + a_1Y_{i-1} + a_2Y_{i-2} + \cdots + a_pY_{i-p} \quad (16.12)$$

***p*th-Order Autoregressive Forecasting Equation**

$$\hat{Y}_{n+j} = a_0 + a_1\hat{Y}_{n+j-1} + a_2\hat{Y}_{n+j-2} + \cdots + a_p\hat{Y}_{n+j-p} \quad (16.13)$$

Mean Absolute Deviation

$$MAD = \frac{\sum_{i=1}^{n} |Y_i - \hat{Y}_i|}{n} \quad (16.14)$$

Exponential Model with Quarterly Data

$$Y_i = \beta_0\beta_1^{X_i}\beta_2^{Q_1}\beta_3^{Q_2}\beta_4^{Q_3}\varepsilon_i \quad (16.15)$$

Transformed Exponential Model with Quarterly Data

$$\begin{aligned}\log(Y_i) &= \log(\beta_0\beta_1^{X_i}\beta_2^{Q_1}\beta_3^{Q_2}\beta_4^{Q_3}\varepsilon_i) \quad (16.16)\\ &= \log(\beta_0) + \log(\beta_1^{X_i}) + \log(\beta_2^{Q_1}) + \log(\beta_3^{Q_2})\\ &\quad + \log(\beta_4^{Q_3}) + \log(\varepsilon_i)\\ &= \log(\beta_0) + X_i\log(\beta_1) + Q_1\log(\beta_2)\\ &\quad + Q_2\log(\beta_3) + Q_3\log(\beta_4) + \log(\varepsilon_i)\end{aligned}$$

Exponential Growth with Quarterly Data Forecasting Equation

$$\log(\hat{Y}_i) = b_0 + b_1X_i + b_2Q_1 + b_3Q_2 + b_4Q_3 \quad (16.17)$$

Exponential Model with Monthly Data

$$Y_i = \beta_0\beta_1^{X_i}\beta_2^{M_1}\beta_3^{M_2}\beta_4^{M_3}\beta_5^{M_4}\beta_6^{M_5}\beta_7^{M_6}\beta_8^{M_7}\beta_9^{M_8}\beta_{10}^{M_9}\beta_{11}^{M_{10}}\beta_{12}^{M_{11}}\varepsilon_i \quad (16.18)$$

Transformed Exponential Model with Monthly Data

$$\begin{aligned}\log(Y_i) &= \log(\beta_0\beta_1^{X_i}\beta_2^{M_1}\beta_3^{M_2}\beta_4^{M_3}\beta_5^{M_4}\beta_6^{M_5}\beta_7^{M_6}\beta_8^{M_7}\beta_9^{M_8}\beta_{10}^{M_9}\beta_{11}^{M_{10}}\beta_{12}^{M_{11}}\varepsilon_i)\\ &= \log(\beta_0) + X_i\log(\beta_1) + M_1\log(\beta_2) + M_2\log(\beta_3)\\ &\quad + M_3\log(\beta_4) + M_4\log(\beta_5) + M_5\log(\beta_6) + M_6\log(\beta_7)\\ &\quad + M_7\log(\beta_8) + M_8\log(\beta_9) + M_9\log(\beta_{10})\\ &\quad + M_{10}\log(\beta_{11}) + M_{11}\log(\beta_{12}) + \log(\varepsilon_i) \quad (16.19)\end{aligned}$$

Exponential Growth with Monthly Data Forecasting Equation

$$\begin{aligned}\log(\hat{Y}_i) &= b_0 + b_1X_i + b_2M_1 + b_3M_2 + b_4M_3 + b_5M_4 + b_6M_5\\ &\quad + b_7M_6 + b_8M_7 + b_9M_8 + b_{10}M_9 + b_{11}M_{10} + b_{12}M_{11} \quad (16.20)\end{aligned}$$

KEY TERMS

autoregressive modeling 627
causal forecasting methods 610
cyclical effect 611
exponential smoothing 614
exponential trend model 620
first-order autocorrelation 627
first-order autoregressive model 628
forecasting 610
irregular effect 611
lagged predictor variable 627
linear trend model 617
mean absolute deviation (*MAD*) 636
moving averages 612
parsimony 636
*p*th-order autocorrelation 627
*p*th-order autoregressive model 628
quadratic trend model 619
qualitative forecasting method 610
quantitative forecasting method 610
random effect 611
seasonal effect 611
second-order autocorrelation 627
second-order autoregressive model 628
time series 610
time-series forecasting methods 610
trend 611

CHECKING YOUR UNDERSTANDING

16.50 What is a time series?

16.51 What are the different components of a time-series model?

16.52 What is the difference between moving averages and exponential smoothing?

16.53 Under what circumstances is the exponential trend model most appropriate?

16.54 How does the least-squares linear trend forecasting model developed in this chapter differ from the least-squares linear regression model considered in Chapter 13?

16.55 How does autoregressive modeling differ from the other approaches to forecasting?

16.56 What are the different approaches to choosing an appropriate forecasting model?

16.57 What is the major difference between using S_{YX} and *MAD* for evaluating how well a particular model fits the data?

16.58 How does forecasting for monthly or quarterly data differ from forecasting for annual data?

CHAPTER REVIEW PROBLEMS

16.59 The data in the following table, stored in Polio, represent the annual incidence rates (per 100,000 persons) of reported acute poliomyelitis recorded over five-year periods from 1915 to 1955:

Year	1915	1920	1925	1930	1935	1940	1945	1950	1955
Rate	3.1	2.2	5.3	7.5	8.5	7.4	10.3	22.1	17.6

Source: Data extracted from B. Wattenberg, ed., *The Statistical History of the United States: From Colonial Times to the Present*, ser. B303.

a. Plot the data.
b. Compute the linear trend forecasting equation and plot the trend line.
c. What are your forecasts for 1960, 1965, and 1970?
d. Using a library or the Internet, find the actually reported incidence rates of acute poliomyelitis for 1960, 1965, and 1970. Record your results.
e. Why are the forecasts you made in (c) not useful? Discuss.

16.60 The U.S. Department of Labor gathers and publishes statistics concerning the labor market. The file Workforce contains data on the size of the U.S. civilian noninstitutional population of people 16 years and over (in thousands) and the U.S. civilian noninstitutional workforce of people 16 years and over (in thousands) for 1984–2011. The workforce variable reports the number of people in the population who have a job or are actively looking for a job. (Data extracted from Bureau of Labor Statistics, U.S. Department of Labor, **www.bls.gov**.)

a. Plot the time series for the U.S. civilian noninstitutional population of people 16 years and older.
b. Compute the linear trend forecasting equation.
c. Forecast the U.S. civilian noninstitutional population of people 16 years and older for 2012 and 2013.
d. Repeat (a) through (c) for the U.S. civilian noninstitutional workforce of people 16 years and older.

16.61 The monthly wellhead and residential prices for natural gas (dollars per thousand cubic feet) in the United States from January 2008 through June 2012 are stored in Natural Gas2. (Data extracted from Energy Information Administration, U.S. Department of Energy, **www.eia.gov**, *Natural Gas Monthly*, August 3, 2012.)

For the wellhead price and the residential price,

a. do you think the price for natural gas has a seasonal component?
b. plot the time series. Does this chart support your answer in (a)?
c. compute an exponential trend forecasting equation for monthly data.
d. interpret the monthly compound growth rate.
e. interpret the month multipliers. Do the multipliers support your answers in (a) and (b)?
f. compare the results for the wellhead prices and the residential prices.

16.62 The data in the following table, stored in McDonalds, represent the gross revenues (in billions of current dollars) of McDonald's Corporation from 1975 through 2011:

Year	Revenues ($billions)	Year	Revenues ($billions)	Year	Revenues ($billions)
1975	1.0	1988	5.6	2001	14.8
1976	1.2	1989	6.1	2002	15.2
1977	1.4	1990	6.8	2003	16.8
1978	1.7	1991	6.7	2004	18.6
1979	1.9	1992	7.1	2005	19.8
1980	2.2	1993	7.4	2006	20.9
1981	2.5	1994	8.3	2007	22.8
1982	2.8	1995	9.8	2008	23.5
1983	3.1	1996	10.7	2009	22.7
1984	3.4	1997	11.4	2010	24.1
1985	3.8	1998	12.4	2011	27.0
1986	4.2	1999	13.3		
1987	4.9	2000	14.2		

Source: Data extracted from *Moody's Handbook of Common Stocks*, 1980, 1989, and 1999; *Mergent's Handbook of Common Stocks*, Spring 2002; and "Investors: About McDonalds," **www.aboutmcdonalds.com/mcd/investors.html**.

a. Plot the data.
b. Compute the linear trend forecasting equation.
c. Compute the quadratic trend forecasting equation.
d. Compute the exponential trend forecasting equation.
e. Determine the best-fitting autoregressive model, using $\alpha = 0.05$.
f. Perform a residual analysis for each of the models in (b) through (e).
g. Compute the standard error of the estimate (S_{YX}) and the *MAD* for each corresponding model in (f).
h. On the basis of your results in (f) and (g), along with a consideration of the principle of parsimony, which model would you select for purposes of forecasting? Discuss.
i. Using the selected model in (h), forecast gross revenues for 2012.

16.63 Teachers' Retirement System of the City of New York offers several types of investments for its members. Among the choices are investments with fixed and variable rates of return. There are several categories of variable-return investments. The Diversified Equity Fund consists of investments that are primarily made in stocks, and the

Stable-Value Fund consists of investments in corporate bonds and other types of lower-risk instruments. The data in TRSNYC represent the value of a unit of each type of variable-return investment at the beginning of each year from 1984 to 2012. (Data extracted from "Historical Data-Unit Values, Teachers' Retirement System of the City of New York," **bit.ly/SESJF5**.)

For each of the two time series,

a. plot the data.
b. compute the linear trend forecasting equation.
c. compute the quadratic trend forecasting equation.
d. compute the exponential trend forecasting equation.
e. determine the best-fitting autoregressive model, using $\alpha = 0.05$.
f. Perform a residual analysis for each of the models in (b) through (e).
g. Compute the standard error of the estimate (S_{YX}) and the *MAD* for each corresponding model in (f).
h. On the basis of your results in (f) and (g), along with a consideration of the principle of parsimony, which model would you select for purposes of forecasting? Discuss.
i. Using the selected model in (h), forecast the unit values for 2013.
j. Based on the results of (a) through (i), what investment strategy would you recommend for a member of the Teachers' Retirement System of the City of New York? Explain.

REPORT WRITING EXERCISE

16.64 As a consultant to an investment company trading in various currencies, you have been assigned the task of studying long-term trends in the exchange rates of the Canadian dollar, the Japanese yen, and the English pound. Data from 1980 to 2011 are stored in Currency, where the Canadian dollar, the Japanese yen, and the English pound are expressed in units per U.S. dollar.

Develop a forecasting model for the exchange rate of each of these three currencies and provide forecasts for 2012 and 2013 for each currency. Write an executive summary for a presentation to be given to the investment company. Append to this executive summary a discussion regarding possible limitations that may exist in these models.

CASES FOR CHAPTER 16

Managing Ashland MultiComm Services

As part of the continuing strategic initiative to increase subscribers to the *3-For-All* cable/phone/Internet services, the marketing department is closely monitoring the number of subscribers. To help do so, forecasts are to be developed for the number of subscribers in the future. To accomplish this task, the number of subscribers for the most recent 24-month period has been determined and is stored in AMS16.

1. Analyze these data and develop a model to forecast the number of subscribers. Present your findings in a report that includes the assumptions of the model and its limitations. Forecast the number of subscribers for the next four months.
2. Would you be willing to use the model developed to forecast the number of subscribers one year into the future? Explain.
3. Compare the trend in the number of subscribers to the number of new subscribers per month stored in AMS13. What explanation can you provide for any differences?

Digital Case

Apply your knowledge about time-series forecasting in this Digital Case.

The *Ashland Herald* competes for readers in the Tri-Cities area with the newer *Oxford Glen Journal* (*OGJ*). Recently, the circulation staff at the *OGJ* claimed that their newspaper's circulation and subscription base is growing faster than that of the *Herald* and that local advertisers would do better if they transferred their advertisements from the *Herald* to the *OGJ*. The circulation department of the *Herald* has complained to the Ashland Chamber of Commerce about *OGJ*'s claims and has asked the chamber to investigate, a request that was welcomed by *OGJ*'s circulation staff.

Open **ACC_Mediation216.pdf** to review the circulation dispute information collected by the Ashland Chamber of Commerce. Then answer the following:

1. Which newspaper would you say has the right to claim the fastest-growing circulation and subscription base? Support your answer by performing and summarizing an appropriate statistical analysis.
2. What is the single most positive fact about the *Herald*'s circulation and subscription base? What is the single most positive fact about the *OGJ*'s circulation and subscription base? Explain your answers.
3. What additional data would be helpful in investigating the circulation claims made by the staffs of each newspaper?

CHAPTER 16 EXCEL GUIDE

EG16.1 The IMPORTANCE of BUSINESS FORECASTING

There are no Excel Guide instructions for this section.

EG16.2 COMPONENT FACTORS of TIME-SERIES MODELS

There are no Excel Guide instructions for this section.

EG16.3 SMOOTHING an ANNUAL TIME SERIES

Moving Averages

Key Technique Use the **AVERAGE(*cell range that contains a sequence of L observed values*)** function to compute moving averages and use the special worksheet value **#N/A** (not available) for time periods in which no moving average can be computed.

Example Compute the three- and five-year moving averages for the movie attendance data that is shown in Figure 16.2 on page 613.

In-Depth Excel Use the **COMPUTE worksheet** of the **Moving Averages workbook** as a template.

The worksheet already contains the data and formulas for the example. For other problems, paste the time-series data into columns A and B and adjust the moving average entries in columns C and D. (Open to the **COMPUTE_FORMULAS worksheet** to examine all formulas the worksheet uses.) To compute five-year moving averages, enter #N/A into the second row cell and the cell that is second from the bottom.

To construct a moving average plot for other problems, open to the adjusted COMPUTE worksheet and:

1. Select the cell range of the time-series data and the moving averages. (For the example, this cell range is **A1:D12.**)
2. Select **Insert → Scatter** and select the second **Scatter** gallery choice in the second row of choices (**Scatter with Straight Lines and Markers**).
3. Relocate the chart to a chart sheet, turn off the gridlines, add axis titles, and modify the chart title by using the instructions in Appendix Section B.6.

Exponential Smoothing

Key Technique Use arithmetic formulas to compute exponentially smoothed values.

Example Compute the exponentially smoothed series ($W = 0.50$ and $W = 0.25$) for the movie attendance data that is shown in Figure 16.3 on page 614.

In-Depth Excel Use the **COMPUTE worksheet** of the **Exponential Smoothing workbook**, as a template.

The worksheet already contains the data and formulas for the example. In this worksheet, cells C2 and D2 contain the formula **=B2** that copies the initial value of the time series. The exponential smoothing begins in row 3, with cell **C3** formula **=0.5 * B3 + 0.5 * C2**, and cell **D3** formula **=0.25 * B3 + 0.75 * D2**. Note that in these formulas, the expression $1 - W$ in Equation (16.1) on page 614 has been simplified to the values 0.5 and 0.75, respectively. (Open to the **COMPUTE_FORMULAS worksheet** to examine all of the exponential smoothing formulas the worksheet uses.)

For other problems, paste the time-series data into columns A and B and adjust the exponentially smoothed entries in columns C and D. For problems with fewer than 11 time periods, delete the excess rows. For problems with more than 11 time periods, select row 12, right-click, and click **Insert** in the shortcut menu. Repeat as many times as there are new rows. Then select cell range **C11:D11** and copy the contents of this range down through the new table rows.

To construct a plot of exponentially smoothed values for other problems, open to the adjusted COMPUTE worksheet and:

1. Select the cell range of the time-series data and the exponentially smoothed values. (For the example, this cell range is **A1:D12.**)
2. Select **Insert → Scatter** and select the second **Scatter** gallery choice in the second row of choices (**Scatter with Straight Lines and Markers**).
3. Relocate the chart to a chart sheet, turn off the gridlines, add axis titles, and modify the chart title by using the instructions in Appendix Section B.6.

Analysis ToolPak Use **Exponential Smoothing.**

For the example, open to the **DATA worksheet** of the **Movie Attendance workbook** and:

1. Select **Data ➔ Data Analysis.**
2. In the Data Analysis dialog box, select **Exponential Smoothing** from the **Analysis Tools** list and then click **OK.**

In the Exponential Smoothing dialog box (shown below):

3. Enter **B1:B12** as the **Input Range.**
4. Enter **0.5** as the **Damping factor.** (The damping factor is equal to 1 − *W*.)
5. Check **Labels**, enter **C1** as the **Output Range**, and click **OK.**

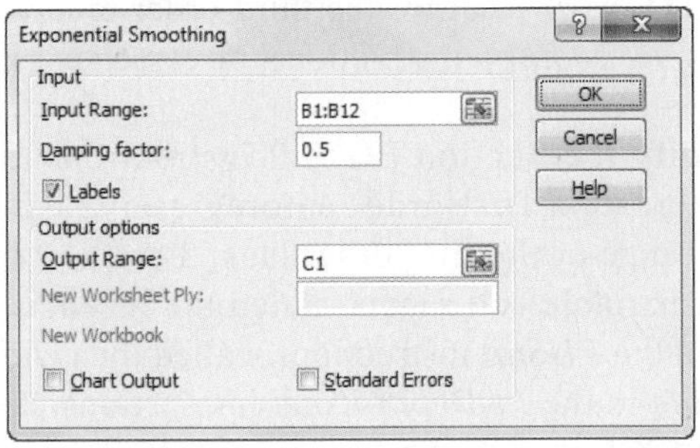

In the new column C:

6. Copy the last formula in cell **C11** to cell **C12.**
7. Enter the column heading **ES(W = .50)** in cell **C1**, replacing the **#N/A** value.

To create the exponentially smoothed values that use a smoothing coefficient of $W = 0.25$, repeat steps 3 through 7 with these modifications: Enter **0.75** as the **Damping factor** in step 4, enter **D1** as the **Output Range** in step 5, and enter **ES(W = .25)** as the column heading in step 7.

EG16.4 LEAST-SQUARES TREND FITTING and FORECASTING

The Linear Trend Model

Modify the Section EG13.2 instructions (see page 520) to create a linear trend model. Use the cell range of the coded variable as the *X* variable cell range (called the **X Variable Cell Range** in the *PHStat* instructions, called the ***cell range of X variable*** in the *In-Depth Excel* instructions, and called the **Input X Range** in the *Analysis ToolPak* instructions). If you need to create coded values, enter them manually in a column. (If you have many coded values, you can use **Home ➔ Fill** (in the Editing group) **➔ Series** and in the Series dialog box, click **Columns** and **Linear**, and select appropriate values for **Step value** and **Stop value.**

The Quadratic Trend Model

Modify the Section EG15.1 instructions (see page 606) to create a quadratic trend model. Use the cell range of the coded variable and the squared coded variable as the *X* variables cell range (called the **X Variables Cell Range** in the *PHStat* instructions and the **Input X Range** in the *Analysis ToolPak* instructions). Use the Section EG15.1 instructions to create the squared coded variable and to plot the quadratic trend.

The Exponential Trend Model

Key Technique Use the **POWER(10, *predicted log*(Y))** function to compute the predicted *Y* values from the predicted log(*Y*) results.

PHStat/In-Depth Excel/Analysis ToolPak Creating an exponential trend model requires more work than creating the other trend models because you must

1. Convert the values of the dependent variable *Y* to log(*Y*) values.
2. Perform a simple linear regression analysis with residual analysis using the log(Y) values.
3. Convert the predicted log(*Y*) results to predicted *Y* results using the **POWER** function.
4. Compute the residuals using the predicted *Y* and original *Y* values.

To complete step 1, use the Section EG15.2 instructions on page 606 to create the log(*Y*) values. To complete step 2, modify the Section EG13.5 "Residual Analysis" instructions on page 521. The Section 13.5 instructions incorporate the Section EG13.2 "Determining the Simple Linear Regression Equation" instructions. For the Section EG13.2 instructions, use the cell range of the log *Y* values as the *Y* variable cell range and the cell range of the coded variable as the *X* variable cell range. (The *Y* variable cell range and the *X* variable cell range are called the **Y Variable Cell Range** and **X Variable Cell Range** in the *PHStat* instructions, called the ***cell range of Y variable*** and ***cell range of X variable*** in the *In-Depth Excel* instructions, and called the **Input Y Range** and **Input X Range** in the *Analysis ToolPak* instructions.)

Using the modified Section EG13.5 instructions will create a simple linear regression results worksheet and a residual worksheet if using the *PHStat* or *In-Depth Excel* instructions, or in the RESIDUAL OUTPUT area in the regression results worksheet, if using the *Analysis ToolPak* instructions. Because you use log(*Y*) values for the regression, the predicted *Y* and residuals listed are log values that need to be converted. [The Analysis ToolPak incorrectly labels the new column for the logs of the residuals as Residuals, and not as LOG(Residuals), as you might expect.]

To complete steps 3 and 4, use empty columns in the residuals worksheet (*PHStat* or *In-Depth Excel*) or empty column ranges to the right of RESIDUALS OUTPUT area (*Analysis ToolPak*) to first add a column of formulas that use the POWER function to compute the predicted *Y* values. Then, add a second column that contains the original *Y* values. (Copy the original *Y* values to this column). Finally, add a third new column that contains formulas in the form

=(*revenue cell* − *predicted revenue cell*) to compute the actual residuals.

Use columns G through I of the **RESIDUALS worksheet** of the **Exponential Trend workbook** as a model. (Use the **Exponential Trend 2007 workbook** if you use an Excel version that is older than Excel 2010.) The worksheet already contains the values and formulas needed to create the Figure 16.9 plot that fits an exponential trend forecasting equation for The Coca-Cola Company revenues (see page 622).

To construct an exponential trend plot, first select the cell range of the time-series data. (For The Coca-Cola Company revenue example, this cell range is **B1:B18** in the **Data worksheet** of the **Coca-Cola workbook.**) Then use the Section EG2.5 instructions to construct a scatter plot. Select the chart. Then select **Layout ➔ Trendline ➔ More Trendline Options** and in the Format Trendline dialog box:

1. Click **Trendline Options** in the left pane.
2. In the Trendline Options right pane, click **Exponential** and click **OK.**

If you use Excel 2013, select **Design ➔ Add Chart Element ➔ Trendline ➔ More Trendline Options**. In the Format Trendline pane, click **Exponential**.

Model Selection Using First, Second, and Percentage Differences

Use arithmetic formulas to compute the first, second, and percentage differences. Use division formulas to compute the percentage differences and use subtraction formulas to compute the first and second differences. Use the **COMPUTE worksheet** of the **Differences workbook**, shown in Figure 16.10 on page 624, as a model for developing a differences worksheet. (Open to the **COMPUTE_FORMULAS worksheet** to see all formulas used.)

EG16.5 AUTOREGRESSIVE MODELING for TREND FITTING and FORECASTING

Creating Lagged Predictor Variables

Create lagged predictor variables by creating a column of formulas that refer to a previous row's (previous time period's) Y value. Enter the special worksheet value **#N/A** (not available) for the cells in the column to which lagged values do not apply.

Use the **COMPUTE worksheet** of the **Lagged Predictors workbook**, shown in Figure 16.12 on page 632 as a model for developing lagged predictor variables for the first-order, second-order, and third-order autoregressive models. (Open to the **COMPUTE_FORMULAS worksheet** to see all formulas used.)

When specifying cell ranges for a lagged predictor variable, you include only rows that contain lagged values. Contrary to the usual practice in this book, you do not include rows that contain **#N/A**, nor do you include the row 1 column heading.

Autoregressive Modeling

Modify the Section EG14.1 instructions (see page 568) to create a third-order or second-order autoregressive model. Use the cell range of the first-order, second-order, and third-order lagged predictor variables as the X variables cell range for the third-order model. Use the cell range of the first-order and second-order lagged predictor variables as the X variables cell range for the second-order model (The X variables cell range is the **X Variables Cell Range** in the *PHStat* instructions and the **Input X Range** in the *Analysis ToolPak* instructions.) If using the *PHStat* instructions, omit step 3 (clear, do *not* check, **First cells in both ranges contain label**). If using the *In-Depth Excel* instructions, use the **COMPUTE3 worksheet** in lieu of the COMPUTE worksheet for the third-order model. If using the *Analysis ToolPak* instructions, do not check **Labels** in step 4.

Modify the Section EG13.2 instructions (see page 520) to create a first-order autoregressive model. Use the cell range of the first-order lagged predictor variable as the X variable cell range (called the **X Variable Cell Range** in the *PHStat* instructions, called the ***cell range of X variable*** in the *In-Depth Excel* instructions, and called the **Input X Range** in the *Analysis ToolPak* instructions). If using the *PHStat* instructions, omit step 3 (clear, do *not* check, **First cells in both ranges contain label**). If using the *Analysis ToolPak* instructions, do not check **Labels** in step 4.

EG16.6 CHOOSING an APPROPRIATE FORECASTING MODEL

Performing a Residual Analysis

To create residual plots for the linear trend model or the first-order autoregressive model, use the instructions in Section EG13.5 on page 521. To create residual plots for the quadratic trend model or second-order autoregressive model, use the instructions in Section EG14.3 on page 569. To create residual plots for the exponential trend model, use the instructions in Section EG16.4 on page 651. To create residual plots for the third-order autoregressive model, use the instructions in Section EG14.3 on page 569 but use the **RESIDUALS3** worksheet instead of the RESIDUALS worksheet if using the *In-Depth Excel* instructions.

Measuring the Magnitude of the Residuals Through Squared or Absolute Differences

To compute the mean absolute deviation (*MAD*), first perform a residual analysis. Then add a formula in the form **=SUMPRODUCT(ABS(*cell range of residual values*)) / COUNT(*cell range of the residual values*)**. In the ***cell range of the residual values*** do not include the column heading as is usual practice in this book. (See Appendix Section F.4 to learn more about the application of **SUMPRODUCT** function in this formula.)

The **RESIDUALS_FORMULAS** worksheet of the **Exponential Trend workbook** shows an example of this formula in cell I19 for The Coca-Cola Company revenues example.

A Comparison of Four Forecasting Methods

Construct a model comparison worksheet similar to the one shown in Figure 16.17 on page 637 by using **Paste Special values** (see Appendix Section B.4) to transfer results from regression results worksheets. For the *SSE* values (row 20 in Figure 16.7), copy the regression results worksheet cell C13, the *SS* value for Residual in the ANOVA table. For the S_{YX} values (row), copy the regression results worksheet cell B7, labeled Standard Error, for all but the exponential trend model. For the *MAD* values, add formulas as discussed in the previous section.

For the S_{YX} value for the exponential trend model, enter a formula in the form **=SQRT(*exponential SSE cell* / (COUNT(*cell range of exponential residuals*) - 2))**. For the Figure 16.8 worksheet, this formula is **=SQRT(H20 / (COUNT(H3:H19) - 2))**. Use the **COMPARE** worksheet of the **Forecasting Comparison workbook** as a model. Open to the **COMPARE_FORMULAS** worksheet to examine all formulas. This worksheet also shows an alternative way that uses a formula to display the *SSE* values.

EG16.7 TIME-SERIES FORECASTING of SEASONAL DATA

Least-Squares Forecasting with Monthly or Quarterly Data

To develop a least-squares regression model for monthly or quarterly data, add columns of formulas that use the **IF** function (see Appendix Section F.4) to create dummy variables for the quarterly or monthly data. Enter all formulas in the form **=IF(*comparison*, 1, 0)**.

Shown below are the first five rows of columns F through K of a data worksheet that contains dummy variables. In the first illustration, columns F, G, and H contain the quarterly dummy variables Q1, Q2, and Q3 that are based on column B coded quarter values (not shown). In the second illustration, columns J and K contain the two monthly variables M1 and M6 that are based on column C month values (also not shown).

	F	G	H
1	Q1	Q2	Q3
2	=IF(B2 = 1, 1, 0)	=IF(B2 = 2, 1, 0)	=IF(B2 = 3, 1, 0)
3	=IF(B3 = 1, 1, 0)	=IF(B3 = 2, 1, 0)	=IF(B3 = 3, 1, 0)
4	=IF(B4 = 1, 1, 0)	=IF(B4 = 2, 1, 0)	=IF(B4 = 3, 1, 0)
5	=IF(B5 = 1, 1, 0)	=IF(B5 = 2, 1, 0)	=IF(B5 = 3, 1, 0)

	J	K
1	M1	M6
2	=IF(C2 ="January", 1, 0)	=IF(C2 = "June", 1, 0)
3	=IF(C3 ="January", 1, 0)	=IF(C3 = "June", 1, 0)
4	=IF(C4 ="January", 1, 0)	=IF(C4 = "June", 1, 0)
5	=IF(C5 ="January", 1, 0)	=IF(C5 = "June", 1, 0)

CHAPTER

17 A Roadmap for Analyzing Data

Learning Objective

In this chapter, you learn:

- The steps involved in choosing which statistical methods to use to conduct data analysis

Angela Waye / Shutterstock

USING STATISTICS

Mounting Future Analyses

Learning business statistics is a lot like climbing a mountain. At first, it may seem intimidating, or even overwhelming, but over time you learn techniques that help make the task much more manageable. In Section LGS.1, you learned how the DCOVA framework can make the big task of applying statistics to business problems more manageable. After learning methods in early chapters to **D**efine, **C**ollect, and **O**rganize data, you have spent most of your time studying ways to **V**isualize and **A**nalyze data.

Determining what methods to use to analyze data may have seemed straightforward when doing homework problems from a particular chapter, but what do you do when you find yourself in new situations, needing to analyze data for another course or to help solve a problem in a real business setting? After all, when you solved a problem from a chapter on multiple regression, you "knew" that multiple regression methods would be part of your analysis. In new situations, you might wonder whether you should use multiple regression—or whether using simple linear regression would be better—or whether *any* type of regression would be appropriate. You also might wonder if you should use a combination of methods from several different chapters to help solve the problems you face.

The question for you becomes: How can you apply the statistical methods you have learned to new situations that require you to analyze data?

Courtesy of Sharyn Rosenberg

Reviewing Table 17.1, which contains a summary of the contents of this book, arranged by data analysis task, would be a good starting point for answering the question posed in the Using Statistics scenario.

TABLE 17.1

Commonly Used Data Analysis Tasks Discussed in This Book

DESCRIBING A GROUP OR SEVERAL GROUPS

For Numerical Variables:

Ordered array, stem-and-leaf display, frequency distribution, relative frequency distribution, percentage distribution, cumulative percentage distribution, histogram, polygon, cumulative percentage polygon **(Sections 2.2 and 2.4)**
Boxplot **(Section 3.3)**
Normal probability plot **(Section 6.3)**
Mean, median, mode, quartiles, geometric mean, range, interquartile range, standard deviation, variance, coefficient of variation, skewness, kurtosis **(Sections 3.1, 3.2, and 3.3)**
Index numbers **(bonus eBook Section 16.8)**

For Categorical Variables:

Summary table, bar chart, pie chart, Pareto chart **(Sections 2.1 and 2.3)**
Contingency tables and multidimensional tables **(Sections 2.1 and 2.7)**

MAKING INFERENCES ABOUT ONE GROUP

For Numerical Variables:

Confidence interval estimate of the mean **(Sections 8.1 and 8.2)**
t test for the mean **(Section 9.2)**
Chi-square test for a variance or standard deviation **(bonus eBook Section 12.7)**

For Categorical Variables:

Confidence interval estimate of the proportion **(Section 8.3)**
Z test for the proportion **(Section 9.4)**

COMPARING TWO GROUPS

For Numerical Variables:

Tests for the difference in the means of two independent populations **(Section 10.1)**
Wilcoxon rank sum test **(Section 12.4)**
Paired *t* test **(Section 10.2)**
F test for the difference between two variances **(Section 10.4)**

For Categorical Variables:

Z test for the difference between two proportions **(Section 10.3)**
Chi-square test for the difference between two proportions **(Section 12.1)**
McNemar test for two related samples **(bonus eBook Section 12.6)**

COMPARING MORE THAN TWO GROUPS

For Numerical Variables:

One-way analysis of variance **(Section 11.1)**
Kruskal-Wallis rank test **(Section 12.5)**
Two-way analysis of variance **(Section 11.2)**
Randomized block design **(bonus eBook Section 11.3)**

For Categorical Variables:

Chi-square test for differences among more than two proportions **(Section 12.2)**

TABLE 17.1

(Continued)

ANALYZING THE RELATIONSHIP BETWEEN TWO VARIABLES

For Numerical Variables:

Scatter plot, time-series plot **(Section 2.5)**

Covariance, coefficient of correlation, t test of correlation **(Sections 3.5 and 13.7)**

Simple linear regression **(Chapter 13)**

Time-series forecasting **(Chapter 16)**

For Categorical Variables:

Contingency table, side-by-side bar chart **(Sections 2.1 and 2.3)**

Chi-square test of independence **(Section 12.3)**

ANALYZING THE RELATIONSHIP BETWEEN TWO OR MORE VARIABLES

For Numerical Dependent Variables:

Multiple regression **(Chapters 14 and 15)**

For Categorical Dependent Variables:

Logistic regression **(Section 14.7)**

Predictive analytics and data mining **(Section 15.6)**

ANALYZING PROCESS DATA

For Numerical Variables:

$\overline{X}$ and R control charts **(bonus eBook Section 18.5)**

For Categorical Variables:

p chart **(bonus eBook Section 18.2)**

For Counts of Nonconformities:

c chart **(bonus eBook Section 18.4)**

Student Tip

Recall that *numerical variables* have values that represent quantities, while *categorical variables* have values that can only be placed into categories, such as yes and no.

In the DCOVA approach, the first thing you do is to *define* the variables that you want to study in order to solve a business problem or meet a business objective. To do this, you must identify the type of business problem (whether you are describing a group or making inferences about a group, among other choices) and then determine the type of variable—numerical or categorical—you are analyzing.

In Table 17.1, the all-uppercase first-level headings identify types of business problems, and the second-level headings always include the two types of variables. The entries in Table 17.1 identify the specific statistical methods appropriate for a particular type of business problem and type of variable.

Choosing appropriate statistical methods for your data is the single most important task you face and is at the heart of "doing statistics." But this selection process is also the single most difficult thing you do when applying statistics! How, then, can you ensure that you have made an appropriate choice? By asking a series of questions, you can guide yourself to the appropriate choice of methods.

The rest of this chapter presents questions that will help guide you in making this choice. Two lists of questions, one for numerical variables and the other for categorical variables, are presented in the next two sections. Having two lists makes the decision you face more manageable while also reinforcing the importance of identifying the type of variable that you seek to analyze.

17.1 Analyzing Numerical Variables

Exhibit 17.1 presents the list of questions to ask if you plan to analyze a numerical variable. Each question is independent of the others, and you can ask as many or as few questions as is appropriate for your analysis. How to go about answering these questions follows Exhibit 17.1.

EXHIBIT 17.1

Questions to Ask When Analyzing Numerical Variables

When analyzing numerical variables, ask yourself these questions:

- Do you want to describe the characteristics of the variable (possibly broken down into several groups)?
- Do you want to reach conclusions about the mean and/or standard deviation of the variable in a population?
- Do you want to determine whether the mean and/or standard deviation of the variable differs depending on the group?
- Do you want to determine which factors affect the value of a variable?
- Do you want to predict the value of the variable based on the values of other variables?
- Do you want to determine whether the values of the variable are stable over time?

Describing the Characteristics of a Numerical Variable

You develop tables and charts and compute descriptive statistics to describe characteristics such as central tendency, variation, and shape. Specifically, you can create a stem-and-leaf display, percentage distribution, histogram, polygon, boxplot, and normal probability plot (see Sections 2.2, 2.4, 3.3, and 6.3), and you can compute statistics such as the mean, median, mode, quartiles, range, interquartile range, standard deviation, variance, coefficient of variation, skewness, and kurtosis (see Sections 3.1, 3.2, and 3.3).

Reaching Conclusions About the Population Mean and/or Standard Deviation

You have several different choices, and you can use any combination of these choices. To estimate the mean value of the variable in a population, you construct a confidence interval estimate of the mean (see Section 8.2). To determine whether the population mean is equal to a specific value, you conduct a t test of hypothesis for the mean (see Section 9.2). To determine whether the population standard deviation or variance is equal to a specific value, you conduct a χ^2 test of hypothesis for the standard deviation or variance (see bonus eBook Section 12.7).

Determining Whether the Mean and/or Standard Deviation Differs Depending on the Group

When examining differences between groups, you first need to establish which categorical variable to use to divide your data into groups. You then need to know whether this grouping variable divides your data in two groups (such as male and female groups for a gender variable) or whether the variable divides your data into more than two groups (such as the four parachute suppliers discussed in Section 11.1). Finally, you must ask whether your data set contains independent groups or whether your data set contains matched or repeated measurements.

If the Grouping Variable Defines Two Independent Groups and You Are Interested in Central Tendency Which hypothesis tests you use depends on the assumptions you make about your data.

If you assume that your numerical variable is normally distributed and that the variances are equal, you conduct a pooled t test for the difference between the means (see Section 10.1). If you cannot assume that the variances are equal, you conduct a separate-variance t test for the difference between the means (see Section 10.1). To test whether the variances are equal, assuming that the populations are normally distributed, you can conduct an F test for the differences between the variances. In either case, if you believe that your numerical variables are not normally distributed, you can perform a Wilcoxon rank sum test (see Section 12.4) and compare the results of this test to those of the t test.

To evaluate the assumption of normality that the pooled t test and separate-variance t test include, you can construct boxplots and normal probability plots for each group.

If the Grouping Variable Defines Two Groups of Matched Samples or Repeated Measurements and You Are Interested in Central Tendency If you can assume that the paired differences are normally distributed, you conduct a paired t test (see Section 10.2).

If the Grouping Variable Defines Two Independent Groups and You Are Interested in Variability If you can assume that your numerical variable is normally distributed, you conduct an F test for the difference between two variances (see Section 10.4).

If the Grouping Variable Defines More Than Two Independent Groups and You Are Interested in Central Tendency If you can assume that the values of the numerical variable are normally distributed, you conduct a one-way analysis of variance (see Section 11.1); otherwise, you conduct a Kruskal-Wallis rank test (see Section 12.5).

If the Grouping Variable Defines More Than Two Groups of Matched Samples or Repeated Measurements and You Are Interested in Central Tendency Say that you have a design where the rows represent the blocks and the columns represent the levels of a factor. If you can assume that the values of the numerical variable are normally distributed, you conduct a randomized block design F test (see bonus eBook Section 11.3).

Determining Which Factors Affect the Value of a Variable

If there are two factors to be examined to determine their effect on the values of a variable, you develop a two-factor factorial design (see Section 11.2).

Predicting the Value of a Variable Based on the Values of Other Variables

When predicting the values of a numerical dependent variable, you conduct least-squares regression analysis. The least-squares regression model you develop depends on the number of independent variables in your model. If there is only one independent variable being used to predict the numerical dependent variable of interest, you develop a simple linear regression model (see Chapter 13); otherwise, you develop a multiple regression model (see Chapters 14 and 15).

If you have values over a period of time and you want to forecast the variable for future time periods, you can use moving averages, exponential smoothing, least-squares forecasting, and autoregressive modeling (see Chapter 16).

Determining Whether the Values of a Variable Are Stable Over Time

If you are studying a process and have collected data on the values of a numerical variable over a time period, you construct R and $\overline{X}$ charts (see bonus eBook Section 18.5). If you have collected data in which the values are counts of the number of nonconformities, you construct a c chart (see bonus eBook Section 18.4).

17.2 Analyzing Categorical Variables

Exhibit 17.2 presents the list of questions to ask if you plan to analyze a categorical variable. Each question is independent of the others, and you can ask as many or as few questions as is appropriate for your analysis. How to go about answering these questions follows Exhibit 17.2.

EXHIBIT 17.2

Questions to Ask When Analyzing Categorical Variables

When analyzing categorical variables, ask yourself these questions:

- Do you want to describe the proportion of items of interest in each category (possibly broken down into several groups)?
- Do you want to reach conclusions about the proportion of items of interest in a population?
- Do you want to determine whether the proportion of items of interest differs depending on the group?
- Do you want to predict the proportion of items of interest based on the values of other variables?
- Do you want to determine whether the proportion of items of interest is stable over time?

Describing the Proportion of Items of Interest in Each Category

You create summary tables and use these charts: bar chart, pie chart, Pareto chart, or side-by-side bar chart (see Sections 2.1 and 2.3).

Reaching Conclusions About the Proportion of Items of Interest

You have two different choices. You can estimate the proportion of items of interest in a population by constructing a confidence interval estimate of the proportion (see Section 8.3). Or, you can determine whether the population proportion is equal to a specific value by conducting a Z test of hypothesis for the proportion (see Section 9.4).

Determining Whether the Proportion of Items of Interest Differs Depending on the Group

When examining this difference, you first need to establish the number of categories associated with your categorical variable and the number of groups in your analysis. If your data contain two groups, you must also ask if your data contain independent groups or if your data contain matched samples or repeated measurements.

For Two Categories and Two Independent Groups You conduct either the Z test for the difference between two proportions (see Section 10.3) or the χ^2 test for the difference between two proportions (see Section 12.1).

For Two Categories and Two Groups of Matched or Repeated Measurements You conduct the McNemar test (see bonus eBook Section 12.6).

For Two Categories and More Than Two Independent Groups You conduct a χ^2 test for the difference among several proportions (see Section 12.2).

For More Than Two Categories and More Than Two Groups You develop contingency tables and use multidimensional contingency tables to drill down to examine relationships among two or more categorical variables (Sections 2.1 and 2.7). When you have two categorical variables, you conduct a χ^2 test of independence (see Section 12.3).

Predicting the Proportion of Items of Interest Based on the Values of Other Variables

You develop a logistic regression model (see Section 14.7).

Determining Whether the Proportion of Items of Interest Is Stable Over Time

If you are studying a process and have collected data over a time period, you can create the appropriate control chart. If you have collected the proportion of items of interest over a time period, you develop a p chart (see bonus eBook Section 18.2).

USING STATISTICS Mounting Future Analyses, Revisited

Angela Waye / Shutterstock

This chapter summarizes all the methods discussed in the first 16 chapters of this book. The data analysis methods discussed in the book are organized in Table 17.1 according to whether each method is used for describing a group or several groups, for making inferences about one group or comparing two or more groups, or for analyzing relationships between two or more variables. Then, sets of questions are listed in Exhibits 17.1 and 17.2 to assist you in determining what method to use to analyze your data.

Digital Case

Whereas other Digital Cases asked you to apply your knowledge about the proper use of statistics, this case helps you remember how to properly apply that knowledge.

Guadalupe Cooper and Gilbert Chandler had worked very hard all semester long in their business statistics course. They now faced a final project in which they had to establish a plan to analyze a set of data that had been assigned to them by their instructor. As they looked through the online materials at the companion website for their statistics textbook, they found **DataAnalysisGuide.pdf** in the Digital Case materials. "Gee, this is like the material in Chapter 17, but in interactive form!" one of them noted. They both then knew what questions they needed to ask in order to get started on their final semester task.

CHAPTER REVIEW PROBLEMS

17.1 In many manufacturing processes, the term *work-in-process* (often abbreviated WIP) is used. At the LSS Publishing book manufacturing plants, WIP represents the time it takes for sheets from a press to be folded, gathered, sewn, tipped on end sheets, and bound together to form a book, and the book placed in a packing carton. The operational definition of the variable of interest, processing time, is the number of days (measured in hundredths) from when the sheets come off the press to when the book is placed in a packing carton. The company has the business objective of determining whether there are differences in the WIP between plants. Data have been collected from samples of 20 books at each of two production plants. The data, stored in WIP, are as follows:

Plant A

5.62	5.29	16.25	10.92	11.46	21.62	8.45	8.58	5.41	11.42
11.62	7.29	7.50	7.96	4.42	10.50	7.58	9.29	7.54	8.92

Plant B

9.54	11.46	16.62	12.62	25.75	15.41	14.29	13.13	13.71	10.04
5.75	12.46	9.17	13.21	6.00	2.33	14.25	5.37	6.25	9.71

Completely analyze the data.

17.2 Many factors determine the attendance at Major League Baseball games. These factors can include when the game is played, the weather, the opponent, whether the team is having a good season, and whether a marketing promotion is held. Popular promotions during a recent season included the traditional hat days and poster days and the newer craze, bobble-heads of star players. (Data extracted from T. C. Boyd and T. C. Krehbiel, "An Analysis of the Effects of Specific Promotion Types on Attendance at Major League Baseball Games," *Mid-American Journal of Business*, 2006, 21, pp. 21–32.) The file Baseball includes the following variables for a recent Major League Baseball season:

TEAM—Kansas City Royals, Philadelphia Phillies, Chicago Cubs, or Cincinnati Reds
ATTENDANCE—Paid attendance for the game
TEMP—High temperature for the day
WIN%—Team's winning percentage at the time of the game
OPWIN%—Opponent team's winning percentage at the time of the game
WEEKEND—1 if game played on Friday, Saturday, or Sunday; 0 otherwise
PROMOTION—1 if a promotion was held; 0 if no promotion was held

You want to predict attendance and determine the factors that influence attendance. Completely analyze the data for the Kansas City Royals.

17.3 Repeat Problem 17.2 for the Philadelphia Phillies.

17.4 Repeat Problem 17.2 for the Chicago Cubs.

17.5 Repeat Problem 17.2 for the Cincinnati Reds.

17.6 The file RealEstate contains data for a sample of 362 single-family homes located in five different communities in a suburban county outside a large city in the northeastern United States. The following variables are included:

Appraised value—$thousands
Lot size—thousands of square feet
Number of bedrooms
Number of bathrooms
Number of rooms
Age in years
Annual real estate taxes—$
Type of Indoor parking facility—None; One-car garage; Two-car garage
Location—A; B; C; D; E
Architectural style—Cape; Expanded ranch; Colonial; Ranch; Split level
Type of heating fuel used—Gas; Oil
Type of heating system—Hot air; Hot water; Other
Type of swimming pool—None; Above ground; In-ground
Eat-in kitchen—Absent; Present
Central air-conditioning—Absent; Present
Fireplace—Absent; Present
Connection to local sewer system—Absent; Present
Basement—Absent; Present
Modern kitchen—Absent; Present
Modern bathrooms—Absent; Present

Prepare a report with the objective of comparing the characteristics of single-family homes in the five communities. In addition, develop models to predict the assessed value of the house and the annual real estate taxes.

17.7 The file Homes contains information on all the single-family houses sold in a small city in the midwestern United States for one year. The following variables are included:

Price—Selling price of home, in dollars
Location—Rating of the location from 1 to 5, with 1 the worst and 5 the best
Condition—Rating of the condition of the home from 1 to 5, with 1 the worst and 5 the best
Bedrooms—Number of bedrooms in the home
Bathrooms—Number of bathrooms in the home
Other Rooms—Number of rooms in the home other than bedrooms and bathrooms

You want to be able to predict the selling price of the homes. Completely analyze the data.

17.8 Zagat's publishes restaurant ratings for various locations in the United States. The file Restaurants2 contains the Zagat rating for food, décor, service, and cost per person for a sample of 50 restaurants located in New York City and 50 restaurants located in suburban areas outside New York City. (Data extracted from *Zagat Survey 2013, New York City Restaurants* and *Zagat Survey 2012–2013, Long Island Restaurants.*)

You want to study differences in the cost of a meal between restaurants in New York City and suburban areas and also want to be able to predict the cost of a meal. Completely analyze the data.

17.9 The data in UsedCars represent characteristics of cars that are currently part of an inventory of a used car dealership. The variables included are car, year, age, price ($), mileage, power (hp), and fuel (mpg).

You want to describe each of these variables, and you would like to predict the price of the used cars. Analyze the data.

17.10 A study was conducted to determine whether any gender bias existed in an academic science environment. Faculty from several universities were asked to rate candidates for the position of undergraduate laboratory manager based on their application. The gender of the applicant was given in the applicant's materials. The raters were from either biology, chemistry, or physics departments. Each rater was to give a competence rating to the applicant's materials on a seven point scale with 1 being the lowest and 7 being the highest. In addition, the rater supplied a starting salary that should be offered to the applicant. These data (which have been altered from an actual study to preserve the anonymity of the respondents) are stored in Candidate Assessment.

Analyze the data. Do you think that there is any gender bias in the evaluations? Support your point of view with specific references to your data analysis.

17.11 Zagat's publishes restaurant ratings for various locations in the United States. The file Restaurants3 contains the Zagat rating for food, décor, service, cost per person, and popularity index (popularity points the restaurant received divided by the number of people who voted for that restaurant) for various types of restaurants in New York City.

You want to study differences in the cost of a meal for the different types of cuisines and also want to be able to predict the cost of a meal. Completely analyze the data. (Data extracted from *Zagat Survey 2012 New York City Restaurants*).

17.12 The data in the file BankMarketing are from a direct marketing campaign conducted by a Portuguese banking institution (Data extracted from S. Moro, R. Laureano and P. Cortez, "Using Data Mining for Bank Direct Marketing: An Application of the CRISP-DM Methodology." in P. Novais et al. (Eds.), *Proceedings of the European Simulation and Modeling Conference—ESM'2011*, pp. 117–121.) The variables included were age, type of job, marital status, education, whether credit is in default, average yearly balance in account in Euros, whether there is a housing loan, whether there is a personal loan, last contact duration in seconds, number of contacts performed during this campaign, and has the client purchased a term deposit.

Analyze the data and assess the likelihood that the client will purchase a term deposit.

17.13 A mining company operates a large heap-leach gold mine in the western United States. The gold mined at this location consists of ore that is very low grade, having about 0.0032 ounce of gold in 1 ton of ore. The process of heap-leaching involves the mining, crushing, stacking, and leaching millions of tons of gold ore per year. In the process, ore is placed in a large heap on an impermeable pad. A weak chemical solution is sprinkled over the heap and is collected at the bottom after percolating through the ore. As the solution percolates through the ore, the gold is dissolved and is later recovered from the solution. This technology, which has been used for more than 30 years, has made the operation profitable. Due to the large amount of ore that is handled, the company is continually exploring ways to improve the process. As part of an expansion several years ago, the stacking process was automated with the construction of a computer controlled stacker. This stacker was designed to load 35,000 tons of ore per day at a cost that was less than the previous process that used manually operated trucks and bulldozers. However, since its installation, the stacker has not been able to achieve these results consistently. Data for a recent 35-day period that indicate the amount stacked (tons) and the downtime (minutes) are stored in the file Mining. Other data that indicate the causes for the downtime are stored in Mining2.

Analyze the data, making sure to present conclusions about the daily amount stacked and the causes of the downtime. In addition, be sure to develop a model to predict the amount stacked based on downtime.

17.14 A survey was conducted on the characteristics of households in the United States. The data (which have been altered from an actual study to preserve the anonymity of the respondents) are stored in Households. The variables are gender, age, Hispanic origin, type of dwelling, age of dwelling in years, years living at dwelling, number of bedrooms, number of vehicles kept at dwelling, fuel type at dwelling, monthly cost of fuel at dwelling ($), U.S. citizenship, college degree, marital status, work for pay in previous week, mode of transportation to work, commuting time in minutes, hours worked per week, type of organization, annual earned income ($), and total annual income ($).

Analyze these data and prepare a report describing your conclusions.

Appendices

APPENDIX A Basic Math Concepts and Symbols

A.1 Rules for Arithmetic Operations

RULE	EXAMPLE
1. $a + b = c$ and $b + a = c$	$2 + 1 = 3$ and $1 + 2 = 3$
2. $a + (b + c) = (a + b) + c$	$5 + (7 + 4) = (5 + 7) + 4 = 16$
3. $a - b = c$ but $b - a \neq c$	$9 - 7 = 2$ but $7 - 9 \neq 2$
4. $(a)(b) = (b)(a)$	$(7)(6) = (6)(7) = 42$
5. $(a)(b + c) = ab + ac$	$(2)(3 + 5) = (2)(3) + (2)(5) = 16$
6. $a \div b \neq b \div a$	$12 \div 3 \neq 3 \div 12$
7. $\frac{a + b}{c} = \frac{a}{c} + \frac{b}{c}$	$\frac{7 + 3}{2} = \frac{7}{2} + \frac{3}{2} = 5$
8. $\frac{a}{b + c} \neq \frac{a}{b} + \frac{a}{c}$	$\frac{3}{4 + 5} \neq \frac{3}{4} + \frac{3}{5}$
9. $\frac{1}{a} + \frac{1}{b} = \frac{b + a}{ab}$	$\frac{1}{3} + \frac{1}{5} = \frac{5 + 3}{(3)(5)} = \frac{8}{15}$
10. $\left(\frac{a}{b}\right)\left(\frac{c}{d}\right) = \left(\frac{ac}{bd}\right)$	$\left(\frac{2}{3}\right)\left(\frac{6}{7}\right) = \left(\frac{(2)(6)}{(3)(7)}\right) = \frac{12}{21}$
11. $\frac{a}{b} \div \frac{c}{d} = \frac{ad}{bc}$	$\frac{5}{8} \div \frac{3}{7} = \left(\frac{(5)(7)}{(8)(3)}\right) = \frac{35}{24}$

A.2 Rules for Algebra: Exponents and Square Roots

RULE	EXAMPLE
1. $(X^a)(X^b) = X^{a+b}$	$(4^2)(4^3) = 4^5$
2. $(X^a)^b = X^{ab}$	$(2^2)^3 = 2^6$
3. $(X^a/X^b) = X^{a-b}$	$\frac{3^5}{3^3} = 3^2$
4. $\frac{X^a}{X^a} = X^0 = 1$	$\frac{3^4}{3^4} = 3^0 = 1$
5. $\sqrt{XY} = \sqrt{X}\sqrt{Y}$	$\sqrt{(25)(4)} = \sqrt{25}\sqrt{4} = 10$
6. $\sqrt{\frac{X}{Y}} = \frac{\sqrt{X}}{\sqrt{Y}}$	$\sqrt{\frac{16}{100}} = \frac{\sqrt{16}}{\sqrt{100}} = 0.40$

A.3 Rules for Logarithms

Base 10

Log is the symbol used for base-10 logarithms:

RULE	EXAMPLE
1. $\log(10^a) = a$	$\log(100) = \log(10^2) = 2$
2. If $\log(a) = b$, then $a = 10^b$	If $\log(a) = 2$, then $a = 10^2 = 100$
3. $\log(ab) = \log(a) + \log(b)$	$\log(100) = \log[(10)(10)] = \log(10) + \log(10)$ $= 1 + 1 = 2$
4. $\log(a^b) = (b)\log(a)$	$\log(1{,}000) = \log(10^3) = (3)\log(10) = (3)(1) = 3$
5. $\log(a/b) = \log(a) - \log(b)$	$\log(100) = \log(1{,}000/10) = \log(1{,}000) - \log(10)$ $= 3 - 1 = 2$

EXAMPLE

Take the base-10 logarithm of each side of the following equation:

$$Y = \beta_0 \beta_1^X \varepsilon$$

SOLUTION: Apply rules 3 and 4:

$$\begin{aligned}\log(Y) &= \log(\beta_0 \beta_1^X \varepsilon)\\ &= \log(\beta_0) + \log(\beta_1^X) + \log(\varepsilon)\\ &= \log(\beta_0) + X\log(\beta_1) + \log(\varepsilon)\end{aligned}$$

Base *e*

ln is the symbol used for base *e* logarithms, commonly referred to as natural logarithms. *e* is Euler's number, and $e \cong 2.718282$:

RULE	EXAMPLE
1. $\ln(e^a) = a$	$\ln(7.389056) = \ln(e^2) = 2$
2. If $\ln(a) = b$, then $a = e^b$	If $\ln(a) = 2$, then $a = e^2 = 7.389056$
3. $\ln(ab) = \ln(a) + \ln(b)$	$\ln(100) = \ln[(10)(10)]$ $= \ln(10) + \ln(10) = 2.302585 + 2.302585 = 4.605170$
4. $\ln(a^b) = (b)\ln(a)$	$\ln(1{,}000) = \ln(10^3) = 3\ln(10) = 3(2.302585) = 6.907755$
5. $\ln(a/b) = \ln(a) - \ln(b)$	$\ln(100) = \ln(1{,}000/10) = \ln(1{,}000) - \ln(10)$ $= 6.907755 - 2.302585 = 4.605170$

EXAMPLE

Take the base *e* logarithm of each side of the following equation:

$$Y = \beta_0 \beta_1^X \varepsilon$$

SOLUTION: Apply rules 3 and 4:

$$\begin{aligned}\ln(Y) &= \ln(\beta_0 \beta_1^X \varepsilon)\\ &= \ln(\beta_0) + \ln(\beta_1^X) + \ln(\varepsilon)\\ &= \ln(\beta_0) + X\ln(\beta_1) + \ln(\varepsilon)\end{aligned}$$

A.4 Summation Notation

The symbol Σ, the Greek capital letter sigma, represents "taking the sum of." Consider a set of n values for variable X. The expression $\sum_{i=1}^{n} X_i$ means to take the sum of the n values for variable X. Thus:

$$\sum_{i=1}^{n} X_i = X_1 + X_2 + X_3 + \cdots + X_n$$

The following problem illustrates the use of the symbol Σ. Consider five values of a variable X: $X_1 = 2, X_2 = 0, X_3 = -1, X_4 = 5$, and $X_5 = 7$. Thus:

$$\sum_{i=1}^{5} X_i = X_1 + X_2 + X_3 + X_4 + X_5 = 2 + 0 + (-1) + 5 + 7 = 13$$

In statistics, the squared values of a variable are often summed. Thus:

$$\sum_{i=1}^{n} X_i^2 = X_1^2 + X_2^2 + X_3^2 + \cdots + X_n^2$$

and, in the example above:

$$\begin{aligned}\sum_{i=1}^{5} X_i^2 &= X_1^2 + X_2^2 + X_3^2 + X_4^2 + X_5^2 \\ &= 2^2 + 0^2 + (-1)^2 + 5^2 + 7^2 \\ &= 4 + 0 + 1 + 25 + 49 \\ &= 79\end{aligned}$$

$\sum_{i=1}^{n} X_i^2$, the summation of the squares, is *not* the same as $\left(\sum_{i=1}^{n} X_i\right)^2$, the square of the sum:

$$\sum_{i=1}^{n} X_i^2 \neq \left(\sum_{i=1}^{n} X_i\right)^2$$

In the example given above, the summation of squares is equal to 79. This is not equal to the square of the sum, which is $13^2 = 169$.

Another frequently used operation involves the summation of the product. Consider two variables, X and Y, each having n values. Then:

$$\sum_{i=1}^{n} X_i Y_i = X_1 Y_1 + X_2 Y_2 + X_3 Y_3 + \cdots + X_n Y_n$$

Continuing with the previous example, suppose there is a second variable, Y, whose five values are $Y_1 = 1, Y_2 = 3, Y_3 = -2, Y_4 = 4$, and $Y_5 = 3$. Then,

$$\begin{aligned}\sum_{i=1}^{n} X_i Y_i &= X_1 Y_1 + X_2 Y_2 + X_3 Y_3 + X_4 Y_4 + X_5 Y_5 \\ &= (2)(1) + (0)(3) + (-1)(-2) + (5)(4) + (7)(3) \\ &= 2 + 0 + 2 + 20 + 21 \\ &= 45\end{aligned}$$

In computing $\sum_{i=1}^{n} X_i Y_i$, you need to realize that the first value of X is multiplied by the first value of Y, the second value of X is multiplied by the second value of Y, and so on. These products are then summed in order to compute the desired result. However, the summation of products is *not* equal to the product of the individual sums:

$$\sum_{i=1}^{n} X_i Y_i \neq \left(\sum_{i=1}^{n} X_i\right)\left(\sum_{i=1}^{n} Y_i\right)$$

In this example,

$$\sum_{i=1}^{5} X_i = 13$$

and

$$\sum_{i=1}^{5} Y_i = 1 + 3 + (-2) + 4 + 3 = 9$$

so that

$$\left(\sum_{i=1}^{5} X_i\right)\left(\sum_{i=1}^{5} Y_i\right) = (13)(9) = 117$$

However,

$$\sum_{i=1}^{5} X_i Y_i = 45$$

The following table summarizes these results:

VALUE	X_i	Y_i	$X_i Y_i$
1	2	1	2
2	0	3	0
3	−1	−2	2
4	5	4	20
5	7	3	21
	$\sum_{i=1}^{5} X_i = 13$	$\sum_{i=1}^{5} Y_i = 9$	$\sum_{i=1}^{5} X_i Y_i = 45$

Rule 1 The summation of the values of two variables is equal to the sum of the values of each summed variable:

$$\sum_{i=1}^{n} (X_i + Y_i) = \sum_{i=1}^{n} X_i + \sum_{i=1}^{n} Y_i$$

Thus,

$$\begin{aligned}\sum_{i=1}^{5} (X_i + Y_i) &= (2 + 1) + (0 + 3) + (-1 + (-2)) + (5 + 4) + (7 + 3) \\ &= 3 + 3 + (-3) + 9 + 10 \\ &= 22\end{aligned}$$

$$\sum_{i=1}^{5} X_i + \sum_{i=1}^{5} Y_i = 13 + 9 = 22$$

Rule 2 The summation of a difference between the values of two variables is equal to the difference between the summed values of the variables:

$$\sum_{i=1}^{n}(X_i - Y_i) = \sum_{i=1}^{n}X_i - \sum_{i=1}^{n}Y_i$$

Thus,

$$\sum_{i=1}^{5}(X_i - Y_i) = (2-1) + (0-3) + (-1-(-2)) + (5-4) + (7-3)$$

$$= 1 + (-3) + 1 + 1 + 4$$

$$= 4$$

$$\sum_{i=1}^{5}X_i - \sum_{i=1}^{5}Y_i = 13 - 9 = 4$$

Rule 3 The sum of a constant times a variable is equal to that constant times the sum of the values of the variable:

$$\sum_{i=1}^{n}cX_i = c\sum_{i=1}^{n}X_i$$

where c is a constant. Thus, if $c = 2$,

$$\sum_{i=1}^{5}cX_i = \sum_{i=1}^{5}2X_i = (2)(2) + (2)(0) + (2)(-1) + (2)(5) + (2)(7)$$

$$= 4 + 0 + (-2) + 10 + 14$$

$$= 26$$

$$c\sum_{i=1}^{5}X_i = 2\sum_{i=1}^{5}X_i = (2)(13) = 26$$

Rule 4 A constant summed n times will be equal to n times the value of the constant.

$$\sum_{i=1}^{n}c = nc$$

where c is a constant. Thus, if the constant $c = 2$ is summed 5 times,

$$\sum_{i=1}^{5}c = 2 + 2 + 2 + 2 + 2 = 10$$

$$nc = (5)(2) = 10$$

EXAMPLE

Suppose there are six values for the variables X and Y, such that $X_1 = 2, X_2 = 1, X_3 = 5, X_4 = -3, X_5 = 1, X_6 = -2$ and $Y_1 = 4, Y_2 = 0, Y_3 = -1, Y_4 = 2, Y_5 = 7$, and $Y_6 = -3$. Compute each of the following:

(a) $\sum_{i=1}^{6}X_i$

(b) $\sum_{i=1}^{6}Y_i$

(c) $\sum_{i=1}^{6}X_i^2$

(d) $\sum_{i=1}^{6}Y_i^2$

(e) $\sum_{i=1}^{6}X_iY_i$

(f) $\sum_{i=1}^{6}(X_i + Y_i)$

(g) $\sum_{i=1}^{6}(X_i - Y_i)$

(h) $\sum_{i=1}^{6}(X_i - 3Y_i + 2X_i^2)$

(i) $\sum_{i=1}^{6}(cX_i)$, where $c = -1$

(j) $\sum_{i=1}^{6}(X_i - 3Y_i + c)$, where $c = +3$

Answers

(a) 4 (b) 9 (c) 44 (d) 79 (e) 10 (f) (13) (g) −5 (h) 65 (i) −4 (j) −5

References

1. Bashaw, W. L., *Mathematics for Statistics* (New York: Wiley, 1969).
2. Lanzer, P., *Basic Math: Fractions, Decimals, Percents* (Hicksville, NY: Video Aided Instruction, 2006).
3. Levine, D. and A. Brandwein, *The MBA Primer: Business Statistics*, 3rd ed. (Cincinnati, OH: Cengage Publishing, 2011).
4. Levine, D., *Statistics* (Hicksville, NY: Video Aided Instruction, 2006).
5. Shane, H., *Algebra 1* (Hicksville, NY: Video Aided Instruction, 2006).

A.5 Statistical Symbols

$+$ add	$\times$ multiply
$-$ subtract	$\div$ divide
$=$ equal to	$\neq$ not equal to
$\cong$ approximately equal to	$<$ less than
$>$ greater than	$\leq$ less than or equal to
$\geq$ greater than or equal to	

A.6 Greek Alphabet

GREEK LETTER		LETTER NAME	ENGLISH EQUIVALENT	GREEK LETTER		LETTER NAME	ENGLISH EQUIVALENT
A	α	Alpha	a	N	ν	Nu	n
B	β	Beta	b	Ξ	ξ	Xi	x
Γ	γ	Gamma	g	O	o	Omicron	ŏ
Δ	δ	Delta	d	Π	π	Pi	p
E	ε	Epsilon	ĕ	P	ρ	Rho	r
Z	ζ	Zeta	z	Σ	σ	Sigma	s
H	η	Eta	ē	T	τ	Tau	t
Θ	θ	Theta	th	Y	υ	Upsilon	u
I	ι	Iota	i	Φ	ϕ	Phi	ph
K	κ	Kappa	k	X	χ	Chi	ch
Λ	λ	Lambda	l	Ψ	ψ	Psi	ps
M	μ	Mu	m	Ω	ω	Omega	ō

APPENDIX B Required Excel Skills

This appendix reviews the Excel skills and operations you need to know in order to make effective use of Microsoft Excel. As stated in Section EG.3 on page 10, if you plan to use the *In-Depth Excel* instructions, you will need to be familiar with the entire contents of this appendix. Mastery of the skills and operations in this appendix is less necessary if you plan to use PHStat (or the Analysis ToolPak), but knowing them will prove useful if you need to customize the worksheets that PHStat creates or plan to create your summary presentations from those results.

If you find the level of this appendix too challenging or are unfamiliar with the skills listed in Table EG.A on page 11, then read the eBook bonus section "Basic Computing Skills" that is mentioned on that page.

B.1 Worksheet Entries and References

As discussed in Section EG.1 on page 10, Microsoft Excel uses worksheets (sometimes called spreadsheets) to both store data and present the results of analyses. A **worksheet** is a tabular arrangement of data, in which the intersections of rows and columns form **cells**, boxes into which you make entries. These entries can be numbers, text that serves to label numbers or title a worksheet, or *formulas*. **Formulas** are instructions that perform a calculation or some other computing task such as logical decision making. Formulas are typically found in worksheets that you use to present intermediate calculations or the results of an analysis. In some cases, formulas can be used to prepare new data to be analyzed.

Formulas typically use values found in other cells to compute a result that is displayed in the cell that stores the formula. This means that when you see that a particular worksheet cell is displaying the value, say, 5, you cannot determine from casual inspection if the worksheet creator typed the number 5 into the cell or if the creator typed a formula that results in the display of the value 5. This trait of worksheets means you should always carefully review the contents of each worksheet you use. In this book, each worksheet with formulas that you might use is accompanied by a "formulas" worksheet that presents the worksheet in a mode that allows you to see all the formulas that have been entered in the worksheet.

Cell References

Most formulas use values that have been entered into other cells. To refer to those cells, Excel uses an addressing, or *referencing*, system that is based on the tabular nature of a worksheet. Columns are designated with letters and rows are designated with numbers such that the cell in the first row and first column is called A1, the cell in the third row and first column is called A3, and the cell in the third column and first row is C1. To refer to a cell in a formula, you use a cell reference in the form *WorksheetName!ColumnRow*. For example, Data!A2 refers to the cell in the Data worksheet that is in column A and row 2.

You can also use only the *ColumnRow* portion of a full address—for example, A2—as a shorthand way of referring to a cell that is on the same worksheet as the one into which you are entering a formula. (Excel calls the worksheet into which you are making entries the **current worksheet**.) If the worksheet name contains spaces or special characters, such as **CITY DATA** or **Figure_1.2**, you must enclose the sheet name in a pair of single quotes, as in 'CITY DATA'!A2 or 'Figure_1.2'!A2.

To refer to a group of cells, such as the cells of a column that store the data for a particular variable, you use a cell range. A cell range names the upper-left cell and the lower-right cell of the group, using the form *WorksheetName!UpperLeftCell:LowerRightCell*. For example, the cell range DATA!A1:A11 identifies the first 11 cells in the first column of the DATA worksheet. Cell ranges can extend over multiple columns; the cell range DATA!A1:D11 would refer to the first 11 cells in the first 4 columns of the worksheet. Cell ranges in the form *Column:Column* (or *Row:Row*) that refer to all cells in a column (or row) are also allowed. In this book, you will occasionally see cell ranges such as B:B that refer to all the cells in a column B for situations in which the number of cell entries in column B would be unknown to the worksheet creator.

As with single cell references, you can skip the *WorksheetName!* part of the reference if you are entering a cell range on the current worksheet. And if a worksheet name contains spaces or special characters, the worksheet name must be enclosed in a pair of single quotes. Note, that in some Excel dialog boxes, you *must* include the worksheet name as part of the cell reference in order to get the proper results. (Such cases are noted in the instructions in this book when they arise.)

Although not used in this book, cell references can include a workbook name in the form *'[WorkbookName]WorksheetName'!ColumnRow* or *'[WorkbookName]WorksheetName'! UpperLeftCell:LowerRightCell*. You might discover such references if you inadvertently copy certain types of worksheets or chart sheets from one workbook to another.

Recalculation

When you use formulas that refer to other cells, the result displayed by the formulas automatically changes as the values in the cells to which the formula refers change.

This process, called **recalculation**, was the original novel feature of worksheet programs and first led to these programs being widely used in accounting.

Recalculation forms the basis for constructing worksheet *templates* and *models*. **Templates** are worksheets in which you only need to enter values to get results. Templates can be reused over and over again, by entering different sets of values. Many of the worksheets illustrated in this book are designed as templates. For those worksheets, you need only to enter new values, typically into cells that are tinted a light turquoise color, to get the results you need. Other worksheets illustrated are **models**, which are similar to templates but require the editing of certain formulas as new values are entered into a worksheet. In this book, worksheet models have been designed to simplify such editing tasks and to provide the most generalized solution.

Worksheets that use formulas capable of recalculation are sometimes called "live" worksheets to distinguish them from worksheets that contain only text and numeric entries ("dead" worksheets), much like a simple word processing table would contain. A novel feature of the PHStat add-in that you can use with this book is that just about every worksheet the add-in constructs for you is a "live" worksheet. This means that, as first noted in Section EG.2 on page 10, you get the same results, the same worksheets, whether you use *PHStat* or the *In-Depth Excel* instructions in the Excel Guides. This is dissimilar to many other add-ins that produce results in the form of dead worksheets that cannot be reused in any way.

B.2 Absolute and Relative Cell References

Many worksheets contain columns (or rows) of similar-looking formulas. For example, column C in a worksheet might contain formulas that sum the contents of the column A and column B rows. The formula for cell C2 would be =**A2** + **B2**, the formula for cell C3 would be =**A3** + **B3**, for cell C4, =**A4** + **B4**, and so on, down column C. To avoid the drudgery of typing many similar formulas, you can copy a formula and paste it into all the cells in a selected cell range. For example, to copy a formula that has been entered in cell C2 down the column through row 12:

1. Right-click cell C2 and press **Ctrl+C** to copy the formula. A movie marquee–like highlight appears around cell C2.
2. Select the cell range **C3:C12**.
3. With the cell range highlighted, press **Ctrl+V** to paste the formula into the cells of the cell range.

When you perform this copy-and-paste operation, Excel adjusts these **relative cell references** in formulas so that copying the formula =**A2** + **B2** from cell C2 to cell C3 results in the formula =**A3** + **B3** being pasted into cell C3, the formula =**A4** + **B4** being pasted into cell C4, and so on.

There are circumstances in which you do not want Excel to adjust all or part of a formula. For example, if you were copying the cell C2 formula =**(A2** + **B2)/B15**, and cell B15 contained the divisor to be used in all formulas, you would not want to see pasted into cell C3 the formula =**(A3** + **B3)/B16**. To prevent Excel from adjusting a cell reference, you use **absolute cell references** by inserting dollar signs ($) before the column and row references of a relative cell reference. For example, the absolute cell reference **$B$15** in the copied cell C2 formula =**(A2** + **B2)/$B$15** will cause Excel to paste the formula =**(A2** + **B2)/$B$15** into cell C3.

For ease of reading, formulas shown in the worksheet illustrations in this book generally show relative cell references, even in cases where using absolute cell references would assist in the physical entry of the formulas. As you review absolute cell references, do not confuse the use of the dollar sign symbol with the worksheet formatting operation that displays numbers as dollar currency amounts. (See Section B.5 to learn how to format cells to display numeric values as dollar currency amounts.)

B.3 Entering Formulas into Worksheets

To enter a formula into a cell, first select the cell and then begin the entry by typing the equal sign (=). What follows the equal sign can be a combination of mathematical and data-processing operations and cell references that is terminated by pressing **Enter**. For simple formulas, you use the symbols +, −, *, /, and ^ for the operations addition, subtraction, multiplication, division, and exponentiation (a number raised to a power), respectively. For example, the formula =**A2** + **B2** adds the contents of cells A2 and B2 displays the sum as the value in the cell containing the formula. To revise a formula, either retype the formula or edit it in the formula bar.

Because formulas display their results and not themselves when entered in a cell, you should always review and verify any formula you enter before you use its worksheet to get results. One way to view all the formulas in a worksheet is to press **Ctrl+`** (grave accent). After your formula review, you can press **Ctrl+`** a second time to restore the normal display of values. (The companion "formulas" worksheets mentioned in Section B.1 were created by pressing **Ctrl+`** one time with a copy of the original worksheet.)

Functions

You can use worksheet functions in formulas to simplify certain arithmetic formulas or to gain access to advanced processing or statistical functions. For example, instead of typing =**A2** + **A3** + **A4** + **A5** + **A6**, you could use the

SUM function to enter the equivalent, and shorter, formula =**SUM(A2:A6)**. Functions are entered by typing their names followed by a pair of parentheses. For almost all functions, you need to make at least one entry inside the pair of parentheses. For functions that require two or more entries, you separate entries with commas, as in the function **QUARTILE (*variable cell range*, *quartile number*)** function that is discussed in Section EG3.3.

To use a worksheet function in a formula, either type the function as shown in the instructions in this book or select a function from one of the galleries in the Function Library group of the Formulas tab. For example, to enter the formula =**QUARTILE(A2:A20, 2)** in cell C2, you could either type these 20 characters directly into the cell or select cell C2 and then select **Formulas → More Functions → Statistical** and click **QUARTILE** from the drop-down list and then enter **A2:A20** and **2** in the Function Arguments dialog box and click **OK**. (For some functions, the selection process is much shorter and, in Excel versions older than Excel 2007, you select **Formulas → Insert Function** and then make the necessary entries and selections in one or more dialog boxes that follow.)

Entering Array Formulas

An **array formula** is a formula that you enter just once but that applies to all of the cells in a selected cell range (the "array"). To enter an array formula, first select the cell range and then type the formula, and then, while holding down the **Ctrl** and **Shift** keys, press **Enter** to enter the array formula into all of the cells of the cell range. (In OS X Excel, you can also press **Command+Enter** to enter an array formula.

To edit an array formula, you must first select the entire cell range that contains the array formula, then edit the formula and then press **Enter** while holding down **Ctrl+Shift** (or press **Command+Enter**). When you select a cell that contains an array formula, Excel adds a pair of curly braces { } to the display of the formula in the formula bar. These curly braces disappear when you start to edit the formula. Including a pair of curly braces around a formula when documenting a worksheet is a convention to indicate that a particular formula is an array formula, but at no time will you ever type the curly braces when you enter an array formula.

B.4 Pasting with Paste Special

While the keyboard shortcuts **Ctrl+C** and **Ctrl+V** to copy and paste cell contents will often suffice, pasting data from one worksheet to another can sometimes cause unexpected side effects. When the two worksheets are in different workbooks, a simple paste creates an external link to the original workbook. This can lead to errors later if the first workbook is unavailable when the second one is being used. Even pasting between worksheets in the same workbook can lead to problems if what is being pasted is a cell range of formulas.

To avoid such side effects, use **Paste Special** in such situations. To use this operation, copy the source cell range using **Ctrl+C** and then right-click the cell (or cell range) that is the target of the paste and click **Paste Special** from the shortcut menu.

In the Paste Special dialog box (shown below), click **Values** and then click **OK**. For the first case, Paste Special Values pastes the current values of the cells in the first workbook and not formulas that use cell references to the first workbook.

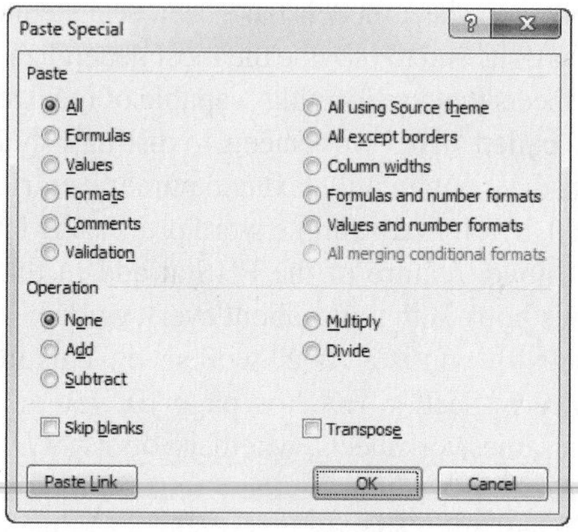

Paste Special can paste other types of information, including cell formatting information. In some copying contexts, placing the mouse pointer over Paste Special in the shortcut menu will reveal a gallery of shortcuts to the choices presented in the Paste Special dialog box. For a full discussion of these additional features of Paste Special, see the Microsoft Excel help system.

If you use PHStat and have data for a procedure in the form of formulas, copy your data and then use Paste Special to paste columns of equivalent *values*. (Click **Values** in the Paste Special dialog box to create the values.) Then use the columns of values as the cell range of the data for the procedure. PHStat will not work properly if the data for a procedure are in the form of formulas.

B.5 Basic Worksheet Formatting

You can change many aspects of how Excel displays the contents of worksheet cells through cell formatting. You format cells either by making entries in the Format Cells dialog box or by clicking shortcut buttons in the Home tab at the top of the Excel window. If you are new to Excel, you may find that using the Format Cells dialog box method to be easier, at least initially. Then, over time, you may want to switch to the Home tab shortcuts discussed on the next two pages.

To use the dialog box, right-click a cell (or cell range) and click **Format Cells** in the shortcut menu. Excel displays the Number tab of the dialog box (partially shown below).

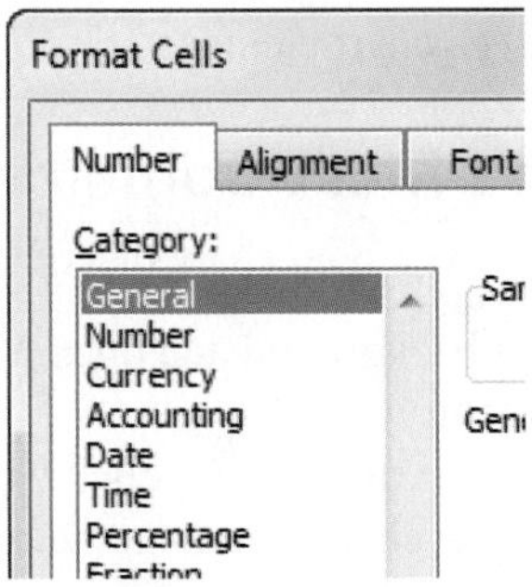

Clicking a **Category** changes the panel to the right of the list. For example, clicking **Number** displays a panel (shown below) in which you can set the number of decimal places. (Many cells in the worksheets used in this book have been set to display four decimal places.)

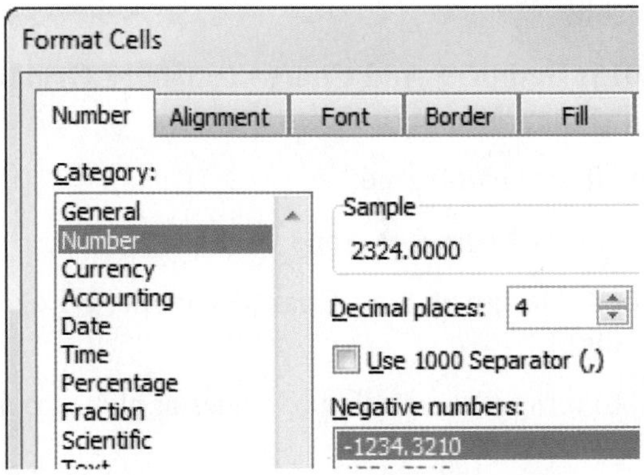

You can also change the numeric formatting of cells by clicking the various buttons of the **Number** group in the Home tab (shown below).

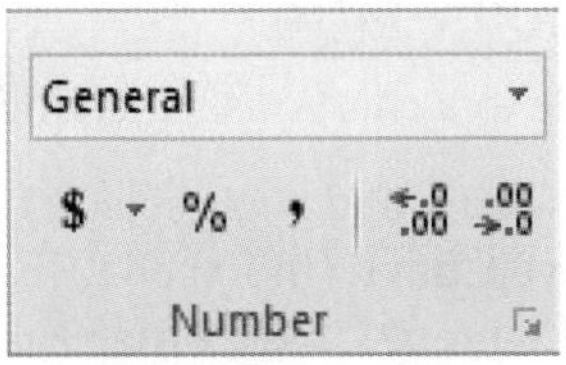

When you click the **Alignment** tab of the Format Cells dialog box (shown at top of right column), you display a panel in which you can control such things such as whether cell contents get displayed centered or top- or bottom-anchored in a cell and whether cell contents are horizontally centered or left or right justified. These choices in this

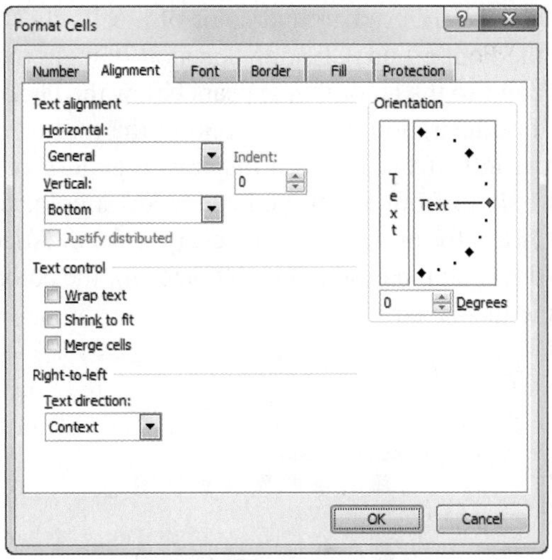

panel are duplicated in the Alignment group of the Home tab (shown below).

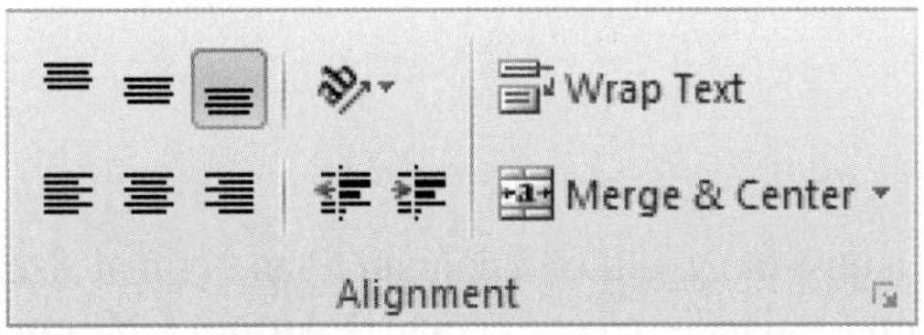

In the Ribbon interface, many buttons, such as **Merge & Center**, have an associated pull-down list that you display by clicking the pull-down arrow at the right. For Merge & Center, this pull-down displays a gallery of similar choices (shown below).

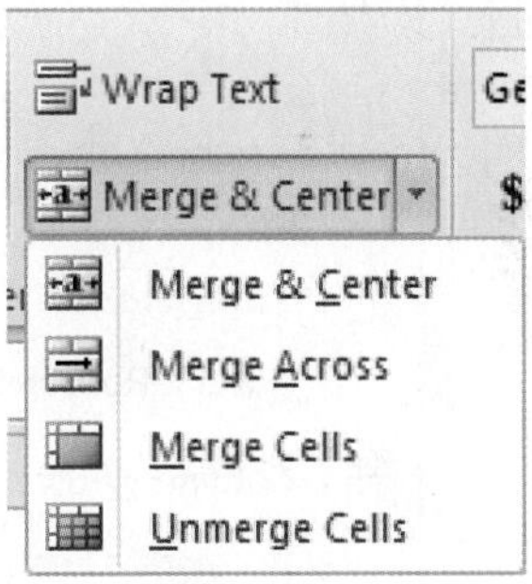

The **Font** tab of the Format Cells dialog box allows you to change the text attributes used to display cell contents, but you will find using the equivalent choices in the Font group of the Home tab (shown below) to be a more convenient way of making choices such as changing the typeface or point size or styling text to be bold or italic.

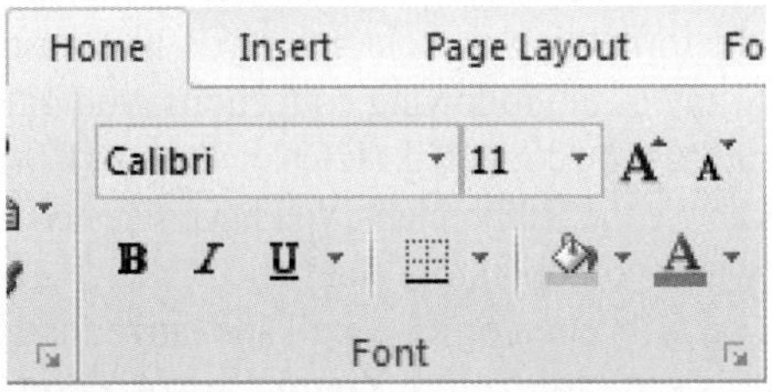

To change the background color of a cell, click the **fill icon** in the Font group. Clicking this icon changes the background color to the color that appears below the bucket (yellow in the illustration below). Clicking the pull-down button to the left of the fill icon displays a gallery of colors (shown below) from which you can select a color or click **More Colors** for even more choices. (The letter A icon and its pull-down button offer similar choices for the color of the text being displayed.)

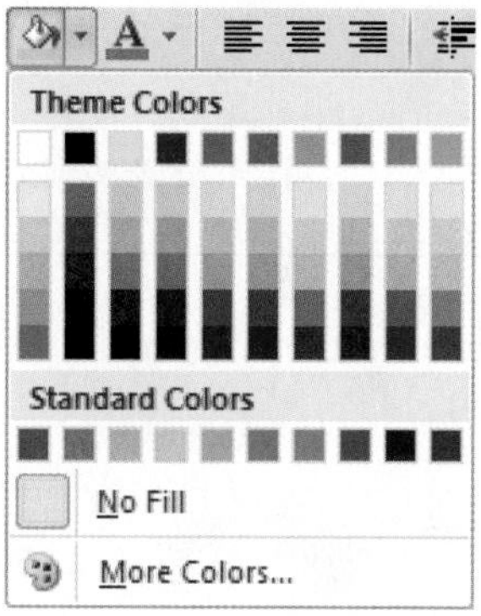

To adjust the width of a column to an optimal size, select the column and then select **Format → Autofit Column Width** (shown below) in the Cells group of the Home tab. Excel will adjust the width of the column to accommodate the display of the values in all of the cells of the column.

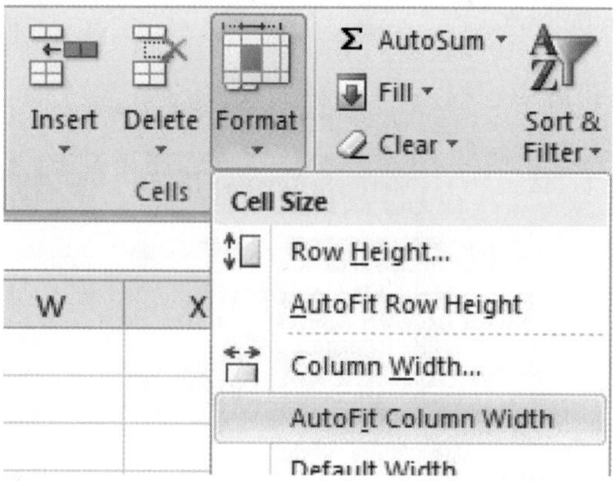

B.6 Chart Formatting

Microsoft Excel often does not use best practices when it creates and formats charts. Many of the *In-Depth Excel* instructions that involve charts, refer you to this section so that you can correct the formatting of a chart that you have just constructed. To apply any of the following corrections, you must first select the chart that to be corrected. (If Chart Tools or PivotChart Tools appears above the Ribbon tabs, you have selected a chart.)

If, when you open to a chart sheet, the chart is either too large to be fully seen or too small and surrounded by a frame mat that is too large, click **Zoom Out** or **Zoom In**, located in the lower-right portion of the Excel window frame, to adjust the chart display.

In the following, instructions preceded with (**2007**) will most likely have to be done only if you are using Excel 2007 and instructions preceded with (**2013**) apply only to Excel 2013. Unlike other Excel versions, in Excel 2013 some of the selections, such as the gridlines selections, are toggles that turn on (or off) a chart element.

Changes You Most Commonly Make

To relocate a chart to its own chart sheet:

1. Click the chart background and click **Move Chart** from the shortcut menu.
2. In the Move Chart dialog box, click **New Sheet**, enter a name for the new chart sheet, and click **OK**.

To turn off the improper horizontal gridlines:

Layout → Gridlines → Primary Horizontal Gridlines → None

(2013) Design → Add Chart Element → Gridlines → Primary Major Horizontal

To turn off the improper vertical gridlines:

Layout → Gridlines → Primary Vertical Gridlines → None

(2013) Design → Add Chart Element → Gridlines → Primary Major Horizontal

To turn off the chart legend:

Layout → Legend → None

(2013) Design → Add Chart Element → Legend → None

(**2007**) To turn off the display of values at plotted points or bars in the charts:

Layout → Data Labels → None

(**2007**) To turn off the display of a summary table on the chart sheet:

Layout → Data Table → None

Chart and Axis Titles

To add a chart title to a chart missing a title:

1. Click on the chart and then select **Layout → Chart Title → Above Chart**. (In Excel 2013, select **Design → Add Chart Element Chart Title → Above Chart.**)
2. In the box that is added to the chart, select the words "Chart Title" and enter an appropriate title.

To add a title to a horizontal axis missing a title:

1. Click on the chart and then select **Layout → Axis Titles → Primary Horizontal Axis Title → Title Below Axis**. (In Excel 2013, select **Design → Add Chart Element → Axis Titles → Primary Horizontal.**)
2. In the box that is added to the chart, select the words "Axis Title" and enter an appropriate title.

To add a title to a vertical axis missing a title:

1. Click on the chart and then select **Layout → Axis Titles → Primary Vertical Axis Title → Rotated Title**. (In Excel 2013, select **Design → Add Chart Element → Axis Titles → Primary Vertical**.)
2. In the box that is added to the chart, select the words "Axis Title" and enter an appropriate title.

Chart Axes

To turn on the display of the *X* axis, if not already shown:

Layout → Axes → Primary Horizontal Axis → Show Left to Right Axis (or **Show Default Axis**, if listed)

(2013) Design → Add Chart Element → Axes → Primary Horizontal

To turn on the display of the *Y* axis, if not already shown:

Layout → Axes → Primary Vertical Axis → Show Default Axis

(2013) Design → Add Chart Element → Axes → Primary Vertical

For a chart that contains secondary axes, to turn off the secondary horizontal axis title:

Layout → Axis Titles → Secondary Horizontal → Axis Title → None

(2013) Design → Add Chart Element → Axis Titles → Secondary Horizontal

For a chart that contains secondary axes, to turn on the secondary vertical axis title:

Layout → Axis Titles → Secondary Vertical Axis Title → Rotated Title

(2013) Design → Add Chart Element → Axis Titles → Secondary Vertical

Correcting the Display of the X Axis

In scatter plots and related lines charts, Microsoft Excel displays the *X* axis at the *Y* axis origin ($Y = 0$). For plots that have negative values, this causes the *X* axis not to appear at the bottom of the chart. To relocate the *X* axis so that it appears at the bottom of a scatter plot or line chart, open to the chart sheet containing the chart and:

1. Right-click the ***Y* axis** and click **Format Axis** from the shortcut menu.

In the Format Axis dialog box:

2. Click **Axis Options** in the left pane. In the Axis Options pane on the right, click **Axis value** and in its box enter the value shown in the dimmed **Minimum box** (near the top of the pane).
3. Click **Close**.

Emphasizing Histogram Bars

To better emphasize each bar in a histogram, open to the chart sheet containing the histogram and:

1. Right-click over one of the histogram bars and click **Format Data Series** in the shortcut menu.

In the Format Data Series dialog box:

2. Click **Border Color** in the left pane. In the Border Color right pane, click **Solid line**. From the Color drop-down list, click t he darkest color in the same column as the currently selected (highlighted) color.
3. Click **Border Styles** in the left pane. In the Border Styles right pane, click the up spinner button to set the **Width** to **3 pt**.
4. Click **OK.**

B.7 Selecting Cell Ranges for Charts

Selecting Cell Ranges for Chart Labels and Series

As a general rule, to enter a cell range in a Microsoft Excel dialog box, you either type that cell range or select the cell range by using the mouse pointer. You are free to choose to enter the cell range either using relative or absolute references (see Section B.2). The Axis Labels and Edit Series dialog box, associated with chart labels and data series, are two exceptions. (These dialog boxes and their contents for the Pareto chart sheet of the Pareto workbook are shown below.)

To enter a cell range into these two dialog boxes, you must enter the cell range as a *formula* that uses absolute cell references in the form *WorksheetName!UpperLeftCell:LowerRightCell*. You should enter such cell ranges using the mouse-pointer method to enter cell ranges in these dialog boxes because that is the easiest way to correctly enter the cell range formula. Typing the cell range, as you might normally do, will often be frustrating, as keys such as the cursor keys will not function as they do in other dialog boxes.

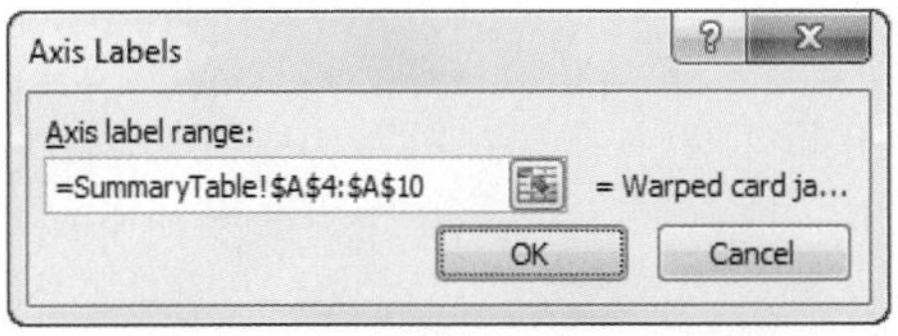

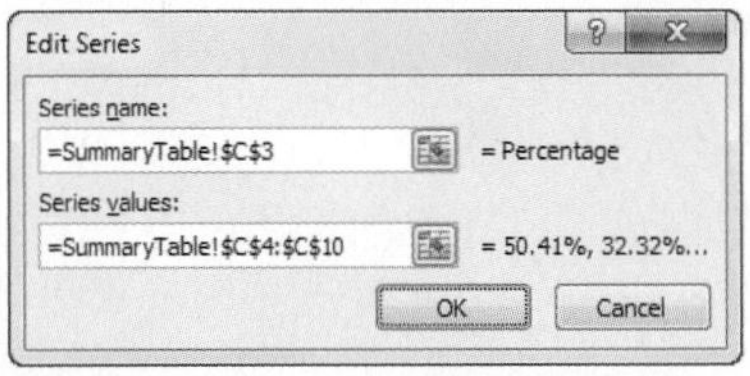

Selecting a Non-contiguous Cell Range

Typically, you enter a non-contiguous cell range such as the cells A1:A11 and C1:C11 by typing the cell range of each group of cells, separated by commas—for example, **A1:A11, C1:C11**. In certain contexts, such as using the dialog boxes discussed in the preceding section, you will need to select that non-contiguous cell range using the mouse pointer method. To use the mouse-pointer method with such ranges, first, select the cell range of the first group of cells and then, while holding down **Ctrl**, select the cell range of the other groups of cells that form the non-contiguous cell range.

B.8 Deleting the "Extra" Bar from a Histogram

As explained in "Classes and Excel Bins" in Section 2.2, you use bins to approximate classes. One result of this approximation is that you will always create an "extra" bin that will have a frequency of zero. Because, by definition, this extra bin considers values that are less than the lowest value that exists in your set of data and therefore will always have the frequency zero, you can safely and properly eliminate the "extra" bar that represents this bin.

To do so, you need to edit the cell range that Excel uses to construct the histogram. Right-click the histogram background and click **Select Data**. In the Select Data Source Data dialog box, first click **Edit** under the **Legend Entries (Series)** heading. In the Edit Series dialog box, edit the **Series values** cell range formula to begin with the second cell of the original cell range and click **OK**. Then click **Edit** under the **Horizontal (Categories) Axis Labels** heading. In the Axis Labels dialog box, edit the **Axis label range** to begin with the second cell of the original cell range and click **OK**.

For these edits, it is possible to type these edits, if you can use the mouse pointer to place the edit cursor exactly before the cell reference to be changed and use **Del** to delete the original reference to the first cell. However, as discussed in Section B.7, you can use the mouse-pointer method to enter the new cell range formulas in these dialog boxes.

B.9 Creating Histograms for Discrete Probability Distributions

You can create a histogram for a discrete probability distribution based on a discrete probabilities table. For example, to create a histogram based on the Figure 5.2 binomial probabilities worksheet on page 199, open to the **COMPUTE worksheet** of the **Binomial workbook**. Select the cell range **B14:B18**, the probabilities in the Binomial Probabilities Table, and:

1. Select **Insert → Column** and select the first **2-D Column** gallery choice **(Clustered Column)**.
2. Right-click the chart background and click **Select Data**.

In the Select Data Source dialog box:

3. Click **Edit** under the **Horizontal (Categories) Axis Labels** heading.
4. In the Axis Labels dialog box, enter the cell range *formula* **=COMPUTE!A14:A18** as the **Axis label range**. (See Section B.7 to learn how to best enter a cell range formula.) Click **OK** to return to the Select Data Source dialog box.
5. Back in the Select Data Source dialog box, click **OK**.

In the chart:

6. Right-click inside a bar and click **Format Data Series** in the shortcut menu.

In the Format Data Series dialog box:

7. Click **Series Options** in the left pane. In the Series Options right pane, change the **Gap Width** slider to **Large Gap**. Click **Close**.

Relocate the chart to a chart sheet and adjust the chart formatting by using the instructions in Section B.5.

APPENDIX C Online Resources

C.1 About the Online Resources for This Book

Online resources support your study of business statistics and your use of this book. Online resources are available from a special download web page for this book as well as in a MyStatLab course for this book. On the download page, these resources are packaged as a series of zip archive files, one zip file for each of the categories listed below. In the MyStatLab course for this book, online resources are also available on a chapter-by-chapter basis. Categories of online resources are:

- **Excel Data Workbooks** The files that contain the data used in chapter examples or named in problems. These data workbooks are available in the **.xlsx** Excel workbook format. A complete list of the data workbooks and their contents appear in *Data Workbooks* in Section C.3.
- **Excel Guide Workbooks** Excel workbooks that contain templates or model solutions for applying Excel to a particular statistical method. A complete list of the Excel Guide Workbooks appear in *Excel Guide Workbooks* in Section C.3.
- **Data Workbooks for the End-of-Chapter Cases** The data workbooks used in the various end-of-chapter cases, including the Managing Ashland MultiComm Services running case. These data workbooks are also included in the set of Excel Data Files and are listed individually in *Data Workbooks* in Section C.3.
- **Files for the Digital Cases** The set of PDF files that support the end-of-chapter Digital Cases. Some of the Digital Case PDF files contain attached or embedded Excel data workbooks for use with particular case questions.
- **Short Takes and eBook Bonus Sections** The set of PDF and Microsoft Word files that expand and extend the discussion of statistical concepts. Included in this set is the full text of two bonus chapters, "Statistical Applications in Quality Management" and "Decision Making." (These sets of files are packaged by chapter.)
- **Visual Explorations Workbooks** The workbooks that interactively demonstrate various key statistical concepts. Three of these workbooks are add-in workbooks stored in the **.xlam** Excel add-in format that are featured in Visual Explorations sections in selected chapters. See "Visual Explorations" in Section C.3 for more information about these workbooks, including Excel security settings that may be necessary if you use a Microsoft Windows computer.
- **PHStat Files** The Microsoft Windows and (Mac) OS X Excel add-in workbook and supporting help files that constitute PHStat, the add-in that simplifies the use of Microsoft Excel with this book, as explained in Section EG.2.

Accessing the Online Resources

Online resources for this book are available either on the student download page for this book or inside the MyStatLab course for this book (see Section C.3). To access resources from the student download page for this book:

1. Open a web browser and go to **www.pearsonhighered.com/levine**.
2. In that web page, find the entries for this book, *Statistics for Managers Using Microsoft Excel*, seventh edition, and click the student download page link.
3. In the download page, click the link for the desired items. Most items will cause the web browser to prompt you to save the (zip archive) file, but several links will open a PDF file directly that you can then save after the entire PDF file loads in your browser.

You can extract and store files in a zip archive in the folder of your choice, but all the files in the PHStat archive must be stored in the same folder.

C.2 Accessing the MyStatLab Course Online

The MyStatLab course for this book contains all the online resources for this book. Log into the course at the CourseCompass website (**www.coursecompass.com**) and in the left panel of the course page for this book, click **Tools for Success**. On that page, click the link for one of the online resource categories listed in Section C.1. Selected Short Takes and eBook bonus section files as well as certain Excel workbooks may also be available in the chapter-by-chapter resource pages.

Using MyStatLab requires that you have an access code for this book. An access code may have been packaged with this book. If your book did not come with an access code, you can obtain one at **mypearson.com**.

C.3 Details of Downloadable Files

Data Workbooks

Data workbooks contain the data used in chapter examples or named in problems. Throughout this book, the names of data workbooks appear in a special inverted color typeface—for example, Retirement Funds.

Data workbooks are stored in the **.xlsx** Excel workbook format. Except where noted, data are stored in a DATA worksheet in the workbook. Worksheets organize the data for each variable by column, using the rules discussed in Section EG.5. In the following alphabetical list, the variables for each data file are presented in the order of their appearance, starting with column A. Chapter references in parentheses indicate the chapter or chapters in which the workbook is used in an example or problem.

ACCOUNTINGPARTNERS Firm and number of partners (Chapter 3)

ACCOUNTINGPARTNERS2 Region and number of partners (Chapter 10)

ACCOUNTINGPARTNERS4 Region and number of partners (Chapter 11)

ACCOUNTINGPARTNERS6 Region, revenue, number of partners, number of professionals, MAS(%), southeast (0 = no, 1 = yes), Gulf coast southeast (0 = no, 1 = yes) (Chapter 15)

ACT Method, ACT scores for condensed course, ACT scores for regular course (Chapter 11)

ACT-ONEWAY Group 1 ACT scores, group 2 ACT scores, group 3 ACT scores, group 4 ACT scores (Chapter 11)

ADVERTISE Sales ($thousands), radio ads ($thousands), and newspaper ads ($thousands) for 22 cities (Chapters 14 and 15)

ADVERTISING Sales ($millions) and newspaper ads ($thousands) (Chapter 15)

AMS2-1 Types of errors and frequency, types of errors and cost, types of wrong billing errors and cost (Chapter 2)

AMS2-2 Days and number of calls (Chapter 2)

AMS8 Rate willing to pay in $ (Chapter 8)

AMS9 Upload speed (Chapter 9)

AMS10 Update times for email interface 1 and email interface 2 (Chapter 10)

AMS11-1 Update time for system 1, system 2, and system 3 (Chapter 11)

AMS11-2 Media (cable or fiber) and interface (system 1, system 2, or system 3) (Chapter 11)

AMS13 Number of hours spent telemarketing and number of new subscriptions (Chapter 13)

AMS14 Week, number of new subscriptions, hours spent telemarketing, and type of presentation (formal or informal) (Chapter 14)

AMS16 Month and number of home delivery subscriptions (Chapter 16)

AMS18 Day and upload speed (Chapter 18)

ANGLE Subgroup number and angle (Chapter 18)

ANSCOMBE Data sets A, B, C, and D, each with 11 pairs of *X* and *Y* values (Chapter 13)

ATM TRANSACTIONS Cause, frequency, and percentage (Chapter 2)

AUDITS Year and number of audits (Chapters 2 and 16)

AUTO2012 Car, miles per gallon, horsepower, and weight (in lb.) (Chapters 14 and 15)

BANK1 Waiting time (in minutes) of 15 customers at a bank located in a commercial district (Chapters 3, 9, 10, and 12)

BANK2 Waiting time (in minutes) of 15 customers at a bank located in a residential area (Chapters 3, 10, and 12)

BANKMARKETING Age, type of job, marital status (divorced, married, or single), education (primary, secondary, tertiary, or unknown), is credit in default, average yearly balance in account, is there a housing loan, is there a personal loan, last contact duration in seconds, number of contacts performed during this campaign, has the client purchased a term deposit (Chapter 17)

BANKTIME Day, waiting times of four bank customers (A, B, C, and D) (Chapter 18)

BASEBALL Team; attendance; high temperature on game day; winning percentage of home team; opponent's winning percentage; game played on Friday, Saturday, or Sunday (0 = no, 1 = yes); and promotion held (0 = no, 1 = yes) (Chapter 17)

BB2011 Team, league (0 = American, 1 = National), wins, earned run average, runs scored, hits allowed, walks allowed, saves, and errors (Chapters 13, 14, and 15)

BBCOST2011 Team and fan cost index (Chapters 2 and 6)

BBREVENUE2012 Team, revenue ($millions), and value ($millions) (Chapter 13)

BBSALARIES Year and average major league baseball salary ($millions) (Chapter 16)

BED & BATH Year, coded year, and number of stores open (Chapter 16)

BESTFUNDS1 Fund type (large cap value, large cap growth), 3-year return, 5-year return, 10-year return, expense ratio (Chapter 10)

BESTFUNDS2 Fund type (foreign large cap blend, small cap blend, midcap blend, large cap blend, diversified emerging markets), 3-year return, 5-year return, 10-year return, expense ratio (Chapter 11)

BESTFUNDS3 Fund type (intermediate municipal bond, short-term bond, intermediate term bond), 3-year return, 5-year return, 10-year return, expense ratio (Chapter 11)

BOOKPRICES Author, title, bookstore price, and online price (Chapter 10)

BRAKES Part, gauge 1, and gauge 2 (Chapter 11)

BRANDZTECHFIN Brand, brand value in 2011 ($millions), % change in brand value from 2010, region, sector (Chapters 10 and 12)

BRANDZTECHFINTELE Brand, brand value in 2011 ($millions), % change in brand value from 2010, region, sector (Chapter 11)

BREAKFAST Menu choice, delivery time difference for early time period, and delivery time difference for late time period (Chapter 11)

BREAKFAST2 Menu choice, delivery time difference for early time period, and delivery time difference for late time period (Chapter 11)

BREAKSTW Operator and breaking strength for machines I, II, and III (Chapter 11)

BRYNNEPACKAGING WPCT score and rating (Chapter 13)

BULBS Manufacturer (1 = A, 2 = B) and length of life in hours (Chapters 2, 10, and 12)

BUNDLE Restaurant, bundle score, cost ($) (Chapters 2 and 3)

BUSINESSVALUATION Drug company name, price to book value ratio, return on equity, growth% (Chapter 14)

BUSINESSVALUATION 2 Drug company name, ticker symbol, SIC 3—Standard Industrial Classification 3 code (industry group identifier), SIC 4—Standard Industrial Classification 4 code (industry identifier), price to book value ratio, price to earnings ratio, natural log of assets (as a measure of size), return on equity, growth (GS5), ratio of debt to earnings before interest, taxes, depreciation, and amortization, dummy variable indicator of SIC 4 code 2834 (1 if 2834, 0 if not), and dummy variable indicator of SIC 4 code 2835 (1 if 2835, 0 if not) (Chapter 15)

CABERNET California and Washington ratings and California and Washington rankings (Chapter 12)

CALLCENTER Month and call volume (Chapter 16)

CAMERAS Battery life of digital cameras (Chapters 10 and 12)

CANDIDATE ASSESSMENT Salary, competence rating, gender of candidate, gender of rater, rater/candidate gender (F to F, F to M, M to M, M to M), school (private, public), department (Biology, Chemistry, Physics), age of rater (Chapter 17)

CANISTER Day and number of nonconformances (Chapter 18)

CARDIOGOODFITNESS Product purchased (TM195, TM498, TM798), age in years, gender (Male, Female), education in years, relationship status (Single, Partnered), average number of times the customer plans to use the treadmill each week, self-rated fitness on a 1-to-5 ordinal scale where 1 = poor shape and 5 = excellent shape, annual household income ($), and average number of miles the customer expects to walk/run each week (Chapters 2, 3, 6, 8, 10, 11, and 12)

CARDSTUDY Upgraded (0 = no, 1 = yes), purchases ($thousands), and extra cards (0 = no, 1 = yes) (Chapter 14)

CARPRODUCTION Year, coded year, number of units produced (Chapter 16)

CATFOOD Ounces eaten of kidney, shrimp, chicken liver, salmon, and beef cat food (Chapters 11 and 12)

CATFOOD2 Piece size (F = fine, C = chunky), coded weight for low fill height, coded weight for current fill height (Chapter 11)

CATFOOD3 Type (1 = kidney, 2 = shrimp), shift, time interval, nonconformances, volume (Chapter 18)

CATFOOD4 Type (1 = kidney, 2 = shrimp), shift, time interval, weight (Chapter 18)

CDRATE One-year and five-year CD rates (Chapters 2, 3, 6, and 8)

CELLSERVICE City, Verizon rating, AT&T rating (Chapter 10)

CEO-COMPENSATION Company, compensation of CEO ($millions), return in 2011 (Chapters 2, 3, and 13)

CEREALS Cereal, calories, carbohydrates, and sugar (Chapters 3 and 13)

CHOCOLATECHIP Cost (cents) of chocolate chip cookies (Chapter 2)

CIGARETTETAX State and cigarette tax ($) (Chapters 2 and 3)

COCA-COLA Year, coded year, revenues ($billions) (Chapter 16)

COFFEE Expert, rating of coffees by brand A, B, C, and D (Chapter 10)

COFFEEPRICESPORTUGAL Year and retail price of coffee in Portugal (€/kg) (Chapter 16)

COFFEESALES Coffee sales at $0.59, $0.69, $0.79, and $0.89 (Chapters 11 and 12)

COFFEESALES2 Coffee sales and price (Chapter 15)

COLA Sales for beverage end-cap and produce end-cap locations (Chapters 10 and 12)

COLASPC Day, total number of cans filled, and number of unacceptable cans (Chapter 18)

COLLEGE BASKETBALL School, coach's total salary ($thousands), expenses, and revenues ($thousands) (Chapters 2, 3, and 13)

COMPLAINTS Day and number of complaints (Chapter 18)

COMPUTERSALES Year, coded year, and computer and software sales ($millions)

CONCRETE1 Sample number and compressive strength after two days and seven days (Chapter 10)

COSTESTIMATION Units produced and total cost (Chapter 15)

CPI-U Year, coded year, value of CPI-U (the consumer price index) (Chapter 16)

CURRENCY Year, coded year, and exchange rates (against the U.S. dollar) for the Canadian dollar, Japanese yen, and English pound (Chapters 2 and 16)

DELIVERY Customer number, number of cases, and delivery time (Chapter 13)

DENSITY Ammonium %, density for stir rate of 100, density for stir rate of 150 (Chapter 11)

DOMESTICBEER Brand, alcohol percentage, calories, and carbohydrates in U.S. domestic beers (Chapters 2, 3, 6, and 15)

DOWDOGS Stock and one-year return (Chapter 3)

DOWMARKETCAP Company and market capitalization ($billions) (Chapters 3 and 6)

DRILL Depth, time to drill additional 5 feet, type of hole (Chapter 14)

DRINK Amount of soft drink filled in 2-liter bottles (Chapters 2 and 9)

DRIVE-THRUSPEED Year and drive-through speed in seconds (Chapter 16)

DRYCLEAN Days and number of items returned (Chapter 18)

ENERGY State and per capita kilowatt hour use (Chapter 3)

ERRORSPC Number of nonconforming items and number of accounts processed (Chapter 18)

ERWAITING Emergency room waiting time (in minutes) at the main facility and at satellite 1, satellite 2, and satellite 3 (Chapters 11 and 12)

ESPRESSO Tamp (the distance in inches between the espresso grounds and the top of the portafilter) and time (the number of seconds the heart, body, and crema are separated) (Chapter 13)

FACEBOOKTIME Gender (F = female, M = male) and amount of time in minutes spent on Facebook per day (Chapter 9)

FACEBOOKTIME2 Gender (F = female, M = male) and amount of time in minutes spent on Facebook per day (Chapter 10)

FASTFOOD Amount spent on fast food in dollars (Chapters 2, 3, 8, and 9)

FEDRECEIPT Year, coded year, federal receipts ($billions current) (Chapter 16)

FIFTEENWEEKS Week number, number of customers, and sales ($thousands) over a period of 15 consecutive weeks (Chapter 13)

FIVEYEARCDRATE Five-year CD rate in New York and Los Angeles (Chapter 10)

FLYASH Fly ash percentage and strength (Chapter 15)

FORCE Force required to break an insulator (Chapters 2, 3, 8, and 9)

FOULSPC Number of foul shots made and number taken (Chapter 18)

FREEPORT Address, appraised value ($thousands), property size (acres), house size, age, number of rooms, number of bathrooms, number of cars that can be parked in the garage (Chapter 15)

FUNDTRAN Day, number of new investigations, and number of investigations closed (Chapter 18)

FURNITURE Days between receipt and resolution of complaints regarding purchased furniture (Chapters 2, 3, 8, and 9)

GASPRICES Month and price per gallon ($) (Chapter 16)

GCFREEROSLYN Address, appraised value, location, property size (acres), house size, age, number of rooms, number of bathrooms, and number of cars that can be parked in the garage in Glen Cove, Freeport, and Roslyn, New York (Chapter 15)

GCROSLYN Address, appraised value ($thousands), location, property size (acres), house size, age, number of rooms, number of bathrooms, and number of cars that can be parked in the garage in Glen Cove and Roslyn, New York (Chapters 14 and 15)

GDP Year and real gross domestic product (Chapter 16)

GLENCOVE Address, appraised value ($thousands), property size (acres), house size, age, number of rooms, number of bathrooms, and number of cars that can be parked in the garage in Glen Cove, New York (Chapters 14 and 15)

GLOBALSOCIALMEDIA Country, GDP, percentage using social media (Chapters 2, 3, and 13)

GOLD Quarter, coded quarter, price ($) (Chapter 16)

GOLFBALL Distance for designs 1, 2, 3, and 4 (Chapters 11 and 12)

GPIGMAT GMAT scores and GPA (Chapter 13)

GRADSURVEY ID number, gender, age (as of last birthday), graduate major (accounting, economics and finance, management, marketing/retailing, other, undecided), current graduate cumulative grade point average, undergraduate major (biological sciences, business, computers, engineering, other), undergraduate cumulative grade point average, current employment status (full-time, part-time, unemployed), number of different full-time jobs held in the past 10 years, expected salary upon completion of MBA ($thousands), amount spent for books and supplies this semester, satisfaction with student advising services on campus, type of computer owned, text messages per week, wealth accumulated to feel rich (Chapters 2, 3, 4, 6, 8, 10, 11, and 12)

GRANULE Granule loss in Boston and Vermont shingles (Chapters 3, 8, 9, and 10)

HARNSWELL Day and diameter of cam rollers (in inches) (Chapter 18)

HEATINGOIL Monthly consumption of heating oil (in gallons), temperature (in degrees Fahrenheit), attic insulation (in inches), style (0 = not ranch, 1 = ranch) (Chapters 14 and 15)

HEMLOCKFARMS Asking price, hot tub, rooms, lake view, bathrooms, bedrooms, loft/den, finished basement, number of acres (Chapter 15)

HOMES Price, location, condition, bedrooms, bathrooms, other rooms (Chapter 17)

HOSPADM Day, number of admissions, mean processing time (in hours), range of processing times, proportion of laboratory rework (over a 30-day period) (Chapter 18)

HOTEL1 Day, number of rooms studied, number of nonconforming rooms per day over a 28-day period, proportion of nonconforming items (Chapter 18)

HOTEL2 Day and delivery time for subgroups of five luggage deliveries per day over a 28-day period (Chapter 18)

HOTELAWAY Nationality and cost in US$ (Chapter 3)

HOTELPRICES City and cost (in English pounds) of two-star, three-star, and four-star hotels (Chapters 2 and 3)

HOUSE1 Selling price ($thousands), assessed value ($thousands), type (new = 0, old = 1), and time period of sale for 30 houses (Chapters 13, 14, and 15)

HOUSE2 Assessed value ($thousands), size of heating area (in thousands of square feet), and age (in years) for 15 houses (Chapters 13 and 14)

HOUSE3 Assessed value ($thousands), size (in thousands of square feet), and presence of a fireplace for 15 houses (Chapter 14)

HOUSEHOLDS Gender, age, Hispanic origin, type of dwelling, age of dwelling in years, years living at dwelling, number of bedrooms, number of vehicles kept at dwelling, fuel type at dwelling, monthly cost of fuel at dwelling ($), U.S. citizenship, college degree, marital status, work for pay in previous week, mode of transportation to work, commuting time in minutes, hours worked per week, type of organization, annual earned income ($), and total annual income ($) (Chapter 17)

ICECREAM Daily temperature (in degrees Fahrenheit) and sales ($thousands) for 21 days (Chapter 13)

INDICES Year, change in DJIA, S&P500, and NASDAQ (Chapter 3)

INSURANCE Processing time in days for insurance policies (Chapters 3, 8, and 9)

INSURANCECLAIMS Claims, buildup (1 if buildup indicated, 0 if not), excess payment in $ (Chapter 8)

INTAGLIO Surface hardness of untreated and treated steel plates (Chapter 10)

INVOICE Number of invoices processed and amount of time (in hours) for 30 days (Chapter 13)

INVOICES Amount recorded (in dollars) from sales invoices (Chapter 9)

LAUNDRY Detergent brand and dirt (in pounds) removed for cycle times of 18, 20, 22, and 24 minutes (Chapter 11)

LUGGAGE Delivery time (in minutes) for luggage in Wing A and Wing B of a hotel (Chapters 10 and 12)

MANAGERS Sales (ratio of yearly sales divided by the target sales value for that region), score from the Wonderlic Personnel Test, score on the Strong-Campbell Interest Inventory Test, number of years of selling experience prior to becoming a sales manager, whether the sales manager has a degree in electrical engineering (0 = no, 1 = yes) (Chapter 15)

MARKETPENETRATION Country and Facebook penetration (in percentage) (Chapters 3 and 8)

MBA Success (0 = did not complete, 1 = completed), GPA, GMAT (Chapter 14)

MCDONALDS Year, coded year, annual total revenues ($billions) at McDonald's Corporation (Chapter 16)

MEDRECORDS Day, number of discharged patients, number of records not processed for a 30-day period (Chapter 18)

METALS Year and the total rate of return (in percentage) for platinum, gold, and silver (Chapter 3)

MINING Day, amount stacked, downtime (Chapter 17)

MINING2 Day, hours of downtime due to mechanical, electrical, tonnage restriction, operator, no feed (Chapter 17)

MOISTURE Moisture content of Boston shingles and Vermont shingles (Chapter 9)

MOLDING Vibration time (seconds), vibration pressure (psi), vibration amplitude (%), raw material density (g/mL), quantity of raw material (scoops), product length (in.) in cavity 1, product length (in.) in cavity 2, product weight (gr.) in cavity 1, and product weight (gr.) in cavity 2 (Chapter 15)

MOTIVATION Motivational factor, global rating of factor, U.S. rating of factor (Chapter 10)

MOVIE Title, box office gross ($millions), DVD revenue ($millions) (Chapter 13)

MOVIE ATTENDANCE Year and movie attendance (billions) (Chapters 2 and 16)

MOVIE REVENUES Year and revenue in $billions (Chapter 2)

MOVING Labor hours, cubic feet, number of large pieces of furniture, availability of an elevator (Chapters 13 and 14)

MYELOMA Patient, measurement before transplant, measurement after transplant (Chapter 10)

NATURAL GAS Month, wellhead, price, residential price (Chapter 2)

NATURAL GAS2 Month, wellhead, price, residential price (Chapter 16)

NBA2011 Team, number of wins, field goal (shots made) percentage (for team and opponent) (Chapter 14)

NBAVALUES Team, annual revenue ($millions), and value ($millions) for NBA franchises (Chapters 2, 3, and 13)

NEIGHBOR Selling price ($thousands), number of rooms, neighborhood location (0 = east, 1 = west) (Chapter 14)

NEWHOMESALES Month, sales in thousands, mean price ($thousands) (Chapter 2)

OIL&GASOLINE Week, price of oil per barrel, price of a gallon of gasoline ($) (Chapter 13)

OMNIPOWER Bars sold, price (cents), promotion expenses ($) (Chapter 14)

ORDER Time in minutes to fill orders for a population of 200 (Chapter 8)

O-RING Flight number, temperature, O-ring damage index (Chapter 13)

PAINRELIEF Temperature and dissolve times for Equate, Kroger, and Alka-Seltzer tablets (Chapter 11)

PALLET Weight of Boston shingles and weight of Vermont shingles (Chapters 2, 8, 9, and 10)

PARACHUTE Tensile strength of parachutes from suppliers 1, 2, 3, and 4 (Chapters 11 and 12)

PARACHUTE2 Loom and tensile strength of parachutes from suppliers 1, 2, 3, and 4 (Chapter 11)

PASTA Type of pasta (A = American, I = Italian), weight for 4-minute cooking time, weight for 8-minute cooking time (Chapter 11)

PEN Gender, ad, product rating (Chapters 11, 12)

PERFORM Performance rating before and after motivational training (Chapter 10)

PETFOOD Shelf space (in square feet), weekly sales ($), aisle location (0 = back, 1 = front) (Chapters 13 and 14)

PHONE Time (in minutes) to clear telephone line problems and location (1 = I, 2 = II) (Chapters 10 and 12)

PHOTO Developer strength, density at 10 minutes, density at 14 minutes (Chapter 11)

PIZZAHUT Gender (0 = female , 1 = male), price, and purchase (0 = the student selected another pizzeria, 1 = the student selected Pizza Hut) (Chapter 14)

PIZZATIME Time period, delivery time for local restaurant, delivery time for national chain (Chapter 10)

POLIO Year and incidence rates per 100,000 persons of reported poliomyelitis (Chapter 16)

POTATO Percentage of solids content in filter cake, acidity (in pH), lower pressure, upper pressure, cake thickness, varidrive speed, and drum speed setting for 54 measurements (Chapter 15)

POTTERMOVIES Title, first weekend gross ($millions), U.S. gross ($millions), worldwide gross ($millions) (Chapters 2, 3, and 13)

PROPERTYTAXES State and property taxes per capita ($) (Chapters 2, 3, and 6)

PROTEIN Type of food, calories (in grams), protein, percentage of calories from fat, percentage of calories from saturated fat, cholesterol (mg) (Chapters 2 and 3)

PTFALLS Month and patient falls (Chapter 18)

PUMPKIN Circumference and weight of pumpkins (Chapter 13)

QSR Company, average sales per unit, market segment (Chapters 11 and 12)

REALESTATE Value ($thousands), lot size (sq. ft.), number of bedrooms, number of bathrooms, age in years, annual taxes ($), type of parking facility (none, one-car garage, two-car garage), location (A, B, C, D, E), style of house (cape, expanded ranch, colonial, ranch, split level), heating fuel (gas, oil), heating system (hot air, hot water, other), swimming pool (none, above ground, in ground), eat-in kitchen (absent, present), central air-conditioning (absent, present), fireplace (absent, present), connection to local sewer system (absent, present), basement (absent, present), modern kitchen (absent, present), modern bathrooms (absent, present) (Chapter 17)

REDWOOD Height (ft.), breast height diameter (in.), bark thickness (in.) (Chapters 13 and 14)

REGISTRATIONERROR Registration error, temperature, pressure, supplier (Chapter 15)

REGISTRATIONERROR-HIGHCOST Registration error and temperature (Chapter 15)

RENT Monthly rental cost ($) and apartment size (sq. ft.) (Chapter 13)

RESTAURANTS Location, food rating, decor rating, service rating, summated rating, coded location (0 = city, 1 = suburban), cost of a meal (Chapters 2, 3, 10, 13, and 14)

RESTAURANTS2 Location, food rating, decor rating, service rating, summated rating, coded location (0 = city, 1 = suburban), cost of a meal (Chapter 17)

RESTAURANT3 Name of restaurant, food rating, decor rating, service rating, summated rating, cost of a meal, popularity index, type of cuisine (Chapter 17)

RETIREMENT FUNDS Fund number, market cap (small, mid-cap, large), type (growth or value), assets ($millions), turnover ratio, beta (measure of the volatility of a stock, standard deviation (measure of returns relative to 36-month average), risk (low, average, high), 1-year return, 3-year return, 5-year return, 10-year return, expense ratio, star rating (Chapters 2, 3, 4, 6, 8, 10, 11, 12, and 15)

ROSLYN Address, appraised value, property size (acres), house size, age, number of rooms, number of bathrooms, number of cars that can be parked in the garage (Chapter 15)

RUDYBIRD Day, total cases sold, cases of Rudybird sold (Chapter 18)

SAFETY Tour and number of unsafe acts (Chapter 18)

SATISFACTION Satisfaction (0 = unsatisfied, 1 = satisfied) and delivery time difference in minutes (0 = no, 1 = yes) (Chapter 14)

SEALANT Sample number, sealant strength for Boston shingles, and sealant strength for Vermont shingles (Chapter 18)

SEDANS Miles per gallon for 2012 family sedans (Chapters 3 and 8)

SILVER Year and price of silver ($) (Chapter 16)

SILVER-Q Quarter, coded quarter, price of silver ($) (Chapter 16)

SITESELECTION Store number, square footage (thousands of sq. ft.), and sales ($millions) (Chapter 13)

SOCCERVALUES2012 Team, country, revenue ($millions), value ($millions) (Chapter 13)

SOLARPOWER Year and amount of solar power generated (in megawatts) (Chapter 16)

SPILLS Year and number of oil spills in the Gulf of Mexico (Chapter 16)

SPONGE Day, number of sponges produced, number of nonconforming sponges, proportion of nonconforming sponges (Chapter 18)

SPORTING Sales ($), age, annual population growth, income ($), percentage with high school diploma, percentage with college diploma (Chapters 13 and 15)

SPWATER Sample number and amount of magnesium (Chapter 18)

STANDBY Standby hours, total staff present, remote hours, Dubner hours, labor hours (Chapters 14 and 15)

STARBUCKS Tear, viscosity, pressure, plate gap (Chapters 13 and 14)

STEEL Error in actual length and specified length (Chapters 2, 6, 8, and 9)

STOCK PERFORMANCE Decade and stock performance (%) (Chapters 2 and 16)

STOCKPRICES2011 Week, and closing weekly stock price for GE, Discovery Communications, and Apple (Chapter 13)

STUDYTIME Gender and study time (Chapter 10)

SUV Miles per gallon for 2012 small SUVs (Chapters 3, 6, and 8)

TABLETS-SEVEN INCH Name and price ($) (Chapter 3)

TARGETWALMART Shopping item, Target price, Walmart price (Chapter 10)

TAX Quarterly sales tax receipts ($thousands) (Chapter 3)

TAXES County taxes ($) and age of house (in years) for 19 single-family houses (Chapter 15)

TEA3 Sample number and weight of tea bags in ounces (Chapter 18)

TEABAGS Weight of tea bags in ounces (Chapters 3, 8, and 9)

TELESPC Number of orders and number of corrections over 30 days (Chapter 18)

TELLER Number of errors by tellers (Chapter 18)

TENSILE Sample number and strength (Chapter 18)

TESTRANK Rank scores and training method used (0 = traditional, 1 = experimental) for 10 people (Chapter 12)

THICKNESS Thickness, catalyst, pH, pressure, temperature, voltage (Chapter 14)

TIMES Times to get ready (Chapter 3)

TOYS R US Quarter, coded quarter, revenue, three dummy variables for quarters (Chapter 16)

TRADE Days, number of undesirable trades, total number of trades made over a 30-day period (Chapter 18)

TRANSMIT Day and number of errors in transmission (Chapter 18)

TRANSPORT Days and patient transport times (in minutes) (Chapter 18)

TRASHBAGS Weight required to break four brands of trash bags (Kroger, Glad, Hefty, Tuff Stuff) (Chapters 11 and 12)

TRAVEL Month and average traffic on Google for searches from the United States on travel, scaled to the average traffic for the entire time period based on a fixed point at the beginning of the time period (Chapter 16)

TROUGH Width of trough (Chapters 2, 3, 8, and 9)

TRSNYC Year, unit value of Diversified Equity funds, and unit value of Stable Value funds (Chapter 16)

TSMODEL1 Year, coded year, and three time series (I, II, and III) (Chapter 16)

TSMODEL2 Year, coded year, and two time series (I and II) (Chapter 16)

TWITTERMOVIES Movie, Twitter activity, and receipts ($) (Chapter 13)

UNDERGRADSURVEY ID number, gender, age (as of last birthday), class designation, major (accounting, computer information systems, economics and finance, international business, management, marketing, other, undecided), graduate school intention (yes, no, undecided), cumulative grade point average, current employment status, expected starting salary ($thousands), number of social networking sites registered for, satisfaction with student advisement services on campus, amount spent on books and supplies this semester, type of computer preferred (desktop, laptop, tablet/notebook/netbook), text messages per week, wealth accumulated to feel rich (Chapters 2, 3, 4, 6, 8, 10, 11, and 12)

UNDERWRITING Score on proficiency exam, score on end of training exam, training method (classroom, online, courseware app) (Chapter 14)

USEDCARS Car, year, age, price ($), mileage, power (hp), fuel (mpg) (Chapter 17)

UTILITY Utilities charges ($) for 50 one-bedroom apartments (Chapters 2 and 6)

VACATION TIME Demands made and percentage (Chapter 2)

VB Time (in minutes) for nine students to write and run a Visual Basic program (Chapter 10)

WAIT Waiting times and seating times (in minutes) in a restaurant (Chapter 6)

WALMART Quarter and Wal-Mart Stores quarterly revenues ($billions) (Chapter 16)

WARECOST Distribution cost ($thousands), sales ($thousands), and number of orders (Chapters 13, 14, and 15)

WAREHSE Day, units handled, and employee number (Chapter 18)

WIP Processing times at each of two plants (1 = A, 2 = B) (Chapter 17)

WORKFORCE Year, population, and size of the workforce (Chapter 16)

YARN Side-by-side aspect and breaking strength scores for 30 psi, 40 psi, and 50 psi (Chapter 11)

Excel Guide Workbooks

Excel Guide workbooks contain templates or model solutions for applying Excel to a particular statistical method. Chapter examples and the *In-Depth Excel* instructions of the Excel Guides feature worksheets from these workbooks and PHStat constructs many of the worksheets from these workbooks for you.

Workbooks are stored in the **.xlsx** Excel workbook format. Most contain a **COMPUTE worksheet** (often shown in this book) that presents results as well as a **COMPUTE_FORMULAS worksheet** that allows you to examine all of the formulas used in the worksheet. The Excel Guide workbooks (with the number of the chapter in which each is first mentioned) are:

Recoded (1)
Random (1)
Summary Table (2)
Contingency Table (2)
Distributions (2)
Pareto (2)
Stem-and-leaf (2)
Histogram (2)
Polygons (2)
Scatter Plot (2)
Time Series (2)
MCT (2)
Slicers (2)
Descriptive(3)
Quartiles (3)
Boxplot (3)
Parameters(3)
VE-Variability (3)
Covariance (3)
Probabilities (4)
Bayes (4)
Discrete Variable (5)
Portfolio (5)
Binomial (5)
Poisson (5)
Hypergeometric (5)
Normal (6)
NPP (6)
Exponential (6)
SDS (7)
CIE sigma known (8)
CIE sigma unknown (8)
CIE Proportion (8)
Sample Size Mean (8)
Sample Size Proportion (8)
Z Mean workbook (9)
T mean workbook (9)
Z Proportion (9)
Pooled-Variance T (10)
Separate-Variance T (10)
Paired T (10)
F Two Variances (10)
Z Two Proportions (10)
One-Way ANOVA (11)
Levene (11)
Chi-Square (12)
Chi-Square Worksheets (12)
Wilcoxon (12)
Kruskal-Wallis Worksheets (12)
Simple Linear Regression (13)
Multiple Regression (14)
Logistic Regression add-in (14)
Moving Averages (16)
Exponential Smoothing (16)
Exponential Trend (16)
Differences (16)
Lagged Predictors (16)
Forecasting Comparison (16)

The **Slicers workbook** works only with Microsoft Windows versions Excel 2010 and Excel 2013. The **Logistic Regression add-in workbook** requires the Solver add-in and, if you use a Microsoft Windows version of Excel, the security settings discussed in Appendix Section D.3. (Appendix Section D.6 discusses how to check for the presence of the Solver add-in.)

In addition to these workbooks, the **Data Cleaning workbook**, mentioned in the Short Takes for Chapter 1, serves as a Excel Guide workbook for Section 1.3 by demonstrating how to implement a number of data cleaning techniques in Microsoft Excel.

PDF Files

PDF files use the Portable Document Format that can be viewed in most web browsers and PDF utility programs, such as Adobe Reader, a free program available for download at **get.adobe.com/reader/**. Both the Digital Case files and the eBook bonus section files use this format. The set of eBook bonus section files includes files that contain the reference tables associated with the binomial and Poisson discrete probability distributions, discussed in Chapter 5, as well as the full text of two chapters titled "Statistical Applications in Quality Management" and "Decision Making."

Visual Explorations

Visual Explorations are workbooks that interactively demonstrate various key statistical concepts. Three of these workbooks are add-in workbooks stored in the **.xlam** Excel add-in format that are featured in Visual Explorations sections in selected chapters. Using these add-in workbooks requires the security settings discussed in Appendix Section D.3 if you use a Microsoft Windows Excel version. The visual exploration workbooks included with this book are:

VE-Normal Distribution (add-in)
VE-Sampling Distribution (add-in)
VE-Simple Linear Regression (add-in)
VE-Variability

PHStat Files

PHStat is the Pearson Education statistics add-in for Microsoft Excel that simplifies the task of operating Excel. PHStat creates *real* Excel worksheets that use in-worksheet calculations. The version of PHStat included with this book requires no setup other than unzipping files from the download zip archive. PHStat consists of the following files:

PHStat.xlam The actual add-in workbook itself. (This file is compatible with current Microsoft Windows and OS X versions of Microsoft Excel as explained in Appendix Section D.2.)

PHStat readme.pdf The readme file, in PDF format, that you should download and read first before using PHStat.

PHStatHelp.chm The help system that provides context-sensitive help for users of Microsoft Windows Excel. (Context-sensitive help is not available for OS X Excel users.) OS X users can use this file as a stand-alone help system by downloading a free CHM reader from the Mac Apps store online.

PHStatHelp.pdf The help system in the form of a PDF file that users of Microsoft Windows and OS X Excel versions can both use.

See Appendix Sections D.2 through D.4 for technical information to configure Microsoft Excel for use with PHStat. See the Appendix G *PHStat FAQs* for answers to frequently asked questions about PHStat.

APPENDIX D Configuring Software

This appendix seeks to eliminate the common types of technical problems that could complicate your use of Microsoft Excel as you learn business statistics with this book. You will want to be familiar with the contents of this appendix—and follow all its directives—if the copy of Microsoft Excel you plan to use runs on a computer system that you control and maintain. If you use a computer system that is maintained by others, such as a computer system in an academic computer lab, this appendix can be a useful resource for those in charge of solving technical issues that may arise.

Not all sections of this appendix apply to all readers. Sections with the code (WIN) apply to you if you use Microsoft Excel with Microsoft Windows, while sections with the code (OS X) apply to you if you use Microsoft Excel with OS X (formerly, Mac OS X). Some sections apply to all readers (ALL).

D.1 Getting Microsoft Excel Ready for Use (ALL)

You must have an up-to-date, properly licensed copy of Microsoft Excel in order to work through the examples and solve the problems in this book as well as to take advantage of the Excel-related free workbooks and add-ins described in Appendix C. To get Microsoft Excel ready for use, follow this checklist:

- ❑ If necessary, install Microsoft Excel on your computer system.
- ❑ Check and apply Microsoft-supplied updates to Microsoft Excel and Microsoft Office.
- ❑ After you first use Microsoft Excel, recheck for Microsoft-supplied updates at least once every two weeks.

If you need to install a new copy of Microsoft Excel on a Microsoft Windows computer system, choose the 32-bit version and not the 64-bit version *even if you have a 64-bit version of a Microsoft Windows operating system*. Many people mistakenly believe that the 64-bit version is somehow "better," not realizing that the OS X Excel 2011 is a 32-bit version and that Microsoft advises you to choose the 32-bit version for reasons the company details on its website. (The 64-bit WIN version exists primarily for users who need to work with Excel workbooks that are greater than 2GB in size. What would a 2GB workbook store? By one informal calculation, the contents of over 60 copies of this book—in other words, *big data*, as defined in Section LGS.3.)

Checking For and Applying Updates

Microsoft Excel updates require Internet access and the process to check for and apply updates differs among Excel versions. If you use a Microsoft Windows version of Excel and use Windows 7 or 8, checking for updates is done by the Windows Update service. If you use an older version of Microsoft Windows, you may have to upgrade to this free service as explained in "Special Note for Microsoft Windows XP and Windows Vista Users" on page 689.

Windows Update can automatically apply any updates it finds, although many users prefer to set Windows Update to *notify* when updates are available and then select and apply updates manually.

In OS X Excel versions and some Microsoft Windows versions, you can manually check for updates. In Excel 2011 (OS X), select **Help → Check for Updates** and in the dialog box that appears, click **Check for Updates**. In Excel 2007 (WIN), first click the **Office Button** and then **Excel Options** at the bottom of the Office Button window. In the Excel options dialog box, click **Resources** in the left pane and then in the right pane click **Check for Updates** and follow the instructions that appear on the web page that is displayed.

You normally do not manually check for updates in either Excel 2010 (WIN) or Excel 2013 (WIN). However, in some installations of these versions, you can select **File → Account → Update Options** (Excel 2013) or **File → Help → Check for Updates** (Excel 2010) and select options or follow instructions to turn on updates or to force the update process to begin.

If all else fails, you can open a web browser and go to the Microsoft Office part of the Microsoft Download Center at **www.microsoft.com/download/office.aspx?q=office** and manually select and download updates. On the web page that gets displayed, filter the downloadable files by specifying the Excel version you use. Discover the version number and update status by these means:

- In Excel 2013 (WIN), select **File → Account** and then click **About Microsoft Excel**. In the dialog box that appears note the numbers and codes that follow the phrase "Microsoft Excel 2013."
- In Excel 2010 (WIN), select **File → Help**. Under the heading "About Microsoft Excel" click **Additional Version and Copyright Information** and in the dialog box that appears note the numbers and codes that follow "Microsoft Excel 2010."
- In Excel 2011 (OS X), click **Excel → About Excel**. The dialog box that appears displays the **Version** and **Latest Installed Update**.
- In Excel 2007 (WIN), first click the **Office Button** and then click **Excel Options**. In the Excel options dialog box, click **Resources** in the left pane. In the right pane note the numbers and codes that follow Microsoft Office Excel 2007 under the "about Microsoft Office Excel 2007" heading.

Special Note for Microsoft Windows XP and Windows Vista Users

If you use a Microsoft Windows XP or Windows Vista system and have previously turned on the Windows Update service, your system has *not* necessarily downloaded and applied all Excel updates. If you use Windows Update on these older systems, you can upgrade for free to the Microsoft Update service that searches for and downloads updates for Microsoft Excel and Microsoft Office.

D.2 Getting PHStat Ready for Use (ALL)

If you plan to use PHStat, the Pearson Education add-in workbook that simplifies the use of Microsoft Excel with this book (see Section EG.2 on page 10), you must first download the PHStat files that are described in Section C.3, using one of the methods discussed in Section C.1. The PHStat download is packaged as a set of files in a zip archive file that you must unzip. You can store the unzip files in the folder of your choice, making sure that files are copied to that folder.

PHStat is fully compatible with these Excel versions: Excel 2007 (WIN), Excel 2010 (WIN), and Excel 2011 (OS X). Most procedures of PHStat are compatible with Excel 2003 (WIN), although opening PHStat in this version will cause a file conversion dialog box to appear as Excel transforms the add-in into a form suitable for use with Excel 2003. PHStat is not compatible with Excel 2008 (OS X), an Excel version that did not include the capability of running add-in workbooks. If you are using Microsoft Excel with Microsoft Windows (any version), then you must first configure the Microsoft Excel security settings as discussed in Section D.3. If you are using Microsoft Excel with OS X, no additional steps are required.

D.3 Configuring Excel Security for Add-In Usage (WIN)

The Microsoft Excel security settings can prevent add-ins such as PHStat and the Visual Explorations add-in workbooks from opening or functioning properly. To configure these security settings to permit proper PHStat functioning:

1. In Excel 2010 and Excel 2013, select **File → Options**. In Excel 2007, first click the **Office Button** and then click **Excel Options**.

In the Excel Options dialog box (see Figure D.1):

2. Click **Trust Center** in the left pane and then click **Trust Center Settings** in the right pane.

In the Trust Center dialog box (partially shown in two views as bottom insets in Figure D.1):

3. Click **Add-ins** in the next left pane, and in the Add-ins right pane clear all of the check-boxes (see the bottom left of Figure D.1).
4. Click **Macro Settings** in the left pane, and in the Macro Settings right pane click **Disable all macros with notification** and check **Trust access to the VBA object model** (see the bottom right of Figure D.1).
5. Click **OK** to close the Trust Center dialog box.

Back in the Excel Options dialog box:

6. Click **OK** to finish.

FIGURE D.1
Microsoft Excel (WIN) security settings

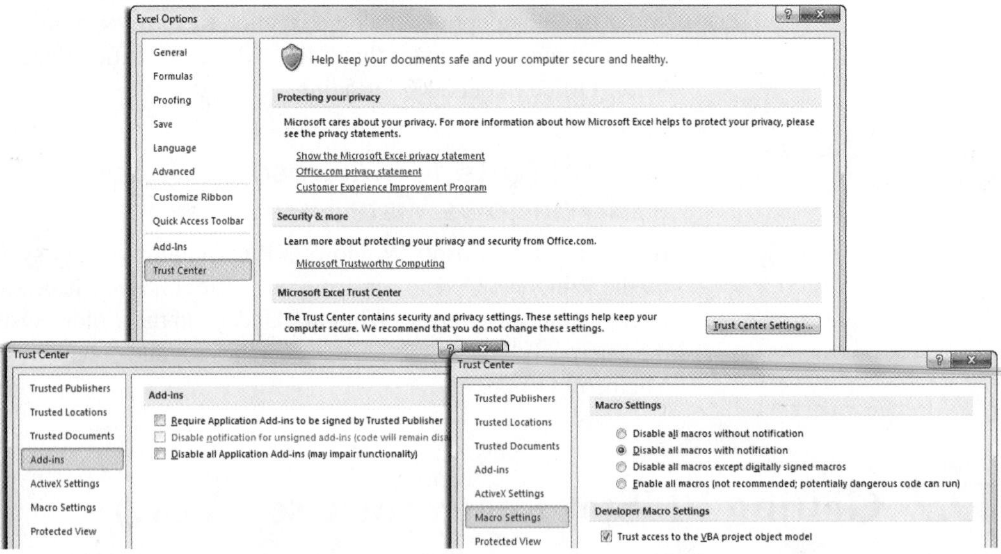

On some systems that have stringent security settings, you might need to modify step 5. For such systems, in step 5, click **Trusted Locations** in the left pane and then, in the Trusted Locations right pane, click **Add new location** to add the folder path that you chose to store the PHStat files and then click **OK**.

D.4 Opening PHStat (ALL)

Open the **PHStat.xlam** file to use PHStat. As you open the file, by any of the means discussed in Section EG.6 on page 13, Microsoft Excel will display a warning dialog box. The dialog boxes for Excel 2010 and Excel 2011 are shown below (the File Path will most likely be different on your

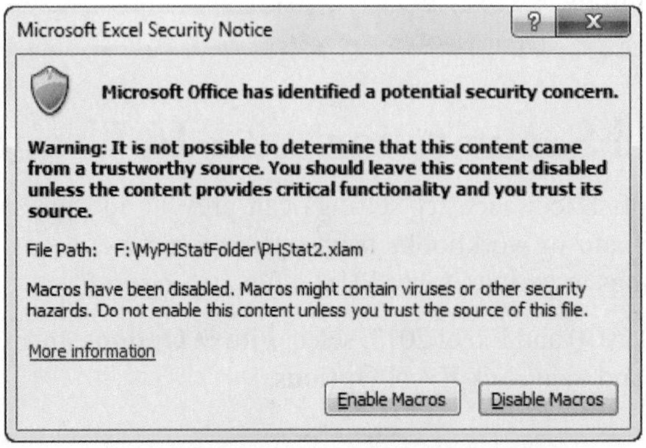

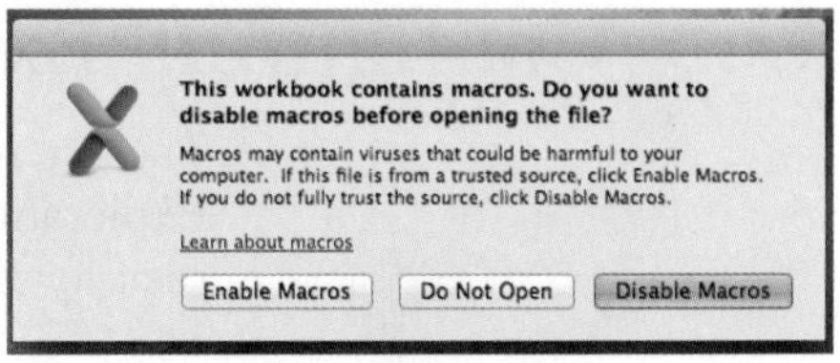

computer system). Click **Enable Macros**, which is not the default choice, to enable PHStat to function properly.

After you click **Enable Macros**, you can verify that PHStat has opened properly by looking for a PHStat menu in the Add-Ins tab of the Office Ribbon (WIN) or in the menu at top of the display (OS X). (In Excel 2003, the PHStat menu will appear in the Excel menu bar.)

If you have skipped checking for and applying necessary Excel updates, or if some of the updates were unable to be applied, when you first attempt to use PHStat, you may see a "Compile Error" message that talks about a "hidden module." If this occurs, repeat the process of checking for and applying updates to Excel. Review the PHStat FAQs in Appendix G for additional assistance, if necessary.

D.5 Using a Visual Explorations Add-in Workbook (ALL)

To use any of the Visual Explorations add-in workbooks, you must first download them using one of the methods discussed in Appendix Section C.1. If your download is packaged as a zip archive file, you must unzip that archive to use the add-in workbook. Store the add-in workbook files together in a folder of your choosing. Then apply the Section D.3 instructions, if necessary. When you open a Visual Explorations add-in workbook, you will see the same type of warning dialog box that is described in Section D.4. As those instructions state, click **Enable Macros** to enable the workbook to function properly.

D.6 Checking for the Presence of the Analysis ToolPak or Solver Add-Ins (ALL)

If you choose to perform logistic regression using the Section EG14.7 *PHStat* or *In-Depth Excel* instructions, you will need to ensure that the Solver add-in has been installed. Similarly, if you choose to use the *Analysis ToolPak* Excel Guide instructions, you will need to ensure that the Microsoft Excel Analysis ToolPak add-in has been installed. (This add-in is not available if you use Microsoft Excel with OS X.)

To check for the presence of the Solver (or Analysis ToolPak) add-in, if you use Microsoft Excel with Microsoft Windows:

1. In Excel 2010 or its successors, select **File → Options**. In Excel 2007, click the **Office Button** and then click **Excel Options** (at the bottom of the Office Button menu window).

In the Excel Options dialog box:

2. Click **Add-Ins** in the left pane and look for the entry **Solver Add-in** (or **Analysis ToolPak**) in the right pane, under **Active Application Add-ins**.
3. If the entry appears, click **OK**.

If the entry does not appear in the **Active Application Add-ins** list, click **Go**. In the Add-Ins dialog box, check **Solver Add-in** (or **Analysis ToolPak**) in the **Add-Ins available** list and click **OK**. If Analysis ToolPak (or Solver Add-in) does not appear in the list, rerun the Microsoft Office setup program to install this component.

To check for the presence of the Solver add-in, if you use Microsoft Excel with OS X, select **Tools → Options**. In the Add-Ins dialog box, check **Solver.Xlam** in the **Add-Ins available** list and click **OK**.

APPENDIX E Tables

TABLE E.1

Table of Random Numbers

	Column							
Row	00000 12345	00001 67890	11111 12345	11112 67890	22222 12345	22223 67890	33333 12345	33334 67890
01	49280	88924	35779	00283	81163	07275	89863	02348
02	61870	41657	07468	08612	98083	97349	20775	45091
03	43898	65923	25078	86129	78496	97653	91550	08078
04	62993	93912	30454	84598	56095	20664	12872	64647
05	33850	58555	51438	85507	71865	79488	76783	31708
06	97340	03364	88472	04334	63919	36394	11095	92470
07	70543	29776	10087	10072	55980	64688	68239	20461
08	89382	93809	00796	95945	34101	81277	66090	88872
09	37818	72142	67140	50785	22380	16703	53362	44940
10	60430	22834	14130	96593	23298	56203	92671	15925
11	82975	66158	84731	19436	55790	69229	28661	13675
12	30987	71938	40355	54324	08401	26299	49420	59208
13	55700	24586	93247	32596	11865	63397	44251	43189
14	14756	23997	78643	75912	83832	32768	18928	57070
15	32166	53251	70654	92827	63491	04233	33825	69662
16	23236	73751	31888	81718	06546	83246	47651	04877
17	45794	26926	15130	82455	78305	55058	52551	47182
18	09893	20505	14225	68514	47427	56788	96297	78822
19	54382	74598	91499	14523	68479	27686	46162	83554
20	94750	89923	37089	20048	80336	94598	26940	36858
21	70297	34135	53140	33340	42050	82341	44104	82949
22	85157	47954	32979	26575	57600	40881	12250	73742
23	11100	02340	12860	74697	96644	89439	28707	25815
24	36871	50775	30592	57143	17381	68856	25853	35041
25	23913	48357	63308	16090	51690	54607	72407	55538
26	79348	36085	27973	65157	07456	22255	25626	57054
27	92074	54641	53673	54421	18130	60103	69593	49464
28	06873	21440	75593	41373	49502	17972	82578	16364
29	12478	37622	99659	31065	83613	69889	58869	29571
30	57175	55564	65411	42547	70457	03426	72937	83792
31	91616	11075	80103	07831	59309	13276	26710	73000
32	78025	73539	14621	39044	47450	03197	12787	47709
33	27587	67228	80145	10175	12822	86687	65530	49325
34	16690	20427	04251	64477	73709	73945	92396	68263
35	70183	58065	65489	31833	82093	16747	10386	59293
36	90730	35385	15679	99742	50866	78028	75573	67257
37	10934	93242	13431	24590	02770	48582	00906	58595
38	82462	30166	79613	47416	13389	80268	05085	96666
39	27463	10433	07606	16285	93699	60912	94532	95632
40	02979	52997	09079	92709	90110	47506	53693	49892
41	46888	69929	75233	52507	32097	37594	10067	67327
42	53638	83161	08289	12639	08141	12640	28437	09268
43	82433	61427	17239	89160	19666	08814	37841	12847
44	35766	31672	50082	22795	66948	65581	84393	15890
45	10853	42581	08792	13257	61973	24450	52351	16602
46	20341	27398	72906	63955	17276	10646	74692	48438
47	54458	90542	77563	51839	52901	53355	83281	19177
48	26337	66530	16687	35179	46560	00123	44546	79896
49	34314	23729	85264	05575	96855	23820	11091	79821
50	28603	10708	68933	34189	92166	15181	66628	58599

TABLE E.1

Table of Random Numbers (*continued*)

	Column							
Row	**00000 12345**	**00001 67890**	**11111 12345**	**11112 67890**	**22222 12345**	**22223 67890**	**33333 12345**	**33334 67890**
51	66194	28926	99547	16625	45515	67953	12108	57846
52	78240	43195	24837	32511	70880	22070	52622	61881
53	00833	88000	67299	68215	11274	55624	32991	17436
54	12111	86683	61270	58036	64192	90611	15145	01748
55	47189	99951	05755	03834	43782	90599	40282	51417
56	76396	72486	62423	27618	84184	78922	73561	52818
57	46409	17469	32483	09083	76175	19985	26309	91536
58	74626	22111	87286	46772	42243	68046	44250	42439
59	34450	81974	93723	49023	58432	67083	36876	93391
60	36327	72135	33005	28701	34710	49359	50693	89311
61	74185	77536	84825	09934	99103	09325	67389	45869
62	12296	41623	62873	37943	25584	09609	63360	47270
63	90822	60280	88925	99610	42772	60561	76873	04117
64	72121	79152	96591	90305	10189	79778	68016	13747
65	95268	41377	25684	08151	61816	58555	54305	86189
66	92603	09091	75884	93424	72586	88903	30061	14457
67	18813	90291	05275	01223	79607	95426	34900	09778
68	38840	26903	28624	67157	51986	42865	14508	49315
69	05959	33836	53758	16562	41081	38012	41230	20528
70	85141	21155	99212	32685	51403	31926	69813	58781
71	75047	59643	31074	38172	03718	32119	69506	67143
72	30752	95260	68032	62871	58781	34143	68790	69766
73	22986	82575	42187	62295	84295	30634	66562	31442
74	99439	86692	90348	66036	48399	73451	26698	39437
75	20389	93029	11881	71685	65452	89047	63669	02656
76	39249	05173	68256	36359	20250	68686	05947	09335
77	96777	33605	29481	20063	09398	01843	35139	61344
78	04860	32918	10798	50492	52655	33359	94713	28393
79	41613	42375	00403	03656	77580	87772	86877	57085
80	17930	00794	53836	53692	67135	98102	61912	11246
81	24649	31845	25736	75231	83808	98917	93829	99430
82	79899	34061	54308	59358	56462	58166	97302	86828
83	76801	49594	81002	30397	52728	15101	72070	33706
84	36239	63636	38140	65731	39788	06872	38971	53363
85	07392	64449	17886	63632	53995	17574	22247	62607
86	67133	04181	33874	98835	67453	59734	76381	63455
87	77759	31504	32832	70861	15152	29733	75371	39174
88	85992	72268	42920	20810	29361	51423	90306	73574
89	79553	75952	54116	65553	47139	60579	09165	85490
90	41101	17336	48951	53674	17880	45260	08575	49321
91	36191	17095	32123	91576	84221	78902	82010	30847
92	62329	63898	23268	74283	26091	68409	69704	82267
93	14751	13151	93115	01437	56945	89661	67680	79790
94	48462	59278	44185	29616	76537	19589	83139	28454
95	29435	88105	59651	44391	74588	55114	80834	85686
96	28340	29285	12965	14821	80425	16602	44653	70467
97	02167	58940	27149	80242	10587	79786	34959	75339
98	17864	00991	39557	54981	23588	81914	37609	13128
99	79675	80605	60059	35862	00254	36546	21545	78179
100	72335	82037	92003	34100	29879	46613	89720	13274

Source: Partially extracted from the Rand Corporation, *A Million Random Digits with 100,000 Normal Deviates* (Glencoe, IL, The Free Press, 1955).

TABLE E.2

The Cumulative Standardized Normal Distribution

Entry represents area under the cumulative standardized normal distribution from $-\infty$ to Z

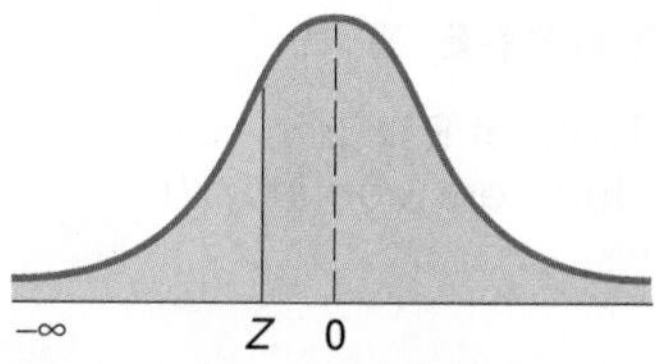

	Cumulative Probabilities									
Z	0.00	0.01	0.02	0.03	0.04	0.05	0.06	0.07	0.08	0.09
−6.0	0.000000001									
−5.5	0.000000019									
−5.0	0.000000287									
−4.5	0.000003398									
−4.0	0.000031671									
−3.9	0.00005	0.00005	0.00004	0.00004	0.00004	0.00004	0.00004	0.00004	0.00003	0.00003
−3.8	0.00007	0.00007	0.00007	0.00006	0.00006	0.00006	0.00006	0.00005	0.00005	0.00005
−3.7	0.00011	0.00010	0.00010	0.00010	0.00009	0.00009	0.00008	0.00008	0.00008	0.00008
−3.6	0.00016	0.00015	0.00015	0.00014	0.00014	0.00013	0.00013	0.00012	0.00012	0.00011
−3.5	0.00023	0.00022	0.00022	0.00021	0.00020	0.00019	0.00019	0.00018	0.00017	0.00017
−3.4	0.00034	0.00032	0.00031	0.00030	0.00029	0.00028	0.00027	0.00026	0.00025	0.00024
−3.3	0.00048	0.00047	0.00045	0.00043	0.00042	0.00040	0.00039	0.00038	0.00036	0.00035
−3.2	0.00069	0.00066	0.00064	0.00062	0.00060	0.00058	0.00056	0.00054	0.00052	0.00050
−3.1	0.00097	0.00094	0.00090	0.00087	0.00084	0.00082	0.00079	0.00076	0.00074	0.00071
−3.0	0.00135	0.00131	0.00126	0.00122	0.00118	0.00114	0.00111	0.00107	0.00103	0.00100
−2.9	0.0019	0.0018	0.0018	0.0017	0.0016	0.0016	0.0015	0.0015	0.0014	0.0014
−2.8	0.0026	0.0025	0.0024	0.0023	0.0023	0.0022	0.0021	0.0021	0.0020	0.0019
−2.7	0.0035	0.0034	0.0033	0.0032	0.0031	0.0030	0.0029	0.0028	0.0027	0.0026
−2.6	0.0047	0.0045	0.0044	0.0043	0.0041	0.0040	0.0039	0.0038	0.0037	0.0036
−2.5	0.0062	0.0060	0.0059	0.0057	0.0055	0.0054	0.0052	0.0051	0.0049	0.0048
−2.4	0.0082	0.0080	0.0078	0.0075	0.0073	0.0071	0.0069	0.0068	0.0066	0.0064
−2.3	0.0107	0.0104	0.0102	0.0099	0.0096	0.0094	0.0091	0.0089	0.0087	0.0084
−2.2	0.0139	0.0136	0.0132	0.0129	0.0125	0.0122	0.0119	0.0116	0.0113	0.0110
−2.1	0.0179	0.0174	0.0170	0.0166	0.0162	0.0158	0.0154	0.0150	0.0146	0.0143
−2.0	0.0228	0.0222	0.0217	0.0212	0.0207	0.0202	0.0197	0.0192	0.0188	0.0183
−1.9	0.0287	0.0281	0.0274	0.0268	0.0262	0.0256	0.0250	0.0244	0.0239	0.0233
−1.8	0.0359	0.0351	0.0344	0.0336	0.0329	0.0322	0.0314	0.0307	0.0301	0.0294
−1.7	0.0446	0.0436	0.0427	0.0418	0.0409	0.0401	0.0392	0.0384	0.0375	0.0367
−1.6	0.0548	0.0537	0.0526	0.0516	0.0505	0.0495	0.0485	0.0475	0.0465	0.0455
−1.5	0.0668	0.0655	0.0643	0.0630	0.0618	0.0606	0.0594	0.0582	0.0571	0.0559
−1.4	0.0808	0.0793	0.0778	0.0764	0.0749	0.0735	0.0721	0.0708	0.0694	0.0681
−1.3	0.0968	0.0951	0.0934	0.0918	0.0901	0.0885	0.0869	0.0853	0.0838	0.0823
−1.2	0.1151	0.1131	0.1112	0.1093	0.1075	0.1056	0.1038	0.1020	0.1003	0.0985
−1.1	0.1357	0.1335	0.1314	0.1292	0.1271	0.1251	0.1230	0.1210	0.1190	0.1170
−1.0	0.1587	0.1562	0.1539	0.1515	0.1492	0.1469	0.1446	0.1423	0.1401	0.1379
−0.9	0.1841	0.1814	0.1788	0.1762	0.1736	0.1711	0.1685	0.1660	0.1635	0.1611
−0.8	0.2119	0.2090	0.2061	0.2033	0.2005	0.1977	0.1949	0.1922	0.1894	0.1867
−0.7	0.2420	0.2388	0.2358	0.2327	0.2296	0.2266	0.2236	0.2206	0.2177	0.2148
−0.6	0.2743	0.2709	0.2676	0.2643	0.2611	0.2578	0.2546	0.2514	0.2482	0.2451
−0.5	0.3085	0.3050	0.3015	0.2981	0.2946	0.2912	0.2877	0.2843	0.2810	0.2776
−0.4	0.3446	0.3409	0.3372	0.3336	0.3300	0.3264	0.3228	0.3192	0.3156	0.3121
−0.3	0.3821	0.3783	0.3745	0.3707	0.3669	0.3632	0.3594	0.3557	0.3520	0.3483
−0.2	0.4207	0.4168	0.4129	0.4090	0.4052	0.4013	0.3974	0.3936	0.3897	0.3859
−0.1	0.4602	0.4562	0.4522	0.4483	0.4443	0.4404	0.4364	0.4325	0.4286	0.4247
−0.0	0.5000	0.4960	0.4920	0.4880	0.4840	0.4801	0.4761	0.4721	0.4681	0.4641

TABLE E.2

The Cumulative Standardized Normal Distribution (*continued*)

Entry represents area under the cumulative standardized normal distribution from $-\infty$ to Z

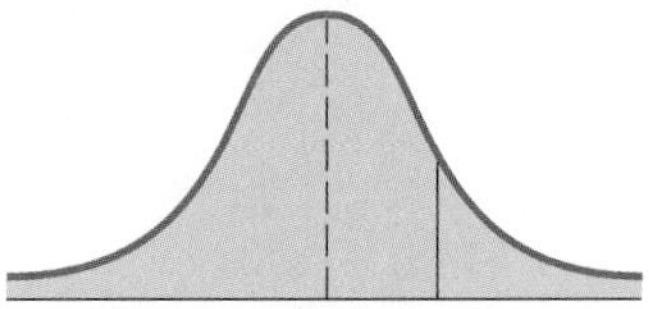

	Cumulative Probabilities									
Z	**0.00**	**0.01**	**0.02**	**0.03**	**0.04**	**0.05**	**0.06**	**0.07**	**0.08**	**0.09**
0.0	0.5000	0.5040	0.5080	0.5120	0.5160	0.5199	0.5239	0.5279	0.5319	0.5359
0.1	0.5398	0.5438	0.5478	0.5517	0.5557	0.5596	0.5636	0.5675	0.5714	0.5753
0.2	0.5793	0.5832	0.5871	0.5910	0.5948	0.5987	0.6026	0.6064	0.6103	0.6141
0.3	0.6179	0.6217	0.6255	0.6293	0.6331	0.6368	0.6406	0.6443	0.6480	0.6517
0.4	0.6554	0.6591	0.6628	0.6664	0.6700	0.6736	0.6772	0.6808	0.6844	0.6879
0.5	0.6915	0.6950	0.6985	0.7019	0.7054	0.7088	0.7123	0.7157	0.7190	0.7224
0.6	0.7257	0.7291	0.7324	0.7357	0.7389	0.7422	0.7454	0.7486	0.7518	0.7549
0.7	0.7580	0.7612	0.7642	0.7673	0.7704	0.7734	0.7764	0.7794	0.7823	0.7852
0.8	0.7881	0.7910	0.7939	0.7967	0.7995	0.8023	0.8051	0.8078	0.8106	0.8133
0.9	0.8159	0.8186	0.8212	0.8238	0.8264	0.8289	0.8315	0.8340	0.8365	0.8389
1.0	0.8413	0.8438	0.8461	0.8485	0.8508	0.8531	0.8554	0.8577	0.8599	0.8621
1.1	0.8643	0.8665	0.8686	0.8708	0.8729	0.8749	0.8770	0.8790	0.8810	0.8830
1.2	0.8849	0.8869	0.8888	0.8907	0.8925	0.8944	0.8962	0.8980	0.8997	0.9015
1.3	0.9032	0.9049	0.9066	0.9082	0.9099	0.9115	0.9131	0.9147	0.9162	0.9177
1.4	0.9192	0.9207	0.9222	0.9236	0.9251	0.9265	0.9279	0.9292	0.9306	0.9319
1.5	0.9332	0.9345	0.9357	0.9370	0.9382	0.9394	0.9406	0.9418	0.9429	0.9441
1.6	0.9452	0.9463	0.9474	0.9484	0.9495	0.9505	0.9515	0.9525	0.9535	0.9545
1.7	0.9554	0.9564	0.9573	0.9582	0.9591	0.9599	0.9608	0.9616	0.9625	0.9633
1.8	0.9641	0.9649	0.9656	0.9664	0.9671	0.9678	0.9686	0.9693	0.9699	0.9706
1.9	0.9713	0.9719	0.9726	0.9732	0.9738	0.9744	0.9750	0.9756	0.9761	0.9767
2.0	0.9772	0.9778	0.9783	0.9788	0.9793	0.9798	0.9803	0.9808	0.9812	0.9817
2.1	0.9821	0.9826	0.9830	0.9834	0.9838	0.9842	0.9846	0.9850	0.9854	0.9857
2.2	0.9861	0.9864	0.9868	0.9871	0.9875	0.9878	0.9881	0.9884	0.9887	0.9890
2.3	0.9893	0.9896	0.9898	0.9901	0.9904	0.9906	0.9909	0.9911	0.9913	0.9916
2.4	0.9918	0.9920	0.9922	0.9925	0.9927	0.9929	0.9931	0.9932	0.9934	0.9936
2.5	0.9938	0.9940	0.9941	0.9943	0.9945	0.9946	0.9948	0.9949	0.9951	0.9952
2.6	0.9953	0.9955	0.9956	0.9957	0.9959	0.9960	0.9961	0.9962	0.9963	0.9964
2.7	0.9965	0.9966	0.9967	0.9968	0.9969	0.9970	0.9971	0.9972	0.9973	0.9974
2.8	0.9974	0.9975	0.9976	0.9977	0.9977	0.9978	0.9979	0.9979	0.9980	0.9981
2.9	0.9981	0.9982	0.9982	0.9983	0.9984	0.9984	0.9985	0.9985	0.9986	0.9986
3.0	0.99865	0.99869	0.99874	0.99878	0.99882	0.99886	0.99889	0.99893	0.99897	0.99900
3.1	0.99903	0.99906	0.99910	0.99913	0.99916	0.99918	0.99921	0.99924	0.99926	0.99929
3.2	0.99931	0.99934	0.99936	0.99938	0.99940	0.99942	0.99944	0.99946	0.99948	0.99950
3.3	0.99952	0.99953	0.99955	0.99957	0.99958	0.99960	0.99961	0.99962	0.99964	0.99965
3.4	0.99966	0.99968	0.99969	0.99970	0.99971	0.99972	0.99973	0.99974	0.99975	0.99976
3.5	0.99977	0.99978	0.99978	0.99979	0.99980	0.99981	0.99981	0.99982	0.99983	0.99983
3.6	0.99984	0.99985	0.99985	0.99986	0.99986	0.99987	0.99987	0.99988	0.99988	0.99989
3.7	0.99989	0.99990	0.99990	0.99990	0.99991	0.99991	0.99992	0.99992	0.99992	0.99992
3.8	0.99993	0.99993	0.99993	0.99994	0.99994	0.99994	0.99994	0.99995	0.99995	0.99995
3.9	0.99995	0.99995	0.99996	0.99996	0.99996	0.99996	0.99996	0.99996	0.99997	0.99997
4.0	0.999968329									
4.5	0.999996602									
5.0	0.999999713									
5.5	0.999999981									
6.0	0.999999999									

TABLE E.3

Critical Values of t

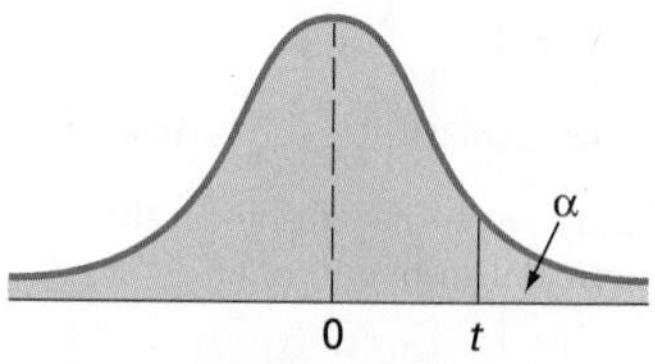

For a particular number of degrees of freedom, entry represents the critical value of t corresponding to the cumulative probability $(1 - \alpha)$ and a specified upper-tail area (α).

	Cumulative Probabilities					
	0.75	0.90	0.95	0.975	0.99	0.995
	Upper-Tail Areas					
Degrees of Freedom	0.25	0.10	0.05	0.025	0.01	0.005
1	1.0000	3.0777	6.3138	12.7062	31.8207	63.6574
2	0.8165	1.8856	2.9200	4.3027	6.9646	9.9248
3	0.7649	1.6377	2.3534	3.1824	4.5407	5.8409
4	0.7407	1.5332	2.1318	2.7764	3.7469	4.6041
5	0.7267	1.4759	2.0150	2.5706	3.3649	4.0322
6	0.7176	1.4398	1.9432	2.4469	3.1427	3.7074
7	0.7111	1.4149	1.8946	2.3646	2.9980	3.4995
8	0.7064	1.3968	1.8595	2.3060	2.8965	3.3554
9	0.7027	1.3830	1.8331	2.2622	2.8214	3.2498
10	0.6998	1.3722	1.8125	2.2281	2.7638	3.1693
11	0.6974	1.3634	1.7959	2.2010	2.7181	3.1058
12	0.6955	1.3562	1.7823	2.1788	2.6810	3.0545
13	0.6938	1.3502	1.7709	2.1604	2.6503	3.0123
14	0.6924	1.3450	1.7613	2.1448	2.6245	2.9768
15	0.6912	1.3406	1.7531	2.1315	2.6025	2.9467
16	0.6901	1.3368	1.7459	2.1199	2.5835	2.9208
17	0.6892	1.3334	1.7396	2.1098	2.5669	2.8982
18	0.6884	1.3304	1.7341	2.1009	2.5524	2.8784
19	0.6876	1.3277	1.7291	2.0930	2.5395	2.8609
20	0.6870	1.3253	1.7247	2.0860	2.5280	2.8453
21	0.6864	1.3232	1.7207	2.0796	2.5177	2.8314
22	0.6858	1.3212	1.7171	2.0739	2.5083	2.8188
23	0.6853	1.3195	1.7139	2.0687	2.4999	2.8073
24	0.6848	1.3178	1.7109	2.0639	2.4922	2.7969
25	0.6844	1.3163	1.7081	2.0595	2.4851	2.7874
26	0.6840	1.3150	1.7056	2.0555	2.4786	2.7787
27	0.6837	1.3137	1.7033	2.0518	2.4727	2.7707
28	0.6834	1.3125	1.7011	2.0484	2.4671	2.7633
29	0.6830	1.3114	1.6991	2.0452	2.4620	2.7564
30	0.6828	1.3104	1.6973	2.0423	2.4573	2.7500
31	0.6825	1.3095	1.6955	2.0395	2.4528	2.7440
32	0.6822	1.3086	1.6939	2.0369	2.4487	2.7385
33	0.6820	1.3077	1.6924	2.0345	2.4448	2.7333
34	0.6818	1.3070	1.6909	2.0322	2.4411	2.7284
35	0.6816	1.3062	1.6896	2.0301	2.4377	2.7238
36	0.6814	1.3055	1.6883	2.0281	2.4345	2.7195
37	0.6812	1.3049	1.6871	2.0262	2.4314	2.7154
38	0.6810	1.3042	1.6860	2.0244	2.4286	2.7116
39	0.6808	1.3036	1.6849	2.0227	2.4258	2.7079
40	0.6807	1.3031	1.6839	2.0211	2.4233	2.7045
41	0.6805	1.3025	1.6829	2.0195	2.4208	2.7012
42	0.6804	1.3020	1.6820	2.0181	2.4185	2.6981
43	0.6802	1.3016	1.6811	2.0167	2.4163	2.6951
44	0.6801	1.3011	1.6802	2.0154	2.4141	2.6923
45	0.6800	1.3006	1.6794	2.0141	2.4121	2.6896
46	0.6799	1.3002	1.6787	2.0129	2.4102	2.6870
47	0.6797	1.2998	1.6779	2.0117	2.4083	2.6846
48	0.6796	1.2994	1.6772	2.0106	2.4066	2.6822
49	0.6795	1.2991	1.6766	2.0096	2.4049	2.6800
50	0.6794	1.2987	1.6759	2.0086	2.4033	2.6778

TABLE E.3

Critical Values of t (*continued*)

	Cumulative Probabilities					
	0.75	0.90	0.95	0.975	0.99	0.995
	Upper-Tail Areas					
Degrees of Freedom	0.25	0.10	0.05	0.025	0.01	0.005
51	0.6793	1.2984	1.6753	2.0076	2.4017	2.6757
52	0.6792	1.2980	1.6747	2.0066	2.4002	2.6737
53	0.6791	1.2977	1.6741	2.0057	2.3988	2.6718
54	0.6791	1.2974	1.6736	2.0049	2.3974	2.6700
55	0.6790	1.2971	1.6730	2.0040	2.3961	2.6682
56	0.6789	1.2969	1.6725	2.0032	2.3948	2.6665
57	0.6788	1.2966	1.6720	2.0025	2.3936	2.6649
58	0.6787	1.2963	1.6716	2.0017	2.3924	2.6633
59	0.6787	1.2961	1.6711	2.0010	2.3912	2.6618
60	0.6786	1.2958	1.6706	2.0003	2.3901	2.6603
61	0.6785	1.2956	1.6702	1.9996	2.3890	2.6589
62	0.6785	1.2954	1.6698	1.9990	2.3880	2.6575
63	0.6784	1.2951	1.6694	1.9983	2.3870	2.6561
64	0.6783	1.2949	1.6690	1.9977	2.3860	2.6549
65	0.6783	1.2947	1.6686	1.9971	2.3851	2.6536
66	0.6782	1.2945	1.6683	1.9966	2.3842	2.6524
67	0.6782	1.2943	1.6679	1.9960	2.3833	2.6512
68	0.6781	1.2941	1.6676	1.9955	2.3824	2.6501
69	0.6781	1.2939	1.6672	1.9949	2.3816	2.6490
70	0.6780	1.2938	1.6669	1.9944	2.3808	2.6479
71	0.6780	1.2936	1.6666	1.9939	2.3800	2.6469
72	0.6779	1.2934	1.6663	1.9935	2.3793	2.6459
73	0.6779	1.2933	1.6660	1.9930	2.3785	2.6449
74	0.6778	1.2931	1.6657	1.9925	2.3778	2.6439
75	0.6778	1.2929	1.6654	1.9921	2.3771	2.6430
76	0.6777	1.2928	1.6652	1.9917	2.3764	2.6421
77	0.6777	1.2926	1.6649	1.9913	2.3758	2.6412
78	0.6776	1.2925	1.6646	1.9908	2.3751	2.6403
79	0.6776	1.2924	1.6644	1.9905	2.3745	2.6395
80	0.6776	1.2922	1.6641	1.9901	2.3739	2.6387
81	0.6775	1.2921	1.6639	1.9897	2.3733	2.6379
82	0.6775	1.2920	1.6636	1.9893	2.3727	2.6371
83	0.6775	1.2918	1.6634	1.9890	2.3721	2.6364
84	0.6774	1.2917	1.6632	1.9886	2.3716	2.6356
85	0.6774	1.2916	1.6630	1.9883	2.3710	2.6349
86	0.6774	1.2915	1.6628	1.9879	2.3705	2.6342
87	0.6773	1.2914	1.6626	1.9876	2.3700	2.6335
88	0.6773	1.2912	1.6624	1.9873	2.3695	2.6329
89	0.6773	1.2911	1.6622	1.9870	2.3690	2.6322
90	0.6772	1.2910	1.6620	1.9867	2.3685	2.6316
91	0.6772	1.2909	1.6618	1.9864	2.3680	2.6309
92	0.6772	1.2908	1.6616	1.9861	2.3676	2.6303
93	0.6771	1.2907	1.6614	1.9858	2.3671	2.6297
94	0.6771	1.2906	1.6612	1.9855	2.3667	2.6291
95	0.6771	1.2905	1.6611	1.9853	2.3662	2.6286
96	0.6771	1.2904	1.6609	1.9850	2.3658	2.6280
97	0.6770	1.2903	1.6607	1.9847	2.3654	2.6275
98	0.6770	1.2902	1.6606	1.9845	2.3650	2.6269
99	0.6770	1.2902	1.6604	1.9842	2.3646	2.6264
100	0.6770	1.2901	1.6602	1.9840	2.3642	2.6259
110	0.6767	1.2893	1.6588	1.9818	2.3607	2.6213
120	0.6765	1.2886	1.6577	1.9799	2.3578	2.6174
∞	0.6745	1.2816	1.6449	1.9600	2.3263	2.5758

TABLE E.4

Critical Values of χ^2

For a particular number of degrees of freedom, entry represents the critical value of χ^2 corresponding to the cumulative probability $(1 - \alpha)$ and a specified upper-tail area (α).

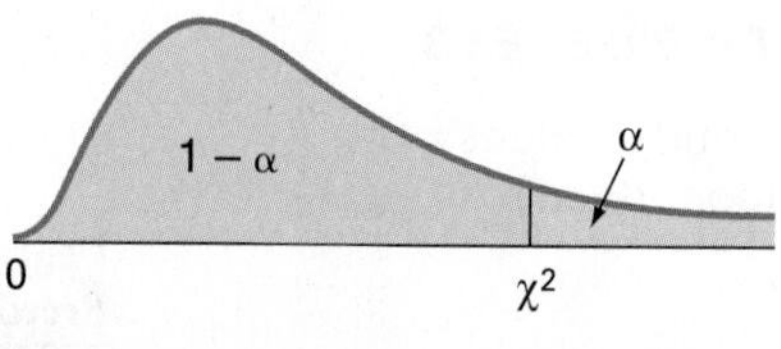

Degrees of Freedom	Cumulative Probabilities											
	0.005	**0.01**	**0.025**	**0.05**	**0.10**	**0.25**	**0.75**	**0.90**	**0.95**	**0.975**	**0.99**	**0.995**
	Upper-Tail Areas (α)											
	0.995	**0.99**	**0.975**	**0.95**	**0.90**	**0.75**	**0.25**	**0.10**	**0.05**	**0.025**	**0.01**	**0.005**
1			0.001	0.004	0.016	0.102	1.323	2.706	3.841	5.024	6.635	7.879
2	0.010	0.020	0.051	0.103	0.211	0.575	2.773	4.605	5.991	7.378	9.210	10.597
3	0.072	0.115	0.216	0.352	0.584	1.213	4.108	6.251	7.815	9.348	11.345	12.838
4	0.207	0.297	0.484	0.711	1.064	1.923	5.385	7.779	9.488	11.143	13.277	14.860
5	0.412	0.554	0.831	1.145	1.610	2.675	6.626	9.236	11.071	12.833	15.086	16.750
6	0.676	0.872	1.237	1.635	2.204	3.455	7.841	10.645	12.592	14.449	16.812	18.548
7	0.989	1.239	1.690	2.167	2.833	4.255	9.037	12.017	14.067	16.013	18.475	20.278
8	1.344	1.646	2.180	2.733	3.490	5.071	10.219	13.362	15.507	17.535	20.090	21.955
9	1.735	2.088	2.700	3.325	4.168	5.899	11.389	14.684	16.919	19.023	21.666	23.589
10	2.156	2.558	3.247	3.940	4.865	6.737	12.549	15.987	18.307	20.483	23.209	25.188
11	2.603	3.053	3.816	4.575	5.578	7.584	13.701	17.275	19.675	21.920	24.725	26.757
12	3.074	3.571	4.404	5.226	6.304	8.438	14.845	18.549	21.026	23.337	26.217	28.299
13	3.565	4.107	5.009	5.892	7.042	9.299	15.984	19.812	22.362	24.736	27.688	29.819
14	4.075	4.660	5.629	6.571	7.790	10.165	17.117	21.064	23.685	26.119	29.141	31.319
15	4.601	5.229	6.262	7.261	8.547	11.037	18.245	22.307	24.996	27.488	30.578	32.801
16	5.142	5.812	6.908	7.962	9.312	11.912	19.369	23.542	26.296	28.845	32.000	34.267
17	5.697	6.408	7.564	8.672	10.085	12.792	20.489	24.769	27.587	30.191	33.409	35.718
18	6.265	7.015	8.231	9.390	10.865	13.675	21.605	25.989	28.869	31.526	34.805	37.156
19	6.844	7.633	8.907	10.117	11.651	14.562	22.718	27.204	30.144	32.852	36.191	38.582
20	7.434	8.260	9.591	10.851	12.443	15.452	23.828	28.412	31.410	34.170	37.566	39.997
21	8.034	8.897	10.283	11.591	13.240	16.344	24.935	29.615	32.671	35.479	38.932	41.401
22	8.643	9.542	10.982	12.338	14.042	17.240	26.039	30.813	33.924	36.781	40.289	42.796
23	9.260	10.196	11.689	13.091	14.848	18.137	27.141	32.007	35.172	38.076	41.638	44.181
24	9.886	10.856	12.401	13.848	15.659	19.037	28.241	33.196	36.415	39.364	42.980	45.559
25	10.520	11.524	13.120	14.611	16.473	19.939	29.339	34.382	37.652	40.646	44.314	46.928
26	11.160	12.198	13.844	15.379	17.292	20.843	30.435	35.563	38.885	41.923	45.642	48.290
27	11.808	12.879	14.573	16.151	18.114	21.749	31.528	36.741	40.113	43.194	46.963	49.645
28	12.461	13.565	15.308	16.928	18.939	22.657	32.620	37.916	41.337	44.461	48.278	50.993
29	13.121	14.257	16.047	17.708	19.768	23.567	33.711	39.087	42.557	45.722	49.588	52.336
30	13.787	14.954	16.791	18.493	20.599	24.478	34.800	40.256	43.773	46.979	50.892	53.672

For larger values of degrees of freedom (*df*) the expression $Z = \sqrt{2\chi^2} - \sqrt{2(df) - 1}$ may be used and the resulting upper-tail area can be found from the cumulative standardized normal distribution (Table E.2).

TABLE E.5

Critical Values of F

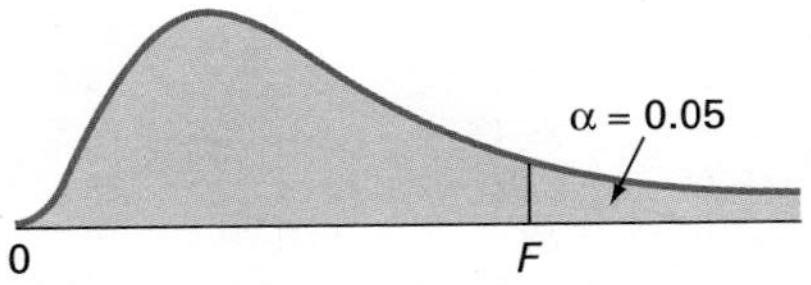

For a particular combination of numerator and denominator degrees of freedom, entry represents the critical values of F corresponding to the cumulative probability $(1 - \alpha)$ and a specified upper-tail area (α).

Cumulative Probabilities = 0.95																			
Upper-Tail Areas = 0.05																			
	Numerator, df_1																		
Denominator, df_2	1	2	3	4	5	6	7	8	9	10	12	15	20	24	30	40	60	120	∞
1	161.40	199.50	215.70	224.60	230.20	234.00	236.80	238.90	240.50	241.90	243.90	245.90	248.00	249.10	250.10	251.10	252.20	253.30	254.30
2	18.51	19.00	19.16	19.25	19.30	19.33	19.35	19.37	19.38	19.40	19.41	19.43	19.45	19.45	19.46	19.47	19.48	19.49	19.50
3	10.13	9.55	9.28	9.12	9.01	8.94	8.89	8.85	8.81	8.79	8.74	8.70	8.66	8.64	8.62	8.59	8.57	8.55	8.53
4	7.71	6.94	6.59	6.39	6.26	6.16	6.09	6.04	6.00	5.96	5.91	5.86	5.80	5.77	5.75	5.72	5.69	5.66	5.63
5	6.61	5.79	5.41	5.19	5.05	4.95	4.88	4.82	4.77	4.74	4.68	4.62	4.56	4.53	4.50	4.46	4.43	4.40	4.36
6	5.99	5.14	4.76	4.53	4.39	4.28	4.21	4.15	4.10	4.06	4.00	3.94	3.87	3.84	3.81	3.77	3.74	3.70	3.67
7	5.59	4.74	4.35	4.12	3.97	3.87	3.79	3.73	3.68	3.64	3.57	3.51	3.44	3.41	3.38	3.34	3.30	3.27	3.23
8	5.32	4.46	4.07	3.84	3.69	3.58	3.50	3.44	3.39	3.35	3.28	3.22	3.15	3.12	3.08	3.04	3.01	2.97	2.93
9	5.12	4.26	3.86	3.63	3.48	3.37	3.29	3.23	3.18	3.14	3.07	3.01	2.94	2.90	2.86	2.83	2.79	2.75	2.71
10	4.96	4.10	3.71	3.48	3.33	3.22	3.14	3.07	3.02	2.98	2.91	2.85	2.77	2.74	2.70	2.66	2.62	2.58	2.54
11	4.84	3.98	3.59	3.36	3.20	3.09	3.01	2.95	2.90	2.85	2.79	2.72	2.65	2.61	2.57	2.53	2.49	2.45	2.40
12	4.75	3.89	3.49	3.26	3.11	3.00	2.91	2.85	2.80	2.75	2.69	2.62	2.54	2.51	2.47	2.43	2.38	2.34	2.30
13	4.67	3.81	3.41	3.18	3.03	2.92	2.83	2.77	2.71	2.67	2.60	2.53	2.46	2.42	2.38	2.34	2.30	2.25	2.21
14	4.60	3.74	3.34	3.11	2.96	2.85	2.76	2.70	2.65	2.60	2.53	2.46	2.39	2.35	2.31	2.27	2.22	2.18	2.13
15	4.54	3.68	3.29	3.06	2.90	2.79	2.71	2.64	2.59	2.54	2.48	2.40	2.33	2.29	2.25	2.20	2.16	2.11	2.07
16	4.49	3.63	3.24	3.01	2.85	2.74	2.66	2.59	2.54	2.49	2.42	2.35	2.28	2.24	2.19	2.15	2.11	2.06	2.01
17	4.45	3.59	3.20	2.96	2.81	2.70	2.61	2.55	2.49	2.45	2.38	2.31	2.23	2.19	2.15	2.10	2.06	2.01	1.96
18	4.41	3.55	3.16	2.93	2.77	2.66	2.58	2.51	2.46	2.41	2.34	2.27	2.19	2.15	2.11	2.06	2.02	1.97	1.92
19	4.38	3.52	3.13	2.90	2.74	2.63	2.54	2.48	2.42	2.38	2.31	2.23	2.16	2.11	2.07	2.03	1.98	1.93	1.88
20	4.35	3.49	3.10	2.87	2.71	2.60	2.51	2.45	2.39	2.35	2.28	2.20	2.12	2.08	2.04	1.99	1.95	1.90	1.84
21	4.32	3.47	3.07	2.84	2.68	2.57	2.49	2.42	2.37	2.32	2.25	2.18	2.10	2.05	2.01	1.96	1.92	1.87	1.81
22	4.30	3.44	3.05	2.82	2.66	2.55	2.46	2.40	2.34	2.30	2.23	2.15	2.07	2.03	1.98	1.91	1.89	1.84	1.78
23	4.28	3.42	3.03	2.80	2.64	2.53	2.44	2.37	2.32	2.27	2.20	2.13	2.05	2.01	1.96	1.91	1.86	1.81	1.76
24	4.26	3.40	3.01	2.78	2.62	2.51	2.42	2.36	2.30	2.25	2.18	2.11	2.03	1.98	1.94	1.89	1.84	1.79	1.73
25	4.24	3.39	2.99	2.76	2.60	2.49	2.40	2.34	2.28	2.24	2.16	2.09	2.01	1.96	1.92	1.87	1.82	1.77	1.71
26	4.23	3.37	2.98	2.74	2.59	2.47	2.39	2.32	2.27	2.22	2.15	2.07	1.99	1.95	1.90	1.85	1.80	1.75	1.69
27	4.21	3.35	2.96	2.73	2.57	2.46	2.37	2.31	2.25	2.20	2.13	2.06	1.97	1.93	1.88	1.84	1.79	1.73	1.67
28	4.20	3.34	2.95	2.71	2.56	2.45	2.36	2.29	2.24	2.19	2.12	2.04	1.96	1.91	1.87	1.82	1.77	1.71	1.65
29	4.18	3.33	2.93	2.70	2.55	2.43	2.35	2.28	2.22	2.18	2.10	2.03	1.94	1.90	1.85	1.81	1.75	1.70	1.64
30	4.17	3.32	2.92	2.69	2.53	2.42	2.33	2.27	2.21	2.16	2.09	2.01	1.93	1.89	1.84	1.79	1.74	1.68	1.62
40	4.08	3.23	2.84	2.61	2.45	2.34	2.25	2.18	2.12	2.08	2.00	1.92	1.84	1.79	1.74	1.69	1.64	1.58	1.51
60	4.00	3.15	2.76	2.53	2.37	2.25	2.17	2.10	2.04	1.99	1.92	1.84	1.75	1.70	1.65	1.59	1.53	1.47	1.39
120	3.92	3.07	2.68	2.45	2.29	2.17	2.09	2.02	1.96	1.91	1.83	1.75	1.66	1.61	1.55	1.50	1.43	1.35	1.25
∞	3.84	3.00	2.60	2.37	2.21	2.10	2.01	1.94	1.88	1.83	1.75	1.67	1.57	1.52	1.46	1.39	1.32	1.22	1.00

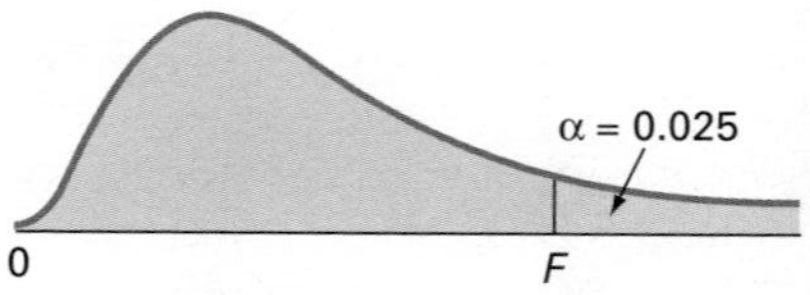

Cumulative Probabilities = 0.975																			
Upper-Tail Areas = 0.025																			
	Numerator, df_1																		
Denominator, df_2	1	2	3	4	5	6	7	8	9	10	12	15	20	24	30	40	60	120	∞
1	647.80	799.50	864.20	899.60	921.80	937.10	948.20	956.70	963.30	968.60	976.70	984.90	993.10	997.20	1,001.00	1,006.00	1,010.00	1,014.00	1,018.00
2	38.51	39.00	39.17	39.25	39.30	39.33	39.36	39.39	39.39	39.40	39.41	39.43	39.45	39.46	39.46	39.47	39.48	39.49	39.50
3	17.44	16.04	15.44	15.10	14.88	14.73	14.62	14.54	14.47	14.42	14.34	14.25	14.17	14.12	14.08	14.04	13.99	13.95	13.90
4	12.22	10.65	9.98	9.60	9.36	9.20	9.07	8.98	8.90	8.84	8.75	8.66	8.56	8.51	8.46	8.41	8.36	8.31	8.26
5	10.01	8.43	7.76	7.39	7.15	6.98	6.85	6.76	6.68	6.62	6.52	6.43	6.33	6.28	6.23	6.18	6.12	6.07	6.02
6	8.81	7.26	6.60	6.23	5.99	5.82	5.70	5.60	5.52	5.46	5.37	5.27	5.17	5.12	5.07	5.01	4.96	4.90	4.85
7	8.07	6.54	5.89	5.52	5.29	5.12	4.99	4.90	4.82	4.76	4.67	4.57	4.47	4.42	4.36	4.31	4.25	4.20	4.14
8	7.57	6.06	5.42	5.05	4.82	4.65	4.53	4.43	4.36	4.30	4.20	4.10	4.00	3.95	3.89	3.84	3.78	3.73	3.67
9	7.21	5.71	5.08	4.72	4.48	4.32	4.20	4.10	4.03	3.96	3.87	3.77	3.67	3.61	3.56	3.51	3.45	3.39	3.33
10	6.94	5.46	4.83	4.47	4.24	4.07	3.95	3.85	3.78	3.72	3.62	3.52	3.42	3.37	3.31	3.26	3.20	3.14	3.08
11	6.72	5.26	4.63	4.28	4.04	3.88	3.76	3.66	3.59	3.53	3.43	3.33	3.23	3.17	3.12	3.06	3.00	2.94	2.88
12	6.55	5.10	4.47	4.12	3.89	3.73	3.61	3.51	3.44	3.37	3.28	3.18	3.07	3.02	2.96	2.91	2.85	2.79	2.72
13	6.41	4.97	4.35	4.00	3.77	3.60	3.48	3.39	3.31	3.25	3.15	3.05	2.95	2.89	2.84	2.78	2.72	2.66	2.60
14	6.30	4.86	4.24	3.89	3.66	3.50	3.38	3.29	3.21	3.15	3.05	2.95	2.84	2.79	2.73	2.67	2.61	2.55	2.49
15	6.20	4.77	4.15	3.80	3.58	3.41	3.29	3.20	3.12	3.06	2.96	2.86	2.76	2.70	2.64	2.59	2.52	2.46	2.40
16	6.12	4.69	4.08	3.73	3.50	3.34	3.22	3.12	3.05	2.99	2.89	2.79	2.68	2.63	2.57	2.51	2.45	2.38	2.32
17	6.04	4.62	4.01	3.66	3.44	3.28	3.16	3.06	2.98	2.92	2.82	2.72	2.62	2.56	2.50	2.44	2.38	2.32	2.25
18	5.98	4.56	3.95	3.61	3.38	3.22	3.10	3.01	2.93	2.87	2.77	2.67	2.56	2.50	2.44	2.38	2.32	2.26	2.19
19	5.92	4.51	3.90	3.56	3.33	3.17	3.05	2.96	2.88	2.82	2.72	2.62	2.51	2.45	2.39	2.33	2.27	2.20	2.13
20	5.87	4.46	3.86	3.51	3.29	3.13	3.01	2.91	2.84	2.77	2.68	2.57	2.46	2.41	2.35	2.29	2.22	2.16	2.09
21	5.83	4.42	3.82	3.48	3.25	3.09	2.97	2.87	2.80	2.73	2.64	2.53	2.42	2.37	2.31	2.25	2.18	2.11	2.04
22	5.79	4.38	3.78	3.44	3.22	3.05	2.93	2.84	2.76	2.70	2.60	2.50	2.39	2.33	2.27	2.21	2.14	2.08	2.00
23	5.75	4.35	3.75	3.41	3.18	3.02	2.90	2.81	2.73	2.67	2.57	2.47	2.36	2.30	2.24	2.18	2.11	2.04	1.97
24	5.72	4.32	3.72	3.38	3.15	2.99	2.87	2.78	2.70	2.64	2.54	2.44	2.33	2.27	2.21	2.15	2.08	2.01	1.94
25	5.69	4.29	3.69	3.35	3.13	2.97	2.85	2.75	2.68	2.61	2.51	2.41	2.30	2.24	2.18	2.12	2.05	1.98	1.91
26	5.66	4.27	3.67	3.33	3.10	2.94	2.82	2.73	2.65	2.59	2.49	2.39	2.28	2.22	2.16	2.09	2.03	1.95	1.88
27	5.63	4.24	3.65	3.31	3.08	2.92	2.80	2.71	2.63	2.57	2.47	2.36	2.25	2.19	2.13	2.07	2.00	1.93	1.85
28	5.61	4.22	3.63	3.29	3.06	2.90	2.78	2.69	2.61	2.55	2.45	2.34	2.23	2.17	2.11	2.05	1.98	1.91	1.83
29	5.59	4.20	3.61	3.27	3.04	2.88	2.76	2.67	2.59	2.53	2.43	2.32	2.21	2.15	2.09	2.03	1.96	1.89	1.81
30	5.57	4.18	3.59	3.25	3.03	2.87	2.75	2.65	2.57	2.51	2.41	2.31	2.20	2.14	2.07	2.01	1.94	1.87	1.79
40	5.42	4.05	3.46	3.13	2.90	2.74	2.62	2.53	2.45	2.39	2.29	2.18	2.07	2.01	1.94	1.88	1.80	1.72	1.64
60	5.29	3.93	3.34	3.01	2.79	2.63	2.51	2.41	2.33	2.27	2.17	2.06	1.94	1.88	1.82	1.74	1.67	1.58	1.48
120	5.15	3.80	3.23	2.89	2.67	2.52	2.39	2.30	2.22	2.16	2.05	1.94	1.82	1.76	1.69	1.61	1.53	1.43	1.31
∞	5.02	3.69	3.12	2.79	2.57	2.41	2.29	2.19	2.11	2.05	1.94	1.83	1.71	1.64	1.57	1.48	1.39	1.27	1.00

continued

TABLE E.5

Critical Values of F (*continued*)

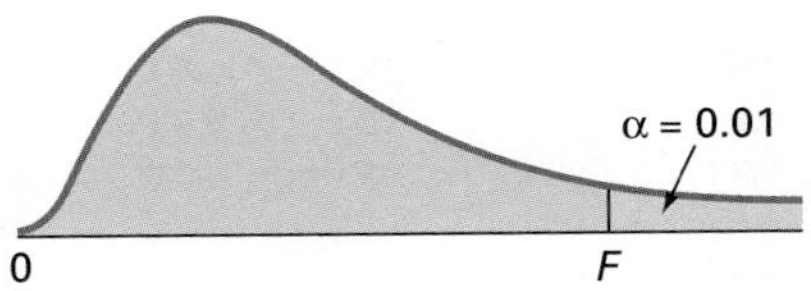

Denominator, df_2	Cumulative Probabilities = 0.99 / Upper-Tail Areas = 0.01 / Numerator, df_1: 1	2	3	4	5	6	7	8	9	10	12	15	20	24	30	40	60	120	∞
1	4,052.00	4,999.50	5,403.00	5,625.00	5,764.00	5,859.00	5,928.00	5,982.00	6,022.00	6,056.00	6,106.00	6,157.00	6,209.00	6,235.00	6,261.00	6,287.00	6,313.00	6,339.00	6,366.00
2	98.50	99.00	99.17	99.25	99.30	99.33	99.36	99.37	99.39	99.40	99.42	99.43	44.45	99.46	99.47	99.47	99.48	99.49	99.50
3	34.12	30.82	29.46	28.71	28.24	27.91	27.67	27.49	27.35	27.23	27.05	26.87	26.69	26.60	26.50	26.41	26.32	26.22	26.13
4	21.20	18.00	16.69	15.98	15.52	15.21	14.98	14.80	14.66	14.55	14.37	14.20	14.02	13.93	13.84	13.75	13.65	13.56	13.46
5	16.26	13.27	12.06	11.39	10.97	10.67	10.46	10.29	10.16	10.05	9.89	9.72	9.55	9.47	9.38	9.29	9.20	9.11	9.02
6	13.75	10.92	9.78	9.15	8.75	8.47	8.26	8.10	7.98	7.87	7.72	7.56	7.40	7.31	7.23	7.14	7.06	6.97	6.88
7	12.25	9.55	8.45	7.85	7.46	7.19	6.99	6.84	6.72	6.62	6.47	6.31	6.16	6.07	5.99	5.91	5.82	5.74	5.65
8	11.26	8.65	7.59	7.01	6.63	6.37	6.18	6.03	5.91	5.81	5.67	5.52	5.36	5.28	5.20	5.12	5.03	4.95	4.86
9	10.56	8.02	6.99	6.42	6.06	5.80	5.61	5.47	5.35	5.26	5.11	4.96	4.81	4.73	4.65	4.57	4.48	4.40	4.31
10	10.04	7.56	6.55	5.99	5.64	5.39	5.20	5.06	4.94	4.85	4.71	4.56	4.41	4.33	4.25	4.17	4.08	4.00	3.91
11	9.65	7.21	6.22	5.67	5.32	5.07	4.89	4.74	4.63	4.54	4.40	4.25	4.10	4.02	3.94	3.86	3.78	3.69	3.60
12	9.33	6.93	5.95	5.41	5.06	4.82	4.64	4.50	4.39	4.30	4.16	4.01	3.86	3.78	3.70	3.62	3.54	3.45	3.36
13	9.07	6.70	5.74	5.21	4.86	4.62	4.44	4.30	4.19	4.10	3.96	3.82	3.66	3.59	3.51	3.43	3.34	3.25	3.17
14	8.86	6.51	5.56	5.04	4.69	4.46	4.28	4.14	4.03	3.94	3.80	3.66	3.51	3.43	3.35	3.27	3.18	3.09	3.00
15	8.68	6.36	5.42	4.89	4.56	4.32	4.14	4.00	3.89	3.80	3.67	3.52	3.37	3.29	3.21	3.13	3.05	2.96	2.87
16	8.53	6.23	5.29	4.77	4.44	4.20	4.03	3.89	3.78	3.69	3.55	3.41	3.26	3.18	3.10	3.02	2.93	2.81	2.75
17	8.40	6.11	5.18	4.67	4.34	4.10	3.93	3.79	3.68	3.59	3.46	3.31	3.16	3.08	3.00	2.92	2.83	2.75	2.65
18	8.29	6.01	5.09	4.58	4.25	4.01	3.84	3.71	3.60	3.51	3.37	3.23	3.08	3.00	2.92	2.84	2.75	2.66	2.57
19	8.18	5.93	5.01	4.50	4.17	3.94	3.77	3.63	3.52	3.43	3.30	3.15	3.00	2.92	2.84	2.76	2.67	2.58	2.49
20	8.10	5.85	4.94	4.43	4.10	3.87	3.70	3.56	3.46	3.37	3.23	3.09	2.94	2.86	2.78	2.69	2.61	2.52	2.42
21	8.02	5.78	4.87	4.37	4.04	3.81	3.64	3.51	3.40	3.31	3.17	3.03	2.88	2.80	2.72	2.64	2.55	2.46	2.36
22	7.95	5.72	4.82	4.31	3.99	3.76	3.59	3.45	3.35	3.26	3.12	2.98	2.83	2.75	2.67	2.58	2.50	2.40	2.31
23	7.88	5.66	4.76	4.26	3.94	3.71	3.54	3.41	3.30	3.21	3.07	2.93	2.78	2.70	2.62	2.54	2.45	2.35	2.26
24	7.82	5.61	4.72	4.22	3.90	3.67	3.50	3.36	3.26	3.17	3.03	2.89	2.74	2.66	2.58	2.49	2.40	2.31	2.21
25	7.77	5.57	4.68	4.18	3.85	3.63	3.46	3.32	3.22	3.13	2.99	2.85	2.70	2.62	2.54	2.45	2.36	2.27	2.17
26	7.72	5.53	4.64	4.14	3.82	3.59	3.42	3.29	3.18	3.09	2.96	2.81	2.66	2.58	2.50	2.42	2.33	2.23	2.13
27	7.68	5.49	4.60	4.11	3.78	3.56	3.39	3.26	3.15	3.06	2.93	2.78	2.63	2.55	2.47	2.38	2.29	2.20	2.10
28	7.64	5.45	4.57	4.07	3.75	3.53	3.36	3.23	3.12	3.03	2.90	2.75	2.60	2.52	2.44	2.35	2.26	2.17	2.06
29	7.60	5.42	4.54	4.04	3.73	3.50	3.33	3.20	3.09	3.00	2.87	2.73	2.57	2.49	2.41	2.33	2.23	2.14	2.03
30	7.56	5.39	4.51	4.02	3.70	3.47	3.30	3.17	3.07	2.98	2.84	2.70	2.55	2.47	2.39	2.30	2.21	2.11	2.01
40	7.31	5.18	4.31	3.83	3.51	3.29	3.12	2.99	2.89	2.80	2.66	2.52	2.37	2.29	2.20	2.11	2.02	1.92	1.80
60	7.08	4.98	4.13	3.65	3.34	3.12	2.95	2.82	2.72	2.63	2.50	2.35	2.20	2.12	2.03	1.94	1.84	1.73	1.60
120	6.85	4.79	3.95	3.48	3.17	2.96	2.79	2.66	2.56	2.47	2.34	2.19	2.03	1.95	1.86	1.76	1.66	1.53	1.38
∞	6.63	4.61	3.78	3.32	3.02	2.80	2.64	2.51	2.41	2.32	2.18	2.04	1.88	1.79	1.70	1.59	1.47	1.32	1.00

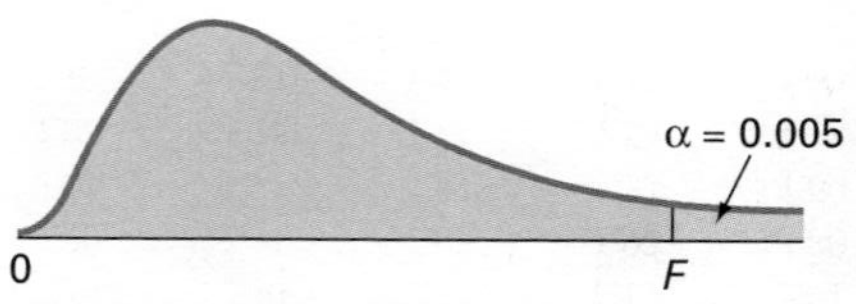

Cumulative Probabilities = 0.995

Upper − Tail Areas = 0.005

Denominator, df_2	Numerator, df_1: 1	2	3	4	5	6	7	8	9	10	12	15	20	24	30	40	60	120	∞
1	16,211.00	20,000.00	21,615.00	22,500.00	23,056.00	23,437.00	23,715.00	23,925.00	24,091.00	24,224.00	24,426.00	24,630.00	24,836.00	24,910.00	25,044.00	25,148.00	25,253.00	25,359.00	25,465.00
2	198.50	199.00	199.20	199.20	199.30	199.30	199.40	199.40	199.40	199.40	199.40	199.40	199.40	199.50	199.50	199.50	199.50	199.50	199.50
3	55.55	49.80	47.47	46.19	45.39	44.84	44.43	44.13	43.88	43.69	43.39	43.08	42.78	42.62	42.47	42.31	42.15	41.99	41.83
4	31.33	26.28	24.26	23.15	22.46	21.97	21.62	21.35	21.14	20.97	20.70	20.44	20.17	20.03	19.89	19.75	19.61	19.47	19.32
5	22.78	18.31	16.53	15.56	14.94	14.51	14.20	13.96	13.77	13.62	13.38	13.15	12.90	12.78	12.66	12.53	12.40	12.27	12.11
6	18.63	14.54	12.92	12.03	11.46	11.07	10.79	10.57	10.39	10.25	10.03	9.81	9.59	9.47	9.36	9.24	9.12	9.00	8.88
7	16.24	12.40	10.88	10.05	9.52	9.16	8.89	8.68	8.51	8.38	8.18	7.97	7.75	7.65	7.53	7.42	7.31	7.19	7.08
8	14.69	11.04	9.60	8.81	8.30	7.95	7.69	7.50	7.34	7.21	7.01	6.81	6.61	6.50	6.40	6.29	6.18	6.06	5.95
9	13.61	10.11	8.72	7.96	7.47	7.13	6.88	6.69	6.54	6.42	6.23	6.03	5.83	5.73	5.62	5.52	5.41	5.30	5.19
10	12.83	9.43	8.08	7.34	6.87	6.54	6.30	6.12	5.97	5.85	5.66	5.47	5.27	5.17	5.07	4.97	4.86	4.75	4.61
11	12.23	8.91	7.60	6.88	6.42	6.10	5.86	5.68	5.54	5.42	5.24	5.05	4.86	4.75	4.65	4.55	4.44	4.34	4.23
12	11.75	8.51	7.23	6.52	6.07	5.76	5.52	5.35	5.20	5.09	4.91	4.72	4.53	4.43	4.33	4.23	4.12	4.01	3.90
13	11.37	8.19	6.93	6.23	5.79	5.48	5.25	5.08	4.94	4.82	4.64	4.46	4.27	4.17	4.07	3.97	3.87	3.76	3.65
14	11.06	7.92	6.68	6.00	5.56	5.26	5.03	4.86	4.72	4.60	4.43	4.25	4.06	3.96	3.86	3.76	3.66	3.55	3.41
15	10.80	7.70	6.48	5.80	5.37	5.07	4.85	4.67	4.54	4.42	4.25	4.07	3.88	3.79	3.69	3.58	3.48	3.37	3.26
16	10.58	7.51	6.30	5.64	5.21	4.91	4.69	4.52	4.38	4.27	4.10	3.92	3.73	3.64	3.54	3.44	3.33	3.22	3.11
17	10.38	7.35	6.16	5.50	5.07	4.78	4.56	4.39	4.25	4.14	3.97	3.79	3.61	3.51	3.41	3.31	3.21	3.10	2.98
18	10.22	7.21	6.03	5.37	4.96	4.66	4.44	4.28	4.14	4.03	3.86	3.68	3.50	3.40	3.30	3.20	3.10	2.99	2.87
19	10.07	7.09	5.92	5.27	4.85	4.56	4.34	4.18	4.04	3.93	3.76	3.59	3.40	3.31	3.21	3.11	3.00	2.89	2.78
20	9.94	6.99	5.82	5.17	4.76	4.47	4.26	4.09	3.96	3.85	3.68	3.50	3.32	3.22	3.12	3.02	2.92	2.81	2.69
21	9.83	6.89	5.73	5.09	4.68	4.39	4.18	4.02	3.88	3.77	3.60	3.43	3.24	3.15	3.05	2.95	2.84	2.73	2.61
22	9.73	6.81	5.65	5.02	4.61	4.32	4.11	3.94	3.81	3.70	3.54	3.36	3.18	3.08	2.98	2.88	2.77	2.66	2.55
23	9.63	6.73	5.58	4.95	4.54	4.26	4.05	3.88	3.75	3.64	3.47	3.30	3.12	3.02	2.92	2.82	2.71	2.60	2.48
24	9.55	6.66	5.52	4.89	4.49	4.20	3.99	3.83	3.69	3.59	3.42	3.25	3.06	2.97	2.87	2.77	2.66	2.55	2.43
25	9.48	6.60	5.46	4.84	4.43	4.15	3.94	3.78	3.64	3.54	3.37	3.20	3.01	2.92	2.82	2.72	2.61	2.50	2.38
26	9.41	6.54	5.41	4.79	4.38	4.10	3.89	3.73	3.60	3.49	3.33	3.15	2.97	2.87	2.77	2.67	2.56	2.45	2.33
27	9.34	6.49	5.36	4.74	4.34	4.06	3.85	3.69	3.56	3.45	3.28	3.11	2.93	2.83	2.73	2.63	2.52	2.41	2.29
28	9.28	6.44	5.32	4.70	4.30	4.02	3.81	3.65	3.52	3.41	3.25	3.07	2.89	2.79	2.69	2.59	2.48	2.37	2.25
29	9.23	6.40	5.28	4.66	4.26	3.98	3.77	3.61	3.48	3.38	3.21	3.04	2.86	2.76	2.66	2.56	2.45	2.33	2.21
30	9.18	6.35	5.24	4.62	4.23	3.95	3.74	3.58	3.45	3.34	3.18	3.01	2.82	2.73	2.63	2.52	2.42	2.30	2.18
40	8.83	6.07	4.98	4.37	3.99	3.71	3.51	3.35	3.22	3.12	2.95	2.78	2.60	2.50	2.40	2.30	2.18	2.06	1.93
60	8.49	5.79	4.73	4.14	3.76	3.49	3.29	3.13	3.01	2.90	2.74	2.57	2.39	2.29	2.19	2.08	1.96	1.83	1.69
120	8.18	5.54	4.50	3.92	3.55	3.28	3.09	2.93	2.81	2.71	2.54	2.37	2.19	2.09	1.98	1.87	1.75	1.61	1.43
∞	7.88	5.30	4.28	3.72	3.35	3.09	2.90	2.74	2.62	2.52	2.36	2.19	2.00	1.90	1.79	1.67	1.53	1.36	1.00

TABLE E.6

Lower and Upper Critical Values, T_1, of the Wilcoxon Rank Sum Test

	α		n_1						
n_2	One-tail	Two-tail	4	5	6	7	8	9	10
4	0.05	0.10	11,25						
	0.025	0.05	10,26						
	0.01	0.02	—,—						
	0.005	0.01	—,—						
5	0.05	0.10	12,28	19,36					
	0.025	0.05	11,29	17,38					
	0.01	0.02	10,30	16,39					
	0.005	0.01	—,—	15,40					
6	0.05	0.10	13,31	20,40	28,50				
	0.025	0.05	12,32	18,42	26,52				
	0.01	0.02	11,33	17,43	24,54				
	0.005	0.01	10,34	16,44	23,55				
7	0.05	0.10	14,34	21,44	29,55	39,66			
	0.025	0.05	13,35	20,45	27,57	36,69			
	0.01	0.02	11,37	18,47	25,59	34,71			
	0.005	0.01	10,38	16,49	24,60	32,73			
8	0.05	0.10	15,37	23,47	31,59	41,71	51,85		
	0.025	0.05	14,38	21,49	29,61	38,74	49,87		
	0.01	0.02	12,40	19,51	27,63	35,77	45,91		
	0.005	0.01	11,41	17,53	25,65	34,78	43,93		
9	0.05	0.10	16,40	24,51	33,63	43,76	54,90	66,105	
	0.025	0.05	14,42	22,53	31,65	40,79	51,93	62,109	
	0.01	0.02	13,43	20,55	28,68	37,82	47,97	59,112	
	0.005	0.01	11,45	18,57	26,70	35,84	45,99	56,115	
10	0.05	0.10	17,43	26,54	35,67	45,81	56,96	69,111	82,128
	0.025	0.05	15,45	23,57	32,70	42,84	53,99	65,115	78,132
	0.01	0.02	13,47	21,59	29,73	39,87	49,103	61,119	74,136
	0.005	0.01	12,48	19,61	27,75	37,89	47,105	58,122	71,139

Source: Adapted from Table 1 of F. Wilcoxon and R. A. Wilcox, *Some Rapid Approximate Statistical Procedures* (Pearl River, NY: Lederle Laboratories, 1964), with permission of the American Cyanamid Company.

TABLE E.7

Critical Values of the Studentized Range, Q

Denominator, *df*	Upper 5% Points ($\alpha = 0.05$) Numerator, *df* 2	3	4	5	6	7	8	9	10	11	12	13	14	15	16	17	18	19	20
1	18.00	27.00	32.80	37.10	40.40	43.10	45.40	47.40	49.10	50.60	52.00	53.20	54.30	55.40	56.30	57.20	58.00	58.80	59.60
2	6.09	8.30	9.80	10.90	11.70	12.40	13.00	13.50	14.00	14.40	14.70	15.10	15.40	15.70	15.90	16.10	16.40	16.60	16.80
3	4.50	5.91	6.82	7.50	8.04	8.48	8.85	9.18	9.46	9.72	9.95	10.15	10.35	10.52	10.69	10.84	10.98	11.11	11.24
4	3.93	5.04	5.76	6.29	6.71	7.05	7.35	7.60	7.83	8.03	8.21	8.37	8.52	8.66	8.79	8.91	9.03	9.13	9.23
5	3.64	4.60	5.22	5.67	6.03	6.33	6.58	6.80	6.99	7.17	7.32	7.47	7.60	7.72	7.83	7.93	8.03	8.12	8.21
6	3.46	4.34	4.90	5.31	5.63	5.89	6.12	6.32	6.49	6.65	6.79	6.92	7.03	7.14	7.24	7.34	7.43	7.51	7.59
7	3.34	4.16	4.68	5.06	5.36	5.61	5.82	6.00	6.16	6.30	6.43	6.55	6.66	6.76	6.85	6.94	7.02	7.09	7.17
8	3.26	4.04	4.53	4.89	5.17	5.40	5.60	5.77	5.92	6.05	6.18	6.29	6.39	6.48	6.57	6.65	6.73	6.80	6.87
9	3.20	3.95	4.42	4.76	5.02	5.24	5.43	5.60	5.74	5.87	5.98	6.09	6.19	6.28	6.36	6.44	6.51	6.58	6.64
10	3.15	3.88	4.33	4.65	4.91	5.12	5.30	5.46	5.60	5.72	5.83	5.93	6.03	6.11	6.20	6.27	6.34	6.40	6.47
11	3.11	3.82	4.26	4.57	4.82	5.03	5.20	5.35	5.49	5.61	5.71	5.81	5.90	5.99	6.06	6.14	6.20	6.26	6.33
12	3.08	3.77	4.20	4.51	4.75	4.95	5.12	5.27	5.40	5.51	5.62	5.71	5.80	5.88	5.95	6.03	6.09	6.15	6.21
13	3.06	3.73	4.15	4.45	4.69	4.88	5.05	5.19	5.32	5.43	5.53	5.63	5.71	5.79	5.86	5.93	6.00	6.05	6.11
14	3.03	3.70	4.11	4.41	4.64	4.83	4.99	5.13	5.25	5.36	5.46	5.55	5.64	5.72	5.79	5.85	5.92	5.97	6.03
15	3.01	3.67	4.08	4.37	4.60	4.78	4.94	5.08	5.20	5.31	5.40	5.49	5.58	5.65	5.72	5.79	5.85	5.90	5.96
16	3.00	3.65	4.05	4.33	4.56	4.74	4.90	5.03	5.15	5.26	5.35	5.44	5.52	5.59	5.66	5.72	5.79	5.84	5.90
17	2.98	3.63	4.02	4.30	4.52	4.71	4.86	4.99	5.11	5.21	5.31	5.39	5.47	5.55	5.61	5.68	5.74	5.79	5.84
18	2.97	3.61	4.00	4.28	4.49	4.67	4.82	4.96	5.07	5.17	5.27	5.35	5.43	5.50	5.57	5.63	5.69	5.74	5.79
19	2.96	3.59	3.98	4.25	4.47	4.65	4.79	4.92	5.04	5.14	5.23	5.32	5.39	5.46	5.53	5.59	5.65	5.70	5.75
20	2.95	3.58	3.96	4.23	4.45	4.62	4.77	4.90	5.01	5.11	5.20	5.28	5.36	5.43	5.49	5.55	5.61	5.66	5.71
24	2.92	3.53	3.90	4.17	4.37	4.54	4.68	4.81	4.92	5.01	5.10	5.18	5.25	5.32	5.38	5.44	5.50	5.54	5.59
30	2.89	3.49	3.84	4.10	4.30	4.46	4.60	4.72	4.83	4.92	5.00	5.08	5.15	5.21	5.27	5.33	5.38	5.43	5.48
40	2.86	3.44	3.79	4.04	4.23	4.39	4.52	4.63	4.74	4.82	4.91	4.98	5.05	5.11	5.16	5.22	5.27	5.31	5.36
60	2.83	3.40	3.74	3.98	4.16	4.31	4.44	4.55	4.65	4.73	4.81	4.88	4.94	5.00	5.06	5.11	5.16	5.20	5.24
120	2.80	3.36	3.69	3.92	4.10	4.24	4.36	4.48	4.56	4.64	4.72	4.78	4.84	4.90	4.95	5.00	5.05	5.09	5.13
∞	2.77	3.31	3.63	3.86	4.03	4.17	4.29	4.39	4.47	4.55	4.62	4.68	4.74	4.80	4.85	4.89	4.93	4.97	5.01

continued

TABLE E.7

Critical Values of the Studentized Range, Q (*continued*)

	Upper 1% Points ($\alpha = 0.01$)																		
Denominator,	**Numerator, *df***																		
df	**2**	**3**	**4**	**5**	**6**	**7**	**8**	**9**	**10**	**11**	**12**	**13**	**14**	**15**	**16**	**17**	**18**	**19**	**20**
1	90.03	135.00	164.30	185.60	202.20	215.80	227.20	237.00	245.60	253.20	260.00	266.20	271.80	277.00	281.80	286.30	290.40	294.30	298.00
2	14.04	19.02	22.29	24.72	26.63	28.20	29.53	30.68	31.69	32.59	33.40	34.13	34.81	35.43	36.00	36.53	37.03	37.50	37.95
3	8.26	10.62	12.17	13.33	14.24	15.00	15.64	16.20	16.69	17.13	17.53	17.89	18.22	18.52	18.81	19.07	19.32	19.55	19.77
4	6.51	8.12	9.17	9.96	10.58	11.10	11.55	11.93	12.27	12.57	12.84	13.09	13.32	13.53	13.73	13.91	14.08	14.24	14.40
5	5.70	6.98	7.80	8.42	8.91	9.32	9.67	9.97	10.24	10.48	10.70	10.89	11.08	11.24	11.40	11.55	11.68	11.81	11.93
6	5.24	6.33	7.03	7.56	7.97	8.32	8.61	8.87	9.10	9.30	9.49	9.65	9.81	9.95	10.08	10.21	10.32	10.43	10.54
7	4.95	5.92	6.54	7.01	7.37	7.68	7.94	8.17	8.37	8.55	8.71	8.86	9.00	9.12	9.24	9.35	9.46	9.55	9.65
8	4.75	5.64	6.20	6.63	6.96	7.24	7.47	7.68	7.86	8.03	8.18	8.31	8.44	8.55	8.66	8.76	8.85	8.94	9.03
9	4.60	5.43	5.96	6.35	6.66	6.92	7.13	7.32	7.50	7.65	7.78	7.91	8.03	8.13	8.23	8.33	8.41	8.50	8.57
10	4.48	5.27	5.77	6.14	6.43	6.67	6.87	7.06	7.21	7.36	7.49	7.60	7.71	7.81	7.91	7.99	8.08	8.15	8.23
11	4.39	5.15	5.62	5.97	6.25	6.48	6.67	6.84	6.99	7.13	7.25	7.36	7.47	7.56	7.65	7.73	7.81	7.88	7.95
12	4.32	5.04	5.50	5.84	6.10	6.32	6.51	6.67	6.81	6.94	7.06	7.17	7.26	7.36	7.44	7.52	7.59	7.66	7.73
13	4.26	4.96	5.40	5.73	5.98	6.19	6.37	6.53	6.67	6.79	6.90	7.01	7.10	7.19	7.27	7.35	7.42	7.49	7.55
14	4.21	4.90	5.32	5.63	5.88	6.09	6.26	6.41	6.54	6.66	6.77	6.87	6.96	7.05	7.13	7.20	7.27	7.33	7.40
15	4.17	4.84	5.25	5.56	5.80	5.99	6.16	6.31	6.44	6.56	6.66	6.76	6.85	6.93	7.00	7.07	7.14	7.20	7.26
16	4.13	4.79	5.19	5.49	5.72	5.92	6.08	6.22	6.35	6.46	6.56	6.66	6.74	6.82	6.90	6.97	7.03	7.09	7.15
17	4.10	4.74	5.14	5.43	5.66	5.85	6.01	6.15	6.27	6.38	6.48	6.57	6.66	6.73	6.81	6.87	6.94	7.00	7.05
18	4.07	4.70	5.09	5.38	5.60	5.79	5.94	6.08	6.20	6.31	6.41	6.50	6.58	6.66	6.73	6.79	6.85	6.91	6.97
19	4.05	4.67	5.05	5.33	5.55	5.74	5.89	6.02	6.14	6.25	6.34	6.43	6.51	6.59	6.65	6.72	6.78	6.84	6.89
20	4.02	4.64	5.02	5.29	5.51	5.69	5.84	5.97	6.09	6.19	6.29	6.37	6.45	6.52	6.59	6.65	6.71	6.77	6.82
24	3.96	4.55	4.91	5.17	5.37	5.54	5.69	5.81	5.92	6.02	6.11	6.19	6.26	6.33	6.39	6.45	6.51	6.56	6.61
30	3.89	4.46	4.80	5.05	5.24	5.40	5.54	5.65	5.76	5.85	5.93	6.01	6.08	6.14	6.20	6.26	6.31	6.36	6.41
40	3.83	4.37	4.70	4.93	5.11	5.27	5.39	5.50	5.60	5.69	5.76	5.84	5.90	5.96	6.02	6.07	6.12	6.17	6.21
60	3.76	4.28	4.60	4.82	4.99	5.13	5.25	5.36	5.45	5.53	5.60	5.67	5.73	5.79	5.84	5.89	5.93	5.97	6.02
120	3.70	4.20	4.50	4.71	4.87	5.01	5.12	5.21	5.30	5.38	5.44	5.51	5.56	5.61	5.66	5.71	5.75	5.79	5.83
∞	3.64	4.12	4.40	4.60	4.76	4.88	4.99	5.08	5.16	5.23	5.29	5.35	5.40	5.45	5.49	5.54	5.57	5.61	5.65

Source: Extracted from H. L. Harter and D. S. Clemm, "The Probability Integrals of the Range and of the Studentized Range—Probability Integral, Percentage Points, and Moments of the Range," *Wright Air Development Technical Report 58–484*, Vol. 1, 1959.

TABLE E.8

Critical Values, d_L and d_U, of the Durbin-Watson Statistic, D (Critical Values Are One-Sided)[a]

	$\alpha = 0.05$										$\alpha = 0.01$									
	$k = 1$		$k = 2$		$k = 3$		$k = 4$		$k = 5$		$k = 1$		$k = 2$		$k = 3$		$k = 4$		$k = 5$	
n	d_L	d_U	d_L	d_U	d_L	d_U	d_L	d_U	d_L	d_U	d_L	d_U	d_L	d_U	d_L	d_U	d_L	d_U	d_L	d_U
15	1.08	1.36	.95	1.54	.82	1.75	.69	1.97	.56	2.21	.81	1.07	.70	1.25	.59	1.46	.49	1.70	.39	1.96
16	1.10	1.37	.98	1.54	.86	1.73	.74	1.93	.62	2.15	.84	1.09	.74	1.25	.63	1.44	.53	1.66	.44	1.90
17	1.13	1.38	1.02	1.54	.90	1.71	.78	1.90	.67	2.10	.87	1.10	.77	1.25	.67	1.43	.57	1.63	.48	1.85
18	1.16	1.39	1.05	1.53	.93	1.69	.82	1.87	.71	2.06	.90	1.12	.80	1.26	.71	1.42	.61	1.60	.52	1.80
19	1.18	1.40	1.08	1.53	.97	1.68	.86	1.85	.75	2.02	.93	1.13	.83	1.26	.74	1.41	.65	1.58	.56	1.77
20	1.20	1.41	1.10	1.54	1.00	1.68	.90	1.83	.79	1.99	.95	1.15	.86	1.27	.77	1.41	.68	1.57	.60	1.74
21	1.22	1.42	1.13	1.54	1.03	1.67	.93	1.81	.83	1.96	.97	1.16	.89	1.27	.80	1.41	.72	1.55	.63	1.71
22	1.24	1.43	1.15	1.54	1.05	1.66	.96	1.80	.86	1.94	1.00	1.17	.91	1.28	.83	1.40	.75	1.54	.66	1.69
23	1.26	1.44	1.17	1.54	1.08	1.66	.99	1.79	.90	1.92	1.02	1.19	.94	1.29	.86	1.40	.77	1.53	.70	1.67
24	1.27	1.45	1.19	1.55	1.10	1.66	1.01	1.78	.93	1.90	1.04	1.20	.96	1.30	.88	1.41	.80	1.53	.72	1.66
25	1.29	1.45	1.21	1.55	1.12	1.66	1.04	1.77	.95	1.89	1.05	1.21	.98	1.30	.90	1.41	.83	1.52	.75	1.65
26	1.30	1.46	1.22	1.55	1.14	1.65	1.06	1.76	.98	1.88	1.07	1.22	1.00	1.31	.93	1.41	.85	1.52	.78	1.64
27	1.32	1.47	1.24	1.56	1.16	1.65	1.08	1.76	1.01	1.86	1.09	1.23	1.02	1.32	.95	1.41	.88	1.51	.81	1.63
28	1.33	1.48	1.26	1.56	1.18	1.65	1.10	1.75	1.03	1.85	1.10	1.24	1.04	1.32	.97	1.41	.90	1.51	.83	1.62
29	1.34	1.48	1.27	1.56	1.20	1.65	1.12	1.74	1.05	1.84	1.12	1.25	1.05	1.33	.99	1.42	.92	1.51	.85	1.61
30	1.35	1.49	1.28	1.57	1.21	1.65	1.14	1.74	1.07	1.83	1.13	1.26	1.07	1.34	1.01	1.42	.94	1.51	.88	1.61
31	1.36	1.50	1.30	1.57	1.23	1.65	1.16	1.74	1.09	1.83	1.15	1.27	1.08	1.34	1.02	1.42	.96	1.51	.90	1.60
32	1.37	1.50	1.31	1.57	1.24	1.65	1.18	1.73	1.11	1.82	1.16	1.28	1.10	1.35	1.04	1.43	.98	1.51	.92	1.60
33	1.38	1.51	1.32	1.58	1.26	1.65	1.19	1.73	1.13	1.81	1.17	1.29	1.11	1.36	1.05	1.43	1.00	1.51	.94	1.59
34	1.39	1.51	1.33	1.58	1.27	1.65	1.21	1.73	1.15	1.81	1.18	1.30	1.13	1.36	1.07	1.43	1.01	1.51	.95	1.59
35	1.40	1.52	1.34	1.58	1.28	1.65	1.22	1.73	1.16	1.80	1.19	1.31	1.14	1.37	1.08	1.44	1.03	1.51	.97	1.59
36	1.41	1.52	1.35	1.59	1.29	1.65	1.24	1.73	1.18	1.80	1.21	1.32	1.15	1.38	1.10	1.44	1.04	1.51	.99	1.59
37	1.42	1.53	1.36	1.59	1.31	1.66	1.25	1.72	1.19	1.80	1.22	1.32	1.16	1.38	1.11	1.45	1.06	1.51	1.00	1.59
38	1.43	1.54	1.37	1.59	1.32	1.66	1.26	1.72	1.21	1.79	1.23	1.33	1.18	1.39	1.12	1.45	1.07	1.52	1.02	1.58
39	1.43	1.54	1.38	1.60	1.33	1.66	1.27	1.72	1.22	1.79	1.24	1.34	1.19	1.39	1.14	1.45	1.09	1.52	1.03	1.58
40	1.44	1.54	1.39	1.60	1.34	1.66	1.29	1.72	1.23	1.79	1.25	1.34	1.20	1.40	1.15	1.46	1.10	1.52	1.05	1.58
45	1.48	1.57	1.43	1.62	1.38	1.67	1.34	1.72	1.29	1.78	1.29	1.38	1.24	1.42	1.20	1.48	1.16	1.53	1.11	1.58
50	1.50	1.59	1.46	1.63	1.42	1.67	1.38	1.72	1.34	1.77	1.32	1.40	1.28	1.45	1.24	1.49	1.20	1.54	1.16	1.59
55	1.53	1.60	1.49	1.64	1.45	1.68	1.41	1.72	1.38	1.77	1.36	1.43	1.32	1.47	1.28	1.51	1.25	1.55	1.21	1.59
60	1.55	1.62	1.51	1.65	1.48	1.69	1.44	1.73	1.41	1.77	1.38	1.45	1.35	1.48	1.32	1.52	1.28	1.56	1.25	1.60
65	1.57	1.63	1.54	1.66	1.50	1.70	1.47	1.73	1.44	1.77	1.41	1.47	1.38	1.50	1.35	1.53	1.31	1.57	1.28	1.61
70	1.58	1.64	1.55	1.67	1.52	1.70	1.49	1.74	1.46	1.77	1.43	1.49	1.40	1.52	1.37	1.55	1.34	1.58	1.31	1.61
75	1.60	1.65	1.57	1.68	1.54	1.71	1.51	1.74	1.49	1.77	1.45	1.50	1.42	1.53	1.39	1.56	1.37	1.59	1.34	1.62
80	1.61	1.66	1.59	1.69	1.56	1.72	1.53	1.74	1.51	1.77	1.47	1.52	1.44	1.54	1.42	1.57	1.39	1.60	1.36	1.62
85	1.62	1.67	1.60	1.70	1.57	1.72	1.55	1.75	1.52	1.77	1.48	1.53	1.46	1.55	1.43	1.58	1.41	1.60	1.39	1.63
90	1.63	1.68	1.61	1.70	1.59	1.73	1.57	1.75	1.54	1.78	1.50	1.54	1.47	1.56	1.45	1.59	1.43	1.61	1.41	1.64
95	1.64	1.69	1.62	1.71	1.60	1.73	1.58	1.75	1.56	1.78	1.51	1.55	1.49	1.57	1.47	1.60	1.45	1.62	1.42	1.64
100	1.65	1.69	1.63	1.72	1.61	1.74	1.59	1.76	1.57	1.78	1.52	1.56	1.50	1.58	1.48	1.60	1.46	1.63	1.44	1.65

[a]n = number of observations; k = number of independent variables.

Source: Computed from TSP 4.5 based on R. W. Farebrother, "A Remark on Algorithms AS106, AS153, and AS155: The Distribution of a Linear Combination of Chi-Square Random Variables," *Journal of the Royal Statistical Society*, Series C (Applied Statistics), 1984, 29, p. 323–333.

TABLE E.9

Control Chart Factors

Number of Observations in Sample/Subgroup (n)	d_2	d_3	D_3	D_4	A_2
2	1.128	0.853	0	3.267	1.880
3	1.693	0.888	0	2.575	1.023
4	2.059	0.880	0	2.282	0.729
5	2.326	0.864	0	2.114	0.577
6	2.534	0.848	0	2.004	0.483
7	2.704	0.833	0.076	1.924	0.419
8	2.847	0.820	0.136	1.864	0.373
9	2.970	0.808	0.184	1.816	0.337
10	3.078	0.797	0.223	1.777	0.308
11	3.173	0.787	0.256	1.744	0.285
12	3.258	0.778	0.283	1.717	0.266
13	3.336	0.770	0.307	1.693	0.249
14	3.407	0.763	0.328	1.672	0.235
15	3.472	0.756	0.347	1.653	0.223
16	3.532	0.750	0.363	1.637	0.212
17	3.588	0.744	0.378	1.622	0.203
18	3.640	0.739	0.391	1.609	0.194
19	3.689	0.733	0.404	1.596	0.187
20	3.735	0.729	0.415	1.585	0.180
21	3.778	0.724	0.425	1.575	0.173
22	3.819	0.720	0.435	1.565	0.167
23	3.858	0.716	0.443	1.557	0.162
24	3.895	0.712	0.452	1.548	0.157
25	3.931	0.708	0.459	1.541	0.153

TABLE E.10

The Standardized Normal Distribution

Entry represents area under the standardized normal distribution from the mean to Z

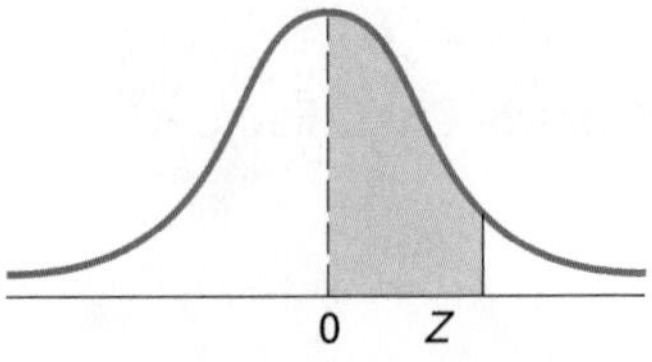

Z	.00	.01	.02	.03	.04	.05	.06	.07	.08	.09
0.0	.0000	.0040	.0080	.0120	.0160	.0199	.0239	.0279	.0319	.0359
0.1	.0398	.0438	.0478	.0517	.0557	.0596	.0636	.0675	.0714	.0753
0.2	.0793	.0832	.0871	.0910	.0948	.0987	.1026	.1064	.1103	.1141
0.3	.1179	.1217	.1255	.1293	.1331	.1368	.1406	.1443	.1480	.1517
0.4	.1554	.1591	.1628	.1664	.1700	.1736	.1772	.1808	.1844	.1879
0.5	.1915	.1950	.1985	.2019	.2054	.2088	.2123	.2157	.2190	.2224
0.6	.2257	.2291	.2324	.2357	.2389	.2422	.2454	.2486	.2518	.2549
0.7	.2580	.2612	.2642	.2673	.2704	.2734	.2764	.2794	.2823	.2852
0.8	.2881	.2910	.2939	.2967	.2995	.3023	.3051	.3078	.3106	.3133
0.9	.3159	.3186	.3212	.3238	.3264	.3289	.3315	.3340	.3365	.3389
1.0	.3413	.3438	.3461	.3485	.3508	.3531	.3554	.3577	.3599	.3621
1.1	.3643	.3665	.3686	.3708	.3729	.3749	.3770	.3790	.3810	.3830
1.2	.3849	.3869	.3888	.3907	.3925	.3944	.3962	.3980	.3997	.4015
1.3	.4032	.4049	.4066	.4082	.4099	.4115	.4131	.4147	.4162	.4177
1.4	.4192	.4207	.4222	.4236	.4251	.4265	.4279	.4292	.4306	.4319
1.5	.4332	.4345	.4357	.4370	.4382	.4394	.4406	.4418	.4429	.4441
1.6	.4452	.4463	.4474	.4484	.4495	.4505	.4515	.4525	.4535	.4545
1.7	.4554	.4564	.4573	.4582	.4591	.4599	.4608	.4616	.4625	.4633
1.8	.4641	.4649	.4656	.4664	.4671	.4678	.4686	.4693	.4699	.4706
1.9	.4713	.4719	.4726	.4732	.4738	.4744	.4750	.4756	.4761	.4767
2.0	.4772	.4778	.4783	.4788	.4793	.4798	.4803	.4808	.4812	.4817
2.1	.4821	.4826	.4830	.4834	.4838	.4842	.4846	.4850	.4854	.4857
2.2	.4861	.4864	.4868	.4871	.4875	.4878	.4881	.4884	.4887	.4890
2.3	.4893	.4896	.4898	.4901	.4904	.4906	.4909	.4911	.4913	.4916
2.4	.4918	.4920	.4922	.4925	.4927	.4929	.4931	.4932	.4934	.4936
2.5	.4938	.4940	.4941	.4943	.4945	.4946	.4948	.4949	.4951	.4952
2.6	.4953	.4955	.4956	.4957	.4959	.4960	.4961	.4962	.4963	.4964
2.7	.4965	.4966	.4967	.4968	.4969	.4970	.4971	.4972	.4973	.4974
2.8	.4974	.4975	.4976	.4977	.4977	.4978	.4979	.4979	.4980	.4981
2.9	.4981	.4982	.4982	.4983	.4984	.4984	.4985	.4985	.4986	.4986
3.0	.49865	.49869	.49874	.49878	.49882	.49886	.49889	.49893	.49897	.49900
3.1	.49903	.49906	.49910	.49913	.49916	.49918	.49921	.49924	.49926	.49929
3.2	.49931	.49934	.49936	.49938	.49940	.49942	.49944	.49946	.49948	.49950
3.3	.49952	.49953	.49955	.49957	.49958	.49960	.49961	.49962	.49964	.49965
3.4	.49966	.49968	.49969	.49970	.49971	.49972	.49973	.49974	.49975	.49976
3.5	.49977	.49978	.49978	.49979	.49980	.49981	.49981	.49982	.49983	.49983
3.6	.49984	.49985	.49985	.49986	.49986	.49987	.49987	.49988	.49988	.49989
3.7	.49989	.49990	.49990	.49990	.49991	.49991	.49992	.49992	.49992	.49992
3.8	.49993	.49993	.49993	.49994	.49994	.49994	.49994	.49995	.49995	.49995
3.9	.49995	.49995	.49996	.49996	.49996	.49996	.49996	.49996	.49997	.49997

APPENDIX F Useful Excel Knowledge

This appendix reviews knowledge that you will find useful if you plan to be more than a casual user of Microsoft Excel. While none of the content in this appendix needs to be mastered in order to use the instructions in the Excel Guides in this book, reviewing this appendix as necessary will help you make better sense of your Excel results. If you are using a version of Excel that is older than Excel 2010, you will need to be familiar with Section F.3 so that you can modify the names of functions used in worksheet templates and models as necessary.

Section F.4 presents an enhanced explanation of some the statistical worksheet functions that recur in two or more chapters. This section also discusses functions that either serve programming purposes or are used in novel ways to compute intermediate results. If you have a particular interest in developing application solutions, you will want to be familiar with this set of functions.

This appendix assumes that you are familiar with Excel and have mastered the concepts presented in Appendix B. If you are a first-time user of Excel, do not make the mistake of trying to comprehend the material in this appendix before you gain experience using Excel and familiarity with Appendix B.

F.1 Useful Keyboard Shortcuts

In Microsoft Excel (and other Microsoft Office programs), certain individual keys or combinations of keys held down as you press another key are shortcuts that allow you to execute common operations without having to select choices from menus or click in the Ribbon. In this book, keystroke combinations are shown using plus signs; for example, **Ctrl+C** means "while holding down the **Ctrl** key, press the **C** key."

Editing Shortcuts

Pressing **Backspace** erases typed characters to the left of the current position, one character at a time. Pressing **Delete** erases characters to the right of the cursor, one character at a time.

Ctrl+C copies a worksheet entry, and **Ctrl+V** pastes that entry into the place that the editing cursor or worksheet cell highlight indicates. Pressing **Ctrl+X** cuts the currently selected entry or object so that you can paste it somewhere else. **Ctrl+C** and **Ctrl+V** (or **Ctrl+X** and **Ctrl+V**) can also be used to copy (or cut) and paste certain workbook objects such as charts. (Using copy and paste to copy formulas from one worksheet cell to another is subject to the adjustment discussed in Section B.2.)

Pressing **Ctrl+Z** undoes the last operation, and **Ctrl+Y** redoes the last operation. Pressing **Enter** or **Tab** finalizes an entry typed into a worksheet cell. Pressing either key is implied by the use of the verb *enter* in the Excel Guides.

Formatting Shortcuts

Pressing **Ctrl+B** toggles on (or off) boldface text style for the currently selected object. Pressing **Ctrl+I** toggles on (or off) italic text style for the currently selected object. Pressing **Ctrl+Shift+%** formats numeric values as a percentage with no decimal places.

Utility Shortcuts

Pressing **Ctrl+F** finds a **Find what** value, and pressing **Ctrl+H** replaces a **Find what** value with the **Replace with** value. Pressing **Ctrl+A** selects the entire current worksheet (useful as part of a worksheet copy or format operation). Pressing **Esc** cancels an action or a dialog box. Pressing **F1** displays the Microsoft Excel help system.

F.2 Verifying Formulas and Worksheets

If you use formulas in your worksheets, you should review and verify formulas before you use their results. To view the formulas in a worksheet, press **Ctrl+`** (grave accent key). To restore the original view, the results of the formulas, press **Ctrl+`** a second time.

As you create and use more complicated worksheets, you might want to visually examine the relationships among a formula and the cells it uses (called the *precedents*) and the cells that use the results of the formula (the *dependents*). Select **Formulas ➔ Trace Precedents** (or **Trace Dependents**) to examine relationships. When you are finished, clear all trace arrows by selecting **Formulas ➔ Remove Arrows**.

After verifying formulas, you should test, using simple numbers, any worksheet that you have modified or constructed from scratch.

F.3 New Function Names

Beginning in Excel 2010, Microsoft renamed many statistical functions and reprogrammed a number of functions to improve their accuracy. Generally, with exceptions noted, this book uses the new function names in worksheet cell formulas. The new functions names used in this book are listed in Table F.1, along with the place of first mention in this book and corresponding older function name.

TABLE F.1

New Function Names Used in This Book and Older ("Compatible") Names

New Name	First Mention	Older Name
BINOM.DIST	EG5.3	BINOMDIST
CHISQ.DIST.RT	EG12.1	CHIDIST
CHISQ.INV.RT	EG12.1	CHIINV
CONFIDENCE.NORM	EG8.1	CONFIDENCE
COVARIANCE.S	EG3.5	none*
EXPON.DIST	EG6.5	EXPONDIST
F.DIST.RT	EG10.4	FDIST
F.INV.RT	EG10.4	FINV
HYPGEOM.DIST	EG5.5	HYPGEOMDIST
NORM.DIST	EG6.2	NORMDIST
NORM.INV	EG6.2	NORMINV
NORM.S.DIST	EG9.2	NORMSDIST
NORM.S.INV	EG6.2	NORMSINV
POISSON.DIST	EG5.4	POISSON
STDEV.S	EG3.2	STDEV
STDEV.P	EG3.2	STDEVP
T.DIST.RT	EG9.3	TDIST
T.DIST.2T	EG9.2	TDIST
T.INV.2T	EG8.2	TINV
VAR.S	EG3.2	VAR
VAR.P	EG3.2	VARP

** COVARIANCE.S is a function that was new to Excel 2010. The COVARIANCE.P function (not used in this book) replaces the older COVAR function.*

Because the new function names are not compatible with Excel versions older than Excel 2010, alternative worksheets have been included in the Excel Guide workbooks, as explained in "Alternative Worksheets," later in this section. If compatibility with older Excel versions is important to you, you should use the older function names (and the alternative worksheets).

Quartile Function

In this book, you will see the older QUARTILE function and not the newer QUARTILE. EXC function. In Microsoft's *Function Improvements in Microsoft Office Excel 2010* (available at **bit.ly/RkoFIf**), QUARTILE.EXC is explained as being "consistent with industry best practices, assuming percentile is a value between 0 and 1, exclusive." Because there are several established but different ways of computing quartiles, there is no way of knowing exactly how the new function works.

Because of this lack of specifics, this book uses the older QUARTILE function, whose programming and limitations are well known, and not the new QUARTILE.EXC function or QUARTILE.INC function, which is the QUARTILES function renamed for consistency with QUARTILES.EXC. As noted in Section EG3.3, none of the three functions compute quartiles using the rules presented in Section 3.3, which are properly computed in the COMPUTE worksheet of the Quartiles workbook that uses the older QUARTILE function. If you are using Excel 2010 or a newer version of Excel, the COMPARE worksheet illustrates the results using the three forms of QUARTILES for the data found in column A of the DATA worksheet.

Alternative Worksheets

If a worksheet in an Excel Guide workbook uses one or more of the new function names, the workbook contains an alternative worksheet for use with Excel versions that are older than Excel 2010. Three exceptions to the rule are the **Simple Linear Regression 2007**, **Multiple Regression 2007**, and **Exponential Trend 2007** ***workbooks.*** As explained in Chapters 13, 14, and 16, respectively, these workbooks serve as alternatives to the Simple Linear Regression, Multiple Regression, and Exponential Trend workbooks. Alternative worksheets and workbooks work best in Excel 2007.

The following Excel Guide workbooks contain an alternative worksheet named COMPUTE_OLDER. Numbers that appear in pare ntheses are the chapters in which these workbooks are first mentioned.

Parameters (3)
Covariance (3)
Hypergeometric (5)
Normal (6)
Exponential (6)
CIE sigma known (8)
CIE sigma unknown (8)
CIE Proportion (8)
Z Mean workbook (9)
T mean workbook (9)
Z Proportion (9)
Pooled-Variance T (10)
Separate-Variance T (10)
Paired T (10)
One-Way ANOVA (11)
Chi-Square (12)

The following Excel Guide workbooks have alternative worksheets with various names:

Descriptive (3)	CompleteStatistics_OLDER
Binomial (5)	CUMULATIVE_OLDER
Poisson (5)	CUMULATIVE_OLDER
NPP (6)	PLOT_OLDER and NORMAL_PLOT_OLDER
One-Way ANOVA (11)	TK4_OLDER
Chi-Square Worksheets (12)	Various worksheets, including ChiSquare2x3_OLDER and Marascuilo2x3_OLDER
Wilcoxon (12)	COMPUTE_ALL_OLDER
Kruskal-Wallis Worksheets (12)	KruskalWallis3_OLDER and KruskalWallis4_OLDER

As explained in Chapters 13, 14, and 16, respectively, the **Simple Linear Regression 2007**, **Multiple Regression 2007**, and **Exponential Trend 2007** ***workbooks*** contain a number of alternative worksheets for Excel versions that are older than Excel 2010. (These alternative workbooks work best in Excel 2007.)

F.4 Understanding the Non-statistical Functions

Although this book focuses on Excel statistical functions, selected Excel Guide worksheets (and worksheets created by PHStat) use a number of non-statistical functions that either compute an intermediate result or perform a mathematical or programming operation. These functions are explained in the following alphabetical list:

CEILING(*cell, round-to value*) takes the numeric value in ***cell*** and rounds it to the next multiple of the ***round-to value***. For example, if the ***round-to value*** is **0.5**, as it is in several column B formulas in the COMPUTE worksheet of the Quartiles workbook, then the numeric value will be rounded either to an integer or a number that contains a half such as 1.5.

COUNT(*cell range*) counts the number of cells in a cell range that contain a numeric value. This function is often used to compute the sample size, *n*, for example, in cell B9 of the COMPUTE worksheet of the Correlation workbook. When seen in the worksheets presented in this book, the ***cell range*** will typically be the cell range of variable column, such as **DATA!A:A**. This will result in a proper count of the sample size of that variable if you follow the Section EG.5 rules for entering data on page 12.

COUNTIF(*cell range for all values, value to be matched*) counts the number of occurrences of a value in a cell range. For example, the COMPUTE worksheet of the Wilcoxon workbook uses **COUNTIF(SortedRanks!A2:A21, "Beverage")** in cell B7 to compute the sample size of the Population 1 Sample by counting the number of occurrences of the sample name Beverage in column A of the SortedRanks worksheet. In the KruskalWallis4 worksheet of the Kruskal-Wallis Worksheets workbook, the function counts the number of occurrences in column A of the SortedRanks worksheet of a supplier name that appears in a column D row.

DEVSQ(*variable cell range*) computes the sum of the squares of the differences between a variable value and the mean of that variable. For example, in Equation (3.6) on page 113 that defines the sample variance, **DEVSQ(*X variable cell range*)** computes the value of the term in the numerator of the fraction.

FLOOR(*cell*, 1) takes the numeric value in ***cell*** and rounds down the value to the nearest integer.

IF(*logical comparison, what to display if comparison holds, what to display if comparison is false*) uses the ***logical comparison*** to make a choice between two alternatives. In the worksheets shown in this book, the IF function typically chooses from two text values, such as **Reject the null hypothesis** and **Do not reject the null hypothesis**, to display, but in Chapter 16, the function is used to create dummy variables for quarterly or monthly data.

MMULT(*cell range* 1, *cell range* 2) treats both ***cell range* 1** and ***cell range* 2** as matrices and computes the matrix product of the two matrices. When each of the two cell ranges is either a single row or a single column, MMULT can be used as part of a regular formula. If the cell ranges each represent rows and columns, then MMULT must be used as part of an array formula (see Appendix Section B.3). One exception to these rules occurs in cell B21 of the CIEandPI worksheet of the Multiple Regression worksheet, in which **MMULT(TRANSPOSE(B5:B7), COMPUTE!B17:B19)** has been entered as part of an array formula because of how Excel treats the results of the TRANSPOSE function.

ROUND(*cell*, 0) takes the numeric value in ***cell*** and rounds to the nearest whole number.

SMALL(*cell range, k*) selects the ***kth*** smallest value in ***cell range***.

SQRT(*value*) computes the square root of ***value***, where ***value*** is either a cell reference or an arithmetic expression.

SUMIF(*cell range for all values, value to be matched, cell range in which to select cells for summing*) sums only those rows in *cell range in which to select cells for summing* in which the value in *cell range for all values* matches the *value to be matched*. SUMIF provides a convenient way to compute the sum of ranks for a sample in a worksheet that contains stacked data. For example, the COMPUTE worksheet of the Wilcoxon workbook uses **SUMIF(SortedRanks!A2:A21,**

"Beverage", SortedRanks!C2:C21) in cell B8 to compute the sum of ranks for the Beverage (End-cap) sample by summing only the rows in the SortedRanks worksheet column C whose column A value is Beverage. In the KruskalWallis4 worksheet of the Kruskal-Wallis Worksheets workbook, SUMIF sums only the rows in the SortedRanks worksheet column C whose column A value matches the value that appears in a column D row.

SUMPRODUCT(*cell range* 1, *cell range* 2) multiplies each cell in ***cell range* 1** by the corresponding cell in ***cell range* 2** and then sums those products. If ***cell range* 1** contains a column of differences between an *X* value and the mean of the variable *X*, and ***cell range* 2** contains a column of differences between a *Y* value and the mean of the variable *Y*, then this function would compute the value of the numerator in Equation (3.16) that defines the sample covariance. In Section EG16.6, **SUMPRODUCT(ABS(*cell range of residual values*))** uses the function in a novel way with only one cell range to efficiently compute the sum of the absolute values of the values found in the ***cell range of residual values***.

TRANSPOSE(*horizontal or vertical cell range*) takes the *cell range*, which must be either a horizontal cell range (cells all in the same row) or a vertical cell range (cells all in the same column) and transposes, or rearranges, the cell in the other orientation such that a horizontal cell range becomes a vertical cell range and vice versa. When used inside another function, Excel considers the results of this function to be an *array*, not a cell range.

VLOOKUP(*lookup value cell*, *table of lookup values*, *table column to use*) function displays a value that has been looked up in a ***table of lookup values***, a rectangular cell range. In the ADVANCED worksheet of the Recoded workbook, the function uses the values in the second column of ***table of lookup values*** (an example of which is shown below) to look up the Honors values based on the GPA of a student (the ***lookup value cell***). Numbers in the first column of ***table of lookup values*** are implied ranges such that No Honors is the value displayed if the GPA is at least 0, but less than 3; Honor Roll is the value displayed if the GPA is at least 3, but less than 3.3; and so on:

0	No Honors
3	Honor Roll
3.3	Dean's List
3.7	President's List

APPENDIX G PHStat and Microsoft Excel FAQs

G.1 PHStat FAQs

What is PHStat?

PHStat is the Pearson Education add-in for Microsoft Excel that makes operating Microsoft Excel as distraction free as possible. As a student studying statistics, you can focus mainly on learning statistics and not worry about having to fully master Excel first. You can consider PHStat a personal assistant that takes your requests and constructs worksheet-based solutions for you.

PHStat executes for you the low-level menu selection and worksheet entry tasks that are associated with implementing statistical analysis in Microsoft Excel. PHStat creates worksheets and chart sheets that are identical to the ones featured in this book. From these sheets, you can learn real Excel techniques at your leisure and give yourself the ability to use Excel effectively outside your introductory statistics course. (Other add-ins that appear similar to PHStat report results as a series of text labels, hiding the details of using Microsoft Excel and leaving you with no basis for learning to use Excel effectively.)

Which versions of Excel are compatible with PHStat?

PHStat works best with Microsoft Windows Excel 2010 (WIN) and its successors and with OS X Excel 2011 and its successors (OS X). PHStat is also compatible with Excel 2007 (WIN), although the accuracy of some Excel statistical functions PHStat uses varies from Excel 2010 and can lead to (minor) changes in the results reported.

PHStat is partially compatible with Excel 2003 (WIN). When you open PHStat in Excel 2003, you will see a file conversion dialog box as Excel translates the .xlam file into a format that can be used in Excel 2003. After this file conversion completes, you will be able to see the PHStat menu and use many of the PHStat procedures. As documented in the PHStat help system some advanced procedures construct worksheets that use Excel functions that were added after Excel 2003 was published. In those cases, the worksheets will contain cells that display the #NAME? error message instead of results.

PHStat is not compatible with Excel 2008 (OS X), which did include the capability of running add-in workbooks.

How do I get PHStat ready for use?

Section D.2 on page 689 explains how to get PHStat ready for use. You should also review the PHStat readme file (available for download as discussed in Appendix C) for any late-breaking news or changes that might affect this process.

When I open PHStat, I get a Microsoft Excel error message that mentions a "compile error" or "hidden workbook." What is wrong?

Most likely, you have not applied the free Microsoft-supplied updates to your copy of Microsoft Excel (see Section D.1 on page 688). If you are certain that your copy of Microsoft Excel is fully up-to-date, verify that your copy is properly licensed and undamaged. (If necessary, you can rerun the Microsoft Office setup program to repair the installation of Excel.)

When I use a particular PHStat procedure, I get an error message that includes the words "unexpected error." What should I do?

"Unexpected error" messages are typically caused by improperly prepared data. Review your data to ensure that you have organized your data according to the conventions PHStat expects, as explained in the Section EG.5 on page 12 and the PHStat help system, and "clean" your data, as discussed in Section 1.3, if necessary.

Where can I get further news and information about PHStat? Where can I get further assistance about using PHStat?

Several websites can provide you with news and information or provide you with assistance that supplements the readme file and help system included with PHStat.

phstat.davidlevinestatistics.com is a website maintained by the authors of this book that contains general news and information about PHStat. This website also contains news about free updates to PHStat as they become available, contains links to the other two websites, and may have content and links to tips for using Microsoft Excel and/or PHStat.

phstatcommunity.org is a new website organized by PHStat users and endorsed by the developers of PHStat. You can click **News** on the home page to display the latest news and developments about PHStat. Other content on the website explains some of the "behind-the-scenes" technical workings of PHStat.

www.pearsonhighered.com/phstat is Pearson Education's official website for PHStat. From the home page, you can click **Contact Pearson Technical Support** to contact Pearson Education Customer Technical Support directly about any technical issue that you cannot resolve. Note that this current news about PHStat gets posted last to this website, and the website contains information about older PHStat versions that is not applicable to the version supplied for use with this book.

How can I make sure that my version of PHStat is up-to-date? How can I get free updates to PHStat when they become available?
PHStat is subject to continuous improvement. When enhancements are made or new issues that have arisen are addressed, a minor version update is produced. When this occurs, the update is announced at the websites listed in the previous answers, and replacement files are posted for download in the locations discussed in Section C.1 on page 679. You can then download those files and overwrite your current files. To discover the exact version number of PHStat, select **About PHStat** from the PHStat menu. (The version number for the PHStat version supplied for use with this book will always be a number that begins with 4.)

G.2 Microsoft Excel FAQs

Do all Microsoft Excel versions contain the same features and functionality? Which Microsoft Excel version should I use?
Unfortunately, features and functionality vary across versions still in use (including versions no longer supported by Microsoft). This book works best with Microsoft Windows versions Excel 2010 and Excel 2013 and OS X version Excel 2011. However, even among these current versions there are variations in features. For example, the slicer functionality discussed in Section 2.8 is found only in Excel 2010 and Excel 2013 and is missing in OS X Excel 2011 as well as in older Microsoft Windows versions. PivotTables have subtle differences across versions, none of which affect the instructions and examples in this book, and PivotCharts, not discussed in this book, are not included in Excel 2011 (see related PivotChart FAQ).

This book identifies differences among versions when they are significant. In particular, this book supplies, when necessary, special instructions and alternative worksheets (discussed in Appendix Section F.3) designed for Excel 2007 and other versions that are older than Excel 2010 and currently supported by Microsoft to be as inclusive as possible. That said, if you plan to use Microsoft Windows Excel 2003, you should consider upgrading to take advantage of new features and improvements and because the official Microsoft support for that product is scheduled to end in early 2014. If you plan to use Microsoft Windows Excel 2007, an upgrade will give you access to the newest features and provide a version with significantly increased statistical accuracy.

If you use OS X Excel 2008, you *must* upgrade to use PHStat or any of the other add-in workbooks mentioned in this book. Even if you plan to avoid using any add-ins, you should consider upgrading to OS X Excel 2011 for the same reasons that Excel 2003 and Excel 2007 face.

What does "Compatibility Mode" in the title bar mean?
Excel displays "Compatibility Mode" when you open and use a workbook that has been previously stored using the older **.xls** Excel workbook file format. Compatibility Mode does not affect Excel functionality but will cause Excel to review your workbook for exclusive-to-xlsx formatting properties and Excel will question you with a dialog box should you go to save the workbook in this format.

To convert a **.xls** workbook to the **.xlsx** format, select **File → Save As** and select **Excel Workbook (*.xlsx)** from the **Save as type** (WIN) or the **Format** (OS X) drop-down list in Excel 2010 or 2011 or their successors. To do so in Excel 2007, click the **Office Button**, move the mouse pointer over **Save As**, and, in the Save As gallery, click **Excel Workbook** to save the workbook in the **.xlsx** file format.

One quirk in Microsoft Excel is that when you convert a workbook by using **Save As**, the newly converted .xlsx workbook stays temporarily in Compatibility Mode. To avoid this outcome, close the newly converted workbook and then reopen it.

Using Compatibility Mode can cause minor differences in the objects such as charts and PivotTables that Excel creates and can cause problems when you seek to transfer data from other workbooks. Unless you need to open a workbook in a version of Excel that is older than Excel 2007, you should avoid using Compatibility Mode.

What Excel security settings will allow the PHStat or a Visual Explorations add-in workbook to function properly when using a Microsoft Windows version of Microsoft Excel?
The security settings are explained in the Appendix Section D.3 instructions on page 689. (These settings do not apply to OS X Excel.)

What is a PivotChart? Why doesn't this book discuss PivotCharts?
PivotCharts are charts that Microsoft Excel creates automatically from a PivotTable. This type of chart is not discussed in this book because Excel will typically create a "wrong" chart that takes more effort to fix than the effort needed to create a proper chart and because PivotChart functionality varies very significantly among the current Excel versions—and is missing from OS X Excel 2011.

The special instructions for selecting a PivotTable cell or cell range that appear in selected Section EG2.3 *In-Depth Excel* instructions help you avoid creating an unwanted PivotChart. (PHStat never creates a PivotChart.)

G.3 FAQs for New Microsoft Excel 2013 Users

When I open Excel 2013, I see a screen that shows panels that represent different workbooks and not the Ribbon interface. What do I do?
Press **Esc**. That screen, called the **Start screen**, will disappear and a screen that contains an Excel window similar to the ones in Excel 2010 and Excel 2011 will appear. For a more permanent solution, select **File → Options** and in the General panel of the Excel Options dialog box that appears clear **Show the Start screen when this application starts** and then click **OK**.

Are there any significant differences between Excel 2013 and its immediate predecessor, Excel 2010?
There are no significant differences, but several File tab commands present restyled panes (with the same or similar information), and opening and saving files differs slightly, as described in the Excel Guide for the Let's Get Started chapter.

The Excel 2013 Ribbon looks slightly different than the Excel 2010 Ribbon that is shown in a number of illustrations in Appendix B. However, these differences are so slight that the Excel 2010 Ribbon illustrations in Appendix B will be recognizable to you if you choose to use Excel 2013.The Excel 2013 Ribbon also contains a number of new icons and groups in some of its tabs, but those additions do not affect any of the Ribbon selection sequences presented in the Excel Guides.

In the Insert tab, what are Recommended PivotTables and Recommended Charts? Should I use these features?
Recommended PivotTables and **Recommended Charts** display one or more "recommended" PivotTables or charts as shortcuts. Unfortunately, the recommended PivotTables can include statistical errors such as treating the categories of a categorical variable as zero values of a numerical variable and the recommended charts often do not conform to best practices (see Appendix Section B.6).

As programmed in Excel 2013, you should ignore and not use these features as they will likely cause you to spend more time correcting errors and formatting mistakes than the little time that you might otherwise save.

What is Microsoft SkyDrive?
Microsoft SkyDrive is an Internet-based service that offers you free online storage that enables you to access and share your files anytime and anywhere there is an Internet connection available. In Excel 2013, you will see **SkyDrive** listed as a choice along with **Computer** in the Open, Save, and Save As panels.

You must sign in to the SkyDrive service using a "Microsoft account," formerly known as a "Windows Live ID." If you use the Microsoft Office Web Excel app, or certain other special versions of Excel, you *may* need to sign into the SkyDrive service to use Excel itself.

Self-Test Solutions and Answers to Selected Even-Numbered Problems

The following sections present worked-out solutions to Self-Test Problems and brief answers to most of the even-numbered problems in the text. For more detailed solutions, including explanations, interpretations, and Excel results, see the *Student Solutions Manual*.

CHAPTER 1

1.2 Small, medium, and large sizes imply order but do not specify how much more soft drink is added at increasing levels.

1.4 (a) The number of cellphones is a numerical variable that is discrete because the outcome is a count. It is ratio scaled because it has a true zero point. **(b)** Monthly data usage is a numerical variable that is continuous because any value within a range of values can occur. It is ratio scaled because it has a true zero point. **(c)** Number of text messages exchanged per month is a numerical variable that is discrete because the outcome is a count. It is ratio scaled because it has a true zero point. **(d)**Voice usage per month is a numerical variable that is continuous because any value within a range of values can occur. It is ratio scaled because it has a true zero point. **(e)** Whether a cellphone is used for email is a categorical variable because the answer can be only yes or no. This also makes it a nominal-scaled variable.

1.6 (a) Categorical, nominal scale. **(b)** Numerical, continuous, ratio scale. **(c)** Categorical, nominal scale. **(d)** Numerical, discrete, ratio scale. (e) Categorical, nominal scale.

1.8 (a) Numerical, continuous, ratio scale. **(b)** Numerical, discrete, ratio scale. **(c)** Numerical, continuous, ratio scale. **(d)** Categorical, nominal scale.

1.10 The underlying variable, ability of the students, may be continuous, but the measuring device, the test, does not have enough precision to distinguish between the two students.

1.18 Sample without replacement: Read from left to right in three-digit sequences and continue unfinished sequences from the end of the row to the beginning of the next row:
Row 05: 338 505 855 551 438 855 077 186 579 488 767 833 170
Rows 05–06: 897
Row 06: 340 033 648 847 204 334 639 193 639 411 095 924
Rows 06–07: 707
Row 07: 054 329 776 100 871 007 255 980 646 886 823 920 461
Row 08: 893 829 380 900 796 959 453 410 181 277 660 908 887
Rows 08–09: 237
Row 09: 818 721 426 714 050 785 223 801 670 353 362 449
Rows 09–10: 406
Note: All sequences above 902 and duplicates are discarded.

1.20 A simple random sample would be less practical for personal interviews because of travel costs (unless interviewees are paid to go to a central interviewing location).

1.22 Here all members of the population are equally likely to be selected, and the sample selection mechanism is based on chance. But selection of two elements is not independent; for example, if *A* is in the sample, we know that *B* is also and that *C* and *D* are not.

1.24 (a)

Row 16: 2323 6737 5131 8888 1718 0654 6832 4647 6510 4877
Row 17: 4579 4269 2615 1308 2455 7830 5550 5852 5514 7182
Row 18: 0989 3205 0514 2256 8514 4642 7567 8896 2977 8822
Row 19: 5438 2745 9891 4991 4523 6847 9276 8646 1628 3554
Row 20: 9475 0899 2337 0892 0048 8033 6945 9826 9403 6858
Row 21: 7029 7341 3553 1403 3340 4205 0823 4144 1048 2949
Row 22: 8515 7479 5432 9792 6575 5760 0408 8112 2507 3742
Row 23: 1110 0023 4012 8607 4697 9664 4894 3928 7072 5815
Row 24: 3687 1507 7530 5925 7143 1738 1688 5625 8533 5041
Row 25: 2391 3483 5763 3081 6090 5169 0546
Note: All sequences above 5000 are discarded. There were no repeating sequences.
(b)

089	189	289	389	489	589	689	789	889	989
1089	1189	1289	1389	1489	1589	1689	1789	1889	1989
2089	2189	2289	2389	2489	2589	2689	2789	2889	2989
3089	3189	3289	3389	3489	3589	3689	3789	3889	3989
4089	4189	4289	4389	4489	4589	4689	4789	4889	4989

(c) With the single exception of invoice 0989, the invoices selected in the simple random sample are not the same as those selected in the systematic sample. It would be highly unlikely that a simple random sample would select the same units as a systematic sample.

1.26 Before accepting the results of a survey of college students, you might want to know, for example: Who funded the survey? Why was it conducted? What was the population from which the sample was selected? What sampling design was used? What mode of response was used: a personal interview, a telephone interview, or a mail survey? Were interviewers trained? Were survey questions field-tested? What questions were asked? Were the questions clear, accurate, unbiased, and valid? What operational definition of "vast majority" was used? What was the response rate? What was the sample size?

1.28 The results are based on an online survey. If the frame is supposed to be small business owners, how is the population defined? This is a self-selecting sample of people who responded online, so there is an undefined nonresponse error. Sampling error cannot be determined since this is not a random sample.

1.30 Before accepting the results of the survey, you might want to know, for example: Who funded the study? Why was it conducted? What was the population from which the sample was selected? What sampling design was used? What mode of response was used: a personal interview, a telephone interview, or a mail survey? Were interviewers trained? Were survey questions field-tested? What other questions were asked? Were the questions clear, accurate, unbiased, and valid? What was the response rate? What was the margin of error? What was the sample size? What frame was used?

1.42 (a) All benefitted employees at the university. **(b)** The 3,095 employees who responded to the survey. **(c)** Gender and marital status are categorical. Age (years), education level (years completed), and household income ($) are numerical.

CHAPTER 2

2.2 **(a)** Table of frequencies for all student responses:

GENDER	STUDENT MAJOR CATEGORIES A	C	M	Totals
Male	14	9	2	25
Female	6	6	3	15
Totals	20	15	5	40

(b) Table based on total percentages:

GENDER	STUDENT MAJOR CATEGORIES A	C	M	Totals
Male	35.0%	22.5%	5.0%	62.5%
Female	15.0	15.0	7.5	37.5
Totals	50.0	37.5	12.5	100.0

Table based on row percentages:

GENDER	STUDENT MAJOR CATEGORIES A	C	M	Totals
Male	56.0%	36.0%	8.0%	100.0%
Female	40.0	40.0	20.0	100.0
Totals	50.0	37.5	12.5	100.0

Table based on column percentages:

GENDER	STUDENT MAJOR CATEGORIES A	C	M	Totals
Male	70.0%	60.0%	40.0%	62.5%
Female	30.0	40.0	60.0	37.5
Totals	100.0	100.0	100.0	100.0

2.4 **(a)** Because the 29% is based on the sample, it is a statistic. (b) Because the 58% is based on the sample, it is a statistic.

2.6 **(a)** The percentages are 4.00, 10.58, 25.91, 59.51. **(b)** More than half the oil produced is from non-OPEC countries. More than 25% is produced by OPEC countries other than Iran and Saudi Arabia.

2.8 **(a)** Table of row percentages:

ENJOY SHOPPING FOR CLOTHING	GENDER Male	Female	Total
Yes	46%	54%	100%
No	53	47	100
Total	50	50	100

Table of column percentages:

ENJOY SHOPPING FOR CLOTHING	GENDER Male	Female	Total
Yes	44%	51%	47%
No	56	49	53
Total	100	100	100

Table of total percentages:

ENJOY SHOPPING FOR CLOTHING	GENDER Male	Female	Total
Yes	22%	25%	47%
No	28	25	53
Total	50	50	100

(b) A higher percentage of females enjoy shopping for clothing.

2.10 Social recommendations had very little impact on correct recall. Those who arrived at the link from a recommendation had a correct recall of 73.07% as compared to those who arrived at the link from browsing who had a correct recall of 67.96%.

2.12 73 78 78 78 85 88 91.

2.14 **(a)** 0 but less than 5 million, 5 million but less than 10 million, 10 million but less than 15 million, 15 million but less than 20 million, 20 million but less than 25 million, 25 million but less than 30 million. **(b)** 5 million. **(c)** 2.5 million, 7.5 million, 12.5 million, 17.5 million, 22.5 million, and 27.5 million.

2.16 **(a)**

Electricity Costs	Frequency	Percentage
$80 up to $99	4	8%
$100 up to $119	7	14
$120 up to $139	9	18
$140 up to $159	13	26
$160 up to $179	9	18
$180 up to $199	5	10
$200 up to $219	3	6

(b)

Electricity Costs	Frequency	Percentage	Cumulative %
$ 99	4	8.00%	8.00%
$119	7	14.00	22.00
$139	9	18.00	40.00
$159	13	26.00	66.00
$179	9	18.00	84.00
$199	5	10.00	94.00
$219	3	6.00	100.00

(c) The majority of utility charges are clustered between $120 and $180.

2.18 **(a)**

Width	Frequency	Percentage
8.310–8.329	3	6.12%
8.330–8.349	2	4.08
8.350–8.369	1	2.04
8.370–8.389	4	8.16
8.390–8.409	5	10.20
8.410–8.429	16	32.65
8.430–8.449	5	10.20
8.450–8.469	5	10.20
8.470–8.489	6	12.24
8.490–8.509	2	4.08

(b)

Width	Percentage Less Than
8.310	0
8.330	6.12
8.350	10.20
8.370	12.24
8.390	20.40
8.410	30.60
8.430	63.25
8.450	73.45
8.470	83.65
8.490	95.89
8.51	100.00

(c) All the troughs will meet the company's requirements of between 8.31 and 8.61 inches wide.

2.20 (a)

Bulb Life (hours)	Percentage, Mfgr A	Percentage, Mfgr B
650–749	7.5%	0.0%
750–849	12.5	5.0
850–949	50.0	20.0
950–1,049	22.5	40.0
1,050–1,149	7.5	22.5
1,150–1,249	0.0	12.5

(b)

% Less Than	Percentage Less Than, Mfgr A	Percentage Less Than, Mfgr B
750	7.5%	0.0%
850	20.0	5.0
950	70.0	25.0
1,050	92.5	65.0
1,150	100.0	87.5
1,250	100.0	100.0

(c) Manufacturer B produces bulbs with longer lives than Manufacturer A. The cumulative percentage for Manufacturer B shows that 65% of its bulbs lasted less than 1,050 hours, contrasted with 92.5% of Manufacturer A's bulbs. None of Manufacturer A's bulbs lasted at least 1,150 hours, but 12.5% of Manufacturer B's bulbs lasted at least 1,150 hours. At the same time, 7.5% of Manufacturer A's bulbs lasted less than 750 hours, whereas none of Manufacturer B's bulbs lasted less than 750 hours.

2.22 (b) The Pareto chart is best for portraying these data because it not only sorts the frequencies in descending order but also provides the cumulative line on the same chart. **(c)** You can conclude that friends/family account for the largest percentage, 45%. When other, news media, and online user reviews are added to friends/family, this accounts for 83%.

2.24 (b) 86%. **(d)** The Pareto chart allows you to see which sources account for most of the electricity.

2.26 (b) Since electricity consumption is spread over many types of appliances, a bar chart may be best in showing which types of appliances used the most electricity. **(c)** Air conditioning, lighting, and clothes washers/other accounted for 58% of the residential electricity use in the United States.

2.28 (b) A higher percentage of females enjoy shopping for clothing.

2.30 (b) Social recommendations had very little impact on correct recall.

2.32 50 74 74 76 81 89 92.

2.34 (a)

Stem Unit	10	Stem Unit	10
12	168	23	
13	0	24	1 2
14	0	25	9
15	9	26	
16	0 0 0 1 2 9	27	
17	1 4 8	28	
18	4	29	
19	6	30	6
20	7 8	31	
21	2 3	32	
22	1 3 6	33	8 9

(b) The results are concentrated between $160 and $178.

2.36 (c) The majority of utility charges are clustered between $120 and $180.

2.38 Property taxes seem concentrated between $1,000 and $1,400 and also between $600 and $800 per capita. There were more states with property taxes per capita below $1,500 than above $1,500.

2.40 (c) All the troughs will meet the company's requirements of between 8.31 and 8.61 inches wide.

2.42 (c) Manufacturer B produces bulbs with longer lives than Manufacturer A.

2.44 (b) Yes, there is a strong positive relationship between X and Y. As X increases, so does Y.

2.46 (c) There appears to be a linear relationship between the first weekend gross and either the U.S. gross or the worldwide gross of Harry Potter movies. However, this relationship is greatly affected by the results of the last movie, *Deathly Hallows, Part II*.

2.48 (a), (c) There appears to be a positive relationship between the coaches' salary and revenue. Yes, this is borne out by the data.

2.50 (b) There is a great deal of variation in the returns from decade to decade. Most of the returns are between 5% and 15%. The 1950s, 1980s, and 1990s had exceptionally high returns, and only the 1930s and 2000s had negative returns.

2.52 (b) There was a slight decline in movie attendance between 2001 and 2011. During that time, movie attendance increased from 2002 to 2004 but then decreased to a level below that in 2001.

2.58 (a) The line that shows the unemployment rate. **(b)** The color under the line is unnecessary.

2.64 (a) Pivot table of tallies in terms of counts:

Count of 3YrReturn%	Star Rating					
Type	Five	Four	One	Three	Two	Grand Total
Growth	**118**	**30**	**6**	**48**	**21**	**223**
Large	51	14	3	25	10	103
Mid-Cap	37	9		13	7	66
Small	30	7	3	10	4	54
Value	**50**	**16**	**2**	**17**	**10**	**95**
Large	31	10	1	8	5	55
Mid-Cap	10	4		3	2	19
Small	9	2	1	6	3	21
Grand Total	**168**	**46**	**8**	**65**	**31**	**318**

Pivot table of tallies in terms of percentage of grand total:

Count of 3YrReturn%	Star Rating					
Type	Five	Four	One	Three	Two	Grand Total
Growth	**37.11%**	**9.43%**	**1.89%**	**15.09%**	**6.60%**	**70.13%**
Large	16.04%	4.40%	0.94%	7.86%	3.14%	32.39%
Mid-Cap	11.64%	2.83%	0.00%	4.09%	2.20%	20.75%
Small	9.43%	2.20%	0.94%	3.14%	1.26%	16.98%
Value	**15.72%**	**5.03%**	**0.63%**	**5.35%**	**3.14%**	**29.87%**
Large	9.75%	3.14%	0.31%	2.52%	1.57%	17.30%
Mid-Cap	3.14%	1.26%	0.00%	0.94%	0.63%	5.97%
Small	2.83%	0.63%	0.31%	1.89%	0.94%	6.60%
Grand Total	**52.83%**	**14.47%**	**2.52%**	**20.44%**	**9.75%**	**100.00%**

(b) Patterns of star rating conditioned on market cap: For the growth funds as a group, most are given a five-star rating, followed by three-star, four-star, two-star, and one-star ratings. The pattern of star rating is the same across the different market cap within the growth funds with most of the funds receiving a five-star rating, followed by three-star, four-star, two-star, and one-star ratings.

The pattern for value funds as a group is the same as the growth funds as a group. However, the pattern across the different market cap is slightly different with most of large and mid-cap funds receiving a five-star rating, followed by four-star, three-star, two-star, and one-star ratings, while most of the small-cap funds received five-star ratings, followed by three-star, two-star, four-star, and one-star ratings.

Patterns of market cap conditioned on star rating: Most of the growth funds are large-cap, followed by mid-cap and small-cap. The pattern is similar among the five-star, four-star, three-star and two-star growth funds but among the one-star growth funds, half are large-cap and half are small-cap, with no mid-cap.

The largest share of the value funds is large-cap, followed by small-cap and mid-cap. The pattern is similar among the three-star and two-star value funds. Among the five-star value funds, most are large-cap, followed by mid-cap and then small-cap, while half of the one-star value funds are large-cap and half are small-cap, with no mid-cap.

(c) Pivot table of the average three-year return for each type, market cap, and rating:

Average of 3YrReturn%	Star Rating					
Type	Five	Four	One	Three	Two	Grand Total
Growth	**22.6507**	**24.3170**	**19.4017**	**22.5215**	**19.2314**	**22.4376**
Large	21.0080	22.4357	15.4300	21.3636	20.1550	21.0431
Mid-Cap	23.1086	25.0600		22.5731	17.8143	22.7077
Small	24.8783	27.1243	23.3733	25.3490	19.4025	24.7674
Value	**19.8206**	**19.8369**	**23.5700**	**22.3324**	**20.5120**	**20.4245**
Large	17.1623	16.1870	14.9300	18.9538	15.7680	17.0782
Mid-Cap	23.3370	23.7175		27.2100	22.2650	23.9158
Small	25.0700	30.3250	32.2100	24.3983	27.2500	26.0300
Grand Total	**21.8084**	**22.7587**	**20.4438**	**22.4720**	**19.6445**	**21.8362**

(d) There are 25 large-cap growth funds with a rating of three, and the summary statistics of their three-year return are given below:

	3YrReturn%
Mean	21.3636
Standard Error	1.9013
Median	19.23
Mode	#N/A
Standard Deviation	9.5065
Sample Variance	90.3734
Kurtosis	16.2970
Skewness	3.7558
Range	50.9700
Minimum	11.9400
Maximum	62.9100
Sum	534.0900
Count	25

The average three-year return is 21.3636%, with a standard deviation of 9.5065%. The median is lower than the mean at 19.23%. The lowest return is 11.94%, while the highest is 62.91%, which yields a range of 50.97%.

2.66 (a) Pivot table of tallies in terms of counts:

Count of 3YrReturn%	Star Rating					
Type	Five	Four	One	Three	Two	Grand Total
Growth	**118**	**30**	**6**	**48**	**21**	**223**
Average	60	15	3	24	11	113
High	27	3	3	11	4	48
Low	31	12		13	6	62
Value	**50**	**16**	**2**	**17**	**10**	**95**
Average	19	2	1	6	4	32
High	11	2	1	8	4	26
Low	20	12		3	2	37
Grand Total	**168**	**46**	**8**	**65**	**31**	**318**

Pivot table of tallies in terms of % of grand total:

Count of 3YrReturn%	Star Rating					
Type	Five	Four	One	Three	Two	Grand Total
Growth	**37.11%**	**9.43%**	**1.89%**	**15.09%**	**6.60%**	**70.13%**
Average	18.87%	4.72%	0.94%	7.55%	3.46%	35.53%
High	8.49%	0.94%	0.94%	3.46%	1.26%	15.09%
Low	9.75%	3.77%	0.00%	4.09%	1.89%	19.50%
Value	**15.72%**	**5.03%**	**0.63%**	**5.35%**	**3.14%**	**29.87%**
Average	5.97%	0.63%	0.31%	1.89%	1.26%	10.06%
High	3.46%	0.63%	0.31%	2.52%	1.26%	8.18%
Low	6.29%	3.77%	0.00%	0.94%	0.63%	11.64%
Grand Total	**52.83%**	**14.47%**	**2.52%**	**20.44%**	**9.75%**	**100.00%**

(b) Patterns of star rating conditioned on risk: For the growth funds as a group, most are given a five-star rating, followed by three-star, four-star, two-star, and one-star ratings. The pattern of star rating is the same among the average-risk and low-risk growth funds. The pattern is different among the high-risk growth funds, with most given a five-star rating, followed by three-star, two-star, and finally equal portions of four- and one-star ratings.

The pattern for value funds as a group is the same as for the growth funds as a group. However, the pattern across the different market caps is different, with most of the average and high-risk funds receiving a five-star rating, followed by three-star, two-star, four-star, and one-star ratings, and most of the low-risk funds receiving a five-star rating, followed by four-star, three-star, two-star, and one-star ratings.

Patterns of risk conditioned on star rating: Most of the growth funds are rated as average risk, followed by low risk and then high risk. The pattern is similar among the five-star, four-star, three-star, and two-star growth funds, but among the one-star growth funds, half are average risk and half are high risk, with no low-risk.

The largest share of the value funds is rated as low risk, followed by average risk and then high risk. The pattern is similar among the five-star value funds. Among the four-star value funds, most are low-risk, followed by equal shares of average risk and high risk. Among the three-star value funds, most are high risk, followed by average risk and then low risk. Among the two-star value funds, the low-risk funds make up the smallest portion, while the average-risk and high-risk funds split the remaining portion; half of the one-star value funds are average risk, and half are high risk, with no low risk.

(c) Pivot table of the average three-year return for each type, risk, and rating:

Average of 3YrReturn%	Star Rating					
Type	Five	Four	One	Three	Two	Grand Total
Growth	**22.6507**	**24.3170**	**19.4017**	**22.5215**	**19.2314**	**22.4376**
Average	23.4607	26.4473	15.4300	21.3446	18.8055	22.7413
High	25.3019	26.2200	23.3733	31.4318	26.6150	26.7529
Low	18.7739	21.1783		17.1546	15.0900	18.5432
Value	**19.8206**	**19.8369**	**23.5700**	**22.3324**	**20.5120**	**20.4245**
Average	19.0800	19.0000	14.9300	20.7650	15.9650	18.8719
High	25.7718	33.5100	32.2100	25.8000	26.4000	26.7200
Low	17.2510	17.6975		16.2200	17.8300	17.3435
Grand Total	**21.8084**	**22.7587**	**20.4438**	**22.4720**	**19.6445**	**21.8362**

(d) There are 11 growth funds with high risk with a rating of three, and the summary statistics of their three-year return are given below:

	3YrReturn%
Mean	31.4318
Standard Error	3.4091
Medain	27.3300
Mode	#N/A
Standard Deviation	11.3068
Sample Variance	127.8431
Kurtosis	7.0378
Skewness	2.4724
Range	41.6800
Minimum	21.2300
Maximum	62.9100
Sum	345.7500
Count	11

The average three-year return is 31.4318%, with a standard deviation of 11.3068%. The median is lower than the mean at 27.33%. The lowest return is 21.23%, while the highest is 62.91%, which yields a range of 41.68%.

2.68

Count of 3YrReturn%	Risk		
	Low	Low Total	Grand Total
Type	Five		
Value	1	1	1
Small	1	1	1
Grand Total	1	1	1

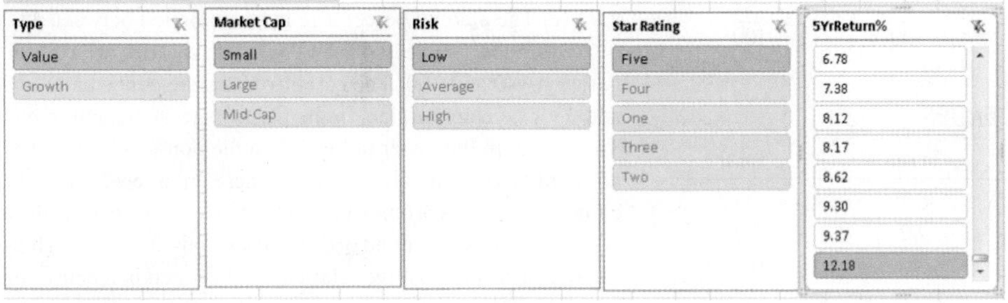

The fund with the highest five-year return is a small-cap, low-risk, five-star-rated value fund.

2.70

Count of 3YrReturn%	Risk		
	High	High Total	Grand Total
Type	Five		
Growth	1	1	1
Small	1	1	1
Grand Total	1	1	1

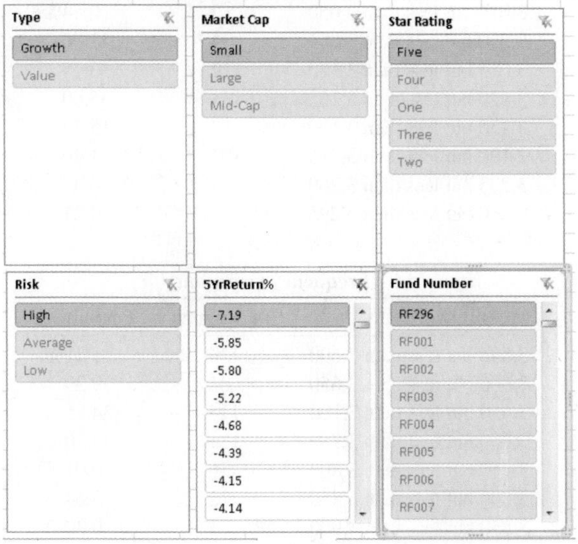

The fund number RF296 in the sample has the lowest five-year return.

2.72

Count of 3YrReturn%	Risk		
	High	High Total	Grand Total
Type	Five		
Growth	1	1	1
Small	1	1	1
Grand Total	1	1	1

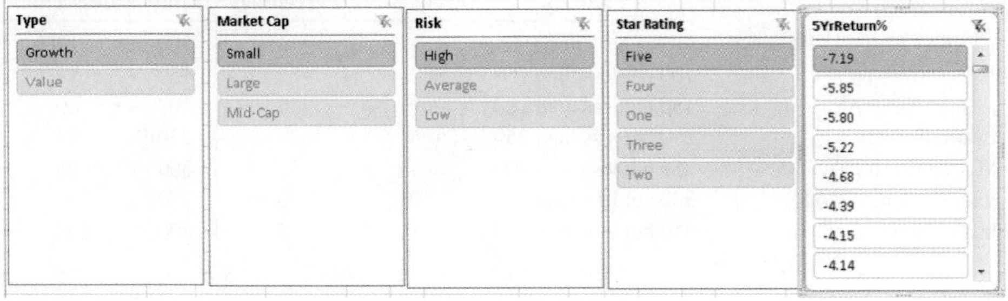

The fund that has the lowest five-year return is a small-cap, high-risk growth fund with a five-star rating.

2.84 (c) The publisher gets the largest portion (64.8%) of the revenue. About half (32.3%) of the revenue received by the publisher covers manufacturing costs. The publisher's marketing and promotion account for the next largest share of the revenue, at 15.4%. Author, bookstore employee salaries and benefits, and publisher administrative costs and taxes each account for around 10% of the revenue, whereas the publisher after-tax profit, bookstore operations, bookstore pretax profit, and freight constitute the "trivial few" allocations of the revenue. Yes, the bookstore gets twice the revenue of the authors.

2.86 (b) The pie chart may be best since with only three categories, it enables you to see the portion of the whole in each category. **(d)** The pie chart may be best since, with only four categories it enables you to see the portion of the whole in each category. **(e)** The online content is not copy-edited or fact-checked as carefully as print content. Only 41% of the online content is copy-edited as carefully as print content, and only 57% of the online content is fact-checked as carefully as the print content.

2.88 (a)

DESSERT ORDERED	GENDER		
	Male	Female	Total
Yes	71%	29%	100%
No	48	52	100
Total	53	47	100

DESSERT ORDERED	GENDER		
	Male	Female	Total
Yes	30%	14%	23%
No	70	86	77
Total	100	100	100

DESSERT ORDERED	GENDER		
	Male	Female	Total
Yes	16%	7%	23%
No	37	40	77
Total	53	47	100

DESSERT ORDERED	BEEF ENTRÉE		
	Yes	No	Total
Yes	52%	48%	100%
No	25	75	100
Total	31	69	100

DESSERT ORDERED	BEEF ENTRÉE		
	Yes	No	Total
Yes	38%	16%	23%
No	62	84	77
Total	100	100	100

DESSERT ORDERED	BEEF ENTRÉE		
	Yes	No	Total
Yes	12%	11%	23%
No	19	58	77
Total	31	69	100

(b) If the owner is interested in finding out the percentage of males and females who order dessert or the percentage of those who order a beef entrée and a dessert among all patrons, the table of total percentages is most informative. If the owner is interested in the effect of gender on ordering of dessert or the effect of ordering a beef entrée on the ordering of dessert, the table of column percentages will be most informative. Because dessert is usually ordered after the main entrée, and the owner has no direct control over the gender of patrons, the table of row percentages is not very useful here. **(c)** 30% of the men ordered desserts, compared to 14% of the women; men are more than twice as likely to order dessert as women. Almost 38% of the patrons ordering a beef entrée ordered dessert, compared to 16% of patrons ordering all other entrées. Patrons ordering beef are more than 2.3 times as likely to order dessert as patrons ordering any other entrée.

2.90 (a) 23575R15 accounts for over 80% of the warranty claims. **(b)** 91.82% of the warranty claims are from the ATX model. **(c)** Tread separation accounts for 73.23% of the warranty claims among the ATX model. **(d)** The number of claims is evenly distributed among the three incidents; other/unknown incidents account for almost 40% of the claims, tread separation accounts for about 35% of the claims, and blowout accounts for about 25% of the claims.

2.92 (c) The alcohol percentage is concentrated between 4% and 6%, with more between 4% and 5%. The calories are concentrated between 140 and 160. The carbohydrates are concentrated between 12 and 15. There are outliers in the percentage of alcohol in both tails. The outlier in the lower tail is due to the non-alcoholic beer O'Doul's, with only a 0.4% alcohol content. There are a few beers with alcohol content as high as around 11%. There are a few beers with calorie content as high as around 302.5 and carbohydrates as high as 31.5. There is a strong positive relationship between percentage of alcohol and calories and between calories and carbohydrates, and there is a moderately positive relationship between percentage alcohol and carbohydrates.

2.94 (c) There appears to be a positive relationship between the yield of the one-year CD and the five-year CD.

2.96 (a)

Frequency (Boston)

Weight (Boston)	Frequency	Percentage
3,015 but less than 3,050	2	0.54%
3,050 but less than 3,085	44	11.96
3,085 but less than 3,120	122	33.15
3,120 but less than 3,155	131	35.60
3,155 but less than 3,190	58	15.76
3,190 but less than 3,225	7	1.90
3,225 but less than 3,260	3	0.82
3,260 but less than 3,295	1	0.27

(b)

Frequency (Vermont)

Weight (Vermont)	Frequency	Percentage
3,550 but less than 3,600	4	1.21%
3,600 but less than 3,650	31	9.39
3,650 but less than 3,700	115	34.85
3,700 but less than 3,750	131	39.70
3,750 but less than 3,800	36	10.91
3,800 but less than 3,850	12	3.64
3,850 but less than 3,900	1	0.30

(d) 0.54% of the Boston shingles pallets are underweight and 0.27% are overweight. 1.21% of the Vermont shingles pallets are underweight and 3.94% are overweight.

2.98 (c)

Calories	Frequency	Percentage	Limit	Percentage Less Than
50 but less than 100	3	12%	100	12%
100 but less than 150	3	12	150	24
150 but less than 200	9	36	200	60
200 but less than 250	6	24	250	84
250 but less than 300	3	12	300	96
300 but less than 350	0	0	350	96
350 but less than 400	1	4	400	100

Cholesterol	Frequency	Percentage	Limit	Percentage Less Than
0 but less than 50	2	8%	50	8%
50 but less than 100	17	68	100	76
100 but less than 150	4	16	150	92
150 but less than 200	1	4	200	96
200 but less than 250	0	0	250	96
250 but less than 300	0	0	300	96
300 but less than 350	0	0	350	96
350 but less than 400	0	0	400	96
400 but less than 450	0	0	450	96
450 but less than 500	1	4	500	100

The sampled fresh red meats, poultry, and fish vary from 98 to 397 calories per serving, with the highest concentration between 150 to 200 calories. One protein source, spareribs, with 397 calories, is more than 100 calories above the next-highest-caloric food. The protein content of the sampled foods varies from 16 to 33 grams, with 68% of the values falling between 24 and 32 grams. Spareribs and fried liver are both very different from other foods sampled—the former on calories and the latter on cholesterol content.

2.100 (b) There is a downward trend in the amount filled. **(c)** The amount filled in the next bottle will most likely be below 1.894 liters. **(d)** The scatter plot of the amount of soft drink filled against time reveals the trend of the data, whereas a histogram only provides information on the distribution of the data.

CHAPTER 3

3.2 (a) Mean = 7, median = 7, mode = 7. **(b)** Range = 9, $S^2 = 10.8$, $S = 3.286$, $CV = 46.948\%$. **(c)** Z scores: 0, −0.913, 0.609, 0, −1.217,1.522. None of the Z scores are larger than 3.0 or smaller than −3.0. There is no outlier. **(d)** Symmetric because mean = median.

3.4 (a) Mean = 2, median = 7, mode = 7. **(b)** Range = 17, $S^2 = 62$ $S = 7.874$, $CV = 393.7\%$. **(c)** 0.635, −0.889, −1.270, 0.635, 0.889. There are no outliers. **(d)** Left-skewed because mean < median.

3.6 −0.085.

3.8 (a)

	Grade *X*	Grade *Y*
Mean	575	575.4
Median	575	575
Standard deviation	6.40	2.07

(b) If quality is measured by central tendency, Grade *X* tires provide slightly better quality because *X*'s mean and median are both equal to the expected value, 575 mm. If, however, quality is measured by consistency, Grade *Y* provides better quality because, even though *Y*'s mean is only slightly larger than the mean for Grade *X*, *Y*'s standard deviation is much smaller. The range in values for Grade *Y* is 5 mm compared to the range in values for Grade *X*, which is 16 mm.

(c)

	Grade *X*	Grade *Y*, Altered
Mean	575	577.4
Median	575	575
Standard deviation	6.40	6.11

When the fifth *Y* tire measures 588 mm rather than 578 mm, *Y*'s mean inner diameter becomes 577.4 mm, which is larger than *X*'s mean inner diameter, and *Y*'s standard deviation increases from 2.07 mm to 6.11 mm. In this case, *X*'s tires are providing better quality in terms of the mean inner diameter, with only slightly more variation among the tires than *Y*'s.

3.10 (a), (b)

	Cost ($)
Mean	7.0933
Standard Error	0.3630
Median	6.8
Mode	6.5
Standard Deviation	1.4060
Sample Variance	1.9769
Kurtosis	−0.5778
Skewness	0.4403
Range	4.71
Minimum	4.89
Maximum	9.6
Sum	106.4
Count	15
First Quartile	5.9
Third Quartile	8.3
CV	19.82%

(c) The mean is only slightly greater than the median, so the data are only slightly right-skewed. **(d)** The mean amount spent is $7.09, and the median is $6.00. The average scatter of the amount spent around the mean is $1.41. The difference between the highest and the lowest amount spent is $4.71.

3.12 (a), (b)

	MPG
Mean	21.6111
Standard Error	0.5122
Median	22
Mode	22
Standard Deviation	2.1731
Sample Variance	4.7222
Kurtosis	2.0493
Skewness	−0.7112
Range	10
Minimum	16
Maximum	26
Sum	389
Count	18
First Quartile	21
Third Quartile	23
CV	10.06%

MPG	Z Score	MPG	Z Score
20	−0.7414	22	0.1790
22	0.1790	22	0.1790
23	0.6391	26	2.0197
22	0.1790	23	0.6391
23	0.6391	24	1.0993
22	0.1790	19	−1.2016
22	0.1790	21	−0.2812
21	−0.2812	22	0.1790
19	−1.2016	16	−2.5821

(c) Because the mean is about the same as the median, the data are symmetrically distributed. **(d)** The distribution of MPG of the sedans is slightly right-skewed, while that of the SUVs is symmetrical. The mean MPG of sedans is 4.14 higher than that of SUVs. The average scatter of the MPG of sedans is almost 3 times that of SUVs. The range of sedans is almost 2 times that of SUVs.

3.14 (a), (b)

Facebook Penetration	
Mean	34.8253
Standard Error	3.3206
Median	37.52
Mode	#N/A
Standard Deviation	12.8607
Sample Variance	165.3968
Kurtosis	0.9334
Skewness	−0.8211
Range	47.99
Minimum	4.25
Maximum	52.24
Sum	522.38
Count	15
First Quartile	28.29
Third Quartile	46.04
CV	36.93%

Country	Facebook Penetration	Z Score
United States	50.19	1.1947
Brazil	25.45	−0.7290
India	4.25	−2.3774
Indonesia	18.04	−1.3052
Mexico	31.66	−0.2461
United Kingdom	49.14	1.1131
Turkey	39.99	0.4016
Philippines	28.29	−0.5082
France	37.52	0.2095
Germany	28.87	−0.4631
Itlay	37.73	0.2259
Argentina	46.04	0.8720
Canada	52.24	1.3541
Colombia	38.06	0.2515
Spain	34.19	0.0066

None of the Z scores are more than 3 standard deviations away from the mean, so there is not any outlier. **(c)** The mean is only slightly smaller than the median, so the data are only slightly left-skewed. **(d)** The mean market penetration value is 34.8253 and the median is 37.52. The average scatter around the mean is 12.8607. The difference between the highest value and the lowest value is 47.99.

3.16 (a), (b)

Cost(U.S. $)	
Mean	155.5
Standard Error	3.3112
Median	153.5
Mode	#N/A
Standard Deviation	9.3656
Sample Variance	87.7143
Kurtosis	−1.0019
Skewness	0.6650
Range	25
Minimum	146
Maximum	171
Sum	1244
Count	8
First Quartile	147
Third Quartile	166

(c) The mean price is $155.5 and the median is $153.5. The average scatter around the mean is $9.37. The difference between the highest and the lowest value is $25.

(d) (a), (b)

Cost(U.S. $)	
Mean	159.125
Standard Error	6.3371
Median	153.5
Mode	#N/A
Standard Deviation	17.9240
Sample Variance	321.2679
Kurtosis	4.6246
Skewness	2.0650
Range	54
Minimum	146
Maximum	200
Sum	1273
Count	8
First Quartile	147
Third Quartile	166

(c) The mean price is $159.13 and the median is $153.5. The average scatter around the mean is $17.92. The difference between the highest and the lowest value is $54. The mean, standard deviation, and range are sensitive to outliers. The higher price at $200 raises the value of mean, standard deviation, and range but has no impact on the median.

3.18 (a) Mean = 7.11, median = 6.68. **(b)** Variance = 4.336, standard deviation = 2.082, range = 6.67, CV = 29.27%. **(c)** Because the mean is greater than the median, the distribution is right-skewed. **(d)** The mean and median are both greater than 5 minutes. The distribution is right-skewed, meaning that there are some unusually high values. Further, 13 of the 15 bank customers sampled (or 86.7%) had waiting times greater than 5 minutes. So the customer is likely to experience a waiting time in excess of 5 minutes. The manager overstated the bank's service record in responding that the customer would "almost certainly" not wait longer than 5 minutes for service.

3.20 (a) $[(1 + 0.0108) \times (1 + 0.0240)]^{1/2} - 1 = 1.0174 - 1 = 1.74\%$ per year. **(b)** $= (\$1{,}000) \times (1 + 0.0174) \times (1 + 0.0174) = \$1{,}035.10$. **(c)** The result for Taser was worse than the result for GE, which was worth $1,193.56.

3.22 (a) Platinum = −3.22%, gold = 16.6%, silver = 16.0% per year. **(b)** Gold had a slightly higher return than silver and a much higher return than platinum. **(c)** Gold and silver had a much higher return than the DJIA, the S&P 500, and the NASDAQ, but platinum's return was worse than the DJIA and the S&P 500, but slightly better than the NASDAQ.

3.24 (a)

Average of 3YrReturn%	Rati n					
Type	Five	Four	One	Three	Two	Grand Total
Growth	**22.6507**	**24.3170**	**19.4017**	**22.5215**	**19.2314**	**22.4376**
Large	21.0080	22.4357	15.4300	21.3636	20.1550	21.0431
Mid-Cap	23.1086	25.0600		22.5731	17.8143	22.7077
Small	24.8783	27.1243	23.3733	25.3490	19.4025	24.7674
Value	**19.8206**	**19.8369**	**23.5700**	**22.3324**	**20.5120**	**20.4245**
Large	17.1623	16.1870	14.9300	18.9538	15.7680	17.0782
Mid-Cap	23.3370	23.7175		27.2100	22.2650	23.9158
Small	25.0700	30.3250	32.2100	24.3983	27.2500	26.0300
Grand Total	**21.8084**	**22.7587**	**20.4438**	**22.4720**	**19.6445**	**21.8362**

(b)

StdDev of 3YrReturn%	Rati n					
Type	Five	Four	One	Three	Two	Grand Total
Growth	**5.9833**	**3.6809**	**4.6102**	**7.8469**	**9.5545**	**6.6408**
Large	7.2865	3.0474	2.0099	9.5065	12.4171	7.9658
Mid-Cap	4.7457	3.4045		5.7344	7.5697	5.3572
Small	3.8454	3.4101	1.3312	4.9093	4.8856	4.2432
Value	**5.1254**	**6.3287**	**12.2188**	**5.7936**	**6.2446**	**5.6783**
Large	3.8638	1.9349	#DIV/0!	4.7559	1.5196	3.5969
Mid-Cap	2.8793	4.4491		6.9632	2.2415	3.9265
Small	4.6636	9.7086	#DIV/0!	4.3233	6.3962	5.2314
Grand Total	**5.8714**	**5.1707**	**6.3429**	**7.3224**	**8.5398**	**6.4263**

(c) The mean three-year return of small-cap value funds is higher than that of the small-cap growth funds across the different star ratings, with the exception of those rated as three-star. On the other hand, the mean three-year return of mid-cap and large-cap value funds is lower than that of the growth funds across the different star ratings with the exception of the mid-cap three-star and four-star funds. The standard deviation of the three-year return of large-cap growth funds is higher than that of the value funds across all the star ratings.

3.26 (a)

Average of 3YrReturn%	Rati n					
Type	Five	Four	One	Three	Two	Grand Total
Growth	**22.6507**	**24.3170**	**19.4017**	**22.5215**	**19.2314**	**22.4376**
Average	23.4607	26.4473	15.4300	21.3446	18.8055	22.7413
High	25.3019	26.2200	23.3733	31.4318	26.6150	26.7529
Low	18.7739	21.1783		17.1546	15.0900	18.5432
Value	**19.8206**	**19.8369**	**23.5700**	**22.3324**	**20.5120**	**20.4245**
Average	19.0800	19.0000	14.9300	20.7650	15.9650	18.8719
High	25.7718	33.5100	32.2100	25.8000	26.4000	26.7200
Low	17.2510	17.6975		16.2200	17.8300	17.3435
Grand Total	**21.8084**	**22.7587**	**20.4438**	**22.4720**	**19.6445**	**21.8362**

(b)

StdDev of 3YrReturn%	Rati n					
Type	Five	Four	One	Three	Two	Grand Total
Growth	**5.9833**	**3.6809**	**4.6102**	**7.8469**	**9.5545**	**6.6408**
Average	4.8351	2.9753	2.0099	2.6636	6.1206	4.8769
High	7.1662	2.5920	1.3312	11.3068	19.1304	9.2959
Low	5.0955	2.3038		3.7787	2.4605	4.4731
Value	**5.1254**	**6.3287**	**12.2188**	**5.7936**	**6.2446**	**5.6783**
Average	4.0668	1.5839	#DIV/0!	3.6059	1.6793	3.7904
High	4.2796	5.2043	#DIV/0!	5.2196	5.4922	5.0234
Low	3.7995	3.5798		5.4001	4.0305	3.7109
Grand Total	**5.8714**	**5.1707**	**6.3429**	**7.3224**	**8.5398**	**6.4263**

(c) The mean three-year return of the average-risk or low-risk growth funds is generally higher than that of the value funds. The mean of the high-risk growth funds is higher than the value funds only for those with two-star or three-star ratings. The standard deviation of the three-year return of growth funds is generally higher than that of the value funds across the various risk levels and star ratings with the exception of the four-star high-risk, two-star, three-star, or four-star low-risk funds.

3.28 (a) 4, 9, 5. **(b)** 3, 4, 7, 9, 12. **(c)** The distances between the median and the extremes are close, 4 and 5, but the differences in the tails are different (1 on the left and 3 on the right), so this distribution is slightly right-skewed. **(d)** In Problem 3.2 (d), because mean = median, the distribution is symmetric. The box part of the graph is symmetric, but the tails show right-skewness.

3.30 (a) −6.5, 8, 14.5. **(b)** −8, −6.5, 7, 8, 9. **(c)** The shape is left-skewed. **(d)** This is consistent with the answer in Problem 3.4 (d).

3.32 (a), (b)

Five-Number Summary	
Minimum	4.25
First Quartile	28.29
Median	37.52
Third Quartile	46.04
Maximum	52.24
Interquartile Range	17.75

The penetration value is left-skewed.

3.34 (a), (b)

Five-Number Summary	
Minimum	16
First Quartile	21
Median	22
Third Quartile	23
Maximum	26
Interquartile Range	2

(c) The MPG is left-skewed.

3.36 (a) Commercial district five-number summary: 0.38 3.2 4.5 5.55 6.46. Residential area five-number summary: 3.82 5.64 6.68 8.73 10.49. **(b)** Commercial district: The distribution is left-skewed. Residential area: The distribution is slightly right-skewed. **(c)** The central tendency of the waiting times for the bank branch located in the commercial district of a city is lower than that of the branch located in the residential area. There are a few long waiting times for the branch located in the residential area, whereas there are a few exceptionally short waiting times for the branch located in the commercial area.

3.38 (a) Population mean, $\mu = 6$. **(b)** Population standard deviation, $\sigma = 1.673$, population variance, $\sigma^2 = 2.8$.

3.40 (a) 68%. **(b)** 95%. **(c)** Not calculable, 75%, 88.89%. **(d)** $\mu - 4\sigma$ to $\mu + 4\sigma$ or −2.8 to 19.2.

3.42 (a)

$$\text{Mean} = \frac{662{,}960}{51} = 12{,}999.22, \text{ variance} = \frac{762{,}944{,}726.6}{51} = 14{,}959{,}700.52,$$

standard deviation $= \sqrt{14{,}959{,}700.52} = 3{,}867.78$. **(b)** 64.71%, 98.04%, and 100% of these states have mean per capita energy consumption within 1, 2, and 3 standard deviations of the mean, respectively. **(c)** This is consistent with 68%, 95%, and 99.7%, according to the empirical rule. **(d) (a)** Mean $= \frac{642{,}887}{50} = 12{,}857.74$, variance $= \frac{711{,}905{,}533.6}{50} = 14{,}238{,}110.67$, standard deviation $= \sqrt{14{,}238{,}110.67} = 3{,}773.34$. **(b)** 66%, 98%, and 100% of these states have a mean per capita energy consumption within 1, 2, and 3 standard deviations of the mean, respectively. **(c)** This is consistent with 68%, 95%, and 99.7%, according to the empirical rule.

3.44 Covariance = 65.2909, $r = +1.0$.

3.46 (a) $$\text{cov}(X, Y) = \frac{\sum_{i=1}^{n}(X_i - \bar{X})(Y_i - \bar{Y})}{n-1} = \frac{800}{6} = 133.3333.$$

(b) $$r = \frac{\text{cov}(X, Y)}{S_X S_Y} = \frac{133.3333}{(46.9042)(3.3877)} = 0.8391.$$

(c) The correlation coefficient is more valuable for expressing the relationship between calories and sugar because it does not depend on the units used to measure calories and sugar. **(d)** There is a strong positive linear relationship between calories and sugar.

3.48 (a) $\text{cov}(X, Y) = 4{,}473{,}270.3$ **(b)** $r = 0.7903$ **(c)** There is a positive linear relationship between the coaches' salary and revenue.

3.64 (a) Mean = 43.89, median = 45, 1st quartile = 18, 3rd quartile = 63. **(b)** Range = 76, interquartile range = 45, variance = 639.2564, standard deviation = 25.28, $CV = 57.61\%$. **(c)** The distribution is right-skewed because there are a few policies that require an exceptionally long period to be approved. **(d)** The mean approval process takes 43.89 days, with 50% of the policies being approved in less than 45 days. 50% of the applications are approved between 18 and 63 days. About 67% of the applications are approved between 18.6 and 69.2 days.

3.66 (a) Mean = 8.421, median = 8.42, range = 0.186, $S = 0.0461$. The mean and median width are both 8.42 inches. The range of the widths is 0.186 inch, and the average scatter around the mean is 0.0461 inch. **(b)** 8.312, 8.404, 8.42, 8.459, 8.498. **(c)** Even though the mean = median, the left tail is slightly longer, so the distribution is slightly left-skewed. **(d)** All the troughs in this sample meet the specifications.

3.68 (a), (b)

	Bundle Score	*Typical Cost ($)*
Mean	54.775	24.175
Standard Error	4.3673	2.8662
Median	62	20
Mode	75	8
Standard Deviation	27.6215	328.6096
Sample Variance	762.9481	18.1276
Kurtosis	−0.8454	2.7664
Skewness	−0.4804	1.5412
Range	98	83
Minimum	2	5
Maximum	100	88
Sum	2191	967
Count	40	40
First Quartile	34	9
Third Quartile	75	31
Interquartile Range	41	22
CV	50.43%	74.98%

(c) The typical cost is right-skewed, while the bundle score is left-skewed. **(d)** $r = 0.3465$. **(e)** The mean typical cost is $24.18, with an average spread around the mean equaling $18.13. The spread between the lowest and highest costs is $83. The middle 50% of the typical cost fall over a range of $22 from $9 to $31, while half of the typical cost is below $20. The mean bundle score is 54.775, with an average spread around the mean equaling 27.6215. The spread between the lowest and highest scores is 98. The middle 50% of the scores fall over a range of 41 from 34 to 75, while half of the scores are below 62. The typical cost is right-skewed, while the bundle score is left-skewed. There is a weak positive linear relationship between typical cost and bundle score.

3.70 (a) Boston: 0.04, 0.17, 0.23, 0.32, 0.98; Vermont: 0.02, 0.13, 0.20, 0.28, 0.83. **(b)** Both distributions are right-skewed. **(c)** Both sets of shingles did quite well in achieving a granule loss of 0.8 gram or less. Only two Boston shingles had a granule loss greater than 0.8 gram. The next highest to these was 0.6 gram. These two values can be considered outliers. Only 1.176% of the shingles failed the specification. Only one of the Vermont shingles had a granule loss greater than 0.8 gram. The next highest was 0.58 gram. Thus, only 0.714% of the shingles failed to meet the specification.

3.72 (a) The correlation between calories and protein is 0.4644. **(b)** The correlation between calories and cholesterol is 0.1777. **(c)** The correlation between protein and cholesterol is 0.1417. **(d)** There is a weak positive linear relationship between calories and protein, with a correlation coefficient of 0.46. The positive linear relationships between calories and cholesterol and between protein and cholesterol are very weak.

3.74 (a), (b)

	Property Taxes per Capita ($)
Mean	1,040.863
Median	981
Standard deviation	428.5385
Sample variance	183,645.2
Range	1,732
First quartile	713
Third quartile	1,306
Interquartile range	593
Coefficient of variation	41.17%

(c), (d) The distribution of the property taxes per capita is right-skewed, with a mean value of $1,040.83, a median of $981, and an average spread around the mean of $428.54. There is an outlier in the right tail at $2,099, while the standard deviation is about 41.17% of the mean. 25% of the states have property tax that falls below $713 per capita, and 25% have property taxes that are higher than $1,306 per capita.

CHAPTER 4

4.2 (a) Simple events include selecting a red ball. **(b)** Selecting a white ball. **(c)** The sample space consists of the 12 red balls and the 8 white balls.

4.4 (a) $60/100 = 3/5 = 0.6$. **(b)** $10/100 = 1/10 = 0.1$. **(c)** $35/100 = 7/20 = 0.35$. **(d)** $9/10 = 0.9$.

4.6 (a) Mutually exclusive, not collectively exhaustive. **(b)** Not mutually exclusive, not collectively exhaustive. **(c)** Mutually exclusive, not collectively exhaustive. **(d)** Mutually exclusive, collectively exhaustive.

4.8 (a) Needs three or more clicks to be removed from an email list. **(b)** Needs three or more clicks to be removed from an email list in 2009. **(c)** Does not need three or more clicks to be removed from an email list. **(d)** "Needs three or more clicks to be removed from an email list in 2009" is a joint event because it consists of two characteristics.

4.10 (a) A marketer who plans to increase use of LinkedIn. **(b)** A B2B marketer who plans to increase use of LinkedIn. **(c)** A marketer who does not plan to increase use of LinkedIn. **(d)** A marketer who plans to increase use of LinkedIn and is a B2C marketer is a joint event because it consists of two characteristics, plans to increase use of LinkedIn and is a B2C marketer.

4.12 (a) $512/660 = 0.7758$. **(b)** $281/660 = 0.4258$. **(c)** $512/660 + 281/660 - 216/660 = 577/660 = 0.8742$. **(d)** The probability of saying that analyzing data is critical *or* is a manager includes the probability of saying that analyzing data is critical plus the probability of being a manager minus the joint probability of saying that analyzing data is critical *and* is a manager.

4.14 (a) $514/1{,}085$. **(b)** $76/1{,}085$. **(c)** $781/1{,}085$. **(d)** $1{,}085/1{,}085 = 1.00$.

4.16 (a) $10/30 = 1/3 = 0.33$. **(b)** $20/60 = 1/3 = 0.33$. **(c)** $40/60 = 2/3 = 0.67$. **(d)** Because $P(A|B) = P(A) = 1/3$, events A and B are independent.

4.18 $\frac{1}{2} = 0.5$.

4.20 Because $P(A \text{ and } B) = 0.20$ and $P(A)P(B) = 0.12$, events A and B are not independent.

4.22 (a) $1,478/1,945 = 0.7599$. **(b)** $1,027/1,868 = 0.5498$.
(c) P(Increased use of LinkedIn) $= 2,505/3,813 = 0.6570$, which is not equal to P(Increased use of LinkedIn | B2B) $= 0.7599$. Therefore, increased use of LinkedIn and business focus are not independent.

4.24 (a) $296/379 = 0.7810$. **(b)** $83/379 = 0.2190$.
(c) $216/281 = 0.7687$. **(d)** $65/281 = 0.2313$.

4.26 (a) $0.025/0.6 = 0.0417$. **(b)** $0.015/0.4 = 0.0375$. **(c)** Because P(Needs warranty repair | Manufacturer based in U.S.) $= 0.0417$ and P(Needs warranty repair) $= 0.04$, the two events are not independent.

4.28 (a) 0.0045. **(b)** 0.012. **(c)** 0.0059. **(d)** 0.0483.

4.30 0.095.

4.32 (a) 0.736. **(b)** 0.997.

4.34 (a) $P(B'|O) = \dfrac{(0.5)(0.3)}{(0.5)(0.3) + (0.25)(0.7)} = 0.4615$.
(b) $P(O) = 0.175 + 0.15 = 0.325$.

4.36 (a) P(Huge success | Favorable review) $= 0.099/0.459 = 0.2157$;
P(Moderate success | Favorable review) $= 0.14/0.459 = 0.3050$;
P(Break even | Favorable review) $= 0.16/0.459 = 0.3486$;
P(Loser | Favorable review) $= 0.06/0.459 = 0.1307$.
(b) P(Favorable review) $= 0.459$.

4.46 (a)

SHARE HEALTH INFORMATION	AGE		
	18–24	45–64	Total
Yes	400	225	625
No	100	275	375
Total	500	500	1,000

(b) Simple event: "Shares health information through social media." Joint event: "Shares health information through social media and is between 18 and 24 years old." **(c)** P(Shares health information through social media) $= 675/1,000 = 0.675$. **(d)** P(Shares health information through social media and is in the 45-to-64-year-old group) $= 225/1000 = 0.225$. **(e)** Not independent.

4.48 (a) 84/200. **(b)** 126/200. **(c)** 141/200. **(d)** 33/200. **(f)** 16/100.

4.50 (a) 0.4712. **(b)** Because the probability that a fatality involved a rollover, given that the fatality involved an SUV, a van, or a pickup is 0.4712, which is almost twice the probability that a fatality involved a rollover with any vehicle type, at 0.24, SUVs, vans, and pickups are generally more prone to rollover accidents.

CHAPTER 5

5.2 (a)
$\mu = 0(0.10) + 1(0.20) + 2(0.45) + 3(0.15) + 4(0.05) + 5(0.05) = 2.0$.

(b) $\sigma = \sqrt{\begin{matrix}(0-2)^2(0.10) + (1-2)^2(0.20) + (2-2)^2(0.45) + \\ (3-2)^2(0.15) + (4-2)^2(0.05) + (5-2)^2(0.05)\end{matrix}} = 1.183$.

5.4 (a)

X	$P(X)$
\$−1	21/36
\$+1	15/36

(b)

X	$P(X)$
\$−1	21/36
\$ + 1	15/36

(c)

X	$P(X)$
\$−1	30/36
\$ + 4	6/36

(d) −\$0.167 for each method of play.

5.6 (a) 2.1058. **(b)** 1.4671.

5.8 (a) 90; 30. **(b)** 126.10, 10.95. **(c)** −1,300. **(d)** 120.

5.10 (a) 9.5 minutes. **(b)** 1.9209 minutes.

5.12

$X \times P(X)$	$Y \times P(Y)$	$(X-\mu_X)^2\ P(X)$	$(Y-\mu_Y)^2\ P(Y)$	$(X-\mu_X)(Y-\mu_Y) \times P(XY)$
−10	5	2,528.1	129.6	−572.4
0	45	1,044.3	5,548.8	−2,407.2
24	−6	132.3	346.8	−214.2
45	−30	2,484.3	3,898.8	−3,112.2

(a) $E(X) = \mu_X = \sum_{i-1}^{N} X_iP(X_i) = 59$, $E(Y) = \mu_Y = \sum_{i-1}^{N} Y_iP(Y_i) = 14$.

(b) $\sigma_X = \sqrt{\sum_{i-1}^{N}[X_i - E(X)]^2P(X_i)} = 78.6702$.

$\sigma_Y = \sqrt{\sum_{i=1}^{N}[Y_i - E(Y)]^2P(Y_i)} = 99.62$.

(c) $\sigma_{XY} = \sum_{i=1}^{N}[X_i - E(X)][Y_i - E(Y)]P(X_iY_i) = -6,306$.

(d) Stock X gives the investor a lower standard deviation while yielding a higher expected return, so the investor should select stock X.

5.14 (a) \$71; \$97. **(b)** 61.88; 84.27. **(c)** 5,113. **(d)** Risk-averse investors would invest in stock X, whereas risk takers would invest in stock Y.

5.16 (a) $E(X) = \$66.20$; $E(Y) = \$63.01$. **(b)** $\sigma_X = \$57.22$; $\sigma_Y = \$195.22$. **(c)** $\sigma_{XY} = \$10,766.44$. **(d)** Based on the expected value criteria, you would choose the common stock fund. However, the common stock fund also has a standard deviation more than three times higher than that for the corporate bond fund. An investor should carefully weigh the increased risk. **(e)** If you chose the common stock fund, you would need to assess your reaction to the small possibility that you could lose virtually all of your entire investment.

5.18 (a) 0.0768. **(b)** 0.9130. **(c)** 0.3370. **(d)** 0.6630.

5.20 (a) 0.40, 0.60. **(b)** 1.60, 0.98. **(c)** 4.0, 0.894. **(d)** 1.50, 0.866.

5.22 (a) 0.0214. **(b)** 0.0001. **(c)** 0.0239. **(d)** $\mu = 1.32$, $\sigma = 1.01477$.
(e) Each adult 55 or older either owns a smartphone or does not own a smartphone and that each person surveyed is independent of every other person.

5.24 (a) 0.5987. **(b)** 0.3151. **(c)** 0.9885. **(d)** 0.0115.

5.26 (a) 0.7217. **(b)** 0.0011. **(c)** 0.9704. **(d)** $\mu = 2.691$, $\sigma = 0.5265$.

5.28 (a) 0.2565. **(b)** 0.1396. **(c)** 0.3033. **(d)** 0.0247.

5.30 (a) 0.0337. **(b)** 0.0067. **(c)** 0.9596. **(d)** 0.0404.

5.32 (a)
$$\begin{aligned} P(X < 5) &= P(X = 0) + P(X = 1) + P(x = 2) + P(X = 3) \\ &\quad + P(X = 4) \\ &= \frac{e^{-6}(6)^0}{0!} + \frac{e^{-6}(6)^1}{1!} + \frac{e^{-6}(6)^2}{2!} + \frac{e^{-6}(6)^3}{3!} + \frac{e^{-6}(6)^4}{4!} \\ &= 0.002479 + 0.014873 + 0.044618 + 0.089235 \\ &\quad + 0.133853 \\ &= 0.2851. \end{aligned}$$

(b) $P(X = 5) = \dfrac{e^{-6}(6)^5}{5!} = 0.1606.$

(c) $P(X \geq 5) = 1 - P(X < 5) = 1 - 0.2851 = 0.7149.$

(d) $P(X = 4 \text{ or } X = 5) = P(X = 4) + P(X = 5) = \dfrac{e^{-6}(6)^4}{4!} + \dfrac{e^{-6}(6)^5}{5!}$
$= 0.2945.$

5.34 (a) 0.1451. **(b)** 0.8549. **(c)** 0.5747.

5.36 (a) 0.0176. **(b)** 0.9093. **(c)** 0.9220.

5.38 (a) 0.4148. **(b)** 0.9404. **(c)** Because Ford had a higher mean rate of problems per car in 2012 than Toyota, the probability of a randomly selected Ford having zero problems and the probability of no more than two problems are both lower than for Toyota.

5.40 (a) 0.3642 **(b)** 0.9179. **(c)** Because Toyota had a lower mean rate of problems per car in 2012 compared to 2011, the probability of a randomly selected Toyota having zero problems and the probability of no more than two problems are both lower in 2011 than in 2012.

5.42 (a) 0.238. **(b)** 0.2. **(c)** 0.1591. **(d)** 0.0083.

5.44 (a) If $n = 6, A = 25$, and $N = 100$,

$$P(X \geq 2) = 1 - [P(X = 0) + P(X = 1)]$$
$$= 1 - \left[\frac{\binom{25}{0}\binom{100-25}{6-0}}{\binom{100}{6}} + \frac{\binom{25}{1}\binom{100-25}{6-1}}{\binom{100}{6}}\right]$$
$$= 1 - [0.1689 + 0.3620] = 0.4691.$$

(b) If $n = 6, A = 30$, and $N = 100$,

$$P(X \geq 2) = 1 - [P(X = 0) + P(X = 1)]$$
$$= 1 - \left[\frac{\binom{30}{0}\binom{100-30}{6-0}}{\binom{100}{6}} + \frac{\binom{30}{1}\binom{100-30}{6-1}}{\binom{100}{6}}\right]$$
$$= 1 - [0.1100 + 0.3046] = 0.5854.$$

(c) If $n = 6, A = 5$, and $N = 100$,

$$P(X \geq 2) = 1 - [P(X = 0) + P(X = 1)]$$
$$= 1 - \left[\frac{\binom{5}{0}\binom{100-5}{6-0}}{\binom{100}{6}} + \frac{\binom{5}{1}\binom{100-5}{6-1}}{\binom{100}{6}}\right]$$
$$= 1 - [0.7291 + 0.2430] = 0.0279.$$

(d) If $n = 6, A = 10$, and $N = 100$,

$$P(X \geq 2) = 1 - [P(X = 0) + P(X = 1)]$$
$$= 1 - \left[\frac{\binom{10}{0}\binom{100-10}{-0\ \ 6}}{\binom{100}{6}} + \frac{\binom{10}{1}\binom{100-10}{6-1}}{\binom{100}{6}}\right]$$
$$= 1 - [0.5223 + 0.3687] = 0.1090.$$

(e) The probability that the entire group will be audited is very sensitive to the true number of improper returns in the population. If the true number is very low ($A = 5$), the probability is very low (0.0279). When the true number is increased by a factor of 6 ($A = 30$), the probability the group will be audited increases by a factor of more than 20 (0.5854).

5.46 (a) $P(X = 4) = 0.00003649$. **(b)** $P(X = 0) = 0.5455$. **(c)** $P(X \geq 1) = 0.4545$. **(d)** $X = 6$. **(a)** $P(X = 4) = 0.0005$. **(b)** $P(X = 0) = 0.3877$. **(c)** $P(X \geq 1) = 0.6123$.

5.48 (a) $P(X = 1) = 0.2424$. **(b)** $P(X \geq 1) = 0.9697$. **(c)** $P(X = 3) = 0.2424$. **(d)** Because there were now 12 funds to consider, the probability that 3 would be growth funds decreased from 0.3810 to 0.2424.

5.54 (a) 0.64. **(b)** 0.64. **(c)** 0.3020. **(d)** 0.0060. **(e)** The assumption of independence may not be true.

5.56 (a) If $\pi = 0.50$ and $n = 12$, $P(X \geq 9) = 0.0730$. **(b)** If $\pi = 0.75$ and $n = 12$, $P(X \geq 9) = 0.6488$.

5.58 (a) 0.0060. **(b)** 0.2007. **(c)** 0.1662. **(d)** Mean = 4.0, standard deviation = 1.5492. **(e)** Since the percentage of bills containing an error is lower in this problem, the probability is higher in (a) and (b) of this problem and lower in (c).

5.60 (a) $\mu = n\pi = 13.6$ **(b)** $\sigma = \sqrt{n\pi(1-\rho)} = 2.0861$. **(c)** $P(X = 15) = 0.1599$. **(d)** $P(X \leq 10) = 0.0719$. **(e)** $P(X \geq 10) = 0.9721$.

5.62 (a) If $\pi = 0.50$ and $n = 39$, $P(X \geq 34) = 0.00000121$. **(b)** If $\pi = 0.70$ and $n = 39$, $P(X \geq 34) = 0.0109$. **(c)** If $\pi = 0.90$ and $n = 39$, $P(X \geq 34) = 0.8097$. **(d)** Based on the results in (a)–(c), the probability that the Standard & Poor's 500 Index will increase if there is an early gain in the first five trading days of the year is very likely to be close to 0.90 because that yields a probability of 80.97% that at least 34 of the 39 years the Standard & Poor's 500 Index will increase the entire year.

5.64 (a) The assumptions needed are (i) the probability that a golfer loses a golf ball in a given interval is constant, (ii) the probability that a golfer loses more than one golf ball approaches 0 as the interval gets smaller, and (iii) the probability that a golfer loses a golf ball is independent from interval to interval. **(b)** 0.0067. **(c)** 0.6160. **(d)** 0.3840.

CHAPTER 6

6.2 (a) 0.9089. **(b)** 0.0911. **(c)** +1.96. **(d)** −1.00 and +1.00.

6.4 (a) 0.1401. **(b)** 0.4168. **(c)** 0.3918. **(d)** +1.00.

6.6 (a) 0.9599. **(b)** 0.0228. **(c)** 43.42. **(d)** 46.64 and 53.36.

6.8 (a) $P(34 < X < 50) = P(-1.33 < Z < 0) = 0.4082$. **(b)** $P(X < 30) + P(X > 60) = P(Z < -1.67) + P(Z > 0.83) = 0.0475 + (1.0 - 0.7967) = 0.2508$. **(c)** $P(Z < -0.84) \cong 0.20$, $Z = -0.84 = \dfrac{X - 50}{12}$, $X = 50 - 0.84(12) = 39.92$ thousand miles, or 39,920 miles. **(d)** The smaller standard deviation makes the absolute Z values larger. **(a)** $P(34 < X < 50) = P(-1.60 < Z < 0) = 0.4452$. **(b)** $P(X < 30) + P(X > 60) = P(Z < -2.00) + P(Z > 1.00) = 0.0228 + (1.0 - 0.8413) = 0.1815$. **(c)** $X = 50 - 0.84(10) = 41.6$ thousand miles, or 41,600 miles.

6.10 (a) 0.9878. **(b)** 0.8185. **(c)** 86.16%. **(d)** Option 1: Because your score of 81% on this exam represents a Z score of 1.00, which is below the minimum Z score of 1.28, you will not earn an A grade on the exam under this grading option. Option 2: Because your score of 68% on this exam represents a Z score of 2.00, which is well above the minimum Z score of 1.28, you will earn an A grade on the exam under this grading option. You should prefer Option 2.

6.12 (a) 0.8847. **(b)** 0.0093. **(c)** 0.0139. **(d)** 27.63.

6.14 With 39 values, the smallest of the standard normal quantile values covers an area under the normal curve of 0.025. The corresponding Z value is −1.96. The middle (20th) value has a cumulative area of 0.50 and a corresponding Z value of 0.0. The largest of the standard normal quantile values covers an area under the normal curve of 0.975, and its corresponding Z value is +1.96.

6.16 (a) Mean = 21.61, median = 22, $S = 2.1731$, range = 10, $6S = 6(2.1731) = 13.0386$, interquartile range = 2.0, 1.33(2.1731) = 2.8861. The mean is slightly less than the median. The range is much less than $6S$, and the interquartile range is less than $1.33S$. **(b)** The normal probability plot appears to be left-skewed. The kurtosis is 2.0493, indicating a distribution that is more peaked than a normal distribution, with more values in the tails.

6.18 (a) Mean $= 1{,}323.784$, median $= 1{,}239$, range $= 2{,}443$, $6(S) = 3{,}378.1338$, interquartile range $= 712{,}1.33(S) = 748.82$. Because the mean is slightly larger than the median, the interquartile range is slightly less than 1.33 times the standard deviation, and the range is much smaller than 6 times the standard deviation, the data appear to deviate from the normal distribution. **(b)** The normal probability plot suggests that the data appear to be right-skewed. The kurtosis is 0.5151 indicating a distribution that is slightly more peaked than a normal distribution, with more values in the tails.

6.20 (a) Interquartile range $= 0.0025$, $S = 0.0017$, range $= 0.008$, $1.33(S) = 0.0023$, $6(S) = 0.0102$. Because the interquartile range is close to $1.33S$ and the range is also close to $6S$, the data appear to be approximately normally distributed. **(b)** The normal probability plot suggests that the data appear to be approximately normally distributed.

6.22 (a) Five-number summary: 82 127 148.5 168 213; mean $= 147.06$, mode $= 130$, range $= 131$, interquartile range $= 41$, standard deviation $= 31.69$. The mean is very close to the median. The five-number summary suggests that the distribution is approximately symmetric around the median. The interquartile range is very close to $1.33S$. The range is about \$50 below $6S$. In general, the distribution of the data appears to closely resemble a normal distribution. **(b)** The normal probability plot confirms that the data appear to be approximately normally distributed.

6.24 (a) $(20-0)/120 = 0.1667$. **(b)** $(30-10)/120 = 0.1667$. **(c)** $(120-35)/120 = 0.7083$. **(d)** Mean $= 60$, standard deviation $= 34.641$.

6.26 (a) 0.10. **(b)** 0.25. **(c)** 0.25. **(d)** Mean $= 50$, standard deviation $= 1.8257$.

6.28 (a) 0.6321. **(b)** 0.3679. **(c)** 0.2326. **(d)** 0.7674.

6.30 (a) 0.7769. **(b)** 0.2231. **(c)** 0.1410. **(d)** 0.8590.

6.32 (a) For $\lambda = 2$, $P(X \le 1) = 0.8647$. **(b)** For $\lambda = 2$, $P(X \le 5) = 0.99996$. **(c)** For $\lambda = 1$, $P(X \le 1) = 0.6321$, for $\lambda = 1$, $P(X \le 5) = 0.9933$.

6.34 (a) 0.6321. **(b)** 0.3935. **(c)** 0.0952.

6.36 (a) 0.8647. **(b)** 0.3297. **(c)(a)** 0.9765. **(b)** 0.5276.

6.46 (a) 0.4772. **(b)** 0.9544. **(c)** 0.0456. **(d)** 1.8835. **(e)** 1.8710 and 2.1290.

6.48 (a) 0.2734. **(b)** 0.2038. **(c)** 4.404 ounces. **(d)** 4.188 ounces and 5.212 ounces.

6.50 (a) Waiting time will more closely resemble an exponential distribution. **(b)** Seating time will more closely resemble a normal distribution. **(c)** Both the histogram and normal probability plot suggest that waiting time more closely resembles an exponential distribution. **(d)** Both the histogram and normal probability plot suggest that seating time more closely resembles a normal distribution.

6.52 (a) 0.0426. **(b)** 0.0731. **(c)** 0.9696. **(d)** 7.2613. **(e)** 1.6891 to 6.7850. **(f)** 0.125, 0.125, 0.90, 1.08, 1.2 to 8.8.

CHAPTER 7

7.2 (a) Virtually 0. **(b)** 0.1587. **(c)** 0.0139. **(d)** 50.195.

7.4 (a) Both means are equal to 6. This property is called unbiasedness. **(c)** The distribution for $n = 3$ has less variability. The larger sample size has resulted in sample means being closer to μ.

7.6 (a) When $n = 2$, because the mean is larger than the median, the distribution of the sales price of new houses is skewed to the right, and so is the sampling distribution of $\overline{X}$ although it will be less skewed than the population. **(b)** If you select samples of $n = 100$, the shape of the sampling distribution of the sample mean will be very close to a normal distribution, with a mean of \$267,900 and a standard deviation of \$9,000. **(c)** 0.9998. **(d)** 0.2081.

7.8 (a) $P(\overline{X} > 3) = P(Z > -1.00) = 1.0 - 0.1587 = 0.8413$. **(b)** $P(Z < 1.04) = 0.85$; $\overline{X} = 3.10 + 1.04(0.1) = 3.204$. **(c)** To be able to use the standardized normal distribution as an approximation for the area under the curve, you must assume that the population is approximately symmetrical. **(d)** $P(Z < 1.04) = 0.85$; $\overline{X} = 3.10 + 1.04(0.05) = 3.152$.

7.10 (a) 0.40. **(b)** 0.0704.

7.12 (a) $\pi = 0.501$, $\sigma_p = \sqrt{\dfrac{\pi(1-\pi)}{n}} = \sqrt{\dfrac{0.501(1-0.501)}{100}} = 0.05$

$$P(p > 0.55) = P(Z > 0.98) = 1.0 - 0.8365 = 0.1635.$$

(b) $\pi = 0.60$, $\sigma_p = \sqrt{\dfrac{\pi(1-\pi)}{n}} = \sqrt{\dfrac{0.6(1-0.6)}{100}} = 0.04899$

$$P(p > 0.55) = P(Z > -1.021) = 1.0 - 0.1539 = 0.8461.$$

(c) $\pi = 0.49$, $\sigma_p = \sqrt{\dfrac{\pi(1-\pi)}{n}} = \sqrt{\dfrac{0.49(1-0.49)}{100}} = 0.05$

$$P(p > 0.55) = P(Z > 1.20) = 1.0 - 0.8849 = 0.1151.$$

(d) Increasing the sample size by a factor of 4 decreases the standard error by a factor of 2.
(a) $P(p > 0.55) = P(Z > 1.96) = 1.0 - 0.9750 = 0.0250$.
(b) $P(p > 0.55) = P(Z > -2.04) = 1.0 - 0.0207 = 0.9793$.
(c) $P(p > 0.55) = P(Z > 2.40) = 1.0 - 0.9918 = 0.0082$.

7.14 (a) 0.7889. **(b)** 0.6746. **(c)** 0.8857. **(d) (a)** 0.9458. **(b)** 0.9377. **(c)** 0.9920.

7.16 (a) 0.3741. **(b)** The probability is 90% that the sample percentage will be contained between 0.0870 to 0.0.1646. **(c)** The probability is 95% that the sample percentage will be contained between 0.08 and 0.172.

7.18 (a) 0.0336. **(b)** 0.0000. **(c)** Increasing the sample size by a factor of 5 decreases the standard error by a factor of $\sqrt{5}$. The sampling distribution of the proportion becomes more concentrated around the true proportion of 0.59 and, hence, the probability in (b) becomes smaller than that in (a).

7.24 (a) 0.4999. **(b)** 0.00009. **(c)** 0. **(d)** 0. **(e)** 0.7518.

7.26 (a) 0.8944. **(b)** 4.617; 4.783. **(c)** 4.641.

7.28 (a) 0.7764. **(b)** 0.8896. **(c)** 0.0029.

CHAPTER 8

8.2 $114.68 \le \mu \le 135.32$.

8.4 Yes, it is true because 5% of intervals will not include the population mean.

8.6 (a) You would compute the mean first because you need the mean to compute the standard deviation. If you had a sample, you would compute the sample mean. If you had the population mean, you would compute the population standard deviation. **(b)** If you have a sample, you are computing the sample standard deviation, not the population standard deviation needed in Equation (8.1). If you have a population and have computed the population mean and population standard deviation, you don't need a confidence interval estimate of the population mean because you already know the mean.

8.8 Equation (8.1) assumes that you know the population standard deviation. Because you are selecting a sample of 100 from the population, you are computing a sample standard deviation, not the population standard deviation.

8.10 (a) $\bar{X} \pm Z \cdot \frac{\sigma}{\sqrt{n}} = 350 \pm 1.96 \cdot \frac{100}{\sqrt{64}}$; $325.50 \leq \mu \leq 374.50$. **(b)** No, the manufacturer cannot support a claim that the bulbs have a mean of 400 hours. Based on the data from the sample, a mean of 400 hours would represent a distance of 4 standard deviations above the sample mean of 350 hours. **(c)** No. Because σ is known and $n = 64$, from the Central Limit Theorem, you know that the sampling distribution of $\bar{X}$ is approximately normal. **(d)** The confidence interval is narrower, based on a population standard deviation of 80 hours rather than the original standard deviation of 100 hours. $\bar{X} \pm Z \times \frac{\sigma}{\sqrt{n}} = 350 \pm 1.96 \times \frac{80}{\sqrt{64}}$, $330.4 \leq \mu \leq 369.6$. Based on the smaller standard deviation, a mean of 400 hours would represent a distance of 5 standard deviations above the sample mean of 350 hours. No, the manufacturer cannot support a claim that the bulbs have a mean life of 400 hours.

8.12 (a) 2.2622. **(b)** 3.2498. **(c)** 2.0395. **(d)** 1.9977. **(e)** 1.7531.

8.14 $-0.12 \leq \mu \leq 11.84$, $2.00 \leq \mu \leq 6.00$. The presence of the outlier increases the sample mean and greatly inflates the sample standard deviation.

8.16 (a) $62 \pm (2.0010)(9)/\sqrt{60}$; $59.68 \leq \mu \leq 64.32$ **(b)** The quality improvement team can be 95% confident that the population mean turnaround time is between 29.44 hours and 34.56 hours. **(c)** The project was a success because the initial turnaround time of 68 hours does not fall within the interval.

8.18 (a) $6.31 \leq \mu \leq 7.87$. **(b)** You can be 95% confident that the population mean amount spent for lunch at a fast-food restaurant is between \$6.31 and \$7.87.

8.20 (a) $20.53 \leq \mu \leq 22.69$. **(b)** You can be 95% confident that the population mean miles per gallon of 2012 small SUVs is between 20.53 and 22.69. **(c)** Because the 95% confidence interval for population mean miles per gallon of 2012 small SUVs overlaps with that for the population mean miles per gallon of 2012 family sedans, you are unable to conclude that the population mean miles per gallon of 2012 small SUVs is lower than that of 2012 family sedans.

8.22 (a) $31.12 \leq \mu \leq 54.96$. **(b)** The number of days is approximately normally distributed. **(c)** No, the outliers skew the data. **(d)** Because the sample size is fairly large, at $n = 50$, the use of the t distribution is appropriate.

8.24 (a) $27.70 \leq \mu \leq 41.95$. **(b)** That the population distribution is normally distributed. **(c)** Both the normal probability plot and the boxplot show that the distribution of the Facebook penetration is left-skewed, so with the small sample size, the validity of the confidence interval is in question.

8.26 $0.19 \leq \pi \leq 0.31$.

8.28 (a) $p = \frac{X}{n} = \frac{135}{500} = 0.27, p \pm Z\sqrt{\frac{p(1-p)}{n}} = 0.27 \pm 2.58\sqrt{\frac{0.27(0.73)}{500}}$; $0.2189 \leq \pi \leq 0.3211$. **(b)** The manager in charge of promotional programs can infer that the proportion of households that would upgrade to an improved cellphone if it were made available at a substantially reduced cost is somewhere between 0.22 and 0.32, with 99% confidence.

8.30 (a) $0.4863 \leq \pi \leq 0.5737$. **(b)** No, you cannot because the interval estimate includes 0.50 (50%). **(c)** $0.5162 \leq \pi \leq 0.5438$. Yes, you can, because the interval is above 0.50 (50%). **(d)** The larger the sample size, the narrower the confidence interval, holding everything else constant.

8.32 (a) $0.3587 \leq \pi \leq 0.4018$. **(b)** $0.2017 \leq \pi \leq 0.2384$. **(c)** Many more people use their phone to keep themselves occupied during commercials or breaks in something they were watching on television.

8.34 $n = 35$.

8.36 $n = 1{,}041$.

8.38 (a) $n = \frac{Z^2\sigma^2}{e^2} = \frac{(1.96)^2(400)^2}{50^2} = 245.86$. Use $n = 246$.

(b) $n = \frac{Z^2\sigma^2}{e^2} = \frac{(1.96)^2(400)^2}{25^2} = 983.41$. Use $n = 984$.

8.40 $n = 97$.

8.42 (a) $n = 167$. **(b)** $n = 97$.

8.44 (a) $n = 246$. **(b)** $n = 385$. **(c)** $n = 554$. **(d)** When there is more variability in the population, a larger sample is needed to accurately estimate the mean.

8.46 (a) $p = 0.18$; $0.1365 \leq \pi \leq 0.2235$. **(b)** $p = 0.13$; $0.0919 \leq \pi \leq 0.1681$. **(c)** $p = 0.09$; $0.0576 \leq \pi \leq 0.1224$. **(d) (a)** $n = 1{,}418$. **(b)** $n = 1{,}087$. **(c)** $n = 787$.

8.48 (a) If you conducted a follow-up study to estimate the population proportion of individuals who say that banking on their mobile device is convenient, you would use $\pi = 0.77$ in the sample size formula because it is based on past information on the proportion. **(b)** $n = 756$.

8.54 (a) $p = 0.88$; $0.8667 \leq \pi \leq 0.8936$
$p = 0.58$; $0.5597 \leq \pi \leq 0.6005$.
$p = 0.61$; $0.5897 \leq \pi \leq 0.6300$.
$p = 0.18$; $0.1643 \leq \pi \leq 0.1961$.
$p = 0.18$; $0.1643 \leq \pi \leq 0.1961$.

(b) Most adults have a cellphone. Many adults have a desktop computer or a laptop computer. Some adults have an e-book reader or a tablet computer.

8.56 (a) $14.085 \leq \mu \leq 16.515$. **(b)** $0.530 \leq \pi \leq 0.820$. **(c)** $n = 25$. **(d)** $n = 784$. **(e)** If a single sample were to be selected for both purposes, the larger of the two sample sizes ($n = 784$) should be used.

8.58 (a) $8.049 \leq \mu \leq 11.351$. **(b)** $0.284 \leq \pi \leq 0.676$. **(c)** $n = 35$. **(d)** $n = 121$. **(e)** If a single sample were to be selected for both purposes, the larger of the two sample sizes ($n = 121$) should be used.

8.60 (a) $0.2459 \leq \pi \leq 0.3741$. **(b)** $3.22 \leq \mu \leq \$3.78$. **(c)** $\$17{,}581.68 \leq \mu \leq \$18{,}418.32$.

8.62 (a) $\$36.66 \leq \mu \leq \$40.42$. **(b)** $0.2027 \leq \pi \leq 0.3973$. **(c)** $n = 110$. **(d)** $n = 423$. **(e)** If a single sample were to be selected for both purposes, the larger of the two sample sizes ($n = 423$) should be used.

8.64 (a) $0.4643 \leq \pi \leq 0.6690$. **(b)** $\$136.28 \leq \mu \leq \$502.21$.

8.66 (a) $8.41 \leq \mu \leq 8.43$. **(b)** With 95% confidence, the population mean width of troughs is somewhere between 8.41 and 8.43 inches. **(c)** The assumption is valid as the width of the troughs is approximately normally distributed.

8.68 (a) $0.2425 \leq \mu \leq 0.2856$. **(b)** $0.1975 \leq \mu \leq 0.2385$. **(c)** The amounts of granule loss for both brands are skewed to the right, but the sample sizes are large enough. **(d)** Because the two confidence intervals do not overlap, you can conclude that the mean granule loss of Boston shingles is higher than that of Vermont shingles.

CHAPTER 9

9.2 Because $Z_{STAT} = +2.21 > 1.96$, reject H_0.

9.4 Reject H_0 if $Z_{STAT} < -2.58$ or if $Z_{STAT} > 2.58$.

9.6 p-value $= 0.0456$.

9.8 p-value $= 0.1676$.

9.10 H_0: Defendant is guilty; H_1: Defendant is innocent. A Type I error would be not convicting a guilty person. A Type II error would be convicting an innocent person.

9.12 H_0: $\mu = 20$ minutes. 20 minutes is adequate travel time between classes. H_1: $\mu \neq 20$ minutes. 20 minutes is not adequate travel time between classes.

9.14 **(a)** $Z_{STAT} = \dfrac{350 - 375}{\dfrac{100}{\sqrt{64}}} = -2.0$. Because $Z_{STAT} = -2.00 < -1.96$, reject H_0. **(b)** p − value $= 0.0456$. **(c)** $325.5 \le \mu \le 374.5$. **(d)** The conclusions are the same.

9.16 **(a)** Because $-2.58 < Z_{STAT} = -1.7678 < 2.58$, do not reject H_0. **(b)** p − value $= 0.0771$. **(c)** $0.9877 \le \mu \le 1.0023$. **(d)** The conclusions are the same.

9.18 $t_{STAT} = 2.00$.

9.20 ± 2.1315.

9.22 No, you should not use a t test because the original population is left-skewed, and the sample size is not large enough for the t test to be valid.

9.24 **(a)** $t_{STAT} = (3.57 - 3.70)/0.8/\sqrt{64} = -1.30$. Because $-1.9983 < t_{STAT} = -1.30 < 1.9983$ and p-value $= 0.1984 > 0.05$, there is no evidence that the population mean waiting time is different from 3.7 minutes. **(b)** Because $n = 64$, the Central Limit Theorem should ensure that the sampling distribution of the mean is approximately normal. In general, the t test is appropriate for this sample size except for the case where the population is extremely skewed or bimodal.

9.26 **(a)** $-1.9842 < t_{STAT} = 1.1364 < 1.9842$. There is no evidence that the population mean retail value of the greeting cards is different from \$2.50. **(b)** p-value $= 0.2585 > 0.05$. The probability of getting a t_{STAT} statistic greater than $+1.1364$ or less than -1.1364, given that the null hypothesis is true, is 0.2585.

9.28 **(a)** Because $-2.1448 < t_{STAT} = 1.6344 < 2.1448$, do not reject H_0. There is not enough evidence to conclude that the mean amount spent for lunch at a fast food restaurant, is different from \$6.50. **(b)** The p-value is 0.1245. If the population mean is \$6.50, the probability of observing a sample of nine customers that will result in a sample mean farther away from the hypothesized value than this sample is 0.1245. **(c)** The distribution of the amount spent is normally distributed. **(d)** With a sample size of 15, it is difficult to evaluate the assumption of normality. However, the distribution may be fairly symmetric because the mean and the median are close in value. Also, the boxplot appears only slightly skewed so the normality assumption does not appear to be seriously violated.

9.30 **(a)** Because $-2.0096 < t_{STAT} = 0.114 < 2.0096$, do not reject H_0. There is no evidence that the mean amount is different from 2 liters. **(b)** p-value $= 0.9095$. **(d)** Yes, the data appear to have met the normality assumption. **(e)** The amount of fill is decreasing over time so the values are not independent. Therefore, the t test is invalid.

9.32 **(a)** Because $t_{STAT} = -5.9355 < -2.0106$, reject H_0. There is enough evidence to conclude that mean widths of the troughs is different from 8.46 inches. **(b)** The population distribution is normal. **(c)** Although the distribution of the widths is left-skewed, the large sample size means that the validity of the t test is not seriously affected. The large sample size allows you to use the t distribution.

9.34 **(a)** Because $-2.68 < t_{STAT} = 0.094 < 2.68$, do not reject H_0. There is no evidence that the mean amount is different from 5.5 grams. **(b)** $5.462 \le \mu \le 5.542$. **(c)** The conclusions are the same.

9.36 p-value $= 0.0228$.

9.38 p-value $= 0.0838$.

9.40 p-value $= 0.9162$.

9.42 $t_{STAT} = 2.7638$.

9.44 $t_{STAT} = -2.5280$.

9.46 **(a)** $t_{STAT} = -1.7094 < -1.6604$. There is evidence that the population mean waiting time is less than 36.5 hours. **(b)** p-value $= 0.0453 < 0.05$. The probability of getting a t_{STAT} statistic less than -1.7094, given that the null hypothesis is true, is 0.0453.

9.48 **(a)** $t_{STAT} = (32-68)/9/\sqrt{50} = -28.2843$. Because $t_{STAT} = -28.2843 < -2.4049$, reject H_0. p-value $= 0.0000 < 0.01$, reject H_0. **(b)** The probability of getting a sample mean of 32 minutes or less if the population mean is 68 minutes is 0.0000.

9.50 **(a)** $t_{STAT} = 1.5713 < 2.4049$. There is insufficient evidence that the population mean one-time gift donation is greater than \$60. **(b)** The probability of getting a sample mean of \$62 or more if the population mean is 60 minutes is 0.0613.

9.52 $p = 0.22$.

9.54 Do not reject H_0.

9.56 **(a)** $Z_{STAT} = 1.4597$, p-value $= 0.0722$. Because $Z_{STAT} = 1.46 < 1.645$ or $0.0722 > 0.05$, do not reject H_0. There is no evidence to show that more than 18.35% of students at your university use the Mozilla Foundation web browser. **(b)** $Z_{STAT} = 2.9193$, p-value $= 0018$. Because $Z_{STAT} = 2.9193 > 1.645$, reject H_0. There is evidence to show that more than 18.35% of students at your university use the Mozilla Foundation web browser. **(c)** The sample size had a major effect on being able to reject the null hypothesis. **(d)** You would be very unlikely to reject the null hypothesis with a sample of 20.

9.58 H_0: $\pi = 0.35$; H_1: $\pi \neq 0.35$. Decision rule: If $Z_{STAT} > 1.96$ or $Z_{STAT} < -1.96$, reject H_0.

$$p = \frac{328}{801} = 0.4095$$

Test statistic:

$$Z_{STAT} = \frac{p - \pi}{\sqrt{\dfrac{\pi(1-\pi)}{n}}} = \frac{0.4095 - 0.35}{\sqrt{\dfrac{0.4095(1-0.4095)}{801}}} = 3.5298.$$

Because $Z_{STAT} = 3.5298 > 1.96$ or p-value $= 0.0004 < 0.05$, reject H_0 and conclude that there is evidence that the proportion of all LinkedIn members who plan to spend at least \$1,000 on consumer electronics in the coming year is different from 35%.

9.60 **(a)** H_0: $\pi \ge 0.31$. The proportion who respond that shared organizational goals and objectives linking the team is the supported driver of alignment is greater than or equal to 0.31. H_1: $\pi < 0.31$. The proportion who respond that shared organizational goals and objectives linking the team is the supported driver of alignment is less than 0.31. **(b)** $Z_{STAT} = -0.6487 > -1.645$; p-value $= 0.2583$. Because $Z_{STAT} = -0.6487 > -1.645$ or p-value $= 0.2583 > 0.05$, reject H_0. There is insufficient evidence that the proportion who respond that shared organizational goals and objectives linking the team is the supported driver of alignment is less than 0.31.

9.70 (a) Concluding that a firm will go bankrupt when it will not. **(b)** Concluding that a firm will not go bankrupt when it will go bankrupt. **(c)** Type I. **(d)** If the revised model results in more moderate or large Z scores, the probability of committing a Type I error will increase. Many more of the firms will be predicted to go bankrupt than will go bankrupt. On the other hand, the revised model that results in more moderate or large Z scores will lower the probability of committing a Type II error because few firms will be predicted to go bankrupt than will actually go bankrupt.

9.72 (a) Because $t_{STAT} = 3.248 > 2.0010$, reject H_0. **(b)** p-value $= 0.0019$. **(c)** Because $Z_{STAT} = -0.32 > -1.645$, do not reject H_0. **(d)** Because $-2.0010 < t_{STAT} = 0.75 < 2.0010$, do not reject H_0. **(e)** Because $Z_{STAT} = -1.61 > -1.645$, do not reject H_0.

9.74 (a) Because $t_{STAT} = -1.69 > -1.7613$, do not reject H_0. **(b)** The data are from a population that is normally distributed. **(d)** With the exception of one extreme value, the data are approximately normally distributed. **(e)** There is insufficient evidence to state that the waiting time is less than five minutes.

9.76 (a) Because $t_{STAT} = -1.47 > -1.6896$, do not reject H_0. **(b)** p-value $= 0.0748$. If the null hypothesis is true, the probability of obtaining a t_{STAT} of -1.47 or more extreme is 0.0748. **(c)** Because $t_{STAT} = -3.10 < -1.6973$, reject H_0. **(d)** p-value $= 0.0021$. If the null hypothesis is true, the probability of obtaining a t_{STAT} of -3.10 or more extreme is 0.0021. **(e)** The data in the population are assumed to be normally distributed. **(g)** Both boxplots suggest that the data are skewed slightly to the right, more so for the Boston shingles. However, the very large sample sizes mean that the results of the t test are relatively insensitive to the departure from normality.

9.78 (a) $t_{STAT} = -21.61$, reject H_0. **(b)** p-value $= 0.0000$. **(c)** $t_{STAT} = -27.19$, reject H_0. **(d)** p-value $= 0.0000$. **(e)** Because of the large sample sizes, you do not need to be concerned with the normality assumption.

CHAPTER 10

10.2 (a) $t = 3.8959$. **(b)** $df = 21$. **(c)** 2.5177. **(d)** Because $t_{STAT} = t_{STAT} = 3.8959 > 2.5177$, reject H_0.

10.4 $3.73 \le \mu_1 - \mu_2 \le 12.27$.

10.6 Because $t_{STAT} = 2.6762 < 2.9979$ or p-value $= 0.0158 > 0.01$, do not reject H_0. There is no evidence of a difference in the means of the two populations.

10.8 (a) Because $t_{STAT} = 5.7883 > 1.6581$ or p-value $= 0.0000 < 0.05$, reject H_0. There is evidence that the mean amount of Goldfish crackers eaten by children is higher for those who watched food ads than for those who did not watch food ads. **(b)** $5.79 \le \mu_1 - \mu_2 \le 11.81$. **(c)** The results cannot be compared because (a) is a one-tail test and (b) is a confidence interval that is comparable only to the results of a two-tail test.

10.10 (a) H_0: $\mu_1 = \mu_2$, where Populations: 1 = Southeast, 2 = Gulf Coast. H_1: $\mu_1 \ne \mu_2$. Decision rule: $df = 26$. If $t_{STAT} < -2.0555$ or $t_{STAT} > 2.0555$, reject H_0.

Test statistic:

$$S_p^2 = \frac{(n_1 - 1)(S_1^2) + (n_2 - 1)(S_2^2)}{(n_1 - 1) + (n_2 - 1)}$$

$$= \frac{(12)(41.8895^2) + (14)(27.9864^2)}{99 + 71} = 1{,}231.619$$

$$t_{STAT} = \frac{(\overline{X}_1 - \overline{X}_2) - (\mu_1 - \mu_2)}{\sqrt{S_p^2\left(\frac{1}{n_1} + \frac{1}{n_2}\right)}}$$

$$= \frac{(40.6923 - 27.6667) - 0}{\sqrt{1231.619\left(\frac{1}{13} + \frac{1}{15}\right)}} = 0.9795.$$

Decision: Because $-2.0555 < t_{STAT} = 0.9795 < 2.0555$, do not reject H_0. There is not enough evidence to conclude that the mean number of partners between the Southeast and Gulf Coast is different. **(b)** p-value $= 0.3364$. **(c)** In order to use the pooled-variance t test, you need to assume that the populations are normally distributed with equal variances.

10.12 (a) Because $t_{STAT} = -4.1343 < -2.0484$, reject H_0. **(b)** p-value $= 0.0003$. **(c)** The populations of waiting times are approximately normally distributed. **(d)** $-4.2292 \le \mu_1 - \mu_2 \le -1.4268$.

10.14 (a) Because $t_{STAT} = 4.10 > 2.024$, reject H_0. There is evidence of a difference in the mean surface hardness between untreated and treated steel plates. **(b)** p-value $= 0.0002$. The probability that two samples have a mean difference of 9.3634 or more is 0.0002 if there is no difference in the mean surface hardness between untreated and treated steel plates. **(c)** You need to assume that the population distribution of hardness of both untreated and treated steel plates is normally distributed. **(d)** $4.7447 \le \mu_1 - \mu_2 \le 13.9821$.

10.16 (a) Because $t_{STAT} = -2.0036 < -2.0017$ or p-value $= 0.0498 < 0.05$, reject H_0. There is evidence of a difference in the mean Facebook time per day between males and females. **(b)** You must assume that each of the two independent populations is normally distributed.

10.18 $df = 19$.

10.20 (a) $t_{STAT} = (-1.5566)/(1.424)/\sqrt{9} = -3.2772$. Because $t_{STAT} = -3.2772 < -2.306$ or p-value $= 0.0112 < 0.05$, reject H_0. There is enough evidence of a difference in the mean summated ratings between the two brands. **(b)** You must assume that the distribution of the differences between the two ratings is approximately normal. **(c)** p-value $= 0.0112$. The probability of obtaining a mean difference in ratings that results in a test statistic that deviates from 0 by 3.2772 or more in either direction is 0.0112 if there is no difference in the mean summated ratings between the two brands. **(d)** $-2.6501 \le \mu_D \le -0.4610$. You are 95% confident that the mean difference in summated ratings between brand A and brand B is somewhere between -2.6501 and -0.4610.

10.22 (a) Because $t_{STAT} = 0.9826 < 1.7291$ do not reject H_0. There is not enough evidence to conclude that the mean at Target is higher than at Walmart. **(b)** You must assume that the distribution of the differences between the prices is approximately normal. **(c)** p-value = 0.1691. The likelihood that you will obtain a t_{STAT} statistic greater than 0.9826 if the mean price at Target is not greater than Walmart is 0.1691.

10.24 (a) Because $t_{STAT} = 1.8425 < 1.943$, do not reject H_0. There is not enough evidence to conclude that the mean bone marrow microvessel density is higher before the stem cell transplant than after the stem cell transplant. **(b)** p-value $= 0.0575$. The probability that the t statistic for the mean difference in microvessel density is 1.8425 or more is 5.75% if the mean density is not higher before the stem cell transplant than after the stem cell transplant. **(c)** $-28.26 \le \mu_D \le 200.55$. You are 95% confident that the mean difference in bone marrow microvessel density before and after the stem cell transplant is somewhere between −28.26 and 200.55. **(d)** That the distribution of the difference before and after the stem cell transplant is normally distributed.

10.26 (a) Because $t_{STAT} = -9.3721 < -2.4258$, reject H_0. There is evidence that the mean strength is lower at two days than at seven days. **(b)** The population of differences in strength is approximately normally distributed. **(c)** $p = 0.000$.

10.28 (a) Because $-2.58 \leq Z_{STAT} = -0.58 \leq 2.58$, do not reject H_0. **(b)** $-0.273 \leq \pi_1 - \pi_2 \leq 0.173$.

10.30 (a) $H_0: \pi_1 \leq \pi_2$. $H_1: \pi_1 > \pi_2$. Populations: 1 = social media recommendation, 2 = web browsing. **(b)** Because $Z_{STAT} = 1.5507 < 1.6449$ or p-value $= 0.0605 > 0.05$, do not reject H_0. There is insufficient evidence to conclude that the population proportion of those who recalled the brand is greater for those who had a social media recommendation than for those who did web browsing. **(c)** No, the result in (b) makes it inappropriate to claim that the population proportion of those who recalled the brand is greater for those who had a social media recommendation than for those who did web browsing.

10.32 (a) H_0: $\pi_1 = \pi_2$. $H_1: \pi_1 \neq \pi_2$. Decision rule: If $|\, Z_{STAT} \,| > 2.58$, reject H_0.

$$\text{Test statistic: } \bar{p} = \frac{X_1 + X_2}{n_1 + n_2} = \frac{930 + 230}{1{,}000 + 1{,}000} = 0.58$$

$$Z_{STAT} = \frac{(p_1 - p_2) - (\pi_2 - \pi_2)}{\sqrt{\bar{p}(1-\bar{p})\left(\frac{1}{n_1} + \frac{1}{n_2}\right)}} = \frac{(0.93 - 0.23) - 0}{\sqrt{0.58(1 - 0.58)\left(\frac{1}{1{,}000} + \frac{1}{1{,}000}\right)}}.$$

$Z_{STAT} = 31.7135 > 2.58$, reject H_0. There is evidence of a difference in the proportion of Superbanked and Unbanked with respect to the proportion that use credit cards. **(b)** p-value $= 0.0000$. The probability of obtaining a difference in proportions that gives rise to a test statistic below −31.7135 or above +31.7135 is 0.0000 if there is no difference in the proportion of Superbanked and Unbanked who use credit cards. **(c)** $0.1570 \leq (\pi_1 - \pi_2) \leq 0.2630$. You are 99% confident that the difference in the proportion of Superbanked and Unbanked who use credit cards is between 0.1570 and 0.2630.

10.34 (a) Because $Z_{STAT} = 7.2742 > 1.96$, reject H_0. There is evidence of a difference in the proportion of adults and users ages 12–17 who oppose ads. **(b)** p-value $= 0.0000$. The probability of obtaining a difference in proportions that is 0.16 or more in either direction is 0.0000 if there is no difference between the proportion of adults and users ages 12–17 who oppose ads.

10.36 (a) 2.20. **(b)** 2.57. **(c)** 3.50.

10.38 (a) Population B: $S^2 = 25$. **(b)** 1.5625.

10.40 $df_{\text{numerator}} = 24$, $df_{\text{denominator}} = 24$.

10.42 Because $F_{STAT} = 1.2109 < 2.27$, do not reject H_0.

10.44 (a) Because $F_{STAT} = 1.2995 < 3.18$, do not reject H_0. **(b)** Because $F_{STAT} = 1.2995 < 2.62$, do not reject H_0.

10.46 (a) $H_0: \sigma_1^2 = \sigma_2^2$. $H_1: \sigma_1^2 \neq \sigma_2^2$.

Decision rule: If $F_{STAT} > 3.0502$, reject H_0.

$$\text{Test statistic: } F_{STAT} = \frac{S_1^2}{S_2^2} = \frac{(41.8895)^2}{(27.9864)^2} = 2.2404.$$

Decision: Because $F_{STAT} = 2.2404 < 3.0502$, do not reject H_0. There is insufficient evidence to conclude that the two population variances are different. **(b)** p-value $= 0.1520$. **(c)** The test assumes that each of the two populations is normally distributed. **(d)** Based on (a) and (b), a pooled-variance t test should be used.

10.48 (a) Because $F_{STAT} = 3.8179 < 4.0721$ or p-value $= 0.0609 < 0.05$, do not reject H_0. There is no evidence of a difference in the variability of the battery life between the two types of digital cameras. **(b)** p-value $= 0.0609$. The probability of obtaining a sample that yields a test statistic more extreme than 3.8179 is 0.0609 if there is no difference in the two population variances. **(c)** The test assumes that each of the two populations are normally distributed. The boxplots appear fairly symmetrical and the skewness and kurtosis statistics are not dramatically different from 0. Thus, the distributions do not appear to be substantially different from a normal distribution. **(d)** Based on (a) and (b), a pooled-variance t test should be used.

10.50 Because $F_{STAT} = 1.6418 < 4.4333$, or p-value $= 0.4988 > 0.05$, do not reject H_0. There is insufficient evidence of a difference in the variance of the yield in the two cities.

10.58 (a) Because $F_{STAT} = 1.4139 < 1.7289$, or p-value $= 0.2150 > 0.05$, do not reject H_0. There is not enough evidence of a difference in the variance of the salary of Black Belts and Green Belts. **(b)** The pooled-variance t test. **(c)** Because $t_{STAT} = 5.0372 > 1.96$ or p-value $= 0.0000 < 0.05$, reject H_0. There is evidence of a difference in the mean salary of Black Belts and Green Belts.

10.60 (a) Because $F_{STAT} = 1.5625 < F_\alpha = 1.6854$, do not reject H_0. There is not enough evidence to conclude that there is a difference between the variances in the talking time per month between women and men. **(b)** It is more appropriate to use a pooled-variance t test. Using the pooled-variance t test, because $t_{STAT} = 11.1196 > 2.6009$, reject H_0. There is enough evidence of a difference in the mean talking time per month between women and men. **(c)** Because $F_{STAT} = 1.44 < 1.6854$, do not reject H_0. There is not enough evidence to conclude that there is a difference between the variances in the number of text messages sent per month between women and men. **(d)** Using the pooled-variance t test, because $t_{STAT} = 8.2456 > 2.6009$, reject H_0. There is enough evidence of a difference in the mean number of text messages sent per month between women and men.

10.62 (a) Because $t_{STAT} = 3.3282 > 1.8595$, reject H_0. There is enough evidence to conclude that the introductory computer students required more than a mean of 10 minutes to write and run a program in Visual Basic. **(b)** Because $t_{STAT} = 1.3636 < 1.8595$, do not reject H_0. There is not enough evidence to conclude that the introductory computer students required more than a mean of 10 minutes to write and run a program in Visual Basic. **(c)** Although the mean time necessary to complete the assignment increased from 12 to 16 minutes as a result of the increase in one data value, the standard deviation went from 1.8 to 13.2, which reduced the value of t statistic. **(d)** Because $F_{STAT} = 1.2308 < 3.8549$, do not reject H_0. There is not enough evidence to conclude that the population variances are different for the Introduction to Computers students and computer majors. Hence, the pooled-variance t test is a valid test to determine whether computer majors can write a Visual Basic program in less time than introductory students, assuming that the distributions of the time needed to write a Visual Basic program for both the Introduction to Computers students and the computer majors are approximately normally distributed. Because $t_{STAT} = 4.0666 > 1.7341$, reject H_0. There is enough evidence that the mean time is higher for Introduction to Computers students than for computer majors. **(e)** p-value $= 0.000362$. If the true population mean amount of time needed for Introduction to Computer students to write a Visual Basic program is no more than 10 minutes, the probability of observing a sample mean greater than the 12 minutes in the current sample is 0.0362%. Hence, at a 5% level of significance, you can conclude that the population mean amount of time needed for Introduction to Computer students to write a Visual Basic program is more than 10 minutes. As illustrated in (d), in which there is not enough evidence to conclude that the population variances are different for the Introduction to Computers students and computer majors, the pooled-variance t test performed is a valid test to determine whether computer majors can write a Visual Basic program in less time than introductory students, assuming that the distribution of the time needed to write a Visual Basic program for both the Introduction to Computers students and the computer majors are approximately normally distributed.

10.64 From the boxplot and the summary statistics, both distributions are approximately normally distributed. $F_{STAT} = 1.056 < 1.89$. There is insufficient evidence to conclude that the two population variances are significantly different at the 5% level of significance. $t_{STAT} = -5.084 < -1.99$. At the 5% level of significance, there is sufficient evidence to reject the null hypothesis of no difference in the mean life of the bulbs between the two manufacturers. You can conclude that there is a significant difference in the mean life of the bulbs between the two manufacturers.

10.66 (a) Because $Z_{STAT} = -4.5867 < -1.96$, reject H_0. There is enough evidence to conclude that there is a difference in the proportion of men and women who order dessert. **(b)** Because $Z_{STAT} = 6.0238 > 1.96$, reject H_0. There is enough evidence to conclude that there is a difference in the proportion of people who order dessert based on whether they ordered a beef entree.

10.68 The normal probability plots suggest that the two populations are not normally distributed. An F test is inappropriate for testing the difference in the two variances. The sample variances for Boston and Vermont shingles are 0.0203 and 0.015, respectively. Because $t_{STAT} = 3.015 > 1.967$ or p-value $= 0.0028 < \alpha = 0.05$, reject H_0. There is sufficient evidence to conclude that there is a difference in the mean granule loss of Boston and Vermont shingles.

CHAPTER 11

11.2 (a) $SSW = 150$. **(b)** $MSA = 15$. **(c)** $MSW = 5$. **(d)** $F_{STAT} = 3$.

11.4 (a) 2. **(b)** 18. **(c)** 20.

11.6 (a) Reject H_0 if $F_{STAT} > 2.95$; otherwise, do not reject H_0. **(b)** Because $F_{STAT} = 4 > 2.95$, reject H_0. **(c)** The table does not have 28 degrees of freedom in the denominator, so use the next larger critical value, $Q_\alpha = 3.90$. **(d)** Critical range $= 6.166$.

11.8 (a) H_0: $\mu_A = \mu_B = \mu_C = \mu_D$ and H_1: At least one mean is different.

$$MSA = \frac{SSA}{c-1} = \frac{1{,}986.475}{3} = 662.1583.$$

$$MSW = \frac{SSW}{n-c} = \frac{495.5}{36} = 13.76389.$$

$$F_{STAT} = \frac{MSA}{MSW} = \frac{662.1583}{13.76389} = 48.1084.$$

$$F_{0.05,3,36} = 2.8663.$$

Because the p-value is approximately 0 and $F_{STAT} = 48.1084 > 2.8663$, reject H_0. There is sufficient evidence of a difference in the mean strength of the four brands of trash bags. **(b)** Critical range $= Q_\alpha \sqrt{\frac{MSW}{2}\left(\frac{1}{n_j} + \frac{1}{n_{j'}}\right)}$

$$= 3.79\sqrt{\frac{13.7639}{2}\left(\frac{1}{10} + \frac{1}{10}\right)} = 4.446.$$

From the Tukey-Kramer procedure, there is a difference in mean strength between Kroger and Tuffstuff, Glad and Tuffstuff, and Hefty and Tuffstuff. **(c)** ANOVA output for Levene's test for homogeneity of variance:

$$MSA = \frac{SSA}{c-1} = \frac{24.075}{3} = 8.025$$

$$MSW = \frac{SSW}{n-c} = \frac{198.2}{36} = 5.5056$$

$$F_{STAT} = \frac{MSA}{MSW} = \frac{8.025}{5.5056} = 1.4576$$

$$F_{0.05,3,36} = 2.8663$$

Because p-value $= 0.2423 > 0.05$ and $F_{STAT} = 1.4576 < 2.8663$, do not reject H_0. There is insufficient evidence to conclude that the variances in strength among the four brands of trash bags are different. **(d)** From the results in (a) and (b), Tuffstuff has the lowest mean strength and should be avoided.

11.10 (a) Because $F_{STAT} = 12.56 > 2.76$, reject H_0. **(b)** Critical range $= 4.67$. Advertisements A and B are different from Advertisements C and D. Advertisement E is only different from Advertisement D. **(c)** Because $F_{STAT} = 1.927 < 2.76$, do not reject H_0. There is no evidence of a significant difference in the variation in the ratings among the five advertisements. **(d)** The advertisements underselling the pen's characteristics had the highest mean ratings, and the advertisements overselling the pen's characteristics had the lowest mean ratings. Therefore, use an advertisement that undersells the pen's characteristics and avoid advertisements that oversell the pen's characteristics.

11.12 (a)

Source	Degrees of Freedom	Sum of Squares	Mean Squares	F
Among groups	2	1.879	0.9395	8.7558
Within groups	297	31.865	0.1073	
Total	299	33.744		

(b) Since $F_{STAT} = 8.7558 > 3.00$, reject H_0. There is evidence of a difference in the mean soft-skill score of the different groups. **(c)** Group 1 versus group 2: $0.072 <$ Critical range $= 0.1092$; group 1 versus group 3: $0.181 > 0.1056$; group 2 versus group 3: $0.109 < 0.1108$. There is evidence of a difference in the mean soft-skill score between those who had no coursework in leadership and those who had a degree in leadership.

11.14 (a) Because $F_{STAT} = 53.03 > 2.92$, reject H_0. **(b)** Critical range $= 5.27$ (using 30 degrees of freedom). Designs 3 and 4 are different from designs 1 and 2. Designs 1 and 2 are different from each other. **(c)** The assumptions are that the samples are randomly and independently selected (or randomly assigned), the original populations of distances are approximately normally distributed, and the variances are equal. **(d)** Because $F_{STAT} = 2.093 < 2.92$, do not reject H_0. There is insufficient evidence of a difference in the variation in the distance among the four designs. **(e)** The manager should choose design 3 or 4.

11.16 (a) 40. **(b)** 60 and 55. **(c)** 10. **(d)** 10.

11.18 (a) Because $F_{STAT} = 6.00 > 3.35$, reject H_0. **(b)** Because $F_{STAT} = 5.50 > 3.35$, reject H_0. **(c)** Because $F_{STAT} = 1.00 < 2.73$, do not reject H_0.

11.20 $df_B = 4$, $df_{TOTAL} = 44$, $SSA = 160$, $SSAB = 80$, $SSE = 150$, $SST = 610$, $MSB = 55$, $MSE = 5$. For A: $F_{STAT} = 16$. For B: $F_{STAT} = 11$. For AB: $F_{STAT} = 2$.

11.22 (a) Because $F_{STAT} = 1.37 < 4.75$, do not reject H_0. **(b)** Because $F_{STAT} = 23.58 > 4.75$, reject H_0. **(c)** Because $F_{STAT} = 0.70 < 4.75$, do not reject H_0. **(e)** Developer strength has a significant effect on density, but development time does not.

11.24 (a) H_0: There is no interaction between brand and water temperature. H_1: There is an interaction between brand and water temperature. Because $F_{STAT} = \frac{253.1552}{12.2199} = 20.7167 > 3.555$ or the p-value $= 0.0000214 < 0.05$, reject H_0. There is evidence of interaction between brand of pain reliever and temperature of the water. **(b)** Because there is an interaction between brand and the temperature of the water, it is inappropriate to analyze the main effect due to brand. **(c)** Because there is an interaction between brand and the temperature of the water, it is inappropriate to analyze the main effect due to water temperature. **(e)** The difference in the mean time a tablet took to dissolve in cold and hot water depends on the brand, with Alka-Seltzer having the largest difference and Equate the smallest difference.

11.26 (a) $F_{STAT} = 0.1523$, p-value $= 0.9614 > 0.05$, do not reject H_0. There is not enough evidence to conclude that there is an interaction between the brake discs and the gauges. **(b)** $F_{STAT} = 7.7701$, p-value is virtually $0 < 0.05$, reject H_0. There is sufficient evidence to conclude that there is an effect due to brake discs. **(c)** $F_{STAT} = 0.1465$, p-value $= 0.7031 > 0.05$, do not reject H_0. There is inadequate evidence to conclude that there is an effect due to the gauges. **(d)** From the plot, there is no obvious interaction between brake discs and gauges. **(e)** There is no obvious difference in mean temperature across the gauges. It appears that Part 1 has the lowest, Part 3 the second lowest, and Part 2 has the highest average temperature.

11.36 (a) Because $F_{STAT} = 1.485 < 2.54$, do not reject H_0. **(b)** Because $F_{STAT} = 0.79 < 3.24$, do not reject H_0. **(c)** Because $F_{STAT} = 52.07 > 3.24$, reject H_0. **(e)** Critical range $= 0.0189$. Washing cycles for 22 and 24 minutes are not different with respect to dirt removal, but they are both different from 18- and 20-minute cycles. **(f)** 22 minutes. (24 minutes was not different, but 22 does just as well and would use less energy.) **(g)** The results are the same.

11.38 (a) Because $F_{STAT} = 0.075 < 3.68$, do not reject H_0. **(b)** Because $F_{STAT} = 4.09 > 3.68$, reject H_0. **(c)** Critical range $= 1.489$. Breaking strength is significantly different between 30 and 50 psi.

11.40 (a) Because $F_{STAT} = 0.1899 < 4.1132$, do not reject H_0. There is insufficient evidence to conclude that there is any interaction between type of breakfast and desired time. **(b)** Because $F_{STAT} = 30.4434 > 4.1132$, reject H_0. There is sufficient evidence to conclude that there is an effect due to type of breakfast. **(c)** Because $F_{STAT} = 12.4441 > 4.1132$, reject H_0. There is sufficient evidence to conclude that there is an effect due to desired time. **(e)** At the 5% level of significance, both the type of breakfast ordered and the desired time have an effect on delivery time difference. There is no interaction between the type of breakfast ordered and the desired time.

11.42 Interaction: $F_{STAT} = 0.2169 < 3.9668$ or p-value $= 0.6428 > 0.05$. There is insufficient evidence of an interaction between piece size and fill height. Piece size: $F_{STAT} = 842.2242 > 3.9668$ or p-value $= 0.0000 < 0.05$. There is evidence of an effect due to piece size. The fine piece size has a lower difference in coded weight. Fill height: $F_{STAT} = 217.0816 > 3.9668$ or p-value $= 0.0000 < 0.05$. There is evidence of an effect due to fill height. The low fill height has a lower difference in coded weight.

11.44 Population 1 = short term 2 = long term, 3 = world; One-year return: Levene test: $F_{STAT} = 50.1527$. Since the p-value $= 0.0000 < 0.05$, reject H_0. There is evidence to show a difference in the variance of return among the three different types of mutual funds at a 5% level of significance. Therefore, the validity of the one-way ANOVA is in serious doubt. A data transformation is necessary, or you can use a nonparametric test such as the Kruskal-Wallis test covered in Section 12.5. Three-year return: Levene test: $F_{STAT} = 1.4796$. Since the p-value $= 0.2456 > 0.05$, do not reject H_0. There is insufficient evidence to show a difference in the variance of return among the three different types of mutual funds at a 5% level of significance. $F_{STAT} = 34.5559$. Since the p-value is virtually zero, reject H_0. There is sufficient evidence to show a difference in the mean three-year returns among the three different types of bond funds at a 5% level of significance. Critical range $= 2.1802$. At the 5% level of significance, there is sufficient evidence that the mean three-year returns of the long-term bond funds is significantly higher than the others. Also, the mean three-year returns of the short-term bond funds are significantly lower than that of the world bond funds.

CHAPTER 12

12.2 (a) For $df = 1$ and $\alpha = 0.05$, $\chi^2_\alpha = 3.841$. **(b)** For $df = 1$ and $\alpha = 0.025$, $\chi^2 = 5.024$. **(c)** For $df = 1$ and $\alpha = 0.01$, $\chi^2_\alpha = 6.635$.

12.4 (a) All $f_e = 25$. **(b)** Because $\chi^2_{STAT} = 4.00 > 3.841$, reject H_0.

12.6 (a) H_0: $\pi_1 = \pi_2$. H_1: $\pi_1 \neq \pi_2$. **(b)** Because $\chi^2_{STAT} = 2.4045 < 3.841$, do not reject H_0. There is insufficient evidence to conclude that the population proportion of those who recalled the brand is different for those who had a social media recommendation than for those who did web browsing. p-value $= 0.1210$. The probability of obtaining a test statistic of 2.4045 or larger when the null hypothesis is true is 0.1210. **(c)** You should not compare the results in (a) to those of Problem 10.30 (b) because that was a one-tail test.

12.8 (a) H_0: $\pi_1 = \pi_2$. H_1: $\pi_1 \neq \pi_2$. Because $\chi^2_{STAT} = (930-580)^2/580 + (70-420)^2/420 + (230-580)^2/580 + (770-420)^2 = 1{,}005.7471 > 6.635$, reject H_0. There is evidence of a difference in the proportion of Superbanked and Unbanked with respect to the proportion that use credit cards. **(b)** p-value $= 0.0000$. The probability of obtaining a difference in proportions that gives rise to a test statistic above 1,005.7471 is 0.0000 if there is no difference in the proportion of Superbanked and Unbanked who use credit cards. **(c)** The results of (a) and (b) are exactly the same as those of Problem 10.32. The χ^2 in (a) and the Z in Problem 10.32 (a) satisfy the relationship that $\chi^2 = 1{,}005.7471 = Z^2 = (31.7135)^2$, and the p-value in (b) is exactly the same as the p-value computed in Problem 10.32 (b).

12.10 (a) Since $\chi^2_{STAT} = 52.9144 > 3.841$, reject H_0. There is evidence that there is a significant difference between the proportion of adults and users ages 12–17 who oppose ads on websites. **(b)** p-value 0.0000. The probability of obtaining a test statistic of 52.9144 or larger when the null hypothesis is true is 0.0000.

12.12 (a) The expected frequencies for the first row are 20, 30, and 40. The expected frequencies for the second row are 30, 45, and 60. **(b)** Because $\chi^2_{STAT} = 12.5 > 5.991$, reject H_0.

12.14 (a) Because the calculated test statistic $\chi^2_{STAT} = 44.6503 > 11.0705$, reject H_0 and conclude that there is a difference in the proportion who bring lunch between the age groups. **(b)** The p-value is virtually 0. The probability of a test statistic greater than 44.6503 or more is approximately 0 if there is no difference between the age groups in the proportion who bring lunch. (c) The 18–24 and 25–34 groups are different from the 45–54, 55–64, and 65+ groups, and the 35–44 group is different from the 65+ group.

12.16 (a) H_0: $\pi_1 = \pi_2 = \pi_3$. H_1: At least one proportion differs.

f_0	f_e	$(f_0 - f_e)$	$(f_0 - f_e)^2/f_e$
118	72	46	29.3889
82	128	−46	16.5313
72	72	0	0
128	128	0	0
26	72	−46	29.3889
174	128	46	16.5313
			91.8403

Decision rule: $df = (c-1) = (3-1) = 2$. If $\chi^2_{STAT} > 5.9915$, reject H_0.

Test statistic: $\chi^2_{STAT} = \sum_{\text{all cells}} \frac{(f_0 - f_e)}{f_e} = 91.8403$.

Decision: Because $\chi^2_{STAT} = 91.8403 > 5.9915$, reject H_0. There is a significant difference in the age groups with respect to using a cellphone to access social networking. **(b)** p-value $= 0.0000$. The probability that the test statistic is greater than or equal to 91.8403 is 0.0000, if the null hypothesis is true.

(c)

Pairwise Comparisons	Critical Range	$\lvert p_j - p_{j'} \rvert$
1 to 2	0.1189	0.23
1 to 3	0.1031	0.46
2 to 3	0.1014	0.23

There is a significant difference between all the groups. **(d)** Marketers can use this information to target their marketing to the 18- to 34-year-old group since they are more likely to use their cellphones to access social media.

12.18 **(a)** Because $\chi^2_{STAT} = 9.0485 > 5.9915$, reject H_0. There is evidence of a difference in the percentage who use their cellphones while watching TV between the groups. **(b)** p-value $= 0.0108$. **(c)** Group 1 versus group 2: $0.0215 < 0.0788$. Not significant. Group 1 versus group 3: $0.0905 > 0.0859$ significant. Group 2 versus group 3: $0.0691 > 0.06457$ significant. The rural group is different from the urban and suburban groups.

12.20 $df = (r-1)(c-1) = (3-1)(4-1) = 6$.

12.22 $\chi^2_{STAT} = 92.1028 > 16.919$, reject H_0 and conclude that there is evidence of a relationship between the type of dessert ordered and the type of entrée ordered.

12.24 **(a)** H_0: There is no relationship between the commuting time of company employees and the level of stress-related problems observed on the job. H_1: There is a relationship between the commuting time of company employees and the level of stress-related problems observed on the job.

f_0	f_e	$(f_0 - f_e)$	$(f_0 - f_e)^2/f_e$
9	12.1379	−3.1379	0.8112
17	20.1034	−3.1034	0.4791
18	11.7586	6.2414	3.3129
5	5.2414	−0.2414	0.0111
8	8.6810	−0.6810	0.0534
6	5.0776	0.9224	0.1676
18	14.6207	3.3793	0.7811
28	24.2155	3.7845	0.5915
7	14.1638	−7.1638	3.6233
			9.8311

Decision rule: If $\chi^2_{STAT} > 13.277$, reject H_0.

$$\text{Test statistic: } \chi^2_{STAT} = \sum_{\text{all cells}} \frac{(f_0 - f_e)^2}{f_e} = 9.8311.$$

Decision: Because $\chi^2_{STAT} = 9.8311 < 13.277$, do not reject H_0. There is insufficient evidence to conclude that there is a relationship between the commuting time of company employees and the level of stress-related problems observed on the job.

(b) Because $\chi^2_{STAT} = 9.831 > 9.488$, reject H_0. There is enough evidence at the 0.05 level to conclude that there is a relationship.

12.26 Because $\chi^2_{STAT} = 6.6876 < 12.5916$, do not reject H_0. There is insufficient evidence of a relationship between consumer segment and geographic region.

12.28 **(a)** 31. **(b)** 29. **(c)** 27. **(d)** 25.

12.30 40 and 79.

12.32 **(a)** The ranks for Sample 1 are 1, 2, 4, 5, and 10. The ranks for Sample 2 are 3, 6.5, 6.5, 8, 9, and 11. **(b)** 22. **(c)** 44.

12.34 Because $T_1 = 22 > 20$, do not reject H_0.

12.36 **(a)** The data are ordinal. **(b)** The two-sample t test is inappropriate because the data can only be placed in ranked order. **(c)** Because $Z_{STAT} = -2.2054 < -1.96$, reject H_0. There is evidence of a significance difference in the median rating of California Cabernets and Washington Cabernets.

12.38 **(a)** H_0: $M_1 = M_2$, where Populations: 1 = Wing A, 2 = Wing B. H_1: $M_1 \neq M_2$.

Population 1 sample: Sample size 20, sum of ranks 561

Population 2 sample: Sample size 20, sum of ranks 259

$$\mu_{T_1} = \frac{n_1(n+1)}{2} = \frac{20(40+1)}{2} = 410$$

$$\sigma_{T_1} = \sqrt{\frac{n_1 n_2 (n+1)}{12}} = \sqrt{\frac{20(20)(40+1)}{12}} = 36.9685$$

$$Z_{STAT} = \frac{T_1 - \mu_{T_1}}{S_{T_1}} = \frac{561 - 410}{36.9685} = 4.0846$$

Decision: Because $Z_{STAT} = 4.0846 > 1.96$ (or p-value $= 0.0000 < 0.05$), reject H_0. There is sufficient evidence of a difference in the median delivery time in the two wings of the hotel.

(b) The results of (a) are consistent with the results of Problem 10.65.

12.40 **(a)** Because $Z_{STAT} = 2.4441 > 1.96$, reject H_0. There is enough evidence to conclude that there is a difference in the median brand value between the two sectors. **(b)** You must assume approximately equal variability in the two populations. **(c)** Using both the pooled-variance t test and the separate-variance t test allowed you to reject the null hypothesis and conclude in Problem 10.17 that the mean brand value is different between the two sectors. In this test, using the Wilcoxon rank sum test with large-sample Z approximation also allowed you to reject the null hypothesis and conclude that the median brand value differs between the two sectors.

12.42 **(a)** Because $-1.96 < Z_{STAT} = 0.7245 < 1.96$ (or the p-value $= 0.4687 > 0.05$), do not reject H_0. There is not enough evidence to conclude that there is a difference in the median battery life between subcompact cameras and compact cameras. **(b)** You must assume approximately equal variability in the two populations. **(c)** Using the pooled-variance t-test, you do not reject the null hypothesis ($t = -2.1199 < -0.6181 < 2.1199$; p-value $= 0.5452 > 0.05$) and conclude that there is insufficient evidence of a difference in the mean battery life between the two types of digital cameras in Problem 10.11 (a).

12.44 **(a)** Decision rule: If $H > \chi^2_U = 15.086$, reject H_0. **(b)** Because $H = 13.77 < 15.086$, do not reject H_0.

12.46 **(a)** $H = 13.517 > 7.815$, p-value $= 0.0036 < 0.05$, reject H_0. There is sufficient evidence of a difference in the median waiting time in the four locations. **(b)** The results are consistent with those of Problem 11.9.

12.48 **(a)** $H = 19.3269 > 9.488$, reject H_0. There is evidence of a difference in the median ratings of the ads. **(b)** The results are consistent with those of Problem 11.10. **(c)** Because the combined scores are not true continuous variables, the nonparametric Kruskal-Wallis rank test is more appropriate because it does not require that the scores be normally distributed.

12.50 **(a)** Because $H = 22.26 > 7.815$ or the p-value is approximately 0, reject H_0. There is sufficient evidence of a difference in the median strength of the four brands of trash bags. **(b)** The results are the same.

12.56 (a) Because $\chi^2_{STAT} = 0.412 < 3.841$, do not reject H_0. There is insufficient evidence to conclude that there is a relationship between a student's gender and pizzeria selection. **(b)** Because $\chi^2_{STAT} = 2.624 < 3.841$, do not reject H_0. There is insufficient evidence to conclude that there is a relationship between a student's gender and pizzeria selection. **(c)** Because $\chi^2_{STAT} = 4.956 < 5.991$, do not reject H_0. There is insufficient evidence to conclude that there is a relationship between price and pizzeria selection. **(d)** p-value $= 0.0839$. The probability of a sample that gives a test statistic equal to or greater than 4.956 is 8.39% if the null hypothesis of no relationship between price and pizzeria selection is true.

12.58 (a) Because $\chi^2_{STAT} = 11.895 < 12.592$, do not reject H_0. There is not enough evidence to conclude that there is a relationship between the attitudes of employees toward the use of self-managed work teams and employee job classification. **(b)** Because $\chi^2_{STAT} = 3.294 < 12.592$, do not reject H_0. There is insufficient evidence to conclude that there is a relationship between the attitudes of employees toward vacation time without pay and employee job classification.

CHAPTER 13

13.2 (a) Yes. **(b)** No. **(c)** No. **(d)** Yes.

13.4 (a) The scatter plot shows a positive linear relationship. **(b)** For each increase in shelf space of an additional square foot, predicted weekly sales are estimated to increase by $7.40. **(c)** $\hat{Y} = 145 + 7.4X = 145 + 7.4(8) = 204.2$, or $204.20.

13.6 (b) $b_0 = -2.37$, $b_1 = 0.0501$. **(c)** For every cubic foot increase in the amount moved, predicted labor hours are estimated to increase by 0.0501. **(d)** 22.67 labor hours.

13.8 (b) $b_0 = -496.3022$, $b_1 = 5.1961$. **(c)** For each additional million-dollar increase in revenue, the value is predicted to increase by an estimated $5.1961 million. Literal interpretation of b_0 is not meaningful because an operating franchise cannot have zero revenue. **(d)** $283.1143 million.

13.10 (b) $b_0 = 14.7756$, $b_1 = 0.0907$. **(c)** For each increase of $1 million of box office gross, the predicted DVD revenue is estimated to increase by $0.0907 million. **(d)** $\hat{Y} = b_0 + b_1X$. $\hat{Y} = 14.7756 + 0.0907(75) = \$21.5760$ million.

13.12 $r^2 = 0.90$. 90% of the variation in the dependent variable can be explained by the variation in the independent variable.

13.14 $r^2 = 0.75$. 75% of the variation in the dependent variable can be explained by the variation in the independent variable.

13.16 (a) $r^2 = \dfrac{SSR}{SST} = \dfrac{20{,}535}{30{,}025} = 0.684$. 68.4% of the variation in sales can be explained by the variation in shelf space.

(b) $S_{YX} = \sqrt{\dfrac{SSE}{n-2}} = \sqrt{\dfrac{\sum_{i=1}^{n}(Y_i - \hat{Y}_i)^2}{n-2}} = \sqrt{\dfrac{9{,}490}{10}} = 30.8058$.

(c) Based on (a) and (b), the model should be useful for predicting sales.

13.18 (a) $r^2 = 0.8892$. 88.92% of the variation in labor hours can be explained by the variation in cubic feet moved. **(b)** $S_{YX} = 5.0314$. **(c)** Based on (a) and (b), the model should be very useful for predicting the labor hours.

13.20 (a) $r^2 = 0.7903$. 79.03% of the variation in the value of a baseball franchise can be explained by the variation in its annual revenue. **(b)** $S_{YX} = 150.9547$. **(c)** Based on (a) and (b), the model should be useful for predicting the value of a baseball franchise.

13.22 (a) $r^2 = 0.1749$. 17.49% of the variation in DVD revenue can be explained by the variation in box office gross. **(b)** $S_{YX} = 21.2824$. The variation of DVD revenue around the prediction line is $21.2824 million. The typical difference between actual DVD revenue and the predicted DVD revenue using the regression equation is approximately $21.2824 million. **(c)** Based on (a) and (b), the model may not be useful for predicting DVD revenue. **(d)** Other variables that might explain the variation in DVD revenue could be the amount spent on advertising, the timing of the release of the DVDs, and the type of movie.

13.24 A residual analysis of the data indicates a pattern, with sizable clusters of consecutive residuals that are either all positive or all negative. This pattern indicates a violation of the assumption of linearity. A curvilinear model should be investigated.

13.26 There does not appear to be a pattern in the residual plot. The assumptions of regression do not appear to be seriously violated.

13.28 Based on the residual plot, there does not appear to be a curvilinear pattern in the residuals. The assumptions of normality and equal variance do not appear to be seriously violated.

13.30 Based on the residual plot, there appears to be an outlier in the residuals, but no evidence of a pattern.

13.32 (a) An increasing linear relationship exists. **(b)** There is evidence of a strong positive autocorrelation among the residuals.

13.34 (a) No, because the data were not collected over time. **(b)** If a single store had been selected and studied over a period of time, you would compute the Durbin-Watson statistic.

13.36 (a)

$$b_1 = \frac{SSXY}{SSX} = \frac{201{,}399.05}{12{,}495{,}626} = 0.0161$$

$$b_0 = \bar{Y} - b_1\bar{X} = 71.2621 - 0.0161\ (4{,}393) = 0.458.$$

(b) $\hat{Y} = 0.458 + 0.0161X = 0.458 + 0.0161(4{,}500) = 72.908$, or $72,908. **(c)** There is no evidence of a pattern in the residuals over time.

(d) $D = \dfrac{\sum_{i=2}^{n}(e_i - e_{i-1})^2}{\sum_{i=1}^{n} e_i^2} = \dfrac{1{,}243.2244}{599.0683} = 2.08 > 1.45$. There is no evidence of positive autocorrelation among the residuals. **(e)** Based on a residual analysis, the model appears to be adequate.

13.38 (a) $b_0 = -2.535$, $b_1 = 0.06073$. **(b)** $2,505.40. **(d)** $D = 1.64 > d_U = 1.42$, so there is no evidence of positive autocorrelation among the residuals. **(e)** The plot shows some nonlinear pattern, suggesting that a nonlinear model might be better. Otherwise, the model appears to be adequate.

13.40 (a) 3.00. **(b)** ± 2.1199. **(c)** Reject H_0. There is evidence that the fitted linear regression model is useful. **(d)** $1.32 \le \beta_1 \le 7.68$.

13.42 (a) $t_{STAT} = \dfrac{b_1 - \beta_1}{S_{b_1}} = \dfrac{7.4}{1.59} = 4.65 > 2.2281$. Reject H_0. There is evidence of a linear relationship between shelf space and sales. **(b)** $b_1 \pm t_{\alpha/2}S_{b_1} = 7.4 \pm 2.2281(1.59)$ $3.86 \le \beta_1 \le 10.94$.

13.44 (a) $t_{STAT} = 16.52 > 2.0322$; reject H_0. There is evidence of a linear relationship between the number of cubic feet moved and labor hours. **(b)** $0.0439 \le \beta_1 \le 0.0562$.

13.46 **(a)** $t_{STAT} = 10.2714 > 2.0484$ or because the p-value is approximately 0, reject H_0 at the 5% level of significance. There is evidence of a linear relationship between annual revenue and franchise value. **(b)** $4.1599 \le \beta_1 \le 6.2324$.

13.48 **(a)** $t_{STAT} = 2.0592 < 2.086$ or because the p-value $= 0.0527 > 0.05$; do not reject H_0. There is insufficient evidence of a linear relationship between box office gross and sales of DVDs. **(b)** $-0.0012 \le \beta_1 \le 0.1825$.

13.50 **(a)** (% daily change in BGU) $= b_0 + 3.0$ (% daily change in Russell 1000 index). **(b)** If the Russell 1000 gains 10% in a year, BGU is expected to gain an estimated 30%. **(c)** If the Russell 1000 loses 20% in a year, BGU is expected to lose an estimated 60%. **(d)** Risk takers will be attracted to leveraged funds, and risk-averse investors will stay away.

13.52 **(a), (b)** First weekend and U.S. gross: $r = 0.7264$, $t_{STAT} = 2.5893 > 2.4469$, p-value $= 0.0413 < 0.05$. reject H_0. At the 0.05 level of significance, there is evidence of a linear relationship between first weekend sales and U.S. gross. First weekend and worldwide gross: $r = 0.8234$, $t_{STAT} = 3.5549 > 2.4469$, p-value $= 0.0120 < 0.05$. reject H_0. At the 0.05 level of significance, there is evidence of a linear relationship between first weekend sales and worldwide gross. U.S. gross and worldwide gross: $r = 0.9629$, $t_{STAT} = 8.7456 > 2.4469$, p-value $= 0.0001 < 0.05$. Reject H_0. At the 0.05 level of significance, there is evidence of a linear relationship between U.S. gross and worldwide gross.

13.54 **(a)** $r = 0.7042$. There appears to be a moderate positive linear relationship between social media networking and the GDP per capita. **(b)** $t_{STAT} = 4.3227$, p-value $= 0.0004 < 0.05$. Reject H_0. At the 0.05 level of significance, there is a significant linear relationship between social media networking and the GDP per capita. **(c)** There appears to be a strong relationship.

13.56 **(a)** $15.95 \le \mu_{Y|X=4} \le 18.05$. **(b)** $14.651 \le Y_{X=4} \le 19.349$.

13.58 **(a)** $\hat{Y} = 145 + 7.4(8) = 204.2\ \hat{Y} \pm t_{\alpha/2} S_{YX} \sqrt{h_i}$

$$= 204.2 \pm 2.2281(30.81)\sqrt{0.1373}$$
$$178.76 \le \mu_{Y|X=8} \le 229.64.$$

(b) $\hat{Y} \pm t_{\alpha/2} S_{YX} \sqrt{1 + h_i}$

$$= 204.2 \pm 2.2281(30.81)\sqrt{1 + 0.1373}$$
$$131.00 \le Y_{X=8} \le 277.40.$$

(c) Part (b) provides a prediction interval for the individual response given a specific value of the independent variable, and part (a) provides an interval estimate for the mean value, given a specific value of the independent variable. Because there is much more variation in predicting an individual value than in estimating a mean value, a prediction interval is wider than a confidence interval estimate.

13.60 **(a)** $20.799 \le \mu_{Y|X=500} \le 24.542$. **(b)** $12.276 \le Y_{X=500} \le 33.065$. **(c)** You can estimate a mean more precisely than you can predict a single observation.

13.62 **(a)** $197.6132 \le \mu_{Y|X=150} \le 368.6155$. **(b)** $-37.7056 \le Y_{X=150} \le 603.9343$. **(c)** Part (b) provides a prediction interval for an individual response given a specific value of X, and part (a) provides a confidence interval estimate for the mean value, given a specific value of X. Because there is much more variation in predicting an individual value than in estimating a mean, the prediction interval is wider than the confidence interval.

13.74 **(a)** $b_0 = 24.84$, $b_1 = 0.14$. **(b)** For each additional case, the predicted delivery time is estimated to increase by 0.14 minute. **(c)** 45.84. **(d)** No, 500 is outside the relevant range of the data used to fit the regression equation. **(e)** $r^2 = 0.972$. **(f)** There is no obvious pattern in the residuals, so the assumptions of regression are met. The model appears to be adequate. **(g)** $t_{STAT} = 24.88 > 2.1009$; reject H_0. **(h)** $44.88 \le \mu_{Y|X=150} \le 46.80$. $41.56 \le Y_{X=150} \le 50.12$.

13.76 **(a)** $b_0 = -122.3439$, $b_1 = 1.7817$. **(b)** For each additional \$1,000 in assessed value, the estimated selling price of a house increases by \$1.7817 thousand. The estimated selling price of a house with a 0 assessed value is \$−122.3439 thousand. However, this interpretation is not meaningful because the assessed value cannot be below 0. **(c)** $\hat{Y} = -122.3439 + 1.78171X = -122.3439 + 1.78171(170) = 180.5475$ thousand dollars. **(d)** $r^2 = 0.9256$. So 92.56% of the variation in selling price can be explained by the variation in assessed value. **(e)** Neither the residual plot nor the normal probability plot reveals any potential violation of the linearity, equal variance, and normality assumptions. **(f)** $t_{STAT} = 18.6648 > 2.0484$, p-value is virtually 0. Because p-value < 0.05, reject H_0. There is evidence of a linear relationship between selling price and assessed value. **(g)** $1.5862 \le \beta_1 \le 1.9773$.

13.78 **(a)** $b_0 = 0.30$, $b_1 = 0.00487$. **(b)** For each additional point on the GMAT score, the predicted GPA is estimated to increase by 0.00487. Because a GMAT score of 0 is not possible, the Y intercept does not have a practical interpretation. **(c)** 3.222. **(d)** $r^2 = 0.798$. **(e)** There is no obvious pattern in the residuals, so the assumptions of regression are met. The model appears to be adequate. **(f)** $t_{STAT} = 8.43 > 2.1009$; reject H_0. **(g)** $3.144 \le \mu_{Y|X=600} \le 3.301$, $2.866 \le Y_{X=600} \le 3.559$. **(h)** $.00366 \le \beta_1 \le .00608$.

13.80 **(a)** There is no clear relationship shown on the scatter plot. **(c)** Looking at all 23 flights, when the temperature is lower, there is likely to be some O-ring damage, particularly if the temperature is below 60 degrees. **(d)** 31 degrees is outside the relevant range, so a prediction should not be made. **(e)** Predicted $Y = 18.036 - 0.240X$, where X = temperature and Y = O-ring damage. **(g)** A nonlinear model would be more appropriate. **(h)** The appearance on the residual plot of a nonlinear pattern indicates that a nonlinear model would be better. It also appears that the normality assumption is invalid.

13.82 **(a)** $b_0 = 17.6465$, $b_1 = 2.7684$. **(b)** For each additional million-dollar increase in revenue, the franchise value will increase by an estimated \$2.7684 million. Literal interpretation of b_0 is not meaningful because an operating franchise cannot have zero revenue. **(c)** \$432.9003 million. **(d)** $r^2 = 0.889$. 88.9% of the variation in the value of an NBA franchise can be explained by the variation in its annual revenue. **(e)** There does not appear to be a pattern in the residual plot. The assumptions of regression do not appear to be seriously violated. **(f)** $t_{STAT} = 14.9779 > 2.0484$ or because the p-value is approximately 0, reject H_0 at the 5% level of significance. There is evidence of a linear relationship between annual revenue and franchise value. **(g)** $417.5025 \le \mu_{Y|X=150} \le 448.2982$. **(h)** $408.8257 \le Y_{X=150} \le 465.9544$. **(i)** The strength of the relationship between revenue and value is stronger for NBA franchises than for European soccer teams and Major League Baseball teams.

13.84 **(a)** $b_0 = -2{,}629.222$, $b_1 = 82.472$. **(b)** For each additional centimeter in circumference, the weight is estimated to increase by 82.472 grams. **(c)** 2,319.08 grams. **(d)** Yes, since circumference is a very strong predictor of weight. **(e)** $r^2 = 0.937$. **(f)** There appears to be a nonlinear relationship between circumference and weight. **(g)** p-value is virtually $0 < 0.05$; reject H_0. **(h)** $72.7875 \le \beta_1 \le 92.156$.

13.86 **(b)** $\hat{Y} = 931{,}626.16 + 21{,}782.76X$. **(c)** $b_1 = 21{,}782.76$. For each increase of the median age of the customer base by one year, the latest one-month sales total is estimated to increase by \$21,782.76. $b_0 = 931{,}626.16$. Since age cannot be 0, there is no direct interpretation for b_0. **(d)** $r^2 = 0.0017$. Only 0.17% of the total variation in the franchise's latest one-month sales total can be explained by using the median age of the customer base. **(e)** The residuals are very evenly spread out across different ranges of median age. **(f)** Because $-2.0281 < t_{STAT} = 0.2482 < 2.0281$, do not reject H_0. There is insufficient evidence to conclude that there is a linear relationship between the one-month sales total and the median age of the customer base. **(g)** $-156{,}181.50 \le \beta_1 \le 199{,}747.02$.

13.88 (a) There is a positive linear relationship between total sales and the percentage of the customer base with a college diploma. **(b)** $\hat{Y} = 789{,}847.38 + 35{,}854.15X$. **(c)** $b_1 = 35{,}854.15$. For each increase of 1% of the customer base having received a college diploma, the latest one-month mean sales total is estimated to increase by \$35,854.15. $b_0 = 789{,}847.38$. Although this is outside the range of the data, it would mean that the estimated sales when the percentage of the customer base with a college diploma was 0 would be \$789,847.38. **(d)** $r^2 = 0.1036$. 10.36% of the total variation in the franchise's latest one-month sales total can be explained by the percentage of the customer base with a college diploma. **(e)** The residuals are evenly spread out around zero. **(f)** Because $t_{STAT} = 2.0392 > 2.0281$, reject H_0. There is enough evidence to conclude that there is a linear relationship between one-month sales total and percentage of customer base with a college diploma. **(g)** $b_1 \pm t_{\alpha/2} S_{b_1} = 35{,}854.15 \pm 2.0281(17{,}582.269)$, $195.75 \le \beta_1 \le 71{,}512.60$.

13.90 (a) The correlation between compensation and stock performance is 0.1457. **(b)** $t_{STAT} = 2.0404 > 1.9724$; p-value $= 0.0427 < 0.05$. The correlation between compensation and stock performance is significant, but only 2.12% of the variation in compensation can be explained by return. **(c)** The small correlation between compensation and stock performance was surprising (or maybe it shouldn't have been!).

CHAPTER 14

14.2 (a) For each one-unit increase in X_1, you estimate that Y will decrease 2 units, holding X_2 constant. For each one-unit increase in X_2, you estimate that Y will increase 7 units, holding X_1 constant. **(b)** The Y intercept, equal to 50, estimates the value of Y when both X_1 and X_2 are 0.

14.4 (a) $\hat{Y} = -2.72825 + 0.047114X_1 + 0.011947X_2$. **(b)** For a given number of orders, for each increase of \$1,000 in sales, the distribution cost is estimated to increase by \$47.114. For a given amount of sales, for each increase of one order, the distribution cost is estimated to increase by \$11.95. **(c)** The interpretation of b_0 has no practical meaning here because it would represent the estimated distribution cost when there were no sales and no orders. **(d)** $\hat{Y} = -2.72825 + 0.047114(400) + 0.011947(4500) = 69.878$, or \$69,878. **(e)** $\$66{,}419.93 \le \mu_{Y|X} \le \$73{,}337.01$. **(f)** $\$59{,}380.61 \le Y_X \le \$80{,}376.33$ **(g)** The interval in (e) is narrower because it is estimating the mean value, not an individual value.

14.6 (a) $\hat{Y} = 156.4 + 13.081X_1 + 16.795X_2$. **(b)** For a given amount of newspaper advertising, each increase by \$1,000 in radio advertising is estimated to result in an increase in sales of \$13,081. For a given amount of radio advertising, each increase by \$1,000 in newspaper advertising is estimated to result in an increase in sales of \$16,795. **(c)** When there is no money spent on radio advertising and newspaper advertising, the estimated mean sales is \$156,430.44. **(d)** Holding the other independent variable constant, newspaper advertising seems to be more effective because its slope is greater.

14.8 (a) $\hat{Y} = 400.8057 + 456.4485X_1 - 2.4708X_2$, where X_1 = land area, X_2 = age. **(b)** For a given age, each increase by one acre in land area is estimated to result in an increase in appraised value by \$456.45 thousands. For a given land area, each increase of one year in age is estimated to result in a decrease in appraised value by \$2.47 thousands. **(c)** The interpretation of b_0 has no practical meaning here because it would represent the estimated appraised value of a new house that has no land area. **(d)** $\hat{Y} = 400.8057 + 456.4485(0.25) - 2.4708(45) = \$403.73$ thousands. **(e)** $372.7370 \le \mu_{Y|X} \le 434.7243$. **(f)** $235.1964 \le Y_X \le 572.2649$.

14.10 (a) $MSR = 15$, $MSE = 12$. **(b)** 1.25. **(c)** $F_{STAT} = 1.25 < 4.10$; do not reject H_0. **(d)** 0.20. **(e)** 0.04.

14.12 (a) $F_{STAT} = 97.69 > 3.89$. Reject H_0. There is evidence of a significant linear relationship with at least one of the independent variables. **(b)** p-value $= 0.0001$. **(c)** $r^2 = 0.9421$. 94.21% of the variation in the long-term ability to absorb shock can be explained by variation in forefoot-absorbing capability and variation in midsole impact. **(d)** $r^2_{adj} = 0.935$.

14.14 (a) $F_{STAT} = 74.13 > 3.467$; reject H_0. **(b)** p-value $= 0$. **(c)** $r^2 = 0.8759$. 87.59% of the variation in distribution cost can be explained by variation in sales and variation in number of orders. **(d)** $r^2_{adj} = 0.8641$.

14.16 (a) $F_{STAT} = 40.16 > 3.522$. Reject H_0. There is evidence of a significant linear relationship. **(b)** p-value < 0.001. **(c)** $r^2 = 0.8087$. 80.87% of the variation in sales can be explained by variation in radio advertising and variation in newspaper advertising. **(d)** $r^2_{adj} = 0.7886$.

14.18 (a)–(e) Based on a residual analysis, there is no evidence of a violation of the assumptions of regression. **(f)** $D = 2.26$ **(g)** $D = 2.26 > 1.55$. There is no evidence of positive autocorrelation in the residuals.

14.20 (a) There appears to be a quadratic relationship in the plot of the residuals against both radio and newspaper advertising. **(b)** Since the data are not collected over time, the Durbin-Watson test is not appropriate. **(c)** Curvilinear terms for both of these explanatory variables should be considered for inclusion in the model.

14.22 (a) The residual analysis reveals no patterns. **(b)** Since the data are not collected over time, the Durbin-Watson test is not appropriate. **(c)** There are no apparent violations in the assumptions.

14.24 (a) Variable X_2 has a larger slope in terms of the t statistic of 3.75 than variable X_1, which has a smaller slope in terms of the t statistic of 3.33. **(b)** $1.46824 \le \beta_1 \le 6.53176$. **(c)** For X_1: $t_{STAT} = 4/1.2 = 3.33 > 2.1098$, with 17 degrees of freedom for $\alpha = 0.05$. Reject H_0. There is evidence that X_1 contributes to a model already containing X_2. For X_2: $t_{STAT} = 3/0.8 = 3.75 > 2.1098$, with 17 degrees of freedom for $\alpha = 0.05$. Reject H_0. There is evidence that X_2 contributes to a model already containing X_1. Both X_1 and X_2 should be included in the model.

14.26 (a) 95% confidence interval on β_1: $b_1 \pm tS_{b_1}$, $0.0471 \pm 2.0796(0.0203)$, $0.0049 \le \beta_1 \le 0.0893$. **(b)** For X_1: $t_{STAT} = b_1/S_{b_1} = 0.0471/0.0203 = 2.32 > 2.0796$. Reject H_0. There is evidence that X_1 contributes to a model already containing X_2. For X_2: $t_{STAT} = b_1/S_{b_1} = 0.0112/0.0023 = 5.31 > 2.0796$. Reject H_0. There is evidence that X_2 contributes to a model already containing X_1. Both X_1 (sales) and X_2 (orders) should be included in the model.

14.28 (a) $9.398 \le \beta_1 \le 16.763$. **(b)** For X_1: $t_{STAT} = 7.43 > 2.093$. Reject H_0. There is evidence that X_1 contributes to a model already containing X_2. For X_2: $t_{STAT} = 5.67 > 2.093$. Reject H_0. There is evidence that X_2 contributes to a model already containing X_1. Both X_1 (radio advertising) and X_2 (newspaper advertising) should be included in the model.

14.30 (a) $227.5865 \le \beta_1 \le 685.3104$. **(b)** For X_1: $t_{STAT} = 4.0922$ and p-value $= 0.0003$. Because p-value < 0.05, reject H_0. There is evidence that X_1 contributes to a model already containing X_2. For X_2: $t_{STAT} = -3.6295$ and p-value $= 0.0012$. Because p-value < 0.05 reject H_0. There is evidence that X_2 contributes to a model already X_2: $F_{STAT} =$ containing X_1. Both X_1 (land area) and X_2 (age) should be included in the model.

14.32 (a) For X_1: $F_{STAT} = 1.25 < 4.96$; do not reject H_0. For X_2: $F_{STAT} = 0.833 < 4.96$; do not reject H_0. **(b)** 0.1111, 0.0769.

14.34 (a) For X_1: $SSR(X_1|X_2) = SSR(X_1 \text{ and } X_2) - SSR(X_2) = 3{,}368.087 - 3{,}246.062 = 122.025$, $F_{STAT} = \dfrac{SSR(X_1|X_2)}{MSE} = \dfrac{122.025}{477.043/21} = 5.37 > 4.325$. Reject H_0. There is evidence that X_1 contributes to a model already containing X_2. For X_2: $SSR(X_2|X_1) = SSR(X_1 \text{ and } X_2) - SSR(X_1) = 3{,}368.087 - 2{,}726.822 = 641.265$, $F_{STAT} = \dfrac{SSR(X_2|X_1)}{MSE} = \dfrac{641.265}{477.043/21} = 28.23 > 4.325$.

Reject H_0. There is evidence that X_2 contributes to a model already containing X_1. Because both X_1 and X_2 make a significant contribution to the model in the presence of the other variable, both variables should be included in the model.

$$\textbf{(b)}\, r^2_{Y1.2} = \frac{SSR(X_1|X_2)}{SST - SSR(X_1 \text{ and } X_2) + SSR(X_1|X_2)} = \frac{122.025}{3{,}845.13 - 3{,}368.087 + 122.025} = 0.2037.$$

Holding constant the effect of the number of orders, 20.37% of the variation in distribution cost can be explained by the variation in sales.

$$r^2_{Y2.1} = \frac{SSR(X_2|X_1)}{SST - SSR(X_1 \text{ and } X_2) + SSR(X_2|X_1)} = \frac{641.265}{3{,}845.13 - 3{,}368.087 + 641.265} = 0.5734$$

Holding constant the effect of sales, 57.34% of the variation in distribution cost can be explained by the variation in the number of orders.

14.36 (a) For X_1: $F_{STAT} = 55.28 > 4.381$. Reject H_0. There is evidence that X_1 contributes to a model containing X_2. For X_2: $F_{STAT} = 32.12 > 4.381$. Reject H_0. There is evidence that X_2 contributes to a model already containing X_1. Because both X_1 and X_2 make a significant contribution to the model in the presence of the other variable, both variables should be included in the model. **(b)** $r^2_{Y1.2} = 0.7442$. Holding constant the effect of newspaper advertising, 74.42% of the variation in sales can be explained by the variation in radio advertising. $r^2_{Y2.1} = 0.6283$. Holding constant the effect of radio advertising, 62.83% of the variation in sales can be explained by the variation in newspaper advertising.

14.38 (a) Holding constant the effect of X_2, for each increase of one unit of X_1, Y increases by 4 units. **(b)** Holding constant the effect of X_1, for each increase of one unit of X_2, Y increases by 2 units. **(c)** Because $t_{STAT} = 3.27 > 2.1098$, reject H_0. Variable X_2 makes a significant contribution to the model.

14.40 (a) $\hat{Y} = 243.7371 + 9.2189X_1 + 12.6967X_2$, where X_1 = number of rooms and X_2 = neighborhood (east = 0). **(b)** Holding constant the effect of neighborhood, for each additional room, the selling price is estimated to increase by 9.2189 thousands of dollars, or \$9,218.9. For a given number of rooms, a west neighborhood is estimated to increase the selling price over an east neighborhood by 12.6967 thousands of dollars, or \$12,696.7. **(c)** $\hat{Y} = 243.7371 + 9.2189(9) + 12.6967(0) = 326.7076$, or \$326, 707.6. $\$309{,}560.04 \le Y_X \le 343{,}855.1$. $\$321{,}471.44 \le \mu_{Y|X} \le \$331{,}943.71$. **(d)** Based on a residual analysis, the model appears to be adequate. **(e)** $F_{STAT} = 55.39$, the p-value is virtually 0. Because p-value < 0.05, reject H_0. There is evidence of a significant relationship between selling price and the two independent variables (rooms and neighborhood). **(f)** For X_1: $t_{STAT} = 8.9537$, the p-value is virtually 0. Reject H_0. Number of rooms makes a significant contribution and should be included in the model. For X_2: $t_{STAT} = 3.5913$, p-value $= 0.0023 < 0.05$. Reject H_0. Neighborhood makes a significant contribution and should be included in the model. Based on these results, the regression model with the two independent variables should be used. **(g)** $7.0466 \le \beta_1 \le 11.3913$. **(h)** $5.2378 \le \beta_2 \le 20.1557$. **(i)** $r^2_{adj} = 0.851$. **(j)** $r^2_{Y1.2} = 0.825$. Holding constant the effect of neighborhood, 82.5% of the variation in selling price can be explained by variation in number of rooms. $r^2_{Y2.1} = 0.431$. Holding constant the effect of number of rooms, 43.1% of the variation in selling price can be explained by variation in neighborhood. **(k)** The slope of selling price with number of rooms is the same, regardless of whether the house is located in an east or west neighborhood. **(l)** $\hat{Y} = 253.95 + 8.032X_1 - 5.90X_2 + 2.089X_1X_2$. For $X_1\,X_2$, p-value $= 0.330$. Do not reject H_0. There is no evidence that the interaction term makes a contribution to the model. **(m)** The model in (b) should be used.

14.42 (a) Predicted time $= 8.01 + 0.00523$ Depth $- 2.105$ Dry. **(b)** Holding constant the effect of type of drilling, for each foot increase in depth of the hole, the drilling time is estimated to increase by 0.00523 minutes. For a given depth, a dry drilling hole is estimated to reduce the drilling time over wet drilling by 2.1052 minutes. **(c)** 6.428 minutes, $6.210 \le \mu_{Y|X} \le 6.646$, $4.923 \le Y_X \le 7.932$. **(d)** The model appears to be adequate. **(e)** $F_{STAT} = 111.11 > 3.09$; reject H_0. **(f)** $t_{STAT} = 5.03 > 1.9847$; reject H_0. $t_{STAT} = -14.03 < -1.9847$; reject H_0. Include both variables. **(g)** $0.0032 \le \beta_1 \le 0.0073$. **(h)** $-2.403 \le \beta_2 \le -1.808$. **(i)** 69.0%. **(j)** 0.207, 0.670. **(k)** The slope of the additional drilling time with the depth of the hole is the same, regardless of the type of drilling method used. **(l)** The p-value of the interaction term $= 0.462 > 0.05$, so the term is not significant and should not be included in the model. **(m)** The model in part (b) should be used.

14.44 (a) $\hat{Y} = 31.5594 + 0.0296X_1 + 0.0041X_2 + 0.000017159X_1X_2$, where X_1 = sales, X_2 = orders, p-value $= 0.3249 > 0.05$. Do not reject H_0. There is not enough evidence that the interaction term makes a contribution to the model. **(b)** Because there is insufficient evidence of any interaction effect between sales and orders, the model in Problem 14.4 should be used.

14.46 (a) The p-value of the interaction term $= 0.002 < 0.05$, so the term is significant and should be included in the model. **(b)** Use the model developed in this problem.

14.48 (a) For $X_1\,X_2$, p-value $= 0.2353 > 0.05$. Do not reject H_0. There is insufficient evidence that the interaction term makes a contribution to the model. **(b)** Because there is not enough evidence of an interaction effect between total staff present and remote hours, the model in Problem 14.7 should be used.

14.50 Holding constant the effect of other variables, the natural logarithm of the estimated odds ratio for the dependent categorical response will increase by 2.2 for each unit increase in the particular independent variable.

14.52 0.4286.

14.54 (a) $\ln(\text{estimated odds ratio}) = -6.9394 + 0.1395X_1 + 2.7743X_2 = -6.9394 + 0.1395(36) + 2.7743(0) = -1.91908$. Estimated odds ratio $= e^{-1.91908} = 0.1470$. Estimated Probability of

Success = Odds Ratio/(1 + Odds Ratio) = 0.1470/(1 + 0.1470) = 0.1260. **(b)** From the text discussion of the example, 70.2% of the individuals who charge $36,000 per annum and possess additional cards can be expected to purchase the premium card. Only 12.60% of the individuals who charge $36,000 per annum and do not possess additional cards can be expected to purchase the premium card. For a given amount of money charged per annum, the likelihood of purchasing a premium card is substantially higher among individuals who already possess additional cards than for those who do not possess additional cards. **(c)** ln(estimated odds ratio) = $-6.9394 + 0.13957X_1 + 2.7743X_2 = -6.9394 + 0.1395(18) + 2.7743(0) = -4.4298$. Estimated odds ratio = $e^{-4.4298} = 0.0119$. Estimated Probability of Success = Odds Ratio/(1 + Odds Ratio) = 0.0119/(1 + 0.0119) = 0.01178. **(d)** Among individuals who do not purchase additional cards, the likelihood of purchasing a premium card diminishes dramatically with a substantial decrease in the amount charged per annum.

14.56 (a) ln(estimated odds) = −121.95 + 8.053 GPA + 0.1573 GMAT. **(b)** Holding constant the effect of GMAT score, for each increase of one point in GPA, ln(estimated odds) increases by an estimate of 8.053. Holding constant the effect of GPA, for each increase of one point in GMAT score, ln(estimated odds) increases by an estimate of 0.1573. **(c)** 0.197. **(d)** Deviance statistic = 8.122 < 40.133, do not reject H_0, so model is adequate. **(e)** For GPA: $Z_{STAT} = 1.60 < 1.96$, do not reject H_0. For GMAT: $Z_{STAT} = 2.07 > 1.96$, reject H_0. **(f)** ln(estimated odds) = 2.765 + 1.02 GPA. **(g)** ln(estimated odds) = −60.15 + 0.099 GMAT. **(h)** Use model in (g).

14.68 (a) $\hat{Y} = -3.9152 + 0.0319X_1 + 4.2228X_2$, where X_1 = number cubic feet moved and X_2 = number of pieces of large furniture. **(b)** Holding constant the number of pieces of large furniture, for each additional cubic foot moved, the labor hours are estimated to increase by 0.0319. Holding constant the amount of cubic feet moved, for each additional piece of large furniture, the labor hours are estimated to increase by 4.2228. **(c)** $\hat{Y} = -3.9152 + 0.0319(500) + 4.2228\,(2) = 20.4926$. **(d)** Based on a residual analysis, the errors appear to be normally distributed. The equal-variance assumption might be violated because the variances appear to be larger around the center region of both independent variables. There might also be violation of the linearity assumption. A model with quadratic terms for both independent variables might be fitted. **(e)** $F_{STAT} = 228.80$, p-value is virtually 0. Because p-value < 0.05, reject H_0. There is evidence of a significant relationship between labor hours and the two independent variables (the amount of cubic feet moved and the number of pieces of large furniture). **(f)** The p-value is virtually 0. The probability of obtaining a test statistic of 228.80 or greater is virtually 0 if there is no significant relationship between labor hours and the two independent variables (the amount of cubic feet moved and the number of pieces of large furniture). **(g)** $r^2 = 0.9327.93.27\%$ of the variation in labor hours can be explained by variation in the number of cubic feet moved and the number of pieces of large furniture. **(h)** $r^2_{adj} = 0.9287$. **(i)** For X_1: $t_{STAT} = 6.9339$, the p-value is virtually 0. Reject H_0. The number of cubic feet moved makes a significant contribution and should be included in the model. For X_2: $t_{STAT} = 4.6192$, the p-value is virtually 0. Reject H_0. The number of pieces of large furniture makes a significant contribution and should be included in the model. Based on these results, the regression model with the two independent variables should be used. **(j)** For X_1: $t_{STAT} = 6.9339$, the p-value is virtually 0. The probability of obtaining a sample that will yield a test statistic farther away than 6.9339 is virtually 0 if the number of cubic feet moved does not make a significant contribution, holding the effect of the number of pieces of large furniture constant. For X_2: $t_{STAT} = 4.6192$, the p-value is virtually 0. The probability of obtaining a sample that will yield a test statistic farther away than 4.6192 is virtually 0 if the number of pieces of large furniture does not make a significant contribution, holding the effect of the amount of cubic feet moved constant. **(k)** $0.0226 \le \beta_1 \le 0.0413$. You are 95% confident that the mean labor hours will increase by between 0.0226 and 0.0413 for each additional cubic foot moved, holding constant the number of pieces of large furniture. In Problem 13.44, you are 95% confident that the labor hours will increase by between 0.0439 and 0.0562 for each additional cubic foot moved, regardless of the number of pieces of large furniture. **(l)** $r^2_{Y1.2} = 0.5930$. Holding constant the effect of the number of pieces of large furniture, 59.3% of the variation in labor hours can be explained by variation in the amount of cubic feet moved. $r^2_{Y2.1} = 0.3927$. Holding constant the effect of the number of cubic feet moved, 39.27% of the variation in labor hours can be explained by variation in the number of pieces of large furniture.

14.70 (a) $\hat{Y} = -120.0483 + 1.7506X_1 + 0.3680X_2$, where X_1 = assessed value and X_2 = time since assessment. **(b)** Holding constant the time period, for each additional thousand dollars of assessed value, the selling price is estimated to increase by 1.7506 thousand dollars. Holding constant the assessed value, for each additional month since assessment, the selling price is estimated to increase by 0.3680 thousand dollars. **(c)** $\hat{Y} = -120.0483 + 1.7506(170) + 0.3680(12) = 181.9692$ thousand dollars. **(d)** Based on a residual analysis, the model appears to be adequate. **(e)** $F_{STAT} = 223.46$, the p-value is virtually 0. Because p-value < 0.05, reject H_0. There is evidence of a significant relationship between selling price and the two independent variables (assessed value and time since assessment). **(f)** The p-value is virtually 0. The probability of obtaining a test statistic of 223.46 or greater is virtually 0 if there is no significant relationship between selling price and the two independent variables (assessed value and time since assessment). **(g)** $r^2 = 0.9430$. 94.30% of the variation in selling price can be explained by variation in assessed value and time since assessment. **(h)** $r^2_{adj} = 0.9388$. **(i)** For X_1: $t_{STAT} = 20.4137$, the p-value is virtually 0. Reject H_0. The assessed value makes a significant contribution and should be included in the model. For X_2: $t_{STAT} = 2.8734$, p-value = 0.0078 < 0.05. Reject H_0. The time since assessment makes a significant contribution and should be included in the model. Based on these results, the regression model with the two independent variables should be used. **(j)** For X_1: $t_{STAT} = 20.4137$, the p-value is virtually 0. The probability of obtaining a sample that will yield a test statistic farther away than 20.4137 is virtually 0 if the assessed value does not make a significant contribution, holding time since assessment constant. For X_2: $t_{STAT} = 2.8734$, the p-value is virtually 0. The probability of obtaining a sample that will yield a test statistic farther away than 2.8734 is virtually 0 if the time since assessment does not make a significant contribution holding the effect of the assessed value constant. **(k)** $1.5746 \le \beta_1 \le 1.9266$. You are 95% confident that the selling price will increase by an amount somewhere between $1.5746 thousand and $1.9266 thousand for each additional thousand-dollar increase in assessed value, holding constant the time since assessment. In Problem 13.76, you are 95% confident that the selling price will increase by an amount somewhere between $1.5862 thousand and $1.9773 thousand for each additional $1,000 increase in assessed value, regardless of the time since assessment. **(l)** $r^2_{Y1.2} = 0.9392$. Holding constant the effect of the time since assessment, 93.92% of the variation in selling price can be explained by variation in the assessed value. $r^2_{Y2.1} = 0.2342$. Holding constant the effect of the assessed value, 23.42% of the variation in selling price can be explained by variation in the time since assessment.

14.72 (a) $\hat{Y} = 163.7751 + 10.7252X_1 - 0.2843X_2$, where X_1 = size and X_2 = age. **(b)** Holding age constant, for each additional 1,000 square feet, the assessed value is estimated to increase by $10.7252 thousand. Holding size constant, for each additional year, the assessed value is estimated to decrease by $0.2843 thousand. **(c)** $\hat{Y} = 163.7751 + 10.7252(1.75) - 0.2843(10) = 179.7017$ thousand dollars. **(d)** Based on a residual analysis, the errors appear to be normally distributed. The equal-variance assumption appears to be valid. There might be a violation of the linearity assumption for age. You might want to include a quadratic term in the model for age. **(e)** $F_{STAT} = 28.58$, p-value $= 0.0000272776$. Because p-value $= 0.0000 < 0.05$, reject H_0. There is evidence of a significant relationship between assessed value and the two independent variables (size and age). **(f)** p-value $= 0.0000272776$. The probability of obtaining an F_{STAT} test statistic of 28.58 or greater is virtually 0 if there is no significant relationship between assessed value and the two independent variables (size and age). **(g)** $r^2 = 0.8265$. 82.65% of the variation in assessed value can be explained by variation in size and age. **(h)** $r^2_{adj} = 0.7976$. **(i)** For X_1: $t_{STAT} = 3.5581$, p-value $= 0.0039 < 0.05$. Reject H_0. The size of a house makes a significant contribution and should be included in the model. For X_2: $t_{STAT} = -3.4002$, p-value $= 0.0053 < 0.05$. Reject H_0. The age of a house makes a significant contribution and should be included in the model. Based on these results, the regression model with the two independent variables should be used. **(j)** For X_1: p-value $= 0.0039$. The probability of obtaining a sample that will yield a test statistic farther away than 3.5581 is 0.0039 if the size of a house does not make a significant contribution, holding age constant. For X_2: p-value $= 0.0053$. The probability of obtaining a sample that will yield a test statistic farther away than -3.4002 is 0.0053 if the age of a house does not make a significant contribution, holding the effect of the size constant. **(k)** $4.1572 \le \beta_1 \le 17.2928$. You are 95% confident that the mean assessed value will increase by an amount somewhere between \$4.1575 thousand and \$17.2928 thousand for each additional 1,000-square-foot increase in the size of a house, holding constant the age. In Problem 13.77, you are 95% confident that the mean assessed value will increase by an amount somewhere between \$9.4695 thousand and \$23.7972 thousand for each additional thousand-square-foot increase in heating area, regardless of the age. **(l)** $r^2_{Y1.2} = 0.5134$. Holding constant the effect of age, 51.34% of the variation in assessed value can be explained by variation in the size. $r^2_{Y2.1} = 0.4907$. Holding constant the effect of the size, 49.07% of the variation in assessed value can be explained by variation in the age. **(m)** Based on your answers to (b) through (k), the age of a house does have an effect on its assessed value.

14.74 (a) $\hat{Y} = 155.4323 - 18.1684X_1 - 5.5176X_2$, where X_1 = ERA and X_2 = league (American = 0 National = 1). **(b)** Holding constant the effect of the league, for each additional ERA, the number of wins is estimated to decrease by 18.1684. For a given ERA, a team in the National League is estimated to have 5.05176 fewer wins than a team in the American League. **(c)** 73.6745 wins. **(d)** Based on a residual analysis, there is no pattern in the errors. There is no apparent violation of other assumptions. **(e)** $F_{STAT} = 10.2272 > 3.35$, p-value $= 0.0005$. Because p-value < 0.05, reject H_0. There is evidence of a significant relationship between wins and the two independent variables (ERA and league). **(f)** For X_1: $t_{STAT} = -4.5171 < -2.0518$, the p-value = 0.0001. Reject H_0. ERA makes a significant contribution and should be included in the model. For X_2: $t_{STAT} = -1.6071 > -2.0518$, p-value $= 0.1197 > 0.05$. Do not reject H_0. The league does not make a significant contribution and should not be included in the model. Based on these results, the regression model with only the ERA as the independent variable should be used. **(g)** $-26.4211 \le \beta_1 \le -9.9157$. **(h)** $-12.5621 \le \beta_2 \le 1.5270$. **(i)** $r^2_{adj} = 0.3889$. 38.89% of the variation in wins can be explained by the variation in ERA and league after adjusting for number of independent variables and sample size. **(j)** $r^2_{Y1.2} = 0.4304$. Holding constant the effect of league, 43.04% of the variation in number of wins can be explained by the variation in ERA. $r^2_{Y2.1} = 0.0873$. Holding constant the effect of ERA, 8.73% of the variation in number of wins can be explained by the variation in league. **(k)** The slope of the number of wins with ERA is the same, regardless of whether the team belongs to the American League or the National League. **(l)** For X_1X_2: $t_{STAT} = -0.2320 > -2.0555$ the p-value is $0.8184 > 0.05$. Do not reject H_0. There is no evidence that the interaction term makes a contribution to the model. **(m)** The model with one independent variable (ERA) should be used.

14.76 The r^2 of the multiple regression is very low, at 0.0645. Only 6.45% of the variation in thickness can be explained by the variation of pressure and temperature. The F test statistic for the model including pressure and temperature is 1.621, with p-value $= 0.2085$. Hence, at a 5% level of significance, there is not enough evidence to conclude that pressure and/or temperature affect thickness. The p-value of the t test for the significance of pressure is $0.8307 > 0.05$. Hence, there is insufficient evidence to conclude that pressure affects thickness, holding constant the effect of temperature. The p-value of the t test for the significance of temperature is 0.0820, which is also > 0.05. There is insufficient evidence to conclude that temperature affects thickness at the 5% level of significance, holding constant the effect of pressure. Hence, neither pressure nor temperature affects thickness individually.

The normal probability plot does not suggest any potential violation of the normality assumption. The residual plots do not indicate potential violation of the equal variance assumption. The temperature residual plot, however, suggests that there might be a nonlinear relationship between temperature and thickness.

The r^2 of the multiple regression model that includes the interaction of pressure and temperature is very low, at 0.0734. Only 7.34% of the variation in thickness can be explained by the variation of pressure, temperature, and the interaction of the two. The F test statistic for the model that includes pressure and temperature and their interaction is 1.214, with a p-value of 0.3153. Hence, at a 5% level of significance, there is insufficient evidence to conclude that pressure, temperature, and the interaction of the two affect thickness. The p-value of the t test for the significance of pressure, temperature, and the interaction term are 0.5074, 0.4053, and 0.5111, respectively, which are all greater than 5%. Hence, there is insufficient evidence to conclude that pressure, temperature, or the interaction individually affects thickness, holding constant the effect of the other variables.

The pattern in the normal probability plot and residual plots is similar to that in the regression without the interaction term. Hence the article's suggestion that there is a significant interaction between the pressure and the temperature in the tank cannot be validated.

CHAPTER 15

15.2 (a) Predicted HOCS is 2.8600, 3.0342, 3.1948, 3.3418, 3.4752, 3.5950, 3.7012, 3.7938, 3.8728, 3.9382, 3.99, 4.0282, 4.0528, 4.0638, 4.0612, 4.045, 4.0152, 3.9718, 3.9148, 3.8442, and 3.76. **(c)** The curvilinear relationship suggests that HOCS increases at a decreasing rate. It reaches its maximum value of 4.0638 at GPA = 3.3 and declines after that as GPA continues to increase. **(d)** An r^2 of 0.07 and an adjusted r^2 of 0.06 tell you that GPA has very low explanatory power in identifying the variation in HOCS. You can tell that the individual HOCS scores are scattered widely around the curvilinear relationship.

15.4 (a) $\hat{Y} = -3.7203 + 22.0215X_1 + 3.9812X_2$ where X_1 = alcohol % and X_2 = carbohydrates. $F_{STAT} = 2{,}177.1912$, p-value $= 0.0000 < 0.05$, so reject H_0. At the 5% level of significance, the linear terms are significant together. **(b)** $\hat{Y} = 11.5227 + 14.9628X_1 + 4.3599X_2 + 0.4817X_1^2 - 0.0134X_2^2$, where X_1 = alcohol % and X_2 = carbohydrates. **(c)** $F_{STAT} = 1{,}144.1146$ p-value $= 0.0000 < 0.05$, so reject H_0. At the 5% level of significance, the model with quadratic terms are significant. $t_{STAT} = 3.0310$, and the p-value $= 0.0029$. Reject H_0. There is enough evidence that the quadratic term for alcohol % is significant at the 5% level of significance. $t_{STAT} = -0.8236$, p-value $= 0.4115$. Do not reject H_0. There is insufficient evidence that the quadratic term for carbohydrates is significant at the 5% level of significance. Hence, since the quadratic term for alcohol is significant, the model in (b) that includes this term is better. The normal probability plot suggests some left-skewness in the errors. However, because of the large sample size, the validity of the results is not seriously impacted. The residual plots of the alcohol percentage and carbohydrates in the quadratic model do not reveal any remaining nonlinearity. **(d)** The number of calories in a beer depends quadratically on the alcohol percentage but linearly on the number of carbohydrates. The alcohol percentage and number of carbohydrates explain about 96.84% of the variation in the number of calories in a beer.

15.6 (b) Predicted cost $= 710.00 + 607.9773$ units $- 1.3693$ units^2. **(c)** Predicted cost $= 710.00 + 607.9773(145) - 1.3693(145)^2$ $=$ \$60.076.79. **(d)** There appears to be a curvilinear pattern in the residual plot of the units and the units squared. **(e)** $F_{STAT} = 320.5955 > 4.74$; reject H_0. **(f)** p-value $= 0.0000 < 0.05$, so the model is significant. **(g)** $t_{STAT} = -5.5790 < -2.3646$; reject H_0. There is a significant quadratic effect. **(h)** p-value $= 0.0008 < 0.05$, so the quadratic term is significant. **(i)** 98.92% of the variation in yield can be explained by the quadratic model. **(j)** 98.61%.

15.8 (a) 215.37. **(b)** For each additional unit of the logarithm of X_1, the logarithm of Y is estimated to increase by 0.9 unit, holding all other variables constant. For each additional unit of the logarithm of X_2, the logarithm of Y is estimated to increase by 1.41 units, holding all other variables constant.

15.10 (a) $\hat{Y} = -151.8524 + 94.1835\sqrt{X_1} + 27.3014\sqrt{X_2}$, where X_1 = alcohol % and X_2 = carbohydrates. **(b)** The normal probability plot suggests that the errors are right-skewed. However, because of the large sample size, the validity of the results is not seriously impacted. The residual plots of the square-root transformation of alcohol percentage and carbohydrates do not reveal any remaining nonlinearity. **(c)** $F_{STAT} = 1{,}021.3978$. Because the p-value is virtually 0, reject H_0 at the 5% level of significance. There is evidence of a significant linear relationship between calories and the square root of the percentage of alcohol and the square root of the number of carbohydrates. **(d)** $r^2 = 0.9329$. So 93.29% of the variation in calories can be explained by the variation in the square root of the percentage of alcohol and the square root of the number of carbohydrates. **(e)** Adjusted $r^2 = 0.9320$. **(f)** The model in Problem 15.4 is slightly better because it has a higher r^2.

15.12 (a) Predicted $\ln(\text{Cost}) = 9.7664 + 0.0080$ Units **(b)** \$55,471.75. **(c)** A quadratic pattern exists, so the model is not adequate. **(d)** $t_{STAT} = 7.362 > 2.306$; reject H_0. **(e)** 87.14%. 87.14 % of the variation in the natural log of the cost can be explained by the number of units. **(f)** 85.53%. **(g)** Choose the model from Problem 15.6. That model has a much higher adjusted r^2 of 98.61%.

15.14 1.25.

15.16 $R_1^2 = 0.64$, $VIF_1 = \dfrac{1}{1 - 0.64} = 2.778$, $R_2^2 = 0.64$,

$VIF_2 = \dfrac{1}{1 - 0.64} = 2.778$. There is no evidence of collinearity.

15.18 $VIF = 1.0 < 5$. There is no evidence of collinearity.

15.20 $VIF = 1.0428$. There is no evidence of collinearity.

15.22 (a) 35.04. **(b)** $C_p > 3$. This does not meet the criterion for consideration of a good model.

15.24 Let Y = selling price, X_1 = assessed value, X_2 = time since assessment, and X_3 = whether house was new (0 = no, 1 = yes). Based on a full regression model involving all of the variables, all the VIF values (1.32, 1.04, and 1.31, respectively) are less than 5. There is no reason to suspect the existence of collinearity. Based on a best-subsets regression and examination of the resulting C_p values, the best models appear to be a model with variables X_1 and X_2, which has $C_p = 2.84$, and the full regression model, which has $C_p = 4.0$. Based on a regression analysis with all the original variables, variable X_3 fails to make a significant contribution to the model at the 0.05 level. Thus, the best model is the model using the assessed value (X_1) and time since assessment (X_2) as the independent variables. A residual analysis shows no strong patterns. The final model is $\hat{Y} = -120.0483 + 1.7506X_1 + 0.3680X_2$, $r^2 = 0.9430$, $r^2_{adj} = 0.9388$. Overall significance of the model: $F_{STAT} = 223.4575$, $p < 0.001$. Each independent variable is significant at the 0.05 level.

15.30 (a) An analysis of the linear regression model with all of the three possible independent variables reveals that the highest VIF is only 1.06. A stepwise regression model selects only the supplier dummy variable for inclusion in the model. A best-subsets regression produces only one model that has a C_p value less than or equal to $k + 1$ which is the model that includes pressure and the supplier dummy variable. This model is $\hat{Y} = -31.5929 + 0.7879X_2 + 13.1029X_3$. This model has $F = 5.1088$ (2 and 11 degrees of freedom) with a p-value $= 0.027$. $r^2 = 0.4816$, $r^2_{adj} = 0.3873$. A residual analysis does not reveal any strong patterns. The errors appear to be normally distributed.

15.32 (a) Best model: predicted appraised value $= 136.794 + 276.0876$ land $+ 0.1288$ house size (sq ft) $- 1.3989$ age. **(b)** The adjusted r^2 for the best model in 15.32 (a), 15.33 (a), and 15.34 (a) are, respectively, 0.81, 0.8117, and 0.8383. The model in 15.34 (a) has the highest explanatory power after adjusting for the number of independent variables and sample size.

15.34 (a) Predicted appraised value $= 110.27 + 0.0821$ house size (sq. ft.). **(b)** The adjusted r^2 for the best model in 15.32(a), 15.33(a), and 15.34 (a) are, respectively, 0.81, 0.8117, and 0.8383. The model in 15.34 (a) has the highest explanatory power after adjusting for the number of independent variables and sample size.

15.36 Let Y = appraised value, X_1 = land area, X_2 = interior, X_3 = age, X_4 = number of rooms, X_5 = number of bathrooms, X_6 = garage size, $X_7 = 1$ if Glen Cove and 0 otherwise, and $X_8 = 1$ if Roslyn and 0 otherwise. **(a)** All VIFs are less than 5 in a full regression model involving all the variables: There is no reason to suspect collinearity between any pair of variables. The following is the multiple regression model that has the smallest $C_p(9.0)$ and the highest adjusted $r^2(0.891)$:

$$\begin{aligned}\text{Appraised Value} = {} & 49.4 + 343\text{ Land} + 0.115\text{ House Size} \\ & -0.585\text{ Age} - 8.24\text{ Rooms} + 26.9\text{ Baths} \\ & +5.0\text{ Garage} + 56.4\text{ Glen Cove} + 210\text{ Roslyn}\end{aligned}$$

The individual t test for the significance of each independent variable at the 5% level of significance concludes that only X_1, X_2, X_5, X_7, and X_8 are significant individually. This subset, however, is not chosen when the C_p criterion is used. The following is the multiple regression result for the model chosen by stepwise regression:

$$\begin{aligned}\text{Appraised Value} = {} & 23.4 + 347\text{ Land} + 0.106\text{ House Size} \\ & -0.792\text{ Age} + 26.4\text{ Baths} + 57.7\text{ Glen Cove} \\ & +213\text{ Roslyn}\end{aligned}$$

This model has a C_p value of 7.7 and an adjusted r^2 of 0.89. All the variables are significant individually at the 5% level of significance. Combining the stepwise regression and the best-subsets regression results along with the individual t test results, the most appropriate multiple regression model for predicting the appraised value is

$$\hat{Y} = 23.40 + 347.02X_1 + 0.10614X_2 - 0.7921X_3 + 26.38X_5 + 57.74X_7 + 213.46X_8.$$

(b) The estimated appraised value in Glen Cove is 57.74 thousand dollars above Freeport for two otherwise identical properties. The estimated appraised value in Roslyn is 213.46 thousand dollars above Freeport for two otherwise identical properties.

15.38 In the multiple regression model with catalyst, pH, pressure, temperature, and voltage as independent variables, none of the variables has a *VIF* value of 5 or larger. The best-subsets approach showed that only the model containing X_1, X_2, X_3, X_4, and X_5 should be considered, where X_1 = catalyst, X_2 = pH, X_3 = pressure, X_4 = temp, and X_5 = voltage. Looking at the p-values of the t statistics for each slope coefficient of the model that includes X_1 through X_5 reveals that pH level is not significant at the 5% level of significance (p-value $= 0.2862$). The multiple regression model with pH level deleted shows that all coefficients are significant individually at the 5% level of significance. The best linear model is determined to be $\hat{Y} = 3.6833 + 0.1548X_1 - 0.04197X_3 - 0.4036X_4 + 0.4288X_5$. The overall model has $F = 77.0793$ (4 and 45 degrees of freedom), with a p-value that is virtually 0. $r^2 = 0.8726$, $r^2_{adj} = 0.8613$. The normal probability plot does not suggest possible violation of the normality assumption. A residual analysis reveals a potential nonlinear relationship in temperature. The p-value of the squared term for temperature (0.1273) in the following quadratic transformation of temperature does not support the need for a quadratic transformation at the 5% level of significance. The p-value of the interaction term between pressure and temperature (0.0780) indicates that there is not enough evidence of an interaction at the 5% level of significance. The best model is the one that includes catalyst, pressure, temperature, and voltage, which explains 87.26% of the variation in thickness.

CHAPTER 16

16.2 (a) 1988. **(b)** The first four years and the last four years.

16.4 (b), (c), (e)

Year	Drive-Thru Speed	*MA*(3)	*ES* ($W = 0.5$)	*ES* ($W = 0.25$)
1998	177.59		177.5900	177.5900
1999	167.02	171.4967	172.3050	174.9475
2000	169.88	169.2500	171.0925	173.6806
2001	170.85	167.8167	170.9713	172.9730
2002	162.72	163.4967	166.8456	170.4097
2003	156.92	157.3867	161.8828	167.0373
2004	152.52	159.1133	157.2014	163.4080
2005	167.90	161.4400	162.5507	164.5310
2006	163.90	166.3000	163.2254	164.3732
2007	167.10	163.2567	165.1627	165.0549
2008	158.77	166.6967	161.9663	163.4837
2009	174.22		168.0932	166.1678

(d) $W = 0.5$: $\hat{Y}_{2010} = E_{2009} = 168.0932$; $W = 0.25$: $\hat{Y}_{2010} = E_{2009} = 166.1678$. **(f)** The exponentially smoothed forecast for 2010 with $W = 0.5$ is higher than that with $W = 0.25$. A smoothing coefficient of $W = 0.25$ smooths out the average time more than $W = 0.50$. The exponential smoothing with $W = 0.5$ assigns more weight to the more recent values and is better for forecasting, while the exponential smoothing with $W = 0.25$, which assigns more weight to more distance values, is better suited for eliminating unwanted cyclical and irregular variations.

16.6 (b), (c), (e)

Decade	Performance (%)	*MA*(3)	*ES*($W = 0.5$)	*ES*($W = 0.25$)
1830s	2.8		2.8000	2.8000
1840s	12.8	7.4000	7.8000	5.3000
1850s	6.6	10.6333	7.2000	5.6250
1860s	12.5	8.8667	9.8500	7.3438
1870s	7.5	8.6667	8.6750	7.3828
1880s	6.0	6.3333	7.3375	7.0371
1890s	5.5	7.4667	6.4188	6.6528
1900s	10.9	6.2000	8.6594	7.7146
1910s	2.2	8.8000	5.4297	6.3360
1920s	13.3	4.4333	9.3648	8.0770
1930s	−2.2	6.9000	3.5824	5.5077
1940s	9.6	8.5333	6.5912	6.5308
1950s	18.2	12.0333	12.3956	9.4481
1960s	8.3	11.0333	10.3478	9.1611
1970s	6.6	10.5000	8.4739	8.5208
1980s	16.6	13.6000	12.5370	10.5406
1990s	17.6	11.2333	15.0685	12.3055
2000s	−0.5		7.2842	9.1041

(d) $\hat{Y}_{2010} = E_{2000} = 7.2842$ **(e)** $\hat{Y}_{2010} = E_{2000} = 9.1041$. **(f)** The exponentially smoothed forecast for the 2010s with $W = 0.5$ is lower than that with $W = 0.25$. The exponential smoothing with $W = 0.5$ assigns more weight to the more recent values and is better for forecasting, while the exponential smoothing with $W = 0.25$ which assigns more weight to more distant values is better suited for eliminating unwanted cyclical and irregular variations. **(g)** According to the exponential smoothing with $W = 0.25$, there appears to be a general upward trend in the performance of the stocks in the past.

16.8 (b), (c), (e)

Year	Audits	*MA*(3)	*ES* ($W = 0.5$)	*ES*($W = 0.25$)
2001	3305		3305.00	3305.00
2002	3749	3461.33	3527.00	3416.00
2003	3330	3821.67	3428.50	3394.50
2004	4386	4191.67	3907.25	3642.38
2005	4859	4407.00	4383.13	3946.53
2006	4276	4186.33	4329.56	4028.90
2007	3424	3784.67	3876.78	3877.67
2008	3654	3616.33	3765.39	3821.76
2009	3771	3625.00	3768.20	3809.07
2010	3450	3630.00	3609.10	3719.30
2011	3669		3639.05	3706.72

(d) $W = 0.5$: $\hat{Y}_{2012} = E_{2011} = 3{,}639.05$; $W = 0.25$: $\hat{Y}_{2012} = E_{2011} = 3706.72$. **(f)** The exponentially smoothed forecast for 2012 with $W = 0.5$ is lower than that with $W = 0.25$. The exponential smoothing with $W = 0.5$ assigns more weight to the more recent values and is better for forecasting, while the exponential smoothing with $W = 0.25$, which assigns more weight to more distant values, is better suited for eliminating unwanted cyclical and irregular variations.

16.10 (a) The Y intercept $b_0 = 4.0$ is the fitted trend value reflecting the real total revenues (in millions of dollars) during the origin, or base year, 1991. **(b)** The slope $b_1 = 1.5$ indicates that the real total revenues are increasing at an estimated rate of \$1.5 million per year. **(c)** Year is 1995, $X = 1995 - 1991 = 4$, $\hat{Y}_5 = 4.0 + 1.5(4) = 10.0$ million dollars. **(d)** Year is 2012, $X = 2012 - 1991 = 21$, $\hat{Y}_{20} = 4.0 + 1.5(21) = 35.5$ million dollars. **(e)** Year is 2015, $X = 2015 - 1991 = 24$, $\hat{Y}_{23} = 4.0 + 1.5(24) = 40$ million dollars.

16.12 (b) Linear trend: $\hat{Y} = 50.1691 + 79.7191X$, where X is relative to 1997. **(c)** Quadratic trend: $\hat{Y} = 35.6532 + 85.9402X - 0.4147X^2$, where X is relative to 1997. **(d)** Exponential trend: $\log_{10}\hat{Y} = 2.1851 + 0.0697X$, where X is relative to 1997. **(e)** Linear trend:

$\hat{Y}_{2013} = 50.1691 + 79.7191(16) = 1{,}325.675 = 1{,}326$

$\hat{Y}_{2014} = 50.1691 + 79.7191(17) = 1{,}405.3941 = 1{,}405$

Quadratic trend: $\hat{Y}_{2013} = 35.6532 + 85.9402(16) - 0.4147(16)^2 = 1{,}304.5232 = 1{,}305$

$\hat{Y}_{2014} = 50.1691 + 79.7191(17) = 1{,}405.3941 = 1{,}405$

Exponential trend: $\hat{Y}_{2013} = 10^{2.1851+0.0697(16)} = 1{,}994.9645 = 1{,}995$

$\hat{Y}_{2014} = 10^{2.1851+0.0697(17)} = 2{,}342.1337 = 2{,}342.$

(f) The linear and quadratic trend model fit the data better than the exponential trend model and, hence, either forecast should be used.

16.14 (b) $\hat{Y} = 310.8862 + 65.6611X$ where X = years relative to 1978. **(c)** $X = 2012 - 1978 = 34$, $\hat{Y} = 310.8862 + 65.6611(34) =$ \$ 2,543.3631 billion $X = 2013 - 1978 = 35$, $\hat{Y} = 310.8862 + 65.6611(35) =$ \$2609.0242 billion.

(d) There is an upward trend in federal receipts between 1978 and 2011. The trend appears to be linear.

16.16 (b) Linear trend: $\hat{Y} = 301.4182 + 113.3515X$, where X is relative to 2002. **(c)** Quadratic trend: $\hat{Y} = 643.1455 - 142.9439X + 28.4773X^2$, where X is relative to 2002. **(d)** Exponential trend: $\log_{10}\hat{Y} = 2.6309 + 0.0530X$, where X is relative to 2002. **(e)** Linear trend:

$\hat{Y}_{2012} = 301.4182 + 113.3515(10) = 1{,}434.9333$ million KWh

$\hat{Y}_{2013} = 301.4182 + 113.3515(11) = 1{,}548.2848$ million KWh

Quadratic trend: $\hat{Y}_{2012} = 643.1455 - 142.9439(10) + 28.4773(10)^2 = 2061.4333$ million KWh

$\hat{Y}_{2013} = 643.1455 - 142.9439(11) + 28.4773(11)^2 = 2{,}516.5121$ millions of KWh

Exponential trend: $\hat{Y}_{2012} = 10^{2.6309+0.0530(10)} = 1{,}447.6883$ million KWh

$\hat{Y}_{2013} = 10^{2.6309+0.0530(11)} = 1{,}635.5060$ million KWh.

16.18 (b) Linear trend: $\hat{Y} = 2.1243 + 0.1135X$, where X is relative to 2000. **(c)** Quadratic trend: $\hat{Y} = 2.0581 + 0.1496X - 0.0030X^2$, where X is relative to 2000. **(d)** Exponential trend: $\log_{10}\hat{Y} = 0.3342 + 0.0181X$, where X is relative to 2000.

(e)

1st Difference	2nd Difference	% Difference
0.30		15.08
0.09	−0.21	3.93
0.20	0.11	8.40
−0.09	−0.29	−3.49
0.14	0.23	5.62
0.20	0.06	7.60
0.09	−0.11	3.18
0.21	0.12	7.19
0.13	−0.08	4.15
0.01	−0.12	0.31
0.05	0.04	1.53
0.06	0.01	1.81

Neither the first differences, second differences, nor percentage differences are constant across the series. Therefore, other models (including those considered in Section 16.5) may be more appropriate.

(f) The forecasts using the three models are:

Linear trend: $\hat{Y}_{2013} = 2.1243 + 0.1135(13) =$ \$3.6 millions

Quadratic trend: $\hat{Y}_{2013} = 2.0581 + 0.1496(13) - 0.0030(13)^2 =$ \$3.4948 millions

Exponential trend: $\hat{Y}_{2013} = 10^{0.3342+0.0181(13)} =$ \$3.7071 millions

16.20 (b) There has been an upward trend in the CPI in the United States over the 47-year period. The rate of increase became faster in the late 70s but tapered off in the early 80s. **(c)** Linear trend: $\hat{Y} = 16.3487 + 4.4858X$. **(d)** Quadratic trend: $\hat{Y} = 19.8135 + 4.0238X + 0.0100X^2$. **(e)** Exponential trend: $\log_{10}\hat{Y} = 1.5569 + 0.0195X$. **(f)** None of the trend models appear appropriate according to the first-, second- and percentage-difference but the second-difference has the smallest variation in general. So a quadratic trend model is slightly preferred over the others. **(g)** Quadratic trend: For 2012: $\hat{Y}_{2012} = 19.8135 + 4.0238(47) + 0.0100(47)^2 = 231.1165$ For 2013: $\hat{Y}_{2013} = 19.8135 + 4.0238(48) + 0.0100(48)^2 = 236.0944$

16.22 (a) For Time Series I, the graph of Y versus X appears to be more linear than the graph of log Y versus X, so a linear model appears to be more appropriate. For Time Series II, the graph of log Y versus X appears to be more linear than the graph of Y versus X, so an exponential model appears to be more appropriate.

(b) Time Series I: $\hat{Y} = 100.0731 + 14.9776X$, where X = years relative to 2000

Time Series II: $\hat{Y} = 10^{1.9982+0.0609X}$, where X = years relative to 2000.

(c) $X = 12$ for year 2012 in all models. Forecasts for the year 2012:

Time Series I: $\hat{Y} = 100.0731 + 14.9776(12) = 279.8045$

Time Series II: $\hat{Y} = 10^{1.9982+0.0609(12)} = 535.6886.$

16.24 $t_{STAT} = 2.40 > 2.2281$; reject H_0.

16.26 (a) $t_{STAT} = 1.60 < 2.2281$; do not reject H_0.

16.28 (a)

	Coefficients	Standard Error	*t* Stat	*P*-value
Intercept	39.9968	16.2961	2.4544	0.0365
YLag1	1.6797	0.3213	5.2277	0.0005
YLag2	−0.6393	0.6135	−1.0421	0.3246
YLag3	−0.0764	0.3271	−0.2336	0.8205

Since the p-value = 0.8205 > 0.05 level of significance, the third-order term can be dropped.

(b)

	Coefficients	Standard Error	*t* Stat	*P*-value
Intercept	30.8885	12.0824	2.5565	0.0267
YLag1	1.8113	0.1397	12.9666	0.0000
YLag2	−0.8407	0.1407	−5.9753	0.0001

Since the p-value = is virtually 0 and is less than 0.05 level of significance, the second-order term cannot be dropped.

(c) It is not necessary to fit a first-order regression model.

(d) The most appropriate model for forecasting is the second-order autoregressive model:

$\hat{Y}_{2013} = 30.8885 + 1.8113Y_{2012} - 0.8407Y_{2011} = 1{,}197.985361 = 1{,}198$ stores.

$\hat{Y}_{2014} = 30.8885 + 1.8113\hat{Y}_{2013} - 0.8407Y_{2012} = 1{,}214.6576 = 1{,}215$ stores.

16.30 (a)

	Coefficients	Standard Error	t Stat	P-value
Intercept	0.3588	0.3237	1.1087	0.3100
YLag1	0.7009	0.4091	1.7131	0.1375
YLag2	0.2013	0.4578	0.4396	0.6756
YLag3	0.0165	0.3456	0.0478	0.9635

Since the p-value = 0.9635 > 0.05 level of significance, the third-order term can be dropped.

(b)

	Coefficients	Standard Error	t Stat	P-value
Intercept	0.3415	0.2413	1.4149	0.1948
YLag1	0.6909	0.3124	2.2112	0.0580
YLag2	0.2334	0.2843	0.8211	0.4354

Since the p-value = 0.4354 > 0.05 level of significance, the second-order term can be dropped.

(c)

	Coefficients	Standard Error	*t* Stat	*P*-value
Intercept	0.4371	0.1858	2.3522	0.0405
YLag1	0.8835	0.0666	13.2587	0.0000

Since the *p*-value is virtually zero, the first-order term cannot be dropped. **(d)** The most appropriate model for forecasting is the first-order autoregressive model:

$$\hat{Y}_{2013} = 0.4371 + 0.8835Y_{2012} = \$3.4233 \text{ million.}$$

16.32 (a) 2.121. **(b)** 1.50.

16.34 (a) The residuals in the linear and exponential trend model show strings of consecutive positive and negative values.

(b), (c)

	Linear	Quadratic	Exponential	AR1
SSE	513,501.8061	85,317.5333	393,163.2638	119,778.7515
Syx	253.3530	110.4003	221.6876	130.8100
MAD	183.1758	87.5145	138.5403	95.8195

(d) The residuals in the linear trend model and exponential trend model show strings of consecutive positive and negative values. The autoregressive model and the quadratic trend model perform well for the historical data and have a fairly random pattern of residuals. The quadratic trend model has the smallest values in MAD and S_{YX}. Based on the principle of parsimony, the quadratic trend model would be the best model for forecasting.

16.36 (b), (c)

	Linear	Quadratic	Exponential	AR1
SSE	26,580.1132	25,597.5921	512,088.5723	1,871.5077
Syx	43.5727	44.3739	191.2531	13.0437
MAD	36.5526	35.4639	123.6300	8.6283

(d) The residuals in the three trend models show strings of consecutive positive and negative values. The autoregressive model performs well for the historical data and has a fairly random pattern of residuals. The autoregressive model also has the smallest values in MAD and S_{YX}. Based on the principle of parsimony, the autoregressive model would be the best model for forecasting.

16.38 (b), (c)

	Linear	Quadratic	Exponential	AR1
SSE	0.0571	0.05686	0.0670	0.0918
Syx	0.0797	0.08430	0.08630	0.1071
MAD	0.0645	0.0649	0.0675	0.0753

(d) The residuals in the linear, quadratic, and exponential trend models show strings of consecutive positive and negative values. The autoregressive model performs well for the historical data and has a fairly random pattern of residuals. The linear trend model, however, has the smallest values in *MAD* and S_{YX}. The autoregressive model would be the best model for forecasting due to its fairly random pattern of residuals even though it has slightly larger *MAD* and S_{YX} than the linear model.

16.40 (a) $\log \hat{\beta}_0 = 2$, $\hat{\beta}_0 = 10^2 = 100$. This is the fitted value for January 2008 prior to adjustment with the January multiplier. **(b)** $\log \hat{\beta}_1 = 0.01$, $\hat{\beta}_1 = 10^{0.01} = 1.0233$. The estimated monthly compound growth rate is 2.33%. **(c)** $\log \hat{\beta}_2 = 0.1$, $\hat{\beta}_2 = 10^{0.1} = 1.2589$. The January values in the time series are estimated to have a mean 25.89% higher than the December values.

16.42 (a) $\log \hat{\beta}_0 = 3.0$, $\hat{\beta}_0 = 10^{3.0} = 1{,}000$. This is the fitted value for the first quarter of 2008 prior to adjustment by the quarterly multiplier. **(b)** $\log \hat{\beta}_1 = 0.1$, $\hat{\beta}_1 = 10^{0.1} = 1.2589$. The estimated quarterly compound growth rate is $(\hat{\beta}_1 - 1)100\% = 25.89\%$. **(c)** $\log \hat{\beta}_3 = 0.2$, $\hat{\beta}_3 = 10^{0.2} = 1.5849$.

16.44 (a) The retail industry is heavily subject to seasonal variation due to the holiday seasons and so are the revenues for Toys R Us. **(b)** There is obvious seasonal effect in the time series. **(c)** $\log_{10}\hat{Y} = 3.6255 + 0.0027X - 0.3660Q_1 - 0.3699Q_2 - 0.3437Q_3$. **(d)** $\log_{10}\hat{\beta}_1 = 0.0027$. $\hat{\beta}_1 = 10^{0.0027} = 1.0062$. The estimated quarterly compound growth rate is $(\hat{\beta}_1 - 1)\,100\% = 0.62\%$. **(e)** $\log_{10}\hat{\beta}_2 = -0.3660$. $\hat{\beta}_2 = 10^{-0.3660} = 0.4305$. $(\hat{\beta}_2 - 1)\,100\% = -56.95\%$. The 1st quarter values in the time series are estimated to have a mean 56.95% below the 4th quarter values.

$\log_{10}\hat{\beta}_3 = -0.3699$. $\hat{\beta}_3 = 10^{-0.3699} = 0.4266$. $(\hat{\beta}_3 - 1)\,100\% = -57.34\%$.

The 2nd quarter values in the time series are estimated to have a mean 57.34% below the 4th quarter values.

$\log_{10}\hat{\beta}_4 = -0.3437$. $\hat{\beta} = 10^{-0.3437} = 0.4532$. $(\hat{\beta}_4 - 1)\,100\% = -54.68\%$.

The 3rd quarter values in the time series are estimated to have a mean 54.68% below the 4th quarter values. **(f)** Forecasts for 2012: $\hat{Y}_{66} = \$2{,}882.0080$ millions; $\hat{Y}_{67} = \$6{,}398.6588$ millions

16.46 (b)

	Coefficients	Standard Error	*t* Stat	*P*-value
Intercept	−0.0916	0.0070	−13.1771	0.0000
Coded Month	−0.0037	0.0001	−64.4666	0.0000
M1	0.1245	0.0086	14.5072	0.0000
M2	0.0905	0.0086	10.5454	0.0000
M3	0.0806	0.0086	9.3975	0.0000
M4	0.0668	0.0086	7.7810	0.0000
M5	0.0793	0.0086	9.2457	0.0000
M6	0.1001	0.0086	11.6725	0.0000
M7	0.1321	0.0086	15.3949	0.0000
M8	0.1238	0.0086	14.4279	0.0000
M9	0.0577	0.0088	6.5372	0.0000
M10	0.0356	0.0088	4.0317	0.0001
M11	0.0103	0.0088	1.1646	0.2472

(c) $\hat{Y}_{103} = 0.4451$.
(d) Forecasts for the last four months of 2012 are 0.3790, 0.3571, 0.3340, and 0.3234.
(e) $\log_{10}\hat{\beta}_1 = -0.0037$; $\hat{\beta}_1 = 10^{-0.0037} = 0.9915$. The estimated monthly compound growth rate is $(\hat{\beta}_1 - 1)\,100\% = -0.8542\%$.
(f) $\log_{10}\hat{\beta}_8 = 0.1321$; $\hat{\beta}_8 = 10^{0.1321} = 1.3554$. $(\hat{\beta}_8 - 1)\,100\% = 35.5382\%$. The July values in the time series are estimated to have a mean 35.5382% above the December values.

16.48 (b)

	Coefficients	Standard Error	*t* Stat	*P*-value
Intercept	0.7827	0.0402	19.4847	0.0000
Coded Quarter	0.0220	0.0016	13.7152	0.0000
Q1	0.0513	0.0419	1.2228	0.2320
Q2	0.0066	0.0418	0.1580	0.8756
Q3	−0.0009	0.0417	−0.0205	0.9838

(c) $\log_{10}\hat{\beta}_1 = 0.0220$; $\hat{\beta}_1 = 10^{0.0220} = 1.0521$; $(\hat{\beta}_1 - 1)\,100\% = 5.2051\%$. The estimated *quarterly* compound mean growth rate in the price of silver is 5.2051%, after adjusting for the seasonal component.
(d) $\log_{10}\hat{\beta}_2 = 0.0513$; $\hat{\beta}_2 = 10^{0.0513} = 1.1253$; $(\hat{\beta}_2 - 1)\,100\% = 12.5311\%$. The first-quarter values in the time series are estimated to have a mean 12.5311% above the fourth-quarter values.
(e) Last quarter, 2011: $\hat{Y}_{31} = \$29.2292$.

(f) 2012: 34.6040, 32.8466, 33.9683, 35.8067
(g) The forecasts in (f) were not accurate because there is not a strong seasonable component in the price of silver.

16.60 (b) Linear trend: $\hat{Y} = 174{,}090.3005 + 2{,}428.0386X$, where X is relative to 1984.

(c)
2012: $\hat{Y}_{2012} = 174{,}090.3005 + 2{,}428.0386(28) = 242{,}075.381$ thousands
2013: $\hat{Y}_{2013} = 174{,}090.3005 + 2{,}428.0386(29) = 244{,}503.4195$ thousands.

(d)

(b) Linear trend: $\hat{Y} = 115{,}282.2734 + 1{,}585.6305X$, where X is relative to 1984.

(c) 2012: $\hat{Y}_{2012} = 115{,}282.2734 + 1{,}585.6305(28) = 159{,}679.9286$ thousands.
2013: $\hat{Y}_{2013} = 115{,}282.2734 + 1{,}585.6305(29) = 161{,}265.5591$ thousands.

16.62 Linear trend: $\hat{Y} = -2.3932 + 0.7037X$, where X is relative to 1975.

	Coefficients	Standard Error	t Stat	P-value
Intercept	−2.3932	0.6080	−3.9358	0.0004
Coded Yr	0.7037	0.0291	24.2199	0.0000

(c) Quadratic trend: $\hat{Y} = 1.2452 + 0.0799X + 0.0173X^2$, where X is relative to 1975.

	Coefficients	Standard Error	*t* Stat	*P*-value
Intercept	1.2452	0.2458	5.0653	0.0000
Coded Yr	0.0799	0.0316	2.5301	0.0162
Coded Yr Sq	0.173	0.0008	20.4209	0.0000

Exponential trend: $\log_{10}\hat{Y} = 0.1678 + 0.0379X$, where X is relative to 1975.

	Coefficients	Standard Error	*t* Stat	*P*-value
Intercept	0.1678	0.0212	7.9231	0.0000
Coded Yr	0.0379	0.0010	37.5036	0.0000

AR(3): $\hat{Y}_i = 0.3823 + 1.3488Y_{i-1} - 1.0019Y_{i-2} + 0.7144Y_{i-3}$

	Coefficients	Standard Error	*t* Stat	*P*-value
Intercept	0.3823	0.1553	2.4611	0.0198
YLag1	1.3488	0.1666	8.0940	0.0000
YLag2	−1.0019	0.2579	−3.8846	0.0005
YLag3	0.7144	0.1731	4.1273	0.0003

Test of A_3: p-value $= 0.0003 < 0.05$. Reject H_0 that $A_3 = 0$. Third-order term cannot be deleted. A third-order autoregressive model is appropriate.

	Linear	Quadratic	Exponential	AR3
SSE	124.6160	9.3943	5,394.9442	6.7002
Syx	1.8869	0.5256	12.4154	0.4726
MAD	1.6072	0.3604	9.2832	0.3081

(h) The residuals in the first three models show strings of consecutive positive and negative values. The autoregressive model performs well for the historical data and has a fairly random pattern of residuals. It also has the smallest values in the standard error of the estimate, *MAD* and *SSE*. Based on the principle of parsimony, the autoregressive model would probably be the best model for forecasting.

(i) $\hat{Y}_{2012} = 0.3823 + 1.3488Y_{2011} - 1.0019Y_{2010} + 0.7144Y_{2009} = \$28.8718$ billions.

CHAPTER 18

18.2 (a) Day 4, Day 3. **(b)** LCL $= 0.0397$, UCL $= 0.2460$. **(c)** No, proportions are within control limits.
18.4 (a) $n = 500$, $\bar{p} = 761/16{,}000 = 0.0476$.

$$\text{UCL} = \bar{p} + 3\sqrt{\frac{\bar{p}(1-\bar{p})}{n}}$$

$$= 0.0476 + 3\sqrt{\frac{0.0476(1-0.0476)}{500}} = 0.0761$$

$$\text{LCL} = \bar{p} - 3\sqrt{\frac{\bar{p}(1-\bar{p})}{n}}$$

$$= 0.0476 - 3\sqrt{\frac{0.0476(1-0.0476)}{500}} = 0.0190$$

(b) Because the individual points are distributed around $\bar{p}$ without any pattern and all the points are within the control limits, the process is in a state of statistical control.

18.6 (a) UCL $= 0.0176$, LCL $= 0.0082$. The proportion of unacceptable cans is below the LCL on Day 4. There is evidence of a pattern over time because the last eight points are all above the mean, and most of the earlier points are below the mean. Therefore, this process is out of control.

18.8 (a) UCL $= 0.1431$, LCL $= 0.0752$. Days 9, 26, and 30 are above the UCL. Therefore, this process is out of control.

18.12 (a) UCL $= 21.6735$, LCL $= 1.3265$. **(b)** Yes, time 1 is above the UCL.

18.14 (a) The 12 errors committed by Gina appear to be much higher than all others, and Gina would need to explain her performance. **(b)** $\bar{c} = 66/12 = 5.5$, UCL $= 12.5356$, LCL does not exist. The number of errors is in a state of statistical control because none of the tellers is outside the UCL. **(c)** Because Gina is within the control limits, she is operating within the system and should not be singled out for further scrutiny. **(d)** The process needs to be studied and potentially changed, using principles of Six Sigma and/or total quality management.

18.16 (a) $\bar{c} = 3.0566$. **(b)** LCL does not exist, UCL $= 8.3015$. **(c)** There are no weeks outside the control limits. Therefore, this process is in control. Note, however that the first eight weeks are below the mean. **(d)** Because these weeks are within the control limits, the results are explainable by common cause variation.

18.18 (a) $d_2 = 2.059$. **(b)** $d_3 = 0.880$. **(c)** $D_3 = 0$. **(d)** $D_4 = 2.282$. **(e)** $A_2 = 0.729$.

18.20 (a) $\bar{R} = 0.247$, R chart: UCL $= 0.636$; LCL does not exist. **(b)** According to the R chart, the process appears to be in control, with all points lying inside the control limits, without any pattern and no evidence of special cause variation. **(c)** $\bar{\bar{X}} = 47.998$, $\bar{X}$ chart: UCL $= 48.2507$; LCL $= 47.7453$. **(d)** According to the $\bar{X}$ chart, the process appears to be in control, with all points lying inside the control limits, without any pattern and no evidence of special cause variation.

18.22 (a) $\bar{R} = \dfrac{\sum_{i=1}^{k} R_i}{k} = 3.275$, $\bar{\bar{X}} = \dfrac{\sum_{i=1}^{k} \bar{X}_i}{k} = 5.941$. R chart: $UCL = D_4\bar{R} = 2.282(3.275) = 7.4736$. *LCL* does not exist. $\bar{X}$ chart: $UCL = \bar{\bar{X}} + A_2\bar{R} = 5.9413 + 0.729(3.275) = 8.3287$. $LCL = \bar{\bar{X}} - A_2\bar{R} = 5.9413 - 0.729(3.275) = 3.5538$. **(b)** The process appears to be in control because there are no points outside the control limits, there is no evidence of a pattern in the range chart, there are no points outside the control limits, and there is no evidence of a pattern in the $\bar{X}$ chart.

18.24 **(a)** $\overline{R} = 0.8794$, LCL does not exist, UCL $= 2.0068$. **(b)** $\overline{\overline{X}} = 20.1065$, LCL $= 19.4654$, UCL $= 20.7475$. **(c)** The process is in control.

18.26 **(a)** $\overline{R} = 8.145$, LCL does not exist, UCL $= 18.5869$; $\overline{\overline{X}} = 18.12$, UCL $= 24.0577$, LCL $= 12.1823$. **(b)** There are no sample ranges outside the control limits, and there does not appear to be a pattern in the range chart. The mean is above the UCL on Day 15 and below the LCL on Day 16. Therefore, the process is not in control.

18.28 **(a)** $\overline{R} = 0.3022$, LCL does not exist, UCL $= 0.6389$; $\overline{\overline{X}} = 90.1312$,UCL $= 90.3060$, LCL $= 89.9573$. **(b)** On Days 5 and 6, the sample ranges were above the UCL. The mean chart may be erroneous because the range is out of control. The process is out of control.

18.30 **(a)** $P(98 < X < 102) = P(-1 < Z < 1) = 0.6826$.
(b) $P(93 < X < 107.5) = P(-3.5 < Z < 3.75) = 0.99968$
(c) $P(X > 93.8) = P(Z > -3.1) = 0.99903$.
(d) $P(X < 110) = P(Z < 5) = 0.999999713$.

18.32 **(a)** $P(18 < X < 22)\%$

$$= P\left(\frac{18-20.1065}{0.8794/2.059} < Z < \frac{22-20.1065}{0.8794/2.059}\right)$$

$$= P(-4.932 < Z < 4.4335) = 0.9999$$

(b)
$$C_p = \frac{(USL-LSL)}{6(\overline{R}/d_2)} = \frac{(22-18)}{6(0.8794/2.059)} = 1.56$$

$$CPL = \frac{(\overline{\overline{X}}-LSL)}{3(\overline{R}/d_2)} = \frac{(20.1065-18)}{3(0.8794/2.059)} = 1.644$$

$$CPU = \frac{(USL-\overline{\overline{X}})}{3(\overline{R}/d_2)} = \frac{22-20.1065}{3(0.8794/2.059)} = 1.477$$

$$C_{pk} = \min(CPL, CPU) = 1.477$$

18.34 $\overline{R} = 0.2248$, $\overline{\overline{X}} = 5.509$, $n = 4$, $d_2 = 2.059$.
(a)
$P(5.2 < X < 5.8) = P(-2.83 < Z < 2.67) = 0.9962 - 0.0023 = 0.9939$.
(b) Because only 99.39% of the tea bags are within the specification limits, this process is not capable of meeting the goal of 99.7%.

18.46 **(a)** The main reason that service quality is lower than product quality is that the former involves human interaction, which is prone to variation. Also, the most critical aspects of a service are often timeliness and professionalism, and it is possible for customers to perceive that the service could be done more quickly and with greater professionalism. For products, customers often cannot perceive a better or more ideal product than the one they are getting. For example, a new laptop is better and contains more interesting features than any laptop the owner has ever imagined. **(b)** Both services and products are the results of processes. However, measuring services is often harder because of the dynamic variation due to the human interaction between the service provider and the customer. Product quality is often a straightforward measurement of a static physical characteristic such as the amount of sugar in a can of soda. Categorical data are also more common in service quality. **(c)** Yes. **(d)** Yes.

18.48 **(a)** $\overline{p} = 0.2702$, LCL $= 0.1700$, UCL $= 0.3703$. **(b)** Yes, RudyBird's market share is in control before the in-store promotion. **(c)** All seven days of the in-store promotion are above the UCL. The promotion increased market share.

18.50 **(a)** $\overline{p} = 0.75175$, LCL $= 0.62215$, UCL $= 0.88135$. Although none of the points are outside the control limits, there is a clear pattern over time, with the last 13 points above the center line. Therefore, this process is not in control. **(b)** Because the increasing trend begins around Day 20, this change in method would be the assignable cause. **(c)** The control chart would have been developed using the first 20 days, and then a different control chart would be used for the final 20 points because they represent a different process.

18.52 **(a)** $\overline{p} = 0.1198$, LCL $= 0.0205$, UCL $= 0.2191$. **(b)** Day 24 is below the LCL; therefore, the process is out of control. **(c)** Special causes of variation should be investigated to improve the process. Next, the process should be improved to decrease the proportion of undesirable trades.

18.54 Separate p charts should be developed for each food for each shift:

Kidney—Shift 1: $\overline{p} = 0.01395$, UCL $= 0.02678$, LCL $= 0.00112$.

Although there are no points outside the control limits, there is a strong increasing trend in nonconformances over time.

Kidney—Shift 2: $\overline{p} = 0.01829$, UCL $= 0.03329$, LCL $= 0.00329$.

Although there are no points outside the control limits, there is a strong increasing trend in nonconformances over time.

Shrimp—Shift 1: $\overline{p} = 0.006995$, UCL $= 0.01569$, LCL $= 0$.

There are no points outside the control limits, and there is no pattern over time.

Shrimp—Shift 2: $\overline{p} = 0.01023$, UCL $= 0.021$, LCL $= 0$.

There are no points outside the control limits, and there is no pattern over time.

The team needs to determine the reasons for the increase in nonconformances for the kidney product. The production volume for kidney is clearly decreasing for both shifts. This can be observed from a plot of the production volume over time. The team needs to investigate the reasons for this.

Index

D

E

N

O

P

Q

W

Y

Z